The Rough
D1050341

Spain

written and researched by

Simon Baskett, Jules Brown, Marc Dubin, Mark Ellingham, John Fisher, Geoff Garvey, AnneLise Sorensen and Greg Ward

with additional contributions by
Phil Lee and Iain Stewart

ROUGH
GUIDES

NEW YORK · LONDON · DELHI
www.roughguides.com

Contents

Fiestas colour section following p.312

Walking in Spain colour section following p.536

Wines of Spain colour section following p.824

3

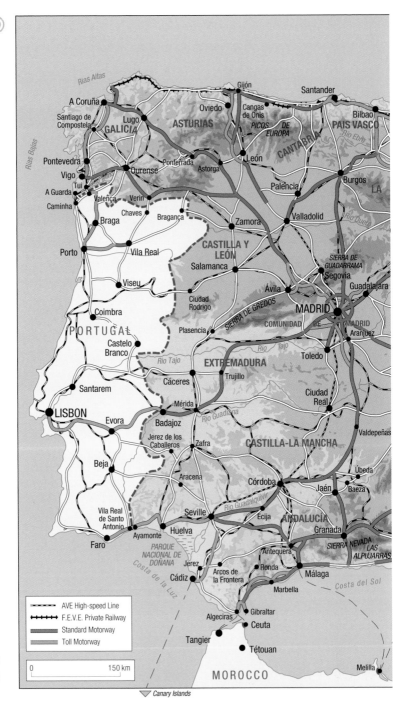

AVE High-speed Line
F.E.V.E. Private Railway
Standard Motorway
Toll Motorway

0   150 km

4

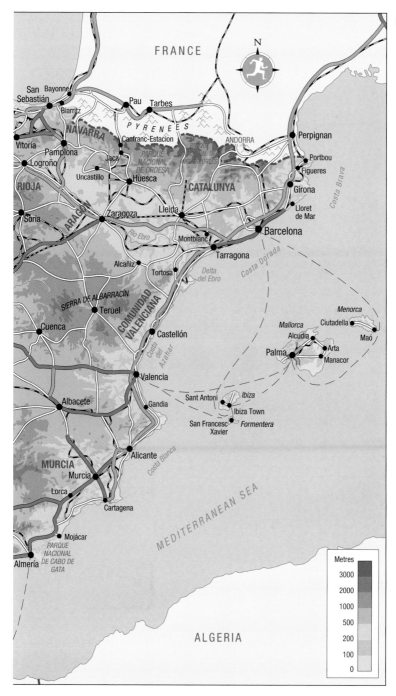

N

FRANCE

San Bayonne
Sebastián
Biarritz
Pau Tarbes
Vitoria
NAVARRA
Canfranc-Estación
ANDORRA
Perpignan
Pamplona
Jaca
PARQUE
NACIONAL
DE ORDESA
PARQUE
NACIONAL DE
AIGÜESTORTES
Portbou
Logroño
Uncastillo
Huesca
Figueres
RIOJA
CATALUNYA
Girona
Soria
ARAGÓN
Zaragoza
Lleida
Lloret
de Mar
Rio Ebro
Montblanc
Barcelona
Alcañiz
Tarragona
Tortosa
Delta
del Ebro
Costa Dorada
SIERRA DE ALBARRACÍN
Teruel
COMUNIDAD
VALENCIANA
Menorca
Mallorca
Ciutadella
Cuenca
Castellón
Alcudia
Maó
Costa
del
Azahar
Palma
Arta
Manacor
Valencia
Albacete
Gandia
Sant Antoni
Ibiza
Ibiza Town
San Francesc
Xavier
Formentera
Alicante
MURCIA
Costa Blanca
Murcia
Lorca
Cartagena
Mojácar
MEDITERRANEAN SEA
PARQUE
NACIONAL
DE CABO DE
GATA
Almería

Costa Brava

Metres	
	3000
	2000
	1000
	500
	200
	100
	0

ALGERIA

Introduction to
Spain

If you're visiting Spain for the first time, be warned: this is a country that fast becomes an addiction. You might intend to come just for a beach holiday, or a tour of the major cities, but before you know it you'll find yourself hooked by something quite different – the celebration of some local fiesta, perhaps, or the amazing nightlife in Madrid, by the Moorish monuments of Andalucía, or maybe Basque cooking or the wild landscapes and birds of prey of Extremadura. And by then, of course, you'll have noticed that there is not just one Spain but many. Indeed, Spaniards often speak of Las Españas (the Spains) and they even talk of the capital in the plural – Los Madriles, the Madrids.

This regionalism is an obsession, and perhaps the most significant change to the country since the 1970s has been the creation of seventeen *autonomías* – autonomous regions – with their own governments, budgets and cultural ministries. The old days of a unified nation, governed with a firm hand from Madrid, seem to have gone forever, as the separate kingdoms that made up the original Spanish state reassert themselves in an essentially federal structure. And the differences are evident wherever you look: in language, culture and artistic traditions, in landscapes and cityscapes, attitudes and politics.

Where to go

The major **cities** are compellingly individual. **Barcelona**, for many, has the edge, thanks to Gaudí's splendid *modernista* architecture, the lively promenades of Las Ramblas, five kilometres of beach, and designer clubs *par excellence*. But **Madrid**, although not as pretty, claims as many devotees. The city, immortalized in the movies of Pedro Almodóvar, has a vibrancy and style that is revealed in a thousand bars and summer *terrazas*. And, of course, it possesses three of the world's finest art museums, not to mention one of the world's most famous football clubs. Then there's **Seville**, home of flamenco and all the clichés of southern Spain; **Valencia**, the vibrant capital of the Levante, with a thriving arts scene and nightlife; and **Bilbao**, a recent entry on Spain's cultural circuit, due to Frank Gehry's astonishing Museo Guggenheim.

Monuments range just as widely from one region to another,

Fact file

• Spain's land area is around half a million square kilometres – about twice the size of the UK or Oregon. Of its 46 million-strong population some eighty percent declare themselves nominally Catholic, though religious observance is patchy.

• Politically, Spain is a parliamentary monarchy; democracy and the monarchy were restored in 1977, after the death of General Franco, the dictator who seized power in the Civil War of 1936–39.

• Regionalism is a major force in Spanish politics; the most powerful of the seventeen *autonomías* are Catalunya and the Basque Country, where nationalism is pushing them towards quasi-independence.

• Spanish (Castilian) is spoken as a first language by 74 percent of the population, while 17 percent speak variants of Catalan (in Catalunya, parts of Valencia and Alicante provinces, and on the Balearic Islands), 7 percent speak Galician and 2 percent Basque. Since regional languages were banned under Franco, the vast majority of the people who speak them are also fluent in Castilian.

• The most important newspapers are *El Pais, La Vanguardia* and *El Mundo*, fairly liberal in outlook. But Spaniards read fewer papers than almost any other Europeans – and the best-selling daily is *Marca*, devoted purely to football.

• A minority of Spaniards attend bullfights; it doesn't rain much on the plains; and they only dance flamenco in the southern region of Andalucía.

◄ Ciudad de las Artes y Ciencias, Valencia

dependent on their history of control and occupation by Romans, Visigoths or Moors, the areas' role in the Golden Age of imperial Renaissance Spain or their later fortunes. Touring **Castile and León**, you can't avoid the stereotypical Spanish image of vast cathedrals and literally hundreds of *reconquista* castles; in northerly, mountainous **Asturias and the Pyrenees**, tiny, almost organically evolved Romanesque churches dot the hillsides and villages; **Andalucía** has the great mosques and Moorish palaces of Granada, Seville and Córdoba; **Castile** boasts the superbly preserved medieval capital,

Tapas

Tapas have become internationalized fare in recent years – yet nothing can prepare you for the variety available on their home soil. The proper way to eat tapas is to wander from one bar to another to sample a particular speciality, for although many bars will have a range of tapas on display or on their menu board, most tend to be known for just one or two dishes ... and the locals would not think of ordering anything else. So you might go to one place for a slice or two of *jamón serrano* (cured ham), another for *pulpo gallego* (deliciously tender pot-cooked octopus), a third for the bizarre *pimientos de Padrón* (small green peppers – about one in ten being fiery-hot), and then maybe on to a smoky old bar that serves just *fino* (dry sherry) from the barrel along with slices of *mojama* (dried, pressed roe).

Toledo, and the gorgeous Renaissance university city of Salamanca; while the harsh landscape of **Extremadura** cradles ornate *conquistador* towns built with riches from the New World.

Not that Spain is predominantly about buildings. The **landscape** holds just as much fascination – and variety. The evergreen estuaries of Galicia could hardly be more different from the high, arid plains of Castile, or the gulch-like desert landscapes of Almería. Agriculture makes its mark in the patterned hillsides of the wine- and olive-growing regions and the rice fields of the Levante. Spain also has some of the finest **mountains** in Europe, with superb walking and **wildlife** in a dozen-plus *sierras* – especially the Picos de Europa and the Pyrenees. The country's unique fauna includes protected species such as brown bears, the Spanish lynx and Mediterranean monk seals, as well as more common wild boar, white storks and birds of prey.

One of Spain's greatest attractions is undeniably its **beaches** – and here, too, there's a lot more variety than the holiday-brochure image might suggest. Long tracts of coastline – along the Costa del Sol in particular – have certainly been steamrolled into concrete hotel and villa complexes, but delightful pockets remain even along the big tourist *costas*. On the Costa Brava, the string of coves between Palamós and Begur is often overlooked, while in Andalucía there are superb windsurfing waters around Tarifa and some decidedly low-key resorts along the Costa de la Luz. In the north, the cooler Atlantic coastline boasts the surfing beaches of Cantabria and Asturias, or the unspoilt coves of Galicia's estuaries. Offshore, the Balearic Islands have some superb sands and, if you're up

▶ Castle, Castilla-La Mancha

Spanish time

Spanish time is notionally one hour ahead of the UK – but conceptually Spain might as well be on a different planet. Nowhere in Europe keeps such late hours. Spaniards may not take a traditional midday siesta as much as they used to, but their diurnal rhythms remain committedly nocturnal. They'll saunter out around 8 or 9pm in the evening for a *paseo*, to greet friends and maybe have a drink and tapas, and if they're eating out, they'll commonly start at 10 or 11pm, often later in Madrid, where it's not unusual for someone to phone around midnight to see if you're going out for the evening.

Like everything else, practices differ somewhat by region. Madrid – its inhabitants nicknamed *los gatos* or "the cats" for their nocturnal lifestyle – is famed for staying up the latest, with Andalucía a close second. In the north, particularly in Catalunya, they keep more northern European hours. And, of course, summer nights never seem to really end.

for it, Ibiza in particular offers one of the most hedonistic backdrops to beachlife in the Mediterranean.

Hedonism, actually, is pretty much unavoidable. Wherever you are in Spain, you can't help but notice the Spaniards' infectious enthusiasm for life. In towns, there's always something happening – in bars and clubs, on the streets, and especially at fiesta times. Even in out-of-the-way places there's a surprising range of nightlife and entertainment, not to mention the daily pleasure of bar-crawling for tapas (see box, p.8), having a drink and a bite of the house speciality.

◀ Beach on the Costa Brava

When to go

Overall, spring, early summer and autumn are ideal times for a Spanish trip – though the **weather** varies enormously from region to region. The high central plains suffer from fierce extremes, stiflingly hot in summer, bitterly cold and swept by freezing winds in winter. The Atlantic coast, in contrast, has a tendency to damp and mist, and a relatively brief, humid summer. The Mediterranean south is warm virtually all year round, and in parts of Andalucía positively subtropical, where it's often balmy enough to wear a t-shirt by day even in the winter months.

In high **summer**, the other factor worth considering is **tourism** itself. As the second most visited country in the world, Spain plays host to about sixty million tourists a year – rather more than the entire population – and all the main beach and mountain resorts are packed in July and August, as are the major sights. August, Spain's own holiday month, sees the coast at its most crowded and the cities, by contrast, pretty sleepy.

Average temperatures

Note that the chart shows **average temperatures** – and while Seville, the hottest city in Spain, can soar high into the 90s at midday in summer, it is a fairly comfortable 23–27°C (75–80°F) through much of the morning and late afternoon. Equally, bear in mind that temperatures in the north

or west, in Extremadura or León for example, can approach freezing at night in winter, while mountainous regions can get extremely cold much of the year.

	Jan	Mar	May	Jul	Sep	Nov
Alicante, Costa Blanca						
(°C)	16	20	26	32	30	21
(°F)	61	68	78	90	86	70
Barcelona, Catalunya						
(°C)	13	16	21	28	25	16
(°F)	56	61	70	83	77	61
Madrid, Castile						
(°C)	9	15	21	31	25	13
(°F)	49	59	70	88	77	56
Málaga, Costa del Sol						
(°C)	17	19	23	29	29	20
(°F)	63	67	74	84	84	68
Mallorca, Balearics						
(°C)	14	17	22	29	27	18
(°F)	58	63	72	84	80	65
Pontevedra, Galicia						
(°C)	14	16	20	25	24	16
(°F)	58	61	68	77	75	61
Santander, Cantabria						
(°C)	12	15	17	22	21	15
(°F)	54	59	63	72	70	59
Seville, Andalucía						
(°C)	15	21	26	35	32	20
(°F)	59	70	78	95	90	68

34

things not to miss

It's not possible to see everything that Spain has to offer in one trip – and we don't suggest you try. What follows is a selection of the country's highlights: outstanding architecture, natural wonders, spectacular festivals and culinary treats. They're arranged, in no particular order, in five colour-coded categories, which you can browse to find the very best things to see and experience. All highlights have a page reference to take you straight to where you can find out more.

01 **La Mezquita, Córdoba** Page **324** • Nothing can prepare you for the breathtaking Grand Mosque of Córdoba – one of the world's most beautiful buildings.

02 Jamón serrano Page **221** • A few thin slices of the best cured *jamón* are a must for any carnivore.

03 Feria de Abril See *Fiestas colour section* • Seville's week-long fiesta is Andalucía at its celebratory best, with flamenco tents, and horsemen and women dressed to kill.

04 Toledo Page **141** • The capital of medieval Spain, Toledo has changed little since its depiction in El Greco's paintings.

05 The Pyrenees Pages **498**, **632**, **769** & *Walking in Spain colour section* • This spectacular range separating France from Spain provides fabulous summer walks, from easy day-hikes in the high valleys to long-distance treks across the mountains, as well as excellent skiing.

06 Ibiza and Formentera's beaches Pages **895** & **898** • The islands' little-developed beaches range from gem-like coves to sweeps of white sand.

07 Seafood in San Sebastián Page **458** • San Sebastián is renowned for its refined Basque cuisine, much of it featuring seafood, served in some of the finest restaurants and tapas bars in the country.

08 Semana Santa See *Fiestas colour section* • Easter Week sees processions of masked penitents parading around villages and towns across Spain, with the biggest events in Seville and Málaga.

09 Fundació Joan Miró Page **692** • The bold paintings and abstract forms of the artist's work are housed in the wonderfully sympathetic building of the Fundació.

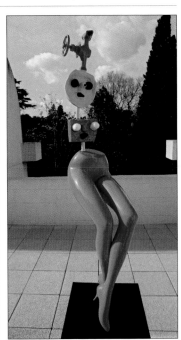

10 Salamanca Page **382** • An ancient university town with beautiful Gothic and Renaissance buildings.

Doñana's unique habitats enable this vast national park to host myriad birds and other wildlife, including the Iberian lynx.

16

11 Clubbing Page **894** • Forget sleep, experience everything else to excess, on Ibiza – the ultimate party island.

13 **Sitges Carnaval** Page **811** • Sitges throws one of the most spectacular carnival parties, in which people – many of them gay – take to the streets with fancy dress and floats.

14 **Museo Guggenheim, Bilbao** Page **475** • Gehry's flagship creation, with its undulating titanium, has become one of the iconic buildings of our age.

15 **A night on the tiles, Madrid** Page **123** • Delight in the capital's most traditional of rituals – a night of bar-hopping and clubbing rounded off by a dawn reviver of *chocolate con churros*.

16 The Prado, Madrid

Page 95 • Paintings such as Goya's powerful *Tres de Mayo*, not to mention outstanding works by Velázquez and El Greco, make the Prado obligatory on any visit to Spain's capital.

17 Flamenco

Page **953** • The stamp of heels and heart-rending lament of a *cante jondo* encapsulate the soul of the Spanish south.

18 Aqueduct, Segovia

Page 175 • Eight hundred metres long, this solid piece of Roman engineering has spanned the Castilian town for nearly two thousand years.

19 Rioja wine

Page **419** & *Wines of Spain* colour section • Spain has a formidable range of quality wines, not least its famous Rioja, which can be sampled in numerous *bodegas* around Logroño, capital of La Rioja province.

20 Picos de Europa

Page **521** • This stunning northern area of mountain peaks and gorges has superb walking, canoeing and rock-climbing.

21 Seville

Page **274** • The quintessential Andalucian city with sun-drenched plazas, winding alleyways, Moorish monuments and more bars than seems remotely feasible.

22 Las Fallas

See *Fiestas* colour section • In March, Valencia erupts in festivities as giant models are burnt and fireworks crackle across town to celebrate San José.

24 Camino de Santiago

Pages **430, 496** & **568** • The medieval pilgrim route to the shrine of Santiago de Compostela left a swathe of Gothic and Renaissance churches, monasteries and inns, not least the great cathedral at the end of the road.

23 Sherry tasting in Jerez

Page **311** & *Wines of Spain* colour **section** • There are few greater pleasures than a chilled glass of fino or manzanilla, and there's no better place to sample this classic Andalucian wine than in the sherry heartland of Jerez.

25 Cádiz Page **303** • Marvellously atmospheric port town built from the proceeds of the colonial trade in precious metals, with an easy-going feel and a great Carnaval.

26 Sagrada Familia, Barcelona Page **698** • One of Spain's truly essential sights – Gaudí's unfinished masterpiece, the church of the "Sacred Family".

28 Teatre-Museu Dalí, Figueres Page **760** • The Dalí museum in Figueres is as surreal as its creator – who lies in a mausoleum within.

27 Paradores Page **39** • Converted castles and monasteries provide an atmospheric setting for many of these luxurious hotels.

21

29 **León Catedral** Page **436** • A vividly painted Romanesque crypt and stained glass up in the Gothic cathedral make this one of the best in Europe, let alone Spain.

30 **Las Alpujarras** Page **358** • Drive over lemons and walk old mule paths in this picturesque region of mountain villages nestled in the southern folds of the Sierra Nevada.

31 **Mérida** Page **222** • The ancient Roman remains of Mérida, including the beautiful Teatro Romano, are impressive for their extent and state of preservation.

32 **Windsurfing**
Page **297** •
Catch the wind in Tarifa at one of the world's top windsurfing spots.

33 **Picasso's Guernica** Page **102** • Picasso's portrayal of Spain's bloody struggle against Fascism and its suffering in Guernica, the showpiece of Madrid's Centro de Arte Reina Sofia.

34 The Alhambra, Granada Page **344** • The legendary Moorish palace complex is a monument to sensuality and contemplative decoration.

Basics

Basics

Getting there

Flying is the quickest way of getting to Spain, with by far the widest choice of routes being from the UK and Ireland. Madrid and Barcelona are the two big gateways, though the summer holiday trade to the costas and the Balearics, and the rapid growth of European budget airlines, has opened up regional airports right across Spain. However, taking the train from London is no longer the endurance test it was, and there's much to be said for waking up refreshed in Madrid or Barcelona after the quick Eurostar service to Paris and the comfortable overnight journey on the "train-hotel". Driving is a bit more of an adventure, but there are several routes that can save you time, like the direct ferry services from Plymouth to Santander and from Portsmouth to Bilbao.

Air, train and ferry fares are seasonal, at their highest in summer (June to end Sept) and around Christmas/New Year and Easter week. You should always book as far in advance as possible to get the best deals. The **cheapest flights** from the UK and Ireland are usually with budget and charter airlines, which are sold direct (by phone or online) on a one-way basis, so you may find one leg of your journey considerably more expensive depending on demand. Be aware, too, that **airport taxes** can cost more than the flight itself, while increasingly things like in-flight meals and luggage allowances are being charged as extra. Cheap flights tend to have fixed dates and are non-changeable and non-refundable, while tickets with holiday charter airlines may limit your stay to one month. Major **scheduled airlines** are usually (though not always) more expensive, but tickets remain valid for three months or more and normally have a degree of flexibility should you need to change dates after booking. You may be able to cut costs by going through a specialist **flight, discount or online agent**, who may also offer special student and youth fares plus a range of other travel-related services.

Flights from the UK and Ireland

Flight time to Spain is two to three hours, depending on the route, and usually the cheapest flights are with the no-frills **budget airlines** such as bmibaby (Ⓦwww.bmibaby.com), easyJet (Ⓦwww.easyjet.com) and Ryanair (Ⓦwww.ryanair.com), who between them fly from over twenty regional UK airports direct to destinations all over Spain. London flights tend to depart from Stansted or Luton; other budget airlines, including Jet2 (from Leeds/Bradford, Manchester, Newcastle and Blackpool; Ⓦwww.jet2.com) or flybe (from Exeter and Southampton; Ⓦwww.flybe.com), concentrate on flights out of particular British regions, while easyJet also flies out of Belfast. In any case, you should be able to find a route that suits you, and not just to the main cities either – many budget airlines offer direct access to smaller regional Spanish airports in the Basque Country, Galicia, the Balearics and Andalucía. It's always worth double-checking the exact airport used, though – Ryanair's "Barcelona" flights, for example, are actually to Girona (1hr to the north) or Reus (1hr 15min to the south). **Fares** for flights on all routes start at around £9.99 each way, or sometimes (depending on the airline) even free with just the taxes to pay. However, book last minute in the summer and you can expect to pay considerably more, up to £100 each way depending on the route.

For convenient flights **to the costas and Balearics**, you can also check the websites of holiday and charter companies such as Monarch (Ⓦwww.flymonarch.com), First Choice (Ⓦwww.firstchoice.co.uk), Thomas Cook (Ⓦwww.flythomascook.com) and Thomson (Ⓦwww.thomsonfly.com). You might not get the rock-bottom deals of the budget airlines, as schedules and prices are geared towards the summer holiday season, but flights depart from regional airports right around the UK.

Iberia (⊛www.iberia.com), Spain's national airline, and British Airways (⊛www.britishair ways.com) have the widest range of **scheduled flights**, with direct services from London Gatwick or Heathrow to half a dozen Spanish cities (most frequently to Madrid and Barcelona, but also Valencia, Malaga and Alicante) and connections on to most other airports in Spain. You'll also be able to arrange add-on sections to London from regional UK airports such as Manchester or Newcastle or from Scotland. Special offers mean prices start at around £100 return, though again a typical late-booking summer rate can be more like £200 return.

From Ireland, you can fly with Iberia from Dublin to Madrid, or with Aer Lingus (⊛www .aerlingus.com) from Dublin or Cork to up to eight Spanish airports (including Barcelona, Bilbao, Malaga and Alicante). Ryanair also connects Dublin and Shannon with most of the same destinations, plus Seville, Valencia, Murcia and Almeria. Prices are highly flexible, starting at around €40 each way, though these rise sharply for last-minute bookings or to popular summer destinations.

Flights from the US and Canada

The widest choice of scheduled flights **from the United States** to Spain is with the national carrier Iberia (⊛www.iberia.com), which flies direct, nonstop from New York to Madrid or Barcelona, and from Miami and Chicago to Madrid. Journey time (typically overnight) is between seven hours ten minutes and eight hours thirty minutes, depending on the route. Fares start at around $600 return, though high-season supplements and taxes can push this up to $1000 or so. The advantage of flying with Iberia is that it offers connecting flights to almost anywhere in Spain, which can be very good value if booked with your transatlantic flight. However, there are other airlines offering Spain routes (some on a code-share basis with Iberia or other airlines), including American Airlines (⊛www.aa.com), Delta (⊛www.delta .com), Continental (⊛www.continental.com), Spanair (⊛www.spanair.com) and United (⊛www.united.com). Or you can fly to Spain with airlines such as Air France, KLM, Lufthansa, TAP or British Airways, for example, which tend to fly via their respective European hubs – in which case, you can add three to fours hours to your total travel time, depending on the connection.

From Canada, there's a direct, nonstop route from Toronto to Madrid with Air Canada (⊛www.aircanada.com), with onward connections across Spain with their partner Spanair. Fares start from CAN$545 one way from Toronto, Montreal or Ottawa, CAN$715 from Calgary or Vancouver. Otherwise, you'll be able to find a route using one of the major European airlines via their respective hubs, with fares starting at around CAN$1100 return.

Flights from Australia, New Zealand and South Africa

There are no direct flights to Spain **from Australia or New Zealand**, but many airlines offer through-tickets with their partners via their European or Asian hubs. Flights via Asia are generally the cheaper option, but fares don't vary as much between airlines as you might think, and in the end you'll be basing your choice on things like flight timings, routes and possible stop-offs on the way. If you're seeing Spain as part of a wider European trip, you might want to aim first for the UK, since there's a wide choice of cheap flights to Spain once there. Or consider a Round-the-World fare, with most basic options able to offer Madrid or Barcelona as standard stopovers.

From **South Africa**, there are direct flights with Iberia (⊛www.iberia.com) from Johannesburg to Madrid, which take around ten hours.

Package holidays, tours and city breaks

The basic, mass-market **package holidays** to the traditional resorts on the Costa del Sol, Costa Brava, Costa Blanca and others are not to everyone's taste, but bargains can be found online or at any UK high-street travel agent, from as little as £99 for a seven-night flight-and-hotel package. There are often really good deals for families, either in hotels or in self-catering apartments, though

Fly less – stay longer! Travel and Climate Change

Climate change is perhaps the single biggest issue facing our planet. It is caused by a build-up in the atmosphere of carbon dioxide and other greenhouse gases, which are emitted by many sources – including planes. Already, **flights** account for three to four percent of human-induced global warming: that figure may sound small, but it is rising year on year and threatens to counteract the progress made by reducing greenhouse emissions in other areas.

Rough Guides regard travel as a **global benefit**, and feel strongly that the advantages to developing economies are important, as are the opportunities for greater contact and awareness among peoples. But we also believe in travelling responsibly, which includes giving thought to how often we fly and what we can do to redress any harm that our trips may create.

We can travel less or simply reduce the amount we travel by air (taking fewer trips and staying longer, or taking the train if there is one); we can avoid night flights (which are more damaging); and we can make the trips we do take "climate neutral" via a carbon offset scheme. **Offset schemes** run by climatecare.org, carbonneutral .com and others allow you to "neutralize" the greenhouse gases that you are responsible for releasing. Their websites have simple calculators that let you work out the impact of any flight – as does our own. Once that's done, you can pay to fund projects that will reduce future emissions by an equivalent amount. Please take the time to visit our website and make your trip climate neutral, or get a copy of the *Rough Guide to Climate Change* for more detail on the subject.

www.roughguides.com/climatechange

the time of year you visit can increase prices significantly (school holidays are always most expensive).

A huge number of **specialist tour operators** offer a wider range of activity holidays or tours, from hiking in the Pyrenees to touring the artistic highlights of Andalucía. We've given a flavour of what's available in the listed reviews at the end of this section, but the options are almost endless. Prices vary wildly depending on the quality of accommodation offered and whether the tours are fully inclusive or not. Many bicycle tours, for example, can either be guided or done on a more independent (and cheaper) self-guided basis. Spanish-based tour operators offer some of the more interesting, off-the-beaten-track options, but for these you'll usually have to arrange your own flights to Spain, while some foreign-based operators also tend to quote for their holidays exclusive of airfares.

Some operators and websites specialize in **city breaks**, with destinations including Barcelona, Madrid, Seville and Granada. UK prices start at around £200 for three-day (two-night) breaks, including return flights, airport transfer and B&B in a centrally located one-, two- or three-star hotel. Adding extra nights or upgrading your hotel is possible, too, usually at a fairly reasonable cost. The bigger US operators, such as American Express and Delta Vacations, can also easily organize short city breaks to Spain on a flight-and-hotel basis, while from Australia Iberian specialist Ibertours (@www.ibertours.com.au) can arrange two- or three-night packages in most Spanish cities.

Other package deals worth considering are **fly-drive** offers, where you'll get a flight, accommodation and car rental arranged through your tour operator. Some companies specialize in villas and apartments, or off-the-beaten-track farmhouses and the like, while on other holiday packages you can tour the country's historic *paradores*, with car rental included.

Trains

Travelling by train from the UK to Spain is a viable option, with total journey times from London of around sixteen hours to Barcelona, eighteen hours to Madrid. You take the afternoon **Eurostar** (@www .eurostar.com) from London St Pancras

International via the Channel Tunnel to Paris and change there for the overnight "train-hotel" for either Barcelona (via Figueres and Girona) or Madrid (via Burgos and Valladolid), with onward connections to Valencia or Andalucía. **Fares** start at £59 return for the Eurostar to Paris (through-tickets available from UK towns and cities), plus £51 each way for the cheapest sleeper accommodation on the overnight train. You'll have to book well in advance on all services to get the lowest prices. There are alternative daytime services through France and Spain, though they don't save you any money. If you don't mind the journey to Spain taking a whole lot longer, there are also minor routes that cross the central Pyrenees (via Canfranc or Puigcerdà), though you may have to spend the night at either of the border towns if you want to see the mountains in daylight.

The best first stop for information about train travel to Spain is the excellent ⓦ**www .seat61.com**, which provides full route, ticket, timetable and contact information. You can book the whole journey **online** with Rail Europe (☎0844/848 5848, ⓦwww .raileurope.co.uk) or call a specialist **rail agent** such as Ffestiniog Travel (☎01766/772050, ⓦwww.ffestiniogtravel .co.uk) or the Spanish Rail Service (☎020/7725 7063, ⓦwww.spanish-rail .co.uk). If you live outside the UK, you can book Eurostar and "train-hotel" tickets through ⓦwww.raileurope.com. These contacts can also advise about **rail passes** (principally InterRail and Eurail), which have to be bought before leaving home – see "Getting around" for more details.

Buses

You can reach most major towns and cities in Spain by bus from the UK with **Eurolines** services (☎08705/808080, ⓦwww.eurolines .co.uk). The main routes are from London (though add-on fares are available from any British city) to Barcelona (25hr), Madrid (27hr) and Valencia (30hr), with connections on to other Spanish destinations, but it's a long time to spend cooped up in a bus. Standard return fares are around £125 to Barcelona, £150 to Madrid, though you'll get better deals if you book seven, fifteen or thirty days in advance or check the website for special offers. You can book tickets online or at any British National Express bus terminal.

Eurolines also has a **Eurolines Pass**, which allows unlimited travel on Eurolines routes between 45 cities, but only between Madrid and Barcelona within Spain, so it's not much use for a Spanish tour. Better value is the **Busabout Explorer** (ⓦwww .busabout.com), a seasonal (May–Oct) hop-on-hop-off backpacker bus service whose "Western Loop" begins in Paris (add-ons from London available) and takes in Barcelona, Valencia, Madrid and San Sebastián (from £299; pass valid for the entire season; other options available).

Driving to Spain

Provided you're not in a hurry, **driving to Spain** from the UK is an interesting way to get there, but with fuel, toll and overnight costs it doesn't compare in terms of price with flying or taking the train. It's about 1600km from London to Barcelona, for example, which, with stops, takes almost two full days to drive, and another 600km on to Madrid.

Many people use the conventional **cross-Channel ferry links**, principally Dover–Calais, though services to Brittany or Normandy might be more convenient depending on where you live (and they cut out the trek around Paris). However, the quickest way of crossing the Channel is to use the **Eurotunnel** (☎08705/353535, ⓦwww.eurotunnel.com), which operates drive-on-drive-off shuttle trains between Folkestone and Calais/Coquelles. The 24-hour service runs every twenty minutes throughout the day; though you can just turn up, booking is advised, especially at weekends and in summer holidays, or if you want the best deals (from £49 one way). French railways run a **Motorail** service (mid-May to mid-Sept; 1–2 departures a week; from £190) from Calais or Paris, where your car is loaded on to the train and you sleep overnight in a couchette, but it only runs as far as Narbonne, on the French Mediterranean side of the Pyrenees, so is a pricey way to save a few hours' driving time.

The best way to cut driving time is to use either of the direct UK–Spain ferry crossings, especially if you're heading for the Basque region, Galicia, Castilla y León or even Madrid. Brittany Ferries (☎0871/244 0744, ⓦwww.brittany-ferries.co.uk) operates a car and passenger ferry from **Plymouth to Santander** in Cantabria (twice weekly; 20hr), or there's a P&O service (☎0871/664 5645, ⓦwww.poferries.com) from **Portsmouth to Bilbao** (twice weekly; 34hr; restricted services Dec & Jan), east of Santander in the Basque Country. Both services are very expensive, especially in summer, when return fares can cost as much as £800 (it's cheaper for foot-passengers, though everyone has to book some form of seating or cabin accommodation).

Any ferry company or travel agent can supply up-to-date schedules and ticket information, or you can consult the encyclopedic ⓦwww.directferries.com, which has details about, and links to, every European ferry service. For driving requirements and regulations in Spain, see "Getting around", p.34.

Booking flights and services online

ⓦwww.cheapflights.co.uk, ⓦwww.cheapflights.com, ⓦwww.cheapflights.ca Price comparison on flights, short breaks, packages and other deals.

ⓦwww.ebookers.com, ⓦwww.ebookers.ie Flights, hotels, cars and holiday packages.

ⓦwww.expedia.co.uk, ⓦwww.expedia.com, ⓦwww.expedia.ca Discount airfares, all-airline search engine, and daily deals on hotels, cars and packages.

ⓦwww.lastminute.com, ⓦwww.us.lastminute.com, ⓦwww.lastminute.com.au Good last-minute flights, holiday packages, hotel bookings and car-rental deals.

ⓦwww.travelocity.co.uk, ⓦwww.travelocity.com, ⓦwww.travelocity.ca, ⓦwww.zuji.com.au Destination guides, hot fares and good deals on car rental, rail passes and accommodation.

Discount travel agents

North South Travel UK ☎01245/608 291, ⓦwww.northsouthtravel.co.uk. Friendly, competitive travel agency, offering discounted fares. Profits are used to support projects in the developing world, especially the promotion of sustainable tourism.

STA Travel UK ☎0871/230 0040, ⓦwww.statravel.co.uk; US ☎1-800/781-4040, ⓦwww.statravel.com; Australia ☎134 782, ⓦwww.statravel.com.au. Worldwide specialists in low-cost flights, and tours for students and under 26s. Also student IDs, travel insurance, car rental, rail passes and more.

Trailfinders UK ☎0845/058 5858, ⓦwww.trailfinders.com; Republic of Ireland ☎01/677 7888, ⓦwww.trailfinders.ie; Australia ☎1300/780 212, ⓦwww.trailfinders.com.au. One of the best-informed and most efficient agents for independent travellers.

Tour operators

Activity and adventure

Adventure Center US ☎1-800/228 8747, ⓦwww.adventurecenter.com. Active vacations in the Picos de Europa, Pyrenees, Catalunya, Andalucía and the Sierra Nevada.

Alto-Aragon UK ☎01869/337 339, ⓦwww.altoaragon.co.uk. An established English-run company offering summer hiking and activity holidays, and winter cross-country skiing programmes in the high Pyrenees.

Exodus Travels UK ☎020/8675 5550, ⓦwww.exodus.co.uk. Walking and cycling in Andalucía, Mallorca, the Picos de Europa and the Pyrenees (and most minor mountain ranges), as well as cycling or multi-adventure (climbing, caving, rafting, etc), cultural and sightseeing trips. There's a big range of trips at all prices, but typical is a week's walking in La Rioja wine country, from around £800 including flights.

Extremely Spanish Adventures UK ☎01691/684 514, ⓦwww.extremelyspanish.com. Canyoning, surfing, canoeing and rock-climbing holidays in and around the Picos de Europa, with a seven-day "Picos Taster" from £350 excluding flights.

Spirit of Adventure UK ☎01822/880 277, ⓦwww.spirit-of-adventure.com. Multi-activity holidays in Catalunya, Andalucía, Galicia and the Picos de Europa. There's trekking, climbing and sea kayaking, with some activity holidays specifically aimed at families (from £650 per person).

Backpacker travel

Busabout UK ☎0207/950 1661, ⓦwww.busabout.com. The European backpacker bus service also offers a seven-day Spain/Portugal bus tour (basically Andalucía and the Algarve; £399) and a six-day San Sebastian surf trip (£299), with prices including hostel accommodation, guides, transport, surf lessons and so on. Also special annual Running of the Bulls and La Tomatina trips, all aimed at a young, party crowd.

Cycling

Bravobike Spain ☎915 595 523, ⓦwww
.bravobike.com. Offers a variety of cycle tours from
one day in Madrid, Segovia or Toledo, for example, to
themed week-long tours in conquistador country, La
Rioja wine country or along the Camino de Santiago.
Prices are variable, but from €30 for a short day-trip,
€650 self-guided per week and from €1000 guided.

Easy Rider Tours US ☎1-800/488 8332, ⓦwww
.easyridertours.com. Guided cycling and sightseeing
tours in Andalucía, Castilla y León, and along the
pilgrims' way to Santiago de Compostela. Tours are
all-inclusive and fully supported, from around $3000
for a week, though airfares are extra.

Iberocycle Spain ☎942 581 085, ⓦwww
.iberocycle.com. An English-run, Spain-based
company specializing in supported or self-guided
cycling tours of northern Spain in particular
(Cantabria, Asturias, Basque Country, Catalunya).
Short five-night trips start at around €430.

Food and drink

A Taste of Spain Spain ☎856 079 626, ⓦwww
.atasteofspain.com. Organizes gourmet culinary tours
of Catalunya, the Basque region/La Rioja, Andalucía
and central Spain, with tastings, meals and cookery
lessons. From around €300 for a day's excursion to
taste Iberico ham to €3000 for a week following La
Mancha's saffron route.

Arblaster & Clarke UK ☎01730/263111,
ⓦwww.arblasterandclarke.com. The most notable
wine-tour specialist, with quality trips to all Spain's
wine-producing regions, including agreeable
accommodation and tastings at both famous and
little-known wineries.

Vintage Spain Spain ☎947 310 126, ⓦwww
.vintagespain.com. Wine-tasting tours of La Rioja,
Ribera del Duero, La Mancha and Penedes, from one-
day excursions to longer tours combining gourmet
wine-tasting trips with activities such as cycling, art
history or yoga.

History, art and culture

Abercrombie and Kent UK ☎0845/618 2203,
ⓦwww.abercrombieandkent.co.uk; US
☎1-800/554 7016, ⓦwww.abercrombiekent.com.
Pricey, upmarket independent or fully escorted tours,

with the ten-day "Signature Spain" trip (Córdoba,
Granada, Seville) typically providing a private guide for
monument visits.

Madrid and Beyond Spain ☎917 580 063,
ⓦwww.madridandbeyond.com. Classy customized
holidays and special experiences, from private gallery
tours to expert-led walks through Gaudí's Barcelona.

Martin Randall Travel UK ☎020/8742 3355,
ⓦwww.martinrandall.com. The leading cultural-tour
specialists, offering small-group, expert-led trips to
Catalunya, Madrid, Toledo, Aragón and Seville, among
others. Departures several times a year on various
trips and themes, from around £1800.

Horseriding

Fantasia Adventure Holidays Spain ⓦwww
.fantasiaadventureholidays.com. British-run
company offering riding breaks on the Costa de la
Luz, from full-board weekends to week-long holidays
(from £655 excluding flights). Contact is best by
email.

Surfing

Surf Spain UK ☎01691/648 514, ⓦwww
.surfspain.co.uk. Surf camps and tailor-made surfing
holidays in the north and south of Spain, with two-
night breaks from £160 per person (excluding flights).

Walking

ATG-Oxford UK ☎01865/315678, ⓦwww
.atg-oxford.co.uk. Sustainable-tourism outfit with
off-the-beaten-track walking holidays in La Rioja
or the volcanic countryside around Girona, plus the
Pyrenees, Catalunya and the Camino de Santiago.
Five-day holidays start from £400.

Olé Spain US ☎1-888/869 7156, ⓦwww
.olespain.com. Small-group cultural walking tours in
Catalunya, Andalucía and Extremadura, with prices
starting at $3300 for an eight-day tour (excluding
airfares).

Ramblers Worldwide Holidays UK
☎01707/331 133, ⓦwww.ramblersholidays
.co.uk. Long-established walking tour operator, with
hiking holidays in most Spanish mountain regions,
as well as vineyard rambles and tours of classical
Andalucía. From around £527 for an all-inclusive
week in the Sierra Nevada.

Getting around

Most of Spain is well covered by public transport. The rail network reaches all the provincial capitals and the main towns along the inter-city lines, and there's an expanding high-speed network that has slashed journey times between Madrid and Seville, Valladolid or Barcelona. Inter-city bus services are often more frequent and cheaper than the regular trains, and will usually take you closer to your destination, as some train stations are a few kilometres from the town or village they serve. Driving a car, meanwhile, will give you the freedom to head away from the major tourist routes and take in some of the spectacular scenery at your own pace.

Approximate journey times and frequencies can be found in the "Travel details" at the end of each chapter, and local peculiarities are pointed out in the text of the Guide. One important point to remember is that all public transport, and the bus service especially, is drastically reduced on Sundays and public holidays – don't even consider travelling to out-of-the-way places on these days. The words to look out for on timetables are *diario* (daily), *laborables* (workdays, including Sat), and *domingos y festivos* (Sun and public hols).

By train

Spanish trains, operated by **RENFE** (☎902 240 202, ⓦwww.renfe.es), tend to be efficient and comfortable, and nearly always run on time. There's a confusing array of services, though the website has a useful English-language version on which you can check timetables and even buy tickets with a credit card (printing them out at home before you travel).

Cercanías are local commuter trains in and around the major cities, while **media distancia** (regional) and **larga distancia** (long-distance) trains go under a bewildering number of names, including Avant, Alaris, Intercity (IC), Regionale and Talgo services. The difference is speed, service and number of stops, and you'll always pay more on the quickest routes (sometimes quite a lot more). The premier services are the high-speed trains, such as the **Euromed** from Barcelona to Alicante, or the expanding **AVE** (Alta Velocidad Española) network from Madrid to Seville, Málaga, Segovia/Valladolid, Zaragoza and Barcelona. The AVE trains have cut travelling times dramatically, with Madrid to Seville, for example, taking two and a half hours compared with six to nine hours on the slower trains. The AVE network is also set to expand to Valencia/Alicante (possibly

All aboard

As well as the main Spanish rail system, there are also several private and regional train lines offering a different view of some spectacular parts of the country, mainly in the north. The best is probably the narrow-gauge **FEVE line** (see p.505), which runs right across the wild northwest, from Santander in Cantabria, through Asturias to Ferrol in Galicia. Catalunya has its own local commuter line, the **FGC** (see p.707), which operates the mountain rack-railway to Montserrat, as well as the **Cremallera**, the "Zipper" (see p.776), another rack-and-pinion line that slinks up a Pyrenean valley to the sanctuary and ski station of Núria. Also in the Pyrenees is the dramatic narrow-gauge carrilet from La Pobla de Lillet to **Castellar de N'Hug** (see p.780). In the Sierra Guadarrama, just north of Madrid, the narrow-gauge line from **Cercedilla** to the ski station at Puerto de Navacerrada and then on to Cotos is a great way to see the mountains (see p.162).

by 2010), Girona and France (2012) and, eventually, to Santander/Bilbao (and on to Oviedo).

Tickets, fares and rail passes

Although you can just turn up at the station for short hops, **advance booking** is essential (and seat reservations obligatory) for long-distance outward and return journeys. Advance tickets can be bought at the stations between sixty days and five minutes before departure, but don't leave it to the last minute, as there are usually long queues (and often separate windows for the different types of train). Automatic **ticket machines** at main stations take some of the hassle out of queueing, or you can buy tickets at **travel agents** that display the RENFE sign – the cost is the same as at the station.

If your Spanish is up to it, you can call RENFE's 24-hour reservation service, or ask at local stations, but the best deals are always available **online** on the RENFE website, where "Web" and "Estrella" fares offer discounts of up to sixty percent on the full fares. Otherwise, **return fares** (*ida y vuelta*) are discounted by ten to twenty percent, depending on the service – you can buy a single, and so long as you show it when you buy the return, you'll still get the discount. There's also a whole range of other **discounted fares** of between 25 and 40 percent for those over 60 or under 26, the disabled, and children aged 4 to 11 years.

Actual fares vary wildly, but as an example, you'll pay around €16.50 on the regional service from Madrid to Salamanca (2hr 30min trip), while on the Madrid to Barcelona route you could pay €40 for the overnight "Estrella" service (9hr 30min) or from €105 on the high-speed AVE service (around 3hr).

The major pan-European **rail passes** (InterRail and Eurail) are only worth considering if you're visiting the country as part of a wider European tour. Both schemes also have single-country Spain rail passes available, which might be better value depending on your Spanish itinerary. The **InterRail Spain Pass** (Ⓦwww.raileurope .co.uk) is only available to European residents and allows three, four, six or eight days' train travel within one month, with under 26, second- and first-class versions available. For anyone else, **Eurail** (Ⓦwww .raileurope.com) has various Spain passes available, typically offering three days' travel in two months, again in various classes. You can check current prices on the websites, but bear in mind that it often works out cheaper to buy individual tickets in Spain as you need them, and it's certainly more convenient to be free to choose long-distance buses on some routes. All passes have to be bought before you leave home, and you'll still be liable for supplements and seat reservations on long-distance and high-speed trains.

By bus

Buses will probably meet most of your transport needs, especially if you're venturing away from the larger towns and cities. Many smaller villages and rural areas are only accessible by bus, almost always originating in the capital of their province. Services are pretty reliable, whether it's the two-buses-a-day school or market run or the regular services between major cities (the latter often far more conveniently scheduled than the equivalent train services). **Fares** are very reasonable, too; Madrid to León (3hr 30min), for example, costs around €20, Madrid to Santander (6hr) around €27. On inter-city runs, you'll usually be assigned a seat when you buy your ticket. Some destinations are served by more than one **bus company**, but main bus stations have posted timetables for all services or you can check timetables on the company websites (given in the Guide where appropriate); Alsa (Ⓦwww.alsa.es) is one of the main companies with nationwide services, and has an English-language version of its website.

There are only a few cities in Spain (Madrid, Barcelona and Valencia, for example) where you'll need to use the **local bus** network, and all the relevant details are given in the accounts. You'll also sometimes need to take a local bus out to a campsite or distant museum or monastery; fares are very cheap, rarely more than a euro.

By car

Spain has an extensive system of highways, both free and with tolls. The **autopistas** are

The Spanish driving experience

If it's your first time out on a Spanish road, especially in one of the bigger cities, you could be forgiven for thinking you've stumbled upon the local chapter of Mad Max devotees, out for a burn-up. In fact, those wild-eyed, dangerously speeding, non-signalling, bumper-hogging, mobile-talking, horn-sounding road warriors are normal law-abiding Spanish citizens on their way to work. **Traffic lights** and **pedestrian crossings** in particular present a difficult conceptual challenge – if you are going to stop at either, make sure you give plenty of warning to avoid another vehicle running into the back of you, and keep an eye out for cars crossing your path who have jumped the lights. **Signposting** is universally poor (yes, *that* was the turn you wanted), even on main roads and highways, while joining and exiting **autopistas/autovias** can be particularly dangerous, as it's almost a point of honour not to let anyone in or out. Many of the worst **accidents** are on the N roads, which have only a single carriageway in each direction, so take particular care on these. Major roads are generally in good **condition**, though some minor and mountain roads can be rather hairy and are little more than dirt tracks in the more remote regions. Sheep, goats and cattle are also regular hazards. Having said all this, things are (slowly) improving and drivers are a bit more careful because of increased use of radar and speed controls. The police are also setting up more **drink-driving** controls than before, though you have to remember that this is a country where it's considered a good idea to have bars in motorway service stations.

the most comfortable and best-kept roads. The second-grade roads, **autovias**, often follow similar routes, but their speed limits are lower. Many *autopistas* and some *autovias* are toll roads, relatively expensive by local standards but worth paying for the lighter traffic encountered. You can usually pay with a credit card, although it would be wise to carry enough cash just in case. Toll roads are usually designated by an "AP" or "R" or the word "*peaje*".

The Spanish **drive on the right**, and **speed limits** are enforced throughout the country. On most *autopistas* it is 120kph, on the *autovia* 90kph, and in towns and villages 50kph. Police have the power to fine drivers on the spot for speeding or any other transgressions, and if you don't have any cash, they will escort you to the nearest cash machine and issue you with a receipt there and then. You can pay by credit card at most petrol stations for **fuel** (*gasolina*), the main companies being Cepsa and Repsol.

An EU **driver's licence** is sufficient to drive in Spain. US, Canadian, Australian and New Zealand licences should also be enough, though you may want to get an International Driver's Licence as well, just to be on the safe side. If you are bringing your own car, you will need your vehicle registration and insurance papers – and check with your insurers that you are covered to drive the car abroad. It's also compulsory to carry two hazard triangles, reflective jackets in case of accident or breakdown, an official first-aid kit and a set of spare bulbs. Rear seat belts are also compulsory, as are child seats for infants.

Parking can be a big pain in the neck, especially in big cities and old-town areas. Metered parking zones usually have stays limited to a couple of hours, though parking between 8pm and 8am, on Saturday afternoons and all Sundays tends to be free. It's always worth double-checking street signs, or ask the locals, that you're allowed to park where you've just left your car, as any illegally parked vehicle will be promptly removed. If your car disappears off the street it is best to assume that it has been towed to the local pound, and enquiries in any hotel, government office or police station should produce the address. In cities it's probably best to pay extra for a hotel with parking or use a pay car park, for which you'll need to budget anything from €12 to €20 a day.

Distance chart (km)

	Alicante	Barcelona	Bilbao	Burgos	Córdoba	Granada	Jaén	León	Madrid	Málaga
Alicante	–	552	814	645	513	372	417	762	420	480
Barcelona	552	–	609	629	893	889	840	818	630	1022
Bilbao	814	609	–	160	795	820	730	350	400	930
Burgos	645	629	160	–	640	664	581	178	245	776
Córdoba	513	893	795	640	–	238	110	736	404	168
Granada	372	889	820	664	238	–	98	761	424	125
Jaén	417	840	730	581	110	98	–	677	342	211
León	762	818	350	178	736	761	677	–	349	871
Madrid	420	630	400	245	404	424	342	349	–	543
Málaga	480	1022	930	776	168	125	211	871	543	–
Murcia	82	602	785	634	482	297	342	749	408	414
Pamplona	723	490	152	210	841	869	791	404	456	993
Salamanca	630	835	398	248	604	634	543	208	219	674
San Sebastián	769	525	249	300	924	949	854	489	534	1065
Santander	837	715	103	186	820	856	762	280	428	967
Santiago de Compostela	1033	1165	596	526	1009	1032	949	364	607	1124
Seville	606	1055	861	711	149	261	300	674	537	231
Toledo	439	710	472	317	391	413	326	412	78	527
Valencia	183	365	651	590	536	510	454	702	361	649

Car rental

The cheapest way to rent a car in Spain is to arrange it before you leave home. The major international chains (Avis, Budget, Europcar, Hertz, Thrifty, for example) charge from around £100/$200 a week for a two-door Ford Ka or Ford Fiesta, more for larger vehicles and in peak holiday periods. Local Spanish companies (such as Pepecar; Ⓦ www.pepecar.com) can sometimes offer better value for money, as can the online rental outfits easyCar (Ⓦ www.easycar.com) and Skycars (Ⓦ www.skycars.com), with high-season prices starting from €25 per day for a small car.

You'll need to be 21 or over (and have been driving for at least a year) to rent a car in Spain. It's essential to check that you have adequate **insurance cover** for your rental car, and that all visible damage on a car you're picking up is duly marked on the rental sheet. It's definitely worth considering paying the extra charge to reduce the "excess" payment levied for any damage, but these waiver charges (by the day) soon add up. However, you can avoid all **excess charges** in the event of damage by taking out an annual insurance policy with Ⓦ www.insurance4carhire.com, which also covers windscreen and tyre damage.

Cycling

Cycling is a great way to see parts of the country that might otherwise pass you by, though bear in mind that Spain is one of the most mountainous countries in Europe and there are often searing high-summer temperatures with which to contend.

For serious cycle touring, you'll need your own bike and to be properly equipped. **Bike rental** itself is not common, save in resort areas or in tourist-oriented cities such as Barcelona and Madrid, where you can expect to pay up to €20 a day, or around €25 for a half-day bike tour. Although the Spanish themselves are keen sport cyclists, other facilities are practically nonexistent. Cycle paths, for example, are rare (again, Barcelona is an exception), and cycling around most major Spanish cities is a hair-raising, if not downright dangerous business.

Most airlines are happy to take bikes as ordinary **baggage**, though it's essential to check first, especially if you're flying with a budget airline, when extra charges may apply. Spanish bus drivers are reasonably amenable, and should let you throw your bicycle in with the baggage. Trains are more problematic, as there are specific trains, times and routes on which bikes are not

Murcia	Pamplona	Salamanca	San Sebastián	Santander	Santiago de Compostela	Seville	Toledo	Valencia
82	723	630	769	837	1033	606	439	183
602	490	835	525	715	1165	1055	710	365
785	152	398	249	103	596	861	472	651
634	210	248	300	186	526	711	317	590
482	841	604	924	820	1009	149	391	536
297	869	634	949	856	1032	261	413	510
342	791	543	854	762	949	300	326	454
749	404	208	489	280	364	674	412	702
408	456	219	534	428	607	537	78	361
414	993	674	1065	967	1124	231	527	649
–	772	604	812	817	1015	531	420	233
772	–	453	97	264	742	924	529	524
604	453	–	554	370	437	467	273	573
812	97	554	–	350	836	2022	631	612
817	264	370	350	–	499	896	508	769
1015	742	437	836	499	–	901	672	970
531	924	467	2022	896	901	–	507	684
420	529	273	631	508	672	507	–	378
233	524	573	612	769	970	684	378	–

allowed. As a rule, local trains are fine but high-speed trains are out, unless your bike is boxed up or you're travelling by overnight sleeper.

You should have no trouble finding bike shops in larger towns, and parts can often be found at auto repair shops or garages. On the road, cars tend to hoot before they pass, which can be alarming at first but is useful once you're used to it. Try not to leave your bike on the street overnight, even with a secure lock, as thieves view them as easy pickings.

Ferries and planes

Anyone heading from the Spanish mainland to the Balearic Islands will probably do so by **ferry** or **catamaran** express ferry (from Alicante, Barcelona, Dénia or Valencia) – all the details are in the relevant city and island chapters. However, there's also an extensive network of internal Spanish **flights**, including to and between the Balearics, with Iberia (Ⓦ www.iberia.com), Spanair (Ⓦ www .spanair.com) and other smaller operators. These can be worth it if you're in a hurry and need to cross the entire peninsula, or if you can snap up a bargain web fare, but otherwise tourists rarely use flights to get around Spain. The main exception has always been Europe's busiest air route, that between Madrid and Barcelona, though this is now facing stiff competition from the high-speed AVE train, which is comparable in overall centre-to-centre journey time, and often cheaper.

Accommodation

There's a great variety of accommodation in Spain, ranging from humble family-run pensions to five-star luxury hotels, often in dramatic historic buildings. The mainstay of the coastal resort is the typical beachfront holiday hotel, though renting an apartment or a villa gives you more freedom, while farm stays, village B&Bs, rural guesthouses and mountain inns are all increasingly popular possibilities.

Compared with other European countries, accommodation in Spain is still pretty good value. In almost any town, you'll be able to get a no-frills double room in a *pensión* or small hotel for around €40, sometimes even less, especially out in the sticks. As a rule, you can expect to pay upwards of €90 for a three-star hotel, from around €120 for four-star and boutique places, and €150–200 for five-star hotels and historic *paradores*. However, the trend is bucked by Madrid and Barcelona, in particular, and some coastal and resort areas, where rooms are often appreciably more expensive in all categories.

If you want to guarantee a room at a particular place, **advance reservations** are essential in major cities and resort areas at peak holiday, festival or convention times. Local festivals and annual events also tend to fill all available accommodation weeks in advance. That said, as a general rule, if you haven't booked, all you have to do is head for the cathedral or main square of any town, which is invariably surrounded by an old quarter full of pensions and hotels. Unlike most countries, you don't always pay more for a central location; indeed, the newer three- and four-star properties tend to be located more on the outskirts. **Families** will find that most places have rooms with three or even four beds at not a great deal more than the double-room price; however, **single travellers** often get a comparatively bad deal, and can end up paying sixty to eighty percent of the price of a double room. Accommodation prices are **seasonal**, but minimum and maximum rates should be displayed at reception. In high season on the *costas*, many hotels only take bookings for a minimum of a week, while some also require at least a half-board stay. However, it's worth noting that high season isn't always summer, in ski resorts for example, while inland cities such as Madrid tend to have cheaper prices in August, when everyone heads for the coast.

Where possible, **website** bookings nearly always offer the best deals, especially with the larger hotel groups that have made big inroads into Spain – it's always worth

Accommodation price codes

All the establishments listed in this book have been coded according to price. They represent the price for the **cheapest available double/twin room in high season** (ie Christmas/New Year, Easter, July & Aug, and other local holidays), which means that at other times you'll often be able to stay for a lower price than that suggested. We've also used price codes for private rooms in youth hostels but have given the per-person euro rate for dorm beds. Note that **seven percent tax** (IVA) is added to all accommodation bills, which might not be specifically stated until it is time to pay, so always ask if you're uncertain.

❶ €35 and under	❹ €71–100	❼ €201–250
❷ €36–50	❺ €101–150	❽ €251–300
❸ €51–70	❻ €151–200	❾ €301 and over

checking NH Hoteles (@www.nh-hotels .com), Accor/Ibis (@www.accorhotels.com) and Sol Meliá (@www.solmelia.com) for current deals.

Rooms, pensiones, hostales and hotels

The cheapest beds are usually in **private rooms**, in someone's house or above a bar or restaurant. The signs to look for are *habitaciones* (rooms) or *camas* (beds), or they might be touted at resort bus and train stations in summer as you arrive. The rooms should be clean, but might well be very simple and timeworn; you'll probably share a communal bathroom. Otherwise, official places to stay are classified as *pensiones*, *hostales* and hotels, though that's just the start of it, as several other names are used to describe accommodation throughout the country.

At the budget end of the scale are **pensiones** (marked P, classified by a two-star system), where straightforward rooms often have shared bathroom facilities (there's usually a washbasin in the room). Other variants are *fondas* (F), which traditionally had a restaurant or dining room attached, and *casas de huéspedes* (CH), literally an old-fashioned "guesthouse". In all such *pensiones*, facilities are likely to be minimal and comforts rationed; things like heating, furniture (other than bed, chair and desk) and even external windows might be too much to hope for. On the other hand, some *pensiones* are lovingly cared for and very good value.

Next step up, and far more common, are **hostales** (Hs) and **hostal-residencias** (HsR), classified from one to three stars. These are not hostels, in any sense, but budget hotels, generally offering good, if functional, rooms, usually with private bathrooms, TV and – in the better places – probably heating and air-conditioning. Many also have cheaper rooms available without private bathrooms. Some *hostales* really are excellent, with good service and up-to-date furnishings and facilities, including wi-fi or internet access.

Fully-fledged **hotels** (H), meanwhile, are graded from one to five stars, with star-rating dependent on things like room size and staffing levels rather than any intrinsic

attraction. There's often not much difference in price between a one-star hotel and a three-star *hostal*, for example, and the *hostal* might be nicer. At three and four stars, prices start to increase and you can expect soundproofing, an elevator, an English-language channel on the TV and a buffet breakfast spread. At five stars, you're in the luxury class, with pools, gyms, jacuzzis, and prices to match, and some hotels differentiate themselves again as five-star "deluxe" or "gran classe" (GL).

You can pick up lists of local accommodation from any Spanish tourist office, and there are countless websites to look at, too, including the excellent Rusticae (@www .rusticae.es), which highlights stylish rural and urban hotels across the country.

Paradores

Spain has over ninety superior hotels in a class of their own, called **paradores** (@www .parador.es), often spectacular lodgings converted from castles, monasteries and other Spanish monuments (although some are purpose-built). They can be really special places to stay, sited in the most beautiful parts of the country, or in some of the most historic cities, and prices are very good when compared with the five-star hotels with which they often compete. They are banded into five categories, depending on location and popularity, with rates starting at around €105 a night, though €150–170 is more typical. That said, a whole host of special offers and web deals (through the official website) offer rooms from as little as €60, or deals for the over 60s, the 20s to 30s or for multi-night stays.

A popular approach is to take a fly-drive holiday based around the *paradores*. There is no end of routes you could choose, but good options include the area around Madrid and through the Sierra de Gredos; along the Cantabrian coast, past the Picos de Europa; or along the French/Spanish border and through the foothills of the Pyrenees. Another popular route takes you through Galicia, and on to one of the most sumptuous *paradores* of all in Santiago de Compostela. Three-night packages, where you stay in a different *parador* every night, start at around €150 per person (based on two sharing, car rental not included). All the details are on the website, or contact the official *parador* agents, Keytel in the UK (Ⓦwww.keytel.co.uk) or Petrabax in the US (Ⓦwww.petrabax.com).

Villas, apartments and rural tourism

Most UK and European tour operators can find you a self-catering **villa** or **apartment**, usually (but not exclusively) on one of the *costas* or in the Balearics. They are rented by the week, and range from simple town-centre apartments to luxury coastal villas with private pools, and prices vary wildly. The best deals are often packages, including flights and car rental, with endless companies like First Choice (Ⓦwww.firstchoice.co.uk/villas), Holiday Villas (Ⓦwww.holiday-villas.com), Iglu Villas (Ⓦwww.igluvillas.com) and Simpson Travel (Ⓦwww.simpsontravel.com).

Casas rurales (rural houses), or *casas de pagès* in Catalunya, are where many Spanish holidaymakers stay if they have the choice. It's a wide-ranging concept, from cave dwellings to restored manor houses, many with pools and gardens, plus all mod cons. You can rent by the room, or by the property, either on a B&B basis or self-catering, depending on the accommodation. Many of the *casas* also come with opportunities to take part in outdoor activities such as horseriding, walking, fishing and cycling. They offer excellent value for money, starting at around €30 per person, even cheaper if you're in a group or staying for longer than a night or two.

ASETUR (Ⓦwww.ecoturismorural.com), the association for rural tourism in Spain, has an excellent website where you can search thousands of properties by region, while many Spanish tourist-office websites also carry information on *casas rurales*. Holiday companies in your own country may also have Spanish rural properties available, or look at the websites of some Spain-based **agencies** such as Ruralia (Cantabria and Asturias; Ⓦwww.ruralia.com), Rustic Blue (Andalucía; Ⓦwww.rusticblue.com) and Top Rural (Spain-wide; Ⓦwww.toprural.com).

Pick of the paradores

Hostal dos Reis Católicos Santiago de Compostela. Apparently the oldest hotel in the world, and certainly one of the most impressive, set in a fifteenth-century hospital at the end of the Camino de Santiago. See p.563.

Parador Condes de Alba y Aliste Zamora. One of the most beautiful *paradores* in Spain, in a fifteenth-century palace in the middle of a quiet town. See p.397.

Parador Hostal San Marcos León. One of León's major historic buildings, once a pilgrims' hostel, later a very grand sixteenth-century monastery. See p.436.

Parador de Lerma Lerma. A remarkable ducal palace facing a broad plaza of elegant beauty. See p.429.

Parador Nacional Castell de la Suda Tortosa. Tortosa's highest point, the splendid Castillo de la Suda, looms majestically over the lush Ebre valley. See p.823.

Youth hostels

There are around 230 youth hostels (*albergues juveniles*) in Spain under the umbrella of the **Red Española de Albergues Juveniles** (REAJ; Ⓦ www.reaj .com), the Spanish youth hostel association that is affiliated to the international organization, Hostelling International (HI; Ⓦ www .hihostels.com). There are full details of each hostel on the REAJ website (English-language version available), and we've included some of the best in the Guide. However, many hostels are only open in the spring and summer, or tend to be inconveniently located in some cities; they also generally have curfews (not so much of a problem in mountain areas) or can be block-booked by school/youth groups. You'll also need an HI membership card, though you can buy one at most hostels on your first night. In the end, it's the price that's the main stumbling block: at €16–25 a night in high season (less for under 26s, and out of season) for a bunk bed with shared facilities, they're no cheaper than a basic double room in a *hostal* or *pensión*. That said, hostels are good places to meet other travellers, and there are some really well-located ones, especially in Andalucía, in the hiking regions of northern Spain, and in Barcelona, Madrid and Valencia.

Some cities – Madrid, Barcelona and Valencia particularly – also have a range of private **backpacker hostels**, not affiliated to the official organizations. Prices are similar, they tend to open all year round and you won't need a membership card; the other advantages are that many are brand-new, often with private rooms as well as dorms, and with excellent facilities (cafés, internet, bike rental, tours, etc).

Mountain refuges, monasteries and pilgrim accommodation

In isolated mountain areas and some of the national parks, climbers and trekkers can stay in **refugios**, basically simple dormitory huts, generally equipped only with bunks and a very basic kitchen. They are run by local mountaineering organizations, mostly on a first-come-first-served basis, which means they fill up quickly in high summer, though you can book in advance at some (or bring a tent and camp outside). Overnight prices start around €14 per person (or €30 with a meal included).

It is sometimes possible to stay at Spanish **monasterios** or **conventos**, which may let empty cells for a small charge. You can just turn up and ask – many will take visitors regardless of sex – but if you want to be sure of a reception, it's best to approach the local *turismo* first, or phone ahead. There are some particularly wonderful monastic locations in Galicia, Castilla y León, Catalunya and Mallorca. If you're following the Camino de Santiago, you can take full advantage of monastic accommodation specifically reserved for **pilgrims** along the route; see p.570 for more information.

Camping

There are literally hundreds of authorized campsites in Spain, mostly on the coast and in holiday areas. They work out at about €4.50 per person plus the same again for a tent, and a similar amount for each car or caravan. The best-located sites, or the ones with top-range facilities (restaurant, swimming pool, bar, supermarket), are significantly more expensive. If you plan to camp extensively, buy the annual *Guía de Campings*, which you can find in large bookshops, or visit Ⓦ www .vayacamping.net.

In most cases, **camping outside campsites** is legal – but there are certain restrictions. You're not allowed to camp "in urban areas, areas prohibited for military or touristic reasons, or within 1km of an official campsite". What this means in practice is that you can't camp on the beach (though you can, discreetly, nearby). In national parks, camping is only allowed in officially designated areas. Aside from these restrictions, however, and with a little sensitivity, you can set up a tent for a short period almost anywhere in the countryside. Whenever possible, ask locally first.

Food and drink

Spanish cuisine has come a long way in recent years, and Spanish chefs are currently at the forefront of contemporary European cooking. You know a power-shift has taken place when what is popularly regarded as the best restaurant in the world, El Bulli, is situated on an isolated stretch of the Catalan coast and it's still booked solid a year in advance. Often, what superchef Ferran Adrià and his disciples all across Spain are doing is arguably less like cooking and more like chemistry, with the foams, gelatins, essences and reductions that are at the heart of much new-wave Spanish cuisine. But there's some fantastic food to be had in every region, and not just the fancy stuff – the tapas, gazpacho, tortilla and paella that you may know from home are simply in a different league when made with the correct ingredients in their natural surroundings.

Of course, not every restaurant is a gourmet experience and not every dish is a classic of its kind. Tourist resorts – after all, where many people go – can be disappointing, especially those aimed at a foreign clientele, and a week on one of the *costas* can just as easily convince you that the Spanish national diet is egg and chips, *sangría*, pizza and Guinness. However, you'll always find a good restaurant where the locals eat, and few places in Europe are still as good value, especially if you have the *menú del día*, the bargain fixed-price lunch that's a fixture across the country.

Each chapter of the Guide highlights the **regional specialities** you'll come across, from Andalucía to Galicia, while for a **menu reader** turn to pp.977–980.

Breakfast, snacks and sandwiches

The traditional Spanish **breakfast** (*desayuno*) is *chocolate con churros* – long, extruded tubular doughnuts served with thick drinking chocolate or coffee. Some places specialize in these but most bars and cafés also serve cakes and pastries (*bollos* or *pasteles*), croissants and toast (*tostadas*), or crusty sandwiches (*bocadillos*) with a choice of fillings (try one with omelette, *tortilla*). A "sandwich", incidentally, is usually a less appetizing ham or cheese sandwich in white processed bread. Other good places for snacks are **cake shops** (*pastelerías* or

confiterías) or the local bakery (*panadería*), where they might also have savoury pasties and turnovers.

Bars, tapas and raciones

One of Spain's glories is the phenomenon of **tapas** – the little portions of food that traditionally used to be served up free with a drink in a bar. (The origins are disputed but the word is from *tapar*, "to cover", suggesting a cover for drinks' glasses, perhaps to keep the flies off in the baking sun.) Tapas can be anything – a handful of olives, a slice or two of cured ham, a little dish of meatballs or *chorizo*, spicy fried potatoes or battered squid. They will often be laid out on the counter, so you can see what's available, or there might be a blackboard menu. Most bars have a speciality; indeed, Spaniards will commonly move from bar to bar, having just the one dish that they consider each bar does well. Conversely, if you're in a bar with just some pre-fried potatoes and day-old Russian salad on display, and a prominent microwave, go somewhere else to eat.

Aside from a few olives or crisps sometimes handed out with a drink, you pay for tapas these days (the cities of Granada and León, are honourable exceptions), usually around €1.50–4 a portion. **Raciones** (around €6–12) are simply bigger plates of tapas, perfect for sharing or enough for a meal – you're sometimes asked if you want a tapa or a *racion* of whatever it is you've chosen.

There are big regional variations in tapas, not least in nomenclature. They are often called **pinchos** (or *pintxos*) in northern Spain, especially in the Basque provinces, where typically tapas comes served on a slice of baguette, held together with a cocktail stick. When you've finished eating, the sticks are counted up to arrive at your bill. This kind of tapas can be as simple as a cheese cube on bread or a far more elaborately sculpted concoction; they are also known as **monta-ditos** (basically, canapés). Famously good places across Spain for tapas-tasting include Madrid, León, Logroño, San Sebastián and Seville.

Most cafés and bars have some kind of tapas available, while you'll also find a decent display in **tascas**, **bodegas** and **tabernas** (kinds of taverns) and **cervecerías** (beer-houses). It's always cheapest to stand at the bar to eat; you'll pay more to sit at tables and more again to sit outside on a terrace.

Restaurants

The simplest kind of restaurant is the **comedor** (dining room), often a room at the back of a bar or the dining room of a *hostal* or *pensión*. Traditionally, they are family-run places aimed at lunching workers, usually offering a straightforward set meal at budget prices. The highway equivalent are known as **ventas**, or inns, dotted along the main roads between towns and cities. These have been serving Spanish wayfarers for centuries – some of them quite literally – and the best places are immediately picked out by the line of cars and trucks outside. Proper restaurants, **restaurantes**, come in a myriad of guises, from rustic village restaurants to stylish Michelin-starred eateries; **asadores** specialize in grilled meats, **marisquerías** in fish and seafood.

Almost every *comedor* and *restaurante* serves a weekday, fixed-price lunchtime meal, the **menú del día**, generally three courses including wine for €9–15, occasionally even cheaper, depending on where you are in Spain (you might also see the words *cubierto* or *menú de la casa*). This is obviously a terrific deal; the *menú del día* is only sporadically available at night, and sometimes prices are slightly higher (and the menu slightly fancier) at weekends. The very cheapest places are unlikely to have a written menu, and the waiter will tell you what the day's dishes are. In smarter restaurants in bigger cities and resorts, there will still be a *menú del día*, though it might be a shadow of the usual à la carte menu, and drinks may be excluded. Even so, it's a way of eating at a restaurant that might normally cost you three or four times as much. Top city restaurants often also feature an upmarket *menú* called a **menú de degustación** (tasting menu), which again can be excellent value, allowing you to try

It's food, Jim, but not as we know it

King of molecular gastronomy, and godfather of Spanish contemporary cuisine, **Ferran Adrià**, started it all, with his liquid-nitrogen-frozen herbs, seafood-reduction Rice Krispies and exploding olive-oil droplets. From his triple-Michelin-starred, world's-best-acclaimed *El Bulli*, near Roses in Catalunya, the influences of Spain's best-known chef have shaken the restaurant scene, as his former employees, acolytes and disciples have gone on to make the country one of the most exciting places to eat in the world. The style-city of Barcelona, not surprisingly, is at the forefront of this innovative form of cooking, with **Carles Abellan**'s *Comerç 24* typical of the breed, while the **Roca brothers**' *El Celler de Can Roca* (Girona) and **Santi Santamaria**'s *Can Fabes* (Sant Celoni) keep Catalunya firmly at the vanguard of new-wave cuisine. However, it's in the Basque Country that many of the hottest chefs are currently in action: **Andoni Aduriz** at *Mugaritz* (Errenteria, San Sebastián), **Juan Mari Arzak** at *Arzak* (San Sebastián), **Martín Berasategui** at *Restaurante Martín Berasategui* (Lasarte-Oria, San Sebastián) are all cooking sensational food in restaurants that regularly feature in lists of the world's best. Maybe it's a northern thing, but there's less fuss in the south of the country about the so-called *cocina de autor*; perhaps only **Sergi Arola** at *La Broche* (Madrid) cuts the new-wave mustard.

out some of the country's finest cooking for anything from €40 to €80 a head.

Otherwise, in bars and so-called cafeterías, meals often come in the form of a **plato combinado** – literally a combined dish – which will be a one-plate meal of something like steak, egg and chips, or

calamares and salad, often with bread and a drink included. This will generally cost in the region of €6–9.

If you want a menu in a restaurant, ask for la carta; menú refers only to the fixed-price meal. In all but the most rock-bottom establishments it is customary to leave a

Spanish cuisine

There really is no such thing as traditional "Spanish" cuisine, since every region claims a quite separate culinary heritage. That said, lots of dishes crop up right across the country, whatever their origin, while the typical Mediterranean staples reflect Spain's rich agricultural backdrop – olive oil, tomatoes, peppers, garlic, onions, lemons and oranges.

It's usual to start your meal with a **salad** or a plate of cold cuts, while **soups** might be fish or seafood or, in the north especially, hearty broths such as the Galician cabbage-and-potato caldo gallego. Boiled potatoes with greens, or a thick minestrone of vegetables, are also fairly standard starters, while depending on the season and region you might be offered grilled asparagus or artichokes, or stewed beans with chunks of sausage.

Fish and **seafood** are ubiquitous, even hundreds of kilometres from the sea. Inland, it might just be salted cod (bacalao), or frozen prawns or squid, though river fish like trout are also common. But anywhere near the coast, you really should make the most of what's on offer, whether it's the fried fish of Málaga, Basque shellfish or the seafood specialities in Galicia, notably the octopus (pulpo). Fish stews (zarzuelas) can be memorable, while seafood rice dishes range from arroz negro ("black rice", cooked with squid ink) to the better-known **paella**. This comes originally from Valencia (still the best place for an authentic one), though a proper paella from there doesn't include fish or seafood at all but things like chicken, rabbit, beans and snails.

Meat is most often grilled and served with a few fried potatoes and a couple of salad leaves. Regional specialities include lamb (cordero) from Segovia, Navarra and the Basque Country, as well as cochinillo (suckling pig) or lechal (suckling lamb) in central Spain. **Cured ham**, or jamón serrano, is superb, produced at its best from acorn-fed Iberian pigs in Extremadura and Andalucía, though it can be extremely expensive. Every region has a local **sausage** in its locker – the best known is the spicy chorizo, made from pork, though others include morcilla (blood sausage; best in Burgos, León and Asturias), and butifarra, a white Catalan sausage made from pork and tripe. **Stews** are typified by the mighty fabada, a fill-your-boots Asturian bean-and-meat concoction.

Cheese is excellent right across the country. Ones to look out for include Cabrales, a tangy blue cheese made in the Picos de Europa; Manchego, a sharp, nutty cheese made from sheep's milk in La Mancha; Mahon, a cow's milk cheese from Menorca, often with paprika rubbed into its rind; Idiazábal, a smoked cheese from the Basque Country; and Zamorano, made from sheep's milk in Old Castile and León.

In most restaurants, **dessert** is nearly always fresh fruit or flan, the Spanish crème caramel, with the regions often having their own versions such as crema catalana in Catalunya and the Andalucian tocino de cielo. There are also many varieties of postre – rice pudding or assorted blancmange mixtures – and a range of commercial ice-cream dishes.

If you want to know more about the food in the region where you're travelling, turn to the special **features** on the cuisine Castilla y León (p.379), the Basque Country (p.458), Asturias (p.548), Galicia (p.555) and Valencia (p.833).

small **tip** (*propina*), though five percent of the bill is considered sufficient and service is normally included in a *menú del día*. IVA, the seven-percent **tax**, is also charged, but it should say on the menu if this is included in the price or not.

Spaniards generally eat very late, with **lunch** served from around 1pm (you'll generally be the first person there at this time) until 4pm, and **dinner** from 8.30pm or 9pm to midnight. Obviously, rural areas are slightly earlier to dine, but making a dinner reservation for 10.30pm or even later is considered perfectly normal in many cities in Spain. Most restaurants **close one day a week**, usually Sunday or Monday or a combination of those evenings.

Vegetarians

Vegetarians generally have a fairly hard time of it in Spain, though there's an increasing number of veggie restaurants in the bigger cities (including some really good ones in Madrid and Barcelona). In more rural areas, there's usually something to eat, but you may get weary of eggs and omelettes. Otherwise, superb fresh fruit and veg, and excellent cheese, is always available in the markets and shops.

In restaurants, you're faced with the extra problem that pieces of meat – especially ham, which the Spanish don't regard as real meat – and tuna are often added to vegetable dishes and salads to "spice them up". You'll also find chunks of *chorizo* and sausage turning up in otherwise veg-friendly soups or bean stews. The phrases to get to know are *Soy vegetariano/a. Como sólo verduras. Hay algo sin carne?* ("I'm a vegetarian. I only eat vegetables. Is there anything without meat?"); you may have to add *y sin marisco* ("and without seafood") and *y sin jamón* ("and without ham") to be really safe.

Some salads and vegetable dishes are strictly **vegan**, but they're few and far between. Fruit and nuts are widely available, nuts being sold by street vendors everywhere.

Coffee, tea and soft drinks

Café (coffee) is invariably an espresso (*café solo*); for a large cup of weaker, black coffee, ask for an *americano*. A *café cortado* is a *café solo* with a drop of milk; a *café con leche* is made with lots of hot milk. Coffee is also frequently mixed with brandy, cognac or whisky, all such concoctions being called *carajillo*. Iced coffee is *café con hielo*. **Chocolate** (hot chocolate) is a popular breakfast drink, or for after a long night on the town, but it's usually incredibly thick and sweet. For a thinner, cocoa-style drink, ask for a brand name, like Cola Cao.

Spaniards usually drink **té** (tea) black, so if you want milk it's safest to ask for it afterwards, since ordering *té con leche* might well get you a glass of warm milk with a tea bag floating on top. Herbal teas (*infusions*) are widely available, like *manzanilla* (camomile), *poleo* (mint tea) and *hierba luisa* (lemon verbena).

Local soft drinks include **granizado** (slush) or **horchata** (a milky drink made from tiger nuts or almonds), available from summer street stalls, and from milk bars (*horchaterías*, also known as *granjas* in Catalunya) and ice-cream parlours (*heladerías*). Although you can drink the **water** almost everywhere, it tastes revolting in some cities and coastal areas – inexpensive *agua mineral* comes either sparkling (*con gas*) or still (*sin gas*).

Wine, beer and spirits

Wine (*vino*) is the invariable accompaniment to every meal, with reasonable-quality wines available in most restaurants and bars, although in budget eating places you'll rarely be offered a wide choice (it's often just straight from the barrel). A small glass of wine in a local bar can cost as little as €0.70, though anywhere serious about wine will have a range by the glass up to €4 or more. At lunchtime, the house wine is usually included in the *menú del día*; otherwise, restaurant wine starts at around €5–10 a bottle, although the sky's the limit for the really good stuff. In recent years, Spanish wine has enjoyed a huge upturn in quality and clout, led largely by the international success of regions like La Rioja, Ribera del Duero and Priorat; in Andalucía, the classic wine is **sherry** (*vino de jerez*), while champagne in Spain means the Catalan sparkling wine, **cava**. For much more on wine, sherry and cava, including recommended vineyards and vintages, see the **Wines of Spain colour section**.

The festival and tourist drink is, famously, **sangría**, a wine-and-fruit punch that's often deceptively strong; a variation in Catalunya is *sangría de cava*. *Tinto de verano* is a similar red wine-and-soda or -lemonade combination; variations on this include *tinto de verano con naranja* (red wine with orangeade) or *con limón* (lemonade).

Beer (*cerveza*) is nearly always lager, though some Spanish breweries also now make stout-style brews, wheat beers and other types. It comes in 300ml bottles (*botellines*) or, for about the same price, on tap – a *caña* of draught beer is a small glass, a *caña doble* larger, and asking for *un tubo* (a tubular glass) gets you about half a pint. Mahou, Cruz Campo, San Miguel, Damm, Estrella de Galicia and Alhambra are all decent beers. A **shandy** is a *clara*, either with fizzy lemon (*con limón*) or lemonade (*con casera*).

In mid-afternoon – or, let's face it, even at breakfast – Spaniards take a *copa* of liqueur with their coffee, such as *anís* (similar to Pernod) or *coñac*, the local **brandy**, which has a distinct vanilla flavour. Most brandies are produced by the great sherry houses in Jerez, but two good ones that aren't are the Armagnac-like Mascaró and Torres, both from Catalunya. Instead of brandy, at the end of a meal many places serve **chupitos** – little shot glasses of flavoured schnapps or local fire water, such as Patxarán in Navarra and the Basque Country, Ratafía in Catalunya or Orujo in Galicia. One much-loved Galego custom is the *queimada*, when a large bowl of *aguardiente* (a herb-flavoured fiery liqueur) with fruit, sugar and coffee-grains is set alight and then drunk hot.

You should order **spirits** by brand name, since there are generally less expensive Spanish equivalents for standard imports, or simply specify *nacional*. Larios gin from Málaga, for instance, is about half the price of Gordon's. Measures are staggeringly generous – bar staff generally pour from the bottle until you suggest they stop. Long drinks include the universal *Gin-Tónic* and the *Cuba Libre* (rum and Coke), and there are often Spanish Caribbean rums (*ron*) such as Cacique from Venezuela or Havana Club from Cuba.

The media

The ubiquitous Spanish newspaper kiosk is your first stop for regional and national newspapers and magazines, though hotels and bars nearly always have a few kicking around for customers. The bigger cities, tourist towns and resorts will also have foreign newspapers available (some of which are actually published in Spain), generally on the day of issue or perhaps a day late. Television is all-pervasive in bars, cafés and restaurants, and you're going to find yourself watching more bullfighting, basketball and Venezuelan soap operas than perhaps you'd bargained for; most pensión and hotel rooms have a TV, too, though only in the fancier places will you get any English-language programming, and then probably only the BBC News, CNN or Eurosport satellite channels.

Newspapers and magazines

Of the Spanish **national newspapers** the best are the Madrid-based centre-left *El País* (ⓦwww.elpais.es) and the centre-right *El Mundo* (ⓦwww.elmundo.es), both of which have good arts and foreign news coverage, including comprehensive regional "what's on" listings and supplements every weekend. Other national papers include the solidly elitist *ABC* and Barcelona's *La Vanguardia*. The **regional press** is generally run by local magnates and is predominantly right of centre, though often supporting local autonomy movements. Nationalist press includes *Avui* in Catalunya, printed in Catalan, and the Basque papers *El Correo Español del Pueblo Vasco*, *Deia* and *Gara*, the last of which has close links with ETA. All that said, the paper with the highest circulation is *Marca* (Ⓦwww.marca.com), the country's top **sports daily**, mainly football-dominated; there's also *As* (Ⓦwww.as.com), *El Mundo Deportivo* (Ⓦwww.elmundodeportivo.es) and *Sport* (Ⓦwww.sport.es). The main cities are also awash with **free newspapers**, which are dished out at bus and metro stops.

There's a bewildering variety of **magazines** specializing in celebrity gossip (known collectively as *la prensa rosa*), ranging from the more traditional *Hola* to the sensationalist *Que me Dices*. *El Jueves* is the Spanish equivalent of *Viz*, while the online daily *El Confidencial* (Ⓦwww.elconfidencial.com) gives the inside track on many serious economic and political stories. There are also various **English-language magazines** and papers produced by and for the expatriate communities in the main cities and on the *costas*, such as *InMadrid* (Ⓦwww.in-madrid.com), *Barcelona Metropolitan* (Ⓦwww.barcelona-metropolitan.com), and *Sur in English* (Ⓦwww.surinenglish.com), which covers southern Spain.

Radio

There are hundreds of local radio channels, broadcasting in Spanish and regional languages, alongside a handful of national ones. The state-run **RNE** (Ⓦwww.rtve.es/radio) network covers five stations: RNE 1, a general news and information channel; Radio Clásica, broadcasting mainly classical music and related programmes; the popular music channel RNE 3; RNE 4, in Catalan; and the rolling news and sports channel RNE 5. Radio Exterior is RNE's international shortwave service. Other **popular channels** include Cadena Ser and Onda Cero (news, talk, sports and culture), the Catholic Church-run COPE, 40 Principales (for the latest hits, Spanish and otherwise) and Cadena 100 (music and cultural programming). Radio Marca (dedicated sports radio) is also very popular. Full listings, local stations and frequencies can be found in *El País* and the local press, or bring a shortwave radio to tune in to the BBC World Service (Ⓦwww.bbc.co.uk/worldservice) or Voice of America (Ⓦwww.voa.gov).

Television

RTV (Ⓦwww.rtve.es/television) provides the main, state-run channels, namely TVE1, a general entertainment and news channel, and its sister La 2 (ie "Dos"), given over to sports and culture. Private national stations are Antena 3, Cuatro (ie Four), Telecinco (Five) and La Sexta (Sixth). There are also plenty of **regional channels**, the most important being Catalunya's TV3 and Canal 33, both broadcast in Catalan, and the Basque Country's ETB1 (in Basque) and ETB2, though there are also stations in Galicia (TVG), Andalucía (Canal Sur) and Valencia (Canal Nou) with local programming. The main satellite channel is Canal+.

Festivals

The fiesta is an absolutely crucial part of Spanish life. Even the smallest village or most modern city suburb devotes at least a couple of days a year to partying, and coinciding with such an event can be huge fun, propelling you right into the heart of Spanish culture. As well as local celebrations, Spain has some really major events worth planning your whole trip around – most famously, the Fiesta de San Fermín at Pamplona (July), Las Fallas in Valencia (March), Seville's Feria de Abril, the pre-Lenten Carnival festivities and the great religious processions of Semana Santa, leading up to Easter. One thing they all tend to have in common is a curious blend of religious ceremony and pagan ritual – sombre processions of statuary followed by exuberant merrymaking – in which fire plays a prominent part.

What follows is a very basic **annual festival calendar**, concentrating mainly on the notable religious, cultural and traditional fiestas. Otherwise, turn to the feature boxes at the beginning of each chapter for more information, where the various regional music and arts festivals are also covered. The **"Fiestas"** colour section also has more on the Spanish "Big Four" of Las Fallas, Semana Santa, Feria de Abril and San Fermín.

Outsiders are always welcome at fiestas, the only problem being that it can be hard to find a hotel, unless you book well in advance. The other thing to note is that not every fiesta is a national public holiday, or vice versa, but even so you might get stuck if you arrive in town in the middle of an annual event, when everything will be closed.

January

5 Cabalgata de Reyes When the Three Magi arrive to bring the children their presents for Epiphany. Any medium-to-large city will stage a spectacular and colourful procession as the Three Kings are driven through the streets throwing sweets to the crowds.
16–17 San Antoni's day Preceded by bonfires and processions, especially on the Balearic Islands.

February

Week preceding Ash Wednesday and Lent Carnaval An excuse for wild partying and masques, most riotous in Cádiz (Andalucía), Sitges (Catalunya) and Águilas (Valencia).

March

12–19 Las Fallas Valencia holds the biggest of the bonfire festivals held for San José, climaxing on the Night of Fire (Nit de Foc) when enormous caricatures are burnt, and firecrackers let off in the streets.

Easter

March/April Semana Santa (Holy Week) Celebrated across Spain with religious processions, at their most theatrical in the cities of Seville, Málaga, Murcia and Valladolid, where *pasos* – huge floats of religious scenes – are carried down the streets, accompanied by hooded penitents atoning for the year's misdeeds. Good Friday sees the biggest, most solemn processions.

April

22–24 Moros y Cristianos Mock battle between Moors and Christians in Alcoy, Valencia. (Similar events take place throughout the year all around Spain.)
23 Sant Jordi (St George's Day) Catalunya's patron saint occasions a big party across the region. Being the birth date of Cervantes, it's also celebrated as National Book Day throughout Spain.
Last week Feria de Abril Spectacular week-long fair in Seville, with a major bullfighting festival.

May

Early May Horse Fair Jerez (Andalucía).
7–22 San Isidro Madrid's patron saint's day (15th) is a signal for parades, free concerts and the start of the bullfight season.
Seventh Sunday after Easter Pentecost (Whitsun) Great pilgrimage to El Rocío, near Huelva (Andalucía).
Thursday after Trinity Sunday Corpus Christi Focus for religious processions, accompanied by floats and penitents, notably in Toledo, Granada and

Valencia. Many town fiestas also take place, including the spectacular costumed events of the Festa de la Patum, in Berga (Catalunya).
Last week Feria de la Manzanilla Celebrates the famous sherry of Sanlúcar de Barrameda (Andalucía).

June

23–24 San Juan/Midsummer's Eve Celebrated with bonfires all over Spain – particularly in San Juan de Alicante, where a local version of Las Fallas takes place, and in Barcelona where the Nit del Foc (Night of Fire) marks a hedonistic welcome to summer.
29 San Pedro The patron saintof fishermen is honoured by flotillas of boats – and partying – all along the coast.

July

7–14 San Fermín The famed Running of the Bulls at Pamplona.
25 Santiago Spain's patron saint, St James, is honoured at Santiago de Compostela, with fireworks and bonfires.
26 Blanes Spectacular week-long fireworks competition on the Costa Brava, with teams from all around the world.
Last three weeks Pirineos Sur World Music festival on a floating stage at Lanuza, near Sallent de Gállego, in the Pyrenees.

August

10–11 Misteri d'Eix Elche (Valencia) hosts mock battles between Christians and Moors, ending with a centuries-old mystery play.
First/second week Descenso Internacional del Sella Mass canoe races down the Río Sella in Asturias.

Last week Gigantones (giant puppets) are paraded in Alcalá de Henares, near Madrid.
Last Wednesday La Tomatina Buñol, near Valencia, hosts the country's craziest fiesta, a one-hour tomato fight.

September

First week Vendimia The grape harvest is celebrated in Valdepeñas (Castilla-La Mancha), Jerez (Andalucía) and other wine towns.
11 Diada Nacional de Catalunya Catalan public holiday commemorating its loss of independence. Various cultural and sporting events over the weekends before and after.
21 Rioja wine harvest Celebrated in Logroño (La Rioja).

October

1 San Miguel Villages across the country celebrate their patron saint's day.
12 La Virgen del Pilar Honouring the patron saint of Aragón is an excuse for bullfights and *jota* dancing at Zaragoza and elsewhere.

December

24 Nochebuena Christmas Eve is particularly exuberant, with parties and carousing early in the evening before it all suddenly stops in time for family dinner or Mass.
31 Nochevieja New Year is celebrated by eating a grape for every stroke of the clock in Plaza del Sol in Madrid, Plaça de Catalunya in Barcelona, and main squares and bars throughout the country.

Culture and etiquette

Spain is a fantastically welcoming, vibrant country, characterized by its love of life. With a population of over 44 million it's a diverse place, too, with regional identities as characteristic as their local landscapes: the Basques, Galicians and Catalans all adding their own languages and cultures to the mix. No matter where you decide to visit though, many of the clichés of Spanish life, such as the siesta, busy bars and restaurants open late into the night, and towns celebrating lively festivals, still pretty much ring true.

Social life and etiquette

One of the most important aspects of Spanish life is the **family**; no celebration would be complete without an extended gathering, although this is more common away from the busy cities where modern life takes its toll. Even so, the elderly are respected, and it's not uncommon to have older relatives being cared for in the family home. Likewise, children are absolutely adored, and included in everything.

Food plays an important part in Spanish family life, with lunch (*la comida*) the biggest meal of the day, often lasting from 2 to 4pm. It's common for shops and whole villages to come to a standstill for the afternoon meal and **siesta**, especially in more out-of-the-way places. Evening meals, which often start as late as 10pm, are usually preceded by a leisurely stroll, or **paseo**, when you may take in an aperitif in a bar or two.

Friends are more likely to meet in restaurants for meals, but if you are **invited to someone's house** for dinner, you should take a small gift for any children, along with chocolates, a bottle of wine, or some flowers (though avoid dahlias, chrysanthemums and flowers in odd numbers as these would only be given at funerals). Also bear in mind that **drinking** too much isn't common, and despite the fact there seems to be a bar on every corner, this is more for coffee and socializing than heavy boozing.

The Spanish are among the biggest **smokers** in Europe, with an estimated thirty percent of the population smoking regularly. Attitudes are changing, however, and the law now bans smoking in workplaces, shops, schools and on public transport. Bars and restaurants that occupy over a hundred square metres now have to have a non-smoking (*Prohibido Fumar*) area and air-conditioning. Bars under a hundred square metres can opt to be either smoking or non-smoking and, tellingly, almost all have chosen the former. Consequently, making a fuss about someone smoking near you when they shouldn't be probably won't get you very far.

Tipping is common in Spain, although not always expected, but locals are small tippers and five percent on a restaurant or bar bill is usually enough. It is also common practice to tip taxi drivers, hotel porters and the like in small change.

If you are planning to indulge in any topless **sunbathing**, consider local feelings first, and try to stick to beaches where people are already doing it. You also need to make sure you are properly covered if you enter a **church**; shorts and sleeveless tops should be avoided.

Greetings

If you're **meeting someone** for the first time, you should shake their hand. If you become friends, you may well move on to hugging (men) or kisses on each cheek (women), starting with the left. Men are also more likely to kiss women hello and goodbye, than shake their hand. To say **hello**, use *Buenos días* before lunch and *Buenos tardes* after that. Bear in mind that in Spain the sense of time is somewhat elastic, so unless you're meeting for business (when being late is very bad form) don't be offended if you are left waiting for a good ten or twenty minutes.

Sports and outdoor activities

Spain is nothing if not enthusiastic about sport, with football and basketball all but national obsessions, and bullfighting – whether or not you agree it's a "sport" – one of its cultural highlights. There are also plenty of opportunities to get out and enjoy the country's stunning outdoors, whether it's ambling around a golf course, skiing in the southern slopes, chasing surf off the Basque Country coast or canyoning in the Pyrenees. For details of tour operators specializing in activity holidays, see "Getting there" on p.31, while for separate information on hiking in Spain, see the "Walking in Spain" colour section.

Basketball

Basketball (*baloncesto*) comes second only to football in national interest, its profile further enhanced in 2006 when Spain won the basketball World Championships for the first time. There are eighteen professional teams competing in the most important league, **ACB** (Ⓦwww.acb.com), whose season runs from September to June. Other big competitions include the Copa del Rey and the Europe-wide Euroleague. The two biggest teams, coincidentally owned by the two most successful football teams, are Barcelona and Real Madrid; they have won the ACB (until 1983 known as the Liga Nacional) some 45 times between them since competition began in 1956. The other most important teams include Adecco Estudiantes from Madrid and Unicaja from Málaga, Tau Ceramica from Vitoria, Pamesa Valencia from Valencia, and DKV Joventut from Barcelona. For more information, see the website of the Federacion Española de Baloncesto (Ⓦwww.feb.es), which has the latest news in English.

Games are broadcast on TV, or match tickets can be bought at individual venues, and cost from around €15.

Basque sports

The Basque sport of **pelota** (a version of which is known as *jai alai*, Basque for "happy party") is played all over Spain, but in Euskal Herria even the smallest village has a *pelota* court or *fronton*, and betting on the sport is rife. **Rowing** is another Basque obsession, and regattas are held every weekend in summer. During local fiestas, you'll also see other unique Basque sports including *aizkolaritza* (log-chopping), *harri-jasotzea* (stone-lifting), *soka-tira* (tug-of-war) and *segalaritza* (grass-cutting). The finest exponents of the first two in particular are popular local heroes (the world champion stone-lifter Iñaki Perurena's visit to Japan resulted in the sport being introduced there – he remains the only lifter to surpass the legendary 315kg barrier).

Bullfighting

The bullfight is a classic image of Spain, and an integral part of many fiestas. In the south, especially, any village that can afford it will put on a *corrida* for an afternoon, while in big cities such as Madrid or Seville, the main festival times are accompanied by a season of prestige fights. However, with the exception of Pamplona, bullfighting is far more popular in Madrid and all points south than it is in the north or on the islands. Indeed, many northern cities don't have bullrings, Barcelona has declared itself an anti-bullfight city, while the Canary Islands' regional government has gone so far as to ban bullfighting. Spain's main opposition to bullfighting is organized by **ADDA** (Asoci-ación para la Defensa del Animal), who coordinate the Anti-Bullfight Campaign (ABC) International and also produce a quarterly newsletter in Spanish and English. Their website (Ⓦwww.addaong.org) has informa-tion (in English) about international campaigns and current actions, while at Ⓦwww.canaryforum.com/gc/bull you'll find a stark description of everything surrounding the spectacle.

Los Toros, as Spaniards refer to bullfighting, is certainly big business. It is said that 150,000 people are involved, in some way, in the industry, and the top performers, the *matadores*, are major earners, on a par with the country's biggest pop stars. To *aficionados* (a word that implies more knowledge and appreciation than "fan"), the bulls are a culture and a ritual – with the emphasis on the way man and bull "perform" together – in which the *arte* is at issue rather than the cruelty. If pressed on the issue of the slaughter of an animal, they generally fail to understand. Fighting bulls are, they will tell you, bred for the industry; they live a reasonable life before they are killed, and, if the bullfight went, so, too, would the bulls.

If you decide to attend a *corrida*, try to see a big, prestigious event, where star performers are likely to despatch the bulls with "art" and a successful, "clean" kill. There are few sights worse than a *matador* making a prolonged and messy kill, while the audience whistles and chucks cushions. The most skilful events are those featuring mounted *matadores*, or *rejoneadores*; this is the oldest form of *corrida*, developed in Andalucía in the seventeenth century.

Popular **matadores** include the veteran Enrique Ponce, José Tomas, César Rincón, Cayetano Rivera, Finito de Cordoba, Litri and Julián "El Juli" López. A complete guide to bullfighting with exhaustive links can be found at ⊛www.mundo-taurino.org.

The corrida

The **corrida** begins with a procession, to the accompaniment of a *paso doble* by the band. Leading the procession are two *algauziles*, or "constables", on horseback and in traditional costume, followed by the three *matadores*, who will each fight two bulls, and their *cuadrillas*, their personal "team", each comprising two mounted *picadores* and three *banderilleros*. At the back are the mule teams who will drag off the dead bulls.

Once the ring is empty, an *algauzil* opens the *toril* (the bulls' enclosure) and the first bull appears, to be "tested" by the *matador* or his *banderilleros* using pink and gold capes.

These preliminaries conducted (and they can be short, if the bull is ferocious), the **suerte de picar** ensues, in which the *picadores* ride out and take up position at opposite sides of the ring, while the bull is distracted by other *toreros*. Once they are in place, the bull is made to charge one of the horses; the *picador* drives his short-pointed lance into the bull's neck, while it tries to toss his padded, blindfolded horse, thus tiring the bull's powerful neck and back muscles. This is repeated up to three times, until the horn sounds for the *picadores* to leave. Cries of "*fuera!*" (out) often greet the overzealous use of the lance, for by weakening the bull too much they fear the beast will not be able to put up a decent fight. For many, this is the least acceptable stage of the *corrida*, and it is clearly not a pleasant experience for the horses, who have their ears stuffed with oil-soaked rags to shut out the noise, and their vocal cords cut out to render them mute.

The next stage, the **suerte de banderillas**, involves the placing of three sets of *banderillas* (coloured sticks with barbed ends) into the bull's shoulders. Each of the three *banderilleros* delivers these in turn, attracting the bull's attention with the movement of his own body rather than a cape, and placing the *banderillas* while both he and the bull are running towards each other. He then runs to safety out of the bull's vision, sometimes with the assistance of his colleagues.

Once the *banderillas* have been placed, the **suerte de matar** begins, and the *matador* enters the ring alone, having exchanged his pink and gold cape for the red one. He (or she) salutes the president and then dedicates the bull either to an individual, to whom he gives his hat, or to the audience by placing his hat in the centre of the ring. It is in this part of the *corrida* that judgements are made and the performance is focused, as the *matador* displays his skills on the (by now exhausted) bull. He uses the movements of the cape to attract the bull, while his body remains still. If he does well, the band will start to play, while the crowd *olé* each pass. This stage lasts around ten minutes and ends with the kill. The *matador* attempts to get the bull into a position where he can drive a sword between its shoulders and through to the heart for a *coup de grâce*. In practice, they rarely succeed in this, instead taking a second sword, crossed at the end, to cut the bull's spinal cord; this causes instant death.

If the audience is impressed by the *matador*'s performance, they will wave their handkerchiefs and shout for an award to be made by the president. He can award one or both ears, and a tail – the better the display, the more pieces he gets – while if the *matador* has excelled himself, he will be carried out of the ring by the crowd, through the *puerta grande*, the main door, which is normally kept locked. The bull, too, may be applauded for its performance, as it is dragged out by the mule team.

The bullfight **season** runs from March to October, and **tickets** for *corridas* start from around €5 – though you pay much more for the prime seats and prestigious fights. The cheapest seats are *gradas*, the highest rows at the back, from where you can see everything that happens without too much of the detail; the front rows are known as the *barreras*. Seats are also divided into *sol* (sun), *sombra* (shade) and *sol y sombra* (shaded after a while), though these distinctions have become less crucial as more and more bullfights start later in the day, at 6pm or 7pm, rather than the traditional 5pm. The *sombra* seats are more expensive, not so much for the spectators' personal comfort as the fact that most of the action takes place in the shade. On the way in, you can rent cushions – two hours' sitting on concrete is not much fun.

Football

Finally, at the 2008 European Championships, the Spanish national football team threw off decades of habitual underperformance and actually won something, beating Germany to become European champions in some style. It's been a good while coming, since although **fútbol** has long been the most popular sport in Spain, it's only recently that Spanish football has made much of an international splash, with the likes of coaches Juande Ramos and Rafa Benitez, and players of the calibre of Fernando Torres, now plying their trade in England's Premier League. Certainly, if you want the excitement

of a genuinely Spanish event, watching a Sunday-evening game in **La Liga** (Ⓦwww .lfp.es) usually produces as much passion as anything you'll find in the Plaza de Toros. Ⓦwww.soccer-spain.com is a very good website in English, where you'll find comprehensive news and articles.

For many years, the country's two dominant teams have been big-spending **Real Madrid** and **FC Barcelona**, and these two have shared domestic league and cup honours more often than is healthy. The pendulum has swung between them in the last few years; as the Real Madrid "Galacticos" era came to an end, Barcelona won back-to-back league titles in 2005 and 2006, as well as their second European Cup, but a chastening Catalan collapse left a revitalized Real Madrid as champions in 2007 and 2008.

The big two have faced serious opposition in recent years from **Valencia** (winners of La Liga in 2002 and 2004), the Andalucian powerhouse of **Sevilla** (UEFA Cup winners in 2006 and 2007) and the emerging force of **Villarreal** (league runners-up in 2008), who have experienced a rags-to-riches success story under president and ceramics tycoon Fernando Roig. Other significant teams include **Athletic Bilbao**, who only draw on players from Euskal Herria (the Basque Country in both Spain and France and Navarra) or who came through the club's youth ranks, while Real Madrid and Barcelona's respective local rivals are **Atlético Madrid** (the third-biggest team in terms of support) and **Espanyol** (Copa del Rey winners in 2006).

The league **season** runs from late August until mid-May or early June, and most games kick off at 5 or 7pm on Sundays, though live TV demands that one key game kicks off at 9 or 10pm on Saturday and Sunday. With the exception of a few big games – mainly those involving Real Madrid and Barcelona – **tickets** are not too hard to get. They start at around €30 for La Liga games, with the cheapest in the *fondo* (behind the goals); *tribuna* (pitchside stand) seats are much pricier. Trouble is very rare (though incidents of racist abuse of black players have become a depressingly common feature of many matches), and there is generally a very easy-going, friendly atmosphere. Many bars advertise the matches they screen, and they will also often feature Sunday-afternoon English league and cup games.

Golf

Stars such as Jose Maria Olazabal, Sergio Garcia, Miguel Angel Jimenez and Severiano Ballesteros have done much to improve the country's golf fortunes in recent years, and interest in the game was boosted by the hosting of the Ryder Cup at Sotogrande in 1997, and the Volvo Masters in Andalucía. Home to around three hundred **golf courses**, Spain has plenty of scope for the amateur golfer, and temperatures, especially favourable in the south, mean that you can play more or less year round. The Costa del Sol is one of the most popular golfing destinations, with Cádiz, Valencia, Marbella and Málaga not far behind. A number of courses are now also being built away from the traditional centres, for example along the Costa de la Luz and the Atlantic coast, which, while not as nice in winter, tend to be a little cheaper. There are increasing concerns, however, about the amount of water used by courses in a country that is experiencing a severe water crisis.

Plenty of tour operators can arrange golf-holiday packages, while for more information visit the very useful **Golf Spain** website (ⓦ www.golfspain.com), in association with the **Real Federacion Espanola de Golf** (ⓦ www .golfspainfederacion.com), which details all the country's golf courses and golf schools, plus green fees and golf-and-resort packages.

Rafting and canyoning

The Pyrenees provide excellent opportunities to indulge in the more white-knuckle sports of canyoning and rafting, although check your insurance policy covers you before you set off. There's **rafting** in various rivers across Spain, though the fast-flowing Noguera Pallaresa in the eastern Pyrenees is the most popular choice for expeditions. The season runs roughly from March to October, during which time you can fling yourself down the rapids in an inflatable raft from around €35 for a two-hour trip, and more like €70 for an all-day trip with lunch. There's more on rafting on p.798.

The Parque Natural Sierra de Guara (ⓦ www.guara.org) and the Parque Nacional de Ordesa (ⓦ www.ordesa.net) provide some of the best locations in Europe for **canyoning**, with plenty of vast caves and fast-flowing rivers to explore. Operators in most of the local villages offer equipment and guides, with prices starting from around €65 for a full day's expedition. The park websites have more information on routes and local organizations.

Skiing and snowboarding

Spain offers a decent range of slopes, and often at lower prices than its more mountainous European neighbours. It is also home to the southernmost skiing in Europe, in the form of the Solynieve resort in the **Sierra Nevada** (Andalucía), which has the longest season in Spain, running from November to April and sometimes even May, allowing you to ski in the morning and head to the beach in the afternoon – really, the only thing the resort's got going for it. Much more challenging skiing is to be had in the north of the country in the Pyrenees. The **Aragonese Pyrenees** are home to a range of resorts catering for beginners to advanced skiers, while the resorts in the **Catalan Pyrenees**, to the east, encompass Andorra; the biggest resort here is Soldeu/El Tarter. Other options include the more intimate **Alto Campoo**, near Santander, and, for a day's excursion, easy-to-intermediate skiing just outside Madrid at **Valdesqui** and **Navacerrada**.

There are ski deals to Spain from tour operators in your home country, though it often works out cheaper if you go through a local Spanish travel agent or even arrange your trip directly with local providers. Many local hotels offer ski deals, and we've covered some options in the Guide. Equipment rental will set you back around €20 a day as a general rule, and daily lift passes around €25–35, although the longer you rent or ski for the cheaper it will be.

Watersports

Spain offers a vast range of watersports, especially along the Mediterranean coast where most resorts offer **pedalo and canoe** rental (from €10/hour), sailing tuition, and **boat rental** (€40/hour) and **waterskiing** (€30/15min).

Surfing is best on the Atlantic coast, backed up by the fact that the area plays regular host to a number of prestigious competitions such as the Billabong Pro, Ferrolterra Pantín Classic and the Goanna Pro. Breaks such as the legendary Mundaka (Costa Vasca), considered by many as the best left-hander in Europe, along with a superb run of picturesque, often near-empty beaches with waves for all abilities, make the region's reputation. The surfing season runs roughly from September to April, meaning that a full wet suit is a basic requirement in the cold Atlantic waters. Equipment can be rented, and advice sought, in local surfing shops, or try asking at tourist information offices. If you prefer to surf in warmer waters, the Andalucian coastline has a few decent spots. For more information, ⓦ www.beachwizard.com is an excellent website giving full details of all the best spots in Spain, along with reviews, maps and travel information.

Tarifa on the Costa de la Luz is *the* spot in Spain – indeed, in the whole of Europe – for **windsurfing and kitesurfing**, with strong winds almost guaranteed, and huge stretches of sandy beach to enjoy, although you'll also find schools dotted around the rest of the coast, with another good spot being the rather colder option of the Atlantic coast in Galicia. Prices are around €25 for an hour's board and sail rental, and €10 for wet suits, while lessons start at €35 an hour including board rental.

Travelling with children

Spain is a good country to travel with children of any age; they will be well received everywhere, and babies and toddlers, in particular, will be the centre of attention. You will probably have to change your usual routine, since young children stay up late in Spain, especially in the summer. It's very common for them to be running around pavement cafés and public squares after 10 or 11pm, and yours will no doubt enjoy joining in. It's expected that families dine out with their children, too, so it's not unusual to see up to four generations of the same family eating tapas in a bar, for example.

Holidays and accommodation

Most tour operators can advise about **family-friendly resorts** in Spain, and many holiday hotels and self-contained club-style resorts offer things like kids' clubs, babysitting, sports and entertainment. The only caveat is that, of course, you're unlikely to see much of Spain on these family-oriented holidays. The country also has various theme parks and leisure activities specifically aimed at kids, most notably **Port Aventura** (Costa Daurada, Catalunya), one of Europe's largest theme parks, and the Western film set of **Mini Hollywood** (Almería). Madrid and Barcelona both have good city amusement/theme parks, as well as a whole range of child-centred attractions, while the long Spanish coastline has a bunch of popular **water parks**.

Museums, galleries and sights throughout Spain either offer **discounts** or **free entry** for children (it's often free for the under 4s), and it's the same on trains, sightseeing tours, boat trips and all the other usual tourist attractions.

If you're travelling independently, finding **accommodation** shouldn't be a problem, as *hostales* and *pensiones* generally offer rooms with three or four beds. Bear in mind that much budget accommodation in towns and cities is located on the upper floors of buildings, often without lifts. It's also worth noting that some older-style *pensiones* don't have heating systems – and it can get very cold in winter. If you want a cot provided, or baby-listening or **baby-sitting** services, you'll usually have to pay the price of staying in a more expensive hotel – and even then, never assume that these facilities are provided, so always check in advance. **Self-catering accommodation** offers the most flexibility, and there's plenty of it in Spain, from seaside apartments to country houses; even in major cities, it's easy to rent an apartment by the night or week and enjoy living like a local with your family.

Products, clothes and services

Baby food, disposable nappies, formula milk and other standard items are widely available in pharmacies and supermarkets, though not necessarily with the same range or brands that you will be used to at home. Organic baby food, for example, is hard to come by away from the big-city supermarkets, and most Spanish non-organic baby foods contain small amounts of sugar or salt. Fresh milk, too, is not always available; UHT is more commonly drunk by small children. If you require anything specific for your baby or child, it's best to bring it with you or check with the manufacturer about equivalent brands. Remember the airline restrictions on carrying liquids in hand luggage if you're planning to bring industrial quantities of Calpol to see you through the holiday.

For **babies' and children's clothing**, Prénatal (ⓦwww.prenatal.es) and Chicco (ⓦwww.chicco.es) are Spain's market leaders, with shops in most towns and cities. Or you can always try the local El Corte Inglés department store.

Families might eat out a lot, but things like **highchairs and special children's menus** are rare, except in the resorts on the *costas* and islands. Most bars and cafés, though, will be happy to heat milk bottles for you. **Baby-changing areas** are also relatively rare, except in department stores and shopping centres, and even where they do exist they are not always up to scratch.

Attitudes

Most establishments are **baby-friendly** in the sense that you'll be made very welcome if you turn up with a child in tow. Many museum cloakrooms, for example, will be happy to look after your pushchair as you carry your child around the building, while restaurants will make a fuss of your little one. However, **breast-feeding** in public is not widespread, though it's more acceptable in big resorts and the main cities; the local village café is probably not the place to test rural sensibilities. **Noise** is the other factor that often stuns visiting parents. Spain is a loud country, with fiesta fireworks, jackhammers, buzzing mopeds and clamouring evening crowds all adding into the mix. Babies sleep through most things, but you might want to pick and choose accommodation with the location of bars, clubs, markets, etc firmly in mind.

Travel essentials

Addresses

Addresses are written as: c/Picasso 2, 4°
izda. – which means Picasso Street (*calle*)
no. 2, fourth floor, left- (*izquierda*) hand flat or
office; dcha. (*derecha*) is right; cto. (*centro*)
centre. Other confusions in Spanish
addresses result from the different spellings,
and sometimes words, used in Catalan,
Basque and Galician – all of which are
replacing their Castilian counterparts; for
example, *carrer* (not *calle*) and *plaça* (not
plaza) in Catalan.

Complaints

By law, all establishments (including hotels)
must keep a *libro de reclamaciones*
(**complaints book**) and bring it out for
regular inspection by the authorities. If you
think you've been overcharged, or have any
other problems, you can usually produce an
immediate resolution by asking for the book.
Most establishments prefer to keep them
empty, thus attracting no unwelcome
attention from officialdom, which, of course,
works in your favour. If you do make an
entry, English is acceptable but write clearly
and simply; add your home address, too, as
you are entitled to be informed of any action,
including – but don't count on it – compensation. You can also take your complaint to
any local *turismo*, which should attempt to
resolve the matter while you wait.

Costs

Prices in Spain have increased considerably
over the last ten years or so, but there are
still few places in Europe where you'll get a
better deal on the cost of simple meals and
drinks, while public transport remains very
good value. Big cities and tourist resorts are
invariably more expensive than remoter
areas, and certain regions tend also to have
higher prices – notably Euskal Herria,
Catalunya and Aragón, and the Balearic
Islands. Prices are hiked, too, to take
advantage of special events, so for example

you'd be lucky to find a room in Seville
during the Feria de Abril, or in Pamplona for
the Running of the Bulls, at less than double
the usual rate.

It's really difficult to come up with **a daily
budget** for the country, as your sixty-cent
glass of wine and €30 *pensión* room in rural
Andalucía might be €3 and €60, respectively,
in Madrid or Barcelona. However, as a very
rough guide, if you always share a room in
the cheapest *pensiones* and hotels, use
public transport and stick to local restaurants
and bars, you could get by on between €50
and €80 a day. Stay somewhere a bit more
stylish or comfortable, eat in fancier restaurants, and go out on the town, and you'll
need more like €100–140 a day, though, of
course, if you're holidaying in Spain's magnificent *paradores* or five-star hotels this figure
won't even cover your room. There's more
detailed information about prices in the
"Accommodation", "Getting around" and
"Food and drink" sections.

Visiting museums, galleries, churches and
monasteries soon adds up – if you visited
every site we cover in Salamanca alone, for
example, you'd be out of pocket by €25 or
so. Accordingly, it pays to take along any
student/youth or senior citizen cards you
may be entitled to, such as the International
Student ID Card (ISIC; Ⓦ www.isiccard.com),
as most attractions offer discounts (and
make sure you carry your passport or ID
card). Some museums and attractions are
free on a certain day of the week or month
(though note that this is sometimes limited to
EU citizens only; you'll need to show your
passport). Any **entrance fees** noted in this
guide are for the full adult price; children (as
well as seniors) usually get a discount, and
the under 4s are often free.

Crime and personal safety

The police in Spain come in various guises.
The **Guardia Civil**, in green uniforms, is a
national police force, formerly a military

Emergency numbers

☎ **112** All emergency services
☎ **061** Ambulance
☎ **080** Fire service
☎ **062** Guardia Civil
☎ **091** Policía Nacional

organization, and has responsibility for national crime, as well as roads, borders and guarding public buildings. There's also the blue-uniformed **Policía Nacional**, mainly seen in cities, who deal with crime, drugs, crowd control, identity and immigrant matters, and the like. Locally, most policing is carried out by the **Policía Municipal**, who wear blue-and-white uniforms, and these tend to be the most approachable in the first instance if you're reporting a crime. There's obviously a certain overlap between regional and municipal forces, and you may be passed from one to another, depending on what you're reporting. In certain of the autonomous regions, there are also regional police forces, which are gradually taking over duties from the Guardia Civil and Policía Nacional. The **Mossos d'Esquadra** in Catalunya (blue uniforms with red-and-white trim) and the Basque **Ertzaintza** (blue and red, with red berets) have the highest profile, though you're most likely to encounter them on traffic and highways duty.

In the unlikely event that you're mugged or otherwise robbed, go straight to the police, where you'll need to make an official statement known as a **denuncia**, not least because your insurance company will require a police report. Expect it to be a time-consuming and laborious business – you can do it by phone, or even online these days (details on ⓦ www.policia.es), but you'll still have to go into the station to sign it. If you have your passport stolen, contact your embassy or consulate (in Madrid, Barcelona, Valencia, Málaga and some other cities; see the relevant "Listings" sections for details).

Avoiding trouble

Petty crime – pickpocketing and bag-snatching – is, unfortunately, a fact of life in Spanish cities and tourist resorts, though no more so than anywhere else in Europe. The usual sensible **precautions** include: carrying bags slung across your neck, not over your shoulder; not putting wallets in your back pocket; leaving passport and tickets in the hotel safe; and keeping a photocopy of your passport, plus notes of your credit card number helplines and so on. Take special care on public transport, and don't leave **bags** unattended anywhere, even if you're looking at rooms upstairs in a *hostal*; know where your belongings are at all times.

On the street, beware of people standing unusually close at street kiosks or attractions, or of those trying to distract you for any reason (pointing out "bird shit" – in reality, planted shaving cream – on your jacket, shoving a card or paper to read right under your nose). Next thing you know, your purse has gone.

Drivers shouldn't leave anything in view in a **parked car**; take the radio/CD player/iPod with you. **On the road**, be cautious about accepting help from anyone other than a uniformed police officer – some roadside thieves pose as "good Samaritans" to persons experiencing car and tyre problems, some of which, such as slashed tyres, may have been inflicted at rest stops or service stations in advance. The thieves typically attempt to divert your attention by pointing out a problem and then steal items from the vehicle while you are looking elsewhere.

Incidentally, if you are stopped by a proper police officer for a **driving offence**, being foreign just won't wash as an excuse. They'll fine you on the spot, cash or card.

Sexual harassment

Spain's macho image has faded dramatically, and these days there are relatively few parts of the country where foreign **women travelling alone** are likely to feel intimidated or attract unwanted attention. There is little of the pestering that you have to contend with in, say, the larger Italian cities, and the outdoor culture of terrazas (terrace bars) and the tendency of Spaniards to move around in large, mixed crowds, help to make you feel less exposed. *Déjame en paz* ("leave me in peace") is a fairly standard rebuff, and if you are in any doubt, take a taxi, always the safest way to travel late at night.

The major **resorts** of the *costas* have their own artificial holiday culture, where problems are more likely to be caused by other alcohol-fuelled holidaymakers. You are actually more vulnerable in isolated, **rural regions**, where you can walk for hours without coming across an inhabited farm or house, though it's rare that this poses a threat – help and hospitality are much more the norm. Many single women happily tramp the long-distance footpaths, from Galicia to the Sierra Nevada, though you are always best advised to stay in rooms and *pensiones* rather than camping wild.

Electricity

The current in most of Spain is 220 or 225 volts AC (just occasionally, it's still 110 or 125V); most European appliances should work as long as you have an adaptor for European-style two-pin plugs. North Americans will need this plus a transformer.

Entry requirements

EU citizens (and those of Norway, Iceland, Liechtenstein and Switzerland) need only a valid national-identity card or passport to enter Spain. Other Europeans, and citizens of the **United States**, **Canada**, **Australia**, **New Zealand and South Africa**, require a passport but no visa, and can stay as a tourist for up to ninety days. Other nationalities may need to get a visa from a Spanish embassy or consulate before departure. Visa requirements do change, and it's always advisable to check the current situation before leaving home.

Most EU citizens who want to stay in Spain for longer than three months, rather than just visit as a tourist, need to register at a provincial **Oficina de Extranjeros** (Foreigners' Office), where they'll be issued with a residence certificate; you'll find a list of offices (eventually) on the Ministry of Interior website (@www.mir.es). You don't need the certificate if you're an EU citizen living and working legally in Spain, or if you're legally self-employed or a student (on an exchange programme or otherwise). US citizens can apply for one ninety-day extension, showing proof of funds, but this must be done from outside Spain. Other nationalities wishing to extend their stay will need to get a special visa from a Spanish embassy or consulate before departure.

Gay and lesbian travellers

Gay and lesbian life in Spain has come a long way in the last three decades, and Spanish attitudes have changed dramatically. Same-sex marriages were made legal in 2005, giving same-sex couples the same rights as heterosexual couples, including the right to adopt, and the age of consent is 16 – the same as for heterosexual couples.

Today, almost every town in Spain has its gay bars and associations, while gay magazines, newspapers and radio programmes are widespread. In 1995, Spain included a clause in its criminal code making it an offence to discriminate in housing and employment based on sexual orientation, and imposing tougher sentences on hate crimes against the gay community.

There's a thriving **gay scene** in most of Spain's main cities, notably, of course, Madrid (p.126) and Barcelona (p.714), the former with its Chueca neighbourhood and annual gay pride parade (June/July), the latter with its "Gaixample" district of bars and clubs and the established International Gay and Lesbian Film Festival (Oct; @www.cinemalambda.com). For gay resorts, **Sitges**, south of Barcelona, is unbeatable, and, as in **Cádiz**, Carnaval is a wonderfully hedonistic time to visit. Ibiza and Torremolinos are two other popular holiday destinations. The Spanish term for the gay scene is "*el ambiente*" ("the atmosphere"), while another useful expression is "*entiendo*", literally, "I understand", but meaning "I'm gay".

There are plenty of **websites** out there for further information, notably @www.cogailes.org (Barcelona-based) and @www.cogam.org (Madrid), which give a good general view of the local scenes and links to other sites.

Health

The **European Health Insurance Card** (EHIC) gives EU citizens access to Spanish state public-health services under reciprocal agreements. While this will provide free or reduced-cost medical care in the event of minor injuries and emergencies, it won't cover every eventuality – and it only applies to EU citizens in possession of the card – so travel insurance (see p.60) is essential.

No **inoculations** are required for Spain, and the worst that's likely to happen to you is that you might fall victim to an upset stomach. To be safe, wash fruit and avoid tapas dishes that look as if they were prepared last week. Water at public fountains is fine, unless there's a sign saying "*auga no potable*", in which case don't drink it.

For minor complaints, go to a **farmacia** – they're easy to find, and pharmacists are highly trained, willing to give advice (often in English) and able to dispense many drugs that would be available only on prescription in other countries. They keep usual shop hours (Mon–Fri 9am–1.30pm & 5–8pm), but some open late and at weekends, while a rota system keeps at least one open 24 hours in every town. The rota is displayed in the window of every pharmacy, or you can check the list in the local newspaper.

If you have special medical or dietary requirements, it is advisable to carry a letter from your doctor, translated into Spanish, indicating the nature of your condition and necessary treatments. With luck, you'll get the address of an English-speaking **doctor** from the nearest *farmacia*, police station or tourist office – it's obviously more likely in resorts and big cities. Treatment at **hospitals** for EU citizens in possession of the EHIC card is free; otherwise, you'll be charged at private-hospital rates, which can be very expensive.

In **emergencies**, dial ☎112 for an ambulance.

Insurance

You should take out a comprehensive **insurance policy** before travelling to Spain, to cover against loss, theft, illness or injury. A typical policy will provide cover for loss of baggage, tickets and – up to a certain limit – cash or traveller's cheques, as well as cancellation or curtailment of your journey. When securing baggage cover, make sure that the per-article limit will cover your most valuable possession. Most policies exclude so-called **dangerous sports** unless an extra premium is paid: in Spain, this can mean most watersports are excluded (plus rafting, canyoning, etc), though probably not things like bike tours or hiking.

If you need to make a claim, you should keep receipts for medicines and medical treatment, and in the event you have anything stolen, you must obtain an official statement from the police – see p.58.

Internet

Internet access is widely available at cafés (often referred to as *cibercafés*), computer shops and phone offices (*locutorios*). You'll pay as little as €1 an hour in many places, though it can cost two or three times as much. Many backpacker hostels and small *pensiones* provide cheap or free internet access for their guests, but hotel business centres or hotel bedrooms wired for access tend to be far more expensive than going out on the street to an internet place. **Wireless access** is increasingly widespread in bars, hotels and other public "hotspots", though if the networks are password-protected you'll have to check first with your host to get online. If you take your own laptop, make sure you've got insurance cover and all the relevant plugs and adaptors for recharging.

Laundry

You'll find a few coin-op self-service laundries (*lavanderías automáticas*) in the major cities,

---

Rough Guides travel insurance

Rough Guides has teamed up with Columbus Direct to offer you tailor-made **travel insurance**. Products include a low-cost **backpacker** option for long stays; a **short break** option for city getaways; a typical **holiday package** option; and others. There are also annual **multi-trip** policies for those who travel regularly. Different sports and activities (trekking, skiing, etc) can usually be included.

See our website (⊛www.roughguides.com/website/shop) for eligibility and purchasing options. Alternatively, UK residents can call ☎0870/033 9988; Australians ☎1300/669 999 and New Zealanders ☎0800/559 911. All other nationalities should call ☎+44 870/890 2843.

but you normally have to leave your clothes for a service wash and dry at a *lavandería*. A dry cleaner is a *tintorería*. Note that by law you're not allowed to leave laundry hanging out of windows over a street, and many *pensiones* and *hostales* expressly forbid washing clothes in the sink. To avoid an international incident, ask first if there's somewhere you can wash your clothes.

Mail

Post offices (*Correos*; ⓦwww.correos.es) are normally open weekdays from 8am to 2pm and again from 5 to 7.30pm, though branches in bigger places may have longer hours, may not close at midday and may open on Saturday mornings. There's an office-finder on the website, which also gives exact opening hours and contact details for each post office in Spain. As you can also pay bills and buy phonecards in post offices, queues can be long – it's often easier to buy **stamps** at tobacconists (look for the brown and yellow *estance* sign).

Outbound mail is reasonably reliable, with letters or cards taking around three days to a week to the UK and the rest of Europe, a week to ten days to North America, New Zealand and Australia, although it can be more erratic in the summer. There's also a whole of host of express-mail services (ask for *urgente* or *exprés*).

Maps

In addition to the maps in this guide, virtually indestructible, waterproof **Rough Guide maps** are available covering Barcelona, Madrid, Mallorca, Northern Spain, the Pyrenees and Andorra, and Spain & Portugal. You'll also find a good selection of **road maps** in most Spanish bookshops, street kiosks and service stations. Most widely available are the regional Michelin maps (1:400,000), covering the country (including the Balearics) in a series of nine maps, though there are also whole-country maps and atlas-format versions available. Other good country and regional maps are those published by Distrimapas Telstar (ⓦwww .distrimapas-telstar.es), which also produces reliable indexed **street plans** of the main cities. Any good book or travel shop in your own country should be able to provide a decent range of Spain maps, or buy online from specialist stores such as ⓦwww .stanfords.co.uk or ⓦwww.randmcnally.com.

You can buy **hiking/trekking maps** from specialist map/travel shops in Spain, including La Tienda Verde in Madrid (ⓦwww .latiendaverde.es), and Librería Quera (ⓦwww .llibreriaquera.com) or Altaïr (ⓦwww.altair.es) in Barcelona. These and bookshops – plus a few overseas specialists – stock the full range of **topographical maps** issued by two government agencies: the IGN (Instituto Geográfico Nacional; ⓦwww.ign.es) and the SGE (Servicio Geográfico del Ejército; ⓦwww .ejercito.mde.es). They are available at scales of 1:200,000, 1:100,000, 1:50,000 and even occasionally 1:25,000. The various SGE series are considered to be more up to date, although neither agency is hugely reliable. A Catalunya-based company, Editorial Alpina (ⓦwww.editorialalpina.com), produces useful 1:40,000 or 1:25,000 map/booklet sets for most of the Spanish **mountain and foothill areas** of interest, and these are also on sale in many bookshops; the relevant editions are noted in the text where appropriate.

Money

Spain's currency is the **euro** (€), with notes issued in denominations of 5, 10, 20, 50, 100, 200 and 500 euros, and coins in denominations of 1, 2, 5, 10, 20 and 50 cents, and 1 and 2 euros. Up-to-the-minute currency **exchange rates** are posted on ⓦwww.oanda.com.

By far the easiest way to get money is to use your bank debit card to withdraw cash from an **ATM**, found in villages, towns and cities all over Spain, as well as on arrival at the airports and major train stations. You can usually withdraw up to €200 a day, and instructions are offered in English once you insert your card. Make sure you have a personal identification number (PIN) that's designed to work overseas, and take a note of your bank's emergency contact number in case the machine swallows your card. Some European debit cards can also be used directly in shops to pay for purchases; you'll need to check first with your bank.

All major **credit cards** are accepted in hotels, restaurants and shops, and for tours, tickets and transport, though don't count on being able to use them in every small *pensión* or village café. You can also use your credit card in an ATM to withdraw cash, though remember that these advances will be treated as loans, with interest accruing daily from the date of withdrawal. If you use a foreign credit card in some shops, you may also be asked for photo ID, so be prepared to show a driving licence or passport. Make sure you make a note of the number for reporting lost or stolen cards to your credit card company.

Spanish **banco** (banks) and **cajas de ahorros** (savings banks) have branches in all but the smallest villages, and most of them are prepared to change traveller's cheques (albeit often with hefty commissions). **Banking hours** are usually Monday to Friday 8.30am–2pm, with some city branches open Saturday 8.30am–1pm (except June–Sept when all banks close on Sat), although times can vary from bank to bank. Outside these times, it's usually possible to change cash at larger hotels (generally with bad rates and low commission) or with travel agents – useful for small amounts in a hurry.

In tourist areas, you'll also find specialist **casas de cambio**, with more convenient hours (though rates vary), while some major tourist offices, larger train stations and most branches of El Corte Inglés department store have exchange facilities open throughout business hours.

Opening hours

Almost everything in Spain – shops, museums, churches, tourist offices – closes for a **siesta** of at least two hours in the middle part of the day. There's a lot of variation (and the siesta tends to be longer in the south), but you'll get far less aggravated if you accept that the early afternoon is best spent asleep, or in a bar, or both.

Basic **working hours** are Monday to Friday 9.30am–2pm and 5–8pm. Many **shops** open slightly later on a Saturday (at 10am) and close for the day at 2pm, though you'll still find plenty of places open in cities, and there are regional variations. Moreover, department and chain stores and shopping malls tend to open a straight Monday to Saturday 10am to 9 or 10pm.

Museums and galleries, with very few exceptions, also have a break between 1 or 2pm and 4pm. On Sundays, most open mornings only, and on Mondays many close all day (museums are also usually closed Jan 1 & 6, May 1, Dec 24, 25 & 31). Opening hours vary from year to year, though often not by more than half an hour or so. Some are also seasonal, and usually in Spain, "summer" means from Easter until September, and "winter" from October until Easter.

The most important **cathedrals, churches and monasteries** operate in much the same way as museums, with regular visiting hours and admission charges. Other churches, though, are kept locked, opening only for worship in the early morning and/or the evening (between around 6 and 9pm), so you'll either have to try at these times, or find someone with a key. A sacristan or custodian almost always lives nearby, and most people will know where to direct you. You're expected to give a small tip, or donation.

Phones

Spanish **telephone numbers** have nine digits; mobile numbers begin with a "6", freephone numbers begin "900", while other "90-plus-digit" and "80-plus-digit numbers are nationwide standard-rate or special-rate services. To **call Spain from abroad**, you dial your country's international access code + 34 (Spain's country code) + the nine-digit Spanish number.

Public telephones have instructions in English, and accept coins, credit cards and phone cards. **Phone cards** (*tarjetas*) with discounted rates for calls are available in tobacconists, newsagents and post offices, issued in various denominations either by Telefónica (the dominant operator) or one of its rivals. Credit cards are not recommended for local and national calls, since most have a minimum charge that is far more than a normal call is likely to cost. It's also best to avoid making calls from the phone in your hotel room, as even local calls will be slapped with a heavy surcharge.

You can make international calls from any public pay-phone, but it's cheaper to go to one of the ubiquitous phone centres, or **locutorios**, which specialize in discounted overseas connections. **Calling home from Spain**, you dial ⊤00 (Spain's international access code) + your country code + city/area code minus initial zero + number. For **reverse-charge calls**, dial the international operator (☎1008 Europe, ☎1005 rest of the world).

Most European **mobile phones** will work in Spain, though it's worth checking with your provider whether you need to get international access switched on and whether there are any extra charges involved. Even though prices are coming down, it's still expensive to use your own mobile extensively while abroad, and you will pay for receiving incoming calls, for example. You could always simply buy a local **SIM card** instead for your mobile, from operators such as Vodafone (ⓦwww.vodafone.es) or Movistar (ⓦwww.movistar.es). Or if you plan to spend some time in Spain, it's almost certainly better to buy a Spanish mobile, as the cheapest non-contract, **pay-as-you-go phones** cost from around €29. You can buy top-up cards, or have them recharged for you, in phone shops, supermarkets and post offices, and from ATMs.

Public holidays

Alongside the Spanish **national public holidays** (see box below) there are scores of regional holidays and local fiestas (often marking the local saint's day), any of which will mean that everything except hotels, bars and restaurants locks its doors.

In addition, **August** is traditionally Spain's own holiday month, when the big cities – especially Madrid and Barcelona – are semi-deserted, with many of the shops and restaurants closed for the duration. In

contrast, it can prove nearly impossible to find a room in the more popular coastal and mountain resorts at these times; similarly, seats on planes, trains and buses in August should if possible be booked in advance.

Shopping

Shopping in Spain can range from digging around in local flea markets to browsing the designer boutiques in Madrid and Barcelona. In the larger towns, most high streets will feature Spanish clothing favourites such as Mango and Zara, along with Camper, the country's most famous shoe brand. For food, supermarkets are easy to locate, while street markets (*mercados*) are held virtually everywhere, and are a great place to pick up fresh produce. The main department store found in most towns is El Corte Inglés, where you can buy almost anything.

Spain is also well known for its local crafts. Leatherwork, such as belts, bags, purses and even saddles, are best sought in Andalucía, where you'll also be able to pick up the most authentic flamenco accessories such as dresses, fans, shawls and lace. The Balearics are renowned for beautiful leather shoes. Ceramics are widely available, but are especially good in the Córdoba region, around Seville and in Catalunya. Textiles such as carpets are also common, but for something special try the handwoven carpets from Andalucía. Sherry is good to seek out in Jerez, and, of course, if you're on a wine trail in La Rioja or Ribera del Deuro, for example, then picking up bottles as you go is an excellent and cost-effective option.

Spanish national public holidays

January 1 *Año Nuevo* New Year's Day

January 6 *Epifanía* Epiphany

March/April *Viernes Santo* Good Friday

May 1 *Fiesta del Trabajo* May Day

August 15 *La Asunción* Assumption of the Virgin

October 12 *Día de la Hispanidad* National Day

November 1 *Todos los Santos* All Saints

December 6 *Día de la Constitución* Constitution Day

December 8 *Inmaculada Concepción*

December 25 *Navidad* Christmas Day

Taxes

Sales tax – **IVA** (pronounced "iba") – often comes as an unexpected surprise when you pay the bill for food or accommodation. It's not always specified, and is seven percent for hotels and restaurants and sixteen percent for other goods and services (though most other prices are quoted inclusive of IVA). **Non-EU residents** are able to claim back the sales tax on purchases that come to over €90. To do this, make sure the shop you're buying from fills out the correct paperwork, and present this to customs before you check in at the airport for your return flight.

Time

Spain is one hour ahead of the UK, six hours ahead of Eastern Standard Time, nine hours ahead of Pacific Standard Time, eight hours behind Australia, ten hours behind New Zealand, and the same time as South Africa. In Spain, the clocks go forward in the last week in March and back again in the last week in October. It's worth noting, if you're planning to cross the border, that Portugal is an hour behind Spain throughout the year.

Toilets

Public toilets are generally reasonably clean but don't always have any paper. They can very occasionally still be squat-style. They are most commonly referred to and labelled *Los Servicios*, though signs may point you to *baños*, *aseos* or *lavabis*. *Damas* (Ladies) and *Caballeros* (Gentlemen) are the usual distinguishing signs for sex, though you may also see the potentially confusing *Señoras* (Women) and *Señores* (Men).

Tourist information

The Spanish national tourist office, **Turespaña** (Ⓦwww.spain.info), is an excellent source of information when planning your trip. The website is full of ideas, information and searchable databases, and there are links to similar websites of Turespaña offices in your own country.

In Spain itself, you'll find **turismos** (tourist offices) in virtually every town, usually open Monday to Friday 9am to 2pm and 4 to 7pm, Saturday and Sunday 9am–2pm, but hours do vary from place to place. In major cities and coastal resorts the offices tend to remain open all day Saturday and on Sunday morning between April and September.

The information and help available in *turismos* also varies: some are very good, and some do little more than hand out a map and ask where you're from. Not all staff speak English, especially in the more rural and out-of-the-way destinations. There's also often more than one information office, especially in bigger towns and cities, where responsibility for local tourism is split between municipal and provincial offices. As a rough rule, the municipal offices are better for specific city information, the provincial offices best for advice about where to go in the region.

Travellers with disabilities

The classic tourist images of Spain – the medieval old towns, winding lanes, the castles and monasteries – don't exactly fill you full of confidence if you're in a wheelchair. However, Spain is changing and facilities are improving rapidly, especially in the more go-ahead, contemporary cities. There are accessible rooms and hotels in all major Spanish cities and resorts and, by law, all new public buildings (including revamped museums and galleries) are required to be fully accessible. Public transport is the main problem, since most local buses and trains are virtually impossible for wheelchairs, though again there are pockets of excellence in Spain. The AVE high-speed train service, for example, is fully accessible, as is every city and sight-seeing bus in Barcelona (and large parts of its metro and tram network, too). In many towns and cities, acoustic traffic-light signals and dropped kerbs are common.

Some organizations at home may be able to advise you further about travel to Spain, like the very useful UK-based **Tourism For All** (Ⓦwww.tourismforall.org.uk). Access Travel (Ⓦwww.access-travel.co.uk) offers Barcelona city breaks and holidays to five other Spanish resorts, and at the very least, local tourist offices in Spain should also be able to recommend a suitable hotel or taxi company. Also in Barcelona, the excellent Ⓦ**www.accessiblebarcelona.com** is the best single source of information for disabled visitors to that city.

Guide

Guide

Madrid

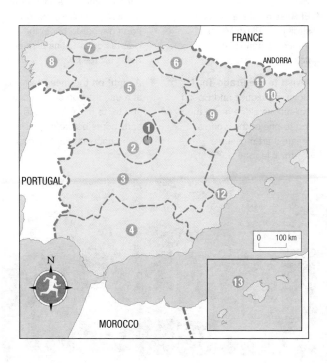

CHAPTER 1 # Highlights

* **Monasterio de las Descalzas Reales** A fascinating hoard of art treasures hidden away in a convent in the centre of Madrid. See p.88

* **Palacio Real** Over-the-top opulence in this grandiose former residence of the Spanish monarchs. See p.89

* **El Rastro** Take a Sunday stroll from Plaza Mayor through Madrid's shambolic flea market. See p.91

* **A visit to the Prado** The Goya, Velázquez and Bosch collections alone make the trip to one of the world's greatest art museums worthwhile. See p.95

* **Guernica** See this icon of twentieth-century art set in context at the Reina Sofía. See p.102

* **Real Madrid** Watch Real's dazzling array of big-name players parade their footballing skills at the Santiago Bernabéu stadium. See p.112

* **Tapas** Sample the vast array of tasty specialities as you hop from bar to bar in the Huertas or La Latina districts. See pp.118–119

* **A night on the tiles** Start late at a bar, then go on to a club and try to make it into the early hours before collapsing over chocolate con churros. See p.123

▲ Palacio Real

1

Madrid

Madrid became Spain's capital simply by virtue of its geographical position at the centre of Iberia. When Felipe II moved the seat of government here in 1561, his aim was to create a symbol of the unification and centralization of the country, and a capital from which he could receive the fastest post and communication from every corner of the nation. The site itself had few natural advantages – it is 300km from the sea on a 650-metre-high plateau, freezing in winter, boiling in summer – and it was only the determination of successive rulers to promote a strong central capital that ensured Madrid's survival and development.

Today, Madrid is a vast, predominantly modern city, with a population of some four million and growing. The journey in – through a stream of soulless suburbs and high-rise apartment blocks – isn't pretty, but the streets at the heart of the city are a pleasant surprise, with pockets of medieval buildings and narrow, atmospheric alleys, dotted with the oddest of shops and bars, and interspersed with eighteenth-century Bourbon squares. Compared with the historic cities of Spain – Toledo, Salamanca, Seville, Granada – there may be few sights of great architectural interest, but the monarchs did acquire outstanding picture collections, which formed the basis of the **Prado** museum. This, together with the **Reina Sofía** and the **Thyssen–Bornemisza** museums, state-of-the-art homes to fabulous arrays of modern Spanish painting (including Picasso's *Guernica*) and European and American masters, has made Madrid a top port of call on the European art tour.

As you get to grips with the place, you soon realize that it's the lifestyle of the inhabitants – the **madrileños** – that is the capital's key attraction: hanging out in traditional cafés or summer terrazas, packing the lanes of the Sunday Rastro flea market or playing hard and very late in a thousand **bars**, clubs, discos and *tascas*. Whatever Barcelona or San Sebastián might claim, the Madrid scene, immortalized in the movies of Pedro Almodóvar, remains the most vibrant and fun in the country. The city centre is also now in better shape than for many years as a result of the ongoing impact of a series of urban rehabilitation schemes – funded jointly by the European Union and local government – in the city's older *barrios* (districts). Improvements have been made to the transport network, with extensions to the metro, the construction of new ring roads, and the excavation of a series of road tunnels designed to bring relief to Madrid's congested streets. The downside is that the city appears to spend much of the time belly-up because of the interminable roadworks and civil-engineering projects.

The city's development

Madrid's great spread to **suburbia** began under Franco, but it has continued unabated ever since, and in recent years unbridled property speculation has

Madrid's fiestas

There are dozens of **fiestas** in Madrid, some of which involve the whole city, others just an individual *barrio*. The more important dates celebrated in the capital are listed below.

Also well worth checking out are cultural festivals organized by the city council, in particular the **Veranos de la Villa** (July–Sept) and **Festival de Otoño** (Sept–Nov) concerts (classical, rock, flamenco). Many events are free and, in the summer, often open air, taking place in the city's parks and squares. Annual festivals for alternative theatre (Feb), flamenco (Feb), books (end May), dance (April–May), photography (mid-June to mid-July) and jazz (Nov) are also firmly established on the cultural agenda. Full **programmes** are published in the monthly *En Madrid* tourist handout, free from any of the tourist offices listed on p.75 and from the city's tourist website (WWw.esmadrid.com).

January
5: Cabalgata de los Reyes To celebrate the arrival of the gift-bearing Three Kings there is a hugely popular evening procession through the city centre in which children are showered with sweets. It's held on the evening before presents are traditionally exchanged in Spain.

February
Week before Lent: Carnaval An excuse for a lot of partying and fancy-dress parades, especially in the gay zone around Chueca. The end of *Carnaval* is marked by the bizarre and entertaining parade, *El Entierro de la Sardina* (The Burial of the Sardine), on the Paseo de la Florida.

March/April
Semana Santa (Holy Week) Celebrated with a series of solemn processions around Madrid, although for a more impressive backdrop head for Toledo (routes and times of processions are available from tourist offices).

---

taken its toll on the green spaces that surround the capital. Franco also extended the city northwards along the spinal route of the Paseo de la Castellana, to accommodate his ministers and minions during development extravaganzas of the 1950s and 1960s. Large, impressive and unappealingly sterile, these constructions leave little to the imagination; but then, you're unlikely to spend much time in these parts of town.

In the centre, things are very different. The oldest streets at the very heart of Madrid are crowded with ancient buildings, spreading out in concentric circles that reveal the development of the city over the centuries. Only the cramped street plan gives much clue as to what was here before Madrid became the **Habsburg** capital (in 1561), but the narrow alleys around the Plaza Mayor are still among the city's liveliest and most atmospheric. Later growth owed much to the French tastes of the **Bourbon** dynasty in the eighteenth century, when for the first time Madrid began to develop a style and flavour of its own.

The early **nineteenth century** brought invasion and turmoil to Spain as Napoleon established his brother Joseph (or José to Spaniards) on the throne. Madrid, however, continued to flourish, gaining some very attractive buildings and squares. With the onset of the twentieth century, the capital became the hotbed of the political and intellectual discussions that divided the country; *tertulias* (political/philosophical discussion circles) sprang up in cafés across the city (some of them are still going) as the country entered the turbulent years of the end of the monarchy and the foundation of the Second Republic.

May

2: Fiesta del Dos de Mayo Held in Malasaña and elsewhere in Madrid. Bands and partying around the Plaza Dos de Mayo, though a bit low-key in recent years.

15: Fiestas de San Isidro Festivities to honour Madrid's patron saint are spread a week either side of this date, and are among the country's biggest festivals. The fiestas also herald the start of the bullfighting season.

June/July

End June/beginning July: La Semana del Orgullo (Gay Pride Week) Week-long party throughout Chueca, culminating in a massive carnival-style parade that brings the city centre to a standstill.

August

6–15: Castizo Traditional fiestas of *San Cayetano*, *San Lorenzo* and *La Virgen de la Paloma* in La Latina and Lavapiés *barrios*. Much of the activity takes place around Calle Toledo, the Plaza de la Paja and the Jardines de las Vistillas.

December

25: Navidad During Christmas, Plaza Mayor is filled with stalls selling festive decorations and displaying a large model of a Nativity scene. El Corte Inglés, at the bottom of c/Preciados, has an all-singing, all-dancing clockwork Christmas scene (*Cortylandia*), which plays at certain times of the day to the delight of assembled children.

31: Nochevieja New Year's Eve is celebrated at bars, restaurants and parties all over the city. Puerta del Sol is the customary place to gather, waiting for the strokes of the clock – it is traditional to swallow a grape on each stroke to bring good luck in the coming year.

The **Civil War**, of course, caused untold damage, and led to forty years of isolation, which you can still sense in Madrid's idiosyncratic style. The Spanish capital has changed immeasurably, however, in the three decades since Franco's death, initially guided by a poet-mayor, the late Tierno Galván. His efforts – the creation of parks and renovation of public spaces and public life – have left an enduring legacy, and were a vital ingredient of the *movida madrileña*, the "happening Madrid", with which the city broke through in the 1980s. Since the early 1990s, the centre-right Partido Popular has been in control of the local council, bringing with it a more restrictive attitude towards bar and club licensing. Unfortunately, there has also been a simultaneous tendency towards homogenization with the rest of Europe as franchised fast-food joints and coffee bars spring up all over the place. Nevertheless, in making the transition from provincial backwater to major European capital, Madrid has still managed to preserve its own stylish and quirky identity.

Orientation, arrival and information

The city's layout is fairly straightforward. At the heart of Madrid – indeed, at the very heart of Spain since all distances in the country are measured from here – is the **Puerta del Sol** (often referred to as just "Sol"). Around it lie the oldest

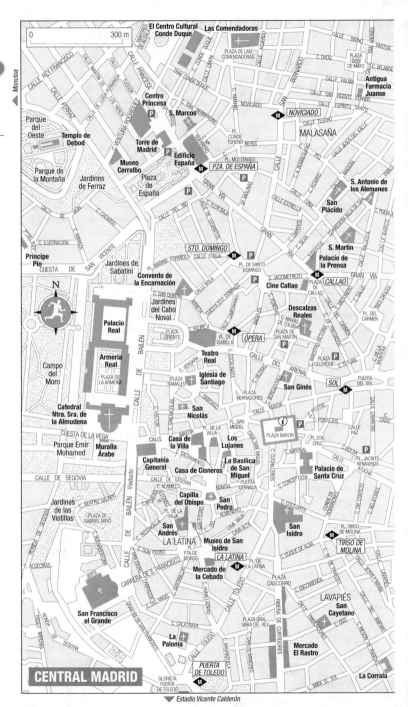

CENTRAL MADRID

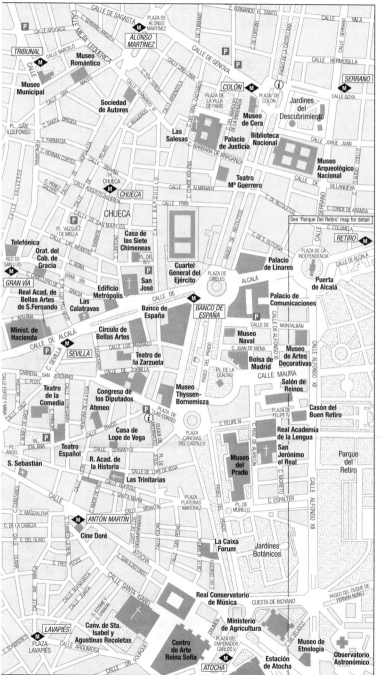

Estación Sur de Autobuses

parts of Madrid, neatly bordered to the west by the **Río Manzanares**, to the east by the park of **El Retiro** and to the north by the city's great thoroughfare, the **Gran Vía**.

The city's three big museums – the **Prado**, **Thyssen-Bornemisza** and **Reina Sofía** – lie in a "golden triangle" just west of El Retiro and centred around Paseo del Prado, while over towards the river are the oldest, Habsburg parts of town surrounding **Plaza Mayor**.

Arrival

If Madrid is your first stop in Spain, by **air**, **train** or **bus**, you are likely to arrive a little way from the centre. Transport into the centre, however, is relatively cheap, easy and efficient.

By plane

The **Aeropuerto de Barajas** (general information ☎902 404 704, Ⓦwww .aena.es) is 16km east of the city, at the end of Avenida de América (the A2 road). It has four terminals, including the vast new T4 building designed by Richard Rogers and Carlos Lamela, which has helped double the capacity to some seventy million passengers a year. All Iberia's domestic and international flights, as well as airlines that belong to the Oneworld group, such as British Airways and American Airways, use T4 (a 10min shuttle-bus ride from the other terminals); other international flights and budget airlines, including easyJet and Ryanair, go from T1, while Air France, KLM and SAS use T2.

From the airport, the **metro** link (Line 8) takes you from T4 and T2 to the city's Nuevos Ministerios station in just twelve minutes (daily 6am–2am; €2) From there it's a fifteen-minute metro ride to most city-centre locations.

The route by road to central Madrid is more variable, depending on rush-hour traffic, and can take anything from twenty minutes to an hour. **Buses** run from each terminal to the terminus at Avenida de América (#200 from T1 and T2, #204 from T4; daily 6am–11.30pm; €1). **Taxis** are always available outside, too, and cost €25–30 (including a €5.25 airport supplement) to the centre, unless you get stuck in traffic.

Half a dozen or so **car rental** companies have stands at the airport terminals and can generally supply clients with maps and directions (see p.137 for addresses and phone numbers of car-rental offices in the city). Other airport facilities include 24-hour currency exchange, ATMs, a post office, left-luggage lockers, a RENFE office for booking train tickets, chemists, tourist offices and hotel reservations desks.

By train

Trains **from France or north and northeast Spain** arrive at the **Estación de Chamartín**, a modern terminal isolated in the north of the city; it has all the usual big-station facilities, including currency exchange. A metro line connects Chamartín with the centre, and there are also regular connections by the commuter trains (*cercanías*) with the more central Estación de Atocha.

The **Estación de Atocha** has two separate terminals: one for local services, the other for all points in **south and eastern Spain**, including the high-speed AVE trains to Toledo, Seville, Malaga, Zaragoza and Lleida.

If you're coming from local **towns around Madrid**, you may arrive at **Príncipe Pío** (aka Estación del Norte), fairly close to the centre below the Palacio Real, which is also connected to the metro network.

For train **information and reservations**, call ℡902 240 202 or go to ⓦwww.renfe.es. Tickets can be bought at the individual stations, at Aeropuerto de Barajas arrivals in T1 and T4 (Mon–Fri 8am–3pm) and at registered travel agents. Bear in mind that you'll need to book in advance for most long-distance trains, especially at weekends or holiday time.

By bus

Bus terminals are scattered throughout the city, but the largest – used by all of the international bus services – is the **Estación Sur de Autobuses** at c/Méndez Álvaro 83 on the corner of c/Retama, 1.5km south of the Estación de Atocha (℡914 684 200, ⓦwww.estaciondeautobuses.com; ⓂMéndez Álvaro). For details of others, see the "Travel details" section at the end of this chapter.

By car

All the main roads into Madrid bring you right into the city centre, although eccentric signposting and even more eccentric driving can be very unnerving. Both ring roads – the M40 and the M30 – and the Paseo de la Castellana are all notorious bottlenecks, although virtually the whole city centre can be close to gridlock during the peak **rush-hour periods** (Mon–Fri 7.30–9.30am & 6–8.30pm). Be prepared for a long trawl around the streets to find **parking**, and even then in most central areas you'll have to buy a ticket at one of the roadside meters (€2.55 for a maximum stay of 2hr in the blue-coloured bays; €1.80 for a maximum stay of 1hr in the green-coloured bays). A better, and safer, option is to put your car in one of the many signposted *parkings* (up to €2/hr and around €25/day). Your own transport is really only of use for out-of-town excursions, so it's advisable to find a hotel with or near a car park and keep your car there during your stay in the city. If you are staying more than a couple of weeks, you can get long-term parking rates at some neighbourhood garages.

Information and maps

There are year-round **turismo offices** at the following locations: Aeropuerto de Barajas in T1 (Mon–Fri 8am–8pm, Sat & Sun 9am–2pm; ℡913 058 656) and T4 (daily 9.30am–8.30pm; ℡901 100 007); Estación de Atocha (Mon–Sat 8am–8pm, Sun 9am–2pm; ℡902 100 007); Estación de Chamartín (Mon–Fri 8am–8pm, Sat 9am–2pm; ℡913 159 976); Casa de la Panaderia, Plaza Mayor 27 (daily 9.30am–8.30pm; ℡915 881 636; ⓂSol, Ópera); Colón (in the underground passageway, accessed at the corner of c/Goya; daily 9.30am–8.30pm; ⓂColón) and c/Duque de Medinaceli 2 (Mon–Sat 8am–8pm, Sun 9am–2pm; ℡914 294 951; ⓂBanco de España). There are also *turismo* booths next to the Reina Sofía, in Plaza de la Cibeles and in Plaza del Callao off Gran Vía (daily 9.30am–8.30pm). The Madrid tourist board has a useful website (ⓦwww .esmadrid.com), while the regional authority has one covering the whole of the province (ⓦwww.turismomadrid.es), and there's a tourist information line on ℡901 300 600, as well as a general number, ℡902 100 007, that links all the *turismo* offices mentioned above.

Free **maps** of the whole central area of Madrid are available from any of the *turismos* detailed above, or there's the *Rough Guide City Map Madrid* that pinpoints most of the sights, hotels, restaurants and bars. The publisher Almax produces a 1:12,000-scale *Madrid Ciudad* (around 55) that goes right out into the suburbs and is widely available at city-centre newspaper kiosks.

City transport and tours

Madrid is a pretty easy city to get around. The central areas are walkable; the metro is modern, extensive and efficient; buses are also good and serve some of the more out-of-the-way districts, and taxis are always available.

If you're using public transport extensively, it could be worth getting a **tourist pass**, recently introduced; these are non-transferable, and you'll need to show your passport or identity card at the time of purchase. **Zone A** cards cover central Madrid on bus, metro and train, **Zone T** cards cover the whole region including buses to Toledo and Guadalajara but not those to the airport. They are available for a duration of one to seven days and range in cost from €5 for a Zone A daily card to €45.20 for a weekly one for Zone T (under-11s are half price; under-4s travel free). If you're staying longer, passes (*abonos*) covering the metro, train and bus, and available for each calendar month, are worthwhile. If you have an InterRail or Eurail pass, you can use the RENFE local trains (*cercanías*) free of charge – they're an alternative to the metro for some longer city journeys.

The metro

The clean and highly efficient **metro** (Ⓦ www.metromadrid.es) is by far the quickest way of getting around Madrid, serving most places you're likely to want to get to. It runs from 6am until 2am, and the flat fare is €1 for the central zone (€1.90 if you want to venture further afield), or €7 for a ten-trip ticket (*bono de diez viajes*), which can be used on buses, too. The network has undergone massive expansion in recent years and some of the outlying commuter districts are now connected by light railways, which link with the existing stations (separate tickets are needed for most of these). Lines are numbered and colour-coded, and the direction of travel is indicated by the name of the terminus station. You can pick up a free colour map of the system (*plano del metro*) at any station.

Buses

The urban **bus network** (Ⓦ www.emtmadrid.es) is comprehensive but a little more complicated than the metro: in the text, where there's no metro stop, we've indicated which bus to take. There are information booths in the Plaza de Cibeles and Puerta del Sol, which dispense a huge route map (*plano de los transportes de Madrid*), and – along with other outlets – sell bus passes. Fares are

---

Madrid discount cards

The **Madrid Card** (☏ 902 877 996, Ⓦ www.madridcard.com; online purchase Ⓦ www.neoturismo.com) gives the holder the right of admission to forty major museums, a tour of the Bernabéu, the use of public transport, the *teleférico*, an open-top bus tour and a guided walking tour of the old city, as well as discounts at a number of shops and restaurants. It costs €42 for one day (€55 for two, €68 for three) and is on sale at the Plaza Mayor and c/Duque de Medinaceli tourist offices. There is a variation known as the **Madrid Card Cultura** directed solely at the museums (from €28/day) and a children's version for under-12s (€32 for three days). Do your sums before you splash out, though, as you would need to cram a lot in to a day's sightseeing to get your money's worth. If you just want to concentrate on the big three art galleries, the Paseo del Arte ticket (see p.95) is far better value, and allows you to take things at a more leisurely pace.

MADRID METRO

Legend:
- Parque de Santa María ●○ Terminus
- Mar de Cristal ●○ Interchange station
- Canillas ●● Station

Metro Oeste light railway connects to Boadilla, Pozuelo de Alarcón & Aravaca

the same as for the metro, at €1 a journey, or €7 for a ten-trip ticket (*bono de diez viajes*), which can be used on both forms of transport, but note that you can only buy the single tickets on the buses themselves (try to have the right money).

Buses run from 6am to 11.30pm. In addition, there are *búho* (owl) night buses that operate on twenty routes around the central area and out to the suburbs: departures are every fifteen to thirty minutes from midnight to 5.30am, from Plaza de Cibeles and Puerta del Sol.

Taxis

One of the best things about getting round Madrid is that there are thousands of **taxis** – white cars with a diagonal red stripe on the side – which are reasonably cheap; €7 will get you to most places within the centre and, although it's common to round up the fare, you're not expected to tip. The minimum fare is €1.95 and supplements are charged for the airport, train and bus stations, the IFEMA congress centre, going outside the city limits, and for night trips (10pm–6am). In any area in the centre, day and night, you should be able to wave down a taxi (available ones have a green light on top of the cab) in a short time, although it is more difficult at weekends when half the population is out on the town. To phone for a taxi, call ☎914 475 180, 914 051 213, 913 712 131 or 915 478 200 (also for wheelchair-friendly cabs). If you leave something in a taxi, ring ☎915 279 590.

Local trains

The **local train** network, or *cercanías*, is the most efficient way of connecting between the main train stations and provides the best route out to many of the suburbs and to nearby towns such as Alcalá de Henares. Most trains are air-conditioned, fares are cheap, and there are good connections with the metro. Trains generally run every fifteen to thirty minutes from 6am to midnight. For more information, go to the RENFE website at ⓦwww.renfe.es and click on the *cercanías* section for Madrid.

City tours

The *turismo* in Plaza Mayor can supply details of a variety of guided English-language **walking tours** around the city on the "Descubre Madrid" programme (from €3.25; info on ☎914 802 036 or 915 882 906 and at ⓦwww .esmadrid.com). For a **bus tour** of all the major city sights, try Madrid Vision, c/Felipe IV (between the Prado and the *Ritz* hotel; ☎917 651 016 or 917 791 888, ⓦwww.madridvision.es; ⓜBanco de España); tickets cost €16 (children €8.50, under-6s free) and allow you to jump on and off throughout the day at various places throughout the city. Pick-up points include Puerta del Sol, Plaza de España and the Prado.

Accommodation

Business hotels apart, most of Madrid's **accommodation** is pretty central. With increasing competition in the sector, many *hostales* and hotels have been busy upgrading their facilities in recent years and a new breed of stylish, design-conscious, medium-priced hotel has emerged. Many of the expensive hotels serving business travellers do special weekend offers. Prices also drop substantially in August when temperatures soar and many people escape to the coast or the mountains. If you prefer to have others find you a room, there are accommodation services at the airport (Viajes Aira in T1, T2 and T4; ☎913 054 224; no fee), the Estación Sur de Autobuses, and Atocha and Chamartín train stations. Brújula is particularly helpful, with offices at Atocha station (daily 8.30am–10pm; ☎915 391 173) and Chamartín (daily 7am–9.30pm; ☎913 157 894), although they sometimes close early in the evenings if business is slow; the service covers the whole of Spain and there is a €2.50 booking fee.

Pensiones, hostales and hotels

If you want to be at the heart of the old town, the areas around **Puerta del Sol**, **Plaza de Santa Ana** and **Plaza Mayor** are the ones to go for; if you're into nightlife, **Malasaña** or **Chueca** may also appeal; for a quieter location and a bit of class, you should opt for the **Paseo del Prado**, **Recoletos** or **Salamanca** areas.

You'll notice that buildings in the more popular hotel/*hostal* areas often house two or three separate establishments, each on **separate floors**; these are generally independent of each other. One thing to bear in mind is **noise**; bars, clubs, traffic and roadworks all contribute to making Madrid a high-decibel city, so avoid rooms on the lower floors, or choose a place away from the nightlife if you want a bit of peace and quiet. As for **facilities**, air-conditioning is a welcome extra in summer when temperatures can soar towards 40°C.

Sol, Ópera and Plaza Mayor

This really is the heart of Madrid, and prices, not surprisingly, are a bit higher than some of the other central areas, though you can still find bargains in the streets around the Plaza Mayor. Be aware that Sol itself is likely to be disrupted by building works in the next few years owing to the construction of a new underground *cercanías* train station.

Hostal Don Alfonso Plaza Celenque 1, 2º ☎915 319 840, Ⓕ915 329 225; Ⓜ Sol/Ópera. Well located just off c/Arenal, this clean, neatly furnished *hostal* has fourteen doubles, two triples and a handful of singles at a competitive price, all with bathrooms, a/c and TV. ❸

Hostal La Macarena Cava de San Miguel 8, 2º ☎913 659 221, Ⓦ www.silserranos.com; Ⓜ Sol. A fine, refurbished, family-run *hostal* in a characterful street just off the Plaza Mayor, though the well-kept rooms are a little on the small side. ❹

Hostal Riesco c/Correo 2, 3º ☎915 222 692, Ⓕ915 329 088; Ⓜ Sol. An old-style, characterful place in a street just off Sol. All rooms in this friendly, family-run *hostal* are en suite and have a/c. ❷

Hostal Tijcal & Hostal Tijcal 2 c/Zaragoza 6, 3º ☎913 655 910, Ⓦ www.hostaltijcal.com; Ⓜ Sol. Situated between Plaza Santa Cruz and Plaza Mayor, this quirky but extremely hospitable *hostal* offers rooms with a/c (€5 supplement), bathroom

and TV (some also have good views). Discounts for cash. There is a sister *hostal*, the *Tijcal 2*, at c/Cruz 26 ☎913 604 628. ❸

Hostal Valencia Plaza de Oriente 23 ☎915 598 450, Ⓦ www.hostalvalencia.tk; Ⓜ Ópera. Fabulous location with great views over the plaza towards the Palacio Real. The seven quiet, traditional-style rooms are very clean, and the owner is charming. ❸

Hotel Meninas c/Campomanes 7 ☎915 412 805, Ⓦ www.hotelmeninas.com; Ⓜ Ópera. A stylish 37-room hotel owned by the same group as the nearby *Ópera*, and similarly good value. Very helpful staff, excellent attic rooms, and free broadband internet access. ❺

Hotel Ópera c/Cuesta de Santo Domingo 2 ☎915 412 800, Ⓦ www.hotelopera.com; Ⓜ Ópera. In a very pleasant location near the Plaza de Oriente, this modern hotel has 79 comfortable, large rooms at a pretty reasonable price. Free broadband internet access. The café downstairs, appropriately enough, offers dinner served by singing waiters. ❺

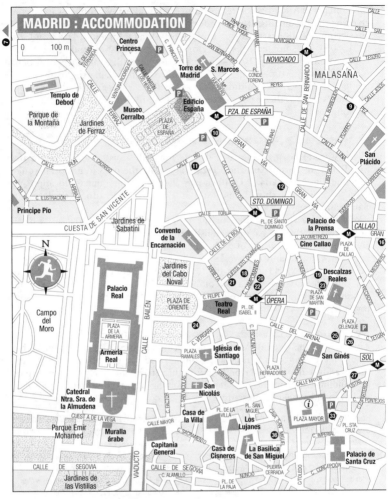

MADRID : ACCOMMODATION

0   100 m

ACCOMMODATION

Los Amigos Backpackers' Hostel	**20**	Hostal Asunción	**6**	Hostal Riesco	**27**
Apartamentos Turísticos	**31**	Hostal Barrera	**42**	Hostal Santa Bárbara	**1**
Aparta-hotel Rosales	**7**	Hostal Don Alfonso	**25**	Hostal Sil/Serranos	**5**
Casón del Tormes	**11**	Hostal Don Diego	**8**	Hostal Tijcal	**33**
Hostal Alaska	**30**	Hostal Gonzalo	**40**	Hostal Tijcal 2	**35**
Hostal Andorra	**16**	Hostal La Macarena	**36**	Hostal Valencia	**24**
		Hostal Persal	**39**	Hostal Zamora	**13**

Hotel Abalú	**9**
Hotel de Las Letras	**17**
Hotel Emperador	**12**
Hotel Galiano	**3**
Hotel Meninas	**18**
Hotel Mora	**43**
Hotel Ópera	**21**

Hotel Palacio de San Martín c/Plaza de San Martín 5 ☎917 015 000, ⓦwww.intur.com; ⓂÓpera/Sol. Situated in a historic building in an attractive square alongside the Monasterío de las Descalzas Reales. Elegant and spacious rooms with period decor, and an attractive rooftop restaurant. ❼

Petit Palace Arenal c/Arenal 16 ☎915 644 355, ⓦwww.hthoteles.com; ⓂSol/ Ópera. A member of the self-styled High-Tech Hotels chain. Sleek, modern decor; all 64 rooms have a/c and free broadband, some have flat-screen TVs and exercise bikes. Two other members of this chain, the *Posada del Peine* and

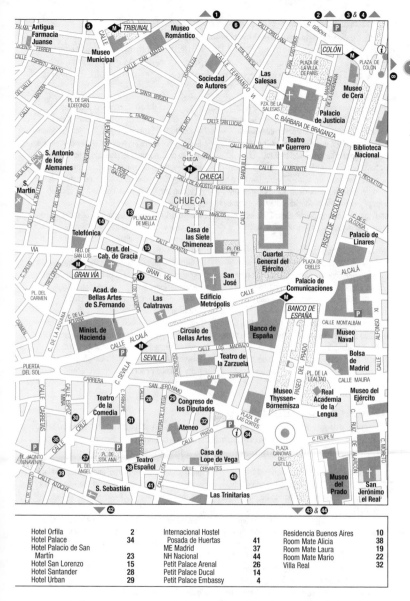

Hotel Orfila	2	Internacional Hostel		Residencia Buenos Aires	10
Hotel Palace	34	Posada de Huertas	41	Room Mate Alicia	38
Hotel Palacio de San		ME Madrid	37	Room Mate Laura	19
Martín	23	NH Nacional	44	Room Mate Mario	22
Hotel San Lorenzo	15	Petit Palace Arenal	26	Villa Real	32
Hotel Santander	28	Petit Palace Ducal	14		
Hotel Urban	29	Petit Palace Embassy	4		

the *Puerta del Sol*, are close at c/Postas 17 and c/Arenal 4. ④–⑤

Room Mate Mario c/Campomanes 4º ☎915 488 548, ⓦ www.room-matehoteles.com; Ⓜ Ópera. Good-value, designer hotel with a perfect spot on a pleasant street close to the opera house and next to the trendy *Viuda Blanca* restaurant

(see p.115). Compact rooms, neat bathrooms, friendly staff and free internet. Buffet breakfast is included. There is another member of the chain, the *Laura*, at nearby Travesía de Trujillos 3 (☎917 011 670). ⑤

Around Plaza de Santa Ana and Huertas

Plaza de Santa Ana and the Huertas area are at the heart of Madrid nightlife, with bars and cafés open until very late at night. The following are all within a few blocks of the square, with the metro stations Antón Martín, Sevilla and Sol close by. Go for rooms on the higher floors if you want to avoid the worst of the noise.

Hostal Alaska c/Espoz y Mina 7, 4º ☎915 211 845, ⓦwww.hostalalaska.com; Ⓜ️Sol. Six brightly decorated doubles and an apartment, all with bathroom and TV, make up this well-run *hostal*, formerly known as the *Hostal Valencia*. ❸

Hostal Barrera c/Atocha 96, 2º ☎915 275 381, ⓦwww.hostalbarrera.com; Ⓜ️Antón Martín. A friendly, good-value fourteen-room *hostal* only a short distance from Atocha station and run by an English-speaking owner. Smart rooms have bath or shower, a/c and TV. Internet access available. ❸

Hostal Persal Plaza del Ángel 12 ☎913 694 643, ⓦwww.hostalpersal.com; Ⓜ️Sol. Affable and excellent-value eighty-room hotel. All the refurbished rooms have a/c, bathroom, TV and free wi-fi. Breakfast is included. Studios and apartments available, too. ❸–❹

Hotel Santander c/Echegaray 1 ☎914 296 644 or 914 299 551, ⓦwww.hotelsantandermadrid.com; Ⓜ️Sevilla. Spacious, spotless rooms – many have a small seating area – in this old-fashioned but pleasant 35-room two-star hotel. No breakfast served. ❹

Hotel Urban Carrera San Jeronimo 34 ☎917 877 770, ⓦwww.derbyhotels.es; Ⓜ️Sevilla/Sol. Extremely stylish, fashion-conscious, five-star hotel offering a glut of designer rooms, a rooftop pool, summer terrace and "pijo" cocktail bar. It even has its own small museum, consisting of items from owner Jordi Clos's collection of Egyptian and Chinese art. Look out for special deals online. ❼

ME Madrid Plaza de Santa Ana 14 ☎917 016 000, ⓦwww.memadrid.travel; Ⓜ️Sol. Once a favourite haunt of bullfighters, this giant cream cake at the top of the plaza has now been refurbished and rebranded as part of Meliá's glamorous new *ME* chain of hotels. Minimalist decor, designer furnishings, hi-tech fittings, a super-cool penthouse bar and a chic restaurant. ❽

Room Mate Alicia c/Prado 2 ☎913 896 095, ⓦwww.room-matehotels.com; Ⓜ️Sol/Sevilla. Perched on the corner of the plaza, the 34-room *Alicia* is in a great location – if a little noisy. Seriously cool decor, stylish rooms and unbeatable value. ❹–❺

Around Paseo del Prado

This is a quieter area, though still very central, and it is close to the main art museums, the Parque del Retiro and Estación de Atocha. Some of the city's most expensive hotels are here – as well as a few more modest options.

Hostal Gonzalo c/Cervantes 34, 3º ☎914 292 714, ⓦwww.hostalgonzalo .com; Ⓜ️Antón Martín. This has to be one of the most welcoming *hostales* in the city. It has fifteen bright, en-suite rooms – all of which have a/c and new bathrooms – and a charming owner. ❸

Hotel Mora Paseo del Prado 32 ☎914 201 569, ⓦwww.hotelmora.com; Ⓜ️Atocha. A good-value, slightly old-fashioned 62-room hotel perfectly positioned for all the galleries on the Paseo del Arte. It's not as smart as the nearby *Nacional*, but it's cheaper, and some of the a/c rooms have pleasant views along the Paseo del Prado. ❹

Hotel Palace Plaza de los Cortes 7 ☎913 608 000, ⓦwww.westinpalacemadrid.com; Ⓜ️Atocha/Banco de España. A colossal, sumptuous hotel with every imaginable facility, a spectacular,

glass-covered central patio, and luxurious rooms – plus none of the snootiness of the *Ritz* across the road. ❼–❾

NH Nacional Paseo del Prado 48 ☎914 296 629, ⓦwww.nh-hoteles.com; Ⓜ️Atocha. A large, plush hotel, part of the NH chain, attractively situated opposite the Jardines Botánicos. Special offers can reduce the price substantially. ❺–❻

Villa Real Plaza de las Cortes 10 ☎914 203 767, ⓦwww.derbyhotels.es; Ⓜ️Sevilla. A high-class, aristocratic hotel with its own art collection owned by Catalan entrepreneur Jordi Clos. Each of the 96 elegant double rooms has a spacious sitting area. The rooftop restaurant, which has some Andy Warhol originals on the wall, affords splendid views over the Congresos de Diputados and down towards the Paseo del Prado. ❺–❽

Plaza de España and Gran Vía

The huge old buildings along the Gran Vía – which stretches all the way from Plaza de España to c/Alcalá – hide a vast array of hotels and *hostales* at every price, often with a delightfully decayed elegance, though they also suffer from traffic noise. After dark, the area can feel somewhat seedy.

Casón del Tormes c/Río 7 ☎915 419 746, ⓦwww.hotelcasondeltormes.com; ⓜPlaza de España. A plush 63-room hotel in a surprisingly quiet street off Plaza de España, the *Casón del Tormes* is a very good option in this price range. Rooms are comfortable, en suite and a/c, and the English-speaking staff are helpful. Discounts in July & Aug. ❹

Hostal Andorra Gran Vía 33, 7º ☎915 323 116, ⓦwww.hostalandorra.com; ⓜCallao. Homely, clean and calm, with bathrooms and a/c in all the rooms. ❸

Hotel Emperador Gran Vía 53 ☎915 472 800, ⓦwww.emperadorhotel.com; ⓜSanto Domingo/ Plaza de España. The main reason to come here is for the stunning rooftop swimming pool with its magnificent views. Otherwise, it is a rather impersonal place, though rooms are large and well decorated. ❺

Hotel de las Letras Gran Vía 11 ☎915 237 980, ⓦwww.hoteldelasletras.com; ⓜGran Vía. A new, design-conscious hotel housed in an elegant, early nineteenth-century building at the smarter end of Gran Vía. The stylish rooms come complete with flat-screen TVs and pillow menus. Downstairs, there's a cool bar and lounge area and a high-quality restaurant with reasonably priced dishes. ❻

Residencia Buenos Aires Gran Vía 61, 2º ☎915 420 102, ⓦwww.hoteleshn.com; ⓜPlaza de España. Thirty pleasantly decorated rooms with a/c, satellite TV and modern bathrooms, plus double-glazing to keep out much of the noise. ❸

North of Gran Vía and Chueca

North of Gran Vía, there are further wedges of *hostales* on and around c/Fuencarral and c/Hortaleza, near ⓜGran Vía. To the east of c/Fuencarral, Chueca is another nightlife centre and the city's *zona gay*, which has been given a new lease of life with the recent opening of numerous bars, clubs and restaurants.

Hostal Zamora Plaza Vázquez de Mella 1, 4º izda. ☎915 217 031, ⓦwww.hostalzamora.com. ⓜGran Vía. Most of the seventeen well-kept, simple rooms in this pleasant *hostal* overlook the recently spruced-up plaza. All have bathrooms, TV and a/c. There are good-value family rooms, too. ❷

Hotel San Lorenzo c/Clavel 8 ☎915 213 057, ⓦwww.hotel-sanlorenzo.com. ⓜGran Vía. A former *hostal* that has been upgraded to a neat and tidy three-star hotel offering clean and comfortable rooms with a/c and bathrooms. Family rooms with two bedrooms are available for €115–165. ❸–❹

Petit Palace Ducal c/Hortaleza 3, 3º ☎915 211 043, ⓦwww.hthoteles.com; ⓜGran Vía. A major upgrading from the old *hostal* that used to occupy this property, this is one of a series of self-styled High-Tech Hotels. Its 58 all-new rooms come complete with all manner of mod cons. ❹–❺

Malasaña and Santa Bárbara

Malasaña, west of c/Fuencarral and centred around Plaza Dos de Mayo, is an old working-class district, and one of the main nightlife areas of Madrid.

Hostal Asunción Plaza Santa Bárbara 8, 2º ☎913 082 348, ⓦwww.hostalasuncion.com; ⓜAlonso Martínez. In a pretty position overlooking the square, this place has small but well-furnished rooms with bath, TV and a/c. Free internet use for guests. ❷

Hostal Santa Bárbara Plaza Santa Bárbara 4, 3º ☎914 457 334 or 914 469 308, ☏914 462 345; ⓜAlonso Martínez. A rather up-market *hostal* in a good location. Tidy little rooms, some with a/c. ❸

Hostal Sil/Serranos c/Fuencarral 95, 2º & 3º ☎914 488 972, ⓦwww.silserranos.com; ⓜTribunal. Two well-managed *hostales*, run by a friendly owner, at the quieter end of c/Fuencarral, with a/c, new bathrooms and TV. ❹

Hotel Abalú c/Pez 19 33, 7º ☎915 314 744, ⓦwww.hotelabalu.com. Another of the new arrivals on the Madrid hotel scene. This one, which is a little north of Gran Vía, has just fifteen specially designed rooms with individual touches such as mini-chandeliers. Great value. ❹

Paseo de Recoletos and Salamanca

This is Madrid at its most chic: the Bond Street/Rue de Rivoli region of smart shops and equally well-heeled apartment blocks. It's a safe, pleasant area, just north of the Parque del Retiro, though a good walk from the main sights.

Hostal Don Diego c/Velázquez 45, 5º ☎914 350 760, ⓦwww.hostaldondiego .com; ⓜVelázquez. Although officially a *hostal*, this is much more like a hotel. All the neat and comfortable rooms are a/c and have satellite TV. Reasonably priced for the area. Some English-speaking staff. ❺

Hotel Galiano c/Alcalá Galiano 6 ☎913 192 000, ⓦwww.hotelgaliano.com; ⓜColón. Hidden away in a quiet street off the Paseo de la Castellana, this small hotel has a sophisticated feel and friendly service. Look out for special offers on the website. Car-parking facilities. ❺

Hotel Orfila c/Orfila 6 ☎917 027 770, ⓦwww .hotelorfila.com; ⓜColón/Alonso Martínez. An exclusive boutique hotel housed in a beautiful nineteenth-century mansion on a quiet street north of Alonso Martínez. Twelve of the exquisite rooms are suites, and there's an elegant terrace for tea and drinks, as well as an upmarket restaurant, too. Of course, none of this comes cheap, with rooms starting at €285 a night. ❽

Petit Palace Embassy c/Serrano 46 ☎914 313 060, ⓦwww.hthoteles.com; ⓜColón/Goya. A member of the sleek High-Tech Hotels chain. This one, which is close to Plaza de Colón and in the middle of the upmarket Salamanca shopping district, has 75 rooms, including ten family rooms for up to four people. Free broadband internet access and flat-screen TVs. ❻

Apartments

If you're travelling as a family or in a group and want to cater a bit more for yourself, there are a few apartments scattered around the city. Below are two of the most convenient.

Apartamentos Turísticos Principe c/Príncipe 11 ☎902 113 311, ⓦwww.atprincipe11.com; ⓜSevilla. A good option for families or groups. The 36 apartments in this centrally located block range from small studios to family suites for up to six. All are a/c and have kitchenettes. Prices range from €107 for a four-person apartment to €160 for a six-person family one.

Aparto-hotel Rosales c/Marqués de Urquijo 23 ☎915 420 351, ⓦwww.apartohotel-rosales.com; ⓜArgüelles. Large, comfortable apartments with separate bedroom, living area and kitchenette. Close to the Parque del Oeste and in one of the quieter areas of town, so a good option if you're travelling with children. Prices are around €150 (2 person) and €190 (4 person).

Youth hostels

Madrid has just one campsite, located well out of the centre, but there are two very handy backpackers' hostels right in the heart of the city.

Summer in Madrid

Although things are beginning to change as Madrid comes into line with the rest of Europe, the Spanish capital experiences a **partial shut-down** in the summer; from the end of July, you'll suddenly find that many of the bars, restaurants and offices are closed, and their inhabitants gone to the coast and countryside. Only in September does the city open properly for business again.

Luckily for visitors, and those *madrileños* who choose to remain, the main sights and museums stay open, and a summer nightlife takes on a momentum of its own in outdoor terrace bars, or *terrazas*. In addition, the city council organizes a major programme of entertainment, **Los Veranos de la Villa**, and overall it's not a bad time to be in town, so long as you can cope with the soaring temperatures and you're not trying to get anything done.

Los Amigos Backpackers' Hostel c/Campomanes 6, 4º ☎915 512 472; c/Arenal 25, 4º ☎915 512 472; Ⓦwww.losamigoshostel.com; ⓂÓpera/Sol. Two great backpacking options, the first in a quiet side street by the Opera House, the second in a busier area close to Sol. Both places have some four-room dorms, others for between four and six people, and more crowded ones catering for up to ten. There are communal rooms, plus internet

access. Friendly staff all speak English. Prices start at €19.

International Hostel Posada de Huertas c/Huertas 21 ☎914 295 526, Ⓦwww.posadadehuertas.com; ⓂAntón Martín/Sevilla. A modern hostel right at the heart of things, close to Plaza de Santa Ana. There's a common room with TV and internet access, plus laundry facilities and individual lockers. Breakfast is included in the €19 price.

The City

Madrid's main sights occupy a compact area between the **Palacio Real** and the gardens of **El Retiro**. The great trio of museums – the **Prado**, **Thyssen-Bornemisza** and **Reina Sofía** – are ranged along the Paseo del Prado, over towards the Retiro. The oldest part of the city, an area known as **Madrid de los Austrias** after the Habsburg monarchs who built it, is centred on the gorgeous, arcaded **Plaza Mayor**, just to the east of the Palacio Real.

If you have very limited time, you might well do no more sightseeing than this. However, monuments are not really what Madrid is about, and to get a feel for the city you need to branch out a little, and experience the contrasting character and life of the various *barrios*. The most central and rewarding of these are the areas around **Plaza de Santa Ana and c/Huertas**, east of Puerta del Sol; **La Latina and Lavapiés**, south of Plaza Mayor, where the Sunday market, **El Rastro**, takes place; and **Malasaña and Chueca**, north of Gran Vía. By happy circumstance, these *barrios* have some of Madrid's finest concentrations of tapas bars and restaurants.

Madrid de los Austrias: Sol, Plaza Mayor and Ópera

Madrid de los Austrias (Habsburg Madrid) was a mix of formal planning – at its most impressive in the expansive and theatrical Plaza Mayor – and areas of shanty town development, thrown up as the new capital gained an urban population. The central area of old Madrid still reflects both characteristics, with its twisting grid of streets, alleyways and steps, and its Flemish-inspired architecture of red brick and grey stone, slate-tiled towers and Renaissance doorways.

Puerta del Sol

The obvious starting point for exploring Habsburg Madrid (and most other areas of the centre) is the **Puerta del Sol** (ⓂSol). This square marks the epicentre of the city – and, indeed, of Spain. It is from this point that all distances are measured, and here that six of Spain's *Rutas Nacionales* officially begin. On the pavement outside the clocktower building on the south side of the square, a stone slab shows **Kilometre Zero**.

The square is a popular meeting place, especially by the fountain, or at the corner of c/Carmen, with its statue of a bear pawing a *madroño* (strawberry tree) – the city's emblem. These apart, there's little of note, though the square fulfils something of a public role when there's a demonstration or celebration; at New Year, for example, it is packed with people waiting for the clock to chime midnight. The square's main business, however, is shopping, with giant branches of the **department stores** El Corte Inglés and the French chain FNAC in

Madrid's freebies

Free entrance can be gained to many of Madrid's premier attractions. Sites classed as *Patrimonio Nacional*, such as the Palacio Real, the Convento de la Encarnación, El Pardo and the Monasterio de las Descalzas, are free to EU citizens on Wednesdays (bring your passport). Seven museums run by Madrid City Council, including the Museo Municipal, the Museo de San Isidro, La Ermita de San Antonio, the Templo de Debod and the Museo de Arte Contemporaneo, no longer charge admission. Most museums are free for under-18s, and give substantial discounts to retirees and students (bring ID in all cases). In addition, many museums and sights that normally charge entry set aside certain times when entrance is free, and nearly all are free on International Museum Day (May 18), the Día de Hispanidad (Oct 12) and Día de la Constitución (Dec 6). The following are free at these times:

Centro de Arte Reina Sofía Sat 2.30–9pm & Sun 10am–2.30pm.

Museo de América Sun 10am–3pm.

Museo Arqueológico Nacional Sat 2.30–8pm & Sun 9.30am–2.30pm.

Museo de Artes Decorativas Sun 10am–3pm.

Museo Cerralbo Wed 9.30am–3pm & Sun 10am–3pm and July 8.

Museo Lázaro Galdiano Sun 10am–4.30pm.

Museo del Prado Tues–Sat 6–8pm, Sun 5–8pm, Nov 19 and May 2.

Museo Sorolla Sun 10am–3pm.

Museo del Traje Sat 2.30–7pm, Sun 10am–3pm.

Real Academia de Bellas Artes Wed 9am–7pm.

---

c/Preciados, at the top end of the square. It is worth noting that in the course of the next few years the area is likely to be heavily disrupted by the construction of a subterranean train station beneath c/Montera.

Plaza Mayor

Follow c/Mayor (the "Main Street" of the medieval city) west from the Puerta del Sol and you could easily walk right past Madrid's most important landmark: **Plaza Mayor**. Set back from the street and entered by stepped passageways, it appears all the more grand in its continuous sweep of arcaded buildings. It was planned by Felipe II – the monarch who made Madrid the capital – as the public meeting place of the city, and was finished thirty years later in 1619 during the reign of Felipe III, who sits astride the stallion in the central statue. The architect was Juan Gómez de Mora, responsible for many of the civic and royal buildings in this quarter.

The square, with its hundreds of balconies, was designed as a theatre for public events, and it has served this function throughout its history. It was the scene of the Inquisition's *autos-da-fé* (trials of faith) and the executions that followed; kings were crowned here; festivals and demonstrations passed through; plays by Lope de Vega and others received their first performances; bulls were fought; and gossip was spread. The more important of the events would be watched by royalty from their apartments in the central **Casa Panadería**, a palace named after the bakery that it replaced. It was rebuilt after a fire in 1692 and subsequently decorated with frescoes. However, the present delightful, and highly kitsch, array of allegorical figures that adorn the facade was only added in 1992. Today, the palace houses municipal offices and a tourist office (daily 9.30am–8.30pm).

Nowadays, Plaza Mayor is primarily a tourist haunt, full of expensive outdoor cafés and restaurants (best stick to a drink), buskers and caricaturists. However,

▲ Plaza Mayor

an air of grandeur clings to the plaza, which still performs public functions. In the summer months and during the major *madrileño* fiestas, it becomes an outdoor **theatre** and **music stage**; and in the winter, just before Christmas, it becomes a **bazaar** for festive decorations and religious regalia. Every Sunday, too, stamp and coin sellers set up their stalls.

In the alleys just below the square, such as c/Cuchilleros and c/Cava de San Miguel, are some of the city's oldest *mesones*, or **taverns**. Have a drink in these in the early evening and you are likely to be serenaded by passing *tunas* – musicians and singers dressed in traditional costume of knickerbockers and waistcoats who wander around town playing and passing the hat. These men-only troupes are attached to various faculties of the university and are usually students supplementing their grants.

Plaza de la Villa, San Miguel and San Ginés

West along c/Mayor, towards the Palacio Real, is **Plaza de la Villa**, an example of three centuries of Spanish architectural development. Its oldest surviving building is the eye-catching fifteenth-century **Torre de los Lujanes**, a fine Mudéjar (Moors working under Christian rule) tower, where Francis I of France is said to have been imprisoned in 1525 after his capture at the Battle of Pavia in Italy. Opposite is the old town hall, the **ayuntamiento** (**Casa de la Villa**), begun in the seventeenth century, but remodelled in Baroque style (tours in Spanish only every Mon at 5pm; free). Finally, fronting the square is the **Casa de Cisneros**, built by a nephew of Cardinal Cisneros in the sixteenth-century Plateresque ("Silversmith") style. Baroque is also seen round the corner in c/San Justo, where the parish church of **La Basílica de San Miguel** (July–Sept 14: Mon–Sat 9.45am–1.40pm & 6–9pm, Sun 9.40am–1.40pm & 6.30–9pm; Sept 15–June 30: Mon–Sat 9.45am–2pm & 5.30–9pm, Sun 9.40am–2.40pm & 6–9pm) shows the imagination of the eighteenth-century Italian architects who designed it.

Another fine – and much more ancient – church is **San Ginés**, north of Plaza Mayor on c/Arenal. This is of Mozarabic origin (built by Christians under

Moorish rule) but was completely reconstructed in the seventeenth century. There is an El Greco canvas of the moneychangers being chased from the temple on show in the **Capilla del Cristo** (on show Mon 12.30pm). The church is open only during services. Alongside, in somewhat uneasy juxtaposition, stands a cult temple of the twentieth century, the *Joy Madrid* disco, and, behind it, the **Chocolatería San Ginés**, a Madrid institution, which at one time catered for the early-rising worker but now churns out *churros* and hot chocolate for the late nightclub crowd (see box, p.127).

Descalzas Reales and Encarnación convents

A couple of blocks north of San Ginés at Plaza de las Descalzas Reales 3 is one of the hidden treasures of Madrid, the **Monasterio de las Descalzas Reales** (Ⓦwww.patrimonionacional.es; ⓂSol/Callao). It was founded in 1557 by Juana de Austria, daughter of the Emperor Carlos V, sister of Felipe II, and, at the age of 19, already the widow of Prince Don Juan of Portugal. In her wake came a succession of titled ladies (*Descalzas Reales* means "Barefoot Royals"), who brought fame and, above all, fortune to the convent, which is unbelievably rich, though beautiful and tranquil, too. It is still in use, with shoeless nuns tending patches of vegetable garden.

Whistle-stop **guided tours** (Tues–Thurs & Sat 10.30am–12.45pm & 4–5.45pm, Fri 10.30am–12.45pm, Sun & some public hols 11am–1.45pm; €5, joint ticket with Convento de la Encarnación €6, valid for a week, free for EU citizens on Wed) conduct visitors (usually in Spanish only) through the cloisters and up an incredibly elaborate stairway to a series of chambers packed with art and treasures of every kind. The former dormitories are perhaps the most outstanding feature, decorated with a series of Flemish tapestries based on designs by Rubens and a striking portrait of St Francis by Zurbarán. These were the sleeping quarters for all the nuns, including St Teresa of Ávila for a time, although the empress María of Germany preferred a little more privacy and endowed the convent with her own luxurious private chambers. The other highlight of the tour is the Joyería (Treasury), piled high with jewels and relics of uncertain provenance. The nuns kept no records of their gifts, so no one is quite sure what many of the things are – there is a bizarre cross-sectional model of Christ – nor which bones came from which saint. Whatever the case, it's an exceptional hoard.

Over towards the Palacio Real in Plaza de la Encarnación is the **Convento de la Encarnación** (same hours as above; €3.60, joint ticket with Monasterio de las Descalzas Reales €6, valid for a week, free for EU citizens on Wed; guided tours only; Ⓦwww.patrimonionacional.es; ⓂÓpera). This was founded a few years after Juana's convent, by Margarita, wife of Felipe III, though it was substantially rebuilt towards the end of the eighteenth century. It houses an extensive but somewhat disappointing collection of seventeenth-century Spanish art, and a wonderfully bizarre library-like reliquary, reputed to be one of the most important in the Catholic world. The most famous relic housed here is a small glass bulb said to contain the blood of the fourth-century doctor martyr, St Pantaleon, whose blood supposedly liquefies at midnight on the eve of his feast day (July 26). The tour ends with a visit to the Baroque-style church featuring a beautifully frescoed ceiling.

Ópera: Plaza de Oriente and the cathedral

West of Sol, c/Arenal leads to the **Teatro Real**, or **Ópera** (tours Mon & Wed–Fri 10.30am–1pm, Sat & Sun 11am–1.30pm; €4; tickets on sale from the box office 10am–1pm, info and reservations ☏915 160 696, Ⓦwww.teatro-real .com; ⓂÓpera), which gives this area its name. Built in the mid-nineteenth century, it almost sank a few decades later as a result of subsidence caused by underground canals and was forced to close in 1925; it finally reopened in 1997 after an epic ten-year refurbishment that ended up costing a mind-boggling €150 million. The interior is suitably lavish and merits a visit in its own right, and it makes a truly magnificent setting for opera, ballet and classical concerts (for details of tickets for performances, see p.131).

Around the back, the opera house is separated from the Palacio Real by the **Plaza Oriente**, one of the most elegant and agreeable open spaces in Madrid and used in the bad old days by Franco as the venue for his public addresses; small groups of neo-Fascists still gather here on the anniversary of his death on November 21. One of the square's main attractions – and the focus of its life – is the elegant *Café del Oriente*, whose summer terraza is one of the stations of Madrid nightlife. The café (which is also a prestigious restaurant) looks as traditional as any in the city but was in fact opened in the 1980s by a priest, Padre Lezama, who ploughs his profits into various charitable schemes.

The café apart, the dominant features of Plaza de Oriente are statues: 44 of them, depicting Spanish kings and queens, which were originally designed to go on the palace facade but found to be too heavy (some say too ugly) for the roof to support. The **statue of Felipe IV** on horseback, in the centre of the square, clearly belongs on a different plane; it was based on designs by Velázquez, and Galileo is said to have helped with the calculations to make it balance.

Facing the Palacio Real to the south, across the shadeless Plaza de la Armería, is Madrid's cathedral, **Nuestra Señora de la Almudena** (daily: summer 10am–2pm & 5–9pm; winter 9am–9pm; not open for visits during Mass; ⓂÓpera). Planned centuries ago, bombed out in the Civil War, worked upon at intervals since, and plagued by lack of funds, it was eventually opened for business in 1993 by Pope John Paul II. The building's bulky Neoclassical facade was designed to match the Palacio Real opposite, while its cold neo-Gothic interior is largely uninspiring; the crypt (daily 10am–8pm; entrance on Cuesta de la Vega), with its forest of columns and dimly lit chapels, is far more atmospheric.

South again from here, c/Bailén crosses c/Segovia on a high **viaduct** (now lined with panes of reinforced glass to prevent once-common suicide attempts); this was constructed as a royal route from the palace to the church of San Francisco el Grande, avoiding the rabble and river that flowed below. Close by is a patch of **Moorish wall** from the medieval fortress here, which the original royal palace replaced. Across the aqueduct, the **Jardines de las Vistillas** ("Gardens of the Views") beckon, with their summer terrazas looking out across the river and towards the distant Sierra.

Palacio Real

The **Palacio Real**, or Royal Palace (April–Sept Mon–Sat 9am–6pm, Sun & hols 9am–3pm; Oct–March Mon–Sat 9.30am–5pm, Sun & hols 9am–2pm; closed occasionally for state visits; Ⓦwww.patrimonionacional.es), scores high on statistics. It claims more rooms than any other European palace; a library with one of the biggest collections of books, manuscripts, maps and musical scores in the world; and an armoury with an unrivalled assortment of weapons dating back to the fifteenth century. If you're around on the first Wednesday of the month (except July & Aug) between 11am and 2pm, look out for the changing of the guard outside the palace, a tradition that has recently been revived.

Optional **guided tours** in various languages (€10; usually with a wait for a group to form) have been abbreviated in recent years, now taking in around 25 (rather than 90) rooms and apartments, including the Royal Armoury Museum and Royal Pharmacy. Nevertheless, they're still a pretty hard slog, rarely allowing much time to contemplate the extraordinary opulence: acres of Flemish and Spanish tapestries, endless Rococo decoration, bejewelled clocks, and pompous portraits of the monarchs, as well as a permanent display of Goya's cartoons and tapestries. You're probably better off going **without a guide** (€8), as each room is clearly signed and described in English anyway, though you'll have to fight your way past the guided groups.

The palace also houses an impressive exhibition space, the **Galería de Pinturas** (same opening hours; €2), which displays work by Velázquez, Caravaggio and Goya among others and is also used for temporary exhibitions.

The palace and outhouses

The Habsburgs' original palace burnt down on Christmas Day, 1734. Its replacement, the current building, was based on drawings made by Bernini for the Louvre. It was constructed in the mid-eighteenth century and was the principal royal residence from then until Alfonso XIII went into exile in 1931; both Joseph Bonaparte and the Duke of Wellington also lived here briefly. The present royal family inhabits a considerably more modest residence on the western outskirts of the city, using the Palacio Real on state occasions only.

The **Salón del Trono** (Throne Room) is the highlight for most visitors, containing the thrones installed for Juan Carlos and Sofía, the current monarchs, as well as the splendid ceiling by Tiepolo, a giant fresco representing the glory of Spain – an extraordinary achievement for an artist by then in his seventies. Look out, too, for the marvellous **Sala de Porcelana** (Porcelain Room) and the incredible oriental-style **Salón de Gasparini**.

The palace outbuildings and annexes include the recently refurbished **Armería Real** (Royal Armoury; separate ticket available if you're not visiting the rest of the palace; €3.40), a huge room full of guns, swords and armour, with such curiosities as the suit of armour worn by Carlos V in his equestrian portrait by Titian in the Prado. Especially fascinating are the complete sets of armour, with all the original spare parts and gadgets for making adjustments. There is also an eighteenth-century **Farmacia**, a curious mixture of alchemist's den and laboratory, whose walls are lined with jars labelled for various remedies. The **Biblioteca Real** (Royal Library) can now only be visited by prior arrangement for research purposes.

The gardens

Immediately north of the palace, the **Jardines de Sabatini** (April–Sept 9am–10pm; Oct–March 9am–9pm) provide a shady retreat and venue for summer concerts, while to the rear the larger, and far more beautiful, park of the **Campo del Moro** (April–Sept Mon–Sat 10am–8pm, Sun 9am–8pm; Oct–March Mon–Sat 10am–6pm, Sun 9am–6pm; occasionally closed for state visits; access only from the far west side, off the Paseo de la Virgen del Puerto) affords shady walks and a splendid view of the western facade of the palace.

South of Plaza Mayor: La Latina, Lavapiés and El Rastro

The areas south of Plaza Mayor have traditionally been tough, working-class districts, with tenement buildings thrown up to accommodate the expansion of the population in the eighteenth and nineteenth centuries. In many places,

El Rastro

Madrid's flea market, **El Rastro**, is as much a part of the city's weekend ritual as a Mass or a *paseo*. This gargantuan, thriving shambles of a street market sprawls south from Metro Latina to the Ronda de Toledo, especially along Ribera de Curtidores. Through it, crowds flood between 10am and 3pm every Sunday – and increasingly on Fridays, Saturdays and public holidays, too. On offer is just about anything you might – or more likely might not – need, from secondhand clothes and military-surplus items to caged birds and antiques.

Some of the goods – broken telephone dials, plastic shampoo bottles half-full of something that may or may not be the original contents – are so far gone that you can't imagine any of them ever selling. Other items may be quite valuable, but on the whole it's the stuff of markets around the world you'll find here: pseudo-designer clothes, bags and T-shirts. Don't expect to find fabulous bargains, or the hidden Old Masters of popular myth; the serious antique trade has mostly moved off the streets and into the surrounding shops, while the real junk is now found only on the fringes. Nonetheless, the atmosphere of the Rastro is always enjoyable, and the bars around these streets are as good as any in the city. One warning: keep a close eye on your bags, pockets, cameras (best left at the hotel) and jewellery. The Rastro rings up a fair percentage of Madrid's tourist thefts.

these old houses survive, huddled together in narrow streets, but the character of **La Latina** and **Lavapiés** has changed as their inhabitants, and the districts themselves, have become younger, more fashionable and more cosmopolitan. The streets of Cava Baja and Cava Alta in La Latina, for example, include some of the city's most popular bars and restaurants. These are attractive *barrios* to explore, particularly for bar-hopping or during the Sunday-morning flea market, **El Rastro**, which takes place along and around the Ribera de Curtidores (Ⓜ La Latina/Tirso de Molina).

Around La Latina

La Latina is a short walk south from Plaza de la Villa and, if you're exploring Madrid de los Austrias, it's a natural continuation, as some of the squares, streets and churches here date back to the early Habsburg period. One of the most attractive pockets is around **Plaza de la Paja**, a delightful square behind the large church of **San Andrés**, and once home to one of the city's medieval markets. In summer, there are a couple of terrazas here, tucked well away from the traffic. The church was badly damaged by an anarchist attack in 1936, and the adjoining **Capilla del Obispo** is undergoing a long-running restoration programme. However, the main church, whose brick cupola has been restored to its former glory, and the richly decorated interior of the Baroque **Capilla de San Isidro** (Mon–Thurs & Sat 8am–1pm & 6–8pm, Fri 8–11.30am & 6–8pm, Sun 9am–2pm) are open to visitors.

Alongside the church of San Andrés is one of the city's newer museums, the **Museo de San Isidro** (Aug Tues–Fri 9.30am–2.30pm, Sat & Sun 10am–2pm; Sept–July Tues–Fri 9.30am–8pm, Sat & Sun 10am–2pm; free; Ⓦ www .munimadrid.es/museosanisidro), housed in a sixteenth-century mansion owned by the counts of Paredes and supposedly once the home of Madrid's patron saint. The city's archeological collection, which consists of relics from the earliest settlements along the Manzanares River and nearby Roman villas, is in the basement. The rest of the museum is given over to exhibits on the later history of the city and also San Isidro and his miraculous activities, including the well from which he is said to have rescued his own son.

A couple of minutes' walk southwest of here down the hill is one of Madrid's grandest, richest and most elaborate churches, **San Francisco el Grande** (ⓂPuerta de Toledo/La Latina). Built towards the end of the eighteenth century as part of Carlos III's renovations of the city, it has a dome even larger than that of St Paul's in London. The interior, which you can only visit with a guided tour (Aug Tues–Sun 11am–12.30pm & 6–7.30pm; rest of year Tues–Fri 11am–1pm & 4–7pm, Sat 11am–1.30pm; €3 with guided tour), contains paintings by, among others, Goya and Zurbarán, and frescoes by Bayeu. After a painfully slow twenty-year restoration programme it is now possible to appreciate this magnificent church in something close to its original splendour.

The Ribera de Curtidores, heart of **El Rastro** (see box, p.91), begins just behind another vast church, **San Isidro** (Mon–Sat 7.45am–1pm & 6–8.45pm, Sun & public hols 8.30am–2pm & 6–8.30pm) which lies at the top of Calle de Toledo. The patron saint's remains are entombed within, and his church acted as the city's cathedral prior to the completion of the Almudena by the Palacio Real. Relics apart, its chief attribute is its size – it's as bleak as it is big. Next door is the **Instituto Real**, a school that has been in existence considerably longer than the church and counts among its former pupils such literary notables as Calderón de la Barca, Lope de Vega, Quevedo and Pío Baroja.

If you continue to the end of Ribera de Curtidores, whose antique shops (some, these days, extremely upmarket) stay open all week, you'll see a large arch, the **Puerta de Toledo**, at one end of the Ronda de Toledo. The only surviving relation to the Puerta de Alcalá in the Plaza de la Independencia, this was built originally as a triumphal arch to honour the conquering Napoleon. After his defeat in the Peninsular Wars, it became a symbol of the city's freedom. Just in front of the arch, the Mercado Puerta de Toledo, once the site of the city's fish market, has pretensions to a stylish arts and crafts centre, though it is still trying to attract business.

Further south, alongside the sorry-looking Río Manzañares, is the **Estadio Vicente Calderón**, home to Atlético Madrid, arch-rivals of the more glamorous Real (see box, p.112 for ticket details). The 54,000-capacity stadium houses a club shop (Mon–Fri 10am–2pm & 5–8pm, Sat & Sun 10am–2pm, match days 11am–45min before kickoff) and a museum (Tues–Sun 11am–7pm, guided visits noon, 1pm, 4.30pm & 5.30pm; €6–8).

Lavapiés and the Cine Doré

A good point to start exploring Lavapiés is the Plaza Tirso de Molina (ⓂTirso de Molina). From here, you can follow c/Mesón de Paredes, stopping for a drink at *Taberna Antonio Sánchez* at no. 13, past rows of wholesale shops to **La Corrala**, on the corner of c/Sombrerete. This is one of many traditional *corrales* – tenement blocks – in the quarter, built with balconied apartments opening onto a central patio. Plays, especially farces and *zarzuelas* (a kind of operetta), used to be performed regularly in Spanish *corrales*, and the open space here usually hosts a few performances in the summer. It has been well renovated and declared a national monument.

From Metro Lavapiés, you can take c/Argumosa towards the Centro de Arte Reina Sofía. Don't miss out on the opportunity to sample some of the excellent local bars on this pleasant tree-lined street while you're here.

To the north of the quarter, near ⓂAntón Martín, is the **Cine Doré**, the oldest cinema in Madrid, dating from 1922, with a late Modernista/Art Nouveau facade. It has been converted to house the Filmoteca Nacional, an art-film centre (see p.132), and it has a pleasant and inexpensive café/restaurant (Tues–Sun 1.30pm–12.30am).

East of Sol: Plaza de Santa Ana to Plaza de Cibeles

The **Plaza de Santa Ana/Huertas** area lies at the heart of a triangle, bordered to the east by the Paseo del Prado, to the north by c/Alcalá and along the south by c/Atocha, with the Puerta del Sol at the western tip. The city reached this district after expanding beyond the Palacio Real and the Plaza Mayor, so the buildings date predominantly from the nineteenth century. Many of them have literary associations: there are streets named after Cervantes and Lope de Vega (where one lived and the other died), and the *barrio* is host to the Atheneum club, Círculo de Bellas Artes (Fine Arts Institute), Teatro Español and the Congreso de los Diputados (parliament). Just to the north, there is also an important museum, the **Real Academia de Bellas Artes de San Fernando**.

For most visitors, though, the major attraction is that this district holds some of the best and most beautiful **bars** and **tascas** in the city. They are concentrated particularly around Plaza de Santa Ana, which – following a rather seedy period – has been smartened up by the council.

Plaza de Santa Ana and around

The bars around **Plaza de Santa Ana** (ⓂSol/Sevilla) really are sights in themselves. On the square itself, the dark-panelled **Cervecería Alemana** was a firm favourite of Hemingway and has hardly changed since the turn of the twentieth century. Opposite, *La Suiza* café is a great place for a coffee and a cake while watching the world go by. Flanking one side of the plaza is the elegant facade of the emblematic *ME Madrid* **hotel**, once a favourite of bullfighters and now the designer showpiece for the Sol-Melía chain.

Viva Madrid, on the northeast corner at c/Manuel Fernández y González 7, should be another port of call, if only to admire the fabulous tilework, original zinc bar and a ceiling supported by wooden caryatids. One block east from here is **c/Echegaray**, home to a string of great bars and restaurants, including the wonderfully delapidated sherry bar, **La Venencia**, at no. 7.

Huertas, El Congreso and the Círculo de Bellas Artes

The area around pedestrianized c/Huertas itself is workaday enough – sleepy by day but buzzing by night – and, again, packed with bars. North of here, and parallel, are two streets named in honour of the greatest figures of Spain's seventeenth-century literary golden age, Cervantes and Lope de Vega. Bitter rivals in life, both are probably spinning in their graves now, since Cervantes is interred in the **Convento de las Trinitarias** on the street named after Lope de Vega, while the latter's house, the **Casa de Lope de Vega**, finds itself at c/Cervantes 11 (Tues–Fri 9.30am–2pm, Sat 10am–2pm, closed mid-July to mid-Aug; €2, Sat free; ⓂAntón Martín). The charming little museum provides a fascinating reconstruction of life in seventeenth-century Madrid; ring the bell and someone will take you on a short tour (usually English is spoken), which includes the delightful little patio garden.

A block to the north is **El Congreso de Los Diputados** (Ⓦwww.congreso.es; ⓂSevilla), an unprepossessing nineteenth-century building where the Congress (the lower house) meets. Sessions can be visited by appointment only, though anyone can turn up (with a passport) for a tour on Saturday mornings (tours every 30min, 10.30am–1pm; closed Aug). You're shown, amongst other things, the bullet holes left by Colonel Tejero and his Guardia Civil associates in the abortive coup attempt of 1981.

Cut across to c/Alcalá from the Plaza de las Cortes and you'll emerge close to the **Círculo de Bellas Artes** at Marqués de Casa Riera 2 (Ⓦwww.circulobellasartes.com; ⓂSevilla), a strange-looking 1920s building crowned by a statue of Pallas Athene. This is Madrid's best arts centre, and includes a theatre, music hall, cinema, exhibition galleries (Tues–Fri 5–9pm, Sat 11am–2pm & 5–9pm, Sun 11am–2pm) and a very pleasant bar (daily 9.30am–1am) – all marble and leather decor, with a nude statue reclining in the middle of the floor. It attracts the capital's arts and media crowd but is not in the slightest exclusive, nor expensive, and there's an adjoining terraza, too. The Círculo is theoretically a members-only club, but it issues €1 day membership on the door, for which you get access to all areas.

Calle Alcalá to Plaza Cibeles

At the Círculo, you are on the corner of Gran Vía and, only a couple of hundred metres to the east, c/Alcalá meets the Paseo del Prado at the **Plaza de la Cibeles**. The monumental wedding-cake building on the far side of this square was until recently Madrid's main post office, the aptly entitled **Palacio de Comunicaciones**. Constructed from 1904 to 1917, it is vastly more imposing than the parliament and runs the Palacio Real pretty close. The local council took a shine to it and is in the process of transferring its offices there.

Awash in a sea of traffic in the centre of the square are a **fountain** and statue of the goddess Cibeles, which survived the bombardments of the Civil War by being swaddled from helmet to hoof in sandbags. It was designed, as were the two other fountains gushing magnificently along the Paseo del Prado, by Ventura Rodríguez, who is honoured in modern Madrid by having a metro station and a street named after him. The fountain is the scene of celebrations for victorious Real Madrid fans (Atlético supporters bathe in the fountain of Neptune just down the road).

Madrid's three principal art museums, the Prado, Thyssen-Bornemisza and Centro de Arte Reina Sofía, all lie to the south of here, along the Paseo del Prado. To the north, on Paseo de Recoletos, are a couple of the city's most lavish **traditional cafés**, the *Café Gijón* at no. 21 and *Café del Espejo* at no. 31 (see box, p.113), and the upmarket Salamanca *barrio*.

Real Academia de Bellas Artes de San Fernando

Art buffs who have some appetite left after the Prado, Thyssen-Bornemisza and Reina Sofía, will find the **Real Academia de Bellas Artes de San Fernando** (Mon & Sat 9am–2.30pm & 4–7pm, Tues–Fri 9am–7pm, Sun & public hols 9am–2.30pm; €3, free Wed; ⓂSevilla) next on their list. Located 200m east of Sol at c/Alcalá 13, it has traditionally been viewed as one of the most important art galleries in Spain. Admittedly, you have to plough through a fair number of dull academic canvases, but there are some hidden gems. These include a group of small panels by **Goya**, in particular *The Burial of the Sardine*; portraits of the monks of the Merced order by Zurbarán and others; and a curious *Family of El Greco*, which may be by the great man or his son. Two other rooms are devoted to foreign artists, especially Rubens. Upstairs, there is a series of sketches by Picasso, and a brutally graphic set of sculptures depicting the *Massacre of the Innocents* by José Ginés – though note that due to staff shortages the second- and third-floor galleries are usually closed between 2 and 4pm. It is also home to the national chalcography (copper or brass engraving) collection (Mon–Fri 10am–2pm, Sat 10am–1.30pm; free), which includes a number of Goya etchings used for his *Capricho* series on show at the Prado.

Museo del Prado

The **Museo del Prado** (Tues–Sun 9am–8pm; Jan 6, Dec 24 & Dec 31 9am–2pm; closed Jan 1, Good Friday, May 1 & Dec 25; €6 (supplement for some temporary exhibitions), free Tues–Sat 6–8pm, Sun 5–8pm; ⓦwww.museodelprado.es; ⓂBanco de España/Atocha) is Madrid's premier attraction – well over two million visitors enter its doors each year – and one of the oldest and greatest collections of art in the world. Built as a natural science museum in 1775, the Prado opened to the public in 1819, and houses the finest works collected by Spanish royalty – for the most part, avid, discerning and wealthy buyers – as well as Spanish paintings gathered from other sources over the past two centuries. Finding enough space for displaying the works has always been a problem, but after fourteen years of arguments, delays and controversy, the €152 million Rafael Moneo-designed **extension**, which includes a stylish glass-fronted building incorporating the eighteenth-century cloisters of the San Jerónimo church, has finally been opened. The new wing houses the restaurant and café areas, an expanded shop, an auditorium, temporary exhibition spaces, restoration and conservation workshops and a new sculpture gallery.

The museum's highlights are its early Flemish collection – including almost all of **Bosch**'s best work – and, of course, its incomparable display of Spanish art, in particular that of **Velázquez** (including *Las Meninas*), **Goya** (including the *Maja*s and the *Black Paintings*) and **El Greco**. There's also a huge section of Italian painters (**Titian**, notably) collected by Carlos V and Felipe II, both great patrons of the Renaissance, and an excellent collection of seventeenth-century Flemish and Dutch pictures gathered by Felipe IV, including **Rubens'** *Three Graces*. The museum has also hosted an increasing number of critically acclaimed temporary displays in recent years. Even in a full day you couldn't hope to do justice to everything here, and it's perhaps best to make a couple of more focused visits.

Organization, catalogues and entrances

The museum is laid out according to national schools, but their location may occasionally be subject to minor changes to make way for temporary shows; any variations will usually be shown on the **free maps** available at the desk on your way into the museum. Start on the ground floor for a more chronological tour spanning the twelfth to sixteenth centuries, while the first floor will take you on to the seventeenth century and beyond, including the main Spanish collections.

What follows is, by necessity, only a brief guide to the museum contents. If you want more background on the key paintings pick up an audioguide (€3.50) or the extensive guide (€24.50) in the bookshop. There are also some useful **colour booklets** (€1) on Velázquez, Goya, El Greco, Titian and Bosch available at the information desk and in their respective galleries.

Tickets are purchased at the Puerta de Goya opposite the *Hotel Ritz* on c/Felipe IV, and the **entrances** are round the back at the Puerta de los

Combined entry ticket

If you plan to visit all three art museums on the Paseo del Prado during your stay, it's well worth buying the under-advertised **Paseo del Arte ticket** (€14.40), which is valid for a year and allows one visit to each museum at a substantial amount, although it does not include the temporary exhibitions. It's available at any of the three museums.

Jerónimos, which leads into the new extension, or at the front at the Puerta de Velázquez. If you want to avoid queuing for tickets, these can now be purchased in advance via the museum website (Ⓦ www.museodelprado.es). The Puerta de Murillo entrance, opposite the botanical gardens, is now for school and university groups only.

A **lunchtime visit** is often a good plan if you want to avoid the worst of the crowds and tour groups.

Spanish painting

The Prado's collections of Spanish painting begin on the ground floor with the cycles of twelfth-century **Romanesque frescoes** (room 51c), reconstructed from a pair of churches from the Mozarabic (Muslim rule) era in Soria and Segovia. **Early panel paintings** – exclusively religious fourteenth- and fifteenth-century works – include a huge *retablo* (altarpiece) by Nicolás Francés; the anonymous *Virgin of the Catholic Monarchs*; Bermejo's *Santo Domingo de Silos*; and Pedro Berruguete's *Auto-da-Fé*.

The Golden Age: Velázquez and El Greco

Upstairs, the collections from Spain's Golden Age – the late sixteenth and seventeenth centuries under Habsburg rule – are prefigured by a fabulous array of paintings by **El Greco** (1540–1614), the Cretan-born artist who worked in Toledo from the 1570s. You really need to have taken in the works in Toledo to appreciate fully his extraordinary genius, but the portraits and religious works here (rooms 16b and 19–23), ranging from the Italianate *Trinity* to the visionary late *Adoration of the Shepherds*, are a good introduction.

In rooms 12, 14, 15, 17, 18 and 27, you confront the greatest painter of Habsburg Spain, **Diego Velázquez** (1599–1660). Born in Portugal, Velázquez became court painter to Felipe IV, whose family is represented in many of the works: "I have found my Titian," Felipe is said to have remarked on his appointment. Velázquez's masterpiece, *Las Meninas* (room 12), is displayed alongside studies for the painting. Manet remarked of it, "After this, I don't know why the

▲ Statue of Diego Velázquez, Museo del Prado

rest of us paint," and the French poet Théophile Gautier asked "But where is the picture?" when he saw it, because it seemed to him a continuation of the room. *Las Hilanderas* and *Vulcan's Forge* showing the royal tapestry factory at work, *Christ Crucified* and *Los Borrachos* (*The Drunkards*) are further magnificent paintings. In fact, almost all of the fifty or so works on display (around half of the artist's surviving output) warrant close attention. Don't overlook the two small panels of the *Villa Medici*, painted in Rome in 1650, in virtually Impressionist style. There are several Velázquez canvases, including *The Surrender at Breda*, in the stunning collection of royal portraits and works depicting Spanish military victories.

In the adjacent rooms are examples of just about every significant Spanish painter of the seventeenth century, including many of the best works of **Francisco Zurbarán** (1598–1664), **Bartolomé Esteban Murillo** (1618–82), **Alonso Cano** (1601–67), **Juan de Valdes Leal** (1622–60) and **Juan Carreño** (1614–85). Note, in particular, Carreño's portrait of the last Habsburg monarch, the drastically inbred and mentally retarded Carlos II, rendered with terrible realism (room 17). There's also a fine selection of paintings by **José Ribera** (1591–1625), who worked mainly in Naples, and was influenced there by Caravaggio. His masterpieces are considered *The Martyrdom of St Philip* and the dark, realist portrait of *St Andrew*, while look out for the bizarre *Bearded Lady* (rooms 25 and 26).

Goya

The final suite of Spanish rooms (16B, 29, 32 and 35–39), which continue up onto the second floor (85 and 90–94), provides an awesome and fabulously complete overview of the output of **Francisco de Goya** (1746–1828), the largest and most valuable collection of his works in the world, with some 140 paintings and 500 drawings and engravings. Goya was the greatest painter of Bourbon Spain, a chronicler of Spain in his time and an artist whom many see as the inspiration and forerunner of Impressionism and modern art. He was an enormously versatile artist: contrast the voluptuous *Maja Vestida* and *Maja Desnuda* (*The Clothed Belle* and *The Naked Belle*) with the horrors depicted in the *Dos de Mayo* and *Tres de Mayo* (moving, on-the-spot portrayals of the rebellion against Napoleon in the streets of Madrid and the subsequent reprisals). Then there is the series of pastoral cartoons – designs for tapestries – and the extraordinary *Black Paintings* (rooms 35–38), a series of disconcerting murals painted on the walls of his home by the deaf and embittered painter in his old age. The many portraits of his patron, Carlos IV, are remarkable for their lack of any attempt at flattery, while those of Queen María Luisa, whom he despised, are downright ugly.

The nineteenth century

The museum's collection of melodramatic nineteenth-century Spanish art was originally housed in the nearby Casón del Buen Retiro, but after a lengthy refurbishment programme that building has now been turned into a research and education centre. The plan is to integrate the paintings, which were given a rare airing in a recent temporary exhibition in the new wing, into the main collection.

Italian painting

The Prado's early Italian galleries on the ground floor (rooms 49, 56B and 75) are distinguished principally by **Fra Angelico**'s *Annunciation* (c.1445) and by a trio of panels by **Botticelli** (1445–1510). The latter illustrate a deeply unpleasant story from the *Decameron* about a woman hunted by hounds; the fourth panel (in a private collection in the US) gives a happier conclusion.

With the sixteenth-century Renaissance, and especially its Venetian exponents, the collection really comes into its own. The Prado is said to have the most complete collection of Titians and painters from the Venetian school of any single museum. There are major works by **Raphael** (1483–1520), including a fabulous *Portrait of a Cardinal*, and epic masterpieces from the Venetians **Tintoretto** (1518–94), such as the beautifully composed *Lavatorio*, bought by Felipe IV when Charles I of England was beheaded and his art collection was auctioned off, and **Veronese** (1528–88), as well as **Caravaggio** (1573–1610), with his brutal *David with the head of Goliath* another highlight. The most important works, however, are by **Titian** (1487–1576) in rooms 75, 8A and 9A. These include portraits of the Spanish emperors *Carlos V* and *Felipe II* (Carlos's suit of armour is preserved in the Palacio Real), and a famous, much-reproduced piece of erotica, *Venus, Cupid and the Organist* (two versions are displayed here), a painting originally owned by a bishop.

Flemish, Dutch and German painting

The biggest name in the **early Flemish collection** (room 56A) is **Hieronymus Bosch** (1450–1516), known in Spain as "El Bosco". The Prado has several of his greatest triptychs: the early-period *Hay Wain*, the middle-period *Garden of Earthly Delights*, and the late *Adoration of the Magi* – all familiar from countless reproductions but infinitely more chilling in the original. Bosch's hallucinatory genius for the macabre is at its most extreme in these triptychs, but is reflected here in many more of his works, including three versions of *The Temptations of St Anthony* (though only the smallest of these is definitely an original). Don't miss, either, the amazing table-top of *The Seven Deadly Sins*.

Bosch's visions find an echo in the works of **Pieter Brueghel the Elder** (1525–69), whose *Triumph of Death* must be one of the most frightening canvases ever painted. Another elusive painter, **Joachim Patinir**, is represented by four of his finest works. From an earlier generation, **Rogier van der Weyden**'s *Descent from the Cross* is outstanding (room 58); its monumental forms make a fascinating contrast with his miniature-like *Pietà*. There are also important works by Memling, Bouts, Gerard David and Massys.

The collection of over 160 works of **later Flemish and Dutch art** has been imaginatively rehoused in a new suite of rooms on the first floor (rooms 8–11). Grouped by themes, such as religion, daily life, mythology and landscape, many of the paintings have also been given a new lease of life by their restoration to their startling original colours. There are enough works here to make an excellent comparison between the flamboyant Counter Reformation propaganda of Flanders and the more austere bourgeois tastes of Holland. **Rubens** (1577–1640) is extensively represented, with the beautifully restored *Three Graces*, *The Judgement of Paris* and a series of eighteen mythological subjects designed for Felipe IV's hunting lodge in El Pardo (though he supervised rather than executed these). There is, too, a fine collection of canvases by his contemporaries, including **Van Dyck**'s dramatic and deeply moving *Piedad*, and his magnificent portrait of himself and Sir Endymion Porter. **Jan Brueghel**'s representations of the five senses and **David Teniers**' scenes of peasant lowlife also merit a closer look. For political reasons, Spanish monarchs collected few works painted from seventeenth-century Protestant Holland; an early **Rembrandt**, *Artemesia*, in which the artist's pregnant wife served as the model, is, however, an important exception (room 7).

The **German room** (55B) on the ground floor is dominated by **Dürer** (1471–1528) and **Lucas Cranach the Elder** (1472–1553). Dürer's magnificent *Adam and Eve* was saved from destruction at the hands of the prudish Carlos III only by the intervention of his court painter, Mengs, whose own paintings are on the second floor in room 89. The most interesting of Cranach's works is a pair of paintings depicting Carlos V hunting with Ferdinand I of Austria.

French and British painting

Most of the **French** work held by the Prado is from the seventeenth and eighteenth centuries (rooms 2–4 on the first floor and room 86 on the second). Among the outstanding painters represented is **Nicolas Poussin** (1594–1665), with his Baroque work shown to best effect in *Triumph of David*, *Landscape with St Jerome* and *Mount Parnassus*. The romantic landscapes and sunsets of **Claude Lorraine** (1600–82) are well represented, and look out for **Hyacinthe Rigaud**'s (1659–1743) portrayal of the imperious *Louis XIV*.

British painting is thin on the ground – a product of the hostile relations between the Spanish and English from the sixteenth to nineteenth centuries. There is, however, a small sample of eighteenth-century portraiture from **Joshua Reynolds** (1723–92) and **Thomas Gainsborough** (1727–88).

The Tesoro del Dauphin and the Casón del Buen Retiro

The museum's basement houses the **Tesoro del Dauphin** (Treasure of the Dauphin), a display of part of the collection of jewels that belonged to the Grand Dauphin Louis, son of Louis XIV and father of Felipe V, Spain's first Bourbon king. The collection includes goblets, cups, trays, glasses and other pieces richly decorated with rubies, emeralds, diamonds, lapis lazuli and other precious stones.

Just east of the Prado, the **Casón del Buen Retiro**, which used to be a dance hall for the palace of Felipe IV, is being converted into the museum's study centre.

Museo Thyssen-Bornemisza

The **Museo Thyssen–Bornemisza** (Ⓜ Banco de España) occupies the old Palacio de Villahermosa, diagonally opposite the Prado, at the end of Plaza de las Cortes. This prestigious site played a large part in Spain's acquisition – for a knock-down $350 million in June 1993 – of what many argue was the world's greatest private art trove after that of the British royals: seven-hundred-odd paintings accumulated by father-and-son German-Hungarian industrial magnates. The son, Baron Hans Heinrich Thyssen, died in April 2002 aged 81. Another trump card was the late baron's fifth wife, Carmen Cervera (aka "Tita" Cervera), a former Miss Spain, who steered the works to Spain against the efforts of Britain's Prince Charles, the Swiss and German governments, the Getty foundation and other suitors.

The museum had no expense spared on its design – again in the hands of the ubiquitous Rafael Moneo, responsible for the remodelling of Estación de Atocha and the current extension at the Prado – with stucco walls (Carmen insisted on salmon pink) and marble floors. A terribly kitsch portrait of Carmen with a lapdog hangs in the great hall of the museum, alongside those of her husband and King Juan Carlos and Queen Sofia. Pass beyond, however, and you are into seriously premier-league art: **medieval to eighteenth-century** on the second floor, **seventeenth–century Dutch** and **Rococo and Neoclassicism to**

Fauves and Expressionists on the first floor, and **Surrealists**, **Pop Art** and the **avant-garde** on ground level. Highlights are legion in a collection that displays an almost stamp-collecting mentality in its examples of nearly every major artist and movement: how the Thyssens got hold of classic works by everyone from Duccio and Holbein, through El Greco and Caravaggio, to Schiele and Rothko, takes your breath away.

Carmen has a substantial collection of her own (over 200 works), which has been housed in the **new extension**, built on the site of an adjoining mansion and cleverly integrated into the original format of the museum. It is particularly strong on nineteenth-century landscape, North American, Impressionist and Post-Impressionist work. The ground floor is home to a large temporary exhibition space, which has staged a number of interesting and highly successful shows (separate entry fee of €5, or €9 for a combined ticket with the main museum). The baroness has recently become a champion for ecologists and local residents for her stand against the plans of the local council to cut down scores of trees as part of their project to remodel the Paseo del Prado, and has even threatened to take the museum elsewhere if the plans go through.

The second floor: European old masters and Carmen's collection

Take a lift to the second floor and you will find yourself at the chronological start of the museum's collections: European painting (and some sculpture) from the fourteenth to the eighteenth century. The core of these collections was accumulated in the 1920s and 30s by the late baron's father, Heinrich, who was a friend of the art critics Bernard Berenson and Max Friedländer. He was clearly well advised. The early paintings include incredibly good (and rare) devotional panels by the Sienese painter **Duccio di Buoninsegna**, and the Flemish artists **Jan van Eyck** and **Rogier van der Weyden**. You then move into a fabulous array of Renaissance portraits (room 5), which include three of the very greatest of the period: **Ghirlandaio**'s *Portrait of Giovanna Tornabuoni*, **Hans Holbein**'s *Portrait of Henry VIII* (the only one of many variants in existence that is definitely genuine) and **Raphael**'s *Portrait of a Young Man. A Spanish Infanta* by **Juan de Flandes** may represent the first of Henry VIII's wives, Catherine of Aragón, while the *Young Knight* by **Carpaccio** is one of the earliest-known full-length portraits. Beyond these is a collection of **Dürer**s and **Cranach**s to rival that in the Prado, and as you progress through this extraordinary panoply, display cases along the corridor contain scarcely less spectacular works of sculpture, ceramics and gold- and silverwork.

Next in line, in room 11, are **Titian** and **Tintoretto**, and three paintings by **El Greco**, one early, two late, which make an interesting comparison with each other and with those in the Prado. **Caravaggio**'s monumental *St Catherine of Alexandria* (room 12) is the centrepiece of an important display of works by followers of this innovator of chiaroscuro. As you reach the eighteenth century, there is a room containing three flawless **Canaletto** views of Venice (room 17).

Tagged onto this floor are the first galleries (lettered A–H) that make up the initial section of Carmen's collection. **Luca Giordano**'s monumental *Judgement of Solomon* (room A) and a **Van Dyck** *Crucifixion* (room B) are two of the early highlights. Gallery C traces the development of landscapes from early Flemish works through to **Constable**'s marvellous *The Lock*, bought in 1910 for £10.8 million. Beyond are some interesting works by North American and European artists that complement the baron's collection and some soothing Impressionist works by **Degas**, **Renoir**, **Pissarro**, **Monet** and **Sisley**.

The first floor: Americans, Impressionists and Expressionists

The route now takes you downstairs through the remainder of Carmen's collection (rooms I–P), beginning with further Impressionist work, taking in some delightful canvases by **Gauguin** and the Post-Impressionists and ending with some striking Expressionist pieces by **Kandinsky** and **Robert Delaunay**.

From room P, walk along the corridor to rejoin the baron's collection. After a comprehensive round of seventeenth-century Dutch painting of various genres, Rococo and Neoclassicism, you reach some **English portraiture** by Gainsborough, Reynolds and Zoffany (room 28) and **American painting** in rooms 29 and 30. The collection, one of the best outside the US, concentrates on landscapes and includes James Goodwyn Clonney's wonderful *Fishing Party on Long Island Sound*, and works by James Whistler, Winslow Homer and John Singer Sargent.

As with Carmen's collection, **Impressionism** and **Post–Impressionism** are another strong point, with a choice collection of paintings by Vincent van Gogh, including one of his last and most gorgeous works, *Les Vessenots* (room 32). **Expressionism**, meanwhile, is represented by some stunning works by Ernst Ludwig Kirchner, Franz Marc, Wassily Kandinsky and Max Beckmann.

The ground floor: avant-gardes

Works on the ground floor run from the beginning of the twentieth century through to around 1970. The good baron didn't, apparently, like contemporary art: "If they can throw colours, I can be free to duck," he explained, following the gallery's opening.

The most interesting work in his "experimental avant-garde" sections is from the **Cubists**. There is an inspired, side-by-side hanging of parallel studies by Picasso (*Man with a Clarinet*) and Braque (*Woman with a Mandolin*). Later choices include a scattering of Joan Miró, Jackson Pollock, Dalí, Rauschenberg and Lichtenstein. In the **Synthesis of Modernity** section, there are some superbly vivid canvases by Max Ernst and Marc Chagall, a brilliant portrait of George Dyer by Francis Bacon, and a fascinating **Lucian Freud**, *Portrait of Baron Thyssen*, posed in front of the Watteau *Pierrot* hanging upstairs.

Centro de Arte Reina Sofía

It is fortunate that the **Centro de Arte Reina Sofía**, facing Estación de Atocha at the end of Paseo del Prado (Mon & Wed–Sat 10am–9pm, Sun

10am–2.30pm; €6, free on Sat after 2.30pm & Sun, see box on p.95 for information on combined ticket; audioguides €5; closed Jan 1 & 6, May 1, Sept 9, Nov 9, Dec 24 & 25; ⓦwww.museoreinasofia.es; ⓂAtocha), keeps slightly different opening hours and days to its neighbours. For this leading exhibition space and permanent gallery of modern Spanish art – its centrepiece is Picasso's greatest picture, *Guernica* – is another essential stop on the Madrid art circuit, and one that really mustn't be seen after a Prado-Thyssen overdose.

The museum, a vast former hospital, is a kind of Madrid response to the Pompidou centre in Paris, with transparent lifts shuttling visitors up the outside of the Sabatini building to the permanent collection. Like the other two great art museums, it has also undergone a major **extension** programme – the French architect Jean Nouvel has added a massive state-of-the-art metal and glass wing behind the main block. If the queues at the main entrance are too long, try the alternative one in the new extension on the Ronda de Atocha.

The Santini building

It is for **Picasso's Guernica** that most visitors come to the Reina Sofia, and rightly so. Superbly displayed, this icon of twentieth-century Spanish art and politics carries a shock that defies all familiarity. Picasso painted it in response to the bombing of the Basque town of Gernika by the German Luftwaffe, acting in concert with Franco, in the Spanish Civil War. In the fascinating preliminary studies, displayed around the room, you can see how he developed its symbols – the dying horse, the woman mourning her dead, the bull, the sun, the flower, the light bulb – and then return to the painting to marvel at how he made it all work.

The work was first exhibited in Paris in 1937, as part of a Spanish Republican Pavilion in the Expo there, and was then loaned to the Museum of Modern Art in New York, until, as Picasso put it, Spain had rid itself of Fascist rule. The artist never lived to see that time, but in 1981, following the restoration of democracy, the painting was, amid much controversy, moved to Madrid to hang (as Picasso had stipulated) in the Prado. Its transfer to the Reina Sofia in 1992 again prompted much soul-searching and protest, though for anyone who saw it in the old Prado annexe, it looks truly liberated in its present setting. Many Basques believe the painting's rightful home is with them, but studies have revealed cracks and fissures that make the painting too fragile to move once again.

Guernica hangs midway around the permanent collection on the second floor. It is preceded by an intriguing introductory room that examines the ground-breaking Basque and Catalan schools and the representation of landscape and the female figure. Strong sections on **Cubism** and the **Paris School** follow, in the first of which Picasso is again well represented, alongside a fascinating straight Cubist work by Salvador Dalí (*Cadaqués Countryside*). There are also good collections of other avant-garde Spaniards of the 1920s and 30s, including Juan Gris.

Dalí and **Miró** make heavyweight contributions to the post-*Guernica* halls. The development of Dalí's work and his variety of techniques are clearly displayed here, with works ranging from the classic *Muchacha en la Ventana* to famous surrealist works such as *El Gran Masturbador* and *El Enigma de Hitler*. There is an impressive collection of Spanish sculpture to be found in the final rooms.

The fourth floor covers Spain's postwar years up to the present day and includes Spanish and international examples of **abstract** and **avant-garde** movements. Outstanding pieces from **Francis Bacon** (*Reclining Figure*), **Henry Moore** and **Graham Sutherland** give a British context, while challenging work from **Antoni Tapiès**, **Antonio Saura** and **Eduardo Chillida** provide the Spanish perspective. If the avant-garde work all gets too much, there are also some more accessible offerings from the Spanish realists.

The Area Nouvel

The extension, or **Area Nouvel** as it is now known, consists of three brand-new buildings built around an open courtyard topped by a striking delta-shaped, metallic, crimson-coloured roof. It is home to the temporary exhibition spaces, which recently hosted an outstanding show featuring the Picasso collection from the Musée National in Paris. There is also an auditorium, a library and a bookshop (Mon–Sat 10am–9pm, Sun 10am–2.30pm) selling a wide range of glossy coffee-table volumes, as well as more academic tomes and the informative museum guidebook (€22), which examines eighty key works in detail.

Also housed in the new wing is *Arola Madrid* (Mon 10am–9pm, Wed–Sat 10am–2.30pm), a café-restaurant run under the auspices of leading Catalan chef Sergi Arola. Coffee and cakes are affordable, but lunch or supper will set you back at least €50 a head.

Parque del Retiro and around

When you get tired of sightseeing, Madrid's many parks are great places to escape for a few hours. The most central and most popular of them is **El Retiro**, a delightful mix of formal gardens and wider open spaces. Nearby, in addition to the Prado, Thyssen-Bornemisza and Reina Sofía galleries, are a number of the city's **smaller museums**, plus the startlingly peaceful **Jardines Botánicos**.

Parque del Retiro

Originally the grounds of a royal retreat (*retiro*) and designed in the French style, the **Parque del Retiro** (ⓜRetiro) has been public property for more than a hundred years. In its 330 acres you can jog, row in the lake (you can rent boats by the Monumento a Alfonso XII), picnic (though officially not on the grass), have your fortune told and – above all – promenade. The busiest day is Sunday, when half of Madrid, replete with spouses, in-laws and kids, turns out for the *paseo*. Dressed for show, the families stroll around, nodding at neighbours and building up an appetite for a long Sunday lunch.

Strolling aside, there's almost always something going on in the park, including a good programme of **concerts** and **fairs** organized by the city council. Concerts tend to be held in the Quiosco de Música in the north of the park. The most popular of the fairs is the *Feria del Libro* (Book Fair), held in early June, when every publisher and half the country's bookshops set up stalls and offer a 25-percent discount on their wares. At weekends, there are **puppet shows** by the Puerta de Alcalá entrance, and on Sundays you can often watch groups of South American musicians performing by the lake.

Travelling art exhibitions are frequently housed in the beautiful **Palacio de Velázquez** (May–Sept Mon & Wed–Sat 11am–8pm, Sun 11am–6pm; Oct–April Mon & Wed–Sat 10am–6pm, Sun 10am–4pm; free) and the nearby **Palacio de Cristal** (during exhibitions same hours; ☎915 746 614 for information) and **Casa de Vacas** (daily 10.30am–2.30pm & 4–8pm; closed Aug; free). Look out, too, for **El Ángel Caído** (Fallen Angel), the world's only public statue to Lucifer, in the south of the park. There is also the **Bosque de los Ausentes**, 192 olive trees and cypresses planted in the Paseo de la Chopera in memory of those who died in the train bombings at the nearby Atocha station on March 11, 2004.

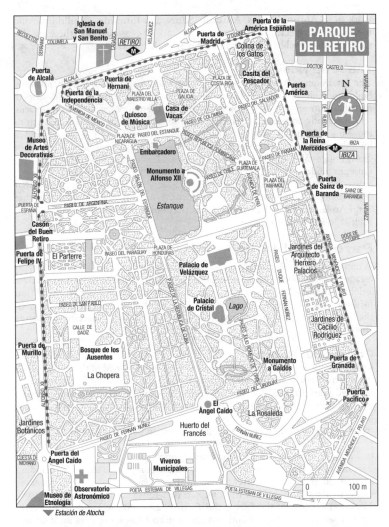

Estación de Atocha

A number of **stalls and cafés** along the Paseo Salón del Estanque sell drinks, *bocadillos* and *pipas* (sunflower seeds), and there are terrazas, too, for *horchata* and *granizados*. The park has a safe reputation, at least by day; in the late evening, it's best not to wander alone, and there are plans to close the park completely at night because of an increase in petty vandalism. Note, too, that the area east of La Chopera is known as a cruising ground for gay prostitutes.

Puerta de Alcalá to San Jerónimo

Leaving the park at the northwest corner takes you to the Plaza de la Independencia, in the centre of which is one of the two remaining gates from the old city walls. Built in the late eighteenth century, the **Puerta de Alcalá** was the biggest in Europe at that time and, like the bear and *madroño* tree, has become one of the city's monumental emblems.

South from here, you pass the **Museo de Artes Decorativas** (Tues–Fri 9.30am–3pm, Sat & Sun 10am–3pm; €2.40, free on Sun; ⓦmnartesdecorativas .mcu.es; ⓂBanco de España/Retiro), which has its entrance at c/Montalbán 12. The furniture and decorations here aren't that spectacular, but there are some superb *azulejos* in a magnificent eighteenth-century tiled Valencian kitchen on the top floor.

A couple of blocks west, in a corner of the Naval Ministry at Paseo del Prado 5, is a **Museo Naval** (Tues–Sun 10am–2pm; closed Aug and public hols; free, though you'll need ID; ⓦwww.museonavalmadrid.com; ⓂBanco de España), strong, as you might expect, on models, charts and navigational aids from or relating to the Spanish voyages of discovery. Exhibits include the first map to show the New World, drawn in 1500, cannons from the Spanish Armada, and part of Cortés' standard used in the conquest of Mexico.

South of here and just behind the Prado is **San Jerónimo el Real** (Mon–Fri 8am–1.30pm & 6–8pm, Sat & Sun 9am–1.30pm & 6.30–8pm, Oct–July opens one hour earlier in the afternoon), Madrid's society church, where in 1975 Juan Carlos (like his predecessors) was crowned. Opposite is the **Real Academía Española de la Lengua** (Royal Language Academy), whose job it is to make sure that the Spanish language is not corrupted by foreign or otherwise unsuitable words; the results are entrusted to their official dictionary – a work that bears virtually no relation to the Spanish you'll hear spoken on the streets.

The Jardín Botánico and Atocha

Immediately south of the Prado is the delightful, shaded **Jardín Botánico** (daily 10am–dusk; €2, under-10s free; ⓦwww.rjb.csic.es; ⓂAtocha). Opened in 1781 by Carlos III (known as *El Alcalde* – "The Mayor" – for his urban-improvement programmes), the garden once contained over 30,000 plants. The numbers are down these days, though the gardens were well renovated in the 1980s, after years of neglect, and the worldwide collection of flora is fascinating for any amateur botanist; don't miss the hothouse with its tropical plants and amazing cacti or the bonsai collection of former prime minister Felipe González. On the other side of the road at Paseo del Prado 36 is **La Caixa Forum** (daily 10am–8pm), an innovative and stylish exhibition space opened in 2008 by the powerful Catalan bank that complements the existing attractions on the Paseo del Arte. The centre, which hosts a variety of high-quality temporary art shows, concerts and workshops, is flanked by an eye-catching vertical garden designed by French botanist Patrick Blanc in which some 15,000 plants form an organic carpet extending across the wall. Inside, there's a decent art bookshop and a neat top-floor café that serves a fine €12 lunchtime *menú*.

On the other side of the botanical gardens is the sloping Cuesta de Moyano, lined with **bookstalls**; although it's at its busiest on Sundays, many of the stalls are open every day. Across the way, the **Estación de Atocha** is worth a look even if you're not travelling out of Madrid. It's actually two stations, old and new, the latter now sadly infamous as the scene of the horrific train bombings that killed 191 people and injured close to 2000 in March 2004. The original station, a glorious 1880s glasshouse, was revamped in the early 1990s with a spectacular tropical-garden centrepiece. It's a wonderful sight from the walkways above, and train buffs and architects will want to take a look at the high-speed AVE trains and the station beyond.

Also in this area, at c/Alfonso XII 68, is the **Museo Nacional de Antro-pología/Etnología** (Tues–Sat 9.30am–8pm, Sun 10am–3pm; €2.40, free Sat after 2.30pm & Sun; Ⓦwww.mnantropologia.mcu.es; ⓂAtocha), designed to give an overview of different cultures of the world, in particular those inter-twined with Spanish history. The most unusual exhibits are to be found in a side room on the ground floor – a macabre collection of deformed skulls, a Guanche (the original inhabitants of the Canary Islands) mummy and the skeleton of a circus giant (2.35m tall). A little farther to the east, the **Real Fábrica de Tapices** at c/Fuenterrabia 2 (Mon–Fri 10am–2pm; closed Aug; €3; Ⓦwww.realfabricadetapices.com; ⓂAtoche Renfe/Menéndez Pelayo) still turns out handmade tapestries, many of them based on the Goya cartoons in the Prado. They are fabulously expensive, but the entrance fee is a bargain with the tour tracing the fascinating manufacturing process, barely changed in the three hundred years of the factory's existence.

The Gran Vía, Chueca and Malasaña

The **Gran Vía**, Madrid's great thoroughfare, runs from Plaza de Cibeles to Plaza de España, effectively dividing the old city to the south from the newer parts northwards. Permanently jammed with traffic and crowded with shoppers and sightseers, it's the commercial heart of the city, and – if you spare the time to look up – quite a monument in its own right, with its early twentieth-century, palace-like banks and offices and the huge hand-painted posters of the cinemas. Look out for the **Edificio Metrópolis** (1905–11) on the corner of c/Alcalá, complete with cylindrical facade, white stone sculptures, zinc-tiled roof and gold garlands, and the towering **Telefónica** building, further up on Redondo de San Luis, which was the chief observation post for the Republican artillery during the Civil War, when the Nationalist front line stretched across the Casa de Campo to the west.

North of the Telefónica, c/Fuencarral heads north to the Glorieta de Bilbao. To either side of this street are two of Madrid's most characterful *barrios*: **Chueca**, to the east, and **Malasaña**, to the west. Their chief appeal lies in an

▲ Edificio Metrópolis

amazing concentration of bars, restaurants and, especially, nightlife. However, there are a few reasons – cafés included – to wander around here by day.

Chueca

Once rather down at heel, Chueca is now one of the city's most vibrant *barrios* and the focal point of Madrid's **gay scene**. At the centre is the lively **Plaza de Chueca** (ⓂChueca), which is fronted by one of the best old-style *vermut* bars in the city, *Bodega Ángel Sierra*, on c/Gravina at the northwest corner. The whole area has become somewhat gentrified in recent years with the rise of a host of stylish bars, cafés and restaurants, many of which have been established by the local gay community.

From Plaza de Chueca east to **Paseo Recoletos** (the beginning of the long Paseo de la Castellana) are some of the city's most enticing streets. Offbeat restaurants, small private art galleries, and odd corner shops are to be found here in abundance, and the **c/Almirante** has some of the city's most fashionable clothes shops, too. On the parallel c/Prim, **ONCE**, the national association for the blind, has its headquarters. ONCE is financed by a lottery, for which the blind work as ticket sellers, and many come here to collect their allocation of tickets. The lottery has become such a major money-spinner that the organization is now one of the wealthiest businesses in Spain.

To the south, the Ministerio de Cultura fronts the **Plaza del Rey**, which is also worth a look for the other odd buildings surrounding it, especially the **Casa de las Siete Chimeneas** (House of Seven Chimneys), which is supposedly haunted by a mistress of Felipe II who disappeared in mysterious circumstances.

To the north, on c/Fernando VI on the edge of the Santa Bárbara *barrio*, is the **Sociedad de Autores** (Society of Authors), housed in the only significant *modernista* building in Madrid designed by José Grasés Riera, who was part of the Gaudí school, and featuring an eye-catching facade that resembles a melted candle. The **Museo Municipal (Museo de Historia)** at c/Fuencarral 78 (Aug Tues–Sun 10am–2pm; Sept–July Tues–Fri 9.30am–8pm; free; ⓦwww .munimadrid.es/museomunicipal; ⓂTribunal) is more interesting for its models and maps of old Madrid, which show the incredible expansion of the city in the last century. It is undergoing refurbishment, but there's an interesting abbreviated exhibition including some of the museum's highlights in the chapel of this former city almshouse. The building itself has a superb Churrigueresque facade by Pedro de Ribera.

Malasaña

The heart, in all senses, of Malasaña is the **Plaza Dos de Mayo**, named after the insurrection against Napoleonic forces on May 2, 1808; the rebellion and its aftermath are depicted in Goya's famous paintings at the Prado (see p.000). The surrounding district bears the name of one of the martyrs of the uprising, 15-year-old Manuela Malasaña, who is also commemorated in a street (as are several other heroes of the time). On the night of May 1, all of Madrid shuts down to honour its heroes, and the plaza is the scene of festivities lasting well into the night.

More recently, the quarter was the focus of the *movida madrileña*, the "happening scene" of the late 1970s and early 80s. As the country relaxed after the death of Franco and the city developed into a thoroughly modern capital under the leadership of the late mayor, Galván, Malasaña became a focal point for the young. Bars appeared behind every doorway, drugs were sold openly in the streets, and there was an extraordinary atmosphere of new-found freedom.

Times have changed and a good deal of renovation has been going on in recent years, but the *barrio* retains a somewhat alternative – nowadays rather grungy – feel, with its bar custom spilling onto the streets, and an ever-lively scene in the Plaza Dos de Mayo terrazas.

One of the few specific sights in this quarter is **San Antonio de los Alemanes** at Corredera de San Pablo 16 (daily 9am–1pm & 6–8pm; free), a delightful, elliptical church with dizzying floor-to-ceiling frescoes by Neapolitan artist Luca Giordano depicting the life of St Anthony. The streets have an interest of their own and are home to some fine traditional bars, while on c/Manuela Malasaña you can take your pick from some of the trendiest cafés in town. There are also some wonderful old shop signs and architectural details, best of all the **Antigua Farmacia Juanse** on the corner of c/San Andrés and c/San Vicente Ferrer, with its irresistible 1920s *azulejo* scenes depicting cures for diarrhoea, headaches and suchlike.

Plaza de España, Parque del Oeste and Casa de Campo

The **Plaza de España** (Ⓜ Plaza de España), at the west end of Gran Vía, was home, until the flurry of corporate building in the north of Madrid, to two of the city's tallest buildings: the **Torre de Madrid** and the **Edificio de España**. These rather stylish 1950s buildings preside over an elaborate monument to Cervantes in the middle of the square, which in turn overlooks the bewildered-looking bronze figures of Don Quixote and Sancho Panza.

The plaza itself is a little on the seedy side, especially at night. However, to its north, **c/Martín de los Heros** is a lively place, day and night, with a couple of the city's best cinemas, and behind them the **Centro Princesa**, with shops, clubs, bars and a 24-hour branch of the ubiquitous VIPS – just the place to have your film developed at 4am, or a bite to eat before heading on to a small-hours club. Up the steps opposite the Centro Princesa is c/Conde Duque, an atmospheric street that contains an intriguing selection of cafés, restaurants and shops and is dominated by the massive former barracks of the royal guard, constructed in the early eighteenth century by Pedro de Ribera. The barracks have been turned into a dynamic cultural centre, **El Centro Cultural de Conde Duque** (Tues–Sat 10am–2pm & 5.30–9pm, Sun & public hols 10.30am–2.30pm; summer: Tues–Sat 10am–2pm & 6–9pm, Sun 10.30am–2pm; Ⓦ www.munimadrid.es/condeduque; free), which is home to the city's collection of contemporary art; it also hosts a variety of temporary exhibitions, and stages concerts, plays and dance as part of the *Veranos de la Villa* season. Just to the east of this, the **Plaza de las Comendadoras** – named after the convent that occupies one side of the square – is a tranquil space bordered by a variety of interesting craft shops, bars and cafés.

A block to the west is the **Museo Cerralbo**, c/Ventura Rodríguez 17 (Tues–Sat 9.30am–3pm, July closes 2pm, Sun 10am–3pm; closed Aug; €2.40, free on Wed & Sun; Ⓦ www.museocerralbo.mcu.es; Ⓜ Ventura Rodríguez; closed for refurbishment), an elegant mansion endowed with its collections by the reactionary politician, poet, traveller and archeologist, the seventeenth Marqués de Cerralbo. The rooms, stuffed with paintings, furniture, armour and artefacts, provide a fascinating insight into the lifestyle of the nineteenth-century aristocracy, though there is little of individual note.

Beyond lies the leafy suburb of **Moncloa** and two of the most pleasant green spaces in the city, the tranquil **Parque del Oeste** and the semi-wild **Casa de Campo**.

Parque del Oeste and La Ermita de San Antonio de la Florida

The **Parque del Oeste** stretches northwest from the Plaza de España, following the rail tracks of Príncipe Pío up to the suburbs of Moncloa and Ciudad Universitaria. On its south side, five-minutes' walk from the square, is the **Templo de Debod** (April–Sept Tues–Fri 10am–2pm & 6–8pm, Sat & Sun 10am–2pm; Oct–March Tues–Fri 9.45am–1.45pm & 4.15–6.15pm, Sat & Sun 10am–2pm; free; ⓦwww.munimadrid.es/templodebod; ⓜPlaza de España), a fourth-century BC Egyptian temple given to Spain in recognition of the work done by Spanish engineers on the Aswan High Dam (which inundated its original site). Reconstructed here stone by stone, it seems comically incongruous, and even more so with a new multimedia exhibition on the culture of Ancient Egypt housed inside. In summer, there are numerous terrazas in the park, while, year-round, a **teleférico** (April–Sept Mon–Fri noon–early eve, Sat & Sun noon–8pm; Oct–March Sat, Sun & public hols noon–dusk; €3.50 single, €5 return; ⓦwww.teleferico.com; ⓜArgüelles/Ventura Rodríguez) shuttles its passengers high over the river from Paseo del Pintor Rosales to the middle of the Casa de Campo, where there's a bar/restaurant with pleasant views back towards the city. Just below the starting point of the *teleférico* is the beautiful **Rosaleda**, a vast rose garden at its best in May and June.

Rail lines from commuter towns to the north of Madrid terminate at the **Príncipe Pío** (aka Estación del Norte), a quietly spectacular construction of white enamel, steel and glass, which has a new shopping and leisure complex tagged alongside. About 400m from the station along the Paseo de la Florida is the *Casa Mingo*, an institution for roast chicken washed down by cider – ideal for take-outs to the Casa de Campo. Almost alongside it, at Glorieta de la Florida 5, is **La Ermita de San Antonio de la Florida** (Tues–Fri 9.30am–2pm & 4–8pm, Sat & Sun 10am–2pm, July 13–23 closed afternoons; free; ⓦwww.munimadrid.es/ermita; ⓜPríncipe Pío). If you can, go on Saturdays, when there are guided tours in English. This little church on a Greek-cross plan was built by an Italian, Felipe Fontana, between 1792 and 1798, and decorated by **Goya**, whose frescoes are the reason to visit. In the dome is a depiction of a miracle performed by St Anthony of Padua. Around it, heavenly bodies of angels and cherubs hold back curtains to reveal the main scene: the saint resurrecting a dead man to give evidence in favour of a prisoner (the saint's father) falsely accused of murder. Beyond this central group, Goya created a gallery of highly realist characters – their models were court and society figures – while for a lesser fresco of the angels adoring the Trinity in the apse, he took prostitutes as his models. The *ermita* also houses the artist's mausoleum, although his head was stolen by phrenologists for examination in the nineteenth century.

Moncloa

The wealthy suburb of **Moncloa** contains the Spanish prime ministerial home and merits a visit even if you are not using the bus terminal for El Pardo and El Escorial. The metro will bring you out next to the mammoth building housing the Air Ministry and the giant Arco de la Victoria, built by Franco in 1956 to commemorate the Nationalist victory in the Civil War. Beyond this lie the leafy expanses of the Parque del Oeste and the campuses of the **Ciudad Universitaria**. During term time, the area becomes one giant student party on weekend evenings, with huddles of picnickers and singing groups under the trees. Take the Plaza de Moncloa metro exit, and the path on your right through the trees will lead you to the **Mirador del Faro** (May to mid-Oct Tues–Sun

10am–2pm & 5pm–dusk; mid-Oct to May Tues–Fri 10am–2pm & 5–7pm, Sat & Sun 10am–6pm; €1.50), a futuristic 92-metre-high tower with great views of the city and the mountains beyond. Just past this, with its main entrance on Avda. Reyes Católicos 6, the **Museo de América** (Tues–Sat 9.30am–3pm, Sun 10am–3pm; €3, free on Sun; ⓦwww.museodeamerica.mcu.es) contains a fine collection of artefacts, ceramics and silverware from Spain's former colonies in Latin America. The highlight is the fabulous Quimbayas treasure – a breathtaking collection of gold objects and figures from the Quimbaya culture of Colombia.

Across the busy road down towards the university is the recently inaugurated **Museo del Traje** (Tues–Sat 9.30am–7pm, Sun 10am–3pm; €3, free for under-18s, Sat after 2.30pm and all day Sun; ⓦwww.museodeltraje.mcu.es; Ⓜ Moncloa), a fascinating excursion through the history of clothes and costume. Exhibits include clothes from a royal tomb dating back to the thirteenth century, some stunning eighteenth-century ball gowns and a selection of Spanish regional costumes, as well as shoes, jewellery and underwear. Modern Spanish and international designers are also featured, with a Paco Rabanne miniskirt and elegant dresses from Pedro del Hierro.

Casa de Campo

If you want to jog, play tennis, swim, picnic, go to the fairground or see pandas, then the **Casa de Campo** is the place to head for. This enormous expanse of heath and scrub is in parts surprisingly wild for a place so easily accessible from the city; other sections have been tamed for more conventional pastimes. The Casa de Campo can be reached by metro (Ⓜ Batán/Lago), various buses (#33 from Príncipe Pío is the easiest) or *teleférico* (see p.109). The walk from the Príncipe Pío station via the Puente del Rey isn't too strenuous, either.

Picnic tables and café-bars are dotted throughout the park and there's a **jogging track** with exercise posts, a municipal open-air **swimming pool** (daily June–Sept 10.30am–8pm; €4) close to Ⓜ Lago, tennis courts, and rowing boats for rent on the **lake** (again near Ⓜ Lago).

Sightseeing attractions include a large and well-organized **zoo** and a popular amusement park, the **Parque de Atracciones** (see p.133), complete with the obligatory selection of heart-stopping, stomach-churning gravity rides. Although some of the **main access roads** through the park are frequented by prostitutes, the city council is taking measures to clamp down on the trade, and there are few problems during daylight hours.

Salamanca and the Paseo de la Castellana

Salamanca, the area north of the Parque del Retiro, is a smart address for apartments and, even more so, for shops. The *barrio* is the haunt of *pijos* – universally denigrated rich kids – and the grid of streets between c/Goya and c/José Ortega y Gasset contains most of the city's designer emporiums. Most of the buildings are modern and undistinguished, though there are some elegant nineteenth-century mansions and apartment blocks. There is a scattering of museums, galleries and exhibition spaces to tempt you up here, too, in particular the **Sorolla** and the **Lázaro Galdiano** museums, two little gems that are often ignored by visitors.

Plaza de Colón

Tackling the area from south to north, the first point of interest is **Plaza de Colón** (Ⓜ Colón), endowed at street level with a statue of Columbus (Cristóbal Colón), and some huge stone blocks arranged as a megalithic monument to the discovery of the Americas. Below the plaza and underneath the cascading waterfall facing the Paseo de la Castellana is the 1970s **Centro Cultural de la Villa**, which is still a good place for film and theatre and occasional exhibitions (Tues–Sat 10am–9pm, Sun 10am–7pm).

Off the square, too, with its entrance at c/Serrano 13, is the **Museo Arqueológico Nacional** (Tues–Sat 9.30am–8pm, Sun 9.30am–3pm; free for duration of ongoing refurbishment programme, otherwise €3, free Sat 2.30–8.30pm & Sun; ⓦwww.man.mcu.es; ⓂColón/Serrano). As the national collection, this has some very impressive pieces, among them the celebrated Celto-Iberian busts known as *La Dama de Elche* and *La Dama de Baza*, and a wonderfully rich hoard of Visigothic treasures found at Toledo. The presentation and layout may be traditional, but the museum contains some outstanding Roman, Egyptian, Greek and Islamic finds. In the gardens, downstairs to the left of the main entrance, is a reconstruction of the Altamira Caves in Cantabria, with their prehistoric wall-paintings. The refurbishment programme means that there are periodic closures of rooms.

The nearby **Biblioteca Nacional** (Tues–Sat 10am–9pm, Sun 10am–2pm; free) contains a museum that displays a selection of the library's treasures including Arab, Hebrew and Greek manuscripts, and has an interesting exhibition on the development of written communication (in Spanish only).

North of Plaza de Colón

North of Plaza de Colón up the Paseo de la Castellana is the **Museo de Escultura al Aire Libre** (free; ⓂRubén Darío), an innovative attempt at using the space underneath the Juan Bravo flyover. However, its haphazard and rather stark collection of sculptures, including the six-tonne suspended block titled *The Meeting* by the late Eduardo Chillada, appears to be more appreciated by the city's skateboard community.

The recently refurbished and extended **Museo Lázaro Galdiano** (Mon & Wed–Sun 10am–4.30pm; €4, free Wed; ⓦwww.flg.es; ⓂGregorio Marañon/ Rubén Darío) is a little farther north at c/Serrano 122. This former private collection was given to the state by José Galdiano in 1948 and spreads over the four floors and thirty-seven rooms of his former home. It is a vast jumble of art works, with some very dodgy attributions, but includes some really exquisite and valuable pieces. Among painters represented are El Greco, Bosch, Gerard David, Dürer and Rembrandt, as well as a host of Spanish artists, including Berruguete, Murillo, Zurbarán, Velázquez and Goya. Other exhibits include a collection of clocks and watches, many of them once owned by Carlos V.

Not far to the west of here, across the Paseo de la Castellana, is another little jewel of a gallery, the **Museo Sorolla**, c/General Martínez Campos 37 (Tues, Thurs–Sat 9.30am–3pm, Wed 9.30am–6pm, July & Aug closes 2.30pm, Sun 10am–3pm; €2.40, free Sun; ⓦwww.museosorolla.mcu.es; ⓂGregorio Marañon/Iglesia). There's a large collection of work by the painter Joaquín Sorolla (1863–1923), tastefully displayed in his beautifully preserved old home; the best of his paintings, which include beach scenes, portraits and landscapes, are striking, impressionistic plays on light and texture. His old studio is much as he left it, and the house itself, with its cool and shady Andalucian-style courtyard and gardens, is worth the visit alone and makes a wonderful escape from the traffic-choked streets.

To the Bernabéu

Farther north along the Paseo de la Castellana, you reach the **Zona Azca** (ⓂNuevos Ministerios/Santiago Bernabéu), a business quarter, once home

Fútbol in Madrid

With the departures of David Beckham, Zinedine Zidane, Ronaldo and Luis Figo, the "Galactico" era is officially over, but **Real Madrid** remains one of the most glamorous teams in club football with an ample quota of superstars. The nine-times winners of the **European Cup** and thirty-times Spanish champions play in the imposing Bernabéu stadium, venue of the 1982 World Cup final and a ground that ranks as one of the world's great sporting arenas.

Tickets to games – which have become more difficult to get hold of in recent years – cost from €40 up to €150 for big matches and usually go on sale in the week before a game; Real runs a telephone and online booking service (☎913 984 300, tickets ☎902 324 324, ⓦwww.realmadrid.com – see section titled "proximo partido" for online bookings). They can be purchased by credit card on the ticket line (best to ignore the options you're given on the line and wait to speak to an operator) or online for all but the biggest matches. You can also get them through online ticket agency ⓦwww.servicaixa.com. Pick the tickets up from Servicaixa cashpoints (11am–8pm) or the automatic tills in the shopping centre at the corner of the Bernabéu (Las Esquina del Bernabéu) on the day of the match. If you don't get lucky, you can still catch a glimpse of the hallowed turf by taking the **stadium tour** (see below).

The capital is also home to another of the country's biggest teams, **Atlético Madrid** (☎913 664 707, ⓦwww.clubatleticodemadrid.com; tickets from around €30, bought via the website or ⓦwww.servicaixa.com), who play at the Estadio Vicente Calderón in the south of the city (ⓜPirámides), and the more modest **Getafe** (☎916 959 771, ⓦwww.getafecf.com; tickets from around €30), who are based at the Coliseo de Alfonso Perez in a working-class satellite town to the south of Madrid (ⓜEspartales on the MetroSur).

to the city's tallest skyscraper, the 157-metre Torre Picasso designed by Minori Yamasaki (also the architect of New York's infamous Twin Towers), although it is now dwarfed by the four new towers being built beyond Plaza Castilla.

Just north of the Azca complex, and easily the most famous sight up here, is the magnificent **Santiago Bernabéu** football stadium, home of Real Madrid. Even if you can't get to see a match, you can take the **stadium tour** (Mon–Sat 10am–7pm, Sun 10.30am–6.30pm, closes 5hr before kickoff on match days; €15, under-14s €10; ⓜSantiago Bernabéu). The tour is very expensive but understandably popular. It starts with a panoramic view of the massive 80,000-capacity stadium and takes in a visit to the dressing rooms and a walk through the tunnel onto the pitch. Also included is the **trophy exhibition**, complete with endless cabinets of gleaming silverware, with pride of place given to the team's nine European Cups and video footage of their greatest triumphs. The tour ends with the obligatory visit to the overpriced club shop – where you soon come to realize why Real is the richest football club in the world. The stadium also has a surprisingly affordable café (*Realcafé*) and a more expensive **restaurant** (*Puerta 57*), both open to the public and affording views over the pitch (though they are not open during games).

El Pardo

Franco had his principal residence at **El Pardo**, a former royal hunting ground, 9km northwest of central Madrid. A garrison still remains at the town – where most of the Generalísmo's staff were based – but the stigma of the place has lessened over the years, and it is now a popular weekend excursion for *madrileños*, who come here for long lunches in the terraza restaurants, or to play tennis or swim at one of the nearby sports centres.

The tourist focus is the **Palacio del Pardo** (April–Sept Mon–Sat 10.30am–5.45pm, Sun 9.30am–1.30pm; Oct–March Mon–Sat 10.30am–4.45pm, Sun 10am–1.30pm; closed occasionally for official visits; guided tours €4; ⓦwww.patrimonionacional.es), rebuilt by the Bourbons on the site of a hunting lodge of Carlos V. The interior is pleasant enough, with its chapel and theatre, a portrait of Isabel la Católica by her court painter Juan de Flandes, and an excellent collection of tapestries, many after the Goya cartoons in the Prado. Guides detail the uses Franco made of the *palacio*, but pass over some of his stranger habits – he kept by his bed, for instance, the mummified hand of St Teresa of Ávila. Tickets to the *palacio* are also valid for the **Casita del Príncipe** (same hours, but undergoing a long-running refurbishment), though this cannot be entered from the gardens and you will need to return to the main road. Like the *casitas* (pavilions) at El Escorial, this was built by Juan de Villanueva, and is highly ornate.

You can reach El Pardo by local **bus** (#601 runs every 15min until midnight from the bus terminal at ⓜMoncloa) or by any city **taxi** (around €15).

Restaurants and tapas bars

Madrid's range of **eating and drinking** establishments are legion, and include bars, cafés, *cervecerías* (beer halls), *marisquerías* (seafood bars) and *restaurantes*. At almost any of our recommendations you could happily eat your fill – money permitting – though at bars, *madrileños* usually eat just a

Madrid's vegetarian restaurants

Madrid has a growing number of good-value **vegetarian restaurants**, scattered about the centre. These include:

Al Natural c/Zorilla 11 ☏913 694 709, ⓦwww.alnatural.biz; ⓜBanco de España. Veggie and non-veggie food, including a very good mushroom and spinach pie and stuffed aubergines. Decent wines and an above-average *menú* at €11.20, and it's non-smoking, too – a rarity for Madrid. Closed Sun eve.

Artemisa c/Ventura de la Vega 4 ☏914 295 092; ⓜSevilla; c/Tres Cruces 4 ☏915 218 721; ⓜGran Vía. Two branches of this long-standing popular vegetarian (you may have to wait for a table), good for veggie pizzas and paellas, superb vegetable dishes and an imaginative range of salads. Reasonable prices at around €20–25 per head. No smoking. Closed Sun eve.

🏃 **El Estragón** Plaza de la Paja 10 ☏913 658 982; ⓜLa Latina. Cosy restaurant enjoying a fine setting on the edge of ancient Plaza de Paja, and dishing up big helpings of hearty vegetarian food and great desserts. *Menú* at €10 (dinner *menú* is €19) during the week.

La Isla del Tesoro c/Manuela Malasaña 3 ☏915 931 440; ⓜBilbao. Tropical beach decor serves as the backdrop for some cosmopolitan vegetarian food at this great-value place on one of the most interesting streets in Malasaña. Constantly changing *menú* for around €10.

Vegaviana c/Pelayo 35 ☏913 080 381; ⓜChueca. A wide range of tasty vegetarian options with an international twist, in the heart of Chueca. There's a free-range chicken option for non-veggies, too. Very good value, with big portions meaning you'll struggle to break the €20 mark. Closed Mon & Sun.

tapa or share a *racion* of the house speciality then move on to repeat the procedure down the road.

Cuisines

Madrid's restaurants and bars offer every regional style of **Spanish cooking**: Castilian, for roasts and stews (such as the meat and chickpea *cocido*); *gallego*, for seafood; *andaluz*, for fried fish; Levantine (Valencia/Alicante), for paella and other rice-based dishes; Asturian, for winter stews like *fabada*; and Basque, for the ultimate gastronomy (and correspondingly high prices).

Over the last few years, dozens of **foreign cuisines** have also appeared. There are some good Peruvian, Argentinian, Middle Eastern and Italian places, a growing number of oriental-influenced restaurants with some inventive fusion-style cuisine, and an explosion of Turkish kebab-houses in the centre of town.

There has also been an unfortunate rise in franchised restaurant chains and coffee bars that have elbowed out some of the more traditional establishments. For more healthy and stylish **fast food**, try the new *Fast Good* (c/Juan Bravo 3; ⓜRubén Darío) or *Iboo* (c/Alcalá 55; ⓜBanco de España) outlets run by celebrity chefs Ferrán Adrià and Mario Sandoval.

Café life

A number of Madrid's **cafés** are institutions. They serve food but are much more places to drink coffee, have a *copa* or *caña*, or read the papers. Some also act as a meeting place for the semi-formal *tertulia* – a kind of discussion/drinking group, popular among Madrid intellectuals of the past and revived in the 1980s. The following are particularly recommended:

Café Barbieri c/Ave María 45; ⓜLavapiés. A relaxed place in the heart of Lavapiés, with unobtrusive music, old-style decor, newspapers and a wide selection of coffees. Open from 3pm.

Café Comercial Glorieta de Bilbao; ⓜBilbao. One of the city's most popular meeting points – a lovely traditional café, well positioned for the Chueca/Santa Bárbara area.

Café del Espejo Paseo de Recoletos 31; ⓜColón. Opened in 1991 but you wouldn't guess it – mirrors, gilt and a wonderful glass pavilion, plus a leafy outside *terraza*.

Café Gijón Paseo de Recoletos 21; ⓜBanco de España. A famous literary café – and a centre of the intellectual/arty *movida* in the 1980s – decked out in Cuban mahogany and mirrors. Has a summer terraza.

Café de Oriente Plaza de Oriente 2; ⓜÓpera. Elegant, Parisian-style affair with a popular terraza looking out towards the Palacio Royal.

Círculo de Bellas Artes c/Alcalá 42; ⓜBanco de España. Day membership to the *Círculo* is €1, which gives you access to exhibitions, and to a stylish bar, where you can loll on sofas and have drinks at "normal" prices. Outside, in summer, there's a comfortable terraza.

La Mallorquina Puerta del Sol 2; ⓜSol. Good for breakfast or snacks – try one of their *napolitanas* (cream slices) in the sunny upstairs salon.

La Suiza Plaza de Santa Ana 2; ⓜSevilla. A classic café serving delicious *leche merengada* (a sort of sweet, whipped-milk ice cream), *chocolate con churros* and a massive selection of cakes. Its year-round terraza on the plaza makes a perfect spot for people-watching.

Sol, Plaza Mayor and Ópera

The central area is the most varied in Madrid in terms of price and food. Indeed, there can be few places in the world that rival the streets around **Puerta del Sol** for sheer number of places to eat and drink. Around the smarter **Ópera** district, you need to be more selective, while on **Plaza Mayor** itself, stick to drinks. Unless indicated otherwise, all these places are easily reached from **Metro Sol**.

Tapas bars

El Abuelo c/Núñez de Arce 3. There's a *comedor* at the back of this down-to-earth bar, where you can order a selection of delicious *raciones* – the *croquetas* are especially good – and a jug of house wine. Closed Mon.

Las Bravas c/Alvarez Gato 3. As the name suggests, *patatas bravas* (spicy potatoes) are the tapa to try at this bar, which has patented its own version of the sauce; the *tortilla* is pretty good, too. On the outside of the bar are novelty mirrors, a hangover from the days when this was a barbers and the subject of a story by Valle Inclán. Standing room only and bright lights mean it is not to everyone's liking, though. Other branches nearby at c/ Espoz y Mina 13, c/Cruz 15 and Pasaje Mathéu 5.

🏃 **Casa del Abuelo** c/Victoria 12. Tiny, highly atmospheric corner bar serving just its cloyingly sweet red house wine, beer and great cooked prawns – try them *al ajilo* (in garlic) or *a la plancha* (fried). You'll be given a voucher for a free glass of wine at the sister bar round the corner in c/Núñez de Arce.

Casa del Labra c/Tetuán 12 ☎915 310 081. A great, traditional place, where the Spanish Socialist Party was founded in 1879. Order a drink at the bar and a *ración* of *bacalao* (cod fried in batter) or some of the best *croquetas* in town at the counter to the right of the door. There's a fairly expensive restaurant at the back with classic *madrileño* food on offer. Closed Sun.

Lhardy Carrera de San Jerónimo 8 ☎915 213 385, ⓦwww.lhardy.com. *Lhardy* is one of Madrid's most famous and expensive restaurants. Once the haunt of royalty, it's a beautiful place but greatly overpriced (minimum €60). Downstairs, however, there's a wonderful bar/shop, where you can snack on canapés, *fino* (dry sherry) and *consommé*, without breaking the bank. Closed Sun eve.

Museo del Jamón Carrera de San Jerónimo 6. The largest branch of this ubiquitous Madrid chain, from whose ceilings are suspended hundreds of *jamones* (hams). The best – and they are not cheap – are the *jabugos* from the Sierra Morena, though a ham croissant is around €3.

La Oreja de Oro c/Victoria 9. Standing room only in this spit-and-sawdust bar just opposite *La Casa del Abuelo*. Try the excellent *pulpo a la Gallega* (sliced octopus layered over a bed of potatoes and seasoned with cayenne pepper) washed down with Ribeiro wine served in terracotta bowls. Plenty of other seafood tapas on offer, too. Closed Aug.

Restaurants

El Botín c/Cuchilleros 17 ☎913 664 217, ⓦwww.botin.es; Ⓜ Sol/Tirso de Molina. Established in 1725, the picturesque *El Botín* is cited in the *Guinness Book of Records* as Europe's oldest restaurant. Favoured by Hemingway, inevitably it's become a tourist haunt but not such a bad one, with quality Castilian roasts – especially suckling pig (*cochinillo*) from Segovia and roast lamb (*cordero asado*). There's a €35 *menú*.

Casa Ciriaco c/Mayor 84 ☎915 480 620; Ⓜ Ópera. An attractive *taberna*, long reputed for traditional Castilian dishes – trout, chicken, partridge and so on, served up in generous portions. The *menú* is €20, main *carta* dishes a bit less. Closed Wed & Aug.

Casa Paco Plaza Puerta Cerrada 11 ☎913 663 166, ⓦwww.amerc.es/casapaco; Ⓜ La Latina/Sol. This classic traditional *comedor*, with no-nonsense service, dishes out some of the best-prepared meat dishes in town. Specializes in sirloin steak (*solomillo*), and another delicious cut known as *cebón de buey*. Count on spending about €35. Closed Sun & Aug.

🏃 **La Finca de Susana** c/Arlabán 4 ⓦwww.lafinca-restaurant.com; Ⓜ Sevilla. One of two great-value restaurants set up by a group of Catalan friends (the other is *La Gloria de Montera* just off Gran Vía). Tasty *menú* for around €9, consisting of simple dishes served with imagination. Arrive early to avoid queuing, as you can't book (opens 1pm for lunch).

Viuda Blanca c/Campomanes 6 ☎915 487 529, ⓦwww.laviudablanca.com; Ⓜ Ópera. A self-consciously super-cool restaurant with *de rigueur* minimalist decor, run by chef César Augusto, the "*White Widow*" serves an inventive €13.15 set lunch (€17 at weekends), which usually includes vegetarian and low-calorie options. On the other side of the bar is *La Viuda Negra* club/cocktail bar. Closed Sun.

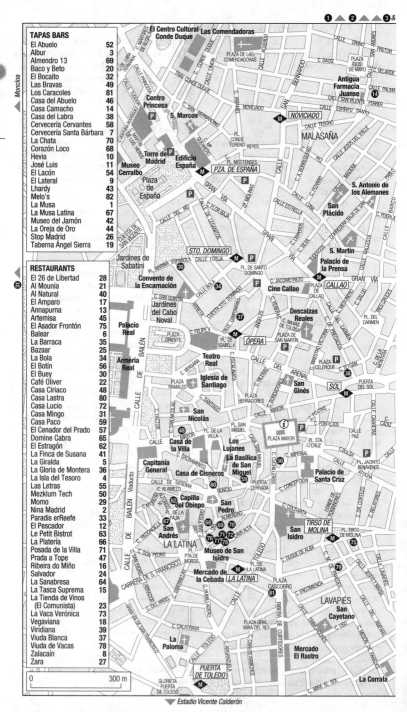

TAPAS BARS

El Abuelo	52
Albur	3
Almendro 13	69
Baco y Beto	20
El Bocaito	32
Las Bravas	49
Los Caracoles	81
Casa del Abuelo	46
Casa Camacho	14
Casa del Labra	38
Cervecería Cervantes	58
Cervecería Santa Bárbara	7
La Chata	70
Corazón Loco	68
Hevia	10
José Luis	11
El Lacón	54
El Lateral	9
Lhardy	43
Melo's	82
La Musa	1
La Musa Latina	67
Museo del Jamón	42
La Oreja de Oro	44
Stop Madrid	26
Taberna Ángel Sierra	19

RESTAURANTS

El 26 de Libertad	28
Al Mounia	21
Al Natural	40
El Amparo	17
Annapurna	13
Artemisa	45
El Asador Frontón	75
Balear	6
La Barraca	35
Bazaar	25
La Bola	34
El Botín	56
El Buey	30
Café Oliver	22
Casa Ciriaco	48
Casa Lastra	80
Casa Lucio	72
Casa Mingo	31
Casa Paco	59
El Cenador del Prado	57
Domine Cabra	65
El Estragón	62
La Finca de Susana	41
La Giralda	5
La Gloria de Montera	36
La Isla del Tesoro	4
Las Letras	55
Mezklum Tech	50
Momo	29
Nina Madrid	2
Paradis erReefe	33
El Pescador	12
Le Petit Bistrot	63
La Platería	66
Posada de la Villa	71
Prada a Tope	47
Ribeira do Miño	16
Salvador	24
La Sanabresa	64
La Tasca Suprema	15
La Tienda de Vinos (El Comunista)	23
La Vaca Verónica	73
Vegaviana	18
Viridiana	39
Viuda Blanca	37
Viuda de Vacas	78
Zalacaín	8
Zara	27

0   300 m

Estadio Vicente Calderón

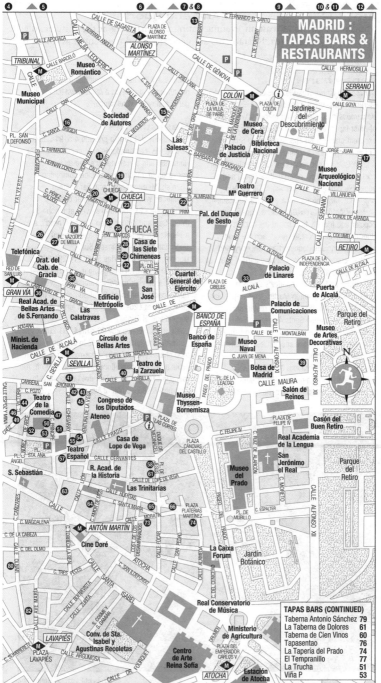

MADRID : TAPAS BARS & RESTAURANTS

TAPAS BARS (CONTINUED)	
Taberna Antonio Sánchez	79
La Taberna de Dolores	61
Taberna de Cien Vinos	60
Tapasentao	76
La Tapería del Prado	74
El Tempranillo	77
La Trucha	51
Viña P	53

Around Plaza de Santa Ana and Huertas

You should spend at least an evening eating and drinking at the historic, tiled bars in this central area. Restaurants are good, too, and frequented as much by locals as tourists.

Tapas bars

Cervecería Cervantes Plaza de Jesús 7; Ⓜ Antón Martín. Prawns are the speciality here – the *tosta de gambas* is delicious – but there's a wide range of other tapas, and the beer is good, too. An excellent place for an aperitivo. Closed Sun eve.

El Lacón c/Manuel Fernández y González 8; Ⓜ Sol. A large Galician bar-restaurant with plenty of seats upstairs. Great *pulpo, caldo gallego* (meat and vegetable broth) and *empanadas*. Closed Aug.

La Taberna de Dolores Plaza de Jesús 4; Ⓜ Antón Martín. Splendid canapés at this popular and friendly tiled bar at the bottom of Huertas. The beer is really good, and the food specialities include Roquefort and anchovy, and smoked-salmon canapés. Get here early if you want a space at the bar.

La Trucha c/Manuel Fernández y González 3 ☎ 914 295 833; Ⓜ Antón Martín. An ever-popular tapas bar and reasonably priced restaurant sandwiched between Santa Ana and c/Echegaray. Andalucian-style *pescaito frito* (smoked fish) and *pimientos de Padrón* are specialities. Usually very crowded. Closed Sun.

Viña P Plaza de Santa Ana 3; Ⓜ Sol/Sevilla. Friendly staff serve a great range of tapas in a bar decked out with bullfighting mementoes and posters. Try the asparagus, stuffed mussels and the mouthwatering *almejas a la marinera* (clams in a garlic and white-wine sauce).

Restaurants

El Cenador del Prado c/Prado 4 ☎ 914 291 561, ⓦ www.elcenadordelprado.com; Ⓜ Sevilla. Romantic and stylish decor serve as the backdrop to imaginative cuisine combining Spanish, Mediterranean and Far Eastern influences with some spectacular desserts. Good-value €21.50 *menú* served at lunch (Mon–Sat) and dinner (Mon–Thurs). There's also a vegetarian version at €19 and a *menú de degustación* at €41. Closed Sun.

Domine Cabra c/Huertas 54 ☎ 914 294 365; Ⓜ Antón Martín. An interesting mix of traditional and modern, with *madrileña* standards given the *nueva cocina* treatment. Smallish helpings but good value at €25–30. Closed Sat lunch, Sun eve & second half of Aug.

Las Letras c/Echegaray 26 ☎ 914 291 206; Ⓜ Sevilla. Designerish touches to the decor and the food characterize this small bar-restaurant, which picks up where its predecessor *Lerranz* left off; the *menú* is €10.50. Closed Sun eve (all day Sun in summer) & second half of Aug.

▲ Tapas at Plaza de Santa Ana

Mezklum Tech c/Príncipe 16 ⏍915 218 911,
ⓦwww.mezklum.com; ⓂSevilla. A hyper-cool
restaurant decked out in shades of mauve and
white and serving a fine array of Mediterranean
dishes, with good salads and pastas. It has two
good-value lunch-time *menús* at €10.90 and
€14.90, while evening meals cost around €25–30.

🏃 Le Petit Bistrot Plaza Matute 5 ⏍914 296
265, ⓦwww.lepetitbistrot.net; ⓂSevilla
Antón Martín. A genuine French bistro in this quiet
plaza just off Huertas. There's a very good €13.20
set lunch (€18.50 on Sat). Classics such as French
onion soup, steak in bearnaise sauce, and profiteroles dripping in chocolate sauce. Closed Sun eve.

Prada a Tope c/Príncipe 11 ⏍914 295 221;
ⓂSevilla. Excellent-quality produce from El Bierzo

in León at this branch of the restaurant chain; the
pimientos asados, *morcilla* and *tortilla* are
extremely tasty. Expect to pay €20–25 for a full
meal. Closed Mon.

La Sanabresa c/Amor de Diós 12 ⏍914 290 338;
ⓂAntón Martín. A real local, with a TV in one corner,
and an endless supply of customers who come for
its good-quality and reasonably priced dishes. Don't
miss the grilled aubergines. Around €20. Closed Sun.

La Vaca Verónica c/Moratín 38 ⏍914 297 827;
ⓂAntón Martín. Excellent Argentinian-style meat,
really good fresh pasta in imaginative sauces,
quality fish dishes and tasty vegetables. Try the
Filet Verónica and the *carabinero con pasta*. The
menú is a good deal at €15, and the service is
friendly. Closed Sat lunch & Sun.

La Latina and Lavapiés

South from Sol and Huertas are the quarters of **La Latina** and **Lavapiés**, whose
patchwork of tiny streets retains an appealing neighbourhood feel, and are home
to a great selection of bars and restaurants.

Tapas bars

🏃 Almendro 13 c/Almendro 13; ⓂLa Latina.
Always packed at weekends, this fashionable
wood-panelled bar serves great *fino* from chilled
black bottles. Tuck into the house specials of *huevos
rotos* (fried eggs on a bed of crisps) and *roscas
rellenas* (rings of bread stuffed with various meats).

Los Caracoles Plaza Cascorro 18; ⓂLa Latina. A
favourite since the 1940s, this does a good range
of tapas as well as its namesake *caracoles* (snails).
The place to come after a trek around the Rastro –
although it will be heaving.

La Chata c/Cava Baja 24; ⓂLa Latina. One of the
most traditional, and popular, tiled tapas bars in
Madrid, with hams hanging from the ceiling,
taurine and football mementoes on the walls, and a
good selection of *raciones*, including *cebolla rellena*
and *pimientos del piquillo rellenos* (stuffed onions
and peppers). Closed Sun eve.

Corazón Loco c/Almendro 22 ⓦwww
.corazonloco.com; ⓂLa Latina. A lively bar just
off the Plaza de San Andrés with a good range of
tapas and a cosy brick-lined dining area at the
back. Two different set lunches are available
(Tues–Fri) for €10 and €12.

Melo's c/Avemaría 44; ⓂLavapíes. It's standing
room only at this very popular Galician bar serving
huge *zapatillas* (slippers of Galician country bread
filled with *lacón* and *queso*) and great *pimientos de
Padrón*. Usually closed Aug.

La Musa Latina c/Costanilla San Andrés 12
ⓦwww.lamusalatina.com; ⓂLa Latina. Another
style-conscious restaurant on the La Latina scene.

Serves a great €11 *menú* and a small selection of
modern tapas.

Taberna de Antonio Sánchez c/Mesón de Paredes
13 ⏍915 397 826; ⓂTirso de Molina. Said to be
the oldest *taberna* in Madrid, this Lavapiés bar has
an appropriately dark, wooden interior complete with
stuffed bulls' heads (one of which killed Antonio
Sánchez, the son of the founder). Lots of *finos* on
offer, plus *jamón* and *queso* tapas or *tortilla de San
Isidro* (with salted cod). Closed Sun eve.

🏃 La Taberna de los Cien Vinos c/Nuncio
16; ⓂLa Latina. A small, friendly wood-
panelled bar with, as the name would suggest, an
excellent selection of wines and a constantly
changing *menú* of inventive and very tasty
raciones. Arrive early if you want a seat for the
evening. Closed Mon & Sun eve.

Tapasentao c/Almendro 27; ⓂLa Latina. On the
corner of the Plaza de San Andrés, this is just the
place for original, seated tapas. Recommended are
the *chorizo* with wafer-thin chips, the three-cheese
salad and the fried mushrooms. There is a less-
crowded branch nearby at c/Príncipe Anglona 1.

🏃 El Tempranillo Cava Baja 38; ⓂLa Latina.
A stylish little bar serving tasty tapas and a
vast range of Spanish wines by the glass – a great
place to discover a new favourite. Closed two
weeks in Aug.

Restaurants

El Asador Frontón Plaza Tirso de Molina 7, 1º
(entrance just off the square) ⏍913 691 617;
ⓂTirso de Molina. A limited but high-quality *menú*

with a wide range of classic Castilian dishes available – red meats, fish and local vegetables. Good home-made desserts. It will cost around €45 for the works. Closed Aug.

Casa Lastra c/Olivar 3 ☎913 690 837, ⓦwww .casalastra.com; ⓂLavapiés/Antón Martín. Very popular local restaurant serving classic Asturian fare, including *entrecot al cabrales* (steak in a strong blue-cheese sauce), *fabada* and, of course, *sidra* (cider). Big portions, and, at around €13, the set lunch is very good value. Closed Wed & Sun eve.

Casa Lucio c/Cava Baja 35 ☎913 653 252, ⓦwww.casalucio.es; ⓂLa Latina. A Madrid institution famous for its Castilian specialities such as *cocido*, *callos* (tripe) and roasts, cooked to perfection. It is where Queen Sofía took George Bush's wife when the First Family visited a few years back.

Booking is essential. Count on around €50 a head. If you can't stretch to a full meal, try some of the specialities in the front bar. Closed Sat lunch & Aug.

🏃 **Posada de la Villa** c/Cava Baja 9 ☎913 661 860, ⓦwww.posadadelavilla.com; ⓂLa Latina. The most attractive-looking restaurant in La Latina, spread over three floors of a seventeenth-century mansion. Cooking is typically *madrileña*, including superb roast lamb. Reckon on a good €50 per person for the works – though you could get away with less. Closed Sun eve & Aug.

Viuda de Vacas c/Aguila 2 ☎913 665 847; ⓂLa Latina. A highly traditional, family-run restaurant, serving good-quality Castilian fare. Has moved to c/Aguila on a temporary basis, but is scheduled to return to its original address at nearby Cava Alta 23 after refurbishment. Closed Thurs & Sun eve.

Gran Vía, Plaza de España and beyond

On the **Gran Vía**, burger bars and fast-food joints tend to fill most of the gaps between shops and cinemas. However, there are a few good restaurants in and around the great avenue.

Restaurants

🏃 **La Barraca** c/Reina 29 ☎915 327 154, ⓦwww.labarraca.es; ⓂGran Vía/Banco de España. Step off the dingy street into this little slice of Valencia for some of the best paellas in town. Service is attentive but not overfussy, the starters are excellent, and there's a refreshing lemon sorbet for dessert. A three-course meal with wine will set you back around €35 a head.

La Bola c/Bola 5 ☎915 476 930, ⓦwww.labola.es; ⓂSanto Domingo. Established in 1870, this is one of the places to go for *cocido madrileño* (soup followed by chickpeas and other vegetables and then a selection of meats), which is only served at lunchtime (€19). Don't plan on doing anything energetic afterwards, as it is incredibly filling. Service can be a little surly. No cards. Closed Sun eve.

El Buey Plaza de la Marina Española 1 ☎915 413 041; ⓂSanto Domingo. A meat-eaters' paradise

specializing in steak – which you fry up yourself on a sizzling hotplate. Very good side dishes, too, including a superb leek and seafood pie, and excellent home-made desserts. All for around €35 a head.

Casa Mingo Paseo de la Florida 34 ☎915 477 918; ⓂPríncipe Pío. Noisy, crowded and fun, *Casa Mingo* is a reasonably priced (around €18 a head) Asturian chicken and cider house just up the road from the Príncipe Pío. Tables are like gold dust, so loiter with your bottle of *sidra* in hand.

La Gloria de Montera c/Caballero de Gracia 10 ⓦwww.lagloriademontera.com; ⓂGran Vía. Sister restaurant to *La Finca de Susana* (see p.115), with the same successful formula. Excellent-value *menú* with imaginative, well-presented dishes – but production-line service – in a cool setting on a gloomy street just off the Gran Vía. *Menú* for around €10.

Chueca and Santa Bárbara

Chueca – and **Santa Bárbara** to its north – have a combination of some superb traditional old bars and stylish new restaurants, as well as a vast amount of nightlife.

Tapas bars

Baco & Beto c/Pelayo 24 ⓦwww.bacoybeto.com; ⓂChueca. Excellent, creative tapas with great *tostas* and canapés. Try the courgette with melted brie and the *croquetas*. An excellent selection of wines, too. Mon–Sat eve & Sat lunch.

🏃 **El Bocaito** c/Libertad 4–6 ⓦwww.bocaito .com; ⓂChueca. Munch away on a variety of delicious canapés and tapas, washed down with a cold beer, at this busy bar; their *Luisito*, is hottest canapé your tastebuds are ever likely to encounter. Closed Sat lunch, Sun & two weeks in Aug.

Cerveceria Santa Bárbara Plaza Santa Bárbara 8; ⓂAlonso Martínez. Popular but rather pricey meeting place, this classic *cervecería* on the plaza serves *cañas* and prawns to keep you going.

Stop Madrid c/Hortaleza 11; ⓂGran Vía. An old-time bar specializing in products from Extremadura, revitalized with Belgian, Mexican and German beers, as well as *vermut* on tap. Tapas are largely *jamón* and *chorizo*, with the *Canapé Stop* of ham and tomato doused in olive oil well worth a try.

🏃 Taberna Angel Sierra c/Gravina 11, Plaza Chueca; ⓂChueca. One of the classic bars of Madrid, with a traditional zinc counter, constantly washed down. Everyone drinks *vermut*, which is on tap and delicious, and free tapas of the most exquisite *boquerones en vinagre* are despatched; *raciones*, however, are a bit pricey.

Restaurants

El 26 de Libertad c/Libertad 26 ☎915 222 522; ⓂChueca. Enjoy creative cuisine at this brightly decorated restaurant popular with the Chueca locals. A good €15 *menú* is available in the week, with more imaginative – and expensive – offerings in the evenings, but service can be slow. Closed Sun eve & Mon eve.

Annapurna c/Zurbano 5 ☎913 198 716; ⓂColón. One of the best Indian restaurants in Madrid, especially if you go for the tandoori dishes or thali. Stylish decor and attentive service. There's a taster *menú* for around €30. Closed Sat lunch & Sun.

Bazaar c/Libertad 21 ⓌWww.restaurantbazaar .com; ⓂChueca. Fusion-style cuisine with Mediterranean and Asian influences from a relatively new arrival that has already become a big hit on the Chueca scene. Very good-value lunchtime *menú* at around €10, though service is impersonal. No reservations, so arrive early to avoid a wait.

Café Oliver c/Almirante 12 ☎915 217 379, Ⓦwww.cafeoliver.com; ⓂChueca. There are strong French and Moroccan influences at this trendy and very popular Chueca restaurant with a quality set lunch at €14. A filling brunch of pastries, eggs and pancakes is on offer on Sun (€24). Closed Sun & Mon eves.

Momo c/Libertad 8 ☎915 327 348; ⓂChueca. Now relocated a few hundred metres from its former home, this well-established eatery is the place to go for a *menú* with that little bit extra. A selection of *menús* available at midday, evening and weekends for €10–14.

Salvador c/Barbieri 12 ☎915 214 524; ⓂChueca. A blast from the past with bullfighting decor and specialities such as *rabo de toro* (bull's tail), *gallina en pepitoria*, fried *merluza* (hake) and *arroz con leche* (rice pudding), all of which are excellent. *Menú* at €20 and á la carte around €35. Closed Sun eve & Aug.

🏃 La Tasca Suprema c/Argensola 7 ☎913 080 347; ⓂAlonso Martínez. This very popular neighbourhood local is worth booking ahead for its Castilian home cooking, done to perfection and including superb *pimientos de piquillo* (piquant red peppers) and *cocido* (Mon & Thurs). Expect to pay around €25 per person. Open for lunch only. Closed Sun & Aug.

La Tienda de Vinos (El Comunista) c/Augusto Figueroa 35; ⓂChueca. A long-established, down-to-earth *comedor*, its unofficial (but always used) name dates back to its time as a student haunt under Franco. The garlic soup is recommended. Most dishes are between €5 and €9.

Zara c/Infantas 5 ☎915 322 074; ⓂChueca/ Gran Vía. Excellent Cuban food at very good prices. *Ropa vieja* (strips of beef), fried yucca, minced beef with fried bananas and other specialities; the *daiquiris* are very good, too. Prices are moderate (under €30). No reservations, so arrive early. Closed weekends and public hols.

Malasaña and Chamberí

Malasaña is another characterful area, with a big nightlife scene and dozens of bars. Farther north, in Chamberí, the area around **Plaza de Olavide** – a real neighbourhood square – offers some good-value places, well off the tourist trail.

Tapas bars

Albur c/Manuela Malasaña 15; ⓂBilbao. Wooden tables, rustic decor and excellent food, although the service can be a little slow. The *champiñones en salsa verde* and the *patatas albur* are both worth sampling; the well-kept wines are the ideal accompaniment.

Casa Camacho c/San Andrés 2 (just off Plaza Dos de Mayo); ⓂTribunal. An irresistible old neighbourhood *bodega*, with a traditional bar counter, *vermut* on tap and basic tapas. An ideal place to start the evening. Packed out at weekends.

🏃 La Musa c/Manuel Malasaña 18 ☎914 487 558; ⓂBilbao. It's easy to see why *La Musa* – a café, bar and restaurant all rolled into one – has become such a firm favourite on the Malasaña scene. A variety of imaginative – and very tasty – tapas, generous helpings, a strong wine list and chic decor are all part of the recipe for success.

Restaurants

Balear c/Sagunto 18 ☎914 479 115; ⓂIglesia. This Levantine restaurant serves only rice-based dishes, but they're superb. There's an inexpensive house *cava*, and you can turn up any time before midnight. Expect to pay around €30 a head. Closed Sun & Mon eve.

La Giralda c/Hartzenbush 12 ☎914 457 779; ⓂBilbao. An *andaluz* fish and seafood restaurant of very high quality: perfectly cooked *chipirones*, *calamares* and all the standards, plus wonderful *mero* (grouper). A second branch, across the road at no. 15, does a similarly accomplished job on *pescados fritos*. Around €30–35 per person. Closed Sun & public hols.

Nina Madrid c/Manuela Malasaña 10 ☎915 910 046; ⓂBilbao. A stylish and modern restaurant serving a very good €11.30 *menú*, excellent weekend brunches (€18) and a tasty evening sampler *menú* for €28. Imaginative dishes such as duck with cauliflower and sea-urchin sauce, crunchy aubergines in honey, and *croquetas* in satay sauce feature on the main menu.

Ribeira do Miño c/Santa Brigida 1 ☎ 915 219 854, ⓦwww.marisqueriaribeiradomino.com; ⓂTribunal. A fabulous-value *marisquería*, serving a seafood platter for two for only €29. Go for the slightly more expensive Galician white wine Albariño to accompany it. Fast, efficient and friendly service.

Paseo del Prado, Paseo de Recoletos and El Retiro

This is a fancier area with few bars of note but some extremely good, if expensive, restaurants, well worth considering, even if you're not staying at the *Ritz*.

Tapas bars

La Platería c/Moratín 49; ⓂAtocha/Banco de España. Just across the square from *La Tapería* (see below), this touristy but conveniently placed bar has an enormously popular summer terraza and a good selection of reasonably priced tapas.

La Tapería del Prado Plaza Platerías de Martínez 1; ⓂAtocha/Banco de España. A modern and slightly pricey bar opposite the Prado serving up an inventive range of tapas and *raciones*.

Restaurants

Al Mounia c/Recoletos 5 ☎914 350 826; ⓂColón/Banco de España. Moroccan cooking at its best in the most established Arabic restaurant in town, offering a romantic setting with impeccable service. Expect to pay around €50 a head. Closed Mon & Aug.

Paradis erReeFe c/Paseo de Recoletos 2 ☎915 754 540; ⓂBanco de España. A wonderful locale with a great summer terraza in the Palacio de Linares, close to Cibeles. Cooking is light, Mediterranean and tasty and not exorbitant given the situation (around €50 per person). Closed Sat lunch, Sun & Aug. There's a branch at c/Marqués de Cubas 14 (☎914 297 303; ⓂBanco de España) and another in the Museo Thyssen-Bornemisza, which does a very reasonable €11.50 *menú*.

Viridiana c/Juan de Mena 14 ☎915 315 222, ⓦwww.restauranteviridiana.com; ⓂRetiro/Banco de España. A bizarre temple of Madrid *nueva cocina*, offering mouthwatering creations from a constantly changing menu, plus a superb selection of wines. Count on around €75 a head, but it's an unforgettable experience. Closed Sun, Easter & Aug.

Salamanca

Salamanca is Madrid's equivalent of Bond Street or Fifth Avenue, full of designer shops and expensive-looking natives. The recommendations below are correspondingly pricey but high quality.

Tapas bars

Hevia c/Serrano 118; ⓂNúñez de Balboa. Plush venue and wealthy clientele for expensive but excellent tapas and canapés – the hot Camembert is a must. Closed Sun & part of Aug.

José Luís c/Serrano 89 ☎915 630 958; ⓂSerrano. An upmarket tapas bar with dainty and delicious sandwiches laid out along the bar. You take what you fancy and cough up at the end, in the safe knowledge that the owner will have notched up another few hundred euros to expand his chain of bars in the Americas.

El Lateral Paseo de la Castellana 134; ⓂSantiago Bernabéu. A swish place serving a good variety of classic dishes such as *croquetas* and *pimientos rellenos* (stuffed peppers) with a modern twist. Other branches at c/Velázquez 57 and c/Fuencarral 43.

Restaurants

El Amparo Callejón Puigcerdá 8 ☎914 316 456; ⓂSerrano. Most critics rate this elegant designer restaurant among the top five in Madrid – and you'll need to book a couple of weeks ahead to get a table. If you strike lucky, the rewards are faultless Basque cooking. Main dishes are around €25–30, so expect a bill of at least €70 a head. Closed Sat lunch & Sun.

El Pescador c/José Ortega y Gasset 75 ☎914 021 290; ⓂLista. One of the city's best seafood restaurants, run by *gallegos* and with specials flown in from the Atlantic each morning. The clientele can be a bit intimidating, but you'll rarely experience better seafood cooking. Around €60. Closed Sun & Aug.

Zalacaín c/Alvarez de Baena 4 ☎915 614 840, Ⓦwww.restaurantezalacain.com; ⓂGregorio Marañon. Luxurious setting for one of the best restaurants in town and the only one that has ever had three Michelin stars. Basque-style, French-influenced cooking for around €100 per person. The nearby *La Broche* and *Santceloni* restaurants are now more famous, but *Zalacain* is more consistent, though it is overly formal (male customers have to wear jacket and tie). Closed Sat lunch, Sun & Aug.

Nightlife

Madrid **nightlife** is a pretty serious phenomenon. This is one of the few cities in Europe where you can get caught in traffic jams in the early hours of the morning when the clubbers are either going home or moving on to the dance-past-dawn discos.

As with everything *madrileño*, there is a bewildering variety of nightlife venues. Most common are the **discobares** – bars of all musical and sexual persuasions, whose unifying feature is background (occasionally live) pop, rock, dance or salsa music. These get going from around 11pm and stay open routinely until 2am, as will the few quieter **cocktail bars** and **pubs**.

For **discotecas**, entry charges are quite common (€5–18), but tend to cover you for a first drink. Free passes can often be picked up from touts in the streets, in tourist offices or bars. Be aware that many *discotecas* are fairly ephemeral institutions and frequently only last a season before opening up somewhere else under a different name, so it's a good idea to consult listing magazines *La Guía del Ocio* or *Metrópoli* or the website Ⓦwww.clubbingspain .com for the very latest information.

Bars

Madrid's bar scene caters to every conceivable taste in terms of drinks, music and atmosphere, though in recent years, the notoriously late opening hours have been somewhat curtailed by the local authorities, who are attempting to get bars to close by 2am.

Sol, Plaza de Santa Ana and Huertas

Alhambra c/Victoria 5; ⓂSol. A friendly tapas bar by day, *Alhambra* transforms itself into a fun *discobar* by night with the crowds spilling over into the *El Buscón* bar next door. Mon–Wed 11am–1.30am, Thurs 11am–2am, Fri & Sat 11am–3.30am.

Cervecería Alemana Plaza de Santa Ana; ⓂSol. A recently refurbished but still stylish old beer house, once frequented by Hemingway. Order a *caña* and go easy on the tapas, as the bill can mount up fast. Daily except Tues 10am–12.30am, Fri & Sat until 2am.

Cervecería Santa Ana Plaza de Santa Ana; ⓂSol. Cheaper than the *Alemana*, with tables outside, friendly service and a good selection of tapas. Daily 11am–1.30am.

La Fidula c/Huertas 57 Ⓦwww.myspace.com /lafidula; ⓂAntón Martín. A fine bar where you can sip *fino* to the accompaniment of live music – classical, jazz, tango and acoustic – performed on the tiny stage (€6 when there's a live act). See website for details. Daily 8pm–3am.

The Glass Bar Carrera San Jeronimo 34; ⓂSevilla. Housed in the ultra-chic five-star *Hotel Urban*, this glamorous glass-fronted cocktail bar

Terrazas and chiringuitos

Madrid is a different city during summer, as temperatures soar, and life moves outside, becoming even more late-night. In July and August, those *madrileños* who haven't headed for the coast meet up with each other, from 10pm onwards, at one or other of the city's immensely popular **terrazas**. These can range from a few tables set up outside a café or alongside a **chiringuito** – a makeshift bar – in one of the plazas, to extremely trendy (and very expensive) designer bars, which form the summer annexe of one or other of the major clubs or *discotecas*. Most places offer cocktails, in addition to regular drinks, and the better or more traditional ones also serve *horchata* (an almond-ish milkshake) and *granizado* (crushed-ice lemon). A few of the terrazas operate year-round.

Be aware that many of the terrazas run by the **clubs** vary their sites year by year as they fall foul of the increasingly strict licensing and noise regulations.

Paseo de Recoletos and Paseo de la Castellana

The biggest concentration of terrazas is to be found along the tree-lined strip in the middle of the Paseo de Recoletos and its continuation, Paseo de la Castellana. On the nearer reaches of **Paseo de Recoletos** is the refined garden terraza at the *Casa de América* (no. 2) and those of the old-style cafés *Gran* (no. 8), *Gijón* (no. 21) and *Espejo* (no. 31), popular meeting points for *madrileños* of all kinds. Beyond **Plaza de Colón** and up to the AZCA centre are the trendier terrazas with music, a posey clientele and higher prices.

Elsewhere in Madrid

Ananda Avda. Ciudad de Barcelona s/n Ⓦwww.ananda.es; ⓂAtocha/Atocha Renfe. A massive multi-terraza close to the main entrance to Estación de Atocha that attracts a glamorous clientele. Get there early to grab one of the comfy sofas in the oriental-style covered area, and if you don't fancy people-watching, there are concerts, talent contests and exhibitions to keep you entertained.

---

has become a compulsory stop for the well-heeled crowd. In summer, there's a terrace bar on the sixth floor. Mon–Sat 11am–3am.

Naturbier Plaza de Santa Ana 9; ⓂSol. Next door to the *cervecerías Alemana* and *Santa Ana*, the *Naturbier* brews its own tasty, cloudy beer and serves a variety of German sausages to accompany it. Daily 8pm–3am.

Reporter c/Fúcar 6; ⓂAntón Martín. The cool terrace garden in this neat bar just off Huertas makes a great place for a relaxing cocktail. It also does tapas and a *menú* during the day. Tues–Sun noon–2.30am.

La Venencia c/Echegaray 7; ⓂSol. For a real taste of old Madrid, this is a must: a rather delapidated wood-panelled bar, serving just sherry – try the extra-dry *fino* or *manzanilla* – cured tuna (*mojama*) and delicious olives. Decoration has remained unchanged for decades, with ancient barrels and posters. Daily 7.30pm–1.30am; closed Aug.

Viva Madrid c/Manuel Fernández y González 7 Ⓦwww.barvivamadrid.com; ⓂAntón Martín.

Another fabulous tiled bar – both outside and in – with quite pricey wines and sherry, plus basic tapas. Nearly always packed. Daily 1pm–2.30am.

Gran Vía

El Cock c/Reina 16 (just behind *Museo Chicote*); ⓂGran Vía. A smart wood-panelled bar styled like a gentlemen's club and popular with the thirty-something crowd. Knock at the door to get in. Daily 7pm–3am; July & Aug Mon–Sat 9pm–4am.

Del Diego c/Reina 12; ⓂGran Vía. An elegant New York-style cocktail bar set up by a former *Museo Chicote* waiter and now better than the original place. There's a friendly, unhurried atmosphere, and it's open until the early hours. The house special is the vodka-based Del Diego, but the mojitos and margaritas are great, too. Mon–Sat 9pm–3am; closed Aug.

El Jardín Secreto c/Conde Duque; ⓂPlaza de España. Cosy, dimly lit bar on the corner of a tiny square close to Plaza de España, serving reasonably priced drinks and cocktails. Service is friendly

Atenas Parque de Atenas (just off c/Segovia); ⓂÓpera – though not very close. Lively summer terraza set in the park down by the river and not far from the bars and clubs of La Latina.

Jardines Las Vistillas c/Bailén (on the south side of the viaduct); ⓂÓpera – though not very close. This popular terraza is good for a relaxing drink while enjoying the *vistillas* ("little vistas") over towards the Almudena cathedral and the Guadarrama mountains to the northwest.

Paseo del Pintor Rosales ⓂArgüelles. There is a clutch of late-night terrazas catering for all tastes and popular with families along this avenue on the edge of the Parque del Oeste.

Plaza de Comendadoras ⓂVentura Rodríguez. One of the city's few traffic-free squares, this has a couple of very popular terrazas – attached to the *Café Moderno* and to the Mexican restaurant next door.

Plaza Dos de Mayo ⓂTribunal. The *chiringuito* on Malasaña's main square is always a lively affair, favoured by a grungy teenage crowd.

Plaza de Olavide ⓂQuevedo. An attractive neighbourhood square, with more or less year-round terrazas belonging to four or five cafés and tapas bars.

Plaza de Oriente ⓂÓpera. The *Café de Oriente* terraza is a station of Madrid nightlife and enjoys a marvellous location next to the opera house, gazing across the plaza to the Palacio Real.

Plaza de la Paja ⓂLa Latina. One of the most pleasant terrazas in the heart of old Madrid in this former market square in La Latina.

Plaza San Andrés ⓂLa Latina. Just the other side of the church of San Andrés a host of bars spill out onto this atmospheric plaza. The place is buzzing in the summer, and makes a great meeting place before a bar crawl around the area.

Plaza de Santa Ana ⓂSol. Several of the *cervecerías* here have outside seating, and there's a *chiringuito* in the middle of the square from June to September.

and the atmosphere unhurried. Mon–Thurs & Sun 5.30pm–12.30am, Fri & Sat 6.30pm–2.30am.
Museo Chicote Gran Vía 12 ⓦwww .museo-chicote.com; ⓂGran Vía. Opened back in 1931, *Chicote* was once a haunt of Buñuel and Hemingway. It's lost some of its charm but is still a very fashionable place, with evening music sessions. Mon–Sat 5pm–1.30am.

La Latina and Lavapiés

🏃 **Aloque** c/Torrecilla del Real 20; ⓂAntón Martín. A relaxed wine bar where you can try top-quality *vino* by the glass; the innovative tapas served up in the tiny kitchen at the back are excellent. Daily 7.30am–1pm; closed Aug.
Delic Plaza de la Paja 8; ⓂAntón Martín. Serving home-made cakes, fruit juices and coffee, this is a pleasant café by day, transforming into a crowded but friendly cocktail bar by night. Mon 8pm–2am, Tues–Sun 11am–2am. Closed first half of Aug.
Montes c/Lavapiés 40; ⓂLavapiés/Tirso de Molina. A Lavapiés favourite for those in search of

a decent glass of wine. Ask owner César for advice and he'll help you find one to suit. A great place to start the evening. Tues–Sat noon–4pm & 7.30pm– midnight; closed Aug.
El Viajero Plaza de la Cebada; ⓂLa Latina. Bar, disco, restaurant and summer terraza on different floors of this fashionable La Latina nightspot. Great views of San Francisco el Grande from the terraza at the top. The food (meat, pizzas and pastas) is good, too. Tues–Sun 2–4pm & 8.30pm–2am, Fri & Sat till 3am.

Chueca, Malasaña and Santa Bárbara

🏃 **La Ardosa** c/Colón 13; ⓂTribunal. One of the city's classic *tabernas*, serving limited but very tasty tapas including great *croquetas*, *salmorejo* and an excellent home-made tortilla. Prides itself on its draught beer and Guinness. Daily 8.30am–2am.
Café del Ruiz c/Ruiz 11; ⓂTribunal/Bilbao. A traditional café, serving coffee, cakes and cocktails. A top spot for a late drink or a pep-up coffee

Gay and lesbian Madrid

Much of Madrid's nightlife has a big gay input and **gay men** especially will feel at home in most of the listings in our "Discotecas" section. However, Plaza Chueca and the surrounding streets, especially c/Pelayo, harbour at least a dozen exclusively gay bars and clubs, as well as a café that's traditionally gay – the *Café Figueroa* at c/ Augusto Figueroa 17. Wandering about, be aware that the area just north of Gran Vía is a red-light and drug centre, so taxis are best late at night. The **lesbian** scene is more disparate.

The main gay organization in Madrid is **Coordinadora Gay de Madrid**, c/Puebla 9 (Mon–Fri 5–9pm; Aug from 7pm; ☎915 230 070, ⓦwww.cogam.org; ⓜGran Vía), which can give information on health, leisure and gay rights. Feminist and lesbian groups are based at the Centro de la Mujer, c/Barquillo 44, 1° izda ☎913 193 689. The *Shangay Express* newspaper, which is given out free in bars and clubs, contains handy information about nightspots.

Gay and lesbian bars and discotecas

Café Acuarela c/Gravina 10; ⓜChueca. Comfortable café, with kitsch Baroque-style decor. The perfect place for a quiet drink, and popular with a mixed crowd.

Cool c/Isabel la Católica 6; ⓜSanto Domingo. Smart, style-conscious mixed club with a large gay following. Expect to pay €10–15 entry fee, and don't arrive until late. Thurs & Sat.

La Lupe c/Torrecilla del Leal 12; ⓜAntón Martín. A mixed gay, lesbian and alternative bar. Good music, cheap drinks and occasional cabaret.

Medea c/Cabeza 33; ⓜTirso de Molina/Antón Martín. A women-only disco with a huge dancefloor and wide-ranging selection of music. Gets going from about 1am.

Ricks c/Clavel 8; ⓜGran Vía. A varied-clientele *discobar* that gets packed at weekends when every available space is used for dancing. Open and light, with a friendly atmosphere – but dinks are pricey.

Stars Dance Café c/Marqués de Valdeiglesias 5; ⓜGran Vía. Quiet and low-key during the day, gradually livening up as the night goes on. It's a popular meeting point for the gay community but the clientele is mixed.

Truco c/Gravina 10; ⓜChueca. A long-established women's bar with a popular summer *terraza* that spills out onto Chueca's main plaza.

---

before going on to one of the nearby clubs. Daily 11am–2am.

Café Libertad c/Libertad 8 ⓦwww.libertad8cafe .es; ⓜChueca. The place to go to listen to budding *cantautores* (singer-songwriters). Some big names – including Rosana and Pedro Guerra – started off in this café, which has been going for over a quarter of a century. Mon–Thurs 5pm–2am, Fri 5pm–3am, Sat 7pm–3am, Sun 6pm–1am.

Finnegans Plaza de las Salesas 9 ⓦwww .finnegansmadrid.com; ⓜColón/Alonso Martínez. A large Irish bar with several rooms, complete with bar fittings and wooden floors brought over from the Emerald Isle. English-speaking staff, and TV sports and a pub quiz on Mon nights. Daily 1pm–2am.

Pepe Botella c/San Andrés 12 (on Plaza Dos de Mayo); ⓜTribunal. An old-style elegance still clings to this little bar with friendly staff, marble-topped

tables, low-volume music and no fruit machines. Daily 11am–3am; Aug from 3pm.

Tupperware c/Corredera Alta de San Pablo 26; ⓜTribunal. You'll find a refreshingly cosmopolitan musical diet at this classic Malasaña nightspot. Daily 9pm–3.30am.

La Vaca Austera c/Palma 20; ⓜTribunal. A refurbished rock bar that made its name in the *movida* and has been a fixture on the Malasaña scene ever since. Punk/indie classics dominate, the clientele is mixed and the atmosphere friendly. Daily 9pm–3am.

Vía Lactea c/Velarde 18; ⓜTribunal. Call in here to see where the *movida* began. *Vía Lactea* was a key meeting place for Spain's designers, directors, pop stars and painters in the 1980s, and it retains its original decor from the time, billiard tables included. There's a stage downstairs. It attracts a young, studenty clientele and is packed at weekends. Daily 8pm–3am.

Salamanca

Alquimia/Alegoría c/Villanueva 2 (entrance on c/Cid) ⊛ www.alegoria-madrid.es; Ⓜ Retiro. A restaurant-bar-club modelled on an English gentlemen's club, with over-the-top Baroque decor. It's a popular backdrop for media presentations and pop videos. Daily 8.30am–5am.

Castellana 8 Paseo de la Castellana 8; Ⓜ Colón. A designer cocktail bar and restaurant with a summer terrace on the first section of the Paseo de la Castellana after the Plaza de Colón. Relaxed music, a fairly *pijo* clientele and decent food served in the restaurant. Daily 1.30–4pm & 9pm–3am.

Teatriz c/Hermosilla 15; Ⓜ Serrano. This former theatre, redesigned by Philippe Starck, is as stylish a bar as any in Europe. There are bars on the main theatre levels, a restaurant in the stalls and a chic tapas bar in the circle. Down in the basement, there's a library-like area and small disco. Drinks are fairly pricey (€9 for spirits), but there's no entrance charge. Bar 9pm–3am, restaurant 1.30–4.30pm & 9pm–1am; closed Sat lunch, Sun & Aug.

Discotecas

Discotecas – or clubs – aren't always that different from *discobares*, though they tend to be bigger and flashier, with a lot of attention to the lighting, sound system and decor. They start late and stay open until around 4am, some till 6am and a couple till noon. In summer, some of the trendier clubs suspend operations and set up outdoor *terrazas* (see box, pp.124–125).

Sol, Ópera and Plaza de Santa Ana

Joy Madrid c/Arenal 11 ⊛ www.joy-eslava .com; Ⓜ Sol/Ópera. *Joy* may not be at the cutting edge of the club scene, but judging by the queues, it remains one of the city's most popular and successful nightspots. If you can't get in, console yourself with the *Chocolatería San Ginés* on the street behind (see box below). Daily 11.30pm–6am; €12–15, including first drink.

🏃 **Palacio de Gaviria** c/Arenal 9 ⊛ www .palaciogaviria.com; Ⓜ Ópera/Sol. Aristocratic nineteenth-century palace where you can wander through a sequence of extravagant Baroque salons, each with its own ambience and style of music. Daily 11pm–late; €10–15 depending on the night of the week and includes a first drink.

The Room/Mondo at Stella c/Arlabán 7 ⊛ www .web-mondo.com; Ⓜ Sevilla. *Stella* has undergone a complete makeover but remains a big favourite with the city's serious partygoers, who are devotees of the *Mondo* (Thurs & Sat) and *Room* (Fri) sessions. €9–11 including first drink.

Torero c/Cruz 26; Ⓜ Sol/Sevilla. A very popular and enjoyable two-floor disco right in the heart of the Santa Ana area, but the door policy is pretty strict and it can become rather overcrowded at weekends. Closed Sun & Mon; €10.

Paseo del Prado/Atocha

Kapital c/Atocha 125 ⊛ www.grupo-kapital.com /kapital; Ⓜ Atocha. A seven-storey macro-disco, complete with three dancefloors, lasers, go-go dancers, a cocktail bar and a top-floor terrace. House, funk and R&B. Thurs–Sat midnight–6am, plus Sun-night session from 8pm; entry can be free but usually around €10.

Gran Vía and Plaza de España

Bash Plaza de Callao 4 ⊛ www.tripfamily.com; Ⓜ Callao. *Bash* is one of the major venues on the Madrid club scene. There's funk and hip-hop on Wed, disco on Thurs and the OHM techno-house session on Fri & Sat, which is popular with a gay crowd. For those with real stamina, there's also a

---

Chocolate before bed

If you stay up through a Madrid night, then you must try one of the city's great institutions – the **Chocolatería San Ginés** (Tues–Sun 6pm–7.30am) on Pasadizo de San Ginés, off c/Arenal between the Puerta del Sol and Teatro Real. Established in 1894, this serves *chocolate con churros* to perfection – just the thing after a night's excess. There's an almost mythical *madrileño* custom of winding up at *San Ginés* after the clubs close (not that they do any longer), before heading home for a shower and then off to work. And why not?

Sun-night session. Sessions usually begin around midnight; around €10.

Sala Heineken c/Princesa 1; (M)Plaza de España. A big, modern and very popular two-floored club in a former cinema. There are frequent live concerts, too – David Gray and the Proclaimers are among the artists that have performed here in recent years. Fri & Sat from midnight; entry can be free but usually €8–10.

El Sol c/Jardines 3 (W)www.elsolmad.com; (M)Gran Vía. Now over 25 years on the scene, this down-to-earth club hosts around twenty live concerts a month, but continues afterwards (usually from about 1.30am) as a disco playing house, soul and acid jazz. Tues–Sat midnight–5.30am; €8.

Tropical House c/Martín de los Heros 14; (M)Ventura Rodríguez. One of the biggest and best salsa venues in the city. Dance the night away or simply enjoy the spectacle as you watch the experts. Wed, Thurs 11.30pm–5am, Fri & Sat midnight–6am; €8 on Wed & Thurs, €12 on Fri & Sat.

Chueca/Santa Bárbara

Pachá c/Barceló 11 (W)www.pacha-madrid.com; (M)Tribunal. An eternal and very popular survivor on the Madrid disco scene. House and techno on Saturdays, with more varied music on other nights. Thurs–Sat midnight–5am; €12 including first drink.

Salamanca and the north

Archy c/Marqués de Riscal 11; (M)Rubén Darío. Frescoed ceilings, columns and classical decor

adorn this *pijo* two-floor club just behind the Paseo de la Castellana. Upstairs is for rock and dance hits, downstairs for house and electronic. Mon–Wed 8pm–3am, Thurs–Sat 8pm–6am; €10.

Macumba Clubbing Estación de Chamartín s/n (W)www.spaceofsound.net; (M)Chamartín. The nearest Madrid gets to Ibiza, *Macumba* holds very popular Fri-and Sat-night sessions on top of the Estación Chamartín. If you've still got energy left, the *Space of Sound* "after hours" club will allow you to strut your stuff from 9am on Sun. Sessions normally begin at midnight; €15.

Moma 56 c/José Abascal 56 (W)www.moma56 .com; (M)Gregorio Marañon. An exclusive, New York-style club, popular with *pijos* and the upmarket glamour crowd. Also inside are the *Moma Gold* restaurant and a bar serving cocktails and light Mediterranean and fusion food. Club Wed–Sun midnight–6am; €10. Bar Mon–Wed 8am–1am, Thurs & Fri 8am–2am, Sat 10am–2am, Sun noon–2am. Restaurant Mon–Fri 1pm–midnight, Sat noon–1am.

Vanitas Vanitatis c/Velásquez 128 (W)www .vanitasvanitatis.com; (M)Núñez de Balboa. A fashionable nightspot that has been a popular stop-off on the Salamanca circuit for the best part of a decade. It attracts a posey clientele, many of whom are thirty-something business people, and there's a pretty strict door policy. Tues & Wed 10pm–2.30am, Thurs 10pm–3.30am, Fri & Sat 10pm–5.30am; around €10.

Music, film and theatre

Most nights in Madrid, you can take in performances of **flamenco**, **salsa**, **rock** (local and imported), **jazz**, **classical music** and **opera** at one or other of the city's venues. Often, it's the smaller, offbeat clubs that are the more enjoyable, though there are plenty of large auditoria for big-name concerts. In summer, events are supplemented by the council's **Veranos de la Villa** cultural programme, and in autumn by the **Festival de Otoño**. These also encompass **theatre** and **film**, both of which have healthy year-round scenes.

Flamenco

Flamenco underwent something of a revival in Madrid in the 1990s, in large part owing to the "new flamenco" artists, like Ketama and Joaquín Cortés, who were unafraid to mix it with a bit of blues, jazz, even rock. A new generation of younger but more traditional artists such as Niña Pastori and Estrella Morente is now more popular. Madrid has its own **flamenco festival** in May, when you stand a chance of catching some of the bigger names. For up-to-date and authoritative information on the flamenco scene, try (W)www .flamenco-world.com, which also has a shop at c/Huertas 62. The club listings

Madrid listings and the madrugada

Listings information is in plentiful supply in Madrid. The **newspapers** *El País* (ⓦwww .elpais.es) and *El Mundo* (ⓦwww.elmundo.es) have excellent daily listings, and on Fridays both publish magazine sections devoted to events, bars and restaurants in the capital.

If your time in Madrid doesn't coincide with the Friday supplements, or you want maximum info, pick up the weekly listings magazine **Guía del Ocio** (ⓦwww.guiadelocio .com; €1) at any kiosk. The *ayuntamiento* publishes a monthly "*What's On*" pamphlet, which is free from any of the tourist offices and lists forthcoming events in the city (also see ⓦwww.esmadrid.com), while the website **La Netro** (ⓦwww.madrid.lanetro.com) has up-to-the-minute information on the latest happenings in the city. *In Madrid* (ⓦwww .in-madrid.com), meanwhile, is a free English-language monthly paper – available in many bars – that features useful reviews of clubs and bars.

One word that might perplex first-timers in Madrid – and which crops up in all the listings magazines – is **madrugada**. This refers to the hours between midnight and dawn and, in this supremely late-night/early-morning city, is a necessary adjunct to announcements of important events. "*Tres de la madrugada*" means an event is due to start at 3am.

below span the range from purist flamenco to crossover experiments, and most artists – even major stars – appear in them. Although the following may open earlier, be aware that in many cases performances won't really get going until around midnight.

Al Andaluz c/Capitán Haya 19 ⓣ915 561 439; ⓂCuzco. A *sala rociera* rather than a professional flamenco joint, with a live show – you can then join in with the rest of the crowd in trying your hand at the dancing. Entry around the €20 mark.

Almonte c/Juan Bravo 35 ⓣ915 632 504, ⓦwww.almontesalarociera.com; ⓂDiego de León. A little slice of Andalucía in this *sala rociera* where it's easy to imagine you've been transported to Sevilla as you watch the locals strut their stuff. A few more *finos* and you'll pluck up the courage to have a go yourself.

Café de Chinitas c/Torija 7 ⓣ915 595 135, ⓦwww.chinitas.com; ⓂSanto Domingo. One of the oldest flamenco clubs in Madrid, with a dinner-dance spectacular. It's expensive, but the music is authentic. Reservations are essential, though you may get in late when people start to leave (at this time, you don't have to eat, and the steep entrance fee of around €30 does at least include your first drink). Mon–Sat 8.30pm–1am.

Candela c/Olmo 2 ⓣ914 673 382; ⓂAntón Martín. A legendary bar frequented by musicians – the late, great Camarón de la Isla is reputed to have sung here until 11am on one occasion. Tues–Sun 10.30pm–2am.

Las Carboneras Plaza Conde de Miranda ⓣ915 428 677, ⓦwww.tablaolascarboneras.com; ⓂSol. A relative newcomer to the restaurant/*tablao* scene, geared to the tourist market and slightly cheaper than its rivals, but a very good alternative if you want to get a taste of flamenco. Mon–Thurs, shows 9pm & 10.30pm, Fri & Sat 8.30pm & 11pm; around €25.

Cardomomo c/Echegaray 15; ⓂSevilla/Sol. A noisy and fun flamenco bar close to Santa Ana with live acts every Wed and Sun. An unpretentious atmosphere that couldn't be more different from the formal *tablaos*. No entry charge, and drinks are standard prices.

Casa Patas c/Cañizares 10 ⓣ913 690 496, ⓦwww.casapatas.com; ⓂAntón Martín. A small but very popular flamenco *tablao* that gets its share of big names. The best nights are Thurs and Fri. Mon–Sat 9pm–2am; €27–30.

Corral de la Morería c/Morería 17 ⓣ913 658 446, ⓦwww.corraldelamoreria.com; ⓂLa Latina. This is a good venue for some serious acts off the tourist circuit but again expensive at about €35 for show plus a drink. Daily 9pm–2am, Sat from 10.45pm.

La Soleá c/Cava Baja 34 ⓣ913 653 308; ⓂLa Latina. This long-established flamenco bar is the genuine article. People sit around in the salon, pick up a guitar or start to sing, and on a good night the atmosphere builds until everyone else is clapping or dancing. Mon–Sat 8.30pm–3am; closed Aug.

Pop, rock and blues

Madrid is very much on the international rock tour circuit and you can catch big (and small) American and British acts in front of enthusiastic audiences. In the smaller clubs, you have a chance of seeing a very wide range of local bands.

Clubs and bars

Chesterfield Café c/Serrano Jover 5 ☎915 422 817; ⓂArgüelles. As well as offering Tex-Mex-style food, this club is a live venue (Wed–Sun) that attracts local acts and some bigger international names. Sets usually begin at midnight (1am on Fri & Sat).

La Coquette c/Hileras 14; ⓂÓpera. A small, smoky basement bar, where people sit around in the near-dark watching the band perform on a tiny stage. Live music most nights with blues on Wed & Thurs. Daily 8pm–2.30am.

Honky Tonk c/Covarrubias 24 ☎914 456 886; ⓂAlonso Martínez. Nightly blues and rock sets in this late-opening bar just north of Alonso Martínez.

Libertad 8 c/Libertad 8 ☎915 321 150, Ⓦwww.libertad8cafe.es; ⓂChueca. *Libertad 8* made its name during the *movida*, but this friendly little bar in Chueca still acts as a venue for up-and-coming singer-songwriters and even has its own record label. Tues–Sun 1pm–2am.

Siroco c/San Dimás 3 ☎915 933 070; ⓂSan Bernardo. Live bands play most nights at this popular little soul club, not far north of the Gran Vía. Closed Sun; €5–10.

El Sol c/Jardines 3 ☎913 611 184, Ⓦwww.elsolmad.com; ⓂSol/Gran Vía. Hosts around twenty live concerts a month; afterwards, it continues as a disco. Very good acoustics. Daily 11.30pm–5am; around €9.

Major concert venues

La Cubierta Plaza de Toros de Leganés ☎917 651890, Ⓦwww.la-cubierta.com; ⓂCasa del Reloj. A bullring in the southern industrial suburb of Leganés, often used as a venue for heavy-rock artists of the Iron Maiden and Megadeth variety, although in a complete contrast a re-formed Soft Cell also made an appearance not that long ago.

Palacio de Deportes Avda. Felipe II s/n ☎912 586 016, Ⓦwww.palaciodedeportes.com; ⓂGoya. The city's all-new sports arena that replaced the old one that burned down in 2001. It's used for visiting groups and big shows. Ricky Martin and Alicia Keys were recent visitors.

Palacio de Vistalegre Avda. Plaza de Toros ☎915 639 493, Ⓦwww.palaciovistalegre.com; ⓂOporto/Vista Alegre. This covered bullring in the south of the city has become one of the favoured venues of touring groups.

Plaza de Toros de las Ventas Las Ventas ☎913 562 200 or 917 264 800, Ⓦwww.las-ventas.com; ⓂVentas. The bullring is a pretty good concert venue, put to use in the summer festival. Tickets are usually one price, though you can pay more for a (good) reserved seat (*asiento reservado*).

La Riviera Paseo Bajo Virgen del Puerto s/n, Puente de Segovia ☎913 652 415, Ⓦwww.salariviera.com; ⓂPuerta del Ángel. A fun disco and concert venue right next to the river, which has hosted Coldplay, Black Eyed Peas and the Hives amongst other recent groups.

Sala Heineken c/Princesa 1 Ⓦwww.salaheineken.com; ⓂPlaza de España. A former cinema turned disco that also acts as a live venue. David Gray and the Proclaimers are among the artists that have performed here.

Tickets

Tickets for most big rock concerts are sold by FNAC, c/Preciados 28 ☎915 956 190 (ⓂCallao), and El Corte Inglés, c/Preciados 1–4 ☎902 400 222, Ⓦwww.elcorteingles.es (ⓂSol). For theatre and concert tickets try Entradas.com ☎902 221 622, Ⓦwww.entradas.com; Caixa Catalunya/Tele Entrada ☎902 101 212, Ⓦwww.telentrada.com; El Corte Inglés; FNAC; TickTackTicket ☎902 150 02, Ⓦwww.ticktackticket.com; and Servi-Caixa ☎902 332 211, Ⓦwww.servicaixa.com. Localidades Galicia, Plaza del Carmen 1 ☎915 312 732 or 915 319131, Ⓦwww.eol.es/lgalicia (ⓂSol), sells tickets for football games, bullfights, theatres and concerts. For last-minute discount tickets to shows and events, try the Taquilla Último Minuto at Plaza del Carmen 1 (ⓂSol) after 5pm. The website Ⓦwww.atrapalo.com also sells discount tickets for the theatre and musicals.

Latin music

Madrid attracts big-name Latin artists, who tend to play at the venues below. The local scene is a good deal more low-key, but there's enjoyable salsa, nonetheless, in a handful of clubs.

Café del Mercado Ronda de Toledo 1 (in the Centro Artesano Puerta de Toledo) ☎913 653 786; ⓂPuerta de Toledo. There's live music every day in this spacious, comfortable club and a *Gran Baile de Salsa* every Fri & Sat at 2am.

Galileo Galilei c/Galileo 100; ⓂIslas Filipinas. A bar, concert venue and disco all rolled into one. Latin music is regularly on offer, but you'll need to check the *Guía del Ocio* to find out which night, as it also hosts cabaret, flamenco and singer-songwriters.

Oba-Oba c/Jacometrezo 4; ⓂCallao. Samba and lambada, with lethal *caiprinhas* from the bar. Daily 11pm–5.30am.

El Son c/ Victoria 6; ⓂSol. Live Cuban music (Mon–Thurs) at this small Latin club, which has picked up where its predecessor *Massai* left off. There's no space to stand and watch, so make sure you bring your dancing shoes. Daily from 7pm.

Jazz

Madrid doesn't rank up there with London, Paris or New York on the jazz front, but the clubs are friendly, unpretentious places. Look out for the annual **jazz festival** staged at a variety of venues in November.

Bogui Jazz c/Barquillo 29 ☎915 211 568, ⓦwww.boguijazz.com; ⓂChueca. Opened in 2005, this club has jazz sets every evening from Mon–Sat (11pm & midnight) with late-night jamming on Mon, Tues & Wed. It also hosts a disco on Fri & Sat after 1.30am.

Café Berlin c/Jacometrezo 4 ☎915 215 753, ⓦwww.cafeberlin.es; ⓂCallao/Santo Domingo. Jazz and blues sessions take place in this elegant Art Nouveau café just off the Gran Vía. Mon–Sat 11pm–5am, Fri & Sat till 6am.

Café Central Plaza del Ángel 10 ☎913 694 143, ⓦwww.cafecentralmadrid.com; ⓂSol. A small and relaxed jazz club that gets the odd big name, plus strong local talent. The Art Deco café is worth a visit in its own right. €6–12 for gigs, otherwise free.

Café Jazz Populart c/Huertas 22 ☎914 298 407, ⓦwww.populart.es; ⓂAntón Martín. Nightly sets from jazz and blues bands. Daily from 6pm, sets start 11pm & 12.30am. €6 for gigs, otherwise free.

Clamores c/Alburquerque 14 ☎914 457 938, ⓦwww.salaclamores.com; ⓂBilbao. A large, low-key and enjoyable jazz bar with accomplished (if not very famous) artists, not too exorbitant drinks and a nice range of snacks. €6–12 for gigs, otherwise free. Sets start around 10.30pm, bar is open until 4am.

Segundo Jazz c/Comandante Zorita 8 ☎915 549 437; ⓂNuevos Ministerios. A typical atmospheric basement club with live music during the week only. Last set at 2.15am.

Classical music and opera

The **Teatro Real** is the city's prestigious opera house and, along with the **Auditorio Nacional de Musica**, is home to the Orquesta Nacional de España. Equally enjoyable are the salons and small auditoria for chamber orchestras and groups.

Auditorio Nacional de Música c/Príncipe de Vergara 146 ☎913 370 140, ⓦwww .auditorionacional.mcu.es; ⓂCruz del Rayo. Home of the Spanish National Orchestra and host to most international visiting orchestras.

Centro de Arte Reina Sofía c/Santa Isabel ☎914 675 062, ⓦwww.museoreinasofia.mcu.es; ⓂAtocha. This arts centre often has programmes of contemporary music.

La Corrala c/Mesón de Paredes ☎915 309 600; ⓂLavapiés. A surviving tenement block, once

typical of working-class Madrid, which stages *zarzuelas* (a sort of operetta) during the Veranos de la Villa summer season.

Teatro Monumental c/Atocha 65 ☎914 291 281; ⓂAntón Martín. A large theatre, offering orchestral concerts, opera, *zarzuela* and flamenco recitals.

Teatro Real Plaza Isabel II, info ☎915 160 660, box office ☎915 160 606, ticket line ☎902 244 848, ⓦwww.teatro-real.com; ⓂÓpera. Madrid's opulent opera house, and a fantastic setting for some prestigious productions. Tickets range from €12 to €150, but you'll need to book well in advance for the best seats.

Teatro Zarzuela c/Jovellanos 4 ☎915 245 410, ⓦwww.teatrodelazarzuela.mcu.es; Ⓜ Sevilla. The main venue for Spanish operetta.

Film

Cines – cinemas – can be found all over the central area, and there's a handful of grand old picture houses strung out along the length of the Gran Vía, some of which still advertise their offerings with the traditional hand-painted posters. These offer major releases dubbed into Spanish, though a number of cinemas have regular **original language** screenings, with subtitles; these are listed in a separate *versión original/subtitulada* (*v.o.*) section in the newspapers. **Tickets** for films cost around €7, but most cinemas have a *día del espectador* (usually Mon or Wed) for the same price. Be warned that on Sunday night half of Madrid goes to the movies, and queues can be long.

Filmoteca/Cine Doré c/Santa Isabel 3; Ⓜ Antón Martín. A beautiful old cinema, now home to an art-film centre, with imaginative programmes of classic and contemporary films, all shown in *v.o.* at an admission price of just €2.50 (closed Mon). In summer, there are open-air screenings on a little terraza – they're very popular, so buy tickets in advance.

Golem, Renoir and Princesa c/Martín de los Heros 12 & 14 and c/Princesa 3 ⓦwww.golem.es, ⓦwww.cinesrenoir.com; Ⓜ Plaza de España. This trio of multiscreen cinemas, within 200m of each

other, show regular *v.o.* films.

Ideal Yelmo Cineplex c/Doctor Cortezo 6 ⓦwww .yelmocineplex.es; Ⓜ Sol/Tirso de Molina. A centrally located, nine-screen complex that shows a good selection of *v.o.* films.

Pequeño Cine Estudio c/Magallanes 1–2 ⓦwww .pcineestudio.com; Ⓜ Quevedo/San Bernardo. A small independent cinema specializing in classic films in *v.o.*

Verdi c/Bravo Murillo 28 ⓦwww.cines-verdi.com; Ⓜ Canal/Quevedo. A newcomer on the scene, which shows an interesting range of *v.o.* films.

Pedro Almodóvar

Arguably Spain's most influential filmmaker, **Pedro Almodóvar** emerged as part of the *movida madrileña*, the thriving alternative cultural scene in Madrid that developed following the death of Franco. He made his feature-film debut in 1980 with the cheap and transgressive **Pepi, Lucy, Bom and a Whole Load of Other Girls**. His prodigious output during the 1980s included **Matador** (1986), a dark thriller linking sexual excitement with the violence of the bullfight; **The Law of Desire** (1987), a story involving a gay film director, his transsexual brother/sister, murder and incest; as well as the internationally successful **Women on the Edge of a Nervous Breakdown** (1988). Madrid was used as the backdrop to many of his films, which reflected the spirit of liberation that reigned in the Spanish capital in the 1980s. His productions have benefited from the performances of actors such as Carmen Maura, Victoria Abril, Rosy de Palma and Antonio Banderas, and over time they have gained in narrative coherence and production values while retaining the capacity to offend – notably with **Tie Me Up, Tie Me Down** (1990). One of the very few directors able to attract audiences across the globe with films in a language other than English, Almodóvar's 1995 **Flower of My Secret** pushed him more into the mainstream, while **All About My Mother** (1999), which marked a return to his trademark obsession with transsexuals, won him an Oscar for Best Foreign Film. **Talk to Her** (2002) was if anything even more successful, and won Almodóvar another Oscar, this time for best screenplay – perhaps marking Spanish cinema's escape from the "foreign films" ghetto. In **Bad Education** (2004), he explored Franco-era religious schooling and the issue of sexual abuse by the Catholic clergy, while in the well-received **Volver** (**Returning**) (2006) he looked to his own childhood in La Mancha and to his sisters and late mother for inspiration.

Theatre and cabaret

Madrid is enjoying a renaissance in theatre; you can catch anything from Lope de Vega to contemporary and experimental productions, and there's also a new wave of cabaret and comedy acts. Look out, too, for the annual **Festival de Otoño** running from September to November, and the alternative **theatre festival** in February.

Centro Cultural de la Villa Plaza de Colón ☏914 800 300; ⓂColón. An arts centre where you're likely to see some of the more experimental companies on tour, as well as popular works and zarzuela performances.

Teatro de la Abadía c/Fernández de los Ríos 42 ☏914 481 181, ⓌWww.teatroabadia.com; ⓂQuevedo/Argüelles. A beautifully decorated theatre set in pleasant grounds just off the main street. It has staged some very successful productions and is especially popular during the Festival de Otoño.

Teatro de Bellas Artes and Círculo de Bellas Artes c/Marqués de Riera 2 ☏915 324 437, Círculo ☏913 605 400 or 902 422 442, ⓌWww.circulobellasartes.com; ⓂBanco de España. The teatro is a beautiful old theatre with a reputation for quality, while the círculo has a theatre staging more adventurous productions.

Teatro Español c/Príncipe 25 ☏913 601 484; ⓂSol/Sevilla. A classic Spanish theatre on the site of one of the city's old corrales.

Teatro de Madrid Avda. de la Ilustracion s/n ☏917 301 750, ⓌWww.teatromadrid.com; ⓂBarrio del Pilar. A large, modern theatre next to the large La Vaguada shopping centre in the north of the city, presenting some excellent ballet, drama and touring cultural shows.

Teatro María Guerrero c/Tamayo y Baus 4 ☏913 102 949 or 913 101 500; ⓂColón. This is the headquarters of the Centro Dramático Nacional, which stages high-quality Spanish and international productions in a beautiful neo-Mudéjar interior.

Teatro Nuevo Apolo Plaza Tirso de Molina 1 ☏913 690 637; ⓂTirso de Molina. Madrid's principal venue for major musicals.

Teatro Valle-Inclán c/Plaza de Lavapiés ☏915 058 800; ⓂLavapiés. Opened in 2006, the state-of-the-art Valle-Inclán provides a second home for the Centro Dramático Nacional.

Children

Many of the big sights may lack children-specific services or activities, but there's plenty to keep kids occupied for a short stay. There are various **parks** (El Retiro being a particular favourite), a host of well-attended public **swimming pools** and an increasing number of **child-oriented attractions**. Children are welcome in nearly all cafés and restaurants. See Ⓦwww.saposyprincesas.com for more ideas.

In the city

Imax Madrid Parque Tierno Galván ☏914 674 800, ⓌWww.imaxmadrid.com; ⓂMéndez Alvaro. Futuristic cinema with three different types of screen showing natural history-style features in Spanish. €7–10.

Museo de Cera (Wax Museum) Paseo de Recoletos 41 ☏913 080 825, ⓌWww.museoceramadrid.com; ⓂColón. Expensive, tacky and the figures bear little resemblance to the originals, but nevertheless popular with children. There's also a chamber of horrors and a film history of Spain. Mon–Fri 10am–2.30pm & 4.30–8.30pm, Sat, Sun & public hols 10am–8.30pm; €15, under-10s & over-65s €9, under-4s free.

Museo del Ferrocarril Paseo de las Delicias 61 ☏902 228 822, ⓌWww.museodelferrocarril.org; ⓂDelicias. An impressive collection of engines, carriages and wagons that once graced the railway lines of Spain. Of more interest to the younger ones is the fascinating collection of model railways and the mini railway (Sat 11.30am–2pm). There's an atmospheric little cafeteria housed in one of the more elegant carriages. The station was used as a backdrop in the film classic Doctor Zhivago. Tues–Thurs 10am–5pm, Fri–Sun 10am–3pm; €4, under-4s free.

Parque de Atracciones Casa de Campo ☏915 268 030 or 914 632 900, ⓌWww.parquedeatracciones.es; ⓂBatán/bus #33 & #65. A theme park packed full of rides, whose attractions include the new Tarantula rollercoaster, a 63-metre vertical drop (La Lanzadera), a whitewater-rafting ride (Los Rápidos), and a haunted mansion (El Viejo Caserón). Oct–March Sat, Sun & public hols noon–7pm; April–Sept most days noon–midnight (consult website); access only

€9.30, €27.50 for a day ticket, which includes most rides, under-7s €18, under-3s free.

Parque Secreto Plaza Conde del Valle de Suchel 3 ⊤915 931 480, Ⓦwww.parquesecreto.com; ⓂSan Bernardo. One of the most central and best-equipped children's playcentres, with a café, too. €2.50–3 for 30min.

Planetario Parque Tierno Galván ⊤914 673 461, Ⓦwww.planetmad.es; ⓂMéndez Álvaro. Exhibition halls, audiovisual displays and projections on a variety of astronomical themes (all in Spanish). €3.45, under-14s €1.50.

Zoo–Aquarium Casa de Campo ⊤917 119 950, Ⓦwww.zoomadrid.com; ⓂCasa de Campo/Batán/ bus #33. Over 2000 different species, including big cats, gorillas, koalas and venomous snakes, plus an impressive aquarium with sharks, a children's zoo, a parrot show and a dolphinarium. Daily 11am–dusk; €16.90, under-7s €13.70, under-3s free.

Out of the city

Cosmo Caixa Pintor Velázquez s/n, Alcobendas ⊤914 845 200, Ⓦwww.fundacio.lacaixa.es; bus #151–154, 156 & 157 from Plaza Castilla, train from Estación de Atocha to Valdelasfuentes, then a 15min walk. A fun, interactive science museum located in the suburb of Alcobendas. Tues–Sun 10am–8pm; €3, under-16s €2. Supplements for the planetarium and special activities.

Faunia Avda. de las Comunidades 28 ⊤913 016 210, Ⓦwww.faunia.es; ⓂValdebernardo, bus #130, 8 & 71. An innovative nature park recreating a series of ecosystems that provide a home to 720 different animal species. Highlights are the Arctic dome with its penguins, and the storms in the indoor tropical rainforest. An entertaining and educational experience for children of all ages. Daily 10.30am–dusk; €23, under-12s €17, under-3s free.

Shopping

Shopping districts in Madrid are pretty defined. The biggest range of stores is along the Gran Vía and the streets running north out of Puerta del Sol, which is where the **department stores** – such as El Corte Inglés – have their main branches. For **fashion** (*moda*), the smartest addresses are calles Serrano, Goya, Ortega y Gasset and Velázquez in the Salamanca *barrio*, while more alternative designers are to be found in Malasaña and Chueca (c/Almirante, especially). For street fashion, there's plenty on offer in and around c/Fuencarral. The **antiques** trade is centred towards the Rastro, on and around c/Ribera de Curtidores and in the Puerta de Toledo shopping centre, while for **general weirdness**, it's hard to beat the shops just off Plaza Mayor, where luminous saints rub shoulders with surgical supports and Fascist memorabilia. The cheapest, trashiest **souvenirs** can be collected at the Todo a un euro ("Everything for a euro", although this isn't true) shops scattered all over the city. If you want international shops or some of the more popular chain stores, head for Madrid 2, a large shopping centre next to ⓂBarrio de Pilar. There is a smaller, more upmarket mall at ABC Serrano, with entrances at c/Serrano 61 and Paseo de la Castellana 34 (ⓂRubén Darío).

Most areas of the city have their own *mercados del barrio* – indoor **markets**, devoted mainly to food. Among the best and most central are those in Plaza San Miguel (just west of Plaza Mayor); La Cebada in Plaza de la Cebada (ⓂLa Latina); and Antón Martín in c/Santa Isabel (ⓂAntón Martín). The city's biggest market is, of course, **El Rastro** – the flea market – which takes place on Sundays in La Latina, south of Plaza Mayor. For details of this great Madrid institution, see the box on p.91.

Other specialized markets include a secondhand **book market** on Cuesta del Moyano, near Estación de Atocha (see p.105), and the stamp and coin markets in Plaza Mayor on Sundays.

Crafts and miscellaneous

Alvarez Gómez c/Serrano 14 Ⓦwww.alvarezgomez .com; ⓂSerrano. Gómez has been making the same perfumes in the same bottles for the past century. The scents – carnations, roses, violets – are as simple and straight as they come. Mon–Sat 10am–2pm & 5–8.30pm.

El Arco Artesania Plaza Mayor 9 🌐www
.elarcoartesania.com; Ⓜ️Sol. This shop may be at
the heart of tourist Madrid, but the goods are a far
cry from the swords, lace and castanets that fill
most stores in the area. Crafts include ceramics,
leather, wood, jewellery and textiles. There's a
gallery space for exhibitions, too. Mon–Sat
11am–8pm, Sun 11am–2.30pm.

Area Real Madrid c/Carmen 3; Ⓜ️Sol. Club store
just off Sol where you can pick up replica shirts
and all manner of – expensive – souvenirs related
to the club's history. There are other branches in
the shopping centre on the corner of Real's
Bernabéu stadium at c/Concha Espina 1 and at
Gate 3 of the stadium itself (Ⓜ️Santiago
Bernabéu). Mon–Sat 10am–9pm, Sun 10am–8pm.

Casa de Diego Puerta del Sol 12 🌐www
.casadediego.com; Ⓜ️Sol. An old-fashioned
shop with helpful staff selling a fantastic array of
Spanish fans (*abanicos*) ranging from cheap
offerings at under €5 to beautifully hand-crafted
works of art costing up to €200.

Casa Jiménez c/Preciados 42; Ⓜ️Callao. Elaborately embroidered *mantones* (shawls) made in
Seville, with prices ranging from €100 to €600, as
well as gorgeous fans from around €40. Mon–Sat
10am–1.30pm & 5–8pm, closed Sat pm in July
and all day Sat in Aug.

Casa Yustas Plaza Mayor 30 🌐www.casayustas
.com; Ⓜ️Sol. Madrid's oldest hat shop, established
in 1894. Pick from traditional designs for men's
and women's hats (*sombreros*), caps (*gorras*) and
berets (*boinas*). There's also a large range of
souvenir-style goods including Lladró porcelain
figurines. Mon–Sat 9.30am–9.30pm, Sun & public
hols 11am–9.30pm.

Contreras c/Mayor 80 🌐www.manuelcontreras
.com; Ⓜ️Sol/Ópera. An award-winning guitar
workshop run on this site for over forty years by
the Contreras family. The perfect place for budding
flamenco artists to buy the genuine article. Mon–Fri
10am–1.30pm & 5–8pm, Sat 10am–1.30pm.

El Flamenco Vive c/Unión 4 🌐www
.elflamencovive.com; Ⓜ️Ópera. A fascinating
little piece of Andalucía in Madrid, specializing
in all things flamenco, from guitars and CDs
to polkadot dresses and books. Mon–Sat
10.30am–2pm & 5–9pm.

Piel de Toro Paseo del Prado 42; Ⓜ️Atocha. Over a
hundred different souvenir T-shirts, nearly all of
which feature the firm's bull logo.

Seseña c/Cruz 23; Ⓜ️Sol. A tailor specializing in
traditional *madrileño* capes for royalty and celebrities. Clients have included Luis Buñuel, Gary
Cooper and Hilary Clinton. Mon–Sat 10am–1.30pm
& 4.30–8pm.

Books and maps

Desnivel Plaza Matute 6 🌐www.libreriadesnivel
.com; Ⓜ️Antón Martín. This centrally located
bookshop stocks a good range of guides and maps
covering mountaineering in all parts of Spain.
Mon–Sat 10am–2pm & 4.30–8.30pm.

FNAC c/Preciados 28 🌐www.fnac.es; Ⓜ️Callao.
The book department of this huge store is a good
place to sit and peruse books and magazines in all
languages. Also sells CDs, computer equipment
and electronic goods.

La Librería c/Mayor 80 🌐www.edicioneslalibreria
.com; Ⓜ️Sol. A tiny place full of books just about
Madrid. Most are in Spanish, but many would serve
as coffee-table souvenirs. It's also a good place to
pick up old prints and photos of the city.

Pasajes c/Genova 3 🌐www.pasajeslibros.com;
Ⓜ️Alonso Martínez/Colón. Specializes in English
and foreign-language books. Also has a useful
noticeboard service for flat-sharing and Spanish
classes. Mon–Fri 10am–2pm & 5–8pm, Sat
10am–2pm.

Clothes and shoes

Adolfo Domínguez c/José Ortega y Gasset 4 &
c/Serrano 96 🌐www.adolfo-dominguez.com;
Ⓜ️Rubén Darío & Ⓜ️Serrano. The classic modern
Spanish look, Domínguez's designs are quite
pricey, but he has a cheaper *Basico* range. Both
branches have men's clothes; women's are only
available at the Ortega y Gasset branch. Mon–Sat
10am–2pm & 5–8.30pm. Other branches at El
Corte Inglés on c/Serrano 47 (Ⓜ️Serrano),
c/Serrano 96 (Ⓜ️Rubén Darío) and c/Fuencarral 5
(Ⓜ️Gran Vía). The branch in El Corte Inglés does not
close for lunch.

Agatha Ruiz de la Prada c/Serrano 2 🌐www
.agatharuizdelaprada.com; Ⓜ️Colón/Goya. Outlet
for the brightly coloured clothes and accessories of
this *movida* designer. There's a children's line,
stationery and household goods, too. Mon–Sat
10am–8.30pm.

Caligae c/Augusto Figueroa 27; Ⓜ️Chueca.
One of a string of shoe shops located on this busy
Chueca street, selling discounted designer
footwear. Mon–Fri 10am–2pm & 5–8pm, Sat
10.30am–2pm & 5–8pm.

Camper c/Gran Vía 54 🌐www.camper.es;
Ⓜ️Callao. Spain's best shoe-shop chain, with
covetable designs at modest prices. There are
lots of other branches around the city. Mon–Sat
10am–2pm & 5–8.30pm.

Ekseptión c/Velázquez 28; Ⓜ️Velázquez. A
dramatic catwalk bathed in spotlights leads into
this shop selling some of the most *moderno* –
and expensive – clothes in Madrid, from Sybilla

and Antoni Miró, among others. Next door are younger, more casual clothes in the *Eks* shop. Men and women. Mon–Sat 10.30am–2.30pm & 5–8.30pm. There's also a branch selling discount last-season fashions at Avda. Concha Espina 14 (MSantiago Bernabéu; Mon–Sat 11.30am–8pm).

Excrupulus Net c/Almirante 7; MChueca. Groovy shoes from Spanish designers Muxart and Looky. Men and women. Mon–Sat 11am–2pm & 5–8.30pm.

Mercado Fuencarral c/Fuencarral 45; MTribunal/Gran Vía. Funky shopping mall catering for the young fashion-conscious crowd, filled with clubwear shops, record stores, jewellers, a café and tattoo parlour. Mon–Sat 10am–10pm.

Sybilla Callejón Jorge Juan 12 www.sybilla.es; MRetiro. Sybilla was Spain's top designer of the 1980s and she remains at the forefront of the scene, with prices to match. Women only. Mon–Sat 10am–2pm & 4.30–8.30pm.

Food and drink

Cacao Sampaka c/Orellana 4 www.cacaosampaka.com; MAlonso Martínez/Colón. Every conceivable colour, shape and flavour of chocolate is available in this chocoholics' paradise. There are even books about the stuff. The only surprise is that the restaurant has some non-chocolate snacks on the menu. Daily 10am–9pm; closed Aug 8–21.

Casa Mira Carrera de San Jerónimo 30; MSol. An old, established *pasteleria*, selling delicious *turrón*, *mazapán*, *frutas glaseadas* and the like. Daily 10am–2pm & 5–9pm.

Lavinia c/José y Gasset 16 www.lavinia.es; MNúñez de Balboa. Massive wine shop in the upmarket *barrio* of Salamanca, with a great selection from Spain and the rest of the world. Mon–Sat 10am–9pm.

Mariano Madrueño c/Postigo San Martín 3; MCallao. The place to get wines and liqueurs such as *Pacharán* sloe gin. Mon–Fri 9.30am–2pm & 5–8pm, Sat 9.30am–2pm.

Reserva y Cata c/Conde de Xiquena 13 www.reservaycata.com; MColón/Chueca. Well-informed staff at this friendly specialist shop will help you select from some of the best new wines in the Iberian Peninsula. Mon–Sat 11am–2.30pm. Another branch at c/Ramiro II 7; MRíos Rosas.

Tienda Olivarero c/Mejia Lequerica 1 www.pco.es; MAlonso Martínez. Outlet for olive growers' cooperative boasting around ninety different varieties of olive oil, and with information sheets to guide you towards purchasing the best ones. Mon–Sat 10am–2pm & 5–8pm.

Records and CDs

Flamenco World c/Huertas 62 www.flamenco-world.com; MBanco España. The place to come for flamenco CDs, DVDs and books. Helpful and highly knowledgeable staff. Mon–Fri 10am–2.30pm & 4.30–8pm.

FNAC c/Preciados 28; MCallao. Large French store with a huge collection of cassettes and CDs.

Children

Imaginarium ABC Serrano, c/Serrano 61/Paseo de la Castellana 64 www.imaginarium.es; MRubén Darío. Toys, games and activities with an educational twist for children of all ages.

Prénatal c/Fuencarral 17 (MQuevedo; c/San Bernardo 97–99 (MSan Bernardo); Madrid 2, La Vaguada, Avda. Monforte de Lemos (MBarrio del Pilar). Spanish equivalent of Mothercare, with more branches around the city – and often a little cheaper.

Puck c/Duque de Sesto 30 www.puck.es; MGoya. An old-fashioned toy shop selling high-quality wooden toys, dolls' houses and puzzles. Mon–Sat 10am–1.30pm & 4.30–8pm.

Listings

Banks and exchange Banks are plentiful throughout the city and are the best place to change money. Branches of El Corte Inglés have exchange offices with long hours and reasonably competitive rates; the most central is on c/Preciados, close to Puerta del Sol.

Bicycles Madrid is a bike-unfriendly city. For tours outside the city, get in touch with Bravi Bike at c/Montera 25–27 (915 595 523/607 448 440,

www.bravobike.com; MSol) or Bike Spain at c/Carmen 17 (915 223 899, www.bikespain.info; MSol).

Bullfights Madrid's main Plaza de Toros, the monumental Las Ventas (c/Alcalá 237; MVentas), hosts some of the year's most prestigious events, especially during the May *San Isidro* festivities, though the main season runs from March to October. Tickets (€3.50–110) are available at the box office at Ventas (March–Oct Fri & Sat 10am–2pm & 5–8pm, from 10am on day of fight; ☏ 917 264 800 or 913 562 200, Ⓦ www .las-ventas.com), the Caja Madrid ticketline (☏ 902 488 488) or at Localidades de Galicia (☏ 915 312 732 or 915 319131, Ⓦ www.eol.es/lgalicia); at this last one, you'll pay around fifty percent more than the printed prices, which are for season tickets sold en bloc.

Car rental Major operators have branches at the airport and train stations. Central offices include: Atesa Atocha ☏ 915 061 846, Ⓦ www.atesa.com (Ⓜ Atocha Renfe; Avis Gran Vía 60 ☏ 915 484 204, reservations ☏ 902 180 854, Ⓦ www .avisworld.com (Ⓜ Plaza de España); Europcar c/San Leonardo 8 ☏ 915 418 892, Ⓦ www .europcar.com (Ⓜ Plaza de España); Hertz Atocha Station ☏ 914 681 318, reservations ☏ 913 729 300, Ⓦ www.hertz.com (Ⓜ Atocha Renfe); Easy-Rent-a-Car (telephone bookings available from Britain only), Ⓦ www.easycar.com. Pepecar at Atocha and Charmartín stations ☏ 807 414 243, Ⓦ www.pepecar.com.

Disabled access Madrid is not particularly well geared up for disabled visitors (minusválidos), although the situation is gradually improving. The Organizacíon Nacional de Ciegos de España (ONCE; National Organization for the Blind c/Prim 3 ☏ 915 325 000, Ⓦ www.once.es) provides specialist advice, as does the Federacion de Asociaciones de Minusválidos Físicos de la Comunidad de Madrid (FAMMA; c/Galileo 69 ☏ 915 933 550, Ⓦ www.famma.org). The website Ⓦ www.discapnet.es is also a useful source of information (Spanish only). Wheelchair-friendly taxis can be ordered from Radio Taxi (☏ 915 478 200/915 478 600).

Embassies Australia, Plaza Descubridor Diego Ordás 3 ☏ 913 536 600, Ⓦ www.embaustralia.es (Ⓜ Ríos Rosas); Britain, c/Fernando el Santo 16 ☏ 917 008 200, Ⓦ www.ukinspain.com (Ⓜ Alonso Martínez); British Consulate Paseo de Recoletos 7–9 ☏ 915 249 700; Canada, c/Núñez de Balboa 35 ☏ 914 233 250, Ⓦ www .canada-es.org (Ⓜ Núñez de Balboa); Republic of Ireland, Paseo de la Castellana 46 ☏ 914 364 093 (Ⓜ Rubén Darío); New Zealand, Plaza Lealtad 2 ☏ 915 230 226, Ⓦ www.nzembassy .com (Ⓜ Banco de España); USA, c/Serrano 75 ☏ 915 872 200, Ⓦ www.embusa.es (Ⓜ Rubén Darío). South Africa, c/Claudio Coello 91 ☏ 914 363 780; Ⓦ www.sudafrica.com (Ⓜ Núñez de Balboa).

Hospitals The most central hospitals are: El Clínico de San Carlos, c/Profesor Martín Lagos s/n ☏ 913 303 747 (Ⓜ Moncloa); Hospital Gregorio Marañon, c/Dr Esquerdo 46 ☏ 915 868 000 (Ⓜ O'Donnell); and Ciudad Sanitaria La Paz, Paseo de la Castellana 261 ☏ 917 277 000 (Ⓜ Diego de León). First-aid stations are scattered throughout the city and are open 24hr a day: one of the most central is at c/Navas de Tolosa 10 ☏ 915 210 025 (Ⓜ Callao). English-speaking doctors are available at the Anglo-American Medical Unit, c/Conde de Aranda 1 ☏ 914 351 823 (Ⓜ Retiro; Mon–Fri 9am–8pm, Sat 10am–3pm).

Internet access Workcenter, Pza. Canalejas ☏ 913 601 395 (Ⓜ Sevilla/Sol; daily 8am–11pm); La Casa de Internet, C/Luchana 20 (Ⓜ Bilbao). Café Comercial on the Glorieta de Bilbao (Ⓜ Bilbao) has an internet café upstairs. Prices are €1–4/hr.

Left luggage There are left-luggage facilties (consignas) at Barajas Airport (open 24hr; €3.60 for up to 24hr and €4.64 per day up to a maximum of fifteen) and lockers at Atocha (daily 6.30am–10.20pm) and Chamartín (daily 7am–11.30pm) train stations.

Pharmacies Farmácias are distinguished by a green cross; each district has a rota with one staying open through the night – for details, ring ☏ 098 (Spanish only) or check the notice on the door of your nearest pharmacy or the listings magazines.

Police Centrally located police stations (comisarías) are at c/Leganitos 19 (☏ 915 417 160; Ⓜ Plaza de España/Santo Domingo), c/Huertas 76 (☏ 913 221 027; Ⓜ Antón Martín) and c/Luna 29 (☏ 915 211 236; Ⓜ Gran Vía).

Post office A central post office can be found in El Corte Inglés, c/Preciados 1 (Ⓜ Sol), and there's another with extended hours at c/Mejía Lequerica 7 (Ⓜ Alonso Martínez).

Telephones International calls can be made from any phone box or locutorio. The main telefónica office at Gran Vía 30 (Ⓜ Gran Vía) has ranks of phones and is open until midnight.

Travel agencies Víajes Zeppelin, Plaza Santo Domingo 2 (☏ 915 477 904; Ⓜ Santo Domingo), are English-speaking and very efficient. The popular high-street agencies Halcón Viajes (c/Goya 23) and Viajes Marsans (Gran Vía 63) have branches scattered all over the city and are good places to find hotel vouchers. For information on student and youth travel, try TIVE, c/Fernando el Católico 88 (☏ 915 437 412; Ⓜ Moncloa; Mon–Fri 10am–2pm).

Travel details

Trains

For information on booking tickets, see p.000; for current timetables and ticket information, consult RENFE ☎ 902 240 202, 🌐 www.renfe.es.

Estación de Atocha (Ⓜ Atocha): Albacete (22 daily; 1hr 56 min–2hr 20min); Alcalá de Henares (every 10–15min; 35min); Algeciras (2 daily; 5hr 35 min); Alicante (8 daily; 3hr 30min–3hr 45min); Almería (2 daily; 6hr 45min); Aranjuez (every \15–20min; 40min); Badajoz (3 daily; 5hr 15min–6hr 45min); Barcelona (16 daily; 2hr 43min–3hr 24min); Cáceres (5 daily; 3hr 20min–4hr); Cádiz (2 daily; 5hr); Cartagena (4 daily; 4hr 35min–5hr 35min); Ciudad Real (20–25 daily; 50min–1hr 10min); Córdoba (30 daily;1hr 50min–2hr); Cuenca (4 daily; 2hr 20min–2hr 45min); Granada (4 daily; 3hr 35min–4hr 35min); Guadalajara (every 30min; 23min AV); Huelva (daily; 4hr 15min); Huesca (2 daily; 2hr 5min–2hr 15min); Jaén (4 daily; 3hr 38min–4hr 20min); Jerez (2 daily; 4hr 10min–4hr 30min); Lleida (7 daily; 2hr 8min); Málaga (14 daily; 2hr 40min); Mérida (5 daily; 4hr 5min–6hr 30min); Seville (24 daily; 2hr 20min–3hr 10min); Toledo (12 daily; 30min); Valencia (14 daily; 3hr 20min–5hr 54min); Zaragoza (18 daily; 1hr 20min). Plus most destinations in the south and west.

Estación de Chamartín (Ⓜ Chamartín): A Coruña (3 daily; 8–10hr); Ávila (29 daily; 1hr 15min–2hr 15min); Bilbao (2 daily; 4hr 46min–6hr); Burgos (7 daily; 2hr 20min–4hr); Ferrol (daily; 10hr 50min); Gijón (3 daily; 5hr 5min–5hr 45min); León (9 daily; 2hr 45min–4hr 15min); Lisbon (daily; 9hr); Lugo (daily; 8hr 30min); Oviedo (3 daily; 4hr 35min–5hr 15min); Pamplona (4 daily; 3hr–3hr 15min); Paris (daily; 13hr 30min); Pontevedra (3 daily; 8hr 20min–9hr 50min); Salamanca (10 daily; 2hr 20min–3hr); San Sebastián (3 daily; 5hr 20min–6hr 30min); Santander (4 daily; 4hr 25min–5hr 45min); Santiago (3 daily; 7hr 10min–8hr 50min); Segovia (18 daily; 35min–1hr); Soria (3 daily; 3hr); Valladolid (18 daily; 1hr 7min–2hr 40min); Vigo (3 daily; 7hr 30min–9hr 30min); Vitoria (5 daily; 3hr 40min–5hr 25min); Zamora (3 daily; 2hr 45min–3hr 15min). Plus most other destinations in the northeast and northwest.

Buses

Estación Sur de Autobuses Albacete (11 daily; 2hr 50min–3hr 20min); Alicante (5–10 daily; 5hr); Almería (5 daily; 7hr); Aranjuez (Mon–Fri every 30min, Sat & Sun hourly; 45min); Ávila (9 daily; 1hr 30min); Badajoz (9 daily; 4hr 30min–5hr); Barcelona (20 daily; 7hr 30min–8hr); Cáceres (7 daily; 4hr–4hr 30min); Ciudad Real (5 daily; 3hr); Córdoba (6 daily; 4hr 45min); Cuenca (9 daily; 2hr–2hr 30min); Gijón (11 daily; 5hr 30min); Granada (14 daily; 4hr 30min–5hr); Jaén (6 daily; 5hr); León (12 daily; 4hr 15min); Málaga (4–8 daily; 6hr); Marbella (2–7 daily; 7hr); Mérida (9 daily; 4–5hr); Oviedo (12 daily; 5hr); Palencia (5 daily; 3hr 15min); Pontevedra (6 daily; 7hr); Salamanca (23 daily; 2hr 30min); Santiago (5 daily; 8–9hr); Seville (8 daily; 6hr); Toledo (every 15–30min; 1hr–1hr 30min); Trujillo (11 daily; 3hr 15min); Valencia (16 daily; 4hr); Valladolid (19 daily; 2hr 15min); Zamora (6 daily; 2hr 45min–3hr 15min) and international services to France and Portugal.

Alsa Avda. de América 9 ☎ 917 456 300, 🌐 www .alsa.es; Ⓜ Avda. de América: Alcalá (every 15min; 45min); Bilbao (6 daily; 4hr 45min); Guadalajara (every 30min; 55min); Logroño (6 daily; 4hr 30min); Pamplona (6 daily; 5hr); San Sebastián (9 daily; 6hr); Santander (6 daily; 5hr 45min); Soria (10 daily; 2hr 30min); Vitoria (5 daily; 4hr 30min); Zaragoza (20 daily; 3hr 45min).

Herranz Intercambiador de Autobuses de Moncloa ☎ 918 904 100, an underground terminal just above Ⓜ Moncloa: El Escorial (approx. every 30min; 55min–1hr). Onward connections to El Valle de los Caídos.

La Sepulvedana Paseo de la Florida 11 ☎ 915 304 800, 🌐 www.lasepulvedana.es; Ⓜ Pío: Segovia (31 daily; 1hr 15min).

La Veloz Avda. Mediterraneo ☎ 914 097 602; Ⓜ Conde Casal: Chinchón (daily every 30min–1hr; 45min).

Around Madrid

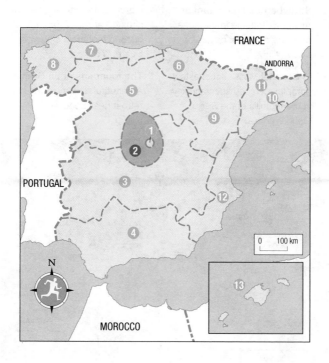

CHAPTER 2 # Highlights

▲ The aqueduct at Segovia

Around Madrid

The lack of historic monuments in Madrid is more than compensated for by the region around the capital. Within a radius of 100km – and within an hour's travel by bus and train – are some of Spain's greatest cities. Not least of these is **Toledo**, which preceded Madrid as the country's capital. Immortalized by El Greco, who lived and worked there for most of his later career, the city is a living museum to the many cultures – Visigothic, Moorish, Jewish and Christian – which have shaped the destiny of Spain. If you have time for just one trip from Madrid, there is really no other choice.

That said, **Segovia**, with its stunning Roman aqueduct and irresistible Disney-prototype castle, puts up strong competition, while Felipe II's vast palace-cum-mausoleum of **El Escorial** is a monument to out-monument all others. And there are smaller places, too, less known to foreign tourists: **Aranjuez**, an oasis in the parched Castilian plain, famed for its asparagus, strawberries and lavish Baroque palace and gardens; the beautiful walled city of **Ávila**, birthplace of St Teresa; and Cervantes' home town, **Alcalá de Henares**, with its sixteenth-century university. For walkers, too, trails amid the sierras of **Gredos** and **Guadarrama** provide enticing escapes from the midsummer heat.

All of the towns in this chapter can be visited as an easy day-trip from Madrid, but they also offer interesting jumping-off points into Castile and beyond.

Toledo

TOLEDO remains one of Spain's great cities. Redolent of past glories, it is packed with memorable sights – hence the whole city's status as a National Monument and UNESCO Patrimony of Mankind – and enjoys an incomparable setting. Be aware, however, that the extraordinary number of day-trippers can take the edge off what was once the most extravagant of Spanish experiences.

Set in a landscape of abrasive desolation, Toledo sits on a rocky mound where every available centimetre has been built upon: churches, synagogues, mosques and houses are heaped upon one another in a haphazard, cobblestoned spiral.

To see the city at its best, it is advisable to avoid peak holiday periods and stay at least a night: a day-trip will leave you hard pressed to see everything. More importantly, in the evening with the crowds gone and the city lit up by flood-lights – resembling one of **El Greco**'s moonlit paintings – Toledo is a different place entirely.

Some history

Toledo was known to the Romans, who captured it in 192 BC, as *Toletum*, a small but well-defended town. Taken by the Visigoths, who made it their capital, it was already an important cultural and trading centre by the time the **Moors** arrived in 712. The period that followed, with Moors, Jews and Mozárabes (Christians subject to Moorish rule) living together in relative equality, was one of rapid growth and prosperity and Toledo became the most important northern outpost of the Muslim emirates. Though there are few physical remains of this period, apart from the enchanting miniature mosque of **Cristo de la Luz**, the long domination has left a clear mark on the atmosphere and shape of the city.

When the Christian king Alfonso VI "reconquered" the town in 1085, with the assistance of El Cid, Moorish influence scarcely weakened. Although Toledo became the capital of Castile and the base for campaigns against the Moors in the south, the city itself was a haven of cultural tolerance. Not only was there a school of translators revealing the scientific and philosophical achievements of the East, but Arab craftsmen and techniques remained responsible for many of the finest buildings of the period: look, for example, at the churches of **San Román** or **Santiago del Arrabal** or at any of the old **city gates**.

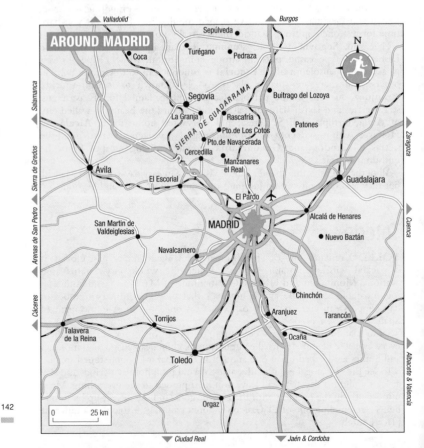

Fiestas

February
First Sunday in the month: Santa Agueda Women's festival when married women take over city administration and parade and celebrate in traditional costume.

March/April
Semana Santa (Holy Week) Formal processions in Toledo and a Passion play on Saturday in the Plaza Mayor at Chinchón.
Mid-April: Fiesta del Anís y del Vino Chinchón.

May/June
Corpus Christi (Thurs after Trinity). Solemn, costumed religious procession in Toledo when the cathedral's magnificent sixteenth-century *custodia* is paraded around.
June 24–29: San Juan y San Pedro Lively procession with floats and music in Segovia.

August
15: Virgen de la Asunción Chinchón's celebrations include an *encierro*, with bulls running through the street.
15: Virgen del Sagrario Amazing fireworks in Toledo.
17–25 Entertaining fiestas in La Granja, (near Segovia) and Orgaz (near Toledo).
Last week in the month: Spectacular parades of giant puppets, and theatre, music and dance in Alcalá de Henares.

September
First weekend of the month: Motín de Aranjuez Re-enactment of the Mutiny of Aranjuez in Aranjuez.
27: La Virgen de la Fuencisla The image of Segovia's patron saint is carried from the sanctuary in the Eresma valley to the cathedral.

October
25: San Frutos Fiestas in Segovia in honour of the patron saint of the city.

At the same time Jewish culture remained powerful. There were, at one time, at least seven **synagogues** – of which two, **Santa María la Blanca** and **El Tránsito**, survive – and Jews occupied many positions of power. The most famous was Samuel Levi, treasurer and right-hand man of Pedro the Cruel until the king lived up to his name by murdering him and stealing his fortune. From this period, too, dates the most important purely Christian monument, Toledo's awesome **Catedral**.

This golden age ended abruptly in the sixteenth century with the transfer of the capital to Madrid, following hard on the heels of the Inquisition's mass expulsion of Muslims and Jews; some of the latter responded by taking refuge in Catholicism, becoming known as *converso*. The city played little part in subsequent Spanish history until the Civil War (see box, p.149) and it remains, despite the droves of tourists, essentially the medieval city so often painted by El Greco.

Arrival

Orientation is pretty straightforward in Toledo, with the compact old city looped by the Tajo, and the new quarters across the bridges. **Getting to the**

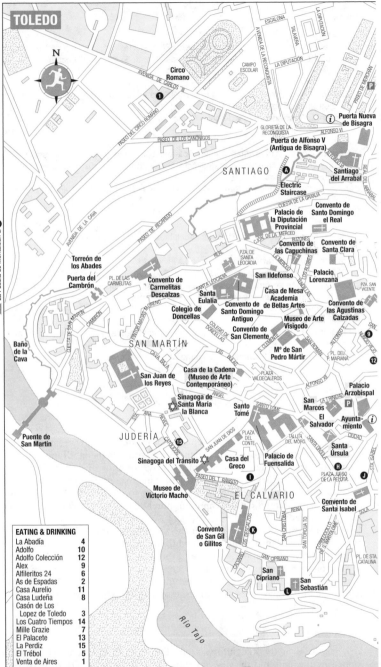

TOLEDO

Ávila ▲

N

Circo Romano ①

Puerta Nueva de Bisagra (i)

Puerta de Alfonso V (Antigua de Bisagra)

SANTIAGO

Santiago del Arrabal

Ⓐ Electric Staircase

Palacio de la Diputación Provincial

Convento de Santo Domingo el Real

Torreón de los Abades

Convento de las Capuchinas

Convento de Santa Clara

Puerta del Cambrón

Convento de Carmelitas Descalzas

San Ildefonso

Palacio Lorenzana

Santa Eulalia

Casa de Mesa Academia de Bellas Artes

Convento de las Agustinas Calzadas

Colegio de Doncellas

Convento de Santo Domingo Antiguo

Museo de Arte Visigodo

⑨

Baño de la Cava

Convento de San Clemente

SAN MARTÍN

Mº de San Pedro Mártir

⑫

Puente de San Martín

San Juan de los Reyes

Casa de la Cadena (Museo de Arte Contemporáneo)

Palacio Arzobispal

San Marcos

Ayuntamiento (i)

El Salvador

Santa Úrsula

Sinagoga de Santa María la Blanca

Santo Tomé

JUDERÍA

⑮

Sinagoga del Tránsito

Casa del Greco

Palacio de Fuensalida

Ⓗ

Ⓙ

Ⓘ

Museo de Victorio Macho

EL CALVARIO

Convento de Santa Isabel

Convento de San Gil o Gilitos

Ⓚ

San Cipriano

San Sebastián

Ⓛ

Rio Tajo

EATING & DRINKING

La Abadía	4
Adolfo	10
Adolfo Colección	12
Alex	9
Alfileritos 24	6
As de Espadas	2
Casa Aurelio	11
Casa Ludeña	8
Casón de Los Lopez de Toledo	3
Los Cuatro Tiempos	14
Mille Grazie	7
El Palacete	13
La Perdiz	15
El Trébol	5
Venta de Aires	1

◀ La Puebla de Montalbán & Ⓑ Ⓓ

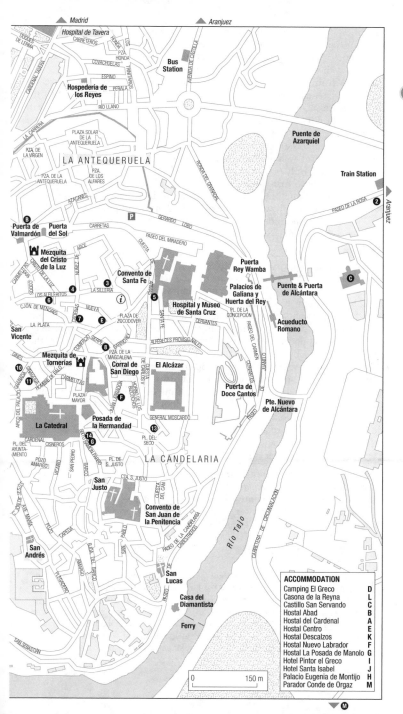

Madrid ▲   Aranjuez ▲

Hospital de Tavera
CARRETEROS
RONDA
LOS
PZA.
HONDA
COVACHUELAS
TRINITARIOS
ESPINO
PERALTA
RÍO LLANO
Hospedería de
los Reyes

Bus
Station

AVENIDA DE CASTILLA

LA CARRERA

CARDENAL TAVERA
DUQUES
DE LERMA

PLAZA SOLAR
DE LA
ANTEQUERUELA
PZA. DE
LA VIRGEN

Puente de
Azarquiel

LA ANTEQUERUELA

PZA. DE LA
ANTEQUERUELA

PZA.
DE LOS
ALFARES

Train Station

PASEO DE LA ROSA

2 ▲ Aranjuez

AZACANES

GERARDO LOBO

P

CARRETAS

RONDA DE GRANADA

Puerta de Puerta
Valmardón del Sol

PASEO DEL MIRADERO

Mezquita
del Cristo
de la Luz

CARRETAS

ARCE

Puerta
Rey Wamba

Palacios de
Galiana y
Huerta del Rey

Puente & Puerta
de Alcántara

C

Convento de
Santa Fe

Hospital y Museo
de Santa Cruz

Acueducto
Romano

CARMELITAS
CRISTO DE LA LUZ
COSO

4
LA SILLERIA

NUEVA

3

5

PL. DE LA
CONCEPCIÓN

CERVANTES

CUESTA

SANTA FE

CJON. DE MENORES

LOS ALFILERITOS

i

E

PLAZA DE
ZOCODOVER

6

7

LA PLATA

8

San
Vicente

Mezquita de
Tornerías

COMERCIO SIERPE

BARRIOS

PZA. DE LA
MAGDALENA

ALFÉREZ PROVISIONALES

El Alcázar

PASEO DEL CARMEN

CERVANTES

Puerta de
Doce Cantos

GINÉS

GRANADA SÁNCHEZ

10

11

Corral de
San Diego

CARMELITAS

HOMBRE DE PALO

CUESTA
DE CARLOS V

CUESTA DE
HORNO DE LOS

F

Pte. Nuevo
de Alcántara

ARCO DEL PALACIO

PLAZA
MAYOR

NUÑEZ DE ARCE

PASEO

La Catedral

Posada de
la Hermandad

GENERAL MOSCARDÓ

13

PL. DEL
SECO

PL. DEL
AYUNTA-
MIENTO

CARDENAL
CISNEROS

14
G

SANTA ÚRSULA

POZO
AMARGO

SAN PEDRO

PL. DE
S. JUSTO

LA CANDELARIA

VICARIO

San
Justo

PL. DE S. JUSTO

CTA. S. JUSTO

COLOR DE JESÚS

AVE. MARÍA

POZO

CAPILLA

San
Andrés

PABLOS

BUEN. DEL TRÁNSITO

BARCO

AMARGO

REYES CATÓLICOS

CUESTA
DEL CAN

Convento de
San Juan de
la Penitencia

PASEO DE LA CANDELARIA

CARRETEROS

CARRETERA DE CIRCUNVALACIÓN

Río Tajo

San
Lucas

Casa del
Diamantista

SAN SEBASTIÁN

Ferry

0   150 m

ACCOMMODATION
Camping El Greco   D
Casona de la Reyna   L
Castillo San Servando   C
Hostal Abad   B
Hostal del Cardenal   A
Hostal Centro   E
Hostal Descalzos   K
Hostal Nuevo Labrador   F
Hostal La Posada de Manolo G
Hotel Pintor el Greco   I
Hotel Santa Isabel   J
Palacio Eugenia de Montijo H
Parador Conde de Orgaz   M

▼ M

2

AROUND MADRID

city is easy, with buses every 30min from the Estación Sur in Madrid (daily 6.30am–10pm; 1hr–1hr 30min; €4.53 single). There's a high-speed **train** service from Atocha station in Madrid (35min; €16.20 return; it's essential to book in advance at the station or from most travel agents in the city).

Toledo's **train station** is some way out on the Paseo de la Rosa, a twenty-minute walk – take the left-hand fork off the dual carriageway and cross the Puente de Alcántara – or a bus ride (#5 or #6 or the tourist shuttle) to the heart of town. The **bus station** is on Avenida de Castilla la Mancha in the modern, lower part of the city; bus #5 runs to Plaza de Zocódover, though if you take shortcuts through the *barrio* at the bottom of the hill just inside the walls, it's a mere ten-minutes' walk to the Puerta Nueva de Bisagra.

Walking is the only way to see the city itself, but be aware that resident cars have a tendency to roar along even the tiniest alleyways in the centre. If you do arrive by **car**, the best places to park are in the streets beyond the Circo Romano in the new town (Mon–Fri 10am–2pm & 5–8pm, Sat 10am–2pm; €0.75/hr) or in the underground car park close to the mechanical staircase (Mon–Fri 7am–10pm, Sat, Sun & hols 8am–10pm) that leads up into the old city.

Information

Toledo's main **turismo** (Mon–Sat 9am–7pm, winter Mon–Fri closes 6pm, Sun & hols 9am–3pm; ℡925 220 843, Ⓦwww.turismocastillalamancha.com) is outside the city walls opposite the Puerta Nueva de Bisagra, where you can pick up information on an array of walking tours (see also Ⓦwww.toledopaisajes .com, Ⓦwww.conocetoledo.com & Ⓦwww.odelotoledo.com). There's another tourist office run by the local *ayuntamiento* in the plaza next to the cathedral (Mon 10.30am–2.30pm, Tues–Sun 10.30am–2.30pm & 4.30–7pm; ℡925 254 030, Ⓦwww.toledo-turismo.com), and an information point in the Zococentro shop at c/Sillería 14 in the centre (daily 10.30am–6pm, till 7pm in the summer, opens at 11am on Sat & Sun; ℡925 220 300). For **internet** access try the *Roscoking* doughnut joint (closed Mon), at c/Armas 9 on the way up to Plaza de Zocódover, or one of the Locutorios in and around Plaza de la Magdalena.

Accommodation

Booking a **room** in advance is important in Toledo, especially at weekends, or during the summer. The *turismo* has a list of all the accommodation available in town, while there is also a **central booking system** (Ⓦwww.loshotelesdetoledo .com, ℡902 513 223). Be aware that prices in many places almost double at Easter, bank holidays and at Corpus Christi.

Toledan steel

Toledo has been a byword for fine **steel** for a thousand years or more, and the glint of knives in souvenir shops is one of the first things you'll notice on arrival. Some have traced the craft back to the Romans, and it was certainly a growth industry when the Moors were here. Hannibal, El Cid and even some Japanese samurai were said to have used Toledan blades. By the seventeenth century, though, Samuel Butler was complaining that "the trenchant blade, Toledo trusty, for want of fighting was grown rusty". Today, it's surprising that, except for a display due to be part of the new military museum in the Alcázar, there's little to see outside the shops; in these, you can still admire attractive damascene steel swords and knives, their handles inlaid with decorative gold and silver filigree.

Casona de la Reyna Carrera de San Sebastián 26 ☎925 282 052, ⓦwww.casonadelareyna.com. Situated in the quiet San Cipriano area of the old town with private parking and 24 spacious, classically decorated rooms all with a/c. ❺

Castillo San Servando Across the Puente de Alcántara and just off Paseo de la Rosa on Cuesta de San Servando ☎925 224 554, 925 221 676, ⓔalbergues@jccm.es. Toledo's youth hostel is across the river from the Alcázar in a wing of the fourteenth-century Mudéjar-style Castillo San Servando, a 15min walk (signposted) from the train station. It has a fine view of the city, and booking is advised. YH card required. Closed mid-Aug to mid-Sept. Under 30s €9.50, over 30s €12.50 in two- or four-bed dormitories.

Hostal Abad c/Real del Arrabal 1 ☎925 283 500, ⓦwww.hotelabad.com. A smart hotel situated in a former ironworks close to the Mezquita de la Luz. The 22 rooms have brick-lined walls and warm colours, and those in the loft are particularly nice. ❹

🏃 Hostal del Cardenal Paseo de Recaredo 24 ☎925 224 900, ⓦwww.hostaldelcardenal.com. A splendid old mansion with a famous restaurant and delightful gardens, located outside the city wall, near Puerta Nueva de Bisagra. ❺

Hostal Centro c/Nueva 13 ☎925 257 091, ⓦwww.hostalcentro.com. Very pleasant, inexpensive a/c 23-room *hostal* situated close to Plaza de Zocódover. ❷–❸

Hostal Descalzos c/Descalzos 30 ☎925 222 888, ⓦwww.hostaldescalzos.com. Very good-value, centrally located *hostal*, handy for the main sights. Some of the modern a/c en-suite rooms have lovely views, plus there's a small open-air pool. ❸

Hostal Nuevo Labrador c/Juan Labrador 10 ☎925 222 620, ⓦwww.nuevolabrador.com. Tucked down a shady street near to the Alcázar,

this friendly and modern *hostal* has twelve good-value rooms and its own restaurant. ❷

🏃 Hostal La Posada de Manolo c/Sixto Ramón Parro 8 ☎925 282 250, ⓦwww.laposadademanolo.com. An atmospheric *hostal* in a carefully refurbished period house close to the cathedral. ❹

Hotel Pintor el Greco c/Alamillos de Transito 13 ☎925 285 191, ⓦwww.hotelpintorelgreco.com. A well-equipped and nicely furnished hotel in a refurbished seventeenth-century bakery situated in the old Jewish quarter. It has 33 comfortable rooms, many with fine views across the Tajo, and private parking. Special offers available. ❺

🏃 Hotel Santa Isabel c/Santa Isabel 24 ☎925 253 120, ⓦwww.santa-isabel.com. The best of the mid-range hotels occupies a converted nobleman's house right in the centre, with airy rooms, wood-panelled floors and safe parking. ❷

Palacio Eugenia de Montijo Plaza del Juego de la Pelota 7 ☎925 274 690, ⓦwww.palacioeugeniademontijo.com. Luxury hotel in the heart of the old town with its own spa and a high-class restaurant run by the Adolfo chain. ❺

Parador Conde de Orgaz Cerro del Emperador s/n ☎925 221 850, ⓦwww.paradores.com. Superb views of the city from the terrace of Toledo's top hotel, but the drawback is that it's a fair walk from the centre. ❻

Campsite

Camping El Greco Ctra. De Toledo-Puebla de Montalbán ☎925 220 090, ⓦwww.campingelgreco.es. A 30min walk from the Puerta de Bisagra: cross the Puente de la Cava towards Puebla de Montalbán, then follow the signs. There are great views of the city from this riverside campsite – and a bar to enjoy them from – plus a swimming pool to cool off in after a hard day's sightseeing.

The City

There are two main entrances to the old city of Toledo: via the mechanical staircase that scales the hill from the Puerta de Bisagra opposite the tourist office and leaves you close to the Convento de Santo Domingo Antiguo, or up Calle Real del Arrabal to the Plaza Zócodover. Once there, the street **layout** can appear confusing, but the old core is so small that it should never take too long to get back on track; part of the city's charm is that it's a place to wander in and absorb, so don't overdose on "sights" if you can avoid it. Don't leave without seeing at least the El Grecos, the cathedral, the synagogues and Alcázar (when it reopens), but give it all time and you may stumble upon things not listed in this or any other guidebook. Enter any inviting doorway and you'll find stunning patios, rooms and ceilings, often of Mudéjar workmanship.

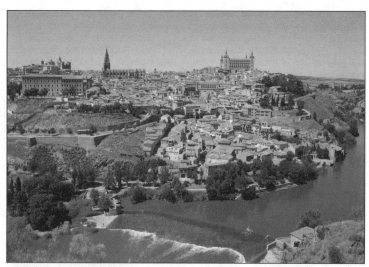

▲ Toledo

Many of the leading sights are undergoing **renovation**, and although this means temporary disruption to some sights, the city should soon be in better shape than it has been for many years.

The Alcázar and the Hospital de Santa Cruz

At the heart of modern Toledo is the **Plaza de Zocódover** (its name derives from the Arabic word *souk*), where everyone converges for an afternoon drink. Dominating this square, indeed all Toledo, is the bluff, striking **Alcázar** (closed for refurbishment). There has probably always been a fortress at this commanding location, and though the present building was originated by Carlos V, it has been burned and bombarded so often that almost nothing remaining is original. The most recent destruction was in 1936 during one of the most symbolic and extraordinary episodes of the Civil War (see box opposite).

After the war, Franco's regime completely rebuilt the fortress as a monument to the glorification of its defenders – the Fascist newspaper *El Alcázar* also commemorates the siege – and their propaganda models and photos are still displayed, as well as the cellars where the besieged families hid. The rest of the building houses an Army Museum that will eventually contain all the exhibits from the former Army Museum in Madrid.

The Alcázar also offers the best views of the town, its upper windows level with the top of the cathedral spire (though in recent years access has been restricted, as part of the building is still occupied by the military).

A couple of blocks to the west of the Alcázar is the **Mezquita de las Tornerías** on c/Tornerías (entrance at Plaza del Solarejo 7; Mon–Fri 10am–2pm; free), a renovated eleventh-century mosque, deconsecrated by the Reyes Católicos around 1500, which also houses occasional displays of beautiful local crafts, mainly pottery.

Just north of the Alcázar and off the Plaza de Zocódover is the **Hospital y Museo de Santa Cruz** (Mon–Sat 10am–6pm, Sun 10am–2pm; free), a superlative Renaissance building with a fine Plateresque facade, housing some of the greatest El Grecos in Toledo, including *The Assumption*, a daringly unorthodox work of feverish spiritual intensity, and a *Crucifixion* with the town as a backdrop. As well as outstanding works by Goya and Ribera, the museum also contains a huge collection of ancient carpets and faded tapestries (including a magnificent fifteenth-century Flemish tapestry called *The Astrolabe*), a military display (note the flags borne by Don Juan of Austria at the Battle of Lepanto), sculpture and a small archeological collection. Don't miss the patio with its ornate staircase – the entrance is beside the ticket office.

The Catedral

In a country overflowing with massive religious institutions, the metropolitan **Catedral** (main body closed noon–3.30pm) has to be something special – and it is. A robust Gothic construction that took over 250 years (1227–1493) to complete, it has a richness of internal decoration in almost every conceivable style, with masterpieces of the Gothic, Renaissance and Baroque periods. The exterior is best appreciated from outside the city, where the hundred-metre spire and the weighty buttressing can be seen to greatest advantage. From the street it's less impressive, so hemmed in by surrounding houses that you can't really sense the scale or grandeur of the whole.

There are eight doorways, but the main entrance is normally through the **Puerta Llana** on the southern side of the main body of the cathedral. Tickets (€7, free Sun pm) for the various chapels, chapterhouses and treasuries that require them will be sold in the cathedral shop opposite when it has been refurbished. The areas that need **tickets** can be visited (Mon–Sat 10am–6.30pm & Sun 2–6.30pm).

The Coro and Capilla Mayor

Inside the cathedral, the central nave is divided from four aisles by a series of clustered pillars supporting the vaults, 88 in all, the aisles continuing around behind the main altar to form an apse. There is magnificent **stained glass** throughout, mostly dating from the fifteenth and sixteenth centuries, particularly

---

The siege of the Alcázar

At the outset of the Spanish Civil War, on July 20, 1936, Colonel José Moscardó – a leading Nationalist rebel – and the cadets of the military academy under his command were driven into the Alcázar. They barricaded themselves in with a large group that included six hundred women and children, and up to a hundred left-wing hostages (who were never seen again).

After many phone calls from Madrid to persuade them to surrender, a Toledo attorney phoned Moscardó with an ultimatum: within ten minutes the Republicans would shoot his son, captured that morning. Moscardó declared that he would never surrender and told his son, "If it be true, commend your soul to God, shout *Viva España*, and die like a hero." (His son was actually shot with others a month later in reprisal for an air raid.) Inside, though not short of ammunition, the defenders had so little food they had to eat their horses.

The number of Republican attackers varied from 1000 to 5000. Two of the three mines they planted under the towers exploded but nothing could disturb the solid rock foundations, while spraying petrol all over the walls and setting fire to it had no effect. Finally, General Franco decided to relieve Moscardó and diverted an army that was heading for Madrid. On September 27, General José Varela commanded the successful attack on the town, which was followed by the usual bloodbath. The day after Franco entered Toledo to consolidate his victory, he was declared head of state.

beautiful in two rose windows above the north and south doors. Beside the south door (Puerto de los Leones) is a huge, ancient **fresco of St Christopher**.

At the physical heart of the church, blocking the nave, is the **Coro** (Choir; closed Sun morning), itself a panoply of sculpture. The wooden stalls are in two tiers. The lower level, carved in 1489–95 by Rodrigo Alemán, depicts the conquest of Granada, with each seat showing a different village being taken by the Christians. The portraits of Old Testament characters on the stalls above were executed in the following century, on the north side by Philippe Vigarni and on the south by Alonso Berruguete, whose superior technique is evident. He also carved the large **Transfiguration** here from a single block of alabaster. The *reja* (grille) that encloses the *coro* is said to be plated with gold, but it was covered in iron to disguise its value from Napoleon's troops and has since proved impossible to renovate.

The **Capilla Mayor** stands directly opposite. Its gargantuan altarpiece, stretching clear to the roof, is one of the triumphs of Gothic art, overflowing with intricate detail and fanciful embellishments. It contains a synopsis of the entire New Testament, culminating in a Calvary at the summit.

Directly behind the main altar is an extraordinary piece of fantasy – the Baroque **Transparente**. Wonderfully and wildly extravagant, with its marble cherubs sitting on fluffy marble clouds, it's especially magnificent when the sun reaches through the hole punched in the roof for just that purpose. You'll notice a red cardinal's hat hanging from the vaulting just in front of this. Spanish primates are buried where they choose, with the epitaph they choose and with their hat hanging above them, where it stays until it rots. One of them chose to be buried here, and there are other pieces of headgear dotted around the cathedral.

Chapels and treasures

There are well over twenty **chapels** around the walls, all of which are of some interest. Many of them house fine tombs, particularly the **Capilla de Santiago**, the octagonal **Capilla de San Ildefonso** and the gilded **Capilla de Reyes Nuevos**.

In the **Capilla Mozárabe**, Mass is still celebrated daily according to the ancient Visigothic rites. When the Church tried to ban the old ritual in 1086 the people of Toledo were outraged. The dispute was put to a combat, which the Mozárabe champion won, but the Church demanded further proof: trial by fire. The Roman prayer book was blown to safety, while the Mozárabe version remained, unburnt, in the flames. Both sides claimed victory, and in the end the two rituals were allowed to coexist. If you want to attend Mass, be there at 9.30am and look out for the priest – you may well be the only congregation.

The Capilla de San Juan houses the riches of the cathedral **Tesoro** (Treasury), most notably a solid silver *custodia* (repository for Eucharist wafers), 3m high and weighing over two hundred kilos. An even more impressive accumulation of wealth is displayed in the **Sacristía** (Sacristy), where paintings include a *Disrobing of Christ* and portraits of the Apostles by El Greco, Velázquez's portrait of Cardinal Borja and Goya's *Christ Taken by the Soldiers*.

In the adjoining rooms, the so-called **New Museums** (closed Mon) house works of art that were previously locked away or poorly displayed. Among them are paintings by Caravaggio, Gerard David and Morales, and El Greco's most important piece of sculpture, a polychromed wooden group of San Ildefonso and the Virgin. The **Sala Capitular** (Chapterhouse) has a magnificent sixteenth-century *artesonado* ceiling and portraits of all Spain's archbishops to the present day.

Santo Tomé and the Casa del Greco

A little way to the west of the cathedral is one of Toledo's outstanding attractions: El Greco's masterpiece, *The Burial of the Count of Orgaz*. It's housed, alone, in a small annexe to the church of **Santo Tomé** (daily 10am–6.45pm, winter closes 5.45pm; €2.30, free Wed after 4pm for EU citizens) and depicts the count's funeral, at which SS Stephen and Augustine appeared in order to lower him into the tomb. It combines El Greco's genius for the mystic, exemplified in the upper half of the picture where the count's soul is being received into heaven, with his great powers as a portrait painter and master of colour. The identity of the sombre-faced figures watching the burial has been a source of endless speculation. On two identities, however, there is universal agreement; El Greco painted himself seventh from the left looking out at the viewer, and his son in the foreground. Less certain are the identities of the rest of the mourners, but the odds are on for Felipe II's presence among the heavenly onlookers, even though he was still alive when it was painted. A search for the count's bones came to an end in early 2001 when they were unearthed from a tomb located, appropriately enough, directly below the painting.

From Santo Tomé the c/de los Alamillos leads down to the old **Judería** (Jewish quarter) and to the **Casa y Museo del Greco**, which despite its name wasn't the artist's actual home. The building, which in fact dates from the beginning of the twentieth century, is currently undergoing an ambitious €1.6 million refurbishment.

The Judería to San Juan de los Reyes

Between Santo Tomé and the Casa del Greco you pass the entrance to the **Palacio de Fuensalida** (undergoing refurbishment; closed to the public), a beautiful fifteenth-century mansion where Carlos V's Portuguese wife Isabel died. A garden separates it from the **Taller del Moro** (closed for restoration), three fourteenth-century rooms of a Mudéjar palace with magnificent decoration and doorways intact. It is approached through its own entrance in the c/Taller del Moro.

A little way to the east at c/Trinidad 7 is the **Centro Cultural de San Marcos** which houses the *Claves de Toledo* (Mon–Sat 10.30am–7.30pm, Sun 10.30am–1.30pm; €4), a multimedia exhibition which details the history of the city and the people who have lived there, but you will only get the best out of it if your Spanish is good.

Almost next door to the Casa del Greco, on c/Reyes Católicos, is the **Sinagoga del Tránsito**, built along Moorish lines by Samuel Levi in 1366. It became a church after the expulsion of the Jews, but is currently being restored to its original form. The interior is a simple galleried hall, brilliantly decorated with polychromed stuccowork and superb filigree windows. Hebrew inscriptions praising God, King Pedro and Samuel Levi adorn the walls. Nowadays it houses a small **Sephardic Museum** (mid-Feb to end Nov Tues–Sat 10am–9pm, Sun 10am–2pm; Dec to mid-Feb Tues–Sat 10am–6pm, Sun 10am–2pm; €2.40, free Sat pm & Sun), tracing the distinct traditions and development of Jewish culture in Spain.

Opposite, splendidly situated on a spur overlooking the Tajo, is the **Museo de Victorio Macho**, Plaza de Victorio Macho 2 (Mon–Sat 10am–7pm, Sun 10am–3pm; €3), which contains the sculptures, paintings and sketches of the Spanish artist Victorio Macho (1887–1966), set in a delightfully tranquil garden. The auditorium on the ground floor shows a documentary film (available in English) about the city and its history.

The only other surviving synagogue, **Santa María la Blanca** (daily 10am–6pm, summer closes 7pm; €2.30, free Wed pm for EU citizens), is a short way further down c/Reyes Católicos. Like El Tránsito, which it pre-dates by over a century, it has been both church and synagogue, though, as it was built by Mudéjar craftsmen, it actually looks more like a mosque. Four rows of octagonal pillars each support seven horseshoe arches, all of them with elaborate and individual designs moulded in plaster, while a fine sixteenth-century *retablo* has been preserved from the building's time as a church. The whole effect is quite stunning, accentuated by a deep-red floor tiled with decorative *azulejos*.

Continuing down c/Reyes Católicos, you come to the superb church of **San Juan de los Reyes** (daily 10am–6.45pm, winter closes 5.45pm; €2.30, free Wed pm), its exterior bizarrely festooned with the chains worn by Christian prisoners from Granada released on the reconquest of their city. It was originally a Franciscan convent founded by the "Catholic Kings", Fernando and Isabel, to celebrate their victory at the Battle of Toro. Designed in the decorative late Gothic style known as Isabelline (after the queen), its double-storeyed cloister is quite outstanding: the upper floor has an elaborate Mudéjar ceiling, and the crests of Castile and Aragón – seven arrows and a yoke – are carved everywhere in assertion of the new unity brought by the royal marriage.

The Museo de Arte Visigodo and the Convento de Santo Domingo de Antiguo

A little way to the north of San Juan de Reyes and close to the mechanical staircase leading out of the old city is the **Convento de Santo Domingo Antiguo**, whose chief claim to fame is that El Greco's remains lie in the crypt, which can be glimpsed through a peephole in the floor. The nuns display their art treasures in the old choir (Mon–Sat 11am–1.30pm & 4–7pm, Sun 4–7pm; €1.90), but more interesting is the high altarpiece of the church, El Greco's first major commission in Toledo. Unfortunately, most of the canvases have gone to museums and are here replaced by copies, leaving only two *St Johns* and a *Resurrection*.

Southeast of here back towards the cathedral is the **Museo de Arte Visigodo** (Tues–Sat 10am–2pm & 4–6.30pm, Sun 10am–2pm; €0.60, free Sat pm & Sun) which can be found in the church of **San Román**. Moorish and Christian elements – horseshoe arches, early murals and a splendid Renaissance dome – combine to make it the most interesting church in Toledo. Visigothic jewellery, documents and archeological fragments make up the bulk of the collection.

The Mezquita del Cristo and beyond the city walls

If you leave the old city by the Cuesta de Armas, which runs out of the Plaza de Zocódover and down the hill, you will come across the battlements of the **Puerta del Sol**, a great fourteenth-century Mudéjar gateway. Tucked behind the gateway on the Cuesta de los Carmelitas Descalzos is the tiny mosque of **Mezquita del Cristo de la Luz** (daily 10am–6pm, summer closes 7pm; €2.30, free on Wed for EU citizens). Although this is one of the oldest Moorish monuments in Spain (it was built by Musa Ibn Ali in the tenth century on the foundations of a Visigothic church), only the nave, with its nine different cupolas, is the original Arab construction. The apse was added when the building was converted into a church, and is claimed to be the first product of the Mudéjar style. According to legend, as King Alfonso rode into the town in triumph, his horse stopped and knelt before the mosque. Excavations revealed a figure of Christ, still illuminated by a lamp, which had burned throughout three and a half centuries of Muslim rule – hence the name *Cristo de la Luz*. The outstandingly elegant mosque is set in a small park and open on all sides to the elements, and is so small that it seems more like a miniature summer pavilion. Occasionally you'll see the mosque used for prayer by visiting Muslims.

Rejoining Calle Real del Arrabal below Puerta del Sol is the intriguing exterior of the Mudéjar church of **Santiago del Arrabal**, while at the foot of the hill and marooned in a constant swirl of traffic is Toledo's main gate, the sixteenth-century **Puerta Nueva de Bisagra**. Its patterned-tile roofs bear the coat of arms of Carlos V. Alongside is the gateway that it replaced, the ninth-century Moorish portal through which Alfonso VI and El Cid led their triumphant armies in 1085.

Beyond and directly in front along the Paseo de Merchán is the **Hospital de Tavera** (daily 10.30am–1.30pm & 3–5.30pm; €4). This Renaissance palace with beautiful twin patios houses the private collection of the duke of Lerma. The gloomy interior is a reconstruction of a sixteenth-century mansion dotted with fine paintings, including a *Day of Judgement* by Bassano; the portrait of Carlos V by Titian is a copy of the original in the Prado. The hospital's archives are kept here, too: thousands of densely handwritten pages chronicling the illnesses treated. The museum contains several works by El Greco, and Ribera's gruesome portrait of a freak "bearded woman". Also here is the death mask of Cardinal Tavera, the hospital's founder, and in the church of the hospital is his ornate marble tomb – the last work of Alonso de Berruguete.

Eating and drinking

Toledo is a major tourist centre and inevitably many of its cafés, bars and restaurants are geared to passing trade. However, the city is also popular with Spanish visitors, so decent, authentic places do exist – and there's a bit of nightlife, too. Most **restaurants** offer the tasty local speciality, *carcamusa* – a meat stew in a spicy tomato sauce, and game such as partridge (*perdiz*), pheasant (*faisán*) and quail (*codorniz*) appear in the more upmarket places.

La Abadía Plaza San Nicolás 3. There's a constantly changing menu in this popular restaurant serving very good specialities such as pheasant *croquetas* and *patatas a lo pobre*.

Adolfo c/Granada 6 ☎ 925 227 321. One of the best restaurants in town, tucked behind a marzipan café, in an old Jewish town house (ask to see the painted ceiling in the eleventh-century cellar downstairs), and serving imaginative, high-quality food. But it comes at a price: the two menus on offer are a hefty €56 or €85. Closed Sun eve & Mon.

Adolfo Colección c/Nuncio Viejo 1. If you can't afford to eat at the *Adolfo* restaurant (above), have a glass of wine and some designer tapas at this elegant little bar run by the same people.

Alex Plaza de Amador de los Ríos 10, at the top end of c/Nuncio Viejo. A reasonable-value restaurant with a much cheaper café at the side. It's in a nice location and has a shady summer terrace. *Conejo* and *perdiz* are the specialities here and you can expect to pay up to €35 a head. Closed Mon.

Alfileritos 24 c/Alfileritos 24. A cool, relaxed, brick-lined bar-restaurant serving an imaginative and very tasty €9.90 *menú*. A good place for a drink, too.

As de Espadas Paseo de la Rosa 64 ☎ 925 212 707. An excellent restaurant close to the railway station serving a €42 *menú de degustación* and imaginative dishes such as chickpeas with spinach and squid. It also does good home-made desserts and has an extensive wine list.

Casa Aurelio c/Sinagoga 1 & 6. Two branches of a popular Toledano group of restaurants (there's another one next to the cathedral in the Plaza del Ayuntamiento) serving up good standard Castilian food. Mains range from €18–25.

Casa Ludeña Plaza Magdalena 13. One of many places around this square, but this is the most authentic. It offers a good-value €10 *menú* and some of the best *carcamusa* in town.

Casón de Los Lopez de Toledo c/Sillería 3. An upmarket restaurant in a quiet street close to Plaza Zocódover with plenty of regional specialities. Main courses cost between €15 and €20.

Los Cuatro Tiempos c/Sixto Ramón Parro 5 (close to the Cathedral) ☎ 925 223 782. An excellent restaurant with local specialities such as *cochinillo*, *perdiz* and *cordero* given a modern twist. The *menú* is around €20, main courses are €18–20. Closed Sun eve.

Mille Grazie c/Cadenas 2. A busy, down-to-earth place with a wide variety of Italian dishes. The tortellini with walnut and cream sauce is particularly good. Closed Mon & Sun eve.

El Palacete c/Soledad 2 ☎ 925 225 375. Located in a beautifully restored building dating back to the eleventh century, this high-quality restaurant serves well-presented meat and fish dishes and offers a fine €40 *menú*. Closed Sun & Mon eve.

La Perdiz c/Reyes Católicos 7. A popular place which does a good *menú de degustación* for €28 and has a fine selection of local wines. Owned by the same people as *Adolfo* (see p.153).

El Trébol c/Santa Fé 15. Very popular bar between Plaza Zocódover and the Museo de Santa Cruz serving some great tapas and the house speciality *bombas* (potatoes stuffed with meat and fried). A tasty range of *bocadillos* and some good tortilla too.

Venta de Aires c/Circo Romano 35 ☎ 925 220 545. A popular restaurant housed in a famous old inn, a little way out of the centre, with outdoor eating in the summer. Allow €35 a head. Closed Sun eve.

Nightlife

By Spanish standards, Toledo's **nightlife** is rather tame. You'll find most late-night bars running along c/Sillería and its extension c/Alfileritos, west of Plaza de Zocódover. *Art-Café* at Plaza San Vicente 6 is a very pleasant early watering hole with good tapas, German beer and art exhibitions. *La Abadia* (see p.153) and the *Enebro* wine bar on Plaza Santiago Balleros also make good early evening stops. Alternative places that frequently offer live music are *Broadway Jazz Club*, on c/Alfonso XII, and *El Último* at Plaza Colegio Infantes 4. In the old core, there are several discobars close to Plaza de Zocódover, while in the new town the area around Plaza de Cuba is packed with bars and clubs.

Out of the tourist season, between September and March, **classical concerts** are held in the cathedral and other churches; details can be obtained from the *turismo*.

Aranjuez and Chinchón

A short train journey from Madrid is **Aranjuez**, a little oasis in the beginnings of New Castile, where the eighteenth-century Bourbon rulers set up a spring and autumn retreat. Their palaces and luxuriant gardens, which inspired the composer Joaquín Rodrigo to write the famous *Concierto de Aranjuez*, and the summer strawberries (served with cream – *fresas con nata* – at roadside stalls), combine to make it an enjoyable stop. Nearby, too, is **Chinchón**, a picturesque village home to Spain's best-known *anís* – a mainstay of breakfast drinkers across Spain.

Aranjuez

The beauty of **ARANJUEZ** is its greenery – it's easy to forget just how dry and dusty most of central Spain is until you come upon this town, with its lavish palaces and luxuriant gardens at the confluence of the Tajo and Jarama rivers. In summer, Aranjuez functions principally as a weekend escape from Madrid and most people come out for the day, or stop en route to or from Toledo.

Arrival and information

An old wooden **steam train** (May–July & Sept to mid-Oct Sat & Sun; €25; ☎902 228 822), the Tren de la Fresa, runs between Madrid and Aranjuez; it leaves Atocha station at 10.05am and returns from Aranjuez at 6pm, arriving back at Atocha at 7pm. The price includes a guided bus tour in Aranjuez, entry to the monuments and *fresas con nata* on the train. The less romantic, but highly efficient, standard trains leave every fifteen to thirty minutes from Atocha, with the last train returning from Aranjuez at about 11.30pm. **Buses** run every half-hour during the week and every hour at weekends from Estación Sur. You'll find a helpful **turismo** in the Casa de Infantes, facing the Plaza de San Antonio (daily 10am–6.30pm, Oct–May closes 5.30pm; ☎918 910 427, ⓦwww.aranjuez.es).

Accommodation

Due to the distinct lack of **accommodation**, it is essential to reserve a room in advance.

Hotels

Castilla Carrera de Andalucía 98 ☎918 912 627, ⓦwww.hostalesaranjuez.com. A straightforward and neat hotel in one of the old courtyarded blocks not far from the main sights. ❸

Hotel Don Manuel c/Príncipe 71 ☎918 754 086, ⓦwww.egidohoteles.com. A comfortable business-style hotel, close to the royal palace and gardens. ❸

NH Príncipe de la Paz c/San Antonio 22 ☎918 099 222, ⓦwww.nh-hoteles.com. A smart NH hotel complete with all the usual facilities and conveniently located next to the palace. ❹–❺

Rusiñol c/San Antonio 76 ☎918 910 155, ⓕ918 916 133. Cheap and cheerful place in the centre of town. ❷

Campsite

Camping Internacional Aranjuez On a far bend of the Río Tajo ☎918 911 395, ⓕ918 914 197. Reopened after a lengthy refurbishment, it's equipped with a swimming pool, and rents out bicycles and rowing boats.

The Town

A bus service occasionally connects the various sights, but all are within easy walking distance of each other, and the town's a very pleasant place to stroll around.

The showpiece eighteenth-century **Palacio Real** (Tues–Sun: April–Sept 10am–6.15pm; Oct–March 10am–5.15pm; €4.50 without a guide, €5 with a guide, free Wed for EU citizens; ⓦwww.patrimonionacional.es) and its **gardens** (daily: April–Sept 8am–8.30pm; Oct–March 8am–6.30pm; free) were an attempt by the Spanish Bourbon monarchs to create a Versailles in Spain; Aranjuez clearly isn't in the same league, but it's a very pleasant place to while away a few hours.

The palace, which is situated alongside the river, is more remarkable for the ornamental fantasies inside than for any virtues of architecture. There seem to be hundreds of rooms, all exotically furnished, most amazingly so the **Porcelain Room**, entirely covered in decorative ware from the factory that used to stand in Madrid's Retiro park. Most of the palace dates from the reign of the "nymphomaniac" Queen Isabel II, and many of the sexual scandals and intrigues that led to her eventual removal from the throne in 1868 were played out here.

Outside, on a small island, are the fountains and neatly tended gardens of the **Jardín de la Isla**. The **Jardín del Príncipe**, on the other side of the main road, is more attractive, with shaded walks along the river and plenty of spots for a siesta. At its far end is the **Casa del Labrador** (June–Sept Tues–Sun 10am–6.15pm; Oct–March Tues–Sun 10am–5.15pm; visits by appointment only ☎918 910 305; €5, free Wed for EU citizens), an opulent house containing more silk, marble, crystal and gold than would seem possible in so small a place, as well as a huge collection of fancy clocks. The guided tour goes into great detail about the weight and value of every item.

Also in the gardens, by the river, is the small **Casa de los Marinos** or **Museo de Faluas** (Tues–Sun: April–Sept 10am–6.15pm; Oct–March 10am–5.15pm; €2 unguided, €3 with guide, free Wed for EU citizens), which houses the brightly coloured launches in which royalty would take to the river. You can do the modern equivalent and take a boat trip through the royal parks from the jetty by the bridge next to the palace (Tues–Sun 11am–sunset; €7).

Look out for the regal eighteenth-century **Plaza de Toros** (summer Tues–Sun 10.30am–2pm & 4.30–7.30pm; winter Tues–Sun 10.30am–2pm & 4–5.30pm; free), part of which is a **museo taurino** with its *trajes de luces*, swords and associated taurine memorabilia; the museum also traces the town's history and royal heritage. Nearby in c/Naranja and c/Rosa are a number of **corralas**, traditional-style wooden-balconied tenement blocks.

Eating and drinking

The splendid nineteenth-century **Mercado de Abastos** on c/Stuart is a good place to buy your own food for a picnic (including, in season, the famous strawberries and asparagus).

La Alegria de la Huerta ☎918 912 938. Near to the bridge across the Tajo on the main road in from Madrid, this place offers a speciality *arroz con bogavante*, pheasant and *cochinillo*. Closed weekday evenings & Tues.

Casa José c/Abastos 32 ☎918 911 488. Renowned restaurant serving high-quality *nouvelle cuisine* at over €50 a head. Closed Sun eve & Mon.

Casa Pablete c/Stuart 108. A traditional bar good for tapas and *raciones*. Closed Tues & Aug.

Casa Pablo c/Almíbar 42 ☎ 918 911 451. Traditional, with walls covered with pictures of local dignitaries and bullfighters. Closed Aug.

El Rana Verde Plaza Santiago Rusiñol s/n ☎918 019 171. Probably the best-known restaurant in the area, the pleasant *El Rana Verde* dates back to the late nineteenth century and serves a wideranging *menú* at around €13.

Chinchón

CHINCHÓN, 45km southeast of Madrid, is an elegant little place, with a fifteenth-century castle. It's connected by sporadic **buses** from Aranjuez at c/Almíbar 138 (Mon–Fri 4 daily, Sat 2 daily) and hourly services from the bus station at Avda. Mediterraneo 49 (Conde Casal) in Madrid.

The town is best-known for being the home of *anís*; your best bet for a sample of the spirit is one of the local bars or the Alcoholera de Chinchón, a shop on the Plaza Mayor. The **Museo Etnológico** (Tues–Sun 11am–2pm & 4–8pm; free), on c/Morata, just off the Plaza Mayor, has some of the traditional *anís*-making machines on show.

If you're visiting over Easter, you'll be treated to the townsfolk's own enactment of the Passion of Christ, though be aware that the small town becomes packed with visitors at this time. Every year in mid-April, the town holds the *Fiesta del Anís y del Vino*, an orgy of *anís*- and wine-tasting. An older annual tradition takes place on July 25, when the feast of St James (*Santiago* in Spanish) is celebrated with a bullfight in the Plaza Mayor.

Practicalities

There is a small **turismo** in the Plaza Mayor (Mon–Fri 10am–6pm, Sat & Sun 11am–3pm & 4–6pm; ☎918 935 323, ⓦwww.ciudad-chinchon.com). If you fancy **staying** you could splash out on the ⌂ *Parador de Chinchón* (☎918 940 836, ⓦwww.paradores.com; ⓞ), in the former Augustinian monastery just off the Plaza Mayor. A more modest but still very pleasant option is the *Hostal Chinchón* (☎918 935 398, ⓦwww.hostalchinchon.com; ❷); it's close to the Plaza Mayor at c/José Antonio 12 and has air conditioning and a pool.

For **food**, try *Mesón del Comendador* (☎918 940 420; closed Wed), one of a cluster of good restaurants serving classic Castilian fare on the Plaza Mayor, or the *Mesón del Duende* (☎918 940 807); both are modestly priced. More expensive is the *Mesón Cuevas del Vino* (☎918 940 206; closed Tues & Aug), in an old olive oil mill at c/Benito Hortelano 13, which has its own *bodega*, while the 🌿 *Casa de Pregonero* (☎918 940 696; closed Tues), again on the Plaza Mayor, adds modern touches to traditional dishes and has some mouthwatering starters and desserts such as *morcilla* with a strawberry-flavoured dressing and mandarin sorbet; reckon on at least €40 a head.

El Escorial and El Valle de los Caídos

Northwest of Madrid, in the foothills of the Sierra de Guadarrama, is one of Spain's best-known and most visited sights – Felipe II's vast monastery-palace complex of **El Escorial**. The vast granite building, which contains a royal palace, a monastery, a mausoleum, 4000 rooms, fifteen cloisters and one of the finest libraries of the Renaissance, embodies all that was important to one of the most powerful rulers in European history. The town around the monastery, **San Lorenzo del Escorial**, is an easy day-trip from Madrid, or if you plan to travel on, rail and road routes continue to Ávila and Segovia. The heart of the **Sierra de Guadarrama** lies just to the north, and is Madrid's easiest mountain escape.

Tours from Madrid to El Escorial often take in **El Valle de los Caídos** (The Valley of the Fallen), 9km north. This is an equally megalomaniac yet far more chilling monument: an underground basilica hewn under Franco's orders, allegedly as a memorial to the Civil War dead of both sides, though in reality as a shrine to the *generalísimo* and his regime.

It's possible to continue on to Ávila in the evening or to just make El Escorial a day-trip from Madrid. Moving on to Segovia by train is a bit trickier as it involves backtracking to Villalba (15min) and hooking up with a Madrid–Segovia train from there.

El Escorial

The monastery of **El Escorial** was the largest Spanish building of the Renaissance: rectangular, overbearing and severe, from the outside it resembles a prison more than a palace. Built between 1563 and 1584 to commemorate the victory over the French at the battle of San Quentin on August 10, 1557 (San Lorenzo's Day), it was originally the creation of Juan Bautista de Toledo, though his one-time assistant, **Juan de Herrera**, took over and is normally given credit for the design. **Felipe II** planned the complex as both monastery and mausoleum, where he would live the life of a monk and "rule the world with two inches of paper". Later monarchs had less ascetic lifestyles, enlarging and richly decorating the palace quarters, but Felipe's simple rooms remain the most fascinating.

There's so much to see that you will need to set out early to do the sight real justice, but despite the size of the task it is still a highly rewarding visit.

Arrival and information

From **Madrid** there are up to 31 **trains** a day (5.45am–11.30pm from Atocha, calling at Chamartín, and up to twelve every weekday going on to Avila), with **buses** (#661 & #664 from the *intercambiador* at Moncloa) running every fifteen minutes on weekdays and hourly at weekends. If you arrive by train, get straight on the local bus that shuttles you up to the centre of town – they leave promptly and it's a long uphill walk. If you're travelling by bus, stay on it and it will take you right up to the monastery. The **turismo** (Mon–Fri 10am–6pm, Sat–Sun 10am–7pm; ℡918 905 313, ⓦwww.sanlorenzoturismo.org) is at c/Grimaldi 4, the small street to the north of the visitors' entrance to the monastery and running into c/Floridablanca.

Accommodation

Most **hotels** are close to the monastery, but in summer it's a favourite retreat from the heat of Madrid, so it's wise to book in advance.

Hotels

El Escorial c/Residencia 14 ℡918 905 924, ⒻF918 900 620. A large 45-room youth hostel situated up on the hill above the monastery. Bed and breakfast €12.50 for over 26's, €8.50 for under 26's. There is another, smaller, hostel down in the park beside the monastery, the *Santa María del Buen Aire* (℡918 903 640, Ⓕ918 903 792), which has a pool and camping space, but it is usually packed with school groups (YH cards needed for both hostels).

Hostal Cristina c/Juan de Toledo 6 ℡918 901 961, ⓦwww.hostalcristina.tk. Old-fashioned and basic, the sixteen-room *Hostal Cristina* tends to be overshadowed by the plush *Hotel Victoria Palace* next door, but is a good-value option. ❸

Hotel Botánico c/Timoteo Padrós 16 ℡918 907 879, ⓦwww.valdesimonte.com. Twenty individually decorated rooms in this plush hotel set in the verdant grounds of a former palace. ❺

Hotel Florida c/Floridablanca 12–14 ℡918 901 520, ⓦwww.hflorida.com. A well-appointed mid-range place, now part of the Best Western chain. There are fifty a/c rooms at €85, or for an extra €16 you get a superior room with views of the monastery. ❹

Hotel Miranda & Suizo c/Floridablanca 18–20 ℡918 904 711, ⓦwww.hotelmirandasuizo.com. A few doors up from the *Florida*, this is a traditional but very comfortable option, with a lively bar and café. ❹

Hotel Parrilla Príncipe c/Mariano Benavente 12 ℡918 901 611, ⓦwww.parrillaprincipe.com. An unflashy, but friendly hotel with a good restaurant located in an eighteenth-century mansion. ❸

Hotel Victoria Palace c/Juan de Toledo 4 ℡918 969 890, ⓦwww.hotelvictoriapalace.com. El Escorial's top hotel with its own pool, views of the monastery and all the facilities you would expect in this category. ❺–❻

Campsite

Caravaning El Escorial Carretera de Guadarrama a El Escorial km 3.5 ℡902 014 900/918 902 412, ⓦwww.campingelescorial.com. A very well-equipped campsite with several swimming pools and three tennis courts situated 6km out on the road back towards Guadarrama. A little noisy during summer weekends.

The monastery

Visits to the **Real Monasterio del Escorial** (Tues–Sun: April–Sept 10am–6pm; Oct–March 10am–5pm; €8, €10 with guided tour; €8.50 combined with monastery and El Valle de los Caídos; free Wed for EU citizens) have become more relaxed in recent years, and you can use your ticket (purchased in the **visitors' entrance**) to enter, in whatever sequence you like, the basilica, sacristy, chapterhouses, library and royal apartments. To escape the worst of the crowds avoid Wednesdays and try visiting just before lunch. For sustenance, you'll find a **cafeteria** near the ticket office; meals are a bit of a rip-off.

The Biblioteca, Patio de los Reyes and Basílica

A good starting point is the west gateway, the traditional **main entrance**, facing the mountains. Above it is a gargantuan statue of San Lorenzo holding the gridiron on which he was martyred.

Within is the splendid **Biblioteca** (**Library**), adorned with shelves designed by Herrera to harmonize with the architecture, and frescoes by Tibaldi and his assistants, showing the seven Liberal Arts. Its collections include the tenth-century *Codex Albeldensis*, St Teresa's personal diary, some gorgeously executed Arabic manuscripts and a Florentine planetarium of 1572 demonstrating the movement of the planets according to the Ptolemaic and Copernican systems.

▲ El Escorial

Beyond is the **Patio de los Reyes**, named after the six statues of the kings of Israel on the facade of the basilica straight ahead. Off to the left is a school, to the right the monastery, both of them still in use.

In the **Basílica**, notice the flat vault of the *coro* above your head as you enter, which is apparently entirely without support, and the white marble Christ carved by Benvenuto Cellini and carried here from Barcelona on workmen's shoulders. The east end is decorated by Italian artists: the sculptures are by the father-and-son team of Leone and Pompeo Leoni, who also carved the two facing groups of Carlos V with his family and Felipe II with three of his wives; Mary Tudor is excluded. The reliquaries near the altar are said to hold the entire bodies of ten saints, plus 144 heads and 306 arms and legs.

The Sacristía, Salas Capitulares and the Panteón Real

The **Sacristía** and **Salas Capitulares** (Chapterhouses) contain many of the monastery's religious treasures, including paintings by Titian, Velázquez and José Ribera. Beside the sacristy a staircase leads down to the **Panteón Real**, the final resting place of all Spanish monarchs since Carlos V, with the exception of Felipe V and Fernando VI. The deceased monarchs lie in exquisite gilded marble tombs: kings (and Isabel II) on one side, their spouses on the other. Just above the entry is the Pudridero Real, a separate room in which the bodies rot for twenty years or so before the cleaned-up skeletons are moved here. The royal children are laid in the **Panteón de los Infantes**; the tomb of Don Juan, Felipe II's bastard half-brother, is grander than any of the kings', while the wedding-cake babies' tomb with room for sixty infants is more than half full.

The Museos Nuevos, Salones Reales and Claustro Grande

What remains of EL Escorial's art collection – works by Bosch, Gerard David, Dürer, Titian, Zurbarán and many others, which escaped transfer to the Prado – is kept in the elegant suite of rooms known as the **Museos**

Nuevos (New Museums). Don't miss the **Sala de las Batallas**, a long gallery lined with an epic series of paintings depicting important imperial battles. Finally, there are the surprisingly modest **Salones Reales** (Royal Apartments) containing the austere **quarters of Felipe II**, with the chair that supported his gouty leg and the deathbed from which he was able to contemplate the high altar of the basilica. If you make a reservation (☏918 905 903; €3.60) for one of the guided tours you can also visit the **Palacio de los Borbones**, the more lavish royal quarters of Felipe's successors that take up the northeastern corner of the complex.

You can also wander at will in some of the El Escorial's courtyards; most notable is the **Claustro Grande**, with frescoes of the Life of the Virgin by Tibaldi, and the secluded gardens of the **Patio de los Evangelistas** which lie within.

Outlying lodges

The **Casita del Príncipe** (aka Casita de Abajo; April–June Sat & Sun, July–Sept Tues–Sun: 10am–1pm & 4–6.30pm; €3.60, free Wed for EU citizens; compulsory tours every 30min for a maximum of 10 people; reservations ☏918 905 903) and the **Casita del Infante** (aka Casita de Arriba; same hours as Casita del Príncipe; €3.40, free Wed for EU citizens) are two eighteenth-century royal lodges, both full of decorative riches, and built by Juan de Villanueva, Spain's most accomplished Neoclassical architect – so worth seeing in themselves as well as for their formal gardens.

The Casita del Infante, which served as the present King Juan Carlos's student digs, is a short way up into the hills and affords a good view of the Escorial complex; follow the road to the left from the main entrance and then stick to the contours of the mountain around to the right – it's well signposted. The Casita del Príncipe, in the Jardines del Príncipe below the monastery, is larger and more worthwhile, with an important collection of Giordano paintings and four pictures made from rice paste.

The Silla de Felipe

Around 3km out of town is the **Silla de Felipe** – "Felipe's Seat" – a chair carved into a rocky outcrop with a great view out towards the palace. His majesty is supposed to have sat here to watch the construction going on. You can reach it on foot by following the path through the arches beyond the main entrance to the monastery by the Biblioteca; keep to the left as you go down the hill and then cross the main road and follow the signs. If you have a car, take the M-505 Ávila road and turn off at the sign after about 3km.

Eating and entertainment

Scattered about town are plenty of small bars, which offer snacks and tapas. For evening entertainment there are several **cinemas**, along with the eighteenth-century **Coliseo** where you'll find jazz and classical **concerts** and theatrical productions year-round. Details of shows can be picked up from the *turismo*, or check out the free weekly *La Semana del Escorial*.

El Charolés c/Floridablanca 24 ☏918 905 975. Renowned for its fish and stews, this restaurant is at the top end of the scale. Expect to pay over €50 a head.

La Cueva c/San Antón 4 ☏918 901 516. An atmospheric wooden-beamed *mesón*, which is a good bet for both tapas and a larger meal (menús at €18 or €30).

La Fonda Genara Plaza de San Lorenzo 2 ☏918 901 636. Enjoyable, low-key place on this lively plaza and inside the *centro coliseo*, which is filled with theatrical mementoes and has a wide-ranging menu of good-quality Castilian fare; expect to pay around €35 per person.

Hotel Parilla Príncipe c/Floridablanca 6 ☏918 901 548. A well-regarded restaurant situated in this small hotel, serving specialities such as roast partridge and goat. Around €35–40. Closed Tues.

Los Pilares c/Juan de Toledo 58 ☎918 961 972. Near the bus station, *Los Pilares* specializes in recreating dishes from the era of Felipe II, such as capon and bean stew, and will cost around €40 per person.

Restaurante Alaska Plaza San Lorenzo 4 ☎918 904 365. Offering Castilian meat specialities, a very good-value €12 *menú* and a more sophisticated special one at €36.

El Valle de los Caídos

The entrance to **El Valle de los Caídos** (Valley of the Fallen) lies 9km north of El Escorial: from here a road (along which you are not allowed to stop) runs 6km to the underground basilica. Above it is a vast 150-metre-high cross, reputedly the largest in the world, and visible far along the road to Segovia. To visit El Valle de los Caídos from El Escorial, you can get a local bus run by Herranz, which starts from the office in Plaza de la Virgen de Gracía, just north of the visitors' entrance to the monastery. The bus runs from El Escorial at 3.15pm, returning at 5.30pm (Tues–Sun; €8 return including entrance to the monument; ☎918 969 028).

The **basilica complex** (Tues–Sun: April–Sept 10am–7pm; Oct–March 10am–6pm; €5, combined ticket with El Escorial €8.50 or €11 guided, free Wed for EU citizens) denies its claims of memorial "to the Civil War dead of both sides" almost at a glance. The debased and grandiose architectural forms employed, the grim martial statuary, the constant inscriptions "Fallen for God and for Spain" and the proximity to El Escorial intimate its true function: the glorification of General Franco and his regime. The dictator himself lies buried behind the high altar, while the only other named tomb, marked simply "José Antonio", is that of his guru, the Falangist leader José Antonio Primo de Rivera, who was shot dead by Republicans at the beginning of the war. The "other side" is present only in the fact that the complex was built by the Republican army's survivors – political prisoners on quarrying duty. It remains a controversial site, although the present government has tried to depoliticize it by passing a law that prevents its use by Falangist supporters keen to glorify the Franco era.

From the entrance, a shaky funicular (Tues–Sun: April–Sept 11am–1.30pm & 4–6pm; Oct–March 11am–1.30pm & 3–5.30pm; €2.50 return) ascends to the base of the **cross**, offering a superlative view over the Sierra de Guadarrama and a closer look at the giant figures propping up the base of the cross.

The Sierra de Guadarrama

The routes from Madrid and El Escorial to Segovia strike through the heart of the **Sierra de Guadarrama**, and it is a beautiful journey. The road is occasionally marred by suburban development, especially around **Navacerrada**, Madrid's main ski station, but from the train it's almost entirely unspoilt. There are plenty of opportunities for walking, but make sure you buy the appropriate maps in Madrid.

If you want to base yourself in the mountains for a while you'd do best to head for **Cercedilla**, 75 minutes by train on the Madrid–Segovia line – and a little way off the main road. Alternatively, over to the east, there is **Manzanares el Real**, with an odd medieval castle and a reservoir-side setting.

In the shadow of the mountains to the north lies the Valle de Lozoya. At the western end are the village of **Rascafría** and the nearby Benedictine monastery of El Paular, and to the east the old fortified town of **Buitrago** with a medieval core and small Picasso museum.

For information about the region as a whole consult the **website** ⓦwww .sierranorte.com.

Cercedilla and the Puerto de Navacerrada

CERCEDILLA is an alpine-looking village perched at the foot of the valley leading up to the Puerto de Fuenfría and makes an excellent base for summer walking. It is much frequented by *madrileños* at weekends, but has the advantage of being accessible by **train** from Madrid (over 20 daily, 6am–11pm from Atocha, calling at Chamartín, and 9 daily going on to Segovia) and buses leaving every half-hour from the Intercambiador de Autobuses de Moncloa. **Accommodation** is limited to the *Hostal El Aribel*, near the station at c/Emilio Serrano 71 (ⓣ918 521 511; ❷); the stylish *Luces del Poniente* at c/Lina de Ávila 4 (ⓣ918 525 587, ⓦwww.lucesdelponiente.com; ❹–❺); and two youth hostels: *Villa Castora* (ⓣ918 520 334, ⓕ918 522 411), which is close to the town and has a pool, and, 2km up the road in the meadows leading up to Fuenfría, *Las Dehesas* (ⓣ918 520 135, ⓕ918 521 836). At both a YH card is needed (€12 for over 26's, €8.50 for under 26's). Places to **eat** include *Los Frutales* on the Carretera de las Dehesas, which does good *croquetas, judías con perdiz* (partridge and beans) and *trucha* (trout); the train station has a restaurant on the first floor; or you could try the restaurant at *Hostal El Aribel*.

The village is the starting point for a very pleasant five-hour round-trip **walk** along the pine-fringed Calzada Romana (old Roman road) up to the Puerto de la Fuenfría (1796m), with its striking views down into Segovia province. Follow the signs up to *Las Dehesas*, where there is an **information centre** (daily 9am–6pm; ⓣ918 522 213), which provides maps and advice on this and other walks in the area. Then head past the meadows and follow the clearly indicated path up to the Puerto.

From Cercedilla, you can embark on a wonderful little train ride to the **Puerto de Navacerrada**, the most important pass in the mountains and the heart of the ski area, or a little farther on to **Cotos** where a number of well-maintained walks around the **Parque Natural de Peñalara** (ⓦwww .parquenaturalpenalara.org) begin. The train runs hourly over weekends and holidays and passes through the *parque natural*, an extension of the upper Manzanares basin: watch out for roe deer and wild boar. In winter it is possible to ski in both Navacerrada and Cotos, but be prepared for long queues and traffic jams at weekends.

Navacerrada is also the starting point for a number of impressive walks along the **high peaks**, while Cotos is the gateway to the highest peak in the Sierra, Peñalara (2430m). It can be reached in about four hours, but is a tough ascent. Less challenging but very enjoyable is the easy hike to the Laguna Grande. There is a small **information booth** just above the small café close to the Cotos train station that will give advice on all routes (summer Mon–Fri 10am–6pm, Sat, Sun & hols 10am–8pm; winter daily 10am–6pm; ⓣ918 520 857).

El Paular and Rascafría

Some 10km below Cotos in the beautiful Valle de Lozoya stands the **Monasterio de Santa María de El Paular**, originally a Carthusian monastery founded at the end of the fourteenth century, and now home to a handful of Benedictine monks who provide guided tours (in Spanish only) of the silent cloisters and the main church (Mon–Sat noon, 1pm & 5pm, Sun 1pm, 4pm &

5pm; free). Part of the monastery has been turned into a *parador*-style hotel, ⚐ *Santa María de El Paular* (☎918 691 011, ⓦwww.hotelsantamariapaular.com; ❻), with a delightful courtyard bar, ideal for cool summer refreshments. Nearby is the pleasant little mountain village of **Rascafría**, where you'll find plenty of **accommodation** and a bus link back to Madrid (twice daily, 2hr 15min). The twelve-room *Los Calizos* (☎918 691 112; ⓦwww.loscalizos.com; ❻) is a tranquil hotel with a fine restaurant and extensive grounds a little way out on the road to Miraflores. The *Hostal Rosali* (☎918 691 213, ⓦwww.hotelrosali.com; ❷) is a cheaper but very cosy option closer to town and also has some apartments.

Manzanares El Real and La Pedriza

Some 50km north of Madrid, on the shores of the Santillana *embalse* (reservoir), lies **Manzanares El Real**, a town which in former times was disputed between the capital and Segovia. Nowadays, it's geared to Madrid weekenders, whose villas dot the surrounding landscape. The one attraction is the **castle** (Tues–Fri 10am–4pm, Sat & Sun 10am–6pm; €3; dramatized visits at noon and 1pm at weekends €6), which despite its eccentric appearance is a perfectly genuine fifteenth-century construction, built around an earlier chapel. It was soon modified into a palace by the architect Juan Guas, who built an elegant gallery on the south side and false machicolations on the other, and studded the tower with stones resembling cannonballs. The interior has been heavily restored, but it makes for an interesting visit.

Nearby is the ruggedly beautiful **La Pedriza**, a spur of the Sierra de Guadarrama that has been declared a regional park (access limited to 350 cars a day at weekends; free; information centre open daily 10am–6pm; ☎918 539 978). There are some enjoyable walks, as well as some much-revered technical climbs, notably the ascent to the jagged Peña del Diezmo. The park is also home to a very large colony of griffon vultures.

Buses from Madrid run hourly (daily 7.30am–9.30pm) from Plaza de Castilla. **Accommodation** is limited to the nine-room *Hostal Tranco* (☎918 530 423; ❷) and the more upmarket *Hotel Parque Real* (☎918 539 912, ⓦwww .hotelparquereal.com; ❸). However, there is usually space at one of the two **campsites**, *El Ortigal* (☎918 530 120), at the foot of La Pedriza and close to the park on c/Montañeros, or the well-equipped *La Fresneda* (☎&ⓕ918 476 523) on the Carretera M608 towards Soto del Real. **Food** is not cheap here, but you'll have a good meal at *Los Arcos* in c/Real, the *Restaurante Parra* in c/Panaderos and *Asador del Carmen* in the *urbanización* Lago Santillana.

Buitrago de Lozoya and Patones

Farther east, beyond the road to Burgos, lies the attractive little town of **Buitrago de Lozoya** (13 buses daily from Plaza de Castilla in Madrid), a fortified settlement with defensive walls that date from the twelfth century, a fine Mudéjar church (daily 9am–2pm & 4–8pm) and, more surprisingly, a small **Picasso museum** (Tues, Thurs & Fri 11am–1.45pm & 4–6pm, Wed 11am–1.45pm, Sat 10am–2pm & 4–7pm, Sun 10am–2pm; free). The collection, based on work donated by the artist to his friend and local barber Eugenio Arias, features an interesting selection of sixty minor pieces dating from between 1948 and 1972.

Nearby on the southern edge of the so-called Sierra Pobre is the picturesque mountain village of **Patones de Arriba** (three buses daily to nearby Patones Abajo from Plaza de Castilla), abandoned in the 1930s but since restored and now a fashionable weekend destination for many *madrileños* who head for a Castilian roast lunch at one of the *mesones* or even stay the night at the luxury boutique hotel *El Tiempo Perdido* (☎918 432 152, ⓦwww.eltiempoperdido .com; ⑥) being refurbished and likely to reopen only at weekends and on fiestas. The black slate architecture of the village is undeniably beautiful, the views are good, and you can be assured of a fine meal, but there is little else to detain the casual visitor. The village is closed to cars, so you will need to leave vehicles in the car park in Patones de Abajo and walk the 2.5km up the signposted path.

Ávila

Two things distinguish **ÁVILA**: its eleventh-century **walls**, two perfectly preserved kilometres of which surround the old town, and the mystic writer **Santa Teresa**, who was born here and whose shrines are a major focus of religious pilgrimage. Set on a high plain, with the peaks of the Sierra de Gredos behind, the town is quite a sight, especially if you approach with the evening sun highlighting the golden tone of the walls and the details of the 88 towers.

Arrival and information

From Madrid (Chamartín station) there are around 25 **trains** a day to Ávila; **buses** are less frequent (Estación del Sur; 8 on weekdays, 4 at weekends). The train station is a fifteen-minute walk to the east of the old town, and a local bus connects it with Plaza de la Victoria, a little west of the cathedral. On foot, follow the broad Paseo de la Estación to its end, by the large church of Santa Ana, and bear left up c/Duque de Alba to reach Plaza Santa Teresa. Buses use a terminal on the Avenida de Madrid, a little closer in: walking from here, cross the small park opposite, then turn right up c/Duque de Alba, or take a local bus to Plaza de la Victoria. **Driving**, follow signs for the walls (*murallas*) or the *parador* and you should be able to park just outside the old town.

The main **turismo** (daily: summer 9am–8pm, Fri & Sat till 9pm; winter 9am–2pm & 5–8pm; ☎920 211 387, ⓦwww.turismocastillayleon.com) is at Plaza de Pedro de Davila 4, and there's a **visitors' centre** (daily: summer 9am–8pm; winter 9am–2pm & 5–8pm; ☎920 225 969, ⓦwww.avilaturismo.com) just beyond the Basílica de San Vicente at Avda. de Madrid 39.

Accommodation

There are numerous cheap *hostales* around the train station and along Avenida José Antonio, but you should be able to find something nearer the walled centre of town.

Las Cancelas c/Cruz Vieja 6 ☎920 212 249, ⓦwww.lascancelas.com. Converted fifteenth-century building. Some of the fourteen a/c rooms have good views of the cathedral and walls. There's a good bar and a nice patio restaurant, too. ❹

Duperier Avda. de Juventud s/n ☎920 221 716. A small youth hostel (with 11pm curfew) out past the monastery, near the local swimming pool. Rooms with bath and meals are available. Open July to mid-Sept. A YH card is needed; €11.60 for over-30, €8.50 under-30.

Hospedería La Sinagoga c/Reyes Católicos 22 ☎920 352 321, ⓦwww .lasinagoga.net. As the name suggests, this marvellous little 21-room hotel was a synagogue in the fifteenth century. Modern, comfortable and good-value rooms in a tastefully restored and atmospheric building. ❹

Hostal Bellas c/Caballeros 19 ☎920 212 910, ⓦwww.hostalbellas.com. Eager-to-please owners run this centrally located *hostal*. Most rooms have showers and there are discounts out of season. ❷

ÁVILA

Segovia (N110) ▲   ▲ Train Station   ▲ Madrid (C505)

◀ Convento de la Encarnación

Parque de San Antonio

Gobierno Civil

Bus Station

Jardín del Recreo

Monasterio de Santa Ana

Convento de las Gordillas

Convento de San José

Ermita de Ntra. Sra. de las Vacas

Santa María de la Antigua

Basílica de San Vicente

Museo Provincial

Santo Tomé el Viejo

San Pedro

Puerta de los Leales

Palacio de los Serrano

Convento de la Concepción

San Andrés

Palacio de los Verdugo

Puerta de S. Vicente

Palacio de los Valderrábanos

Catedral

Palacio de los Valderrábanos

Convento de Ntra. Sra. de Gracia

San Martín

Puerta del Mariscal

Palacio de los Águila

Palacio de los Dávila

Puerta del Alcázar

Ermita de Santa María de la Cabeza

Capilla de Mosén Rubí

Ayuntamiento

San Juan

Puerta del Rastro

Santiago

Puerta del Carmen

Palacio de los Polentinos

Torreón de los Guzmanes

Parque del Rastro

San Nicolás

San Esteban

Casa de los Superunda

Convento Santa Teresa

Puerta de Sta. Teresa

Palacio de los Núñez-Vela

Puerta del Puente

Ermita de San Segundo

Puente Romano

Río Adaja

▶ Toledo (N403)

◀ Cáceres

◀ ① Los Cuatro Postes & Salamanca (N 501)

▶ ② Monasterio de Santo Tomás, Museo Oriental & ③

N

100 m

ACCOMMODATION
Las Cancelas   I
Duperier   J
Hospedería La Sinagoga   H
Hostal Bellas   B
Hostal Don Diego   F
Hostería de Bracamonte   C
Palacio de Valderrábanos   E
Palacio de los Velada   D
Parador Raimundo de Borgoña   A

EATING & DRINKING
El Almacén   2
Bar El Rincón   3
Las Cancelas   I
Casa Patas   6
La Casona   5
Hostería de Bracamonte   C
El Molino de la Losa   1
La Posada de la Fruta   4

Hostal Don Diego c/Marqués de Canales y Chozas 5 ☎ 920 255 475, ⓕ 920 254 549. A friendly, very good-value *hostal* just opposite the *parador*. All thirteen rooms have bath or shower. ❸

Hostal San Juan c/Comuneros de Castilla 3 ☎ 920 251 475, ⓦ www.hostalsanjuanavila.com. There are thirteen comfortable, pine-furnished double rooms with bathrooms in this pleasant *hostal* in the centre of the old town. ❷

Hostería de Bracamonte c/Bracamonte 6 ☎ 920 251 280, ⓦ www.hospederiadebracamonte.com. An atmospheric and attractive hotel, between the city walls and the Plaza de la Victoria, created from a number of converted Renaissance mansions. It has a decent restaurant but rooms have no a/c. ❷–❸

Palacio de Valderrábanos Plaza de la Catedral 9 ☎ 920 211 023, ⓦ www.palaciovalderrabanoshotel .com. This former bishop's palace beats the *parador* for ambience and its rooms are just as good. ❹–❺

Palacio de los Velada Plaza de la Catedral 10 ☎ 920 255 100, ⓦ www.veladahoteles.com. A beautifully converted sixteenth-century palace and the priciest hotel in town, but look out for deals that can bring the price down to around €100. ❺

Parador Raimundo de Borgoña c/Marqués de Canales y Chozas 2 ☎ 920 211 340, ⓦ www .paradores.com. A converted fifteenth-century mansion – not the most exciting *parador* in Spain, but pleasant enough, with the usual comforts. ❺

The Town

Ávila's walls make orientation straightforward, with the **cathedral** and most other sights contained within. Just outside the southeast corner of the walls is the city's main square, **Plaza Santa Teresa**, and the most imposing of the old gates, the **Puerta del Alcázar**. Within the walls, the old market square, **Plaza de la Victoria**, fronts the *ayuntamiento* at the heart of the old city.

Santa Teresa in Ávila

The obvious place to start a tour of Teresa's Ávila is the **Convento de Santa Teresa** (daily 9am–1pm & 3.30–8.30pm; free), built over the saint's birthplace just inside the south gate of the old town and entered off the Paseo del Rastro. Most of the convent remains *de clausura* but you can see the very spot where she was born, now an elaborate chapel in the Baroque church, which is decorated with scenes of the saint demonstrating her powers of levitation to various august bodies. In a small reliquary (daily 9.30am–1.30pm & 3.30–7.30pm; free), beside the gift shop, is a **museum** (daily: summer 10am–2pm & 4–7pm; winter 10am–1.30pm & 3.30–5.30pm; €2) containing memorials of Teresa's life, including not only her rosary beads, but also one of the fingers she used to count them with.

Santa Teresa de Ávila

Santa Teresa (1515–82) was born to a noble family in Ávila and from childhood began to experience visions and religious raptures. Her religious career began at the Carmelite convent of La Encarnación, where she was a nun for 27 years. From this base, she went on to reform the movement and found convents throughout Spain. She was an ascetic, but her appeal lay in the mystic sensuality of her experience of Christ, as revealed in her autobiography, for centuries a bestseller in Spain. As joint patron saint of Spain (together with Santiago), she remains a central pillar in Spanish Catholicism and schoolgirls are brought into Ávila by the busload to experience first-hand the life of the woman they are supposed to emulate. She died in Alba de Tormes just outside Salamanca, and the Carmelite convent, which contains the remains of her body and a dubious reconstruction of the cell in which she passed away, is another major target of pilgrimage. On a more bizarre note, one of Santa Teresa's mummified hands has now been returned to Ávila after spending the Franco years by the bedside of the dictator.

Heading through the old town, and leaving by the Puerta del Carmen, you can follow a lane, c/Encarnación, to the **Monasterio de la Encarnación** (summer: Mon–Fri 9.30am–1pm & 4–6pm, Sat & Sun 10am–1pm & 4–6pm; winter Mon–Fri 9.30am–1.30pm & 3.30–6pm, Sat & Sun 10am–1.30pm & 4–6pm; €1.50). Teresa lived here for much of the time between 1535 and 1574; each room is labelled with an act she performed, while everything she might have touched or looked at is on display. A small museum section also provides a reasonable introduction to the saint's life, with maps showing the convents, and a selection of her sayings – the pithiest, perhaps, "Life is a night in a bad hotel."

A third Teresan sight lies a couple of blocks east of the Plaza de Santa Teresa. This is the **Convento de San José** (daily: summer 10am–1.30pm & 4–7pm; winter 10am–1.30pm & 3–6pm; €1), the first monastery that the saint founded, in 1562. Its museum contains relics and memorabilia, including the coffin in which Teresa once slept. The tomb of her brother Lorenzo is in the larger of the two churches.

Lastly, you might want to make your way up to **Los Cuatro Postes**, a little four-posted shrine, 1.5km along the Salamanca road west of town and a fine vantage point from which to admire the walls of the town. It was here, aged 7, that the infant Teresa was recaptured by her uncle, running away with her brother to seek Christian martyrdom fighting the Moors.

The cathedral

Ávila's **Catedral** (summer Mon–Fri 10am–7.30pm, Sat 10am–8pm, Sun noon–6.30pm; winter Mon–Fri 10am–5pm, Sat 10am–6pm, Sun noon–5pm; last tickets given out 45min before closing; €4) was started in the twelfth century but has never been finished, as evidenced by the missing tower above the main entrance. The earliest Romanesque parts were as much fortress as church, and the apse actually forms an integral part of the city walls.

Inside, the succeeding changes of style are immediately apparent; the **Roman-esque** parts are made of a strange red-and-white mottled stone, then there's an abrupt break and the rest of the main structure is pure white stone with **Gothic** forms. Although the proportions are exactly the same, this newer half of the cathedral seems infinitely more spacious. The *coro*, whose elaborate carved back you see as you come in, and two chapels in the left aisle, are **Renaissance** additions. Here you can admire the elaborate marble tomb of a fifteenth-century bishop known as El Tostado (the "toasted" or "swarthy"), while the thirteenth-century *sacristía* with its star-shaped cupola and gold inlay decor, and the treasury-museum with its monstrous silver *custodía* and ancient religious images are also worth a visit.

Basilíca de San Vicente and San Pedro

The **Basilíca de San Vicente** (Mon–Sat, summer: 10am–6.30pm; winter 10am–1pm & 4–6.30pm; €1.60) marks the site where San Vicente was martyred, and his tomb narrates the gruesome story of torture and execution by the Romans. Legend has it that following the martyrdom a rich Jew who had been poking fun at the martyrs was enveloped and suffocated by a great serpent that miraculously emerged from the rocks. On the verge of asphyxiation he repented and converted to Christianity, later building the church on the very same site, and he, too, is said to be buried here. In the crypt you can see part of the rocky crag where San Vicente and his sisters were executed and from which the serpent later supposedly appeared. Like the cathedral, the building is a mixture of architectural styles. The warm pink glow of the sandstone of the church is a

▲ Ávila city walls

characteristic feature of Ávila, also notable in the church of **San Pedro** (daily 10.30am–noon & 7–8pm), on Plaza de Santa Teresa.

The city walls and around

The walls were built under Alfonso VI, following his capture of the city from the Moors in 1090; they took his Muslim prisoners nine years to construct. At closer quarters, they prove a bit of a facade, as the old city within is sparsely populated and a little dishevelled, most of modern life having moved into the new developments outside the fortifications. It's possible to walk along the **city walls** from Puerta del Alcázar to Puerta del Rastro (summer daily 10am–8pm; winter Tues–Sat 11am–6pm; €3.50); the view of the town is stunning. There have been some experiments with night-time opening in the summer (usually 10pm–12.30am Sun–Wed), but check with the *turismo*. Tickets are available from the green kiosk by the Puerta del Alcázar.

Just outside the city walls, through the Puerta del Peso de la Harina, is the small **Museo Provincial**, housed in the sixteenth-century Palacio de los Deanes (Tues–Sat 10am–2pm & 5–8pm; winter 4–7pm; Sun 10am–2pm; €1.20, free Sat & Sun) where the cathedral's deans once lived. Today, its eclectic exhibits include collections of archeological remains, ceramics, agricultural implements and traditional costumes, as well as some fine Romanesque statues and a wonderful fifteenth-century triptych depicting the Life of Christ. The ticket also allows you entry to the museum storeroom in the church of Santo Tomé El Viejo just opposite.

The **Monasterio de Santo Tomás** (daily 10am–1pm & 4–8pm; €3; closed Feb 1–6, Oct 15 & Dec 25) is a fifteen-minute walk south of the old city. Established by the Reyes Católicos Fernando and Isabel in the later fifteenth century, the monastery is set around three cloisters and contains a fine carved Gothic choir in the main church. Within are the tombs of Don Juan, the only son of the Reyes Católicos, and Isabel's confessor and later head of the Inquisition Torquemada. Alongside is the **Museo Oriental** (same hours as monastery except closed on Mon & Tues mornings in summer; €3), which contains memorabilia brought back from the Far East by Dominican missionaries.

Eating and drinking

Ávila has a decent if unexceptional array of **bars** and **restaurants**, some of them sited just outside the walls. **Local specialities** include the Castilian *cordero asado* (roast lamb), *judias del barco con chorizo* (haricot beans with sausage), *mollejas* (cow's stomach) and *yemas de Santa Teresa* (candied egg-yolk) – the last of these sold in confectioners all over town. For **nightlife** head outside the city walls to c/Capitán Peña where the strip of four *bares de copas* next to each other keeps the walking to a minimum.

El Almacén Ctra Salamanca 6 ☎920 254 455. One of the best restaurants in the province situated in a former storehouse across the river, close to Los Cuatro Postes, with great views of the city walls. It serves quality meat and fish dishes with a creative touch and excellent desserts, and boasts a lengthy wine list. But somewhat overpriced at around €50 a head. Closed Sun eve & Mon.

Bar El Rincón Plaza Zurraquín 6. To the north of Plaza de la Victoria, this bar serves a generous three-course *menú* for around €10.

Las Cancelas c/Cruz Vieja 6 ☎920 212 249. Next to the cathedral and in the hotel of the same name, this friendly restaurant is popular with locals and serves some great *cordero asado* (roast lamb). Á la carte will cost around €35.

Casa Patas c/San Millán 4. A pleasant bar, with good tapas, and a little *comedor* (evenings only), near the church of San Pedro. Closed Wed & Sept.

La Casona Plaza de Pedro Dávila 6 ☎920 256 139. Popular restaurant specializing in lamb, with *menús* starting at around €10.

Hostería de Bracamonte c/Bracamonte 6 ☎920 251 280. A comfy, rustic atmosphere reigns in this restaurant housed within the walls of a converted Renaissance mansion. The speciality is *cordero asado*. Closed Tues.

El Molino de la Losa c/Bajada de la Losa 12 ☎920 211 101. A converted fifteenth-century mill out by Los Cuatro Postes, with a deserved reputation and handy if you're with kids (there's a play area in the garden). Expect to pay around €50. Closed Mon & mid-Oct to mid-March.

La Posada de la Fruta Plaza de Pedro Dávila 8 ☎920 254 702. With an attractive, sunny, covered courtyard, this is a nice place for a drink, and also serves some good standard Castilian fare with a good-value €12 *menú*.

The Sierra de Gredos

The **Sierra de Gredos** continues the line of the Sierra de Guadarrama, enclosing Madrid to the north and west. A major mountain range, with peaks in excess of 2500m, Gredos offers the best trekking in central Spain, including high-level routes across the passes, as well as more casual walks around the villages.

By bus, the easiest access is from Madrid to **Arenas de San Pedro**, from where you can explore the range, and then move on west into the valley of La Vera in Extremadura. If you have your own transport, you could head into the range south from Ávila along the N502, and you might prefer to base yourself in one of the villages on the north side of the range, along the **Tormes valley** such as Hoyos del Espino or Navarredonda and explore circular walks from there. The *casas rurales* that are scattered throughout the villages often make a good base, especially if you are travelling in a group (information line ☎902 424 141, ⓦwww.casasgredos.com and ⓦwww.gredos.com).

Arenas de San Pedro and Mombeltran

ARENAS DE SAN PEDRO is a sizeable town with a somewhat prettified fifteenth-century castle and a Gothic church. The main reason to stop here is

Walks in the Gredos

The two classic walks in the Gredos are best approached from the so-called **Plataforma**, at the end of a twelve-kilometre stretch of paved road running from the village of Hoyos del Espino (see opposite), where you can purchase detailed maps of the area. You could also reach this point by walking up from El Hornillo or El Arenal on the southern side of the range, although it makes for a tougher challenge.

Circo de Laguna Grande

The **Circo de Laguna Grande** is the centrepiece of the Gredos range, with its highest peak, Almanzor (2593m), surrounded by pinnacles sculpted into utterly improbable shapes. The path begins at the car park at the end of the road coming from Hoyos and climbs towards the high Pozas meadow. From there you can reach the large glacial lake at the end of the valley, a spectacular two-hour walk that winds its way down the slopes on a well-defined path. The route is best done in late spring, summer or early autumn, as snow makes it a treacherous walk in winter.

Circo de las Cinco Lagunas

For a tougher and much longer route – the **Circo de las Cinco Lagunas** – you can continue on from the Laguna Grande, where there is a *refugio* and camping area, to the Cinco Lagunas (allow 8hr from the Plataforma). Take the signposted path to the right just before the lake, which follows an old hunting route used by Alfonso XIII, up to the Portilla del Rey pass. From there you will be able to look down on the lakes – which are reached along a sharp, scree-laden descent. The drop is amply rewarded by virtual solitude, even in midsummer, and sightings of *Capra pyrenaica victoriae*, the graceful (and almost tame) Gredos mountain goat. There are also species of salamanders and toads found only in the area. It is another four to five hours on to the village of Navalperal de Tormes, which is 14km west of Hoyos del Espino.

---

to make your way up to the villages of **EL HORNILLO** and **El ARENAL**, respectively 6km and 9km to the north, the trailheads for **walks** up to the Gredos watershed. There are no buses but it's a pleasant walk up from Arenas to El Arenal on a track running between the road and the river – start out past the sports centre and swimming pool in Arenas.

Pleasant **accommodation** options include the three-star *Hostería Los Galayos* (T&F 920 371 379, W www.losgalayos.com; ❷–❸), which also has a reliable restaurant; the rustic *Posada de la Triste Condesa* (T 920 372 567; ❸) with three roomy doubles; the more basic *Hostal Castillo* (T 920 370 091; ❶); and the cosy *El Canchal* (T 920 370 958, W www.elcanchal.com; ❸). If you haven't already obtained **maps** of Gredos, you can pick up a functional pamphlet from the **turismo** (Mon–Fri 9.30am–1.30pm & 4.30–7.30pm, Sat 9.30am–1.30pm; T 920 372 368, W www.aytoarenas.com) on the main street c/Triste Condesa.

MOMBELTRÁN, 12km north (an enjoyable, mainly downhill, walk from Arenas), is an attractive alternative stop, with its fifteenth-century **castle** of the dukes of Albuquerque set against a stunning mountain backdrop. The village has one **hostal**, the *Marji* (T 920 386 031; ❸), while 4km south of the centre towards Arenas de San Pedro is the *Prados Abiertos hostal* (T 920 386 131; ❶) with a **campsite** and pool alongside.

The Tormes valley

On the north side of Gredos is the beautiful Tormes valley, which enjoys spectacular views across to the highest peaks in the range. The village of

HOYOS DEL ESPINO, 20km west along the AV941, makes a good base, as there are several places to stay, a few decent bars, and shops where you can stock up on supplies. *Aparthotel Gredos* (☎920 349 252 or 653 161 069, Ⓦwww .apartahotelgredos.com) offers studio apartments for two or three at €50 and for four to six people at €75. On the outskirts of the village is the wonderful 🍴 *Hotel Milano Real* (☎920 349 108, Ⓦwww.elmilanoreal.com; ⑤), which has thirteen comfortable doubles and eight suites (€187). It also has a high-quality restaurant with an excellent gourmet menu at €40 and a *menú de degustación* at €58. A riverside **campsite**, *Camping Gredos*, is on the road towards the Plataforma (☎920 207 585; Easter to mid-Oct) by the Puente del Duque.

A few kilometres to the east is **Navarredonda**, another good base from which to explore the area. **Accommodation** includes a youth hostel (☎920 348 005; €11.60, €8.50 under 30; YH card needed) with a pool, a very pleasant campsite, *Camping Navagredos* (☎920 207 476; May–Sept), an atmospheric *casa rural*, the 🍴 *Casa de Arriba* (☎920 348 024, Ⓦwww.casadearriba .com; ④), and Spain's first ever *parador* at km 43 on the AV941 (☎920 348 048, Ⓦwww.paradores.com; ⑤), which has undergone a major refurbishment programme and enjoys some great views across the mountains.

Segovia and around

After Toledo, **SEGOVIA** is the outstanding trip from Madrid. A relatively small city, strategically sited on a rocky ridge, it is deeply and haughtily Castilian, with a panoply of squares and mansions from its days of Golden Age grandeur, when it was a royal resort and a base for the Cortes (parliament). It was in Segovia that Isabel la Católica was proclaimed queen of Castile in 1474.

For a city of its size, there are a stunning number of outstanding architectural monuments. Most celebrated are the **Roman aqueduct**, the **cathedral** and the fairy-tale **Alcázar**, but the less obvious attractions – the cluster of ancient churches and the many mansions found in the lanes of the old town, all in a warm, honey-coloured stone – are what really make it worth a visit. Just a few kilometres outside the city and reasonably accessible from Segovia are two Bourbon palaces, **La Granja** and **Riofrío**, while routes to the north, towards the Río Duero and Castilla y León, run past a succession of mighty **castles**.

Arrival and information

Well connected by road and rail, Segovia is easily accessible from Madrid. The **high-speed train** from Chamartín (return tickets from €16.20) takes just 35minutes, though the train station is quite a way out of town (take the #11 bus, which goes to the aqueduct every 15min). If you take a **regional train** it will take you a lot longer (1hr 50min–2hr) but it goes to the old station nearer to the centre (then take bus #8). There are regular **buses** from Madrid (operated by La Sepulvedana, Paseo de la Florida 11; Ⓜ Príncipe Pío) that drop you at the **bus station** to the west of the aqueduct.

There are two main **turismos** in Segovia, a regional one at Plaza Mayor 10 (summer Mon–Thurs & Sun 9am–8pm, Fri & Sat 9am–9pm; winter 9am–2pm & 5–8pm; ☎921 460 334, Ⓦwww.turismocastillayleon.com) and a visitors' reception office run by the local council in the busy Plaza de Azoguejo (Mon–Fri & Sun 10am–7pm, Sat 10am–8pm; ☎921 466 720, Ⓦwww.turismodesegovia.com) just beneath the aqueduct. There is an **internet café** close by at c/Teodosio Garcia 10 (Mon–Sat 9am–11pm).

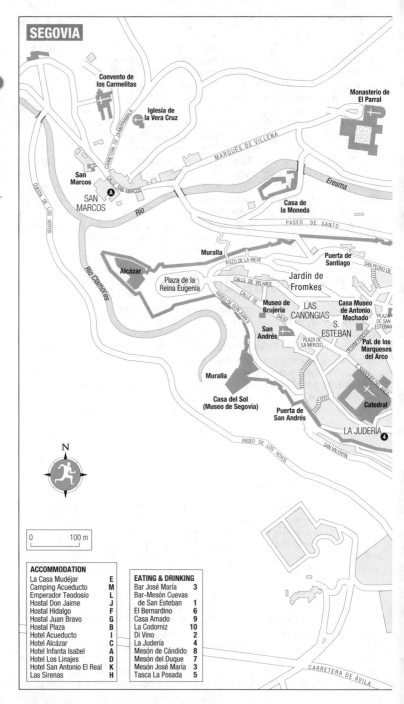

SEGOVIA

Convento de
los Carmelitas

Iglesia de
la Vera Cruz

Monasterio de
El Parral

MARQUÉS DE VILLENA

Eresma

CARRETERA DE ZAMARRAMALA

CALLE SAN MARCOS

San
Marcos
Ⓐ

SAN
MARCOS

Río

CUESTA DE LOS HOYOS

Casa de
la Moneda

PASEO DE SANTO

Muralla

Río Clamores

Alcázar

POZO DE LA NIEVE

Puerta de
Santiago

SAN PEDRO DE

Plaza de la
Reina Eugenia

CALLE DE VELARDE

Jardín de
Fromkes

CALLE DE

PASEO DE DON JUAN II

DAOIZ

Museo de
Brujería

San
Andrés

LAS
CANONGIAS

S.
ESTEBAN

PLAZA DE
LA MERCED

Casa Museo
de Antonio
Machado

PLAZA
DE SAN
ESTEBAN

DESAMPARADOS

Pal. de los
Marqueses
del Arco

C. MARQUÉS DEL ARCO

Muralla

Casa del Sol
(Museo de Segovia)

Puerta de
San Andrés

PASEO DE LOS HOYOS

SAN VALENTÍN

Catedral

LA JUDERÍA
❹

N

0   100 m

CARRETERA DE ÁVILA

ACCOMMODATION
La Casa Mudéjar	E
Camping Acueducto	M
Emperador Teodosio	L
Hostal Don Jaime	J
Hostal Hidalgo	F
Hostal Juan Bravo	G
Hostal Plaza	B
Hotel Acueducto	I
Hotel Alcázar	C
Hotel Infanta Isabel	A
Hotel Los Linajes	D
Hotel San Antonio El Real	K
Las Sirenas	H

EATING & DRINKING
Bar José María	3
Bar-Mesón Cuevas de San Esteban	1
El Bernardino	6
Casa Amado	9
La Codorniz	10
Di Vino	2
La Judería	4
Mesón de Cándido	8
Mesón del Duque	7
Mesón José María	3
Tasca La Posada	5

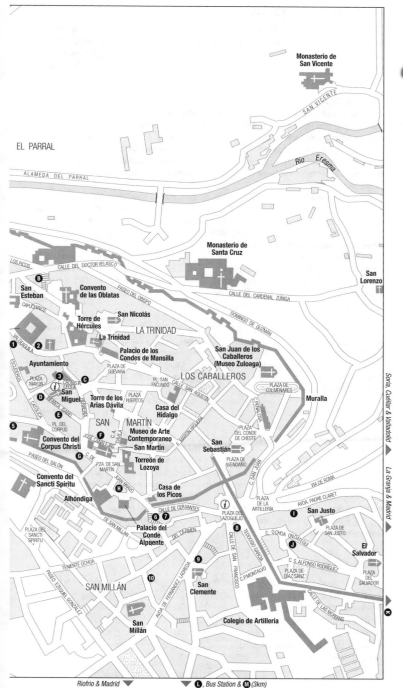

EL PARRAL

Monasterio de
San Vicente

Río Eresma

ALAMEDA DEL PARRAL

Monasterio de
Santa Cruz

San
Lorenzo

LOS PICOS

CALLE DEL DOCTOR VELASCO

B

San
Esteban

Convento
de las Oblatas

PASEO DEL OBISPO

CALLE DEL CARDENAL ZUÑIGA

CAPUCHINOS

Torre de
Hércules

San Nicolás

DOMINGO DE GUZMAN

LA TRINIDAD

1   2

La Trinidad

Palacio de los
Condes de Mansilla

San Juan de los
Caballeros
(Museo Zuloaga)

VALDEAGUILA

Ayuntamiento

3

PLAZA DE
GUEVARA

PL SAN
FACUNDO

LOS CABALLEROS

Muralla

PLAZA DE
COLMENARES

CRONISTA LECEA

i

PLAZA
MAYOR

San
Miguel

D

CALLE SAN AGUSTIN

INFANTA ISABEL

Torre de los
Arias Dávila

PLAZA
HUERTOS

Casa del
Hidalgo

CALLE REAL

ESCUDEROS

CATALICA

E

PL. DEL
CORPUS

SAN   MARTÍN

Museo de Arte
Contemporaneo

San Martín

E. MARTIN HIGUERA

PLAZA
DEL CONDE
DE CHESTE

5

Convento del
Corpus Christi

F

JOSE CANALEJAS

C.A. DAVILA

San
Sebastián

PLAZA DE
AVENDAÑO

PASEO DEL SALÓN

G

C. DE

PZA. DE SAN
MARTIN

Torreón de
Lozoya

JUAN BRAVO

SAN JUAN

VIA DE ROMA

Convento del
Sancti Spiritu

H

Casa de
los Picos

i

PLAZA
DE LA
ARTILLERIA

AVDA. PADRE CLARET

Alhóndiga

DE SAN MILLAN

CALLE DE CERVANTES

PLAZA DEL
AZOGUEJO

I

San Justo

PLAZA DEL
SANCTI
SPIRITU

6   7

Palacio del
Conde
Alpuente

DEL CARMEN

CALLE DE SAN FRANCISCO

TEODORO GARCIA

C. OCHOA ONDATEGUI

8

PLAZA DE
SAN JUSTO

J

TENIENTE OCHOA

PASEO EZEQUIEL GONZALEZ

SAN MILLÁN

AVDA. DE FERNANDEZ LADREDA

9

San
Clemente

C.P.MONTALVO

C.S. ALFONSO RODRIGUEZ

El
Salvador

PLAZA DE
DIAZ SANZ

PLAZA
DEL
SALVADOR

10

San
Millán

Colegio de Artillería

CALLE DE LAS MORERAS

K

Soria, Cuéllar & Valladolid

La Granja & Madrid

173

Accommodation

Most of the **accommodation** is to be found in the streets around the Plaza Mayor and Plaza de Azoguejo, but rooms can be hard to come by even out of season, so it's worth booking ahead. Be warned that in winter, at over 1000m, the nights can be very cold and sometimes snowy, and the more basic rooms generally aren't heated.

La Casa Mudéjar c/Isabel Católica 8 ☎921 466 250, ⓦwww.lacasamudejar.com. Characterful hotel located in a restored mansion sandwiched between the Plaza Mayor and the Judería. Well-appointed rooms with historic touches such as beautiful carved *artesonado* ceilings and a restaurant that serves some traditional *sefardi* dishes with fruit sauces. ❺

Emperador Teodosio Paseo Conde de Sepúlveda 4 ☎921 441 111, ⓕ921 441 047. Located between the train and bus stations, this pleasant, spacious student residence becomes a youth hostel between July and Sept 15. €11.60 over-30, €8.50 under-30. YHA card needed.

Hostal Don Jaime c/Ochoa Ondategui 8 ☎921 444 787, ⓦwww.viasegovia.com/hostaldonjaime. An excellent, very comfortable sixteen-room *hostal* near the aqueduct. All doubles have their own bathroom.

Hostal Hidalgo c/José Canalejas 3 & 5 ☎921 463 529, ⓦwww.el-hidalgo.com. A small, beautiful old building overlooking the church of San Martín, with a good restaurant and decent a/c rooms. *El Hidalgo 2,* the sister *hostal* nearby at c/Juan Bravo 21, is cheaper and also worth a try. Both ❷

Hostal Juan Bravo c/Juan Bravo 12 ☎921 463 413. A good budget option with lots of big, comfortable rooms and plant-festooned bathrooms. ❷

Hostal Plaza c/Cronista Lecea 11 ☎921 460 303, ⓦwww.hostal-plaza.com. A clean *hostal*, centrally located just off the Plaza Mayor, with a/c rooms. It also has a garage. ❷

Hotel Acueducto Avda. Padre Claret 10 ☎902 250 550, ⓦwww.hotelacueducto.com. A pleasant eighty-room hotel outside the city walls with a terraza overlooking the aqueduct. The restaurant gets busy with bus parties during the day, but is quiet most evenings. ❹

Hotel Alcázar c/San Marcos 5 ☎921 438 568, ⓦwww.alcazar-hotel.com. A tranquil, upmarket boutique hotel situated next to the River Eresma with a relaxing garden affording views of the Alcázar. ❺–❻

Hotel Infanta Isabel Plaza Mayor 12 ☎921 461 300, ⓦwww.hotelinfantaisabel.com. A comfortable hotel with 37 classically decorated rooms and ideally positioned on Plaza Mayor. ❹–❺

Hotel Los Linajes c/Dr Velasco 9 ☎921 460 475, ⓦwww.loslinajes.com. A good-value cosy hotel set in part of an old palace in a quiet corner of the walled city. It has a fine garden overlooking the river valley, and all rooms have a/c. ❹–❺

Hotel San Antonio El Real San Antonio El Real s/n ☎921 413 455, ⓦwww.sanantonioelreal.es. Luxury hotel located inside a splendid old convent just up from the aqueduct. The 51 rooms are large, sumptuously decorated and with all the facilities you could want. ❹–❻

Las Sirenas c/Juan Bravo 30 ☎921 462 663, ⓦwww.hotelsirenas.com. Classic decor, big rooms, a neat garden and terrace all at a very reasonable price. ❸–❹

Campsite

Camping Acueducto Avda. Don Juan de Borbón 49 ☎921 425 000, ⓦwww.campingacueducto.com. The nearest campsite, 3km out on the road to La Granja; take a #6 "Nueva Segovia" bus from the Plaza Mayor. A quiet site with a swimming pool and plenty of shade. Closed Oct–Easter.

The City

Segovia has more than a full day's worth of sights. If you're on a flying visit from Madrid, obvious priorities are the breathtaking Roman **aqueduct**, the Gothic **cathedral** and **Alcázar** in the old town, and the church of **Vera Cruz**, which lies just to the north in the valley beyond the city walls. Given more time, take a walk out of the city for the **views**, or just wander at will through the **old quarters** of the city, away from the centre: each has a village atmosphere of its own.

The aqueduct

The most photographed sight in Segovia is the stunning **aqueduct**. Over 800m of granite, supported by 166 arches and 120 pillars and at its highest point towering some 30m above the Plaza de Azoguejo, it stands up without a drop of mortar or cement. No one knows exactly when it was built, but it was probably around the end of the first century AD under either Emperor Domitian or Trajan. It no longer carries water from the Río Acebeda to the city, and in recent years traffic vibration and pollution have been threatening to undermine the entire structure, but the completion of a meticulous restoration programme should ensure it remains standing for some time to come. If you climb the stairs beside the aqueduct you can get a view looking down over it from a surviving fragment of the city walls.

Around the aqueduct

Some 200m up the hill to the right of the aqueduct and nestled against the walls is the **Museo Zuloaga** (July–Sept Tues–Sat 10am–2pm & 5–8pm, Sun 10am–2pm; rest of year Mon–Sat 10am–2pm & 4–7pm, Sun 10am–2pm; €1.20), a museum dedicated to the ceramicist Daniel Zuloaga and housed in the Romanesque Iglesia San Juan de los Caballeros, where the noble families of the city used to meet.

Passing under the aqueduct and up the hill along c/Cervantes, you will be directed from La Trinidad to Casa de los Picos towards the old city past the curious fifteenth-century **Casa de los Picos** (House of Spikes), with its waffle-like facade made up of pyramid-shaped stones to your right and the former corn exchange, the **Alhóndiga**, down a few steps on your left.

A little farther on is the **Plaza de San Martín**, one of the city's grandest squares, whose ensemble of buildings includes the fourteenth-century **Torreón de Lozoya** (open for exhibitions Mon–Fri 5–9pm, Sat & Sun noon–2pm & 5–9pm), and the twelfth-century church of **San Martín**, which demonstrates all the local stylistic peculiarities. It has the characteristic covered portico, a fine arched tower and a typically Romanesque aspect; like most of Segovia's churches, it can be visited only when it's open for business, during early morning or evening services. In the middle of the plaza is a **statue of Juan Bravo**, a local folk hero who led the *comuneros* rebellion against Carlos V in protest against tax increases, the undermining of local power and the influence of foreign advisers. On the northern side of the square is the **Museo de Arte Contemporáneo** (Tues–Fri 11am–2pm & 4–7pm, til 8pm Thurs & Fri, Sat 11am–7pm, Sun 11am–3pm; €2.40, free Thurs), dedicated to local artist Esteban Vicente (1903–2000) who produced some interesting and striking abstract expressionist work.

North of here, the church of **La Trinidad** (daily 10am–2pm & 4–7pm) preserves the purest Romanesque style in Segovia: each span of its double-arched apse has intricately carved capitals, every one of them unique. Nearby – and making a good loop to or from the Alcázar – is the **Plaza San Esteban**, worth seeing for its superb, five-storeyed, twelfth-century church tower.

Plaza Mayor and around

Calle Juan Bravo eventually leads on to the bar-filled **Plaza Mayor**. Dominating one corner of the plaza are the exuberant lines of the **Catedral** (daily spring/summer: 9.30am–6.30pm, autumn/winter: 9.30am–5.30pm, except during Mass). Construction began in 1525, on the orders of Carlos V, to make amends for the damage done to the city during the *comuneros* revolt. However, it was not completed for another two hundred years, making it the last major Gothic building in Spain. Accordingly it takes the style to its logical – or perhaps illogical – extreme, with pinnacles and flying buttresses tacked on at every conceivable point. Though impressive for its size alone, the interior is surprisingly bare for so florid a construction and its space is cramped by a great green marble *coro* at its very centre. The treasures are almost all confined to the museum (April–Oct Mon–Sat 9am–6.30pm, Sun 1.15–6.30pm; Nov–March Mon–Sat 9.30am–5.30pm, Sun 1.30–5.30pm; €3), which opens off the cloisters. On the opposite side of the plaza is the Iglesia San Miguel, the church where Isabel la Católica was crowned queen of Castile in 1474.

Down beside the cathedral, c/Daoiz leads past a line of souvenir shops to the twelfth-century Romanesque church of San Andrés. Off to the right at c/Desamparados 5 is the **Casa-Museo de Antonio Machado** (mid-March to mid-Sept: Tues 4–7pm, Wed–Sun 10am–2pm & 4.30–7.30pm, mid-Sept to mid-March: Wed–Sun 11am–2pm & 4.30–7.30pm; €1.50, free Wed). This little house displays the spartan accommodation and furnishings of one of Spain's greatest poets of the early twentieth century; Machado is generally more associated with Soria, but spent the last years of his life teaching here.

The Judería

Segovia was once home to one of Spain's biggest Jewish communities and there are several interesting remnants from that period tucked away in the streets of the old Judería to the south of the Plaza Mayor. The **synagogue**, which now serves as the convent church of **Corpus Christi** (Tues 4–7pm, Wed–Sun 10am–2pm & 4–7pm; donation), is in a little courtyard at the end of c/Juan Bravo near the east end of the cathedral. You can see part of its exterior from the Paseo del Salón. During the nineteenth century it was badly damaged by fire, so what you see now is a reconstruction. Close by is the **Centro Didáctico de la Judería** (Mon 10am–2pm, Wed–Sun 10am–2pm & 4–7pm; €1.50), which houses a limited exhibition about Jewish culture and is located in the former house of Abraham Senneor, a rabbi who lived in Segovia in the fifteenth century. Just south of here is the **Puerta de San Andrés** (summer Mon 11am–2pm, Wed–Sun 11am–2pm & 4–8pm, winter Thurs, Sat & Sun 11am–2pm & 4–7pm; €1.50), the old gate into the Judería and back towards the Alcázar in the old Jewish slaughterhouse, now the **Provincial museum** (July–Sept Tues–Sat 10am–2pm & 5–8pm, Sun 10am–2pm, Oct–June Tues–Sat 10am–2pm & 4–7pm, Sun 10am–2pm; €1.20, free Sat & Sun), which contains an interesting and comprehensive range of exhibits detailing the history of Segovia from prehistoric times to the present day.

The Alcázar

Beyond the Plaza Mayor and the Judería, perched on the northwestern tip of the city walls, is the **Alcázar** (daily: April–Sept 10am–7pm; Oct–March 10am–6pm; €4, access to the tower an additional €2, free third Tues in the month for EU citizens). An extraordinary fantasy of a castle, with its narrow towers and flurry of turrets, it will seem eerily familiar to just about every visitor, having apparently served as the model for the original Disneyland castle in California. It is itself a bit of a sham; although it dates from the fourteenth and fifteenth centuries, it was almost completely destroyed by a fire in 1862 and rebuilt as a deliberately hyperbolic version of the original. Still, it should be visited if only for the splendid *artesonado* ceilings and the magnificent panoramas from the tower.

Walks around Segovia

Segovia is an excellent city for **walks**. Drop down onto the path that winds its way down into the valley from the Alcázar on the north side of the city wall and you'll reach the Río Eresma. Head west and you'll pass close to Vera Cruz and the Convento de los Carmelitas, with some great views of the Alcázar, before turning back towards the city; head east and you can follow the beautiful tree-lined path alongside the river and wend your way back up the hill to the old town in a round-trip of a little over an hour. On your way round you can visit the **Monasterio de El Parral** (July & Aug Tues 4–7pm, Wed–Sun 10am–2pm & 4–7pm; rest of year Tues–Sat 10am–12.30pm & 4.15–6.30pm, Sun 10–11.30am & 4.15–6.30pm; donation); or better still, follow the track that circles behind Vera Cruz to the monastery. El Parral is a sizeable and partly ruined complex occupied by Hieronymites, an order found only in Spain. Ring the bell for admission and you will be shown the cloister and church; the latter is a late Gothic building with rich sculpture at the east end. Gregorian Masses can be heard during the week at 1pm in spring and summer and on Sundays at noon.

For the **best view** of all of Segovia, take the main road north for 2km or so towards Cuéllar. A panorama of the whole city, including the aqueduct, gradually unfolds.

Vera Cruz

The best of Segovia's ancient churches is undoubtedly **Vera Cruz** (Tues–Sun 10.30am–1.30pm & 4–7pm, winter closes 6pm; closed Nov; €1.75), a remarkable twelve-sided building outside town in the valley facing the Alcázar, which can be reached by taking the path down to Paseo San Juan de la Cruz. It was built by the Knights Templar in the early thirteenth century on the pattern of the church of the Holy Sepulchre in Jerusalem, and once housed part of the True Cross (hence its name; the sliver of wood itself is now in the nearby village church at Zamarramala). Inside, the nave is circular, and its heart is occupied by a strange two-storeyed chamber – again twelve-sided – in which the knights, as part of their initiation, stood vigil over the cross. Climb the tower for a highly photogenic vista of the city.

While you're over here you could take in the prodigiously walled **Convento de las Carmelitas** (summer Mon 10am–1.30pm, Tues–Sun 10am–1.30pm & 4–8pm; winter same times, but closes an hour earlier in the evening; free/ voluntary donation), which is also referred to as the monastery of San Juan de la Cruz, and contains the gaudy mausoleum of its founder saint.

Beyond the aqueduct

If you follow the line of the aqueduct away from the old city you will come to the **Convento de San Antonio Real** (Tues–Sat 10am–2pm & 4–6.30pm, open til 7pm in summer; €2), a little gem of a palace (and now also a luxury hotel), originally founded by Enrique IV in 1455 and containing an intriguing collection of Mudéjar and Hispano-Flemish art, some outstanding *artesonado* ceilings and a wonderful fifteenth-century wooden calvary.

Back towards the city, but still outside the old walls, stand two fine Romanesque churches. Between the bus station and the aqueduct is the church of **San Millán** (daily 10am–2pm & 4.30–7.30pm), with a fine Mozárabe tower and open porticoes. Its interior has been restored to its original form. Facing the aqueduct is **San Justo** (summer Tues–Sat: 10am–2pm & 4–7pm, winter Mon–Sat 11am–2pm & 4–6pm), which has a wonderful Romanesque wall-painting in the apse and a twelfth-century sculpture of Christ complete with hinged arms.

Eating and drinking

Segovia takes its cooking seriously, with restaurants of Madrid quality – and prices to match. **Culinary specialities** include roast suckling pig (*cochinillo asado*) and the rather healthier *judiones*, large white beans from La Granja. Cheaper **bar-restaurants** cluster on c/Infanta Isabel, off the Plaza Mayor, and late-night bars are on c/Escuderos, c/Herrería and c/Judería Vieja, and along Avenida Fernández Ladreda.

Bar José María c/Cronista Lecea 11, just off Plaza Mayor. Bar-annexe to one of Segovia's best restaurants, serving delicious and modestly priced tapas.

Bar-Mesón Las Cuevas de San Esteban c/Valdelaguila 15, off the top end of Plaza San Esteban. A cavern-restaurant and bar (serving draught beer), popular with locals and excellent value. There are *menús* at €9.50 and €15.

El Bernardino c/Cervantes 2 ☏ 921 462 477, ⓦ www.elbernardino.com. A friendly place serving the Castilian classics of *cochinillo* and *cordero*, but better value than some of the city's more famous restaurants. The *menú segoviano* with *cochinillo* is €27.50, while they also do a kids' *menú* at €7.50.

Casa Amado Avda. Fernández Ladreda 9 ☏ 921 432 077. A small but popular local restaurant serving traditional dishes, near the Plaza Azoguejo. Allow €35 per head, although there are also *menús* at around half this price. Closed Wed & the second half of Oct.

La Codorniz c/Aniceto Marinas 1. Inexpensive *menús*, some great *tortilla* and lots of *combinados* involving *codorniz* (quail) at this unpretentious place opposite San Millán church.

Di Vino c/Valdeáguila 7 ☏ 921 460 789 & 921 460 650. A high-class restaurant housed in an old convent owned by the same people as *Las Cuevas de San Esteban*. Expect excellent food, good service and imaginative touches to Castilian classics. There's a tourist *menú* for €22 and a *menú de degustación* for €48. Closed Tues.

La Judería c/Judería Vieja 5 ☏ 921 461 402. Close to the *catedral*, this is another good option for Castilian specialities. Does a decent tourist *menú* for €20. Closed Wed.

Mesón de Cándido Plaza Azoguejo 5 ☏ 921 428 103. In the shadow of the aqueduct you will find the city's most famous restaurant: the place for *cochinillo* and other roasts. The *cochinillo* is €19 and the *cordero* €39 for two people.

Mesón del Duque c/Cervantes 12 ☏ 921 462 487. Rival to the nearby *Cándido*, and also specializing in Castilian roasts. The Segovian *menú* is €35 and includes *cochinillo*, while there's a more sophisticated *menú gastrónomico* at €43.

Mesón José María c/Cronista Lecea 11, just off Plaza Mayor ☏ 921 461 111. Reckoned to be the city's best and most imaginative restaurant, run by a former *Cándido* protégé, with modern variations on Castilian classics. The *menú gastrónomico* is €42, but individual mains cost around €20.

Tasca La Posada c/Judería Vieja 19. A fine *bar-mesón* for tapas, *raciones* or a *menú*.

Out of town

La Posada de Javier in the village of Torrecaballeros, 8km northeast on the N110 ☏ 921 401 136. Serious *madrileño* – and *segoviano* – gourmands eat out in the neighbouring villages, and this lovely old farmhouse is one of the most popular choices. It isn't cheap, however, with a *menú* costing at least €30. Booking is essential at weekends. Closed eves Mon–Thurs & Sun & July.

La Granja and Riofrío

Segovia has a major outlying attraction in the Bourbon summer palace and gardens of **La Granja**, 10km southeast of the town on the CL601 Madrid road, and connected by regular bus services. True Bourbon aficionados, with time and transport, might also want to visit a second palace and hunting museum 12km west of La Granja at **Riofrío**.

La Granja

La Granja (full name, San Ildefonso de la Granja) was built by the reluctant first Bourbon king of Spain, Felipe V, no doubt homesick for the luxuries of Versailles. Its glories are the mountain setting and the extravagant wooded grounds and gardens, but it's also worth casting an eye over the **palace**

(April–Sept Tues–Sun 10am–6pm; Oct–March Tues–Sat 10am–1.30pm & 3–5pm, Sun 10am–2pm; guided tour €5, unguided €4.50, free Wed for EU citizens). Though destroyed in parts and damaged throughout by a fire in 1918, much has been well restored and is home to a superlative collection of sixteenth-century tapestries, one of the most valuable in the world. Everything is furnished in plush French imperial style, but it's almost all of Spanish origin; the majority of the huge chandeliers, for example, were made in the **glass factory** in the village of San Ildefonso (mid-June to mid-Sept Tues–Fri 10am–6pm, Sat, Sun & hols 10am–7pm; mid-Sept to mid-June Tues–Sat 10am–6pm, Sun 10am–3pm; €4). Here you can visit an exhibition on the history of the craft and still see the glass being blown and decorated in the traditional manner.

The highlight of the **gardens** (daily: summer 10am–7pm; winter 10am–6pm) is its series of **fountains**, which culminate in the fifteen-metre-high jet of La Fama. They're fantastic and really not to be missed, which means timing your visit for 5.30pm on Wednesdays or weekends (€3.40) when some are switched on (they may not be switched on during periods of water shortage, so it's best to check on ☎921 470 019 beforehand). Only on three saints' days in the year – normally May 30 (San Fernando), July 25 (Santiago) and August 25 (San Luis) – are all of the fountains set to work, with accompanying crowds to watch.

Practicalities

The **village** of San Ildefonso de la Granja is a pleasant place to spend some time, with a range of accommodation: try the new *Parador*, which is in the eighteenth-century Casa de los Infantes at at c/Fuentes 3 (☎921 010 750; ❻), *Las Fuentes* at c/Padre Claret 8 (☎921 471 024; ❹), the friendly *Hotel Roma* at c/Guardas 2 (☎921 470 752, ⓦwww.hotelroma.org; ❸), right outside the palace gates, or the cheaper, but less welcoming, *Pensión Pozo de la Nieve*, c/Baños 4 (☎921 470 598; ❶). Decent **bars** and **restaurants** include the *Bar La Villa* off the main square for tapas, *Casa Zaca*, also off the square, for lunch, or *Bar Madrid*, near the palace.

Riofrío

The palace at **Riofrío** (April–Sept Tues–Sun 10am–6pm; Oct–March Tues–Sat 10am–1.30pm & 3–5pm, Sun 10am–2pm; €4, €2.25 toll for cars, free Wed for EU citizens) was built by Isabel, the widow of Felipe V, in the fear that she would be banished from La Granja by her stepson Fernando VI. He died, however, leaving the throne for Isabel's own son, Carlos III, and Riofrío was not occupied until the nineteenth century, when Alfonso XII moved in to mourn the death of his young queen Mercedes. He, too, died pretty soon after, which is perhaps why the palace has a spartan and slightly tatty feel.

The complex, painted in dusty pink with green shutters, is surrounded not by manicured gardens but by a **deer park**, into which you can drive but not wander. Inside the palace, you have to join a guided tour, which winds through an endless sequence of rooms, none stunningly furnished. About half the tour is devoted to a **museum of hunting**; the most interesting items here are reconstructions of cave paintings, including the famous Altamira drawings.

North from Segovia: a castle tour

It is said there were once ten thousand castles in Spain. Of those that are left, some five hundred are in a reasonable state of repair, and Segovia province has an especially rich selection. Drivers en route to Valladolid and the Río Duero (see Chapter 5) can construct an enjoyable route to see the best of them; there are buses (from Segovia or Valladolid), but you may end up spending the night in places that really only warrant a quick stop and a cup of coffee.

Fifty kilometres northwest of Segovia, the **fortress** (Mon–Fri 10.30am–1pm & 4.30–6/7pm, Sat & Sun 11am–1pm & 4/4.30–6/7pm, closed first Tues of each month; €2.50) at the small town of **COCA** is the prettiest imaginable, less a piece of military architecture than a country house masquerading as one. Built in about 1453, as the base of the powerful Fonseca family, it's constructed from pinkish bricks, encircled by a deep moat and fantastically decorated with octagonal turrets and elaborate castellation – an extraordinary design strongly influenced by Moorish architecture. There are five **buses** a day here from Segovia, though Coca itself is fairly unremarkable; drivers should push on to Medina del Campo for lunch (in Castilla y León), itself the site of another fabulous castle.

The castle at **TURÉGANO**, 28km north of Segovia, is essentially a fifteenth-century structure enclosing an early thirteenth-century church. However, it's east of here, off the main Segovia–Soria road (N110), that the most rewarding diversions are to be made. Eight kilometres east of Turégano, **PEDRAZA** in particular is almost perfectly preserved from the sixteenth century. The village is protected on three sides by a steep valley; the only entrance is the single original gateway (which used to be the town prison), from where the narrow lanes spiral up towards a large Plaza Mayor, still used for a bullfighting festival in the first week in September. The **Castillo de Pedraza** is where the eight-year-old dauphin of France and his younger brother were imprisoned in 1526, given up by their father François I who swapped his freedom for theirs after he was captured at the battle of Pavia. **SEPÚLVEDA**, a little further north (and off the highway between Madrid and Burgos), is less of a harmonious whole, but has an even more dramatic setting, strung out high on a narrow spit of land between the Castilla and Duratón river valleys. Its physical and architectural high point is the distinctive Romanesque church of **El Salvador**, perched high above its ruined castle.

Both Pedraza and Sepúlveda have become rather upmarket getaways for wealthy Castilians; there are infrequent bus services from Segovia, but the villages are best avoided altogether at weekends when every *madrileño* with a Mercedes seems to descend on them to sample the (delicious) local roast lamb. Sepúlveda is probably the better bet for accommodation – the **turismo**, on the central Plaza del Trigo (closed Mon & Tues; ☎921 540 237, ⊛www.sepulveda.es), has a list on its website. Castle-hunters, meanwhile, will bowl up the highway to Aranda del Duero, where – east or west along the Río Duero – more stunning examples await.

East of Madrid

The only tempting day-trip east of the capital is to the old university town of **Alcalá de Henares**, Cervantes' birthplace. Farther afield, the **Alcarria**, the region southwest of Guadalajara, has its charms, especially if you want to follow in the footsteps of Spain's Nobel prizewinner, Camilo José Cela, who described his wanderings here in the 1940s in his book, *Viaje a la Alcarria*.

Alcalá de Henares

ALCALÁ DE HENARES, a little over 30km from Madrid, is one of Europe's most ancient university towns, and renowned as the birthplace of **Miguel de Cervantes**. In the sixteenth century, the university was a rival to Salamanca's, but in 1836 the faculties moved to Madrid and the town went into decline. Nowadays, it's virtually a suburb of Madrid and not somewhere you'd want to stay longer than it takes to see the sights.

The **Universidad Antigua** (regular 45min guided tours usually in Spanish; €3) stands at the heart of the old town, in Plaza San Diego. It was endowed by Cardinal Cisneros (also known as Cardinal Jiménez) at the beginning of the sixteenth century and features a fabulous Plateresque facade and a Great Hall, the **Paraninfo**, with a gloriously decorated Mudéjar *artesonado* ceiling. Next door, the **Capilla de San Ildefonso** has another superb ceiling, intricately stuccoed walls and the Italian marble tomb of Cardinal Cisneros, although his actual remains are buried in the cathedral in Plaza de los Santos Niños.

The **Museo Casa Natal de Cervantes** on the porticoed c/Mayor (Tues–Sun 10am–6pm; free) claims to have been the birthplace of Cervantes in 1547: though the house itself is hardly thirty years old, it's authentic in style, furnished with genuine sixteenth-century objects and contains a small museum with a few early editions of *Don Quixote* and other curiosities related to the author. Next door is the **Hospital de Antezana** (daily 10am–2pm & 4.30–8pm; free) with its beautiful Mudéjar-style patio. Founded in 1493, it claims to be the oldest hospital in Europe and Cervantes' father Rodrigo was said to have worked here.

Just off the central Plaza Cervantes is the oldest surviving public theatre in Europe, the **Corral de Comedias** (regular guided tours with English usually spoken; €2.50; reservations ℡918 821 354), which has been brought to life once more after a twenty-year restoration programme. Originally dating from 1601, the theatre was discovered beneath a crumbling old cinema by three drama students in 1980.

On the outskirts of town are the foundations of a Roman villa, the **Casa de Hippolytus** (Tues–Fri 10am–2pm, Sat & Sun 10am–2pm & 4–7pm; free), originally a school for the children of wealthy Romans, complete with temple, baths, and a garden containing exotic animals. The centrepiece is a magnificent mosaic signed by Hippolytus, depicting a vast array of aquatic life.

Practicalities

Regular **trains** (Chamartín or Atocha; daily every 15–30min from 5.30am–11.45pm) and Continental Auto **buses** (Avda. de América bus station; daily every 15min) run from Madrid. Alternatively, the **Tren de Cervantes** leaves Atocha at 11am on Saturday and Sunday (mid-April to late June & late Sept to early Dec; €19; ℡918 892 694), complete with staff in period costume, and includes a guided tour of the main sights, before returning at 7pm.

The **turismo** is just off central Plaza de Cervantes (daily 10am–2pm & 5–6.30pm, until 7.30pm in summer; ℡918 892 694, ⓦwww.turismoalcala .com), can arrange tours and has maps and other handy information. The best **restaurant** in town is the ⚑ *Hostería del Estudiante*, situated in part of the old university (℡918 880 330; closed Aug).

The Alcarria

The **Alcarria** has few particular monuments, but the wild scenery and sporadic settlements are eerily impressive, especially coming upon them so close to Madrid. The largest town in the region is **PASTRANA**, 15km south of the N320. The museum of its vast **Colegiata** church (daily 11.30am–2pm & 4–6pm; €3) contains some wonderful fifteenth-century tapestries depicting the conquest of Tangier and Asilah by Alfonso V of Portugal. A ten-minute walk out of town, the Carmelite **Convento del Carmen** was founded by Santa Teresa;

within is a small museum of assorted religious art and relics of the saint (Tues–Sun 11am–1.30/2pm & 3.30/4–6.30pm; €2.40).

The **turismo** is in the Plaza de la Hora (Tues–Fri 10am–2pm & 4–6pm, Sat 10am–2pm & 4–8pm, Sun 10am–2pm; ☎949 370 672, ⓦwww.pastrana.org). Part of the Convento del Carmen is an excellent-value *parador*-style **hotel**, the *Hospedería Real de Pastrana* (☎949 371 060, ⓦwww.hosteriasreales.com; ❹), which has its own restaurant, too. For good-value local **food** try the *Convento de San Francisco*, which offers a varied *menú* in atmospheric surroundings.

Travel details

Trains

For current timetables and ticket information, consult RENFE ☎902 240 202, ⓦwww.renfe.es.

Atocha, Madrid (ⓂAtocha) to: Alcalá (every 15–30min; 30min); Aranjuez (every 15–30min; 45min); El Escorial via Chamartín (25 daily; 1hr); Guadalajara via Chamartín (every 15–30min; 55min); Toledo (12 daily; 30min).

Chamartín, Madrid (ⓂChamartín) to: Ávila (24 daily; 1hr 20min–2hr 10min); Cercedilla (23 daily; 1hr 15min); Segovia (27 daily; 35min–2hr).

Aranjuez to: Madrid (every 15–30min; 45min).

Ávila to: Madrid (35 daily; 1hr 20min–2hr 10min); El Escorial (9 daily; 1hr); Medina del Campo (15 daily; 20–40min); Salamanca (6 daily; 1hr 30min).

Cercedilla to: Cotos (6 daily; 40min); Madrid (21 daily; 1hr 15min); Puerto de Navacerrada (6 daily; 25min); Segovia (9 daily; 40–50min).

El Escorial to: Ávila (9 daily; 1hr); Madrid (21 daily; 1hr).

Segovia to: Cercedilla (9 daily; 40min); Madrid (27 daily; 35min–2hr).

Toledo to: Madrid (12 daily; 30min).

Buses

Estación Sur de Autobuses, Madrid c/Méndez Álvaro s/n (ⓂMéndez Álvaro) to: Aranjuez (Mon–Fri every 30min, Sat & Sun hourly; 45min); Arenas de San Pedro (9–14 daily; 2hr 15min); Ávila (5–10 daily; 1hr 20min–1hr 40min); Toledo (every 15–30min; 1hr 15min).

Auto-Res, Madrid Plaza Conde de Casal (ⓂConde de Casal) to: Cuenca (4–9 daily; 2hr–2hr 30min); Salamanca (8–20 daily; 2hr 30min–3hr).

La Veloz, Madrid Avda. del Mediterráneo 49 (ⓂConde de Casal) to: Chinchón (10–15 daily; 45min).

Herranz, Madrid Intercambiador de Autobuses, Moncloa (ⓂMoncloa) to: El Escorial (every 15–30min; 1hr).

La Sepulvedana, Madrid Intercambiador de Autobuses, Moncloa (ⓂMoncloa) to: Cercedilla (every 30min; 50min–1hr 10min).

La Sepulvedana, Madrid Paseo de la Florida 11 (ⓂPríncipe Pío) to: Segovia (every 15min–1hr; 1hr 15min).

Continental Auto, Madrid Avda. de América 9 (ⓂAvda. de América) to: Alcalá (every 15min; 40min); Guadalajara (every 30min; 45min).

Intercambiador de Autobuses, Madrid Plaza de Castilla (ⓂPlaza de Castilla) to: Manzanares del Real (hourly; 40min).

Ávila to: Arenas de San Pedro (daily Mon–Fri; 1hr 30min); Madrid (8 daily; 1hr 30min); Salamanca (2–3 daily; 1hr 30min); Segovia (2–7 daily; 1hr 30min).

El Escorial to: Guadarrama (every 30min–1hr; 15min); Madrid (every 15–30min; 1hr); Valle de los Caídos (daily; 15min).

Segovia to: Ávila (2–3 daily; 1hr); La Granja (12 daily; 20min); Madrid (every 30min; 1hr 15min); Salamanca (1–3 daily; 2–3hr); Valladolid (5–9 daily; 2hr 30min).

Toledo to: Ciudad Real, for the south (daily; 2hr); Cuenca (Mon–Fri 1 daily; 2hr 30min); Guadamur (7 daily; 20min); Madrid (every 30min; 1hr 15min); Orgaz (3–10 daily; 30min); La Puebla de Montalbán (5 daily Mon–Fri, daily Sat; 40min); Talavera de la Reina, for Extremadura (10 daily; 1hr).

③

Castilla-La Mancha and Extremadura

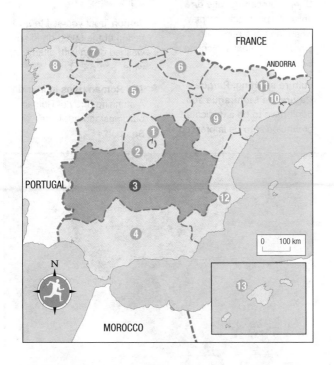

CHAPTER 3 # Highlights

✳ **Museo de Arte Abstracto, Cuenca** One of the famous hanging houses is the wonderful setting for this gem of a museum. See p.193

✳ **La Ciudad Encantada** Weird and wonderful limestone formations near Cuenca. See p.195

✳ **Cherry blossom, Valle de Jerte** A spectacular display when the trees burst into bloom for ten days in spring. See p.206

✳ **Vulture spotting, Parque Natural de Monfragüe** You don't have to be a dedicated ornithologist to be impressed by these prehistoric-looking creatures. See p.210

✳ **Trujillo** A visit to the birthplace of Pizarro is worthwhile for the view of the town from the Cáceres road alone. See p.211

✳ **Cáceres** Wander around the atmospheric historic core at night. See p.218

✳ **Jamón** Treat yourself to a ración of the cured dried ham washed down with pitarra wine. See p.221

✳ **The Roman ruins in Mérida** A stunning array of Roman buildings and artefacts. See p.224

▲ Vulture, Parque Natural de Monfragüe

Castilla-La Mancha
and Extremadura

The vast area covered by this chapter is some of the most travelled, yet least visited, country in Spain. Once south of Toledo, most tourists thunder nonstop across the plains of Castilla-La Mancha to Valencia and Andalucía, or follow the great rivers through Extremadura into Portugal. At first sight this is understandable. **Castilla-La Mancha**, in particular, is Spain at its least welcoming: a huge, bare plain – the name La Mancha comes from the Arab *manxa*, meaing steppe – burning hot in summer, chillingly exposed in winter. But this impression is not an entirely fair one – away from the main highways the villages are as friendly as any in the country, and in the northeast, where the mountains start, are the extraordinary cliff-hanging city of **Cuenca** and the historic cathedral town of **Sigüenza**. Castilla-La Mancha is also the agricultural and wine-growing heartland of Spain and the country through which Don Quixote cut his despairing swathe.

It is in **Extremadura**, though, that there is most to be missed by just passing through. This harsh environment was the cradle of the *conquistadores*, men who opened up a new world for the Spanish empire. Remote before and forgotten since, Extremadura enjoyed a brief golden age when its heroes returned with their gold to live in splendour. **Trujillo**, the birth-place of Pizarro, and **Cáceres** were built with *conquistador* wealth, the streets crowded with an array of perfectly preserved and very ornate mansions of returning empire builders. Then there is **Mérida**, the most completely preserved Roman city in Spain, and the monasteries of **Guadalupe** and **Yuste**, the one fabulously wealthy, the other rich in imperial memories. Finally, for some wild scenery and superb fauna, northern Extremadura has the **Parque Natural de Monfragüe**, where even the most casual birdwatcher can look up to see eagles and vultures circling the cliffs.

Castilla-La Mancha

The region that was for so long called **New Castile** – and that until the 1980s held Madrid in its domain – is now officially known as **Castilla-La**

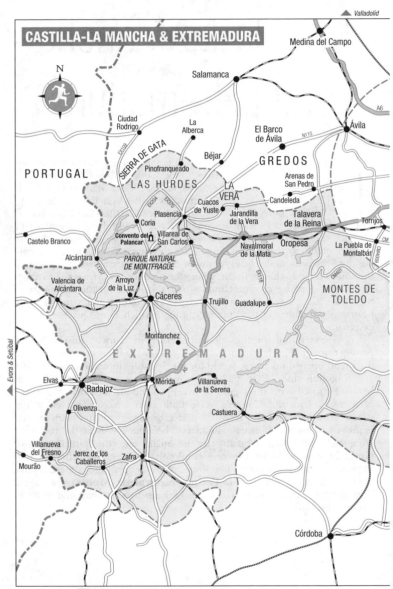

CASTILLA-LA MANCHA & EXTREMADURA

▲ Valladolid

Medina del Campo

N

Salamanca

Ciudad Rodrigo

La Alberca

El Barco de Ávila

N110

Ávila

A6

SIERRA DE GATA

Béjar

GREDOS

EX109

PORTUGAL

Pinofranqueado

LAS HURDES

LA VERA

Arenas de San Pedro

EX204

EX370

Cuacos de Yuste

Candeleda

Plasencia

Jarandilla de la Vera

Talavera de la Reina

Torrijos

Coria

EX108

Castelo Branco

Convento del Palancar

Villareal de San Carlos

Navalmoral de la Mata

Oropesa

La Puebla de Montalbán

CM

Alcántara

PARQUE NATURAL DE MONTFRAGÜE

EX208

EX118

CM4013

EX207

Valencia de Alcántara

Arroyo de la Luz

Cáceres

Trujillo

Guadalupe

MONTES DE TOLEDO

CM401

Évora & Setúbal ▲

Montanchez

EXTREMADURA

A5

Elvas

Badajoz

Mérida

Villanueva de la Serena

Olivenza

Castuera

Villanueva del Fresno

Jerez de los Caballeros

Zafra

Mourão

Córdoba

▼ Seville

Mancha. The main points of interest are widely spaced on an arc drawn from Madrid, with little between. If you are travelling east on **trains and buses** towards Aragón, the only worthwhile stops are Sigüenza (en route to Zaragoza) or Cuenca (en route to Teruel). To the south, Toledo has bus links within its own province, but heading for Andalucía or Extremadura you'd do better returning to Madrid and starting out again; the Toledo rail line stops at the town.

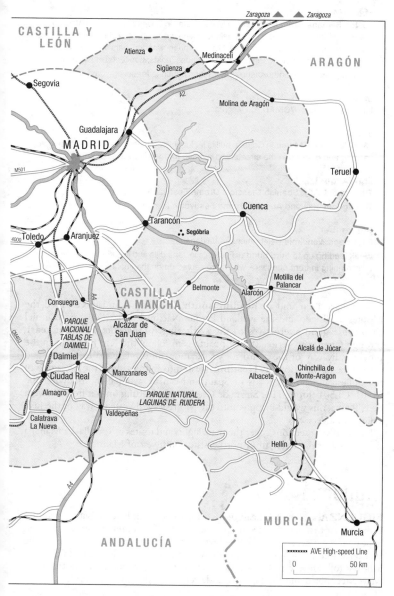

Fiestas

February
First weekend: La Endiablada Ancient festival in Almonacid Marquesado (near Cuenca), when all the boys dress up as devils and parade through the streets.
Week before Lent Carnaval everywhere.

March/April
Easter: Semana Santa (Holy Week) Major fiestas in Cáceres and Trujillo. Valverdede la Vera has the tradition of Los Empalaos, men who re-enact Jesus's journey to the Cross by roping their outstretched arms to huge wooden bars as they walk the streets of town at night. Magnificent celebrations (floats, penitents) in Cuenca.
April 23: San Jorge Enthusiastic celebrations continue for several days in Cáceres.

May
First half of May: WOMAD At Cáceres.

June
23–27: San Juan Manic In Coria, a bull is let loose for a few hours a day, with people dancing and drinking in the streets and running for their lives when it appears.

July/August
Throughout July: Spanish Classical Drama Festival At Almagro.
Throughout July and August: Drama Festival In Mérida.

September
First week: Vendimia Celebrations at Valdepeñas.
Week leading up to third Sunday Festivals in Jarandilla and Madrigal de la Vera with bulls running in front of cows – which are served up on the final day's feast.

If you have a **car**, and are **heading south**, the Toledo–Ciudad Real road, the Montes de Toledo and the wetland Parque Nacional de las Tablas de Daimiel all provide good alternatives to the sweltering A4 *autopista*. **Heading east**, through Cuenca to Teruel, the best route is to follow the Río Júcar out of the province, by way of the weird rock formations in the Ciudad Encantada and the source of the Río Tajo. **Heading west**, into Extremadura, the A5 is one of the dullest and hottest roads in Spain and can be avoided by following the M501/CL501 through the Sierra de Gredos or by cutting onto it from Talavera de la Reina; this would bring you to the Monastery of Yuste by way of the lush valley of La Vera.

The following sections cover the main sights and routes of Castilla-La Mancha in a clockwise direction, from northeast to southwest of Madrid.

Sigüenza

SIGÜENZA, 120km northeast of Madrid, is a sleepy little town with a beautiful cathedral. At first glance it seems quite untouched by contemporary life, though appearances are deceptive: taken by Franco's troops in 1936, the town was on the Nationalist front line for most of the Civil War, and its people and buildings paid a heavy toll. However, the postwar years saw the cathedral restored, the Plaza Mayor recobbled and the bishop's castle rebuilt, so that the only evidence of its troubled history is in the facades of a few buildings, including the pencil-thin cathedral belltower, pockmarked by bullets and shrapnel.

Arrival and information

Around seven **trains** a day run from Madrid to Sigüenza (1hr 30min). Renfe operates a special "tren medieval" excursion which leaves Chamartín station in Madrid (most Sat March–July; departs Chamartín 10am, arrive Sigüenza 11.25am, return 6.10pm or 7.40pm arriving at Chamartín 7.30pm or 9pm; Sept–Nov €25; price includes a guided tour of the town and entry to the main sights). The train station is five minutes from the centre of this compact town. There is a **turismo** to the west of the cathedral at c/Serrano Sanz 9 (Mon–Thurs 10am–2pm & 4–6pm, Fri 10am–2pm & 4–8pm, Sat 10am–2.30pm & 4–7pm, Sun 10am–2pm; ☏949 347 007, ⊛www.siguenza.es) and another in La Ermita del Humilladero (same hours). Between May and September the offices run guided **tours** of the town for groups of six or more people (Mon–Sat 11.30am & 5.15pm, Sun 11.30am; €7).

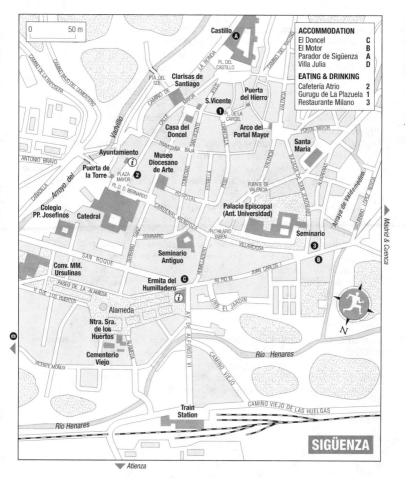

ACCOMMODATION
El Doncel	C
El Motor	B
Parador de Sigüenza	A
Villa Julia	D

EATING & DRINKING
Cafetería Atrio	2
Gurugu de La Plazuela	1
Restaurante Milano	3

SIGÜENZA

▼ Atienza

Accommodation

The town makes for a relaxing stopover en route to Soria and the north or as a base for exploring the rest of the region.

Hostal El Doncel Paseo de la Alameda 1 ☎949 390 001, ⓦ www.eldoncel.com. A smart eighteen-room *hostal* with a very good restaurant serving some high-quality regional cuisine. ❸

El Motor Avda. Juan Carlos I 2 ☎949 390 827, ⓦ www.hostalelmotor.com. A neat and simple, a/c two-star *hostal*, with its own bar and restaurant, on the road coming into town from Madrid. ❷

Parador de Sigüenza Plaza del Castillo s/n ☎949 390 100, ⓦ www.paradores.com. Located in the town's twelfth-century castle, the *parador* enjoys a stunning hilltop location, with fine views from the rooms on the upper floors. ❻

Villa Julia Paseo de las Cruces 27 ☎949 393 339. Extremely comfortable *casa rural* with just five double en-suite rooms. ❸

The Town

Sigüenza's main streets lead you towards the hilltop **Catedral** (daily 9.30am–2pm & 4.30–8pm; frequent guided tours of chapels Tues–Sun; €4), built in the pinkish yellow stone that characterizes the town. Begun in 1150 by the town's first bishop, Bernardo of Toledo, it is essentially Gothic, with three rose windows, though it has been much altered over the years. Facing the main entrance is a huge marble *coro* with an altar to a thirteenth-century figure of the Virgin. To the right of the *coro* is the cathedral's principal treasure, the alabaster tomb of Martín Vázquez de Arce, known as *El Doncel* (the page boy); a favourite of Isabel la Católica, he was killed fighting the Moors in Granada. On the other side of the building is an extraordinary doorway: Plateresque at the bottom, Mudéjar in the middle and Gothic at the top – an amazing amalgam, built by a confused sixteenth-century architect. Take a look, too, at the sacristy, whose superb Renaissance ceiling has 304 heads carved by Covarrubias. In a chapel opening off this (with an unusual cupola, best seen in the mirror provided) is an El Greco *Annunciation*.

More treasures are displayed in the **cloister**, while further artworks from local churches and convents, including a saccharine Zurbarán of *Mary as a Child*, are displayed in the nearby **Museo Diocesano del Arte** (Tues–Fri 11am–2pm & 4–7pm, Sat, Sun & hols 11am–2pm & 5–8pm; €3, Wed free).

The cathedral looks out over the **Plaza Mayor** from where c/Mayor leads up to the castle, passing close by the church of **San Vicente**.

The **castle** started life as a Roman fortress, was adapted by the Visigoths and further improved by the Moors as their Alcazaba. Reconquered in 1124, it became the official residence of the warlike Bishop Bernardo and his successors. The Civil War virtually reduced the castle to rubble, but it was almost completely rebuilt in the 1970s and converted into a *parador*. You can still visit the central patio even if you are not staying at the hotel.

Eating

For **meals**, try the hotel restaurants at *El Motor* and *El Doncel*, or the *Restaurante Milano* at Avda. Juan Carlos I, 31, which has a €20 *menú*. Alternatively, go for tapas at the *Cafetería Atrio* on the Plaza Mayor or the *Gurugu de la Plazuela* (ⓦ www. gurugudelaplazuela.com), next to the Plazuela de la Cárcel, which specializes in wild mushrooms with some sixteen different varieties on the menu.

Around Sigüenza

Northeast from Sigüenza, just over the border in the Soria province of Castilla y León, is the picturesque town of **MEDINACELI**, perched in an exhilarating, breezy position above the Río Jalón. Highly evocative of its former glory as a Roman and Moorish stronghold, the original old town is sited 3km above the dull modern village, which lies on the main Madrid–Barcelona rail and road routes. Straight up the hill from the new village is the distinctive **Arco Romano** – a triple arch, in fact – that's unique in Spain. Its presence is something of a mystery: such monuments were usually built to commemorate military triumphs, but the cause of celebration at Medinaceli is unknown. A bit further along the road stands the dilapidated Moorish **castle**, now a mere facade sheltering a Christian cemetery. The quiet streets are full of ancient mansions with proud coats of arms, the grandest of which is the Palacio del Duque de Medinaceli on the Plaza Mayor that not long ago featured in a David Beckham Pepsi commercial set in the Middle Ages. It's an easy day-trip from Sigüenza, around a twenty-kilometre drive.

To the northwest is **Atienza**, an atmospheric former fortress town with five Romanesque churches and an almost impregnable castle perched high on the hill above. A good route for drivers heading south is to make for **Cuenca**, past great reservoirs watered by the Tajo and Guadiela rivers, and skirting around the **Alcarria** region.

Cuenca and around

The mountainous, craggy countryside around **CUENCA** is as dramatic as any in Spain. The city, the capital of a sparsely populated province, is an extraordinary-looking place, enclosed on three sides by the deep gorges of the Huécar and Júcar rivers, with balconied houses hanging over the cliff top – the finest of them tastefully converted into a wonderful museum of abstract art. No surprise, then, that this is a popular weekend outing from Madrid; to get the most from a visit, try to come on a weekday, and stay overnight; with this much time, you can make the short trip to see the bizarre limestone formations of the **Ciudad Encantada** and visit the picturesque source of the Río Cuervo.

Arrival and information

The old town of Cuenca – the **Ciudad Antigua** – stands on a high ridge, looped to the south by the Río Huécar and the **modern town** and its suburbs. If you're driving in, follow signs for the *catedral* and try one of the car parks beyond that up at the top of the old town. The **train and bus stations** are next to each other at the southern edge of the modern part of town. To get to the old town from here, head to the Puerta de Valencia, from where it's a steep climb; bus #1 or #2 will save you the twenty-minute walk.

Cuenca's helpful **turismo** is in the Plaza Mayor (summer Mon–Sat 9am–9pm, Sun 9am–2.30pm; winter Mon–Sat 9am–2pm & 5–8pm, Sun 9am–2pm; ☎969 241 051, ⓦwww.cuenca.org and www.turismocuenca.com). There is another office in the new town at Plaza Hispanidad (summer daily 9am–9pm, winter Mon–Sat 9am–2pm & 4–6.30pm, Sun 10am–2pm). **Internet** is available at *Cyber Viajero* at Avda. República Argentina 3 in the new town (Mon–Fri 10am–2pm & 5–11pm).

Accommodation

You'll find many **places to stay** in the new town, with a concentration of *hostales* along c/Ramón y Cajal, but there are several reasonably priced options in the old town.

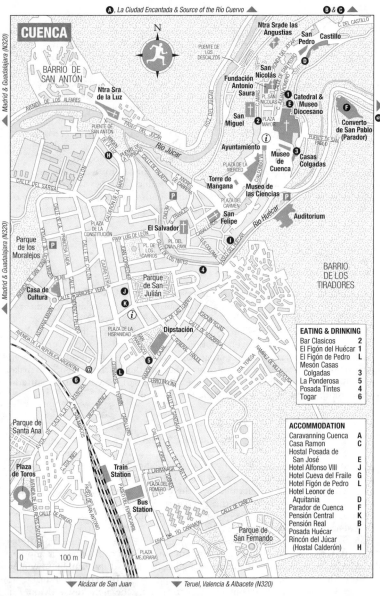

EATING & DRINKING

Bar Clasicos	2
El Figón del Huécar	1
El Figón de Pedro	L
Mesón Casas Colgadas	3
La Ponderosa	5
Posada Tintes	4
Togar	6

ACCOMMODATION

Caravanning Cuenca	A
Casa Ramon	C
Hostal Posada de San José	E
Hotel Alfonso VIII	J
Hotel Cueva del Fraile	G
Hotel Figón de Pedro	L
Hotel Leonor de Aquitania	D
Parador de Cuenca	F
Pensión Central	K
Pensión Real	B
Posada Huécar	I
Rincón del Júcar (Hostal Calderón)	H

▼ Alcázar de San Juan   ▼ Teruel, Valencia & Albacete (N320)

Casa Ramon c/La Paz s/n ☎659 066 204, ⓦwww.casa-ramon.com. Two modern apartments that can accommodate up to five people up at the top of the old town by the castle. €140 for five people, €90 for two, but rates are cheaper outside the peak holiday periods.

Hostal Posada de San José c/Julián Romero 4 ☎969 211 300,

ⓦwww.posadasanjose.com. A lovely old building with a tranquil garden in the old town near the cathedral. It has only 22 stylishly decorated rooms, so be sure to book ahead. There's a good-quality restaurant, too, and an extra €12 will get you a room with a view over the gorge. ❹

Hotel Alfonso VIII c/Parque de San Julián 3 ☎969 212 512, ⓦwww.hotel-alfonsoviii.com.

A nicely located hotel in the new town, facing the park. They also offer two-room apartments for between €80 and €150 depending on the time of year. ②–⑤ depending on season.

Hotel Cueva del Fraile Ctra. Cuenca-Buenache km 7 ☎969 211 571, ⓦ www.hotelcuevadelfraile .com. A sixteenth-century former monastery 5km out from Cuenca. The rooms are pleasantly furnished in antique style and the extensive grounds include a pool. It also has its own restaurant serving local specialities. ④–⑤

🏃 **Hotel Leonor de Aquitania** c/San Pedro 58–60 ☎969 231 000, ⓦ www.hotelleonor deaquitania.com. Cuenca's prime hotel, beautifully situated in an eighteenth-century nobleman's house in the old town. Tastefully decorated rooms with superb views and prices to match. A great spot for a meal, too. ④–⑤

Parador de Cuenca Convento de San Pablo ☎969 232 320, ⓦ www.paradores.com. Expensive, but not that special, although it does have a pool and great views across the gorge to the *Casas Colgadas*. ⑥

Pensión Central c/Dr Chirino 7, 2° ☎969 211 511. A basic but very good-value *pensión* offering fifteen large rooms with separate bath. ①

Pensión Real c/Larga 41 ☎969 229 977. The last building in the old town, with commanding views of Cuenca. Six rooms, with shared bathroom. ①

Posada Huécar c/Paseo del Huécar 3 ☎&ⓕ969 214 201, ⓦ www.posadahuecar.com. A characterful inn on the banks of the Río Huécar with pleasantly furnished rooms, all with en-suite bathrooms. Provides free cots for babies. ②

Rincón del Júcar (Hostal Calderón) Avda Virgen de la Luz 3 ☎969 238 365, ⓦ www.hostalcalderon .net. A neat well-appointed *hostal* with 10 en-suite rooms and its own cafetería located close to a park down by the rivers in the new town. ③

Campsite

Carvanning Cuenca 6km north of the city on the CM 2105 (no bus) ☎969 231 656. A riverside location for this extremely well-appointed campsite with a great pool, surrounded by shady pines. Closed mid-Oct to mid-March.

The Ciudad Antigua

At the centre of the rambling **Ciudad Antigua** is the Plaza Mayor, a fine space, entered through the arches of the Baroque *ayuntamiento* and ringed by cafés and ceramic shops. Occupying most of its east side is the **Catedral** (daily 10.30am– 2pm & 4–6.30pm, July & Aug closes 7pm and open all day on Sat & Sun, closed some feast days; €2.80), whose incongruous, unfinished facade betrays a misguided attempt to beautify a simple Gothic building after the tower collapsed. The interior is much more attractive, especially the carved Plateresque arch at the end of the north aisle and the chapel next to it, with distinctly un-Christian carvings round its entrance.

Alongside is a small **Tesoro Catedralicio** (same hours and entry fee), which contains some beautiful gold and silver work, as well as wooden doors by Alonso Berruguete. Further religious treasures are to be found in the adjacent **Museo Diocesano** (Tues–Sat 10am–2pm & 4–7pm, Sun 11am–2pm; €2) on c/Obispo Valero, including two canvases by El Greco, a magnificent *Crucifixion* by Gerard David and a Byzantine diptych unique in Spain. Right opposite is the excellent **Museo de Cuenca** (summer Tues–Sat 10am–2pm & 5–7pm, Sun 11am–2pm; winter Tues–Sat 10am–2pm & 4–7pm, Sun 11am–2pm; €1.20), which traces the city's history from prehistoric times and showcases a good local Roman collection from local finds.

The artistic highlight of Cuenca, however, has to be the nearby **Museo de Arte Abstracto** (Tues–Fri 11am–2pm & 4–6pm, Sat 11am–2pm & 4–8pm, Sun 11am–2.30pm; €3), a gallery established in the 1960s by Fernando Zóbel, one of the leading artists in Spain's "abstract generation". It is now run by the prestigious Fundación Juan March, which displays works from a core collection of abstract painting and sculpture by, among many others, Eduardo Chillida, José Guerrero, Lucio Muñoz, Antonio Saura, Antonio Tàpies and Fernando Zóbel, and hosts some of the best exhibitions to be found in provincial Spain. The museum itself is a stunning conversion from the extraordinary *Casas Colgadas* ("Hanging Houses"), a pair of fifteenth-century houses, with cantilevered

▲ Hanging Houses, Cuenca

balconies, literally hanging from the cliff face. A little further up the hill from here in the Casa Zavala on Plaza de San Nicolás is the **Fundación Antonio Saura** (Mon, Wed–Sat 11am–2pm & 5–9pm, winter 4–8pm, Sun 11am–2pm; free), which contains some important and striking work by the renowned Spanish surrealist who died in Cuenca in 1998. There are also excellent **views** from the top of the old city; just follow the road out of the Plaza Mayor or take bus #1 or #2 until you reach the castle.

Back down the hill in Plaza de la Merced is the **Museo del las Ciencias** (Tues–Sat 10am–2pm & 4–7pm, Sun 10am–2pm; €1.20 for museum, €1.20 for the planetarium). Housed in an old convent and an adjoining modern extension, it is an ambitious, and largely successful, attempt to explain the origins of the universe and the history of the earth in the context of the local region.

Eating, drinking and nightlife

The Plaza Mayor is the place to head for evening *copas*, with its vibrant and diverse range of **bars**. The liveliest joints are on c/Severo Catalina and in the little alleyways overlooking the Río Júcar, where you'll find the *Taberna-Artistica*

Los Elefantes, a long-time artists' hangout playing a good range of alternative music, and the excellent *Las Tortugas* at no. 39. Another popular area is on and around c/Parque del Huécar, where the crowds start off around midnight, moving on later to c/Alferez Rubianes. A host of bars around the stations and c/Fermin Caballero play salsa.

Bar Clasicos c/Severo Catalina 5. A cosy little place in the street below the Plaza Mayor. It does a good-value *menú* and has a small terrace that overlooks the Río Júcar.

🏃 **El Figón del Huécar** c/Julián Romero 6 ☎969 240 062. Inventive cuisine in this place up in the old town, dishes range from quail stuffed with grapes to pork steak with aroma of truffles. Mains €15–20.

El Figón de Pedro c/Cervantes 13 ☎969 226 821. A renowned restaurant, serving classic Castilian roasts, regional specialities and superb fish dishes at moderate to expensive prices. Closed Sun eve.

🏃 **Mesón Casas Colgadas** c/Canónigos 3 ☎969 223 509. A classy restaurant in the old town run by the same people as *El Figón de Pedro* and housed in a fine hanging house. The menu features suckling pig and other Castilian specialities. Expect to pay around €40 a head. Closed Mon eve.

La Ponderosa c/San Francisco 20. The best tapas selection in a street full of worthwhile *mesónes*. Closed Sun & July.

Posada Tintes c/Tintes 7. This popular and atmospheric local serves up a wide range of moderately priced dishes. Closed Mon.

Togar Avda. República Argentina 1. Well-prepared, moderately priced home-style cooking draws diners to this friendly little place near the train station.

La Ciudad Encantada

The classic excursion from Cuenca is to the **Ciudad Encantada**, a twenty-square-kilometre "park" of karst limestone outcrops, sculpted by erosion into a bizarre series of abstract, natural and animal-like forms. A few of the names – "fight between an elephant and a crocodile", for example – stretch the imagination a little, but the rocks are certainly amazing, and many of the creations really do look knocked into shape by human hands. The fantasy landscape was used as a backdrop for Arnold Schwarzenegger's first major film *Conan the Barbarian*.

The most interesting area of sculptures is enclosed (daily 10am–dusk; €3), and the extensive car park and restaurants outside testify to its popularity with weekending *madrileños*. However, off season, or during the week, you can have the place almost to yourself. Just outside the entrance there are signs to the **Mirador de Uña**, providing excellent views over the valley. You will need your own transport to get to the park, which is around 20km northeast of Cuenca, on signed backroads towards Albarracín. If you get stuck, there is a quiet and comfortable **hostal**, the *Ciudad Encantada* (☎969 288 194, ⓦwww .hotelciudadencantada.com; ❸), opposite the entrance gate.

Another 30km farther north on the CM 2106 past Tragacete is the **source of the Río Cuervo**, a moss-covered crag peppered with waterfalls.

East into Teruel

If you have transport, the route east from the Ciudad Encantada towards Albarracín is a delight, edging through the verdant **Júcar Gorge** and across the wild, scarcely populated Serranía de Cuenca. En route, still in Cuenca Province, you might stop at **Uña**, a village sited between a lagoon and barrage, where the lakeside *Hotel Agua Riscas* (☎969 282 852, ⓦwww.hotelaguariscas.es; ❸) at c/Egido 23 has decent rooms, a panoramic restaurant and a garden bar.

Just over the provincial border, in Teruel Province, the road between Uña and Frías de Albarracín runs past a point known as García, close to the **source of the Río Tajo** where the great river begins its journey across Iberia to the Atlantic.

Segóbriga and Alarcón

Travelling south with your own transport from Cuenca, you'll find Cuenca Province has a couple more places where you might consider breaking your journey: the impressive Roman ruins at **Segóbriga** (just off the A3 back towards Madrid) and the castle village of **Alarcón** (just off the NIII to Valencia).

Segóbriga

Just south of the NIII, near the village of Saelices, **SEGÓBRIGA** (April–Sept Tues–Sun 9am–9pm; Oct–March 10am–6pm; €4) makes a worthy detour for anyone interested in Roman ruins. References to the town date back to the second century BC and it developed into a prosperous settlement largely thanks to the presence of nearby gypsum mines. The town reached its peak about four hundred years later, but declined under the Visigoths and was effectively abandoned during the Arab occupation. The best-preserved structures are the theatre and amphitheatre – which had a capacity for 5500 people – but there are also some interesting additions made by the Visigoths. There is a small museum on the site that recounts the history of what was a fairly important settlement.

Alarcón

Lively **ALARCÓN** occupies an imposing defensive site sculpted by the burrowing of the Río Júcar. Almost completely encircled and walled, the village is accessible by a spit of land just wide enough to take a road that passes through a succession of **fortified gateways**.

At the top of the village is an exquisite **castle**, eighth-century in origin and captured from the Moors in 1184 after a nine-month siege. This has been converted into **accommodation**, the ⚐ *Parador Marqués de Villena* (☎969 330 315, ⓦwww.paradores.com; ❼), one of the country's smallest and most characterful *paradores*. More affordable is the *Pensión El Infante*, c/Dr Tortosa 6 (☎969 330 323, ⓦwww.posadaelinfante.com; ❷). Either option should be booked ahead in summer or at weekends. The *parador*, with its atmospheric dining hall, is the best place to **eat**, and there is cheaper fare served at the bars on the main Plaza de Don Juan Manuel.

Albacete province

Travelling between Madrid or Cuenca and Alicante or Murcia, you'll pass through **Albacete province**, one of Spain's more forgettable corners. Hot, arid plains for the most part, the province shelters the lovely **Alcalá del Júcar** and the humdrum provincial capital, **Albacete**. Scenically, the only relief is in the hyperactive **Río Júcar**, which, in the north of the province, sinks almost without warning into the plain.

Alcalá del Júcar

If you are driving, it's certainly worth making a detour off the main roads east to take the scenic route along the banks of the Río Júcar, between Valdeganga and the stunning village of **ALCALÁ DEL JÚCAR**. Almost encircled by the river, the village is an amazing sight, with its houses built one on top of the other and burrowed into the white cliff face. Several of these **cuevas** (caves)

3

have been converted into bars and restaurants and make a great place for a drink, with rooms carved up to 170m through the cliff and windows overlooking the river on each side of the loop. They're open daily in summer but otherwise only at weekends.

Alcalá also boasts a **castle** – adapted at intervals over the past 1500 years, though today just a shell – with great views. There are two simple **hostales** on the main road at the bottom of the village – *Hermanos Plaza* (℡967 473 029, Ⓦwww.hermanosplaza.com; ❷) and the *Júcar* (℡967 473 055; ❷) – and the rather nicer *Hostal Pelayo* (℡967 473 099; Ⓦwww.hotel-restaurante-pelayo .com; ❷), Avda. Constitución 4, which has its own restaurant. There is also a popular campsite, *El Berrocal*, with a swimming pool on the banks of the river on the outskirts of town (℡967 473 212).

Albacete

ALBACETE was named *Al-Basit* – "the plain" – by the Moors, but save for a few old backstreets, it is basically a modern city. The **Catedral** is not of any great interest and is noteworthy only for the presence of Ionic columns instead of normal pillars astride its nave. The **Museo Provincial de Albacete** (Tues–Sat 10am–2pm & 4.30–7pm, Sun 10am–2pm, open mornings only in summer; €1.20), however, has a more than respectable archeological and ethnographical collection, whose prize exhibits are five small Roman dolls, perfectly sculpted and jointed, and an array of local Roman mosaics. For Spaniards, Albacete is synonymous with high-quality knives, a speciality that, as with Toledo, can be traced back to the Moors: if you're after some top cutlery, this is your chance. There's even a **Museo de la Cuchillería** (Knife Museum) by the cathedral (Tues–Sat 10am–2pm & 5.30–8pm, Sun 10am–2pm; €2). A more family-oriented visit is the **Museo del Niño** (Museum of Children) in c/Méjico (Mon–Fri 9.30am-1.30pm; free) next to the Los Llanos shopping centre, which has exhibits on the history of childhood including school, recreation and home.

Practicalities

Albacete's **turismo** is at c/Tinte 2 (Mon–Fri: 10am–2pm & 4.30–7.30pm, Sat & Sun 10am–2pm; ℡967 580 522). There's no real reason to **stay**, unless you want to break a longer journey, in which case, try the modern *Hotel San José* (℡967 507 402, Ⓦwww.hotelsanjose-albacete.es; ❹–❺) in c/San José de Calasanz 12, close to the pleasant city-centre park. Don't be tempted by signs to Albacete's *parador*, a modern creation southeast of the town, right on the flight path of a military airfield.

The city is full of **tapas bars** and **restaurants** serving high-quality local produce with several good options to be found in the streets around the cathedral.

Ciudad Real and the heartland of La Mancha

There is a huge gap in the middle of the tourist map of Spain between Toledo and the borders of Andalucía, and from Extremadura almost to the east coast. This, the province of **Ciudad Real**, comprises the heartland of **La Mancha**. The tourist authorities try hard to push their *Ruta de Don Quixote* across the plains, highlighting the windmills and other Quixotic sights: the signposted route, which starts at Belmonte and finishes at Consuegra, can be done in a day, but much of it is fanciful and, unless you're enamoured with the book, it's only of passing interest.

Nonetheless, there are a few places that merit a visit if you've got time to spare, most notably **Consuegra**, for the best windmills, **Almagro**, for its arcaded square and medieval theatre, and **Calatrava**, for the castle ruins of its order of knights. It is also the heart of wine-producing country, and many of the *bodegas* in **Valdepeñas** offer free tastings. The **websites** ⓦwww.elquijote .com and ⓦwww.castillalamancha.es/turismo both give more information about the area.

Consuegra

CONSUEGRA lies just to the west of the A4 *autovía*, roughly midway from Madrid to Andalucía, and has the most picturesque and typical of Manchegan settings, below a ridge of eleven restored (and highly photogenic) windmills. The first of these is occupied by the town's **turismo**, with uncertain – indeed, truly Quixotic – opening hours (usually Mon–Fri 9am–2pm & 3.30–6pm, Sat 10.30am–2pm & 3.30–6pm, Sun 10.30am–2pm; ⓦwww.consuegra.es), but good for information on the *Ruta de Don Quixote*, while others house shops and workshops. They share their plateau with a ruined **castle**, which was once the headquarters of the order of St John in the twelfth century and offers splendid views of the plain from its windswept ridge. The town below is also attractive, with a lively Plaza Mayor and many Mudéjar churches.

Don Quixote

Not a novel in the modern sense, **Miguel Cervantes'** *Don Quijote de La Mancha* (published in 1604) is a sequence of episodes following the adventures of a country gentleman in his fifties, whose mind has been addled by romantic tales of chivalry. In a noble gesture, he changes his name to Don Quixote de La Mancha, and sets out on horseback, in rusty armour, to right the wrongs of the world. At his side throughout is **Sancho Panza**, a shrewd, pot-bellied rustic given to quoting proverbs at every opportunity. During the course of the book, Quixote, an instantly sympathetic hero, charges at windmills and sheep (mistaking them for giants and armies), makes ill-judged attempts to help others and is mocked by all for his efforts. Broken-hearted but wiser, he returns home and, on his deathbed, pronounces: "Let everyone learn from my example … look at the world with common sense and learn to see what is really there."

Cervantes' life was almost as colourful as his hero's. The son of a poor doctor, he fought as a soldier in the sea battle of **Lepanto**, where he permanently maimed his left hand and was captured by pirates and put to work as a slave in Algiers. Ransomed and sent back to Spain, he spent the rest of his days writing novels and plays in relative poverty, dying ten years after the publication of *Don Quixote*, "old, a soldier, a gentleman and poor".

Spanish academics have spent as much time dissecting the work of Cervantes as their English counterparts have Shakespeare's. Most see *Don Quixote* as a satire on the popular romances of the day, with the central characters representing two forces in Spain; Quixote the dreaming, impractical nobility, and Sancho the wise and down-to-earth peasantry. There are also those who read in it an ironic tale of a visionary or martyr frustrated in a materialistic world, while others see it as an attack on the Church and establishment. Debates aside, this highly entertaining adventure story is certainly one of the most influential works to have emerged from Spain.

Places to stay are limited to two friendly options, the *Vida de Antes* (☎925 480 609, ⓦwww.lavidadeantes.com; €65–80) at c/Colón 2, a cosy hotel with nine individually designed rooms, and the busy and comfortable *Hotel Las Provincias* (☎925 482 000, ⓦwww.restaurantelasprovincias.com; €50), which has a good restaurant and is within walking distance on the main road north of town.

Ciudad Real

The city of **CIUDAD REAL**, capital of the province at the heart of this flat country, makes a good base for excursions and has connections by bus with most villages in the area. It has a few sights of its own, too, including a Mudéjar gateway, the **Puerta de Toledo**, which fronts the only surviving fragment of its medieval walls, at the northern edge of the city on the Toledo road. Further in, take a look at the fourteenth-century church of **San Pedro**, an airy, Gothic edifice, housing some exquisite chapels and an elaborate fifteenth-century alabaster *retablo*, and the **Museo Provincial** (July–Aug Tues–Sat 10am–2pm; Sept–July Tues–Sat 10am–2pm & 5–8pm, Sun 10am–2pm; free), a modern building opposite the cathedral, with two floors of local archeology (the second also has some stuffed local wildlife) and a third devoted to artists of the region. More entertaining is the **Museo de Don Quijote** (July–Aug daily 10am–2pm; Sept–June Mon–Sat 10am–2pm & 5–8pm, Sun 10am–2pm; free), where personalities from the story guide you round the exhibits that include some smart audiovisuals bringing the tale to life.

Practicalities

The two local **turismos** (Mon–Sat 10am–2pm & 4–7pm, Sun 10am–2pm; ☎926 200 037) are at c/Alarcos 21 in the centre of town, a ten-minute walk from the **bus station** on the Ronda de Ciruela and on the Plaza Mayor (Tues–Sat 10am–2pm & 5–9pm, Sat & Sun 10am–2pm; ☎926 210 044, ⓦwww.ciudadreal.es, ⓦwww.tierradecaballeros.com). Ciudad Real's **train station**, with high-speed AVE connections to Madrid and south to Seville and Córdoba, lies out of town at the end of Avenida de Europa; bus #5 connects with the central Plaza de Pilar.

Accommodation is not always easy to find, so it's worth booking ahead. The *Pensión Escudero*, c/Galicia 48 (☎926 252 309; ❷), is one of the cheapest options, the *Hostal Plaza* (☎926 923 500, ⓦwww.hostalplazacr.es; ❸) is a more comfortable well-equipped option, while the four-star *Hotel Santa Cecilia*, c/Tinte 3 (☎926 228 545, ⓦwww.santacecilia.com; ❸–❹), is also reasonably priced. An impressive range of **tapas bars** includes *Casa Lucio*, off c/Montesa at Pasaje Dulcinea del Toboso, and *Gran Mesón*, Ronda Ciruela 34, which also has a swankier restaurant, *Miami Park*, down the road at no. 48. Look out for local specialities like *migas* (breadcrumbs, garlic, chorizo and pepper) and *atascaburras* (pureed potato, garlic and cod) in the *Mesón El Ventero* in the Plaza Mayor. The town's **nightlife** at the weekend generally starts off with tapas on c/Palma, carrying on to the bars along Avenida Torreón del Alcázar and around.

Almagro

Twenty kilometres east of Ciudad Real is **ALMAGRO**, an elegant little town, which for a period in the fifteenth and sixteenth centuries was quite a metropolis in southern Castile, partly thanks to the influence of the Fuggers, bankers to the Habsburg king and Holy Roman Emperor Carlos I (Charles V).

National parks and reserves in La Mancha

A respite from the arid monotony of the Castilian landscape, and a treat for bird-watchers, is provided by the oasis of **La Mancha Húmeda** ("Wet La Mancha"). This is an area of lagoons and marshes, both brackish and fresh, along the high-level basin of the **Río Cigüela** and **Río Guadiana**. Drainage for agriculture has severely reduced the amount of water in recent years, so that the lakes effectively dry up in the summer, but there is still a good variety of interesting plant and bird life. You're best off visiting from April to July when the water birds are breeding, or from September to midwinter when migrating birds pass through.

Major parks between Ciudad Real and Albacete include the **Parque Nacional de las Tablas de Daimiel**, 11km north of Daimiel itself, which is renowned for its bird life. There's an **information centre** (daily: summer 8.30am–8pm; winter 8am–6.30pm; ☏ 926 693 118) alongside the marshes. The park is accessible only by car or taxi, and Daimiel has little **accommodation** on offer outside the upmarket *Hotel Las Tablas* (☏ 926 852 108, ⓦ www.hotellastablas.com; ❸–❹).

Rather more traveller-friendly, but more crowded in the summer months, is the **Parque Natural de las Lagunas de Ruidera**, which lies northeast of Valdepeñas (frequent buses from Albacete). You'll find an **information centre** (July & Aug daily 10am–9pm; Sept–June Wed–Sun 10am–2pm & 4–6pm; ☏ 926 528 116) on the roadside, as you enter Ruidera from Manzanares, and several nature trails inside the park, as well as swimming and boating opportunities. **Accommodation** here ranges from a campsite, *Los Molinos* (☏ 926 528 089; Easter & July to mid-Sept), with a pool, and the friendly *Hostal La Noria* (☏ 926 528 032; ❷), to the good-value *Don Quijote Aparthotel* (☏ 625 406 772; ❸) and the comfortable *Hotel Entrelagos* (☏ 926 528 022, ⓦ www.entrelagos.com; ❷–❸).

Arrival and information

There's a small **turismo** just south of Plaza Mayor on c/Bernadas 2 (April–June & Aug–Oct Tues–Fri 10am–2pm & 5–8pm, Sat 10am–2pm & 5–7pm, Sun 11am–2pm; July Tues–Fri 10am–2pm & 6–9pm, Sat 10am–2pm & 6–8pm, Sun 11am–2pm; Nov–March Tues–Fri 10am–2pm & 4–7pm, Sat 10am–2pm & 4–6pm, Sun 11am–2pm; ☏ 926 860 717, ⓦ www.ciudad-almagro.com).

Almagro is connected to Madrid with two direct **trains** a day and to Ciudad Real with five trains and **buses**; the train station is a short distance from the centre of town along the Paseo de la Estación, while buses stop near the *Hotel Don Diego* on the Ronda de Calatrava.

Accommodation

Almagro is a great place to **stay**, although accommodation can be fairly limited during the theatre festival and at holiday weekends, so make sure you book ahead.

🏃 **Casa del Rector** c/Pedro Oviedo 8 ☏ 926 261 259, ⓦ www.lacasadelrector.com. Some delightful and atmospheric rooms, each with their own individual decor, set around a beautiful interior patio. ❹–❺

Hospedería Almagro Ejido de Calatrava s/n ☏ 926 882 087, ⓕ 926 882 122. Over forty simple and functional rooms in this neat hotel located next to the convent. A pleasant patio bar and restaurant. ❷

Hostal Los Escudos c/Bolaños 55 ☏ 926 861 574, ⓦ www.hostallosescudos.es. Thirteen individually decorated, a/c rooms in this upmarket little *hostal* well located for all the main sights. ❶–❷

Hotel Don Diego c/Bolaños 1 ☏ 926 861 287, ⓕ 926 860 574. A recently refurbished two-star hotel due east of the plaza. ❹

Parador de Almagro c/Gran Maestre ☏ 926 860 100, ⓦ www.paradores.com. Housed in a sixteenth-century Franciscan convent, this historic *parador* features some peaceful interior courtyards and a great swimming pool. ❻

The Town

Today, its main claim to fame is the **Corral de las Comedias**, in the Plaza Mayor, a perfectly preserved sixteenth-century open-air theatre, unique in Spain. Plays from its sixteenth- and seventeenth-century heyday – the golden age of Spanish theatre – are performed regularly in the tiny auditorium, and throughout July it hosts a fully fledged theatre festival (Ⓦ www.festivaldealmagro.com). By day the theatre is open to visitors though the visiting hours are complex and can be subject to variation (as at the tourist office, but usually Tues–Sun 10am–2pm & evening; €2.50). Across the square on Callejon de Villar, the **Museo del Teatro** (Tues–Fri 10am–2pm & 4–7pm, Sat 11am–2pm & 4–6pm, Sun 11am–2pm, July Tues–Fri 11am–2pm & 6–9pm, Sat 11am–2pm & 7–9pm, Sun 11am–2pm; €1.20) houses photos, posters, model theatres and other paraphernalia, but is probably only of passing interest to anyone other than theatre buffs.

The **Plaza Mayor** itself is magnificent: more of a wide street than a square, it is arcaded along its length, and lined with rows of green-framed windows – a north European influence brought by the Fugger family, Carlos V's bankers, who settled here. Also resident in Almagro for a while were the Knights of Calatrava (see below), though their power was on the wane by the time the **Convento de la Asunción de Calatrava** was built in the early sixteenth century. Further traces of Almagro's former importance are dotted throughout the town in the grandeur of numerous **Renaissance mansions**.

Back in the Plaza Mayor, you can have an open-air snack or browse among the shops in the arcades, where **lacemakers** at work with bobbins and needles are the main attraction. On Wednesday mornings there's a lively **market** in c/Ejido de San Juan.

Eating and drinking

Tapas **bars** cluster around the Plaza Mayor; and the *bodega* at the *parador* is worth a stop for a drink, too.

La Cuerda Plaza del General Jorreto 6. Just in front of the train station, this is a cheap option with a good *menú* specializing in fish and *arroz* for around €10 (closed Mon eve and first 2 weeks in Sept).

 Mesón El Corregidor c/Jerónimo Ceballos 2. The best restaurant in town, although somewhat overpriced at around €50 per head. Specialities include game and locally grown vegetables. Closed Mon & first week in Aug.

La Posada de Almagro c/Gran Maestre 5. There are two beautiful interior patios in this restaurant that specializes in local delicacies and roast lamb. A meal costs in the region of €35 a head.

Calatrava La Nueva

The area known as the **Campo de Calatrava**, south of Almagro and Ciudad Real, was the domain of the **Knights of Calatrava**, a Cistercian order of soldier-monks at the forefront of the reconquest of Spain from the Moors. So influential were they in these parts that Alfonso X created Ciudad Real as a royal check on their power. Even today, dozens of villages for many kilometres around are suffixed with their name.

In the opening decades of the thirteenth century, the knights pushed their headquarters south, as land was won back, from Calatrava La Vieja, near Daimiel, to a commanding hilltop 25km south of Almagro, protecting an important pass – the Puerto de Calatrava – into Andalucía. Here, in 1216, they founded **Calatrava La Nueva**, a settlement that was part monastery and part castle, and whose main glory was a great Cistercian church. The site (Tues–Sun: summer 10am–2pm & 5–7pm; winter 10am–6pm; free) is reached by turning west off the main road (CM410) and following the signposts uphill. Once there, you will get a good idea of what must have been an enormously rich and well-protected fortress. The church itself is now completely bare but preserves the outline of a striking rose window and has an amazing stone-vaulted entrance hall.

On the hill opposite is a further castle ruin, known as **Salvatierra**, which the knights took over from the Moors.

Valdepeñas and beyond

The road from Ciudad Real through Almagro continues to **VALDEPEÑAS**, centre of the most prolific wine region in Spain and handily situated just off the main Madrid–Andalucía motorway. You pass many of the largest **bodegas** on the slip road into town coming from the north and Madrid; most of them offer free tastings – ask at the **turismo** on the Plaza España (summer Tues–Sat 10am–2pm & 5–7pm, Sun 11.30am–1.30pm winter same hours but 4–6pm; ☎926 312 552, ⓦwww.valdepenas.es). Another option is the hi-tech **museo del vino** at c/Princesa 39, close to Plaza de España (May–Sept Tues–Sat 10.30am–2pm & 6–8.30pm, Sun noon–2pm; free). The town holds a popular wine **festival** at the beginning of September. Wine aside, there are few other sights. There is a **windmill**, again on the Madrid road, which the tourist office says "could be the biggest in Europe", and a museum dedicated to the abstract drawings and other work of local artist Gregorio Prieto (Tues–Sat 10am–1.30pm & 5–8pm, Sun 11.30am–2pm; free). If you choose to **stay** here try the neat and tidy *Hostal Valdepeñas* (☎926 322 328; ❷) at Avda. Gregorio Prieto 47 or the more upmarket *Hospedería Museo Valdepeñas* (☎926 310 795, ⓕ926 310 882; ❸) at c/Unión 98.

Heading south beyond Valdepeñas, you enter Andalucía through the **Gorge of Despeñaperros** (literally, "Throwing Over of the Dogs"), a narrow mountain gorge once notorious for bandits and still a dramatic natural gateway that signals a change in both climate and vegetation, or as Richard Ford put it (travelling south to north), "exchanges an Eden for a desert".

The Montes de Toledo

The **Montes de Toledo** cut a swathe through the upper reaches of La Mancha, between Toledo, Ciudad Real and Guadalupe. If you're heading into Extremadura, and have time and transport, the deserted little roads across these hills (they rise to just over 1400m) provide an interesting and atmospheric alternative to the main routes. This is an amazingly remote region to find so close to the centre of Spain: its people are so unused to visitors that in the smaller villages you'll certainly get a few odd looks.

Toledo to Navalmoral de la Mata

The CM4000, west of Toledo, provides a direct approach into **Extremadura**, linking with the A5 from Madrid to Trujillo, and with roads north into the valley of **La Vera** (see p.204). It follows the course of the Río Tajo virtually all the way to uninspiring **TALAVERA DE LA REINA**, known for its manufacture of ceramics; 33km farther west lies **OROPESA**, the best place to stay in this area: the *Parador Virrey de Toledo* (☎925 430 000, ⓦwww .parador.es; ❺) is installed in part of the village **castle**, a warm, stone building on a Roman site, rebuilt from Moorish foundations in the fifteenth century by Don García Álvarez de Toledo. Below it, stretches of the old town walls survive, along with a few noble mansions and a pair of Renaissance churches. There are great views from the neatly manicured gardens across to the hulking silhouettes of the Gredos mountain range on the horizon, beyond which an attractive minor road, from **Oropesa**, with its castle *parador*, runs to **El Puente del Arzobispo** and south of the river to the Roman site of **Los Vascos**. West again, **Navalmoral de la Mata** has nothing to offer other than its road, rail and bus connections to more engrossing places such as the **Monasterio de Yuste** across the rich tobacco-growing area to the north, **Plasencia** to the west, and **Trujillo** and **Guadalupe** to the south.

Into the hills

The most accessible route into the Montes de Toledo from Talavera is via the CM4000 and then the CM4009 and CM403 south of La Puebla de Montalbán, which runs through the backwater village of **Las Ventas Con Peña Aguilera**, overlooked by rock-studded hills, including a curious outcrop shaped like three fat fingers – the name Peña Aguilera means "Crag of Eagles". Southwest of Las Ventas, a tiny road leads to **San Pablo de los Montes**, a delightful village of fine stone houses nestling against the mountains. Beyond here, you can walk over the hills to the spa of **Baños del Robledillo**, a spectacular five- to six-hour trek (get directions locally or at the *turismo* in the Museo La Celestina in Puebla de Montalbán at Avda. de Madrid 1; ☎925 776 542).

If you keep to the CM403 south of Las Ventas, you will come to the main pass over the Montes de Toledo, the **Puerto del Milagro**, with great views of the hills dipping down on either side to meet the plain. Past the Puerto del Milagro, you can drive through lovely scenery towards Ciudad Real, or turn right along the CM4017 at the El Molinillo junction to follow a road through the hills via Retuerta del Bullaque to **Navas de Estena**. Here the road curves round to the north, passing a large crag with caves 5km beyond Navas, allowing you to loop round to Navahermosa and on to the CM401 to Guadalupe.

Extremadura

Once neglected and overlooked by many visitors, **Extremadura** has established itself on the tourist trail – and deservedly so. The grand old *conquistador* towns of **Trujillo** and **Cáceres** are excellent staging posts en route south from Madrid or Salamanca; **Mérida** has numerous Roman remains and an exemplary museum of local finds; and there is superb bird life in the **Parque Natural de Monfragüe**. Almost inaccessible by public transport, but well worth visiting, is the great **monastery of Guadalupe**, whose revered icon of the Virgin has attracted pilgrims for the past five hundred years. The lush hills and valley of **La Vera** are the first real patch of green you'll come to if you've driven along the A5 west from Madrid.

La Vera

Characterized by its lovely *gargantas* – streams – **La Vera** lies just south of the Sierra de Gredos, a range of hills tucked above the **Río Tiétar** valley. In spring and summer, the area attracts bands of weekenders from Madrid to the picturesque villages of **Candeleda** and **Jarandilla**. At the heart of the region is the **Monasterio de Yuste**, the retreat chosen by Carlos V to cast off the cares of empire.

Jarandilla and around

The main village in these parts is **JARANDILLA DE LA VERA**, with some good, affordable places to **stay**, among them the comfortable *Ruta Imperial* (☎927 561 330, ⓦwww.hotelruralrutaimperial.com; ❸–❹) and *Posada de Pizarro* (☎927 560 727, ⓦwww.laposadadepizarro.com; ❷–❸), with frescoes on the bedroom walls. There is also a wonderful fifteenth-century *parador*, the 🛪 *Parador Carlos V* (☎927 560 117, ⓦwww.paradores.com; ❻), in the castle where the emperor stayed during the construction of Yuste, and the *Don Juan de Austria* spa hotel (☎927 560 206, ⓦwww.hoteljaranda.com; from €100 per person). If you've got a tent to pitch, head for the attractive *Camping Jaranda* (☎927 560 454; mid-March to Sept). In the village there are several decent **restaurants** (try *Leti* and *Casa Tarra* for regional dishes) and a scattering of **bars**. Buses run through here, en route between Madrid and Plasencia; the stop is outside *Bar Charly* on the main road.

There is good **walking** around Jarandilla. A track into the hills leads to the village of **El Guijo de Santa Barbara** (4.5km) and then ends, leaving the ascent of the rocky valley beyond to walkers. An hour's trek away is a pool known as *El Trabuquete* and a high meadow with shepherds' huts known as *Pimesaíllo*. On the other side of the valley – a serious trek needing a night's camping and good area maps – is the *Garganta de Infierno* (Stream of Hell) and natural swimming pools known as *Los Pilones*.

▲ Parador Carlos V, Jarandilla

The *gargantas* are flanked in summer by some superb **campsites**: *Minchones* (℡927 565 403; Easter & June to mid-Sept) is just outside **Villanueva de la Vera**, a village to the east of Jarandilla along the EX 203 that has gained a certain amount of notoriety for its *Pero Palo* fiesta, in which donkeys are horribly mistreated. It seems strange to imagine any cruelty, given the rural idyll hereabouts and the incredibly house-proud appearance of the villages, especially **Losar**, which has an almost surreal display of topiary.

The Monasterio de Yuste

There is nothing especially dramatic about the **Monasterio de Yuste** (Tues–Fri 10.30am–1.30pm & 3–5.15pm, Sat, Sun & hols 10.30am–5.15pm; compulsory guided tour in Spanish €2.50, free Wed), the retreat created by Carlos V after renouncing his empire: just a simple beauty and the rather stark accoutrements of the emperor's last years. The monastery, which is signposted from Cuacos de Yuste on the Jarandilla-Plasencia road, had existed here for over a century before Carlos's retirement and he had earmarked the site for some years, planning his modest additions – which included a pleasure garden – while still ruling his empire from Flanders. He retired here with a retinue that included an Italian clockmaker, Juanuelo Turriano, whose inventions were his last passion.

The imperial apartments are draped throughout in black, and exhibits include the little sedan chair in which Carlos was brought here, and another designed to support the old man's gouty legs. If you believe the guide, the bed and even the sheets are the very ones in which the emperor died, though since the place was sacked during the Peninsular War and deserted for years after the suppression of the monasteries, this seems unlikely. A door by the emperor's bed opens out over the church and altar so that even in his final illness he never missed a service. Outside, there's a snack bar and picnic spots, and you'll find a track signposted through the woods to Garganta La Olla (see below).

Cuacos de Yuste

The monastery is 2km into the wooded hills from **CUACOS DE YUSTE**, an attractive village with a couple of squares, including the tiny Plaza de Don Juan de Austria, named after the house (its upper floor reconstructed) where Carlos's illegitimate son Don Juan lived when visiting his father. The surrounding houses, their overhanging upper floors supported on gnarled wooden pillars, are sixteenth-century originals, and from the beams underneath the overhang tobacco is hung out to dry after the harvest. There are several **bars**, a good family-run **hotel**, ☆ *La Vera* (℡927 172 178, @www.verahotel.com; ❸–❹), with a swimming pool, and a shady **campsite**, *Carlos I* (℡927 172 092; late March to mid-Sept).

Garganta La Olla

Just beyond Jaraíz de la Vera, a left turning leads for around 5km to **GARGANTA LA OLLA** a beautiful, ramshackle mountain village set among cherry orchards. There are several things to look out for: the **Casa de Putas** (a brothel for the soldiers of Carlos V's army, now a butcher's but still painted the traditional blue) and the **Casa de la Piedra** (House of Stone), a house whose balcony is secured by a three-pronged wooden support resting on a rock. The latter is hard to find; begin by taking the left-hand street up from the square and then ask. If you want to spend the night here, it's either the tiny *Hostal Yuste*

(☎&ⓕ927 179 604; ❷) or the larger and more comfortable *Hotel Rural Carlos I* (☎927 179 678, ⓦwww.hotelcarlosprimero.com; ❸).

From Garganta, there is a signposted short-cut track to the Monasterio de Yuste.

El Valle de Jerte

Immediately north of La Vera, the main Plasencia–Ávila road follows the valley of the **Río Jerte** (from the Greek *Xerte*, meaning "joyful") to the pass of Puerto de Tornavacas, the boundary with Ávila Province. The villages here are more developed than those of La Vera but the valley itself is stunning and renowned for its orchards of cherry trees, which for a ten-day period in spring cover the slopes with white blossom. If you're anywhere in the area at this time, it's a beautiful spectacle.

If you have transport, you can follow a minor road across the sierra to the north of the valley from **Cabezuela del Valle** to **Hervás**, where there's a fascinating former Jewish quarter. This is the highest road in Extremadura, rising to 1430m.

On the **southern side** of the valley, the main point of interest is the **Puerto del Piornal** pass, just behind the village of the same name. The best approach is via the villages of **Casas del Castañar** and **Cabrero**. Once at the pass you can continue over to Garganta La Olla in La Vera.

Plasencia

Set in the shadow of the Sierra de Gredos, and surrounded on three sides by the Río Jerte, **PLASENCIA** looks more impressive from afar than it actually is. Once you get up into the old city the walls are hard to find – for the most part they're propping up the backs of houses – and the cathedral is barely half-built, but it still merits a visit. Plasencia has some lively bars, delightful cafés and a fine, arcaded **Plaza Mayor**, the scene of a farmers' **market** every Tuesday morning, held here since the twelfth century.

Arrival and information

If you arrive by **bus**, you'll be about fifteen-minutes' walk from the centre, along the gently inclining Avenida del Valle to the west; the **train station** is much farther out – take a taxi (around €5) unless you fancy the hike. If you're **driving**, be warned that navigation in and around town is notoriously difficult.

Plasencia's **turismo** is at c/Santa Clara 2 (Mon–Fri 9am–2pm & 4–9pm, Sat & Sun 9am–2pm & 4–8pm; ☎927 423 843, ⓦwww.aytoplasencia.es), just off the Plaza de la Catedral, and there's a **provincial office** in the Torre Lucia next to the city walls (Mon–Fri 9am–2pm & 4–6pm, Sat & Sun 9.45am–2pm; ☎927 017 840, ⓦwww.turismodeextremadura.com).

Accommodation

Hostal La Muralla c/Berrozana 6 ☎927 413 874. A professionally run *hostal* with a/c rooms and a central location. ❶

Hotel Los Álamos Avda. Martín Palomino s/n ☎927 411 550, ⓦwww.hotellosalamos.es.

A clean, modern but unflashy hotel, with its own bar and restaurant, on the Cáceres road, facing the tobacco factory. ❷

Hotel Alfonso VIII c/Alfonso VIII 32 ☎927 410 250, ⓦwww.hotelalfonsoviii.com. A smart four-star hotel with classically decorated rooms, located on the main road near the post office. All the facilities you'd expect. ⑤

Parador Plaza de San Vicente Ferrer s/n ☎927 425 870, ⓦ www.paradores.com. Housed in a beautiful restored fifteenth-century Gothic convent, this *parador* has a convenient central location. ⑥

Campsite

La Chopera 2.5km out on the Ávila road ☎927 416 660, ⓦ www.campinglachopera.com. A large riverside campsite with decent facilities and a swimming pool. Closed Oct–April.

The Town

Plasencia's **Catedral** is in fact two churches – old and new – built back-to-back. Work began on the second, **La Nueva** (summer Mon–Sat 9am–1pm & 5–7pm, Sun 9am–1pm; winter Mon–Sat 9am–1pm & 4–6pm, Sun 9am–1pm; free) at the end of the fifteenth century, but after numerous technical hitches it was eventually abandoned in 1760 when the open end was simply bricked up. It does have some redeeming features, however, most notably the Renaissance choirstalls intricately carved by Rodrigo Alemán and described with some justice by the National Tourist Board as "the most Rabelaisian in Christendom". The older, Romanesque part of the cathedral, known as **La Vieja** (summer Mon–Sat 9am–12.30pm & 5–6.30pm, Sun 9–11.30am; winter Mon–Sat 9am–12.30pm & 4–5.30pm, Sun 9–11.30am; €2), was built between the thirteenth and fourteenth centuries and now houses the obligatory **museum**, and the entrance fee includes access to the similarly aged **cloisters**.

Opposite the cathedral is the **Casa del Deán** (Dean's House), with an intriguing balcony like the prow of a ship. Continuing away from the cathedral along c/Blanca you come out at the **Plaza de San Nicolás**, where, according to local tradition, the church was built to prevent two local families from shooting arrows at each other from adjacent houses. On c/Trujillo, near the hospital, the **Museo Etnográfico Textil Provincial** (July to mid-Sept Wed–Sun 11am–2.30pm; mid-Sept to June Wed–Sat 11am–2pm & 5–8pm, Sun 11am–2pm; free) contains some colourful costumes and local crafts. Many of the exhibits are still much in evidence in the more remote villages in the north of Plasencia Province.

At the entrance to the city on the main road in from Ávila is the very pleasant **Parque de la Isla** on the banks of the Río Jerte; head here for a relaxing walk or picnic. A little north of here are the remaining 55 arches of the sixteenth-century aqueduct, designed by Juan de Flandes, that used to bring in the city's water supply.

Eating and drinking

This is the land of the **pincho**, a little sample of food provided free with your beer or wine – among which is the local *pitarra* wine. Finding good **restaurants** is not as easy as finding bars in Plasencia: there are over fifty **bars** in the old town alone, mostly found in c/Patalón (go down c/Talavera from the main square and it's the second turning on the left); *La Herradura* is good for *pinchos* and *pitarra*, and the *Asador el Refugio* for fish, squid and octopus *pinchos*.

For restaurants, try the area between the cathedral and the Plaza Mayor. The *Restaurante Los Monges*, c/Sor Valentina Mirón 24, just up from Puerta Berronzana, has a decent *menú*, and the *Mesón Chamizo* at Plaza de Ansano is a good option, as are *La Catedral* at c/Calvo Sotelo 23 and *La Taberna Extremeña* on c/Vidriera 2.

Las Hurdes and the Sierra de Gata

Las Hurdes, the abrupt rocky lands north of Plasencia, have always been a rich source of mysterious tales. According to legend, the region was unknown to the outside world until the time of Columbus, when two lovers fleeing from the court of the Duke of Alba chanced upon it. The people who welcomed them were supposedly unaware of the existence of other people or other lands. Shields and other remnants belonging to the Goth Rodrigo and his court of seven centuries earlier were discovered by the couple, giving rise to the saying that the *Hurdanos* are descendants of kings.

Fifty years ago, the inhabitants of the remoter areas were still so unused to outsiders that they hid in their houses if anyone appeared. In 1932, **Luis Buñuel** filmed an unflatteringly grotesque documentary, *Las Hurdes: Tierra Sin Pan* ("Land Without Bread"), here, in which it was hard to discern any royal descent in his subjects. Modernity has crept up on the villages these days, though they can still feel wild and very remote, and the soil is so barren that tiny terraces have been constructed on the riverbeds as the only way of getting the stubborn land to produce anything.

The **Sierra de Gata** creates a westerly border to Las Hurdes, in a series of wooded hills and odd outcrops of higher ground, in parts stunningly beautiful. To explore the whole region, you need your own transport and certainly a detailed local **map** – regular Spanish road maps tend to be pretty sketchy.

Las Hurdes villages

You could approach Las Hurdes from Plasencia, Salamanca or Ciudad Rodrigo (the region borders the Sierra de Francia – see p.394). From Plasencia the approach is along the EX370 and then the EX204. The village of **PINOF-RANQUEADO** marks the start of the region and has a campsite, *hostales* and a natural swimming pool. Fifteen kilometres farther along on the road at Vegas de Coria you can turn off to reach **NUÑOMORAL**, a good base for excursions, with an excellent and inexpensive **hostal**, *El Hurdano* (☎927 433 012; ●); this does big dinners, and there is a bank alongside – not a common sight in these parts. Nuñomoral is also the village best connected to the outside world, with early-morning buses to both Ciudad Rodrigo and Plasencia.

A few kilometres to the north of Nuñomoral, the tiny village of **LA HUETRE** is worth a visit; take a left fork just before the village of Casares de las Hurdes. The typical slate-roofed houses are in decent condition and have an impressive setting, surrounded by steep rocky hills. Walkers might also head for the remote and disarmingly primitive settlement of **El Gasco**, at the top of Valle de Malvellido, the next valley to the south, where there is a huge waterfall beneath the Meancera Gorge.

Sierra de Gata villages

The **Sierra de Gata** is almost as equally isolated as Las Hurdes – in some of the villages the old people still speak *maniego*, a mix of Castilian Spanish and Portuguese. For a trip into the heart of the region, take the EX204 south from Las Hurdes to **Villanueva de la Sierra** and follow the EX205 west. A couple of kilometres past the Río Arrago, a very minor road veers north towards **Robledillo de Gata**, a village of old houses packed tightly together. A shorter, easier detour, south of the EX205, around 5km on, goes to the hilltop village of **Santibáñez el Alto**, whose oldest houses are built entirely of stone, without windows. At the top of town, look out for a tiny bullring, castle remains and the old cemetery – there's a wonderful view over the Borbollón reservoir from here. Another 3km along the EX205, a turn-off to the north takes you on a winding road up to **Gata**, a pretty village with rooms at the *Pensión Las Ruedas* (☎927 672 903; ➊). Farther west on the EX205 is **Hoyos**, the largest village of the region, with some impressive mansions. There's one *hostal*, *Pensión El Redoble*, c/La Paz 14 (☎927 514 665; ➌), and a pleasant **campsite**, 3km below the village by a natural swimming pool, created by the damming of the river. Lastly, farther along the EX205, another turning leads north to **San Martín de Trevejo**, one of the prettiest of the many lonely villages around.

South to Cáceres

South from the Sierra de Gata towards Cáceres along the EX109, **CORIA** makes an interesting stop. It looks nothing much from the main road, but it's actually a cool, quiet old town with lots of stately whitewashed houses and a fifteenth-century **convent** (daily 10am–1pm & 4–6.45pm; €1.50), enclosed within third- and fourth-century **Roman walls**. For the most part the walls are built into and around the houses, but a good stretch is visible between the deserted tower of the fifteenth-century castle, built by the dukes of Alba, and the cathedral.

The **Catedral** (daily 10am–1.30pm & 4–6.30pm; summer opens and closes an hour later in the afternoons; museum same hours but closed Mon; €2) has beautifully carved west and north portals in the Plateresque style of Salamanca and, inside, the choirstalls and *retablo* are worth seeing. The building overlooks a striking medieval bridge across fields, the river having changed course three hundred years ago.

Coria has a small **turismo** (usually Mon–Fri 9.30am–2pm & 5–7.30pm, Sat & Sun 10am–2pm, winter opens and closes an hour earlier in the afternoons; ☎927 501 351, ⓦwww.coria.org) inside the *ayuntamiento* on Avenida de Extremadura, as well as plenty of **accommodation**. Try comfortable *Hotel Los Kekes* (☎&Ⓕ927 504 080; ➍–➐), Avda. Sierra de Gata 49, with a decent restaurant; *Pensión Bravatas* (☎927 500 401; ➊) at Avda. Sierra de Gata 32; or the *San Cristobal* (☎927 501 412, ⓦwww.hotelsancristobal.net; ➋), a good-value two-star on the outskirts of town.

Convento del Palancar

A detour off the EX109, south of Coria, will take you to the **Convento del Palancar**, a monastery founded by San Pedro de Alcántara in the sixteenth century and said to be the smallest in the world at only seventy square metres. It's hard to imagine how a community of ten monks could have lived in these cubbyholes, though San Pedro himself set the example, sleeping upright in his cubicle. A small monastic community today occupies a more modern monastery alongside; ring the bell (daily except Wed 10am–1pm & 4.30–6.45pm; voluntary contribution) and a monk will come and show you around.

To reach Palancar, turn left off the EX109 just after Torrejoncillo and follow the road towards **Pedroso de Acim**; a left turn just before the village leads to the monastery.

Parque Natural de Monfragüe

South of Plasencia a pair of dams, built in the 1960s, has turned the **ríos Tajo and Tiétar** into a sequence of vast reservoirs. It's an impressive sight and a tremendous area for wildlife: almost at random here, you can look up to see storks, vultures and even eagles circling the skies. The best area for concerted wildlife viewing – and some very enjoyable walks – is the **PARQUE NATURAL DE MONFRAGÜE**, Extremadura's only protected area, which extends over 44,000 acres to either side of the Plasencia–Trujillo road.

Park practicalities

The park's headquarters are at **Villarreal de San Carlos**, which has a couple of bars and a restaurant, plus an **information centre** (daily: summer 9am–7.30pm; winter 9am–6pm; ☎927 199 134, ⓦwww.monfrague.com), where you can pick up a leaflet with a map detailing three colour-coded walks from the village and details about activities like horseriding and walking in the park. There is also a seasonal shop, selling wildlife T-shirts and the like, and a useful guide to the park (in Spanish).

The easiest **approach to the park** is along the EX208 from Plasencia to Trujillo, which runs past the park headquarters at Villarreal de San Carlos. Transport of your own is an advantage unless you are prepared to do some walking. There is just one **bus** along the road, which runs daily between Plasencia and Torrejón El Rubio, and on Mondays and Fridays covers the whole distance to Trujillo. The nearest **train station** is Monfragüe, 18km from Villarreal de San Carlos and a stop for slow trains on the Madrid–Cáceres line.

There are three *casas rurales* in Villarreal, the *Al-Mofrag* (☎927 199 205/686 454 393, ⓦwww.casaruralalmofrag.com; ❸), *El Cabrerin* (☎927 199 002, ⓦwww.elcabrerin.com; ❸) and the *Monfragüe* (☎927 199 003; ❸). In **TORREJÓN EL RUBIO** there is the *Pensión Monfragüe* (☎927 455 026; ❷) and the more expensive, but still good value for money *Hotel Carvajal*, Plaza de Pizarro 54 (☎927 455 254, ⓦwww.hotelcarvajal.es; ❸), while at the top end is the luxurious *Hospedería Parque de Monfragüe* (☎927 455 278, ⓦwww.hospederiasdeextreamadura.es; ❹), which has an upmarket offering a range of local specialities and barbecues on the terrace in summer. The nearest **campsite** is *Camping Monfragüe* (☎927 459 233, ⓦwww.campingmonfrague.com), a well-equipped, year-round site with a swimming pool and restaurant, 12km north of Villarreal on the Plasencia road. It is near the turning to the Monfragüe train station and it also has **bikes for rent** to get to Monfragüe.

Walking in the park

If you're **walking** in Monfragüe, it's best to stick to the colour-coded paths leading from Villarreal de San Carlos. Each of them is well paint-blobbed and leads to rewarding birdwatching locations. Elsewhere, it is not easy to tell where you are permitted to wander – it's very easy to find yourself out of the park area

---

Monfrague's wildlife

There are over two hundred **species of animals** in the park, including reptiles, deer, wild boar and the ultra-rare Spanish lynx. Most important is the **bird population**, especially the black stork – this is the only breeding population in western Europe – and birds of prey such as the black vulture (not averse to eating tortoises), the griffon vulture (partial to carrion intestine), the Egyptian vulture (not above eating human excrement), the rare Spanish imperial eagle (identifiable by its very obvious white shoulder patches), the golden eagle and the eagle owl (the largest owl in Europe). Ornithologists should visit Monfragüe in May and June, botanists in March and April, and everybody should avoid July to September, when the heat is stifling.

in a private hunting reserve. The **Green Route**, to the Cerro Gimio, is especially good – a two-and-a-half-hour stroll looping through woods and across streams, in a landscape unimaginable from Villarreal, to a dramatic clifftop viewing station. The longer **Red Route** heads south of Villarreal, over a bridge across the Río Tajo, and past a fountain known as the *Fuente del Francés* after a young Frenchman who died there trying to save an eagle. Two kilometres farther is a great crag known as the *Peñafalcón*, which houses a large colony of griffon vultures, and the Castillo de Monfragüe, a castle ruin high up on a rock, with a chapel next to it; there is an observation post nearby. All these places are accessible from the EX208 and if you're coming in on the bus, you could ask to get off here. There are also two routes of 8km and 12km respectively that have been designed for **cars** and include a number of viewing points.

On the south side of the park, towards Trujillo, you pass through the **dehesas**, strange Africa-like plains, among the oldest woodlands in Europe. The economy of the *dehesas* is based on grazing, and the casualties among the domestic animals provide the vultures of Monfragüe with their daily bread. The information centre in Villarreal also provides details of routes that can be done on horseback or bicycle.

Trujillo

TRUJILLO is the most attractive town in Extremadura: a classic *conquistador* stage set of escutcheoned mansions, stork-topped towers and castle walls. Much of it looks virtually untouched since the sixteenth century, and it is redolent above all of the exploits of the conquerors of the Americas; Francisco Pizarro, the conqueror of Peru, was born here, as were many of the tiny band who with such extraordinary cruelty aided him in defeating the Incas.

Arrival and information

Trujillo could be visited easily enough as a day-trip from Cáceres, but it's worth staying the night. There is no train station, but the town is well served by **buses**, with up to ten a day to and from Madrid. Coming in by bus, you'll arrive in the lower town, just five-minutes' walk from the Plaza Mayor, where there is a **turismo** (daily 11am–2pm & 4–7pm; ☏927 322 677, ⓦ www.trujillo.es), which gives discount tickets for combined visits to some of the main sites (€4.70–6.75) and provides information on guided tours. If you're **driving**, follow the signs to the Plaza Mayor, and with luck you should be able to park beyond the square and farther along c/García de Paredes. There is an internet café at c/Judería 18 just below the Plaza Mayor.

Accommodation

Places to stay are in high demand – so book ahead if you can. The *turismo* can provide accommodation lists. The best rooms are in the old town close to the Plaza Mayor.

Casa de Orellana c/Palamos 5–7 ☏927 659 265, ⓦ www.casadeorellana.com. Just four doubles and a single in this delightful and exclusive little hotel located in a fabulous refurbished fifteenth-century mansion close to the Plaza Mayor. Price includes breakfast. ❻

Hostal La Cadena Plaza Mayor 8 ☏927 321 463. An attractive *hostal*, with simple a/c rooms overlooking all the action and a decent restaurant. ❷

Hostal Trujillo c/Francisco Pizarro 4–6 ☏927 322 274, ⓦ www.hostaltrujillo.com. A pleasant *pensión*

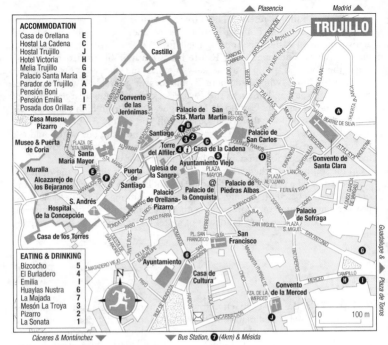

situated in a fifteenth-century building between the Plaza Mayor and the bus station. Twenty a/c rooms and a good restaurant. ②

Hotel Victoria Plaza de Campillo 22 ☏ 927 321 819, ℱ 927 323 084. A modern and friendly hotel, with a pool, restaurant and comfortable en-suite rooms. ④

Melia Trujillo Plaza del Campillo 1 ☏ 927 458 900, ⒲ www.solmelia.com. Situated in the converted *convento* de San Antonio, this swish hotel has 72 double rooms and a swimming pool. ⑤

Palacio Santa María c/Ballesteros 6 ☏ 927 659 190, ⒲ www.nh-hotels.com. A chain hotel, but more atmospheric than its brethren; set in a beautiful refurbished sixteenth-century mansion and tucked down a small street behind the Plaza Mayor. Slick, modern facilities, including a rooftop pool. ④–⑥

Parador de Trujillo Plaza Santa Beatriz de Silva ☏ 927 321 350, ⒲ www.paradores.com. Upmarket accommodation in a sixteenth-century former *convento* north of the Plaza Mayor. ⑥

Pensión Boni c/Domingo de Ramos 11 ☏ 927 321 604. Cheap and meticulously run, just off the northeast corner of the Plaza Mayor. ①

Pensión Emilia c/Plaza Campillo 28 ☏ 927 320 083, ⒲ www.laemilia.com. A clean and comfortable *pensión* located down by the main road into town with warm, classical decor and a restaurant and bar downstairs. ②

Posada dos Orillas c/Cambrones 6 ☏ 927 659 079, ⒲ www.dosorillas.com. Thirteen individually designed rooms in this converted inn in the heart of the old quarter. It has a delightful patio area where you can have breakfast and a restaurant serving up some imaginative, well-presented salads and local specialities. ③–④

The Town

Trujillo is a very small place, still only a little larger than its extent in *conquistador* times. At the centre of a dense web of streets is the **Plaza Mayor**, a grand square overlooked by a trio of palaces and churches, and ringed by a half-dozen cafés and restaurants, around which life for most visitors revolves. In the centre is a bronze statue of Pizarro – oddly, the gift of an American sculptor, one Carlos Rumsey, in 1929. In the square's southwest corner is the **Palacio de la**

Conquista (closed for long-term restoration), the grandest of Trujillo's mansions with its roof adorned by statues representing the twelve months. Just one of many built by the Pizarro clan, it was originally inhabited by Pizarro's half-brother and son-in-law Hernando, who returned from the conquests to live here with his half-Inca bride (Pizarro's daughter). Diagonally opposite, and with a skyline of storks, is the bulky church of **San Martín** (Mon–Sat 10am–2pm & 4.30–6.30pm, Sun 10am–1.30pm & 4.30–6.30pm; €1.40). Its tombs include, among others, that of the family of Francisco de Orellana, the first explorer of the Amazon. Adjacent is the **Palacio de los Duques de San Carlos** (Mon–Sat 10am–1pm & 4.30–6.30pm, Sun 10am–12.30pm; €1.20), home to a group of nuns who moved out of their dilapidated convent up the hill and restored this palace in return for the lodgings. The chimneys on the roof boast aggressively of cultures conquered by Catholicism in the New World – they are shaped like the pyramids of Aztecs, Incas and others subjected to Spanish rule.

Of the many other town mansions, or *solares*, the most interesting is the **Palacio de Orellana-Pizarro**, just west of the main square (Mon–Fri 10am–1pm & 4–6pm, Sat & Sun 11am–2pm & 4.30–6.30pm; free). Go in through the superb Renaissance arched doorway to admire the courtyard, an elegant patio decorated with the alternating coats of arms of the Pizarros – two bears with a pine tree – and the Orellanas.

North of Plaza Mayor

From the plaza, c/Ballesteros leads up to the walled upper town, past the domed **Torre del Alfiler** with its coats of arms and storks' nests, and through the fifteenth-century gateway known as the Arco de Santiago. Built up against the walls is the **Iglesia de Santiago** (daily: summer 10am–2pm & 5–8pm; winter 10am–2pm & 4–7pm; €1.40), which dates from the thirteenth century and was sometimes used as a venue for council meetings in the Middle Ages, while opposite it is the Palacio de los Chaves, which was where the Reyes Católicos, Fernando and Isabel, stayed when they were in town. A short way up the hill is **Santa María Mayor** (daily 10am–2pm & 4–7pm, summer closes 7.30pm; €1.25), the most interesting and important of the town's many churches. The building is basically Gothic but contains a beautiful raised Renaissance *coro* noted for the technical mastery of its almost flat vaults. There is a fine Hispano-Flemish reredos by Fernando Gallego, and tombs including those of the Pizarros – Francisco was baptized here – and Diego García de Paredes, a man known as the "Sansón Extremeño" (Extremaduran Samson). Among other exploits, this giant of a man, armed only with his gargantuan sword, is said to have defended a bridge against an entire French army and to have picked up the font, now underneath the *coro*, to carry holy water to his mother. You are allowed to clamber up the **tower**, which provides magnificent views of the town, the parched plains over towards Cáceres and the Sierra de Gredos.

Farther up the hill, in the Pizarros' former residence, the **Casa Museo Pizarro** (daily 10am–2pm & 4–7pm, summer opens and closes an hour later in the afternoons; €1.40) is a small, relatively dull affair, with little beyond period furniture and a few panels on the conquest of Peru. More detailed exhibits on the conquest are to be found in the nearby **Museo de la Coria** (Sat, Sun & public hols 11.30am–2pm; free), which is housed in an old Franciscan convent.

The Castle

The **castle** (daily 10am–2pm & 4–7pm, summer opens and closes an hour later in the afternoons; €1.40) is now virtually in open countryside; for the last hundred metres of the climb you see nothing but the occasional broken-down remnant of a wall clambered over by sheep and dogs. The **fortress** itself, Moorish in origin but much reinforced by later defenders, has been restored, and its main attraction is the panoramic view of the town and its environs from the battlements. As you look out over the barren heath that rings Trujillo, the extent to which the old quarter has fallen into disrepair is abundantly evident, as is the castle's superb defensive position.

Eating, drinking and nightlife

There are plenty of **bar-restaurants** on the Plaza Mayor, and for budget eating, all the *pensiones* around Plaza Campillo have reasonably priced *menús* on offer. At the weekend, **nightlife** revolves around the streets splaying out of Plaza Mayor and down in the newer parts of town.

Bizcocho Plaza Mayor 11 ☎ 927 322 017. A reliable restaurant serving regional specialities and good meat dishes. It has two separate dining areas and a summer terrace looking out on to the plaza. Around €40 a head.

El Burladero Plaza Mayor 7. A good bar to start the night, serving imaginative tapas and a decent selection of wine.

Emilia c/Plaza Campillo 28 ☎ 927 321 216. A *pensión* located down towards the main road, which offers one of the most competitive *menús* in town.

Huaylas Nustra Hotel Isla del Gallo Plaza Aragón 2 ☎ 927 320 423. Named after Pizarro's second wife, this hotel restaurant has some very good-value creative food based on regional dishes. Expect to pay around €50 a head.

La Majada ☎ 927 320 349. Situated some 4km south of town on the road to Mérida in a pleasant garden with a play area for children. Good fish, local sausages and partridge. Around €35–40 a head.

Mesón La Troya Plaza Mayor 10 ☎ 927 321 364. Trujillo's best-known restaurant. Offers a huge *menú* for €15, although it is a case of quantity over quality and they'll probably serve you a giant tortilla as a starter before you have even ordered.

Pizarro Plaza Mayor 13 ☎ 927 310 925. Rather better-quality food than *La Troya* and more manageable quantities, costing €20–30 *à la carte*, and about half that for the *menú*.

La Sonata c/Ballesteros 10 ☎ 927 322 884. Tucked away in a street just north of the Plaza Mayor, this serves some well-presented Extremeño specialities. It does a tasty *menú* for €14 and a more sophisticated version featuring mains such as wild boar, lamb and salmon for €23.

Guadalupe

The small town of **GUADALUPE**, perched up in the sierra to the west of Trujillo, is dominated in every way by the great **Monasterio de Nuestra Señora de Guadalupe**, which for five centuries has brought fame and pilgrims to the area. It was established in 1340, on the spot where an ancient image of the Virgin, said to have been carved by St Luke, was discovered by a shepherd fifty or so years earlier. The delay was simply a question of waiting for the Reconquest to arrive in this remote sierra, with its lush countryside of forests and streams.

Arrival and information

Guadalupe's **turismo** is in the arcaded Plaza Mayor (summer Tues–Fri 10am–2pm & 5–7pm, Sat & Sun 10am–2pm; winter Tues–Fri 10am–2pm & 4–6pm, Sat & Sun 10am–2pm; ☎ 927 154 128, ⓦ www.puebladeguadalupe .net). **Buses** leave from either side of Avenida de Barcelona, uphill from the *ayuntamiento*, 200m from the Plaza Mayor: Mirat operates services to Trujillo and Cáceres, Doalde runs buses to Madrid (though you might have to change at Talavera de Reina).

Accommodation

There are plenty of **places to stay** in Guadalupe and the only times you're likely to have difficulty finding a room are during Easter Week or around September 8, the Virgin's festival day.

Hospedaría del Real Monasterio Plaza Juan Carlos s/n ☎ 927 367 000. Housed in a wing of the monastery and popular with Spanish pilgrims, it's better value than the *parador*, very atmospheric and serves excellent food, too. ❸

Hostal Alfonso XI c/Alfonso Onceno 21 ☎&☏ 927 154 184. A comfortable, nicely furnished *hostal* with a/c in most rooms. ❷

Hostal Isabel Plaza Santa María 13 ☎ 927 367 126. A modern *hostal* offering rooms with bath, and a bar downstairs. They have another branch with the same name next to the *parador* with antique furnished rooms and a/c for the same price. ❶

Hostal Taruta c/Alfonso Onceno 16 ☎ 927 254 144. This *hostal* can arrange rooms in private houses if its own are fully booked, and it offers discounts for full board, with meals in a *comedor* downstairs, which also serves an inexpensive range of *platos*. ❷

Parador de Guadalupe c/Marqués de la Romana 12 ☎ 927 367 075, ⓦ www.paradores.com. A beautiful *parador*, housed in a fifteenth-century hospital, with a swimming pool and immaculate patio gardens. ❺

Campsite

Las Villuercas ☎ 927 367 139. Some 2km out of town towards Trujillo, close to the main road. A quiet campsite with a pool. Open all year.

The Town

In the fifteenth and sixteenth centuries, Guadalupe was among the most important pilgrimage centres in Spain: Columbus named the Caribbean island in honour of the Virgin here, and a local version was adopted as the patron saint of Mexico. Much of the monastic wealth, in fact, came from returning *conquistadores*, whose successive endowments led to a fascinating mix of styles. The **monastery** was abandoned in the nineteenth-century dissolution, but was later reoccupied by Franciscans, who continue to maintain it.

The town itself is a fitting complement to the monastery and countryside: a net of narrow cobbled streets and overhanging houses constructed around the Plaza Mayor, the whole overshadowed by the monastery's bluff ramparts. There's a timeless feel, only slightly diminished by modern development on the outskirts, and a brisk trade in plastic copies of religious treasures.

The church and monastery

The **monastery church** (daily 8.30am–8pm, closes 9pm in summer; free) opens onto the Plaza Mayor (aka Plaza de Santa María). Its gloomy Gothic interior is, like the rest of the monastery, packed with treasures from generations of wealthy patrons.

The entrance to the **monastery** proper (daily 9.30am–1pm & 3.30–6.30pm; €4) is to the left of the church. The (compulsory) guided tour begins with a Mudéjar **cloister** – two brick storeys of horseshoe arches with a strange pavilion or tabernacle in the middle – and moves on to the **museum**, with an apparently endless collection of rich vestments, early illuminated manuscripts and religious paraphernalia, along with some fine artworks including a triptych by Isenbrandt and a small Goya. The **Sacristía**, beyond, is the finest room in the monastery. Unaltered since it was built in the seventeenth century, it contains eight paintings by Zurbarán, which, uniquely, can be seen in their original context – the frames match the window frames and the pictures themselves are a planned part of the decoration of the room.

Climbing higher into the heart of the monastery, you pass through various rooms filled with jewels and relics before the final ascent to the Holy of Holies.

From a tiny room high above the main altar you can look down over the church while a panel is spun away to reveal the highlight of the tour – the bejewelled and richly dressed **image of the Virgin**. The Virgin is one of the few black icons ever made – originally carved out of dark cedarwood, its colour has further deepened over the centuries under innumerable coats of varnish. The story goes that the image was originally carved by St Luke, made its way to Spain and was then hidden during the Arab occupation for over five hundred years. It was eventually rediscovered by a local cowherd on the banks of the Río Guadalupe at the beginning of the thirteenth century.

On the way out, drop in at the **Hospedaría del Real Monasterio**, around to the right. The bar, in its Gothic cloister, with lovely gardens outside, is one of the world's more unusual places to enjoy a *Cuba libre*.

Eating and drinking

You can **eat** at most *hostales* and *pensiones*, with just about everywhere – including the restaurants on Plaza Mayor – serving *menús* for around €10. *Restaurante Lujuan* is particularly good value, while the *Hospedaria del Real Monasterio* has a pricier €17 *menú* but with a great courtyard setting. The *Mesón del Cordero* at c/Alfonso Onceno 27 serves good home cooking with grand views from the dining room thrown in.

The Sierra de Guadalupe

A truly superb view of Guadalupe set in its sierra can also be enjoyed from the road (EX118) north to Navalmoral. Five kilometres out of town, the **Ermita del Humilladero** marks the spot where pilgrims to the shrine traditionally caught their first glimpse of the monastery.

The surrounding **Sierra de Guadalupe** is a wild and beautiful region, with steep, rocky crags abutting the valley sides. If you have your own transport, you could strike northwest of the EX102 at Cañamero, up to the village of **Cabañas del Castillo**, nestling against a massive crag and ruined castle; the handful of houses are mostly empty, as only twelve inhabitants remain. Beyond here, you can reach the main **Navalmoral–Trujillo road** close to the **Puerto de Miravete**, a fabulous viewpoint, with vistas of Trujillo in the far distance. Another great driving route, again leaving the EX102 at Cañamero, is to follow the narrow road **through Berzocana** to Trujillo.

Cáceres

CÁCERES is in many ways remarkably like Trujillo. It features an almost perfectly preserved walled town, the Ciudad Monumental, packed with *solares* built on the proceeds of American exploration, while every available tower and spire is crowned by a clutch of storks' nests. As a provincial capital, however, Cáceres is a much larger and livelier place, especially in term time, when the students of the University of Extremadura are in residence. With its Roman, Moorish and *conquistador* sights, and a number of great bars and restaurants, it is an absorbing and highly enjoyable city. It also provides a dramatic backdrop for an annual **WOMAD** festival, held over the second weekend in May and attracting up to 70,000 spectators.

The walled **Old Town** stands at the heart of Cáceres, with a picturesque **Plaza Mayor** just outside its walls. Almost everything of interest is contained within – or a short walk from – this area; try and base yourself as close to it as possible.

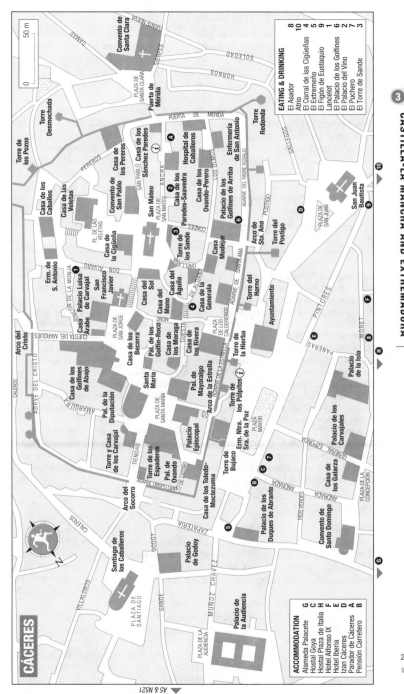

CÁCERES

ACCOMMODATION

Alameda Palacete	G
Hostal Goya	C
Hostal Plaza de Italia	H
Hotel Alfonso IX	F
Hotel Iberia	E
Izan Cáceres	D
Parador de Cáceres	A
Pensión Carretero	B

EATING & DRINKING

El Asador	8
Atrio	10
El Corral de las Cigüeñas	4
El Extremeño	5
El Figón de Eustaquio	9
Lancelot	1
El Palacio de los Golfines	6
El Palacio del Vino	2
El Puchero	7
El Torre de Sande	3

Arrival and information

If you arrive by **train or bus**, you'll be around 3km out from the old town, at the far end of the Avenida de Alemania. It's not a particularly enjoyable walk, so it's best to take bus #1, which runs down the *avenida* to Plaza de San Juan, a square adjoining the Plaza Mayor; an irregular shuttle bus from the train station (free if you show a rail ticket) also runs into town, to the Plaza de América, a major traffic junction west of the old town. If you're driving, be warned that increasing pedestrianization is making access to some streets impossible by car; your best bet is to park on Avenida de España, on the main road in from Madrid, or outside the old town.

Cáceres has a helpful regional **turismo** (Mon–Fri 9am–2pm & 4–6pm, summer 8am–3pm, Sat & Sun 10am–2pm; ☎927 010 834, ⓦwww.turismoextremadura.com & ⓦturismo.caceres.es) in the Plaza Mayor, with a municipal office (summer Tues–Sun 10am–2pm & 5.30–8.30pm, winter Tues–Sun 10am–2pm & 4.30–7.30pm) opposite the *parador* in the old town.

Accommodation

It's worth noting that **accommodation** right on the Plaza Mayor can get rather noisy at night.

Alameda Palacete c/Margallo 45 ☎927 211 674, ⓦwww.alamedapalacete.com. Nine fascinatingly decorated rooms, each with its own individual ambience in this delightful little hotel not far from the Plaza Mayor. Suites are available from €85–100. Breakfast included. ❸–❹
Hostal Goya Plaza Mayor 11 ☎927 249 950, ⓦwww.hotelgoya.net. A good-value *hostal* on the Plaza Mayor, with en-suite rooms. Those with views over the plaza are an extra €10. ❸
Hostal Plaza de Italia c/Constancia 12 ☎927 627 294, ⓦwww.hotelplazaitalia.com. A very friendly and clean option, a 5min walk from the Plaza Mayor. ❷
Hotel Alfonso IX c/Moret 20 ☎927 246 400, ⓦwww.hotelalfonsoix.com. Well located on a pedestrianized street off c/Pintores, this hotel offers decent en-suite rooms with a/c and satellite TV. ❹

Hotel Iberia c/Pintores 2 ☎927 247 634, ⓦwww.iberiahotel.com. A tastefully restored building in a corner of the Plaza Mayor. ❷–❹
Izan Cáceres Plaza de San Juan 11 ☎927 215 800, ⓦwww.sercotelhoteles.com. Part of the Sercotel chain, this hotel is in a sixteenth-century palace, just outside the walls of the old town, and is in many ways a nicer and certainly better value place than the *parador*. ❹
Parador de Cáceres c/Ancha 6 ☎927 211 759, ⓦwww.paradores.com. The *parador* occupies a *conquistador* mansion in the Ciudad Monumental – the only hotel within the walls. ❻
Pensión Carretero Plaza Mayor 22–23 ☎927 247 482, ⓦwww.caceresjoven.com. Best value in town – very basic, large rooms, spotless bathrooms and a TV lounge – though some rooms can be noisy at the weekend. ❶

The Town

The **walls** of the Ciudad Monumental are basically Moorish in construction, though parts date back to the Romans – notably the **Arco del Cristo** – and they have been added to, refortified and built against throughout the centuries. The most intact section, with several original adobe Moorish towers, runs in a clockwise direction, facing the walls from the Plaza Mayor.

Around the Old Town

Entering the Old Town – the **Parte Vieja**, as it's also known – from the Plaza Mayor, you pass through the low **Arco de la Estrella**, an entrance built by Manuel Churriguera in the eighteenth century. To your left, at the corner of the walls, is one of the most imposing *conquistador solares*, the **Casa de Toledo-Moctezuma** with its domed tower. It was to this house that a follower of Cortés brought back one of the New World's more exotic prizes, a daughter of the Aztec emperor, as his bride. The building houses the provincial historical archives, and also stages occasional exhibitions.

Walking straight ahead through the Arco de la Estrella brings you into the **Plaza de Santa María**, flanked by another major *solar*, the Casa de los Golfines de Abajo, the Palacio Episcopal and the Gothic church of **Santa María** – Cáceres's finest (Mon–Fri 9.30am–12.30pm & 4–6.15pm, Sat 9.30am–12.50pm & 4–6.15pm, Sun 9.30–11.50am & 5–6.15pm, open an hour later in the afternoons in summer; €1 for museum). Inside, you can illuminate a fine sixteenth-century carved wooden *retablo*, while in the surrounding gloom are the tombs of many of the town's great families.

Plaza San Mateo and Plaza de las Veletas

A couple of blocks west, at the town's highest point, is the Plaza de San Mateo, flanked by the church of **San Mateo**, another Gothic structure with fine chapels, and the **Casa de la Cigüeña** (House of the Stork), whose narrow tower was the only one allowed to preserve its original battlements when the rest were shorn by royal decree. It is now a military installation. On the other side of the square, notice the **family crests** on the **Casa del Sol**, and indeed on many of the other buildings within the walls.

Just behind, in the Plaza de las Veletas, is the **Casa de las Veletas**, which houses the archeology and ethnology sections of the **Museo de Cáceres** (mid-April to Sept Tues–Sat 9am–2.30pm & 5–8.15pm, Sun 10.15am–2.30pm; Oct to mid-April Tues–Sat 9am–2.30pm & 4–7.15pm, Sun 10.15–2.30pm; €1.20, EU citizens free). The collections here take second place to the building itself: its beautifully proportioned rooms are arrayed around a small patio and preserve the *aljibe* (cistern) of the original Moorish Alcázar with its horseshoe arches. It also has an extraordinary balustrade, created from Talavera ceramic jugs.

From here, a footbridge leads to the museum's art collection in the **Casa de los Caballos** (House of Horses), open mornings only. The modern art and sculpture includes works by Miró, Picasso and Eduardo Arroyo, while the highlight of the medieval section is El Greco's *Jesús Salvador*. There is also a temporary exhibition space for contemporary artists.

Something could be said about almost every other building, but look out, too, for the **Casa de los Golfines de Arriba** on c/Adarve Padre Rosalío, the alleyway that runs alongside the walls parallel to the Plaza Mayor. It was in this latter *conquistador* mansion that Franco had himself proclaimed Generalísimo and head of state in October 1936. Near the Casa del Sol is another *solar*, the **Casa del Mono** (House of the Monkey), which is now a public library; the facade is adorned with grotesque gargoyles and a stone monkey is chained to the staircase in the courtyard.

Plaza San Jorge

You might take time, too, for the **Casa Árabe** (variable hours but generally Tues–Sun winter 10.30am–2pm & 4.30–7.30pm, summer 10.30am–8.30pm; €1.50), off Plaza San Jorge at Cuesta del Marqués 4. The owner of this Moorish house has had the bright idea of decorating it more or less as it would have been when occupied by its original owner. The Alhambra it's not, but it at least provides a context for all the horseshoe arches and curving brick ceilings and it still possesses the original cistern supplied by water from the roof.

Outside the walls

Outside the walls, it's worth wandering up to the sixteenth-century church of **Santiago de los Caballeros**, which fronts the plaza of the same name, opposite a more or less contemporary mansion, **Palacio de Godoy**, with its corner balcony. The church, open only for Masses, has a fine *retablo* by Alonso Berruguete.

For a good view of the old town, exit the walls through the Arco del Cristo down to the main road and turn right onto c/Fuente Concejo, following the signs for about five minutes or so.

Eating, drinking and nightlife

There is a good range of **bars, restaurants** and **bodegas** in and around the Plaza Mayor, while the old town offers a bit more style at modest prices. Cáceres has the best **nightlife** in the region – especially during term time – with the night starting off in the bars along c/Pizarro, south of Plaza de San Juan, moving on to c/Dr Fleming and the discos in the nearby Plaza de Albatros. There are several late-night bars around Plaza Mayor and a string of interesting watering holes in and around c/Donoso Cortés, while live music can be heard in many places along the nearby c/General Ezponda.

Restaurants

El Asador c/Moret 34. A reasonably priced restaurant, off c/Pintores, serving local dishes and fronted by a popular tapas bar.

Atrio Avda. de España 30, block B ☏ 927 242 928. An exclusive Michelin-starred restaurant, southwest of Plaza Mayor, with an extensive menu and sophisticated food. Allow at least €60 per head and the *menú de degustación* is double that. Closed Sun eve.

🏃 **El Figón de Eustaquio** Plaza de San Juan 12. This features an extensive list of regional dishes, cooked with care. Large helpings. Allow €25–30 a head, although there is also a €17 lunchtime *menú*.

El Palacio de los Golfines c/Adarve Padre Rosalío 2 ☏ 927 242 414. Stylishly presented food in a magnificent setting in an old palace just inside the city walls. There's an extensive wine list, too. Expect to pay around €35. Closed Sun eve.

🏃 **El Palacio del Vino** c/Ancha 4. A pleasant, traditional *mesón* near the *parador* in the old town with a nice summer terrace; reckon on around €25–30 a head.

El Puchero Plaza Mayor 10. The cheapest restaurant on the plaza, with an ever-popular terraza, but as you would expect the food is not outstanding.

El Torre de Sande c/Los Condes 3 ☏ 927 211 147. Another top-class restaurant in the middle of the old town, It has refined food and attentive service for around €50 a head and a delightful summer terrace too. Closed Sun eve & Mon.

Bars

El Corral de las Cigüeñas Cuesta de Aldana 6. A beautiful spot in the old town with tables in a large, palm-shaded courtyard. A great place to enjoy a breakfast snack, a lunchtime *aperitivo* or a night-time cocktail. Live music and other acts.

El Extremeño Plaza del Duque 10, off the Plaza Mayor. A student favourite, with Guinness on tap and beer sold by the metre.

Lancelot Rincon de la Monja 2. A relaxed English-run bar close to Plaza de las Veletas.

Northwest of Cáceres

Northwest of Cáceres is the vast **Embalse de Alcántara**, one of a series of reservoirs harnessing the power of the Río Tajo in the last few kilometres before it enters Portugal. The scheme swallowed up large tracts of land and you can see the old road and railway to Plasencia disappearing into the depths of the reservoir (their replacements cross the many inlets on double-decker bridges), along with the tower of a castle.

The EX207 loops away to the south of the reservoir, through **Arroyo de la Luz** and **Brozas**, each with fine churches, before reaching **Alcántara**, with its superb Roman bridge across the Tajo. The Portuguese border – and the road to Costelo Branco and Coimbra – is just a dozen kilometres beyond.

Alcántara

The name **ALCÁNTARA** comes from the Arabic for "bridge" – in this case a beautiful six-arched **Puente Romano** spanning a gorge of the Río Tajo. Completed in 105 AD, and held together without mortar, it was reputed to be the loftiest bridge ever built in the Roman Empire, although it's far from certain which bits, if any, remain genuinely Roman.

The bridge is quite a distance from the town itself, which is built high above the river; if you're on foot, don't follow the signs via the road – instead, head to the far side of the town and down the steep cobbled path.

Further Roman remains include a **triumphal arch** dedicated to Trajan and a tiny **classical temple**. The dominating landmark, however, is the restored **Convento San Benito**, erstwhile headquarters of the Knights of Alcántara, one of the great orders of the Reconquest. For all its enormous bulk, the convent and its church are only a fragment; the nave of the church was never built. Outside, the main feature is the double-arcaded Renaissance gallery at the back; it serves as the backdrop for a season of classical plays, which moves here from Mérida in August. Entry to the convent (frequent guided tours all day Tues–Sat & Sun morning; free) is through the adjacent Fundación de San Benito, which has been making attempts to restore the cloister and the Plateresque east end with its elaborate wall tombs.

Alcántara also contains the scanty remains of a **castle**, numerous **mansions** and street after street of humble whitewashed houses. The place is marvellous for scenic walks, whether in the town, along the banks of the Tajo or – best of all – in the hills on the opposite bank.

Practicalities

The **turismo**, Avda. de Mérida 21 (May–Sept Tues–Fri 10am–2pm & 5–7pm, Sat & Sun 10.30am–2.30pm; Oct–April Tues–Fri 10am–2pm & 4–6pm, Sat & Sun 10.30am–12.30pm; ☎927 390 863, ⓦwww.alcantara.es), is very helpful and can provide a town map. **Buses**, which run twice a day to and from Cáceres, stop at a little square ringed by cafés at the entrance to the historic part of the town.

For **accommodation** there's the *Kantara Al Saif*, just out of town on the Avenida de Mérida (☎927 390 246, ⓦwww.hotelpuenteromanosl.com; ❹), with an adjoining restaurant and café. A more luxurious option is the *Hospedería Conventual*, housed in a beautifully restored fifteenth-century convent (☎927 390 367, ⓦwww.hospederiasdeextremadura.es; ❹) a little way to the north of the town.

Jamón Serrano: a gastronomic note

Extremadura, to many Spaniards, means **ham**. Together with the Sierra Morena in Andalucía, the Extremaduran sierra is the only place in the country that supports the pure-bred Iberian pig, source of the best *Jamón Serrano*. For its ham to be as flavoursome as possible, the pig, a subspecies of the European wild boar exclusive to the Iberian peninsula, is allowed to roam wild and eat acorns for several months of the year. The undisputed kings of hams in this area, praised at length by Richard Ford in his *Handbook for Travellers*, are those that come from Montánchez, in the south of the region. The village is midway between Cáceres and Mérida, so if you're in the area try some in a bar, washed down with local red wine – but be warned that the authentic product is extremely expensive, a few thinly cut slices often costing as much as an entire meal. The local wine, *pitarra*, is an ideal accompaniment.

Or you could try the well-kept *casa rural*, the *Casa La Cañada* (☎927 390 298; ❸), and a campsite, the *Puente de Alcántara* (☎927 390 934, ⓦwww.campingalcantara. com), which can help organize birdwatching trips, hikes and excursions on bikes and horseback.

Mérida

Some 70km to the south of Cáceres on the N630, the former capital of the Roman province of Lusitania, **MÉRIDA** (the name is a corruption of *Augusta Emerita*), contains more **Roman remains** than any other city in Spain. Even for the most casually interested, the extent and variety of the remains here are compelling, with everything from engineering works to domestic villas, by way of cemeteries and places of worship, entertainment and culture. With a little imagination, and a trip to the wonderful modern museum, the Roman city is not difficult to evoke – which is just as well, for the modern city, in which the sites are scattered, is no great shakes.

Each July and August, the Roman theatre in Mérida hosts a **theatre festival** (ⓦwww.festivaldemerida.es), including performances of classical Greek plays and Shakespeare's Roman tragedies.

Arrival and information

Mérida sees a lot of visitors and has plenty of facilities to cater for them. The **turismo** (summer daily 9.30am–2pm & 5–8pm; winter daily 9.30am–2pm & 4.30–7pm; ☎924 009 730, ⓦwww.turismoextremadura.com) is just outside the gates to the theatre and amphitheatre site. There is another office run by the local *ayuntamiento* (daily 9.30am–2pm & 5–9pm; ☎924 330 722, ⓦwww .merida.es) just off Plaza Puerta de la Villa.

The **train station** is pretty central, with the theatre site and Plaza de España no more than ten-minutes' walk away. The **bus station** is on the other side of the river and is a grittier twenty-minutes' walk from the town centre, along Avenida de Libertad, which extends from the new single-arch bridge. You can get inexpensive **internet** access at the *Escuela de Idiomas* at c/Santa Eulalia 19, 1º (Mon–Fri 11am–1.30pm & 5.30–10pm).

Accommodation

There is no shortage of **places to stay**, though prices tend to be high.

Hostal El Alfarero c/Sagasta 40 ☎924 303 183, ⓦwww.hostalelalfarero.com. A very cosy *hostal* with nine a/c doubles all with their own bathroom. ❷

Hostal Bueno c/Calvario 9 ☎924 302 977. A basic but clean *hostal* – all the rooms have tiny bathrooms. ❷

Hotel Cervantes c/Camilo José Cela 8 ☎924 314 961, ⓦwww.hotelcervantes.com. A comfortable hotel, off c/Cervantes, with large rooms, secure parking and its own café. ❸

Hostal Senero c/Holguin 12 ☎924 317 207, ⓦwww.hostalsenero.com. A long-established, friendly *hostal* with neat rooms situated around a quiet courtyard close to the main plaza. ❷

Hotel Mérida Palace Plaza de España 19 ☎924 383 800, ⓦwww.hotelmeridapalace .com. A swish, upmarket hotel located in a former palace bang on the city's main plaza. It's part of the MCA chain. ❹–❻

Hotel Nova Roma c/Suavez Somontes 42 ☎924 311 261, ⓦwww.novaroma.com. A large, modern hotel in a central location. Book ahead if you're coming during the theatre festival. ❹

Parador Vía de la Plata Plaza Constitución 3 ☎924 313 800, ⓦwww.paradores.com. Well-run and friendly *parador* in an eighteenth-century Baroque convent, near the Arco de Trajano. ❻

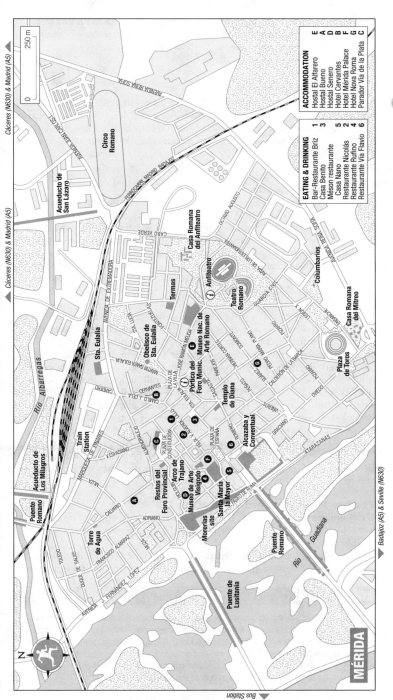

MÉRIDA

ACCOMMODATION
Hostal El Alfarero	E
Hostal Bueno	A
Hostal Senero	D
Hotel Cervantes	B
Hotel Mérida Palace	F
Hotel Nova Roma	G
Parador Vía de la Plata	C

EATING & DRINKING
Bar-Restaurante Briz	1
Casa Benito	3
Mesón restaurante	
Casa Nano	5
Restaurante Nicolás	2
Restaurante Rufino	4
Restaurante Vía Flavio	6

Cáceres (N630) & Madrid (A5)

Cáceres (N630) & Madrid (A5)

Badajoz (A5) & Seville (N630)

Bus Station

223

Campsite

Camping Lago de Proserpina ☎ 924 123 055. Signposted off the A5 and the road to Cáceres, this is a pleasant site by the Embalse de Prosperina reservoir 5km north of town, offering swimming, fishing and windsurfing. Closed mid-Sept to March.

The Roman sites

Built on the site of a Celto-Iberian settlement and founded by Emperor Augustus in 25 BC as a home for retired legionaries, Mérida became the tenth city of the Roman Empire and the final stop on the Vía de la Plata, the Roman road that began in Astorga in northern Castile. The old city stretched as far as the modern bullring and Roman circus, covering only marginally less than the triangular area occupied by the modern town.

The Puente Romano and Alcazaba

The obvious point to begin your tour is the magnificent **Puente Romano**, the bridge across the islet-strewn Río Guadiana. It is sixty arches long (the seven in the middle are fifteenth-century replacements) and was still in use until the early 1990s, when the new **Puente de Lusitania** – itself a structure to admire – was constructed.

Defence of the old bridge was provided by a vast **Alcazaba** (combined ticket or €4), built by the Moors to replace a Roman construction. The interior is a rather barren archeological site, although in the middle there's an *aljibe* to which you can descend by either of a pair of staircases.

Northeast of the Alcazaba, past the airy sixteenth-century Plaza de España, the heart of the modern town, is the so-called **Templo de Diana**, adapted into a Renaissance mansion, and farther along are remains of the **Foro**, the heart of the Roman city. To the west of the plaza, the Convento de Santa Clara houses the **Museo de Arte Visigodo** (Tues–Sun: summer 10am–2pm & 5–7pm; winter 10am–2pm & 4–6pm; free), with a collection of about a hundred lapidary items. It will eventually be housed alongside the Museo Nacional de Arte Romano (see opposite). Just behind here is the great **Arco Trajano**, once wrongly believed to be a triumphal arch; it was, in fact, a marble-clad granite monumental gate to the forum. Heading to the river from here you'll also discover the **Morerías archeological site** (combined ticket or €4) along c/ Morerías, where you can watch the digging and preservation of houses and factories from Roman through Visigoth to Moorish times – particularly of interest are the well-preserved Roman mosaics.

Teatro Romano and Anfiteatro

A ten-minute walk east of the Plaza de España will take you to Mérida's main archeological site (combined ticket or €7), containing the theatre and amphitheatre.

The elaborate and beautiful **Teatro Romano** is one of the best preserved anywhere in the Roman Empire. Constructed around 15 BC, it was a present

Combined ticket

The best way to see the Roman sights is to buy the excellent-value **combined ticket**, costing €10 and valid over a number of days. It covers the Teatro Romano and Anfiteatro, the Roman villas Casa del Anfiteatro and Casa del Mitreo, the Columbarios burial ground, the Circo Romano, the archeological site at Morerías, the Alcazaba and the Basílica de Santa Eulalia (all daily: summer 9.30am–1.45pm & 5–7.15pm; winter 4–6.15pm), and is available at any of the sites.

▲ Teatro Romano, Mérida

to the city from Agrippa, as indicated by the large inscription above the passageway to the left of the stage. The stage itself, a two-tier colonnaded affair, is in particularly good shape, and many of the seats have been entirely rebuilt to offer more comfort to the audiences of the annual July and August season of classical plays.

Adjoining the theatre is the **Anfiteatro**, a slightly later and very much plainer construction. As many as 15,000 people – almost half the current population of Mérida – could be seated to watch gladiatorial combats and fights with wild animals. The **Casa Romana del Anfiteatro** (combined ticket or €4) lies immediately below the museum, and offers an approach to it from the site. It has wonderful mosaics, including a vigorous depiction of grape-treading.

The Museo Nacional de Arte Romano

The **Museo Nacional de Arte Romano** (March–Nov Tues–Sat 10am–2pm & 4–9pm, Sun 10am–2pm; Dec–Feb Tues–Sat 10am–2pm & 4–6pm, Sun 10am–2pm; €2.40, free Sat pm & Sun am), constructed in 1986 above the Roman walls, is a wonderfully light, accessible building, using a free interpretation of classical forms to present the mosaics and sculpture as if emerging from the ruins. The exhibits, displayed on three levels of the basilica-like hall, include statues from the theatre, the Roman villa of **Mithraeus** (Mitreo; see p.226) and the vanished forum, and a number of mosaics – the largest being hung on the walls so that they can be examined at each level. Individually, the finest exhibits are probably the three statues, displayed together, depicting Augustus, the first Roman emperor; his son Tiberius, the second emperor; and Drusus, Augustus's heir apparent until (it is alleged) he was murdered by Livia, Tiberius's mother.

Outside the centre

The remaining monuments are on the other side of the train tracks. From the museum, it's a fifteen-minute walk if you cut down the streets towards Avenida de Extremadura and then head east out of the city to the **Circo Romano**, essentially an outline, where up to 30,000 spectators could watch horse and chariot races. Across the road from here, a stretch of the **Acueducto de San Lázaro** leads off towards the Río Albarregas.

The more impressive aqueduct, however, is the **Acueducto de los Milagros**, of which a satisfying portion survives in the midst of vegetable gardens, west of the train station. Its tall arches of granite, with brick courses, brought water to the city in its earliest days from the reservoir at Proserpina, 5km away. The best view of the aqueduct is from a low and inconspicuous **Puente Romano** across the Río Albarregas; it was over this span that the Vía de la Plata entered the city.

Two further sights are the church of **Santa Eulalia** (combined ticket or €4), by the train station, which has a porch made from fragments of a former temple of Mars, and a second Roman villa, the **Mitreo** (combined ticket or €4), in the shadow of the Plaza de Toros, south of the museum and theatres. The villa has a magnificent but damaged mosaic depicting the cosmos. A short walk away is the Columbarios burial ground with two family sepulchres and an interesting series of exhibits on Roman death rites.

Proserpina and Cornalvo reservoirs

You can swim in the **Embalse de Proserpina**, a Roman-constructed reservoir 5km north of town (special buses from Paseo de Roma in July & Aug; €1), and a popular escape to cool off in summer; it's lined with holiday homes, has a campsite and a small beach area but is best avoided at weekends. Alternatively, if you have transport, head to the **Embalse de Cornalvo**, 18km east of Mérida (turn left after the village of Trujillanos). There's a Roman dyke here, and a small national park has been created in the area with walking trails in the surrounding forest.

Eating and drinking

The whole area between the train station and the Plaza de España is full of **bars** and **cheap restaurants**, flyers for many of which will be stuffed into your hands outside the theatre site entrance.

Bar-Restaurante Briz c/Félix Valverde Lillo 7, just off Plaza de España. A reliable restaurant offering the local speciality *raciones* and a good-value €10.60 *menú*. Closed Sun eve.

Casa Benito c/San Francisco 3. Bullfighters' ephemera line the walls of this bar, which serves the local speciality tapas, *pitarra* wine and good breakfasts. Closed Sun.

Mesón Restaurante Casa Nano c/Castelar 3. Pleasant restaurant, offering good fish dishes and two decent *menús* at €12 and €23.

Restaurante Nicolás c/Félix Valverde Lillo 13. A good range of Extremaduran dishes such as migas and gazpacho stew with a *menú* at €13, otherwise allow €25 a head. Located close to the Mercado Municipal. Closed Sun eve.

Restaurante Rufino Plaza de Santa Clara 2. Traditional dishes in lovely surroundings at this centrally located restaurant, opposite the Museo Visigodo. Allow €15–20 a head or try the substantial €14 *menú*.

Restaurante Vía Flavia Plaza del Rastro 1. A friendly place next to the central plaza serving a good range of local dishes. The *menú* is very good value at €10.60.

Badajoz

The valley of the Río Guadiana, followed by road and rail, waters rich farmland between Mérida and **BADAJOZ**. The main reason for visiting this provincial capital, traditional gateway to Portugal and the scene of innumerable sieges, is still to get across the border. It's not somewhere you'd want to stay very long – crude modern development has largely overrun what must once have been an attractive old centre, and few of the monuments have survived – but food and lodging are cheap, and it does serve as a useful stopover. The city's troubled history, springing from its strategically important position on the Río Guadiana, is its main claim to fame. Founded by the Moors in 1009, the city was taken by the Christian armies of Alfonso IX in 1230, used as a base by Felipe II against the Portuguese in 1580, stormed by British forces under the Duke of Wellington in 1812 and taken by Franco's Nationalist troops in 1936.

Arrival and information

If you're arriving by **bus**, you'll have a fifteen-minute-plus walk to the centre, as the station is awkwardly located in wasteland beyond the ring road at the southern edge of the city. Your best bet is to hop on city bus #3 or #4 to Avenida de Europa or #6 to the Plaza de la Libertad. The **train station** is still farther from the action, on the far side of the river, up the road that crosses the Puente de Palmas. Buses #1 and #2 go to the Plaza de la Libertad, or it's around

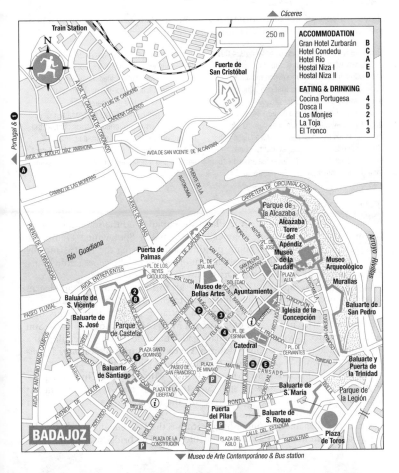

▲ Cáceres

ACCOMMODATION

Gran Hotel Zurbarán	B
Hotel Condedu	C
Hotel Río	A
Hostal Niza I	E
Hostal Niza II	D

EATING & DRINKING

Cocina Portugesa	4
Dosca II	5
Los Monjes	2
La Toja	1
El Tronco	3

BADAJOZ

▼ Museo de Arte Contemporáneo & Bus station

The **Portuguese frontier** is 4km west of Badajoz. You can get to Elvas, the first sizeable town on the Portuguese side of the border, by local bus (Mon–Fri 5 daily 6.30am–8.30pm). From here there are eleven long-distance buses (2hr 45min) and two trains per day to Lisbon (4hr 30min).

€4 in a taxi. If you're looking for **parking**, follow the signs to Plaza de Minayo where you'll find an attended underground car park.

The town has two tourist offices. The efficient municipal **turismo** (June–Sept Mon–Fri 10am–2pm & 6–8pm, Sat 10am–2pm; Oct–May Mon–Fri 10am–2pm & 4.30–6.30pm, Sat 10am–2pm; ☎924 224 981, ⓦwww.turismobadajoz .com) is in c/San Juan, just off Plaza de España, while the **Junta de Extremadura** office (Mon–Fri 10am–2pm & 5–7pm, Sat & Sun 10am–2pm; ☎924 013 659, ⓦwww.turismoextremadura.com), good for information on the whole region, is down the hill on Plaza de la Libertad – follow the signs from any approach to the town.

Accommodation

There's plenty of **accommodation** available in Badajoz, much of it inexpensive, if you want to use the city as a stopover on the way into Portugal.

Gran Hotel Zurbarán Paseo Castelar ☎924 001 400, ⓦwww.husa.es. A sleek, business-style hotel, with swimming pool and renowned restaurant. Look out for weekend deals that can bring the price down to as low as €60. ❹

Hostal Niza I and II c/Arco Agüero 34 & 45 ☎924 223 881, ⓦwww.hostal-niza.com. Simple, clean rooms in these two *hostales*. The *Niza I* used to be cheaper and less well equipped but has been upgraded recently and both now cost around €40 for a double room with en-suite bathroom. ❷

Hotel Condedu c/Muñoz Torrero 27 ☎ 924 207 247, ⓦwww.condedu.com. A simple, but comfortable and well-located hotel (aka *Hotel Conde Duque*), handy for the museum and cathedral and with its own garage. ❸

Hotel Río Avda. Adolfo Díaz Ambrona s/n ☎924 272 600, ⓦwww.gruporiodehoteles.com. At the far end of Puente de la Universidad, this upmarket 101-room hotel has a swimming pool, parking and a good restaurant. Closed weekends & Aug. ❸–❺

The Town

At the heart of old Badajoz is the **Plaza de España** and the squat thirteenth-century **Catedral** (Tues–Sat: summer 11am–1pm & 6–8pm; winter 11am–1pm & 5–7pm), a fortress-like building, prettified a little during the Renaissance by the addition of a portal and embellishment of the tower. The *museo* (same hours; €3) contains work by local-born artist Luís de Morales (1520–86).

Northeast of the square, c/de San Juan leads to **Plaza Alta**, once an elegant arcaded concourse and what remains of the town's fortress, the **Alcazaba**. This is largely in ruins but preserves Moorish entrance gates and fragments of a Renaissance palace inside. Part of it houses a **Museo Arqueológico** (Tues–Sun 10am–3pm; free), with local Roman and Visigothic finds. Defending the townward side is the octagonal Moorish **Torre del Aprendiz**, or *Torre Espantaperros* ("dog-scarer" – the dogs in question being Christians).

Nearby in the Plaza de Santa María is the new **Museo de la Ciudad** (April–Sept Tues–Sat 10am–2pm & 5–8pm, Sun 10am–2pm; free), which presents an interesting and well-thought-out survey of the city's chequered history from prehistoric times to the present day.

The city's other main distinguishing feature is the Río Guadiana, spanned by the graceful **Puente de Palmas**, or Puente Viejo. The bridge was designed by

Herrera (architect of El Escorial) as a fitting first impression of Spain, and leads into the city through the **Puerta de Palmas**, once a gate in the walls, now standing alone as a sort of triumphal arch.

From the plaza behind this arch, c/Santa Lucía leads to c/Duque de San Germán where you'll find the **Museo de Bellas Artes** (Sept–May Tues–Fri 10am–2pm & 4–6pm, Sat & Sun 10am–2pm, June–Aug Tues–Sat 10am–2pm & 6–8pm, Sun 10am–2pm; free), which includes works by Morales and a couple of good panels by Zurbarán. Near Plaza de la Constitución and off Avenida Calzadillas Maestre is the **Museo de Arte Contemporáneo** (Tues–Sat 10am–1.30pm & 5–8pm, Sun 10am–1.30pm; free). This striking circular, rust-coloured building houses a wealth of modern paintings, installations and sculpture, by artists from Spain, Portugal and Latin America.

Eating, drinking and nightlife

The area around c/Muñoz Torrero, a couple of blocks below the Plaza de España, is the most promising for reasonably priced food and tapas. For **nightlife**, *Mercantil* (daily 4.30pm–2/5am), off Plaza España at c/Zurbarán 10, is a stylish bar that hosts live guitar-based music at the weekend.

Cocina Portuguesa c/Muñoz Torrero 7. The best budget bet in Badajoz, with tasty, reasonably priced Portuguese cooking and a selection of good-value *menús*.

Dosca II Avda. de Colón 3. Just off Plaza Santo Domingo, this place is very popular with locals, serving a wide range of generous, well-cooked specialities in the nautically themed restaurant. Does a generous €11 *menú*.

Los Monjes *Gran Hotel Zurbarán*, Paseo Castelar ☎924 223 741. Probably the best food in town, with a pricey range of Spanish dishes, but it's a slightly characterless place. *À la carte* will probably

set you back over €40, though there's also a lunchtime buffet at half the price. Reservation recommended.

La Toja c/Sanchez de la Rocha 22 – the Portugal road. A good-quality restaurant, run by a *gallego*, so serving food from Extremadura and Galicia. A bit of a trek from the centre, though if you drive it has its own parking. Allow around €35 a head. Closed Sun eve & 15 days in Feb.

El Tronco c/Muñoz Torrero 16. Perhaps the best reason to stay in town – this has a vast range of superb-value bar snacks and excellent regional food and wine in the restaurant. Closed Sun eve.

Southern Extremadura

The routes **south from Mérida** or **Badajoz** cross territory that is mostly harsh and unrewarding, fit only for sheep and the odd cork or olive tree, until you come upon the foothills of the Sierra Morena, on the borders of Andalucía. En route, **Olivenza**, a town that has spent more time in Portugal than Spain, is perhaps the most attractive stop, and offers a road approach to Évora, the most interesting city of southern Portugal.

Olivenza

Twenty-five kilometres southwest of Badajoz, whitewashed **OLIVENZA** seems to have landed in the wrong country; long disputed between Spain and Portugal, it has been Spanish since 1801. Yet not only are the buildings and the town's character clearly Portuguese, the oldest inhabitants still cling to this language. There's a local saying here: "the women from Olivenza are not like the rest, for they are the daughters of Spain and the granddaughters of Portugal."

The town has long been strongly fortified, and traces of the **walls and gates** can still be seen, even though houses have been built up against them.

They extend up to the **castle**, which has three surviving towers and holds an ethnographic **museum** (winter Tues–Fri 11am–2pm & 4–7pm, Sat 10am–2pm & 4–7pm, Sun 10am–2pm, summer Tues–Fri 11am–2pm & 5–8pm, Sat 10am–2pm & 5–8pm, Sun 10am–2pm; €1) displaying an interesting and comprehensive range of exhibits detailing all aspects of life in the region. Right beside the castle is the seventeenth-century church of **Santa María del Castillo** (Tues–Sat 11am–2pm & 4–7pm, opens and closes an hour later in the afternoon in summer, Sun 11am–2pm), and around the corner, **Santa María Magdalena** (same hours), built a century later. The latter is in the distinctive Portuguese Manueline style, with arcades of twisted columns; the former is a more sober Renaissance affair with three aisles of equal height and a notable work of art in the huge "Tree of Jesse" *retablo*. Just across the street from Santa María Magdalena is a former **palace**, now the public library, with a spectacular Manueline doorway.

There's a **turismo** kiosk on the Plaza de España (summer Tues–Fri 10am–2pm & 5–7pm, Sat & Sun 10am–2pm; winter Tues–Fri 10am–2pm & 4–6pm, Sat & Sun 10am–2pm; ☎924 490 151). Should you want to **stay** in Olivenza, make for the hotel-restaurant *Heredero*, a large, modern place on the fringes of town, at the exit to Badajoz (☎924 490 835, ⓦwww.hotelheredero.net; ❹). You'll find a public **swimming pool** by the football ground, on Avenida Portugal, near the Badajoz exit, with its own restaurant.

Jerez de los Caballeros

The road from Badajoz to Jerez de los Caballeros is typical of southern Extremadura, striking across a parched landscape whose hamlets – low huts and a whitewashed church strung out along the road – look as if they have been dumped from some low-budget Western set of a Mexican frontier town. It's a cruel country that bred cruel people, if we are to believe the names of places like Valle de Matamoros (Valley of the Moorslayers), and one can easily understand the attraction that the New World and the promise of the lush Indies must have held for its inhabitants.

It is hardly surprising, then, that **JEREZ DE LOS CABALLEROS** produced a whole crop of *conquistadores*. The two most celebrated are Vasco Núñez de Balboa, discoverer of the Pacific, and Hernando de Soto (also known as the Conqueror of Florida), who in exploring the Mississippi became one of the first Europeans to set foot in North America. You're not allowed to forget it either – the bus station is in the Plaza de Vasco Núñez de Balboa, complete with a statue of Vasco in the very act of discovery, and from it the c/Hernando de Soto leads up into the middle of town.

It's a quiet, friendly place, through which many tourists pass but few stay. The church towers dominate the walled old town: a passion for building spires gripped the place in the eighteenth century, when three churches had new ones erected; the first is **San Miguel**, in the central Plaza de España, made of carved brick; the second is the unmistakable red-, blue- and ochre-glazed tower of **San Bartolomé**, on the hill above it, with a striking tiled facade; and the third, rather dilapidated, belongs to **Santa Catalina**, outside the walls.

Above the Plaza de España the streets climb up to the restored remains of a **castle** of the Knights Templar (this was once an embattled frontier town), mostly late thirteenth century but with obvious Moorish influences. Adjoining the castle, and pre-dating it by over a century (as do the town walls), is the church of **Santa María**. Built on a Visigothic site, it's more interesting seen from the battlements above than from the inside. In the small park below the castle walls, a café commands fine views of the surrounding countryside and the magnificent sunsets.

There's a small **turismo** in the *ayuntamiento* on Plaza de San Agustín (daily 9.30am–2.30pm & 4.30–6.30pm; ☎924 730 372). There aren't many places to **stay**: the *Casa Ramos*, Ctra. Badajoz 26 (☎924 730 983; ❶–❷), with its modest en-suite rooms is a good-value option. More upmarket alternatives are the *Hotel Oasis*, c/El Campo 18 (☎924 731 836; ❷–❸), and *Los Templarios* on the carretera Villanueva (☎924 731 636, ⓦwww.hoteltemplarios.net; ❹). For some tasty regional tapas and *pitarra* wine, try *La Ermita*, an old chapel on c/Dr Benitez.

Zafra

If you plan to stick to the main routes or are heading south from Mérida, **ZAFRA** is rather less of a detour, though it's also much more frequented by tourists. It's famed mainly for its **castle** – now converted into a *parador* – which is remarkable for the white marble Renaissance patio.

Two beautiful arcaded plazas, the Plaza Grande and the Plaza Chica, adjoin each other in the town centre. The most attractive of several interesting churches is **Nuestra Señora de la Candelaria** (summer Mon, Tues, Thurs, Fri 10.30am–1pm & 6.30–8.30pm, Sat & Sun 11am–1pm; winter opens and closes an hour earlier in the afternoons), with nine panels by Zurbarán in the *retablo* and a chapel by Churriguera; the entrance is on c/José through a small gateway, around the side of the church. Also worth a look are the tombs of the Figueroa family (the original inhabitants of the castle) in the **Convento de Santa Clara** (Mon–Fri 5–7pm, Sun & hols 10.30am–1pm & 4–6pm), just off the main shopping street, c/Sevilla; ring the bell to get in. Like many convents it also sells home-made cakes and biscuits.

This region is famous for its wines, and you can visit the **Bodega Medina**, c/Cestria (Mon–Fri 10.30am–2pm & 5–8pm, Sat 10am–2pm; ☎924 575 060, ⓦwww.bodegasmedina.net); call in at the **turismo** in the Plaza de España (Mon–Fri 9.30am–2pm & 5–8pm, Sat & Sun 10am–1.30pm & 6–8pm, winter opens and closes an hour earlier in the afternoons; ☎924 551 036, ⓦwww .ayto-zafra.com, ⓦwww.rutadelaplata.com) to make an appointment.

Accommodation options include the splendid *parador* (☎924 554 540, ⓦwww.paradores.com; ❻), housed in a fifteenth-century castle in the centre; the beautiful and luxurious boutique-style 🎗 *Casa Palacio Conde de la Corte*, at c/Pilar Redondo 2 (☎924 563 3811, ⓦwww.condedelacorte.com; ❹); the well-appointed *Hotel Las Palmeras*, Plaza Grande 14 (☎924 552 208, ⓦwww.hotellaspalmeras.net; ❷); and the small but very tidy *Hostal Carmen*, Avda. Estación 9 (☎924 551 439, ⓦwww.hostalcarmen.com; ❸), which also boasts an excellent medium-priced restaurant. For food, *La Rebotica* (☎924 554 289), at c/Boticas 12, has a wide selection of high-quality local dishes for which you'll pay around €35 a head.

Travel details

Trains

For current timetables and ticket information, consult RENFE ☎902 240 202, ⓦwww.renfe.es.
Albacete to: Alicante (10 daily; 1hr 30min); Madrid (23 daily; 2hr 10min–3hr); Valencia (15 daily; 1hr 20min–2hr).

Badajoz to: Cáceres (2 daily; 1hr 55min); Madrid (3 daily; 5hr 15min–6hr 15min); Mérida (7 daily; 40min–1hr).
Cáceres to: Badajoz (3 daily; 2hr); Lisbon (daily; 5hr 15min); Madrid (5 daily; 2hr 20min–3hr 55min); Mérida (5 daily; 50min–1hr); Plasencia (2 daily; 1hr 20min); Sevilla (daily; 5hr 40min); Zafra (2 daily; 2hr 10min).

Ciudad Real to: Almagro (5 daily; 1hr 15min); Madrid (25 daily; 50min–1hr).

Cuenca to: Madrid (5 daily; 2hr 30min–2hr 55min); Valencia (4 daily; 2hr 45min–3hr 10min).

Madrid to: Albacete (22 daily; 2hr–2hr 20min); Almagro (daily; 2hr 40min); Badajoz (4 daily; 5hr 40min–7hr); Cáceres (6 daily; 3hr 20min–5hr); Ciudad Real (2 daily, 3hr; 20 daily AVE, 55min); Cuenca (4 daily; 2hr 30min); Mérida (5 daily; 4hr 10min–4hr 50min); Navalmoral (7 daily; 2hr–2hr 20min); Plasencia (4 daily; 3hr 10min–3hr 30min); Sigüenza (6 daily; 1hr 40min); Talavera de la Reina (7 daily; 1hr 30min).

Mérida to: Badajoz (7 daily; 45min); Cáceres (4 daily; 1hr); Madrid (4 daily; 4hr 30min–5hr 50min); Plasencia (2 daily; 2hr 25min); Seville (daily; 4hr 35min).

Plasencia to: Badajoz (daily; 3hr 30min); Cáceres (3 daily; 1hr 20min); Madrid (up to 5 daily; 3hr 20min); Mérida (3 daily; 2hr 20min).

Sigüenza to: Barcelona (daily; at least 6hr 30min), via Zaragoza (3–4hr); Madrid (7 daily; 1hr 40min); Medinaceli (4 daily; 15–20min).

Buses

Albacete to: Alicante (7 daily; 1hr 50min–2hr 25min); Cuenca (2–3 daily; 2hr 45min); Madrid (19 daily; 3hr 10min–3hr 30min); Murcia (11 daily; 1hr 45min–2hr 30min); Parque Natural de las Lagunes de Ruidera (Mon–Sat daily; 2hr); Valencia (6 daily; 2hr 5min–3hr 15min).

Badajoz to: Cáceres (7 daily; 2hr); Córdoba (3 daily; 5hr); Madrid (7 daily; 4hr 30min–5hr); Mérida (8 daily; 45min); Murcia (daily; 9hr 20min); Olivenza (12 daily; 30min); Seville (2–5 daily; 4hr 30min); Zafra (8 daily; 1hr 30min).

Cáceres to: Alcántara (2 daily; 1hr 30min); Arroyo de la Luz (8–15 daily; 30min); Badajoz (4 daily; 1hr 15min–1hr 45min); Coria (4 daily; 1hr 15min); Guadalupe (2 daily; 2hr 30min); Madrid (8 daily; 4hr); Mérida (4 daily; 1hr); Plasencia (4–5 daily; 1hr 20min); Salamanca (4 daily; 3hr 30min); Seville (8 daily; 4hr); Trujillo (8 daily; 45min).

Ciudad Real to: Almagro (6 daily; 1hr); Córdoba (daily; 4hr 30min); Jaén (2 daily; 4hr); Madrid (4 daily; 4hr); Toledo (daily; 3hr); Valdepeñas (3 daily; 2hr).

Cuenca to: Albacete (2–3 daily; 2hr 45min); Barcelona (daily; 9hr); Madrid (9 daily; 2hr–2hr 30min); Teruel (daily; 2hr 30min); Valencia (2–3 daily; 2hr 30min–3hr 30min).

Guadalupe to: Cáceres (2 daily; 2hr 30min); Madrid (2 daily; 4hr); Trujillo (2 daily; 2hr–2hr 30min).

Madrid to: Albacete (11 daily; 3hr); Badajoz (9 daily; 4hr 30min–5hr); Cáceres (7–10 daily; 3hr 50min–4hr 30min); Cuenca (10 daily; 2hr–2hr 30min); Jarandilla (daily; 3hr 30min); Mérida (10 daily; 4–5hr); Plasencia (2 daily; 4hr); Talavera de la Reina (15 daily; 1hr 30min); Trujillo (10 daily; 4–5hr).

Mérida to: Badajoz (8 daily; 45min); Cáceres (7 daily; 1hr); Guadalupe (4 daily; 2hr); Jerez de los Caballeros (1–3 daily; 2hr); Madrid (8–9 daily; 4hr 20min); Murcia (daily; 9hr); Salamanca (5 daily; 4hr); Seville (6–8 daily; 3hr 15min, some stopping in Zafra); Trujillo (4 daily; 2hr); Zafra (1–3 daily; 1hr 10min).

Navalmoral to: Jarandilla (2 daily; 3hr); Plasencia (2 daily; 2–4hr); Trujillo (6 daily; 1hr).

Plasencia to: Cáceres (4–5 daily; 1hr 20min); Jarandilla (2 daily; 2hr); Madrid (2 daily; 4hr); Salamanca (4 daily; 2hr).

Talavera de la Reina to: Guadalupe (2 daily; 2hr 30min); Madrid (15 daily; 1hr 30min); Toledo (10 daily; 1hr 30min).

Trujillo to: Cáceres (8 daily; 45min); Guadalupe (2 daily; 2hr); Madrid (13–16 daily; 3hr–3hr 30min); Mérida (4 daily; 2hr).

Andalucía

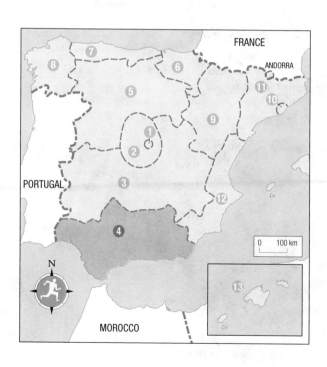

CHAPTER 4

Highlights

* **Semana Santa** Andalucía's major Holy Week festival is memorably celebrated in Seville, Málaga, Córdoba and Granada. See p.238

* **Seville** Andalucía's pulsating capital city is a treasure house of churches, palaces and museums. See p.274

* **Flamenco** The passionate dance, song and music of the Spanish south. See p.293

* **Sherry** Andalucía's classic wine makes the perfect partner for tapas. See "Wines of Spain" colour section

* **Coto de Doñana** Europe's largest and most important wildlife sanctuary. See p.312

* **Mezquita, Córdoba** This 1200-year-old Moorish mosque is one of the most beautiful ever built. See p.324

* **Alhambra** Granada's Moorish palace is the pinnacle of Moorish architectural splendour in Spain. See p.344

* **Las Alpujarras** A wildly picturesque region dotted with traditional mountain villages. See p.358

▲ Alcázar, Seville

Andalucía

T he popular image of Spain as a land of bullfights, flamenco, sherry and ruined castles derives from **Andalucía**, the southernmost territory of the country and the most quintessentially Spanish part of the Iberian peninsula. Above all, it's the great Moorish monuments that compete for your attention in this part of Spain. The Moors, a mixed race of Berbers and Arabs who crossed into Spain from Morocco and North Africa, occupied *al-Andalus* for over seven centuries. Their first forces landed at Tarifa in 710 AD, and within four years they had conquered virtually the entire country; their last kingdom, Granada, fell to the Christian Reconquest in 1492. Between these dates, they developed the most sophisticated civilization of the Middle Ages, centred in turn on the three major cities of Córdoba, Seville and Granada. Each one preserves extraordinarily brilliant and beautiful monuments, of which the most perfect is Granada's Alhambra palace, arguably the most sensual building in all of Europe. Seville, not to be outdone, has a fabulously ornamented Alcázar and the grandest of all Gothic cathedrals. Today, Andalucía's capital and seat of the region's autonomous parliament is a vibrant contemporary metropolis that's impossible to resist. Córdoba's exquisite Mezquita, the grandest and most beautiful mosque constructed by the Moors, is a landmark building in world architecture and not to be missed.

These three cities have, of course, become major tourist destinations, but it's also worth leaving the tourist trail and visiting some of the smaller **inland towns** of Andalucía. Renaissance towns such as **Úbeda**, **Baeza** and **Osuna**, Moorish **Carmona** and the stark white hill towns around **Ronda** are all easily accessible by local buses. Travelling for some time here, you'll get a feel for the landscape of Andalucía: occasionally spectacularly beautiful but more often impressive on a huge, unyielding scale.

The province also takes in mountains – including the **Sierra Nevada**, Spain's highest range. You can often ski here in March, and then drive down to the coast to swim the same day. Perhaps more compelling, though, are the opportunities for walking in the lower slopes, **Las Alpujarras**. Alternatively, there's good trekking amongst the gentler (and much less-known) hills of the **Sierra Morena**, north of Seville.

On the **coast**, it's easy to despair. Extending to either side of **Málaga** is the **Costa del Sol**, Europe's most heavily developed resort area, with its poor beaches hidden behind a remorseless density of concrete hotels and apartment complexes. However, the province offers two alternatives, much less developed and with some of the best beaches in all Spain. These are the villages **between**

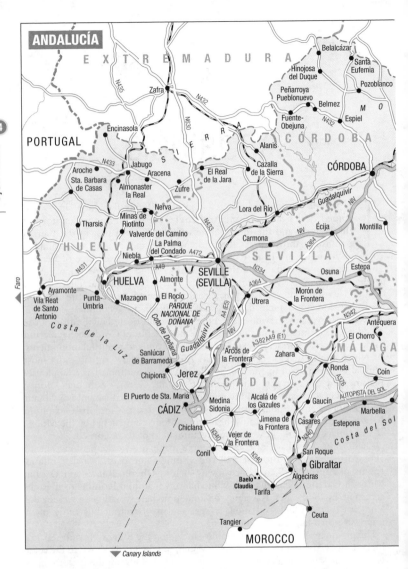

▼ *Canary Islands*

Tarifa and Cádiz on the Atlantic, and those **around Almería** on the southeast corner of the Mediterranean. The latter allow warm swimming in all but the winter months; those near Cádiz, more easily accessible, are fine from about June to September. Near Cádiz, too, is the **Parque Nacional Coto de Doñana** national park, Spain's largest and most important nature reserve, which is home to a spectacular range of flora and fauna.

The realities of life in contemporary Andalucía can be stark. **Unemployment** in the region is the highest in Spain – over twenty percent in some areas – and a large proportion of the population still scrapes a living from

seasonal agricultural work. The *andaluz* villages, bastions of anarchist and socialist groups before and during the Civil War, saw little economic aid or change during the Franco years, and although much government spending has been channelled into improving infrastructure such as hospitals, road and rail links, the lack of employment opportunities away from the coastal tourist zones persists. For all its poverty, however, Andalucía is also Spain at its most exuberant – those wild and extravagant clichés of the Spanish south really do exist and can be absorbed at one of the hundreds of annual **fiestas**, **ferias** and **romerías**.

4

Fiestas

January
1–2: La Toma Celebration of the entry of Los Reyes Católicos into the city – at Granada.

6: Romería de la Virgen del Mar Pilgrimage procession from Almería.

17: Romería del Ermita del Santo Similar event at Guadix.

February
1: San Cecilio Fiesta in Granada's traditionally gypsy quarter of Sacromonte.

Week before Lent: Carnaval An extravagant week-long event in all the Andalucian cities. Cádiz, above all, celebrates, with uproarious street parades, fancy dress and satirical music competitions.

March/April
Easter: Semana Santa (Holy Week) You'll find memorable processions of floats and penitents at Seville, Málaga, Granada and Córdoba, and to a lesser extent in smaller towns such as Jerez, Arcos, Baeza and Úbeda. All culminate with dramatic candle-light processions at dawn on Good Friday, with Easter Day itself more of a family occasion.

Last week of April: Feria de Abril Week-long fair at Seville: the largest fair in Spain.

Last week of April Small fair in vejer de la Frontera, featuring bull-running.

May
First week: Cruces de Mayo Celebrated in Córdoba and includes a "prettiest patio" competition in a town full of prize examples.

Early May (week after Feria de Abril): Feria del Caballo A somewhat aristocratic horse fair is held at Jerez de la Frontera.

3: Moros y Cristianos "Moors and Christians" carnival at Pampaneira (Las Alpujarras).

Pentecost: Romería del Rocío Horse-drawn carriages and processions converge from all over the south on El Rocío (Huelva).

Corpus Christi (Thurs after Trinity) Bullfights and festivities at Granada, Seville, Ronda, Vejer and Zahara de la Sierra.

Last week: Feria de la Manzanilla Prolonged binge in Sanlúcar de Barrameda to celebrate the town's major product, with flamenco and sporting events on the river beach.

June
Second week: Feria de San Bernabé At Marbella, this fair is often spectacular since this is the richest town in Andalucía.

The Costa del Sol

The outstanding feature of the **Costa del Sol** is its ease of access. Hundreds of flights arrive here every week, and **Málaga airport** is positioned midway between **Málaga**, the main city on the coast, and **Torremolinos**, its most grotesque resort.

13: San Antonio Fiesta at Trevélez (Las Alpujarras) with mock battles between Moors and Christians.

Third week The Algeciras *Feria Real* is another major event of the south.

23–24: Candelas de San Juan Bonfires and effigies at Vejer and elsewhere.

30 Conil *feria*.

End June/early July: International Festival of Music and Dance Major dance/flamenco groups and chamber orchestras perform in Granada's Alhambra palace, Generalife and Carlos V palace.

July

Early July: International Guitar Festival Brings together top international acts from classical, flamenco and Latin American music in Córdoba.

End of month: Virgen del Mar Almería's major annual shindig, with parades, horseriding events, concerts and lots of drinking.

August

First week The first cycle of horse races along Sanlúcar de Barrameda's beach, with heavy official and unofficial betting; the second tournament takes place two weeks later.

5 Trevélez observes a midnight *romería* to Mulhacén.

13–21: Feria de Málaga One of Andalucía's most enjoyable fiestas for visitors, who are heartily welcomed by the ebullient *malagueños*.

15: Ascension of the Virgin Fair With *casetas* (dance tents) at Vejer and elsewhere.

Noche del Vino Riotous wine festival at Competa (Málaga).

23–25: Guadalquivir festival Bullfights and an important flamenco competition, at Sanlúcar de Barrameda.

September

First two weeks: Feria de Ronda. Ronda's annual *feria*, with flamenco contests and *Corrida Goyesca* – bullfights in eighteenth-century dress.

1–3: Virgen de la Luz Processions and horseback riding in Tarifa.

First/second week: Vendimia Celebrating the vintage at Jerez.

27–Oct 1: Feria de San Miguel In Órgiva (Las Alpujarras).

October

1: San Miguel Fiesta in Granada's Albaicín quarter and elsewhere, including Torremolinos.

15–23: Feria de San Lucas Jaén's major fiesta, dating back to the fifteenth century.

You can easily reach either town by taking the electric train (*cercanía*) that runs every thirty minutes (daily 7am–11.45pm) along the coast between Málaga and **Fuengirola**, 20km to the southwest. Frequent bus connections also link all the major coastal resorts, while a toll *autopista* (motorway) between Málaga and Sotogrande has taken the strain off the often-overloaded coastal highways. Inland, Granada, Córdoba and Seville are all within easy reach of Málaga; so, too, are **Ronda** and the beautiful "White Towns" to the west, and a handful of relatively restrained coastal resorts, such as **Nerja**, to the east. The **beaches** here are generally grit-grey rather than golden, but the sea is reliably clean.

Málaga

MÁLAGA seems at first an uninviting place. It's the second city of the south (after Seville), with a population of half a million, and is also one of the poorest: an estimated one in four of the workforce are jobless. Though the clusters of high-rises look pretty grim as you approach, the city does have some compelling attractions. The recently renovated and elegant central zone has a number of interesting churches and museums, not to mention the **birthplace of Picasso** and the **Museo Picasso Málaga**, housing an important collection of works by Málaga's most famous son. Perched on the hill above the town are the formidable citadels of the **Alcazaba** and **Gibralfaro**, magnificent vestiges of the seven centuries that the Moors held sway here. Málaga is also renowned for its **fish** and **seafood**, which can be sampled at tapas bars and restaurants throughout the city, as well as at the old fishing villages of **El Palo** and **Pedregalejo**, now absorbed into the suburbs, where there's a seafront *paseo* lined with some of the best **marisquerías** and **chiringuitos** (seafood cafés) in the province.

Arrival

From the **airport** (T 952 048 804), the **electric train** (*ferrocarril*) provides the easiest approach to Málaga (every 30min 7am–11.45pm; €1.20). The Málaga platform is the one farthest away and reached by an underpass; stay on the train right to the end of the line – the **Centro–Alameda** stop (12min). Alternatively, city **bus** #19 leaves from outside the Arrivals hall (every 30min 7am–midnight; €1), stopping at the train and bus stations en route to the centre and the Paseo del Parque near the port, from where you can also pick it up in the opposite direction when you're returning to the airport. A **taxi** into town from the rank outside the Arrivals hall will cost around €15 depending on traffic and time of day and takes roughly fifteen minutes.

The city's impressive new RENFE **train station** is southwest of the heart of town; bus #3 runs from here to the centre every 10min or so. The **bus station** is just behind the RENFE station, from where all buses (run by a number of different companies) operate. In summer, it's best to arrive an hour or so early for the bus to Granada, since tickets can sell out.

Arriving in Málaga **by car** you face the serious problem of parking and will have little choice but to use one of the many signed car parks around the centre or use a garage connected to your accommodation (for which you will still need to pay). Note that **theft** from cars is rampant in Málaga.

Málaga has the remnants of a **passenger ferry port**, the Estación Marítima, though these days there's a service only to the Spanish enclave of Melilla in Morocco, with Trasmediterranea (7hr; T 902 454 645, W www .trasmediterranea.es). If you're heading for Fes and eastern Morocco, this is a useful connection – particularly so for taking a car over – though most people go for the quicker services at Algeciras and Tarifa to the west.

Information

The **turismo**, Pasaje de Chinitas 4 (Mon–Fri 9am–8pm, Sat & Sun 10am–2pm; T 952 213 445), can provide information on cultural events and accommodation, and sells a detailed map of the city. There's also a very helpful **turismo municipal** on Plaza de la Marina (Mon–Fri 9am–7.30pm, Sat 10am–7pm, Sun 10am–2pm; T 952 122 020), with other branches at the bus station and in the airport Arrivals hall.

One way to get to grips quickly with the city is on an **open-topped bus tour**. This hop-on hop-off service is operated by Málagatour (℡902 101 081, Ⓦwww.city-ss.com; €15, tickets valid 24hr); buses leave the bus station every half-hour (9.15am–7pm) with about a dozen stops around the centre, including the cathedral, Plaza de la Merced, the Alameda and the Gibralfaro.

Accommodation

Málaga boasts dozens of hotels and *hostales* in all budget categories. The best places to start looking for budget **accommodation** are the area just south of the Alameda Principal and the streets east and west of c/Marques de Larios, which cuts between the Alameda and Plaza de la Constitución. The nearest **campsite** lies 10km west along the coast towards Torremolinos.

Budget

Albergue Juvenil Málaga Plaza de Pio XII ℡952 308 500. Modern youth hostel on the western outskirts of town, with double and single rooms, disabled facilities and its own sun terrace. Tends to fill up in season, so book ahead. Bus #18 heading west across the river from the Alameda will drop you nearby. Under-26 €16, over-26 €20.

Hostal El Cenachero c/Barroso 5 ℡952 224 088. Clean, quiet, friendly and reasonably priced *hostal*; left off the seafront end of c/Córdoba. Most rooms en suite. ❸

Hostal Derby c/San Juan de Dios 1 ℡952 221 301. Excellent-value fourth-floor *hostal*, just off the Plaza de la Marina, with some en-suite rooms overlooking the harbour. ❷

Hostal La Hispanidad Explanada de la Estación 5 ℡952 311 135, Ⓦwww.hostalhispanidad.com. Facing the train station, this is a useful sleepover if you've got an early train (or bus) to catch. The labyrinthine interior has refurbished en-suite rooms named after different countries of the Americas, with a/c and TV, and there are plenty of eating places nearby. ❸

Hostal La Palma c/Martínez 7 ℡952 226 772. One of the best budget places in town with new a/c en-suite doubles in addition to simpler rooms sharing bath; sometimes gives discounts. ❷–❸

Hostal Victoria c/Sancha de Lara 3 ℡952 224 223. Pleasant *hostal* with good-value double and single rooms, just north of the Alameda. ❸

Pensión Juanita c/Alarcón Luján 8 ℡952 213 586. Central and friendly *pensión* offering rooms with or without bath on the fourth floor (with a lift). Large family rooms also available. ❷

Moderate and expensive

Hotel California Paseo de Sancha 17, 500m east of the bullring ℡952 215 164, Ⓦwww.costadelsol .spa.es/hotel/california. Charming small hotel near the beach with a flower-bedecked entrance and safe parking; well-appointed rooms come with a/c

and strongbox. Buses #11, #34 and #35 from the Alameda will drop you outside. ❹

Hotel Don Curro c/Sancha de Lara 7 ℡952 227 200, Ⓦwww.hoteldoncurro.com. Central and comfortable, if rather featureless, hotel with a/c rooms and its own car park. Some views from top-floor rooms. ❺

Hotel Larios c/Marqués de Larios 2 ℡952 222 200, Ⓦwww.hotel-larios.com. Modern, upmarket and central hotel inside the shell of an original Art Deco edifice; satellite TV, room safes and a panoramic rooftop bar are among the features. Does frequent special offers. B&B ❺

Hotel Lola c/Casas de Campos 17 ℡952 579 300, Ⓦwww.room-matehotels.com. New designer-chic boutique hotel where rooms come with plasma TV, free internet, DVD player, minibar and room safe. Also has own bar-restaurant and garage. ❺

Hotel Málaga Palacio Cortina del Muelle 1 ℡952 215 185, Ⓦwww.ac-hotels.com. This central four-star hotel with sea-view rooms pampers its guests with free minibar and bathrobes. Facilities include rooftop pool and gym. Online special offers. ❺

Hotel Montevictoria c/Conde de Ureña 58 ℡952 656 525, Ⓦwww.hotelmontevictoria .com. Sweet little hotel with friendly proprietors in an elegant garden villa in the hills above Málaga, with great views over the city. Slightly pricier rooms 104 & 105 have their own private terrace. Bus #36 from the Alameda (ask for the c/Conde de Ureña stop) stops almost outside. ❹

Hotel Sur c/Trinidad Grund 13 ℡952 224 803, Ⓕ952 212 416. Quiet, efficient and central hotel with secure garage; all rooms have bath and TV. ❹

Parador Gibralfaro Monte de Gibralfaro ℡952 221 902, Ⓦwww.paradores.es. You won't get a better panoramic view of the coast than from this eagle's nest on top of the Gibralfaro hill; it's quite small as *paradores* go, which adds to its charm, plus there's a pretty good restaurant (see p.247) and it also squeezes in a pool. Own garage. ❻

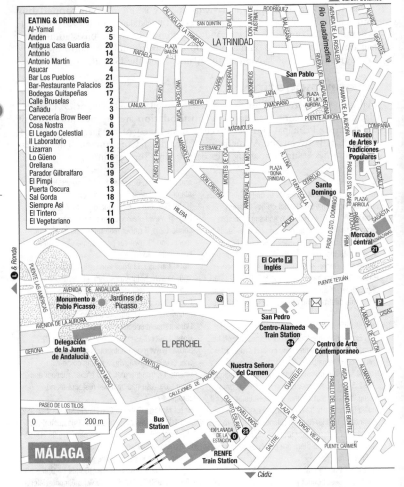

EATING & DRINKING

Al-Yamal	23
Anden	5
Antigua Casa Guardia	20
Antonio	14
Antonio Martín	22
Asucar	4
Bar Los Pueblos	21
Bar-Restaurante Palacios	25
Bodegas Quitapeñas	17
Calle Bruselas	2
Cañadu	3
Cervecería Brow Beer	9
Cosa Nostra	6
El Legado Celestial	24
Il Laboratorio	1
Lizarran	12
Lo Güeno	16
Orellana	15
Parador Gilbralfaro	19
El Pimpi	8
Puerta Oscura	13
Sal Gorda	18
Siempre Asi	7
El Tintero	11
El Vegetariano	10

MÁLAGA

The City

Over the last few years, Málaga has raised its game and a once grimy reputation is largely a thing of the past. A costly face-lift of the central zone, focused on the elegant marble-paved and pedestrianized **Calle Marqués de Larios** – now a fashionable shopping street – leading into a revamped Plaza de la Constitución, has improved things immensely and given the *malagueños* a rejuvenated sense of civic pride. From Plaza de la Constitución the Moorish **Alcazaba**, the towering **cathedral** and the spectacular **Museo Picasso Málaga** all lie within a few minutes' walk. The seafront has also been revamped, with new hotels and restaurants lining promenades along the beaches east and west of the centre.

The Alcazaba and Gibralfaro

The impressive **Alcazaba** (Tues–Sun: April–Sept 9.30am–8pm; Oct–March 8.30am–5.45pm; €2, €3.30 combined ticket with Gibralfaro) is the place to

242

ANDALUCÍA | Málaga

4

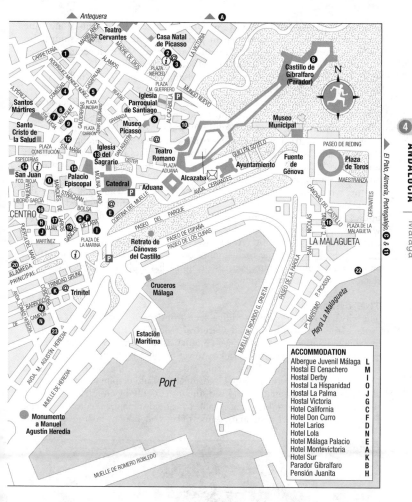

ACCOMMODATION

Albergue Juvenil Málaga	L
Hostal El Cenachero	M
Hostal Derby	I
Hostal La Hispanidad	O
Hostal La Palma	J
Hostal Victoria	G
Hotel California	C
Hotel Don Curro	F
Hotel Larios	D
Hotel Lola	N
Hotel Málaga Palacio	E
Hotel Montevictoria	A
Hotel Sur	K
Parador Gibralfaro	B
Pensión Juanita	H

make for if you're killing time between connections. It's just fifteen-minutes' walk (or 5min bus ride) from the train or bus stations, and can be clearly seen from most central points. To the left of its entrance on c/Acazabilla stands the **Teatro Romano** (Roman Theatre) accidentally discovered in 1951, and – following excavation and restoration – now a venue for various outdoor entertainments. The citadel, too, is Roman in origin, with blocks and columns of marble interspersed among the Moorish brick of the double- and triple-arched gateways.

The main structures, reopened in 2002 following a three-year restoration, were begun by the Moors in the eighth century, probably soon after their conquest, but the palace higher up the hill dates from the early decades of the eleventh century. This was the residence of the Arab emirs of Málaga, who carved out an independent kingdom for themselves upon the break-up of the Western Caliphate. Their independence lasted a mere thirty years, but for a while their kingdom included Granada, Carmona and Jaén. The complex's **palace** was heavily restored in the 1930s, but some fine stuccowork, the ceilings and elegant patios give a flavour of the sumptuous edifice it must once have been. The interior displays Moorish ceramics found during the archeological excavations. You can avoid the climb up to the palace by taking a **lift** built into the hill and accessed on c/Guillen Sotelo, directly behind the *ayuntamiento*.

Above the Alcazaba, and connected to it by a long double wall (the *coracha*), is the **Gibralfaro castle** (same hours and entry fee). It's reached by climbing a twisting path that skirts the southern walls, passing bougainvillea-draped ramparts and sentry-box-shaped Moorish wells. You can also approach from the town side, as the urban buses and tourist coaches do, but this is a rather unattractive walk and not one to be done alone after sundown. If you want to avoid the climb altogether, you can take bus #35 east from the Paseo del Parque, which stops just outside the entrance. Last used in 1936 during the Civil War, the castle, like the Alcazaba, has been wonderfully restored and now houses an interesting **museum** devoted to its history – a scale model lets you see how the city would have looked in Moorish times. A walk around the battlements affords terrific **views** over the city, while the nearby *parador* (reached by following the road leading out of the castle's car park for 100m and turning right into the *parador's* grounds) has a pleasant terrace café and restaurant with more fine views.

The catedral

The city's most conspicuous edifice seen from the heights of the Gibralfaro castle is the peculiar, unfinished **Catedral** (Mon–Fri 10am–6pm, Sat 10am–5pm, closed Sun except for services; €3.50). Constructed between the sixteenth and eighteenth centuries, it still lacks a tower on the west front because a radical *malagueño* bishop donated the earmarked money to the American War of Independence against the British. Unfortunately – and despite its huge scale – it also lacks any real inspiration and is distinguished only by an intricately carved seventeenth-century *sillería* (choirstall) by noted sculptor Pedro de Mena. However, **Iglesia del Sagrario** (same ticket and hours), on the cathedral's

▲ Málaga Catedral

northern flank, is worth a look, if only for its fine Gothic portal, dating from an earlier, uncompleted Isabelline church. Inside, a restored and magnificent gilded Plateresque **retablo**, which is brilliantly illuminated during services, is the work of Juan Balmaseda.

Museo Picasso Málaga and Casa Natal de Picasso

Just around the corner from the cathedral on c/San Agustín is the **Museo Picasso Málaga** (Tues–Sun 10am–8pm; permanent collection €6, temporary collection €4.50; combined ticket €8; ⓦ www.museopicassomalaga.org), housed in the elegant sixteenth-century mansion of the counts of Buenavista. It was opened by the king and queen in 2003, 112 years after Picasso left Málaga at the age of 10 and to where he returned only once for an unhappy, fleeting visit in his late teens. In later life, he toyed with the idea of "sending two lorries full of paintings" to set up a museum in Málaga but vowed never to set foot in Spain while the ruling General Franco was still alive. Picasso died in 1973 and was outlived by the dictator by two years.

The **permanent collection** consists of 204 works donated by Christine and Bernard Ruiz-Picasso, the artist's daughter-in-law and grandson, while the **temporary collection** comprises loaned works and special exhibitions (not necessarily connected with Picasso). Though not on a par with the Picasso museums in Paris and Barcelona, the museum does allow you to see some of the lesser-known works that Picasso kept for himself or gave away to his lovers, family and friends – rather harshly described as the "less saleable stuff" by one critic. Among the highlights are, in Room 2, *Olga Koklova con Mantilla* (a portrait of his first wife, draped in a hotel tablecloth) and a moving portrait of his son Paul, painted in 1923. Other rooms have canvases from the breadth of Picasso's career including his Blue, Pink and Cubist periods, as well as sculptures in wood, metal and stone and a few ceramics. Two other influential women who figured prominently in the artist's long and turbulent love life are also the subject of powerful images: in Room 5, *Cabeza de Mujer 1939* is a portrait of the beguiling yet tragic Dora Maar, and in Room 8, *Jacqueline Sentada* is a seated representation of his second wife, Jacqueline Roque.

An unexpected surprise lies in the museum's basement – **archeological remains** revealed during the construction of the building. These include substantial chunks of a Phoenician city wall and tower, which date from the seventh century BC and would have protected these early colonists from attacks by the Iberian tribes. From later periods there are parts of a Roman *salazones* factory used to produce the famous *garum*, a fish-based sauce and Roman delicacy, and vestiges of the cellar of the sixteenth-century Palacio de Buenavista. A case nearby displays some of the finds unearthed in the excavations, including Phoenician, Greek and Roman pottery fragments and a sixth-century BC Egyptian scarab.

The museum also has a good, if cramped, **bookshop** and an equally cramped **café**, although this spills out onto a pleasant garden terrace in fine weather. The museum opens on certain Saturday evenings throughout the summer (€2; details from museum), with live music in the garden and other events.

The **Museo de las Bellas Artes** that was formerly housed here is due to be relocated to the Aduana (the old customs building on the Paseo del Parque). Either of the tourist offices should have the latest news on this. The collection includes significant works by Murillo and Zurbarán.

Picasso was born a couple of hundred metres away from the museum in the Plaza de la Merced, where the **Casa Natal de Picasso** (daily 10am–8pm; €1) is home to the Fundación Picasso, a centre for scholars researching the painter's life and work. A recently revamped exhibition space now displays lithographs, etchings and washes by Picasso – mainly with women as the subject matter – while on the stairs are photos of the artist at various stages in his long life. The stairs lead to a reconstructed reception room, furnished as it might have looked when Picasso was growing up here at the end of the late nineteenth century. Among the items on display are some embroidered bed linen by the artist's mother, a canvas by his art-teacher father, and the infant Picasso's christening robe used in the ceremony at the nearby Iglesia de Santiago.

Centro de Arte Contemporaneo and Museo Carmen Thyssen Bornemisza

Building on the success of the Picasso museum, the city is now turning itself into an art lover's hot spot with a modern art museum and the soon to open Museo Carmen Thyssen Bornemisza.

Sited on the east bank of the Río Guadalmedina, the **Centro de Arte Contemporaneo** on c/Alemania (July & Aug daily 10am–2pm & 5–9pm; Sept–June Tues–Sun 10am–8pm; free; Ⓦ www.cacmalaga.org) is an impressive modern art museum housed in a former market building. The permanent collection displays works by international artists Louise Bourgeois, Cindy Sherman and Damien Hirst, while Spain is represented by Juan Muñoz, Miguel Barcelo and Juan Uslé among others. Check out the centre's website for information on frequent temporary exhibitions. A **cafetería** has a pleasant riverview terrace.

Just off the west side of Plaza de la Constitución and housed in the refurbished sixteenth-century Palacio de Villalón, in c/Compañia, is the **Museo Carmen Thyssen Bornemisza** (scheduled to open end 2009; details from either *turismo*), named after the spouse of the late baron whose collection forms the core of the similarly named museum in Madrid. Another donation by the family, this museum will display Spanish art of the nineteenth century, but other periods will also be represented with works by artists such as Zurbarán and Juan Gris.

Jardín Botánico La Concepción

A pleasant trip out of town is to the **Jardín Botánico La Concepción** (guided tours Tues–Sat: April–Sept 9.30am–8.30pm; Oct–March 9.30am–4pm; last visit 90min before closing; €4), 5km north of the city and signposted off the N331 *autovía*. A spectacular tropical garden, much of which was planted in the nineteenth century, this formerly private estate was founded in the 1850s by Amelia Loring, granddaughter of the British consul, and purchased in 1990 by the Málaga city council, since when it has been open to the public. Specimens on view include exotic blooms, thirty species of palm, and other trees of all shapes and continents, such as the Australian banyan with its serpentine aerial roots.

Bus #61 from the north side of the Alameda Principal will drop you at the gates (Sat & Sun), or at its terminus 700m short (Mon–Fri). Another way of visiting the garden by bus is to use the Málagatour sightseeing bus (see p.241), which has a stop here. A **taxi** costs about €8 one way from the centre.

Eating and drinking

Málaga has no shortage of **places to eat and drink**, and, though it's hardly a gourmet paradise, the city has a justified reputation for seafood. Its greatest claim to fame is undoubtedly its **fried fish**, acknowledged as the best in Spain. You'll find many fish restaurants grouped around the Alameda, although for some of the very best you need to head out to the suburbs of Pedregalejo and El Palo, served by bus #11 (from Paseo del Parque). On the seafront *paseo* at **Pedregalejo**, almost any of the cafés and restaurants will also serve up terrific seafood. Farther on, after the *paseo* disappears, you find yourself amid fishing shacks and smaller, sometimes quite ramshackle, cafés in **El Palo**, an earthier sort of area for the most part, with a beach and huts, and – in summer or at weekends – an even better place to eat.

Málaga has plenty of good **tapas bars**: *Bar Lo Güeno*, c/Marín García 9, off c/Marqués de Larios is a popular place at *aperitivo* time, whilst the diminutive size of the bustling ⚒ *Orellana* at c/Moreno Monroy 5, nearer to Plaza de la Constitución, is in inverse proportion to its reputation as one of the best in town. Other good options include *Bodegas Quitapeñas* (aka *La Manchega*), c/Marín García 4; the Basque *pinxtos* bar *Lizarran*, c/Sanchez Pastor 2, northeast of Plaza de la Constitución; and *Antigua Reja* on Plaza de Uncibay.

A number of **traditional bars** serve the sweet **Málaga wine** (Falstaff's "sack"), made from muscatel grapes and dispensed from huge barrels; try it with shellfish at *Antigua Casa Guardia*, a great old nineteenth-century bar at the corner of c/Pastora, on the Alameda's north side. The new-season wine, *Pedriot*, is incredibly sweet; much more palatable is *Seco Añejo*, which has matured for a year.

Al-Yamal c/Blasco de Garay 3, near *Hostal El Cenachero*. Good Arabic restaurant serving up pricey but authentic meat in spicy sauces, *couscous – cordero* (lamb) *couscous* is a house special – and other typical dishes. Good selection of Moroccan wines. Closed Sun.

Antonio Fernando Lesseps 7. Popular small and central restaurant serving well-prepared *malagueño* dishes with an outdoor terrace in an atmospheric cul-de-sac off the north end of c/ Nueva; *menú* for around €12.

⚒ **Antonio Martín** Paseo Maritimo ☏952 227 398. One of Málaga's renowned fish restaurants and the traditional haunt of *matadores* celebrating their successes in the nearby bullring. *Fritura malagueña* or *rape a la marinera* are signature dishes (mains around €11–20). Has a sea-view terrace.

Bar Los Pueblos c/Ataranzas, almost opposite the market. Serves satisfying, inexpensive food all day – bean soups and *estofados* are its specialities; *gazpacho* is served in half-pint glasses.

Bar-Restaurante Palacios c/Eslava 4, near the train station. Plain, honest food in a vibrant *comedor popular* with friendly waiters; has a *menú* for €9, and specialities include *jamón iberico*, fish *surtido* and a mean *paella*.

Cañadu Plaza de la Merced 21. Vegetarian place serving a good selection of salad- and pasta-based dishes accompanied by organic wines and beers. Has a *menú* for €8.40.

Il Laboratorio Plaza San Pedro de Alcántara, off c/Carretería. Great little Italian-style pizzeria-trattoria serving (besides pizzas) salads and daily specials. There's a small outdoor terrace under the trees on this charming *plazuela*.

El Legado Celestial c/Peregrino 2, at the back of the *Correo*. Delightful vegetarian and vegan self-service restaurant with an Asian slant. Standard charge of €8, and the *menú* includes a large selection of salads and a dozen or so hot dishes, as well as some tempting desserts. Drinks are squeezed juices (the lemon, orange, apple and carrot cocktail is recommended) and teas, but no alcohol.

⚒ **Parador Gilbralfaro** Monte Gilbralfaro ☏952 221 902. Superior dining on the terrace with spectacular views over the coast and town. The house specialities are *malagueño* fish and meat dishes, and the *menú* is excellent value at around €23.50 (lunch) or €31 (dinner). Ring to book a frontline table. If you can't face the climb, take a taxi or bus #35 east along Paseo del Parque.

⚒ **Sal Gorda** Avda. Canovas de Castillo 12. Excellent little *raciones* (and *media raciones*) bar-restaurant serving up a mouthwatering range of seafood and shellfish. Their *arroz marinero* at €26 (for two) is recommended. Also has outstanding Asturian *sidra* (cider) on draught.

El Tintero El Palo. Right at the far eastern end of the seafront, just before the *Club Náutico* (bus #11; ask for "*Tintero*"), this is a huge beach restaurant where the waiters charge round with plates of fish (around €7) and you shout for, or grab, anything you like. The fish to go for are, above all, *mero* (a kind of gastronomically evolved cod) and *rosada* (dogfish and catfish), along with Andalucian regulars such as *boquerones* (fresh anchovies), *gambas* (prawns) and *sepia* (cuttlefish). Haute cuisine it certainly isn't, but for sheer entertainment it's a must.

El Vegetariano Pozo del Rey 5, Just north of the Teatro Romano. Atmospheric little veggie place offering a variety of imaginative pasta-, cheese- and salad-based dishes. Closed Sun.

Nightlife

Most of Málaga's **nightlife** is northeast of the cathedral along and around **calles Granada** and **Beatas** and the streets circling the nearby **Plaza de Uncibay**. In the summer months, there's also a scene at **Malagueta**, south of the bullring. At weekends and holidays, dozens of youth-oriented disco-bars fill the crowded streets in these areas, and over the summer – though it's dead out of season – the scene spreads out along the seafront to the suburb of **Pedregalejo**. Here the streets just behind the beach host most of the action, and dozens of *discotecas* and smaller music bars lie along and off the main street, Juan Sebastián Elcano.

Málaga's daily paper, *Sur*, is good for local entertainment **listings**; there's also an English edition (*Sur in English*) on Fridays, available from *turismos* and hotels.

Anden Plaza de Uncibay. Fri & Sat only disco-bar with a wild crowd. Open till very late.

Asúcar Junction of c/Juan de Padilla & c/Lazcano west of Plaza de Uncibay. The place to come for salsa in Málaga.

La Botellita Pasaje Mitjana, slightly west of Plaza Uncibay. Wild place packed to the rafters with young local revellers dancing to the tunes of the Spanish Top 40. Daily till late.

Calle de Bruselas Plaza de la Merced 16. A laid-back, largely gay, Belgian-style bar with lively terrace that stays open into the small hours.

Cervecería Brow Beer c/Ángel 3 off c/Granada. Bar specializing in a wide variety of world beers. Serious drinkers at midday, youthful revellers at night. Also serves tapas.

Cosa Nostra c/Lazcano 5, slightly west of Plaza de Uncibay. Music bar with a mafia theme, which regularly stages live bands. Thurs–Sun 11pm–6am.

Luna Rubia Pasaje Mitjana 4, slightly west of Plaza de Uncibay. Wide range of international sounds and open till dawn. At the end of this alley, the tiny Plaza Marqués Vado del Maestre is filled with drinking bars and plenty of night-time action.

El Pimpi c/Granada 62. Cavernous and hugely popular *bodega*-style bar serving up (among other concoctions) tasty *vino dulce* by the glass or bottle. Do a bit of celebrity-spotting on their wall of photos (including a young Antonio Banderas) and don't miss a superb terrace (with Alcazaba view) out the back. A great place to kick-start the evening.

Puerta Oscura c/Molina Lario 5 near the cathedral. Slightly incongruous classical-music bar – sometimes with live performers – which also mounts art exhibitions; serves cocktails, ices and baguettes. T-shirts are definitely a no-no here. Daily till 3am.

Siempre Asi c/Convalecientes, north of Plaza Uncibay. Another late-opening bar specializing in Spanish rock and techno. Thurs–Sat 11pm–3.30am.

Listings

Airport Málaga's airport (℡ 952 048 838) is Andalucía's busiest and set to get busier once its new terminal is completed in 2010. See p.240 for details on transport to and from the airport.

Banks Numerous banks all over town have ATMs, especially along c/Marqués de Larios and on Plaza de la Constitución. El Corte Inglés will also change currency free of charge.

Books Málaga's best travel bookshop is Mapas y Compañía, c/Compañía 33, west of Plaza de la Constitución – they sell IGN walking maps, as well as 1:50,000 Mapas Cartografía Militar (military maps).

Consulates UK, Edificio Eurocom, c/Mauricio Moro Pareto 2 ℡ 952 352 300; US, Avda. Juan Goméz 8, Fuengirola ℡ 952 474 891; Republic of Ireland, Galería Santa Monica, Fuengirola ℡ 952 475 108.

Football After spending a few seasons in Division 2, in 2008 C.F. Málaga were promoted back into the top flight. Games are at La Rosaleda stadium, Paseo de Martiricos s/n, at the northern end of the Río Guadalmedina. Tickets can be purchased from the stadium (℡ 952 614 210, ⓦ www.malagacf.es).

Hospital Hospital Carlos Haya, Avda. Carlos Haya, 2km west of the city centre ℡ 951 290 000.

Internet Free wi-fi connection is available in the vicinity of the Teatro Cervantes and along the central c/Marqués de Larios. Conventional cyber cafés near the centre include *Meeting Point*, Plaza de la Merced 20 (daily 10am–11pm), and *Cibercafé Teatro Romano*, c/Alcazabilla s/n (10am–midnight).

Left luggage There are lockers and a *consigna* at the train station (daily 6.15am–12.45am), and

lockers at the bus station (daily 6.30am–11pm).
Pharmacy Farmacia Caffarena (24hr) on the
Alameda at no. 2, near the junction with c/Marqués
de Larios ☏952 212 858.
Police The Policía Local are at Avda. La Rosaleda
19 (☏952 126 500); in emergencies, dial ☏092
(local police) or 091 (national).
Post office Avda. de Andalucía 1, on the left
across the bridge at the end of the Alameda
(Mon–Fri 8.30am–8pm, Sat 8.30am–2pm).

Shopping El Corte Inglés, Avda. de Andalucía 4,
is a great department store and its basement
supermarket has a terrific selection of the nation's
wines and spirits. La Mallorquina, Plaza Felix Saenz
(near the market), is a good place to pick up
malagueño cheeses, wines, almonds and dried fruit.
Flamenca, c/Caldería 6, north of the cathedral
(🌐www.flamenka.com), stocks a range of *trajes de
flamenco* (costumes), as well as shoes, instruments
and flamenco CDs, DVDs and books.

El Chorro, Antequera and El Torcal

North of Málaga are two impressive sights: the magnificent limestone **gorge**
near **El Chorro** and the prehistoric **dolmen caves** at **Antequera**. Located
close to the junction of roads inland to Seville, Córdoba and Granada and on
direct train lines, both are possible as day-trips from Málaga but also offer
overnight accommodation. Approaching Antequera along the old road from
Málaga (MA424) via Almogía and Villenueva de la Concepción, you pass the
entrance to the popular natural park famed for its haunting rock sculptures,
El Torcal.

Garganta del Chorro

Fifty kilometres northwest of Málaga, **Garganta del Chorro** is an amazing place
– an immense five-kilometre-long cleft in a vast limestone massif, which has
become Andalucía's major centre for rock climbers. The gorge's most stunning
feature, however, is a concrete catwalk, *El Camino del Rey*, which threads the
length of the gorge, hanging precipitously halfway up its side. Built in the 1920s
as part of a hydroelectric scheme, it was one of the wonders of Spain, but it has
fallen into disrepair, and access to the catwalk has finally been cut at each end of
the gorge, making it impossible to reach without a guide and climbing gear. It's
still possible to explore the rest of the gorge, however, and get a view of the
Camino by doing the walk described below. A glimpse of both gorge and *Camino*
can also be had from any of the trains going north from Málaga – the line, slipping
in and out of tunnels, follows the river for a considerable distance along the gorge,
before plunging into a last long tunnel just before its head.

One of the best ways of viewing the gorge is to follow a twelve-kilometre
walk (vehicles should follow the same route) from the village of **EL
CHORRO**. Take the road from the train station, signposted *Pantano de Guadalhorce*, reached by crossing over the dam and turning right, then following the
road north along the lake towards the hydroelectric plant. After 8km turn right
at a junction to reach – after 2km – the bar-restaurant *El Mirador*, poised above
a road tunnel and overlooking the various lakes and reservoirs of the Guadalhorce scheme. From the bar (where you should leave any transport) a dirt track
on the right heads towards the gorge. Follow this and take the first track on the
right after about 700m. This climbs for some 2km to where it splits into two
small trails. The trail to the left leads after 300m to a magnificent **viewpoint**
over the gorge from where you can see the *Camino del Rey* clinging to the rock
face. The right-hand track climbs swiftly to an obvious peak, the **Pico de
Almochon**, with more spectacular views, this time over the lakes of the
Embalse de Guadalhorce.

Practicalities

El Chorro is served by a couple of daily direct **trains** (45min), but no buses, from Málaga. To get there with your own transport, take the MA402 heading west from Málaga towards Álora (where the road is titled the A343) and turn west at Valle de Abdalajís along the minor MA226, a journey of around 65km.

In the village, there's an excellent **campsite** with a pool and restaurant, reached by heading downhill to your right for 400m after getting off the train (T952 495 244, W www.alberguecampingelchorro.com). The campsite also rents out wood cabins sleeping up to six (②). Near the station, *Bar-Restaurante Garganta del Chorro* (T952 497 219, W www.lagarganta.com; ③) has pleasant **rooms** inside a converted mill and overlooking a pool. Signs from the station will also direct you 2km to ᚷ *Finca La Campana* (mobile T626 963 942, W www.el-chorro.com), a farmhouse set in rural surroundings with a bunkhouse (€12 per bunk) and a couple of pleasant cottages (②). Run by Swiss climber Christine Hofer, the place also offers courses in rock climbing and caving, rents out mountain bikes and can arrange horseriding and hiking excursions, as well as **guided trips** along the *Camino del Rey* using ropes to gain access. For **food**, besides the campsite and the *Garganta*'s decent restaurant, *Bar Isabel* on the station platform does tapas, where there's also a **shop** selling provisions.

Antequera and around

ANTEQUERA, some 55km north of Málaga on the main rail line to Granada, is an undistinguished, modern town, but it does have peripheral attractions in a Baroque church, **Nuestra Señora del Carmen** (Mon–Sat 10am–2pm & 4–7pm, Sun 10am–2pm; €2), which houses one of the finest *retablos* in Andalucía, and a group of three prehistoric **dolmen caves**, among the most important in Spain. Now enclosed in a futuristic new "dolmen park" with visitor centre, car park and a Centro de Interpretación (opening 2010), the most impressive and famous of these is the **Cueva de Menga** (Tues–Sat 9am–6pm, Sun 9.30am–2.30pm; free), its roof formed by an immense 180-tonne monolith. To reach this, and the nearby **Cueva de Viera** (same hours), take the Granada road out of town – the turning, rather insignificantly signposted, is after about 1km on the left. Two kilometres away, a third cave, **El Romeral** (same hours), is different (and later) in structure, with a domed ceiling of flat stones; get instructions (and a map) of how to reach it from the visitor centre. The **Plaza de Toros** (museum Tues–Sat 10am–2pm & 4–7pm; Sun 10am–2pm; free) in the newer part of town is also worth a look and staged its first *corrida* in 1848.

If you want to **stay** in Antequera – which also makes a good base for visits to El Torcal – just west of Plaza de San Francisco, the market square, there's a good-value new *pension*, *Número Uno*, at c/Lucena 40 (T952 843 134, W www.hotelnumerouno.com; ①), with pleasant air-conditioned en-suite rooms, above a great restaurant and tapas bar. The cheapest beds in town are on offer at the excellent ᚷ *Camas El Gallo* (T952 842 104; ①), at c/Nueva 2, off Plaza San Sebastián; this friendly place has simple, spotless rooms (with fans in summer) and equally pristine shared bathrooms. A plusher option is the central *Hotel Plaza San Sebastián* (T952 844 239; ②), with air-conditioned en-suite rooms facing the church of San Sebastián. Camping is no longer allowed inside the natural park, but there's a **campsite**, *Camping Torcal*, just off the C3310, 6km south of Antequera (T95 211 16 08; closed Oct–March).

Town maps and information on El Torcal are available from a helpful **tourist office** on the central Plaza San Sebastián (June–Sept Mon–Sat 11am–2pm &

5–8pm, Sun 11am–2pm; Oct–May Mon–Sat 10.30am–1.30pm & 4–7pm, Sun 11am–2pm; ☎952 702 505, ⓦwww.turismoantequera.com), alongside the church of the same name.

Parque Natural de El Torcal

Parque Natural de El Torcal, 13km south of Antequera, is one of the most geologically arresting of Spain's natural parks. A massive high plateau of glaciated limestone tempered by a lush growth of hawthorn, ivy and wild rose, it can be painlessly explored using the three walking routes that radiate from the centre of the park, outlined in a leaflet available from the **Centro de Recepción** (daily 10am–5pm; ☎952 702 505 or 649 472 688).

The best-designed and most exciting **trails** are the yellow and red routes, the former climaxing with suitable drama on a cliff edge with magnificent views over a valley. The latter gives fantastic vantage points of the looming limestone outcrops, eroded into vast, surreal sculptures. Because of the need to protect flora and fauna, the red route is in a restricted zone and can only be visited with a **guide** (ask at the *centro*). The **green** and **yellow routes** (waymarked) can be walked without a guide, the former taking about forty minutes if you don't dawdle, the latter about two hours. In early summer on the popular green route you may find yourself competing with gangs of schoolkids, who arrive en masse on vaguely educational trips, excitedly trying to spot La Copa (the wineglass), El Lagarto (the lizard) and La Loba (the she-wolf), as well as other celebrated **rock sculptures**. Keep an eye on the skies while you're here, for griffon vultures are frequent visitors and, with their huge wingspans, make a spectacular sight as they glide overhead.

Buses run from Málaga (Mon–Fri 5 daily, Sat & Sun daily); ask the driver to drop you at the road for El Torcal from where it's a four-kilometre uphill slog to the visitor centre. The most convenient way to visit the park without your own transport, however, is to take the **taxi turistico**, which can be arranged through the *turismo* in Antequera; for €32, a taxi will drop up to four passengers off at the Centro de Recepción and wait until you have completed the green route before returning you to Antequera.

East from Málaga: the coast to Almería

The eastern section of the **Costa del Sol**, from Málaga to Almería, is uninspiring. Though far less developed than the stretch of wall-to-wall concrete from Torremolinos to Marbella in the west, it's not exactly unspoilt. If you're looking for a village and a beach and not much else, then after the pleasant resorts of **Nerja**, **Almuñecar** and **Salobreña** you'll probably want to keep going at least to beyond the city of Almería.

Nerja and around

East of Málaga there's certainly little to tempt anyone to stop before **NERJA**. Nestling in the foothills of the Almijara range, this was a village before it was a resort, so it has some character, and villa development has been shaped around it.

The focus of the whitewashed old quarter is the **Bálcon de Europa**, a striking palm-fringed belvedere overlooking the sea. The beaches flanking this are also reasonably attractive, with a series of quieter coves within walking distance. There are plenty of other great **walks** around Nerja, too, well documented in the *turismo*'s own leaflets; or, at Smiffs you can buy individual leaflets detailing walks in the area by local resident and hiker Elma Thompson.

Nerja's chief tourist attraction, the **Cuevas de Nerja** (daily July & Aug 10am–7.30pm; rest of year 10am–2pm & 4–6.30pm; €7; Ⓦwww .cuevadenerja.es), 3km east from the town, are a heavily commercialized series of caverns, impressive in size – and home to the world's longest-known **stalactite** at 63m – though otherwise not tremendously interesting. They also contain a number of prehistoric paintings, but these are not currently on public view.

Practicalities

The main **bus station** (actually a stand) is on c/San Miguel at the north end of town close to Plaza Cantarero; from here hourly buses leave for the *cuevas*. It's a five-minute walk south from the station to the beach and centre, where you'll find the helpful **turismo**, c/Puerta del Mar 2 (July–Sept daily 10am– 2pm & 6–10pm; Oct–June Mon–Fri 10am–2pm & 5–8pm, Sat 10am–1pm; ℡952 521 531, Ⓦwww.nerja.org), just to the east of the Balcón de Europa. West of the centre, at Avda. Castilla Pérez 2, Club Nautico de Nerja (℡952 524 654) rents out **mopeds** and **bikes**, and also offers horseriding and diving tuition.

Central budget **accommodation** choices include the excellent new *Hostal Marissal*, Paseo Balcón de Europa 3 (℡952 520 199 Ⓦwww.marissal .com; ❸), actually on the belvedere with air-conditioned en-suite rooms, many (try for rooms 102–5 or 204–5) with sea view; it also rents apartments (❹) in the same location. Nearby, the very pleasant *Hostal Mena*, c/El Barrio 15 (℡952 520 541; ❷), has more sea-view en-suite rooms with a garden. Overlooking one of Nerja's most popular beaches, Playa de Burriana, are the *Parador Nacional*, c/Almuñécar 8 (℡952 520 050, Ⓦwww.parador.es; ❻), with a pool set in attractive gardens and a lift to the beach, and the nearby and cheaper *Hotel Paraiso del Mar*, c/Carabeo 22 (℡952 521 621, Ⓦwww .hotelparaisodelmar.es; ❺), with similar facilities plus a sauna dug out of the cliff face. The **campsite**, *Nerja Camping*, with pool, bar and restaurant, is 4km east of town along the N340 (℡952 529 714).

Almuñécar

The lively resort of **ALMUÑÉCAR** is marred by a number of towering holiday apartments, and the rocky grey-sand beaches are rather cramped, but the esplanade behind them, with palm-roofed bars (many serving free tapas with each drink) and restaurants, is fun, and the old quarter – clustered around a sixteenth-century castle – attractive.

The **bus station**, which has frequent connections to Málaga and Granada, is located at the junction of *avenidas* Juan Carlos I and Fenicia, northeast of the centre, while the **turismo** can be found in an imposing neo-Moorish mansion on Avda. de Europa (daily 10am–2pm & 5–8pm, July & Aug 6–9pm; ℡958 631 125, Ⓦwww.almunecar.info), behind the Playa San Cristóbal beach at the west end of the town.

Half a dozen good-value **hostales** and **hotels** ring the central Plaza de la Rosa in the old part of town; the cosy and recently refurbished *Hostal Plaza Damasco*, c/Cerrajos 8 (℡958 630 165; ❸), and the decent-value *Hotel Victoria II*, Plaza de la Victoria (℡958 631 734; ❷), are two of the best, both offering air-conditioned en-suite rooms. If you want to be closer to the beach, try the excellent *Hotel Casablanca*, Plaza San Cristóbal 4 (aka Plaza

Abderramán; ☎958 635 575, ⓦwww.almunecar.info/casablanca; ❸), with a flamboyant neo-Moorish facade and interior, offering balcony en-suite rooms with sea views.

Places worth seeking out for **eating and drinking** include *Bar-Taberna El Cortijillo*, Plaza Kelibia 4, near the centre, a lively *freiduría* and *raciones* bar popular with young locals, in an attractive square. For tapas and *platos combinados*, *Bodega Francisco*, c/Real 15, north of Plaza de la Rosa, is a wonderful old bar with barrels stacked up to the ceiling behind the counter and walls covered with ageing *corrida* posters and mounted boars' heads. More upmarket, the excellent ⚒ *Horno de Candida*, c/Orovia 3, close to the *ayuntamiento*, is the restaurant of the town's hotel and catering school, with a delightful roof terrace and a recommended *menú* for €29. Near the Parque Botanico, the new *Manjar*, Avda. Europa 9, is a very welcome **vegetarian** restaurant with a creative kitchen.

Salobreña

SALOBREÑA, 10km farther east on the coast road, is compact and more laid-back. A white hilltop town gathered beneath the shell of a Moorish castle and surrounded by fields of sugar cane, it's set back 2km from the sea and is thus comparatively little developed. Its beach – a black sandy strip – is only partially fronted by hotels and *chiringuitos*.

Buses arrive at and leave from Plaza de Goya, close to the **turismo** (daily 9.30am–1.30pm, Tues–Sun also 4.30–6.30pm; ☎958 610 314, ⓦwww.ayto–salobrena.org). Along and off Avenida García Lorca, the main avenue that winds down from the town to the beach, are a few **pensiones** and **hostales**: *Pensión Castellmar*, c/Nueva 21 (☎958 610 227; ❶), has the best views, while the similarly priced *Pensión Mari Carmen* over the road (☎958 610 906; ❶–❷) is equally good, with fans in the rooms; both have some en-suite rooms. An attractive new arrival located two-minutes' walk from the *turismo* is ⚒ *Hostal San Juan*, c/Jardines 1 (☎958 611 729, ⓦwww.hostalsanjuan.com; ❸), situated in a beautifully restored townhouse where en-suite rooms come with air-conditioning and TV. The most atmospheric **places to eat** are the restaurants and *chiringuitos* lining the seafront, notably *El Peñon*, on the promontory from which it takes its name, serving up great paella, and the nearby – and more reasonably priced – *La Bahía*.

The Costa del Sol resorts

West of Málaga – or more correctly, west of Málaga airport – the real **Costa del Sol** gets going, and if you've never seen this level of tourist development, it's quite a shock. These are certainly not the kind of resorts you could envisage anywhere else in Europe. The 1960s and 1970s hotel and apartment tower-blocks were followed by a second wave of property development in the 1980s and 1990s, this time villa homes and leisure complexes, funded by massive international investment. It's estimated that 300,000 foreigners now live on the Costa del Sol, the majority of them British and other northern Europeans, though marina developments such as Puerto Banús have also attracted Arab and Russian money.

Approached in the right kind of spirit, it is possible to have fun in **Fuengirola** and, at a price, in **Marbella**. But if you've come to Spain to be in Spain, put on the shades and keep going at least until you reach Estepona.

Fuengirola

Twenty kilometres southwest of Málaga, beyond the vast, bizarre resort of **Torremolinos**, lies **FUENGIROLA**, very slightly less developed and infinitely more staid than its neighbour. It's not so conspicuously ugly, but it is distinctly middle-aged and family-oriented. The huge, long beach has been divided up into restaurant-beach strips, each renting out lounge chairs and pedal-boats.

An efficient **turismo** is located at Avda. Jesús S. Rein 6 (Mon–Fri 9.30am–2pm & 5–7pm, Sat 10am–1pm; ☎952 467 457, ⓦwww.fuengirola.org), close to the **train** (☎952 128 080) and **bus** (☎952 475 066) stations. A good **place to stay** is *Hostal Italia*, off the east side of the focal Plaza de la Constitución (☎952 474 193, ⓦwww.hostal-italia.com; ❸), offering en-suite rooms with balcony, or the nearby *Hostal Cuevas*, c/Capitan 7 (☎952 460 606; ❸), which also has pleasant air-conditioned rooms with bath. Moving upmarket, *Hotel Las Piramides*, Paseo Marítimo s/n, at the western end of the seafront (☎952 583 297, ⓦwww.hotellaspiramides.com; ❻), has its own pool and all the four-star frills. Fuengirola's nearest **campsite** lies 2km to the east of the centre (☎952 474 108) and is reached by a turn-off near the junction of the N340 and the road to Mijas; bus "Línea Roja" from Avenida Ramón y Cajal on the main Marbella road will take you there.

For excellent **seafood**, you could try the mid-priced *Bar La Paz Garrido* on Avenida de Mijas, just north of the main square, Plaza de la Constitución. Slightly pricier but well worth it is *Mesón del Mar*, Paseo Marítimo Rey de España, at the extreme western end of the seafront and 100m from the *Hotel Piramides*. Equally good, the French-style 🌿 *Restaurante Guy Massey* (☎952 585 120; eves only), Rotonda de la Luna, a couple of blocks to the north of the *turismo*, has rapidly become one of the town's top dining venues, whose eponymous chef has worked with Gordon Ramsey; there's a recommended *menú de degustación* for €25.

Marbella and around

Sheltered by the hills of the Sierra Blanca, **MARBELLA**, 25km farther west, stands in considerable contrast to most of what's come before. Since it attracted the attentions of the smart set in the 1960s the town has zealously polished its reputation as the Costa del Sol's most stylish resort. Glitz comes at a price, of course: many of the chic restaurants, bars and cafés cash in on the hype, and everything costs considerably more. Marbella has the highest per capita income in Europe and more Rolls-Royces than any European city apart from London. Recently, the Spanish government and authorities have been exercised by the arrival in Marbella of Russian and Italian mafia bosses

---

The Costa del Sol's main highway, the *carretera nacional* **N340**, is one of the **most dangerous roads in Europe**. The accident count is extremely high (particularly on the stretch west of Marbella) and includes, on average, over a hundred fatalities a year. You can avoid it altogether by using the recently completed Autopista del Sol (A7-E15), a four-lane toll motorway linking Málaga with Estepona in the west, but if you do decide to use the N340:

- don't make dangerous (and illegal) left turns from the fast lane – use the "Cambio de Sentido" junctions, which also allow you to change direction.

- be particularly careful after heavy rain, when the hot, oily road surface can easily send you into a skid.

- watch out for pedestrians, who should only cross at traffic lights, a bridge or an underpass.

who have been buying up property and using the town as a base to control their criminal empires, activities that led to the discovery by police in 2005 of Europe's biggest-ever money-laundering operation, channelling billions of dollars from worldwide crime syndicates into Marbella-registered companies. In an ironic twist of history, there's been a massive return of Arabs to the area, especially since the late King Fahd of Saudi Arabia built a White House lookalike, complete with adjacent mosque, on the town's outskirts, where the Saudi royal family and a veritable army of courtiers and servants spend the summer months.

To be fair, the town has been spared the worst excesses of concrete architecture and also retains the greater part of its **old town** – set back a little from the sea and the new development. Centred on the attractive Plaza de los Naranjos and still partially walled, the old town is hidden from the main road and easy to miss. Slowly, this original quarter is being bought up and turned into clothes and jewellery boutiques and restaurants, but the process isn't that far advanced. You can still sit in an ordinary bar in a small old square and look up beyond the whitewashed alleyways to the mountains of Ronda. South of the centre, there are three excellent **beaches** stretching east from Playa de la Badajilla and Playa de Venus to Playa de la Fontanilla to the west, which gets progressively less crowded the farther west you go.

The seriously rich don't stay in Marbella itself. They secrete themselves away in villas in the surrounding hills or laze around on phenomenally large and luxurious yachts at the marina and casino complex of **Puerto Banús**, 6km west of town. As you'd expect, Puerto Banús has more than its complement of designer boutiques and cocktail bars, most of them very pricey.

Practicalities

From the new **bus station** (☎952 764 400) in the north of the town, buses #2 or #7 will drop you close by the old town; otherwise, it's a twenty-minute walk south along c/Trapiche.

Marbella's only budget **pensiones** are on the eastern flank of the old town. The lowest priced are the friendly *Hostal Juan*, c/Luna 18 (☎952 779 475; ❶), with some en-suite rooms, and *Hostal Guerra*, Llanos de San Ramón 2 (☎952 774 220; ❶), on opposite sides of the main road as you come into town from the east. At c/Trapiche 2 to the north of the old town, the *Albergue Juvenil* (☎952 771 491; under-26 €14, over-26 €19) has even cheaper beds in smart double and four-person en-suite rooms, and there's also a pool. There are plenty of more expensive places, too: the central and welcoming *Hostal Berlin* c/San Ramón 21 (☎952 821 310, ⓦwww.hostalberlin.com; ❸), has sparkling air-conditioned en-suite rooms and free internet access for guests. To the north of Plaza de los Naranjos, ☘ *Hotel La Morada Mas Hermosa*, c/Montenebros 16, (☎952 924 467, ⓦwww.lamoradamashermosa.com; ❹), is an enchanting small hotel in a refurbished eighteenth-century town house with elegant, individually styled air-conditioned rooms (most with terraces). The most central upmarket option is *Hotel El Fuerte*, Avda. Severo Ochoa 10 (☎952 861 500, ⓦwww .hotel-elfuerte.es; ❼), with beach access, gardens and a pool. If you need help in finding a room, call in at the **turismo** in Plaza de los Naranjos (Mon–Fri 9am–9pm, Sat 10am–2pm; ☎952 823 550), which provides a street-indexed town map and list of addresses.

Avoid the overpriced **restaurants** on the Plaza de los Naranjos, which turn the whole square into their dining terrace after dark – you're better off seeking out some of Marbella's excellent **tapas bars** such as ☘ *Bar Altamarino*, Plaza de Altamarino 4, just west of Plaza de los Naranjos, for mouthwatering seafood; nearby *Bar California* at the junction of c/Málaga and Avda. Severo Ochoa, east of the old town; or *El Estrecho*, c/San Lazaro 12, a narrow alley to the southeast of Plaza de los Naranjos, where a clutch of other bars is also to be found. For a splurge, head for ✝ *Santiago*, Avda. Duque de Ahumada s/n (℡952 772 369), near the Puerto Deportivo, one of Marbella's swankiest and oldest restaurants, founded in the 1950s, with excellent food, an attractive seafront terrace and a recommended *menú de degustación* (€48 including wine).

There are plenty of **late-night bars** and **clubs** around Plaza de Olivos on the old town's eastern flank, including *Club Premiere*, at Plaza de Olivos 2, a popular venue staging live gigs ranging from pop to electronica and acid-jazz.

Estepona and around

The coast continues to be upmarket (or "money-raddled", as Laurie Lee put it) until you reach **ESTEPONA**, about 30km west, which is about as Spanish as the resorts round here get. It lacks the enclosed hills that give Marbella character, but the hotel and apartment blocks that sprawl along the front are restrained in size, and there's space to breathe. The fine sand beach has been enlivened a little by a promenade studded with flowers and palms, and, away from the seafront, the old town is very pretty, with cobbled alleyways and two delightful plazas.

From May onward, Estepona's **bullfighting** season gets under way in a modern bullring reminiscent of a Henry Moore sculpture. This building has now taken on an additional role as the location for no fewer than four museums (all Mon–Fri 9am–3pm, Sat 10am–2pm; free): the **Museo Etnográfico** (folk museum), the **Museo Arqueológico**, the **Museo Paleontológico** (paleontology) and, perhaps the most interesting, the **Museo Taurino** (bullfighting), with fascinating exhibits and photos underlining the importance of *taurinismo* in Andalucian culture. At the beginning of July, the *Fiesta y Feria* week transforms the place, bringing out whole families in flamenco-style garb.

The **Selwo Adventure Park** (daily 10am–8pm; €23.50, children €16; Ⓦwww.selwo.es) is a landscaped zoo 6km to the east of town where the two-thousand-plus resident animals are allowed to roam in "semi-liberty" and there are re-creations of African Zulu and Masai villages. To reach the park, there are signed exits indicated from the N340 and the A7-E15 Autopista del Sol, plus regular buses from all the major Costa del Sol resorts.

Beyond Estepona, 8km along the coast, a minor road (the MA546) climbs a farther 13km into the hills to **CASARES**, one of the classic *andaluz* White Towns. In keeping with the genre, it clings tenaciously to a steep hillside below a castle, and has attracted its fair share of arty types and expats. But it remains comparatively little known; bus connections are just about feasible for a day-trip (leaving 1pm, returning 4pm; further details from the *turismo*).

Practicalities

Estepona's **bus station** is on Avenida de España, to the west of the centre behind the seafront. The efficient and centrally located **turismo** at Avda. San Lorenzo 1, west of the centre near the seafront (Mon–Fri 9.30am–2pm, Sat 10am–1.30pm; ℡952 802 002), will supply town maps and can help you find a **room**. Otherwise, *Hostal El Pilar* on the pretty Plaza Las Flores (℡952 800 018, Ⓔhostalpilar@telefonica.net; ❸), and the nearby *Pensión San Miguel*, c/Terraza 16 (℡952 802 616; ❷), with its own bar, are both good bets, as is the seafront *Hotel Mediterráneo*, Avda. de España 68 (☎952 793 393, ⓦwww .mediterraneo-estepona.com). Estepona's nearest **campsite** is *Camping Parque Tropical* (☎952 793 618) 6km to the north on the N340 (km.162).

The town is well provided with **places to eat**, among them a bunch of excellent *freidurías* and *marisquerías*, located on c/Terraza, the main street that cuts through the centre – try *La Gamba* at no. 25 or *La Palma* at no. 57. Estepona's **nightlife** centres on the pedestrianized c/Real, running behind and parallel to the seafront; its **clubs** and **music bars** – with plenty of terrace tables on hot summer nights – compete for the custom of a mainly local clientele.

San Roque and La Línea de la Concepción

Situated 35km beyond Estepona in Cádiz province, **SAN ROQUE** was founded in 1704 by the people of Gibraltar fleeing the British, who had captured the Rock and looted their homes and churches. The Rock's inhabitants expected to return within months, since the troops had taken the garrison in the name of Archduke Carlos of Austria, whose rights Britain had been promoting in the War of the Spanish Succession. But it was the British flag that was raised on the conquered territory – and so it has remained. C/San Felipe leads up from the main square to a **mirador** with views of the Rock of Gibraltar and the hazy coast of Africa beyond.

The "**Spanish-British frontier**" is 8km away at **LA LÍNEA DE LA CONCEPCIÓN**, obscured by San Roque's huge oil refinery. In February 1985, the gates were reopened after a sixteen-year period of Spanish-imposed isolation, and since then crossing has been a routine affair of passport stamping, except for the odd diplomatic flare-up when the Spanish authorities decide to operate a go-slow to annoy the Rock's inhabitants. There are no sights as such; it's just a fishing village that has exploded in size owing to the job opportunities in Gibraltar and Algeciras.

Practicalities

At the heart of La Línea is the large, modern and undistinguished Plaza de la Constitución, where you'll find the post office. The friendly **turismo** (Mon–Sat 9am–3pm; ☎956 784 138), which provides a useful town map, and the **bus station** are both on Avda. 20 Abril, to the south of the square. The closest mainline **train station** is San Roque-La Línea, 12km away, from where you can pick up a train to Ronda and beyond. Buses link La Línea with Seville, Málaga, Cádiz (via Tarifa), and as far as Ayamonte on the Portuguese border. Local **buses** depart hourly to Algeciras (30min).

La Línea has plenty of budget **hostales**, making it a cheaper alternative to staying in Gibraltar; most are around Plaza de la Constitución. The friendly *La Campana*, c/Carboneras 3, just off the square (☎956 173 059; ❷), is clean and has rooms with bath and TV; if this is full, try the slightly cheaper *Hotel-Restaurante Carlos*, almost opposite (☎956 762 135; ❷). For **eating and drinking**, both the *hostales* above have good, inexpensive restaurants. Off the east side of Plaza de la Constitución an archway leads to the smaller, pedestrianized Plaza Cruz de Herrera (undergoing refurbishment at the time of writing), which is packed with lots of reasonably priced bars and restaurants. Slightly north of here lies c/Real, the main pedestrianized shopping street, offering plenty of bars and cafés – good for breakfast pastries – as well as restaurants. *D'Antonio*, c/Dr Villar 19, just off the north side of the same street, does decent tapas and *raciones*.

Gibraltar

GIBRALTAR's interest is essentially its novelty: the genuine appeal of the strange, looming physical presence of its rock, and the dubious one of its preservation as one of Britain's last remaining colonies. For most of its history it has existed in a limbo between two worlds without being fully part of either. It's a curious place to visit, not least to witness the bizarre process of its opening to mass tourism from the Costa del Sol. Ironically, this threatens both to destroy Gibraltar's highly individual hybrid society and at the same time to make it much more British, after the fashion of the expat communities and huge resorts of the Costa. In recent years, the economic boom Gibraltar enjoyed throughout the 1980s, following the reopening of the border with Spain, has started to wane, and the future of the colony – whether its population agrees to it or not – is almost certain to involve closer ties with Spain.

Arrival, information and orientation

Owing to the relatively scarce and pricey accommodation, you're far better off visiting the Rock on a day-trip from La Línea or Algeciras, from where there are **buses** on the hour and half-hour (30min). If you have a **car**, don't attempt

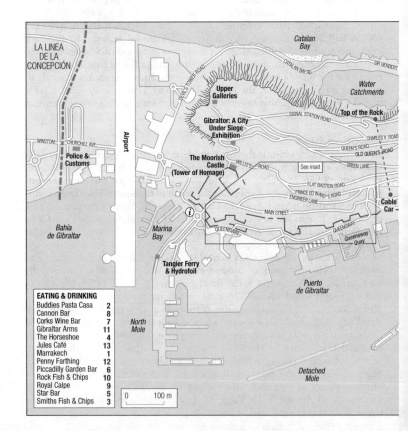

Phoning Gibraltar

From Spain, the UK and Europe dial 00 + 350 + number

From North America dial 011 + 350 + number

to bring it to Gibraltar – the queues at the border are always atrocious and parking is a nightmare owing to lack of space. Use the underground car parks in La Línea – there's one beneath the central Plaza de la Constitución – and either catch the **bus** (#9, every 15min) from the border, or take an easy ten-minute **walk** across part of the airport runway to the town centre.

The town has a necessarily simple layout, as it's shoehorned into the narrow stretch of land on the peninsula's western edge in the shadow of the towering Rock. **Main Street** (La Calle Real) runs for most of the town's length, a couple of blocks back from the port. On and around Main Street are most of the shops, together with many of the British-style pubs and hotels. You'll find the main **tourist office** in the focal Casemates Square (Mon–Fri 9am–5.30pm, Sat & Sun 10am–3pm; ⓣ74982, ⓦwww.gibraltar.gi/tourism), and there's a sub-office in the customs and immigration building at the border (Mon–Fri 9am–4.30pm, Sat 10am–3pm; ⓣ50762). Much of Gibraltar – with

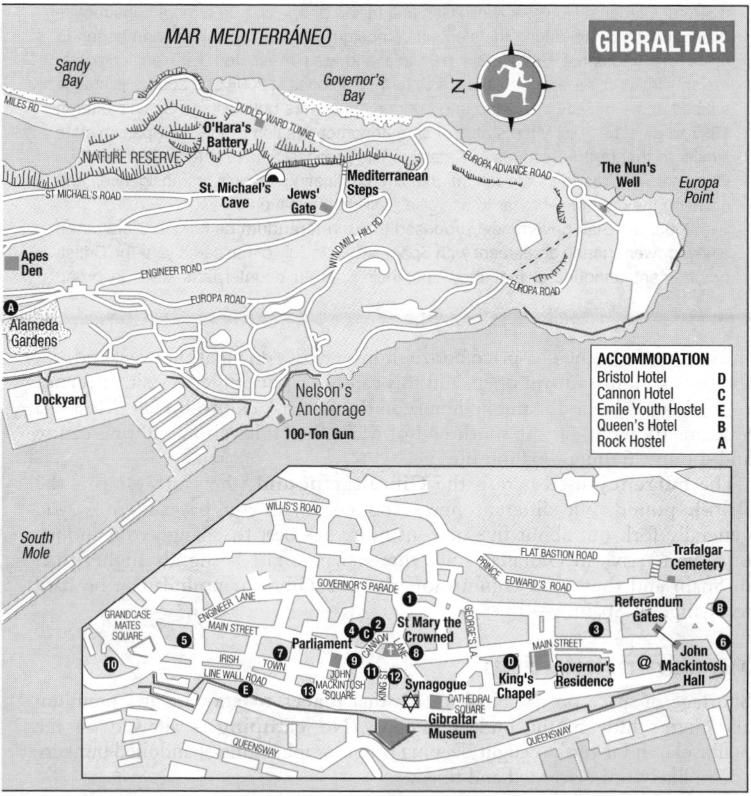

British sovereignty in Gibraltar

Sovereignty of the Rock (a land area smaller than the city of Algeciras across the water) will doubtless eventually return to Spain, but at present a **stalemate** exists regarding the colony's future. For Britain, it's a question of divesting itself of the colony without incurring the wrath of Gibraltar's citizens who are implacably opposed to any further involvement with Spain. For Spain, there are unsettling parallels with the *presidios* (Spanish enclaves) on the Moroccan coast at Ceuta and Melilla – both at present part of Andalucía. Nonetheless, the British presence is in practice waning and the British Foreign Office clearly wants to steer Gibraltar towards a new, harmonious relationship with Spain. To this end, they are running down the significance of the military base, and now only a token force of under a hundred British troops remains – most of these working in a top-secret high-tech bunker buried deep inside the Rock from where the Royal Navy monitors sea traffic through the Strait (accounting for a quarter of the world's movement of all shipping).

In 1967, just before Franco closed the border in the hope of forcing a quick agreement, the colony voted on the return to Spanish control of the Rock – rejecting it by 12,138 votes to 44. Most people would probably sympathize with that vote – against a Spain that was then still a dictatorship – but more than forty years have gone by, Spanish democracy is now secure, and the arguments are becoming increasingly tenuous. May 1996 saw a change in the trend of internal politics, with the defeat of the colony's pugnaciously anti-Spanish Labour government (following two previous landslide victories) and the election of a new **Social Democratic administration** led by Peter Caruana. However, while Caruana talked of opening up a more constructive dialogue with Spain during the election campaign, once in control he soon began to voice the traditional Gibraltarian paranoia and was re-elected with an increased majority in 2000, repeating this feat with further victories in 2004 and 2007. His stance caused some dismay in Madrid and London, who were both behind Spain's offer in 1997 to give the colony the status of an autonomous region inside the Spanish state similar to that of the Basques or Catalans. The proposal was rejected out of hand by Caruana who made a speech at the UN castigating Spain's intransigence, and claiming the right of Gibraltar to exercise "self-determination".

In 2002, the Blair government proposed that a **referendum** be held in Gibraltar on a new power-sharing agreement with Spain. When in July of the same year the British government announced that they and their Spanish counterparts were in broad

the exception of the cut-price booze shops – closes down at the weekend, but the tourist sights remain open, and this can be a quiet time to visit. **Internet** access is available at the public library in the John Mackintosh Hall (Mon–Fri 9.30am–10.30pm), at the south end of Main Street; it's also a cultural centre and mounts frequent exhibitions.

The **currency** used here is the **Gibraltar pound** (the same value as the British pound, but different notes and coins); if you pay in euros, you generally fork out about five percent more. It's best to change your money once you arrive in Gibraltar, since the exchange rate is slightly higher than in Spain and there's no commission charged. Gibraltar pounds can be hard to change in Spain.

Accommodation

Shortage of space on the Rock means that **places to stay** are at a premium and there's little in the budget category. No **camping** is allowed on the peninsula, and if you're caught sleeping rough or inhabiting abandoned bunkers, you're likely to be arrested and fined.

agreement regarding how they should share the sovereignty of Gibraltar, Caruana denounced this as an act of treachery. His campaign to kill any idea of ever sharing sovereignty with Spain – which resurrected the old slogan "Give Spain No Hope!" – resulted in a referendum on the issue on November 7, 2002. The predictable result turned out to be a 99 percent vote against any sharing of sovereignty with Spain, in an 88 percent turnout that sent shockwaves through the diplomatic corridors in London and Madrid.

The **new Spanish administration** elected in 2004 has repeated the claims over Gibraltar voiced by all its predecessors, and the political stalemate seems set to continue for as long as Britain uses the wishes of the Gibraltarians as a pretext for blocking any change in the colony's status – a policy that infuriates the Spanish government, whose former foreign minister, Abel Matutes, stated that the wishes of the residents "did not apply in the case of Hong Kong".

What most outsiders don't realize about the political situation is that the Gibraltarians feel very vulnerable, caught between the interests of two big states; they are well aware that both governments' concerns are primarily strategic and political rather than with the wishes of the people of Gibraltar. Until very recently, people were sent over from Britain to fill all the top civil-service and Ministry of Defence jobs, a practice that, to a lesser degree, still continues – the current governor is Sir Robert Fulton, an old Etonian and former commanding officer in the Royal Marines. Large parts of the Rock are no-go areas for "natives"; the South District in particular is taken up by military facilities. Local people also protest about the Royal Navy nuclear-powered submarines that dock regularly at the naval base, and secrecy surrounds the issue of whether nuclear warheads and/or chemical and biological weapons are stored in the arsenal, probably deep inside the Rock itself.

Yet Gibraltarians stubbornly cling to British status, and all their institutions are modelled on British lines. Contrary to popular belief, however, they are of neither mainly Spanish nor British blood, but an ethnic mix descended from Genoese, Portuguese, Spanish, Menorcan, Jewish, Maltese and British forebears. **English** is the official language, but more commonly spoken is what sounds to an outsider like perfect Andalucian Spanish. It is, in fact, *llanito*, an Andalucian dialect with the odd borrowed English and foreign words reflecting its diverse origins – only a Spaniard from the south can tell a Gibraltarian from an Andalucian.

Cannon Hotel 9 Cannon Lane ☎51711, ⓦwww
.cannonhotel.gi. Small, pleasant hotel close to Main
St with a/c rooms. B&B £37.50–46.
Emile Youth Hostel Montagu Bastion, Line Wall Rd
☎51106, ⓦwww.emilehostel.com. Gibraltar's
privately run youth hostel has the cheapest beds
(dorms £15, shared-bathroom doubles £35) in
town. Prices include breakfast.
Hotel Bristol Cathedral Square ☎76800, ⓦwww
.bristolhotel.gi. Long-established place with
recently refurbished rooms and a pool. Currently
charges £81 for the cheapest non-sea view double
(supplement for sea view).

Queen's Hotel Boyd St ☎74000, ⓦwww
.queenshotel.gi. Decent traditional hotel offering
comfortable rooms many with terrace balconies.
Charges £70 for the cheapest non-sea view double
(supplement for sea view).
Rock Hotel 3 Europa Rd ☎73000, ⓦwww
.rockhotelgibraltar.com. Flagship hotel immediately
below the Apes' Den, trading on its imperial
connections – rooms are decorated in "colonial
style" and come with ceiling fans and a trouser
press. Doubles from £160.

Around the Rock

From near the southern end of Main Street you can hop on a **cable car** (daily 9.30am–6pm, last trip down 5.45pm; £8 return, £6.50 one way), which will carry you up to the summit – **The Top of the Rock** as it's logically known

– via **Apes' Den** halfway up, a fairly reliable viewing point to see the tailless monkeys. Although the cable car's fare structure militates against it, after riding to the top it's possible to walk back down, a pleasant twenty- to thirty-minute stroll. From The Top of the Rock you can look over the Strait of Gibraltar to the Atlas Mountains of Morocco and down to the town, the elaborate water-catchment system cut into the side of the rock, and ponder whether it's worth heading for one of the beaches such as Catalan Bay (see opposite). Entry to the **Upper Rock Nature Reserve** (as the area at the top of the Rock, containing the Apes' Den, St Michael's Cave and other sights, is designated) costs £0.50, but the attractions in this zone cost extra and can all be accessed with an **inclusive ticket** (£8, under-12s half-price) available from tourist offices or at each attraction. A grand tour of the Rock takes a half to a full day, and all sites on it are open daily from 9.30am to 7pm in summer, 10am to 5.30pm in winter.

From the cable-car stop at The Top of the Rock, it's an easy walk south along St Michael's Road through the Nature Reserve, home to six-hundred-plus plant and tree species, to **St Michael's Cave** (inclusive ticket), an immense natural cavern that led ancient people to believe the rock was hollow and gave rise to its old name of *Mons Calpe* (Hollow Mountain). The cave was used during the last war as a bomb-proof military hospital and nowadays hosts occasional concerts. If you're adventurous, you can arrange at the tourist office for a guided visit to Lower St Michael's Cave, a series of chambers going deeper down and ending in an underground lake.

If you walk rather than take the cable car to the top, you could visit the **Tower of Homage** (inclusive ticket), reached via Willis's Road. Dating from the fourteenth century, this is the most visible surviving remnant of the old **Moorish Castle**. Nearby on Willis's Road itself is the **Gibraltar: A City Under Siege** exhibition (inclusive ticket), housed in a former ammunition store. Farther up you'll find the **Upper Galleries** (aka the Great Siege Tunnels; inclusive ticket), blasted out of the rock during the Great Siege of 1779–82, in order to point guns down at the Spanish lines.

To **walk down** from The Top of the Rock (20min), follow Signal Station Road and St Michael's Road to O'Hara's Road and the **Mediterranean Steps** – a very steep descent most of the way down the east side, turning the southern corner of the Rock. You'll pass through the **Jews' Gate** and into Engineer Road, from where the return to town is through the Alameda Gardens and past the evocative **Trafalgar Cemetery**, with a good line in imperial epitaphs and where many of those who perished at the Battle of Trafalgar are buried.

Back in town, the **Gibraltar Museum**, in Bomb House Lane (Mon–Fri 10am–6pm, Sat 10am–2pm; £2), is mainly concerned with gilding the imperial story, although the building also holds two well-preserved and beautiful fourteenth-century **Moorish baths**. The only other sight of possible interest is **Nelson's Anchorage** (Mon–Sat 9.30am–5.15pm; £1, free with inclusive Rock ticket), on Rosia Road, where a monstrous **100-ton Victorian gun** marks the site where Nelson's body was brought ashore – preserved in a barrel of rum – from HMS *Victory* after the Battle of Trafalgar in 1805.

Offshore excursions include daily dolphin-spotting **boat trips**, run by companies operating from Marina Bay, including Dolphin Safari (£20, children £15; ☎71914) and Dolphin World (£20, children £10; mobile ☎54481000), which offers a money-back guarantee should you not see dolphins. You should ring first to book places or ask the tourist office to do it for you.

Gibraltar has plans to reclaim an area equivalent to that of the present town from the sea, and is currently doing feasibility surveys on pumping up sand from the seabed. But at present, there's just the one tiny fishing village at **Catalan Bay**, which is where you'll find the Rock's best **beach** backed by a characterless stretch of seafront reminiscent of a hum-drum British holiday resort. The inhabitants of the village like to think of themselves as very distinct from the townies on the other side of the Rock. It's easily reached by following Devil's Tower Road from near the airport (20min walk) or on bus #4 from the centre.

Eating and drinking

Restaurants are far more plentiful than places to stay, though by Spanish standards are still relatively expensive: pub snacks or fish and chips are reliable standbys. Main Street is crowded with touristy places, among which *Smiths Fish and Chip Shop*, at no. 295 near the Convent, is a long-established institution. Other good choices are *Penny Farthing* on King Street, always busy for home-cooked food at reasonable prices, plus, a couple of blocks north of here, *Jules Café*, 30 John Mackintosh Square, a decent lunch stop with a *menú* for £12.50 (excluding wine) and an outdoor terrace. *Buddies Pasta Casa* on Cannon Lane serves up decent pasta in all its varieties, while *Corks Wine Bar*, 79 Irish Town, is a pleasant place for light meals, and nearby, at no. 78, *The Clipper* serves pub grub in a varnished lounge. An interesting option in the centre of town is the Moroccan *Marrakech Restaurant*, 9 Governor's Parade, with a pleasant terrace serving couscous, tagines and other Maghrebi dishes with a *menú* for under £10.

Pubs all tend to mimic traditional English styles, the difference being that they are often open into the wee hours; another drawback is that few of them have terraces and many resemble saunas in high summer. For pub food, the *Royal Calpe*, 176 Main St, *Gibraltar Arms*, 14 Main St, and *The Horseshoe*, 193 Main St, are among the best, all offering hearty meals. For a quieter drink, try the *Cannon Bar* in Cannon Lane near the cathedral, or the *Piccadilly Garden Bar*, 3 Rosia Rd, just beyond the Referendum Gates (aka South Port). The *Star Bar*, 12 Parliament Lane, off the west side of Main Street near the post office, is reputedly Gibraltar's oldest and was a favourite hang-out of Lord Nelson when it traded under its original name, *La Estrella*.

Moving on

One decidedly functional attraction of Gibraltar is its role as a port for **Morocco**. A catamaran service, the *Tanger Jet*, sails to Tangier (Fri 6pm; 1hr) and back (Sun 8pm local time); check with the agent for the current timetable. Tickets – available from the agent Turner, 65/67 Irish Town (☎78305, ✉turner@gibtelecom.net) – cost £25 one way and £45 return for a foot passenger, and £65 one way and £117 return for a car.

Bland Travel, Cloister Building, Irish Town (☎77012, ⊕www.blands.gi; closed Sat & Sun), is the leading travel agent in Gibraltar and runs twice-weekly **day-trips to Morocco** on Wednesday (Tangier; £45) and Friday (Tetouan & Tangier; £47), which include guided tour and lunch. They can also assist with booking easyJet (2 daily), British Airways (daily) and Monarch Airlines (daily) **flights** to London and the latter's (4 weekly) flights to Manchester.

Gibraltar has plans to reclaim an area equivalent to that of the present town from the sea, and is currently doing feasibility surveys on pumping up sand from the seabed. But at present, there's just the one tiny fishing village at **Catalan Bay**, which is where you'll find the Rock's best **beach** backed by a characterless stretch of seafront reminiscent of a hum-drum British holiday resort. The inhabitants of the village like to think of themselves as very distinct from the townies on the other side of the Rock. It's easily reached by following Devil's Tower Road from near the airport (20min walk) or on bus #4 from the centre.

Algeciras

ALGECIRAS occupies the far side of the bay from Gibraltar, spewing out smoke and pollution in the direction of the Rock. The last town of the Spanish Mediterranean, it must once have been an elegant resort; today, it's unabashedly a port and industrial centre, its suburbs extending on all sides. When Franco closed the border with Gibraltar at La Línea it was Algeciras that he decided to develop to absorb the Spanish workers formerly employed in the British naval dockyards, thus breaking the area's dependence on the Rock.

Most travellers are scathing about the city's ugliness, and unless you're waiting for a bus or train, or heading **for Morocco**, there's admittedly little reason to stop. Yet some touch of colour is added by the groups of Moroccans in transit, dressed in flowing *jallabahs* and slippers, and lugging unbelievable amounts of possessions. Algeciras has a real port atmosphere, and even passing through it's hard to resist the urge to get on a boat south, if only for a couple of days in Tangier. Once you start to explore, you'll also discover that the **old town** has some very attractive corners that seem barely to have changed in fifty years, especially around Plaza Alta.

Practicalities

Algeciras' **turismo** is on c/Juan de la Cierva (Mon–Fri 9am–7.30pm, Sat & Sun 9.30am–3pm; ℡956 572 636, ⓦwww.ayto-algeciras.es), south of the train track near the port. There's **internet** access at *Locutorio Central*, c/Teniente Maroto 2 (Mon & Wed–Sun 10am–10pm), southwest of the market.

There are plenty of **places to stay** in the grid of streets to the north of the railway line between the port and the train station. In c/José Santacana, there's basic but clean *González* at no. 7 (℡956 652 843; ❶) where all rooms are en suite, or nearby on Plaza Palma, the market square, there's the surprisingly spruce *Hostal*

Moving on

Morocco is easily visited from Algeciras: in summer, there are **crossings to Tangier** (hourly: fast-ferry 1hr, normal ferry 2hr 30min) and to the Spanish *presidio* of **Ceuta** (at least 10 daily; fast ferry 35min), little more than a Spanish Gibraltar with a brisk business in duty-free goods, but a relatively painless way to enter Morocco. **Tickets** cost €38 (normal ferry) or €40 (fast) one way to Tangier or Ceuta, and are sold at scores of travel agents along the waterfront and on most approach roads. For up-to-date **information** on hydrofoils and fast-ferries, check with the *turismo* or with the ferry companies: Trasmediterránea, on the harbourfront (℡956 583 400, ⓦwww.trasmediterranea.es), or Viajes Transafric at Avda. Marina 4 (℡956 654 311, ⓦwww.transafric.com), fronting the port, both of which have frequent special offers (which can reduce a round-trip ticket to €40). Viajes Transafric also do a daily all-inclusive **day-trip to Tangier** by fast-ferry, which includes a guided tour, lunch and time for shopping (€48). Wait till Tangier – or if you're going via Ceuta, Tetouan – before buying any **Moroccan currency**; rates in the embarkation building kiosks are very poor.

At Algeciras, the **train line** begins again, heading north to Ronda, Córdoba and Madrid. The route to Ronda – one of the best rail journeys in Andalucía – is detailed on p.265; there are four departures a day. For **buses** to all parts of Andalucía as well as destinations further afield such as Madrid and Barcelona, you'll need the newly reconstructed **main bus station** (℡956 653 456), in c/San Bernardo, behind the port, next to *Hotel Octavio* and just short of the **train station**: to get there, follow the train tracks from the harbour. The bus to La Línea also goes every half-hour from here.

Nuestra Señora de la Palma (☎956 632 481; ❶) for good air-conditioned en-suite rooms with TV. A very pleasant hotel close to the waterfront is the *Marina Victoria*, Avda. de la Marina 7 (☎956 650 111, ⓦwww.hotelmarinavictoria.com; ❸), whose high, air-conditioned balcony rooms overlook the bay, with great views towards Gibraltar. Algeciras' luxurious **youth hostel**, Ctra. Nacional 340 (☎956 679 060; under-26 €14, over-26 €19), has a pool, tennis courts and double rooms with bath, but lies 8km west of town on the Tarifa road; buses heading for Tarifa will drop you there if you ask.

The huge number of people passing through the port area guarantees virtually limitless possibilities for **eating and drinking**, but it's worth venturing a short distance away from here for a bit more quality. A little north of the bus station, the excellent ✠ *Restaurante Montes*, c/Juan Morrison 27, is a traditional, slightly upmarket place but has a great-value *menú* for €9.50 and an equally excellent **tapas** bar lower down the hill on the same street, at the junction with c/Emilio Castelar. The bustling and colourful daily **market** in the nearby Plaza Palma is a useful place to buy food for travelling or picnics. For a change of scene from the harbour zone head uphill along c/Castillo, just north of the market, to Algeciras' elegant main square, **Plaza Alta**, where there are more bars, cafés and *heladerías*.

Ronda and the White Towns

Andalucía is dotted with small, brilliantly whitewashed settlements – the **Pueblos Blancos** or "**White Towns**" – most often straggling up hillsides towards a castle or towered church. Places such as **Mijas**, up behind Fuengirola, are solidly on the tourist trail, but even here the natural beauty is undeniable. All of them look great from a distance, though many are rather less interesting on arrival. Arguably the best lie in a roughly triangular area between Málaga, Algeciras and Seville; at its centre, in a region of wild, mountainous beauty, is the spectacular town of **Ronda**.

To Ronda from the coast

Of several possible approaches to Ronda from the coast the stunningly scenic route up **from Algeciras**, via Gaucín, is the most rewarding – and worth going out of your way to experience. It's possible by either bus or train (a spectacularly scenic option), or, if you've time and energy, can be walked in four or five days. En route, you're always within reach of a river and there's a series of hill towns, each one visible from the next, to provide targets for the day. Casares is almost on the route, but more easily reached from Estepona.

From Málaga, most buses to Ronda follow the coastal highway to San Pedro before turning into the mountains via the modern A376 *autovía*, dramatic enough, but rather a bleak route, with no villages and only limited views of the sombre rock face of the Serranía; an alternative route, via Álora and Ardales, is far more attractive and is taken by a couple of daily buses. The two-hour train ride up from Málaga is another scenic option with three connecting services daily, including a convenient early-evening departure (6.43pm).

Castellar de la Frontera

The first White Town on the route proper is **CASTELLAR DE LA FRONTERA**, 27km north of Algeciras, a bizarre village enclosed within the walls of a striking thirteenth-century Moorish castle, whose population, in accord with some grandiose scheme, was moved downriver in 1971 to the "new" town of Nuevo Castellar, turning the castle settlement into a ghost village. Inside the castle walls there's actually a **place to stay**: *Casas Rurales de Castellar* (℡956 236 620, ⓦwww.tugasa.com; ❸) consists of a number of restored village houses with a decent **restaurant** attached.

Jimena de la Frontera and Gaucín

JIMENA DE LA FRONTERA, 20km farther north along the A369, is a far larger and more open hill town, rising to a grand Moorish castle with a triple-gateway entrance. Of a number of **places to stay**, the charming and friendly *Hostal El Anon*, c/Consuelo 34 (℡956 640 113, ⓦwww.hostalanon.com; B&B ❸) is perhaps the best, comprising a series of tastefully renovated houses and stables with bar, restaurant and rooftop pool. Jimena's **campsite**, *Camping Los Alcornocales* (℡956 640 060), occupies a suberb location with great views on the north side of town (reached by following c/Sevilla to the end), and has its own restaurant. Other **places to eat** include *Bar Ventorrillero*, Plaza de la Constitución 2, at the foot of c/Sevilla, with a lunchtime *menú* for around €8, and the equally good *Restaurante Bar Cuenca*, Avenida de los Deportes, on the way into town, which also serves tapas and has a pretty terrace patio at the rear.

Beyond Jimena, it's 23km farther along the A369 passing through woods of cork oak and olive groves to reach **GAUCÍN**. Almost a mountain village, Gaucín commands tremendous views (to Gibraltar and the Moroccan coast on a very clear day), and makes a great place to stop over. There are **rooms** and food to be had at *Hostal Santa Isabel*, c/Luís Armiñian (℡952 151 324; ❷), with rooms above its restaurant next to the *gasolinera* (where you should enquire; get a room at the back for a view) as you come into the village from Jimena. A more upmarket option in the village proper is the charming *Hotel Rural Fructuosa*, c/Covento 67 (℡952 151 072, ⓦwww.lafructuosa.com; B&B ❹), with its own restaurant nearby.

You can reach Gaucín by **bus** or by train, but the **train station** (at El Colmenar on the fringes of the Cortés nature reserve) is 13km away. It's a bracing and mostly uphill hike to the village; a **taxi** (around €20 one way) can be arranged at *Bar-Restaurante Flores* fronting the station (℡952 153 026). They also do decent meals (€10 *menú*), and there are several other bars here. The train line between Gaucín and Ronda passes through a handful of tiny villages. En route, you can stop off at the station of Benaoján-Montejaque, from where it's an hour's trek to the prehistoric **Cueva de la Pileta** (see p.271). From Benaoján, Ronda is just three stops (30min) down the line.

Ronda

The full natural drama of **RONDA**, rising amid a ring of dark, angular mountains, is best appreciated as you enter the town. Built on an isolated ridge of the *sierra*, it's split in half by a gaping river gorge, **El Tajo**, which drops sheer for 130m on three sides. Still more spectacular, the gorge is spanned by a stupendous eighteenth-century arched bridge, the **Puente Nuevo**, while tall, whitewashed houses lean from its precipitous edges.

Much of the attraction of Ronda lies in this extraordinary view, or in walking down by the Río Guadalévin, following one of the donkey tracks through the rich green valley. Birdwatchers should look out for the lesser kestrels nesting in the cliffs beneath the Alameda; lower down you can spot crag martins. The town has a number of **museums** and, surprisingly, has sacrificed little of its character to the flow of day-trippers from the Costa del Sol.

Arrival and information

Ronda's **train** and **bus stations** are both in the Mercadillo quarter to the northeast of the bullring. Trains arrive at the station on Avenida Andalucía, a ten-minute walk or easy bus ride from the centre, and all the bus companies use the terminal close by on Plaza Redondo. Arriving **by car**, your best bet for street parking is to park as far out as possible (near the train station is usually feasible), or head straight for one of the pay car parks (clearly signed).

The **turismo** is at the northern end of the focal Plaza de España (Mon–Fri 9am–7.30pm, Sat & Sun 9.30am–3pm; ☎952 871 272), and can help with accommodation and provide a map. A useful **municipal tourist office** lies nearby, opposite the south side of the bullring (Mon–Fri 10am–7.15pm, Sat & Sun 10.15am–2pm & 3.30–6.30pm; ☎952 187 119). Ronda's official **website** ⓦwww.turismoderonda.es is also a good source of information on all aspects of the town. **Internet** access is available at *El Molino*, c/Molino 6, to the north of Plaza del Socorro.

Accommodation

Most of the places to stay are in the **Mercadillo** quarter, although some more-upmarket hotels have recently opened up in the old Moorish quarter, **La Ciudad**, on the south side of El Tajo. Both zones are within easy walking distance of Plaza de España. Ronda's **campsite**, *Camping El Sur*, with pool, bar and restaurant, lies 2km out of town along the road to Algeciras (☎952 875 939).

Budget

Hostal Águilar c/Naranja 28 ☎952 871 994. Clean, welcoming, family-run *hostal* for rooms with or without bath, off c/Cristo. ❶–❷

Hostal Andalucía c/Martínez Astein 19 ☎952 875 450. Pleasant rooms in leafy surroundings opposite the train station. ❶

Hostal Ronda Sol c/Cristo 11, near the intersection with c/Seville ☎952 874 497. Good-value (doubles €20) budget *hostal* for rooms with shared bath, but check what you're offered as two interior rooms (lacking windows) are a bit claustrophobic. ❶

Hotel Colón c/Pozo 1, on the Plaza de la Merced ☎952 870 218, ⓦwww.hotelcolon.es. Charming small hotel with a/c en-suite facilities and – in rooms 301 & 302 – your own spacious roof terrace. ❷

Hotel Morales c/Sevilla 51 ☎952 871 538, ⓦwww.hotelmorales.es. Welcoming small hotel where en-suite rooms come with TV and a/c and there's free internet access for clients. ❷

Moderate to expensive

Alavera de los Baños c/San Miguel s/n, next door to the Baños Arabes ☎952 879 143, ⓦwww.alaveradelosbanos.com. Enchanting small hotel with stylish rooms, garden, pool, restaurant, and views from rear rooms of grazing sheep on the hill across the river. B&B ❹

En Frente Arte c/Real 40 ☎952 879 088, ⓦwww.enfrentearte.com. Stylish hotel inside a restored mansion with distinctive and elegant rooms.

Breakfast is included in the price, as are soft drinks and draught beer. Additional luxuries include a delightful garden pool, games room, free sauna and internet access. Reductions for longer stays. ❹

Hotel San Gabriel c/José Holgado 19, La Ciudad ☎952 190 392, ⓦwww.hotelsangabriel.com. One of the recently arrived hotels in La Ciudad, this is a stunning restoration of an eighteenth-century mansion, with beautifully furnished a/c rooms, an amusing five-seater cinema for guests (library of classic DVDs) and welcoming proprietors. ❹

Jardín de la Muralla c/Espíritu Santo 13 ☎952 872 764, ⓦwww.jardindelamuralla.com. New hotel in La Ciudad situated in a wonderful eighteenth-century *casa palacio* with classically furnished rooms, many overlooking a delightful leafy garden with pool. Ten percent discount for Rough Guide readers with this guide. ❹

Parador de Ronda Plaza de España ☎952 877 500, ⓦwww.parador.es. Ronda's imposing *parador* has spectacular views overlooking El Tajo, plus a pool, terrace bar and restaurant. ❻

Los Pastores 4km outside town along the Algeciras road (A369), take right turn 400m after 4km sign ☎952 114 464, ⓦwww.lospastores.com. Very pleasant rural option in a remodelled former farmhouse surrounded by fine walking country and offering attractively furnished a/c apartment-rooms, many with terraces. All are provided with DVD & CD player, and activities include horseriding lessons and hiking; breakfast available. ❹

The Town

Ronda divides into three parts: on the south side of the bridge is the old Moorish town, **La Ciudad**, and farther south still, its **San Francisco** suburb. On the near north side of the gorge, and where you'll arrive by public transport, is the largely modern **Mercadillo** quarter.

La Ciudad

The **Ciudad** retains intact its Moorish plan and a great many of its houses, interspersed with a number of fine Renaissance mansions. It is so intricate a maze that you can do little else but wander at random. However, at some stage, make your way across the eighteenth-century **Puente Nuevo** bridge, peering down the walls of limestone rock into the yawning Tajo and the Río Guadalvín, far below. The bridge itself is a remarkable construction and now has its own **Centro de Información** (Mon–Fri 10am–9pm, until 6pm Nov–March, Sat 10am–1.45pm, Sun 10am–3pm; €2), housed in a former prison above the central arch; entry is to the side of the *parador* in Plaza de España. Once you're across the bridge, veering left along c/Santo Domingo, also known as c/Marqués de Parada, will bring you, at no. 17, to the somewhat arbitrarily named **Casa del Rey Moro** (House of the Moorish King), an early eighteenth-century mansion built on Moorish foundations. The gardens (but not the house itself) have recently been opened to the public (daily 10am–7pm; €4), and from here a remarkable underground stairway, the *Mina*, descends to the river; these 365 steps (which can be slippery after rain), guaranteeing a water supply in times of siege, were cut by Christian slaves in the fourteenth century. There's a viewing balcony at the bottom where you can admire El Tajo's towering walls of rock and its bird life, although the long climb back up will make you wonder whether it was worth it.

Farther down the same street is the **Palacio del Marqués de Salvatierra**, a splendid Renaissance mansion with an oddly primitive, half-grotesque frieze of Adam and Eve on its portal. Just down the hill you reach the two old town bridges – the **Puente Viejo** of 1616 and the single-span Moorish **Puente de San Miguel**; nearby, on the southeast bank of the river, are the distinctive

▲ Puente Nuevo and El Tajo gorge

hump-shaped cupolas and glass roof-windows of the old **Baños Árabes** (Mon–Fri 10am–7pm, Sat 10am–1.45pm, Sun 10am–3pm; €2, free on Sun). Dating from the thirteenth century and recently restored, the complex is based on the Roman system of cold, tepid and hot baths and is wonderfully preserved; note the sophisticated barrel-vaulted ceiling and brickwork octagonal pillars supporting horseshoe arches.

At the centre of La Ciudad, on Ronda's most picturesque square, the Plaza Duquesa de Parcent, stands the cathedral church of **Santa María La Mayor** (daily 10am–7pm; €3), originally the Moorish town's Friday mosque. Externally, it's a graceful combination of Moorish, Gothic and Renaissance styles with the belfry built on top of the old minaret. The interior is decidedly less interesting, but you can see an arch covered with Arabic calligraphy, and just in front of the street door, a part of the old Arab *mihrab*, or prayer niche, has been exposed. Slightly west of the square on c/Montero lies the fourteenth-century **Casa de Mondragón**, probably the real palace of the Moorish kings (Mon–Fri 10am–7pm, Oct–March until 6pm, Sat & Sun 10am–3pm; €3). Inside, three of the patios preserve original stuccowork and there's a magnificent carved ceiling, as well as a small museum covering local archeology and aspects of Moorish Ronda.

To the northeast of the Plaza Duquesa de Parcent, on c/Armiñan, which bisects La Ciudad, you'll find the new **Museo Lara** (daily 11am–8pm, Oct–March until 7pm; €4), containing the collection of *rondeño* Juan Antonio Lara, a member of the family that owns and runs the local bus company of the same name. An avid collector since childhood, Señor Lara has filled the spacious museum with a fascinating collection of antique clocks, pistols and armaments, musical instruments and archeological finds, as well as early cameras and cinematographic equipment. Nearby, at no. 65, the **Museo del Bandolero** (daily 10.30am–8pm; €3) is largely devoted to celebrating the Serranía's illustrious, mainly nineteenth-century bandits and includes displays of their weapons, as well as tableaux and audiovisual presentations.

Farther along the same street, near the southern end of La Ciudad, to the right, are the ruins of the **Alcázar**, once impregnable until razed by the French ("from sheer love of destruction", according to the nineteenth-century hispanist Richard Ford) in 1809. Beyond here the principal gates of the town, the magnificent Moorish **Puerto de Almocabar**, through which passed the Christian conquerors (led personally by Fernando), and the triumphal **Puerta de Carlos V**, erected later during the reign of the Habsburg emperor, stand side by side at the entrance to the suburb of San Francisco.

Mercadillo

The **Mercadillo** quarter, which grew up in the wake of the Reconquest, is of comparatively little interest, with only one genuine monument, the eighteenth-century **Plaza de Toros** (daily 10am–8pm, Oct–March until 6pm; €6). It's sited close by Plaza de España and the beautiful cliff-top *paseo*, from which you get good views of the old and new bridges. Ronda played a leading part in the development of bullfighting and was the birthplace of the modern *corrida* (bullfight). The ring, built in 1781, is one of the earliest in Spain and the fight season here is one of the country's most important. At its September *feria*, the *corrida goyesca*, honouring Spain's great artist Goya, who made a number of paintings of the fights at Ronda, takes place in eighteenth-century costume. You can wander around the arena, and there's a **museum** inside stuffed with memorabilia such as famous bullfighters' *trajes de luces* (suits) and photos of the ubiquitous Ernest Hemingway and Orson Welles visiting the ring.

The **Puente Nuevo** bridge was originally the town prison (now housing an information centre; see p.268), which last saw use during the Civil War, when Ronda was the site of some of the south's most vicious massacres. Hemingway, in *For Whom the Bell Tolls*, recorded how prisoners were thrown alive into the gorge.

Eating and drinking

Most of Ronda's bargain **restaurants** are grouped round Plaza del Socorro and nearby Plaza Carmen Abela, though there are also some to be found near Plaza de España. Many of the regional specialities served in the more upmarket places consist of hearty mountain fare, including *cocidos* (stews), *conejo* (rabbit), *perdiz* (partridge) and other game dishes.

Bar Faustino c/Santa Cecilia 4, off Plaza Carmen Abela. Lively place for tapas, *raciones* and *platos combinados*. Stays open until well beyond midnight and has an open-air patio. Closed Mon.

Bar Maestro c/Espinel 7, near Plaza de Toros. Great hole-in-the-wall (and one of Ronda's oldest tapas venues) with a tempting menu recited verbally by the proprietor. It's also a bar *taurino*, so the photos of past *torero* greats plus Hemingway and Welles (all one-time customers) gaze down from the walls.

Café Alba c/Espinel 44, the main pedestrianized shopping street. Piping-hot *churros* and delicious breakfast coffee. If this popular place is too packed, the nearby *Cafetería La Ibense* is a good alternative.

Casa Santa Pola c/Santo Domingo 3, La Ciudad ℡952 879 208. Impressive and pricey restaurant in a former *casa señorial* containing bits of the ninth-century house that preceded it. On three floors, with views over El Tajo, it has a wide range of local dishes – the speciality is *carnes asados* (roasted meats) cooked in a wood-burning oven.

Doña Pepa Plaza del Socorro. Family-run and reliable restaurant with some vegetarian possibilities and offering a variety of *menús* on a shaded terrace.

Mesón Rondeño Plaza de la Merced 4. Inviting new restaurant offering a wide-choice *menú* (€9), well-prepared fish and meat dishes, and a range of paellas, with a vegetarian version (€14 for two).

Parador de Ronda Plaza de España ℡952 877 500. The *parador*'s upmarket restaurant has an excellent choice of local and regional dishes such as *rabo de toro* (bull's tail), many of them appearing on a bargain *menú gastronomico* for around €30.

Patatín Patatán c/Borrego 7, off the east side of Plaza del Socorro. Popular tapas bar with a buzzing *ambiente* and a wide range of specials, including *conejo en salsa* and *habas a la rondeña* (broad beans). *La Viña*, next door at no. 9, is also good.

El Portón c/Pedro Romero 7, off the west side of Plaza del Socorro. Great little tapas bar and favourite haunt of bullfighting aficionados; does good *jamón* and *cazón* (shark) tapas and serves a cheap *menú* at terrace tables.

Restaurante del Escudero Paseo de Blas Infante 1, near the Plaza de Toros ℡952 871 367. Superb, stylish new restaurant housed in an elegant mansion with Ronda's best garden terrace, offering views towards the Serranía de Ronda. There's a *menú* for around €17. Closed Sun eve.

SonArte c/Santa Cecilia 1, off Plaza Carmen Abela. Smart new place serving Mediterranean meat and fish dishes, salads and fresh pasta as well as authentic pizzas. Mains €7.50–20.

Tragabuches c/José Aparicio 1 ℡952 190 291. Ronda's most stylish (and acclaimed) restaurant is named after a celebrated eighteenth-century *rondeño* bullfighter-turned-bandit, and, with an adventurous menu and minimalist decor, is worth a splurge. For €75, the *menú de degustación* is one of the most expensive in Andalucía. Booking advised. Closed Sun eve & Mon.

Around Ronda

Ronda makes an excellent base for exploring the superb countryside of the Serranía de Ronda to the south or for visiting the remarkable **Cueva de la Pileta**, with prehistoric cave paintings, and the Roman ruins of **Ronda la Vieja**.

Ronda la Vieja

Some 12km northwest of Ronda are the ruins of a town and **Roman theatre** at a site known as **Ronda la Vieja**, reached by turning right 6km down the main A376 road to Arcos/Seville. At the site (Wed–Sun 10am–2pm; free) a friendly farmer, who is also the guardian, will present you with a plan (in Spanish). Based on Neolithic foundations – note the recently discovered prehistoric stone huts beside the entrance – it was as a Roman town in the first century AD that Acinipo (the town's Roman name) reached its zenith. Immediately west of the theatre, the ground falls away in a startlingly steep escarpment offering fine views all around, taking in the picturesque hill-village of Olvera to the north.

Cueva de la Pileta

West from Ronda is the prehistoric **Cueva de la Pileta** (daily guided visits on the hour 10am–1pm & 4–6pm; €8; limit of 25 persons per tour, booking essential at peak times ☎952 167 343), a fabulous series of caverns with some remarkable paintings of animals (mainly bison), fish and what are apparently magic symbols. These etchings and the occupation of the cave date from about 25,000 BC – hence predating the more famous caves at Altamira in Northern Spain – to the end of the Bronze Age. The tour lasts an hour on average, but can be longer, and is in Spanish – though the guide does speak a little English. There are hundreds of bats in the cave, and no artificial lighting, so visitors carry lanterns; you may also want to take a jumper, as the caves can be extremely chilly. Be aware if you leave a car in the car park that thieves are active here.

To **reach the caves** from Ronda, take either an Algeciras-bound local train to Estación Benaoján-Montejaque (4 daily; 25min), or a bus, which drops you a little closer in Benaoján. There's a bar at the train station if you want to stock up on drink before the six-kilometre walk (1hr) to the caves. Follow the farm track from the right bank of the river until you reach the farmhouse (30min). From here, a track goes straight uphill to the main road just before the signposted turning for the caves. If you're driving, follow the road to Benaoján and take the signed turn-off, from where it's about 4km.

Towards Cádiz and Seville

Ronda has good transport connections in most directions. Almost any route to the north or west is rewarding, taking you past a whole series of White Towns, many of them fortified since the days of the Reconquest from the Moors – hence the mass of "de la Frontera" suffixes.

Grazalema and Ubrique

Perhaps the best of all the routes, though a roundabout one, and tricky without your own transport, is to **Cádiz** via Grazalema, Ubrique and Medina Sidonia. This passes through the spectacular **Parque Natural Sierra de Grazalema** before skirting the nature reserve of **Cortes de la Frontera** (which you can drive through by following the road beyond Benaoján) and, towards Alcalá de los Gazules, running through the northern fringe of **Parque Natural de los Alcornocales**, which derives its name from the forests of cork oaks, one of its main attractions and the largest of its kind in Europe.

Twenty-three kilometres from Ronda, **GRAZALEMA** is a striking white village at the centre of the magnificent Parque Natural Sierra de Grazalema, a paradise for hikers and naturalists. A **turismo** on the main square, Plaza de España (Mon–Fri 10am–2pm & 5–9pm, Sat & Sun 10am–9pm; ☎956 132 073), can provide information about the park, accommodation in the village and activities such as horseriding and also sells good walking maps. The only budget **place to stay** is the hospitable *Casa de las Piedras*, c/Las Piedras 32 (☎956 132 014, ⓦwww.casadelaspiedras.org; ❷), above the main square, which has rooms with and without bath – all have heating, which you'll be glad of outside high summer. One of the most attractive of the upmarket alternatives is 🖈 *La Mejorana*, c/Santa Clara 6 (☎956 132 327, 🌐www.lamejorana.net; B&B ❸), housed in an elegant *casa señorial* and replete with pool. Grazalema's **campsite**, *Tajo Rodillo*, is located above the village at the end of c/Las Piedras (☎956 132 063). The **bars and restaurants** on and around Plaza de España are reasonably priced for *raciones* and *menús*; three places worth singling out for value are *Cádiz El Chico*, on Plaza de España; the excellent *Torreón*, c/Agua 44, just north of it; and the *Casa de las Piedras* (see above).

The **Puerto de las Palomas** (Pass of the Doves – at 1350m the second-highest pass in Andalucía) rears up behind the village. Cross this (a superb walk or drive), and you descend to Zahara de la Sierra and the main road west (see below).

From Grazalema, following the scenic A374 towards Ubrique takes you through the southern sector of the natural park, a landscape of dramatic vistas and lofty peaks. The road snakes through the charming ancient villages of Villaluenga del Rosario and Benaocaz with plenty of opportunities for hikes – perhaps down Benaocaz's six-kilometre-long paved Roman road – along the way. **UBRIQUE**, 20km southwest of Grazalema, is a natural mountain fortress and was a Republican stronghold in the Civil War. Today, it's a prosperous and bustling town, owing its wealth to the medieval guild craft of **leather working**. Shops selling the output of numerous workshops (footwear and bags, often at bargain prices) line the main street, Avenida Dr Solis Pascual.

Zahara de la Sierra

Heading directly to Jerez or Seville from Ronda, a scenic rural drive along the Grazalema park's eastern fringes, you pass below **ZAHARA DE LA SIERRA** (or *de los Membrillos* – "of the Quinces"), perhaps the most perfect example of these fortified hill towns. Set above a lake (in reality, the man-made *embalse*, or reservoir, which has dramatically changed the landscape to the north and east of town), Zahara is a landmark for many kilometres around, its red-tiled houses huddling round a church and castle perched on a stark outcrop of rock. Once an important Moorish citadel, the town was captured by the Christians in 1483, opening the way for the conquest of Ronda – and ultimately Granada.

There's a clutch of **places to stay**: towards the swimming pool on the eastern edge of the village, the *Hostal Los Tadeos*, Paseo de la Fuente s/n (☎956 123 086; ❷), has rooms with bath and views, or there's the more central *Hotel Marqués de Zahara*, c/San Juan 3 (☎956 123 061; B&B ❷), with a good **restaurant**. Zahara has a new **campsite** (with its own decent restaurant) on the reservoir's shore: *Camping Entre Olivos* is located 2km south of the village (☎956 234 044, 🌐www.entreolivos.net), reached by following the old Ronda road (C339) and turning off along a signed road to Arroyo Molinos.

Arcos de la Frontera

Of more substantial interest, and another place to break the journey, is **ARCOS DE LA FRONTERA**, taken from the Moors in 1264, over two centuries before Zahara fell – an impressive feat, for it stands high above the Río Guadalete on a double crag and must have been a wretchedly impregnable fortress. This dramatic location, enhanced by low, white houses and fine sandstone churches, gives the town a similar feel and appearance to Ronda – only Arcos is poorer and, quite unjustifiably, far less visited. The streets of the town are if anything more interesting, with their mix of Moorish and Renaissance buildings. At its heart is the Plaza del Cabildo, easily reached by following the signs for the *parador*, which occupies one side of it. Flanking another two sides are the castle walls and the large Gothic-Mudéjar church of **Santa María de la Asunción**; the last side is left open, offering plunging views to the river valley. Below the town to the north lies **Lago de Arcos** (actually a reservoir) where locals go to cool off in summer.

Practicalities

A **turismo** on the west side of Plaza del Cabildo (Mon–Sat 10am–2.30pm & 5–8pm, Sun 10.30am–1.30pm; ☎956 702 264, ⓦwww.ayuntamientoarcos .org) can provide a town map and also does guided tours of the old town (Mon–Fri 11am; €7).

Budget **accommodation** in the old town is confined to the *Pensión de Callejón de las Monjas*, immediately behind the church of Santa María (☎956 702 302; ❶–❷), and the very friendly *Hostal San Marcos*, c/Marquéz de Torresoto 6 (☎956 700 721; ❶), the better alternative, with its own restaurant. More upmarket options are the elegant *Parador de Arcos de la Frontera* (☎956 700 500, ⓦwww.parador.es; ❾), perched on a rock pedestal with stunning views, plus a new hotel, *La Casa Grande*, c/Maldonado 10 (☎956 703 930, ⓦwww .lacasagrande.net; ❹), with beautiful rooms inside an eighteenth-century mansion and a stunning terrace view across the river valley.

Eating and drinking tends to be expensive in the old quarter, where most of the hotels have their own restaurants. A more modest, good-value option is *La Terraza* in the gardens of the Paseo de Andalucía to the southwest of Plaza del Cabildo, which serves a wide variety of *platos combinados* at outdoor tables, while *Alcaraván*, c/Nueva 1, close to the castle walls, is an interesting cave restaurant that does tapas and *platos asados* (roasted meats). The small and inexpensive restaurant of the *Hostal San Marcos* is also recommended. If you're looking to push the boat out, Arcos's top table is at the elegant restaurant of the *parador*, serving regional specialities on a *menú* for around €30.

Just out of town, towards Ronda, a road leads down to a couple of sandy **beaches** on Lago de Arcos (hourly buses from the bus station), where there's a pleasant two-star waterfront *hostal*, *La Molinera* (☎956 708 002, ⓦwww .mesondelmolinera.com; ❹), and a **campsite**, *Lago de Arcos* (☎956 708 333); bring mosquito protection if you stay at either, and if you swim here, or farther along towards the village of Bornos, take care – there are said to be whirlpools in some parts.

Seville, the west and Córdoba

With the major exception of **Seville** – and to a lesser extent **Córdoba** – the west and centre of Andalucía are not greatly visited. The coast here, certainly the Atlantic **Costa de la Luz**, is a world apart from the Mediterranean resorts, with the entire stretch between Algeciras and Tarifa designated a "potential military zone". This probably sounds grim – and in parts, marked off by *Paso Prohibido* signs, it is – but the ruling has also had happier effects, preventing foreigners from buying up land, and placing strict controls even on Spanish developments. So, for 100km or more, there are scarcely any villa developments and only a modest number of hotels and campsites – small, easy-going and low-key even at the growing resorts of breezy **Tarifa**, one of Europe's prime windsurfing locations, and **Conil**. On the coast, too, there's the attraction of **Cádiz**, one of the oldest and most elegant seaport towns in Europe.

Inland rewards include the smaller towns between Seville and Córdoba, Moorish **Carmona** particularly, and in the sherry zone of Cádiz province, where **Jerez** and its neighbours have plenty of *bodegas* to visit. But the most beautiful – and neglected – parts of this region are the dark, ilex-covered hills and poor rural villages of the **Sierra Morena** to the north and northwest of Seville. Perfect walking country with its network of streams and reservoirs between modest peaks, this is also a botanist's dream, brilliant with a mass of spring flowers.

On a more organized level, though equally compelling if you're into bird-watching or wildlife, is the huge nature reserve of the **Parque Nacional Coto de Doñana**, spreading back from Huelva in vast expanses of *marismas* – sand dunes, salt flats and marshes. The most important of the Spanish reserves, Doñana is vital to scores of migratory birds and to endangered mammals such as the Iberian lynx.

Seville (Sevilla)

"Seville," wrote Byron, "is a pleasant city, famous for oranges and women." And for its heat, he might perhaps have added, since **SEVILLE**'s summers are intense and start early, in May. But the spirit, for all its nineteenth-century chauvinism, is about right. Seville has three important monuments and an illustrious history, but what it's essentially famous for is its own living self – the greatest city of the Spanish south, of Carmen, Don Juan and Figaro, and the archetype of Andalucian promise. This reputation for gaiety and brilliance, for theatricality and intensity of life does seem deserved. It's expressed on a phenomenally grand scale at the city's two great festivals – **Semana Santa** (Holy Week at Easter) and the **Feria de Abril** (which starts two weeks after Easter Sunday and lasts a week). Either is worth considerable effort to get to. Seville is also Spain's second most important centre for **bullfighting**, after Madrid.

Despite its elegance and charm, and its wealth, based on food processing, shipbuilding, aircraft construction and a thriving tourist industry, Seville lies at the centre of a depressed agricultural area and has an unemployment rate of nearly twenty percent – one of the highest in Spain. The total refurbishment of the infrastructure boosted by the 1992 Expo – including impressive new roads, seven bridges, a high-speed rail link and a revamped airport – was intended to regenerate the city's (and the region's) economic fortunes, but has hardly turned out to be the catalyst for growth and prosperity promised at the time. Indeed, some of the colossal debts are still unpaid almost two decades later.

Meantime, **petty crime** (usually bag-snatching or breaking into cars) is a big problem. Be careful, but don't be put off – despite a worrying rise in the number of muggings in recent years, when compared with cities of similar size in northern Europe, violent crime is still relatively rare.

Moorish Seville

Seville was one of the earliest Moorish conquests (in 712) and, as part of the **Caliphate of Córdoba**, became the second city of *al-Andalus*. When the caliphate broke up in the early eleventh century it was by far the most powerful of the independent states (or *taifas*) to emerge, extending its power over the Algarve and eventually over Jaén, Murcia and Córdoba itself. This period, under a series of three Arabic rulers from the **Abbadid dynasty** (1023–91), was something of a golden age. The city's court was unrivalled in wealth and luxury and was sophisticated, too, developing a strong chivalric element and a flair for poetry – one of the most skilled exponents being the last ruler, al-Mu'tamid, the "poet-king". But with sophistication came decadence, and in 1091 Abbadid rule was overthrown by a new force, the **Almoravids**, a tribe of fanatical Berber Muslims from North Africa, to whom the Andalucians had appealed for help against the rising threat from the northern Christian kingdoms.

Despite initial military successes, the Almoravids failed to consolidate their gains in *al-Andalus* and attempted to rule through military governors from Marrakesh. In the middle of the twelfth century, they were in turn supplanted by a new Berber incursion, the **Almohads**, who by about 1170 had recaptured virtually all the former territories. Seville had accepted Almohad rule in 1147 and became the capital of this last real empire of the Moors in Spain. Almohad power was sustained until their disastrous defeat in 1212 by the combined Christian armies of the north, at Las Navas de Tolosa. In this brief and precarious period, Seville underwent a renaissance of public building, characterized by a new vigour and fluidity of style. The Almohads rebuilt the Alcázar, enlarged the principal mosque – later demolished to make room for the Christian cathedral – and erected a new and brilliant minaret, a tower over 100m tall, topped with four copper spheres that could be seen for miles around: the Giralda.

Arrival and information

Points of arrival are straightforward, though the **train station**, Santa Justa, is a fair way out on Avenida Kansas City, the airport road. Bus #32 will take you from here to Plaza de la Encarnación, from where all sights are within easy walking distance; alternatively, buses #70 and #C1 will take you to the Prado de San Sebastián bus station. A bus map detailing all routes is available from the *turismo*. The **airport** bus, operated by Amarillos (every 30min; €2.10), takes thirty minutes to the centre and terminates at the Puerta de Jerez, near the Alcázar, stopping at the train station en route. A taxi from the airport into the centre costs €20 (for up to 4 people) plus €1 per bag (slightly more Sun and after 10pm). The current fare can be obtained from the taxi authority ☏954 505 840 or any *turismo*.

The **main bus station** is at Prado de San Sebastián (☏954 417 111), from where most destinations are served; exceptions include buses for Badajoz, Extremadura (the provinces of Cáceres and Badajoz), Huelva, Madrid and international destinations, which arrive at and depart from the station at Plaza de Armas (☏954 908 040) by the Puente del Cachorro on the river.

Arriving by car, your best plan is to store your vehicle in one of the central underground pay car parks (which are well signed) or choose a hotel with a garage (where you'll still need to pay).

The city is engaged in constructing a **metro system** that will crisscross Seville. The first sections – due to be opened in 2009 – will link the southern suburbs to the Puerto de Jerez and Triana, with a stop near the old Expo '92 site on the west bank of the river. A new **tram** system will also be expanded in the years to come but presently runs only from Plaza Nueva to the Prado de San Sebastián bus station.

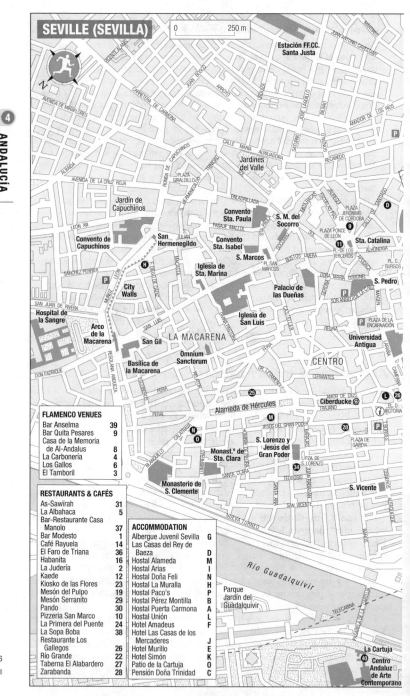

SEVILLE (SEVILLA)

0 ——— 250 m

Estación FF.CC.
Santa Justa

Jardines
del Valle

Convento
Sta. Paula

S. M. del
Socorro

Sta. Catalina

San
Hermenegildo

Convento
Sta. Isabel

S. Marcos

Iglesia de
Sta. Marina

S. Pedro

Jardín de
Capuchinos

Convento de
Capuchinos

City
Walls

Palacio de
las Dueñas

Hospital de
la Sangre

Arco
de la
Macarena

Iglesia de
San Luis

LA MACARENA

San Gil

Universidad
Antigua

Omnium
Sanctorum

CENTRO

Basílica de
la Macarena

Ciberducke @

Alameda de Hércules

S. Lorenzo y
Jesús del
Gran Poder

Monast.º de
Sta. Clara

Monasterio de
S. Clemente

S. Vicente

Río Guadalquivir

Parque
Jardín del
Guadalquivir

La Cartuja

Centro
Andaluz
de Arte
Contemporáneo

FLAMENCO VENUES

Bar Anselma	39
Bar Quita Pesares	9
Casa de la Memoria de Al-Andalus	8
La Carbonería	4
Los Gallos	6
El Tamboril	3

RESTAURANTS & CAFÉS

As-Sawirah	31
La Albahaca	5
Bar-Restaurante Casa Manolo	37
Bar Modesto	1
Café Rayuela	14
El Faro de Triana	36
Habanita	16
La Judería	2
Kaede	12
Kiosko de las Flores	23
Mesón del Pulpo	19
Mesón Serranito	29
Pando	30
Pizzeria San Marco	10
La Primera del Puente	24
La Sopa Boba	38
Restaurante Los Gallegos	26
Río Grande	22
Taberna El Alabardero	27
Zarabanda	28

ACCOMMODATION

Albergue Juvenil Sevilla	G
Las Casas del Rey de Baeza	D
Hostal Alameda	M
Hostal Arias	I
Hostal Doña Feli	N
Hostal La Muralla	H
Hostal Paco's	P
Hostal Pérez Montilla	B
Hostal Puerta Carmona	A
Hostal Unión	L
Hotel Amadeus	F
Hotel Las Casas de los Mercaderes	J
Hotel Murillo	E
Hotel Simón	K
Patio de la Cartuja	O
Pensión Doña Trinidad	C

4

ANDALUCÍA

Jeréz, Cádiz & G

Remedios

SAN BERNARDO

AVENIDA DE LA BORBOLLA

JIMÉNEZ ARANDA

SAN BERNARDO

DEMETRIO DE LOS RÍOS

AVENIDA DE MENÉNDEZ

AVENIDA DE CARLOS V

Prado de San Sebastián

Plaza de España

Main Bus Station

AVENIDA DE PORTUGAL

Parque de María Luisa

Internetia @

PLAZA DE S. AGUSTÍN

A

MENÉNDEZ PELAYO

PL. DON JUAN DE AUSTRIA

AVENIDA DEL CID

GLORIETA SAN DIEGO

AVENIDA DE M. LUISA

AVENIDA DE ISABEL LA CATÓLICA

B C

PLAZA DE STA. CRUZ

Jardines de Murillo

Fábrica de Tabacos

Casino-Teatro Lope de Vega

Casa de Pilatos

PLAZA DE PILATOS

SANTA CRUZ

Cvto. San Leandro

Jardines de los Reales Alcázares

PLAZA DE LOS VENERABLES

Alcázar

Hotel Alfonso XIII

Palacio de San Telme

Iglesia de Sta. Cruz

Museo del Baile Flamenco

PLAZA ALFALFA

Palacio Arzobispal

PL. VIRGEN DE LOS REYES

PL. DEL TRIUNFO

Archivo de las Indias

PUERTA DE JEREZ

AV. DE ROMA

San Salvador

Catedral

PLAZA DEL SALVADOR

Casa de la C. de Lebrija

Ayuntamiento

PLAZA DE SAN FRANCISCO

Hospital de la Caridad

Torre del Oro

PLAZA DE CUBA

EL ARENAL

AV. REP. ARGENTINA

S. Buenaventura

Plaza de Toros de la Maestranza

Igl. de la Magdalena

'See 'Seville: The Old City' map

Santa Ana

Capilla de los Marineros

TRIANA

Museo de Bellas Artes

Mercado del Barranco

P. DE ISABEL II (TRIANA)

PL. DEL ALTOZANO

San Jacinto

Río Guadalquivir

PLAZA DE ARMAS

Mercado de Triana

Plaza de Armas Bus Station

Nuestra Señora de la 'O'

PUERTO FLUVIAL

Puerta Triana

PUERTA SUR

BARS	
Bulebar	25
El Capote	35
Embarcadero	21
El Paseo	33
Ritual	40

TAPAS BARS	
Bar Bistec	32
Bar Europa	17
Bar Giralda	13
Casa Morales	18
Eslava	34
El Rinconcillo	11
Sopa de Ganso	15
Taberna Coloniales II	20
Las Teresas	7

The main **turismo** is at Avda. de la Constitución 21 (Mon–Fri 9am–7.30pm, Sat 10am–3.30pm; ☎954 787 578); they have accommodation lists and can give you a copy of the very useful free listings magazine *El Giraldillo*. There's also a less chaotic **municipal tourist office** at c/Arjona 28, near the river by the Puente de Triana (Mon–Fri 9am–7.30pm, Sat & Sun 10am–2pm; ☎954 221 714, ⓦwww.turismosevilla.org), with a sub-office at Santa Justa train station.

One way to get to grips with the city is to take an **open-top bus tour** – especially good if you're pressed for time. This hop-on hop-off service is operated by Sevirama (☎954 560 693); buses leave half-hourly from the riverside Torre del Oro, stopping at or near the main sites (all-day ticket €15).

Accommodation

Seville has some of the finest hotels in Andalucía. The most attractive area to stay is undoubtedly the **Barrio Santa Cruz**, though this is reflected in the prices, particularly during high season (April–June). Nonetheless, there are a few reasonably priced places to be found in the *barrio* and on its periphery (especially immediately north, and south towards the bus station) and they're at least worth a try before heading elsewhere. Slightly farther out, another promising area is to the north of the Plaza Nueva, and especially over towards the river and the Plaza de Armas bus station. The once drab **Alameda de Hercules** is now one of the city's foremost up and coming zones.

If you're arriving during any of the major **festivals**, particularly Semana Santa or the Feria de Abril (April fair), you're strongly advised to book ahead.

Budget

Albergue Juvenil Sevilla c/Isaac Peral 2 ☎954 613 150 (they tend not to answer). Leafy, if often crowded, youth hostel some way out in the university district; take bus #34 from the Puerta de Jerez by the *turismo* or Plaza Nueva. Under-26 €16, over-26 €20.

Hostal Alameda Alameda de Hércules 31 ☎954 900 191, ⓦwww.hostalalameda.es. Modern, pleasant and very friendly *hostal* overlooking the tree-lined Alameda. En-suite rooms come with a/c and TV. ❸

Hostal Arias c/Mariana de Pineda 9 ☎954 218 389, ⓦwww.hostalarias.com. Cosy *hostal* with smart if simple rooms – all en suite with a/c and TV – in a quiet pedestrian street close to the Alcázar's doorstep. ❸

🏃 **Hostal Doña Feli** Jesus del Gran Poder 130 ☎954 901 048, ⓦwww.hostaldfeli.com. At the northern end of the atmospheric Alameda de Hércules this is a very pleasant (and economically priced) small *hostal* with cosy en-suite rooms equipped with a/c and TV. Own garage with low rates. ❷

Hostal La Muralla c/Macarena 52 ☎954 371 049, Ⓔhmuralla@terra.es. Very pleasant and good-value residential *hostal* facing the medieval walls in La Macarena *barrio*. All rooms come with bath, a/c and TV. Own garage. ❷

Hostal Paco's c/Pedro del Toro 7, off c/Gravina ☎954 217 183, ⓦwww.sol.com/hostales-sp.

Friendly place with clean and economical en-suite rooms. The same proprietor has a number of similar *hostales* nearby (some sharing bath are even cheaper). ❷

Hostal Pérez Montilla Plaza Curtidores 13 ☎954 421 854, Ⓔperezmontilla@hotmail.com. Spotless *hostal* on a tranquil square. Cheaper rooms come without bath; those with have a/c. Prices can drop dramatically when business is slack. ❷

Hostal Puerta Carmona Plaza de San Agustín 5 ☎954 988 310, ⓦwww.hostalpuertacarmona.es. Very pleasant *hostal* with good-value modern en-suite rooms with a/c and TV; they will advise on where to park nearby. ❸

Hostal Unión c/Tarifa 4 ☎954 229 294. Slightly east of the Plaza Duque de la Victoria and one of the best-value places in this area. Decent a/c rooms with bath. ❷

Pensión Doña Trinidad c/Archeros 7 ☎954 541 906, ⓦwww.donatrinidad.com. Sparkling new Santa Cruz *hostal* with tastefully decorated en-suite rooms (some single) around a central patio. ❸

Moderate and expensive

🏃 **Las Casas del Rey de Baeza** Plaza Jesús de la Redención 2 ☎954 561 496, ⓦwww .hospes.es. Wonderful hotel with rooms arranged around an eighteenth-century *sevillano corral*. The plant-bedecked interior patio is a picture, and stylishly furnished pastel-shaded rooms come with traditional exterior *esparto* blinds, a neat finishing touch – and there's a rooftop pool to cool off in. ⑥

Hotel Amadeus c/Farnesio 6, near the Iglesia de Santa Cruz ☏ 954 501 443, Ⓦ www.hotelamadeussevilla.com. Welcoming hotel – housed in an eighteenth-century *casa señorial* – owned by an *aficionada* of the great composer. There's a *sala de musica,* and the soundproofed and stylish rooms come with a/c, satellite TV, wi-fi and free internet access. The house is topped off with a stunning roof terrace (with telescope) for breakfasting. ④

Hotel Las Casas de los Mercaderes c/Álvarez Quintero 12 ☏ 954 225 858, Ⓦ www.casasypalacios .com. Near the cathedral, this converted former *bodega* has been transformed into a very comfortable hotel with a delightful seventeenth-century patio, a roof terrace and great views from some rooms (especially nos. 201–206). ⑥

Hotel Murillo c/Lope de Rueda 7 ☏ 954 216 095, Ⓦ www.hotelmurillo.com. Traditional hotel in a restored mansion close to Plaza Santa Cruz with all facilities plus amusingly kitsch features, including suits of armour and paint-palette key rings. ④

Hotel Simón c/García de Vinuesa 19 ☏ 954 226 660, Ⓦ www.hotelsevilla.com. Well-restored mansion in an excellent position across from the cathedral. All rooms are en suite and a/c, and this can be a bargain out of high season. ④

Patio de la Cartuja c/Lumbreras 8, off west side of Alameda's northern end ☏ 954 900 200, Ⓦ www.patiosdesevilla.com. Stylish and excellent-value apartment-hotel created from an old *sevillano corral*; en-suite apartments with balconies, kitchen and lounge are set around a tiled patio. Own garage. ④

Camping

Camping Villsom 10km out of town on the main Cádiz road ☏&Ⓕ 954 720 828. Recently overhauled campsite with a pool. Half-hourly buses from c/La Rabida (near the Fábrica de Tabacos) take 20min – the M-132 signed "Dos Hermanas por Barriadas" will drop you outside.

Club de Campo ☏ 954 720 250. About 12km south of the centre in Dos Hermanas, with a pool. Half-hourly Amarillos buses from the main bus station or c/Palos de la Frontera, south of the cathedral.

The City

Seville's **old city** – where you'll want to spend most of your time – is sited along the east bank of the Guadalquivir. At its heart, side by side, stand the three great monuments: the **Giralda tower**, the **Catedral** and the **Alcázar**, with the cramped alleyways of the **Barrio Santa Cruz**, the medieval Jewish quarter and now the heart of tourist life, extending east of them.

North of here is the main shopping and commercial district, its most obvious landmarks **Plaza Nueva**, **Plaza Duque de la Victoria** and the smart, pedestrianized **c/Sierpes**, which runs roughly between them. From **La Campana**, the small square at the northern end of c/Sierpes, c/Alfonso XII runs down towards the river by way of the **Museo de Bellas Artes**, second in importance in Spain only to the Prado in Madrid. Across the river is the earthier, traditionally working-class district of **Triana**, flanked to the south by the **Los Remedios** *barrio*, the city's wealthier residential zone where the great April *feria* takes place.

The Catedral

Seville's **Catedral** (July & Aug Mon–Sat 9.30am–4pm, Sun 2.30–6pm; Sept–June Mon–Sat 11am–5pm, Sun 2.30–6pm; ticket valid for Catedral and the Giralda; €7.50, under-16s free; Ⓦ www.catedraldesevilla.es) was conceived in 1402 as an unrivalled monument to Christian glory – "a building on so magnificent a scale that posterity will believe we were mad". To make way for this new monument, the Almohad mosque that stood on the proposed site was almost entirely demolished. Meanwhile, the canons, inspired by their vision of future repute, renounced all but a subsistence level of their incomes to further the building.

The cathedral was completed in just over a century (1402–1506), an extraordinary achievement, as it's the largest Gothic church in the world. As Norman Lewis says, "It expresses conquest and domination in architectural terms of

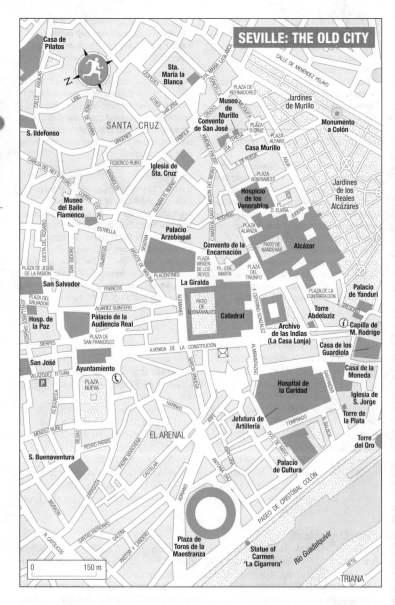

SEVILLE: THE OLD CITY

sheer mass." Though it is built upon the huge, rectangular base-plan of the old mosque, the Christian architects (probably under the direction of the French master architect of Rouen cathedral) added the extra dimension of height. Its central nave rises to 42m, and even the side chapels seem tall enough to contain an ordinary church. The total area covers 11,520 square metres, and new calculations, based on cubic measurement, have now pushed it in front of St Paul's in London and St Peter's in Rome as the largest church in the world, a claim upheld by the *Guinness Book of Records*, a copy of whose certificate is proudly displayed in the church.

From the old mosque, the magnificent **Giralda** and the Moorish entrance court, the **Patio de los Naranjos**, were spared, though the patio is somewhat marred by Renaissance embellishments. The patio was originally entered from c/Alemanes, through the **Puerta del Perdón**, the original main gateway and now the visitor exit – the **main visitor entrance** is on the cathedral's south side, through the Puerta de San Cristóbal.

The interior

Entering the cathedral, you are guided through a reception area that brings you into the church to the west of the portal itself. Turn right once inside to head east, where you will soon be confronted by the **Monument to Christopher Columbus** (*Cristóbal Colón* in Spanish), actually the explorer's tomb. Columbus' remains were originally interred in the cathedral of Havana, on the island that he had discovered on his first voyage in 1492. But during the upheavals surrounding the declaration of Cuban independence in 1902, Spain transferred the remains to Seville, and the monumental tomb – in the late Romantic style by Arturo Mélida – was created to house them. However, doubts have always been voiced concerning the authenticity of the remains, and in 2002 scientists from the University of Granada carried out DNA tests in an attempt to confirm that they are those of Columbus – but these proved inconclusive. The mariner's coffin is held aloft by four huge allegorical figures, representing the kingdoms of León, Castile, Aragón and Navarra; the lance of León should be piercing a pomegranate (now inexplicably missing), symbol of Granada (and the word for the fruit in Spanish), the last Moorish kingdom to be reconquered.

As you move into the **nave**, sheer size and grandeur are, inevitably, the chief characteristics of the cathedral. But once you've grown accustomed to the gloom, two other qualities stand out with equal force: the rhythmic balance and interplay between the parts, and an impressive overall simplicity and restraint in decoration. All successive ages have left monuments of their own wealth and style, but these have been limited to the two rows of side chapels. In the main body of the cathedral only the great box-like structure of the **coro** stands out, filling the central portion of the nave.

The *coro* extends and opens onto the **Capilla Mayor**, dominated by a vast **Gothic retablo** composed of 45 carved scenes from the Life of Christ. The lifetime's work of a single craftsman, Fleming Pieter Dancart, this is the supreme masterpiece of the cathedral – the largest and richest altarpiece in the world and one of the finest examples of Gothic woodcarving. The guides provide staggering statistics on the amount of gold involved.

Before proceeding around the edge of the nave in a clockwise direction it's best to backtrack to the church's southeast corner to take in the **Sacristía de los Cálices** where many of the cathedral's main art treasures are displayed, including a masterly image of *Santas Justa y Rufina* by Goya, depicting Seville's patron saints, who were executed by the Romans in 287. Should you be interested in studying the many canvases here or the abundance of major artworks placed in the various chapels, it's worth calling at the bookshop near the entrance to purchase a copy of the official *Guide to the Cathedral of Seville*, which deals with them in detail. Alongside this room is the grandiose **Sacristía Mayor**, housing the treasury. Embellished in the Plateresque style, it was designed in 1528 by Diego de Riaño, one of the foremost exponents of this predominantly decorative architecture of the late Spanish Renaissance. Amid a confused collection of silver reliquaries and monstrances – dull and prodigious wealth – are displayed the **keys** presented to Fernando by the Jewish and Moorish communities on the surrender of the city; sculpted into the metal in stylized Arabic script are the words "May Allah render eternal the dominion of Islam in this city". Through a small antechamber here you enter the oval-shaped **Sala Capitular** (chapterhouse), with paintings by Murillo and an outstanding **marble floor** with geometric design.

Continuing to the southwest corner and the **Puerta del Nacimiento** – the door through which pass all the *pasos* and penitents who take part in the Semana Santa processions – you then turn right (north) along the west wall, passing the Puerta Principal. In the northwest corner, the **Capilla de San Antonio** has Murillo's *Vision of St Anthony* depicting the saint in ecstatic pose before an infant Christ. The nave's north side leads to the Puerta de la Concepción, through which you will exit – but before doing so, continue to the northeast corner to view the domed Renaissance **Capilla Real** (not always open), built on the site of the original royal burial chapel and containing the body of Fernando III (*El Santo*) in a suitably rich, silver shrine in front of the altar. The large tombs on either side of the chapel are those of Fernando's wife, Beatrice of Swabia, and his son, Alfonso the Wise. You are now close to the entry to the Giralda tower.

La Giralda

The **entrance to the Giralda** (same ticket as cathedral) lies to the left of the Capilla Real in the cathedral's northeast corner. Unquestionably the most beautiful building in Seville, the **Giralda**, named after the sixteenth-century *giraldillo*, or weather vane, on its summit, dominates the city skyline. From the entrance you can ascend to the **bell chamber** for a remarkable **view** of the city – and, equally remarkable, a glimpse of the Gothic details of the cathedral's buttresses and statuary. But most impressive of all is the tower's inner construction, a series of 35 gently inclined ramps wide enough to allow two mounted guards to pass.

The **minaret** was the culmination of Almohad architecture, and served as a model for those at the imperial capitals of Rabat and Marrakesh. It was used by the Moors both for calling the faithful to prayer (the traditional function of a minaret) and as an observatory, and was so venerated that they wanted to destroy it before the Christian conquest of the city. This they were prevented from doing by the threat of Alfonso (later King Alfonso X) that "if they removed a single stone, they would all be put to the sword". Instead, it became the belltower of the Christian cathedral.

The Moorish structure took twelve years to build (1184–96) and derives its firm, simple beauty from the shadows formed by blocks of brick trelliswork (a style known as *sebka*), different on each side, and relieved by a succession of arched niches and windows. The original harmony has been somewhat spoiled by the Renaissance-era addition of balconies and, to a still greater extent, by the four diminishing storeys of the belfry – added, along with the Italian-sculpted bronze figure of "Faith" which surmounts them, in 1560–68, following the demolition by an earthquake of the original copper spheres. Even so, it remains in its perfect synthesis of form and decoration one of the most important and beautiful monuments of the Islamic world.

To reach the cathedral's **exit**, retrace your steps to Puerta de la Concepción and beyond this cross the **Patio de los Naranjos** to the Puerta del Perdón, the former main entrance. In the centre of the patio remains a **Moorish fountain** where worshippers carried out the ritual ablutions before entering the mosque. Interestingly, it incorporates a sixth-century font from an earlier Visigothic cathedral, which was in its turn levelled to make way for the mosque.

▲ La Giralda

Archivo de las Indias and Ayuntamiento

If the Columbus monument has inspired you, or you have a keen interest in the navigator's travels, visit the sixteenth-century **Archivo de las Indias** (Mon–Sat 10am–4pm, Sun 10am–2pm; free), between the cathedral and the Alcázar. Originally called La Casa Lonja, it served as the city's old stock exchange (*lonja*). Built in the severe and uncompromising style of El Escorial near Madrid, and designed by the same architect, Juan de Herrera, in the eighteenth century it was turned into a storehouse for the archive of the Spanish empire – a purpose it served for almost three hundred years. In 2006, this mountain of documentation (of vital importance to scholars) was moved to another building around the corner and the Archivo was renovated, enabling visitors to enjoy Herrera's masterpiece in all its splendour once again. The exterior is defined by four identical facades, while corner pyramids supporting weather vanes are the main decorative feature. Inside, the sumptuous marble floors, bookcases in Cuban wood, arcaded central patio, and grand staircase in pink and black marble are a visual feast. The upper floor houses temporary **exhibitions** of interesting documents from the archive; these frequently include items such as Columbus's log and a letter from Cervantes (pre-*Don Quixote*) petitioning the king for a position in the Americas – fortunately for world literature, he was turned down.

Another building worth a look and sited slightly to the north of the cathedral is the sixteenth-century **Ayuntamiento** on Plaza de San Francisco, with a richly ornamented Plateresque facade by Diego de Riaño. The interior is open for guided visits (Tues, Wed & Thurs 5.30pm, Sat noon; closed Aug; free).

The Alcázar

Rulers of Seville have occupied the site of the **Alcázar** (April–Sept Tues–Sat 9.30am–7pm, Sun 9.30am–5pm; Oct–March Tues–Sat 9.30am–5pm, Sun 9.30am–1.30pm; €7; ⓦwww.patronato-alcazarsevilla.es) from the time of the Romans. Here was built the great court of the **Abbadids**, which reached a peak of sophistication and exaggerated sensuality under the cruel and ruthless al-Mu'tadid – a ruler who enlarged the palace in order to house a harem of eight hundred women, and who decorated the terraces with flowers planted in the skulls of his decapitated enemies. Later, under the **Almohads**, the complex was turned into a citadel, forming the heart of the town's fortifications. Its extent was enormous, stretching to the Torre del Oro on the bank of the Guadalquivir.

Parts of the Almohad walls survive, but the present structure of the palace dates almost entirely from the Christian period. Seville was a favoured residence of the Spanish kings for some four centuries after the Reconquest – most particularly of **Pedro the Cruel** (Pedro I; 1350–69) who, with his mistress María de Padilla, lived in and ruled from the Alcázar. Pedro embarked upon a complete rebuilding of the palace, employing workmen from Granada and utilizing fragments of earlier Moorish buildings in Seville, Córdoba and Valencia. Pedro's works form the nucleus of the Alcázar as it is today and, despite numerous restorations necessitated by fires and earth tremors, it offers some of the best surviving examples of **Mudéjar architecture** – the style developed by Moors working under Christian rule. Later monarchs, however, have left all too many traces and additions. Isabel built a new wing in which to organize expeditions to the Americas and control the new territories; Carlos V married a Portuguese princess in the palace, adding huge apartments for the occasion; and under Felipe IV (c.1624) extensive renovations were carried out to the existing rooms. On a more mundane level, kitchens were installed to provide for General Franco, who stayed in the royal apartments whenever he visited Seville.

Entry: the Salón del Almirante

The Alcázar is entered from the Plaza del Triunfo, adjacent to the cathedral. The gateway, flanked by original Almohad walls, opens onto a courtyard where Pedro I (who was known as "the Just" as well as "the Cruel", depending on one's fortunes) used to give judgement; to the left is his **Sala de Justicia** and beyond this the **Patio del Yeso**, the only surviving remnant of the Almohads' Alcázar. The main facade of the palace stands at the end of an inner court, the **Patio de la Montería**; on either side are galleried buildings erected by Isabel.

This principal facade is pure fourteenth-century Mudéjar and, with its delicate, marble-columned windows, stalactite frieze and overhanging roof, is one of the finest things in the whole Alcázar. But it's probably better to look round the **Salón del Almirante** (or Casa de Contración de Indias), the sixteenth-century building on the right, before entering the main palace. Founded by Isabel in 1503, this gives you a standard against which to assess the Moorish forms. Here most of the rooms seem too heavy, their decoration ceasing to be an integral part of the design. The only notable exception is the **Sala de Audiencias** (or Capilla de los Navigantes, Chapel of the Navigators) with its magnificent *artesonado* ceiling inlaid with golden rosettes; within is a fine sixteenth-century *retablo* by Alejo Fernández depicting Columbus (in gold) and Carlos V (in a red cloak) sheltering beneath the Virgin. In the rear, to the left, are portrayed the kneeling figures of the Indians to whom the dubious blessings of Christianity had been brought by the Spanish conquest.

The **royal apartments**, known as the **Palacio Real Alto**, have now been opened for visits when not in use, and a temporary desk located in front of the Salón del Almirante sells tickets (€4) for a guided tour lasting about thirty minutes. This takes in the **royal chapel** with a fine early sixteenth-century *retablo* by Nicola Pisano, the so-called **bedroom of Pedro I**, with fine early Mudéjar plasterwork, and the equally splendid **Sala de Audiencias** – with more stunning plaster and tile decoration – which is still used by the royal family when receiving visitors in Seville.

Palacio de Pedro I

As you enter the main palace, the **Palacio de Pedro I**, the "domestic" nature of Moorish and Mudéjar architecture is immediately striking. This involves no loss of grandeur but simply a shift in scale: the apartments are remarkably small, shaped to human needs, and take their beauty from the exuberance of the decoration and the imaginative use of space and light. There is, too, a deliberate disorientation in the layout of the rooms, which makes the palace seem infinitely larger and more open than it really is. From the entrance court a narrow passage leads straight into the central courtyard, the **Patio de las Doncellas** (Patio of the Maidens), its name recalling the Christians' tribute of one hundred virgins presented annually to the Moorish kings. The heart of the patio has recently been restored to its fourteenth-century original state after having been buried under a tiled pavement for four centuries. Archeologists have replanted the six orange trees that once grew in sunken gardens to either side of a central pool. The pool is now filled with goldfish – as it was in the time of Pedro I – a medieval way of eliminating mosquitoes in summer. The court's stuccowork, *azulejos* and doors are all of the finest Granada craftsmanship. Interestingly, it's also the only part of the palace where Renaissance restorations are successfully fused – the double columns and upper storey were built by Carlos V, whose *Plus Ultra* ("yet still farther") motto recurs in the decorations here and elsewhere.

Past the **Salón de Carlos V**, distinguished by a superb ceiling, are three rooms from the original fourteenth-century design built for María de Padilla (who was popularly thought to use magic in order to maintain her hold over Pedro – and perhaps over other gallants at court, too, who used to drink her bath water). These open onto the **Salón de Embajadores** (Salon of the Ambassadors), the most brilliant room of the Alcázar, with a stupendous *media naranja* (half-orange) wooden dome of red, green and gold cells, and horseshoe arcades inspired by the great palace of Medina Azahara outside Córdoba. Although restored, for the worse, by Carlos V – who added balconies and an incongruous frieze of royal portraits to commemorate his marriage to Isabel of Portugal here – the salon stands comparison with the great rooms of Granada's Alhambra. Adjoining are a long dining hall (*comedor*) and a small apartment installed in the late sixteenth century for Felipe II.

Beyond is the last great room of the palace – the **Patio de las Muñecas** (Patio of the Dolls), which takes its curious name from two tiny faces decorating the inner side of one of the smaller arches. It's thought to be the site of the harem in the original palace. In this room, Pedro is reputed to have murdered his brother Don Fadrique in 1358; another of his royal guests, Abu Said of Granada, was murdered here for his jewels (one of which, an immense ruby that Pedro later gave to Edward, the "Black Prince", now figures in the British crown jewels). The upper storey of the court is a much later, nineteenth-century restoration. On the other sides of the patio are the **bedrooms** of Isabel and of her son Don Juan, and the arbitrarily named **Dormitorio del los Reyes Moros** (Bedroom of the Moorish Kings).

Palacio de Carlos V and the gardens

To the left of the main palace loom the large and soulless apartments of the **Palacio de Carlos V** – something of an endurance test, with endless tapestries (eighteenth-century copies of the sixteenth-century originals now in Madrid) and pink, orange or yellow paintwork. Their classical style asserts a different and inferior mood.

It's best to hurry through to the beautiful and rambling **Jardines de los Reales Alcázares** (gardens), the confused but enticing product of several eras, where you can take a well-earned rest from your exertions. Here you'll find the vaulted baths in which María de Padilla is supposed to have bathed (in reality, an auxiliary water supply for the palace), and the **Estanque de Mercurio** with a bronze figure of the messenger of the gods at its centre. This pool was specially constructed for Felipe V in 1733, who whiled away two solitary years at the Alcázar fishing here and preparing himself for death through religious flagellation. Just to the left of the pool a path beyond the Puerta de Marchena leads to a pleasant **cafetería** with a terrace overlooking the gardens. South of here towards the centre of the gardens there's an unusual and entertaining **maze** of myrtle bushes and, nearby, the **pavilion** (*pabellón*) **of Carlos V**, the only survivor of several he built for relaxation.

Plaza de España and Parque de María Luisa

Ten-minutes' walk to the south of the Alcázar, Plaza de España was laid out in 1929 for an ill-fated "Fair of the Americas". Both this and the adjoining Parque de María Luisa are among the most pleasant – and impressive – public spaces in Spain. En route you pass by the **Antigua Fábrica de Tabacos**, the city's old tobacco factory and the setting for Bizet's *Carmen*. Now part of the university, this massive structure was built in the 1750s and for a time was the largest building in Spain after El Escorial. At its peak in the following century, it was also the country's largest single employer, with a workforce of some four thousand women *cigarreras* – "a class in themselves," according to Richard Ford, who were forced to undergo "an ingeniously minute search on leaving their work, for they sometimes carry off the filthy weed in a manner her most Catholic majesty never dreamt of."

Plaza de España, beyond, was designed as the centrepiece of the Spanish Americas Fair, which was somewhat scuppered by the 1929 Wall Street crash. A vast semicircular complex, with its fountains, monumental stairways and mass of tile work, it would seem strange in most Spanish cities, but here it looks entirely natural, carrying on the tradition of civic display. At the fair, the plaza was used for the Spanish exhibit of industry and crafts, and around the crescent are *azulejo* scenes representing each of the provinces – an interesting record of the country at the tail end of a moneyed era.

Both *sevillanos* and tourists alike come to the plaza to potter about in the little boats rented out on its tiny strip of canal, or to hide from the sun and crowds amid the ornamental pools and walkways of the **Parque de María Luisa**. The park is designed, like the plaza, in a mix of 1920s Art Deco and mock-Mudéjar. Scattered about, and round its edge, are more buildings from the fair, some of them amazingly opulent. Towards the end of the park, the grandest mansions from the fair have been turned into **museums**. The farthest now houses the city's **Museo Arqueológico** (Tues 2.30–8.30pm, Wed–Sat 9am–8.30pm, Sun 9am–2.30pm; €1.50, free with EU passport), the most important archeology collection in Andalucía. The main exhibits include a hoard of prehistoric treasure found in the Seville suburb of Camas in 1958, as well as Roman mosaics and artefacts from nearby Italica and a unique Phoenician statuette of Astarte-Tanit, the virgin goddess once worshipped throughout the Mediterranean. Opposite, the fabulous-looking **Museo de Costumbres Populares** (Popular Arts Museum; same hours and entry) is often besieged by schoolkids but has interesting displays relating to traditional arts and crafts and the April *feria*.

Barrio Santa Cruz, the river and Triana

The **Barrio Santa Cruz** is very much in character with the city's romantic image, its streets narrow and tortuous to keep out the sun, the houses brilliantly whitewashed and barricaded with *rejas* (iron grilles), behind which girls once kept chaste evening rendezvous with their *novios*. Of the numerous mansions, by far the finest is the so-called **Casa de Pilatos** (daily 9am–7pm, Oct–Feb until 5.30pm; €5 ground floor only, both floors €8, Tues 1–5pm free), built by the Marqués de Tarifa on his return from a pilgrimage to Jerusalem in 1519 and popularly thought to have been in imitation of the house of Pontius Pilate. In fact, it's an interesting and harmonious mixture of Mudéjar, Gothic and Renaissance styles, featuring brilliant *azulejos*, a tremendous sixteenth-century stairway and one of the most elegant domestic patios in the city.

Patios are a feature of almost all the houses in Santa Cruz: they are often surprisingly large and in summer they become the principal family living room. One of the most beautiful is within the Baroque **Hospicio de los Venerables Sacerdotes** (daily 10am–2pm & 4–8pm; guided visits every 30min; €4.75), near the centre in a plaza of the same name – one of the few buildings in the *barrio* worth actively seeking out. The former hospice also displays some outstanding artworks including **sculptures** by Martínez Montañés and a painting of the *Last Supper* by Roelas, plus some wonderfully restored **frescoes** by Lucás Valdés and Valdés Leal as well as a recently acquired work, *Santa Rufina*, by Velázquez.

A few minutes' walk north of here lies the new **Museo del Baile Flamenco**, c/Manuel Rojas Marcos 3 (daily 9am–7pm; €10; ☎954 340 311, ⓦwww .museoflamenco.com), an innovative and entertaining museum dedicated to the history and evolution of this emblematic *andaluz* art form. Set up in collaboration with celebrated flamenco dancer Cristina Hoyos, the museum is interactive (and multilingual), employing the latest sound and image technology to familiarize visitors with the origins of flamenco and the range of dance styles or "*palos*", which can all be seen at the touch of a button.

Down by the **Río Guadalquivir** are pedal-boats for idling away the afternoons, and at night a surprising density of local couples. The main riverside landmark here is the twelve-sided **Torre del Oro**, built by the Almohads in 1220 as part of the Alcázar fortifications. It was connected to another small fort across the river by a chain that had to be broken by the Castilian fleet before their conquest of the city in 1248. The tower was later used as a repository for the gold brought back from the Americas – hence its name. It now houses a small **naval museum** (Tues–Fri 10am–2pm, Sat & Sun 11am–2pm; closed Aug; €1, free with EU passport). A couple of hundred metres upriver from the Torre del Oro lies the **Plaza de Toros de la Maestranza** (daily 9.30am–7pm, fight days until 3pm; €5), one of the top three bullrings in Spain and the setting for the tragic finale of Bizet's *Carmen*. Guided visits (in English) allow you to see the impressive interior and a museum documenting its history.

One block away, with its entry on c/Temprado, is the **Hospital de la Caridad** (Mon–Sat 9am–1.30pm & 3.30–7.30pm, Sun 9am–1pm; €5; ⓦwww .santa-caridad.org), founded in 1676 by Don Miguel de Mañara, the inspiration for Byron's *Don Juan*. According to the testimony of one of Don Miguel's friends, "there was no folly which he did not commit, no youthful indulgence into which he did not plunge … (until) what occurred to him in the street of the coffin." What occurred was that Don Miguel, returning from a reckless orgy, had a vision in which he was confronted by a funeral procession carrying his own corpse. He repented his past life, joined the Brotherhood of Charity (whose task was to bury the bodies of vagrants and criminals), and later set up this hospital for the relief of the dying and destitute, for which purpose it is still used. Don Miguel commissioned a series of eleven paintings by Murillo for the chapel; six remain, including a superlative image of *San Juan de Dios* for which Mañara himself posed as the model. Alongside them hang two *Triumph of Death* pictures by Valdés Leal. One, depicting a decomposing bishop being eaten by worms (beneath the scales of justice labelled *Ni más, Ni menos* – No More, No Less), is so powerfully repulsive that Murillo declared that "you have to hold your nose to look at it". The mood of both works may owe a lot to the vivid memory of the 1649 plague that killed almost half the population of the city.

Museo de Bellas Artes

North of the hospital, near the Plaza de Armas bus station, is one of Spain's most impressive art galleries, the **Museo de Bellas Artes** (Tues 2.30–8.30pm, Wed–Sat 9am–8.30pm, Sun 9am–2.30pm; €1.50, free with EU passport), housed in recently modernized premises in a beautiful former convent. The collection is frequently rotated, so not all the works mentioned here may be on show.

Among the highlights is a wonderful late fifteenth-century sculpture in painted terracotta in Room 1, *Lamentation over the Dead Christ*, by the Andalucian **Pedro Millán**, the founding father of the Seville school of sculpture. A marriage of Gothic and expressive naturalism, this style was the starting point for the outstanding seventeenth-century period of religious iconography in Seville. A later example, in Room 2, is a magnificent *San Jerónimo* by the Italian **Pietro Torrigiano**, who spent the latter years of his life in the city. Room 3 has a *retablo* of the *Redemption* (c.1562), with fine woodcarving by Juan Giralte, while a monumental *Last Supper* by Alonso Vázquez covers an end wall of Room 4.

Beyond a serene patio and cloister, Room 5 is located in the monastery's former church, where the recently restored paintings on the vault and dome by the eighteenth-century *sevillano*, Domingo Martínez, are spectacular. Here also is the nucleus of the collection: **Zurbarán**'s *Apotheosis of St Thomas Aquinas*, as well as a clutch of works by **Murillo** in the apse, crowned by the great *Immaculate Conception* – known as "*La Colosal*" to distinguish it from the other work here with the same name. In an alcove nearby you'll see the same artist's *Virgin and Child*; popularly known as *La Servilleta* because it was said to have been painted on a dinner napkin, the work is one of Murillo's greatest.

Upstairs, Room 6 (quadrated around the patio) displays works from the Baroque period, among which a moving *Santa Teresa* by **Ribera** – Spain's master of *tenebrismo* (darkness penetrated by light) – and a stark *Crucifixion* by Zurbarán stand out. Room 10 contains more imposing canvases by Zurbarán, including *St Hugo visiting the Carthusian Monks at Supper* and another almost sculptural *Crucifixion* to compare with the one in Room 6. Here also are sculptures by **Martínez Montañés**, the sixteenth-century "Andalucian Lysippus", whose early *St Dominic in Penitence* and *San Bruno* from his mature period display mastery of technique.

The collection ends with works from the Romantic and Modern eras. In Room 11, an austere late canvas by **Goya** of the octogenarian *Don José Duaso* compensates for some not terribly inspiring works accompanying it. In Room 12, Gonzalo Bilbao's *Las Cigarreras* is a vivid portrayal of the wretched life of women in the tobacco factory during the early years of the last century, while Room 13 has an evocative image of *Sevilla en Fiestas* dated 1915 by Gustavo Bacarisas and the monumental canvas by José Villegas Cordero, *La Muerte del Maestro*, depicting the death of a *torero*, which was purchased by the Junta de Andalucía in 1996. Finally, in Room 14 there's *Juan Centeño y su cuadrilla* by Huelvan artist Daniel Vásquez Díaz, who worked in Paris and was a friend of Picasso. This stirring image of the *torero* and his team provides an appropriately *andaluz* conclusion to a memorable museum.

Triana and La Cartuja

Over the river is the **Triana** *barrio*, scruffy, lively and well away from the tourist trails. This was once the heart of the city's *gitano* community and, more specifically, home of the great flamenco dynasties of Seville who were kicked out by developers early last century and are now scattered throughout the city. The *gitanos* lived in extended families in tiny, immaculate communal houses called *corrales* around courtyards glutted with flowers; today, only a handful remain intact. Triana is still, however, the starting point for the annual pilgrimage to El Rocío (end of May), when a myriad painted wagons leave town, drawn by oxen. It houses, too, the city's oldest working **ceramics factory**, Santa Ana, where the tiles, many still in the traditional, geometric Arabic designs, are hand-painted in the adjoining shop.

At Triana's northern edge lies **La Cartuja** (April–Sept Tues–Fri 10am–9pm, Sat 11am–9pm; Oct–March Mon–Fri 10am–8pm, Sat 11am–8pm, Sun 10am–3pm; €3, free on Tues with EU passport), a fourteenth-century former Carthusian monastery expensively restored as part of the Expo '92 World Fair. Part of the complex is now given over to the **Centro Andaluz de Arte Contemporáneo** (same hours and ticket as La Cartuja; ⓦ www.caac.es), which stages rotating exhibitions from a large and interesting collection of contemporary work by *andaluz* artists, including canvases by Antonio Rodríguez de Luna, Joaquín Peinado, Guillermo Pérez Villalta, José Guerrero and Daniel Vásquez Díaz. Two other galleries stage temporary exhibitions by international artists and photographers (see website for details).

The remnants of much of the **Expo '92 site** itself have been incorporated into the **Isla Mágica** (April–Nov daily 11am–7pm, closes later in summer; €27; evening-only tickets €19; reductions for kids; ⓦ www.islamagica.es), an amusement park based on the theme of sixteenth-century Spain, with water and rollercoaster rides, shows and period street animations (included in ticket price).

Outside the city: Itálica and around

The Roman ruins and remarkable mosaics of **Itálica** and the exceptional Gothic **Monasterio San Isidoro del Campo** lie some 9km to the north of Seville, just outside the village of **Santiponce**.

To get here by public transport, take a **bus** from the Plaza de Armas station (bay 34; every 30min, Sun every hour), a journey of about twenty minutes. The easiest way to see both monuments (noting the opening hours) is to ask the bus to drop you at the monastery stop ("*Parada Monasterio*") on the outward journey. You can then cover the 1.5km (15min walk or take a later bus) through Santiponce to the Itálica site entrance (from where buses return to the city).

Itálica and Santiponce

Itálica (April–Sept Tues–Sat 8.30am–8.30pm, Sun 10am–3pm; Oct–March Tues–Sat 9am–5.30pm, Sun 10am–4pm; €1.50, free with EU passport) was the birthplace of two emperors (Trajan and Hadrian) and one of the earliest Roman settlements in Spain, founded in 206 BC by Scipio Africanus as a home for his veterans. It rose to considerable military importance in the second and third centuries AD, was richly endowed during the reign of Hadrian (117–138) and declined as an urban centre only under the Visigoths, who preferred Seville, then known as *Hispalis*. Eventually, the city was deserted by the Moors after the river changed its course, disrupting the surrounding terrain.

Throughout the Middle Ages, the ruins were used as a source of stone for Seville, but somehow the shell of its enormous **amphitheatre** – the third largest in the Roman world – has survived. Today, it's crumbling perilously, but you can clearly detect the rows of seats, the corridors and the dens for wild beasts. Beyond, within a rambling and unkempt grid of **streets** and **villas**, about twenty **mosaics** have been uncovered. Most are complete, including excellent coloured floors depicting birds, Neptune and the seasons, and several fine black-and-white geometric patterns.

There's also a well-preserved **Roman theatre** in **SANTIPONCE** itself, signposted from the main road. Santiponce is not well endowed with facilities, but the *Ventarillo Canario* **restaurant** almost opposite the Itálica site entrance does good *platos combinados* and is famous for its grilled steaks served on wooden slabs with *papas arrugadas* – small baked potatoes in *mojo* spicy sauce.

Monasterio San Isidoro del Campo

A little over 1km to the south of Santiponce on the road back to Seville lies the former Cistercian **Monasterio San Isidoro del Campo** (Wed & Thurs 10am–2pm, Fri & Sat 10am–2pm & 5.30–8.30pm, Sun 10am–3pm; €2, Wed free). Closed for many years, it has now been painstakingly and gloriously restored and shouldn't be missed.

Founded by the thirteenth-century monarch Guzmán El Bueno of Tarifa, the monastery is a masterpiece of Gothic architecture, which, prior to its confiscation during the nineteenth-century Disentailment, was occupied by a number of religious orders. Among these were the *ermitaños jerónimos* (Hieronymites) who, in the fifteenth century, decorated the central cloister and the Patio de los Evangelistas with a remarkable series of **mural paintings** depicting images of the saints – including scenes from the life of San Jerónimo – as well as astonishingly beautiful floral and Mudéjar-influenced geometric designs. In the seventeenth century, the monastery employed the great *sevillano* sculptor Martínez Montañés to create the magnificent **retablo mayor** in the larger of the complex's twin churches.

Eating and drinking

Seville is packed with lively and enjoyable bars and restaurants, and you'll find somewhere to eat and drink at just about any hour. With few exceptions, anywhere around the major sights and the **Barrio Santa Cruz** will be expensive. The two most promising central areas are down **towards the bullring** and north of here towards the Plaza de Armas bus station. The **Plaza de Armas** area is slightly seedier but has the cheapest *comidas* this side of the river. Wander down c/Marqués de Paradas, and up c/Canalejas and c/San Eloy, and find out what's available. Across the river in **Triana**, c/Betis and c/Pureza are also good hunting grounds.

Barrio Santa Cruz and around the Catedral

La Albahaca Plaza Santa Cruz 29 ☎954 220 714. Charming traditional restaurant housed in a converted mansion where three intimate period rooms hung with paintings provide the ambience. Fairly expensive, but there's a *menú* for around €30. Closed Sun.

Bar Modesto c/Cano y Cueto. At the north end of Santa Cruz, this mid-priced bar-restaurant offers a tempting *menú* (€20) and great tapas. House specials include *punta de solomillo* (pork tenderloin) and *coquinas* (clams).

Café Rayuela c/Miguel de Mañara 9. Pleasant lunchtime venue serving value-for-money *raciones* and salads at outdoor tables in a pedestrianized street behind the *turismo*.

La Judería c/Cano y Cueto 13 ☎954 412 052. Solid mid-priced restaurant with a good-value daily *menú* for €20. *Revueltos* are a speciality here.

Kaede *Hotel Alfonso XIII*, c/San Fernando 2. In the gardens of the town's swishest address, this is an authentic and entertaining Japanese restaurant. Sushi and sashimi are included on a good-value *menú* for around €18.

Mesón del Pulpo c/Tomás Ibarra 10. Excellent little Galician restaurant popular with locals. Specializes (as the name implies) in *pulpo a la gallega* (octopus), and there's a decent *menú* for €12.

Pizzeria San Marco c/Mesón del Moro 4. Good, cheap Italian pasta and pizzas served inside a remarkable twelfth-century Moorish bathhouse.

Triana and the Río Guadalquivir

As-Sawïrah c/Galera 5. Superb Moroccan restaurant offering a variety of North African dishes including a delicate couscous and their house special *tajín de cordero con membrillos* (lamb with quinces). Lunch *menú* €12. Closed Sat eve & Sun.

Bar-Restaurante Casa Manolo c/San Jorge 16. Buzzing Triana bar-restaurant with tapas and *raciones* (or breakfast) in the bar or economical *platos combinados* in a dining room just off it.

El Faro de Triana Puente de Triana ☎954 331 251. Sitting atop the western end of the Puente de Triana (aka Puente de Isabel II), the dining room and roof terrace here give amazing river views.

Tapas at the bar and *raciones* at the tables consist of fish, meat and seafood.

Kiosko de las Flores c/Betis near to the *Río Grande*. One of Seville's best-loved fried-fish emporia on the riverside, with a delightful terrace; tapas are served in the bar and moderately priced *raciones* on the terrace – just the place on a summer night. Closed Mon.

La Primera del Puente c/Betis 66. The riverside terrace of the restaurant over the road has one of the city's best vistas; soft-talk a waiter to get a frontline table. You can enjoy low-priced, generous *raciones* or *media raciones* of fish, meat and seafood.

Río Grande c/Betis 70 ☎954 273 956. This mid-priced Triana restaurant has the best view in town from its terrace on the river's west bank facing the Torre del Oro, and is the ideal venue for a lunchtime feast of traditional meat and fish dishes. Their next-door tapas bar is also worth a visit. Mains €12–20.

La Sopa Boba c/Torneo 85 ☎954 379 784. Mid-priced, modern and attractive place with a creative approach; specials include *manzana con bacalao y cabrales* (cod with apples and goat's cheese). Closed Sun eve & Mon.

🏃 **Taberna El Alabardero** c/Zaragoza 20 ☎954 502 721. Elegant nineteenth-century *casa-palacio sevillana* with attractive decor and an upmarket clientele. Pricey – and outstanding – restaurant upstairs where the *menú de degustación* costs €60; however, a daily €17.50 lunchtime *menú* in the patio bar below comes from the same kitchen.

Centro, La Macarena, Alameda and Santa Justa

Habanita c/Golfo s/n, a small street off c/Pérez Galdos. Meat, fish and vegetarian dishes with a Caribbean slant are served up at this inexpensive diner; try their *yuca con salsa mojito* (sweet potato with spicy sauce) and *berenjenas Habanita* (aubergine house-style). Has a pleasant terrace.

Mesón Serranito Alfonso XII 9, behind the El Corte Inglés department store. Cosy little restaurant beyond a lively tapas bar out front, with excellent fish and meat dishes and a *menú* for €9.

Pando c/San Eloy 47. Lively, stylish tapas and *raciones* restaurant, which also does salads. An ideal lunch stop.

Restaurante Los Gallegos c/Capataz Franco. Friendly and inexpensive Galician restaurant in a tiny alley off c/Martín Villa, serving *gallego* specialities (try their *tarta de Santiago* dessert). *Menú* for €14.

Zarabanda c/Padre Tarín 6. Friendly little family restaurant cooking pizzas and traditional dishes to a high standard. Also does salads and is just the place for a lunch stop.

Bars

For casual eating and drinking and taking tapas – Seville's great speciality – there are **bars** all over town. The tapas venues all serve barrelled sherries from nearby Jerez and Sanlúcar (the locals drink the cold, dry *fino* with their tapas, especially *camarones*, or shrimps); a *tinto de verano* is the local version of *sangría* – wine with lemonade, a great summer drink.

Outside the centre, you'll find lively bars in the **Plaza Alfalfa** area, and across the river in **Triana** – particularly in and around c/Castilla and c/Betis. Over recent years, a zone that has emerged as a focus for artistic, student and gay barhoppers is the **Alameda** (de Hércules). In summer, much of the action emigrates to the bars along the **river's east bank** to the north of the Triana bridge as far as the spectacular Puente de la Barqueta, built for Expo '92. Many of these open for a season only, springing up the following year under a new name and ownership. Tapas bars tend to close around 9pm but many drinking bars keep going until well beyond midnight.

Barrio Santa Cruz and around the Catedral

Bar Europa Junction of c/Alcaicería de Loza and c/Siete Revueltas. Fine old watering hole with lots of cool tiled walls, plus excellent *manzanilla* and a variety of tapas served on marble-topped tables.

Bar Giralda c/Mateus Gagos 1. Excellent and popular bar in a converted ancient Moorish bathhouse, with a wide selection of tapas.

Casa Morales c/García de Vinuesa 11. Atmospheric traditional bar (founded 1850) with barrelled wine and a few *tablas* (tapas served on wooden boards).

Las Teresas c/Santa Teresa 2. Good beer and sherry served in this atmospheric bar with hanging cured hams and tiled walls lined with faded *corrida* photos. It's also worth stopping here for breakfast the morning after.

Taberna Coloniales II c/Fernandez y González 36. Offspring of the similarly named establishment in Plaza Cristo de Burgos, this is up to the same high standard. Tapas are served at the bar, but cornering a table will allow you to feast on a wide (and fair-priced) range including *solomillo al whisky* (pork loin); and they also let you round it off with coffee and *desserts de la casa.*

Triana and the Río Guadalquivir

Bar Anselma c/Pagés del Corro 49. Fine old place with a neo-Moorish facade owned by a *dueña* with many Rocío connections (every night at midnight the lights are dimmed and the Rocío hymn is sung). If you're lucky, you may just catch some of the best impromptu flamenco in town. House specials include *caldereta* (lamb stewed in *fino*), and *pisto* (stewed vegetables). Doesn't open till 11pm. Closed Sun.

Bar Bistec c/Pelay y Correa 34. Ancient and hearty Triana hostelry, with outdoor tables in summer. Specials include *cabrillas* (spicy snails), *codorniz en salsa* (quail) and *pan de mi pueblo* (cod *gazpacho*). Closed Wed.

El Capote c/Radio Sevilla off c/Arjona. Popular summer terrace bar with a varied clientele that gets younger as the night wears on. Sometimes has live music.

El Paseo c/Paseo de Colón 2. Small gay bar playing 1970s, 80s and 90s music.

Embarcadero c/Betis 69. Down a narrow passage to the side of the *Río Grande* restaurant, this is a great little *copas* bar with a riverside terrace and a stunning view towards the Torre del Oro and cathedral across the river. Daily 5pm until late.

Ritual c/José de Gálvez s/n, in La Cartuja. This Indian-inspired terrace is decorated with Hindu art and whimsical swings. You can cozy up in one of many secluded corners or do your moves to techno music on a dancefloor. A surprise here is a miniature model of Andalucía rescued from Expo '92.

Centro, La Macarena, Almeda and Santa Justa

Bar Eslava c/Eslava 3–5. Very good and extremely popular – which often means you can't get through the door – tapas bar with an outstanding, equally excellent restaurant attached.

Bulebar Alameda de Hércules 83. Lively *copas* bar that does good tapas and stays open late, with an outdoor plant-filled terrace looking onto the Alameda. They often stage theatre or other music shows.

🏃 **El Rinconcillo** c/Gerona 32. Seville's oldest bar (founded in 1670) does a fair tapas selection as well as providing a hang-out for the city's literati.

Sopa de Ganso ("Duck Soup") c/Pérez Galdos 8. Young, lively bar in one of the city's main nightlife zones. On offer are *tagarninas* (a pastie) and *pudín de verduras* (vegetable bake). Until midnight it operates as a tapas bar and – on the stroke of twelve – the illumination changes from orange to blue, the food stops and it becomes a late-night *copas* bar with cool sounds.

Nightlife

Seville is a wonderfully late-night city, and in summer and during fiestas, the streets around the central areas – particularly the Plaza de Alfalfa, Alameda de Hércules and Triana riverfront zones – are often packed out until the small hours.

Flamenco

Flamenco music and dance is on offer at dozens of places in the city, some of them extremely tacky and expensive. Unless you've heard otherwise, avoid the fixed "shows", or *tablaos* (many of which are a travesty, even using recorded music) – the spontaneous nature of flamenco makes it almost impossible to timetable into the two-shows-a-night cabaret demanded by impresarios. The nearest you'll get to the real thing is at *Los Gallos* (Ⓦ www.tablaolosgallos.com), on Plaza Santa Cruz, which has a professional cast. However, it's pricey (€30 incl. one drink), and you'd probably do just as well at *El Tamboril*, a renowned flamenco bar in the opposite corner of the same square. Singers and dancers aren't guaranteed to drop in (around midnight is best), but when they do, you're in for an unforgettable night.

Another excellent bar that often has spontaneous flamenco (try Thurs after 10pm) is *La Carbonería* at c/Levies 18. It used to be the coal merchants' building (hence the name) and is a large, simple and welcoming place. *Bar Quita Pesares*, on Plaza Jerónimo de Córdoba, is run by a flamenco singer, and is a chaotic place where there's often impromptu music, especially at weekends, when things get lively around midnight. The *Casa de la Memoria de Al-Andalus*, c/Jiménez de Enciso 28 (tickets must be booked in advance; ☎954 560 670), has concerts most nights and charges around €14 for entry, whilst regular concerts are also staged at the Museo del Baile Flamenco (see p.287).

Live music and clubs

For **rock and pop music**, the bars around Plaza Alfalfa and the Alameda de Hércules generally have the best action. Recommended music bars on the Alameda include *Bulebar* at Alameda de Hércules 83 and *Fun Club* at no. 86; the latter is a weekends-only (Thurs–Sat) music and dance bar with live bands. *Abril*, c/Luis Montoto 118 near Santa Justa, is the ultimate in chic, trendy *sevillano* nightlife and known for hosting international DJs. *Antique*, Avda. Matemáticos Rey Pastor y Castro s/n, near the south edge of the Isla Mágica theme park, is popular with Seville's smart set, comes with transparent dancefloor and plays Latin pop "early on", giving way to heavier stuff later (Thurs–Sat from midnight). South of here, *Boss*, c/Betis 67, is a cavernous disco that takes off after midnight and has a penchant for house. *Urbano Comix*, c/Matahacas 5, near the Convento de Santa Paula in La Macarena is a popular student bar with zany urban decor for rock, punk and R&B sounds plus live bands, staying open till dawn. *Buddha del Mar*, Plaza Legión 8, inside the Plaza de Armas shopping mall, is a three-storey Asian-fusion resto-lounge-*discoteca* where you can follow a meal by smoking a hookah on terrace loungers or take a drink in the *discoteca*.

Major **concerts**, whether touring international bands or big Spanish acts, often take place in one or other of the football stadiums, but more frequently these days in the Auditorio de La Cartuja across the river. La Teatral, c/Velázquez 12, near Plaza Duque de la Victoria (☎954 228 229), is the official ticket agent for many concerts, and tickets are also sold by the El Corte Inglés department store in Plaza Duque de la Victoria itself. Throughout the summer, the Alcázar, the Prado de San Sebastián gardens and other squares host occasional **free concerts**. Information on these and most of the above should be available from the *turismo*, the local press and the *El Giraldillo* listings magazine.

Listings

Airport For flight information, call ☎954 449 000.

Banks and currency exchange ATMs are located throughout the centre of town, including around Avda. de la Constitución and Plaza Duque de la Victoria. Bureaux de change can be found on Plaza Nueva.

Books and newspapers A wide range of books in English (and other languages) is stocked by Casa del Libro, c/Velázquez 8, just east of c/Sierpes. Vértice, c/San Fernando 33, near the Alcázar, is also good, and the Beta chain also stocks guides and maps: a central branch is at Avda. Constitución 20. El Corte Inglés, Plaza Duque de la Victoria, also stocks English titles as well as international press. A more comprehensive range of international newspapers is stocked by Esteban, c/Alemanes 15, next to the cathedral.

Bullfights The main *corridas* are staged during the April *feria*, but not regularly outside this month. Details and tickets from the Plaza de Toros (☎954 223 506) on fight days from 4.30pm or in advance (with commission) from the Impresa Pagés ticket office at c/Adriano 37.

Football Seville has two major *Primera Division* teams: Sevilla CF plays at the Sánchez Pizjuán stadium (☎954 535 353, ⓦ www.sevillafc.es) and Real Betis uses the Manuel Ruiz de Lopera stadium (☎902 191 907, ⓦ www.realbetisbalompie.es), in the southern suburbs. Match schedules are in the local or national press, and tickets are surprisingly easy to get hold of for many matches (check the stadium or *turismos*).

Hiking maps The excellent LTC, Avda. Menéndez Pelayo 42 in Santa Cruz (☎954 425 964), and Risko, Avda. Kansas City 26, close to Santa Justa train station (☎954 570 849), stock maps, and the latter has a wide range of outdoor equipment.

Hospital English-speaking doctors are available at Hospital Universitario Virgen Macarena, c/Dr Marañon s/n (☎955 008 000), behind the Andalucía parliament building to the north of the centre. For emergencies, dial ☎061.

Internet access Almost opposite the cathedral's main entrance, *Seville Internet Center*, c/Almirantazgo 2, on the first floor (daily 9am–10pm), is probably the most central location. An alternative is the cheaper *Ciberducke*, c/Trajano 8 (daily 10am–11pm).

Left luggage There are coin-operated lockers at the Santa Justa train station in a basement (to the right as you enter). There are *consignas* at the Prado de San Sebastián (daily 7am–10pm; €2 per day for a standard item), and Plaza de Armas (9am–1.30pm & 3.30–7pm) bus stations; note that the latter one is not inside the bus station but around the right side of the building where there are taxis.

Lost property Oficina de Objetos Perdidos, c/Manuel V. Sagastizabál 3, next to the Prado de San Sebastián bus station (Mon–Fri 9.30am–1.30pm; ☎954 420 403).

Markets Entertaining Sunday *mercadillos* (roughly 10am–2pm depending on weather) take place on Plaza del Cabildo opposite the cathedral (stamps, coins, pins, ancient artefacts), and on Plaza del Museo in front of the Museo de las Bellas Artes (various art, tiles and woodcarvings). Calle Feria's long-standing *El Jueves* (Thursday market) with secondhand articles and antiques, east of the Alameda de Hércules, is another good one.

Police Central local police stations are at c/Arenal 1 (☎954 590 558) and c/Credito 11 (☎954 378 496), off the north end of the Alameda de Hércules. Dial ☎092 (local police) or ☎091 (national) in an emergency.

Post office Avda. de la Constitución 32, by the cathedral; *Lista de Correos* (poste restante) Mon–Fri 8.30am–8.30pm, Sat 9.30am–2pm.

Taxis The main central ranks are in Plaza Nueva, the Alameda de Hércules and the Plaza de Armas and Prado de San Sebastián bus stations. The basic charge for a short journey is around €4. A reliable taxi service, Radio Taxi, will come and collect you if you ring them on ☎954 580 000.

The Sierra Morena

The longest of Spain's mountain ranges, the **Sierra Morena** extends almost the whole way across Andalucía – from Rosal on the Portuguese frontier to the dramatic pass of Despeñaperros, north of Linares. Its hill towns marked the northern boundary of the old Moorish Caliphate of Córdoba, and in many ways the region still signals a break, with a shift from the climate and mentality of the south to the bleak plains and villages of Extremadura and Castilla-La Mancha. The range is not widely known – with its highest point a mere 1110m, it's not a dramatic *sierra* – and even Andalucians can have trouble placing it.

Aracena and around

Some 90km northwest of Seville, **ARACENA** is the highest town in the Sierra Morena with sharp, clear air, all the more noticeable after the heat of the city. A substantial but pretty place, it rambles partly up the side of a hill topped by the **Iglesia del Castillo**, a Gothic-Mudéjar church built by the Knights Templar around the remains of a Moorish castle. The town is flanked to the south and west by a small offshoot of the Sierra Morena – the **Sierra de Aracena** – a wonderfully verdant corner of Andalucía with wooded hills and cobble-streeted villages.

Although the church is certainly worth the climb, Aracena's principal attraction is the **Gruta de las Maravillas** (daily 10.30am–1.30pm & 3.30–6pm; guided hourly visits, half-hourly at weekends; €7.70), the largest and arguably the most impressive cave in Spain. Supposedly discovered by a local boy in search of a lost pig, the cave is now illuminated and there are guided tours as soon as a couple of dozen or so people have assembled; to protect the cave there's now a strict limit of 35 persons per visit. At weekends and holiday periods, try to visit before noon – coach parties with advance bookings tend to fill up the afternoon allocation. On Sunday, there's a constant procession, but usually plenty of time to gaze and wonder. The cave is astonishingly beautiful, and funny, too – the last chamber of the tour is known as the Sala de los Culos (Room of the Buttocks), its walls and ceiling an outrageous, naturally sculpted exhibition, tinged in a pinkish orange light. Close by the cave's entrance are a couple of excellent **restaurants**, open lunchtime only (meaning until 4pm in Andalucía). Aracena is at the heart of a prestigious *jamón*-producing area, so try to sample some, and, when they're available, the delicious wild asparagus and local snails – in the fields in spring and summer, respectively.

Practicalities

Aracena's **turismo** is at the Gruta (daily 10am–1.30pm & 3.30–6pm; ☎959 128 206, ⓦwww.sierradearacena.net). The **bus station**, Avda. de Sevilla s/n, lies on the southeast side of town close to the Parque Municipal. The town's solitary **internet** café, *Servicio Informatica*, is on Calle Constitución, near the main Plaza Marqués de Aracena (Mon–Fri 10.30am–2pm & 5.30–9pm, Sat 11am–2pm).

There are limited **places to stay**, the best of which, at the bottom end of the scale, is *Casa Manolo*, below the main square at c/Barberos 6 (☎959 128 014; ❶). Alternatively, the *Hotel Sierra de Aracena*, Gran Vía 21 (☎955 126 175, ⓦwww .sierradearacena.es; ❸), offers relative luxury. There's also a **campsite** with pool (☎959 501 005; closed Oct–March), about 3km out along the Seville road, then left for 500m on the road towards Corteconcepción. For **meals**, the mid-priced ⚒ *Restaurante José Vicente*, Avda. Andalucía 51 (☎959 128 455), opposite the park, specializes in *jamón* and pork dishes, including a mouthwatering *solomillo* (pork loin); a recent addition here is an outstanding tapas bar. Good tapas and *platos*

Sierra Morena practicalities

The Morena's **climate** is mild – sunny in spring, hot but fresh in summer – but it can be very cold in the evenings and mornings. A good **time to visit** is between March and June, when the flowers, perhaps the most varied in the country, are at their best. You may get caught in the odd thunderstorm, but it's usually bright and hot enough to swim in the reservoirs or splash about in the clear springs and streams, all of which are good to drink. If your way takes you along a river, you'll be entertained by armies of frogs and turtles plopping into the water as you approach, by lizards, dragonflies, bees, hares and foxes peering discreetly from their holes – and, usually, no humans for miles round.

The locals maintain that, while the last bears disappeared only a short time ago, there are still a few wolves in remoter parts. Of more concern to trekkers, however, are the **fighting bulls**, since you are quite likely to come across them. They should always be in fenced-off pastures with explicit signs warning you to keep out (*toros bravos* or *peligros* are the words to look out for), but these often disappear or are not put up in the first place. Apparently, a group of bulls is less to be feared than a single one, and a single one only if he directly bars your way and looks mean. The thing to do, according to expert advice, is to stay calm, and without attracting the bull's attention, go round. If you even get a whiff of a fighting bull, though, it might well be best to adopt the time-honoured technique – drop everything and run.

Getting around
East–west **transport** in the *sierra* is very limited. Most of the bus services are radial and north–south, with Seville as the hub, and this leads to ridiculous situations where, for instance, to travel from Aracena to Cazalla de la Sierra, a distance of some 80km, you must take a bus to Seville, 70km away, and then another up to Cazalla – a full day's journey of nearly 150km. The best solution is to organize your routes round **treks**. A bicycle, too, could be useful, but your own car much less so – this is not Michelin car-window-view territory. If you have a **bike**, you'll need plenty of gears, while the roads round Almonaster, and between Cazalla and Constantina, are very bad for cycling.

Buses from Seville to the *sierra* leave from the Plaza de Armas station. If you just want to make a quick foray into the hills, **Aracena** is probably the best target (and the most regularly served town). If you're planning on some walking, it's also a good starting point: before you leave Seville, however, be sure to get yourself a decent **map** (see below) which, though it will probably be crammed with misleading information, should point you in the right direction to get lost somewhere interesting.

combinados are on offer at the more basic *Café-Bar Manzano*, at the southern end of Plaza Marqués de Aracena.

If you intend to do some **walking in the sierra**, you can get useful information (including maps and leaflets on flora and fauna) on the surrounding Parque Natural Sierra de Aracena y Picos de Aroche from an **information centre** in the ancient *cabildo* (town hall), Plaza Alta 5 (Tues–Sun 10am–2pm & 4–6pm, July & Aug 6–8pm). You should also ask at the Aracena *turismo* for the free *Senderos de la Sierra de Aracena y Picos de Aroche* map listing 23 waymarked routes, and they also sell a more detailed *Mapa Guía de la Sierra de Aracena y Picos de Aroche*. A good **hiking guide**, *Sierra de Aracena* by David & Ros Brawn (Discovery Walking Guides), details 27 clearly described walks in the *sierra* ranging between four and fourteen kilometres. An accompanying map for the book is sold separately, and all walks have GPS waypoints identifying key locations en route.

Villages around Aracena
Surrounding Aracena is a scattering of attractive but economically depressed villages, most of them dependent on the **jamón industry** and its curing factory

at Jabugo. *Jamón serrano* (mountain ham) is a *bocadillo* standard throughout Spain, and some of the best, *jamón de bellota* (acorn-fed ham), comes from the Morena, where herds of sleek grey pigs grazing beneath the trees are a constant feature. In October, the acorns drop and the pigs, waiting patiently below, gorge themselves, become fat and are promptly whisked off to be slaughtered and then cured in the dry mountain air.

The **sierra villages** – Jabugo, Aguafría, Almonaster La Real – all make rewarding bases for walks, though all are equally ill-served by public transport (details from the Aracena *turismo*). The most interesting is **ALMONASTER LA REAL**, whose castle encloses a tiny ninth-century mosque, **La Mezquita** (daily 9am–7pm; free), with what is said to be the oldest mihrab in Spain. Tacked onto the mosque is the village bullring, which sees action once a year in August during the annual fiesta. The village also has a couple of **places to eat and stay**: the very hospitable *Hostal La Cruz*, Plaza El Llano 8 (☏959 143 135; ❷), in the centre with a good restaurant, and *Hotel Casa García*, at the entrance to the village (☏955 143 109, ⓦwww.hotelcasagarcia.com; ❸), which also has a good restaurant, with great *jamón* and *ensaladilla*.

The Costa de la Luz

Stumbling on the villages along the **Costa de la Luz**, between Algeciras and Cádiz, is like entering a new land after the dreadfulness of the Costa del Sol. The journey west from Algeciras seems in itself a relief, the road climbing almost immediately into rolling green hills, offering fantastic views down to Gibraltar and across the Strait to the just-discernible white houses and tapering minarets of Moroccan villages. Beyond, the Rif Mountains hover mysteriously in the background, and on a clear day, as you approach **Tarifa**, you can distinguish Tangier on the edge of its crescent-shaped bay. Beyond Tarifa lies a string of excellent golden-sand beaches washed by Atlantic breakers and backed by a clutch of low-key resorts such as **Conil**. Inland, the haunting Moorish hill town of **Vejer de la Frontera** beckons, while set back from the sea at Bolonia is the ancient Roman settlement of **Baelo Claudia**.

Tarifa and around

TARIFA, spreading out beyond its Moorish walls, was until the mid-1980s a quiet village, known in Spain, if at all, for its abnormally high suicide rate – a result, it is said, of the unremitting winds that blow across the town and its environs. Today, it's a prosperous, popular and, at times, very crowded resort, following its discovery as Europe's prime **windsurfing** and **kitesurfing** spot. There are equipment-rental shops along the length of the main street, and regular competitions are held year-round. Development is moving ahead fast as a result of this new-found popularity, but for the time being it remains an attractive place for a stopover.

Arrival and information

At the northern end of town near the *gasolinera* (petrol station) you'll find the **bus station** (frequent services to Seville, Málaga, Cádiz and points in between), from where the main Algeciras–Cádiz road (c/Batalla del Salado) leads to the walled old town, a five- to ten-minute walk. Along here there's a supermarket, fried-fish and *churro* stalls, and windsurfing-equipment shops.

The welcoming **turismo**, on the central Paseo la Alameda (Mon–Fri 10am–2pm & 4–6pm, Oct–March 5–7pm, Sat & Sun 10am–2pm; ☏956 680 993,

@www.aytotarifa.com), can help with maps and accommodation. The independently run **websites** @www.tarifainfo.com and @www.tarifaweb.com are also useful sources of information. **Internet** access is available at *Ciber Pandor@*, c/Sancho IV El Bravo 5, fronting the church of San Mateo.

Accommodation

Tarifa has plenty of **places to stay**, though finding a bed in summer can often be a struggle, with crowds of windsurfers often packing out every available *hostal*. A little way out of town, there are plenty of **campsites** (see opposite).

Casa Facundo c/Batalla del Salado 47 ☎956 684 298, ©h.facundo@terra.es. Reliable *hostal* on the main road into town just outside the walls, offering en-suite rooms with TV. ❹

Hostal Africa c/María Antonia Toledo 12 ☎956 680 220, ©hostal_africa@hotmail .com. Charming, small *hostal* with clean and simple en-suite rooms and spectacular sea views from a communal terrace. ❷–❸

Hostal La Calzada c/Justina Pertiñez 7 ☎956 680 366. Popular and friendly *hostal* in the centre of the old town, close by the church of San Mateo, offering a/c en-suite rooms with TV. ❹

Hostal-Restaurante Villanueva Avda. Andalucía 11 ☎956 684 149. Welcoming and good-value *hostal*, with en-suite rooms and a good restaurant below (see opposite). ❸

Hotel Misiana c/Sancho IV El Bravo 18 ☎956 627 083, @www.misiana.com. Central, stylish place with arty decor whose rooms are decorated with modern art and Moroccan furnishings. ❺

The Town

If windsurfing is not your motive for visiting, there can still be an appeal in wandering the crumbling ramparts, gazing out to sea or down into the network of lanes that surround the fifteenth-century, Baroque-fronted church of **San Mateo** (daily 9am–1pm & 5.30–8.30pm; free), which has a beautiful late Gothic interior. Also worth a look is the **Castillo de Guzman** (Tues–Sun 11am–2pm & 5–7pm; €2), the site of many a struggle for this strategic foothold into Spain. It's named after Guzmán el Bueno (the Good), Tarifa's infamous commander during the Moorish siege of 1292, who earned his tag for a superlative piece of tragic drama. Guzmán's 9-year-old son had been taken hostage by a Spanish traitor, and surrender of the garrison was demanded as the price of the boy's life. Choosing "honour without a son, to a son with dishonour", Guzmán threw down his own dagger for the execution. The story – a famous piece of heroic resistance in Spain – had echoes in the Civil War siege of the Alcázar at Toledo, when the Nationalist commander defied similar threats, an echo much exploited for propaganda purposes.

Whale and dolphin-watching trips

A recent innovation in Tarifa is **whale- and dolphin-watching** excursions in the Strait of Gibraltar, which leave daily from the harbour. The trip is a fairly steep €30 (reductions for under-14s), but this includes another trip free of charge if there are no sightings. Places must be booked in advance from either of two non-profit-making organizations: **Whale Watch**, Avda. de la Constitución 6, close to the *turismo* (☎956 682 247, reservations ☎639 476 544, @www.whalewatchtarifa.com), and **FIRMM** (Foundation for Information and Research on Marine Mammals), c/Pedro Cortés 3, slightly west of the church of San Mateo (☎956 627 008, @www.firmm.org). A more commercial operation, **Turmares**, with an office on the beach road near the foot of the Paseo de la Alameda (☎956 680 741, @www.turmares.com), also runs whale-spotting trips (€27, kids €18) with a glass-bottomed boat.

Eating, drinking and nightlife

For **meals**, the restaurant of the *Hostal Villanueva*, specializing in *urta* (Cádiz sea bream), is a good bet, as is the pricier *Restaurante Alameda*, Paseo Alameda 4, near the *turismo*, which does a variety of *platos combinados* and has a pleasant terrace. Towards the church of San Mateo, one place definitely worth seeking out is ⚓ *Bar El Francés*, Paseo c/Sancho IV El Bravo 21, a highly popular French tapas and *raciones* bar adding a subtly Gallic touch to such staples as *calamares, rabo de toro* and *tortilla de camarones*. Another good place is the atmospheric *Mandragora*, c/Independencía 3, behind the church, offering dishes from both sides of the strait; as well as Moroccan couscous, it does excellent tapas (*raciones* only in the evenings), including *boquerones rellenos* (stuffed anchovies). Another interesting new arrival just outside the walls is ⚓ *Tarifa Eco Centre*, c/San Sebastián 4; this complex has an organic vegetarian restaurant (pasta, pizzas, quiches, *taboulé*, etc) out front, an eco-shop at the rear and a chill-out zone serving herbal and other teas to the side. Off a courtyard terrace, further rooms offer yoga and other courses.

Of the dozen or so **bars** dotted around the centre, the German-run *Bistro Point* on c/San Francisco is a windsurfers' hang-out and a good place for finding long-term accommodation, as well as secondhand windsurfing gear. *Bar Morilla*, c/Sancho IV El Bravo 2, facing San Mateo's main entrance, is a favourite meeting place with locals and a good breakfast and tapas stop. Apart from bars staging live music to keep the windsurfers happy, there's little in the way of entertainment beyond style **bars** such as that attached to the hotel *Misiana* and *Bamboo*, Paseo de la Alameda 2, plus a couple of *discotecas*. Tarifa's main summer **nightlife** scene happens when the town council erects *carpas* (disco tents) on the Playa de los Lances beach at the eastern end of town. It's also worth finding out what's happening at the *Tarifa Eco Centre* (ⓦ www.tarifaecocentre.com), as they stage frequent concerts and show films.

Tarifa Beach

Heading northwest from Tarifa, you find the most spectacular **beaches** of the whole of the Costa de la Luz – wide stretches of yellow or silvery-white sand, washed by some magical rollers. The same winds that have created such perfect conditions for windsurfing can, however, sometimes be a problem for more casual enjoyment, sandblasting those attempting to relax on towels or mats and whipping the water into whitecaps.

The beaches lie immediately west of town. They get better as you move past the tidal flats and the mosquito-ridden estuary – until the dunes start and the first camper vans lurk among the bushes. At **TARIFA BEACH**, a little bay 9km from town, there are restaurants, a windsurfing school, campsites and a string of pricey hotels, including the *Hurricane Hotel*, Ctra. Cádiz s/n (☎956 684 919, ⓦ www.hotelhurricane.com; ❺), set in dense gardens at the ocean's edge. A cluster of **beach campsites** fronts the strand, all signposted from the main road or accessible by walking along the coast. All of these – the main ones are *Río Jara* (☎956 680 570), *Tarifa* (☎956 684 778), *Torre de la Peña* (☎956 684 903) and *Paloma* (☎956 684 203) – are well equipped and inexpensive.

The coast west of Tarifa

Around the coast from the *Paloma* campsite are extensive ruins of the Roman town of **BOLONIA,** or *Baelo Claudia* as the Romans knew it, where you can make out the remains of three temples and a theatre, as well as a forum and numerous houses (Tues–Sun 10am–7pm, June–Sept until 8pm, Nov–Feb until 6pm; €1.50, free with EU passport). The site can be reached down a small side road that turns off the

▲ Kitesurfing near Tarifa

main Cádiz road 15km after Tarifa. There's also a fine **beach** here with bars and eating places and a few **places to stay**, including the excellent *Hostal La Hormiga Voladora*, c/El Lentiscal 15 (☎956 688 562; ❸), with garden rooms (some en suite) close to the beach. It's located at the eastern end of the village next to the *Panadería Beatriz*. Alternatively, it's a good walk along the coast from *Paloma*.

Vejer de la Frontera

While you're on the Costa de la Luz, be sure to take time to visit **VEJER DE LA FRONTERA**, a classically white, Moorish-looking hill town set in a cleft between great protective hills that rear high above the road from Tarifa to Cádiz. The drama of Vejer is in its isolation and elevated position, both easily appreciated from an approach road that winds upwards for a dizzying 4km. This eventually arrives at the Parque de los Remedios and a **car park**, which, given Vejer's tortuously narrow streets, one-way system and traffic congestion, you'd be strongly advised to make use of if you've arrived by car; this is also where the **bus** drops you. From here you'll need to ascend a further 300m along c/Los Remedios to reach La Plazuela, the effective centre of town.

Until the end of the twentieth century, the women of Vejer wore long, dark cloaks that veiled their faces like nuns' habits; despite being adopted as the town's tourist icon, this custom seems now to be virtually extinct, but the place has a remoteness and Moorish feel as explicit as anywhere in Spain. There's a castle and a church of curiously mixed styles (mainly Gothic and Mudéjar), but the main fascination lies in exploring the brilliant white and labyrinthine alleyways, wandering past iron-grilled windows, balconies and patios and slipping into a succession of bars.

Practicalities

There's a **turismo** in the Parque de los Remedios, Avda. de los Remedios 2 (April–Sept Mon–Fri 10am–2pm & 6–8pm, Sat 11am–1pm & 6–8pm, Sun 11am–1pm; Oct–March Mon–Fri 10am–2pm & 5–7pm, Sat 10am–2pm; ☎956 451 736, ⓦwww.turismovejer.com), which can provide a useful town map, accommodation list and information on the budget *casas particulares* nearby.

A good place to start looking for **accommodation** is at the delightful *Hotel Convento de San Francisco* on La Plazuela (☎956 451 001, ⓦwww.tugasa .com; ❸), where you can also get town maps if the *turismo* is closed; it's rather hidden away, so ask for directions. One of Vejer's most striking hotels is *La Casa del Califa*, Plaza de España 16 (☎956 447 730, ⓦwww.lacasadelcalifa.com; ❹), occupying a refurbished, rambling house, parts of which date back to Moorish times; the stylish rooms are decorated with Moroccan fittings and guests have use of two patios with fine views and a library. The price includes buffet breakfast, and *Rough Guide* readers with this guide can claim (at check-in) a ten-percent reduction. Not far away, *Casa Rural Leonor*, c/Rosario 25 (☎956 451 085, ⓦwww.casaleonor.com; ❷), is another possibility, offering pleasant en-suite rooms. Cheaper options are available at nos. 7 or 14 c/Filmo, around the corner from the *turismo*, where families let out rooms during the summer. Vejer's **campsite** lies below town on the main N340 Málaga to Cádiz road (☎956 450 098; closed Oct–May).

There are budget **places to eat** scattered all around the old town. Two slightly more upmarket places worth the extra are *El Refectorio*, the restaurant of the *Hotel Convento de San Francisco* (with a *menú* for €16.50), and *El Jardín del Califa*, the restaurant of *La Casa del Califa* (see above for both), where – in keeping with the house style – the kitchen offers Spanish-North African cuisine served on a tree-shaded courtyard terrace. A couple of the best **tapas bars** are *Mesón Pepe Julián*, c/Juan Relinque 7, just off La Plazuela, or, at the other end of town, *Bar Peneque* on Plaza de España, almost opposite *La Casa del Califa*.

Conil

Back on the coast, a dozen or so kilometres on, lies the increasingly popular resort of **CONIL**. Outside July and August, though, it's still a good place to

On to Morocco

Tarifa offers the tempting opportunity of a quick approach **to Morocco** – Tangier is feasible as a day-trip on a daily catamaran ferry (departs 11.30am & 6pm, Fri 7pm; returns 8.15am & 5.30pm; 40min; book a few days in advance), though an overnight stay would give you more time to look around, and might be a better way of justifying the price (€55 return). Note, too, that the return times are local (2hr behind Spanish time in summer, 1hr in winter). Tickets are available from FRS (Ferrys Rápido del Sur) at the Estación Maritimo building in the harbour (☎956 681 830, ⓦwww.frs.es), Viajes Marruecotur, Avda. Constitución 5, near the *turismo* (☎956 681 821, ⓔmcotur1 @mcotur1.e.telefonica.net; English spoken), or travel agents along c/Batalla del Salado. Catamaran-based one- or two-day **excursions** to Tangier are also available, starting at €56 for the one-day package, which includes a sightseeing tour, lunch and all transport. The two-day tour (€93) adds a night in a four-star hotel. Details of these and all other ferry information, including current timetables, are available from the helpful Viajes Marruecotur. This crossing is significantly more expensive than going from Algeciras (see p.264), but might be a better bet if the latter is chock-a-block, which usually happens in summer or when Moroccans are returning home for the two major Islamic festivals (which rotate between Jan, Feb & March).

ANDALUCÍA | The Costa de la Luz

relax, and in mid-season the only real drawback is trying to find a room. Conil town, once a poor fishing village, now seems entirely modern as you look back from the beach, though when you're actually in the streets you find many older buildings, too. The majority of the tourists are Spanish (with a lesser number of Germans), so there's an enjoyable atmosphere, and, if you are here in mid-season, a very lively nightlife.

The **beach**, Conil's *raison d'être*, is a wide bay of brilliant yellow stretching for many kilometres to either side of town and lapped by an amazingly, not to say disarmingly, gentle Atlantic – you have to walk halfway to Panama before it reaches waist height. The area immediately in front of town is the family beach; up to the northwest you can walk to some more sheltered coves, while across the river to the southeast is a topless and nudist area. Walking along the coast in this direction, the beach is virtually unbroken until it reaches the cape, the familiar-sounding **Cabo de Trafalgar**, off which Lord Nelson achieved victory and met his death on October 21, 1805. If the winds are blowing, this is one of the most sheltered beaches in the area. It can be reached by road, save for the last 400m across the sands to the rock.

Practicalities

Most **buses** use the Transportes Comes station on c/Carretera; walk towards the sea and you'll find yourself in the centre of town. There's a helpful **turismo** along the way at the junction of c/Carretera and c/Menéndez Pidal (May–Oct daily 8am–2pm & 5.30–8.30pm; Nov–April Mon–Sat 8am–2pm, Sun 8.30am–2pm; ☎956 440 501, ⓦwww.conil.org); it's worth picking up a copy of their useful free booklet *Conil en su Bolsillo*, which details all the town's tapas bars, restaurants and much more.

Accommodation needs are served by numerous hotels and *hostales*, augmented in high season by a multitude of private rooms for rent; full details on all of these are available from the *turismo*. The central *Hostal La Villa*, Plaza de España 6 (☎956 441 053; ❷), is one of the most reasonable options, and nearby is the even cheaper and more atmospheric *Pensión Los Hermanos*, c/Virgen 2 (☎956 440 196; ❷), Conil's oldest *fonda*. Near the Torre del Guzmán in the old quarter, *Hostal Santa Catalina*, c/Carcel 2, just off Plaza Santa Catalina (☎956 441 583, ⓦwww.hostalsantacatalina.webconil.com; ❸), is another decent place for air-conditioned rooms with TV. Conil also has a number of luxury hotels, the best value of which is the refurbished *Hotel Flamenco* on the Fuente del Gallo beach (☎956 440 711, ⓦwww.hipotels.com; B&B ❺), where well-appointed rooms have balcony terraces and sea views and features include two garden pools and steps down to a fine strand. **Campsites** include *Fuente del Gallo* in the nearby *urbanización*, Fuente del Gallo (☎956 440 137; closed Nov–Feb), a three-kilometre walk despite all signs to the contrary.

Seafood is king here and Conil has lots of good **restaurants** along the front; try the *ortiguillas* – deep-fried sea anemones – which you see only in the Cádiz area. Two of the best restaurants, *Francisco* and *La Fontanilla*, are to be found side by side on the Playa de la Fontanilla, the town's northernmost beach. During the summer, Conil's great **nightlife** attraction is *Las Carpas* ("the tents"), a huge triple entertainment complex on the central Playa de Los Bateles beach that caters for all ages and features techno, salsa, dance bands and flamenco shows, often all in action at the same time in the separate venues. The whole attraction is provided by the town council and, best of all, it's absolutely free.

Cádiz and around

CÁDIZ is among the oldest settlements in Spain, founded about 1100 BC by the Phoenicians and one of the country's principal ports ever since. Its greatest period, however, and the era from which the central part of town takes most of its present appearance, was the eighteenth century. Then, with the silting up of the river to Seville, the port enjoyed a virtual monopoly on the Spanish-American trade in gold and silver, and on its proceeds were built the cathedral – itself golden-domed (in colour at least) and almost oriental when seen from the sea – grand mansions, public buildings, dockyards, warehouses and the smaller churches.

Inner Cádiz, built on a peninsula-island, remains much as it must have looked in those days, with its grand, open squares, sailors' alleyways and high, turreted houses. Literally crumbling from the effect of the sea air on its soft limestone, it has a tremendous atmosphere – slightly seedy, definitely in decline, but still full of mystique.

Within easy reach of Cádiz are the pretty sherry towns of **El Puerto de Santa María** and, further north along the coast, **Sanlúcar de Barrameda**, which also provides an easy entry point into the wonderful Parque Nacional Coto de Doñana.

Arrival and information

Arriving by **train**, you'll find yourself on the periphery of the old town, close to Plaza de San Juan de Dios, busiest of the city's many squares. By **bus**, you'll arrive either at the Los Amarillos terminal between Plaza San Juan de Dios and the port (serving Rota, Chipiona and the resorts west of Cádiz) or on the north side of the port at the Autobuses Comes station on Plaza de la Hispanidad (used by buses from Seville, Tarifa and most other destinations toward Algeciras). Coming **by car**, you'll soon discover sea-locked Cádiz's acute lack of parking space, and if you don't want to spend an age searching you'd be best off taking accommodation with a garage (all the hotels will assist with parking) or heading for a car park – two of the most central inside the city walls are by the train station and along Paseo de Canalejas near the port.

There's a **turismo** on Avda. Ramón de Carranza (Mon–Fri 9am–7.30pm, Sat–Sun 9am–5pm; ☎956 203 191) near to Plaza San Juan de Dios; there's also a useful **turismo municipal** on the Paseo de Canalejas (Mon–Fri 8.30am–6pm & 4–8pm, Sat & Sun 10am–1.30pm & 4–7pm; ☎956 241 001). **Internet** access is available at *Novap Computers*, Cuesta de las Calesas 45 (daily 10am–11pm), and *Ciber Columela*, c/Columela 2 (daily 9am–10.30pm).

One way to get to grips with the city is to do an **open-top bus tour**; two competing companies do the same hop-on, hop-off clockwise route around the peninsula. Tour por Cádiz (10am–11pm; €10) and Cádiz Tour (10am–9pm; €12 with a slightly longer route) both have stops at or near Plaza San Juan de Dios, the cathedral, Parque Genoves, Playa de la Victoria and places in between. With Cádiz Tour, your ticket is valid for 24 hours from the time you board; Tour por Cádiz tickets are valid only on the day of purchase.

Accommodation

In tune with the city itself, much of Cádiz's budget **accommodation** has seen better days. Although things are slowly improving, there's still a shortage of good-quality accommodation in all categories. Radiating out from the Plaza

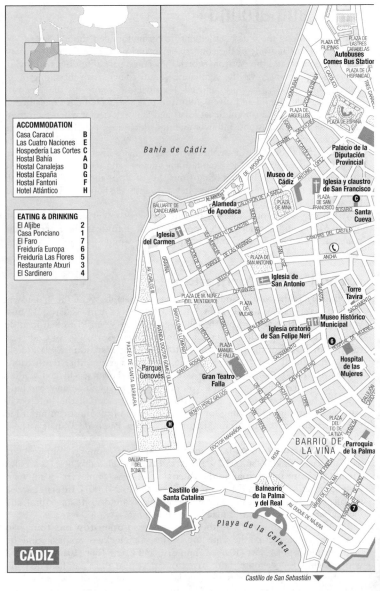

ACCOMMODATION
Casa Caracol	B
Las Cuatro Naciones	E
Hospedería Las Cortes	C
Hostal Bahía	A
Hostal Canalejas	D
Hostal España	D
Hostal Fantoni	F
Hotel Atlántico	H

EATING & DRINKING
El Aljibe	2
Casa Ponciano	1
El Faro	7
Freiduría Europa	6
Freiduría Las Flores	5
Restaurante Atxuri	3
El Sardinero	4

CÁDIZ

Castillo de San Sebastián ▼

San Juan de Dios is a dense network of alleyways crammed with **hostales** and **fondas** and a few less inviting options. More salubrious places to stay are to be found a couple of blocks away, towards the cathedral or Plaza de Candelaria.

🏃 **Casa Caracol** c/Suárez de Salazar 4 ☎956 261 166, ⊛www.caracolcasa.com. Friendly backpackers' place with dorm beds (€16 per person) in a large house near Plaza San Juan de Dios. Price includes breakfast, free internet access and use of kitchen. ②

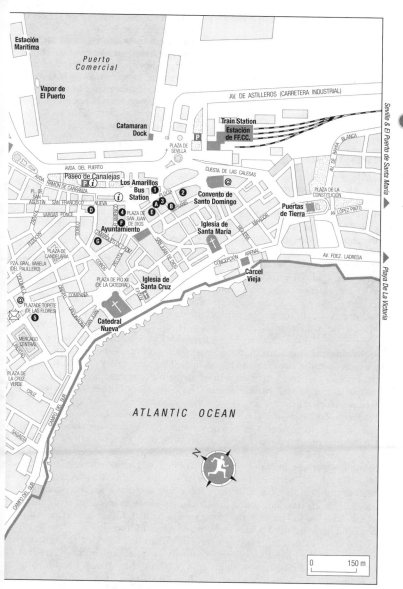

Las Cuatro Naciones c/Plocia 3 ☎956 255 539. Clean, unpretentious place with low-priced rooms, close to Plaza San Juan de Dios. ❷

Hospedería Las Cortes c/San Francisco 9 ☎956 212 668, ⓦwww.hotellascortes .com. Splendid newish hotel in a stylishly restored *casa señorial*. Elegant rooms have a/c and minibar

and come internet-connected. Facilities include sauna and gym, and there's a *cafetería* and restaurant. Can advise on parking. High-season price Aug only. ❺

Hostal Bahía c/Plocia 5 ☎956 259 061, ⓔhostalbahia@hostalbahia.info. Reasonable-value and conveniently located *hostal*, offering rooms with bath. Request their more attractive balcony rooms. ❹

Hostal Canalejas c/Cristóbal Colón 5 ☏ 956 264 113. Pleasant two-star *hostal* in completely restored town-house. En-suite rooms come with a/c and TV, and there's a pay car park nearby. Avoid the windowless interior rooms though. ❸

Hostal España Marqués de Cádiz 9 ☏ 956 285 500. Pleasant *hostal* inside a restored *casa palacio*

with reasonable rooms with fans (some en suite) ranged around a patio. ❷–❸

Hostal Fantoni c/Flamenco 5 ☏ 956 282 704. Good-value *hostal* in renovated town-house with lots of *azulejos* and cool marble, offering simple and en-suite rooms, the latter with a/c and TV. ❷–❹

Hotel Parador Atlántico Parque Genovés 9 ☏ 956 226 905, ⊛ www.paradores.es. Functional, if somewhat charmless, modern *parador* with Atlantic views and an outdoor pool. ❺

The Town

Unlike most other ports of its size, Cádiz seems immediately relaxed, easy-going and not at all threatening, even at night. Perhaps this is due to its reassuring shape and compactness, the presence of the sea, and the striking **sea fortifications** and waterside **alamedas** making it impossible to get lost for more than a few blocks. But it probably owes this tone as much to the town's tradition of liberalism and tolerance – one maintained through the years of Franco's dictatorship even though this was one of the first towns to fall to his forces, and was the port through which the Nationalist armies launched their invasion. In particular, Cádiz has always accepted its substantial gay community, who are much in evidence at the city's brilliant **Carnaval** celebrations.

Cádiz is more interesting for its general ambience – its blind alleys, cafés and backstreets – than for any particular buildings. As you wander, you'll find the **Museo de Cádiz**, at Plaza de Mina 5 (Tues 2.30–8.30pm, Wed–Sat 9am–8.30pm, Sun 9.30am–2.30pm; €1.50, free with EU passport), incorporating the **archeological museum** on the ground floor with many important finds and artefacts from the city's lengthy history, including two remarkable fifth-century BC Phoenician carved sarcophagi in white marble (one male, the other female), unique to the western Mediterranean. The upper floor houses the **Museo de Bellas Artes**. This contains a quite exceptional series of saints painted by Francisco Zurbarán, brought here from the Carthusian monastery at Jerez and one of only three such sets in the country (the others are at Seville and Guadalupe) preserved intact, or nearly so. With their sharply defined shadows and intense, introspective air, Zurbarán's saints are at once powerful and very Spanish – even the English figures such as Hugh of Lincoln, or the Carthusian John Houghton, martyred by Henry VIII when he refused to accept him as head of the English Church. Perhaps this is not surprising, for the artist spent much of his life travelling round the Carthusian monasteries of Spain and many of his saints are in fact portraits of the monks he met. Other important artists displayed here include Murillo, Rubens and Alonso Cano.

Even if you don't normally go for High Baroque, it's hard to resist the attraction of the huge and seriously crumbling eighteenth-century **Catedral Nueva** (Mon–Fri 10am–6.30pm & 4.30–7pm, Sat 10am–4.30pm, Sun 1–6.30pm; €5 including museum, free Tues–Fri 7–8pm), now coming to the end of a belated (and astronomically expensive) restoration. The cathedral is decorated entirely in stone, with no gold in sight, and in absolutely perfect proportions. In the crypt, you can see the tomb of Manuel de Falla, the great *gaditano* (as inhabitants of Cádiz are known) composer of such Andalucía-inspired works as *Nights in the Gardens of Spain* and *El Amor Brujo*. For a magnificent view over the city, you can also climb the **Torre de Poniente** (guided visits daily: June–Sept 10am–8pm; Oct–May 10am–6pm; €4), one of the cathedral's twin towers.

Over on the seaward side of the mammoth complex, the "old" cathedral, **Santa Cruz** (Tues–Sat 10am–2pm & 5–8pm, Sun 10am–2pm; free), was one of the buildings severely knocked about by the Earl of Essex during the English assault on Cádiz in 1596, causing the thirteenth-century church to be substantially rebuilt. A fine Gothic entry portal survived, and inside there's a magnificent seventeenth-century *retablo* with sculptures by Martínez Montañés. A first-century BC **Roman theatre** (daily 10am–2.30pm; free) has been excavated behind. To the north of the cathedral along c/Sacramento, the **Torre Tavira** (daily: June–Sept 10am–8pm; Oct–May 10am–6pm; €3.50), c/Marqués del Real Tesoro 10, is an eighteenth-century mansion with the tallest tower in the city, from where there are great **views** over the rooftops to the sea beyond; it also houses an entertaining **camera obscura**. Lastly, there are two churches of note for the paintings they contain. Foremost of these is the chapel of the **Hospital de las Mujeres** (Mon–Sat 10am–1.30pm; €0.80; ask the porter for admission), which has a brilliant **El Greco**, *St Francis in Ecstasy*. The other, an oval, eighteenth-century chapel, **Santa Cueva** (Tues–Fri 10am–1pm & 4.30–7.30pm, Sat & Sun 10am–1pm; €2.50), on c/Rosario, has three fine frescoes on Eucharistic themes by **Goya**.

Cádiz has two main **beaches** – the excellent **Playa de la Victoria** (and its less commercial continuation the Playa de la Cortadura), to the left of the promontory approaching town (reached from the centre on bus #1 from Plaza de España), and the often overcrowded **Playa de la Caleta** on the peninsula's western tip.

Eating and drinking

Takeaway **fried fish** was invented in Cádiz (despite English claims to the contrary), and there are numerous *freidurías* (fried-fish shops) around the town, as well as stands along the beach in season; few eating experiences here can beat strolling the city streets while dipping into a *cartucho* (paper funnel) of *pescado frito*. In the bars, *tortilla de camarones* (shrimp omelette) is another superb local speciality. Worth seeking out are the *Freiduría Las Flores* on the square of the same name and the nearby, equally good *Freiduría Europa*, c/Hospital de Mujeres 21.

Plaza San Juan de Dios has several cafés and inexpensive **restaurants**. On the square's west side, *Restaurante El Sardinero* is a traditional *gaditano* fish restaurant offering good-quality fish dishes served on a pleasant terrace, while nearby *Casa Ponciano*, c/Lazaro Dou, near the train station, is a lively bar-restaurant for tapas, fish and meat dishes; there's also a three-course *menú* for €7. Superior-quality fare is to be had at the very popular *Restaurante Atxuri*, c/Plocia 15, off the square's northern end (☎956 253 613; closed Mon–Wed & Sun eves), serving up excellent Basque and *andaluz*-inspired fish dishes in a smart new restaurant. When closed, the nearby *El Aljibe*, c/Plocia 25 (☎956 266 656; closed Sun eve), with its own tapas bar, is a good substitute.

For fish, you must also visit tiny **Plaza Tío de la Tiza**, in the old fishing quarter near Playa de la Caleta beach, which has dozens of good seafood places, with outdoor tables filling the surrounding streets (particularly c/Virgen de la Palma) in summer. The more upmarket *El Faro*, c/San Félix 15, nearby, is one of the best fish restaurants in Andalucía – their weekday €20 *menú* is very good value – with an equally outstanding tapas bar attached.

El Puerto de Santa María

Just 10km across the bay, **EL PUERTO DE SANTA MARÍA** is the obvious choice for a day-trip from Cádiz, a traditional family resort for both *gaditanos* and *sevillanos* – many of whom have built villas and chalets along the fine **Playa**

Puntillo. This strand is a little way out from town (10–15min walk or local bus ride), a pleasant place to while away an afternoon; there are friendly beach bars where for ridiculously little you can nurse a litre of *sangría* (bring your own food). In the town itself, the principal attraction is a series of **sherry bodegas** – long, whitewashed warehouses flanking the streets and the banks of the river. Until the train was extended to Cádiz, all shipments of sherry from Jerez came through Santa María, and its port is still used to some extent. Many of the firms offer tours and tastings to visitors – the most worthwhile tours are offered by two of the town's major producers, Osborne & Duff Gordon, c/Los Moros 7 (visits: in English Mon–Fri 10.30am; in Spanish Mon–Fri 11am & midday; ☎956 869 100; €6; booking required), and Fernando de Terry, c/Santísima Trinidad 2 (Mon–Thurs 10.30am–12.30pm; €8; Fri guided visit, including stables 11am; €15; ☎956 857 780), situated in a beautiful, converted, seventeenth-century convent. The *turismo* can provide details of visits to smaller *bodegas*.

The **ferry** from Cádiz (known locally as *El Vapor*, alluding to the earlier steamboats) is quicker and cheaper than the bus at €3 one way (€4 return); the forty-minute trip across the bay departs from the Estación Marítima at 10am, noon, 2pm, 6.30pm and 8.30pm (summer only), returning to Cádiz at 9am, 11am, 1pm, 3.30pm, 5.30pm and 7.30pm (summer only), with extra sailings in season according to demand (especially in the evening). A faster **catamaran** service (roughly hourly; ☎902 450 550; €1.95 one way) leaves from the Muelle Reina Victoria jetty near the train station. El Puerto's helpful **turismo** is situated close to the ferry quay at c/Luna 22 (daily 10am–2pm, May–Sept also 6–8pm; ☎956 542 413, ⓦwww.turismoelpuerto.com) and can provide a useful town map plus a complete accommodation list. **Internet** access is available at *Ciber Rapido*, c/Ricardo Alcon 12, to the north of the centre (Mon–Sat 10am–10pm, Sun 4–10pm).

There are plenty of **places to stay** – decent budget options include the pleasant *Hostal Loreto*, c/Ganado 17 (☎956 542 410; ❷), and the welcoming *Pensión Santa María*, c/Pedro Muñoz Seco 38 (☎956 857 525; ❶); both are close to the *turismo* and have rooms with and without bath. A good upmarket choice is *Hotel Santa María*, Avda. Bajamar s/n (☎956 873 211, ⓦwww .hotelsantamaria.es; ❺), with air-conditioned rooms fronting the river (where there's a convenient car park) and a rooftop pool. Bus #2 from the Plaza de las Galeras Reales (ferry quay) goes to the **campsite** at Playa Las Dunas (☎956 872 210), near the beach with plenty of shade.

Close by and a little upstream from the centre you'll also find some excellent seafood **restaurants**, including the justly famous and great fun ⚒ *Romerijo*, c/Ribera del Marisco, one of the most popular *marisquerías* in town, where you can buy your choice of shellfish in a *cartucho* (paper funnel) and eat it on their terrace with a beer. The same outfit has a *freiduría* bar-restaurant over the road from here where a generous *frito variado* (assorted fried fish) easily serves two. A delightful, if slightly more upmarket, alternative is *La Solera*, c/Ganado 17, next to the *Hostal Loreto*, a quality restaurant with fair-priced dishes such as *brocheta de rape con langostinos* (skewer-grilled monkfish) and a delicious *peras al rioja* (pears in wine) dessert, with a lunch *menú* for €7.50 (lunch) or €11.75 (dinner).

Sanlúcar de Barrameda

Like Santa María, **SANLÚCAR DE BARRAMEDA**, 15km to the northwest, also has its sherry connections. Nine kilometres east of Chipiona and set at the mouth of the Guadalquivir, it's the main depot for **manzanilla** wine, a pale, dry variety much in evidence in the bars, which you can also sample during visits to the town's **bodegas**. *Bodega Antonio Barbadillo*, near the castle at c/Sevilla 25 (visits in English Tues–Sat 11am; €3; ☎956 385 500, ⓦwww.barbadillo.com), the town's major producer, is the most interesting; a list of other *bodegas* is available from the *turismo* (see below). Sanlúcar is also the setting for some exciting **horse races** along the beach in the first and third weeks of August (check with the *turismo* for exact dates), the best time to be here.

There's not a great deal to see, although the attractive old quarter in the upper town, or **Barrio Alto**, is worth taking time to explore. The town's port was the scene of a number of important maritime exploits: Magellan set out from here to circumnavigate the globe; Pizarro embarked to conquer Peru; and 4km upriver, from the fishing harbour of Bonanza, Columbus sailed on his third voyage to the Americas. The few buildings of interest are all located in the Barrio Alto, reached by following the Cuesta de Belén from the lower town. The most significant is the magnificent sixteenth- to eighteenth-century ducal palace of **Medina Sidonia** (visits Sun 11am & noon; €3; book in advance ☎956 360 161, ⓦwww.fcmedinasidonia.com), stuffed with paintings by Spanish masters, including Goya. Nearby, the **Palacio de Orleáns y Borbón** (Mon–Fri 10am–1.30pm; free), built by the dukes of Montpensier and decorated in a wild neo-Mudéjar style, is also worth a look, as is the thirteenth-century church of **Nuestro Señora de la O** (Tues–Sat 10am–1pm, Sun 10am–noon; also open for daily Mass at 8pm or can be visited on a *turismo* tour) with its fine Gothic-Mudéjar portal and *artesonado* ceiling within. Just along the c/Eguilaz from here, the newly renovated Moorish **Castillo de Santiago** (Tues–Sat 11am–1pm; €5, kids €3) has guided visits enabling you to see the castle's barbicans, Plaza de Armas and towers with stunning views.

One of the best things about Sanlúcar is its shell-encrusted **river beach** and warm waters, a couple of kilometres' walk from the town centre and usually quite deserted. This is flanked, on the opposite shore, by the beginnings of the **Parque Nacional Coto de Doñana**, whose vast marshy expanses (strictly regulated access) signal the end of the coast road to the west. Visits to the park from Sanlúcar are now possible with a boat cruise, which, while it doesn't allow for serious exploration, is nevertheless a wonderful introduction to this remarkable area. The trip lasts approximately four hours and allows two short guided walks inside the park to spot wildlife. The *Real Fernando* – which has a *cafetería* on board – leaves daily from the Bajo de Guía quay (Mon–Sat June–Sept 10am & 5pm; March, April, May & Oct daily 10am & 4pm; Nov–Feb daily 10am; €16.20, under-12s half-price; booking essential on ☎956 363 813, ⓦwww.visitasdonana.com). Tickets should be collected (at least 30min before sailing) from the Fábrica de Hielo, Bajo de Guía s/n, the national park's **exhibition centre** (daily 9am–8pm) opposite the *Real Fernando*'s jetty. Also note that binoculars are pretty essential, and, while they can be hired on board, having your own is a distinct advantage.

Practicalities

The helpful **turismo** is at Calzada del Ejército (April–Sept Mon–Fri 10am–2pm & 6–8pm, Sat & Sun 10am–2pm; rest of year Mon–Fri only; ☎956 366 110, ⓦwww.turismosanlucar.com), on the avenue leading to the river estuary. They can provide a good town map, and also offer a guided walking **tour of the town** in English and Spanish (Thurs 10.30am; €3), which includes a *bodega* visit.

Accommodation is limited. For central budget options try the basic but clean *Pensión Blanca Paloma*, Plaza San Roque 9 (☎956 363 644, ⓔhostalblancapaloma @msn.com; ❶), or *Pensión Bohemia* c/Don Claudio 5 (☎956 369 599; ❷). Moving upmarket, the new *Hotel Barrameda*, c/Ancha 10, just off the main square (☎956 385 878, ⓦwww.hotelbarrameda.com; ❹), is very comfortable, while in the Barrio Alto, the charming ⚐ *Posada de Palacio*, c/Caballeros 11

(☎956 364 840, ⊛www.posadadepalacio.com; ➎), is housed in an elegantly converted eighteenth-century *casa palacio* with attractive rooms, delightful patio and rooftop terraces. For **eating and drinking**, you shouldn't miss the central 🍴 *Casa Balbino*, Plaza del Cabildo 11, one of the best tapas bars in Andalucía and famed for their *tortillita de camarones* (shrimp in batter). For more elaborate fare, head to the Bajo de Guía – a river beach backed by a line of great seafood restaurants. You can take a taxi or walk there by continuing past the *turismo* to the end of the Calzada del Ejército and turning right (or east) when you hit the river, about 1km from the town centre. 🍴 *El Bigote* and 🍴 *Mirador de Doñana* are outstanding – serving up some of the finest seafood in the region.

Jerez de la Frontera

JEREZ DE LA FRONTERA, 30km inland towards Seville, is the home and heartland of sherry (itself an English corruption of the town's Moorish name – *Xerez*) and also, less known but equally important, of Spanish brandy. An elegant and prosperous town, it's a tempting place to stop, arrayed as it is round the scores of wine *bodegas*, with plenty of sights to visit in between.

Life is lived at a fairly sedate pace for most of the year here, although things liven up considerably when Jerez launches into one or other of its two big **festivals** – the May Horse Fair (perhaps the most snooty of the Andalucian *ferias*), or the celebration of the vintage towards the end of September.

Arrival and information

The **turismo** is attached to the Covento de Santo Domingo (June–Sept Mon–Fri 10am–3pm & 5–7pm, Sat & Sun 10am–2.30pm; Oct–May Mon–Fri 9.30am–3pm & 4.30–6.30pm, Sat & Sun 9.30am–2.30pm; ☎956 341 711, ⊛www.turismojerez.com) and reached by following the pedestrianized main street, c/Larga, north from the centre; it's well stocked with information about the town and the area and can supply a detailed town map.

The **train** and **bus** stations are next door to each other, eight blocks (10min walk) east of the town's central square, Plaza del Arenal. Coming **by car**, you'll meet the familiar problem of finding a place to park; to avoid being clamped or towed, use the pay car parks signed in the centre or park farther out and walk in. Arriving at Jerez **airport** (7km out of town on the NIV; ☎956 150 083), there are daily buses to the centre between 6.30am and 9.45pm (€0.90) with a less frequent service from the bus station in the reverse direction. A taxi from the airport costs approximately €12–15. **Internet** access is available a little to the northwest of Plaza del Arenal at *Ciber Jerez*, c/Santa María 3, near the market (Mon–Sat 10am–10.30pm, Sun 5–10.30pm).

Accommodation

There's usually no problem finding **rooms** in Jerez except during April and May, when Semana Santa, the Festival de Jerez, the World Motorcycle Championship (held at the town's Formula 1 racing circuit) and the Fería del Caballo (May Horse Fair) come one after the other and fill the town to bursting point.

Albergue Juvenil Avda. Blas Infante 30 ☎856 814 001. Good-value hostel, with a pool, but out in the suburbs; take bus #9 from outside the bus station. Under-26 €14, over-26 €18.

Hostal Las Palomas c/Higueras 17 ☎956 343 773, ⊛www.hostal-las-palomas.com. The most central budget option, with clean and simple rooms, some en suite. ➊

Hotel Al Andalus Jerez c/Arcos 29 ☏956 323 400, Ⓦwww.alandalusjerez.com. Comfortable hotel with two pretty patios. Recently refurbished rooms – the better ones lie off the inner patio – are equipped with a/c and TV, and garage too. ❸

Hotel El Ancla c/Mamelón 15 ☏956 321 297, Ⓦwww.helancla.com. Welcoming and good-value place, fronting the upper end of the Alameda Cristina on the north side of the centre. Some rooms overlooking the noisy street (not so at night) are compensated for by views of square and fountains. ❸

Hotel Chancilleria c/Chancilleria 21 in the Barrio de Santiago ☏956 301 038, Ⓦwww.hotelchancilleria.com. Delightful new hotel with excellent rooms equipped with CD and DVD players, plus there's a very good restaurant and a fine roof terrace to take breakfast. B&B ❹

AP Hotel-Hostal San Andrés c/Morenos 12 ☏956 340 983, Ⓦwww.hotelsanandres.info. Excellent and friendly hotel-hostal offering both en suite and rooms sharing bath, with a charming patio below. ❶–❷

The Town

Jerez is famous throughout Spain for a long and distinguished **flamenco** tradition, and if you're interested in finding out more about Andalucía's great folk art, then a visit to the **Centro Andaluz de Flamenco**, Plaza de San Juan (Mon–Fri 9am–2pm; free; Ⓦwww.caf.cica.es), in the atmospheric *gitano* quarter, the Barrio de Santiago, is a must. There's an audiovisual introduction to *El Arte Flamenco* (hourly on the half hour), plus videos of past greats and information on flamenco venues in the town.

The **tours of the sherry and brandy processes** can be interesting – almost as much as the sampling that follows – and, provided you don't arrive in August when much of the industry closes down, there are a great many firms and *bodegas* to choose from. The visits are conducted either in English (very much the second language of the sherry world) or a combination of English and Spanish and last for about an hour. Jerez's "big two" are **González Byass**, c/Manuel González s/n (daily except Sun afternoon 11.30am, 12.30pm, 1.30pm, 2pm, 3.30pm, 4.30pm, 5.30pm; €10 with wine tasting; ☏902 440 077, Ⓦwww.bodegastiopepe.com), makers of the famous *Tío Pepe* brand, and the neighbouring **Pedro Domecq**, c/San Ildefonso 3 (reservation required; Mon–Fri 4 visits on the hour 10am–1pm, Tues & Thurs extra visit at 2pm, Sat noon & 2pm; €8; ☏956 151 500, Ⓦwww.bodegasfundadorpedrodomecq.com), producers of La Ina; besides manufacturing sherry, both *bodegas* are also major brandy producers. Many of these firms were founded by British Catholic refugees, barred from careers at home by the sixteenth-century Supremacy Act, and even now they form a kind of Anglo-Andalucian tweed-wearing, polo-playing aristocracy (on display, most conspicuously, at the Horse Fair). The González cellars – the *soleras* – are perhaps the oldest in Jerez and, though it's no longer used, preserve an old circular chamber designed by Eiffel (of the tower fame). If you feel you need comparisons, you can pick up a list of locations and opening times of the other *bodegas* from the *turismo*.

The most attractive of the town's buildings – including the imposing Gothic-Renaissance **Catedral de San Salvador** (Mon–Sat 11am–1pm & 6.30–8pm, Sun 11am–1.30pm; free) and the impressive eleventh-century Moorish **Alcázar** (May–Sept Mon–Sat 10am–8pm, Sun 10am–3pm; Oct–April daily 10am–6pm; €3 or €5.40 including *camera obscura*) next to the González *bodega* – are within a couple of minutes' walk of central Plaza del Arenal. An excellent **Archeological Museum** (June–Aug Tues–Sun 10am–2.30pm; Sept–May Tues–Fri 10am–2pm & 4–7pm, Sat & Sun 10am–2.30pm; €3) lies five minutes north of the centre in the Plaza del Mercado on the edge of the Barrio de Santiago; star exhibits include a seventh-century BC Greek military helmet, a Visigothic sarcophagus and a fine caliphal bottle vase. Evidence of Jerez's great enthusiasm for horses can be seen at the **Real Escuela Andaluz del Arte Ecuestre** (Royal Andalucian School of Equestrian Art), Avda. Duque de Abrantes s/n, which offers the chance to watch them performing to music (Tues & Thurs noon, plus July 15–Oct 15 Fri noon; €18–24; information & reservations ☎956 318 008, ⓦwww.realescuela.org). Training, rehearsals (without music) and visits to the stables take place on other weekdays (10am–1pm; €10).

Eating and drinking

There are tapas bars and **eating places** all over the central zone; one of the best tapas venues is *Juanito*, c/Pescadería Vieja 4 (off the west side of Plaza del Arenal), and, close to the Covento de Santo Domingo, *Bar El Poema* is another excellent place on Plaza Rafael Rivero, an atmospheric square that it shares with three other bars. More upmarket options include *La Carbona*, c/San Francisco de Paula 2, slightly northwest of the bus station, where in a wonderfully cavernous room (actually an old *bodega*) they serve up delicious charcoal-grilled fish and meat dishes; in the same street, the excellent mid-priced *Bodegon El Patio* c/San Francisco de Paula 7, is also worth a try as is the neighbouring *Mesón Restaurante Alcazaba* at no. 6 with a more economical menu (mains under €10) and *menús* for €8 and €11. Finally, *Restaurante Gaitán*, c/Gaitán 3 (closed Sun), slightly northwest of the Covento de Santo Domingo, is one of the best places in town specializing in Basque and *andaluz* dishes.

Huelva province

The **province of Huelva** stretches between Seville and Portugal, but aside from its scenic section of the Sierra Morena to the north and a chain of fine **beaches** to the west of the provincial capital, it's a pretty dull part of Andalucía, laced with large areas of swamp – the *marismas* – and notorious for mosquitoes. This distinctive habitat is, however, particularly suited to a great variety of wildlife, especially birds, and over 60,000 acres of the delta of the Río Guadalquivir (the largest roadless area in western Europe) have been fenced off to form the **Parque Nacional Coto de Doñana**. Here, amid sand dunes, pine woods, marshes and freshwater lagoons, live scores of flamingos, along with rare birds of prey, thirty pairs of the endangered Spanish lynx, mongooses and a startling variety of migratory birds.

Parque Nacional Coto de Doñana

The seasonal pattern of its delta waters, which flood in winter and then drop in the spring, leaving rich deposits of silt, raised sandbanks and islands, gives **Coto de Doñana** its uniqueness. Conditions are perfect in winter for ducks and geese, but spring is more exciting; the exposed mud draws hundreds of flocks of breeding birds. In the marshes and amid the cork-oak forests behind, you've a good chance of seeing squacco herons, black-winged stilts, whiskered terns, pratincoles and sand grouse, as well as flamingos, egrets and vultures. There are, too, occasional sightings of the Spanish imperial eagle, now reduced to a score of breeding pairs. Conditions are not so good in late summer and early autumn, when the *marismas* dry out and support far less bird life.

The park, however, is under threat from development. Even at current levels the drain on the water supply is severe, and made worse by **pollution** of the Guadalquivir by farming pesticides, Seville's industry and Huelva's mines. The

Fiestas

It's hard to beat the experience of arriving in some small
Spanish village, expecting no more than a bed for the night,
to discover the streets decked out with flags and streamers,
a band playing in the plaza and the entire population out
celebrating the local fiesta. Everywhere in Spain, from the
tiniest hamlet to the great cities, devotes at least a couple of
days a year to its festivals. Usually, it's the local saint's day
or some event in the church calendar, such as **Semana Santa**
(Holy Week), but there are also fiestas celebrating deliverance
from the Moors, safe return from the sea – any excuse will do.

Cofradías, Seville ▲

Hooded penitent ▼

Semana Santa

Semana Santa is celebrated throughout Spain with processions of *pasos*, huge floats carrying statues of Christ or the Virgin and borne by hooded penitents. The most spectacular processions are staged in Andalucía, especially Málaga, Granada, Córdoba and, above all, Seville, where the last lap of the official route for every *paso* goes from La Campana south along c/Sierpes – the most awe-inspiring venue – through the cathedral and around the Giralda and the Bishop's Palace.

Each town has a number of brotherhoods, or *cofradías*, and each processes with its own float – the Virgin draped in beautiful robes and decked in valuable jewels, and the whole glittering *paso* adorned with flowers – usually accompanied by several hundred penitents.

La salida, the moment when the *paso* emerges from the church, is an occasion of great emotion and attracts huge crowds. The floats weigh up to two tons and can only be carried for a short distance before the *costaleros* – the men who are carrying the *paso* – have to rest.

The climax of Semana Santa takes place during the early hours of Good Friday, when the candlelit floats depicting the Crucifixion leave their churches at midnight and move through the darkened streets watched by sombre crowds and followed by a band playing traditional dirges. In Seville, the image of Christ on the Cross is accompanied by the most important of the city's virgins, *La Macarena*. As she nears the cathedral, individuals will often step out in front of the *paso* and erupt into an impromptu lament delivered in flamenco style. When it's over, there's a ripple of applause and the *paso* moves on.

La Macarena paso, Seville ▼

Feria de Abril

Held in Seville barely two weeks after Semana Santa, the **Feria de Abril** is the country's largest fair – a week-long, nonstop celebration in which locals dress up in traditional costume, the women in vibrantly coloured gypsy dresses.

During the day, they parade around the fairground in carriages or on horseback, an incredible extravaganza with subtle but distinct gradations of dress and style. Bullfights are held daily in the Maestranza bullring, with big-name *matadores* performing in some of the best line-ups of the season.

In the evenings (and most of the night), thousands throng the *casetas* – canvas pavilions or tents of varying size set up along the banks of the Río Guadalquivir – to eat, drink sherry and dance *sevillanas* (a variation of flamenco).

▲ Horsemen, Feria de Abril

▼ Traditional dress at Feria de Abril

Fiesta de San Fermín

The **Fiesta de San Fermín** is held in Pamplona from midday on July 6 until midnight on July 14. The main event, memorably evoked in Hemingway's *The Sun Also Rises*, is the *encierro*, or Running of the Bulls, when six bulls are released from a pen at one end of the city and run through the streets to the bullring, accompanied by hundreds of locals and tourists, hardy enough to test their daring against the bulls. Despite the very real dangers (each year there is at least one serious injury, sometimes a fatal one), it's an undeniably thrilling spectacle, usually all over in two to three chaotic minutes.

See p.490 for more information.

▼ The Running of the Bulls

A falla ▲

Falleros ▼

Las Fallas

From March 12 to 19, around the saint's day of San José, Valencia erupts in a blaze of colour and noise for the **Fiesta de las Fallas**. During the year, each *barrio* or neighbourhood builds a satirical caricature or *falla*, some as tall as buildings. These begin to appear in the plazas at the beginning of March and are judged and awarded prizes before being set alight at midnight on March 19, the Nit de Foc – traditionally, carpenters celebrated the beginning of spring by decorating torches (*foc* in Valenciano) they used over winter and adding them to a ritual bonfire. The *fallas* are ignited in succession, the last to go up being the prizewinners. Each *falla* has a small model or *ninot* beside it, usually created by the children of the *barrio*. These are exhibited in La Lonja before the fiesta begins, and the best added to the Museu Faller; the rest are burned with the *fallas*.

During the fiesta, processions of *falleros*, dressed in traditional costume and accompanied by bands, carry flowers to the Plaza de la Virgen, where they are massed to create the skirt of a huge statue of La Virgen. The daily Las Mascaletas firecracker display takes place at 2pm in the Plaza del Ayuntamiento – when the whole city races to the central square for a ten-minute series of body-shuddering explosions. There are also nightly fireworks, bullfights, paella contests in the streets and *chocolate y buñuelos* stalls. Finally, around 1am on March 19, the *falla* of the Plaza del Ayuntamiento goes up in flames, set off by a string of firecrackers, followed by the last thunderous firework display of the fiesta.

Visiting Parque Nacional Coto de Doñana

Visiting Doñana involves (perhaps understandably) a certain amount of frustration. At present, it's open only to a **boat cruise** from Sanlúcar (see p.309) and to brief, organized **tours** (April–Sept daily 8.30am & 5pm; Oct–March Tues–Sun 8.30am & 3pm; €25) by all-terrain 24-seater buses – four hours at a time along one of five charted, eighty-kilometre routes. The starting point for these, and the place to book them (essential, and as far ahead as possible in high season), is at the Centro de Recepción de Acebuche, 4km north of Matalascañas towards El Rocío and Almonte (daily 9am–8pm; ☎959 439 627, English spoken; ⊛www.parquenacionaldonana .com), or at the Cooperativa Marismas del Rocío, Plaza del Acebuchal 16, El Rocío (☎959 430 432). The tours are quite tourist-oriented and point out only spectacular species such as flamingos, imperial eagles, deer and wild boar (binoculars are pretty essential). If you're a serious ornithologist, enquire instead at the *centro* about organizing a private group tour. There are excellent birdwatching **hides** (daily 8am–8pm) at the El Acebuche, La Rocina and El Acebron reception centres, as well as a 1.5-kilometre footpath from El Acebuche, which creates a mini-trek through typical *cotos*, or terrains, to be found in the reserve. Although binoculars are on hire, they sometimes run out, and you're advised to bring your own. All three centres have exhibitions and displays covering the species to be seen in the park and the history of human activity within its boundaries.

seemingly inevitable disaster finally occurred in 1998 when an upriver mining dam used for storing toxic waste burst, unleashing millions of litres of pollutants into the Guadiamar, which flows through the park. The noxious tide was stopped just 2km from the park's boundary, but catastrophic damage was done to surrounding farmland, with nesting birds decimated and fish poisoned. What is even more worrying is that the mining dams have not been removed (the mines are a major local employer) but merely repaired.

Equally disturbing are the proposals for a huge new tourist centre to be known as the Costa Doñana, on the very fringes of the park. Campaigning by national and international environmental bodies resulted in this project being shelved, but the threat remains, much of the pressure stemming from local people who see much-needed jobs in this or similar proposals.

Matalascañas

Birds and other wildlife apart, the resort settlement of **MATALASCAÑAS** on the park's coastal edge is utterly characterless, with its large hotel complexes and a concrete shopping centre. The **beach**, it must be said though, is attractive and you're allowed to use the strand inside the national park, too: you enter by a gate at the eastern end of the seafront and can walk along the sand (but not into the park proper) with plenty of opportunities for birdwatching; no vehicles or camping are allowed.

In summer, the few *hostal* rooms are generally booked solid and you'll probably end up camping – either unofficially at the resort itself, or at the vast *Camping Rocío Playa*, 1.5km down the road towards Huelva (☎959 430 238). This site is a little inconvenient without your own transport if you're planning to take regular trips into the Doñana zone, but if you just want a beach, it's not a bad option. Playa Doñana and its continuation Playa Mazagón (with another campsite, *Doñana Playa* ☎959 536 281) are fine strands stretching the whole distance to Huelva, and with hardly another foreign tourist in sight. This route is covered by three daily buses in both directions in summer, with a less frequent service the rest of the year.

El Rocío

Set on the northwestern tip of the *marismas*, **EL ROCÍO** is a tiny village of white cottages and a church stockade where perhaps the most famous pilgrimage-fair of the south takes place annually at Pentecost. This, the **Romería del Rocío**, is an extraordinary spectacle, with whole village communities and local "brotherhoods" from Huelva, Seville and even Málaga converging in lavishly decorated ox carts and on horseback. Throughout the procession, which climaxes on the Saturday evening, there is dancing and partying, while by the time the carts arrive at El Rocío they've been joined by busloads of pilgrims swelling numbers in recent years to close on half a million. The fair commemorates the miracle of Nuestra Señora del Rocío (Our Lady of the Dew), a statue found – so it is said – on this spot and resistant to all attempts to move it elsewhere. The image, credited with all kinds of magic and fertility powers, is paraded before the faithful early on the Sunday morning.

In spring, as far as **birdwatching** goes, the town is probably the best base in the area. The adjacent *marismas* and pine woods are teeming with birds, and following tracks east and southeast of El Rocío, along the edge of the reserve itself, you'll see many species (up to a hundred if you're lucky). It's a nice **place to stay**, with wide, sandy streets, cowboy-hatted horseriding farmers and a frontier-like feeling, and prices for most of the year are reasonable; however, don't even think about getting a room during the *romería* as they not only cost over ten times normal prices, but are booked up years ahead. Worth a try in quieter times are the pleasant *Hostal Isidro*, Avda. los Ansares 59 (℡959 442 242; **❸**), and the more central *Hostal Cristina*, c/Real 32 (℡959 406 513; **❷**), with en-suite rooms and its own restaurant. Moving up a notch in price, there's a choice between the inviting ⅍ *Hotel Toruño*, Plaza Acebuchal 22 (℡959 442 323, ⓦwww.toruno.es; B&B **❹**), with *marismas* views, and the mammoth complex of apartments and rooms at the *Hotel Rocío de Doñana*, Avda. Canaliega 1 (℡959 442 575, ⓦwww.rociodonana.com; **❹**), at the entrance to the town.

Huelva and the coast to Portugal

Large, sprawling and industrialized, **HUELVA** is the least attractive and least interesting of Andalucía's provincial capitals. It has claims as a "flamenco capital", but unless you're really devoted it's unlikely you'll want to stop long enough to verify this. By day – and in the evening as well – the most enticing thing to do is to head 21km south via an impressive road bridge spanning the marshlands of the Río Odiel estuary, now designated the Paraje Natural Marismas del Odiel, an important wildlife sanctuary, to **Punta Umbría**, the local resort. This is hardly an over-inspiring place either, but it does at least have some life, a fair beach, numerous *hostales* and seafood restaurants and a campsite. One trip well worth doing by bus or with your own transport is along the Columbus Trail: a clutch of locations associated with the fifteenth-century **voyages of Christopher Columbus**.

The Columbus Trail

Across the Río Tinto estuary from Huelva, the monastery of La Rábida and the villages of Palos and Moguer are all places connected with the voyages of Columbus (*Cristóbal Colón* in Spanish) to the New World. Frequent buses from Huelva's main bus station at Avda. Dr Rubio s/n (℡959 256 900) link all three places, and both Palos and Moguer have accommodation. **La Rábida** (Tues–Sat guided tours hourly 10am–1pm & 4–7pm, Sun 10.45am–1pm & 4–7pm; €3; ⓦwww.monasteriodelarabida.com), 8km from Huelva and easily reached by bus, is a charming and tranquil fourteenth-century Franciscan monastery whose fifteenth-century abbot was instrumental in securing funds for the voyage from the monarchs Fernando and Isabel.

Nearby, on the estuary, the **Muelle de la Carabelas** (Harbour of the Caravels; June–Sept Tues–Fri 10am–2pm & 5–9pm, Sat & Sun 11am–8pm; Oct–May Tues–Sun 10am–7pm; €3.40) has impressive full-size replicas of the three caravels that made the epic voyage to the New World, and an adjoining museum features a replica geography book annotated in Columbus's own surprisingly delicate hand among its displays. At **Palos**, 4km to the north, is the church of **San Jorge** (Mon–Fri 10am–noon & 6–7.30pm) where, in August 1492, Columbus and his crew heard Mass before setting sail from the now silted-up harbour. Should you want to stay, the welcoming *Cafetería Pensión Rábida*, c/Rábida 9 (℡959 350 163; ❷), is a good bet for economical en-suite rooms and serves tapas and *platos combinados* in its *cafetería*. A further 8km north, at the whitewashed town of **MOGUER**, is the fourteenth-century **Convent of Santa Clara** (hourly guided tours Tues–Sat 11am–7pm; €2), in whose church Columbus spent a whole night in prayer as thanksgiving for his safe return. The small town is a beautiful place, the birthplace of the Nobel prize-winning poet Juan Ramón Jiménez (1881–1958), and boasts a scaled-down, whiter version of Seville's Giralda attached to the church of **Nuestra Señora de la Granada**. If you want to stay overnight, head for the delightful *Hostal Pedro Alonso Niño*, c/Pedro Alonso Niño 13 (℡959 372 392; ❶), with excellent-value en-suite rooms. One bar worth seeking out is *Mesón El Lobito* at c/La Rábida 31, which is in a league of its own when it comes to decor: the smoke-blackened walls covered with graffiti are only the start of it; it also sells wine at crazy prices (€0.20 per glass) and does decent fish and meat dishes *a la brasa*.

West to Portugal

From Huelva it's best either to press on inland to the Sierra Morena or straight **along the coast to Portugal**. There are a number of good beaches and some low-key resorts noted for their seafood, such as **Isla Cristina**, along the stretch of coastline between Huelva and the frontier town of **Ayamonte**, but not much more to detain you. A good bus service along this route and a new road suspension bridge across the Río Guadiana estuary and border, linking Ayamonte and **Vila Real de Santo Antonio** in Portugal, make for a relatively painless crossing of the country border. From this approach, a good first night's target in Portugal is **Tavira**, on the Algarve train line. Note that Portugal is an hour behind Spain throughout the year.

Seville to Córdoba

The direct route from **Seville to Córdoba**, 135km along the valley of Guadalquivir, followed by the train and some of the buses, is a flat and rather unexciting journey. There's far more to see following the route just to the south of this, via **Carmona** and **Écija**, both interesting towns, and more still if you detour further south to take in **Osuna** as well. There are plenty of buses along these roads, making travel between the villages easy. Overnighting, too, is possible, with plenty of places to stay – although Carmona is an easy day-trip from Seville.

Carmona

Set on a low hill overlooking a fertile plain, **CARMONA** is a small, picturesque town made recognizable by the fifteenth-century tower of the Iglesia de San Pedro, built in imitation of the Giralda. The tower is the first thing you catch sight of and it sets the tone for the place – an appropriate one, since the town shares a similar history to Seville, less than 30km distant. It was an important Roman city (from which era it preserves a fascinating subterranean necropolis), and under the Moors was often governed by a brother of the Sevillen ruler. Later, Pedro the Cruel built a palace within its castle, which he used as a "provincial" royal residence.

Arrival and information

Buses from Seville stop on the central Paseo del Estatuto in sight of the landmark Moorish Puerta de Sevilla; if you're arriving **by car**, your best bet is to use the reasonably priced **car park** beneath the Paseo de Estatuto. The Puerta de Sevilla also houses an efficient **turismo** (Mon–Sat 10am–6pm, Sun 10am–3pm; ☎954 190 955, ⓦwww.turismo.carmona.org), which is well stocked with information and can provide a town map and guide to Carmona's tapas bars.

Accommodation

Budget **accommodation** is limited: the best bet is *Pensión El Comercio* (☎954 140 018; ❸), built into the Puerta de Sevilla gateway, with air-conditioned en-suite rooms, or the nearby *Hotel San Pedro*, c/San Pedro 17 (☎954 190 087; ❸), close to the church of the same name. An attractive new arrival in the old town is the *Hospedería Palacio Marques de las Torres*, c/Fermín Molpeceres 2 (☎954 196 248, ⓦwww.hospederiamarquesdelastorres.com; ❸–❹), a converted eighteenth-century *palacio* where in addition to pleasant en-suite doubles there are dormitories divided into two- and four-bed partitioned cubicles (€23 per bed) sharing bath. *Parador Alcázar del Rey Don Pedro*, in the ruins of the palace (☎954 141 010, ⓦwww.parador.es; ❻), is Carmona's most atmospheric upmarket hotel, and even if you don't stay it's worth calling at the bar for a drink to enjoy the fabulous views from its terrace.

The Town

The **Iglesia de San Pedro** (Mon & Thurs–Sun 11am–2pm plus Wed–Mon service at 8.30pm; €1.20) is a good place to start exploring the town; it dominates Carmona's main thoroughfare, c/San Pedro, and has a splendid Baroque *sagrario* (sacristy) within. From the nearby Paseo del Estatuto, looking east, you get a view of the magnificent Moorish **Puerta de Sevilla**, a grand, fortified Roman gateway (with substantial Carthaginian and Moorish elements) to the old town; it now houses the *turismo*, which organizes guided tours of the gate's upper ramparts (Mon–Sat 10am–6pm, Sun 10am–3pm; €2, Mon free). The **old town** is circled by 4km of ancient walls, inside which narrow streets wind up past Mudéjar churches and Renaissance mansions. Follow c/Prim uphill to **Plaza San Fernando** (or Plaza Mayor), modest in size but dominated by splendid Moorish-style buildings. Behind it there's a bustling fruit and vegetable **market** most mornings.

Close by, to the east, is **Santa María la Mayor** (Mon–Sat 9am–2pm & 5.30–7.30pm, Sat 10am–2pm, closed second half Aug; €3), a fine Gothic church built over the former main mosque, whose elegant patio it retains; like many of Carmona's churches, it is capped by a Mudéjar tower, possibly utilizing part of the old minaret. Slightly east of here and housed in the graceful eighteenth-century Casa del Marqués de las Torres is the **Museo de la Ciudad** (Mon 11am–2pm, Tues–Sun 11am–7pm; €2, Tues free), documenting the history of the town with mildly interesting displays of artefacts from the prehistoric, Iberian, Carthaginian, Roman, Moorish and Christian epochs. Dominating the ridge of the town are the massive ruins of **Pedro's Alcázar**, destroyed by an earthquake in 1504 and now taken over by a remarkably tasteful *parador*. To the left, beyond and below, the town comes to an abrupt and romantic halt at the Roman **Puerta de Córdoba**, from where the ancient Córdoba road (once the mighty Via Augusta heading north to Zaragoza and Gaul, now a dirt track) drops down to a vast plain.

The extraordinary **Roman necropolis** (guided tours only, English spoken: Tues–Fri 9am–6pm, Sat & Sun 9.30am–2.30pm; €2, free with EU passport) lies on a low hill at the opposite end of Carmona; walking out of town from San Pedro, take c/Enmedio, the middle street (parallel to the main Seville road) of three that leave the western end of Paseo del Estatuto and follow this for about 450m. Here, amid the cypress trees, more than nine hundred family tombs dating from the second century BC to the fourth century AD can be found. Enclosed in subterranean chambers hewn from the rock, the tombs are often frescoed and contain a series of niches in which many of the funeral urns remain intact. Some of the larger tombs have vestibules with stone benches for funeral banquets, and several retain carved family emblems (one is of an elephant, perhaps symbolic of long life). Most spectacular is the **Tumba de Servilia** – a huge colonnaded temple with vaulted side chambers. Opposite the site is a partly excavated **amphitheatre**.

Eating and drinking

Both the new and old towns have plenty of places for **eating and drinking**; in the old town, the cheapest places are the tapas bars on c/Prim, off the west side of Plaza de San Fernando: the excellent *Bar Goya*, with a pleasant terrace, and *El Tapeo*, almost opposite, are two worth seeking out (the latter also offers a good-value *menú* for €10). For more elaborate fare, 🌟 *Molino de la Romera*, c/Pedro s/n, near the *parador*, serves up tasty regional dishes, has a great terrace view across the plain and offers an excellent-value *menú* for around €18 (including wine). The restaurant of the *parador* is also outstanding, with a *menú* (€34) that includes many local dishes; they also offer vegetarian and diabetic *menús*, a laudable initiative.

Écija

Lying midway between Seville and Córdoba in a basin of low sandy hills, **ÉCIJA** is known, with no hint of exaggeration, as *la sartenilla de Andalucía* ("the frying pan of Andalucía"). In mid-August, it's so hot that the only possible strategy is to slink from one tiny shaded plaza to another, or with a burst of energy to make for the riverbank.

The heat is worth enduring, since this is one of the most distinctive and individual towns of the south, with eleven superb, decaying church towers, each glistening with brilliantly coloured tiles. It has a unique domestic architecture, too – a flamboyant style of twisted and florid forms, best displayed on c/Castellar, where the magnificent painted and curved frontage of the huge **Palacio de Peñaflor** (interior currently closed; enquire at the *turismo*) runs along the length of the street; the building has a fine patio and until recently housed Écija's public library. Other sights not to be missed are the beautiful polychromatic tower of the church of **Santa María**, overshadowing the main Plaza de España, and the **Palacio de Benamejí**, a stunning eighteenth-century palace on c/Castillo, south of Plaza de España, with a beautiful interior patio, now declared a national monument. This building houses the town museum, the **Museo Historico Municipal** (June–Sept Tues–Sun 10am–2.30pm; Oct– May Tues–Sat 10am–1.30pm & 4.30–6.30pm, Sun 10am–2pm; free), displaying archeological finds from all periods, with a particularly interesting section on

Astigi's (the town's Roman name) role in the olive-oil trade. One sensational recent addition is the **Amazona de Écija**, a stunning, two-metre high, almost totally intact first-century AD Roman statue discovered in the 2002 excavations of Plaza de España, depicting an Amazon resting against a pillar.

The town's focal **Plaza Mayor** (Plaza de España) was a building site for seven years during the construction of a subterranean car park, a work held up by archeologists who demanded time to investigate the area (which was the centre of both the Moorish and Roman towns). Following this upheaval, the revamped square has been turned into a rather desolate and controversial modern architectural eyesore jarring with the Baroque splendours surrounding it. A **Roman bath** discovered in the course of these works – just one of many archeological discoveries – can now be viewed from a walkway in the plaza's southeast corner.

Practicalities

Overlooking Plaza de España, the *ayuntamiento* houses the **turismo** (Mon–Fri 9.30am–3pm, Sat & Sun 10am–2pm; ☎955 902 933, ⓦwww.turismoecija .com); an additional feature here is a **camera obscura** (same hours; €2.50), which is an effortless way to appreciate Éjica's marvellous collection of church towers.

The most economical of the **hotels** – there are no *hostales* – is *Hotel Platería*, c/Garcilópez 1, just off the east side of Plaza de España (☎955 902 754, ⓦwww.hotelplateria.net; ❸), with excellent modern rooms around a central patio, while the *Hotel Sol Pirula*, south of the centre at c/Cervantes 50 (☎954 830 300, ⓦwww.hotelsolpirula.com; ❸), has comfortable air-conditioned rooms and a restaurant. The town has plenty of places for **eating and drinking**, and one of the nicest is mid-priced *Las Ninfas*, using the Palacio de Benamejí's patio as its terrace. On Plaza de España, *Casa Emilio*, on the south side, does tapas and *platos combinados*, or there's more choice at *La Reja*, c/Garcilopez 1, close to the *Hotel Platería*. The latter hotel's restaurant isn't a bad choice either, with a bargain weekday *menú* for €7.

Osuna

OSUNA (like Carmona and Écija) is one of those small Andalucian towns that are great to explore in the early evening: slow in pace and quietly enjoyable, with elegant streets of tiled, whitewashed houses interspersed with fine **Renaissance mansions**. The best of these are off the main street, c/Carrera, which runs down from the central Plaza Mayor, and in particular on c/San Pedro, which intersects it; at no. 16, the **Cilla del Cabildo** has a superb geometric relief round a carving of the Giralda, and, farther along, the eighteenth-century **Palacio de el Marqués de la Gomera** – now a hotel and restaurant (see opposite) – is a stunning Baroque extravaganza. There's also a marvellous **casino** on Plaza Mayor, with 1920s Mudéjar-style decor and a grandly bizarre ceiling, which is open to all visitors and makes an ideal place for a cool drink.

Two huge stone buildings stand on the hilltop: the **old university** (suppressed by reactionary Fernando VII in 1820; patio open term-time Mon–Fri 10am–7pm; closed July & Aug) and the lavish sixteenth-century **Colegiata** (guided tours only, English spoken, Mon–Sat 10am–1.30pm & 4–7pm, Sun 10am–1.30pm plus Sept–June 3.30–6.30pm; €2.50), which contains the gloomy but impressive **pantheon and chapel** of the dukes of Osuna, descendants of the kings of León and once "the lords of Andalucía", as well as a **museum** displaying some fine artworks, including imposing canvases by Ribera. Opposite the entrance to the Colegiata is the Baroque convent of **La Encarnación** (same hours as Colegiata; €2), which has a fine plinth of Sevillan *azulejos* round its cloister and gallery.

Practicalities

The **turismo** lies 300m northwest of the Plaza Mayor at c/Carrera 83 (Tues–Sat 9.30am–1.30pm & 4–6pm, Sun 9.30am–1.30pm; ℡954 815 732, Ⓦwww.ayto-osuna.es) and can provide a town map.

Osuna has plenty of **accommodation** but not a lot of budget options. Among the lowest priced is the pleasant *Hostal Caballo Blanco*, c/Granada 1 (℡954 810 184; ❸), in a restored coaching inn with a decent restaurant off the northern end of c/Carrera. Slightly cheaper is the *Hostal Granadino*, Plaza Salitre 1 (℡954 810 000; ❷), a bit further away from the centre to the southwest of the Plaza Mayor, with air-conditioned en-suite rooms above a restaurant. The standout upmarket option is the ⚜ *Hotel Palacio Marqués de la Gomera*, c/San Pedro 20 (℡954 812 223, Ⓦwww.hotelpalaciodelmarques.com; ❹), housed inside one of the most beautiful *casas palacios* in the country. There are plenty of **food and drink** possibilities along c/Carrera and around Plaza Mayor – one restaurant worth seeking out is the *Mesón del Duque*, Plaza de la Duquesa 2, uphill behind the casino, offering an inexpensive *menú* on its jasmine-fringed terrace. For **tapas**, don't miss ⚜ *Casa Curro*, Plaza Salitre 5 (near the *Hostal Granadino*), the town's best (and liveliest) tapas and *raciones* bar, which cooks up a tasty range of seafood and meat dishes. There's a superb restaurant in the back, too.

Córdoba

CÓRDOBA lies upstream from Seville beside a loop of the Guadalquivir, which was once navigable as far as here. It is today a minor provincial capital, prosperous in a modest sort of way. Once, however, it was the largest city of Roman Spain, and for three centuries it formed the heart of the western Islamic empire, the great medieval caliphate of the Moors.

It is from this era that the city's major monument dates: the **Mezquita**, the grandest and most beautiful mosque ever constructed by the Moors in Spain. It stands right in the centre of the city, surrounded by the old Jewish and Moorish quarters, and is a building of extraordinary mystical and aesthetic power. Make for it on arrival and keep returning as long as you stay; you'll find its beauty increases with each visit, as, of course, is proper, since the mosque was intended for daily attendance.

The Mezquita apart, Córdoba itself is a place of considerable charm. It has few grand squares or mansions, tending instead to introverted architecture, calling your attention to the tremendous and often wildly extravagant **patios**. These have long been acclaimed, and they are actively encouraged and maintained by the local council, which runs a "Festival of the Patios" in May.

Just 7km outside the town, more Moorish splendours are to be seen among the ruins of the extravagant palace complex of **Medina Azahara**, undergoing fascinating reconstruction.

Arrival and information

From the magnificent new combined **train and bus station** on Plaza de las Tres Culturas, on Avda. de America at the northern end of town, head east to the junction with broad Avda. del Gran Capitán; this leads down to the old quarters and the Mezquita (15min walk or bus #3 from outside the station).

Arriving **by car** can be a pain, especially during rush hour in the narrow streets around the Mezquita. Parking in the centre is also a major headache, and it's worth considering staying somewhere that doesn't require traversing the old

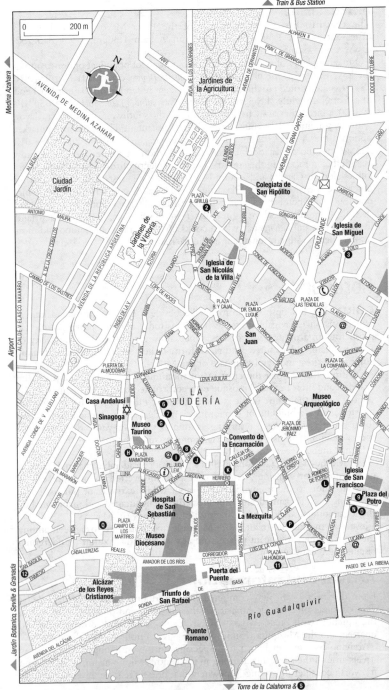

Train & Bus Station

Medina Azahara

Airport

Jardín Botánica, Seville & Granada

0   200 m

N

AVENIDA DE MEDINA AZAHARA

Ciudad
Jardín

Jardines de
la Agricultura

Jardines de
la Victoria

Colegiata de
San Hipólito

PLAZA
A. GRILLO
②

Iglesia de
San Miguel
③

Iglesia de
San Nicolás
de la Villa

PLAZA DE
LAS TENDILLAS
ⓘ

PLAZA
R. Y CAJAL

PLAZA
DR. EMILIO
LUQUE

San
Juan

PLAZA DE
LA COMPAÑÍA

PUERTA DE
ALMODÓVAR

LA
JUDERÍA

Museo
Arqueológico

Casa Andalusi
Sinagoga
ⓖ

⑥
⑦

PLAZA DE
JERÓNIMO
PÁEZ

Museo
Taurino
ⓗ

Convento de
la Encarnación

PLAZA
MAIMÓNIDES
ⓘ

Ⓙ

ⓘ
PL. JUDÁ
LEVÍ

Ⓚ

Iglesia de
San Francisco
ⓛ

Plaza del
Potro
⑨
Ⓝ Ⓞ

Hospital
de San
Sebastián
ⓘ

Ⓜ

PLAZA
CAMPO DE
LOS
MÁRTIRES

Museo
Diocesano

La Mezquita

Ⓠ

Ⓡ

ⓞ

PLAZA
ALHÓNDIGA
⑪

⑫

AMADOR DE LOS RÍOS

Puerta del
Puente

PASEO DE LA RIBERA

Alcázar
de los Reyes
Cristianos

Triunfo de
San Rafael

Rio Guadalquivir

Puente
Romano

AVENIDA DEL ALCÁZAR

Torre de la Calahorra & ⓢ

CÓRDOBA

Convento de la Merced

ACERA GUERRITA

Torre de la Malmuerta

❶

ALONSO

DE STA. MARINA

REYES CATÓLICOS

PLAZA DE COLÓN

JUAFRE

MARROQUIES

AVENIDA DE LAS OLLERÍAS

SANTA MARINA

MURO DE LA MISERICORDIA

CARCAMO

ONCINO

VIEJAS

PLAZA DOBLAS

OSARIO

Hospital de San Juan y San Jacinto

Iglesia del Cristo de los Faroles

PLAZA DEL CONDE PRIEGO

LOS MORISCOS

Iglesia de Santa Marina de Aguas Santas

COSTANILLAS

SIMANCAS

CJ. MELLADOS

NEVES

ANGLERA

PUERTA DEL RINCÓN

BARGS. LUIS

MORALES

Convento de Santa Isabel

Palacio del Marqués de Viana

OBISPO OSIO

OSARIO

HORNILLO

ZAMORANO

IMAGENES

Iglesia de San Agustín

HUMOSA

Círculo de la Amistad

SANTA

MARTA

RUFO

JUAN

ENRIQUE REDEL

CAPILLA

REJAS DE DON GOME

MONTERO

ROSAS

FRAILES

CARBONELL Y MORAND

ALFAROS

CABRERA

ARROYO

Convento-Hospital de Jesús Nazareno

CUSTODIO

COSTAS

SAN LORENZO

PEDRO FDEZ.

SAN ANDRÉS

ISAAC PERAL

ROELAS

Iglesia de San Lorenzo

④

Templo Romano

CRISTO

MARCELO

CAPITULARES

SAN PABLO

VILLALONES

REALEJO

ARROYO

SANTA MARÍA

DE GRACIA

Iglesia de San Rafael

PLAZA DE SAN LORENZO

MARIA AUXILIADORA

DOMINGO SBRIO

TUNDIDORES

Ⓔ

COLÓN

RODRÍGUEZ

PEDRO

LÓPEZ

DE LOS

RÍOS

BERMEJO

Iglesia de San Pablo

Iglesia de San Andrés

MUÑICES

ABEJAR

LORENZO

ESCAÑUELA

SAN FRANCISCO DE SALES

Ⓕ

REGINA

D. VICTORIA

D. MENDEZ

MUÑOZ

KARION

PLAZA DE LA CORREDERA

E. REGISTINA

PLAZA DE LA MAGDALENA

GOLONDRINA

CERRO

HISTORIADOR DOMÍNGUEZ ORTIZ

TOBIL

ALCANTARA

PATRIARCA

C. DE ISABEL II

ARENILLAS

FRANCISCO ROMERO

RONDA DE ANDUJAR

DOMINGO BADÍA

PLAZA CAÑAS

LUIS

TORRILLO

GUTIÉRREZ DE LOS RÍOS

S. ELOY

ALFONSO XII

MAGDALENA

CAMPO SAN ANTÓN

Museo de Bellas Artes y Museo Julio Romero de Torres

FERIAS

CARCEL LA ROSA

PLAZA AGUAYOS

PLAZA VIZCONDE MIRANDA

CRUZ VERDE

BARROSO

CAMPO MADRE DE DIOS

DON RODRIGO

AGUSTÍN MORENO

BADANAS

MUCHO TRIGO

SIETE REVUELTAS

NOGUES

❿

VALDERRAMA

RONQUILLO BRICEÑO

CLAUSTRO

▶ Jaén & Madrid

321

EATING & DRINKING

Albergue Juvenil	F
Amaltea	11
Bar Plateros	9
Bar-Restaurante Barril	2
Casa Paco Acedo	1
El Choto	6
El Churrasco	7
El Gallo	4
Mesón San Basilio	12
Los Mochuelos	10
El Rincón del Carmen	8
Taberna Salinas	5
Taberna San Miguel (El Pisto)	3

ACCOMMODATION

Albergue Juvenil	I
Campamento Municipal	A
Camping Los Villares	C
Casa de los Azulejos	E
Fonda Agustina	P
Hospedería de Churrasco	G
Hostal Alcázar	Q
Hostal Almanzor	R
Hostal El Portillo	L
Hostal & Hotel Maestre	N
Hostal Plaza Corredera	F
Hostal Séneca	J
Hotel Amistad Córdoba	H
Hotel Hespería Córdoba	S
Hotel Marisa	K
Hotel Mezquita	M
Los Villares	D
Parador La Arruzafa	B
Pensión Los Arcos	O

quarter. Better still is if you park up for the duration of your stay – Avda. de la República Argentina bordering the Jardines de la Victoria on the western edge of the old quarter, and across the river in the streets either side of the *Hotel Hespería Cordoba* are possible places – and get around the city on foot, which is both easy and enjoyable.

The main **turismo** is at the Palacio de Congresos y Exposiciones at c/Torrijos 10 (Mon–Fri 9am–7.30pm, Sat & Sun 9.30am–3pm; ☏957 355 179), alongside the Mezquita. Córdoba's municipal tourist office (ⓦwww .turismodecordoba.org) has joined forces with a private company to provide tourist information from three central **kioskos**: at Plaza Campo de los Martires, almost facing the Alcázar (daily 9.30am–2pm & 4.30–7.30pm); in Plaza de las Tendillas in the centre of the modern town (daily 10am–1.30pm & 6–9.30pm); and on the main concourse of the train station (daily 9.30am–2pm & 4.30–7.30pm). The same company also offers guided **walks** around the old city (*Paseos por Córdoba*; English spoken; €15); the walks last an hour and a half and end up at a typical *cordobés* taverna. Córdoba changes its **monument timetables** more than any other town in Andalucía – always check with one of the tourist offices. Córdoba's most central **internet** cafés are *Ch@t*, c/ Claudio Marcelo 15, near the focal Plaza Tendillas (Mon–Sat 10am–2pm & 5–9.30pm) in the new town, and, in the old quarter, *Hostal El Pilar del Potro* at c/ Lucano 12 (daily 10am–1pm & 5–10pm).

Accommodation

The majority of **places to stay** are concentrated in the narrow maze of streets to the north and east of the Mezquita. Finding a room at any time of the year – except during Semana Santa and the May festivals (the city's busiest month) – isn't usually a problem, and it's also worth bearing in mind that Córdoba's high season is April–June, while July and August are the hotel trade's low-season months when the more upmarket places often drop their prices considerably.

Budget

Albergue Juvenil Plaza Judá Levi ☏957 355 040, reservations ☏902 510 000, ⓦwww.inturjoven .com. Excellent and superbly located modern youth hostel (with twin, triple and four-person en-suite rooms), which also serves meals and has wi-fi throughout. It's a prime destination for budget travellers, so you may need to book ahead at busy periods. Under-26 €16, over-26 €20.

Fonda Agustina c/Zapatería Vieja 5 ☏957 470 872. Charming and spotlessly clean little *fonda*, with basic rooms in a tranquil location. ❷

Hostal Alcázar c/San Basilio 2 ☏957 202 561, ⓦwww.hostalalcazar.com. Comfortable and welcoming family-run *hostal* with a nice patio and a range of rooms (most en suite) with a/c and TV. Also has some good-value apartments opposite (€75 for up to four; two-night minimum stay). B&B ❷–❸

Hostal Almanzor Corregidor Luís de la Cerda 10 ☏957 485 400, ⓦwww.hostal-almanzor.es. East of the Mezquita, a pleasant and recently refurbished *hostal* for a/c, en-suite rooms with TV. Free use of car park. ❷–❸

Hostal & Hotel Maestre c/Romero Barros 4 & 16 ☏957 475 395 for the *hostal*, ☏957 472 410 for the hotel, ⓦwww.hotelmaestre .com. Excellent *hostal* between c/San Fernando and the Plaza del Potro – all rooms en suite – and neighbouring hotel with attractive a/c rooms with TV. *Rough Guide* readers with this guide get free underground parking (except April & May). ❷–❸

Hostal Plaza Corredera c/Rodríguez Marín 15 ☏957 470 581, ⓦwww.hostallacorredera.com. Clean, friendly and recently refurbished place with rooms sharing bath, and great views over the plaza from some. ❷

Hostal El Portillo c/Cabezas 2 ☏957 472 091, ⓦwww.hostalelportillo.com. Beautiful, recently refurbished and friendly old *hostal* with elegant patio, offering en-suite a/c singles and doubles. ❷

Hostal Séneca c/Conde y Luque 7 ☏957 473 234, Ⓔhostalseneca@eresmas.com. Wonderful place to stay, with simple and en-suite rooms around a stunning patio with Moorish pavement where you can take breakfast. Very popular, so book ahead. B&B ❸

Pensión Los Arcos c/Romero Barros 14 ☎957
485 643, Ⓦ www.pensionlosarcos.com. Excellent
hostal with simple rooms (some en suite) around a
delightful patio. ❷

Moderate and expensive

🏃 Casa de los Azulejos c/Fernando Colón 5
☎957 470 000, Ⓦ www.casadelosazulejos
.com. Stylish small boutique hotel with distinctively
furnished rooms, featuring iron bedsteads and
artworks, ranged around a leafy patio, itself used
for art shows. Car park. B&B ❹
Hospedería de Churrasco c/Romero 38 ☎957
294 808, Ⓦ www.elchurrasco.com. Elegant new
nine-room hotel in the Judería belonging to the
restaurant of the same name. Entry is through

a double patio, and rooms are classically furnished
with chintz drapes and bedcovers, and some have
terraces. Facilities include minibar, in-room internet
(free) and rooftop terrace/solarium. B&B ❺
Hotel Amistad Córdoba Plaza de Maimónides 3
☎957 420 335, Ⓦ www.nh-hoteles.com. Stylish
upmarket hotel with comfortable rooms incorporating two eighteenth-century mansions, near the
old wall in the Judería. Car park available. ❼
Hotel Hesperia Córdoba Avda. de la Confederación
s/n ☎957 421 042, Ⓦ www.hoteles-hesperia.es.
Luxurious four-star hotel with great views across the
river towards the Mezquita and city from rooms at
the front. Features include restaurant, *cafetería*, pool
and rooftop bar (with the same view) and easy
access to the town across the pedestrianized Puente

Moorish Córdoba

Córdoba's **domination of Moorish Spain** began thirty years after its conquest – in
756, when the city was placed under the control of **Abd ar-Rahman I**, the sole
survivor of the Umayyad dynasty, which had been bloodily expelled from the eastern
caliphate of Damascus. He proved a firm but moderate ruler, and a remarkable
military campaigner, establishing control over all but the north of Spain and
proclaiming himself *emir*, a title meaning both "king" and "son of the caliph". It was
Abd ar-Rahman who commenced the building of the Great Mosque (*La Mezquita*, in
Spanish), purchasing from the Christians the site of the cathedral of St Vincent
(which, divided by a partition wall, had previously served both communities). This
original mosque was completed by his son **Hisham** in 796 and comprises about one-
fifth of the present building, the first dozen aisles adjacent to the Patio de los
Naranjos.

The **Cordoban emirate**, maintaining independence from the eastern caliphate,
soon began to rival Damascus both in power and in the brilliance of its civilization.
Abd ar-Rahman II (822–52) initiated sophisticated irrigation programmes, minted his
own coinage and received embassies from Byzantium. He in turn substantially
enlarged the mosque. A focal point within the culture of *al-Andalus*, this was by now
being consciously directed and enriched as an alternative to Mecca; it possessed an
original script of the Koran and a bone from the arm of Mohammed and, for the
Spanish Muslim who could not get to Mecca, it became the most sacred place of
pilgrimage. In the broader Islamic world, it ranked third in sanctity after the Kaaba of
Mecca and the Al Aksa mosque of Jerusalem.

In the tenth century, Córdoba reached its zenith under a new *emir*, **Abd
ar-Rahman III** (912–61), one of the great rulers of Islamic history. He assumed power
after a period of internal strife and, according to a contemporary historian, "subdued
rebels, built palaces, gave impetus to agriculture, immortalized ancient deeds and
monuments, and inflicted great damage on infidels to a point where no opponent or
contender remained in *al-Andalus*. People obeyed en masse and wished to live with
him in peace." In 929, with Muslim Spain and part of North Africa firmly under his
control, Abd ar-Rahman III adopted the title of "caliph". It was a supremely confident
move and was reflected in the growing splendour of Córdoba, which had become the
largest, most prosperous city of Europe, outshining Byzantium and Baghdad (the
new capital of the eastern caliphate) in science, culture and scholarship. At the turn
of the tenth century, Moorish sources boast of the city's 27 schools, 50 hospitals
(with the first separate clinics for the leprous and insane), 900 public baths, 60,300
noble mansions, 80,455 shops and 213,077 houses.

Romano. Own car park or easy parking nearby. Does frequent special offers. ⑥

Hotel Marisa c/Cardenal Herrero 6 ☎957 473 142, ⓦwww.hotelmarisacordoba.com. Two-star hotel with a superb position immediately outside the Mezquita. Rooms come with a/c but not TV. Own garage. ④

Hotel Mezquita Plaza Santa Catalina 1 ☎957 475 585, ⓦwww.hotelmezquita.com. Atmospheric and central hotel in a converted sixteenth-century mansion with excellent a/c rooms. ④

Parador La Arruzafa Avda. de la Arruzafa s/n, off Avda. El Brillante ☎957 275 900, ⓦwww.parador .es. Córdoba's modern *parador* is located on the outskirts of the city 5km to the north of the

Mezquita, but compensates with pleasant gardens, a pool and every other amenity (including a shooting range). ⑤

Camping

Campamento Municipal Avda. El Brillante 50 ☎957 403 836. Córdoba's local campsite (with restaurant and pool) is 2km north of the centre in the El Brillante *barrio*, and served by bus #10 or #11 from the bus station. Tents and equipment for hire.

Camping Los Villares ☎957 330 145. If you have your own transport, this site (7km north of the city along a minor road to Santo Domingo; the campsite lies just beyond this) is a better option, set in woodland with nature trails and a restaurant.

La Mezquita

The **development of the Mezquita** paralleled the new heights of confidence and splendour of ninth- and tenth-century Córdoba. Abd ar-Rahman III provided it with a new minaret (that has not survived but which provided the core for the later belfry), 80m high, topped by three pomegranate-shaped spheres, two of silver and one of gold and each weighing a ton. But it was his son, **al-Hakam II** (961–76), to whom he passed on a peaceful and stable empire, who was responsible for the most brilliant expansion. He virtually doubled its extent, demolishing the south wall to add fourteen extra rows of columns, and employed Byzantine craftsmen to construct a new *mihrab*, or prayer niche; this remains complete and is perhaps the most beautiful example of all Moorish religious architecture.

Al-Hakam had extended the mosque as far to the south as was possible. The final enlargement of the building, under the chamberlain-usurper **al-Mansur** (977–1002), involved adding seven rows of columns to the whole east side. This spoiled the symmetry of the mosque, depriving the *mihrab* of its central position, but Arab historians observed that it meant there were now "as many bays as there are days of the year". They also delighted in describing the rich interior,

▲ La Mezquita

with its 1293 marble columns, 280 chandeliers and 1445 lamps. Hanging inverted among the lamps were the bells of the pilgrimage cathedral of Santiago de Compostela. Al-Mansur made his Christian captives carry them on their shoulders from Galicia – a process that was to be observed in reverse after Córdoba was captured by Fernando el Santo (the Saint) in 1236.

Entering the Mezquita

As in Moorish times, the **Mezquita** (Mon–Sat 10am–7pm, Sun 2–7pm; Oct–March until 5pm; free entrance at side doors 8.30am–10am for services but without lighting; €8, kids €4) is approached through the **Patio de los Naranjos**, a classic Islamic ablutions court that preserves its orange trees, although the fountains for ritual purification before prayer are now purely decorative. Originally, when in use for the Friday prayers, all nineteen naves of the mosque were open to this court, allowing the rows of interior columns to appear an extension of the trees with brilliant shafts of sunlight filtering through. Today, all but one of the entrance gates is locked and sealed, and the mood of the building has been distorted from the open and vigorous simplicity of the mosque to the mysterious half-light of a cathedral.

Nonetheless, a first glimpse inside the Mezquita is immensely exciting. "So near the desert in its tentlike forest of supporting pillars," Jan Morris found it, "so faithful to Mahomet's tenets of cleanliness, abstinence and regularity." The mass of supporting pillars was, in fact, an early and sophisticated innovation to gain height. The original architect had at his disposal columns from the old Visigothic cathedral and from numerous Roman buildings; they could bear great weight but were not tall enough, even when arched, to reach the intended height of the ceiling. His solution (which may have been inspired by Roman aqueduct designs) was to place a second row of square columns on the apex of the lower ones, serving as a base for the semicircular arches that support the roof. For extra strength and stability (and perhaps also deliberately to echo the shape of a date palm, much revered by the early Spanish Arabs), the architect introduced another, horseshoe-shaped arch above the lower pillars. A second and purely aesthetic innovation was to alternate brick and stone in the arches, creating the red-and-white striped pattern that gives a unity and distinctive character to the whole design.

The mihrab

The uniformity was broken only at the culminating point of the mosque – the domed cluster of pillars surrounding the sacred **mihrab**, erected under al-Hakam II. The *mihrab* had two functions in Islamic worship: it indicated the direction of Mecca (and hence of prayer) and it amplified the words of the *imam*, or prayer leader. At Córdoba, it was also of supreme beauty. As Titus Burckhardt wrote, in *Moorish Art in Spain*:

"The design of the prayer niche in Córdoba was used as a model for countless prayer niches in Spain and North Africa. The niche is crowned by a horseshoe-shaped arch, enclosed by a rectangular frame. The arch derives a peculiar strength from the fact that its central point shifts up from below. The wedge-shaped arch stones or voussoirs fan outwards from a point at the foot of the arch and centres of the inner and outer circumferences of the arch lie one above the other. The entire arch seems to radiate, like the sun or the moon gradually rising over the edge of the horizon. It is not rigid; it breathes as if expanding with a surfeit of inner beatitude, while the rectangular frame enclosing it acts as a counterbalance. The radiating energy and the perfect stillness form an unsurpassable equilibrium. Herein lies the basic formula of Moorish architecture."

The inner vestibule of the niche (frustratingly fenced off) is quite simple in comparison, with a shell-shaped ceiling carved from a single block of marble. The chambers to either side – decorated with exquisite Byzantine mosaics of gold, rust-red, turquoise and green – constitute the *maksura*, where the caliph and his retinue would pray.

The cathedral and other additions

Originally, the whole design of the mosque would have directed worshippers naturally towards the *mihrab*. Today, though, you almost stumble upon it, for in the centre of the mosque squats a Renaissance **cathedral coro**. This was built in 1523 – nearly three centuries of enlightened restraint after the Reconquest – and in spite of fierce opposition from the town council. The erection of a *coro* and *capilla mayor*, however, had long been the "Christianizing" dream of the cathedral chapter and at last they had found a monarch – predictably Carlos V – who was willing to sanction the work. Carlos, to his credit, realized the mistake (though it did not stop him from destroying parts of the Alhambra and Seville's Alcázar); on seeing the work completed, he told the chapter, "You have built what you or others might have built anywhere, but you have destroyed something that was unique in the world." To the left of the *coro* stands an earlier and happier Christian addition – the Mudéjar **Capilla de Villaviciosa**, built by Moorish craftsmen in 1371 (and now partly sealed up). Beside it are the dome and pillars of the **earlier mihrab**, constructed under Abd ar-Rahman II.

The belfry, the **Torre del Alminar** (currently closed), at the corner of the Patio de los Naranjos, is contemporary with the cathedral addition. Close by, the **Puerta del Perdón**, the main entrance to the patio, was rebuilt in Moorish style in 1377. It's worth making a tour of the Mezquita's **outer walls** before leaving; parts of the original "caliphal" decoration surrounding the portals (in particular, some exquisite lattice work) are stunning.

The rest of town

After the Mezquita, Córdoba's other remnants of Moorish – and indeed Christian – rule are not individually very striking. The river, though, with its great **Arab waterwheels** and recently restored and pedestrianized **Roman bridge** (the Puente Romano), is an attractive area in which to wander.

At the bridge's eastern end the medieval **Torre de la Calahorra** (daily: May–Sept 10am–2pm & 4.30–8.30pm; Oct–April 10am–6pm; €4.50) houses a gimmicky, hi-tech museum containing models of the pre-cathedral Mezquita, weird talking tableaux and a rather incongruous multimedia presentation on the history of man; there's a great panoramic **view**, though, from the top of the tower towards the city. On the western riverbank, the wheels, and the ruined mills, were in use for several centuries after the fall of the Muslim city, grinding flour and pumping water up to the fountains of the Alcázar. This originally stood beside the Mezquita – on the site now occupied by the **Museo Diocesano** (July & Aug Mon–Sat 9.30am–3pm; Sept–June 9.30am–1.30pm & 4–6pm; €1.50, free with Mezquita ticket), now a museum of religious art with some fine examples of medieval wood sculpture. After the Christian conquest, the Alcázar was rebuilt a little to the west by Fernando and Isabel, hence its name, **Alcázar de los Reyes Cristianos**. The buildings (July & Aug Tues–Sun 10am–2pm; Sept–June Tues–Sat 10am–2pm & 5.30–7.30pm, Sun 9.30am–2.30pm; gardens only Tues–Sun 8pm–midnight; €4, evening gardens visit €2; free on Fri) are a bit dreary, having served as the residence of the Inquisition from 1428 to 1821. However, they display some fine mosaics from Roman Córdoba, among which is one of the largest complete Roman mosaics in existence, and the wonderful **gardens** are a great place to get your breath back. Three hundred metres downriver from the Alcázar on the opposite bank lies the university's **Jardín Botánico** (April–June Tues–Sun 10am–9pm; July & Aug Tues–Sat 10am–3pm & 7pm–midnight, Sun 10am–3pm; Sept–March Tues–Sat 10am–7.30pm, Sun 10am–3pm; €2; @www.jardinbotanicodecordoba.com), displaying exotic trees, shrubs and plants from all over the world, including Andalucía's very own arboreal rarity, the **pinsapo Spanish fir**, a pre-Ice Age survivor transplanted from its only European habitat in the Sierra de Grazalema. The garden has a pleasant **cafetería**.

To the northeast of the Mezquita, near the Museo Arqueológico and in an area that was once the *plateros* or silversmiths' quarter, you'll find **Plaza de la Corredera**, a once ramshackle but now wonderfully refurbished colonnaded square, much resembling Madrid's or Salamanca's Plaza Mayor. Unique in Andalucía, the square's complete enclosure occurred in the seventeenth century and presented the city with a suitable space for all kinds of spectacles. These have included burnings by the Inquisition as well as bullfights, from which event the tiny Callejón Toril (Bull Pen) on the square's eastern side takes its name. After decades of delay, the city has finally rescued this remarkable construction, and now bars and restaurants have opened and their terraces have become popular places to sit out on summer evenings.

La Judería

Between the Mezquita and the beginning of Avda. del Gran Capitán lies **La Judería**, Córdoba's old Jewish quarter, and a fascinating network of lanes – more atmospheric and less commercialized than Seville's Barrio Santa Cruz, though tacky souvenir shops are beginning to gain ground. Near the heart of the quarter, at c/Judías 20, is a **sinagoga** (Tues–Sat 9.30am–2pm & 3.30–5.30pm, Sun 9.30am–1.30pm; €0.30, free with EU passport), one of only three synagogues in Spain – the other two are in Toledo – that survived the Jewish expulsion of 1492. This one, built in 1316, is minute, particularly in comparison with the great Santa María in Toledo, but it has some fine stuccowork elaborating on a Solomon's-seal motif and retains its women's gallery. Outside is a statue of Maimónides, the Jewish philosopher, physician and Talmudic jurist, born in Córdoba in 1135. Just along from the synagogue, at c/Judíos 12, there's a restored twelfth-century mansion, **La Casa Andalusí** (daily 10.30am–7.30pm; €2.50), which attempts to recreate the atmosphere of the Moorish period with furniture and a variety of exhibits.

Nearby is a small **Museo Taurino** (Bullfighting Museum; Tues–Sat 10am–2pm & 5.30–7.30pm, Sun 9.30am–2.30pm; €3, free on Fri). It warrants a look, if only for the kitschy nature of its exhibits: row upon row of bulls' heads, two of them given this "honour" for having killed matadors. Beside a copy of the tomb of Manolete – most famous of the city's *toreros* – is exhibited the hide of his taurine nemesis, Islero.

Other museums and mansions

More interesting, perhaps, and more rewarding, is the **Museo Arqueológico** (Tues 2.30–8.30pm, Wed–Sat 9am–8.30pm, Sun 9am–2.30pm; €1.50, free with EU passport). During its original conversion, this small Renaissance mansion was revealed as the unlikely site of an original Roman patio. Incorporating the Roman elements, it is now one of the most imaginative and enjoyable small museums in the country, with good local collections from the Iberian, Roman and Moorish periods. Outstanding is an inlaid tenth-century bronze stag found at the Moorish palace of Medina Azahara (see p.329) where it was used as the spout of a fountain.

A couple of blocks below the archeological museum, back towards the river, you'll come upon **Plaza del Potro**, a fine old square named after the colt (*potro*) that adorns its fountain. This, as a wall plaque proudly points out, is mentioned in *Don Quixote*, and indeed Cervantes himself is reputed to have stayed at the inn opposite, the **Posada del Potro**, which has an atmospheric cattle yard within; recently restored, it is currently being transformed into a centre for the study of flamenco (details from the *turismo*). On the other side of the square is the **Museo de Bellas Artes** (Tues 2.30–8.30pm, Wed–Sat 9am–8.30pm, Sun 9am–2.30pm; €1.50, free with EU passport), with paintings by Ribera, Valdés Leal and Zurbarán, and, across its courtyard, the small **Museo Julio Romero de Torres** (May–Sept Tues–Sat 10am–2pm & 5.30–7.30pm, Sun 9.30am–2.30pm; Oct–April Tues–Sat 8.30am–2.30pm, Sun 9.30am–2.30pm; €4, free on Fri), devoted to the Córdoban artist Romero de Torres (1885–1930), a painter of some sublimely dreadful canvases, many of which depict reclining female nudes with furtive male guitar players.

In the north of town, towards the train station, are numerous Renaissance churches – some converted from mosques, others showing obvious influence in their minarets – and a handful of convents and palaces. The best of these, still privately owned, is the **Palacio del Marqués de Viana** (guided tours Mon–Fri 10am–1pm & 4–6pm, Sat 10am–1pm; €6, patios only €3; last entry 15min before closing), whose main attraction for many visitors is its twelve flower-filled patios.

Eating and drinking

Bars and **restaurants** are on the whole reasonably priced – you need only to avoid the touristy places round the Mezquita. There are lots of good places to eat in La Judería and in the old quarters off to the east, above Paseo de la Ribera. Two celebrated specialities worth trying here are *rabo de toro* (slow-stewed bull's tail) and *salmorejo*, the deliciously hunky *cordobés* variant of gazpacho, made with bread, tomatoes, oil and chopped *jamón* often topped off with sliced hard-boiled eggs.

Albergue Juvenil Plaza Judá Leví s/n. The youth hostel's *cafetería* (open to all) has some of the cheapest food in town, with hearty three-course lunch (2–3pm) and dinner (8.30–9.30pm) *menús* a bargain €7.

Amaltea c/Ronda de Isasa 10 ☎957 491 968. Excellent organic restaurant with lots of veggie options, run by a charming Wolverhampton-educated *cordobésa*. Specialities of the house include *tabulé de cous-cous* and *calabacín con cabrales* (courgettes with strong cheese). Plenty of organic wines and a few special beers, too – try the *Alhambra 1925*. Some dishes are pricier, but it's possible to eat here for under €15. Closed Mon.

Bar Plateros c/San Francisco 6. Specializes in Montilla-Moriles, the local barrelled wine (vaguely similar to a mellow, dry sherry), and is a good spot to try *fiti-fiti*, a half-and-half combo of white and sweet white wine. Also turns out great tapas.

Bar-Restaurante Barril c/Concepción 16. Efficient tapas and breakfast bar with a small terrace and serving all-day *platos combinados*. Some vegetarian dishes.

Casa Paco Acedo Beneath the Torre de la Malmuerta. The house specialities at this celebrated, good-value *cordobés* institution include *salmorejo* and a memorable *rabo de toro*.

El Choto c/Almanzor 10 ☎957 760 115. Attractive, small and serious restaurant offering a range of well-prepared fish and meat dishes including its signature dish *choto asado* (roast kid). There's a four-course *menú de degustación* for €35 including wine and a *menú de la casa* for around €18 (both Tues–Fri). Closed Sun eve & Mon.

El Churrasco c/Romero 16 (not c/Romero Barros) ☎957 290 819. This renowned restaurant with attractive rooms and patio is famous for its *churrasco* (a grilled pork dish, served with pepper sauces) and *salmorejo* (a thick Córdoban version of *gazpacho* with hunks of ham and egg). Expensive but offers an interesting *menú de degustación* for around €30. Closed Aug.

El Gallo c/María Cristina 6. Another classic old *cordobés* drinking hole, which has changed little since it opened at the turn of the twentieth century; try their *gambas rebozadas* (fried prawns) washed down with outstanding *amargoso* Montilla from their own *bodega*.

Mesón San Basilio c/San Basilio 19. Good and unpretentious busy local restaurant offering well-prepared fish and meat *raciones* and *platos combinados*, plus a weekday *menú* for €12.

Los Mochuelos c/Agustín Moreno 51. Traditional tapas and *raciones* restaurant with large variety of dishes including *revuelto de setas con salmón* and *mochuelitos* (spicy meat); plenty of atmosphere, stacked sherry butts, bullfight posters and a pleasant patio.

El Rincón del Carmen c/Romero 4. Small, pleasant café-restaurant with a charming patio terrace below and restaurant upstairs, serving inexpensive *raciones* and *media raciones*.

Taberna Salinas c/Tundidores 3. Century-old, reasonably priced *taberna* with dining rooms around a charming patio. Good *raciones* place – try their *naranjas con bacalao* (cod with oranges) – and serves a great *salmorejo*.

Taberna San Miguel (El Pisto) Plaza San Miguel 1. Known to all as *El Pisto* (*The Barrel*), this is one of the city's legendary bars – over a century old – and not to be missed. Wonderful *montilla* and tapas; *rabo de toro* and *callos en salsa picante* (tripe in spicy sauce) are house specials. Closed Aug.

Nightlife

Córdoba takes its tranquillity seriously, especially after dark, when La Judería and the old quarter turn very quiet.

Conventional **discotecas** are in the centre of town around c/Cruz Conde, north of Plaza Tendillas. *Gongora*, c/Góngora 10, is an all-day *copas* café playing blues and other sounds, which transmutes nightly into an all-night dance venue, often staging live gigs. Nearby, *Underground*, c/Conde de Robledo 1 (Thurs–Sun), plays Latin and rock until the early hours. The ♪ *Jazz Café*, c/Espartería s/n (50m from the Templo Romano), is a great and atmospheric jazz and blues bar, staying open till the early hours; it regularly stages live bands and is famous for its jam sessions. Slightly north from here *Soul*, c/Alfonso XIII 3, with a wide variety of sounds, is also good. The rest of Córdoba's **nightlife** scene centres on the **Ciudad Jardín** zone between c/Albeniz and the bullring a few blocks further west, and the streets to the south of c/Antonio Maura, in a quarter with plenty of music and drinking bars favoured by the city's student set. Popular long-standing bars here include *Galía* at c/Alcalde de la Cruz Ceballos 3, and the Lilliputian but lively *La Quadra* at c/de los Alderetes 25, off c/Antonio Maura.

You'll find the most authentic **flamenco** in town at *Tablao Cardenal*, c/Torrijos 10 (next to the *turismo*; ⓦ www.tablaocardenal.com), though it doesn't come cheap at €25 a ticket (includes one drink). Performances begin at 10.30pm and you can book a good table by phone (☏ 957 483 320; closed Sun).

Medina Azahara

Seven kilometres to the northwest of Córdoba lie the vast and rambling ruins of **Medina Azahara**, a palace complex built on a dream scale by **Caliph Abd ar-Rahman III**. Naming it after a favourite, az-Zahra (the Radiant), he spent one-third of the annual state budget on its construction each year from 936 until his death in 961. Ten thousand workers and 1500 mules and camels were employed on the project, and the site, almost 2km long by 900m wide, stretched over three descending terraces. In addition to the palace buildings, it contained a zoo, an aviary, four fishponds, three hundred baths, four hundred houses, weapons factories and two barracks for the royal guard. Visitors, so the chronicles record, were stunned by its wealth and brilliance: one conference room was provided with pure crystals, creating a rainbow when lit by the sun; another was built round a huge pool of mercury.

Medina Azahara was a perfect symbol of the western caliphate's extent and greatness, but it was to last for less than a century. **Al-Hakam II**, who succeeded Abd ar-Rahman, lived in the palace, continued to endow it, and enjoyed a stable reign. However, distanced from the city, he delegated more and more authority, particularly to his vizier Ibn Abi Amir, later known as **al-Mansur** (the Victor). In 976, al-Hakam was succeeded by his eleven-year-old son Hisham II and, after a series of sharp moves, al-Mansur assumed the full powers of government, keeping Hisham virtually imprisoned at Medina Azahara, to the extent of blocking up connecting passageways between the palace buildings.

Al-Mansur was equally skilful and manipulative in his wider dealings as a dictator, retaking large tracts of central Spain and raiding as far afield as Galicia and Catalunya; consequently, Córdoba rose to new heights of prosperity. But with his death in 1002 came swift decline, as his role and function were assumed in turn by his two sons. The first died in 1008; the second, Sanchol, showed open disrespect for the caliphate by forcing Hisham to appoint him as his successor. At this, a popular revolt broke out and the caliphate disintegrated into civil war and a series of feudal kingdoms. Medina Azahara was looted by a mob at the outset, and in 1010 was plundered and burned by retreating Berber mercenaries.

The site

For centuries, **the site** (April–Sept Tues–Sat 10am–8.30pm, Sun 10am–2pm; Oct–March Tues–Sat 10am–2pm & 5–6.30pm, Sun 10am–1.30pm; confirm winter hours with site ☏957 355 506; €1.50, free with EU passport) continued to be looted for building materials; parts, for instance, were used in the Seville Alcázar. But in 1944 excavations unearthed the remains of a crucial part of the palace – the **Royal House**, where guests were received and meetings of ministers held. This has been meticulously reconstructed and, though still fragmentary, its main hall must rank among the greatest of all Moorish rooms. It has a different kind of stuccowork from that at Granada or Seville – closer to natural and animal forms in its intricate Syrian *Hom* (Tree of Life) motifs. Unlike the later Spanish Arab dynasties, the Berber Almoravids and the Almohads of Seville, the caliphal Andalucians were little worried by Islamic strictures on the portrayal of nature, animals or even men – the beautiful hind in the Córdoba museum is a good example – and it may well have been this aspect of the palace that led to such zealous destruction during the civil war.

The reconstruction of the palace gives a scale and focus to the site. Elsewhere, you have little more than foundations to fuel your imaginings, amid an awesome area of ruins, hidden beneath bougainvillea and rustling with cicadas. Perhaps the most obvious of the outbuildings yet excavated is the **mosque**, just beyond the Royal House, which sits at an angle to the rest of the buildings in order to face Mecca.

A decade ago, biologists from Córdoba University carried out a study of soil samples from the site to gain an understanding of exactly which plants and flowers the Moors had cultivated in the extensive **gardens**. When the study was completed, reconstructive planting began, and the trees, shrubs and herbs are now maturing into a delightful and aromatic garden the caliphs would recognize.

To reach Medina Azahara, follow Avda. de Medina Azahara west out of town, onto the road to Villarubia and Posadas. About 4km down this road, make a right turn, after which it's another 3km to the site. City **bus** #01 from a stop on the Avda. de la Republica Argentina (at the northern end, near a petrol station) will drop you off at the intersection for the final three-kilometre walk to the site – ask the driver for "El Cruce de Medina Azahara". A **dedicated bus service** also links the city with the site (Tues–Sun 11am & 6pm, Oct–March 4pm, Sat, Sun & public hols 10am & 11am; €6.50 return). The bus departs from a signed stop on Avda. del Alcázar directly below the Alcázar, but tickets must be purchased in advance from any municipal tourist office *kiosko* (see p.322). An alternative way to make a visit without your own transport is with the **bus tour** organized by the municipal tourist authority. Buses to the site (Tues–Fri 11am & 6pm, Sat 10am, 11am & 6pm, Sun 10am & 11am; Oct–March 6pm services depart at 4.30pm; €6.50; book in advance from a *kiosko*) leave from a stop at the northern end of Paseo de la Victoria (just above Plaza A. Grillo) and return to the city two hours later. The trip includes a free map-guide to the site, and your return bus ticket is valid only for the bus you arrived with, so ensure that you don't miss it.

A **taxi** will cost you about €25 one way for up to five people, or there's a special round-trip deal ("Taxi-Tour Córdoba") for €40, which includes a one-hour wait at the site while you visit. A convenient taxi rank is located outside the *turismo* on the west side of the Mezquita. Alternatively, Córdoba Vision also runs **guided trips** to the site (Tues–Sun 11am; €18; ☎957 299 777, English spoken); buses leave from the same stop on Avda. del Alcázar as the dedicated bus service.

Eastern Andalucía

There is no more convincing proof of the diversity of Andalucía than its eastern provinces: **Jaén**, with its rolling, olive-covered hills; **Granada**, dominated by the peninsula's highest peaks, the Sierra Nevada; and **Almería**, waterless and in part semi-desert.

Jaén is slightly isolated from the main routes around Andalucía, but if you're coming down to Granada from Madrid you might want to consider stopping over in the small towns of **Úbeda** or **Baeza**, both crammed with Renaissance architectural jewels and served on the main train line by their shared station of Linares-Baeza. Úbeda also serves as the gateway to **Cazorla** and its neighbouring natural park, Andalucía's largest.

Granada, a prime target of any Spanish travels, is easily reached from Seville, Córdoba, Ronda, Málaga or Madrid. When you've exhausted the city, there are dozens of nearby possibilities, perhaps the most enticing being the walks in the **Parque Nacional de Sierra Nevada**, created in 1999, and its lower southern slopes, **Las Alpujarras**. The **Almería beaches**, least developed of the Spanish Mediterranean, are also within striking distance.

Jaén province

There are said to be over 150 million olive trees in the province of Jaén. They dominate the landscape as infinite rows of green against the orange-red earth, occasionally interspersed with stark white farm buildings. It's beautiful on a grand, sweeping scale, though concealing a bitter and entrenched economic reality. The majority of the olive groves are owned by a mere handful of families, and for most residents this is a very poor area.

Sights may not be as plentiful here as in other parts of Andalucía, but there are a few gems worth going out of your way to take in. Fairly dull in itself, the provincial capital of **Jaén** merits a visit for its fine cathedral and Moorish baths, while farther to the northwest **Baeza** and **Úbeda** are two remarkable Renaissance towns. Extending northeast from the town of Cazorla, **Parque Natural de Cazorla**, Andalucía's biggest natural park, is a vast expanse of dense woodlands, lakes and spectacular crags.

Jaén

JAÉN, the provincial capital and by far the largest town, is an uneventful sort of place with traces of its Moorish past in the winding, narrow streets of the old quarter and in the largest surviving Moorish baths in Spain. Activity is centred on Plaza de la Constitución and its two arterial streets, Paseo de la Estación and Avda. de Madrid. The town is overlooked by the Cerro de Santa Catalina, a wooded hill topped by a recently restored Moorish fort, now partly transformed into a spectacular *parador*.

West of the main plaza is the imposing seventeenth-century Renaissance **Catedral** (Mon–Sat 8.30am–1pm & 5–8pm, Sun 9am–1.30pm & 5–7pm; museum daily 10.30am–1pm & 5–8pm; church free, museum €3), by the great local architect Andrés de Vandelvira, with a dramatic west facade flanked by twin towers. To the north of the cathedral, between the churches of San Andrés and Santo Domingo, you'll find the painstakingly restored Moorish *hammam* in the **Baños Árabes** (Tues–Sat 8.45am–9.30pm, Sun 9.30am–2.45pm; free). Among the finest of their kind in Spain, the baths were originally part of an eleventh-century Moorish palace, and are now located inside the sixteenth-century Palacio de Villardompardo, which was constructed over it. On view are the various rooms (containing hot, tepid and cold baths), with pillars supporting elegant horseshoe arches and brickwork ceilings pierced with distinctive star-shaped windows. Jaén's **Museo Provincial**, Paseo de la Estación 29 (Tues 2.30–8.30pm, Wed–Sat 9am–8.30pm, Sun 9am–2.30pm; free), has a large archeological collection including some remarkable fifth-century BC Iberian sculptures, now set to become the centrepiece of a major new museum of Iberian art.

Practicalities

The **bus station** (℡953 250 106) is at Plaza Coca de la Pinera, 300m northeast of Plaza de la Constitución, while the **train station** (℡953 270 202) lies to the left a further 1km or so beyond, along Paseo de la Estación (bus #19 from the centre). Jaén's **turismo** is to the rear of the cathedral on c/Ramon y Cajal (Mon–Fri 9am–7.30pm, Sat & Sun 9.30am–3pm; ℡953 190 455). **Internet** access is available at the central Almadena Telecom, c/Hurtado 18 (daily 11am–3pm & 5–11pm).

There are only two budget **accommodation** options worth considering. The first is the sparkling new ⚑ *Albergue Inturjoven*, c/Borja s/n (℡953 313 540, ⓦwww.inturjoven.com; under-25 €16, over-25 €20), where a former eighteenth-century hospital has been converted into a youth hostel with minimalist air-conditioned en-suite rooms; there's also a pool and, somewhat incongruously, a full-blown spa with a variety of detox and anti-ageing cures. The other option is the Spanish rail company's *Hostal Estación RENFE*, attached to the train station (℡953 274 614, ⓦwww.hostalrenfejaen.cjb.net; ❸); despite the location, it's a rather swish affair with comfortable air-conditioned rooms with TV, wi-fi throughout and a car park. There are more expensive places on the Paseo de la Estación and Avda. de Madrid, including *Hotel Europa*, Plaza de Belén 1, just off Avda. de Madrid (℡953 222 700, ⓦwww.gremiodehospedaje. com; B&B ❹), which has modern air-conditioned rooms and its own garage. Overlooking the town, and built in the shell of a Moorish castle with stunning

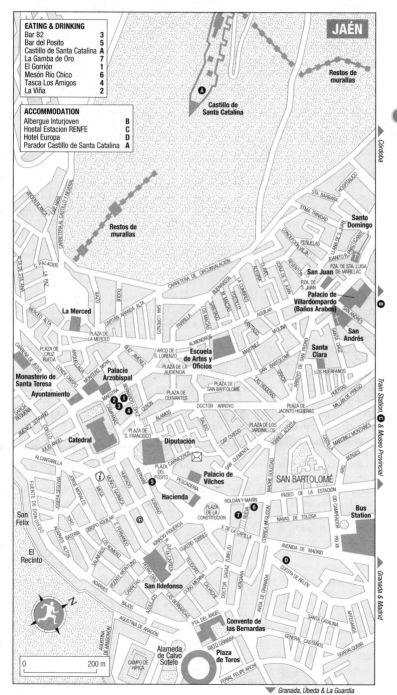

JAÉN

EATING & DRINKING

Bar 82	3
Bar del Posito	5
Castillo de Santa Catalina	A
La Gamba de Oro	7
El Gorrión	1
Mesón Río Chico	6
Tasca Los Amigos	4
La Viña	2

ACCOMMODATION

Albergue Inturjoven	B
Hostal Estacion RENFE	C
Hotel Europa	D
Parador Castillo de Santa Catalina	A

Castillo de
Santa Catalina

Restos de
murallas

Restos de
murallas

Córdoba

Train Station **C** *& Museo Provincial*

Granada & Madrid

Santo
Domingo

San Juan

Palacio de
Villardompardo
(Baños Arabes)

San
Andrés

Santa
Clara

La Merced

Escuela
de Artes y
Oficios

Monasterio de
Santa Teresa

Palacio
Arzobispal

Ayuntamiento

Catedral

Diputación

Palacio de
Vilches

SAN BARTOLOMÉ

Hacienda

Bus
Station

San Félix

El
Recinto

San Ildefonso

Convento de
las Bernardas

Alameda
de Calvo
Sotelo

Plaza
de Toros

0   200 m

Granada, Úbeda & La Guardia

views, is the ♣ *Parador Castillo de Santa Catalina* (☎ 953 230 000, ⊛ www.parador
.es; ⑤), one of the most spectacularly sited hotels in Spain.

Calle Nueva, off the east side of Plaza Constitución, has a whole bunch of
places to eat; *Mesón Río Chico* and *La Gamba de Oro* are both good tapas bars.
Above the west side of the Plaza de la Constitución, you'll find *Bar del Posito*, a
popular tapas and *raciones* venue on Plaza Deán Mazas with outdoor tables.
More bars for tapas around the centre include cosy *Tasca Los Amigos*, c/Bernardo
López, where there's good *jamón* and *morcilla* (blood pudding); the nearby *Bar
82* and *El Gorrión* on c/Arcos del Consuelo (this street is a tapas hot spot) are
also worth a visit. Nearby *La Viña*, c/Maestra 8, is a stylish new *cervecería*, restaurant and *raciones* bar with a pleasant street terrace.

Baeza and Úbeda

Less than an hour from Jaén are the elegant twin towns of **Baeza** and **Úbeda**.
Each has an extraordinary density of exuberant Renaissance palaces and richly
endowed churches, plus fine public squares. Both towns were captured from the
Moors by Fernando el Santo and, repopulated with his knights, stood for two
centuries at the frontiers of the reconquered lands facing the Moorish kingdom
of Granada.

Baeza

BAEZA is tiny, compact and provincial, with a perpetual Sunday air about it.
At its heart are the Plaza Mayor – comprised of two linked plazas, Plaza de la
Constitucíon at the southern end with a garden, and smaller Plaza de España to
the north – and *paseo*, flanked by cafés and very much the hub of the town's
limited animation.

Plaza de Leones, an appealing cobbled square enclosed by Renaissance
buildings, stands slightly back at the far end. Here, on a rounded balcony, the
first Mass of the Reconquest is reputed to have been celebrated. There are no
charges to enter any of Baeza's monuments (except the cathedral), but you may
offer the guardian a small *propina* (tip). Finest of the town's mansions is the
Palacio de Jabalquinto (patio open Mon–Fri 9am–2pm), now a seminary,
with an elaborate "Isabelline" front (showing marked Moorish influence in its
stalactite decoration). Close by, the sixteenth-century **Catedral de Santa
María** (daily 10.30am–1pm & 5–7pm; church free, museum €2), like many of
Baeza and Úbeda's churches, has brilliant painted *rejas* (iron screens) created in
the sixteenth century by Maestro Bartolomé, the Spanish master of this craft. In
the cloister, part of the old mosque has been uncovered, but the cathedral's real
novelty is a huge silver *custodia* – cunningly hidden behind a painting of St Peter,
which whirls aside for a €1 coin.

There are some good **walks** around town; wandering up through the Puerta
de Jaén on Plaza de los Leones and along Paseo Murallas/Paseo de Don Antonio
Machado takes you round the edge of Baeza with fine views over the
surrounding plains. You can cut back to Plaza Mayor via the network of narrow
stone-walled alleys – with the occasional arch – that lies behind the cathedral.

Practicalities

The **bus station** (☎ 953 740 468) is at the end of c/San Pablo and along Paseo
Arca del Agua. The nearest **train station** is Linares-Baeza, 14km from Baeza
and served by frequent trains from Seville, Córdoba and Granada (there's a
connecting bus for most trains, except on Sun; €20 taxi ride). Most bus connections are via Úbeda. The **turismo** is on Plaza de Leones, in a mansion beneath

the Mass balcony (Mon–Fri 9am–7.30pm, Sat & Sun 9.30am–3pm; ℡953 779 982), where you can pick up a map; they can also provide details of daily **guided tours** of the town. **Internet** access is available at the central *Micro Ware*, c/Portales Tundidores 13, facing Paseo de la Constitución (Mon–Thurs 10.30am–2pm & 5–9.30pm, Fri–Sun 11am–2pm & 5–10pm).

Baeza has a range of **accommodation** with considerably more choice at the upmarket end: the only budget option is the *Hotel El Alcázar*, Paseo Arca del Agua s/n, north of the bus station (℡953 740 028; ➋), with decent if unadorned en-suite rooms above a restaurant. Best of the central pricier places is the new *Hotel Baeza Monumental*, c/Cuesta de Prieto 6, to the northeast of Plaza de la Constitución (℡953 737 282, ⓦwww.hotelbaezamonumental.com; B&B ➌), with attractive rooms equipped with plasma satellite TV, minibar and strongbox, and there's a car park; higher rates apply Friday and Saturday. Nearer the centre, *Hotel Baeza*, c/Concepción 3, near the Plaza de España (℡953 748 130, ⓦwww .trhhoteles.com; B&B ➍), is partly set inside a former Renaissance palace, and the splendid ⚲ *Hotel Puerta de la Luna*, c/Canónigo Melgares Raya s/n, near Plaza del Populo (℡953 747 019, ⓦwww.hotelpuertadelaluna.com; ➍), is a beautiful four-star hotel in a refurbished seventeenth-century *casa palacio*, with two delightful patios, a restaurant, gym and small pool; prices rise slightly Friday and Saturday.

Good bets for **food and drink** include the more-than-a-century-old *Cafetería Mercantil*, on Plaza de España, which, besides being the best place for a lazy terrace breakfast, offers decent tapas and *raciones* later in the day. More formal dining is on offer at *El Sarmiento*, Plaza del Ardeciano 10, behind the cathedral, an excellent new restaurant specializing in roasted meat dishes with a terrace on this attractive square; there's a weekday *menú* for €17 (closed Sun eve & Mon). Another good place for dining alfresco is the pleasant terrace of the mid-priced *Restaurante El Sali* around the corner at c/Benavides 15, with a view of Baeza's magnificent sixteenth-century *ayuntamiento* (weekday *menú* around €11).

Úbeda

ÚBEDA, 9km east of Baeza, is a larger town with modern suburbs. Follow the signs to the Zona Monumental and you'll eventually reach the **Plaza de Vázquez de Molina**, a tremendous Renaissance square and one of the most impressive of its kind in Spain. Most of the buildings round the square are the late sixteenth-century work of Andrés de Vandelvira, the architect of Baeza's cathedral and numerous churches in both towns. One of these buildings, the **Palacio de las Cadenas**, originally a palace for Felipe II's secretary, houses Úbeda's *ayuntamiento* and features a magnificent facade fronted by monumental lions. At the opposite end of the square, the **Capilla del Salvador** (Mon–Sat 10am–2pm & 4.30–6.30pm, Sun 11.15am–2pm & 4–7pm; €3), erected by Vandelvira, though actually designed by Diego de Siloé, architect of the Málaga and Granada cathedrals, is the finest church in Úbeda. It's a masterpiece of Spanish Renaissance architecture with a dazzling Plateresque facade, its highlight a carving of the Transfiguration of Christ flanked by statues of San Pedro and San Andrés. Inside, the Transfiguration theme is repeated in a brilliantly animated *retablo* by Alonso de Berruguete, who studied under Michelangelo. Entry to the church is via a doorway on the south side.

Following c/Horno Contado out of Plaza de Vázquez de Molina leads to yet another delightful square, Plaza del Primero de Mayo, with a superb arcaded sixteenth-century **Ayuntamiento Viejo** (old town hall) and the idiosyncratic church of **San Pablo** (Mon–Wed 11am–noon, Thurs–Sat 11am–1pm, Sun 11am–1.30pm, plus Mon & Sat 7–8pm), with a thirteenth-century balcony and various Renaissance additions.

Practicalities

The **turismo** is housed in its own Renaissance mansion, the Palacio del Marqués de Contadero, c/Baja Marqués 4, just to the west of the Plaza de Vázquez de Molina (Mon–Fri 8.30am–7.30pm, Sat & Sun 9.30am–3pm; ☎953 729 204), and can provide a town map.

Most of the limited budget **accommodation** options are grouped around the main **bus station** on Avda. de Ramón y Cajal, in the modern part of town – east of the station *Hostal Victoria*, c/Alaminos 5 (☎953 791 718; ❷), is a welcoming, refurbished *hostal* offering air-conditioned en-suite rooms; it also has its own car park. In the Zona Monumental, among a number of inviting upmarket options, the 🔆 *Parador Condestable Dávalos*, Plaza de Vázquez de Molina 1 (☎953 750 345, ⓦwww.parador.es; B&B ❺), housed in yet another fabulous sixteenth-century Renaissance mansion, is outstanding. A good-value alternative is nearby *Hotel María de Molina*, Plaza del Ayuntamiento s/n (☎953 795 356, ⓦwww.hotel-maria-de-molina.com; ❸), occupying a magnificent sixteenth-century *casa palacio* with a superb patio, where rooms come with air-conditioning, room safe, satellite TV and terraces or balconies.

There are plenty of **places to eat** around Avda. Ramón y Cajal in the new town: *El Gallo Rojo*, c/Torrenueva 3, has outdoor tables in the evening and a *menú* for €15, while just north from here along c/Virgen de Guadalupe, *Pintor Orbaneja* at no. 5 does pretty good tapas in its bar and fish and meat dishes in its restaurant. In the Zona Monumental, a couple of restaurants worth seeking out are the *Restaurante Marqués*, Plaza Marqués de la Rambla 2, which serves up a good-value *menú*, and, slightly east of here, the mid-priced *El Seco*, c/Corazón de Jesús 8, close to Plaza del Ayuntamiento, which is noted for its tasty *potaje carmelitano* (chickpea, leek and cod soup) but also does excellent meat and game dishes. For a special treat, the elegant restaurant of the *parador* is worth a visit and, although expensive, offers regional dishes on good-value lunchtime (€23.50) and evening (€31) *menús*.

Cazorla

During the Reconquest of Andalucía, **CAZORLA** acted as an outpost for Christian troops, and the two castles that still dominate the town testify to its turbulent past – both were originally Moorish but later altered and restored by their Christian conquerors. Today, it's the main base for visits to the **Parque Natural de las Sierras de Segura y Cazorla**, a vast protected area of magnificent river gorges and forests. Cazorla also hosts the **fiesta de Cristo del Consuelo**, with fairgrounds, fireworks and religious processions on September 16–21.

Cazorla itself is constructed around three main squares. Buses arrive in the busy, commercial **Plaza de la Constitución**, linked by the main c/de Muñoz to the second square, **Plaza de la Corredera** (or *del Huevo*, "of the Egg", because of its shape). The *ayuntamiento* is here, a fine Moorish-style palace at the far end of the plaza. Beyond, a labyrinth of narrow, twisting streets descends to Cazorla's liveliest square, **Plaza Santa María**, which takes its name from the old cathedral that, damaged by floods in the seventeenth century, was later torched by Napoleonic troops. Its ruins, now preserved, and the fine open square form a natural amphitheatre for concerts and local events as well as being a popular meeting place. The square is dominated by **La Yedra**, an austere, reconstructed castle tower, which houses the **Museo de Artes y Costumbres** (Tues 2.30–8pm, Wed–Sat 9am–8pm, Sun 9.30am–2.30pm; free), an interesting folklore museum displaying domestic utensils and furniture.

Cazorla's official **turismo** is at Paseo del Santo Cristo 17, 100m north of Plaza de la Constitución (April–Sept Wed–Sun 10am–2pm; ☎953 710 102, Ⓦwww.cazorla.es), and can provide a useful town map. There's also a privately run office inside a shop called La Despensa del Parque in Plaza de la Constitución (daily 10am–1pm & 5.30–8pm; ☎953 721 351, Ⓦwww.turisnat .org); this also acts as an agent for Turisnat, one of the major providers of activities in the park, and ostensibly exists to promote Land Rover excursions, photo safaris and the like. However, they do sell the Editorial Alpina hiking maps for the *parque natural*.

There's a surprising range of **accommodation** in Cazorla. At the bottom end is the cosy *Pensión Taxi*, Travesía de San Antón 7 (☎953 720 525; ❷), off Plaza de la Constitución; as a resident, you can also eat for very little in their *comedor*. Better facilities (all rooms en suite with a/c) are available at the friendly *Hotel Guadalquivir*, c/Nueva 6 (☎953 720 268, Ⓦwww.hguadalquivir.com; ❸), off Plaza de la Corredera. There's also a clutch of more upmarket places, of which the *Villa Turística de Cazorla*, Ladera de San Isidro s/n (☎953 710 100, Ⓦwww .villacazorla.com; ❹), is one of the best; it's a five-minute walk from Plaza de la Constitución and reached by crossing the bridge over the river below the square. If you have a car, there are some very attractive alternatives out in the *sierra*, including the *Hotel Sierra de Cazorla*, 2km outside town (☎953 720 015, Ⓦwww.hotelsierradecazorla.com; ❸–❹), with a pool, and the *Parador El Adelantado*, a well-designed modern building with pool in a wonderful setting, 25km away in the park (☎953 727 075, Ⓦwww.parador.es; ❻). Cazorla also has an

4

ANDALUCÍA | Jaén province

Parque Natural de las Sierras de Segura y Cazorla

Even casual visitors to **Parque Natural de las Sierras de Segura y Cazorla** are likely to see a good variety of wildlife, including *Capra hispanica* (Spanish mountain goat), deer, wild pig, birds and butterflies. Ironically, though, much of the best viewing will be at the periphery, or even outside the park, since the wildlife is most successfully stalked on foot and walking opportunities within the park itself are surprisingly limited.

The main **information centre** inside the park is the Torre del Vinagre Centro de Interpretación (Tues–Sun 10am–2pm & 5–8pm, Oct–March 4–6pm; ☎953 713 040). It's worth getting hold of a good **map** from here (also available from Despensa del Parque in Cazorla): the 1:100,000 map, *Parque Natural de las Sierras de Cazorla y Segura*, and the 1:50,000 version, *Cazorla*, are recommended, but best of all is the 1:40,000 set of map and guide packs to the Sierras de Cazorla and Segura (divided into three zones), published by Editorial Alpina, which are the most accurate maps available, detailing *senderos* (footpaths), mountain-bike routes, refuges, campsites and hotels. In addition to the hiking routes marked on the maps above, Guy Hunter-Watts' *Walking in Andalucía* details five clearly described walks in the park of between 5km and 19km.

Two daily **buses** link Cazorla with **Coto Ríos** (Mon–Fri only depart 7.15am & 2.30pm, return 9am & 4.15pm; 1hr 15min) in the middle of the park (confirm timetable on ☎953 721 142). Distances between points are enormous, so to explore the park well you'll need a car or to be prepared for long treks.

There are ten official **campsites** throughout the park, which are accurately marked on the Editorial Alpina map. There's more accommodation at Coto Ríos, with three privately run campsites and a succession of *hostales*. Before setting out, you can also get the latest update on transport, campsites and accommodation from the *turismo* in Cazorla.

efficient **youth hostel**, at Mauricio Martínez 2 (☎953 711 301; under-26 €14, over-26 €19), reached by walking along c/Juan Domingo from Plaza de la Constitución for five minutes.

On Plaza Corredera, the popular ⚔ *Bar La Montería* is one of the best of Cazorla's clutch of outstanding **tapas bars**. *Bar Rincón Serrano* on the same square is also good. There are also several spit-and-sawdust bars with good tapas clustered round Plaza Santa María – rustic *Mesón la Cueva* offers authentic local food cooked on a wood-fired range; the *conejo* (rabbit) is recommended. Other places where you can eat well are *Mesón Don Chema*, down some steps off c/Muñoz, serving *platos combinados* and a cheap *menú*, and, at the bottom of the same steps, in Plaza del Mercado, ⚔ *La Sarga* (☎953 721 507), Cazorla's top **restaurant**; *lomo de jabali en salsa de castañas* (wild boar with chestnut sauce) is one of a number of game options prepared here, and there's also a *menú de degustación* for around €28. At the southern end of the same square, *Juan Carlos* is similar but slightly cheaper, serving up delicious trout and game dishes with a *menú* for around €12.

Granada

If you see only one town in Spain, it should be **GRANADA**. For here, extraordinarily well preserved and in a tremendous natural setting, stands the **Alhambra** – the most exciting, sensual and romantic of all European monuments. It was the palace fortress of the Nasrid sultans, rulers of the last Spanish Moorish kingdom, and in its construction Moorish art reached a spectacular and serene climax. But the building seems to go further than this, revealing something of the whole brilliance and spirit of Moorish life and culture. There's a haunting passage in Jan Morris's book, *Spain*, which the palace embodies:

"Life itself, which was seen elsewhere in Europe as a kind of probationary preparation for death, was interpreted [by the Moors] as something glorious in itself, to be ennobled by learning and enlivened by every kind of pleasure."

Built on the slopes of three hills, the rest of the city basks in the Alhambra's reflected glory. Because the Moorish influence here was so ruthlessly extinguished following capitulation to the Catholic monarchs Fernando and Isabel, Granada tends to be more sober in character and austere in its architecture than Andalucía's other provincial capitals. Many visitors, once they've viewed the Alhambra, are too jaded or can't be fussed to take in the city's other sights, which is a pity, for Granada has much to offer. The hilltop **Albaicín**, the former Moorish town, is a fascinating quarter full of narrow alleyways and small squares, and a great place for an hour's stroll. Not far away, too, is the cathedral with the gem of the **Capilla Real** attached to it, the final resting place of the Catholic monarchs who ended Moorish rule in Spain. Add in an **archeological museum**, **Moorish baths** and some fine churches, including a spectacular **La Cartuja** monastery, and you have more than enough to start you thinking about extending your stay.

Arrival and information

Virtually everything of interest in Granada – including the hills of the **Alhambra** (to the east) and **Sacromonte** (to the north) – is within easy walking distance of the centre.

Granada's glory was always precarious. It was established as an independent kingdom in 1238 by **Ibn al-Ahmar**, a prince of the Arab Nasrid tribe that had been driven south from Zaragoza. He proved a just and capable ruler, but all over Spain the Christian kingdoms were in the ascendant. The Moors of Granada survived only through paying tribute and allegiance to Fernando III of Castile – whom they were forced to assist in the conquest of Muslim Seville – and by the time of Ibn Ahmar's death in 1275 theirs was the only surviving Spanish Muslim kingdom. It had, however, consolidated its territory (stretching from just north of the city down to a coastal strip between Tarifa and Almería) and, stimulated by refugees, developed a flourishing commerce, industry and culture.

By a series of shrewd manoeuvres Granada maintained its autonomy for two and a half centuries, its rulers turning for protection, in turn as it suited them, to the Christian kingdoms of Aragón and Castile and to the Merinid Muslims of Morocco. The city-state enjoyed a particularly confident and prosperous period under **Yusuf I** (1334–54) and **Mohammed V** (1354–91), the sultans responsible for much of the existing Alhambra palace. But by the mid-fifteenth century, a pattern of coups and internal strife became established and a rapid succession of rulers did little to stem Christian inroads. In 1479, the kingdoms of Aragón and Castile were united by the marriage of Fernando and Isabel, and within ten years they had conquered Ronda, Málaga and Almería. The city of Granada now stood completely alone, tragically preoccupied in a civil war between supporters of the sultan's two favourite wives. The Reyes Católicos made escalating and finally untenable demands upon it, and in 1490 war broke out. **Boabdil**, the last Moorish king, appealed in vain for help from his fellow Muslims in Morocco, Egypt and Ottoman Turkey, and in the following year **Fernando and Isabel** marched on Granada with an army said to total 150,000 troops. For seven months, through the winter of 1491, they laid siege to the city, and on January 2, 1492, Boabdil formally surrendered its keys. The Christian Reconquest of Spain was complete.

The **airport** is 17km west of the city on the A92 *autovía*; buses connect with Plaza Isabel La Católica in the centre of town (14 daily; 30min; €3 one way). Buses run out to the airport from a stop on the east side of Gran Vía opposite the cathedral. Check with the operator (Gonzalez S.L.; ☏958 490 164) for the latest timetable. Alternatively, a taxi costs about €20–25.

The **train station** (☏902 432 343) is 1km or so out on Avda. de Andaluces, off Avda. de la Constitución; to get into town, take bus #3, #4, #6 or #9, which run direct to Gran Vía de Colón and the centre, or bus #11, which takes a circular route – inbound on the Gran Vía and back out via the Puerta Real and Camino de Ronda. The most central stop is by the cathedral on the Gran Vía. The city's main **bus station** is on Carretera de Jaén (☏958 185 480), some way out of the centre in the northern suburbs – bus #3 from outside will drop you near the cathedral (15min) – and handles all services except those to the Lorca museum at Fuente Vaqueros (see p.354). For departure information, check with the individual companies: Alsina Graells (serving Madrid, Jaén, Úbeda, Córdoba, Seville, Málaga, Las Alpujarras, Motril, Guadix, Almería & the coast; ☏958 185 480); Empresa Bonal (the north side of the Sierra Nevada; ☏958 465 022); Empresa Autedia (Guadix; ☏902 422 242); and Empresa Bacoma (Valencia/Alicante & Barcelona; ☏902 422 242). All terminals are on bus routes #3, #4 and #11.

Arriving **by car** you'll face the usual snarl-ups in the centre of town (try to time your arrival with the *siesta*) and the near-impossibility of finding on-street

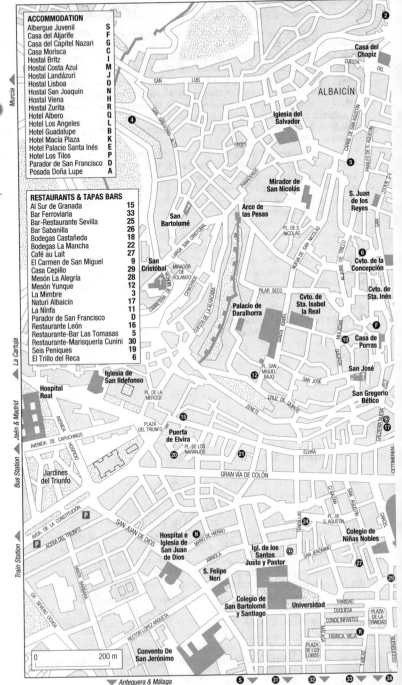

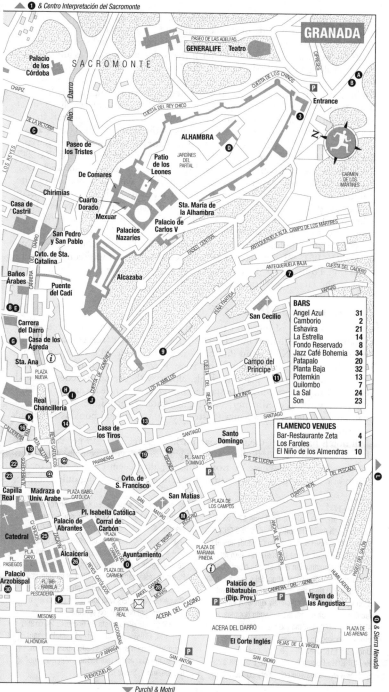

① & Centro Interpretación del Sacromonte

GRANADA

PASEO DE LAS ADELFAS

GENERALIFE Teatro

Ⓐ
Ⓑ

Palacio de los Córdoba

SACROMONTE

CUESTA DE LOS CHINOS

Ⓟ

Entrance

CHAPIZ

CUESTA DEL REY CHICO

③

DE LA VICTORIA

Ⓒ

Paseo de los Tristes

ALHAMBRA

Ⓓ

N

Chirimias

Patio de los Leones

JARDINES DEL PARTAL

CARMEN DE LOS MÁRTIRES

Casa de Castril

De Comares

Cuarto Dorado

Mexuar

Sta. María de la Alhambra

San Pedro y San Pablo

Palacios Nazaríes

Palacio de Carlos V

Cvto. de Sta. Catalina

ANTEQUERUELA ALTA CAMPO DE LOS MÁRTIRES

Baños Árabes

Puente del Cadí

Alcazaba

ANTEQUERUELA BAJA CUESTA DEL CAIDERO

Ⓔ
⑧

⑦

VARGAS

San Cecilio

BARS

Angel Azul	31
Camborio	2
Eshavira	21
La Estrella	14
Fondo Reservado	8
Jazz Café Bohemia	34
Patapalo	20
Planta Baja	32
Potemkin	13
Quilombo	7
La Sal	24
Son	23

Carrera del Darro

Ⓖ

Casa de los Ágreda

Sta. Ana

ⓘ

PLAZA NUEVA

Campo del Príncipe

⑨

⑪

Ⓗ Ⓘ

Real Chancillería

Ⓙ

LOS ALAMILLOS

SANTIAGO

Ⓚ

⑯

Casa de los Tiros

⑬

FLAMENCO VENUES

Bar-Restaurante Zeta	4
Los Faroles	1
El Niño de los Almendras	10

⑱

SANTIAGO

Santo Domingo

②②

②③

Capilla Real

Madraza o Univ. Arabe

PAVANERAS

⑲

Cvto. de S. Francisco

Pl. SANTO DOMINGO

P. S. DE LUCENA

DEL PESCADO

Ⓛ

PLAZA ISABEL CATÓLICA

San Matías

CUARTO REAL

Catedral

②⑤

Palacio de Abrantes

Pl. Isabella Católica

Corral de Carbón

San Matías

Ⓜ

PLAZA DE LOS CAMPOS

Catedral

Alcaicería

②⑥

Ayuntamiento

ⓘ

PLAZA DE MARIANA PINEDA

Ⓞ

Palacio Arzobispal

③⓪

Pl. BIB RAMBLA

②⑧

Palacio de Bibataubín (Dip. Prov.)

Ⓟ

Virgen de las Angustias

Ⓟ

MESONES

PUERTA REAL

ACERA DEL CASINO

Ⓞ & Sierra Nevada

ACERA DEL DARRO

ALHÓNDIGA

Ⓟ

El Corte Inglés

REJAS DE LA VIRGEN

PLAZA DE LAS ARENAS

▼ Purchil & Motril

parking. Underground **car parks** (*parking subterráneo*) are located at Puerta Real (down the right-hand side of the post office); La Caleta, near the train station; and on c/San Agustín, beneath the new municipal market off the west side of Gran Vía near the cathedral. Long-term free street parking places are often to be found along Carrera del Genil and the Paseo del Salón, slightly southwest of the centre.

The city's **turismo**, c/Santa Ana 2 (Mon–Fri 9am–7.30pm, Sat 9.30am– 3pm & 4–7pm, Sun 9.30am–3pm; ☏958 575 202), is up steps to the right of the church of Santa Ana off Plaza Nueva. They have a sub-office in the Alhambra's ticket office (open same hours as the monument). There's also a very helpful, and less frenetic, **municipal tourist office** at Plaza Mariana Pineda 10 (Mon–Fri 9am–8pm, Sat 10am–7pm, Sun 10am–3pm; ☏958 247 128, ⓦwww.granadatur.com). For listings, the monthly *Guía del Ocio* (available from newspaper *kioscos*) details most of what's happening on the cultural and entertainment front, though it tends to be less up to date than the city's daily paper, *Ideal*, which is particularly good in its weekend editions. One way to get to grips with the city – especially if it's your first visit – is with a **guided walk**; Cicerone Granada's tour (daily 10.30am, 11am Nov–Feb; 2hr; English & Spanish; €12, under-14 free; book in high season; ☏600 412 051, ⓦwww.ciceronegranada.com) starts at the green and white "Meeting Point" kiosk in the northeast corner of Plaza Bib Rambla and takes in the city's major sights (but not the Alhambra).

Accommodation

Granada has some of the most beautiful **hotels** in Spain, most noticeably in the atmospheric Albaicín but also along the Gran Vía, c/Reyes Católicos, in and around Plaza Nueva and Puerta Real and off Plaza del Carmen (particularly c/Las Navas). In the university zone, Plaza de la Trinidad (and east of here) is another good place to look, along with the semi-pedestrianized (taxis and minibuses only) Cuesta de Gomérez, which leads up from Plaza Nueva towards the Alhambra. In high season (April–June & Sept) and especially during Semana Santa (Easter week), you should book as far ahead as possible.

All hotels have either their own **car park** or garage (€10–15 per vehicle per day) or can advise on finding a parking place for your vehicle. The main problem, almost anywhere, is **noise**, though the recently built road to the Alhambra, diverting traffic away from the centre, has made a big difference.

Budget

Albergue Juvenil Camino de Ronda 171, at the junction with Avda. Ramón y Cajal ☏958 002 900, ⓦwww.inturjoven.com. Granada's youth hostel is conveniently close to the train station: turn left onto Avda. de la Constitución and left again onto Camino de Ronda. From the bus station, take bus #3 to the cathedral and then the circular #11, which will drop you outside. It's efficiently run with lots of facilities, and all rooms are en-suite doubles; the staff are friendly but the food is institutional; it can also be booked up for days ahead in summer. Under-26 €16, over-26 €20.

Hostal Britz Cuesta de Gomérez 1 ☏958 223 652, ⓦwww.lisboaweb.com. Very comfortable,

welcoming and well-placed *hostal*, en route to the Alhambra. Some rooms en suite, and some singles. ❷

Hostal Costa Azul c/Rosario 5 ☏958 222 298, ⓦwww.hostalcostaazul.com. Friendly, central, small *hostal* for pleasant a/c en-suite rooms. Has own restaurant and free internet for guests. Also rents out some luxurious apartments (❹) nearby. *Rough Guide* readers with this guide can claim a fifteen-percent discount on apartments. ❷

Hostal Landázuri Cuesta de Gomérez 24 ☏958 221 406, ⓦwww.hostallandazuri.com. Pleasant, good-value rooms, some en suite, plus its own restaurant, bar and a roof terrace with a view of the Alhambra. Some singles. ❷

Hostal Lisboa Plaza del Carmen 27 ☎958 221 413, ⓦwww.lisboaweb.com. Clean and comfortable central *hostal*, offering rooms with and without bath. Has wi-fi and internet access. ❷–❸

Hostal San Joaquin c/Mano de Hierro 14 ☎958 282 879, ⓦwww.pensionsanjoaquin.com. Great, rambling old *hostal* with simple rooms (some en suite with TV) and charming patios. ❷

Hostal Viena c/Hospital de Santa Ana 2 ☎958 221 859, ⓦwww.hostalviena.com. In a quiet street, this is a pleasant, efficient, Austrian-run *hostal* offering a/c rooms with and without bath. If full, they have other places nearby. Own garage. ❷–❸

Hostal Zurita Plaza de la Trinidad 7 ☎958 275 020, ⓦwww.pensionzurita.com. Friendly place where immaculate rooms come with and without bath, and all have TV and a/c. Own garage. ❷

Hotel Albero Avda. Santa María de La Alhambra 6 ☎958 226 725, ⓦwww.hotelalbero.com. Excellent-value and friendly small hotel on the access road to the Alhambra to the south of the centre. Sparkling a/c balcony rooms come with TV, and there's easy parking. Ring if you have problems finding them (English spoken). ❶

Posada Doña Lupe Avda. del Generalife s/n ☎958 221 473, ☏958 221 474. A stone's throw from the Alhambra, this rambling and potentially inviting place is blighted by a rule-ridden student hostel atmosphere (toilet paper and towels are doled out at check-in); numerous price permutations for rooms with and without bath, some exceptionally cheap. Has a small rooftop pool. ❶–❷

Moderate and expensive

Casa del Aljarife Placeta de la Cruz Verde 2 ☎958 222 425, ⓦwww.casadelaljarife.com. This welcoming upmarket Albaicín *hostal* occupies a restored sixteenth-century mansion near the heart of the *barrio*, has three attractive en-suite a/c rooms (two with Alhambra views) around a patio, and there's free internet access. ❹

Casa del Capitel Nazari Cuesta de Aceituneros 6 ☎958 21 52 60, ⓦwww.hotelcasacapitel.com. Another beautiful sixteenth-century *palacio* transformed into an enchanting small hotel with rooms overlooking a triple-tiered patio; room 22 has Alhambra view. Special offers in July, Aug, Jan & Feb can cut prices significantly. Parking nearby. ❹

Casa Morisca Cuesta de la Victoria 9 ☎958 215 796, ⓦwww.hotelcasamorisca.com. Stunningly romantic small Albaicín hotel inside an immaculately renovated fifteenth-century Moorish mansion with exquisite patio; there are

recreated Moorish furnishings throughout, and room 15 (with Alhambra views) is the one to go for. Exterior rooms cost more. ❺

Hotel América Real de la Alhambra 53 ☎958 227 471, ⓦwww.hamerica.com. Charming one-star hotel in the Alhambra grounds; you're paying for location rather than creature comforts (a/c but no TV) and prices have risen steeply (and unjustifiably) here. Booking essential. ❺

Hotel Los Angeles Cuesta Escoriaza 17 ☎958 221 423, ⓦwww.hotellosangeles.net. Pleasant and good-value modern hotel on a leafy, quiet avenue within easy walking distance of the Alhambra. All rooms come with minibar and terrace balcony, and there's a garden, pool and car park. ❹

Hotel Guadalupe Paseo de la Sabica s/n ☎958 223 423, ⓦwww.hotelguadalupe.es. Comfortable and well-appointed hotel a stone's throw from the Alhambra's entrance – some of the a/c rooms have partial Alhambra views. Clients get reduced-rate parking in Alhambra car park, or the Alhambra bus from Plaza Nueva drops you nearby. In July and Aug, rates are cut by thirty percent.

Hotel Macía Plaza Plaza Nueva 4 ☎958 227 536, ⓦwww.maciahoteles.com. Centrally located hotel, with pleasant rooms overlooking this atmospheric square. Does frequent discounts and special offers. If full, they have a couple of other same-standard hotels nearby. ❹

Hotel Palacio Santa Inés Cuesta de Santa Inés 9 ☎958 222 362, ⓦwww.lugaresdivinos.com. Sumptuous six-room hotel in a restored sixteenth-century Mudéjar mansion on the edge of the Albaicín, with views of the Alhambra. The nearby, slightly cheaper but equally attractive *Carmen de Santa Inés* (same phone no.) is owned by the same proprietors and occupies a restored Moorish *carmen* (garden villa). ❺

Hotel Los Tilos Plaza de Bib-Rambla 4 ☎958 266 712, ⓦwww.hotellostilos.com. Pleasant, two-star hotel well located near the cathedral on an atmospheric square; make sure you request an exterior room if you don't want to overlook a gloomy light well. All rooms a/c, and some higher ones (try 301 & 302 or 401 & 402) have great Alhambra views. ❹

Parador de San Francisco Real de la Alhambra ☎958 221 440, ⓦwww.paradores.com. Without question the best – and most expensive – place to stay in Granada; a fifteenth-century converted monastery in the Alhambra grounds. The cheapest rooms are €310. Booking (at least three months ahead) is essential. If you aren't staying, call in for a drink at the attractive terrace bar. ❾

Camping

Camping Reina Isabel 4km along the Zubia road to the southwest of the city ⊤958 590 041. With a pool, this is a less noisy and shadier site than the *Sierra Nevada*, making a pleasant rural alternative; can be reached by the Zubia-bound bus from the bus station, but with your own transport the city is still in easy reach.

Camping Sierra Nevada Avda. de Madrid 107 ⊤958 150 062. Closest site to the centre (bus #3 from the centre or 3min walk south from the bus station), and with a welcome pool. Closed Nov–Feb.

The Alhambra

There are three distinct groups of buildings on the Alhambra hill: the **Palacios Nazaríes** (Royal Palace, or Nasrid Palaces), the palace gardens of the **Generalife** and the **Alcazaba**. This last, the fortress of the eleventh-century Ziridian rulers, was all that existed when the Nasrid ruler Ibn al-Ahmar made Granada his capital, but from its reddish walls the hilltop had already taken its name: *Al Qal'a al-Hamra* in Arabic means literally "the red fort". Ibn al-Ahmar rebuilt the Alcazaba and added to it the huge circuit of walls and towers that forms your first view of the castle. Within the walls he began a palace, which he supplied with running water by diverting the River Darro nearly 8km to the foot of the hill; water is an integral part of the Alhambra and this engineering feat was Ibn al-Ahmar's greatest contribution. The Palacios Nazaríes was essentially the product of his fourteenth-century successors, particularly Yusuf I and Mohammed V, who built and redecorated many of its rooms in celebration of his accession to the throne (in 1354) and the taking of Algeciras (in 1369).

After their conquest of the city, **Fernando and Isabel** lived for a while in the Alhambra. They restored some rooms and converted the mosque but left the palace structure unaltered. As at Córdoba and Seville, it was **Emperor Carlos V**, their grandson, who wreaked the most insensitive destruction, demolishing a whole wing of rooms in order to build a Renaissance palace. This and the Alhambra itself were simply ignored by his successors, and by the eighteenth century the Palacios Nazaríes was in use as a prison. In 1812, it was taken and occupied by **Napoleon's forces**, who looted and damaged whole sections of the

▲ The Alhambra

Admission to the Alhambra

To protect the Alhambra, only 8100 daily admissions are allowed (daily 8.30am–8pm, Nov–March until 6pm; last admission 1hr before closing time; €12). If you're **buying tickets in person**, you have two options: you can buy them at the entrance (ticket office opens at 8am), where queues can be long, or by credit card from a number of *ServiCaixa* machines in a small building signed off the car park nearby; insert your card into the machine and request a day and time. All tickets will state whether they are for morning (8.30am–2pm) or afternoon (2–8pm, Oct–March until 6pm) sessions, and you must enter between the stated times (once inside, you may stay as long as you wish). However, you should bear in mind that tickets put on sale in the manners above are only what remain after pre-booked ticket sales (see below), which could well mean in high season that **no tickets** are on sale at the entrance.

Alternatively, and this is the method strongly recommended by the Alhambra to guarantee entry on a specific day, you can **book in advance**, either online (ⓦwww .alhambra-tickets.es or ⓦ www.servicaixa.com; €1 booking fee) or by **phone** on (from Spain) ☎902 888 001 or (from abroad) ☎934 923 750 (24hr service). Tickets should then be collected (at least 1hr before your time slot for the Palacios Nazaríes, allocated when booking; see below) from the Alhambra ticket office. You will need your credit card and passport for identification.

The tickets have **sections** for each part of the complex – Alcazaba, Palacios Nazaríes, Generalife – which must be used on the same day. Note that you will not be allowed to enter the complex (even with pre-booked tickets) less than an hour before closing time. To alleviate the severe overcrowding that used to occur, tickets are stamped with a half-hour **time slot** during which you must enter the Palacios Nazaríes. You will not be allowed to enter before or after this time, but once inside the palace you can stay as long as you like: any waiting time can be spent in the Alcazaba, museums or at one of the numerous cafés dotted around the complex. Note, too, that the Museo de la Alhambra and the Museo de las Bellas Artes, both in the Palacio de Carlos V, have different hours and admission fees to those of the Alhambra. It's also worth pointing out that only the palaces, museums and Generalife gardens require a ticket to gain entry – the rest you are allowed to wander around freely.

The Alhambra is also open for **floodlit visits**, limited to the Palacios Nazaríes (March–Oct Tues–Sat 10–11.30pm, ticket office open 9.45–10.15pm only; Nov–Feb Fri & Sat 8–9.30pm, ticket office open 7.45–8.15pm only; €12), and occasional **concerts** are held in its courts (details from the *turismo*). Availability of tickets (which can be pre-booked) is subject to the same terms as for daytime visits.

To check any changes to opening times, admission charges or booking procedures, visit the Alhambra's **website** ⓦwww.alhambra-patronato.es.

palace, and on their retreat from the city tried to blow up the entire complex. Their attempt was thwarted only by the action of a crippled soldier (José García) who remained behind and removed the fuses; a plaque honouring his valour has been placed in the Plaza de los Aljibes.

Two decades later, the Alhambra's "rediscovery" began, given impetus by the American writer **Washington Irving**, who set up his study in the empty palace rooms and began to write his marvellously romantic *Tales of the Alhambra* (on sale all over Granada – and good reading amid the gardens and courts). Shortly after its publication, the Spaniards made the Alhambra a **national monument** and set aside funds for its restoration. This continues to the present day and is now a highly sophisticated project, scientifically removing the accretions of later ages in order to expose and meticulously restore the Moorish creations.

Approaches and orientation

The standard **approach** to the Alhambra is along the Cuesta de Gomérez, the semi-pedestrianized road that climbs uphill from Granada's central Plaza Nueva. The only vehicles allowed to use this road are taxis and the **Alhambrabus** (line #30), a dedicated minibus service (daily 7am–10pm, every 10min; €1.10). To get there **by car**, you'll need to use the route that is signed from the Puerta Real, to the south of the cathedral; this guides you along *paseos* del Salón and de la Bomba, eventually bringing you to the Alhambra's car park, close to the entrance and ticket office on the eastern edge of the complex.

Should you decide to **walk** up the hill along the Cuesta de Gomérez (20min from Plaza Nueva), after a few hundred metres you reach the **Puerta de las Granadas**, a massive Renaissance gateway erected by Carlos V. Here two paths

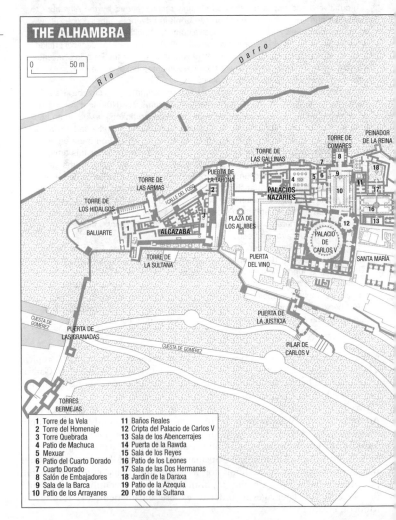

THE ALHAMBRA

1 Torre de la Vela	**11** Baños Reales
2 Torre del Homenaje	**12** Cripta del Palacio de Carlos V
3 Torre Quebrada	**13** Sala de los Abencerrajes
4 Patio de Machuca	**14** Puerta de la Rawda
5 Mexuar	**15** Sala de los Reyes
6 Patio del Cuarto Dorado	**16** Patio de los Leones
7 Cuarto Dorado	**17** Sala de las Dos Hermanas
8 Salón de Embajadores	**18** Jardín de la Daraxa
9 Sala de la Barca	**19** Patio de la Azequia
10 Patio de los Arrayanes	**20** Patio de la Sultana

diverge to either side of the road: the one on the right climbs up towards a group of fortified towers, the **Torres Bermejas**, which may date from as early as the eighth century. The left-hand path leads through the woods past a huge terrace-fountain (again courtesy of Carlos V) to the main gateway – and former entrance – of the Alhambra. This is the **Puerta de la Justicia**, a magnificent tower that forced three changes of direction, making intruders hopelessly vulnerable. It was built by Yusuf I in 1340 and preserves above its outer arch the Koranic symbol of a key (for Allah the Opener) and an outstretched hand, whose five fingers represent the five Islamic precepts: prayer, fasting, alms-giving, pilgrimage to Mecca and the oneness of God. The **entrance and ticket office** to the Alhambra – at the eastern end, near to the Generalife – lies a further five-minute walk uphill, reached by following the wall to your left.

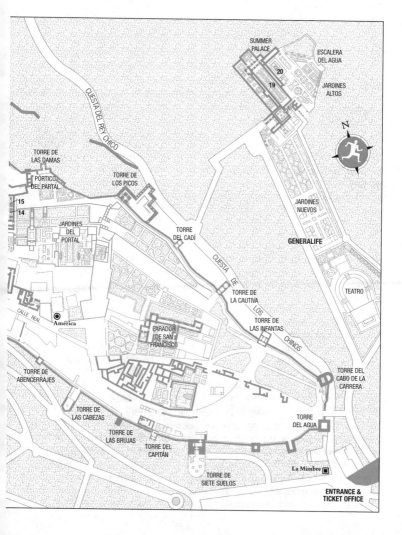

Within the citadel stood a complete "government city" of mansions, smaller houses, baths, schools, mosques, barracks and gardens. Of this only the **Alcazaba** and the **Palacios Nazaríes** remain; they face each other across a broad terrace (constructed in the sixteenth century over a dividing gully), flanked by the majestic though incongruous **Palacio de Carlos V**.

Within the walls of the citadel, too, are the beautiful *Parador de San Francisco* (a converted monastery, where Isabel was originally buried – terrace bar open to non-guests), and the *Hotel América*. There are a handful of **drinks stalls** around as well, including one, very welcome, in the Plaza de los Aljibes, just beyond the Puerta del Vino, and another in the Portal gardens (towards the Palacio de Carlos V after you leave the Palacios Nazaríes).

The Alcazaba

The entrance to the Alhambra brings you into the complex at the eastern end, near to the Generalife gardens. However, as you will have a time slot for entering the Palacios Nazaríes (usually up to an hour ahead), it makes sense chronologically and practically to start your visit with the **Alcazaba** at the Alhambra's opposite, or western, end, entered through the **Puerta del Vino** – named from its use in the sixteenth century as a wine cellar.

The Alcazaba is the earliest and most ruined part of the fortress. At its summit is the **Torre de la Vela**, named after a huge bell on its turret, which until recent years was rung to mark the irrigation hours for workers in the *vega*, Granada's vast and fertile plain. It was here, at 3pm on January 2, 1492, that the Cross was first displayed above the city, alongside the royal standards of Aragón and Castile and the banner of St James. Boabdil, leaving Granada for exile in the Alpujarras, turned and wept at the sight, earning from his mother Aisha the famous rebuke: "Do not weep like a woman for what you could not defend like a man." To gain access to the Palacios Nazaríes you need to recross the **Plaza de los Aljibes**. In Nasrid times, this area was a ravine dividing the hill between the Royal Palace on one side, and the Alcazaba on the other. Following the *reconquista*, the ravine was filled in to hold two rainwater cisterns (*aljibes*) and the surface above laid out with fortifications. During the construction of Carlos V's palace in the sixteenth century, the area was cleared to create a parade ground, the rather desolate form it retains today.

The Palacios Nazaríes

It is amazing that the **Palacios Nazaríes** has survived, for it stands in utter contrast to the strength of the Alcazaba and the encircling walls and towers. It was built lightly and often crudely from wood, brick and adobe, and was designed not to last but to be renewed and redecorated by succeeding rulers. Its buildings show a brilliant use of light and space, but they are principally a vehicle for ornamental stucco decoration. This, as Titus Burckhardt explains in *Moorish Culture in Spain*, was both an intricate science and a philosophy of abstract art in direct contrast to pictorial representation:

With its rhythmic repetition, [it] does not seek to capture the eye to lead it into an imagined world, but, on the contrary, liberates it from all pre-occupations of the mind. It does not transmit any specific ideas, but a state of being, which is at once repose and inner rhythm.

Burckhardt adds that the way in which patterns are woven from a single band, or radiate from many identical centres, served as a pure simile for Islamic belief in the oneness of God, manifested at the centre of every form and being. Arabic inscriptions feature prominently in the ornamentation. Some are poetic eulogies to the buildings and builders, others to various sultans (notably Mohammed V). Most, however, are taken from the Koran, and among them the phrase *Wa-la ghaliba illa-Llah* (There is no Conqueror but God) is tirelessly repeated. This became the battle cry (and family motto) of the Nasrids upon Ibn al-Ahmar's return in 1248 from aiding the Castilian war of Fernando III against Muslim Seville; it was his reply to the customary, though bitterly ironic, greetings of Mansur (Victor), ridiculing his role as a feudal puppet of the Christian enemy.

The palace is structured in three parts, each arrayed round an interior court and with a specific function. The sultans used the **Mexuar**, the first series of rooms, for business and judicial purposes. In the **Serallo**, beyond, they received embassies and distinguished guests. The last section, the **Harem**, formed their private living quarters and would have been entered by no one but their family or servants.

The Mexuar

The council chamber, the main **reception hall** of the Mexuar, is the first room you enter. It was completed in 1365 and hailed (perhaps formulaically) by the court poet and vizier Ibn Zamrak as a "haven of counsel, mercy, and favour". Here the sultan heard the pleas and petitions of the people and held meetings with his ministers. At the room's far end is a small oratory, one of a number of prayer niches scattered round the palace and immediately identifiable by their distinctive alignment (to face Mecca). This "public" section of the palace, beyond which few would have penetrated, is completed by the Mudéjar **Cuarto Dorado** (Golden Room), decorated under Carlos V, whose *Plus Ultra* motif appears throughout the palace, and the **Patio del Cuarto Dorado**. This has perhaps the grandest facade of the whole palace, for it admits you to the formal splendour of the Serallo.

The Serallo

The Serallo – the part of the complex where important guests were received – was built largely to the design of Yusuf I, a romantic and enlightened sultan who was stabbed to death by a madman while worshipping in the Alhambra mosque. Its rooms open out from delicate marble-columned arcades at each end of the long **Patio de los Arrayanes** (Patio of the Myrtles).

At the court's north end, occupying two floors of a fortified tower, is the royal throne room, known as the **Salón de Embajadores** (Hall of the Ambassadors). As the sultan could be approached only indirectly, it stands at an angle to the entrance from the Mexuar. It is the largest room of the palace, perfectly square and completely covered in tile and stucco decoration. Among the web of inscriptions is one that states simply "I am the Heart of the Palace." Here Boabdil signed the terms of his city's surrender to the Catholic kings, whose motifs (the arms of Aragón and Castile) were later worked into the room's stunning wooden dome, a superb example of *lacería*, the rigidly geometric "carpentry of knots". Here, too, so it is said, Fernando met Columbus to discuss his plans for finding a new sea route to India – which led to the discovery of the Americas. The dome itself, in line with the mystical-mathematical pursuit of medieval Moorish architecture, has a complex symbolism representing the seven heavens. Carlos V tore down the rooms at the southern end of the court; from the arcade there is access (frequently closed) to the gloomy **Chapel Crypt** (*cripta*) of his palace, which has a curious "whispering gallery" effect.

The **Patio de los Leones** (Court of the Lions), which has become the arche-typal image of Granada, constitutes the heart of the harem. The stylized and archaic-looking lions beneath its fountain (due to be returned to their place in 2009 after a lengthy restoration) probably date, like the patio itself, from the reign of Mohammed V, Yusuf's successor; a poem inscribed on the bowl tells how much fiercer they would look if they weren't so restrained by respect for the sultan. The court was designed as an interior garden and planted with shrubs and aromatic herbs; it opens onto three of the palace's finest rooms, each of which looks onto the fountain.

The most sophisticated rooms in this part of the complex, apparently designed to give a sense of the rotary movement of the stars, are the two facing each other across the court. The largest of these, the **Sala de los Abencerrajes**, has the most startlingly beautiful ceiling in the Alhambra: sixteen-sided, supported by niches of stalactite vaulting, lit by windows in the dome and reflected in a fountain on the floor. This light and airy quality stands at odds with its name and history, for here Abu'l-Hasan (Boabdil's father) murdered sixteen princes of the Abencerraje family, whose chief had fallen in love with his favourite, Zoraya; the crimson stains in the fountain are popularly supposed to be the indelible traces of their blood, but are more likely to be from rust.

At the far end is the **Sala de los Reyes** (Hall of the Kings), whose dormitory alcoves preserve a series of unique paintings on leather. These, in defiance of Koranic law, represent human scenes; it's believed that they were painted by a Christian artist in the last decades of Moorish rule. The second of the two facing chambers on the court's north side, the **Sala de las Dos Hermanas** (Hall of the Two Sisters), is more mundanely named – from two huge slabs of marble in its floor – but just as spectacularly decorated, with a dome of over five thousand "honeycomb cells". It was the principal room of the sultan's favourite, opening onto an inner apartment and balcony, the **Mirador de Daraxa** (known in English as the "Eyes of the Sultana"); the romantic garden patio below was added after the Reconquest.

Beyond, you are directed along a circuitous route through **apartments** redecorated by Carlos V (as at Seville, the northern-reared emperor installed fireplaces) and later used by Washington Irving. Eventually you emerge at the **Peinador de la Reina**, or Queen's Tower, a pavilion that served as an oratory for the sultanas and as a dressing room for the wife of Carlos V; perfumes were burned beneath its floor and wafted up through a marble slab in one corner.

From here, passing the **Patio de la Lindaraja** (added in the sixteenth century – though the basin of its marble fountain was taken from outside the Mexuar), you reach the **Baños Reales** (Royal Baths). These are tremendous, decorated in rich tile mosaics and lit by pierced stars and rosettes once covered by coloured glass. The central chamber was used for reclining and retains the balconies where singers and musicians – reputedly blind to keep the royal women from being seen – would entertain the bathers. At present, entry is not permitted to the baths, though you can make out most of the features through the doorways. The visit route exits via the exquisite **Pórtico del Partal**, with the **Torre de las Damas** (Ladies' Tower) and elegant portico overlooking a serene pool. What appears no more than a garden pavilion today is in fact the surviving remnant of the early fourteenth-century Palace of the Partal, a four-winged structure originally surrounding the pool, the Alhambra's largest expanse of water. The **Jardines del Partal** lie beyond this, and the nearby gate brings you out close to the entrance to the Palacio de Carlos V.

Palacio de Carlos V

The grandiose **Palacio de Carlos V** seems totally out of place here, its austere stone-built architecture jarring with the delicate oriental style and materials of the Moorish palace. Begun in 1526 but never finished, it is in fact a distinguished piece of Renaissance design in its own right – the only surviving work of Pedro Machuca, a former pupil of Michelangelo. On its upper floors – reached by steps from a circular central courtyard where bullfights were once held – is a mildly interesting **Museo de Bellas Artes** (Tues 2.30–8pm, Wed–Sat 9am–8pm, Sun 9am–2.30pm; Nov–March Tues–Sat until 6pm; €1.50, free with EU passport) with some notable examples of *andaluz* wood sculpture. The lower floor holds the **Museo de la Alhambra** (aka Museo Hispano-Musulman; Tues noon–2.30pm; Wed–Sat 9am–2.30pm; €1.50, free with EU passport), a small but fascinating collection of Hispano-Moorish art, displaying many items discovered during the Alhambra restoration; the star exhibit is a beautiful fifteenth-century metre-and-a-half-high **Alhambra vase** (Jarrón de las Gacelas), made from local red clay enamelled in blue and gold and decorated with leaping gazelles. Note, however, that both museums frequently fail to open on their advertised days and are liable to close early in slack periods.

The Generalife

Paradise is described in the Koran as a shaded, leafy garden refreshed by running water where the "fortunate ones" may take their rest. It is an image that perfectly describes the **Generalife**, the gardens and summer palace of the sultans. Its name means literally "Garden of the Architect", and the grounds consist of a luxuriantly imaginative series of patios, enclosed gardens and walkways.

By chance, an account of the gardens during Moorish times, written rather poetically by the fourteenth-century court vizier and historian Ibn Zamrak, survives. The descriptions that he gives aren't all entirely believable, but they are a wonderful basis for musing as you lie around by the patios and fountains. There were, he wrote, celebrations with horses darting about in the dusk at speeds that made the spectators rub their eyes (a form of festival still indulged in at Moroccan *fantasías*); rockets shot into the air to be attacked by the stars for their audacity; tightrope walkers flying through the air like birds; and men bowled along in a great wooden hoop, shaped like an astronomical sphere.

Today, devoid of such amusements, the gardens are still evocative – above all, perhaps, the **Patio de los Cipreses** (aka Patio de la Sultana), a dark and secretive walled garden of sculpted junipers where the Sultana Zoraya was suspected of meeting her lover Hamet, chief of the unfortunate Abencerrajes. Nearby, too, is the inspired flight of fantasy of the **Escalera del Agua**, a staircase with water flowing down its stone balustrades. From here you can look down on the wonderful old Arab quarter of the Albaicín.

The rest of town

If you're spending just a couple of days in Granada, it's hard to resist spending both of them in the Alhambra. You shouldn't miss, however, the run-down medieval streets of the **Albaicín**, Spain's largest and most characteristic surviving Moorish *barrio*, or the cave-quarter of **Sacromonte** extending up from the Río Darro. And while the cathedral is not one of Andalucía's finest, the **Capilla Real** attached to it is a flamboyant Gothic masterpiece and demands to be seen.

Security in the Albaicín

Although you certainly shouldn't let it put you off visiting the atmospheric Albaicín quarter, it's worth bearing in mind that the area has been the scene of repeated **thefts** from tourists. To ensure your visit is a happy one, take all the usual precautions: avoid carrying around large amounts of money or valuables (including airline tickets and passports – a photocopy of the latter will satisfy museums), and keep what you have in safe pockets instead of shoulder bags. If you do get something snatched, don't offer resistance; crime in these streets rarely involves attacks to the person, but thieves will be firm in getting what they want. Finally, try not to look like an obvious tourist (map/guidebook in hand is a dead giveaway) or flaunt expensive-looking photographic equipment, and keep to the streets where there are other people about, particularly at night.

The Albaicín

Declared a UNESCO World Heritage Site in 1994, the Albaicín stretches across a fist-shaped area bordered by the river, the Sacromonte hill, the old town walls and the winding Calle de Elvira (parallel to the Gran Vía de Colón). The best approach is along Carrera del Darro, beside the river. At no. 31 on this street are the remains of the **Baños Árabes** (Tues–Fri 10am–2pm; €1.50, free with EU passport), marvellous and little-visited Moorish public baths. Nearby, and just to the east of Plaza Nueva behind the church of Santa Ana, the Baños Arabes Al Andalus, c/Santa Ana 16 (reservation required ⊤958 229 978; bath €17), gives you some idea of what a **Moorish bathhouse** would have been like when functioning. Here you can wallow in the graded temperatures of the recreated traditional baths – decorated with mosaics and plaster arabesques – or take tea in the peaceful *tetería* (tea room) upstairs.

Continuing along Carrera del Darro, you come to the **Casa de Castril** (Tues 2.30–8.30pm, Wed–Sat 9.30am–8.30pm, Sun 9.30am–2.30pm; €1.50, free with EU passport), at no. 43, a Renaissance mansion housing the town's **archeological museum**. Of particular note here are some remarkable finds from the Neolithic Cueva de los Murciélagos (Cave of the Bats) in the Alpujarras; there are also exhibits from Granada's Phoenician, Roman, Visigothic and Moorish periods. Beside the museum, a road ascends to the churches of **San Juan** (with an intact thirteenth-century minaret) and **San Nicolás**, whose square offers a stunning **view of the Alhambra**, considered the best in town.

Sacromonte

Continuing parallel with the river takes you up into the gypsy cave-quarter of Sacromonte. Like many cities in Andalucía, Granada has an ancient and still considerable *gitano* population, from whose clans many of Spain's best flamenco guitarists, dancers and singers have emerged. They have traditionally lived in caves in this area, although these days the *barrio* is better known for its nightlife. If you wander up here in the daytime, take a look at the old **caves** on the far side of the old Moorish wall – most of them deserted after severe floods in 1962. There are fantastic views from the top. Sacromonte now has its own museum, the **Centro Interpretación del Sacromonte**, Barranco de los Negros s/n (Tues–Sun 10am–2pm & 5–9pm, Nov–Feb 4–7pm; €5), depicting the life and times of the *barrio*.

The Capilla Real, cathedral and churches

In addition to the city's Moorish legacy, it's worth the distinct readjustment and effort of will to appreciate the city's later Christian monuments, notably the **Capilla Real** (Royal Chapel; daily 10.30/11am–12.45pm & 4–7pm, Nov–Feb 3.30–6.15pm; €3.50), in the centre of town at the southern end of Gran Vía de Colón. It's an impressive building, flamboyant late Gothic in style and built ad hoc in the first decades of Christian rule as a mausoleum for Los Reyes Católicos, the city's "liberators". The actual **tombs** are as simple as could be imagined: Fernando (marked with a not-easily-spotted "F" on the left of the central pair) and Isabel, flanked by their daughter Joana ("the Mad") and her husband Felipe ("the Handsome"), resting in lead coffins placed in a plain crypt. But above them – the response of their grandson Carlos V to what he found "too small a room for so great a glory" – is a fabulously elaborate **monument** carved in Carrara marble by Florentine Domenico Fancelli in 1517, with sculpted Renaissance effigies of the two monarchs; the tomb of Joana and Felipe alongside is a much inferior work by Ordoñez. In front of the monument is an equally magnificent **reja**, the work of Maestro Bartolomé of Jaén, and a splendid **retablo** behind depicts Boabdil surrendering the keys of Granada.

Isabel, in accordance with her will, was originally buried on the Alhambra hill (in the church of San Francisco, now part of the *parador*), but her wealth and power proved no safeguard for her wishes. The queen's final indignity occurred during the 1980s when the candle that she asked should perpetually illuminate her tomb was replaced by an electric bulb – it was restored in 1999 following numerous protests. In the Capilla's **Sacristy** is displayed the sword of Fernando, the crown of Isabel and her outstanding personal collection of **medieval Flemish paintings** – including important works by Memling, Bouts and van der Weyden – and various Italian and Spanish paintings, including panels by Botticelli, Perugino and Pedro Berruguete.

For all its stark Renaissance bulk, Granada's **Catedral**, adjoining the Capilla Real and entered from the door beside it (Mon–Sat 10.45am–1.30pm & 4–8pm, Sun 4–8pm; Nov–Feb until 7pm; €3.50), is a disappointment. It was begun in 1521, just as the chapel was finished, but was then left incomplete well into the eighteenth century. At least it's light and airy inside, though, and it's fun to go round putting coins in the slots to light up the chapels, where an El Greco *St Francis* and sculptures by Pedro de Mena and Martínez Montañés will be revealed.

Other churches have more to offer, and with sufficient interest you could easily fill a day of visits. Northwest of the cathedral, ten-minutes' walk along c/San Jerónimo, the Baroque **San Juan de Dios**, with a spectacular *retablo*, is attached to a majestically portalled hospital (still in use; porter will allow a brief look) with two marvellous **patios**. Close by is the elegant Renaissance **Convento de San Jerónimo** (daily 10am–2.30pm & 4–7.30pm, Nov–Feb until 6.30pm; €3), founded by the Catholic Monarchs, though built after their death, with two imposing patios and a wonderful frescoed church.

Lastly, on the northern outskirts of town, is **La Cartuja** (Mon–Sat 10am–1pm & 4–8pm, Sun 10am–noon & 4–8pm; Nov–March until 6pm; €3.50), perhaps the grandest and most outrageously decorated of all the country's lavish Carthusian monasteries. It was constructed at the height of Baroque extravagance – some say to rival the Alhambra – and has a chapel of staggering wealth, surmounted by an altar of twisted and coloured marble. It lies a further ten- to fifteen-minute walk beyond San Juan de Dios; bus line #8, going north along the Gran Vía, also passes by.

Casa Museo Federico García Lorca

To the west of the city, in the pleasant *vega* village of **FUENTE VAQUEROS**, the birthplace of Federico García Lorca, Andalucía's greatest poet and dramatist, has been transformed into a museum, the **Casa Museo Federico García Lorca** (April, May, June & Sept Tues–Sat 10am–2pm & 5–6pm, Sun 10am–1pm; July & Aug Tues–Sun 10am–2pm; Oct–March Tues–Sat 10am–1pm & 4–5pm, Sun 10am–1pm; guided visits on the hour; €1.80; ☎958 516 453, ⓦwww.museogarcialorca.org), and contains a highly evocative collection of Lorca memorabilia. Buses (hourly from 9am, last bus returns 8pm; 20min) leave from Granada's Avda. de Andaluces, fronting the train station. The village makes a pleasant overnight stop, and **accommodation** is available at *Hostal-Restaurante Moli-Lorc*, c/Ancha Escuelas 11 (☎958 516 532; ➋), next to the church, which incidentally holds the font where Lorca was baptized.

Eating

When it comes to **restaurants**, Granada certainly isn't one of the gastronomic centres of Spain, possibly due in part to the *granadino* **tapas bars** that tempt away potential diners by giving out some of the most generous tapas in Andalucía – one comes free with every drink.

A flavour of North Africa is to be found along **c/Calderería Nueva** and its surrounds in "Little Morocco", where you'll find health-food stores, as well as numerous Moroccan tearooms and eating places. This street is useful for assembling picnics for Alhambra visits, as is the revamped ultramodern **Mercado Municipal** in Plaza San Agustín just north of the cathedral (Mon–Sat early until 1.30pm). The warren of streets between **Plaza Nueva** and the **Gran Vía** has plenty of good-value places, particularly tapas bars, as does the area around **Plaza del Carmen** (near the *ayuntamiento*) and along c/Navas. Another good location is the **Campo del Príncipe**, a pleasant square below the south side of the Alhambra hill, with a line of open-air restaurant terraces, highly popular on summer nights.

City centre and Albaicín

Bar-Restaurante Sevilla c/Oficios 12 ☎958 221 223. One of the few surviving prewar restaurants, and once a haunt of Lorca's, this is a pleasant restaurant with a *menú* for around €40, and an outdoor terrace – beneath the walls of the Capilla Real – in the evenings. Closed Mon.

Café au Lait Callejón de los Franceses 31. Laid-back French-style café-bar with pleasant palm-shaded terrace; serves a good-value breakfast complete with domestic or foreign newspapers, and later does economical pizzas, tapas and *crêpes*.

Casa Cepillo c/Pescadería 8, off c/Príncipe. Cheap and cheerful *comedor* with an excellent-value *menú* for €9.50; the soups are especially good.

Mesón La Alegría c/Moras 4. This economical *mesón* is a favourite of *granadinos* working nearby and specializes in *carnes a la brasa* (charcoal grilled meats).

Mesón El Trillo del Reca Callejón del Aljibe del Trillo 3 ☎958 225 182. Enchanting little mid-priced restaurant in an Albaicín *carmen* offering

Basque-influenced cuisine: *bacalao al pil-pil* (salted cod with garlic) is a signature dish. Has outdoor tables on a delightful garden patio shaded by pear and quince trees.

Mesón Yunque Plaza San Miguel Bajo. Owned by a flamenco singer, this medium-priced place has a great atmosphere, with tasty meat and fish dishes served at indoor and outdoor tables on a delightful square.

Naturi Albaicín c/Calderería Nueva 10. Imaginative vegetarian cooking, such as fine salads and stuffed mushrooms, at reasonable prices (€7 *menú*). Take tea or coffee afterwards at the nearby tea-houses.

Restaurante León c/Pan 3. Long-established *cordobés* restaurant (occupying premises on both sides of the street) and serving many *carne de monte* (game) dishes, with a good-value *menú* for €10.

Restaurante-Bar Las Tomasas Carril de San Agustín 4 ☎958 224 108. Mid-priced restaurant serving *cocina andaluz* in a huge and beautiful *carmen* with a stunning terrace view of the floodlit Alhambra at night. *Ajo blanco* (white *gazpacho*) is a speciality. You can also nurse a *tinto de verano* here if you don't want to eat. Closed Sun, also lunch in July & Aug.

🍤 **Restaurante-Marisquería Cunini** c/Pescadería 9 ☎958 267 587. One of Granada's most established and outstanding upmarket restaurants (booking advised), serving mainly fish, with a superb tapas bar attached.

Around town

Bar Ferroviaria c/Lavadero Tablas 1, off c/Tablas. This is in fact a pensioners' club for former railway workers, but don't let that put you off – behind the anonymous exterior you'll find an amazingly cheap *menú* (€4.50) that attracts workers and students for miles around; if the paella is on, it's your lucky day. Daily 9.30am–8.30pm (lunch 1.30–4pm). Closed Aug.

El Carmen de San Miguel Plaza Torres Bermejas 3 ☎958 226 723. One of Granada's noted places to eat, with a fabulous terrace looking out over the city (book a frontline table). The restaurant's signature dish, *conejo relleno de langostinos escabechados con ostras y limón* (rabbit with prawns and oysters),

typifies its innovative approach (occasionally overdone) to *andaluz* cuisine. Seasonal menu; mains €16–25. Closed Sun.

La Mimbre Paseo del Generalife s/n. With a delightful terrace shaded by willows (*mimbres*), this is one of the best restaurants on the Alhambra hill. The food is good, but they are sometimes overwhelmed in high season. There's a decent *menú* for around €17.50, which you may need to ask for.

La Ninfa Campo del Principe. Popular Italian restaurant for pizzas, pasta and salads that puts out tables on this pleasant plaza, and is often full to bursting at weekends.

Parador de San Francisco Alhambra ☎958 221 440. The *parador*'s restaurant is one of the best in an upmarket chain often noted for its blandness. There's a pleasant dining room plus a terrace with fine views, and it offers a varied and not-too-bank-breaking *menú* (around €32). Laudably, they also do equally good vegetarian (€24.50) and diabetic (€32) *menús*.

Seis Peniques Plaza de Padre Suárez. Quite a good little bar-restaurant with a small terrace facing the Casa de los Tiros; serves a decent *menú* for €8.50.

Drinking and nightlife

Enjoyable central **tapas bars** include *Bodegas Castañeda* on the corner of c/Elvira and c/Almireceros, a traditional, though modernized, *bodega*; the lively *Bodegas La Mancha*, around the corner at c/Joaquín Costa 10; and the earthy *Bar Sabanilla*, c/San Sebastián 14, up an alley off the southeast corner of Plaza Bib Rambla, which claims to be the oldest bar in Granada, and serves a free tapa with every drink. Recent arrival *Al Sur de Granada*, c/Elvira 150, is a thoroughly modern bar-shop serving delicious cheese, *jamón* and *salchichón* tapas, and they often stage exhibitions of work by local artists. All these stay open until around midnight.

If you want to go on **drinking through the early hours**, head out to the student areas round the university; c/Pedro Antonio de Alarcón – particularly the stretch between Plaza Albert Einstein and c/Obispo Hurtado – is extremely lively, while the streets to the east (c/Casillas de Prats, c/Trajano and Plaza Menorca) are another hot spot for **pubs** and **disco-bars**. When the university is in session, several of the cave dwellings in Sacromonte are turned into **disco-tecas**, packed with students at weekends.

Angel Azul c/Lavadero de Tablas 15, west of Plaza Trinidad. Along with the nearby *Tic Tac* (c/Horno de Haza 19), this is the most gay of Granada's gay bars with lots of action at weekends (Spanish-language skills not required).

Babylon c/Silleria (between Plaza Nueva and Gran Via). Reggae club and popular pick-up venue – much favoured by US students.

Camborio Camino del Sacromonte s/n. Fashionable *discobar* housed in a cave, which is especially

lively at weekends and lifts off about 4am. Be alert for bag-snatchers in this area.

Eshavira c/Postigo de la Cuna 2, a tiny alley off c/Azacayas. Jazz/flamenco bar that gets quite lively. Wed, Thurs & Sun nights only.

La Estrella c/Cuchilleros. Congested, smoky disco-bar with great sounds.

Fondo Reservado c/Santa Ines 4. Funky gay and straight bar with a hilarious drag show every weekend.

Granada 10 c/Carcél Baja 10, off Gran Vía near the cathedral. Small and popular central *discoteca* inside a beautifully restored old retro cinema.

Jazz Café Bohemia c/Santa Teresa 17, west of Plaza Trinidad. Relaxed jazz bar with cool sounds, and walls lined with photos and memorabilia.

Patapalo c/Naranjos 2. Stylish *discobar* appealing to a younger crowd.

Peatón Pub c/Socrates 25, off c/Pedro Antonio de Alarcón. Rock bar popular with a student crowd. Other lively places nearby include *Babel*, *Van Gogh* and *Genesis*.

Planta Baja Horno de Abad, off Carril del Picón. Long-established *discobar* – garage and lounge are big here – now in a new home.

Potemkin Plaza Hospicio Viejo s/n. Great new pint-sized *copas* bar with cool sounds run by Richard Dudanski, former drummer with J. Rotten of London's punk era. He's calmed down a bit since, and has discovered a great Japanese chef, whose mouthwatering tapas are the icing on the cake of a night out here.

Quilombo c/Carril de San Cecilio 21. With a pool table and big dancefloor that starts humming around 3am. Sometimes stages live music.

La Sal c/Santa Paula 11. Originally a lipstick lesbian dance bar, but now attracting male gays, too.

Son c/Joaquín Costas 3. Ultra-cool bi-level bar with older salsa upstairs and younger heavy-metal scene in the smoky (not tobacco smoke) downstairs.

Flamenco

When it comes to **flamenco**, finding anything near the real thing in Granada is not as easy as you might think. Shows in Sacromonte, traditionally the home of the city's flamenco performers, are generally shameless rip-offs – one exception is *Los Faroles*, almost at the very end of the line of "caves" (ask anyone for directions as it's well known) and owned by Quiqui, a genial flamenco singer. If the mood is favourable, impromptu flamenco often happens here after dark. This place is also good for a lunchtime or evening drink, with a view of the Alhambra from its terrace.

In the Albaicín, tiny *El Niño de los Almendras*, a signless place in c/Muladar de Doña Sancha owned by the flamenco singer of the same name, is done up inside to resemble a cave. It's only open Friday nights (starts around midnight), but if you're in luck you may see some *inolvidable* flamenco here. *Bar-Restaurante La Zeta*, c/Pages 10 (⊤958 294 860), a couple of blocks northwest of Plaza Larga, is another venue that stages frequent flamenco shows.

Listings

Airport Granada airport (⊤958 245 200) handles domestic flights to Madrid and Barcelona as well as European budget airlines.

Books, newspapers and maps Metro, c/Gracia 31, off c/Alhóndiga, to the southwest of Plaza de la Trinidad, is the best international bookshop, with a wide selection of books on Granada, Lorca, etc, plus walking maps. For maps, try also the Librería Dauro at c/Zacatín 3 (a pedestrian street between the cathedral and c/Reyes Católicos), or for a more specialist selection Cartografica del Sur, c/Valle Inclán 2, southwest of the train station. Foreign press is sold by the *kioscos* in Plaza Nueva and Puerta Real.

Hospital Cruz Roja (Red Cross), c/Escoriaza 8 ⊤958 222 222; Hospital Clinico San Cecilio, Avda.

del Doctor Olóriz, near the Plaza de Toros ⊤958 023 000. For advice on emergency treatment, phone ⊤061.

Internet access *Uninet* Plaza del la Encarnación 2 (Mon–Sat 9.30am–10pm, Sun 4.30–10pm) to the east of the cathedral; *Locutorio Azahara* c/Colcha s/n (daily 9am–midnight), southwest of Plaza Nueva.

Police For emergencies, dial ⊤091 (national) or ⊤092 (local). The Policía Local station is at Plaza de Campos 3 ⊤958 808 502. There's also a property lost-and-found section in the *ayuntamiento* building on Plaza del Carmen (⊤958 248 103).

Post office Puerta Real (Mon–Fri 9am–8pm, Sat 9am–2pm).

Parque Nacional Sierra Nevada

The mountains of the **Sierra Nevada**, designated Andalucía's second national park in 1999, rise to the south of Granada, a startling backdrop to the city, snowcapped for much of the year and offering good trekking and also skiing from late November until late May. The ski slopes are at **Solynieve**, an unimaginative, developed resort just 28km away from the city centre. From here, you can make the two- to three-hour trek up to **Veleta** (3400m), the second-highest peak of the range (and of the Iberian peninsula); this is a perfectly feasible day-trip from Granada by bus.

The Veleta ascent

From the *Albergue Universitario* (see box below), the Capileira road (closed to vehicles) runs past the **Pico Veleta**; now asphalted, it is perfectly – and tediously – walkable. With your own transport, it's possible to shave a couple of kilometres off the walk to the summit by ignoring the no-entry signs at the car park near the *Albergue* and continuing on to a second car park farther up the mountain, from which point the road is then barred. Although the peak of the mountain looks deceptively close from here, you should allow two to three hours up to the summit and two hours down. There is no water en route so you'd be advised

Sierra Nevada practicalities

Flora and fauna

The Sierra Nevada is particularly rich in **wild flowers**, with fifty varieties unique to these mountains. **Wildlife** abounds away from the roads; one of the most exciting sights is the *Cabra hispanica*, a wild horned goat that (with luck) you'll see standing on pinnacles, silhouetted against the sky. Birdwatching is also superb, with the colourful hoopoe – a bird with a stark, haunting cry – a common sight.

Information and transport

The best **map** of the Sierra Nevada including the lower slopes of the Alpujarras is the one co-produced by the Instituto Geográfico Nacional and the Federación Española de Montañismo (1:50,000), generally available in Granada. A 1:40,000 **map and guide set**, *Sierra Nevada and La Alpujarra*, published in English by Editorial Alpina, is also good and comes with a booklet describing walks in the park and information on flora and fauna.

To reach the *parque nacional* with your **own transport**, take the Acera del Darro and follow signs for the Sierra Nevada. The park's **visitor centre**, "El Dornajo", is signposted just off the road, at the 22km mark (daily 10am–2pm & 6–8pm, Oct–March 4–6pm; ☏958 340 625, ⊛www.mma.es). It sells guidebooks, maps and hats (sun protection is vital at this altitude), and has a permanent exhibition on the park's flora and fauna. They can provide hiking information (English spoken) and rent out horses and mountain bikes. The centre also has a pleasant **cafetería** with a stunning terrace view. Beyond the visitor centre, the route into the park continues for a further 10km to pass the Solynieve ski resort, and 2km farther on lies the *Albergue Universitario*, where the bus terminates.

Buses from Granada are operated by Autocares Bonal (☏958 465 022) with a daily service to Solynieve (€8 return) and, just above this, the *Albergue Universitario* (departs 9am, returns from *Albergue Universitario* 5pm, Solynieve 5.10pm). Tickets should be bought in advance at the bus station, although you can pay on board if the bus isn't full. For the winter service (Oct–March), ring the bus company or check with the *turismo*.

to take some along; the summit makes a great place for a picnic. Weather permitting, the **views** beyond the depressing trappings of the ski resort are fabulous: the Sierra Subbética of Córdoba and the Sierra de Guadix to the north, the Mediterranean and Rif Mountains of Morocco to the south, and nearby to the southeast, the towering mass of **Mulhacén** (3483m), the Spanish peninsula's highest peak.

Solynieve

SOLYNIEVE ("Sun and Snow" aka Pradollano), which lies outside the boundaries of the national park, is a hideous-looking ski resort regarded by serious alpine skiers as something of a joke, but with snow lingering so late in the year, it does have obvious attractions. For budget **accommodation**, try the modern and comfortable *Albergue Juvenil*, c/Peñones 22 (☎958 575 116, ⓦwww.inturjoven.com; summer/winter under-26 €10/€25, over-26 €14/€30), on the edge of the ski resort, where you can get great-value (outside the Nov–March ski season) double and four-bed rooms, all en suite. They also rent out skis and equipment. Other places here are pricey in winter (and often closed outside it); the *turismos* in Granada have complete accommodation lists.

Three kilometres away in isolated Peñones de San Francisco lies one more option: the *Albergue Universitario* (☎958 481 003, ⓦwww.nevadensis.com; B&B ❷), with bunk rooms, doubles sharing bath, and a restaurant. The only **campsite** in this area is at the Ruta del Purche, 15km out of Granada and halfway to Solynieve (☎958 340 407), with a supermarket and restaurant. The bus will drop you at the road leading to the site, from where it's a good kilometre walk.

Las Alpujarras

Beyond the mountains, farther south from Granada, lie the great **valleys of the Alpujarras**, first settled in the twelfth century by Berber refugees from Seville, and later the Moors' last stronghold in Spain.

The valleys are bounded to the north by the Sierra Nevada, and to the south by the lesser *sierras* of Lujar, La Contraviesa and Gador. The eternal snows of the high *sierras* keep the valleys and their seventy or so villages well watered all summer long. Rivers have cut deep gorges in the soft mica and shale of the upper mountains, and over the centuries have deposited silt and fertile soil on the lower hills and in the valleys; here the villages have grown, for the soil is rich and easily worked. The intricate terracing that today preserves these deposits was begun as long as two thousand years ago by Visigoths or Ibero-Celts, whose remains have been found at Capileira.

The **Moors** carried on the tradition, and modified the terracing and irrigation in their inimitable way. They transformed the Alpujarras into an earthly paradise, and here they retired to bewail the loss of their beloved lands in *al-Andalus*, resisting a series of royal edicts demanding their forced conversion to Christianity. In 1568, they rose up in a final, short-lived revolt, which led to the expulsion of all Spanish Moors. Even then, however, two Moorish families were required to stay in each village to show the new Christian peasants, who had been marched down from Galicia and Asturias to repopulate the valleys, how to operate the intricate irrigation systems.

Through the following centuries, the land fell into the hands of a few wealthy families, and the general population became impoverished labourers. The Civil

There are several **buses** a day from both Granada and Motril to **Lanjarón** and **Órgiva**, and one a day from Almería in the east. There are also buses from Granada (daily 8.30am & 5.30pm) to Ugíjar (4hr), in the **"Low" Alpujarras**, via a less scenic route through Lanjarón, Órgiva, Torvizcón, Cadiar, Yegen and Valor.

A direct **bus** from Granada to the more spectacular **"High" Alpujarras** (daily 10am, noon & 5pm) runs via Trevélez to Bérchules (returns 5.35am & 5.05pm, passing Trevélez 6.05am & 6.35pm). The return buses arrive in Granada at 8.45am and 8.45pm respectively (with another service from Trevélez to Granada at 4pm). Further information is available from the bus operator Alsina Graells (☎902 422 242).

War passed lightly over the Alpujarras: the occasional truckload of Nationalist youth trundled in from Granada, rounded up a few bewildered locals and shot them for "crimes" of which they were wholly ignorant; Republican youths came up in their trucks from Almería and did the same thing. Under Franco, the stranglehold of the landlords increased and there was real hardship and suffering. Today, the population has one of the lowest per capita incomes in Andalucía, with – as a recent report put it – "a level of literacy bordering on that of the Third World, alarming problems of desertification, poor communications and a high degree of underemployment".

Ironically, the land itself is still very fertile – oranges, chestnuts, bananas, apples and avocados grow here – while the recent influx of **tourism** is bringing limited wealth to the region. The so-called "High" Alpujarras have become popular with Spanish tourists and also with migrants from northern Europe who have purchased property here; Pampaneira, Bubión and Capileira, all within half an hour's drive from Lanjarón, have been scrubbed and white-washed. Though a little over-prettified, they're far from spoilt, and have acquired shops, lively bars, good, unpretentious restaurants and small, family-run *pensiones*. Other villages, less picturesque or less accessible, have little employment, and are sustained only by farming.

Walkers' guides to the Alpujarras are now beginning to mushroom; useful recent publications are listed in the "Books" section on pp.969–970.

Approaches: Lanjarón and Órgiva

The road **south from Granada to Motril** climbs steeply after leaving the city, until at 860m above sea level it reaches the **Puerto del Suspiro del Moro** – the Pass of the Sigh of the Moor. Boabdil, last Moorish king of Granada, came this way, having just handed over the keys of his city to the Reyes Católicos (see p.339). From the pass you catch your last glimpse of the city and the Alhambra. Just beyond Béznar is the turning to **Lanjarón** and **Órgiva**, the market town of the region.

Lanjarón

LANJARÓN has been subject to tourism and the influence of the outside world for longer than anywhere else in the Alpujarras owing to the curative powers of its **spa waters**, sold in bottled form throughout Spain. Between March and December, the spa baths are open, and the town fills with the aged and infirm – should you wish to try a cure at the **Balneario** at the village's western end (March–Dec; ☎958 770 137, ⊛www.balneariodelanjaron.com), a basic soak will cost €13.50, with add-ons for massage, mud baths and all kinds of other alarming-sounding *tracciónes* and *inyecciónes*.

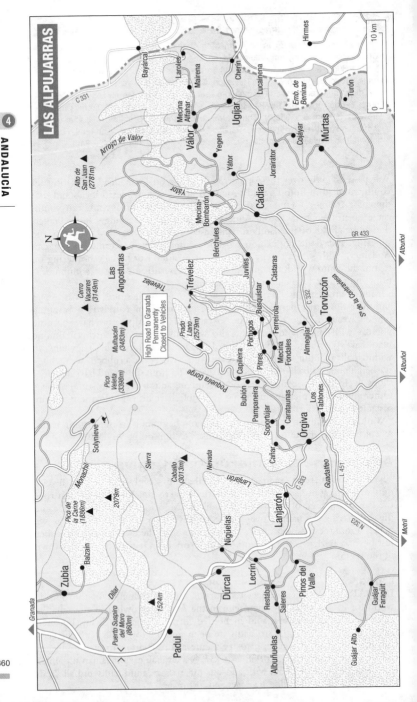

LAS ALPUJARRAS

High Road to Granada
Permanently
Closed to Vehicles

0 — 10 km

Lanjarón itself is little more than a ribbon of buildings, mostly modern, flanking the road through the village, the Avda. Alpujarra, and its continuation, the Avda. Andalucía. Below this thoroughfare, marking Lanjarón's medieval status as the gateway to the Alpujarras, is a **Moorish castle**, newly refurbished and due to open in 2009 (details from the *turismo*). A ten-minute stroll reveals its dramatic setting – follow the signs down the hill from the main street and out onto the terraces and meadows below the town.

The countryside and mountains within a day's walk of Lanjarón, however, are beyond compare. A track off the backstreets behind town takes you steeply up to the vast spaces of the **Reserva Nacional de la Sierra Nevada**. For a somewhat easier day's walk out of Lanjarón, go to the bridge just east of town and take the sharply climbing, cobbled track that parallels the **river**. After two to two-and-a-half hours through small farms, with magnificent views and scenery, a downturn to a small stone bridge permits return to Lanjarón on the opposite bank. Allow a minimum of six hours.

Practicalities

Opposite the Balneario is Lanjarón's **municipal tourist office**, Avda. Andalucía s/n (Mon–Sat 10am–2pm & 6.30–8.30pm, Sun 10–2pm; ℡958 770 462). Midway along the same street (now c/Real) is the **bus stand** with a ticket office at no. 123 (℡958 770 003) near the Caja Rural bank. **Internet** access is available at *Cyberplay Lanjarón*, Avda. de Andalucía 30, at the eastern end of the main street to the side of the La Caixa bank (daily except Wed 6pm–midnight).

There's no shortage of **hotels** and **pensiones** in the town. The grand-looking *Hotel España*, Avda. Alpujarra 42 (℡958 770 187, ⓦwww.lanjaron .biz; ❷), next door to the Balneario, is good value, very friendly and has a pool. Farther along the road, a signed turn-off leads downhill to the excellent *Hotel Alcadima*, c/Francisco Tarrega 3 (℡958 770 809, ⓦwww.alcadima.com; ❸), with the best pool and restaurant terrace in town, and many of the comfortable rooms have stunning balcony views towards the castle. A kilometre farther east – on the road out – the refurbished *Venta El Buñuelo* (℡958 770 461; ❶) has air-conditioned en-suite rooms with great views, a decent terrace restaurant below and easy parking.

Lanjarón has plenty of **restaurants** and tapas bars, too, many attached to the hotels (the *España*'s is worth trying), which often offer a good-value *menú*. Best choice for dining out, however, has to be the terrace restaurant of the *Hotel Castillo Alcadima*, a perfect place to while away a summer evening with a superb terrace view of the castle and a *menú* for €15. *Bar Galvez*, c/Real 95, is a good choice if you're on a tighter budget.

Órgiva

Heading east out of Lanjarón brings you after 11km to **ÓRGIVA** (also spelled Órjiva), the "capital" and market centre of the western Alpujarras. It is closer to the heart of the valley but is still really only a starting point; if the bus goes on to Capileira, you may want to stay on it. If you're **driving**, it's worth noting that petrol stations become scarcer from this point on.

Órgiva is a lively enough town, though, with plenty of bars and hotels and an animated **Thursday market** that draws in shoppers from far and wide. On the main street is an over-restored *Mudéjar* Moorish palace, now housing the *ayuntamiento*, and the sixteenth-century church of **Nuestra Señora de la Expectación**, whose towers add a touch of fancy to the townscape.

Houses in the Alpujarras

Houses in the valleys are built of grey stone, flat-roofed and low; whitewashing them is a recent innovation. The coarse walls are about 75cm thick, for summer coolness and protection from winter storms. Stout beams of chestnut, or ash in the lower valleys, are laid from wall to wall; on top of these is a mat of canes or split chestnut; upon this, flat stones are piled, and on the stones is spread a layer of *launa*, the crumbly grey mica found on the tops of the Sierra Nevada. It must – and this maxim is still observed today – be laid during the waning of the moon for the *launa* to settle properly and thus keep rain out. Gerald Brenan wrote in *South from Granada* of a particularly ferocious storm: "As I peered through the darkness of the stormy night, I could make out a dark figure on every roof in the village, dimly lit by an *esparto* torch, stamping clay into the holes in the roof."

Practicalities

For budget **accommodation**, one of the nicest places is the pretty *Alma Alpujarreña*, a little beyond the traffic lights at the town's main (and solitary) intersection (☎958 784 085; ❷), with simple and en-suite rooms plus a leafy terrace restaurant. Good-value rooms are available at *Hotel-Hostal Mirasol*, Avda. González Robles 3, on the way in from Lanjarón (☎958 785 159, @www .hotelmirasol.es; ❶–❷). Close to here, *Casa Rural El Molino*, Avda. González Robles 12 (☎646 616 628, @www.casaruralelmolino.com; ❸), has attractive en-suite rooms in a refurbished old olive-oil mill. Órgiva's **campsite**, with a pool, bar and restaurant, lies 2km south of town (☎958 784 307), reached by continuing along the road where the bus drops you. It also rents out cabins (❷) and bungalows (❸), has its own restaurant and pool and can advise on **walking routes** and renting horses in the nearby Sierra de Lújar.

For **food**, both the *Alma Alpujarreña* (*menú* €8.50) and the *Hostal Mírasol* (*menú* €8) are worth a try, have terraces and offer tapas, too. Other good places to eat are *Pizzería Almazara* on the main street (c/González Robles) below the church, *El Limonero* in c/Yanez (off the main road close to the *Almazara*), which has music on Wednesday nights, and *Café Libertad* in c/Libertad at the top of the main street behind the church.

The High (Western) Alpujarras

The best way to experience the **High Alpujarras** is to walk, and there are a number of paths between Órgiva and Cadiar, at the farthest reaches of the western valleys. Equip yourself with a compass and the Instituto Geográfico Nacional/Federación Española de Montañismo 1:50,000 map or the Editorial Alpina map (see p.357), which cover all the territory from Órgiva up to Bérchules (Alpina) and Berja (IGN/FEM) respectively. Alternatively, a bus from Lanjarón (daily 1pm) winds through all the upper Alpujarran villages.

Cañar, Soportújar and Carataunas

On from Órgiva, the first settlements you reach, almost directly above the town, are **CAÑAR** and **SOPORTÚJAR**, the latter a maze of sinuous white-walled alleys. Like many of the High Alpujarran villages, they congregate on the neatly terraced mountainside, planted with poplars and laced with irrigation channels. Both have bars where you can get a **meal**, and Soportújar can provide excellent-value en-suite **rooms** at *Bar Correillo* (☎958 787 578; ❶) on c/Real (behind the church). Both villages are perched precariously on the steep hillside with a rather sombre view of Órgiva in the valley below, and the mountains of Africa over the ranges to the south.

Just below the two villages, the tiny hamlet of **CARATAUNAS** is particularly pretty and puts on a lively start to its Semana Santa on Palm Sunday, when an effigy of Judas is tossed on a bonfire. Two kilometres out of Carataunas a turn-off on the left (signed "*Camino Forestal*") beyond the *Los Llanos* restaurant ascends 6km (the last three a rugged unpaved track) to the Buddhist monastery of Osel Ling (see below).

Poqueira Gorge and up to Capileira

Shortly after Carataunas the road swings to the north, and you have your first view of the **Poqueira Gorge**, a huge, sheer gash into the heights of the Sierra Nevada. Trickling deep in the bed of the cleft is the Río Poqueira, which has its source near the peak of Mulhacén. The steep walls of the gorge are terraced and wooded from top to bottom, and dotted with little stone farmhouses. Much of the surrounding country looks barren from a distance, but close up you'll find it's rich with flowers, woods, springs and streams.

A trio of villages – three of the most spectacular and popular in the Alpujarras – teeters on the steep edge of the gorge. The first is neat, prosperous and pretty **PAMPANEIRA**. On its leafy main square, Plaza de la Libertad, is Nevadensis, an **information centre** for the Natural and National Parks of the Sierra Nevada (Mon & Sun 10am–3pm, Tues–Sat 11am–2pm & 4–6pm; ☏958 763 127, ⓦwww.nevadensis.com); they also sell large-scale topographical maps of the zone, and offer horseriding tours and **guided treks**, including an ascent of Mulhacén. Other activities on offer include mountain biking, climbing, canyoning and cross-country skiing. If you're thinking of a longer stay, this is also where you can pick up a list of hostels, village houses and farmhouses for rent throughout the Alpujarras.

Rooms are available as you enter the village at the homely *Hostal Pampaneira*, c/José Antonio 1 (☏958 763 002; B&B ❷), with some en-suite rooms, or, continuing up the road for a couple of hundred metres, at the plush new *Hotel Estrella de las Nieves* (☏958 763 322, ⓦwww.estrelladelasnieves.com; ❸). On Plaza de la Libertad, *Bar Belezmín* is one of the village's **best places to eat**, offering a menu filled with hearty *alpujarreña* dishes. Nearby *Casa Diego* has a terrace and a *menú* for €9, while another good bet is *Casa Julio*, up some steps near the *Hostal Pampaneira*, offering solid mountain fare with an €8 *menú*.

Above Pampaneira, on the very peak of the western flank of the Poqueira Gorge, is the **Tibetan Buddhist Monastery of Osel Ling** ("Place of Clear Light"), founded in 1982 by a Tibetan monk on land donated by the communities of Pampaneira and Bubión. The simple, stone-built monastery, complete with stupas and stunning **views** across the Alpujarras, welcomes visitors between 3pm and 6pm daily; lectures on Buddhism are held regularly and facilities exist for those who want to visit for periods of retreat in cabins dotted around the site (☏958 343 134 for details).

BUBIÓN is the next of the three villages up the hill, backed for much of the year by snowcapped peaks. The village has a private **museum**, the Casa Alpujarreña (Mon–Thurs & Sun 11am–2pm, Fri, Sat & Sun also 5–7pm; €1.80), just off Plaza de la Iglesia, the main square, displaying aspects of the folklore, daily life and architecture of the Alpujarras in a traditional house. For **places to stay**, there's a comfortable *pensión*, *Las Terrazas* (☏958 763 034, ⓦwww.terrazasalpujarra .com; ❶–❷), which has en-suite rooms with views. *Los Tinaos*, downhill from here at c/Parras s/n (☏958 763 217, ⓦwww.lostinaos.com; ❷), offers some excellent apartments that come with garden terrace, kitchen, satellite TV and fine views.

A decent **restaurant**, *La Artesa*, at c/Carretera 2, turns out *alpujarreño* speciali-ties and has an €8.50 *menú*. *Teide*, just over the road, is another good place for solid mountain cooking with a pleasant leafy terrace. For **horseriding trips** of one to five days, contact the friendly *Rancho Rafael Belmonte* (☎958 763 135, ⓦwww.ridingandalucia.com), at the bottom of the village near *Rustic Blue*, or Dallas Love (☎958 763 038, ⓔdallaslove@arrakis.es). *Rustic Blue* (☎958 763 381, ⓦwww.rusticblue.com), a privately run **information office** on the main road to the right as you enter the village, can also book horseriding and walking tours and help with accommodation in fully equipped houses across the Alpujarras.

Capileira

Two kilometres north of Bubión, **CAPILEIRA** is the highest of the three villages and the terminus of the road – Europe's highest, but now closed to traffic – across the heart of the Sierra Nevada from Granada. In addition to the direct daily afternoon **bus** from Granada, anything going to Ugíjar and Berja will come very close to Capileira; buses to Granada and Órgiva pass by at 6.35am, 4.45pm and 6.15pm. If you're thinking of doing any walking in this zone, this is probably the best village in which to base yourself.

There's an **information kiosk** for the national park at the centre of the village (daily 9am–2pm & 5–8pm), near where the bus drops you, which hands out a **village map** and sells newspapers and large-scale walking maps. Just downhill from here lies the village's interesting **museum** (Tues–Sun 11.30am–2.30pm), containing displays of regional dress and handicrafts, as well as various bits and pieces belonging to, or produced by, Pedro Alarcón, the nineteenth-century Spanish writer who made a trip through the Alpujarras and wrote a (not very good) book about it. There are numerous **places to stay**, starting with, as you enter the village to the right, *Hostal Atalaya* (☎958 763 025, ⓦwww.hostalatalaya.com; B&B ❶–❷), with en-suite rooms and terrific views from those at the front. Near the bus stop, the friendly *Mesón-Hostal Poqueira*

Walks from Capileira

Capileira is a handy base for easy **day walks** in the **Poqueira Gorge**. For a not-too-strenuous hike, take the northernmost of three paths below the village, each with bridges across the river. This sets off from alongside the *Pueblo Alpujarreño* villa complex. The path winds through the huts and terraced fields of the river valley above Capileira, ending after about an hour and a half at a dirt track within sight of a power plant at the head of the valley. You can either retrace your steps or cross the stream over a bridge to follow a dirt track back to the village. In May and June, the fields are tended laboriously by hand, as the steep slopes dictate.

Reasonably clear paths or tracks also lead to **Pampaneira** (2–3hr, follow lower path to the bridge below Capileira), continuing to Carataunas (1hr, mostly road) and Órgiva (45min, easy path), from where you can get a bus back. In the other direction, taking the Sierra Nevada road and then the first major path to the right, by a ruined stone house, you can reach **Pitres** (2hr), Pórtugos (2hr 30min) and Busquístar (2hr 45min). Going in the same direction but taking the second decent-sized path (by a sign encouraging you to "conserve and respect nature"), you'll get to **Trevélez** (5hr) – you can also get to Pórtugos this way.

More fine walking routes in this zone are detailed in *34 Alpujarras Walks* by Charles Davis, *Landscapes of Andalucía* by John and Christine Oldfield, *Walking in Andalucía* by Guy Hunter-Watts and *Holiday Walks in the Alpujarra* by Jeremy Rabjohns.

(☎958 763 048, Ⓦwww.hotelpoqueira.com; ❷), offers en-suite heated rooms, some with terraces and views, and has a pool and good restaurant with a substantial *menú* for around €10. It also has some attractive apartments sleeping up to four (❹) for longer stays. The new *El Cascapeñas*, also near the bus stop (☎958 763 011, Ⓦwww.elcascapeñas.com; ❷), has good-value en-suite rooms with TV. Continuing uphill, you come to the more luxurious *Finca Los Llanos* (☎958 763 071, Ⓦwww.hotelfincalosllanos.com; B&B ❹), with apartment-style rooms with kitchenettes and terraces, a pool and a good restaurant.

In addition to the **restaurants** mentioned above, other places worth seeking out are *Mesón Rural Panjuila*, a little way uphill from the bus stop to the right with a €9 *menú*, and, further uphill near the *Finca Los Llanos*, *La Casa de Paco y Pilar*, Ctra. Sierra Nevada 16, serving well-prepared mountain fare (with some vegetarian options) on a pleasant garden terrace. *Restaurante El Tilo*, on the focal Plaza Calvario in the lower village, is a decent place for *platos combinados* or watching-the-world-go-by drinks on its tranquil terrace shaded by a lime tree. Near the museum, the tangerine-tinted dining room of *Casa Ibero*, c/Parra 1 (open evenings only), is another good place for vegetarian dishes such as very tasty couscous, Indian and other adventurous concoctions.

The High Route to Trevélez

PITRES and **PÓRTUGOS**, 6km east of Pampaneira and the next two villages on the High Route, are perhaps more "authentic" and less polished. You're more likely to find rooms here during the summer months, while all around you is some of the best Alpujarran walking country. For **accommodation** in Pitres, you could try the *Hotel San Roque*, c/Cruz 1 on the east side of the village (☎958 857 528; ❸), which has decent rooms with (on the south side) views. On the village's eastern edge, the *Refugio de los Albergues* (☎958 343 176; ❶) is an old Civil War hostel with dormitory beds (€10) and cooking facilities. Pitres's **campsite**, *Balcón de Pitres* (☎958 766 111), with restaurant and pool, is located in a stunning position 1km west of the village. A couple of kilometres east, Pórtugos has the good-value *Hostal Mirador* on the main square (☎958 766 014; ❶), with en-suite rooms above a decent restaurant.

Down below the main road (GR421) linking Pitres and Pórtugos are the three villages of Mecina Fondales (and its offshoot, Mecinilla), Ferreirola and Busquístar; along with Pitres, these formed a league of villages known as the *Taha* under the Moors. **FERREIROLA** and **BUSQUÍSTAR** are especially attractive, as is the path between the two, clinging to the north side of the valley of the Río Trevélez. You're out of tourist country here and the villages display their genuine characteristics to better effect. For **rooms**, Ferreirola has the delightful Scandinavian-run 🍴 *Sierra y Mar*, c/Albaycin 3 (☎958 766 171, Ⓦwww.sierraymar.com; B&B ❸), with fine views and where the owners – enthusiastic walkers – will advise on routes in the area, whilst Busquístar has the charming new *Casa Sonia*, at c/San Francisco 5, in the heart of the village near the church (☎958 857 503, Ⓦwww.casasonia.eu; ❸), with elegant en-suite air-conditioned rooms, some with great views. In **MECINA FONDALES**, there are **rooms** at the very pleasant upmarket *Hotel Albergue de Mecina* (☎958 766 241, Ⓦwww.hoteldemecina.com; ❸), a delightful hideaway with an excellent garden pool where you can also rent horses and mountain bikes. The hotel has its own decent restaurant, but the best place for **food** here is a few minutes' walk away in the adjoining hamlet of **Mecinilla** at the French-run 🍴 *L'Atelier*, a charming restaurant specializing in vegetarian/vegan cuisine, located in the old village bakery on c/Alberca (☎&Ⓕ958 857 501). Booking is advised at weekends. It also lets a few rooms (B&B ❷) and has singles.

TREVÉLEZ, at the end of an austere ravine carved by the Río Trevélez, is purportedly Spain's highest permanent settlement, with cooler temperatures year-round than its neighbours. In traditional Alpujarran style, it has lower, middle and upper quarters (*barrios bajo*, *medio* and *alto*) overlooking a grassy, poplar-lined valley where the river starts its long descent. The village is well provided with **hostales**: in the *barrio medio*, Hostal Fernando (☎958 858 565; ❶) is friendly, good value and has heated (useful outside July & Aug) en-suite rooms, as does the comfortable 🗲 Hotel La Fragua, c/Antonio 4 (☎958 858 626, ⓌＷwww.hotellafragua.com; ❷–❸), in the *barrio alto*, which also has an excellent restaurant and tapas bar with vegetarian options. Trevélez's **campsite** lies 1km out along the Órgiva road (☎958 858 735); conditions are arctic in midwinter, but it also rents out some heated cabins (❷).

Besides the *Fragua*'s restaurant, other **places to eat** include the *Río Grande*, down near the bridge in the *barrio bajo*, which serves good, solid mountain food. The great-value *Mesón Haraicel*, in c/Real just above the *barrio bajo*'s main square, Plaza Francisco Abellán, also offers tasty tapas and *raciones* in its bar. Trevélez's **jamón serrano** is a prized speciality and an obsession throughout eastern Andalucía; good places to try it include *Mesón del Jamón* above the Plaza de la Iglesia or *Mesón Joaquín* in the lower *barrio*, which also has a decent restaurant.

East from Trevélez

Heading east from Trevélez, you come to **Juviles**, an attractive village straddling the road, followed, 5km further on, by **BÉRCHULES**, a high village of grassy streams and chestnut woods, also famous for its *jamón*. It is a large, abruptly demarcated settlement, three streets wide, on a sharp slope overlooking yet another canyon. For **accommodation**, *Alojamiento Rural La Tahoma* (☎958 769 051; ❶), c/Baja de la Iglesia s/n, which (as the street name implies) is just below the church offers excellent-value apartments with kitchen, *salon* and TV, and one-night stays are possible. Fully equipped apartments (sleeping up to 4) are also on offer at *El Mirador de Berchules*, Plaza de Zapata 1 (☎958 767 690, Ⓦwww .miradordeberchules.com; ❹), with terraces and views; it also has its own good restaurant, tapas bar and pool. On the main road into the village, the more upmarket *Hotel Bérchules* (☎958 852 530, Ⓦwww.hotelberchules.com; ❷) has comfortable rooms above its own restaurant and there's also a pool. For **food**, *Bar Vaqueras*, on the focal Plaza Victoria, does decent tapas and *raciones*.

Just below Bérchules, **CÁDIAR**, the central town of the Alpujarras, is more attractive than it seems from a distance, and springs into life when a colourful **produce market** is held on the 3rd and 18th of every month, sometimes including livestock. The annual **Fuente del Vino** wine and cattle fair (Oct 5–9) turns the waters of the fountain literally to wine. The most tempting **place to stay** here is an out-of-town option, 2km away along the A348 towards Torvizcón, where the excellent-value apart-hotel 🗲 *Alquería de Morayma* (☎958 343 303, Ⓦwww.alqueriamorayma.com; ❸), is a converted Alpujarran *cortijo* sited in 86 acres of farmland; there are charmingly rustic rooms and apartments (almost same price) many with terraces, and it has its own good restaurant (open to non-guests). Guests can go mountain biking and horseriding, and there are also plenty of hiking trails. The *Morayma*'s own organic farm and vineyard on the estate, the *bodega* of which is open to visitors, also supplies the restaurant and provides its virgin olive oil and bottled wine.

Eastern Alpujarras

The villages of the eastern Alpujarras display many of the characteristics of those to the west, but as a rule they are poorer and much less visited by tourists. In

YEGEN, one of the most famous, some 7km northeast of Cádiar, there's a plaque on the house (just along from the central fountain) where **Gerald Brenan** lived during his ten or so years of Alpujarran residence. His autobiography of these times, *South from Granada*, is the best account of rural life in Spain between the wars, and describes the visits made here by Virginia Woolf, Bertrand Russell and the arch-complainer Lytton Strachey. Disillusioned with the strictures of middle-class life in England after World War I, Brenan rented a house in Yegen and shipped out a library of two thousand books, from which he was to spend the next eight years educating himself. He later moved to the hills behind Torremolinos, where he died in 1987, a writer better known and respected in Spain (he made an important study of St John of the Cross) than in his native England.

Brenan connections aside, Yegen is one of the most characteristic Alpujarran villages, with its two distinct quarters, cobbled paths and cold-water springs. It has a **fonda**, *Bar La Fuente*, opposite the fountain in the square (☎958 851 067, ⓦwww.pensionlafuente.com; ❶), offering rooms with and without bath and whose bar is decorated with some old photos of Brenan. There are more en-suite rooms at the similarly priced *El Tinao* on the main road (☎958 851 212, ⓔloranne123@hotmail.com; ❶), which also rents a couple of fully equipped houses in the village (❹). Heading east out of Yegen, you'll find more upmarket accommodation at *El Rincón de Yegen* (☎620 446 872, ⓦwww.aldearural.com/rincondeyegen; ❷), where heated rooms come with TV and there are apartments (❹) for longer stays, as well as a pool and a good, inexpensive restaurant. Other places serving **food** are thin on the ground, but *Bar La Fuente* does tapas and *raciones*.

Towards Almería

If you don't enter Almería province via the Alpujarras following the winding A348 that eventually arrives at Almería city, the most straightforward route from Granada – and that followed by buses – is along the A92 *autovía*. The main landmark, 16km beyond the town of Guadix, famous for its cave dwellings, is a magnificent sixteenth-century castle on a hill (15min hike) above the village of **La Calahorra**, one of the finest in Spain, with a remarkable Renaissance patio within (Wed 10am–1pm & 4–6pm; €3). If it's closed, visit the guardian's house – avoiding *siesta* time – at c/de los Claveles 2 (☎958 677 098; Spanish only), and he will open it up for a consideration. For **rooms**, you could try the central *Hostal-Restaurante La Bella*, Crta. de Aldeire 1 (☎958 677 000; ❶) which, in addition to en-suite rooms, also has a **restaurant** with a decent weekday €9 *menú*.

From La Calahorra a minor mountain road, the A337, climbs dizzily and scenically to the **Puerto de la Ragua**, at 1993m Andalucía's highest all-weather pass. It's another route into the Alpujarras, and once through the pass the road descends to Yegen. If you're driving, you might want to keep going straight on the *autovía*, meeting the Almería–Sorbas road at what has become known as **Mini Hollywood** (see p.370), the preserved film set of *A Fistful of Dollars*.

Almería province

The **province of Almería** is a strange corner of Spain. Inland, it has an almost **lunar landscape** of desert, sandstone cones and dried-up riverbeds. The coast to the east of the provincial capital is still largely unspoilt; lack of water and roads frustrated development in the 1960s and 70s and it is only now beginning to take off. Limited development allowed the creation in the 1980s of the **Parque Natural de Cabo de Gata**, a haven for flora and fauna. To the west of Almería is another story, though, with a sea of plastic greenhouses spreading for a good 30km across the Campo de Dalías, the source of much of Almería's new-found wealth.

A number of **good beaches** are accessible by bus, and in this hottest province of Spain they're worth considering during what would be the off-season elsewhere, since Almería's summers start well before Easter and last into November. In midsummer, it's incredibly hot (frequently touching 38°C/100°F in the shade and often well above), while all year round there's an intense, almost luminous, sunlight. This and the weird scenery have made Almería one of the most popular **film locations** in Europe – much of *Lawrence of Arabia* was shot here, along with scores of spaghetti Westerns.

Almería

ALMERÍA is a pleasant, modern city, spread at the foot of a stark grey mountain. At the summit is a tremendous **Alcazaba** (Tues–Sun 9am–8.30pm, Nov–March until 6.30pm; €1.50, free with EU passport), probably the best surviving example of Moorish military fortification, with three huge walled enclosures, in the second of which are the remains of a mosque, converted to a chapel by the Reyes Católicos. In the eleventh century, when Almería was an independent kingdom and the wealthiest, most commercially active city of Spain, this citadel contained immense gardens and palaces and some 20,000 people. Its grandeur was reputed to rival the court of Granada, but comparisons are impossible since little beyond the walls and towers remains, the last remnants of its stuccowork having been sold off by the locals in the eighteenth century.

From the Alcazaba, however, you do get a good view of the coast, of Almería's **cave quarter** – the Barrio de la Chanca on a low hill to the left – and of the city's strange, fortified **Catedral** (Mon–Fri 10am–2pm & 4–5.30pm, Sat 10am–1pm; €2), built in the sixteenth century at a time when the southern Mediterranean was terrorized by the raids of Barbarossa and other Turkish and North African pirate forces; its corner towers once held cannons. Almería's splendid new **Museo Arqueológico** (Tues 2.30–8.30pm, Wed–Sat 9am–8.30pm, Sun 9am–2.30pm; €1.50, free with EU passport), Ctra. de Ronda 13, off the east side of Avenida Federico García Lorca, is also worth a visit and has an impressive collection of important artefacts from the prehistoric site of Los Millares, as well as interesting Roman and Moorish collections, including some fine Moorish ceramics.

There's little else to do in town, and your time is probably best devoted to sampling the cafés, tapas bars and terrazas in the streets circling the Puerta de Purchena, the focal junction of the modern town, strolling along the main Paseo de Almería down towards the harbour and taking day-trips out to the beaches along the coast. The city's own **beach**, southeast of the centre beyond the train lines, is long but dismal.

Practicalities

Almería's international **airport** is 8km out of town with a connecting bus service (#14 or #20, labelled "El Alquián") every half-hour from the junction of Avda. Federico García Lorca and c/Gregorio Marañon.

There are **boats to Melilla** on the Moroccan coast throughout summer (fewer out of season), a journey that can pay dividends in both time and money over Algeciras if you're driving (daily; 6hr; June–Sept high-speed ferry 4hr): For information and tickets, contact *Compañía Trasmediterránea*, Parque Nicolás

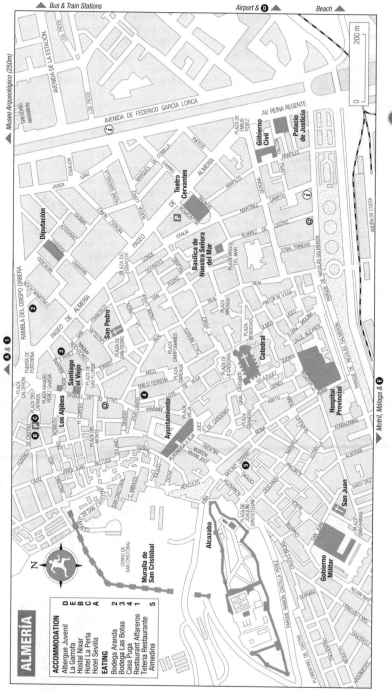

ALMERÍA

ACCOMMODATION
Albergue Juvenil	D
La Garrofa	E
Hostal Nixar	B
Hotel La Perla	C
Hotel Sevilla	A

EATING
Bodega Aranda	2
Bodega Las Botas	3
Casa Puga	4
Restaurant Alfareros	1
Tetería Restaurante Almedina	5

Bus & Train Stations

Airport & **D**

Beach

Museo Arqueológico (250m)

A & 1

ANDALUCÍA

369

Salmerón 19, near the port (☎950 236 956, ⊛www.trasmediterranea.es). The **boat to Nador** in Morocco (daily April–Sept; 6hr) is run by *Ferrimaroc*, which has an office at the port (☎950 274 800, ⊛www.ferrimaroc.com).

Almería's **bus station** (☎950 262 098) and **train station** (☎902 240 202) have been combined into a striking Estación Intermodal, on Carretera de Ronda, a couple of blocks east of Avda. de Federico García Lorca, with the bus terminals and train platforms side by side.

The **turismo** is on c/Parque de Nicolás Salmerón (Mon–Fri 9am–7.30pm, Oct–May 8.30am–2pm, Sat & Sun 9.30am–3pm; ☎950 175 220). They have a list of most buses out of Almería, as well as train and boat schedules. *Locutorio del Puerto*, near the *turismo* (daily 10am–10pm), is a handy place for **internet** access.

A good place to start looking for **rooms** is around Puerta de Purchena, where, just off this intersection, *Hotel La Perla*, Plaza del Carmen 7 (☎950 238 877, ⊛www.githoteles.com; ❸), is Almería's oldest hotel and once played host to big-name stars making Westerns at Mini Hollywood. Just behind is a cheaper option, *Hostal Nixar*, c/Antonio Vico 24 (☎&℉950 237 255; ❷); ask for a higher, airy room. Slightly east of the Puerta de Purchena junction, *Hotel Sevilla*, c/Granada 25 (☎950 230 009; ❸), is a modern, small hotel with comfortable rooms equipped with air-conditioning and TV. The *Albergue Juvenil Almería*, c/Isla de Fuerteventura s/n (☎950 269 788; under-26 €16, over-26 €20), is a swish 150-double-roomed affair on the east side of town next to the Estadio Juventud sports arena; take bus #1 from the junction of Avda. Federico García Lorca and c/Gregorio Marañon. The nearest **campsite**, *La Garrofa*, is on the coast at La Garrofa, some 5km west (☎950 235 770), easily reached by the buses to Aguadulce and Roquetas de Mar.

When it comes to **eating and drinking**, the Puerta de Purchena is a great place to head for, particularly at night. On the north side, in a small street, *Restaurante Alfareros*, c/Marcos 6, has an excellent-value *menú* for around €10. Just east of the junction, *Bodega Aranda*, c/Obispo Orbera 8, is a popular tapas bar that fairly hums at lunchtime when local professionals come to grab a bite; in former days, this was the "sordid" *pensión* where a penurious Gerald Brenan put up in 1921. On the opposite side of the junction, *Bodega Las Botas*, c/Fructuoso Perez 3, is well worth seeking out. A few blocks south of here the atmospheric ⚘ *Casa Puga*, at the corner of c/Lope de Vega and c/Jovellanos, is the city's outstanding tapas outlet, founded in 1870. Just below the Alcazaba, ⚘ *Tetería-Restaurante Almedína*, c/Paz 2, is a friendly little Moroccan-run *tetería* serving full meals later in the day, including couscous and chicken and lamb tagines, and often stages concerts of flamenco and North African music at weekends. For **bars**, try the streets around Plaza Masnou, off the southern end of the Alameda, and c/Trajano slightly northeast of here, both areas bouncing with action, especially at weekends. To move the night-time scene away from the residential area in summer, the city council erects a line of **discoteca marquees** at the start of the Paseo Marítimo, near the beach.

Inland: Mini Hollywood and Níjar

The N-340a northwest from Almería towards Tabernas follows the Andarax riverbed before forking right into the badlands, an area resembling Arizona, which looks as if it should be the backdrop for a Hollywood Western. Just beyond the fork, at **Mini Hollywood** (aka Oasys Parque Temático; daily 10am–9pm, Nov–May until 7pm; €19, under-12s €9), you discover that someone else had the same idea first. This is a full-blown Western movie set, and a visit here is hard to resist – especially if you're travelling with kids – although it's probably better value if you time your arrival to coincide with one of the shows. Once

▲ Mini Hollywood

inside you can walk around the set of *A Fistful of Dollars* and various other spaghetti Westerns that were filmed here, and wander down Main Street into the *Tombstone Gulch* saloon for a drink. The fantasy is carried a step further with acted-out "shows" (noon & 5pm, June–Sept also 8pm), when actors in full cowboy rig blast off six-guns during a mock bank raid or re-enact the "capture, escape and final shooting of Jesse James." The complex has also added a somewhat incongruous **zoo**, featuring birds and reptiles, as well as rhinos, lions and other big cats prowling depressingly small cages. Further along the road towards Tabernas, **Texas Hollywood** (April–Oct daily 9am–8pm; 3 shows morning and afternoon; €16.50, kids €9.50), location for the shooting of *Once Upon a Time in the West*, and **Western Leone** (similar hours and prices), are a couple of less commercialized film sets in spectacular desert scenery.

Following the A7-E15 east from Almería brings you, after 24km, to the turn-off for **NÍJAR**, famed throughout Andalucía for its pottery. A neat, white and typically Almerian town, with – in the upper *barrio* – narrow streets designed to give maximum shade, it makes a good base from which to explore the coast and Parque Natural de Cabo de Gata to the south (see p.372). Níjar's **turismo** is sited at the junction of c/Real with Avda. García Lorca (daily 9am–2pm, Tues–Sun also 4–8pm; ☎950 612 243, ⒲www.nijar.es), and can provide literature on the town and region. Níjar is firmly on the tourist trail owing to the inexpensive **handmade pottery** manufactured in workshops and sold in the shops along the broad main street – Avda. García Lorca – and c/Real to the west, where many of the potters have their workshops. The more authentic potters, however, are located in the **barrio alfarero**, along c/Real running parallel to the main street, where the workshops of Gongora, Granados, El Oficio and the friendly and cheaper Angel y Loli (at no. 54) are located; also, in a tiny street off the southern end of c/Real, is the studio-shop (named "La Tienda de los Milagros") of talented English ceramic artist Matthew Weir. Níjar is known, too, for its *jarapas*: quilts, curtains and rugs made from rags, and widely on sale around the town.

There are a couple of **places to stay** on the main street; try *Montes* at no. 26 (☎950 360 157; ❷), with good-value en-suite rooms. Further up the same street, at no. 6, *Bar La Untá* is a very good **bar-restaurant** with a street terrace, and there are more tapas and *raciones* bars in the upper square, Plaza La Glorieta, beyond the church – of which *El Pipa* is the best.

El Cabo de Gata to Mojácar

Almería's best **beaches** lie on its eastern coast; those to the west of the city, particularly surrounding the "ugly sisters" resorts of Aguadulce and Roquetas de Mar, have already been exploited, and what remains is rapidly being covered with *invernaderos*, or plastic tents, for fruit and vegetable production. In stark contrast, the eastern stretch of the Almerian coastline offers some of the most relaxing beaches left in Spain: half-abandoned fishing communities that have only begun to be promoted for tourists relatively recently. Outside the centres of **Mojácar** and **San José** development is low-key, and with a short walk along the coast you should be able to find plenty of relatively secluded spots to lay your towel.

El Cabo de Gata

The closest resort with any appeal is the modest **EL CABO DE GATA**, now inside the **Parque Natural de Cabo de Gata**, where there is a long expanse of coarse sand. Five buses a day run between here and Almería. Arriving at El Cabo, you pass a lake, the **Laguna de Rosa**, protected by a conservation society and home to flamingos and other waders throughout the summer. Around the resort are plentiful bars, cafés and shops, plus a fish market. There's little **accommodation**; you'll need to head inland to the friendly but pricey *Hostal Las Dunas*, c/Barrionuevo 58 (℡950 370 072; ❸), 100m back from the beach, offering air-conditioned en-suite rooms with TV. On the coast 2km northwest of the village there's a campsite, *Cabo de Gata* (℡950 160 443), with its own pool and restaurant. The beach gets windy in the afternoons, and it's a deceptively long walk eastwards to **Las Salinas** (The Salt Pans) for a couple of bar-restaurants and a café.

A few kilometres south of here, the **Faro de Cabo de Gata** (lighthouse) marks the cape's southern tip. In the lighthouse car park an **information cabin** (June–Sept daily 10am–2pm & 6–8pm) has maps and information on the natural park. There's also a friendly tapas bar here, *El Faro*, serving up tasty, locally caught fried fish, as well as a **mirador** from where you can get a great view of the rock cliffs and – on clear days – Morocco's Rif mountains.

San José

Ten kilometres east of the lighthouse lies **SAN JOSÉ**, also reached by bus from Almería. Although it's possible to hike to the resort along a coastal track from the lighthouse, this is now closed to vehicles and to get there by road entails retracing your route to El Cabo de Gata and following the inland road via the village of El Pozo de los Frailes.

San José is an established and popular family resort, set back from a sandy beach in a small cove, with shallow water. More fine **beaches** lie within easy walking distance and one of the best – Playa de los Genoveses – a kilometre-long golden strand, can be reached by a track to the southwest. On the main street, Avda. de San José, near the centre of the village, you'll find a **Centro de Información** for the natural park (daily 10am–2pm & 5–8pm; ℡950 380 299), which has lots of information on guided walks and horse treks, plus a complete list of accommodation. They also have a couple of screens for **internet** access, which is also available at the nearby *Bla Bla Bla*, Pasaje Curry s/n (daily 9am–midnight). David the Bookman (daily 11am–2pm & 4.30–9pm), on the main street up some steps opposite *Hostal Costa Rica*, is a good source of paperback **books** in English and will exchange any books you wish to offload.

Practicalities

Accommodation can be hard to come by in summer, but outside high season (Aug only) rates fall sharply. On the main road to the right as you come in (5min walk from the village), the *Hotel Agades Agidir* (☎950 380 390, Ⓦwww.hotelagades.com; ❹) has air-conditioned en-suite balcony rooms, plus garden pool, bar and restaurant. Along the main road into the village and off to the left *Hostal Brisa del Mar*, c/Ancla s/n (☎950 380 431, Ⓦwww.brisamar .com; ❸), is a recent arrival with bright and spacious air-conditioned en-suite balcony rooms and a pretty garden. Continuing along the same street will bring you to the good-value *Hostal Aloha*, c/Higuera s/n (☎950 380 461, Ⓦwww.hostalaloha.com; ❸), with refurbished air-conditioned en-suite rooms with terrace balcony and the bonus of a fine palm-fringed pool at the rear; they also have a very good tapas bar below. Near to the village's main junction, *Hostal Sol Bahía*, c/Correos 5 (☎950 380 307, Ⓦwww.solbahiasanjose.es; ❸), is a comfortable modern *hostal* with air-conditioned en-suite facilities. San José also has a good beachfront **campsite**, *Camping Tau* (☎950 380 166; closed Nov–March), and an equally pleasant, privately run **Albergue Juvenil** (☎950 380 353, Ⓦwww.alberguesanjose.com; €12 per person), both reached by a signed road on the left as you enter the village.

There are numerous **places to eat** around the beach and harbour zones, plus a couple of well-stocked supermarkets. For fresh fish, try the restaurants overlooking the harbour – *La Cueva* is noted for its *salmonetes* (red mullet fried with garlic) and *El Tempranillo* next door is also good for tasty paellas. Near the main junction, the friendly and good-value *Bar-Restaurante El Emigrante*, facing the *Hostal Sol Bahía*, also does good fish and has a *menú* for €10.

Los Escullos to Las Negras

Next along the coast is the isolated and peaceful resort of **LOS ESCULLOS**, with a reasonable sandy beach fronted by a formidable eighteenth-century fort, the recently refurbished **Castillo de San Felipe**. There's a **campsite**, *Camping Los Escullos* (☎950 389 811), set back from the sea with limited shade and, closer to the beach, the pleasant beachfront hotel-restaurant, *Casa Emilio* (☎950 389 761; ❸).

Two kilometres farther east, **LA ISLETA** is another fishing hamlet, and although development is happening it's still a place with a sleepy atmosphere and lots of charm. There's a rather scruffy village beach but a much better one a few minutes' walk away in the next bay to the east – the Playa la Ola. A **hostal** overlooking the harbour, *Hostal Isleta de Moro* (☎951 389 713; ❸), has reasonably priced en-suite balcony rooms with sea view, plus a popular **bar-restaurant** for tapas and good fish meals below.

LAS NEGRAS, 5km farther on, is another place with a decidedly Spanish feel, where there's a cove with a pebbly beach and a few bars and restaurants plus an attractive **hostal**, *Arrecife*, close to the village shop (☎950 388 140; ❷). If the *hostal* is full, you can enquire here (English spoken) about a room in a private house or renting an apartment nearby. A **campsite**, *La Caleta*, set in a tranquil location with its own bay, is reached via a one-kilometre road just outside the village on the way in (☎950 525 237).

Agua Amarga

There's no road from Las Negras to Agua Amarga (10km north as the crow flies); to reach it by road you'll need to head 5km inland to the village of Fernan Pérez from where a new road heads east for 11km to reach the small resort. Agua Amarga is served by frequent direct **buses** from Almería.

ANDALUCÍA | Almería province

AGUA AMARGA is a one-time fishing hamlet that has transformed itself into a pleasant and easy-going resort. A fine sand EU-blue-flagged beach is the main attraction, and this is backed by a tasteful crop of villas. The best-value **place to stay** is the French-run ⚓ *Hotel Family* (☎950 138 014, ⓦwww .hotelfamily.es; B&B ❹–❺), set back from the south end of the beach with a pool and very good restaurant. On a rise behind, *Hotel El Tío Kiko* (☎950 138 080, ⓦwww.eltiokiko.com; B&B ❺) is one of a clutch of new luxury hotels here. Back a little way from the beach, *Apartamentos Playa* (☎950 138 202, ⓦwww.aguamarga.net; ❸) has some good-value apartments sleeping up to four. In addition to the above, another place well worth a visit for **food** is the reasonably priced restaurant of the *Hotel las Calas*, c/Desagüe s/n, near *Hotel Family*, with good fish and a pleasant terrace.

Mojácar

MOJÁCAR, 22km north of Carboneras, is eastern Almería's main resort, hugely popular with Spaniards and foreign visitors throughout summer. The coastal strip takes its name from the ancient hill village that lies a couple of kilometres back from the sea – Mojácar Pueblo – a striking agglomeration of white cubist houses wrapped round a harsh outcrop of rock. In the 1960s, when the main Spanish *costas* were being developed, this was virtually a ghost town, its inhabitants having long since taken the only logical step and emigrated. The town's fortunes suddenly revived, however, when the local mayor, using the popularity of other equally barren spots in Spain as an example, offered free land to anyone willing to build within a year. The scheme was a modest success, attracting one of the decade's multifarious "artist colonies", now long supplanted by package-holiday companies and second-homers. The long and sandy **beach**, down at the development known as Mojácar Playa, is excellent and the waters (like all in Almería) are warm and brilliantly clear.

Mojácar Pueblo

MOJÁCAR PUEBLO is linked to the coastal resort 2km below by a road that climbs from a prominent seafront junction called "El Cruce"; hourly **buses** also make the climb from here until 11.30pm, after which it's a punishing hike or a taxi. The **turismo** is located just below the main square (Mon–Fri 10am–2pm & 5–7pm, Sat 10am–1.30pm; ☎950 615 025, ⓦwww .mojacarviva.com) – you'll need their free map to negotiate the maze of narrow streets – with the **post office** in the same building and a convenient **ATM** next door. The village is more about atmosphere than sights, and once you've cast an eye over the heavily restored fifteenth-century church of **Santa María**, the main diversion is to wander the narrow streets with their flower-decked balconies and cascading bougainvillea, and call in at the numerous boutiques and bars.

There are a handful of small **hostales**. You could try *Hostal Arco Plaza*, just off the main square (☎950 472 777, ⓔarcoplazam@yahoo.es; ❷), which is a reasonable deal for air-conditioned en-suite rooms with TV. The more upmarket but good-value ⚓ *Mamabel's* at c/Embajadores 3 (☎950 472 448, ⓦwww.mamabels.com; ❸–❹) is the best of the fancier places, with beautiful en-suite rooms, some with stunning views.

Rincón de Embrujo, on the *plazuela* fronting the church, does decent *platos combinados*, but for something more memorable the mid-priced **restaurant** of *Mamabel's* is worth a meal for its spectacular terrace views alone, and has a good-value *menú* for €18.

Mojácar Playa

The beach resort of **MOJÁCAR PLAYA** is a refreshingly brash alternative to the upper village and caters to a mix of mainly Spanish tourists who fill its four-kilometre-long beach all summer. The busy road behind the strand is lined with hotels, restaurants and bars stretching north and south of the main junction, El Cruce, marked by a large *centro comercial*. Just south of here **internet** access is available at *Indal-futur*, Paseo del Mediterráneo 293 (Mon–Fri 9am–2pm & 5–10pm, Sat & Sun 11am–2pm & 6–11pm). The turismo's **map** also covers the coastal strip and is a useful aid to getting your bearings.

There are plenty of **places to stay**, including rooms and a good **campsite**, *El Cantal de Mojácar* (T950 478 204). South of El Cruce, *Hotel Sal Marina* (T950 472 404; ●) has very pleasant air-conditioned balcony rooms with sea views and drops prices by thirty percent outside August. Close by, the simpler *Hostal Bahía*, Paseo del Mediterráneo 295 (T951 478 010; ●), has en-suite rooms ranged around a charming patio. Of the more upmarket places, you could try the seafront *Hotel El Puntazo* (T951 478 229, Wwww.hotelelpuntazo.com; ●) for air-conditioned sea-view terrace rooms with minibar and strongbox.

Places to eat along the seafront are fairly dismal and standards tend to fall markedly in high season. A kilometre south of the El Cruce junction, places worth a try include the seafront *Albatros*, close to the *Hotel El Puntazo* and, on the landward side of the road, *Restaurante Sal Marina* attached to the hotel of the same name; both do good fish and paella. A kilometre farther south again, *Omega* and its neighbour *Casa Egea*, Playa Las Ventanicas 127, are a couple of other long-established and reliable seafront places. **Nightlife** is centred along the coastal strip for 3km to the south of El Cruce; first on the left comes the huge *Mandila Beach*, with numerous bars and dancefloors, followed by *Maui Beach Bar* and – a couple of kilometres further south – *Buddha Bar*. All three are flanked by late-night *copas* and music bars that plug away till dawn in high summer.

Travel details

Trains

For current timetables and ticket information, consult RENFE T902 240 202, Wwww.renfe.es.

Algeciras to: Córdoba (2 daily; 3hr 15min); Granada (3 daily; 4hr 20min); Madrid (2 daily; AVE 5hr 20min); all Algeciras northbound trains go via Ronda (1hr 40min) and Bobadilla.

Almería to: Granada (4 daily; 2hr 15min); Madrid (2 daily; 7hr); Seville (4 daily; 4hr 30min).

Cádiz to: Córdoba (3 daily; 3hr); Granada (5 daily, change at Seville; 5hr); Madrid (2 daily; 5hr); Seville (17 daily; 5hr).

Córdoba to: Algeciras (2 daily; 3hr 30min); Cádiz (2 daily; 3hr); Granada (2 daily; 2hr 45min); Jaén (4 daily; 1hr 45min); Madrid (19 daily; AVE 1hr 50min); Málaga (13 daily; 1hr 20min, AVE 1hr); Ronda (2 daily; 2hr); Seville (22 daily; 1hr 15min, AVE 45min).

Granada to: Algeciras (3 daily, 4hr 15min); Almería (4 daily, 2hr 15min); Antequera (daily; 2hr 20min); Córdoba (daily; 2hr 30min); Linares-Baeza (2 daily; 2hr 20min); Madrid (daily; 4hr 50min); Málaga (5 daily, change at Bobadilla; 2hr 40min); Ronda (3 daily; 2hr 45min); Seville (4 daily; 2hr 45min); Valencia (2 daily, change at Madrid/Córdoba; 15hr, 1 daily direct Mon, Thurs & Fri 8hr 20min).

Jaén to: Cádiz (3 daily, change at Córdoba; 4hr 30min); Córdoba (4 daily; 1hr 30min); Madrid (3 daily Mon–Sat, daily Sun); Seville (3 daily; 2hr 50min).

Huelva to: Madrid (daily; 4hr 25min); Seville (3 daily; 1hr 30min); Zafra (daily; 5hr).

Málaga to: Algeciras (2 daily, change at Bobadilla; 4hr 30min); Córdoba (15 daily; 2hr 20min, AVE 1hr); Fuengirola (every 30min from airport; 35min); Granada (2 daily, change at Bobadilla; 3hr 30min); Madrid (9 daily; 2hr 40min); Ronda (6 daily, change at Bobadilla; 3hr); Seville (6 daily; 2hr 30min).

Seville to: Algeciras (8 daily, change at Córdoba/ Bobadilla; 5hr); Badajoz (3 daily, change at Puertollano; 5hr 15min); Cádiz (10 daily; 2hr); Córdoba (20 daily; 1hr 45min, AVE 45min); Granada (5 daily; 3hr); Huelva (3 daily; 1hr 35min); Madrid (AVE 14 daily; 3hr 20min); Málaga (10 daily; 2hr 30min); Mérida (daily; 4hr 20min).

Buses

Algeciras to: Cádiz (hourly 7am–10pm; 2hr 15min); La Linea (for Gibraltar: hourly; 30min); Madrid (4 daily; 8hr); Seville (11 daily; 2hr 30min); Tarifa (10 daily; every 30min).

Almería to: Agua Amarga (2–4 daily; 1hr 30min); Alicante (6 daily; 5hr 10min); Cabo de Gata/San José (6 daily; 55min); Carboneras (2–4 daily; 1hr 15min); Córdoba (daily; 5hr); Granada (2 daily; 4hr); Madrid (5 daily; 7hr); Málaga (9 daily; 3hr 30min); Jaén (3 daily; 4hr); Mini Hollywood, now Oasis (from Tabernas; 2–4 daily; 40min); Mojácar (3 daily; 1hr 30min); Nijar: (2 daily Mon–Fri; 35min); Seville (3 daily; 5hr 45min); Tabernas (2 daily Mon–Fri); Ugíjar (2 daily; 2hr 45min).

Cádiz to: Algeciras (10 daily; 2hr 15min); Arcos de la Frontera (5 daily; 1hr 30min); Chipiona (9 daily; 1hr 15min); Conil (13 daily; 1hr); Granada (4 daily; 5hr); Jerez de la Frontera (20 daily; 40min); Málaga (6 daily; 3hr 45min); El Puerto de Santa María (20 daily; 30min); Sanlúcar de Barrameda (5–9 daily; 1hr); Seville (12 daily; 1hr 45min); Tarifa (5 daily; 2hr); Vejer de la Frontera (13 daily; 1hr 10min).

Córdoba to: Badajoz (2 daily; 4hr 25min); Écija (5 daily; 55min); Granada (9 daily; 4hr); Jaén (6 daily; 1hr 30min); Málaga (7 daily; 2hr); Madrid (7 daily; 4hr 50min); Seville (7 daily; 2hr).

Granada to: Alicante (4 daily; 4hr 15min); Almería (8 daily; 3hr 45min); Cádiz (4 daily; 5hr); Cazorla (2 daily; 4hr); Córdoba (4 daily; 2hr 45min); Jaén (12 daily; 1hr 15min); Madrid (13 daily; 5hr); Málaga (21 daily; 2hr); Mojácar (2 daily; 4hr); Motril (11 daily; 1hr 45min); Ronda (2 daily; 3hr 45min); Seville (9 daily; 3hr 40min); Sierra Nevada (daily; 45min); Lanjarón & Órgiva (6 daily; 1hr 30min; 2 daily to other villages in the Alpujarras); Solynieve (Pradollana) (3–4 daily in winter, daily in summer; 25min); Valencia (5 daily; 9hr 20min); Úbeda/Baeza (9 daily; 2hr 20min).

Huelva to: Aracena (2 daily; 2hr); Huelva Ayamonte/Portuguese border (6 daily; 1hr); Granada (daily; 4hr); Matalascañas (2 daily; 50min); Moguer/Palos (15 daily; 40/30min); Punta Umbría (17 daily; 30min); Seville (20 daily; 1hr 15min).

Jaén to: Almería (2 daily; 4hr); Baeza/Úbeda (14 daily; 1hr 25min); Cazorla (3 daily; 2hr 30min); Córdoba (8 daily; 2hr); Granada (11 daily; 1hr

10min); Madrid (5 daily; 4hr 20min); Málaga (4 daily; 3hr 15min); Seville: (daily; 4hr).

Jerez to: Algeciras (11 daily; 1hr 30min); Arcos de la Frontera (17 daily; 35min); Cádiz (12 daily; 45min); Chipiona (10 daily; 40min); Córdoba (daily; 3hr 30min); Málaga (daily; 5hr); El Puerto de Santa María (15 daily; 30min); Ronda (7 daily; 3hr 30min); Sanlúcar de Barrameda (16 daily; 30min); Seville (7 daily; 1hr 30min); Vejer de la Frontera (2 daily; 1hr 30min).

Málaga to: Algeciras (15 daily; 2–3hr); Almería (8 daily; 3hr 30min); Almuñécar (9 daily; 2hr); Cádiz (7 daily; 3hr 45min); Córdoba (5 daily; 2hr); Fuengirola (8 daily; 45min); Gibraltar (stops at La Linea border; 4 daily; 3hr); Granada (20 daily; 1hr 30min); Huelva (daily; 4hr 30min); Jaén (4 daily; 3hr); Jerez de la Frontera (3 daily; 4hr 30min); Madrid (11 daily; 6hr); Marbella (25 daily; 45min); Motril (8 daily; 2hr); Nerja (17 daily; 1hr 30min); Ronda (18 daily; 1hr 45min); Salobreña (6 daily; 1hr 45min); Seville (11 daily; 2hr 30min); Úbeda/Baeza (3 daily; 4hr).

Ronda to: Arcos de la Frontera (6 daily; 2hr 30min); Cádiz (6 daily; 3hr 15min); Grazalema (2 daily; 35min); Jerez de la Frontera (6 daily; 2hr 30min); Málaga (6 daily; 2hr); Marbella (2 daily; 1hr); San Pedro de Alcantara (2 daily; 45min); Seville (3 daily; 2hr 30min); Ubrique (2 daily; 1hr 30min); Zahara de la Sierra (daily; 55min).

Seville to: Albufeira, Portuguese Algarve (via Ayamonte and Faro; 4 daily; 2hr 30min); Algeciras (3 daily; 3hr 30min); Almería (3 daily; 5hr 45min); Aracena (2 daily; 1hr 20min); Badajoz (4 daily; 3hr 30min); Cádiz (10 daily; 1hr 45min); Carmona (10 daily; 30min); Córdoba (10 daily; 1hr 45min); Écija (7 daily; 1hr 15min); El Rocío (4 daily; 1hr 30min); Granada (8 daily; 3hr); Huelva (24 daily; 1hr 15min); Jerez de la Frontera (8 daily; 1hr 15min); Madrid (8 daily; 6hr); Málaga (9 daily; 2hr 30min); Matalascañas (4 daily; 2hr); Mérida (5 daily; 1hr 15min); Ronda (6 daily; 2hr).

Ferries

A useful site for checking the latest ferry schedules is Ⓦ www.directferries.co.uk.

Algeciras to: Ceuta (up to 25 daily; 35min); Tangier (up to 30 daily; 35min–1hr 30min).

Almería to: Melilla (11 weekly; 3hr); Nador (12 weekly; 6hr).

Cádiz to: El Puerto de Santa María (El Vapor: 5 daily; 40min; Catamaran: 12–18 daily; 25min); Las Palmas (weekly on Tues; 48hr); Tenerife (weekly on Tues; 48hr).

Gibraltar to: Tangier (weekly on Fri; 1hr 20min).

Málaga to: Melilla (2 daily; 3hr 45min–8hr).

Tarifa to: Tangier (3–5 daily; 35min).

Castilla y León and La Rioja

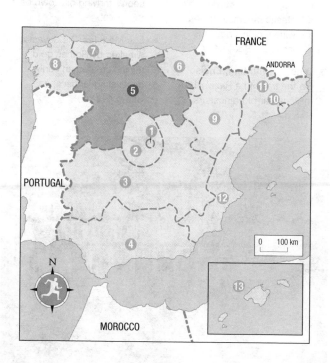

CHAPTER 5 # Highlights

* **Plaza Mayor, Salamanca**
Perhaps the most graceful
and beautiful of all Spanish
plazas. See p.386

* **Museo Nacional de
Escultura, Valladolid**
The finest collection of
Renaissance sculpture in
Spain. See p.403

* **La Rioja's monasteries** Take
a fantastic mountain drive to
the wine region's peerless
monasteries. See p.420

* **Dinosaur-hunting, Enciso**
On the trail of La Rioja's 120-
million-year-old dinosaurs.
See p.421

* **Burgos Cathedral** An
extraordinary masterpiece of
Gothic art. See p.425

* **Covarrubias** Possible winner
of the "most charming small
town in Castile" award?
See p.428

* **A tapas crawl, León** You still
get free tapas with drinks in
León's thriving old-town bars.
See p.439

* **Las Médulas** The devastation
wreaked by Roman gold
mining created an eerily
captivating landscape.
See p.442

▲ Plaza Mayor, Salamanca

Castilla y León and La Rioja

The foundations of modern Spain were laid in the kingdom of Castile. Incorporated within the modern *comunidad* of **Castilla y León** (Ⓦ www.turismocastillayleon.com), it's a land of frontier fortresses – the *castillos* from which it takes its name – and became the most powerful force of the Reconquest, extending its domination through military gains and marriage alliances. By the eleventh century, Castile had merged with and swallowed León; through Isabel's marriage to Fernando in 1469 it encompassed Aragón, Catalunya and eventually the entire peninsula. The monarchs of this triumphant age were enthusiastic patrons of the arts, endowing their cities with superlative monuments, above which, quite literally, tower the great Gothic cathedrals of **Salamanca**, **León** and **Burgos**.

These three cities are the major draws of the region, though in **Valladolid**, **Zamora** and even unsung **Palencia** and **Soria** are outstanding reminders of the glory days of Old Castile. But equally in many lesser towns – notably **Ciudad Rodrigo**, **El Burgo de Osma** and **Covarrubias** – you'll be struck by a wealth of art and architecture incongruous with present.

Castilian soil is fertile, and the vast central plateau – the 700- to 1000-metre-high **meseta** – is given over almost entirely to grain. Huge areas stretch to the horizon without a single landmark, not even a tree, though each spring a vivid red carpet of poppies decorates fields and verges. The sporadic and depopulated villages, bitterly cold in winter, burning hot in summer, are rarely of interest – travel consists of getting as quickly as you can from one grand town to the next. That said, there are a few enclaves of mountain scenery,

---

Castilian cuisine

Castilian cuisine is based upon the traditional produce of the **meseta** – white, crusty bread is especially good here. The most celebrated dishes comprise sumptuous **roast meats**: you'll find *cochinillo* (suckling pig) and *lechazo* or *cordero asado* (lamb) almost everywhere, as well as thick *sopas castellanos*, usually containing chickpeas or white haricot beans (*alubias blancas*), both staple Castilian crops. Freshwater fish, particularly trout (*trucha*), is popular, while Salamanca province is known for its *jamones* (hams) and *embutidos* (sausages).

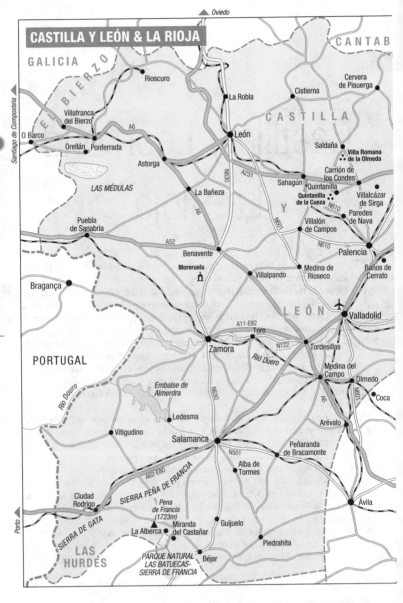

CASTILLA Y LEÓN & LA RIOJA

from the **Sierra de Francia** in the deep southwest to the lakeland of the **Sierra de Urbión** in the east. Moreover, the **Río Duero** runs right across the province and into Portugal, with the river at the heart of one of Spain's great wine-producing regions, Ribera del Duero; another, more famous wine region lies to the north in the autonomous *comunidad* of **La Rioja**, whose *bodegas* line the banks of the Río Ebro, spreading out from the likeable provincial capital of **Logroño**.

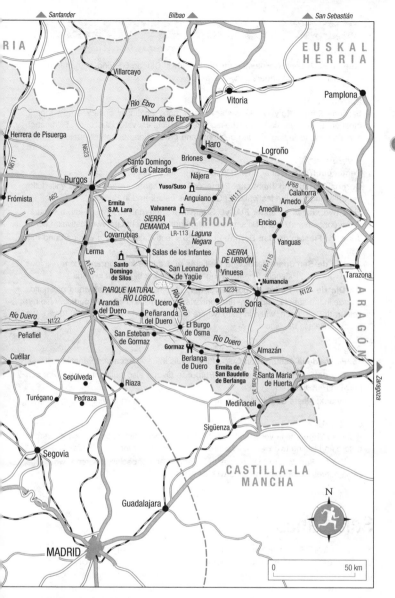

The final feature of the region is the host of Romanesque churches, monasteries and hermitages, a legacy of the **Camino de Santiago**, the great pilgrim route from the Pyrenees to the shrine of St James at Santiago de Compostela in Galicia. It cuts through La Rioja and then heads west across the upper half of Castilla y León (see feature on p.430), taking in the great cathedral cities of Burgos and León, but also many minor places of great interest, from **Frómista** in the central plains to **Astorga** and **Villafranca del Bierzo**, en route to the Galician mountains.

Fiestas

February
Week before Lent: Carnaval Particularly lively in Ciudad Rodrigo, with bull-running and bullfights in the streets and squares.

March/April
Semana Santa (Holy Week) Easter is even more fanatically observed here than in most areas – celebrations in all the big cities, particularly Valladolid, León, Salamanca and Zamora, including hooded penitents and processions of holy statues.

May/June
Pentecost (7th Sun after Easter) Week-long *Feria Chica* in Palencia.

Corpus Christi (2nd Thurs after Pentecost) Celebrations in Palencia and Valladolid; the following day, the festival of *El Curpillos* is celebrated in Burgos.

First two weeks of June: FIACyL Salamanca's International Arts Festival features street concerts, urban art, DJ sets and neighbourhood events (Ⓦwww.festivalcyl.com).

June 11: Fiestas de San Bernabé Logroño's festivities run for a week around this date.

24: Día de San Juan Fiesta with bullfights and dance in León and more religious observances in Palencia. The following week there's a big fiesta in Soria.

29: Día de San Pedro Burgos starts a vibrant two-week fiesta, when *gigantillos* parade in the streets, and there are concerts, bullfights and all-night parties. Also big celebrations in León, while in Haro (where festivities started on the 24th) there's the drunken *Batalla del Vino*.

August
15: Fiesta de la Assumption Colourful festivals in La Alberca and Peñafiel.

16: Día de San Roque Fiesta in El Burgo de Osma; also bullfights in the wooden plaza in Penafiel.

Last week: Fiesta de San Agustín In Toro, with the "fountain of wine" and *encierros*.

September
8: Fiesta Virgen de la Vega First day of the fiesta in Salamanca, beginning the evening before and lasting two weeks, as well as the famous bull-running in Tordesillas.

21: Día de San Mateo Major *ferias* in Valladolid and especially Logroño, where the Rioja harvest is celebrated with a week's worth of hijinks.

Salamanca

SALAMANCA is the most graceful city in Spain. For four centuries, it was the seat of one of the most prestigious universities in the world, and at the intellectual heart of the burgeoning Spanish crown's enterprise – Cortes and St Ignatius of Loyola were students, while Columbus came here in 1486 in an initially unsuccessful attempt to persuade a university commission of inquiry to back his exploration plans. City and university declined in later centuries, and there was much damage done during the Napoleonic Wars, but the Salamanca of today presents a uniformly gorgeous ensemble from Spain's Golden Age, given a perfect harmony by the warm golden sandstone, known as Villamayor, with which its finest buildings were constructed. It's still a relatively small place, with a population of 160,000, but an awful lot of those are students, both Spanish and foreign, which adds to the general level of gaiety.

Arrival and information

The compact **Casco Histórico**, with the Plaza Mayor at its heart, spreads back from the Río Tormes, bounded by a loop of avenues and *paseos*. Bus and train stations are on opposite sides of the city, each about fifteen-minutes' walk from the centre or a €5 taxi ride. From the **bus station** (Avda. de Filiberto Villalobos) turn right and keep going straight until you reach Plaza Mayor. From the **train station**, go left down the Paseo de la Estación to Plaza de España, from where c/Azafranal or c/Toro lead directly to the Plaza Mayor. **Driving** into the centre, all the main hotels and car parks are clearly signposted. You'll be able to unload outside most hotels (though not on every street in the old centre), but street **parking** is usually restricted to two hours, so it's best to use one of the garages or car parks (around €16–20 per day).

The main city **turismo** is at Plaza Mayor 32 (Mon–Fri 9am–2pm & 4.30–8pm, Sat 10am–8pm, Sun 10am–2pm; winter Mon–Sat closes 6.30pm; ☏923 218 342, ⊛www.salamanca.es); there are also seasonal offices (July–Sept) inside the train and bus stations.

Accommodation

With the exception of the *parador*, all the places reviewed below are in the **Casco Histórico**, and you'll be able to walk to everything in five minutes or so. There are some splendid boutique and classy lodgings, but many budget *pensiones* are more or less permanently occupied by students during the academic year. You may be approached at the train or bus station and offered **private rooms**, which will usually be the lowest-priced options available. Otherwise, c/Meléndez and c/Jesus (both just south of Plaza Mayor) are good places to look for cheap rooms.

Hostal Catedral Rúa Mayor 46, 1° ☏923 270 614. Clean, bright, budget *hostal* with modern bathrooms. It's in a great location, and most rooms have cathedral views. ❷

Hostal Plaza Mayor Plaza del Corillo 20 ☏923 262 020, ⊛www.hostalplazamayor.es. Just behind Plaza Mayor, this *hostal* has nineteen small, plain rooms (including five singles). It can get noisy at weekends, as you're right in the thick of things. ❸

Hostal Sara c/Meléndez 11 ☏923 281 140, ⊛www.hostalsara.org. The best – and friendliest – budget option on this busy street, 100m from Plaza Mayor. Its fifteen rooms are comfortably furnished, and feature wood floors and tiled bathrooms. Internal rooms are nice and quiet. ❷

Hotel Abba Fonseca Plaza San Blas 2 ☏923 011 010, ⊛www.abbafonsecahotel.com. A contemporary four-star hotel on a tranquil square a 10min walk from Plaza Mayor. Many rooms have lovely views across the city (though there are cheaper rooms without the views). ❺

Hotel Emperatriz I c/La Compañía 44 ☏923 219 200, ⊛www.emperatrizhotel.com. A two-star hotel in an old mansion, part of a chain of three in the city (the other central location is Rúa Mayor 18). Rooms are comfortable, and good value, even if they don't quite live up to the historic setting. ❸

Hotel Estrella Albatros c/Grillo 18 ☏923 266 033, ⊛www.estrellaalbatros.com. A terrific four-star boutique hotel, whose secret is its sweeping city-view from the roof. Spacious, contemporary rooms are in soft colours and blond wood, while classy bathrooms have smoked-glass sinks and jacuzzi-baths. Garage parking underneath. ❺

Hotel San Polo c/Arroyo de Santo Domingo 2 ☏923 211 177, ⊛www.hotelsanpolo.com. A charming hotel arranged around the ruins of a sixth-century Roman church – there are terrace tables in the ruined nave. The only downside is the traffic noise from the front-facing rooms. ❺

Meliá Las Claras c/Marquesa Almarza 31 ☏923 128 500, ⊛www.solmelia.com. Very comfortable contemporary four-star hotel in a quiet corner of town. Spacious rooms in muted colours provide a tranquil base, the buffet breakfast is excellent, and there's a good restaurant. The same group also has the nearby business-oriented, four-star *Tryp Salamanca* – both hotels offer online deals, from as little as €60 (*Tryp*) or €75 (*Las Claras*), and both are easy to find by car and have garage parking. ❺

Palacio de Castellanos c/San Pablo 58–64 ☏923 261 818, ⊛www.nh-hotels.com. An opulent, marbled four-star hotel set in a fifteenth-century

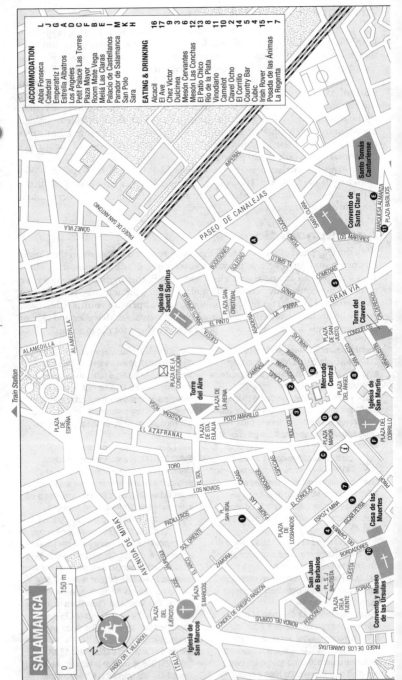

SALAMANCA

0   150 m

N

▲ Train Station

▼ Van Dyck Tapas Bars

ACCOMMODATION

Abba Fonseca	L
Catedral	J
Emperatriz I	G
Estrella Albatros	A
Los Angeles	D
Petit Palace Las Torres	C
Plaza Mayor	F
Room Mate Vega	B
Meliá Las Claras	E
Palacio de Castellanos	I
Parador de Salamanca	M
San Polo	K
Sara	H

EATING & DRINKING

Alcacil	16
El Ave	17
Chez Victor	9
Dulcinea	3
Mesón Cervantes	6
Mesón Las Conchas	12
El Patio Chico	13
Río de la Plata	8
Vinodiario	11
Camelot	10
Clavel Ocho	2
El Corrillo	14
Country Bar	5
Cubic	4
Irish Rover	15
Posada de las Ánimas	1
La Regenta	7

Iglesia de San Marcos

PLAZA DEL EJÉRCITO

PLAZA DE ESPAÑA

ALAMEDILLA

PASEO DE SAN ANTONIO

GÓMEZ VILA

Iglesia de Sancti Spíritus

PLAZA DE LA CONSTITUCIÓN

Torre del Aire

PASEO DE CANALEJAS

IMPERIAL

PEDRO COJOS

SANTA CLARA

LOS MÁRTIRES

Convento de Santa Clara

Santo Tomás Cantuariense

GRAN VÍA

Torre del Clavero

MARQUESA ALMARZA

PLAZA BASILIOS

Convento y Museo de las Ursulas

San Juan de Barbalos

Casa de las Muertes

Mercado Central

Iglesia de San Martín

PLAZA MAYOR

PLAZA DEL CORRILLO

EL AZAFRANAL

PLAZA DE STA. EULALIA

POZO AMARILLO

PLAZA DE LA REINA

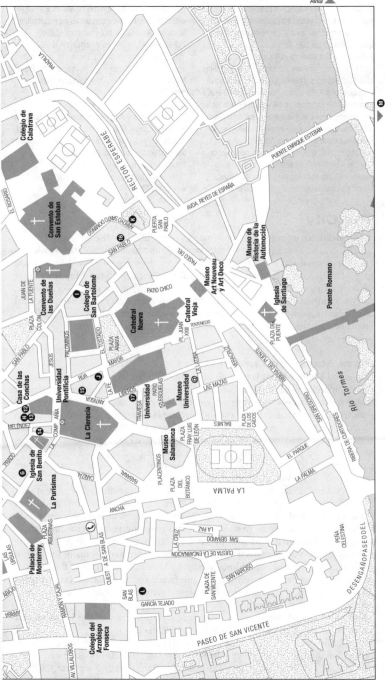

Colegio de Calatrava

Convento de San Esteban

EL ROSARIO

RECTOR ESPERABÉ

PRADILLA

ARROYO SANTO DOMINGO

K

PUERTA SAN PABLO

SAN PABLO

16

Convento de las Dueñas

JUAN DE LA FUENTE

PLAZA COLÓN

SAN PABLO

JESÚS

Colegio de San Bartolomé

I

PATIO CHICO

PALOMINOS

EL TOSTADO

PLAZA ANAYA

MAYOR

Catedral Nueva

Catedral Vieja

PL. JUAN XXIII

TENTENECIO

AVDA. REYES DE ESPAÑA

PUENTE ENRIQUE ESTEBAN

M

▶

Museo de Historia de la Automoción

PASEO DEL

Museo Art Nouveau y Art Deco

Iglesia de Santiago

PLAZA DEL PUENTE

Puente Romano

RÍO Tormes

Casa de las Conchas

13 12

MELÉNDEZ

11

Universidad Pontificia

RÚA

7

LA FE

ANTIGUA

ANA

LA COMP.

15

LIBREROS

TRAVESÍA

17

Universidad

PATIO ESCUELAS

Museo Universidad

@ LA LATINA

LAS MAZAS

CORDEL

PLAZA DE LOS CAÍDOS

BALMES

RIBERA DE CURTIDORES

SAN GREGORIO

RÍO Tormes

La Clerecía

Iglesia de San Benito

G

PRADO

CAÑIZAL

La Purísima

FRAGANAL

Museo Salamanca

PLACENTINOS

PLAZA FRAY LUIS DE LEÓN

EL PARQUE

LA PALMA

Palacio de Monterrey

PLAZA AGUSTINAS

LAS URSULAS

ANCHA

PLAZA DEL BOTÁNICO

LA PALMA

RAMÓN Y CAJAL

ARRIBA

ABAJO

AV. VILLALOBOS

Colegio del Arzobispo Fonseca

OESTE A DE SAN BLAS

OESTE

✆

SAN BLAS

L

GARCÍA TEJADO

LA CRUZ

SAN GERARDO

CUESTA DE LA ENCARNACIÓN

LA PAZ

PLAZA DE SAN VICENTE

SAN NARCISO

PEÑA CELESTINA

PASEO DEL DESENGAÑO

PASEO DE SAN VICENTE

◀ Bus Station

palace. The entrance area – a glassed-in Renaissance cloister converted into a drawing room – is stunning, and it has a very fine restaurant, *Trento*. Internet rates from €99. ⑥

Parador de Salamanca c/Teso de la Feria 2 ⓣ923 192 082, ⓦwww.parador.es. The best thing about Salamanca's modern *parador* is the magnificent view of the city across the river. There's also a very welcome swimming pool with the same views, and parking available, but the location does mean a trip into the centre each day for sightseeing. ⑥

Pensión Los Angeles Plaza Mayor 10, 2 & 3º ⓣ923 218 166, ⓦwww.pensionlosangeles.com. The city's best-sited *pensión*, with four en-suite rooms boasting stunning views over the Plaza Mayor (the most expensive), plus another five shared-bath doubles with rooftop views. It's distinctly no-frills, and room prices vary according to aspect and season, but start from €25. ❸

Petit Palace Las Torres c/Concejo 4 ⓣ923 212 100, ⓦwww.hthoteles.com. Three-star hotel with stylish, minimalist rooms. Some overlook the Plaza Mayor, as does the breakfast room. Internet deals from €70. ❺

Room Mate Vega Plaza del Mercado 16 ⓣ923 272 250, ⓦwww.room-matehotels.com. Part of a young and funky boutique chain, *Vega* is a classy restoration of an old building opposite the market and just a stone's throw from Plaza Mayor. Rooms are all nice, bright and chic, but "executive" rooms are more spacious. ❹, weekends ❺

The City

You'll need to set aside the best part of two full days to see everything in Salamanca, and even then you might struggle – time has a habit of flashing by in a city so easy on the eye that simply strolling around often seems like the best thing to do. Highlights are many, starting with the most elegant **Plaza Mayor** in Spain before moving on to the two **cathedrals**, one Gothic and the other Romanesque, and the beautiful surviving **university buildings**. After this, it's down to individual taste when it comes to deciding exactly how many stately Renaissance palaces, embellished churches, sculpted cloisters, curio-filled museums and religious art galleries you'd like to see.

Plaza Mayor and around

The grand **Plaza Mayor** is the hub of Salamantine life; its bare central expanse, in which bullfights were staged as late as 1863, is enclosed by a continuous four-storey building, broken only by the grand *ayuntamiento* on its northern side. Decorated with iron balconies and medallion portraits, the building was the work of Andrea García Quiñones and Alberto Churriguera, younger brother of José, and nowhere is the Churrigueras' inspired variation of Baroque (see box opposite) so refined as here. Cafés and restaurants ring the arcades, and some *pensiones* and hotels occupy parts of the upper storeys, but signs, advertising, lights and other modern clutter are not allowed to intrude upon the harmonious facades.

Arches from Plaza Mayor lead out into the surrounding shopping streets, including, on the east side, to Plaza del Mercado and the red-brick-and-iron **Mercado Central**, the city's small two-tier market, surrounded by lively restaurants and tapas bars. On the west side, you can wander through the charming streets to find the **Convento y Museo de las Úrsulas** (daily 11am–1pm & 4.30–6pm; €2), recognizable by its unusual open-topped tower; its church contains the superb marble tomb of Archbishop Alonso Fonseca by Diego de Siloé. Facing the east wall of this church is the impressive Plateresque facade of the **Casa de las Muertes** (House of the Dead), the mansion of leading Salamantine architect Juan de Álava, named for the four small skulls at the base of the upper windows.

South of Plaza Mayor, on c/La Compañia, the main draw of the **Universidad Pontifícia de Salamanca** (Tues–Fri 10.30am–12.45pm & 5–6.45pm, Sat 10am–1.15pm & 5–7.15pm, Sun 10am–1.15pm; €2.50; ⓦwww.upsa.es) is its central building, a former Jesuit college founded in 1617. Although linked originally to the university proper, it was formally established as a separate religious college in 1940 by Pope Pius XII, with faculties of theology and canon law (excluded from the main university in 1852). Obligatory Spanish-only guided tours set off every 45 minutes, starting at a magnificent stone staircase, *la escalera noble*, that seems to hang suspended in the air, then taking in the richly decorated main hall and the grandiose cloister, before ending in the vast Baroque church of **La Clerecía** next door.

Opposite stands the early sixteenth-century mansion called the **Casa de las Conchas** (House of Shells), named after the rows of carved scallop shells, symbol of the pilgrimage to Santiago, which decorate its facade. It's now partly a public library and exhibition space, but you can look into the courtyard (Mon–Fri 9am–9pm, Sat 9am–2pm & 4/5–7/8pm; free) and enjoy a good view of the towers of La Clerecía from the upper storey.

Universidad de Salamanca

The historic core of the **Universidad de Salamanca** (Mon–Fri 9.30am–1.30pm & 4–7pm, Sat until 6.30pm, Sun 10am–1pm; €4, free Mon morning; Ⓦwww.usal.es), also known as the Universidad Civil, is reached down c/Libreros. You'll recognize it by the milling tour groups, all straining their necks to examine the magnificent **facade**, the ultimate expression of Plateresque. It's covered with medallions, heraldic emblems and floral decorations, amid which lurks a hidden frog said to bring good luck and marriage within the year to anyone who spots it unaided. The centre is occupied by a portrait of Isabel and Fernando, surrounded by a Greek inscription commemorating their devotion to the university.

Inside, the old lecture rooms are arranged round a courtyard. The **Aula Fray Luís de León** preserves the rugged original benches and the pulpit where this celebrated professor lectured. In 1573, the Inquisition muscled its way into the room and arrested Fray Luís for alleged subversion of the faith; five years of torture and imprisonment followed, but upon his release he calmly resumed his lecture with the words "*Dicebamus hesterna die...*" ("As we were saying yesterday..."). An elegant Plateresque stairway leads to the upper floor, where you'll find the old university **library**, stuffed with thousands of antiquated books on wooden shelves and huge globes of the world, whose faded magnificence gives some idea of Renaissance Salamanca's academic splendour.

Facing the university entrance is the **Patio de las Escuelas**, a small, enclosed square housing the **Museo de Salamanca** (Tues–Sat 10am–2pm & 4–7pm, July–Sept till 8pm, Sun 10am–2pm; €1.20, free weekends). This occupies an exquisite fifteenth-century mansion – originally the home of Isabel's personal physician – which is at least as interesting as the collection of Spanish religious

La Universidad de Salamanca

The **Universidad de Salamanca** was founded by Alfonso IX in 1218, and, after the union of Castile and León, became the most important in Spain. Its rise to international stature was phenomenal, and within thirty years Pope Alexander IV proclaimed it equal to the greatest universities of the day. As at Oxford, Paris and Bologna, theories formulated here were later accepted as fact throughout Europe. The university continued to flourish under the Reyes Católicos, and in the sixteenth century it was powerful enough to resist the orthodoxy of Felipe II's Inquisition, but, eventually, freedom of thought was stifled by the extreme clericalism of the seventeenth and eighteenth centuries. Books were banned for being a threat to the Catholic faith, and mathematics and medicine disappeared from the curriculum. During the Peninsular War, the French demolished 20 of the 25 colleges, and by the end of the nineteenth century there were no more than three hundred students (compared to 6500 in the late sixteenth century). The university saw a revival in the early part of the twentieth century, particularly under the rectorship of celebrated philosopher and man of letters Miguel de Unamuno. Today, numbers are higher than ever (around 30,000 students) and Salamanca Uni has a certain social cachet, though it ranks academically well behind Madrid, Barcelona and Seville. It does, however, run a highly successful **language school** – nowhere else in Spain will you find so many young foreigners.

paintings and sculpture contained within. At the back of the square, an arch leads through to the cloistered Renaissance courtyard of the **Escuelas Menores**, which served as a kind of preparatory school for the university proper. A succession of weekend newlyweds poses here for photographs while, on the far side of the courtyard, the building marked **Museo de la Universidad** (Tues–Sat noon–2pm & 4–8.30pm, Sun 10am–2pm; free) features a remarkable zodiacal ceiling, the so-called *Cielo de Salamanca*, once housed in the university chapel. As your eyes adjust to the light, centaurs, serpents and the Grim Reaper all come into focus amid the twinkling stars.

The cathedrals

The **Catedral Nueva** (daily: summer 9am–8pm; winter 9am–1pm & 4–6pm; free), begun in 1512, was a glorious last-minute assertion of Gothic architecture. The main entrance is contemporary with that of the university and equally dazzling in its wealth of ornamental detail, while the doorways on the north side facing Plaza de Anaya are scarcely less fine. For financial reasons, construction spanned two centuries and thus the building incorporates a range of styles; if you stand under the dome, you can clearly see the transition from Gothic at the bottom to late Baroque at the top. Alberto Churriguera and his brother José both worked here – the former on the choirstalls, the latter on the dome.

The earlier, Romanesque **Catedral Vieja** (daily: summer 10am–7.30pm; winter 10am–12.30pm & 4–5.30pm; €4.25) is dwarfed by its neighbour, through which it's entered. The chapels opening off the cloisters were used as university lecture rooms until the sixteenth century and one, the **Capilla de Obispo Diego de Anaya**, contains the oldest organ in Europe (mid-fourteenth century). Otherwise, the cathedral's most distinctive feature is its dome, known as the **Torre de Gallo** (Cock Tower) on account of its rooster-shaped weather vane. Fashioned like the segments of an orange, the dome derives from Byzantine models and is similar to those at Zamora and Toro; there's a good view of it from Patio Chico around the back of the cathedrals. Also at the rear is the entrance to the **Exposición Ieronimus** (enter from Plaza Juan XXIII; daily 10am–7.15pm; €3.25; ⓦ www.ieronimus.com), primarily a collection of rare documents relating to the cathedral and named after the first bishop of Salamanca. However, it occupies the medieval Torre Mocha, through which you get to clamber, and has outstanding views over the city.

Museo Art Nouveau y Art Deco

Down c/Tentenecio, behind the Catedral Vieja, you'll stumble upon possibly Salamanca's quirkiest museum, the **Museo Art Nouveau y Art Deco** (April to mid-Oct Tues–Fri 11am–2pm & 5–9pm, Sat & Sun 11am–9pm; mid-Oct to March Tues–Fri 11am–2pm & 4–7pm, Sat & Sun 11am–8pm; €3, free Thurs 11am–2pm; Ⓦwww.museocasalis.org), contained within the Casa Lis, built for an Art Nouveau enthusiast at the turn of the twentieth century and partly constructed from vibrantly painted glass (the best views of the house are actually from the ring road below). There's a terrific miscellany of objects inside, from bronze statues and porcelain figures to jewellery and furniture, with notable exhibits including the famous scent bottles René Lalique designed for Guerlain and Worth.

The Puente Romano and the river

For a terrific city view up to the walls and spires, walk down below the cathedrals to the river and cross the arched **Puente Romano**, built in the first century AD (don't look back until you're most of the way across). Back on the city side of the **Río Tormes**, there's a riverside promenade that runs east past the other main city bridges; it starts behind the **Museo de Historia de la Automoción** (April–Sept Tues–Sun 11am–2pm & 5–9pm; Oct–March Tues–Sun 10.30am–2pm & 4.30–8pm; €3; Ⓦwww.museoautomocion.com), which does exactly what it says – provides a brief overview of the history of automobiles before presenting ninety gleaming vintage vehicles on three floors.

The convents: San Esteban, Las Dueñas and Santa Clara

The final historic grouping lies across c/San Pablo, east of the cathedrals. Start with the facade of the **Convento de San Esteban** (daily 10am–2pm & 4–8pm, winter until 7pm; €3), another faultless example of Plateresque art, the central panel of which depicts the stoning of its patron saint, St Stephen. If you pay to go inside, you get to see the lavish Baroque *retablo* by José Churriguera as well as the choir, cloister and museum of sacred art (museum closed Sun pm, Mon, & Tues am).

The most beautiful cloisters in the city, however, stand across the road in the **Convento de las Dueñas** (Mon–Fri 10.30am–12.45pm & 4.30–6.45pm, Sat 10.30am–12.45pm; €1.50). Built in the sixteenth century on an irregular pentagonal plan, the imaginative upper-storey capitals are wildly carved with rams' heads, scallop shells, winged cherubs, mythical beasts and an extraordinary range of human faces. The nuns sell boxes of crumbly almond pastries from a booth next to the entrance.

Just north of here, the thirteenth-century **Convento de Santa Clara** (Mon–Fri 9.30am–2pm & 4–7pm, Sat & Sun 9.30am–3pm; €2, guided tours only) was found to be concealing unsuspected treasure when the whitewash was taken off the chapel walls in 1976. Underneath was an important series of frescoes from the thirteenth to the eighteenth century, while Romanesque and Gothic columns and a stunning sixteenth-century polychrome ceiling were also uncovered in the cloister. But the most incredible discovery was made in the church, where the Baroque ceiling constructed by Joaquín Churriguera was found to be false; rising above this, you can see the original fourteenth-century beams, decorated with heraldic motifs of the kingdoms of Castile and León.

Eating and drinking

Salamanca is a great place for hanging out in bars and cafés, but not so great for eating, at least at the budget end of the scale. *Menús* start at around €12–15, and you can easily spend €50 in the better **restaurants**, while sitting outside to eat in the Plaza Mayor or anywhere nearby attracts a hefty mark-up. Just south of Plaza Mayor, the adjacent c/Meléndez and Rúa Mayor are packed with bars and restaurants, with enticing tables set out in the pedestrianized streets. There's another bunch of popular restaurants and tapas places near the market (around Plaza del Mercado and up c/Pozo Amarillo), but the best **tapas bars** in the city are a fifteen-minute walk north of the old centre, along c/Van Dyck (follow Paseo Doctor Torres Villaroel, cross Avda. Portugal, and Van Dyck is two streets up, on the right). A score of bars and restaurants along this street serve tapas and *raciones*, specializing in sausages, grills and Castilian meats, at considerably better prices than down in the tourist zone.

Alcacil c/San Pablo 49 ☎923 280 590. Veggies need look no further, a smart restaurant serving dishes such as seasonal risotto or spinach-and-pine-nut stuffed peppers. Lunch dishes are €7–10; at night, there's a €17 tasting *menú* that lets you choose five tapas from a changing list, with puds and drinks extra. Closed Sun eve & Mon.

El Ave c/Libreros 24 ☎923 264 511. Right by the university, and with long opening hours (daily 8am to midnight). Breakfast, tapas, sandwiches and *platos* are standard (most things cost €3–8), but you can also get shakes, juices and a choice of teas, and it's another euro to sit outside under the shady parasols. Closed last week Dec & first week Jan.

Chez Victor c/Espoz y Mina 26 ☎923 213 123. A French-influenced restaurant, specializing in seasonal market cuisine, including fish and game. It's been at the forefront of Salamanca dining for years; at least €50 per head. Closed Sun eve, Mon & Aug.

Dulcinea c/Pozo Amarillo 5 ☎923 217 843. Probably the best-value restaurant in the centre, this reliable, old-fashioned place near the market has two straightforward *menús* at €10 and €20, and an *à la carte* menu of meat and fish that won't break the bank.

Mesón Cervantes Plaza Mayor 15 ☎923 217 213. Two selling points here: a prime position overlooking Plaza Mayor (arrive early at meal times for a window seat) and all-day food service from 10am onwards. Serves *platos combinados* from around €9 or €10, or drinks, tapas and *raciones*.

Mesón Las Conchas Rúa Mayor 16 ☎923 212 167. Reasonable prices and reliable food, especially the *platos combinados* (from €8) or the set lunch *menú* (€13). You can sit outside, while two nice dining rooms upstairs are linked by the city's most amusingly low doorway.

El Patio Chico c/Meléndez 13 ☎923 265 103. A typical brick-walled tavern with rear dining room, where *raciones*, sandwiches, grills and salads are served throughout the day. The food isn't the greatest, but there's lots of choice and prices are pretty fair, from around €8 for the *platos combinados* and with a €13 *menú* that's also available at night.

Río de la Plata Plaza Peso 1 ☎923 210 005. The well-regarded regional Castilian cuisine here is a real step up in quality from most in the area, as are the prices – mains from €14–25, or a full meal at around €40 or more, depending on how far you investigate the enticing wine list. Closed Mon & July.

Vinodiario Plaza de los Basilios 1 ☎923 614 925. Terrific contemporary wine bar with food, just off the main tourist track. There are good wines by the glass and superior meals and *raciones*, including brochette of mozzarella and cherry tomatoes, smoked salmon, grilled peppers, and a ground-beef-and-herb hamburger (most dishes €5–10).

Nightlife

Bars open between 5pm and 8pm, though many don't get going till after midnight (clubs are best after 4am), and it tends to be quieter Monday to Wednesday in winter. There's a whole host of student-oriented **bars and clubs** on the southeast edge of the Casco Histórico, particularly in the arcades of the Gran Vía, in Plaza de San Justo and near the market (near c/Varillas). Another area for bars and clubs is around the Convento de las Úrsulas, while if you're looking for quantity over quality try the infamous **bar de litros** just to the north of here, which sell drinks in litre "buckets" – you'll find several around Plaza de San Juan de Bautista.

Camelot c/Bordadores 3. A fun *discoteca*, housed in part of the Convento de las Úrsulas. The interior, an ex-church, is a mix of medieval and industrial decor, with a bar on the first floor, above the dance-floor. The bar's open from 6pm.

Clavel Ocho c/Clavel 6. One of several amenable bars that put out tables in two interlinked squares just below the market, underneath the San Julian church walls. A good place to start the evening.

El Corrillo c/de Meléndez 18. This arty café-restaurant morphs into a hip jazz club at night, with other live acts ranging from blues bands to poetry readings. It's open from 9am for drinks and food, and there's a terraza around the back on Plaza San Benito.

Country Bar c/Arco de la Lapa 5. Good for folk, rock, punk and anything vaguely alternative; downstairs you'll find an atmospheric tavern

covered wall-to-wall in swirling mosaics (the owner is a Gaudí fanatic).

Cubic Club c/Iscar Peyra 30. Salamanca's electro-techno joint, with international guest DJs, open from 11pm till very late.

Irish Rover Rua Antigua 11. The Irish pub opposite La Clerecía is known as "The Rov", by its expat and student fans. It opens around 5pm, puts on up-and-coming Spanish bands, and converts to a raucous late-night *discoteca* at weekends.

Posada de las Ánimas Plaza San Boal 7. The terraza is a bit hidden away from the main drag (and shared with the equally likeable bar *Juanita*), and don't miss the weird interior of cherubs, chandeliers and dolls' houses.

La Regenta c/Espoz y Mina 25. A stylish recreation of a nineteenth-century literary café and bar, with thick red velvet drapes and wood panelling, and tables lit by dripping candles.

Listings

Bookshop Librería Portonaris, Rúa Mayor 35, has a reasonable selection of English-language books.

Bus station Information on ☎ 923 236 717. Companies with ticket offices at the bus station include Vivas (for Zamora/León and Astorga/Ponferrada; ☎ 923 223 587, @ www.autocaresvivas.es); El Pilar (Ciudad Rodrigo; ☎ 923 222 608, @ www.elpilar-arribesbus.com); Auto-Res/Avanza (Valladolid/Madrid; ☎ 923 232 266, @ www.avanzabus.com); and Alsa (Ávila/Madrid, Valladolid /Burgos and Portugal; ☎ 902 422 242, @ www.alsa.es).

Hospitals Hospital Clínico, Paseo San Vicente 182 ☎ 923 291 100; Hospital Virgen de la Vega, Paseo San Vicente 58–182 ☎ 923 291 200.

Internet access At Plaza Mayor 10, underneath *Pensión Los Angeles* (daily noon–midnight).

Language courses Spanish-language courses offered by the Universidad de Salamanca (@ www.usal.es/curespus; look under "Español para extranjeros") are heavily subscribed, but there are loads of other schools.

Laundry At Pasaje Azafranal 19, off c/Azafranal (daily: summer 10am–8pm; winter 9.30am–2pm & 4–8pm).

Police Policía Nacional, Ronda Sancti Spiritus 8–12 ☎ 923 127 700. In an emergency, call ☎ 091.

Post office The main *correos* is at Gran Vía 25 (Mon–Fri 8.30am–8.30pm, Sat 9.30am–2pm).

Taxis Radio Tele-Taxi ☎ 923 250 000.

Ciudad Rodrigo

The unspoiled frontier town of **CIUDAD RODRIGO** – 90km southwest of Salamanca, astride the road to Portugal – is worth a detour even if you don't plan to cross the border. It's an endearingly sleepy place, which, despite an orgy of destruction during the Peninsular War, preserves streets full of Renaissance mansions.

Arrival and information

Ciudad Rodrigo's **bus station** is a five-minute walk north of the old town. There is a **train station**, though there's only one train a day to Lisbon (at 6.05am), and another to Hendaye in France (10.52pm; via Salamanca, Valladolid and Burgos, all in the dead of night). You can easily **park** outside the walls, or try your luck with the limited spaces on Plaza Mayor. The **turismo** is on Plaza de Amayuelas (Mon–Fri 9am–2pm & 5–7pm, Sat & Sun 10am–2pm & 5–8pm; ☎923 460 561, ⓦwww.ciudadrodrigo.net), just through the rampart tunnel. There's a daily market outside the walls, and a Tuesday **market** within, in the arcaded Plaza del Buen Alcalde, where you can pick up fruit, veg and flowers from local smallholders and greengrocers. The **Carnaval del Toro** (Feb; ⓦwww.carnavaldeltoro.es), with bull running in the streets and fights in the Plaza Mayor, is one of the most dramatic in Spain, whilst Semana Santa (Easter) sees processions of hooded penitents.

Accommodation

Reservations are best for the popular *parador*, but otherwise, outside festival time, you should always be able to find a **hotel** room right in the old centre.

Hostal Puerta del Sol c/Rúa del Sol 33 ☎923 460 671, ⓦwww.puertadelsolhostal.com. Trim little en-suite rooms by the Puerta del Sol gate, and a cosy feel throughout. Public parking 1min away through the gate. ❸

Hotel Conde Rodrigo I Plaza de San Salvador 9 ☎923 461 404, ⓦwww .conderodrigo.com. An old mansion loaded with character – check out the period-piece panelled bar. Decent rooms with good bathrooms, very quiet at the rear, plus private garage parking nearby (you can unload outside). ❹

Parador de Ciudad Rodrigo Plaza Castillo 1 ☎923 460 150, ⓦwww.parador.es. Has an unrivalled location in the old castle, which has been beautifully restored. There are views to all sides, and some very grand rooms and public spaces, as well its own restaurant and car park. ❻

Pensión Madrid c/Madrid 20, 1º ☎923 462 467. Reasonable budget *pensión*, offering doubles with shared bathrooms and a few rooms with private facilities. ❶

The Town

The best way to get an overview of town is by making the thirty-minute circuit of the encircling **walls** and ramparts – originally twelfth century, with seventeenth-century additions. Inside the walls, all roads lead sooner or later to the elongated **Plaza Mayor**, while to the northwest is the **Catedral** (daily 9am–1pm & 4–6pm; €1.50, free Wed), with its unusual eight-part vaults, dome-like in shape, and a *coro* with wonderfully grotesque stalls carved by Rodrigo Alemán, who also created those at Toledo and Plasencia.

Ciudad Rodrigo was a crucial border point in the **Peninsular War**, guarding the route between Spain and Portugal. The town fell to the French in 1810, despite valiant resistance from General Herrasti's Spanish garrison – a four-cornered monument to the general and his men stands in the little square beside the cathedral. In front of the walls near here is another memorial, to Julián Sánchez, "El Charro", who led the local guerillas against the French, and beyond this, up on the wall itself, is a tiny plaque marking the site of the **Great Breach** through which the British retook Ciudad Rodrigo with a devastatingly rapid siege in 1812. A triumphant rampage of looting followed, and, when order was restored, the troops paraded out dressed in a ragbag of stolen French finery. A bemused Wellington muttered to his staff, "Who the devil are those fellows?" The British guns were on the two ridges opposite town (the lower one with the block of flats, the other higher up beyond the rail line) – you can still see the cannonball dents above the doorway on this side of the cathedral.

Eating and drinking

The Plaza Mayor is ringed with regular **cafés**, but the town also has a growing reputation as a weekend retreat, so some fancier **restaurants** offer more refined fare.

Estoril c/General Pando 11 ☏ 923 460 550. The best place in town for modern interpretations of regional cuisine – marinated quail salad, milk-fed lamb, duck with blackberry sauce, etc. Café at the front, plus formal, but unstuffy, restaurant to the rear (mains €13–20).

El Rodeo c/Gigantes 10 ☏ 923 482 017. Simple, old-fashioned restaurant offering hearty local specialities, such as scrambled eggs with *farinato* (pork and bread sausage). There's a *menú* for €10, or you can eat in the evening for €15–20.

El Sanatorio Plaza Mayor 13–15. Atmospheric little bar-restaurant whose walls are covered in bullfighting photos from decades of *corridas* and fiestas. Dishes €5–8.

El Zascandil c/Correo Viejo 5 ☏ 665 635 884. A contemporary place for creative *pinchos* and good wine, with a jazzy, laid-back vibe. You need to reserve for the more elaborate meals in the small restaurant upstairs.

La Alberca and Parque Natural Las Batuecas-Sierra de Francia

The protected mountain region of the **Sierra de Francia** marks the southern region of Salamanca province, with the most obvious target the captivating "national monument" village of **La Alberca**. It makes a good walking base for the surrounding hills and valleys, notably the stunning **Valle de Las Batuecas**, with its isolated monastery and ancient rock art.

There are daily buses to La Alberca from Salamanca, but the area is otherwise best explored by car, in which case you'll also be able to make a half day's circuit via the equally venerable hill-town of **Miranda del Castañar**.

La Alberca

Although ringed by the trappings of mass tourism these days, the centre of **LA ALBERCA** still maintains an extraordinary collection of late medieval, half-timbered houses. It's very pretty, and an obvious honeytrap for weekenders and coach parties who trawl the rather-too-clean cobbled lanes shopping for basketware and other souvenirs. The smell and dirt of the farmyard may be long gone, but La Alberca is still known for its *embutidos* and *jamones* and every second shop displays the rich, nutty hams, smoked pork and cured sausages. A granite porker stands outside the church, while the most elegant houses are found in the arcaded **Plaza Mayor**, which is ringed by cafés and restaurants and dominated by a stone cross.

The village is 45km southeast of Ciudad Rodrigo, and 73km southwest of Salamanca. Cosme **buses** run here daily in the afternoon from Salamanca – the only day with a possible day-return service is Sunday – stopping on the edge of the old quarter. You should eventually find somewhere to park on the main through-roads, though there's also a large **car park** a few hundred metres out on the Batuecas road, just past the *Hotel Antiguas Eras* and right next to the Casa del Parque **information office** (Mon–Fri 10am–2pm & 5–7pm, Sat & Sun 10am–2pm & 4–8pm; ☏ 923 415 213). Half a dozen **bars and restaurants** ring Plaza Mayor, and there are a few more down neighbouring streets, serving tapas and meals, none particularly cheap, all agreeably rustic. *La Fuente*, c/Tablao 8

(☎923 415 399), just off the plaza, is typical, a good place to eat milk-fed lamb or the local pork.

Accommodation

Accommodation is expensive for what you get, though there are a few cheaper *pensiones*, with the best deals further up the Batuecas road, a few minutes' walk from the centre. There's also the Al-Bereka **campsite**, 2km out on the Salamanca road (☎923 415 195; closed Nov–April).

Hotel Antiguas Eras Batuecas road ☎923 415 113, ⓦwww.antiguaseras.com. Agreeable three-star hotel with spacious, pleasantly furnished rooms, distant hill views and a family-friendly welcome. The simple *Hostal San Blas*, next door, is a cheap stand-by. ❸

Hotel Las Batuecas Batuecas road ☎923 415 188, ⓦwww.hotellasbatuecas.com. Three-star hotel and restaurant with a rustic *ambiente clasico*

and old-fashioned rooms that may or may not appeal. ❺

Hostal El Castillo Mogarraz road ☎923 415 001. Basic rooms above a restaurant. ❷

Hotel Doña Teresa Mogarraz road ☎923 415 308, ⓦwww.hoteldeteresa.com. The smartest choice in town, this four-star hotel has a spa and restaurant at the hotel, and landscaped pool and gardens nearby. ❺

Parque Natural Las Batuecas-Sierra de Francia

La Alberca sits in the middle of the **PARQUE NATURAL LAS BATUECAS-SIERRA DE FRANCIA**, and at the centre of an excellent network of hiking trails. These are well signposted and easily followed, especially if you've already stopped for maps at the Casa del Parque information office in La Alberca.

The most obvious route on a clear day is up to the summit of **Peña de Francia** (1723m), not quite the highest point in the range but the most panoramic. The trail is signposted a couple of hundred metres outside La Alberca (Batuecas road), by the Cooperativa Chacinera (across from the *Hotel Antiguas Eras*); it's a very specific 8.3km on foot (6hr round trip) or 17km by road. There's the church and sanctuary of Our Lady of the Peña de Francia at the windswept summit, along with a welcome *cafeteria* and even lodgings at the *Hospedería del Santuario Peña de Francia*.

The Batuecas road out of La Alberca climbs in 3.5km to the pass of **El Portillo** (1247m), surrounded by rugged hills. From here, the road drops sharply for another 9km, via a series of hairpin bends, into the **Valle de las Batuecas**, where a signpost points you up a short track to a parking area outside the **Monasterio San José de las Batuecas**. There's also a more direct seven-kilometre path (3hr 30min each way) from La Alberca, over the pass and down to the monastery. This sylvan retreat in a hidden valley was founded at the beginning of the seventeenth century, and is a closed Carmelite order (no public access). However, a signposted path around the side of the monastery leads along the babbling river to a series of three **rock-art** sites dating from between 5000 and 2500 BC, depicting hunting and pastoral scenes of goats and deer, and even human figures. The closest site, Cabras Pintadas, is an enjoyable half-hour's walk and scramble from the monastery gate.

Other **walking trails** from La Alberca head east, out towards Mogarraz and Miranda del Castañar, and there's a direct road this way, too, but with a car it's a good half-day's excursion to continue on from the monastery south for 5km to the junction at **Las Mestas**, just across the border in Extremadura. Following signs for Cepeda and Salamanca then takes you around the eastern edge of the *parque natural*, eventually arriving (after 27km) at **Miranda del Castañar**, a similarly ancient town to La Alberca, though this time set within the walls of a honey-coloured castle. There are sweeping views to all sides, a couple of rather nice *casas rurales* and upmarket restaurants, and a boho café-jazz bar, *La Mandrágora* (signposted by the gateway to the old town), which can provide a superior toastie or pizza to munch on its vista-laden terrace.

Zamora and around

ZAMORA, 62km north of Salamanca and only 50km from the Portuguese border, is the quietest of the great Castilian cities, with a population of just 65,000. In medieval romances, it was known as *la bien cercada* (the well-enclosed) on account of its strong fortifications; one siege here lasted seven months. Its old quarters, still walled and medieval in appearance, are spread out along the top of a ridge that slopes down to the banks of the Río Duero. The city's surviving Romanesque churches are its most distinctive feature, while the beguiling streets and squares of the old town make for an attractive overnight stay. When it's time to move on, the obvious routes are east to Valladolid, with a stop in the small town of Toro, or north to León, via Benavente and its *parador*; Bragança, the first main town over the border in Portugal, is just over 100km away on a good, fast road.

Arrival and information

The **train station** and **bus terminal** are close to each other, thirty-minutes' walk north of Plaza Mayor. From the bus station, turn right out of the main entrance then right again around the side of the terminal to reach the main road; turn left here and follow the Avenida Tres Cruces all the way in to town. From the train station walk straight out over the roundabout in front to join the Avenida Tres Cruces. Alternatively, it's a ten-minute ride on bus #4 (every 20min), which leaves from outside the bus station and runs down Avenida Tres Cruces, dropping you at Plaza Sagasta by Plaza Mayor; note the return bus departs from outside the market. Some of the old town is residents-only access and parking, but the main central **car parks** are well signposted.

There are two useful **turismos**: a municipal office at Plaza de Arias Gonzalo 6, near the cathedral (daily: April–Sept 10am–2pm & 5–8pm; Oct–March 10am–2pm & 4–7pm; ☎980 533 694, ⓦwww.zamoradipu.es), and the regional office at Avda. Príncipe de Asturias 1 (daily: July to mid-Sept 9am–8pm, Fri & Sat until 9pm; mid-Sept to June 9am–2pm & 5–8pm; ☎980 531 845 or 902 203 030), on the edge of the old town.

Accommodation

Zamora has a reasonable spread of accommodation, most of it within a short walk of the old quarter.

Hostal La Reina c/La Reina 1, 1º ☎980 533 939. The best budget accommodation, with mostly bright, spacious rooms in an unbeatable location right by Plaza Mayor. Some rooms overlook the square, some are en suite, and some a bit dowdier than others, so it pays to specify or look at a couple. ❷

Hostal Sol c/Benavente 2, 3º ☎980 533 152, ⓦwww.hostal-sol.com. Regular *hostal* rooms in an apartment building, a little on the small side, but reasonably smart and all with private bathroom. The similar *hostales Luz* (under the same management) and *Chiqui* are in the same block. ❷

Hostería Real de Zamora c/Cuesta del Pizarro 7 ☎ 980 534 545, ⓦwww.hosteriasreales.com. The poor man's *parador* is set in the 400-year-old Palacio de Inquisidores, complete with tiled staircases, a cobbled Renaissance patio and goldfish pond. Pretty rooms are ranged around the patio gallery, and some

Valladolid (N620) & Tordesillas (N122)

Bus & Train Stations

Portugal (N122)

Salamanca (N630)

Ledesma

ACCOMMODATION
Hostal La Reina   B
Hostal Sol   A
Hostería Real de   E
Zamora   C
Meliá Horus Zamora   D
Parador Condes de
Alba y Aliste

EATING & DRINKING
El Jardín   1
Paris   2
El Rincón de   3
Antonio

Parque de la Marina
Española

Mercado

San Andrés

Muralla

Santo Tomé

La Horta

San Leonardo

Santa Lucía

San Cipriano

Museo
Provincial

Casa de
Cultura

La Concepción

Museo
Etnográfico

San
Juan

Ayuntamiento

S. Vicente

Palacio
de los Momos

Teatro
Principal

San Esteban

San Antolín

San Torcuato

Santiago
del Burgo

Sta. María
la Nueva

Museo de la
Semana Santa

San Ildefonso

La
Magdalena

San Isidoro

Los Remedios

Bosque de
Valorio

Valderrey

Espíritu
Santo

Santiago
el Viejo

Castillo

Catedral

Palacio
Episcopal

Parque del Castillo

Puente de
Piedra

Río Duero

200 m

0

ZAMORA

have river views, while simple meals (*menú* €12, available lunch & dinner) are served around the patio or in the beamed dining room. ❹

Meliá Horus Zamora Plaza del Mercado 20 ☏ 980 508 282, Ⓦ www.solmelia.com. Handsome boutique lodgings right opposite the market, in a restored mansion. Most of the rooms are nice and quiet, with some set in the eaves, and there's a good contemporary restaurant and garage parking – though there's also restricted street parking outside in the market square. Website rates from as low as €70. ❹

Parador Condes de Alba y Aliste Plaza de Viriato 5 ☏ 980 514 497, Ⓦ www.parador.es. Zamora's classy *parador* is a stunning conversion of a fifteenth-century palace in the heart of town, mixing lovely rooms with princely trappings throughout, from the heroic medallions surmounting the internal courtyard to the idly positioned suits of armour. A fine restaurant serves updated regional cuisine (mains €16–20), or you can just call in for a drink – the bar (open, like the restaurant, to non-guests) has a garden terrace. ❻

The City

The joy of Zamora lies in its quiet, western old-town quarter – looking decidedly spruce and scrubbed these days – and, above all, in its dozen **Romanesque churches** (all Tues–Sun: Feb–Sept 10am–1pm & 5–8pm; Oct–Dec 10am–2pm & 4.30–6.30pm; free), with their unassumingly beautiful architecture, and towers populated by colonies of storks. The majority date from the twelfth century and reflect Castile's sense of security following the victorious campaigns against the Moors by Alfonso VI and El Cid. All are worthy of a closer look, though **San Juan de Puerta Nueva** (Plaza Mayor), **La Magdalena** (Rua de los Francos) and **Santiago del Burgo** (c/Santa Clara) are considered the highlights. Opposite Santa María la Nueva, slightly west of Plaza Mayor, the **Museo de la Semana Santa** (Tues–Sat 10am–2pm & 5–8pm, Sun 10am–2pm; €3) contains the *pasos* – statues depicting the Passion of Christ – which are paraded through the streets during Zamora's famous Holy Week processions (Ⓦ www.ssantazamora.es).

The **Catedral** (Tues–Sun: April–Sept 10am–2pm & 5–8pm; Oct–March 10am–2pm & 4.30–6.30pm; €3), enclosed within the ruined citadel at the far end of town, is now shining very brightly after restoration. Begun in 1151, its mainly Romanesque body is largely hidden behind an overbearing Renaissance facade, above which the building's most striking feature – a Byzantine-inspired dome similar to that of the Catedral Vieja at Salamanca – perches in incongruous splendour. However, it springs a surprise inside, with its famous carved **choirstalls**, which depict devout scenes and mystical animals as well as lusty carryings-on between monks and nuns. Access to the cathedral is through the associated **Museo Catedralicio**, on the other side of the cloisters, which houses the city's celebrated "Black Tapestries", a series of fifteenth-century Flemish masterpieces woven in stunning detail.

Next to the cathedral are the impressive moated remains of the **Castillo**, now laid out as a shady park; wander round the back for majestic views over the surrounding countryside and Río Duero, along with Zamora's burgeoning suburbs. Back towards town, **Rua de los Francos** and **c/Ramon Carrión** have a mix of traditional shops, antique stores and a few more contemporary delis and galleries. Pedestrianized c/Santa Clara is the main shopping street, with the daily **Mercado de Abastos** tucked in between here and the church of San Andrés.

Eating and drinking

Most **restaurants and cafés** are found around the Plaza Mayor and in the side streets and squares off c/Santa Clara. Zamora's most celebrated dishes are *sopas de ajo* (garlic soup) and *arroz de la Zamorana*, rice flavoured with pigs' trotters. There's also a cluster of no-nonsense **tapas bars** in the alleys around Plaza del

▲ Zamora's Catedral

Maestro (east end of c/Santa Clara, by the church of San Torcuato), while a lively run of twenty or so music and drinking **bars** down the narrow c/de los Herreros, just off Plaza Mayor, is where the weekend starts.

El Jardín Plaza del Maestro 8 ☏ 980 531 827. The best of the cheap and cheerful bunch at this end of town serves tapas, sandwiches, *platos combinados* (from €7) and gargantuan *menús* (€8.50), either out in the sunny square or in the *comedor* upstairs.

Paris Avda. de Portugal 14 ☏ 980 514 325. The traditional port of call for locals on the trail of regional meat specialities, such as *lechazo de Castille* and *cochinillo* (mains €12–19), though

there's also some fish, and a choice of *menú* from €15.

El Rincon de Antonio Rua de los Francos 6 ☏ 980 535 370. The town's most inventive restaurant takes Castilian cuisine to a different level. With classy mains at €25 or so, and the *menú degustación* at €55, it's a special-occasion place, but you can drop in for fancy tapas at the bar (what they call *cocina en miniatura*) at a couple of euros a pop.

North to León

It's 140km north to León from Zamora, or a two-hour bus ride, on a fast road (N630 then A66) through the baking wheat fields of the *meseta*. Drivers can at least break the journey at a couple of interesting places, the first a marked turn-off from the N630 (on the left) at the dusty roadside village of Granja de Moreruela, around 40km north of Zamora. "Granja" means farm, meaning the village was originally an outlying property of the medieval **Monasterio de Moreruela**, which lies 3.7km from the highway, down a paved country lane. It's now in ruins, and home to a large colony of storks, but is an evocative sight nonetheless, under a carpet of daisies and poppies, with rolling farmland to all sides.

Thirty kilometres further north, the small town of **BENAVENTE** is rather charming once you penetrate the outskirts, with busy pedestrianized shopping streets set around a honey-coloured stone church or two. A broad landscaped *paseo* on a bluff offers extensive views over the surrounding countryside, while, at the end of the gardens, the *Parador de Benavente* (☏980 630 300, ⓦ www.parador .es; ⓖ) occupies the remains of the town's impressive castle.

Toro

TORO, 30km east of Zamora, looks dramatic seen from below: "an ancient, eroded, red-walled town spread along the top of a huge flat boulder", as Laurie Lee described it in *As I Walked Out One Midsummer Morning*. At closer quarters it turns out to be a rather ordinary provincial town, though embellished with one outstanding Romanesque reminder of past glory. This is the **Colegiata de Santa María la Mayor** (Tues–Sun: March–Sept 10.30am–2pm & 5–7.30pm; Oct–Dec 10am–2pm & 4.30–6.30pm; free, cloisters €1), whose west portal (c.1240), inside the church, is one of the most beautiful examples of Romanesque art in the region. Its seven recessed arches carved with royal and biblical themes still retain much of their colourful original paint. Also inspect the *Virgin of the Fly*, a notable fifteenth-century painting hanging in the sacristy – the eponymous insect perches on the Virgin's robes. Around the back of the church is a wide terrace with a famous view over the *meseta*, with the Río Duero far below.

Toro is increasingly well known for its gutsy red **wines**, and the **turismo** on Plaza Mayor (☏980 694 747, ⓦ www.toroayto.es; closed Mon) can point you in the direction of local wineries open to the public.

Practicalities

Buses to Toro are reasonably frequent (Zamora–Valladolid route, hourly service, fewer at weekends) and stop on the main road that skirts the north side of town – it's best to **park** outside town here, too. Walk through the big arch and straight on for about five minutes, through the clock tower, to reach Plaza Mayor, with

The Battle of Toro

Toro – an historic military stronghold – played a role of vital significance in both Spanish and Portuguese history. The **Battle of Toro** in 1476 effectively ended Portugal's interest in Spanish affairs and laid the basis for the unification of Spain. On the death of Enrique IV in 1474, the Castilian throne was disputed: almost certainly his daughter Juana la Beltraneja was the rightful heiress, but rumours of illegitimacy were stirred up and Enrique's sister Isabel seized the throne. Alfonso V of Portugal saw his opportunity and supported Juana. At Toro, the armies clashed in 1476 and the Reyes Católicos – Isabel and her husband Fernando – defeated their rivals to embark upon one of the most glorious periods in Spanish history.

the Colegiata immediately behind. Staying the night is hardly necessary, though the *Hotel Juan II*, Paseo del Espolón 1 (☎980 690 300, ⓦwww.hoteljuanii .com; ❹), right by the Colegiata, has pleasant **rooms**, a pool, and a terrace bar with fantastic views. Between church and clock tower, Plaza Mayor is lined with characteristic red-brick houses and stone arcades, with many enticing **tapas bars** and **restaurants**.

Valladolid and around

VALLADOLID, at the centre of the *meseta* and capital of the Castilla y León region, ought to be dramatic and exciting. Many of the greatest figures of Spain's Golden Age – Fernando and Isabel, Columbus, Cervantes, Torquemada, Felipe II – lived in the city at various times, and for five years at the turn of the seventeenth century it vied with Madrid as the royal capital. It had wealth and prestige, yet modern Valladolid – a busy, working city of 400,000 – lost much that was irreplaceable, as many of its finest palaces and grandest streets were swept away during subsequent centuries. Nonetheless, much remains that is appealing in a city centre of restored squares and gleaming churches, including a series of excellent art museums, notably the finest collection of religious sculpture assembled anywhere in Spain. While it doesn't have the overriding beauty of Salamanca, or the stand-out monumental presence of Burgos or León, Valladolid is an easy city to like – whether it's the pretty shaded gardens of the Campo Grande, or the student bars lined up under the shadow of a majestic Gothic church. The best time to get a sense of the city's historic traditions is **Semana Santa** (Holy Week), when Valladolid is host to some of the most extravagant and solemn processions in Spain.

Outside the city, there are easy side trips to two handsome small towns, **Tordesillas** and **Medina del Campo**, both now on the quiet and sleepy side but that, like Valladolid, also boast significant histories.

Arrival and information

Arrival points are centred on the large triangular park that is the Campo Grande: the **train station** is at the foot of the park, and the **bus station** a few minutes' walk west, at c/Puente Colgante 2; the AVE high-speed train service now makes Valladolid just over an hour's jump from Madrid. It's a fifteen-minute walk up to Plaza Mayor from the train station, or there are taxis outside. There's also a small **airport** 15km outside the city (served by domestic flights and Ryanair services from London Stansted); buses (€3) run to the centre, while a taxi should cost €20. Driving in, it's easiest to use one of the signposted **car parks** for overnight stays – there's one under Plaza Mayor (hotels round here all offer overnight parking for around €12). The **turismo** is near the top of the Campo Grande (daily 9am–2pm & 5–8pm; ☎983 219 310, ⓦwww.valladolidturismo.com).

Accommodation

The main concentration of **accommodation** – in all price ranges – is in the pleasant area around Plaza Mayor, though there are also some nicely sited places down the east side of Campo Grande.

Hostal París c/Especería 2 ☎983 370 625, ⓦwww.hostalparis.com. The best mid-range place, with very agreeable rooms that are well equipped (flat-screen TV, a/c, wi-fi enabled) and well soundproofed, the front ones with glassed-in street balconies. Two cafés immediately downstairs have good breakfast deals. ❹

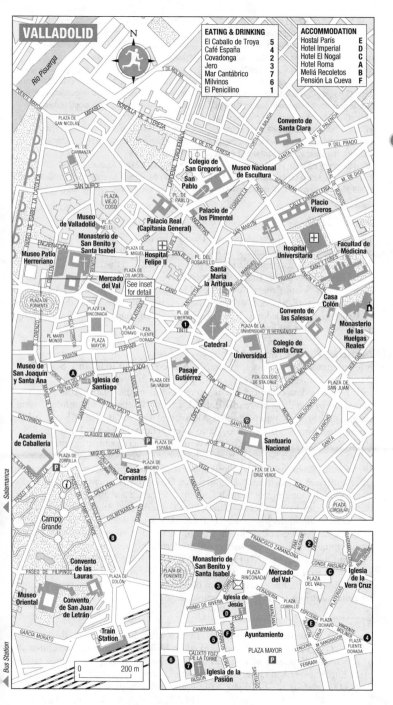

VALLADOLID

See inset for detail

EATING & DRINKING

El Caballo de Troya	5
Café España	4
Covadonga	2
Jero	3
Mar Cantábrico	7
Milvinos	6
El Penicilino	1

ACCOMMODATION

Hostal París	E
Hotel Imperial	D
Hotel El Nogal	C
Hotel Roma	A
Meliá Recoletos	B
Pensión La Cueva	F

Río Pisuerga

PUENTE MAYOR

PASEO DE ISABEL LA CATÓLICA

RONDILLA DE S. TERESA

T. DE MOLINA

MIRABEL

PLAZA DE SAN NICOLÁS

PL. DE CARRANZA

SAN QUIRCE

PLAZA VIEJO COSO

AV. DE STA. TERESA

PORTILLO DE BALBOA

Convento de Santa Clara

P. DEL PRADO

AV. DE PALENCIA

SANTA CLARA

REAL DE BURGOS

M. DE DIOS

GONDOMAR

Colegio de San Gregorio

San Pablo

Museo Nacional de Escultura

PL. DE S. PABLO

CARDENAL TORQUEMADA

PL. F. NELLI

Museo de Valladolid

TORRECILLA

PADILLA

CADENA

CALLE CHANCILLERÍA

Palcio Viveros

Palacio Real (Capitania General)

ENCARNACIÓN

Monasterio de San Benito y Santa Isabel

Palacio de los Pimentel

SAN MARTÍN

Hospital Universitario

Facultad de Medicina

Museo Patio Herreriano

PLAZA DE S. MIGUEL

Hospital Felipe II

SAN BLAS

PL. DEL ROSARILLO

Santa María la Antigua

PARAÍSO

MARQUÉS DEL DUERO

SANZ Y FORÉS

RAMÓN Y CAJAL

Mercado del Val

PLAZA DE LOS ARCES

L. CANO

ANGUSTIAS

Casa Colón

PLAZA DE PONIENTE

PLAZA LA RINCONADA

PLATERÍAS

PLAZA OCHAVO

PL. DE LIBERTAD

TINTE

PLAZA DE LA UNIVERSIDAD R. HERNÁNDEZ

COLÓN

Convento de las Salesas

Monasterio de las Huelgas Reales

FRUELAS

PL MARTI MONSO

PLAZA MAYOR

PZA. FUENTE DORADA

FERRARI

PASIÓN

Catedral

Universidad

Colegio de Santa Cruz

PZA. COLEGIO DE STA. CRUZ

CARDENAL MENDOZA

PLAZA DE SAN JUAN

Museo de San Joaquín y Santa Ana

ZORRILLA

MARÍA DE MOLINA

REGALADO

DUQUE DE LA VICTORIA

Pasaje Gutiérrez

FRAY LUIS DE LEÓN

LÓPEZ GÓMEZ

MENDEZ

MALDONADO

DON SANCHO

SANTA

Iglesia de Santiago

MONTERO CALVO

SANTIAGO

PLAZA DEL SALVADOR

SANTUARIO

Salamanca

DOCTRINOS

CLAUDIO MOYANO

Academia de Caballería

MIGUEL ISCAR

P PLAZA DE ESPAÑA

JOSÉ M. LACORT

Santuario Nacional

PLAZA DE ZORRILLA

P

PASEO DE ZORRILLA

ACERA DE RECOLETOS

Casa Cervantes

PLAZA DE MADRID

VEGA

PZA. DE LA CRUZ VERDE

TUDELA

i

Campo Grande

PASEO DEL CAMPO GRANDE

COLMENARES

GAMAZO

PANADEROS

PLAZA CIRCULAR

PASEO DE FILIPINOS

Convento de las Lauras

PLAZA DE COLÓN

Museo Oriental

Convento de San Juan de Letrán

GARCÍA MORATO

Train Station

Bus Station

0   200 m

[Inset map]

FRANCISCO ZARANDONA

Monasterio de San Benito y Santa Isabel

PLAZA DE PONIENTE

PLAZA RINCONADA

CORREOS

CEBADERÍA

Mercado del Val

PLAZA DEL VAL

CONDE ANSÚREZ

PLAZA CORRILLO

Iglesia de la Vera Cruz

GUADAMACILES

RUA OSCURA

Iglesia de Jesús

PRIMO DE RIVERA

PESO

CORREOS

MANZANA

PLATERÍAS

ESPECERÍA

PLAZA OCHAVO

VINCENTE MOLINER

PLAZA FUENTE DORADA

CAMPANAS

CORREOS

REINA

Ayuntamiento

LENCERÍA

M SANGRADOR

CALIXTO FDEZ DE LA TORRE

PLAZA MAYOR

P

SANTIAGO

FERRARI

Iglesia de la Pasión

PASIÓN

Hotel Imperial c/del Peso 4 ☏ 983 330 300, ⓦ www.himperial.com. Old-fashioned hotel in a beautiful Renaissance mansion right by Plaza Mayor. Everything is a bit on the fussy side, and the columned bar is certainly a talking point. Rates drop quite a bit outside summer. ❺

Hotel El Nogal c/Conde Ansúrez 10 ☏ 983 340 333, ⓦ www.hotelelnogal.com. A smart three-star hotel, offering tasteful rooms with crimson drapes and wood floors, and up-to-date, if rather small, bathrooms (the single rooms are a bit on the pokey side, too). The attached restaurant is a nice find, facing the pretty Plaza del Val around the back. ❹

Hotel Roma c/Héroes del Alcázar de Toledo 8 ☏ 983 351 833, ⓦ www.hotelromavalladolid.com.

Rather charming hotel in a great location (some rooms throw their French windows open onto a little square opposite a church), plus there's a restaurant and its own parking. ❹

Meliá Recoletos c/Acera de Recoletos 13 ☏ 983 216 200, ⓦ www.solmelia.com. The finest boutique lodgings are opposite Campo Grande, not far from the train station, in this handsomely restored mansion. Upper-floor "loft" rooms have particularly good views. Website deals are from €75, while the same chain also has a cheaper city-centre hotel, the *Meliá Olid*. ❺

Pensión La Cueva c/Correos 4 ☏ 983 330 072. Simple *pensión* with en-suite doubles and cheaper singles, above a lively tapas bar and restaurant. ❷

The City

The heart of Valladolid is the spacious **Plaza Mayor**, a broad expanse surrounded by arcaded buildings painted a striking, uniform red. Originally laid out in the sixteenth century after a fire had devastated the city, it was the first plaza of its kind in the country, becoming the model for countless similar civic centrepieces in both Spain and its South American colonies. Though much rebuilt since, it's still one of the grandest urban spaces in Spain and a pleasant place to watch the world go by, while many of Valladolid's best tapas bars and restaurants can be found in the narrow streets just off its western edge.

Around Plaza Mayor

A few minutes' walk west of the plaza, the **Museo de San Joaquín y Santa Ana** (Mon–Fri 10am–1.30pm & 5–7/8pm, Sat 10am–2.30pm; free) is filled mostly with religious dust-collectors but has three Goyas in the chapel. After that, you can swing by the daily **Mercado del Val**, a rather impressive 112m long, before circling the brilliant white restored Monasterio de San Benito y Santa Isabel, whose annex houses the **Museo Patio Herreriano** (Tues–Fri 11am–8pm, Sat 10am–8pm, Sun 10am–3pm; €3; ⓦ www.museopatioherreriano.org), entered from c/Jorge Guillén. It's a beautiful space dedicated to contemporary Spanish art (from 1918 to the present day), with galleries on several floors wrapped around a Renaissance courtyard of luminous pale gold stone. There's a permanent display of works by artists at the forefront of Spanish Cubism, Surrealism and abstract art, including Rafael Barradas, Joaquin Torres-García, Julio González and Ángel Ferrant, but also temporary exhibitions by young contemporary artists and sculptors, sometimes of the light-flashing-pointlessly-in-a-room variety but often with bouts of real quality, too. A stylish café-bar sits on the modern patio outside.

Continuing north up c/San Ignacio brings you to the **Museo de Valladolid** in Plaza de Fabio Nelli (Tues–Sat 10am–2pm & 4–7pm, July–Sept till 8pm, Sun 10am–2pm; €1.20, free weekends), an old-fashioned archeological museum and art gallery set in a Renaissance mansion.

The catedral

The city's **Catedral** was designed but not completed by Juan de Herrera (architect of El Escorial) and later worked on by Alberto Churriguera. Only half of it was ever built and what stands is something of a disappointment – rather plain, rather severe and rather hard to view as a whole. Inside (entrance on Plaza de la Universidad), the highlight is the *retablo mayor* by Juan de Juni (which was actually made for the Gothic Santa María la Antigua in the plaza behind). You should be able to duck in to see this, but you're officially supposed to stump up for a tour of both cathedral and the treasures of the diocesan museum, the **Museo Diocesano y Catedralicio** (Tues–Sat 10am–1.30pm & 4.30–7pm, Sun 10am–2pm; €2.50).

San Pablo and San Gregorio

Altogether more enticing than the cathedral are the facades of the two churches at Plaza San Pablo, five-minutes' walk to the north. The exuberant **San Pablo** betrays a wild mixture of styles: the lower part is a product of the lavish form of late Gothic known as Isabelline, whereas the upper part is a Plateresque confection, similar to the Catedral Nueva and Convento de San Esteban at Salamanca. Wilder still is the facade of the adjacent **Colegio de San Gregorio**, adorned not just with coats of arms and crowned lions, but sculpted twigs, naked children clambering in the branches of a pomegranate tree and long-haired men carrying maces. Considered to be from the workshop of master sculptor Gil de Silóe, it's very much like icing on a cake – Jan Morris, for one, was convinced that the flamboyant facade must be edible.

Museo Nacional de Escultura

Valladolid's best museum stands directly opposite San Gregorio, housed in the sixteenth-century Palacio de Villena. The beautifully presented **Museo Nacional de Escultura** (Tues–Sat 10am–2pm & 4–9pm, Oct to mid-March afternoons 4–6pm, Sun 10am–2pm; €2.40, free Sat pm & Sun am; Ⓦmuseoescultura.mcu.es) contains a renowned collection of Spanish religious sculpture of the sixteenth to eighteenth centuries, including some of the most brilliant works of the Spanish Renaissance – often commissioned for churches and monasteries, rarely do you see such vibrant pieces at these close quarters. Sixteenth-century artists such as **Alonso Berruguete** (1486–1561), **Diego de Siloé** (1495–1565) and the Frenchman **Juan de Juni** (1507–77) adapted the classical revival to the religious intensity of the Spanish temperament, and the results are often magnificent and sometimes quite beautifully brutal, as weeping wounds, agonized faces and rapt expressions echo around the galleries. There are good English notes throughout, and you can pick up a leaflet at the desk detailing the highlights, while in an extraordinary flourish at the last you're confronted by a remarkable sculpted **Nativity tableau** – in an eighteenth-century Neapolitan street, between the hanging laundry, itinerant musicians and fruit sellers, the three Wise Men troop towards the manger on camels. The city's processional Easter figures, or *pasos*, are also part of the museum's remit – they're on display in a separate building, to which you can be directed from the front desk.

Eating and drinking

Plaza Mayor has the best outdoor **cafés** for a drink with views, while c/Correos, just to the west, is packed with largely upscale **tapas bars and restaurants** (though you'll still get a *menú* here for €15). There are two good areas for late-opening **bars**: either around the small modern square of Plaza Marti y Monso, just off Plaza Mayor, or the more student-oriented cluster around the back of the cathedral, by the Santa María de la Antigua church (around c/Antigua and c/Paraíso).

Cafés and bars

Café España Plaza Fuente Dorada 8. A nice, straight-up café-bar with black-and-white photos on the walls and a small stage at the back, serving as a regular venue for live jazz.

Mar Cantábrico c/Caridad. It's just down a side-alley from the square with all the bars, but it's a great place for a beer and a seafood snack.

El Penicilino Plaza de la Libertad. Studenty, yes, but a fine bar, with a bit more about it than the nearby identikit c/Antigua places. You'll be lucky to score an outdoor table, but it's nice and pub-like inside.

Tapas bars and restaurants

El Caballo de Troya c/Correos 1 ☎983 339 355. An enticing blend of historic *palacio* and contemporary design, with meals either in the award-winning restaurant or slightly cheaper taverna, both with *menús* (€22 in the restaurant; €12.50 in the taverna) and pricier *à la carte* dishes. Alternatively,

you might just be able to have a drink in the gem of a Renaissance courtyard.

Covadonga c/Zapico 1 ☎983 330 798. A straightforward place dishing up home-cooked meals at bargain prices, with nothing much over €6 or €7 (only a huge *chuletón* at €12.50, and lots for considerably less). You can hardly go wrong – only the television, broadcasting to Mars, spoils the experience.

Jero c/Correos 11. Valladolid has a creative tapas competition every year and *Jero* often comes out on top, with its remarkable sculpted canapés called things like "Matrix", "Galactico" or "Mission Impossible" (this last, for example, a *bacalo*-and mushroom *montadito* topped with tomato confit, prawn and almond crunch), sold at €2 a pop.

Milvinos Plaza Marti y Monso ☎983 344 336. Very slick contemporary grill-house with a terrific wine list. Anything from a house burger to tuna steak or a *chuletón*, plus carpaccios and salads, but you'll easily spend €50 if you're not careful.

Listings

Airport Information on ☎983 415 500, ⊛www.aena.es.
Buses Companies include Auto Res/Avanza to Tordesillas/Salamanca (☎983 220 274, ⊛www.avanzabus.com) and La Regional to Tordesillas, Toro, Zamora, Palencia, Peñafiel and the Duero (☎983 308 088, ⊛www.laregionalvsa.com).
Hospital Hospital de Valladolid Felipe II, c/Felipe II 9 ☎983 358 000.

Internet Happy Net, c/Santuario 15 (10am–2pm & 4.30–10.30pm; closed Sun am).
Laundry Lavandería San Benito, c/Fray Antonio Alcalde, by the market.
Post office Plaza de la Rinconada, near Plaza Mayor.
Trains The train is most convenient for services to Palencia, Burgos, León, Medina del Campo and Madrid. Reservations recommended for AVE services.

Tordesillas

The quiet riverside town of **TORDESILLAS**, 30km southwest of Valladolid, boasts an important place in Spain's (indeed, the world's) history. It was here, with papal authority, that the **Treaty of Tordesillas** (1494) divided "All Lands Discovered, or Hereafter to be Discovered in the West, towards the Indies or the Ocean

Seas" between Spain and Portugal, along a line 370 leagues west of the Cape Verde Islands. Brazil, allegedly discovered six years later, went to Portugal – though it was claimed that the Portuguese already knew of its existence but had kept silent to gain better terms. The rest of the New World, including Mexico and Peru, became Spanish, with the consequences to play out across the generations.

Further fame of sorts was brought to Tordesillas by the unfortunate **Juana la Loca** (Joanna the Mad), daughter of Fernando and Isabel, who spent 46 years in a windowless cell. After Isabel's death, she had ruled Castile jointly with her husband Felipe I from 1504–06 but was devastated by his early death and for three years toured the monasteries of Spain, keeping the coffin perpetually by her side and stopping from time to time to inspect the corpse. In 1509, she reached the convent of Santa Clara in Tordesillas, where first Fernando and, later, her son, Carlos V, declared her insane, imprisoning her for half a century and assuming the throne of Castile for themselves.

Juana's place of confinement could have been worse. The **Real Convento de Santa Clara** (Tues–Sat 10am–1.30pm & 4–5.45pm, April–Sept until 6.30pm, Sun 10.30am–1.30pm & 3.30–5.30pm; €3.60; joint ticket with Las Huelgas at Burgos €6) overlooks the Duero and is known as "The Alhambra of Castile" for its delightful Mudéjar architecture. The rest of the old town is a low-key delight of faded red-brick buildings set around a charming, arcaded **Plaza Mayor**. There's a museum or two, though nothing essential, and several timeworn churches, while a long medieval bridge extends across the wide Río Duero. There's swimming from a small beach on the other side, and a bar that's handily sited for an evening breeze off the river.

Practicalities

Tordesillas is on the Valladolid–Zamora/Salamanca routes (hourly service, slightly fewer at weekends; 30min) and the **bus station** is just outside the old centre. The Plaza Mayor is easy to find, from where there are signs pointing you towards both the Convento de Santa Clara and the **turismo** (Tues–Sat 10am–1.30pm & 4/5–6.30/7.30pm, Sun 10am–2pm; ☎983 771 067, ⓦwww.tordesillas.net), which overlooks the river. **Parking** is easy near the bridge, beneath the old town.

If you fancied a quiet night, there are several modest **places to stay**, though only one actually in the old streets: the good-value *Hostal San Antolín*, c/San Antolín 8, between Plaza Mayor and the *turismo* (☎983 796 771; ❸). Otherwise, the very tranquil *Parador Nacional de Tordesillas* lies 1km out on the Salamanca road (☎983 770 051, ⓦwww.parador.es; ❻), almost country-club in feel, with shaded grounds, a sizeable outdoor pool and comfortable, rustic-style rooms. Inexpensive **cafés and restaurants** ring Plaza Mayor, particularly along c/San Antón and c/Santa María; *Palacio del Corregidor*, c/San Pedro 14 (☎983 796 849; closed Wed), is for rather finer dining in a nice old building, while the restaurant at the *parador* is a treat.

Medina del Campo

MEDINA DEL CAMPO, 23km south of Tordesillas and around 55km from Valladolid, stands below one of the region's great castles, the Moorish, brick-built **Castillo de la Mota** (Mon–Sat 11am–2pm & 4–7pm, Sun 11am–2pm; free). A classic child's design if there ever was one – four square towers, battlements and a deep moat – it often hosted the court of Queen Isabel, and later served as both prison and girls' boarding school. Visitors are only allowed inside the main courtyard and lower rooms, including the brick-vaulted chapel, though the surrounding grounds are open all day. The castle sits on one side of the train line, the town on the other, and it's worth walking into the centre to see what's left of Renaissance Medina del Campo (Market of the Field), which in the fifteenth and sixteenth centuries was one of the most important market towns in Europe. Merchants came from as far afield as Italy and Germany to attend its *ferias* (fairs), and the handsome **Plaza Mayor de la Hispanidad** is still evocative of the days when the town's bankers determined the value of European currencies; a nearby **Museo de las Ferias**, c/San Martín 26 (Tues–Sat 10am–1.30pm & 4–7pm, Sun 11am–2pm; €2; ⓦwww.museoferias.net) puts plenty of flesh on the story. There's a **turismo** on the plaza at no. 48 (ⓣ983 811 357, ⓦwww.turismomedina.net), and several cafés and restaurants that are good for a sunny outdoor lunch. The quickest way here is by **train** from Valladolid; turn right out of the station and keep walking for the castle and underpass to town.

Palencia

PALENCIA, 47km north of Valladolid, is Castile's least-known city, and capital of a small province of the same name, equally unheralded. That it has a rich past goes without saying, especially in Roman and medieval times – Spain's oldest university was founded in 1208, though it was later swallowed up by that of Salamanca. But today's modest city of 80,000 has no great sights, though the authorities are working hard to promote what little is left: there are pretty riverside gardens, famous Semana Santa processions and numerous restored plazas, most dominated by churches built in a rather gaunt white stone, but while all are diverting, none – save the cathedral – is outstanding. It's actually in the wider province that Palencia reveals its charms, especially in the north in the so-called Montaña Palentina – a region of peaks, lakes and Romanesque churches – but also along the Palencian section of the Santiago pilgrimage route (see p.430).

The city and around

The older part of the city centre is at its most attractive near the Gothic **Catedral** (Mon–Sat 10.30am–1.30pm & 4.30–7.30pm, Sun 9am–1.30pm; €1.50, guided tours €3), which faces a large open square surrounded by restored buildings. The exterior is plain by Spanish standards, while soon after the cathedral's completion Palencia fell into decline, which explains the almost complete absence of Baroque trappings inside. In fact, this simply focuses attention on the highlights within, notably the stunning *retablo mayor*, which contains twelve beautiful little panels, ten of them painted by Juan de Flandes, court painter to Isabel – it's the best collection of his work anywhere. A staircase leads down into the atmospheric crypt, containing the worn, carved columns of the earlier Visigothic and Romanesque churches on this site and an ancient well. You can also have a peek at the enclosed cloisters, but to see any more, including the treasures of the **Museo Catedralicio**, you'll have to join a guided tour.

With a map from the *turismo*, you can then track down the various Romanesque and Gothic churches worth a second glance, notably San Pablo, San Lázaro, San Miguel and San Francisco, followed by a coffee in the attractive **Plaza Mayor** and a poke around the adjacent **Mercado**, housed in an old cast-iron market hall. There are charming riverside gardens behind the cathedral, with two old stone bridges, while further up, at the top of town, is extensive parkland.

Just north of the city, on a hill off the road to Frómista/Santander (N611), sits the striking **Cristo del Otero**, a twenty-metre-high sculpture of Christ with the best views of the city from its base.

Meanwhile, 7km south, the village of Baños de Cerrato contains the oldest church in the entire peninsula – *Monumento Nacional 1* in the catalogue. The seventh-century **Basílica de San Juan de Baños** (Tues–Sun 10am–1.30pm & 5–8pm, Oct–March afternoons 4–6pm), established by the Visigoth King Recesvinto in 661, has tiny lattice windows and horseshoe arches and incorporates materials from Roman buildings. Roughly hourly buses from Palencia bus station (only 3 or 4 at weekends) run out to Baños in around fifteen minutes or so.

Practicalities

Short-term street parking is easy, or head for one of the signposted **car parks**, like that at Plaza Pio XII (c/Mayor), by the river at the southern end of town. Palencia's **bus and train stations** are both located off the Plaza de los Jardinillos, at the north end of the city centre. The roundabout of Plaza León is over on the far side of the gardens to your left as you leave either terminal; from here the long, pedestrianized c/Mayor – the main shopping street – runs up past the Plaza Mayor (5min), with the provincial **turismo** at c/Mayor 31 (Mon–Fri 9am–3pm & 5–8pm, Sat 10.30am–2.30pm; ℡979 706 523, Ⓦwww.palenciaturismo.com).

It's hard to come up with convincing reasons to stay the night, given that Palencia is only half an hour from Valladolid and an hour from Burgos. **Accommodation** is at least reasonably priced and rarely full, starting with the convenient *Hotel Plaza Jardinillos*, c/Eduardo Dato 2 (℡979 750 022; ❷), right by Plaza León and across from the stations – if not quite the "máximo confort" promised, the stylish lobby and glass reception table suggest they might get around to upgrading the functional rooms at some point. There's agreed *confort* (and some very good web deals) at the four-star *Diana Palace*, Avda. de Santander 12 (℡979 018 050, Ⓦwww.eurostarshotels.com; ❸), opposite the train station.

You'll get a €12 lunch at two or three places around the Plaza Mayor, while the city's top **restaurant** is *La Rosario*, c/La Cestilla 3 (℡979 740 936), with a weekday €16 *menú* and pricey, seasonal *à la carte* meals (up to €50 a head). For a good steak in a noisy bar, try *Meson La Cantina*, c/Mayor 4 (℡979 741 662). Plaza Mayor comes into its own in the early evening, as families come out for a stroll and a drink; later on, head for the small, modern courtyard of bars known as **Plaza Seminario**, a short walk west of Plaza Mayor, off c/Cardenal Almaraz.

Along the Río Duero to Soria

The **Río Duero** long marked the frontier between Christian and Arab territory. It meanders right across central Castile, between Zamora and Soria, with the eastern section in particular, from Valladolid, marked by a series of spectacular castles and old market towns, some restored as tourist attractions, others crumbling to dust. This part of the river is also at the heart of one of Spain's greatest wine-producing areas, the **Ribera del Duero** (see box, p.408). It's a fine route to follow by car (N122), stopping off for lunch in rustic *posadas* and for walks in the beautiful surroundings. You can make the trip by bus, but if you do, realistically, you'll only be able to see the major towns of Peñafiel and El Burgo de Osma.

Peñafiel

First stop beyond Valladolid is **PEÑAFIEL**, 60km to the east, whose fabulous castle is visible long before you reach the town. Standing on a narrow ridge, and at 210m long but only 23m across, it bears an astonishing resemblance to a huge ship run aground. It's quite a hike up to the **Castillo** (Tues–Sun: April–Sept 11am–2.30pm & 4.30–8.30pm; Oct–March 11.30am–2pm & 4–7pm; €3) – it's

The wines of the Ribera del Duero

Some of Spain's most celebrated red wine comes from the demarcated region of **Ribera del Duero** (ⓦwww.riberadelduero.es), including the country's best-known and most expensive wine, Vega Sicilia. Recent excellent vintage years were 2001 and 2004. Around 170 wineries are found along the Duero, with many of the *bogedas* concentrated between Peñafiel and Aranda del Duero, 40km to the east. If you'd like to make winery visits (not all are open for tours, including Vega Sicilia), the comprehensive website is a good place to start – some wineries require advance reservations, though many have shops that are open to casual buyers mornings and afternoons. **Bodegas Alejandro Fernandez** (ⓦwww.pesqueraafernandez.com) makes its fabulous Tinto Pesquera at Pesquera de Duero, 4km north of Peñafiel, while the acclaimed **Senorio de Nava** (ⓦwww.senoriodenava.es) is based at Nava de Roa, 13km to the east.

far easier to drive – which was built in the mid-fifteenth century out of the region's distinctive white stone. The views aside, visits here revolve around the castle's **Museo Provincial del Vino** (combined ticket with castle €6, or €15 with wine-tasting), where you can learn all about the Ribera del Duero wines. The other extraordinary sight in Peñafiel is **Plaza del Coso**, at the edge of town, entirely surrounded by balconied wooden buildings that make the most spectacular bullring in Spain (Aug only, during Día de San Roque).

Buses from Valladolid drop you on the west side of the Río Duratón – walk down to the river and cross the bridge, then turn right and walk up to the central Plaza de España. The street off the top of this square leads in five minutes to Plaza del Coso. Parking's not usually a problem, but if town's no good, there's a massive free **car park** just outside the centre on the road up to the castle.

There are a couple of cheapish **places to stay**, including *Hostal Chicopa*, visible off Plaza de España, right in the centre (☎983 880 782; ❶), but Peñafiel probably only warrants a night if you can run to one of the grander choices, such as the riverside four-star *Convento Las Claras*, a restored seventeenth-century convent by the bridge (☎938 878 168, ⓦwww.hotelconventolasclaras.com; ❺). There's also the *Hotel Ribera de Duero*, Avda. Escalona 17 (☎983 873 111, ⓦwww.hotelriberadelduero.com; ❹), a contemporary three-star set in a rather grand old flour mill on the edge of town (Soria road), whose stylish rooms almost all have castle views. Both places have good **restaurants**, and there are more modest places in the centre, while the *Molino de Palacios*, Avda. de la Constitución 16 (☎983 880 505), serves traditional, wood-fired Castilian dishes in a converted sixteenth-century watermill over the Río Duratón.

Peñaranda del Duero

Past Aranda del Duero, a short eight-kilometre detour from the highway at La Vid leads through rolling vineyards to the gorgeous, honey-toned town of **PEÑARANDA DEL DUERO**, whose restored historic kernel sits beneath another battlemented castle. It's a popular weekend getaway, hence the rather upmarket accommodation and pristine houses, but nothing detracts from the first view of the picture-perfect Plaza Mayor – Renaissance palace on one side, bulky church the other and flower-decked wooden houses in the lanes beyond. You can **stay** and eat at either *La Posada Ducal* (☎947 552 347, ⓦwww.laposadaducal.com; ❹) or *Hotel Señorío de Velez* (☎947 552 202, ⓦwww.hotelvelez.com; ❹), both on the square and both agreeably chic-rustic affairs with their own **restaurants**. With a day to spare, there's a signposted local **walk** (21km) that leads up hill and down dale from Peñaranda, through the pinewoods. Back at La Vid, by the highway, marvel how such a small village with such a small name has quite such a large monastery.

El Burgo de Osma and around

There's more of the almost absurdly picturesque at **EL BURGO DE OSMA**, once a very grand place boasting both cathedral and university. Today, there are gleaming town walls, a lovely riverside promenade and ancient colonnaded streets overhung by houses supported on precarious wooden props. The **Catedral** (Tues–Sun 10.30am–1.30pm & 4.30–6pm, mid-July to mid-Sept afternoons 4–8pm; free) seems more ostentatious than usual, embellished over the centuries, culminating in the superb Baroque tower decorated with pinnacles and gables that dominates the town. If quiet square and cathedral make a glorious ensemble, then more is at hand a couple of minutes' walk up the quaintly arcaded c/Mayor, where Osma's other main square, **Plaza Mayor**, is flanked by the former Hospital de San Agustín of 1699 (the *turismo* is inside here). On summer nights, as the temperature drops, the families of El Burgo use the Plaza Mayor and its cafés and tree-shaded benches as playground, exercise yard and social club.

Practicalities

El Burgo is 63km east of Aranda del Duero, and around 160km from Valladolid. The **bus station** is on the main Valladolid–Soria road through town, with free street parking along the road here, and the Plaza Mayor just a minute or two's walk away. There's lots of **accommodation** and much incentive to stay the night; at the bottom of the cathedral square, atmospheric *Posada del Canónigo*, c/San Pedro de Osma 19 (T975 360 362, Wwww.posadadelcanonigo.es; ❹), has rustic rooms and a pretty courtyard, while the town's best hotel is reckoned to be the four-star *Hotel Virrey* (T975 341 311, Wwww.virreypalafox.com; ❹), entered from either the main road through town or Plaza Mayor, complete with baronial fittings that are virtually tourist attractions in their own right. You can save money next door at the very reasonable *Hospedería El Fielato* (T975 368 236, Wwww.hospederiaelfielato.es; ❸), though the rooms aren't quite as glam. At all three, you can park virtually outside.

El Burgo is a pork and steak town, and you can eat big, expensive meaty **meals** at a number of *asadores*, including those at c/Mayor 71 and at the *Hotel Virrey* – the latter even has a "pork museum" and an annual spring pig slaughter (*matanza*). *Café 2000*, in a corner of Plaza Mayor, is a less rarified place, with café tables on the square and an excellent-value upstairs dining room (*menú* €9).

Parque Natural Cañon del Río Lobos

Don't miss the excursion north of El Burgo de Osma to the impressive **Parque Natural del Cañón del Río Lobos**. It's a quick fourteen-kilometre drive on a ruler-straight road to the small village of Ucero, just outside which (under the ruined castle) is the Casa del Parque **visitor centre** (daily: April–Sept 10am–8pm; Oct–March 10am–2pm & 5–8pm, Sat & Sun 10am–8pm; T975 363 564). From the centre the main road runs another kilometre or so up to the stone bridge over the source of the Río Ucero, where you've a choice. The signposted left turn runs along the valley floor towards the Romanesque **Ermita de San Bartolomé**. There's a bar-restaurant near the turn, and plenty of parking and picnic places further in among the trees, from where paths run into the gorge – one of the walks from the visitor centre runs to the hermitage and back. The main road, meanwhile, twists up for 3km to the top of the canyon and the **Mirador de la Galiana** (1122m), affording mesmerizing views of the canyon walls and the circling eagles and vultures. It's worth noting that everything is very busy in August, at Easter and on bank holidays, when it's not particularly *tranquilo* anywhere – the size of the car parks gives the game away.

Calatañazor

Halfway between El Burgo de Osma and Soria, just off the N122, lies tiny **CALATAÑAZOR**, a sleepy medieval village overseen by skimpy castle ruins and some remarkable old houses, with their distinctive conical chimneys, decorative coats of arms and wooden balconies. It often seems deserted, though there's enough weekend and holiday trade to warrant several shops selling local honey, dried wild mushrooms and cheese, while *Casa del Cura* (☎975 183 631, Ⓦwww.casadelcuraposadas.com; ❸) offers chic lodgings and a rather fancy restaurant (meals around €30), with outdoor terrace overlooking the gorge.

Fortaleza de Gormaz

The stupendous **Fortaleza de Gormaz** (always open; free) lies on the back route to Berlanga de Duero (Recuerda road), 15km southeast of El Burgo de Osma. Again, you'll see the fortress long before you climb to it, past the nondescript village of Gormaz. It was originally built by the Moors in the tenth century, and two keyhole doorways survive, as well as a later medieval tower dating from after the castle was captured and modified by the Christians. Gormaz was one of the largest fortified buildings in Spain – the inside is now a shell, albeit an enormous one, hundreds of metres across, and there are 28 towers in all, ruined but still mightily impressive. There are magnificent panoramas from here, down to the snaking Río Duero and the giant patchwork of fields in the cultivated plains below.

Berlanga de Duero and around

The next historic stop lies south of the N122 (Soria road), and a fair way south of the Río Duero as well, although it still takes its name. **BERLANGA DE DUERO** stands just off the CL116 between El Burgo de Osma and Almazán (27km from the former); coming from Gormaz (14km), follow the signs for Recuerda and then Morales. The **Plaza Mayor** is another that's arcaded by precarious wooden posts sitting on stone pillars and, once again, the main sight is a **castle**, whose massive cylindrical towers and older double curtain wall, reminiscent of Ávila, loom above the town. The way up is through a doorway in a ruined Renaissance palace, just a few minutes' walk from the plaza. The other dominant monument is the **Colegiata de Nuestra Señora del Mercado**, one of the last flowerings of the Gothic style. Its unusually uniform design is a consequence of rapid construction – it was built in just four years. Berlanga also has several fine mansions, some pretty arcaded streets and **La Picota**, a "pillar of justice" to which offenders were tied (it's just outside the old town, on the El Burgo road, where the buses stop).

Only students of (very) small town life will be taken sufficiently with Berlanga to want to stay; the best **accommodation** is the two-star *Hotel Fray Tomás*, c/Real 16 (☎975 343 033; ❸) – middle left street off Plaza Mayor – a palatial townhouse with bright, modern rooms, though the better **restaurant** is at the *Posada Los Leones*, c/Los Leones (☎975 343 275, Ⓦwww.posadalosleones.com; ❸) – top right off the plaza.

Ermita de San Baudelio de Berlanga

Eight kilometres south of Berlanga, the **Ermita de San Baudelio de Berlanga** (Wed–Sat 10am–2pm & 4–8pm, Oct–March afternoons 4–6pm, Sun 10am–2pm; €0.60, free Sat & Sun) is the best-preserved and most important example of Mozarabic style in Spain. Five years after being declared a national monument, in the 1920s, its marvellous cycle of frescoes was acquired by an international art dealer and exported to the US. After much fuss, the Spanish government got some of them back on indefinite loan, but they are now kept in the Prado. In spite of this loss, the hermitage remains a beauty. Its eight-ribbed interior vault springs from a central pillar, while much of the space is taken up by the tribune gallery of horseshoe arches. Some original frescoes do remain, including two bulls from the great sequence of animals and hunting scenes.

Almazán

For the full set of handsome Duero towns, you need to divert south of the main N122 and Soria to **ALMAZÁN**, 32km east of Berlanga de Duero, which, despite a lot of unsightly modern development, still possesses surviving medieval walls, pierced by three gateways. Several Romanesque churches also stand out, while on the Plaza Mayor is the fine Renaissance Palacio de los Hurtado de Mendoza, with a Gothic *loggia* at the rear, visible from the road around the walls. Almazán is reached by public transport from Soria; between the few daily train (Madrid line) and bus departures, you should be able to make a half-day trip of it. Heading south by car instead, towards Madrid, you won't want to miss the interesting town of Medinaceli (see p.190), 40km south of Almazán.

Soria and around

SORIA is a modest provincial capital of around 40,000 – an attractive place, despite encroaching suburbs, and the inspiration behind much of Antonio Machado's best-loved verse (the Seville-born poet lived here from 1907 to 1912). It stands between a ridgeback of hills on the banks of the Duero, with a castle ruin above and a medieval centre dotted with mansions and Romanesque churches. You can see all the sights easily in a day, but a quiet night or two has its attractions, especially if you use the city as a base to explore some of Castile's loveliest countryside. The Roman site of **Numancia**, in particular, is an easy side trip, while to the northwest rises the **Sierra de Urbión**, the weekend getaway of choice for Soria's inhabitants.

Arrival, information and accommodation

Soria's **train station** is at the extreme southwest of the city, but limited services mean you're far more likely to arrive by bus; the **bus station** is on Avenida de Valladolid on the western side of the city, a fifteen-minute walk from the centre. Street **parking** is easy to find, but is limited to the usual two hours in metered zones, so follow the signs to central car parks for overnight parking. There's a **turismo** at c/Medinaceli 2, near the Parque Alameda de Cervantes (July to mid-Sept Mon–Thurs & Sun 9am–8pm, Fri & Sat 9am–9pm; mid-Sept to June daily 9am–2pm & 5–8pm; ☏975 212 052, ⊛www.sorianitelaimaginas.com).

Accommodation

Soria's tourists are rarely great in number, so finding a place to stay shouldn't be a problem. There are plenty of centrally located budget options, and a reasonable choice of mid-range and four-star hotels.

Hostal Alvi c/Alberca 2 ☏975 228 112, ⊛www .hostalalvi.com. Nice en-suite *hostal* rooms on a quiet side street in a good central location, with free wi-fi and garage parking. ❸

Hosteria Solar de Tejada c/Claustrilla 1 ☏975 230 054, ⊛www.hosteriasolardetejada.com. With its exposed wood and old stone walls, and charmingly decorated rooms all painted in different colours with

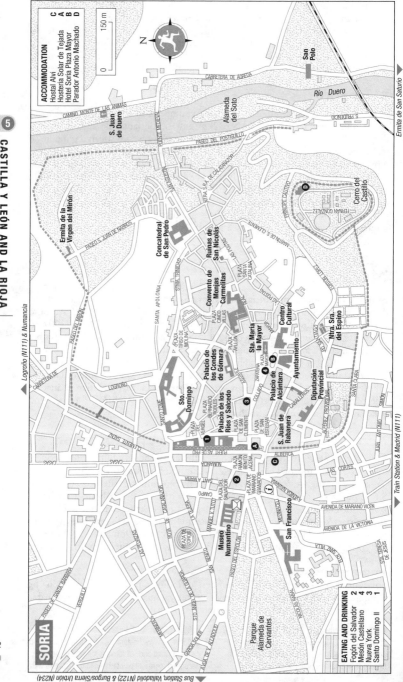

SORIA

ACCOMMODATION
Hostal Alvi	C
Hostería Solar de Tejada	A
Hotel Soria Plaza Mayor	B
Parador Antonio Machado	D

EATING AND DRINKING
Fogón del Salvador	2
Mesón Castellano	4
Nueva York	3
Santo Domingo II	1

0 — 150 m

Zaragoza (N122)

Río Duero

Ermita de San Saturio

San Polo

Alameda del Soto

CARRETERA DE ÁGREDA

CAMINO MONTE DE LAS ÁNIMAS

S. Juan de Duero

PASEO DEL POSTIGUILLO

PUENTE MEDIEVAL

Cerro del Castillo

FERNÁN GONZÁLEZ

PRÍNCIPE CARLITO

MARTÍN DE S. CLEMENTE

Ermita de la Virgen del Mirón

PASEO S. JUAN DE BARRIOS

Concatedral de San Pedro

Ruinas de San Nicolás

Convento de Monjas Carmelitas

SANTA APOLONIA

STMA. TRINIDAD

PLAZA CINCO VILLAS

PLAZA CATALINA

Logroño (N111) & Numancia

PASEO DEL MIRÓN

CARRETERA DE

LOGROÑO

SANTO TOMÉ

CLEMENTE SÁENZ

PUENTE SÁENZ

Sto. Domingo

PLAZA SAN JORGE

PLAZA BERNARDO ROBLES

Palacio de los Condes de Gómara

Palacio de los Ríos y Salcedo

Sta. María la Mayor

Centro Cultural

Palacio de Alcántara

Ayuntamiento

Diputación Provincial

Ntra. Sra. del Espino

S. Juan de Rabanera

PLAZA TIRSO DE MOLINA

PLAZA ZAPATERÍA

COLLADO

PLAZA RAMÓN BENITO ACEÑA

PLAZA DE SAN CLEMENTE

PLAZA DE SAN ESTEBAN

SANTA CLARA

CABALLEROS

AGUIRRE

SANTA TERESA DE JESÚS

ALBERCA

ALFÉREZ PROVISIONAL

LAS CORTES

AVENIDA DE MARIANO VICÉN

AVENIDA DE LA VICTORIA

Train Station & Madrid (N111)

NUMANCIA

PLAZA DEL SALVADOR

PLAZA DE MARIANO GRANADOS

San Francisco

Museo Numantino

Parque Alameda de Cervantes

PASEO DEL ESPOLÓN

CAMPO

PLAZA DE LEÓN

CASAS

SANTA MARÍA

CANALEJAS

NICOLÁS RABAL

PASEO DE SANTA BÁRBARA

VENERILLA

SAN BENITO

MANUEL VII LUJO

GARCÍA SOLIER

Bus Station, Valladolid (N122) & Burgos/Sierra Urbión (N234)

coordinated fabrics, it's the best mid-range option in the city. ❸

Hotel Soria Plaza Mayor Plaza Mayor 10 ☎975 240 864, ⓦwww.hotelsoriaplazamayor.com. This small boutique townhouse two-star has pride of place in Soria's prettiest old-town square. Some rooms in the eaves retain their old beams, while decor, fabrics, bathrooms and public areas are all in the best contemporary style. ❹

Parador Antonio Machado Parque del Castillo ☎975 240 800, ⓦwww.parador.es. Soria's modern red-brick and glass *parador* has a beautiful hilltop location in the grounds of the ruined castle – there are steps down the hillside into the town centre (15min). Rooms are very spacious, with wooden floors and glassed-in balconies with stunning countryside views, an aspect shared by the good restaurant, which highlights regional dishes. ❻

The City

The city centre is rather elongated, with sights split between the old centre and further down by the Río Duero. For once, the **Plaza Mayor** – quiet and handsome – isn't the focal point. Instead, all the bustle is to the west along the pedestrianized shopping street of c/El Collado and its offshoots and little side squares, while Soria decamps for strolls, games and chats into the lovely **Parque Alameda de Cervantes** – the city centre's best feature. Just back from here you'll find the excellent **Museo Numantino** (Tues–Sat 10am–2pm & 4–7pm, July–Sept afternoons 5–8pm, Sun 10am–2pm; €1.20, free Sat & Sun), which gathers together the region's major archeological finds, from Neolithic bones to medieval ceramics. The Celtic-Iberian and Roman displays do much to illuminate a visit to the nearby site of Numancia.

Of the central churches, the highlight is the rose-coloured facade of the twelfth-century convent church of **Santo Domingo**, on c/Santo Tomé, a few minutes' walk north of the main drag. The recessed arches of the main portal are magnificently sculpted with scenes from the Life of Christ, surrounded by a wonderful gallery of heavily bearded musicians who resemble the lost medieval ancestors of ZZ Top – look out, in particular, for the fetching three-in-a-bed scene.

The rest of the sights lie down towards the river, starting with Soria's now rather isolated cathedral, the **Concatedral de San Pedro** (July–Sept Tues–Sun 11am–2pm & 5–7pm; rest of the year, weekdays open for services, Sat 11am–2pm & 4–6pm, Sun 11am–2pm; free, cloisters €1), whose interior takes the Spanish penchant for darkness to a ridiculous extreme. However, light and harmony are restored in the three bays of a superb Romanesque cloister, which belonged to the cathedral's predecessor.

It's another five-minutes' walk to the old bridge over the Duero, where you suddenly realize that you're out of the city and in the country. Just over the bridge stands the **Monasterio de San Juan de Duero** (July–Sept Tues–Sat 10am–2pm & 5–8pm, Oct–June afternoons 4–7pm, Sun 10am–2pm; €0.60, free Sat & Sun), whose ruined cloister is one of the most striking medieval monuments you'll ever see. Built in the thirteenth century by Mudéjar masons, each of the four sides of the cloister is in a different style, mixing Moorish, Romanesque and Gothic elements, with keyhole doorways and beautifully interlinked arches. The bare church, meanwhile, is now a **museum**, with two unusual freestanding temples inside boasting vivid carved capitals.

From here, there's a good walk south along the banks of the river, passing the former Templar church of **San Polo** (now a private home), and arriving, after 2km, at the **Ermita de San Saturio**, a two-tiered complex including an octagonal chapel with thirteenth-century frescoes (Tues–Sat 10.30am–2pm & 4.30–6.30/7.30pm, July & Aug till 8.30pm, Sun 10.30am–2pm; free).

Eating and drinking

Soria's dining scene is pretty diverse, with good **tapas** the norm and **restaurant** menus – here on the edge of Castile – showing welcome Basque and Riojan influences, with fish and vegetables suddenly much more in evidence. The best selection of tapas bars is in **Plaza Ramón Benito Aceña**, at the end of the main drag, where the locals stand around outside at big wooden barrels. There's a grungier set of bars in nearby **Plaza San Clemente** (just behind Citibank, off c/El Collado), while **c/Manuel Vicente Tutot**, behind the Museo Numatino, has a line of old-fashioned bars for Soria's cheapest eats. There are kiosk cafés in the **Parque Alameda de Cervantes**, nice for an early evening drink.

Fogón del Salvador Plaza del Salvador 1 ☎975 230 194. An excellent *asador*, with wood-fired grilled meats and vegetables, a decent range of tapas and a long regional wine list. Mains and *menú* from around €15.

Mesón Castellano Plaza Mayor 2 ☎975 213 045. Specializing in a fairly rich form of Castilian cuisine and located in a cosy building of warm brick, with hams hanging from the wooden beams. Eat tapas at the bar or big meals in the *comedor*, where meat and fresh fish dishes (including trout from the Río Ucero) run from between €11 and €22.

Nueva York Plaza San Blas y el Rosel. The city's best pastry and cake place, also nice for breakfast, has tables outside on an old-town square.

Santo Domingo II Plaza de Vergel 1 ☎975 211 717. With a terraza on the square, this upmarket restaurant concentrates on solid, traditional Castilian fare, from oxtail in red wine (*rabo de buey al vino tinto*) to goat fried with red peppers and garlic (*cabrito frito con ajillos*). €26 buys you a six-course *menú*; otherwise, €15–20.

Numancia

Around 7km north of Soria, off the N111 to Logroño and just outside the village of Garray, lie the evocative ruins of **Numancia** (Tues–Sat 10am–2pm & 4–8pm, Oct–March until 6pm, Sun 10am–2pm; €0.60, free weekends), a hilltop Celtic-Iberian (third to second century BC) and later Roman settlement. Numancia was one of the last towns to hold out against the Romans, falling to Scipio in 133 BC; its long and fierce resistance was turned into a tragic play by Cervantes and dubbed "a sort of Vietnam for Rome" by novelist Carlos Fuentes. It's a stunningly sited spot, with extensive remains of streets, drains, courtyards and public baths, some reconstructed houses and a stretch of wall, and a good English-language leaflet available.

Sierra de Urbión

Summer weekends and holidays see locals flock to the tranquil slopes of the **Sierra de Urbión**, northwest of Soria, with its network of hiking and cycling trails, and even skiing at Santa Inés. The lower section of what is a protected "reserva nacional" is focused on the shores of an enormous reservoir, the **Embalse de la Cuerda del Pozo**, where there are pinewood and beachside picnic areas, watersports and a café-restaurant at **Playa Pita**. The real highlight, however, is **Laguna Negara**, an alpine glacial lake hemmed in by a dramatic amphitheatre of granite cliffs. There's a lakeside boardwalk here, and more hiking trails, including the serious ascent from the lake to the summit of **Pico Urbión** (2229m), just over the border in La Rioja. The *laguna* is reached from the village of Vinuesa (see below), which lies just north of the reservoir and 33km from Soria (N234). Follow the signs (18km) from Vinuesa until you reach a small upper car park just 300m from the *laguna*; at busy times, or if the barrier is closed, you'll have to park at the much larger car park, 1km back down the road (20min walk), near the seasonal café-restaurant.

VINUESA makes the most obvious base; there are daily buses from Soria or Burgos. It's a pleasant village, attuned to tourists, with many restored old houses, a church adopted by nesting storks, a suspicious number of banks and ATMs and even a late-night bar or two. Half a dozen **accommodation** options (mostly two-star-*hostal* standard) line the main road that leads down to the Laguna Negara turn-off, with the *Virginia*, c/Castillo de Vinuesa 21 (☎975 378 555, ⓦwww.virginiarh.net; ❸), easily the pick of the bunch. It's close to the bridge near the turn-off, with stylish rooms and a good-value restaurant of the same name just across the road (lunch around €12, dinner €20). Most of the other *hostales* also have their own restaurants. *Camping Cobijo* is 2km along the Laguna Negara road (☎975 378 331, ⓦwww.campingcobijo.com; closed Nov–Easter), and also has rooms (❷), cabins (❹) and bikes for rent.

Logroño and La Rioja province

One of Spain's most famous wine regions, La Rioja takes its name from the Río Oja, which flows from the mountains down to the Río Ebro, the latter marking the northern border of **La Rioja province** (ⓦwww.lariojaturismo.com). Confusingly, the demarcated wine region and province are not quite the same thing, since many of the best vineyards are on the north bank of the Ebro, in the Basque province of Araba (Alava in Castilian, the so-called Rioja Alavesa, covered on p.485). Nevertheless, the main wine towns are all in La Rioja proper, starting with the enjoyable provincial capital, **Logroño**, which is a great place to spend a couple of days eating and drinking. The province is traditionally divided further into two parts, with the busy little wine town of **Haro** being the mainstay of the **Rioja Alta**. This makes the best base for any serious wine touring, though there are *casas rurales* in many of the surrounding villages, too. It's also here, west of Logroño, that the Camino de Santiago winds on towards Burgos. East of Logroño is the **Rioja Baja**, the southeastern part of La Rioja province, which has quite a different feel – there are vineyards, but the main attraction is following in the footsteps of La Rioja's ancient dinosaurs.

Logroño is the hub for all local bus and train services, but if you want to do any more than see the towns of Nájera, Haro and Calahorra, it's far better to have your own transport, as connections to the smaller villages are rarely convenient for day-trips.

Logroño

LOGROÑO, lying on the Río Ebro some 100km north of Soria, and 115km east of Burgos, is a prosperous city of around 150,000, a pleasant place of elegant streets, open squares and riverside parkland. The wine trade is not as immediately apparent here as in, say, Haro, but the big draw is its lively old quarter with an unparalleled selection of excellent tapas bars, for which it's worth making a considerable detour. The two big annual events are **Fiestas San Bernabé** (June), a week's worth of enjoyable local festivities, from street fairs and *pelota* tournaments to folk concerts and costumed processions, and the even more exuberant **Fiesta de San Mateo** (Sept), which coincides with the *vendimia* (grape harvest).

Arrival and information

The heart of modern Logroño is the gardens of the **Paseo del Espolón**, but it's in the **Casco Antiguo** that you'll find the liveliest bars and restaurants and the lowest-priced accommodation. It's a five-hundred-metre walk (10min) up

EATING & DRINKING
Bar García	7
Café Moderno	1
Casa Pali	8
Las Cubanas	4
La Cueva	3
Lorenzo	6
La Taberna de Baco	2
La Taberna del Laurel	9
Vinissimo	5

ACCOMMODATION
Hostal Niza	E
La Redonda	B
Marqués de Vallejo	F
Pensión La Bilbaina	A
Pensión Sebastián	D
Portales	C

LOGROÑO

0   200 m

Bus Station (250m) ▼   Train Station (500m) ▼

to the centre along c/General Vara de Rey from the **bus station**; the **train station** is 400m south of the bus station, down Avenida de España. Street parking and signposted garages are easy to find, though there's a large free **car park** just opposite the surviving bit of medieval wall known as Murallas del Revellín, on the edge of the old town. The **turismo**, stocked with useful information on the whole Rioja region, is in a modern building on the edge of the Paseo del Espolón (Mon–Fri 10am–2pm & 4–7pm, Sat & Sun 10am–2pm & 5–7pm; ☏941 291 260).

Accommodation

You shouldn't have trouble finding **accommodation**, except during the week-long Fiesta de San Mateo, which starts on September 21, for which rooms are booked months in advance.

Hostal Niza c/Capitán Gallarza 13 ☏941 206 044, ⓦwww.hostalniza.com. A reasonable mid-range *hostal* in the heart of the old town, by the market and tapas bars, with decent en-suite rooms that do the job. ❸

Hotel Marqués de Vallejo c/Marqués de Vallejo 8, ☏941 248 333, ⓦwww.hotelmarquesdevallejo .com. This old-town hotel has been given a

thorough makeover, giving it something of a boutique feel. Soundproofed rooms have polished wood floors and contemporary furnishings, and bathrooms are very swish. ❺

Hotel Portales c/Portales 85 ☏941 502 794, ⓦwww.hotelportales.es. Smart three-star hotel in contemporary style, right on the edge of the old town, with garage parking. The website has some good deals, including free midweek breakfast if you book online. ④

🏃 **Pensión La Bilbaina** c/Capitán Gallarza 10 ☎941 254 226. Very smart en-suite rooms (including singles) at excellent prices. Everything is freshly painted and squeaky clean, though furnishings are a bit ascetic (bed, wardrobe, chair). They have more rooms in the same vein at *Pensión La*

Redonda, c/Portales 21 (☎941 272 409). Both are in the bar zone, and street-facing rooms are apt to be noisy at weekends. ❸

Pensión Sebastián c/San Juan 21 ☎941 242 800. Old-fashioned *pensión* on a busy tapas street, with ageing rooms and shared bathrooms. There's also the *Daniel*, in the same building. ❷

The Town

Before the wine trade brought prosperity to Logroño, it owed its importance for some six centuries to the Camino de Santiago, hence the church dedicated to the saint, which stands close to the iron bridge over the Río Ebro. High on the south side (ie not the side facing the river) of the lofty sixteenth-century **Santiago el Real**, above the main entrance, is a magnificent eighteenth-century Baroque equestrian statue of St James, mounted on a stallion that Edwin Mullins (in *The Pilgrimage to Santiago*) describes as "equipped with the most heroic genitals in all Spain, a sight to make any surviving Moor feel inadequate and run for cover".

Other fine Logroño churches include **San Bartolomé**, which has an unrefined but richly carved Gothic portal, and the mouthful of a cathedral, the **Concatedral Santa María de la Redonda**, which faces the old market square. The cathedral was originally a late Gothic hall church with a lovely sweeping elevation that was extended at both ends in the eighteenth century – the twin-towered facade is a beautiful example of the Churrigueresque style.

Other than that, you're free to potter about and ponder the wine trade, since the art museum, the **Museo de la Rioja**, was still under renovation at the time of writing. The **Mercado de Abastos** (Mon–Sat 7.30am–1.30pm & 4–7.30pm) is worth a visit (it's right by many of the best tapas bars), and on the corner here you'll also find *Vinos El Peso*, at c/Peso 1, a wine shop with a decent selection of regional wines. For traditional *botas de vino* (leather flagons filled with wine), stroll down and have a look at *Felix Barbero Botas Rioja* at c/Sagasta 8. The evening *paseo*, meanwhile, fills the pedestrianized main street, c/Portales, packing out the bars and cafés under the arcades.

Eating and drinking

Logroño's old town is thick with bars and restaurants, and the local **cuisine** is celebrated for its potato and bean dishes, seasonal vegetables (particularly peppers, asparagus and mushrooms) and thick steaks. But Logroño's mini masterpieces are its **tapas bars**, clustered in the bar-run alleys of c/Laurel and Travesia de Laurel, and the similar c/San Juan. In these two locales alone are around fifty different bars, each with their own advertised speciality. Punters spill out in the alleys at the drop of a hat, washing it all down with a glass of the superb local Rioja wine.

What's yours?

Cosecha (which literally means "harvest"), when used on its own, refers to young wines in their first or second year, which tend to have a fresh and fruity flavour – you'll also see these wines advertised as the *vino de año*. **Crianzas** are wines that are at least in their third year, having spent at least one year in an oak cask and several months in the bottle. **Reservas** are vintages that have been aged for three years with at least one year in oak; and **gran reservas** have spent at least two years in oak casks and three years in the bottle. Recent Rioja **years** classified as "excellent" are '94, '95, '01, '04 and '05, while '96, '98 and '06 were "very good".

Tapas bars and restaurants

Bar García c/San Juan 28. It's hanging hams here that indicate the speciality – try the *zapato* (literally "shoe"), ham and tomato with bread. Closed Wed.

Café Moderno c/Francisco Martínez Zaporta 9. A gloriously ornate café, established in 1912, with an antique bar, and locals playing board games inside. It's a good spot for breakfast, or a glass of *tinto* in the evening; there are meals, too.

Casa Pali c/Laurel 11. An old-town classic, knocking out tapas treats such as fried asparagus or *berenjena con queso* (aubergine with melted cheese). Closed Tues.

Las Cubanas c/San Agustín 17 ☎941 220 050. For a more refined night out – this classy restaurant dates from the 1920s, but the interior is sleek and contemporary, with a choice of dishes from a modish Riojan menu (mains €16–25). Closed Tues.

La Cueva c/San Juan 13. A few tapas bars claim the mantle of mushroom king (the *Angel* on c/Laurel has its admirers), but this is the place for grilled mushroom *pinchos* par excellence.

Lorenzo Traversía Laurel 4. A no-nonsense, stand-up place specializing in *pinchos morunos* (mini pork kebabs) and grilled kidneys, washed down with four grades of Rioja wine, all absurdly cheap.

La Taberna de Baco c/San Agustín 10. A truly excellent tapas bar, with a range of delicious specialities: try the *bombita* (potato-and-mushroom ball) or the *migas* (garlic and breadcrumb mixture with a fried egg) and brilliant fried green tomatoes. There are a few tables if you want to make a meal of it.

La Taberna del Laurel c/Laurel 9. Often bursting at the seams with patrons eagerly stuffing themselves with the house speciality, *patatas bravas*.

Vinissimo c/San Juan 23. Fantastic home-made tapas (*brochetas* of chicken, prawn or even wild boar are a speciality), plus a carefully selected wine list add up to a more refined tapas bar than usual along here. A small dining room out back offers a good-value *menú* and various *à la carte* options.

Haro

The capital of Rioja Alta is **HARO**, a modern, working town 44km northwest of Logroño. It's entirely devoted to the wine trade, but has some lovely reminders of a grand past, notably the Renaissance church of Santo Tomás, with its 68-metre-high wedding-cake tower. The very small old quarter around it is attractive in a faded kind of way, its lower margins marked by the **Plaza de la Paz**, a glass-balconied square whose mansions overlook an archaic bandstand. The **Centro de Interpretación del Vino de la Rioja** (Tues–Fri 10am–2pm & 4–7pm, Sat & Sun 10am–7pm, closed Sun pm Nov–March; €3) is on c/Breton de los Herreros, behind the bus station; for the wines themselves, you need to visit the **bodegas** (see box opposite), though you can also buy quality wines at the **wine shops** up c/Santo Tomás (just off Plaza de la Paz); Juan González at no. 22 is particularly good.

Apart from harvest time (Sept), the best time to be in Haro is in June, starting with the **Semana del Vino** (Wine Week, usually second week), when the bars and restaurants come together to offer *crianza* and *reserva* wine-tastings at bargain prices. There's more of the same during the continuous **fiestas** of San Juan, San Felices (the town's patron saint) and San Pedro (June 24–29), when there are outdoor concerts, street parades and the climactic **Batalla del Vino** (June 29), when thousands of people climb the Riscos de Bilibio (a small mountain near the town) to be drenched from head to foot in wine.

Practicalities

Haro is only small, and **parking** isn't usually a problem. The **train station** is a fifteen-minute walk from the centre, down over the bridge on the other side of the river. That said, services from Logroño by bus are far more frequent and the **bus station** is slightly closer in: from the traffic circle, follow the sign for "Centro Ciudad", straight up c/La Ventilla, bearing left for Plaza de la Paz at the *Casa Terete* restaurant. The **turismo** is on Plaza Florentino Rodríguez (Mon–Fri

10am–2pm, Sat 10am–2pm & 4–7pm; ☎941 303 366, ⓦwww.haro.org), opposite *Hotel Los Agustinos*.

The best budget **accommodation** choice is *Pensión La Peña*, c/La Vega 1, just off Plaza de la Paz (☎941 310 022; ❷), which has cosy, well-kept rooms, some of them en suite and many with a balcony overlooking the plaza. Finest lodgings, though, are at the four-star *Hotel Los Agustinos*, c/San Agustín 2 (☎941 311 308, ⓦwww.hotellosagustinos.com; ❺), a converted Augustinian convent founded in 1373 whose centrepiece is a magnificent glass-covered cloister.

Even the humblest *tapa* is transformed by a glass of Rioja, and you'll get plenty – and very cheaply – in the half-dozen **bars and restaurants** that lie the short distance between Plaza de la Paz and Santo Tomás. *El Portillo*, Plaza San Martín 3 (☎941 305 025), in a cute little square below the church, is less rustic and more contemporary than most, with fancy tapas (including a carpaccio of artichoke and *bacalao*), a good lunchtime *menú* for €12 and *à la carte* meals for around €30. *Los Caños*, right opposite, is a fine, stone-walled bar, while at *Meson Los Berones*, c/Santo Tomás 23, there's traditional Riojan tapas and good-value meals, day and night. If you're staying at *Los Agustinos*, you're unlikely to eat anywhere other than its fine restaurant, *Las Duelas* (closed Jan), which is a contemporary Spanish place (mains from around €23) with dining in the hotel cloister.

Touring the wine region

Wine is at the very heart of La Rioja's identity (ⓦwww.riojawine.com), and few people will pass through without wanting to visit a *bodega* and taste a few *vinos*. You can pick up lots of useful **information** at the *turismos* in Logroño and Haro, and in some of the smaller towns, too, such as Nájera and Santo Domingo de la Calzada – the Haro office, in particular, is very helpful.

In **Haro** itself, there are a dozen *bodegas* within walking distance of town, most clustered around the train station, including the famous houses of Bodegas Bilbaínas (☎941 310 147, ⓦwww.bodegasbilbainas.com), La Rioja Alta (☎941 310 346, ⓦwww.riojalta.com), Bodegas CVNE (pronounced Cune; ☎941 304 809, ⓦwww.cvne.com) and Bodegas Muga (☎941 310 498, ⓦwww.bodegasmuga.com). There are daily tours at all these (not always on Sun; usually in English in the mornings), but you have to call and make a reservation; Haro *turismo* can advise about current tour times and details. Some are free, some charge €3–5 for tours and tastings lasting from ninety minutes to two hours. At López de Heredia (☎941 310 244, ⓦwww.lopezdeheredia.com), the stand-out attraction is the eye-catching Modernist wine shop designed by Zaha Hadid.

With a car, you're able to tour La Rioja more thoroughly and visit some of the more interesting, contemporary wineries, all within half an hour's drive of Haro or Logroño. They've got wine shops attached, and some have excellent restaurants, and the out-of-town *bodegas* tend to be open for drop-in visits without appointment. The striking village of **San Vicente de la Sonsierra** – you'll have seen its hilltop church and castle on the drive across to Haro – has no fewer than sixteen wineries around and about, while just to the north of Haro at **Briñas** is the classy, minimalist winery of La Encina Bodegas y Viñedos (☎941 305 630, ⓦwww.laencinabodegas.com). You also shouldn't miss the **Museo de la Cultura del Vino** (June–Sept Tues–Sun 10am–8pm; Oct–May Tues–Thurs & Sun 10am–6pm, Fri & Sat 10am–8pm; last entry 1hr 30min before closing; ☎941 322 323 or 902 320 001, ⓦwww.dinastiavivanco.com; €7.50 includes a tasting; reservations needed for guided tour), housed in impressive premises at the Bodega Dinastía Vivanco on the edge of **Briones**, 6km southeast of Haro (N232 road).

However, it's just across the Río Ebro, in the Basque **Rioja Alavesa** region, that some of the most celebrated vineyards are found, close to the town of **Laguardia**, 19km northwest of Logroño or 26km east of Haro (see p.486).

▲ Bodega La Rioja

Nájera and beyond

The Camino de Santiago sweeps through Logroño and on towards Burgos, passing to the south of Haro. At the small riverside town of **NÁJERA**, 15km south of Haro, dramatically sited below a pink, cave-riddled rock formation, you're ostentatiously welcomed to the "Capital of Furniture" (Nájera is known for its fixtures and fittings), though it's more likely that you're here for the stork-topped Gothic **Monasterio Santa María la Real** (Tues–Sat 10am–1pm & 4–7pm, Oct–April until 5.30pm, Sun 10am–12.30pm & 4–6pm; €3). This contains a royal pantheon of ancient monarchs of Castile, León and Navarra, though best of all is the cloister of rose-coloured stone and elaborate tracery. Old and modern Nájera are separated by the grassy riverbanks of rippling Río Najerilla – there's plenty of free parking on either side – and just across the footbridge from the charming old town stands the two-star *Hotel San Fernando*, Paseo San Julián 1 (☏941 363 700, Ⓦwww.sanmillan.com; ❹), with reasonable rooms and a rather unexpected traditional red English phone box in the lobby. A riverside **market** takes place behind the hotel every Thursday.

Next stop for pilgrims, the last in La Rioja, is **SANTO DOMINGO DE LA CALZADA**, 20km west of Nájera, another handsome small town with a beckoning cathedral – you might prefer to stay overnight here instead, at the majestic *Parador Santo Domingo de la Calzada* (☏941 340 300, Ⓦwww.parador .es; ❻), once the medieval pilgrims' hospital.

The best driving route, however, is south, up into the hills, following signs for 18km to the stone village of **San Millán de la Cogolla**, which serves the two greatest Riojan monasteries of all, twin establishments known as Yuso and Suso. The immense lower **Monasterio de Yuso** (Easter–Sept Tues–Sun 10.30am–1.30pm & 4–6.30pm, also Mon in Aug same times; rest of the year until 1pm & 6pm; guided 50min visits €4; Ⓦwww.monasteriodeyuso.org) dominates the valley, built in the sixteenth and seventeenth centuries to house the relics of the crowd-pulling sixth-century saint, San Millán. It's at the centre of some fairly big tourist business, with one wing of the monastery housing a four-star hotel, the *Hostería del Monasterio* (☏941 373 277, Ⓦwww.sanmillan .com; ❻), while in front of the complex is the simpler *La Posada de San Millán* (☏941 373 161, Ⓦwww.vallesanmillan.com; ❸), a couple of big restaurants and enough parking to accommodate the entire Spanish nation, should it choose to all come at once. To see the much older **Monasterio de Suso** (Tues–Sun 9.30am–1.30pm & 3.30–6.30pm, half-hourly tours from 9.55am and 3.55pm; €3), a few hundred metres up in the hills, you must book first at the lower ticket office at Yuso (access from the hotel courtyard). The earlier monastery is hidden out of public view and you're taken up by shuttle bus to see the beautiful, haunting building, the original site of Millán's burial before he was sanctified in 1030 and later transferred down the hill into surroundings more in keeping with a patron saint.

There's another wonderfully sited monastery, the **Monasterio de Valvanera**, 35km further south, whose location is even more dramatic, 1000m above a steep-sided valley, with the tidy terraces of the Benedictine monks' vegetable gardens below. There's simpler accommodation here, as well as a bar and restaurant, though none of the crowds of Yuso and Suso. It's a five-kilometre detour off the **LR-113 mountain road**, which makes a magnificent journey south and west between Nájera and Salas de los Infantes (90km; 2hr drive), twisting ever higher up the glorious, lush valley of the Río Najerilla, hugging the sides of the huge hydroelectric Mansilla dam, before careering across the bare uplands of the **Sierra de la Demanda** to cross into Castilla y León. This makes a great roundabout approach to Burgos, and you'll emerge close to the equally magnificent monastery of Santo Domingo de Silos (see p.428).

La Rioja Baja

Forty kilometres from Logroño, **Calahorra** is the main town of La Rioja Baja, the southeastern part of the province. After the wine towns of the Rioja Alta it's a disappointment, and there's no pressing need to stop, though its *parador* brings some out this way. However, it does offer an attractive back-country route to Soria, via **Arnedo**, 12km southwest of Calahorra, where the scenery suddenly changes from cultivated flatland to vivid red rock, punctured by hundreds of caves, both natural and man-made, used in the past as houses and hermitages. From here until the tiny valley-bottom village of **Yanguas**, 30km southwest, the LR-115 makes a twisting journey through the narrow Río Cidacos gorge, before climbing up over the bare tops for the sweeping run into Soria, another 50km to the south. It takes a couple of hours all told from Calahorra to Soria, though it's much the best idea to break in the middle for a spot of dinosaur-hunting.

Enciso, Arnedillo and La Rioja's dinosaurs

A hundred and twenty million years ago (early Cretaceous period), the south-eastern part of La Rioja was a steamy marshland where **dinosaurs** roamed, leaving their footprints in mud that later fossilized. You can spend an enjoyable day tracking the tracks, and in Arnedillo, 24km southwest of Calahorra, there's also a pretty village base for overnight stays. It's the village of **ENCISO**, however, 35km southwest of Calahorra, that's the main dinosaur centre and the easiest place to see some footprints. A jumble of houses on the hillside shelters the **Centre Paleon-tológico** (June to mid-Sept daily 11am–2pm & 5–8pm; rest of the year Mon–Sat 11am–2pm & 3–6pm, Sun 11am–2pm; €3; ☎941 396 093, ⓦ www.dinosaurios-larioja.org), where there's information about all of the region's dinosaur sites. Parking is just over the old bridge (Soria side of the village), where it's planned to build an even larger *paleoaventura* centre, and brown signposts here point you to the nearby sites of **Virgen del Campo** and **Valdecevillo**, both featuring lots of visible tracks in the stone as well as huge replica dinos to thrill the kids. A well-signposted six-kilometre circular **walk** from Enciso tours these sites, too, if you fancy leaving the car behind.

There are lots of other signposted dinosaur sites in the vicinity, at Munilla or Préjano, for example, though many are on 4WD dirt tracks. A mountain bike would be ideal, or pack your hiking boots. At **ARNEDILLO**, 11km north of Enciso, it's only around thirty minutes on foot to the local footprint site, and the village has the advantage of being the one place you might be tempted to stay the night. It's a pretty spot, a minor spa, set in a deep river valley beneath spiky crags, with the church at the very bottom by the river. *Hospederia Las Pedrolas* (☎941 394 401; ④) is a charming, rustic house right outside the church: the rest of the facilities are up on the main through road, above the village, where several restaurants, and another *hostal* or two, line the road. At ⚔ *Casa Cañas* (☎941 394 022; closed Wed & Sun) they are very proud of their "century at your service", and so they should be – the food is excellent, with succulent grills the speciality, alongside Riojan staples like *pochas* (stewed white beans) and vegetable *minestra*. The *menú* is €12, or eat *à la carte* for €20. You can walk it all off in Arnedillo's lovely surroundings, up the side valleys and along the river, past the ruined water-mills, restored hermitages and waterside allotments.

Burgos

BURGOS was the capital of Old Castile for almost five hundred years, the home of El Cid in the eleventh century, and the base, two centuries later, of Fernando III, the reconqueror of Murcia, Córdoba and Seville. It was Fernando who began the city's famous Gothic cathedral, one of the greatest in all Spain, and Burgos is a firm station on the pilgrim route. During the Civil War, Franco temporarily installed his Fascist government in the city and Burgos owes much of its modern expansion to Franco's "Industrial Development Plan", a strategy to shift the country's wealth away from Catalunya and the Basque Country and into Castile. Even now, such connotations linger – the Capitanía General building still displays a 1936 plaque (admittedly, under protective glass) honouring Franco, the "supreme authority of the nation".

But Burgos is also a changed city, much scrubbed and restored over the last few years, due to its candidature for European City of Culture for 2016. Every paving stone in the centre looks to have been relaid, and while it's no longer a clearly medieval city, the handsome buildings, squares and riverfront of the old town are an attractive prospect for a night's stay.

Arrival and information

The Río Arlanzón bisects the city and neatly delimits the Casco Histórico, or old quarter, on the north bank. You'll be able to park out of the centre along the river, though there are large central signposted **car parks**, including under Plaza Mayor and at Plaza de España. **Bus** and **train stations** are on the south side of the river, but it's only a short walk up to cross the bridges into town. The city **turismo** is on Plaza Rey San Fernando, opposite the cathedral (July–Sept daily 10am–8pm; Oct–June Mon–Fri 10am–2pm & 4.30–7.30pm, Sat & Sun 10am–1.30pm & 4–7.30pm; ☎947 288 874, ⓦwww.aytoburgos.es). The office at Plaza de Alonso Martínez 7 (daily: July–Sept 9am–8pm, Fri & Sat until 9pm; Oct–June 9am–2pm & 5–8pm; ☎947 203 125), a five-minute walk northeast of the cathedral, also has information on Burgos province. A **Trén Turistico** (trolley-train) rumbles around town hourly at weekends (daily July–Sept), departing from outside the cathedral, with tickets available inside the *turismo* – it's €4, though the evening, floodlit tours (€5) might be the better choice.

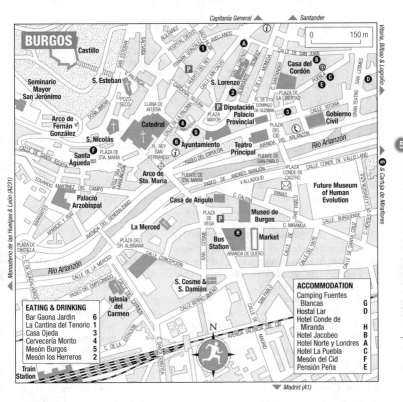

Map labels:

BURGOS

Castillo

Capitanía General ▲   ▲ Santander

0   150 m

Vitoria, Bilbao & Logroño ▶

Seminario Mayor San Jerónimo

S. Esteban

Casa del Cordón

Arco de Fernán González

S. Lorenzo

Santa Águeda

Diputación
Palacio Provincial

Palacio Arzobispal

Catedral

Ayuntamiento

Teatro Principal

Gobierno Civil

Arco de Sta. María

Río Arlanzón

Casa de Angulo

Future Museum of Human Evolution

Museo de Burgos

La Merced

Bus Station

Market

Río Arlanzón

◀ Monasterio de las Huelgas & León (A231)

G & Cartuja de Miraflores ▶

S. Cosme & S. Damián

Iglesia del Carmen

EATING & DRINKING
Bar Gaona Jardin	6
La Cantina del Tenorio	1
Casa Ojeda	3
Cervecería Morito	4
Mesón Burgos	5
Mesón los Herreros	2

ACCOMMODATION
Camping Fuentes Blancas	G
Hostal Lar	D
Hotel Conde de Miranda	H
Hotel Jacobeo	B
Hotel Norte y Londres	A
Hotel La Puebla	C
Mesón del Cid	F
Pensión Peña	E

Train Station

N

Madrid (A1) ▼

Accommodation

It's generally nicest to stay over the river, closer to the old town, though many of the new three- and four-star hotels are on the outskirts or even further out.

Hostal Lar c/Cardenal Benlloch 1, 2º ☎ 947 209 655. A reasonable *hostal*, just outside the old quarter (and with a few similar places nearby). The rooms are nothing special, and en-suite shower-rooms are a tight squeeze, but the owners are friendly. ❸

Hotel Conde de Miranda c/Miranda 4 ☎ 947 265 267, ⓦ www.abc-hoteles.com. Right on top (literally) of the bus station might not be your first choice of location, but this smart little two-star has bright, stylish rooms with squeaky laminate floors, wi-fi access and cute marble bathrooms. There's street parking right outside, or a garage nearby. ❹

Hotel Jacobeo c/San Juan 24 ☎ 947 260 102, ⓦ www.hoteljacobeo.com. It might only have one star, but the *Jacobeo* is a snazzy outfit with budget-boutique style, and very good value for most of the year. Small, trim rooms are in muted, contemporary colours, and there's a breakfast bar downstairs, though you're very close to all the cafés and restaurants. ❹

Hotel Norte y Londres Plaza Alonzo Martínez 10 ☎ 947 264 125, ⓦ www .hotelnorteylondres.com. A two-star hotel in a very attractive *belle époque* house, right in the centre. Rooms are comfortable and modern, but with antique furniture and wood floors, and there's a cosy feel throughout. ❹

Hotel La Puebla c/Puebla 20 ☎ 947 200 011, ⓦ www.hotellapuebla.com. Small hotel with just fifteen rooms (including four singles) sporting elegant, contemporary design. Free bikes available for guests. ❹

Mesón del Cid Plaza de Santa María 8 ☎ 947 208 715, ⓦ www.mesondelcid.es. Facing the cathedral and set apart from its restaurant, this is the most traditional hotel in the old town, a three star in a handsome old building, with its own parking. ❺

Pensión Peña c/Puebla 18 ☎ 947 206 323. The top budget option in Burgos is this welcoming and immaculate *pensión*; advance reservations are essential. ❶

Campsite

Camping Fuentes Blancas ☎947 486 016, ⓦwww.campingburgos.com. Out along the river at the Parque de Fuentes Blancas, a 45min walk or a bus ride from the centre (from Avda. del Arlanzón, along the river by the Cid statue) – excellent facilities, including a pool and restaurant, bikes for rent, and bungalows (from €40 per night). Closed Oct–March.

The City

Despite the encroaching suburban sprawl and a population of almost 200,000, when it comes down to it, Burgos really isn't that big. You can see everything in the centre easily in a day, and while its lesser churches inevitably tend to be eclipsed by the cathedral, on the outskirts are two monasteries that are by no means overshadowed. Museums tend to be an afterthought here, though that will possibly change with the construction of a new cultural centre and Museum of Human Evolution that's currently under way on the river's south bank.

Puenta de Santa María and the riverside

The main approach to the old town and cathedral is across the **Puenta de Santa María**, where you're confronted by the **Arco de Santa María** (Tues–Sat 11am–2pm & 5–9pm, Sun 11am–2pm; free), a gateway that originally formed part of the town walls. There are temporary art exhibitions held inside, and you can also view its exquisite Mudéjar ceiling, but it's the exterior that catches the eye. It was embellished with statues in 1534–36 in order to appease Carlos V after Burgos's involvement in a revolt by Spanish noblemen against their new Flemish-born king. Carlos's statue is glorified here in the context of the greatest Burgalese heroes: Diego Porcelos, founder of the city in the late ninth century; Nuño Rasura and Laín Calvo, two early magistrates; Fernán González, founder of the Countship of Castile in 932; and, above all, **El Cid Campeador**, who is surpassed in popular sentiment only by Santiago *Matamoros* in his legendary exploits against the Moors. There's a splendid equestrian **statue** of him, too – with flying cloak, flowing beard and raised sword – lording over the **Puente de San Pablo**, the next bridge up along the river. The statue, one of the city's principal landmarks, stands at the end of the **Paseo del Espolón**, a tree-lined riverside promenade along which much of the evening strolling takes place. On the river's south bank, a footpath starts

---

El Cid Campeador

Burgos lays full claim to the Castilian nobleman, soldier and mercenary **El Cid**, born Rodrigo Díaz in the nearby village of Vivar in 1040 or thereabouts. Actually, his most significant military exploits took place around Valencia, the city he took back briefly from the Moors after a long siege in 1094, but no matter – El Cid (from the Arabic *sidi* or lord) is a local boy, whose heroic feats (not all strictly historically accurate) have been celebrated in Spain since the twelfth century. His honorific title, **Campeador** ("Supreme in Valour"), is some indication of the esteem in which he's always been held, though there's generally a veil drawn over his avarice and political ambition, not to mention the fact that, as an exiled sword-for-hire in the 1080s, El Cid turned out for Moorish princes as easily as for Christian kings. He died in Valencia in 1099, and the city fell again to the Moors in 1102, after which his wife Jimena took El Cid's body to the monastery of San Pedro de Cardeña, south of Burgos, where it rested for centuries. The body disappeared to France after the ravages of the Peninsular War, but husband and wife were reburied together in Burgos cathedral in 1921.

at Plaza de Santa Teresa and follows the river through parkland all the way to pretty **Parque de Fuentes Blancas** (45min), a popular target for a Sunday stroll.

The Catedral

The Casco Histórico is totally dominated by the **Catedral** (daily 9.30am–7.30pm, last entrance at 6.30pm, closed Sun between 3pm and 3.30pm; €4, free second and fourth Sun of month in the afternoon), one of the most extraordinary achievements of Gothic art. It has emerged from a lengthy period of restoration, looking cleaner than it has for centuries, though visiting it has been reduced to something of a production line, with a separate visitor centre, well-stocked gift-shop and one-way flow inside to keep tourists from worshippers.

The most striking thing about the vast interior is the size and number of side chapels. The official tourist route passes two of the most important, around the back of the choir. The **Capilla del Santísimo Cristo de Burgos** contains a cloyingly realistic image of Christ (c.1300), endowed with real human hair and nails and covered with the withered hide of a water buffalo, still popularly believed to be human skin. Legend has it that the icon was modelled directly from the Crucifixion and that it requires a shave and a manicure every eighth day. The **Capilla de Santa Tecla**, opposite, has a distinctive star-shaped vault, a form adapted from the Moorish "honeycomb" vaults of Granada. Note that both chapels are highly venerated places of worship and closed to anyone clutching a cathedral ticket – worshippers enter via the Puerta de Santa María outside.

At the **Capilla de Santa Ana**, the magnificent *retablo* is by Gil de Siloé, a Flanders-born craftsman whose son Diego crafted the glorious **Escalera Dorada**, a double stairway next door and one of the crowning achievements of the cathedral. Moorish influences can also be seen in the cathedral's central dome (1568), supported on four thick piers that fan out into remarkably delicate buttresses – a worthy setting for the **tomb of El Cid** and his wife Jimena, marked by a simple slab of pink veined marble in the floor below, opposite the magnificent **Coro**.

The octagonal **Capilla del Condestable**, behind the high altar, is possibly the most splendid chapel of all, with a ceiling designed to form two eight-pointed stars, one within the other. From here the route leads out of the main body of the cathedral and into the spacious two-storey **cloisters**, and beyond this to a series of chapels that house the **Museo Catedralício** with its collection of religious treasures and two El Cid mementoes, namely his marriage contract and a wooden trunk. The light-filled lower cloister also has an audio-visual history of the church and its architecture, including a look at the various restoration projects.

San Nicolás, San Esteban and Castillo de Burgos

Overlooking the plaza in front of the cathedral stands the fifteenth-century church of **San Nicolás**, which has an altarpiece within that's as rich as anything in the city. At the side of San Nicolás, c/Pozo Seco ascends to the early Gothic church of **San Esteban**, from where steps climb up the hillside to the **Castillo de Burgos** (April–June Sat & Sun 11am–2pm & 4–7pm; July–Sept daily 11am–2pm & 5–8.30pm; Oct–March Sat & Sun 11am–2pm; €3.50), a huge fortress that was largely destroyed by the French in 1813. The walls, battlements and staircases have been restored, and there's also an innovative museum inside covering the history of the town, but even if you don't plan to visit it's worth the short climb up the hill anyway, for the views from a *mirador* over the cathedral and town. Beyond stretch the shaded green spaces of the town's parkland.

Monasterio de las Huelgas

The Cistercian **Monasterio de las Huelgas** (Tues–Sat 10am–1pm & 3.45–5.30pm, Sun 10.30am–2pm; €5, free Wed) is remarkable for its wealth of Mudéjar craftsmanship. It's under 1.5km from the city centre (a 20min walk): cross Puente de Santa María, turn right and follow the signs along the riverbank, soon bearing left through a well-to-do suburb. Founded in 1187 as the future mausoleum of Alfonso VIII (who died in 1214) and his wife Eleanor, daughter of Henry II of England, it became one of the most powerful convents in Spain. It was popularly observed that "if the pope were to marry, only the abbess of Las Huelgas would be eligible!" A community of nuns still lives here (making pottery that's for sale), and though you can enter through the gatehouse into the impressive courtyard, you have to pay to go any further.

It's very definitely worth it. The main **church**, with its typically excessive Churrigueresque *retablo*, contains the tombs of no fewer than sixteen Castilian monarchs and nobles, including Eleanor and Alfonso. Napoleon's troops paid their usual violent courtesy visit, and robbed the convent of its valuables, but remarkably, when the surviving tombs were later opened, many were found to contain regal clothes, embroidery and jewellery, now on display in a small **museum**. Other highlights include a set of delicate Romanesque cloisters, **Las Claustrillas**, and the ceiling of the main Gothic cloisters, which is adorned with patches of Mudéjar decoration. The **Capilla de Santiago** also has a fine Mudéjar ceiling and pointed horseshoe archway. Its cult statue of St James has an articulated right arm, which enabled him to dub knights of the Order of Santiago (motto: "The Sword is Red with the Blood of Islam") and on occasion even to crown kings.

Cartuja de Miraflores

The second of the town's two notable monastaries, the **Cartuja de Miraflores** (daily 10.15am–3pm, Sun from 11am, & 4–6pm; €1), famous for its three dazzling masterpieces by sculptor Gil de Siloé, lies in a secluded spot about 4km from the centre. It's a very pleasant hour's walk, following the path along the south bank of the river (towards *Camping Fuentes Blancas*), then bearing right up the hill at the Fuente del Prior park (45min) and crossing the road for the monastery (or it's well signposted by road all the way from town).

The monastery buildings are still in use and you can only visit the **church** (1454–1488), which is divided, in accordance with Carthusian practice, into three sections: for the public, the lay brothers and the monks. In front of the high altar lies the star-shaped carved alabaster tomb of Juan II of Castile (1405–1454) and Isabel of Portugal, of such perfection that it forced Felipe II and Juan de Herrera to admit "we did not achieve very much with our Escorial". Isabel la Católica, a great patron of the arts, commissioned it from Gil de Siloé in 1489 as a memorial to her parents. The same sculptor carved the magnificent altarpiece, plated with the first gold shipped back from the Americas and featuring scores of figures with expressive faces, so delicately carved that even the open pages of a Bible and parchment rolls are depicted. Finally comes the smaller but no less intricate tomb of the Infante (Crown Prince) Alfonso, brother of Queen Isabel, through whose untimely death in 1468 she was later able to claim the throne of Castile.

Eating, drinking and nightlife

You'll find plenty of **restaurants** in Burgos serving traditional Castilian dishes, including the local speciality, *morcilla* (a kind of black pudding or blood sausage, mixed with rice). Good **tapas bars** are legion, especially down the narrow bar-run of c/San Lorenzo (off Plaza Mayor), but also along c/Avellanos, and near the cathedral around c/de la Paloma. Burgos **nightlife**, meanwhile, is mainly generated by the local students, who hang out in the lively "pubs" and music bars in the open spaces of c/Huerto del Rey and c/Llana de Afuera, behind the cathedral – just follow the crowds. There's a more stylish scene over on c/Puebla and c/San Juan, where some fancier *copas* places hide behind smoked glass. After 3am, check out the late-night bars and **clubs** around the modern courtyard known as Plaza de Las Bernardas, just off c/Las Calzadas, east of the Casco Histórico, which are usually open till 7am.

Tapas bars and restaurants

Bar Gaona Jardin c/Sombrerería 29 ☎947 206 191. Tucked down a dead-end alley, with an interior modelled on an *andaluz* garden. Beautifully sculpted bite-sized *pinchos* line the bar, or order specialities such as the signature foie-gras with apple purée. Around the block (on c/de la Paloma, by the cathedral) another entrance leads to the *Gaona*'s more mainstream tapas bar and restaurant (€15 *menú*). Closed Mon.

La Cantina del Tenorio c/Arco del Pilar 10 ☎947 269 781. Atmospheric stone tavern with a nice line in creative fish *pinchos*, including anchovy and pickled peppers, smoked salmon and cherry tomatoes, and razor clams and olives. Closed Sun eve.

Casa Ojeda c/Vitoria 5 ☎947 209 052. One of the oldest and grandest places in town, dividing its efforts between deli, café, beer-house and restaurant. It's an ornately decorated space, with a smart Castilian restaurant upstairs and cheaper eats in the *comedor* or at the bar, though you're looking at *platos combinados* from €12.50 and *à la carte* dishes in the restaurant for around €20. Closed Sun eve.

Cervecería Morito c/Sombrerería 27 ☎947 429 062. The best budget dining spot in town – permanently rammed with locals at meal times, even when the spillover marquee across the lane is in use. Huge, freshly cooked, meal-in-one platters for around €8 (tuna tortilla, calamari and salad, say), or big stuffed sandwiches, *raciones*, salads and cheap drinks. If there are queues, *La Mejillonera* next door is great for stand-up mussels and beer.

Mesón Burgos c/Sombrerería 8 ☎947 206 150. A small, old-fashioned tapas bar with exposed stone and wooden beams – the speciality is scrumptious *patatas bravas* – while the snug restaurant behind serves Castilian classics (such as *cordero* and *cochinillo*) from €12. Closed Tues.

Mesón los Herreros c/San Lorenzo 20 ☎947 202 448. At busy times, you have to perch around the barrel table-tops outside on the street at this classic old-town tapas bar. There's a famously wide range of tapas (snails to stuffed mussels) and, like the other places along here, there's also an upstairs *comedor* for meals.

South and east of Burgos

South and east of Burgos lies a quartet of renowned sights – ancient hermitage, lavish abbey cloister and two very different restored towns – that are all easy excursions by car. They would make a fine, if busy, day's tour from Burgos, or can be seen en route to Soria, down the N234, though for an alternative overnight stop it's a hard choice between the dramatic *parador* at Lerma and the small-town charms of Covarrubias.

Ermita de Santa María de Lara

Down the N234 towards Soria, past the first signposted turn-off for Covarrubias, there's a detour after 34km to the dusty village of Quintanilla de las Viñas, which retains a rare Visigothic church and hermitage, the **Ermita de Santa María de Lara** (May–Sept Wed–Sun 10am–2pm & 4–8pm; Oct–April Wed–Sun 10am–5pm, closed last weekend in each month; custodian on site, free). It's a remarkable survivor, a simple stone building on a bare hillock outside the village, dating back to around 700 AD. Only a third of its original size (the ground plan is still shown in the stone foundations outside), it nonetheless packs an emotive punch, not least in the delicately carved exterior friezes depicting grapes, animals, birds and a scallop shell over the door – centuries of pilgrims have left cruder scratched crosses on the walls. Inside, there's a stone arch with capitals representing the sun and moon, and a block that is believed to be the earliest representation of Christ in Spanish art. You can see the exterior outside official visiting times.

Covarrubias

The small town – village really – of **COVARRUBIAS**, 40km south of Burgos, is superbly preserved, with many white half-timbered houses and an air of sleepy gentility throughout. Set by an old bridge overlooking the Río Arlanza, the *casco histórico* is arranged around three adjacent plazas of ever increasing prettiness. The late Gothic **Colegiata de San Cosme y San Damián** is the main church, crammed with tombs, giving an idea of the grandeur of the town in earlier times. The whole ensemble is studiously quaint, and attracts weekend tourists in number, but it's not yet overwhelmed – there's an antiques shop and a classy butcher-deli or two, but there are also locals tending to brimming flower boxes and children playing around the worn stone crosses.

The limited **bus** service from Burgos means you'll probably have to stay the night. There's plenty of **parking** outside the village – you're not supposed to drive inside. Everything is within two- or three-minutes' walk, and easy to find. The best-value **hotel**, with charming owners and rustic wood-trimmed rooms, is the ✻ *Hotel Rey Chindasvinto*, Plaza del Rey Chindasvinto 5 (☎947 406 560; ❸), right next to the Colegiata, while in the main Plaza Mayor there's budget accommodation at *Pension El Galin* (☎947 406 552; ❶), above the restaurant, and fancier three-star lodgings at *Hotel Nuevo Arlanza* (☎947 400 511, ⓦwww.hotel nuevoarlanza.com; ❹), also with its own restaurant. *Los Castros*, c/Los Castros 10 (☎947 406 368; ❸), with good rooms, is one of several *casas rurales* in town. The bar and **restaurant** at *El Galin* (restaurant closed Tues, & Sun eve) is a good-value choice for a straightforward meal (*menú*, lunch and dinner, €11), though the more renowned local choice is *Restaurante de Galo*, just up from the main square (☎947 406 393), with classier traditional Castilian dishes from €13.

Santo Domingo de Silos

The Benedictine abbey of **Santo Domingo de Silos**, 18km southeast of Covarrubias, is one of Spain's greatest Christian monuments. Surrounded by the fawn stone buildings of a small village of the same name, its defining feature is a double-storey eleventh-century **Romanesque cloister** (Tues–Sat 10am–1pm & 4.30–6pm, Sun 4.30–6pm; €3), with eight graphic sculpted reliefs on the corner pillars. They include *Christ on the Road to Emmaus*, dressed as a pilgrim to Santiago (complete with scallop shell), in solidarity with pilgrims that make a hefty detour from the main route to see the tomb of Santo Domingo, the eleventh-century abbot after whom the monastery is named. The same sculptor was responsible for about half of the **capitals**, which besides a famous bestiary include many Moorish motifs, giving rise to speculation that he may have been a Moor. Whatever the case, it is an early example of the effective mix of Arab and Christian cultures, which was continued in the fourteenth century with the vivid, painted Mudéjar wood-beamed ceiling. A quite different sculptor carved many of the remaining capitals, including the two that ingeniously tell the stories of the Nativity and the Passion in a very restricted space.

Visits to the monastery also usually include entry to the eighteenth-century pharmacy, which has been reconstructed in a room off the cloister. The bare church itself is an anticlimax, though the monks who sing here are considered one of the top three **Gregorian choirs** in the world – you may remember

▲ Santo Domingo de Silos

their 1994 platinum-selling CD *Chant*. If you can, make a point to attend *eucaristía* (Mon–Fri 9am) or vespers (daily 7pm), while the best singing of all can be heard at noon on Sundays.

The village really just exists to serve, with half a dozen small **hotels** and a few cafés and **restaurants**, all rather overpriced, but there's no great reason to stay (nearby Covarrubias is far nicer). The best sited is *Hotel Arco de San Juan* (☎947 390 074; ❺), with a pleasant garden and restaurant by the river, 200m or so downhill from Plaza Mayor, past the cloister entrance.

Lerma

The upper town of **LERMA**, high above the Río Arlanza, takes some beating as a piece of vanity building, constructed almost entirely between 1606 and 1617 at the behest of the Duke of Lerma, court favourite of the weak Felipe III. A pious man, Lerma established no fewer than six monasteries and convents in town, while on the site of the former castle he erected an enormous ducal palace, fronted by a sweeping, arcaded plaza. This is now the superb *Parador de Lerma* (☎947 177 110, ⓦwww.parador.es; ❻), beautifully restored – like the entire upper town – and with a stunning central courtyard around which are the public areas and restaurant (open to non-guests); the ducal-sized, terracotta-tiled rooms look directly out on to the burned countryside far below. You can park right outside in the vast square, except Wednesdays (during the day) when the weekly **market** takes place. Lerma's pricey **restaurants** around the plaza all specialise in *lechazo asado* (roast suckling lamb), cooked in wood-fired ovens – around €35 or so for a serving for two people. The *Mercado Viejo* bar, in the nearby old market square, is a cheaper place for **tapas** and **drinks**, or walk straight down the steep hill from the main plaza and out through the town gate to the main road, where a handful of less rarified restaurants and *hostales* offer reasonable meals. There are daily **buses** from Burgos, 37km to the north, but realistically Lerma is a stop for drivers, overnight or otherwise, in combination with Covarrubias, 23km to the east, and Santo Domingo de Silos beyond.

The Camino de Santiago: Burgos to León

The central section of the great pilgrim route, the **Camino de Santiago**, cuts across the northern plains of Castilla y León, with the stretch from Burgos to León seen as one of the most rewarding – not for the walking but in terms of the art and architecture encountered along the way. From Burgos the *camino* runs south of the main road, via Castrojeriz and, more importantly, **Frómista**, before running up to **Carrión de los Condes** and **Sahagún**, the latter two towns both on the A231 Burgos–León road. With a car, rather than a rucksack and boots, there are also a couple of possible short detours off the main road to see the **Roman remains** on either side of Carrión de los Condes.

Frómista

FRÓMISTA still trades on the *camino*, but today's small crossroads of a town has only a fraction of the population of medieval times. Its undisputed highlight is the church of **San Martín** (daily: summer 10am–2pm & 4.30–8pm; winter 10am–2pm & 3–6.30pm; €1), which was originally part of an abbey that no longer exists. Carved representations of monsters, human figures and animals run right around the roof of the eleventh-century church, which was built in a Romanesque style unusually pure for Spain, with no traces of later additions. A couple of other churches in Frómista are also associated with the *camino*, and there's usually a steady trail of walkers and cyclists passing through, taking advantage of the simple **accommodation** here. Opposite the church of San Pedro, the *Hostería de Los Palmeros*, Plaza San Telmo 4 (☎979 810 067), is a former medieval pilgrims' hostel, now a rather nice café and rustic restaurant. There's a daily **bus** to Frómista from Burgos, although it's reached more easily from Palencia (in whose province it lies) by bus or train.

The Camino de Santiago in Castilla y León

With the vineyards and well-watered countryside of La Rioja behind you, the **Camino de Santiago** arrives at Burgos and the start of the plains of Castile. Pilgrims are sharply divided about the *meseta*. Fans praise the big skies and the contemplative nature of the unchanging views, while detractors bemoan the bone-chilling wind that blows for nine months of the year, and the depressing way that you can see your destination hours before you reach it. It's certainly the flattest, driest part of the path and, if it's cold in winter, the lack of shade makes it uncomfortably hot in summer. The route often shadows the main road along a purpose-built gravel track, but there are many well-marked detours along isolated tracks crunchy with wild thyme.

Highlights are, of course, the glorious Gothic cathedrals of Burgos and León, after which the *meseta* ends at the town of Astorga, 50km west of León. From here you'll climb to the highest pass of the *camino* (1517m), where mist and fog can descend year-round and snow makes winter travel difficult. Traditionally, pilgrims bring a stone from home to leave on a massive pile at Cruz de Hierro, just before the pass. Things warm up considerably as you descend through gorgeous scenery to the Bierzo valley, 50km from Astorga, where the charming riverside town of Villafranca del Bierzo is an ideal place to rest before heading uphill into Galicia. For practicalities on the *camino*, see p.570.

▲ Walkers on the Camino de Santiago

Villalcázar de Sirga

Thirteen kilometres along the *camino* from Frómista (the route shadows the road), **VILLALCÁZAR DE SIRGA** has another notable church, Santa María La Blanca, built by the Knights Templar in the heart of the village. The Gothic style here begins to assert itself over the Romanesque, as witnessed by the figure sculpture on the two portals and the elegant pointed arches inside. There's a comfortably rustic **place to stay**, *Hostal Infanta Doña Leonor* (☎979 888 048, ⓦwww.hostalinfantaleonor.com; ❸), while in the main square are a few medieval houses, one of which has been converted into an atmospheric, medieval-style restaurant, *El Mesón de Villasirga*. Meanwhile, as pilgrims strike onwards past the village they are confronted by surely one of the most depressing signposts along the whole route – "Carrión de los Condes, 6km" (oh good), "Santiago de Compostela, 463km" (oh heck).

Carrión de los Condes

If the myths are to be believed, quiet, conservative **CARRIÓN DE LOS CONDES**, 80km west of Burgos and 40km north of Palencia, has a sensational past. In typically inflammatory fashion, it was reputed to be the place where, before the Reconquest, Christians had to surrender one hundred virgins annually to the Moorish overlords – a scene depicted on the badly worn portal of the church of **Santa María del Camino**, situated at the edge of the old town (where the *camino* comes into Carrión). There's finer sculpture over the doorway of the church of **Santiago** in the centre of town, overlooking the main square, Plaza del Generalísmo, still named for Franco after all these years. Burned out during the last century, the church has been restored and now contains the **Museo Parroquial** of sacred art (daily 11am–2pm & 4.30–8pm; €1). Its pilgrim days have bestowed another dozen churches and monasteries upon Carrión, but it's the riverside park that is most tempting on hot days, especially if you've just walked here. Across the sixteenth-century bridge look in at least at the **Monasterio de San Zoilo** (May to mid-Oct Tues–Sun 10.30am–2pm & 4.30–8pm; mid-Oct to April Tues–Fri 10.30am–2pm, Sat & Sun 10.30am–2pm & 4–6.30pm; €2); a side room off the cloister contains the tombs of the counts (*condes*) of Carrión, from whom the town's name comes.

Buses (from Burgos, León and, more frequently, Palencia) stop on the main road at the edge of town, near the seasonal kiosk **turismo** (☎979 880 932). By far the most atmospheric **accommodation** is at the *Hotel Real Monasterio San Zoilo* (☎979 880 049, ⓦwww.sanzoilo.com; ❹), converted from part of the monastery; it's also the best (though by no means the cheapest) place to eat in town. On a budget, try *Hostal La Corte*, c/Santa María 34 (☎979 880 138; ❶), opposite Santa María del Camino church (which has its own good-value restaurant), or the better *Hostal Santiago*, at nearby Plaza de los Regents (☎979 881 052; ❷). There are plenty of other *pensiones* and pilgrim *albergues* as well, while a decent municipal **campsite**, *El Edén* (☎979 881 152), lies in the parkland down by the river.

Villa Romana de la Olmeda and Quintanilla de la Cueza

Located outside the village of Pedrosa de la Vega, 22km northwest of Carrión (CL-615), the **Villa Romana de la Olmeda** is considered one of the most important domestic Roman sites in Spain. Dating from the late Roman period (fourth century AD), the villa boasts more than 1000 square metres of well-preserved mosaics, but the site is unfortunately still closed while works continue on an ambitious redevelopment project. However, finds from the site are currently displayed at the **Museo de la Olmeda** (Tues–Sun 10am–1.30pm & 4.30–8pm; mid-Oct to March afternoons 4–6pm; closed Jan; €2.40) in the Iglesia de San Pedro in **Saldaña**, 4km to the north. There's a second Roman villa that is open to the public, that of **Quintanilla de la Cueza** (same hours and entrance fee), though this lies in completely the opposite direction, around 17km southwest of Carrión de los Condes (N120). It's contemporary with La Olmeda and also has impressive mosaics, as well as a surviving hypocaust heating system.

Sahagún

From Carrión de los Condes the direct *camino* route west continues 35km to the small town of **SAHAGÚN**, once the seat of the most powerful monastery in all Spain, San Benito, which is now little more than a ruined shell. Right beside its surviving gateway and belfry is the most delicate of Sahagún's churches, the beautifully restored twelfth-century **San Tirso** (Tues–Sat 10.30am–1.30pm & 4.30–8pm, Oct–March afternoons 4.30–6pm, Sun 10.30am–1.30pm; free), a Mudéjar brick church. It's a style that appears again and again in Sahagún, and walking across town you'll see the grand brick towers of further Mudéjar edifices rising incongruously above its otherwise modern skyline. The most imposing is the church of **San Lorenzo** (services only), just off the Plaza Mayor.

Sahagún is an easy side trip from either Palencia or León; it's on the **train** route between the two (around 40min from either) and the station is a ten-minute walk from Plaza Mayor, down Avenida Constitución. There's convenient **parking** near ruined San Benito. *La Codorniz*, c/Arco 84 (☎987 780 276; ❷), has reasonable **rooms** and a nice faux-medieval restaurant attached, while the smart **restaurant** *Luís* at Plaza Mayor 4 (☎987 781 085) is the best place to try Sahagún's famous leeks (*puerros*).

León

Even if they stood alone, the stained glass in the cathedral of **LEÓN** and the Romanesque wall paintings in its Pantéon Real would merit a very considerable journey, but there's much more to the city than this. An attractive provincial capital that welcomes *camino* pilgrims by the thousand, it also presents itself as a lively university town with one of the best tapas bar scenes in the whole of Spain. Handsome old- and new-town areas complement each other, set back from extensive riverside gardens, and, while the city's major monuments are renowned, León is a fine place simply to spend a relaxed, casual day or two.

Aside from an early Roman presence, its **history** is that of the Reconquest. In 914, as the Christians edged their way south from Asturias, Asturian king Ordoño II transferred his capital from Oviedo to León. Despite being sacked by the dreaded al-Mansur in 996, the new capital rapidly eclipsed the old, and as more and more territory came under the control of León it was divided into new administrative groupings: in 1035, the county of Castile matured into a fully fledged kingdom with its capital at Burgos. For the next two centuries, León and Castile jointly spearheaded the war against the Moors until, by the thirteenth century, Castile had come finally to dominate her mother kingdom. These two centuries were nevertheless the period of León's greatest power, from which date most of her finest buildings.

Arrival and information

León's Casco Antiguo, with most of the historic sights and best bars and restaurants, lies east of the Río Bernesga, with the modern part of the city laid out in between. The old town is the big attraction; that said, the modern district has the bulk of the shops and services, and **parking** is much easier. Car parks are signposted as you drive in, or there's plenty of short-term street parking.

The **train** and **bus stations** are on the river's west bank, from where it's a twenty-minute walk up to the cathedral, or catch the minibus shuttle (#14), which runs on the hour between 8am and 10pm (Mon–Fri only) between the bus station and Plaza de Santo Domingo, c/Ancha and Plaza Mayor. Trains from the cute yellow **FEVE station** on the north side of town run a long daily route to and from Bilbao. The main **turismo** is on Plaza Regia, opposite the cathedral (July & Aug Mon–Thurs & Sun 9am–8pm, Fri & Sat 9am–9pm; Sept–June Mon–Fri 9am–2pm & 5–8pm, Sat & Sun 10am–2pm & 5–8pm; ☎987 237 082, ⓦwww.aytoleon.com).

Accommodation

There's a cluster of budget places around the atmospheric **Plaza Mayor**, though anything without double-glazing close to the bars and restaurants can be very noisy at night. If you're on a bigger budget, you might prefer one of the decent mid-range options nearby. The **new town** offers a greater choice of cheaper places, as well as the luxurious *parador*, and you're only ever a fifteen-minute walk or less from all the action.

Casco Antiguo

Boccalino Plaza de San Isidoro 1 ☎987 220 017. Sits on a lovely square overlooking San Isidoro church. The rooms are above a café-bar, and have parquet floors, good bathrooms with decent showers, double-glazing and church views;

across the square is the associated restaurant, a good-value pizza and pasta place. Internet access available. ❸

🏃 **Hostal Albany** c/la Paloma 13 ☎987 264 600, ⓦwww.albanyleon.com. One of the best in town, right opposite the cathedral, a spiffy,

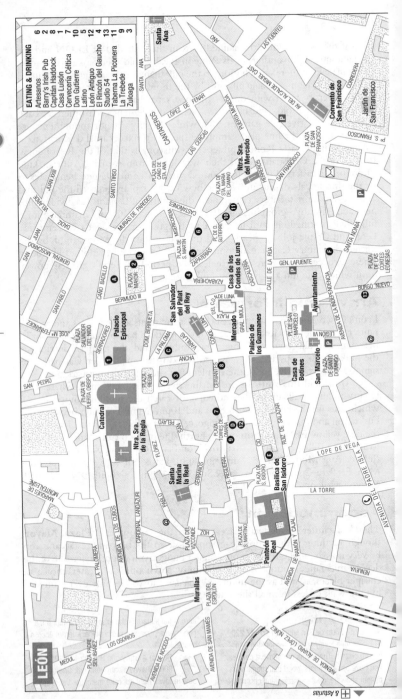

LEÓN

EATING & DRINKING	
Artesanos	6
Barry's Irish Pub	2
Capitán Haddock	8
Casa Luisón	1
Cervecería Céltica	7
Don Gutierre	10
Latino	5
León Antiguo	12
El Rincón del Gaucho	4
Studio 54	13
Taberna La Piconera	11
La Trébede	9
Zuloaga	3

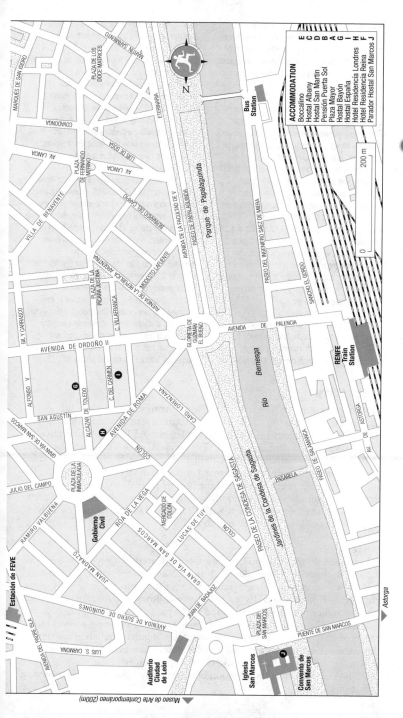

5

N

ACCOMMODATION
Boccalino E
Hostal Albany C
Hostal San Martín D
Pensión Puerta Sol B
Plaza Mayor A
Hostal Bayón I
Hostal España G
Hotel Residencia Londres H
Hotel Residencia Reina F
Parador Hostal San Marcos J

0   200 m

Astorga

modern two-star *hostal* with compact en-suite rooms with a/c and flat-screen TVs. It also has a great café on the square (good cakes and home-made ice cream) and the fine attached restaurant, *Las Termas*, which serves more inventive meals than most (*menú* €13). ❸

🏃 **Hostal San Martin** Plaza Torres de Omaña 1, 2º ☎987 875 187, Ⓦwww .sanmartinhostales.com. An excellent *hostal* with simple but stylish rooms painted in pastel shades – there's a choice of shared or private bathrooms, and wi-fi is available. ❷

Pensión Puerta Sol c/Puerta del Sol 1 2º ☎987 211 966. Reasonable *pensión* rooms in an excellent location overlooking Plaza Mayor; however, if you're looking for quiet, early nights, this is not the part of town for you. ❶

Plaza Mayor Plaza Mayor 15–17 ☎987 344 357, Ⓦwww.nh-hotels.com. Chic boutique style in a classy refit of one of the square's handsome arcaded buildings. Facilities and services are four-star standard, and include one of superchef Ferran Adrià's *Nhube* contemporary bistro-style restaurants. Best rates are online. ❺

New town

🏃 **Hostal Bayón** c/Alcázar de Toledo 6, 2º ☎987 231 446. Handsome budget *hostal*: stripped-pine floors, high ceilings, large windows, quiet rooms and firm beds throughout. There are only five rooms, so it's essential to book ahead. ❶

Hostal España c/del Carmen 3, 1º ☎987 236 014. A cheap standby, located in a quiet side street. It's a bit dowdy, and there aren't any en-suite rooms, but you can't argue with the price. ❶

Hotel Residencía Londres Avda. de Roma 1, 1º ☎987 222 274, Ⓦwww.hostallondres.com. Large, spotless singles and doubles with cork-tile floors, some with particularly spacious bathrooms, and big windows onto the street. For breakfast, you can pop over the road to the fabulously retro *Cantabrico* café. ❷

🏃 **Hotel Residencía Reina** c/Puerto de la Reina 2 ☎987 205 212, Ⓦwww.hotelreina .com. A surprisingly funky one-star hotel, quite centrally located, with excellent-value rooms, some en suite. The cheery, English-speaking hosts have taken some care with the decor and furnishings, and there's a really laidback feel. ❷

Parador Hostal San Marcos Plaza San Marcos 7 ☎987 237 300, Ⓦwww.parador.es. The sensational *parador* occupies one of León's oldest and most dramatic buildings. Bedrooms are of the antiques and four-poster kind, though with all mod cons, and there's a sense of calm and majesty throughout. The restaurant is also good, with mains from €25. It's one of only a handful of the *paradores* with no off-season prices. ❼

The City

Almost everything to see is in the **Casco Antiguo**, on either side of the pedestrianised c/Ancha, which arrows straight up to the cathedral. In fact, the stand-out buildings are few, if spectacular, but old León is a fine place for strolling, with large parts of the encircling medieval walls still intact. The tangle of narrow streets is shabby in part, though the ramshackle buildings in faded ochre and rose pink give the old *barrio* a charm all of its own. It bursts into life at night when the streets throng and the bars are packed out. By day, apart from the crowds around the cathedral and San Isidoro, it's much quieter in the pretty lanes and squares, though always with the accompanying footfall of arriving *camino* hikers making their way into town.

Catedral

All eyes are drawn to León's mighty Gothic **Catedral** (July–Sept: Mon–Sat 8.30am–1.30pm & 4–8pm, Sun 8.30am–2.30pm & 5–8pm; Oct–June until 7pm; Ⓦwww.catedraldeleon.org; free), which dates from the final years of the city's period of greatness. Its stained-glass **windows** in particular (thirteenth century and onwards) are equal to the masterpieces in any European cathedral – a stunning kaleidoscope of light streaming in through soaring walls of multi-coloured glass. While such extensive use of glass is purely French in inspiration, the colours used here – reds, golds and yellows – are essentially Spanish. The glass screen added to the otherwise obscuring *coro* gives a clear view up to the altar, and only enhances the sensation of all-pervasive light with its bewildering refractions.

To see the rest of the cathedral – basically, the cloisters, carved choir stalls and museum treasures – you have to pay, though you can opt for a partial visit (€2) or just the **cloisters** alone (€1). With the full-on visit to the **Museo Catedralicio Diocesano** (Mon–Sat 9.30am–1.30pm & 4–7pm, closed Sat pm Oct–May; €4), you get a guided tour of the whole complex (in Spanish), though it does tend to go on a bit. It also includes the climb to the platform erected above the central nave, for a closer look at the stained glass, though this is something you can do separately anyway from the entrance around the side of the cathedral (*Plataforma*; visits on the half-hour during opening times, though closed Mon & Sun; €2).

Take a moment outside to appreciate the magnificent triple-arched **west facade** (on Plaza Regia), dominated by a massive rose window and comprising two towers and a detached nave supported by flying buttresses – a pattern repeated at the south angle. Above the central doorway, the Last Judgement is in full swing, with the cooking pots of Hell doing a roaring trade in boiled sinners.

Plaza Mayor to Santo Domingo

A couple of minutes' walk south of the cathedral lies the elegant, arcaded **Plaza Mayor**, for once not the absolute focus of attention in town and all the quieter for it, during the day at least. It's on the edge of the nightlife zone, which spills out from nearby **Plaza de San Martín**, also rather charming, though every building here is a bar or restaurant. Come the evening, and out come the pan-handlers, cigarette bums and dodgy DVD merchants, mingling with the crowds. Hands-down plaza winner, though, is **Plaza de Santa Maria del Camino**, a gorgeous cobbled square with two big shady trees, a surviving wooden arcade and the pretty Romanesque church of Nuestra Señora del Mercado – the name a reminder that the square was once the site of the city's grain market (it's still known as Plaza del Grano). You can wind back towards c/Ancha via the daily **mercado** itself in Plaza del Conde Luna, which is surrounded by the old town's most characteristic shopping streets, such as c/de la Rúa and c/Azabachería – on the latter, at no. 20, for example, is the beautiful Don Queso cheese shop.

Emerging on c/Ancha you're confronted by a series of striking buildings ranged around **Plaza de Santo Domingo**. The modest *ayuntamiento* sits back in its own square, across the road from the Renaissance **Palacio de los Guzmanes**. But it's the mock-Gothic, exuberantly turreted **Casa Botines** that steals the show, an early (1892–93) work of *modernista* architect Antoni Gaudí, now an exhibition space and Caja España bank building. Saint George (the Catalan patron saint) is doing his best to subdue a dragon above the entrance.

Basílica de San Isidoro and the Pantéon Real

The city's other prominent sight is the **Basílica San Isidoro** (open all day; free), a five-minute walk from the cathedral or Plaza de Santo Domingo. It was founded by Fernando I, who united the two kingdoms of León and Castile in 1037. He commissioned the complex both as a shrine for the bones of San Isidoro and as a mausoleum for himself and his successors. Backing into the very walls of the city, it's a beautiful construction, dating mainly from the mid-twelfth century and thus one of the earliest Romanesque buildings in Spain. Two adjacent doorways show fine sculpted reliefs, of the Descent from the Cross (right) and the Sacrifice of Abraham (left), the latter surmounted by a later Renaissance pediment topped by the horse-riding San Isidoro himself. Inside, the saint's bones lie in a reliquary on the high altar.

The royal bones, however (of eleven kings and twelve queens), were laid to rest in tombs in the adjacent **Pantéon Real** (July & Aug Mon–Sat 9am–8pm, Sun

9am–2pm; Sept–June Mon–Sat 10am–1.30pm & 4–6.30pm, Sun 10am–1.30pm; €4, free Thurs pm), essentially two crypt-like chambers constructed between 1054 and 1063 as a portico of the church. It's a deeply atmospheric space, with two squat columns in the middle of the Panteón carved with thick foliage, rooted in Visigothic tradition. Moreover, towards the end of the twelfth century, these extraordinarily well-preserved vaults were then covered in some of the most significant **frescoes** in Spanish Romanesque art. These present a vivid splash of colour, not just biblical scenes and stories but also an agricultural calendar, for example (on the underside of one entire arch). The central dome is occupied by Christ Pantocrator surrounded by the four Evangelists depicted with animal heads – allegorical portraits that stem from the apocalyptic visions in the Bible's Book of Revelation. Your ticket also allows you to visit the cloister, as well as the small museum of glittering church treasures and the impressive library.

Convento de San Marcos and around

At the opulent **Convento de San Marcos** (15min walk from the old town), and on presentation of the relevant documents, pilgrims were allowed to regain their strength before the gruelling Bierzo mountains west of León. The original pilgrims' hospital and hostel was built in 1168 for the Knights of Santiago, one of several chivalric orders founded in the twelfth century to protect pilgrims and lead the Reconquest. In the sixteenth century, it was rebuilt as a kind of palatial headquarters, its massive one-hundred-metre-long facade lavishly embellished with Plateresque appliqué designs: over the main entrance, Santiago is depicted swatting Moors with ease.

The monastery is now a *parador*, and is strictly off-limits to non-guests beyond its foyer and (modern) bar and restaurant. However, there's unimpeded access to the adjacent **Iglesia San Marcos**, vigorously speckled with the scallop-shell motif of the pilgrimage. Follow the signs through the side-chapels to the **Museo de León** (Tues–Sat 10am–2pm & 4–7pm, July–Sept afternoons 5–8pm, Sun 10am–2pm; €0.60), housed in the sacristy. This is a collection of monumental statuary and paintings, as well as church treasures including a thirteenth-century processional cross made of rock crystal. There are also guided visits from here to see the celebrated *coro alto* of the church (Tues, Wed & Fri 1pm, Thurs 5.30pm), which has a fine set of carved stalls by Renaissance sculptor Juan de Juni.

Just up from San Marcos stands the **Auditorio Ciudad de León** (Ⓦwww .auditoriociudaddeleon.net), a striking series of white cubes facing a contemporary plaza. The concert and exhibition venue was designed by Luis Moreno Mansilla and Emilio Tuñón, the award-winning Spanish architects also responsible for the dazzling **Museo de Arte Contemporáneo** (Tues–Sun 10am–3pm & 4–9pm; free; Ⓦwww.musac.es), at Avenida de los Reyes Leoneses 24, a fifteen-minute walk north of San Marcos. The multicoloured glass facade was inspired by the stained-glass windows in the cathedral, and regularly changing exhibitions inside feature work by contemporary Spanish artists.

Eating, drinking and nightlife

The liveliest **tapas bars and restaurants** are those in and around Plaza de San Martín – an area known as the **Barrio Húmedo** (the Wet Quarter) for the amount of liquid sloshing around. Scores of bars here will give you a free *pincho* with every drink, so you can eat pretty well if you hop from bar to bar ordering *cortos* – small tumblers of beer for a euro a pop. The other good area for bars is across c/Ancha, along c/Cervantes and in the surrounding little squares, where there's a mix of traditional tapas places and more contemporary *copas* and music bars. Music **bars and clubs** tend to open Thursday to Saturday, between 11pm and 5am. Things really take off during **Semana Santa**, and for the **fiestas** of San Juan and San Pedro in the last week of June. The celebrations, concentrated around the Plaza Mayor, get pretty riotous, with an enjoyable blend of medieval pageantry and buffoonery.

Tapas bars

Don Gutierre Plaza Don Gutierre 4. Quality *raciones* and wine in a quieter square on the edge of the main bar zone – you can drink and eat inside or out, sampling things such as *chorizo* in cider, *pimientos* with anchovies or *calamares* in ink, with most *raciones* costing €6–12.

Latino Plaza San Martín 10. A popular tapas bar that's serious about its food and wine, with usually a choice of a couple of free snacks with a drink, as well as a restaurant at the back that serves a wide variety of Leonese dishes (€8–16).

El Rincón del Gaucho c/Azabachería 1. Tucked in a back alley off San Martín, this classic old-town tapas bar is best known for its delicious, garlicky *patatas gauchos*, served with every drink.

La Trebede Plaza Torres de Omaña. A cosy bar that's a bit of an Old Curiosity Shop, once you start to examine the shelves and ornaments. There's always a good *tapa* served with your drink, plus more than thirty wines by the glass.

Restaurants

Artesanos c/Juan de Arfe 2 ☎987 215 322. Set on the first floor around the courtyard of the seventeenth-century Palacio Jabalquinto, with an innovative, seasonal menu of *nouveau* Leonese cuisine, including lots of fresh fish. Mains €15–20.

Casa Luisón Plaza Puerta Obispo 16 ☎987 254 029. A real find for a reliable cheap meal in the heart of the tourist zone, by the cathedral. Old-time bar out front, and *comedor* in the back serving a good €9 *menú*, plus inexpensive snacks and *à la carte* dishes.

Taberna La Piconera Plaza Santa María del Camino 2 ☎987 212 607. Lunch on the pretty cobbled square is a treat, enjoying a simple but tasty €10.50 *menú*. It's a contemporary place inside, with dishes to share – prawns to carpaccio, mussels to tempura veg – and a good line in grilled meats. Around €30 and upwards.

Zuloaga c/Sierra Pambley 3 ☎987 237 814. Sophisticated, stylish restaurant, with romantic candlelit garden terrace, which produces a seasonal menu of Leonese cuisine with an unusual amount of flair and imagination. Main courses start at €16, though there's a lunchtime *menú* for around the same price.

Bars and clubs

Barry's Irish Pub Plaza Mayor 23. The main Irish pub in town, on the central plaza, part bar and part *discoteca* at the weekends.

Capitán Haddock c/de Ancha 8. Terrible name, but not a bad bar as the night wears on, with the outside world screened off by heavy red curtains. A bit further up c/Cervantes is the similarly rock-and-roll *El Gran Café*.

Cervecería Céltica c/Cervantes 10. Noisy beer-house that's all the rage for foreign and Spanish beers on tap, including the knock-your-socks-off Belgian brews.

León Antiguo Plaza Ordoño IV. A good place to start the night, with an outdoor terrace overlooking the El Cid gardens and the Gaudí towers.

Studio 54 c/Burgo Nuevo 18. A popular club in a small residential courtyard off the main street in the new town, with a few other late-opening bars nearby. Open from midnight weekends, usually with cover.

Listings

Buses Bus station information ☎987 211 000. Alsa (☎902 422 242, ⊛www.alsa.es) has services to Burgos and Astorga; Abel (⊛www.autocaresabel .com) to Sahagún and Palencia; Vivas (☎987 252 560, ⊛www.autocaresvivas.es) to Zamora/Salamanca.

Hospital Hospital San Juan de Dios, Avda. San Ignacio de Loyola 73 ☎987 232 500.

Internet access Arco Park, c/Pablo Flórez 26 (till midnight, closed Sun am); basement of the *cafetería* at Avda. de Ordoño II 3 (daily 8am–11pm).

Laundry Lavandería La Paloma, c/Paloma 6 (closed Sat pm).

Police Policía Municipal, Paseo del Parque ☎987 255 500, emergency ☎092; Policía Nacional, Villa Benavente 6 ☎987 218 900, emergency ☎091.

Post office Main branch at the southern end of Avda. de Independencia, by Plaza de San Francisco (Mon–Fri 10am–2pm & 4.30–8.30pm, Sat 10am–2pm).

Taxis Radio Taxi León ☎987 261 415; Taxi Trabajo Villaquilambe ☎987 285 355.

Astorga and beyond

For the very fittest of the pilgrims, it was one day's walk, 50km, west of León to the next major stop at **Astorga**; it's an easy day-trip today and, if you go by car, you can call in at **Hospital de Órbigo**, 36km from León, where legend has it that Don Suero de Quiñones, a jilted knight, defeated three hundred men in a jousting tournament at the town's famous twenty-arch medieval bridge. Beyond the valley town of **Ponferrada**, weary pilgrims confronted the mountains of El Bierzo, where the pretty *camino* town of **Villafranca del Bierzo** is the obvious target, while any circuit by car should definitely include the old Roman mines of **Las Médulas**, south of Ponferrada.

Astorga

ASTORGA was originally settled by the Romans, sacked by the Moors in the eleventh century, then rebuilt and endowed with the usual hospices and monasteries, but as the pilgrimage lost popularity in the late Middle Ages, the place fell into decline. It's now a small provincial capital with an incongruously grand cathedral and the bizarre *modernista* **Palacio Episcopal** – commissioned by a Catalan bishop from his countryman Antoni Gaudí in 1887, and resembling some kind of horror-movie castle. It houses the excellent **Museo de los Caminos** (Tues–Sat: summer 10am–2pm & 4–8pm, Sun 10am–2pm; winter 11am–2pm & 4–6pm, Sun 11am–2pm; €2.50, €4 joint ticket with Museo Catedralicio), which throws interesting sidelights on the story of the pilgrimage: hanging on the wall are examples of the documents issued at Santiago to certify that pilgrims had "travelled, confessed and obtained absolution".

Opposite stands the florid **Catedral** (Mon–Sat 9–11am, Sun 11am–1pm; free). Built between 1471 and 1693, it combines numerous architectural styles, but still manages to be totally upstaged by the palace. The **Museo Catedralicio** (daily: summer 10am–2pm & 4–8pm; winter 11am–2pm & 3.30–6.30pm; €2.50; entrance to the left of the main facade) is interesting, however, especially for its beautiful twelfth-century wooden tomb painted with scenes from the lives of Christ and the Apostles.

While you're in town you could take in the **Museo del Chocolate**, on c/José María Goy (Tues–Sat 10.30am–2pm & 4–6pm, Sun 11am–2pm; €2), which charts the growth of Astorga's flourishing chocolate industry during the eighteenth and nineteenth centuries. You can also trace Astorga's Roman past on the **Ruta Romana**, picked out on the *turismo*'s map of town, which passes the remnants of city walls, thermal bath complex and sewer system (*cloacas*), among other sites. The theme is developed in the **Museo Romano** on Plaza de San Bartolomé (Tues–Sat 10am–1.30pm & 4–6/7pm, Sun 10am–1.30pm; free), which displays local Roman finds and special exhibitions.

Practicalities

The **train station** is a long way from the centre of town, and it makes far more sense to arrive and depart by **bus**; services are very frequent from León and Ponferrada, and the station is centrally located, right opposite the Palacio Episcopal. **Parking** is easy, also right by the *palacio*. The **turismo** is on the opposite side of the Palacio Episcopal at c/Eduardo de Castro 5 (Tues–Sat 10am–1.30pm & 4–6.30pm, Sun 10am–1.30pm; ☏987 618 222, ⓦwww.ayuntamientodeastorga.com).

Astorga is an easy day-trip from León, but there's some agreeable central **accommodation**, including the smart *La Peseta*, a two-star *hostal* on Plaza de

The Maragatos

Astorga is the traditional market town of the **Maragatos**, a distinct ethnic group of unknown origin, possibly descended from the Berbers of North Africa, who crossed into Spain with the first Moorish incursions of the early eighth century. For several centuries, they dominated the Spanish carrying trade with their mule trains. Marrying only among themselves, they maintained their traditions and individuality well into recent decades. Along with the Maragato *cocido*, a typically hearty stew made with assorted meats and sausage, chickpeas and cabbage, their only obvious legacy to the town is a pair of colourful clockwork figures dressed in traditional costume who jerk into action to strike the hour on the town-hall clock in Plaza Mayor.

San Bartolomé, next to the Museo Romano (℡987 617 275, Ⓦwww.restaurant elapeseta.com; ❸), with an excellent, moderately priced restaurant (which is closed Tues eve & Sun eve). *Hotel Gaudí*, Plaza Eduardo de Castro 6 (℡987 615 654, Ⓦwww.hotelgaudiastorga.com; ❹), is a bit classier, and rooms look directly onto Gaudí's *palacio*, though most atmospheric of all is *Casa de Tepa*, c/Santiago 2 (℡987 603 299, Ⓦwww.casadetepa.com; ❺), a beautifully restored eighteenth-century townhouse with some lovely rooms and an enclosed terrace-garden.

Local **restaurants** all advertise the delights of the *cocido maragato* (see box above), for around €16 or so – you eat the meats first, then the veg, then drink the broth, and good luck in finishing what tend to be gigantic portions. There are plenty of **cafés** and **bars** around Plaza Mayor especially.

Ponferrada

At first sight, the heavily industrialized, bowl-shaped valley centred on the large town of **PONFERRADA** seems to have little to offer, but the mountainous terrain of the Bierzo has scenery as picturesque as any in Spain. The town itself sums up this dichotomy, dominated by a huge slag heap and spreading suburbs, yet with a charming, unspoiled old quarter. The two are separated by the Río Sil, spanned by the iron bridge that gave Ponferrada its name.

The heart of the *casco antiguo* is the restored **Plaza del Ayuntamiento**, named for its late seventeenth-century town hall. Ponferrada's museum, the **Museo del Bierzo** (Tues–Sat 11am–2pm & 4–7pm, May–Sept 5–8.30pm, Sun 11am–2pm; €3), is housed in an old prison just off the plaza, through the quaint Puerta del Reloj (Clock Gateway). A bit further along is the prettier central square, Plaza de la Encina, overlooked by the **Basílica de la Encina**, the town's finest Renaissance church, and beyond here, above the river, stands the **Castillo de los Templarios** (Tues–Sat 11am–2pm & 4.30–6.30pm, May–Sept till 8.30pm, closed Sun pm; €3). Established by the Knights Templars in the thirteenth century, it's a textbook castle with fancy turrets and battlements, all gleaming after a handsome restoration.

Practicalities

If you're driving from Astorga, you'll hit the old town first, on the east side of the Río Sil, and can avoid the new section altogether. There's **parking** on the edge of the old town, as well as under Plaza del Ayuntamiento, or free street parking on the bridge, below the castle. From the **bus station**, head across the open space outside to the far left-hand corner to pick up c/General Gomez Nuñez (subsequently Avda Perez Colino) and walk straight down it for ten minutes to reach the river, from where you'll see the castle up on your left. The **train station** is more centrally located, on the edge of the town centre.

There are plenty of **hotels** and *hostales* in the new town, all signposted as you drive in (and detailed on the tourist office website, ⓦwww.ponferrada .org/turismo). But it's nicest to stay in the old quarter, where you can choose between *Hotel Bierzo Plaza*, on Plaza del Ayuntamiento (☎987 409 001, ⓦwww .hotelbierzoplaza.com; ❹), which boasts characterful rooms with big windows overlooking the city, and the smaller, simpler *Hotel Los Templarios*, just through the clock gateway at c/Flórez Osorio 3 (☎987 411 484, ⓦwww.hotellostemplarios .info; ❸). There are some pleasant *tabernas* and café-bars on Plaza de la Encina, with shaded seating in the square, and both hotels also have decent **restaurants**, particularly *Los Arcos* in the *Hotel Bierzo Plaza*, which serves meals in an airy, subterranean cavern or out on the plaza itself.

Las Médulas

Twenty kilometres southwest of Ponferrada lie **Las Médulas**, the jagged remains of hills ravaged by Roman strip-mining. Nine hundred thousand tonnes of gold were ripped from the hillsides using specially constructed canals, leaving an eerie, mesmerizing landscape reminiscent of Arizona, peppered with caves and needles of red rock. Just outside Carucedo (on the N536), the road splits, with the right fork leading 3km up to the village of Las Médulas, a pretty place of restored stone houses, climbing roses and spreading chestnut trees set behind the largest rock outcrops. You have to park just outside, by the visitor centre, the **Aula Arquelógica** (April–Sept daily 10am–1.30pm & 4–8pm; Oct–March Sat 10am–1.30pm & 3.30–6pm, Sun 10am–2pm; €1.50), and then walk 200m into the village, from where various signposted **trails** lead into the dramatic workings. The shortest are to Somido lake (3km return; 45min), for great views of the outcrops, and the Las Valiños trail (4km; 1hr 15min), which takes you partly inside the old mines themselves. There's a detour off this latter route up to the **Mirador de Orellán**, which offers the most spectacular panorama over the whole area of crumbling peaks. You can also drive here directly by taking the left fork out of Carucedo and winding up for 4.5km, through the village of Orellán. It's a steep six-hundred-metre walk from the car park to the viewing platforms. A gaggle of studiously rustic cafés and bars in Las Médulas caters for day-trippers, and there's also a similar place to eat in Orellán, before you reach the *mirador*.

Villafranca del Bierzo

The last halt before the climb into Galicia, **VILLAFRANCA DEL BIERZO**, 22km from Ponferrada, was where pilgrims on their last legs could chicken out of the final trudge. Those who arrived at the Puerta del Perdón (Door of Forgiveness) at the simple Romanesque **church of Santiago** could receive the same benefits of exemption of years in Purgatory as in Santiago de Compostela itself. The town itself is quietly enchanting, with a jumble of old-town streets, slate-roofed houses, encircling hills, cool mountain air and the clear Río Burbia providing a setting vaguely reminiscent of the English Lake District. The historic pilgrim connection makes it a great place to stop for the night, with plenty of reasonably priced accommodation and a multitude of restaurants offering good-value pilgrim *menús*.

Hourly **buses** from Ponferrada stop near the *parador*, on the edge of town as you drive in. For **parking**, keep straight on right through Plaza Mayor to reach the parking spaces by the town gardens. For traditional **lodgings**, what could be more appropriate in a pilgrim town than the *Hospedería San Nicolas*, a massive seventeenth-century Jesuit monastery right in the centre by the town gardens (☎987 540 483, ⓦwww.hospederiasannicolas.com; ❹), with serviceable rooms and a decent restaurant. The *Hotel San Francisco* on the central plaza (☎987 540 465, ⓦ www.hotelsanfrancisco.org; ❸) is a decent bet, though the most charming option is the *Parador de Villafranca del Bierzo*, Avenida Calvo Sotelo (☎987 540 175, ⓦ www.parador.es; ❺), just three-minutes' walk from Plaza Mayor. Clad in creepers, it's country-house in feel, with comfortable rooms looking out over the local hills and a small vine-shaded terrace.

Plaza Mayor has a line of **cafés and restaurants**, nearly all offering a €10 or €11 *menú del día*, served at night too, though the *parador* has the best restaurant in town.

Travel details

Trains

For current timetables and ticket information, consult RENFE ☎902 240 202, ⓦ www.renfe.es or FEVE ☎987 271 210, ⓦ www.feve.es.

Burgos to: Bilbao (5 daily; 2hr 30min–4hr 30min); León (4 daily; 2hr); Logroño (4 daily; 2hr 15min); Madrid (7 daily; 2hr 30min–4hr 15min); Palencia (9 daily; 45min–1hr); Salamanca (4 daily; 2hr 30min); Valladolid (up to 13 daily; 1hr–1hr 20min); Vitoria (10 daily; 1hr 15min–1hr 30min); Zaragoza (4 daily; 4hr).

León to: Astorga (9 daily; 40min); Bilbao (daily; 5hr); Burgos (4 daily; 2hr); Logroño (2 daily; 4hr); Madrid (up to 11 daily; 3hr–4hr 30min); Oviedo (9 daily; 2hr); Palencia via Sahagún (up to 12 daily; 1hr–1hr 30min); Ponferrada (8 daily; 1hr 30min–2hr); Valladolid (up to 10 daily; 1hr 30min–2hr); Vigo (3 daily; 6hr 30min).

Logroño to: Burgos (4 daily; 2hr 15min); Haro (2 daily; 40min); Madrid (daily; 3hr 15min); Palencia (daily; 3hr); Valladolid (daily; 3hr 45min); Vitoria (daily; 1hr 30min); Zaragoza (6 daily; 2hr).

Salamanca to: Ávila (9 daily; 1hr); Burgos (4 daily; 2hr 30min); Madrid (8 daily; 2hr 30min); Valladolid (10 daily; 1hr 15min–1hr 30min).

Soria to: Almazán (4 daily; 30min); Madrid (4 daily; 3hr).

Valladolid to: Burgos (up to 13 daily; 1hr–1hr 20min); León (up to 10 daily; 1hr 30min–2hr); Madrid (AVE 6 daily, 1hr; other services at least hourly, 1hr 30min–2hr 45min); Medina del Campo (hourly; 20–30min); Palencia (hourly; 30min); Salamanca (10 daily; 1hr 15min–1hr 30min); Zamora (daily; 1hr 40min).

Zamora to: Madrid (3 daily; 3hr 30min–4hr); Santiago de Compostela (3 daily; 4hr 30min); Valladolid (daily; 1hr 40min); Vigo (3 daily; 5hr).

Buses

Astorga to: León (hourly; 50min); Ponferrada (hourly; 1hr); Villafranca del Bierzo (4–6 daily; 1hr 40min).

Burgos to: Bilbao (8 daily; 2hr); Carrión de los Condes (daily; 1hr 20min); Covarrubias (Mon–Fri 2 daily, Sat daily; 1hr); Frómista (daily; 1hr); León (4–5 daily, 2hr direct, otherwise up to 3hr); Logroño via Nájera (Mon–Fri 7 daily, Sat & Sun 3–4 daily; 2hr); Madrid (10 daily; 2hr 45min); Palencia (up to 3 daily; 1hr 15min); Pamplona (4 daily; 3hr 30min); Salamanca (3 daily; 3hr 30min); San Sebastián (7 daily; 3hr 30min); Santander (4 daily; 3hr); Soria (up to 3 daily; 2hr–2hr 30min); Santo Domingo de Silos (Mon–Sat daily; 1hr 30min); Valladolid (5 daily; 2hr 30min); Vinuesa (2–3 daily; 2hr 15min); Zaragoza (4 daily; 4hr).

León to: Astorga/Ponferrada (hourly; 50min/2hr); Burgos (4–5 daily, 2hr direct, otherwise up to 3hr); Carrión de los Condes (daily; 2hr); Madrid (12 daily; 3hr 30min); Oviedo (9 daily; 1hr 30min); Salamanca (4–5 daily; 2hr); Valladolid (8 daily; 2hr); Zamora (4–6 daily; 2hr).

Logroño to: Bilbao (4–6 daily; 2hr 30min); Burgos (Mon–Fri 7 daily, Sat & Sun 3–4 daily; 2hr); Calahorra (Mon–Sat 6–7 daily; Sun 3 daily; 1hr); Haro (Mon–Fri 7 daily, Sat & Sun 3–4 daily; 1hr); Nájera (Mon–Fri every 30–60min, Sat & Sun roughly hourly; 30min); Pamplona (up to 6 daily; 2hr); Soria (up to 5 daily; 1hr 30min); Vitoria (6–7 daily; 1hr).

Palencia to: Burgos (up to 3 daily; 1hr 15min); Carrión de los Condes (3 daily; 45min); Frómista (Mon–Sat 3–4 daily; 30min); Madrid (6 daily; 3hr); Salamanca (up to 7 daily; 2hr 15min); Valladolid (hourly; 1hr); Zamora (2 daily; 2hr 15min).

Salamanca to: Astorga/Ponferrada (1–2 daily; 2hr 40min/3hr 30min); Ávila (8 daily; 1hr 30min); Burgos (3 daily; 3hr 30min); Cáceres (8 daily; 3hr 45min); Ciudad Rodrigo (Mon–Fri hourly, Sat 6 daily, Sun 4 daily; 1hr); León (4–5 daily; 3hr–3hr 30min); Madrid (hourly; 2hr 30min); Palencia (up to 7 daily; 2hr 15min); Porto/Lisbon, Portugal (1–2 daily; 6hr/9hr); Valladolid (up to 8 daily; 1hr 15min–1hr 40min); Zamora (hourly; 1hr 10min).

Soria to: Almazán (4 daily; 45min); Burgos (1–3 daily; 2hr–2hr 30min); El Burgo de Osma (Mon–Sat 2 daily, Sun daily; 1hr); Logroño (up to 5 daily; 1hr 30min); Madrid (8 daily; 2hr 30min); Medinaceli (2 daily; 1hr); Pamplona (5 daily; 2hr); Valladolid via Peñafiel (3 daily; 3hr); Vinuesa (2–3 daily; 35min); Zaragoza (9 daily; 2hr).

Valladolid to: El Burgo de Osma (3 daily; 2hr); Burgos (5 daily; 2hr 30min); León (8 daily; 2hr); Madrid (hourly; 2hr 15min); Palencia (Mon–Fri hourly, Sat 6 daily, Sun 3 daily; 1hr); Peñafiel (Mon–Sat 7 daily, Sun 4 daily; 1hr); Salamanca (up to 8 daily; 1hr 15min–1hr 40min); Segovia (hourly; 2hr); Soria (3 daily; 3hr); Zamora (Mon–Fri hourly, Sat & Sun 4–6 daily; 1hr 30min).

Zamora to: León via Benavente (4–6 daily; 2hr); Madrid (6 daily; 2hr 45min–3hr 15min); Palencia (2 daily; 2hr 15min); Salamanca (hourly; 1hr 10min); Toro (Mon–Sat roughly hourly, Sun 3 daily; 30min); Valladolid (Mon–Fri hourly, Sat & Sun 4–6 daily; 1hr 30min).

6

Euskal Herria: the País Vasco & Navarra

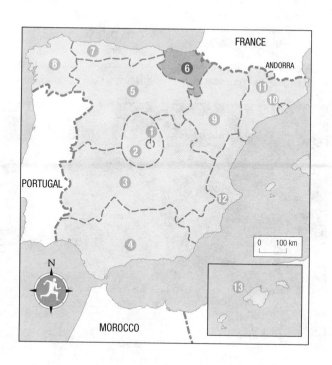

CHAPTER 6

Highlights

* **Playa de la Concha, San Sebastián** Admire the *belle époque* elegance of one of the world's great urban beaches. See p.457

* **Pintxos** Basque gourmet tapas, the best in Spain, are the way to dine in the *cascos viejos* throughout the region. See p.458

* **Mundaka estuary** Sublime scenery, world-class surfing and Gernika, the Basque spiritual capital. See p.469

* **Museo Guggenheim, Bilbao** This giant titanium sculpture has become the symbol of the regenerated city. See p.475

* **Zalduondo** Catch the traditional carnaval parade in this tiny Araban village. See p.485

* **Fiestas de San Fermín** Pamplona's famous fiesta is rowdy, dirty and lunatic, but for once the bulls get a fair shot. See p.490

* **Olite** Delightful village of ochre-coloured stone mansions on the edge of the Navarran plains. See p.493

▲ Surfing at Mundaka

Euskal Herria: the País Vasco & Navarra

E uskal Herria is the name the Basque people give to their own land, an area that includes the three Basque provinces of **Gipuzkoa**, **Bizkaia** and **Araba** (which today form the *Comunidad Autónoma del País Vasco*, or "Euskadi" in Basque), **Navarra** (Nafarroa) and part of southwestern France. It's an immensely beautiful region – mountainous, green and thickly forested. It rains often, and much of the time the countryside is shrouded in a fine mist. But the summers – if you don't mind the occasional shower – are a glorious escape from the unrelenting heat of the south.

Despite some of the heaviest industrialization on the peninsula (making it one of the wealthiest regions of Spain), Euskal Herria is remarkably unspoilt – neat and quiet inland, rugged and wild along the coast. **San Sebastián** is a major resort, with superb if crowded beaches and magnificent food, but any number of lesser-known, equally attractive villages line the coast all the way to **Bilbao**, home to the magnificent **Museo Guggenheim**. Inland, **Pamplona** boasts its exuberant **Fiestas de San Fermín**, while many other destinations have charms of their own, from the drama of the **Pyrenees** to the laidback elegance of **Vitoria-Gasteiz**.

Choice, quiet **accommodation** in rural spots abounds all over the region, thanks to the Basque government's **nekazalturismoa** (*agroturismo* or homestay) programme, which offers the opportunity to stay in traditional Basque farmhouses and private homes, usually in areas of outstanding beauty, at very reasonable cost (€35–60). In Navarra, as in much of the country, these are known as **casas rurales**, or *landa exteak*. You can get details from the region's many excellent local **tourist offices** (which also handle bookings), or on ⓦwww.nekatur.net, and ⓦwww .ecoturismorural.com for Navarra.

Some history

At the time of the **Roman invasion**, large areas of southwestern Gaul and parts of northern Iberia were inhabited by an ethnic group called the Aquitani, who spoke an ancestral version of Basque. Most of the Aquitani were defeated and Romanized, but the invaders, for once, saw little to gain from subjugating the Vascones, wild tribes living in the mountains of Euskal Herria. In exchange for allowing the Romans trading rights and free passage through their territory, the Vascones were allowed to retain their tribal customs, language and independence.

The Basques

The origin of **the Basques** is something of a mystery. They are a distinct people, generally with a different build from the French and Spanish and a different blood group distribution from the rest of Europe. Their language, the complex **Euskara**, is unrelated to any other, and was already spoken here when Indo-European languages such as Celtic and Latin began to arrive from the East some three thousand years ago. Written records were scarce until the first books in Euskara were published in the mid-sixteenth century; language and culture were maintained instead through oral traditions, including that of the *bertsolariak*, popular poets specializing in improvised verse, a tradition still alive today.

Archeological and genetic evidence suggests that the Basque people may be the last surviving representatives of Europe's first modern human population, commonly known as **Cro-Magnon man**. Skull fragments, believed to date from around 9000 BC, have been shown to be identical to present-day Basque cranial formation. Much anthropological work, above all by the revered José Miguel de Barandiarán (who died in 1991, aged 101), lends itself to the view that the Basques have continuously inhabited the western Pyrenees for thousands of years.

After the fall of Rome, the new rulers were not so accommodating. Successive **Visigoth** kings tried and failed to eradicate the Basques. The **Moors**, as they stormed through Spain, conquered the lowlands of Araba (Alava in Castilian) and Navarra as far north as Pamplona, but never really had a firm grip on the mountainous north. This new enemy, however, forced the Basques, hitherto a collection of more or less allied tribes, to unite, and in 818 one Basque leader, Iñigo Iñiguez, was proclaimed the first ruler of the **Kingdom of Navarre**. Inevitably, in the context of the holy wars sweeping Europe, the Basques at last embraced Christianity, while maintaining many ancestral beliefs and customs. Chief among these customs were the ancient laws by which the Basques governed themselves, maintained by oral tradition until the twelfth century, when they were first written down (in Castilian) and known as **fueros**.

Once the Reconquest was complete and Spain was being welded into a single kingdom, Navarre (by now ruled by French monarchs) was one of the missing pieces. The Reyes Católicos persuaded the Bizkaians, Gipuzkoans and Arabans to split away from Navarre and join Castile. In return, their ancient laws and privileges, the *fueros*, including exemption from customs duty, conscription and central taxation, would be respected. Under duress, the Navarrese agreed to the same deal, and by 1512 all four territories were subject to rule from Madrid.

Having given up their political independence in return for the right to self-government, the Basques jealously defended that right for the next four centuries. Not until 1876, and the final defeat of the **Carlists**, whom most Basques supported, did the victorious Liberals finally abolish the *fueros* altogether. However, this only served to inflame the Basque desire for self-government, and the late nineteenth and early twentieth centuries saw the emergence of Basque nationalism as an ideology. The conservative **Basque Nationalist Party** (PNV) was founded in 1895 by Sabino Arana, the son of a Carlist shipbuilder.

At the start of the Civil War, the Nationalists quickly seized control of predominantly rural, conservative Navarra and Araba. Bizkaia and Gipuzkoa, dominated by left-leaning industrial cities, supported the Republic, in return for promises of autonomy. Irun was quickly captured by Navarrese troops in 1936, cutting off the northern Republican zone from France. San Sebastián was rapidly surrendered to spare its avenues from bombardment. An autonomous Basque government, in practice limited to Bizkaia, was declared, with José Antonio Aguirre as *lehendakari*

Fiestas

January
19–20: Festividad de San Sebastián Twenty-four hours of festivities, including *tamborrada* (a march with pipes and drums).

February
Weekend before Ash Wednesday: Carnaval Throughout the region, but especially Bilbao, San Sebastián and Tolosa; traditional parade in Zalduondo.

March/April
March 4–12 A series of pilgrimages to the castle at Javier, birthplace of San Francisco Javier.
Semana Santa (Holy Week) Extensive Easter celebrations in Vitoria, also Segura.
Easter Sunday: Aberri Eguna The Basque National Day celebrated particularly in Bilbao.
April 28: Fiesta de San Prudencio is celebrated with *tamborradas*, and a re-enactment of the retreat is staged in Vitoria.

June
24: Fiestas de San Juan In Lekeitio, Laguardia and Tolosa.
Last week: Fiesta de San Pedro In Mundaka, with Basque dancing.

July
First week: Fiesta at Zumaia with dancing, Basque sports and an *encierro* on the beach.
7–14: Fiestas de San Fermín In Pamplona, featuring the famous Running of the Bulls.
22: Fiesta de la Magdalena In Bermeo, with torch-lit processions of fishing boats and the usual races and Basque sports.
24–28: *Encierro* in Tudela.
31: Día de San Ignacio Loyola Celebrated throughout, but above all in Loyola.

August
First weekend: Patron saint's celebration in Estella.
4–9: Fiesta de la Virgen Blanca In Vitoria, with bullfights, fireworks and *gigantones*.
14–17: Fiestas de Andra Mari In Ondarroa.
15: Semana Grande An explosion of celebration, notably in Bilbao, with Basque games and races, Gernika with an *encierro* and San Sebastián where the highlight is an International Fireworks Competition.

September
First week: Euskal Jaiak Basque games in San Sebastián.
4: Fiesta de San Antolín In Lekeitio, where the local youth attempt to knock the head off a goose.
9: Día del Pescador In Bermeo.
12: *Encierro* in Sangüesa.
14: Patron saint's day Olite, with yet more bulls.
Last two weeks: International Film Festival In San Sebastián.

(president); it lasted just nine months. After failing to capture Madrid, Franco turned on the Basques, who were finally conquered in June 1937, after a vicious campaign that included the infamous German bombing of **Gernika**.

After the war, Franco's boot went in hard, and as many as 21,000 people died in his attempts to tame the Basques. Public use of the language was forbidden

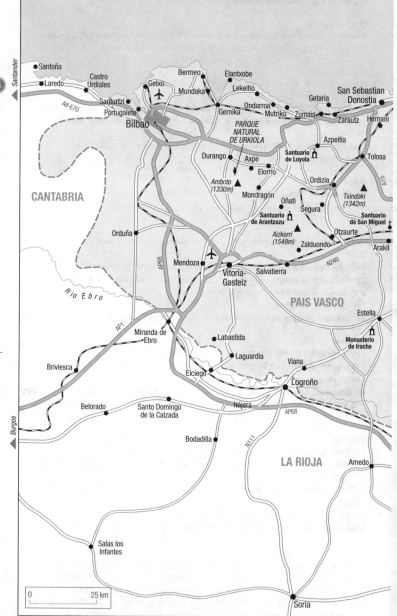

EUSKAL HERRIA: THE PAÍS VASCO & NAVARRA

MAR CANTÁBRICO

Santander

Santoña
Laredo
Castro Urdiales
A8-E70
Santurtzi
Portugalete
Getxo
Bilbao
Bermeo
Mundaka
Elantxobe
Lekeitio
Gernika
Ondarroa
Mutriku
Zumaia
Getaria
San Sebastian Donostia
Zarautz
Hernani
Azpeitia

PARQUE NATURAL DE URKIOLA

Durango
Axpe
Elorrio
Santuario de Loyola
Amboto (1330m)
Mondragón
Oñati
Ordizia
Txindoki (1342m)
Tolosa
Santuario de Arantzazu
Segura
Santuario de San Miguel
Aizkorri (1549m)
Zalduondo
Otzaurte
Arakil

CANTABRIA

Orduña

Mendoza
Vitoria-Gasteiz
Salvatierra
N240

PAIS VASCO

Rio Ebro

AP68

Miranda de Ebro
AP1

Briviesca

Belorado

Santo Domingo de la Calzada

Labastida
Laguardia
Elciego
Viana
Logroño
Nájera
AP68
Estella
Monasterio de Irache

Burgos

Bodadilla

N111

LA RIOJA

Arnedo

Salas los Infantes

Soria

0   25 km

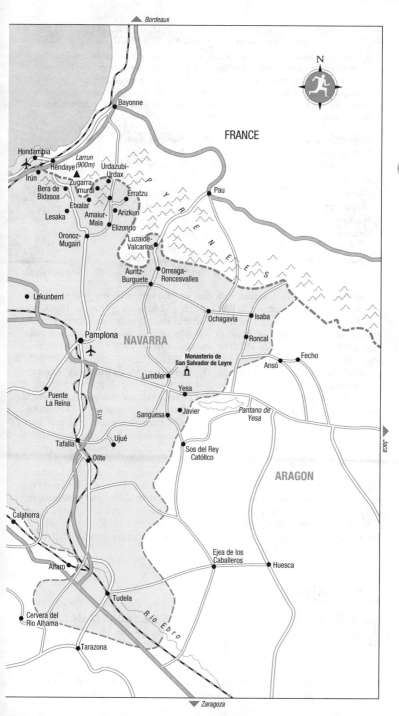

Bordeaux

N

FRANCE

Bayonne

Hondarribia
Larrun *(900m)*
Hendaye   Urdazubi-
Irún   Urdax
Bera de   Zugarra-
Bidasoa   murdi
Etxalar   Erratzu
Lesaka   Amaiur-   Arizkun
              Maia
                  Elizondo
Oronoz-   Luzaide-
Mugairi   Valcarlos

P
Y
R
E
N
E
E
S

Pau

Auritz-   Orreaga-
Burguete   Roncesvalles

Lekunberri

Ochagavia   Isaba

Pamplona   NAVARRA

Roncal

Monasterio de
San Salvador de Leyre   Fecho

Lumbier   Ansó

Yesa

Puente
La Reina   Javier
                Sangüesa   *Pantano de*
                          Yesa

Ujué

Tafalla

Olite   Sos del Rey
              Católico

ARAGON

Calahorra

Ejea de los
Caballeros   Huesca

Alfaro

Tudela

Cervera del   R i o   E b r o
Rio Alhama

Tarazona

A15

Jaca

Zaragoza

Basque names

Almost everywhere in Euskadi, street and road signs are in both Basque and Castilian, but the latter is often painted over. Many town halls have officially chosen to use the Basque names and this is reflected on new tourist brochures and maps. We have, therefore, used the Basque name for these towns. Some cities, however, including Pamplona and Bilbao, are still generally referred to by their Castilian names and in these cases we have supplied the Basque name in brackets.

Castilian name	Basque name
Bilbao	Bilbo
San Sebastián	Donostia
Pamplona	Iruña/Iruñea
Álava	Araba
Guipúzcoa	Gipuzkoa
Navarra	Nafarroa
Vizcaya	Bizkaia
Guernica	Gernika
Pasajes San Juan	Pasai Donibane

and central control was asserted with the gun. But state violence succeeded only in nurturing a new resistance, **ETA** (*Euskadi ta Askatasuna* – "Basque Homeland and Freedom"), founded in 1959 and whose most spectacular success was the assassination in Madrid of Franco's right-hand man and probable successor, Admiral Carrero Blanco in 1973. In contrast to the PNV, ETA became increasingly identified with the radical left.

Things started to change following the **transition to democracy**. The new constitution granted the Basques limited autonomy, with their own parliament and tax collection. Today, there's a regional police force, the red-bereted *ertzaintza*, much in evidence in the streets, and the Basque language is taught in schools and universities. The Basque flag (*ikurriña*), banned under Franco, flies everywhere. Basque demands for independence have not ended, however, and the violence has continued. Since 1968, ETA is estimated to have killed around 850 people, with targets ranging from members of the Spanish police and armed forces to Basque businessmen and politicians, academics, journalists, the tourist industry and random civilians. Assorted ceasefires have come and gone, most recently the so-called "**permanent ceasefire**" declared in March 2006, and Batasuna, the political party most closely identified with ETA, has been officially banned since 2002. Meanwhile, human rights organizations continue to denounce not only ETA's activities, but also police brutality and alleged torture, and the dispersal of ETA prisoners to jails around Spain.

San Sebastián

The undisputed queen of the Basque resorts, **SAN SEBASTIÁN** (Donostia) is a picturesque city, with magnificent beaches and some of the best **food** in Spain. It's also the capital of Gipuzkoa, and has been a fashionable place to escape the southern heat since the royal family made it their summer residence in the nineteenth century – in July and August, it's packed. Set around the deep, still bay of La Concha and enclosed by rolling low hills, the city is beautifully situated; the **Parte Vieja** (Old Quarter) sits on the eastern promontory, its back to the wooded slopes of Monte Urgull, while newer development has spread along the banks of the Urumea, home to the city's wonderful *belle époque* architecture, and around the edge of the bay to the foot of Monte Igeldo.

Arrival and information

Most **buses** arrive at Plaza Pío XII (the ticket office is around the corner facing the river), fifteen-minutes' walk from **Centro**, the city's commercial heart. To get to the **Parte Vieja**, farther north, take bus #28 (€1.20) to Alameda del Boulevard. Buses from Pasaia San Pedro and Hernani arrive on c/Okendo, just below the Parte Vieja, and from the airport, Irun and Hondarribia on nearby Plaza de Gipuzkoa. RENFE's main-line **Estación del Norte** is across the Río Urumea on Paseo de Francia, in the area known as **Gros**, although local lines of the EuskoTren from Hendaia, or Bilbao via Zumaia, have their terminus on Plaza Easo at the **Estación de Amara** in Centro. The small **airport** serving domestic flights is 22km from the city centre, just outside Hondarribia; an airport bus plies back and forth as necessary (30min; €3). Taxis should be around €25. Direct buses also run to San Sebastián from the airport at Bilbao.

San Sebastián's helpful **turismo** is at c/Regina Regente 3 (June–Sept Mon–Sat 8.30am–8pm, Sun 10am–2pm & 3.30–7pm; Oct–May Mon–Sat 9am–1.30pm & 3.30–7pm, Sun 10am–2pm; ☎943 481 166, ⓦwww.sansebastian turismo.com), by the Puente de Zurriola. Donosti Tour runs daily guided **bus tours** around the city from Teatro Victoria (☎696 429 847, ⓦwww.busturistikoa .com; no tours Feb; €12).

Accommodation

Rates in the **Parte Vieja** are not especially higher than elsewhere, but there's often more availability in **Centro** or **Gros**.

Parte Vieja

Hotel Parma Paseo de Salamanca 10 ☎943 428 893, ⓦwww.hotelparma.com. Nicely located between the Parte Vieja and Paseo Nuevo, this rather characterless modern building offers comfortable rooms with all amenities, including free wi-fi; the best overlook the sea. ❺

Pensión Amaiur c/31 de Agosto 44, 2º ☎943 429 654, ⓦwww.pensionamaiur.com. A justly popular *pensión* in one of the few houses to survive the 1813 fire. Eleven attractive bedrooms, with an immaculate tiled bathroom for every two rooms; pay a little extra for a room with external window. Guests can access two kitchens with microwave, fridge and free coffee, and internet. ❷

Pensión Anne c/Esterlines 15, 2º ☎943 421 438, ⓦwww.pensionanne.com. Renovated *pensión* with friendly, English-speaking staff. Most rooms share bathrooms, but you can have one en suite. It tends to get booked up fast. ❸

Pension Edorta c/Puerto 15, 1–2º ☎943 423 773, ⓦwww.pensionedorta.com. Friendly, attractive *pensión* in a nice old house, where the colourful, fresh decor includes exposed stone walls and wooden beams. Some rooms have small balconies, while you can also pay less for a room with shared bath. ❹

Pensión Kaia c/Puerto 12, 2º ☎943 431 342, ⓦwww.pensionkaia.com. A comfortable two-star *pensión*, with pleasant, brightly painted but smallish en-suite modern rooms. Single rates are good value. ❹

Pensión San Lorenzo c/San Lorenzo 2, 1º ☎943 425 516, ⓦwww.pensionsanlorenzo.com. Clean, if unexciting, modernized *pensión* with just five en-suite rooms, bare wood floors, free wi-fi and a self-catering kitchen. Reserve well in advance. ❸

Centro

Hostal Alemana c/San Martín 53, 1º ☎943 462 544, ⓦwww.hostalalemana.com. Great location behind La Concha, housed in a fine *belle époque* building with spacious but fairly average, modern rooms, and a bit overpriced in the summer. Parking €11.50 daily. ❹

Hotel de Londres y de Inglaterra c/Zubieta 2 ☎943 440 770, ⓦwww.hlondres.com. This imposing yet charming nineteenth-century hotel, facing the beach, is the best luxury choice in the centre, with large, comfortable en-suite rooms, and wonderful sea views. Extras include satellite TV and parking on site. **7**

Hotel María Cristina c/Okendo 1 ⌕943 437 600, ⓦwww.luxurycollection.com/mariacristina. A city landmark, this magnificent hotel was built in 1912. Rooms are tastefully decorated in *belle époque*

style, with extra-comfy beds and marble-clad bathrooms. **7**

Hotel Niza c/Zubieta 56 ⌕943 426 663, ⓦwww .hotelniza.com. Stylish hotel, in a 1920s building right across from the beach. Rooms are simply decorated in modern style, with bare wood floors and wi-fi; all cost the same, though only half have sea views. **5**

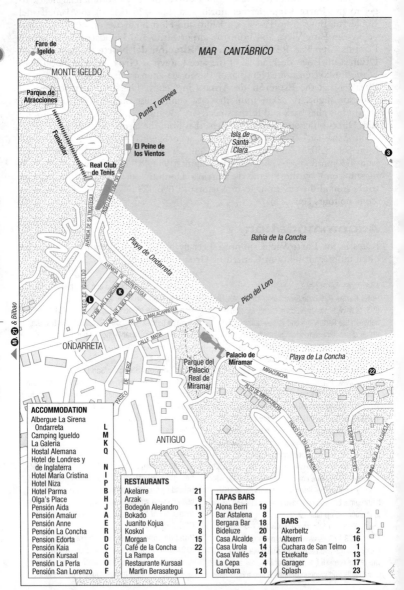

MAR CANTÁBRICO

Faro de Igeldo

MONTE IGELDO

Parque de Atracciones

Funicular

Punta Torrepea

El Peine de los Vientos

Real Club de Tenis

PASEO DE EDUARDO CHILLIDA

Isla de Santa Clara

Bahía de la Concha

Playa de Ondarreta

AVENIDA DE SATRÚSTEGUI

PASEO DE IGELDO

AVENIDA DE SATRÚSTEGUI

L **K**

CALLE ANZA AROSTEGI

CALLE ANZA BEATRIZ

AV. DE ZUMALACÁRREGUI

CALLE MATÍA

Pico del Loro

Playa de La Concha

ONDARRETA

Parque del Palacio Real de Miramar

Palacio de Miramar

MIRACONCHA

ALTO DE MIRACONCHA

PASEO DE

ANTIGUO

PASEO DE HÉRO

PASEO DE ALFEREZA

PASEO DE JOSÉ ITURRA DE PRADA

◀ **M**, **21** & Bilbao

22

ACCOMMODATION	
Albergue La Sirena Ondarreta	**L**
Camping Igueldo	**M**
La Galeria	**K**
Hostal Alemana	**Q**
Hotel de Londres y de Inglaterra	**N**
Hotel María Cristina	**I**
Hotel Niza	**P**
Hotel Parma	**B**
Olga's Place	**H**
Pensión Aida	**J**
Pensión Amaiur	**A**
Pensión Anne	**E**
Pensión La Concha	**R**
Pension Edorta	**D**
Pensión Kaia	**C**
Pensión Kursaal	**G**
Pensión La Perla	**O**
Pensión San Lorenzo	**F**

RESTAURANTS	
Akelarre	21
Arzak	9
Bodegón Alejandro	11
Bokado	3
Juanito Kojua	7
Koskol	8
Morgan	15
Café de la Concha	22
La Rampa	5
Restaurante Kursaal Martín Berasategui	12

TAPAS BARS	
Alona Berri	19
Bar Astalena	8
Bergara Bar	18
Bideluze	20
Casa Alcalde	6
Casa Urola	14
Casa Vallés	24
La Cepa	4
Ganbara	10

BARS	
Akerbeltz	2
Altxerri	16
Cuchara de San Telmo	1
Etxekalte	13
Garager	17
Splash	23

Pensión La Concha c/San Martín 51 ☏ 943 450 389, ⓦ www.pensionlaconcha.net. Bright, modern, but rather characterless en-suite rooms with TV and internet access – you're paying for the location, a few steps from La Concha beach. ④

Pensión La Perla c/Inazio Loiola 10 ☏ 943 428 123, ⓦ www.pensionlaperla.com.

Excellent-value *pensión*, near Catedral del Buen Pastor, offering spotless en-suite rooms, simply decorated. Some have balconies. ③

Gros

Olga's Place c/Zabaleta 49, 4º ☏ 943 326 725, ⓔ olgatalaya@hotmail.com. This simple private

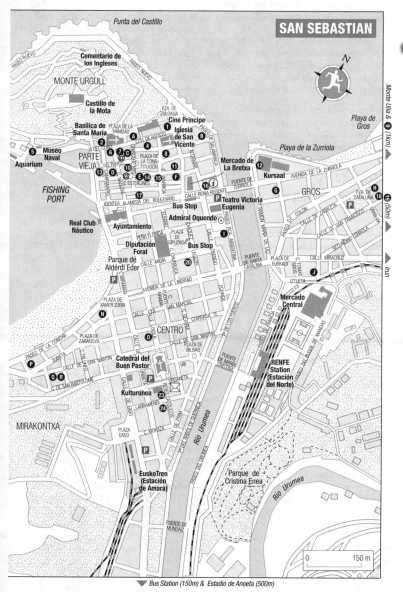

Monte Ulia & ⑨ (1km)

Playa de Gros

Playa de la Zurriola

GROS

⑱ (50m)

Irun

SAN SEBASTIAN

Punta del Castillo

Cementario de los Ingleses

MONTE URGULL

Castillo de la Mota

Basilica de Santa María

Cine Principe

Iglesia de San Vicente

Museo Naval Aquarium

PARTE VIEJA

PLAZA DE LA CONSTITUCIÓN

Mercado de La Bretxa

Kursaal

FISHING PORT

Teatro Victoria Eugenia

Bus Stop

Admiral Oquendo

Real Club Náutico

Ayuntamiento

Diputación Foral

Bus Stop

Parque de Alderdi Eder

Mercado Central

CENTRO

MIRAKONTXA

Catedral del Buen Pastor

Kulturunea

RENFE Station (Estación del Norte)

Río Urumea

EuskoTren (Estación de Amara)

Parque de Cristina Enea

Río Urumea

0   150 m

▼ Bus Station (150m) & Estadio de Anoeta (500m)

hostel is hugely popular with surfers heading for nearby La Zurriola beach, and it's also a short walk from the Parte Vieja and the train and bus stations. Beds in four- to six-person dorms cost just under €30, and the shared lounges have free internet access. ❶

Pensión Aida Iztueta 9, 1º, Gros ☏ 943 327 800, ⓦ www.pensionesconencanto.com. Friendly *pensión* with cheerful pastel decor and exposed stonework. Rooms have tiled bathrooms and showers. Free wi-fi. ❹

Pensión Kursaal c/Peña y Goñi 2, 1º ☏ 943 292 666, ⓦ www.pensionesconencanto.com. Co-managed with the similar *Aida*, this is in a superb location just a few steps from the Kursaal itself, with large, modern rooms and bathrooms. ❸

The rest of the city

Albergue La Sirena Ondarreta Paseo de Igeldo 25 ☏ 943 310 268. San Sebastián's popular youth hostel is a long, long way from the Parte Vieja,

though at least it's just a few minutes' walk from the end of Ondarreta beach (bus #5, #16 or #25). En-suite six-bunk rooms are €16.50 for under 25s and €18.05 for everyone else. There's a 2am curfew and 11pm "quiet" rule.

Camping Igueldo Paseo Padre Orkolaga 69, Barrio de Igueldo ☏ 943 214 502, ⓦ www.campingigueldo .com. San Sebastián's campsite is excellent, but it's 5km from the centre on the landward side of Monte Igeldo (up a steep hill), reached by bus #16 from Alameda del Boulevard (every 30min; 30min). €15 for a tent pitch in summer, €29 if you have a car.

La Galeria c/Infanta Cristina 1–3 ☏ 943 317 559, ⓦ www.hotellagaleria.com. Although it's a long walk from the Parte Vieja, this hotel is a gem, set in a beautifully restored *belle époque* house just back from Ondarreta beach. Rooms are simply but stylishly decorated, each with a different theme based on a painter such as Picasso, Dalí or Miró. Free parking and wi-fi. ❺

The City

The **Parte Vieja**, or Old Quarter, at the base of Monte Urgull, is the most fascinating and enjoyable part of San Sebastián. In its cramped and lively pedestrian streets, crowds congregate in the evenings to wander among numerous bars and shops or sample the shellfish from the traders down by the fishing point. Much of this area was destroyed by a fire in 1813 (started by British troops) and subsequently restored, though the old medieval wall was swept away to allow expansion later the same century – the Alameda del Boulevard marks its former course. San Sebastián's chief sights are the elaborate Baroque facade of the eighteenth-century **Basílica de Santa María** (Mon–Sat 8am–2pm & 4–8pm) and the more elegantly restrained sixteenth-century Gothic **Iglesia de San Vicente** (Mon–Sat 8.30am–1pm & 6.30–8.30pm). The centre of the old quarter is the **Plaza de la Constitución** (known by the locals simply as *La Consti*) – the numbers on the balconies around the square date from the days when it was used as a bullring. Set around the cloisters of a former convent, just off c/31 de Agosto on Plaza Zuloaga, is the excellent **Museo San Telmo**; closed for renovation at the time of writing, it centres on a fine collection of local art, but also includes displays on Basque ethnography.

For a lovely stroll, especially at sunset, it's well worth following the coastal footpath that leads around **Monte Urgull** at sea level. Alternatively, a stairway off the plaza flanking the museum rises to the top of the hill, crisscrossed by winding paths. From the mammoth figure of Christ and the **Castillo de la Mota** (summer 8am–8pm; winter 8am–6pm) on its summit, a forty-five-minute climb, there are great views out to sea and back across the bay to town. On the way down you can stop at the **Cementerio de los Ingleses**, an overgrown but atmospheric patch of ground dedicated to British soldiers killed in the First Carlist War, or the **Aquarium** (April–June & Sept Mon–Fri 10am–8pm, Sat & Sun 10am–9pm; July & Aug daily 10am–9pm; Oct–March Mon–Fri 10am–7pm, Sat & Sun 10am–8pm; €10, under-13s €6; ⓦ www.aquariumss.com) on the harbour; it contains the skeleton of a whale caught in the last century and an extensive history of Basque navigation. There aren't that many fish to see, though you can have fun walking through the middle of a giant aquarium in a perspex tube.

Though its summit is smothered by a tacky amusement park, **Monte Igeldo**, around the bay, affords still better views: stroll round the bay to its base near Real Club de Tennis, from where the **funicular** (daily: summer 10am–8pm; winter 11am–7pm; every 15min; €1.20), built in 1912, will carry you to the top (bus #16 stops at the funicular). Continuing along the *paseo* past the tennis club, you end up at Eduardo Chillida's striking iron **sculpture**, *El Peine de los Vientos* (The Comb of the Winds), looking as if it is trying to grasp the waves in its powerful rusting arms. More of Chillida's work is on display at the Museo Chillida-Leku in Hernani (see p.463).

Beaches

San Sebastián boasts four **beaches**: Playa de la Concha, Playa de Ondarreta, Playa de la Zurriola and Playa de Gros. **La Concha**, the most central, is deservedly the most celebrated; indeed, it ranks among the very finest city beaches in the world. A wide crescent of yellow sand, stretching around the bay from the old quarter, it's filled with an almost impenetrable mass of flesh during much of the summer, enlivened by sellers of peeled prawns and cold drinks, and offering great swimming out to the diving platforms moored in the Bahía La Concha. The small island out in the bay, **Isla de Santa Clara**, makes a good spot for picnics; a boat leaves from the port at the edge of the old town every half-hour in the summer (daily 10am–8pm; €2 round-trip).

La Concha and **Ondarreta** are the best beaches for swimming – the latter is a continuation of the same strand beyond the rocky outcrop that supports the **Palacio de Miramar** (daily 8am–9pm; free), once the summer home of Spain's royal family. You can walk around the pleasant gardens, but the house itself – now a posh *conservatori* – is off limits.

Far less crowded, and popular with surfers, are **Playa de la Zurriola** and the adjacent **Playa de Gros**, across the river. Surfers should make for Pukas at Avda. de la Zurriola 24 (Ⓦwww.pukassurf.com), which rents boards (€30/day, €10/1hr) and offers lessons. The giant translucent glass blocks of Rafael Moneo's **Kursaal** appeared on the elegant promenade at the turn of the millennium (Ⓦwww .kursaal.org; guided tours Fri–Sun 1.30pm; tickets on sale at noon; €2). In addition to an auditorium and art gallery, the building houses a pleasant café–restaurant (see p.459) with an outside terrace in summer.

Eating and drinking

San Sebastián is home to some of the finest **restaurants** and **tapas bars** in the country, ranging from traditional, earthy Basque *tabernas* to celebrated houses of *nueva cocina vasca* (new Basque cuisine).

Tapas bars

San Sebastián produces the best **tapas** in Spain (*pintxos* in Basque), and the **Parte Vieja** is crammed with an astonishing range of *pintxos* bars, each with an overwhelming array of snacks and specialities (typically €1.50–4.50). Do as the locals do and head out between 8 and 9pm on a *txikiteo*, or bar crawl, spending around ten minutes at each place; it's usual to try just one *pintxo*, preferably standing and washed down with a small glass (or *txikitos*) of red wine, a *zurito* of beer or a glass of *txakoli*, a fizzy, dry white wine made exclusively in the Basque Country. Real connoisseurs should head to **Gros**, noted for its innovative, high-quality *pintxos*. Things start to wind down by 11pm.

Alona Berri c/Bermingham 24. One of the most popular tapas bars in Gros, this is an upscale place with award-winning *pintxos* from €2.

Bar Astalena c/Iñigo 1. Tapas bar in a great old-quarter location, serving a mouthwatering selection of *pintxos*, cold at one end of the bar and hot at the other, with all sorts of ham and shellfish delights, and delicious pistachio croquettes for vegetarians.

Bergara Bar c/Gral. Artetxe 8. Crammed with drinkers most nights, this swanky bar in Gros has bottles of wine set on the tables and a fabulous array of lavish *pintxos*.

Bideluze Plaza Gipuzkoa 14. Friendly, relaxed café-pub, overlooking the pretty green Plaza Gipuzkoa, with a warren of little nooks and crannies and overflowing with train memorabilia and other junk. The *pintxos* are great, with plenty of eggy concoctions at breakfast time, while in the evening it attracts a mixed crowd of drinkers.

Casa Alcalde c/Mayor 19. Large, elegant *belle époque* bar, with hams hanging from the ceiling and a vast selection of *pintxos* from €1.35, including thinly sliced ham (€4), *bacalao* (cod) in *pil-pil* sauce, cheese and shellfish – a good place for

Basque cuisine

Basque cuisine is accepted as Spain's finest, and the people here are compulsive eaters: try *bacalao* (cod) *a la vizcaina* or *al pil-pil*, *merluza* (hake) *a la vasca*, *txipirones en su tinta* (squid cooked in its ink) or *txangurro* (spider crab), which you'll find in reasonably priced roadside *caseríos* (*baserri* in Basque) throughout the region. In earthy cider-houses (*sidrerías* or *sagardotegiak*), slabs of beef, *bacalao* and chorizo are washed down with all the cider you can drink, served straight from the barrel (see box, p.460). You'll also come across traditional Basque food in the form of tapas (known in the Basque Country as **pintxos**) in virtually every bar, freshly cooked and usually excellent.

The tradition of **gastronomic societies** (*txokos*) is unique to the Basque Country. They were first founded in the mid-nineteenth century, as socializing places for different craftsmen. Controversy has surrounded the traditional barring of women (which is now changing); all cooking is done by men who pay a token membership fee for the facilities. Members prepare elaborate dishes to perfection as a hobby, and it could be said that true Basque cookery has largely retreated to these societies. The so-called **nueva cocina vasca** (new Basque cuisine), heavily influenced by French cuisine, is increasingly evident on menus throughout the country. Note also that in most Basque towns you'll find **local taverns** affiliated to the major political parties – fascinating, cheap (and perfectly safe) places to eat and drink. Batasuna bars go by the name *Herriko*, while PNV taverns are known as *Batzoki*.

beginners. You can also have full meals in a small restaurant at the back. Daily 10am–4pm & 6–11pm.

Casa Urola c/Fermín Calbetón 20. Classic Basque restaurant, with mains from €18, where the tiny tapas bar at the front serves elaborate and unusual *pintxos*, including goose liver in port sauce, plus the best *txakoli* in town (€1.50 per glass). Daily 1–4pm & 8–11.30pm.

Casa Vallés Reyes Católicos 10. An attractive bar with wood panels, tables and benches, established in 1942. It tends to stay busier longer than those in the old quarter mid-week, with tapas that are just as good – mainly fresh fish (hake and eel) and ham-based *pintxos* from €1.50. Daily 8.30am–11pm.

La Cepa c/31 de Agosto 7. Inexpensive *raciones* are served amid a decor of bullfighting posters and dangling hams; little compartments below the glass table-tops hold all sorts of treasures. The most celebrated snack is *jamón jabugo*, the most sought-after cured ham in Spain (€4.50), but the grilled squid and salt-cod omelette is also excellent. Mon & Wed–Sun 11am–midnight.

Cuchara de San Telmo c/31 de Agosto. Bright, lively and very narrow bar with a hippy-esque edge, where the tables spill out into an otherwise empty square at the foot of Monte Urgull. The *pintxos* are irresistible.

Ganbara c/San Jerónimo 21. A small but popular bar with quality tapas, the highlight being the *kokotxas de bacalao con almejas* (cod with clams). Tues, Wed & Fri–Sun 11am–3.15pm & 6–11.45pm.

Restaurants

Most **restaurants** are in the **Parte Vieja**, but there are also a few in **Centro** and farther afield, especially at the top end. Prices in the old quarter tend to reflect the area's popularity, but lunchtime *menús* are generally good value.

Akelarre Paseo Padre Orkolaga 56 ☎943 311 209, ⓦwww.akelarre.net. On the far side of Monte Igeldo – take a taxi – *Akelarre* is home of lauded chef Pedro Subijana, and a trend-setter for *nueva cocina vasca*. Enjoy magnificent views, a real fireplace and exquisite dishes – the *foie gras* is especially renowned, and watch out for creations such as pepper ice cream. Reckon on €135 per head.

Arzak Avda Alcalde Elosegui 273 ☎943 285 593, ⓦwww.arzak.es. On the lower slopes of Monte Ulia, 1km east of the centre. A shrine of *nueva cocina vasca*, named after Michelin-star winning chef Juan Mari Arzak, who serves up a creative menu designed to mesmerize in an antique dining room with first-class service – expect to pay around €145 per head for the experience. Closed Nov and second half of June.

Bokado Plaza Jacques Cousteau 1 ☎943 431 842. Stylish new restaurant in an unbeatable setting – alongside the aquarium right at the mouth of the bay – with tables on a large sea-view terrace as well as indoors. The full menu features meat dishes from €25 and fish from €33, but you can also sample *pintxos*, such as spider crab and leek ravioli (€3).

Bodegón Alejandro c/Fermín Calbetón 4 ☎943 427 158, ⓦwww.bodegonalejandro.com. An excellent restaurant from the stable of celebrated Basque chef Martin Berasategui, with two pale-yellow dining rooms and an exceptional tasting *menú* (€35.70) which changes every other day, featuring Basque classics such as peppers stuffed with cod, and roast veal.

Café de la Concha Paseo de La Concha s/n. Splendidly perched above La Concha beach, the terrace of this café-restaurant makes a great spot for a people-watching breakfast or lunch; the food is unexceptional, but the location makes it worth it. Closed Sun.

Juanito Kojua c/Puerto 14 ☎943 420 180, ⓦwww.juanitokojua.com. An exceptional top-notch seafood restaurant, off Plaza de la Constitución, holding two basic dining areas with wooden beams, and traditional decor behind the bar. Sublime fresh fish from €18, or €29.50 dinner *menú*.

Koskol c/Iñigo 5. A very simple place with a decent spread of *pintxos* (try the tasty omelettes), and a cheap *menú* (€9 weekdays, €12 weekends) that's a bargain.

Morgan c/Narrika 7. A bohemian clientele and a jazz soundtrack set the tone for this *cafetería* specializing in cheaper *nueva cocina vasca* dishes, emphasizing lighter first courses – stuffed aubergin, venison carpaccio – and creative desserts, rather than the traditional hearty main meals. Lunch *menú* €15, dinner *menú* €22. Closed Tues eve & Sun.

La Rampa Muelle 30. The best (and last) of a string of seafood restaurants on the old fishing harbour, with tables on the quayside and straightforward, tasty seafood, best sampled in the afternoons with a glass of wine. Reckon on around €40 for a meal. Closed Tues eve & Wed.

Restaurante Kursaal Martin Berasategui c/Zurriola 1, Kursaal ☎943 003 162, ⓦwww.restaurantekursaal.com. Chef Berasategui now has two outlets at the Kursaal; in addition to this superb restaurant upstairs, which serves sumptuous tasting menús at €48.50 and €64.50, there's also a less formal *cafetería* downstairs. Wed–Sat 11.30am–1.30pm & 8.30–10.30pm, Sun 11.30am–1.30pm.

Bars and clubs

In the evenings, you'll find no shortage of action, with **clubs** and **bars** everywhere. The two main areas are the **Parte Vieja**, especially along Fermín Calbetón, Puerto and Juan de Bilbao, and in **Centro** around the intersection of c/Reyes Católicos and c/Larramendi, where a large number of the city's more expensive music pubs and cafés are located.

Akerbeltz c/Virgin de Coro 10. A cosy bar with exposed stone walls and decent beers (Paulaner on tap), usually filled with amicable locals all day. Daily 11am–3am.

Altxerri c/Reina Regente 2. Long-established, stylish jazz bar with a slightly older crowd. Tues–Thurs & Sun 4pm–2am, Fri & Sat 4pm–3am.

Etxekalte c/Mari 11. A fashionable bar near the harbourfront, with a mix of jazz, fusion and soul, and live sets most weekends from around midnight. Tues–Thurs & Sun 6pm–4am, Fri & Sat 6pm–5am.

Garager Alameda del Boulevard 22. Large, friendly pub, with wood beams, slot machines and Murphys and Guinness on tap (€5.50 per pint). There's a late-night club upstairs. Daily 10am–2am.

Splash c/Sanchez Toca 7. Chic bar in Centro, behind the cathedral, with minimalist decor, stylish seating, soft lighting and a mix of garage and hip-hop. Noon–3.30am.

Zibbibo Club Centro de Ocio Illumbe, Paseo Miramón 2. One of the best clubs in the city lies in Illumbe, on the southern edge of town, with a warehouse feel and big sound system. It's definitely worth the cab fare if you fancy dancing till the early hours. Don't bother turning up before midnight.

Festivals

The summer sees a constant succession of **fiestas**, many involving Basque sports including the annual rowing (*trainera*) races between the villages along the coast, which culminate in a final regatta on September 9. The **Jazz Festival** (T 943 481 900, W www.jazzaldia.com), held all over town for six days during the latter half of July, invariably attracts top jazz and blues names, as well as hordes of people on their way home from the Fiesta de San Fermín in Pamplona. During the week around August 15 – known as **Semana Grande** or Aste Nagusia – numerous concerts, special events and fireworks are laid on. San Sebastián's **Film Festival** takes place in the second half of September (W www.sansebastian festival.com).

Sidrerías

If you're in San Sebastián between late January and early May, a visit to one of the many **sidrerías** (*sagardotegiak* in Basque, or cider houses) in the area between **Astigarraga and Hernani**, about 6km from town, is a must. Several now stay open all year, so it's worth checking at the *turismo* even in summer.

Cider production is one of the oldest traditions in the Basque Country – until the Civil War and the subsequent move towards industrialization, practically every farmhouse in Gipuzkoa and, to a lesser extent, the other provinces produced cider. A valuable commodity, it was used for barter, which remained the main form of exchange in rural communities until comparatively recently, and the farms were practically open houses where local people drank cider and socialized – the *bertsolariak* tradition of oral poetry originated in such places.

Cider houses are again flourishing, and for €15–25 you can feast on *bacalao*, *chuleton* and cheese, washed down with unlimited quantities of cider straight from the barrel, and enjoy the raucous atmosphere in general. Of the seventy or so *sidrerías*, some of the most accessible include *Petritegi* and *Gartziategi*, just a few kilometres out of town in Astigarraga, while many of the more rustic and authentic ones, such as *Sarasola* and *Oiarbide*, are on the *ruta de las sidrerías* (cider trail) just beyond Astigarraga. Check in the *turismo* for a full list, or visit W www.sagardotegiak.com.

Listings

Books For maps and books on travel and all things related to the Basque Country, head for Graphos on the corner of Alameda del Boulevard and c/Nagusia (Mon–Fri 10am–1.30pm & 4–7.30pm, Sat 10am–2pm).

Car rental Operators include Avis, Triunfo 2 ☎943 461 527; Budget, Alcalde José Elosegui ☎943 392 945; Europcar, RENFE train station ☎943 322 304; and Hertz, Travesía de Garbera 1 ☎943 392 223.

Emergency Call ☎112 for accident, police or fire emergencies.

Film Venues include the ten-plex Cine Principe, on the Plaza de Zuloaga by San Telmo in the Parte Vieja, and the Cine Trueba at Secundino Esnaola 2,

across the Puente Santa Catalina in Gros, which often shows art and *versión original* movies.

Football San Sebastián's Primera Division side, Real Sociedad, play at the Estadio Anoeta, a short walk south of the main bus station, served by bus #28.

Hospital Hospital Complex Donostia, Dr Begiristain 114 ☎943 007 000.

Internet access *Donosti-Net* at c/Embeltrán 2 (daily 9am–9pm; €3/hr) and *Internet-Locutorio Puerto* c/Puerto 14 (daily 11am–11pm; €2/hr).

Post office The main office is at c/Urdaneta 7.

Taxis Radio-Taxi Donostia ☎943 464 646, Tele-Taxi Vallina ☎943 404 040.

East to the French border

San Sebastián is 21km from the **French frontier**, with all routes to Biarritz and Paris channelled through the dull border town of **Irún**. The attractive fishing port of **Hondarribia**, north of Irún, is well worth a look, while the main route south from Irún crosses quickly into Navarra, and leads initially via the beautiful **Valle de Bidasoa** to Pamplona.

Hondarribia

Set along the Bidasoa river mouth and facing the French town of Hendaye across Bahía de Txingudi, the town of **HONDARRIBIA** lies 35km east of San Sebastián, and 6km north of the rail line at Irún. It comprises two main areas: the picturesque, walled **Casco Antiguo**, the medieval upper town, and just to the north the commercial centre known as **La Marina**. The Casco Antiguo can be approached from c/Jabier Ugarte and the *turismo*, or up c/Nagusia from the more traditional entrance to the south, the fifteenth-century **Puerta de Santa María**. Climbing to the **Plaza de Armas**, the central square, you'll pass fine half-timbered houses with painted balconies and studded doors, some displaying family coats of arms above doorways. The plaza itself is dominated by the gorgeous **Castille de Carlos V**, now one of the finest *paradors* in Spain. It was started in the tenth century by Sancho the Strong of Navarra and subsequently extended by Carlos V in the sixteenth. Just down from here, the smaller, arcaded **Plaza Gipuzkoa** is worth seeking out, as are the streets in La Marina just inland from the waterfront, where traditional, wood-beamed Basque houses are interspersed with bars offering some of the best seafood and *pintxos* around. During the summer, **Playa Hondartza**, immediately north of town, is an alternative beach to ultra-crowded San Sebastián.

Practicalities

The helpful **turismo** is on c/Javier Ugarte 6, just off Plaza San Kristobal, at the base of the road up to the Casco Antiguo (July–Sept Mon–Fri 10am–7.30pm, Sat & Sun 10am–2pm & 4–8pm; Oct–June Mon–Fri 9.30am–1.30pm & 4–6.30pm, Sat & Sun 10am–2pm; ☎943 645 458, ⓦwww.bidasoaturismo.com).

Hondarribia makes a comfortable day-trip from San Sebastián, but it's also a lovely spot to spend the night, with plenty of characterful **accommodation**.

Options in the heart of the Casco Antiguo include the pretty *Hotel San Nikolas* at Plaza de Armas 6 (☎943 644 278, ⓦwww.hotelsannikolas.com; ④), with its blue balconies and en-suite rooms, and *Hotel Palacete* at Plaza Gipuzkoa 5 (☎943 640 813, ⓦwww.hotelpalacete.net; ⑤), with tasteful modern rooms and a nice little courtyard. Best of all is the magnificent *Parador de Hondarribia* (*El Emperador*), in the Castille de Carlos V on Plaza de Armas (☎943 645 500, ⓦwww.parador.es; ⑧), with its opulent rooms, great views and smart restaurant.

Apart from the formal hotel restaurants, the upper town holds very few **places to eat**, though the *Mamutzar*, c/Eguzki 10 (closed Tues), serves a good-value *menú* (€10). Alternatively, head down to c/Santiago and parallel c/San Pedro and c/Zuloaga, a couple of short blocks inland from the water in La Marina; *Lekuona*, at no. 45, is one of several good *pintxos* bars on c/San Pedro, for example. For something special, join the crowds on the wooden benches of the classic *Hermandad de Pescadores* at c/Zuloaga 12 (☎943 642 738; closed Sun eve & Mon).

Inland to Pamplona

The N121a follows the attractive **Valle de Bidasoa** down from Irún towards Pamplona. Several well-preserved towns lie just off the highway, including **Bera de Bidasoa**, **Lesaka** and **Etxalar** – all just over the border in Navarra and often swarming with French tourists at the weekends. Turn left at Oieregi, just under halfway to Pamplona, to reach the Valle de Baztán, where the Navarran Pyrenees really start (see p.499).

Bera (Vera) de Bidasoa and around

BERA (VERA) DE BIDASOA offers some of the finest old wood-beamed and traditional stone houses in the region. The highway passes through the newer part of the village; head left, following signs for Lizuniaga, and you'll find yourself on the main road through the older part of town, where you'll pass through the delightful main square, Plaza Juan de Altzate, before eventually crossing a little stream at the eastern end of the village. When local politics finally permits, the **Itzea Baroja** here, the former home of the Basque writer Pío Baroja, just past the old customs house at c/Itzea 24, is expected to reopen as a museum.

The local **turismo** is on the Lizuniaga road, a few hundred metres before Plaza Juan de Altzate (Easter & mid-June to mid-Sept Tues–Sat 10am–2pm & 4–7pm, Sun 10am–2pm; ☎948 631 222, ⓦwww.berakoudala.net). The fanciest **place to stay** is the big pink *Hotel Churrut*, c/Fueros 2 (☎948 625 540, ⓦwww.hotel churrut.com; ⑤), while *Hostal Auzoa*, just across the stream at c/Illekueta 11 (☎948 631 584, ⓦwww.hotelchurrut.com; ③), has simple rooms and serves reasonable meals out on its terrace.

Six kilometres northeast of Bera, straddling the French border, **Larrun** (900m) is an easy climb; from the summit you'll get spectacular views across the Pyrenees and the French Basque coast. There's a bar-restaurant at the top of the **rack-railway** that climbs up from the French side (Le Petit Train de La Rhune, ⓦwww.rhune.com; €14 return).

Lesaka

Some 4km south of Bera along the Valle de Bidasoa, a right turn leads to **LESAKA**. Despite the large, eyesore factory and lumber depots on the outskirts of town, the centre is a delight, dominated by the hilltop parish church in which the pews bear family names of the local farms and mansions. Twenty little stone footbridges cross the various streams in the middle of town, beside one of which stands a fine *casa torre* (fortified private house) of a design peculiar to the Basque Country, dating back to the days when north Navarra was in the hands of a few powerful and constantly feuding families. Lesaka also celebrates its own remarkable **San Fermín** festival in early July, lacking the bulls of Pamplona but featuring elaborate rituals and dancing. *Hostal Ekaitza* at no. 13 in the central Plaza Berria (☎948 637 559, Ⓦwww.ekaitzalesaka.com; ❷) has good-value **rooms** and a pleasant terrace café, and there are several small **restaurants** around town.

Etxalar
ETXALAR is a small, bucolic place, 4km above the Valle de Bidasoa on the way up to a minor border crossing at the Lizarrieta pass, but it is perhaps the best-preserved village of the valley, famous for an impressive array of Basque funerary stelae in the churchyard. Among numerous **casas rurales** here, two good ones with rooms available for short stays are the central *Casa Domekeneko Borda* (☎948 635 031, Ⓦwww.domekenekoborda.com; ❹) and the *Casa Herri-Gain* (☎948 635 208; ❸), the latter perched on a steep hill with fantastic views of the surrounding area. There are also a couple of **restaurants** and **bars** near the giant church.

Inland from San Sebastián: a circuit through Gipuzkoa

Gipuzkoa is in many ways the heartland of Basque language and culture. Medieval towns such as **Tolosa**, with its traditional *Carnaval*, and **Oñati**, famous for its ancient university, and well-preserved villages like **Segura**, are set in spectacular mountain scenery, with excellent walking in the Sierra de Aralar near the market town of **Ordizia**. In the nearby Sierra de Urkilla, the **Santuario de Arantzazu** is a prime pilgrimage destination for Basques.

Gipuzkoa is the smallest province in Spain, and good public **transport** connections make it possible to visit most places as day-trips from San Sebastián. Alternatively, the circuit set out below can act as a stepping stone to Vitoria-Gasteiz and places farther south.

Hernani

The reason to visit **HERNANI**, 7km south of San Sebastián, is its wonderful **Museo Chillida-Leku** (July & Aug Mon–Sat 10.30am–8pm, Sun 10.30am–3pm; Sept–June Mon & Wed–Sun 10.30am–3pm; €8; Ⓦwww.eduardo-chillida.com), the open-air museum dedicated to the life and work of the internationally renowned sculptor Eduardo Chillida, whose massive works can be seen all over the Basque Country and farther afield, including San Sebastián, Gernika and Gijón. Buses leave every half-hour from c/Okendo in San Sebastián, near the main *turismo*. The sculptures, housed in a beautifully refurbished sixteenth-century farmhouse and the surrounding field (which can be muddy), present an elemental solidity that almost seems to capture the essence of Basqueness.

Tolosa and around

TOLOSA, 24km south of San Sebastián, is famous for its **carnival**, celebrated with fervour over six days in February. Considered by Basques to be superior to San Sebastián's, it was the only one whose tradition was maintained throughout the Franco era. Although fairly industrialized, Tolosa has an extensive **Casco Histórico** with an impressive town square, Plaza Euskal Herria, and is also well known for its *pintxos*: sample the *guindillas de Ibarra* (pickled green chilli peppers), and the *alubias de Tolosa* (kidney beans, usually served with blood sausage, cabbage and pork), considered the best in the region. The **turismo** is at Plaza Santa María 1 (Mon 9.30am–1.30pm ℡ 943 697 413, Ⓦ www.tolosaldea .net), in the centre of the old town, near the river. **Accommodation** options include the upmarket *Hotel Oria*, c/Oria 2 (℡ 943 654 688, Ⓦ www.hoteloria .com; ❸), which has its own restaurant and *asador* with a €27 cider-house *menú* (closed Sun), and *Hostal Oyarbide*, Plaza Gorriti 1 (℡ 943 670 017; ❷). Plaza Euskal Herria holds two good, inexpensive **restaurants**: *Agustin Enea* at no. 6 (℡ 943 650 986) and *Astelena* at no. 4 (℡ 943 650 996). Tolosa has the largest **market** in the Basque Country, held on Saturday; and it also boasts one of the most famous **chocolate** and sweet shops in Spain, Gorrotxategi, at Plaza Zaharra 3, not far from the *turismo*.

A farther 20km south, on the main railway line to Vitoria-Gasteiz, **ORDIZIA** is a prosperous town with a well-preserved historical centre dating from 1512. If your visit coincides with a Wednesday, don't miss the weekly **market**, when farmers from the region converge on the town to buy and sell livestock, cheese and the like. Ordizia is backed by the impressive peak of **Txindoki** (1342m), rising above the town like a mini-Matterhorn. You can climb it in about two hours from the tiny village of **Larraitz**, 7km southeast of Ordizia. Another option is to continue walking across the **Sierra de Aralar** to the Santuario de San Miguel (7–8hr in all; see p.492).

SEGURA, 5km southwest of Ordizia, ranks among the most attractive inland villages in Gipuzkoa. It was originally a seigneurial village from where the powerful Guevara family wielded power, and old mansions proudly displaying their coats of arms line the long, winding main street. Today, this sleepy backwater comes alive during the **Easter processions** (not otherwise much celebrated in Euskal Herria) and hosts one of the best village **fiestas** in the region in mid-June.

Oñati

OÑATI, 65km southwest of San Sebastián, is without doubt the most interesting inland town in Gipuzkoa, with some fine examples of Baroque architecture among its many historic buildings; indeed, the Basque painter Zuloaga described it as the "Basque Toledo".

The **University of Sancti Spiritus** (Mon–Fri 9am–5pm, Sat & Sun 11am–2pm; free) dominates the town. Open from 1548 to 1901, it was the only functioning university in Euskal Herria for hundreds of years. The facade, with its four pilasters adorned with figures, and the serene courtyard, are particularly impressive. The Baroque town hall and parish church of **San Miguel** (Sun 10am–2pm, otherwise enquire at the *turismo*) are at opposite ends of the arcaded Foruen Enparantza. In the church crypt are buried all the counts of Oñati from 988 to 1890; the cloister is unusual in that it is actually built over the river. Other fine buildings around the town include various *casas torres* of the type also found in northern Navarra, private family mansions, and the Plateresque-style sixteenth-century monastery of **Bidaurreta** (Mon–Fri 10am–noon & 3.30–8.30pm, Sat 3.30–8.30pm, Sun 10am–12.30pm & 3.30–8.30pm; free). Staff at the very helpful **turismo**, opposite Sancti Spiritus at c/San Juan 14 (April–Sept Mon–Fri 10am–2pm & 3.30–7.30pm, Sat 10am–2pm & 4.30–6.30pm, Sun 10am–2pm; Oct–March Mon–Fri 10am–1pm & 4–7pm, Sat & Sun 11am–2pm; ℡ 943 783 453, Ⓦ www.oinati.org), can arrange guided visits to the university and church.

Accommodation is fairly limited in town; *Hotel Ongi Ostatua* (℡ 943 718 285; ❷), just behind the university at c/Zaharra 19, is a solid choice. If you'd prefer to stay in an **agroturismo**, try *Arregi*, Garagaltza 19 (℡ 943 780 824; ❷), run by a

friendly family, or the attractive *Etxe-Aundi* (℡943 781 956, Ⓦwww.etxeaundi
.com; ❸), housed in a sixteenth-century tower in Torre Auzu, 2km northwest
of town, with its own good restaurant. There are surprisingly few **places to eat**
in Oñati itself, but the *Taberna Oñati*, no. 10 in the Foruen Enparantza near the
university, offers a decent selection of *pintxos*.

Santuario de Arantzazu

A prime pilgrimage site for Basques, the **Santuario de Arantzazu** (daily
9.30am–9.30pm; free) clings spectacularly to the mountainside above a gorge
9km south of Oñati. **Our Lady of Arantzazu** (Santa María) is the patron saint
of Gipuzkoa. Although a monastery on this site dates back to the fifteenth century,
the present spiky building was built in 1950 and features contemporary work by
the sculptors Chillida (the doors) and Sáenz de Oteiza (part of the facade). The
severe, Modernist architecture might not be to everyone's taste, but it's worth
looking inside for the soaring stained-glass windows. The cheapest **accommodation** is in the basic *Hospedería de Arantzazu* (℡943 781 313, Ⓔostatua
@euskalnet.net; ❷), which is popular with hiking groups and pilgrims; the newer
Sindika next door (℡943 781 303; ❸) has better views and its own swimming
pool; both places offer meals. There is ample **parking** near the church, while
buses ply to and from Oñati every Sunday between April and November
(7.30am–7.30pm, hourly; €1 return).

The Costa Vasca

West from San Sebastián, both road and rail run inland, following the Río Oria,
then towards the coast at Zarautz, some 20km from San Sebastián. From here on,
the **Costa Vasca** is glorious – a rocky and wild coastline, with long stretches of
road hugging the edge of the cliffs – all the way to Bilbao. The hillsides, particularly
around Getaria, are also famous for the production of *txakoli*, a fizzy wine popular
in the summer. The farther you go, the less developed the resorts become.

Getaria

GETARIA, a tiny fishing port 25km from San Sebastián that's sheltered by the
hump-backed islet of **El Ratón** (The Mouse), was once a major whaling centre.
Founded in 1209, it preserves the magnificent fourteenth-century church of **San
Salvador**, whose altar is raised theatrically above the heads of the congregation.
The first man to sail around the world, Juan Sebastián Elcano, was born here
around 1487 – his ship was the only one of Magellan's fleet to make it back
home. Every four years on August 6, during the village's **fiestas**, Elcano's landing
is re-enacted on the beach; the next will be in 2011. **Cristóbal Balenciaga**
(1895–1972), the fashion designer, was also born in Getaria – a lavish
new museum dedicated to his work has long been promised, but the futuristic shell
of the building has languished incomplete on the hillside for several years, amid
allegations of corruption by local politicians, including charges that several prize
items from the collection were given to the wives of councillors.

Even if there's little to do in Getaria apart from surf from its crescent beach, it
makes a much nicer **place to stay** than sprawling Zarautz on the main highway
– get details from the small **turismo** at Aldamar Parkea 2 (Easter to mid-Sept
Tues–Sun 10am–1.30pm & 4.30–7.30pm; ℡943 140 957, Ⓦwww.getaria.net).
The stylish ⚲ *Saiaz Getaria* offers lovely sea-view rooms at Roke Deuna 25

(☎943 140 143, ⓦwww.saiazgetaria.com; ❺), while the comfortable *Pensión Iribar* is higher up, near the church at c/Nagusia 34 (☎943 140 451, ⓦwww.come .to/iribar; ❸). There are slightly cheaper *agroturismos* a few kilometres up the hillside on the way to Meagas, including the *Casa Rural Itsas-Lore* (☎943 140 619, ⓦwww.itsaslore.com; ❸), with great views of the sea and the mountains. In town, the *Elkano* at c/Herrerieta 2 (☎943 140 614, ⓦwww.restauranteelkano .com) does truly excellent fresh fish and seafood **meals** for around €60 a head. Alternatively, *The Mayflower*, overlooking the harbour at Katrapuna 4, has superb sardines, and the daily *menú* is a bargain. Though the local speciality, *chipirones a lo Pelayo* (tiny cuttlefish with onion), is served all along the coast, Getaria is the best place to try it.

Zumaia

The coast becomes still more rugged on the way to **ZUMAIA**, 6km from Getaria – an industrial-looking place at first sight, but with an attractive centre and pleasant waterfront along the estuary of the Río Urola. Zumaia's local **fiesta** in the first days of July is one of the region's most exuberant, with Basque sports, dancing, and bullocks let loose on the beach to test the mettle of the local youth.

Zumaia has two very different beaches – **Playa Itzurun**, over the hill behind the town, is a large splash of grey sand enclosed by extraordinary sheer cliffs of layered slate-like rock, which channel the waves in to produce some of the best surfing on the coast. The other beach, **Playa Santiago**, across the river from the port, is yellow and flat, sheltered by a little pine forest. Behind Santiago, on the road to Getaria, you'll find the **Villa Zuloaga** (April to mid-Sept Wed–Sun 4–8pm; €6), former home of the nineteenth-century-born Basque painter Ignacio Zuloaga, and now a small art museum displaying his work alongside that of other Basque artists, together with a rather bizarre exhibition of bullfighting memorabilia.

A very helpful **turismo** stands across the river from the old town on the road to Getaria, at Kantauri Enparantza 13 (mid-June to mid-Sept daily 10am–2pm & 4–8pm; mid-Sept to mid-June Tues 4–7pm, Wed–Sat 10am–2pm & 4–7pm, Sun 10am–2pm; ☎943 143 396, ⓦwww.zumaiaturismoa.com). Zumaia holds a couple of **hotels**: the *Zumaia* at Alai 13 (☎943 143 441, ⓔzumaiahotela @euskalnet.net; ❹), in between the train station and the centre, and the pricier *Zelai*, Larretzo 16 (☎943 865 100, ⓦwww.talasozelai.com; ❺), above Playa Itzurun, with a sea-water therapy centre. Cheaper rooms can be found at the quiet, friendly *Agroturismo Jesuskoa*, at Oikia Auzoa, 3km along the Meagas road (☎943 143 209, ⓦwww.jesuskoa.net; ❸), with a renowned restaurant specializing in grilled lamb. Recommended **places to eat** include *Algorri*, a *sidrería* near the marina at Kirol Portua (☎943 865 617). Try the traditional Basque dessert of *queso con membrillo y nueces* (cheese with quince jelly and walnuts) if you get the chance.

Santuario de Loyola

Sixteen kilometres inland from Zumaia and 1.5km south of the town of **Azpeitia** is the grandiose **Santuario de Loyola** (daily 7.30am–9pm; ⓦwww .santuariodeloyola.com; free), built as a monument to local son Ignacio (Iñigo) López de Loyola, better known as **St Ignatius of Loyola** (1491–1556). Loyola founded the Society of Jesus, or **Jesuits**, in 1534, and this is a major Catholic pilgrimage site. The complex, which includes an imposing eighteenth-century Baroque basilica, is arranged around the medieval tower-house and museum, **Casa Natal de San Ignacio** (daily 7.30am–1pm & 3–7pm), where Loyola was born and the scene of his spiritual rebirth in 1521. A major pilgrimage celebrates St Ignatius Day, July 31.

Mutriku and around

Despite some ugly recent construction above the town, **MUTRIKU**, 10km west of Zumaia, has some attractive narrow streets leading steeply down to the fishing harbour. Admiral Churruca, the "Hero of Trafalgar" to locals, was born here in 1761; his imposing statue faces the incongruous church of **Nuestra Señora de la Asunción** (Mon–Sat 45min before Mass at 6.15pm & Sun 9.30am 1hr before Mass), built along the lines of a Greek temple, with a painting attributed to Zurbarán inside. If you're **driving**, it's best to use the underground car park behind the church. Mutriku has a **turismo** in front of the church (mid-June to mid-Sept Tues–Sun 10am–2pm & 4–6pm; mid-Sept to mid-June Tues–Sat 11am–1pm & 4–6pm, Sun 11am–2pm; ☎943 603 378, ⓦwww.mutriku.net) and no fewer than four campsites around several small beaches.

The newly restored *Zumalabe*, at c/Bajada Puerto 2, is a nice **hotel** overlooking the port; all rooms are en suite, some have balconies (☎943 604 617, ⓦwww.hotelzumalabe.com; ④). Nearby *agroturismos* include *Casa Matzuri*, 1km beyond town on the road to Ondarroa (☎943 603 001; ②), with lovely sea and mountain views, and the self-catering *Koostei* (☎943 583 008; ②), perched high up in the hills several kilometres from the main road, which offers horseriding. Beyond Mutriku, the road temporarily turns inland until it reaches the coast 2km farther on at the beach of **Saturrarán**, which gets very crowded in summer, when there's a campsite (☎943 603 847, ⓦwww.campingseuskadi.com/saturraran; closed Oct–May).

Ondarroa

Around the headland from Saturrarán, **ONDARROA**, the first coastal town in Bizkaia, looks very different to the small resorts farther east. Here, the usual town beach and attractive tree-lined *rambla* end at a no-nonsense **fishing port** filled with an eclectic set of trawlers. In the early morning, trucks file in from the coastal road to fill up with fish – the traffic is so great that a large bridge has been built across the bay to channel the fishing trucks directly to the port. Ondarroa is an interesting place to stop over, particularly during its mid-August **fiestas**. Founded in 1327, it was razed to the ground by French troops in 1794, but the late Gothic church of **Santa María**, in the centre, survived; its extremely ornate facade includes flower and animal motifs and a "court" of twelve figures including a king, queen, pilgrims, crossbowmen, a minstrel and a wet nurse. Ondarroa's **turismo** is nearby on the port at Kofradi Zaharra-Erribera 9 (Fri & Sat 10.30am–1.30pm & 4–7pm, Sun 10.30am–2.30pm, ☎946 831 951, ⓦwww.learjai.com). Since the local hotel closed at the end of 2007, the one **place to stay** in town is the simple but good-value *Pensión Patxi*, c/Artabide 2 (☎609 986 446; ②). **Bars** such as *Kulixka* and *Gau Argi* at the harbour stay open late, stuffed with a tempting array of seafood *pintxos*.

Lekeitio

LEKEITIO, 10km west from Ondarroa, is an active fishing port with two fine **beaches** – one beside the harbour, the other, much better, across the river to the east of town. Stop in at the **church of Santa María** (daily 8am–noon & 5–7.30pm), in the town centre, to see its magnificent sixteenth-century Flemish Gothic altarpiece, the third largest on the peninsula after those of the cathedrals of Seville and Toledo.

Lekeitio's **turismo** is on Independentziaren Enparantza (mid-June to mid-Sept daily 10am–2pm & 4–8pm; mid-Sept to mid-June Mon–Sat 10.30am–1.30pm & 4–7pm, Sun 10.30am–2.30pm; ☎946 844 017, ⓦwww.lekeitio.com). The best

accommodation option is the *Hotel Emperatriz Zita*, Santa Elena s/n (☎946 842 655, Ⓦwww.aisiahoteles.com/ing_zita.asp; ❹), where some rooms enjoy superb sea views; it also has a restaurant and seawater therapy centre. Another excellent choice is the elegant *Hotel Zubieta*, Portal de Atea s/n (☎946 843 030, Ⓦwww.hotelzubieta.com; ❹), set in the gardens of an old palace at the edge of town. The cheaper *Piñupe* is in the town centre at Paskual Abaroa 10 (☎946 842 984, Ⓔpinupehotela@euskalnet.net; ❸). **Campsites** include *Endai*, on the main road to Ondarroa (☎946 842 469; closed mid-Sept to mid-June), and the year-round *Leagi* in little Mendexa, 3km inland between Ondarroa and Lekeitio (☎946 842 352, Ⓦwww.campingleagi.com). Lekeitio is literally teeming with **bars**, with harbourfront places such as *Itxas Alde* and *La Marina* offering delicious *pintxos*, while good seafood **restaurants** include *Kaia* at Txatxo Kaia 5 (☎946 840 204; closed Sun pm & Mon), and *Goitiko* on Independentziaren Enparantza (☎946 843 103).

Elantxobe

Though the road turns inland from Lekeitio, the well-preserved fishing village of **ELANTXOBE**, 10km farther west, merits a detour back to the coast. The road forks just before you reach it; head left for the main village, or right to drop down to the harbour. You can **park** just before the former, but spaces are limited. From the main square (where buses stop) an incredibly steep cobbled street lined with attractive fishermen's houses, c/Nagusia, connects the village to the harbour below – in the other direction, it continues 2km up to the cemetery from where a signposted track leads to **Mount Ogoño**, at 280m the highest cliff on the Basque coast. Elantxobe has a couple of small **restaurants** including the recommended *Makues*, Bide 1, just below the square (☎946 276 513), and one central *pensión* nearby, *Itsasmin Ostatua*, at c/Nagusia 32 (☎946 276 174, Ⓦwww.itsasmin.com; ❸). Alternatively, you can **stay** at the *agroturismo* located in Ibarrangelu, 1km from the crossroads towards Gernika – *Caserio Arboliz*, at c/Arboliz 12 (☎946 276 283, Ⓦwww.arboliz.com; ❸).

Gernika and around

Immortalized by Picasso's nightmare painting, **GERNIKA**, inland and west of Lekeitio, is the traditional heart of Basque nationalism. It was here that the Basque parliament met until 1876, and here, under the **Tree of Gernika** (*Gernikako Arbola*), that their rights were reconfirmed by successive rulers. It was more for its symbolic importance than the presence of a small-arms factory that Gernika was chosen during the Civil War as the target for one of the first-ever saturation bombing raids on a civilian centre. In just four hours on April 27, 1937, planes from the Condor Legion (lent to Franco by Hitler) destroyed the town centre and killed more than 1600 people, many of them attending the weekly market (still held every Monday in the Plaza de Gernika). The nearby town of Durango had, in fact, been bombed a few days earlier, but because there were no foreign observers, the reports were simply not believed.

For a Basque, at least, a visit to Gernika is more pilgrimage than tourist trip. The parliament, church and tree remained miraculously unscathed by the bombing, but the rest of the town was destroyed and has been rebuilt. It's now rather nondescript, and not really a place to spend much time on a holiday trip, though the arcaded main street, Artekalea, has a certain appeal. As for Picasso's picture, it was finally brought "home" to Spain after the death of Franco, and is now exhibited in the Centro de Arte Reina Sofía in Madrid.

Just opposite the *turismo*, on Artekalea, the **Gernika Peace Museum** (July & Aug Tues–Sat 10am–8pm, Sun 10am–3pm; Sept–June Tues–Sat 10am–2pm & 4–7pm, Sun 10am–2pm; ☎946 270 213, ⓦwww.peacemuseumguernica.org; €4) contains a moving display about the bombing, explores various concepts of peace and has a section on ETA and the Basque conflict. Exhibits in the neighbouring **Museo Euskal Herria** (Tues–Sat 10am–2pm & 4–7pm, Sun 11am–3pm; free) depict the history of the Basque Country (Basque/Spanish only), while the adjacent church of **Santa María la Antigua** is adorned with portraits of the various nobles of Bizkaia who pledged allegiance to the *fueros*. The church traditionally served as a meeting house, although in fine weather, assemblies were held under the tree. The **tree** itself is nearby (now just a stump – a new one was planted in 2005), in the grounds of the parliament building, the **Batzarretxea**, or Casa de las Juntas (daily 10am–2pm & 4–7pm, until 6pm in winter; free). The Bizkaia parliament was reactivated in 1979 and still meets here (though the government is in Vitoria-Gasteiz). Behind the Batzarretxea, **Europa Park** (daily 10am–7pm, until 9pm in summer) contains ornamental gardens, a fast-flowing stream, and peace sculptures by Henry Moore and Eduardo Chillida. Housed in the Palacio Udetxea next to the park is the headquarters of the **Urdaibai Biosphere Reserve** (Mon–Thurs 9am–1.30pm & 3–5pm, Fri & Sat 9am–2.30pm; free), which often holds exhibitions on environmental and cultural themes. The reserve itself, which encompasses the watershed of the Mundaka estuary, was declared a UNESCO World Heritage Site in 1984; it includes the most diverse range of habitats in Euskal Herria and is the resting place for hosts of migrating birds.

Practicalities

The helpful **turismo** at Artekalea 8 (mid-June to mid-Sept daily 10am–7pm; mid-Sept to mid-June Mon–Sat 10am–2pm & 4–7pm, Sun 10am–2pm; ☎946 255 892, ⓦwww.gernika-lumo.net) has details of **places to stay**. Don't reckon on more than a single night here; *Pensión Akelarre Ostatua*, behind the *turismo* at Barrenkale 5 (☎946 270 197, ⓦwww.hotelakelarre.com; ❸), and the *Hotel-Restaurante Boliña*, next door at Barrenkale 3 (☎946 250 300, ⓦwww.hotelbolina .net; ❸), are cheap and central, while *Gernika*, on the Bermeo road at Carlos Gangoiti 17 (☎946 254 948, ⓦwww.hotel-gernika.com; ❹), is more comfortable. **Places to eat** in town include *Julen*, c/Industria 14 (☎946 254 927), and the *Boliña*, Barrenkale 3. If you have transport, it's worth heading for ⚘ *Baserri Maitea*, a three-hundred-year-old Basque farmhouse a few kilometres off the Bermeo road in Fortua (☎946 253 408; closed Sun eve all year & Mon–Thurs eve Nov–April) serving dishes roasted in a wood-fired oven, or the inexpensive *Zallo Barri* (☎946 251 800), Juan Kaltzada 79, off the Bilbao road, home to another highly acclaimed Basque chef, Iñigo Ordorica.

Mundaka

Continuing the route west, the Río Mundaka flows from Gernika into a broad estuary fringed by hilly pinewoods and dotted with islets. There's a succession of sandy coves to swim in, but the best spots are at Sukarrieta and especially **MUNDAKA**. This lovely little village remains amazingly unspoiled, despite having achieved legendary status for its magnificent **surfing**, which includes the longest left break in the world. Since Mundaka was first chosen in 1999 as one of only eleven sites to feature on the Billabong Pro World Championship circuit, it has become clear that its "Wave" varies considerably from year to year; it disappeared altogether as a result of dredging work but returned in full force in 2008. During peak season (Sept–Dec), you can often watch the surfers battle the waves from the plaza next to the church. The Mundaka Surf Shop, close to the port (℡946 876 721, Ⓦwww.mundakasurfshop.com), sells and rents equipment and offers surf lessons. A passenger ferry plies across the river (June–Sept 10am–8pm; every 20min; €1.20) to **Playa de Laída**, an enormous area of white sand, which at low tide stretches across the mouth of the bay in an unbroken crescent.

Mundaka's **turismo** is next to the harbour (Tues–Sat 10.30am–1.30pm & 4–7pm, Sun 11am–2pm; ℡946 177 201, Ⓦwww.mundaka.org). For **accommodation**, the delightful ⚓ *Hotel el Puerto*, right on the fishing port at Portu 1 (℡946 876 625, Ⓦwww.hotelelpuerto.com; ❹), has a lovely shaded terrace and great sea views, while *Hotel Mundaka*, just off the main square at Florentino Larriñaga 9 (℡946 876 700, Ⓦwww.hotelmundaka.com; ❹), is also attractive and surfer-friendly. Surfers fill the *Portuondo* **campsite** (℡946 877 701, Ⓦwww.campingportuondo.com), perched high above the water with steps leading down to a rocky beach. In the absence of fancy **restaurants**, the *pintxos* at *Bar Txopos*, Portu 2, are irresistible.

Bermeo

The local EuskoTren train line from Bilbao and Gernika gives good access to the estuary beaches and continues beyond Mundaka for 3km to **BERMEO**, whose fishing fleet is the largest remaining in these waters, a riot of red, green and blue boats in the harbour. Worth checking out while you're here is the **Museo del Pescador** near the harbour (Tues–Sat 10am–2pm & 4–7pm, Sun 10am–2.15pm; free), which is full of local interest and more general maritime displays. Apart from a stroll through the narrow, cobbled streets, there's not much else to see, and no beach worth the name.

Bermeo's **turismo** at Parque de Lamera, on the waterfront (Mon–Fri 10am–2pm & 4–7pm, Sat 10am–1pm & 4–7pm, Sun 10am–2pm; ℡946 179 154, Ⓦwww.bermeo.org), can put you in touch with the several *agroturismos* in the area, though there's top-notch inexpensive **accommodation** a few streets up from the port behind Santa María church in ⚓ *Hostal Torre Ercilla*, Talaranzko 14, 1° (℡946 187 598, Ⓔbarrota@piramidal.com; ❷); ask for the spacious corner room, with a balcony and glassed-in gallery as well as en-suite bathroom. The main square facing the harbour, Parque de la Lamera, is lined with inexpensive **tapas bars**; the atmospheric *Taberna Sollube* has the best selection.

Bilbao

Stretching for some 14km along the narrow valley of the formerly polluted Río Nervión, **BILBAO** (Bilbo) is a large city that rarely feels like one, its urban sprawl having gradually engulfed a series of once-separate communities. Even in the city centre you can always see the green slopes of the surrounding mountains beyond the high-rise buildings. Prosperous and modern, with a busy and attractive centre, surrounded by smoke-belching factories, Bilbao has reinvented itself since the collapse of its traditional industrial base in the 1980s and 90s. Steel mills and shipyards have been transformed into conference centres and luxury flats, and the **Museo Guggenheim**, which opened in 1997, has sparked a tourism boom. The new metro, airport and celebrations of Bilbao's seven-hundredth anniversary in 2000 brought new impetus to the redevelopment programme. Today, Bilbao is the biggest city in the Basque Country with a population of around 450,000, and the capital of Bizkaia province. It also holds some of the best places to eat and drink in Spain, and very open, friendly inhabitants with an abundance of civic pride.

Arrival

Bilbao's spanking new **airport**, 12km north of town, is served by flights from London Heathrow, London Gatwick and Barcelona (all Clickair), and London Stansted (easyJet); though heralded as an architectural gem, it's not a pleasant place to use, with minimal seating space or facilities inside the terminal. A **taxi** into town costs around €20, while **Bizkaiabus** services (€1.25) run every twenty minutes, calling at the Plaza Moyúa in the centre of the new town (Ensanche) and terminating further west at the **Termibús station** (Ⓜ San Mamés), which fills an entire block between Luis Briñas and Gurtubay. Most long-distance and international **bus** companies also use this terminal.

If you're **driving** into Bilbao, the motorways are very efficient at delivering you to the centre, but once there traffic is consistently dreadful; you're better off parking straight away in the car park nearest your accommodation, and walking from there.

The main RENFE train station is the **Estación de Abando** on Plaza Circular, but EuskoTren services to San Sebastián, Gernika, Bermeo and Durango use the **Estación de Atxuri**, on the other side of the river, to the south of the Casco Viejo. FEVE services, along the coast to Santander and beyond, stop at the highly decorative **Estación de Santander**, on the riverbank right below the Estación de Abando.

The **P&O ferry** from Portsmouth in the UK docks at **Santurtzi**, across the river from Getxo, 14km north of the city centre; regular buses and trains run from the docks to the centre of town.

Information

Bilbao's main **turismo** is inconveniently located at Plaza Ensanche 11 (Mon–Fri 9am–2pm & 4–7.30pm; ☎944 795 760, Ⓦ www.bilbao.net; Ⓜ Abando or Moyúa), but there are two useful, if a little overstretched, offices closer to the main sights, on the corner of the Teatro Arriaga (Mon–Fri 9am–2pm & 4–7.30pm, Sat 9.30am–2pm & 5–7.30pm, Sun 9.30am–2pm; Ⓜ Casco Viejo), and outside the Museo Guggenheim (July & Aug Mon–Sat 10am–7pm, Sun 10am–3pm; Sept–June Tues–Fri 11am–6pm, Sat 11am–7pm, Sun 11am–3pm). There's also a booth at the airport (Mon–Fri 7.30am–11pm, Sat & Sun 8.30am–11pm; ☎944 710 301). The *turismo* offers **guided tours** of the city at the weekends (10.30am & noon; €3).

City transport

Central Bilbao is small enough to **walk** around comfortably; indeed, the riverside stroll between the Casco Viejo and the Guggenheim is a highlight for many visitors. The city does, however, boast the modern **Metro Bilbao**, designed by Norman Foster. An easy, efficient service runs every four minutes from Plentzia (northeast of Getxo) to Extebarri, south of the city centre; a second line runs from here to Portugalete on the southern bank of the river, with an extension in the works as far as Santurzi. Free metro maps are available from the tourist offices. The 34 stops are divided into three zones, but all journeys in the city centre (including the Casco Viejo) are within one zone (€1.20). For parts the metro doesn't reach, there are red municipal **buses** (€1) with route maps at the green bus shelters, or for longer journeys (including to the airport) the blue and yellow Bizkiabuses. The green Euskotran **trams** (€1) run along a single line, linking the Casco Viejo and the Museo Guggenheim with San Mamés and the bus station.

If you plan to use the transport system frequently, buy a **BilbaoCard** from any *turismo* (€6/10/12 for one/two/three days), which provides unlimited travel on all Bilbao's various modes of transport in the Creditrans network – the metro, tram,

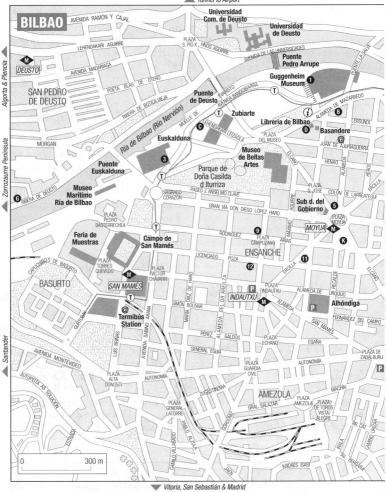

Tunnel to Airport

Universidad
Com. de Deusto

Universidad
de Deusto

AVENIDA RAMÓN Y CAJAL

LEHENDAKARI AGUIRRE

PLAZA
S. PÍO X

HNOS. AGUIRRE

AVENIDA DE LAS UNIVERSIDADES

M DEUSTO

AVENIDA MADARIAGA

Puente
Pedro Arrupe

POETA BLAS DE OTERO

SAN PEDRO
DE DEUSTO

RIBERA DE BOTICA VIEJA

Puente
de Deusto

AVENIDA BANDOIBARRA

Guggenheim
Museum 1

T

ALAMEDA DE MAZARREDO

B

MUELLE DE

Zubiarte

T

Librería de Bilbao

i

D

Basandere

MORGAN

Ría de Bilbao (Río Nervión)

LEHENDAKARI LEIZAOLA

C

Euskalduna

PLAZA
DEL MUSEO

JUAN DE AJURIAGUERRA

HENAO

ELCANO

3

Museo
de Bellas
Artes

PLAZA
S. JOSÉ

COLÓN DE LARREATEGUI

Puente
Euskalduna

RIBERA DE DEUSTO

G

Parque de
Doña Casilda
d Iturriza

PASEO J. ANSELMO CLAVE

Sub d. del
Gobierno 5

Museo
Marítimo
Ría de Bilbao

PLAZA
PEDRO
BASTERRECHEA

SAGRADO
CORAZÓN

T

GRAN VÍA DON DIEGO LÓPEZ HARO

AGUIRRE

PLAZA
MOYUA

MOYUA M

K

Feria de
Muestras

RODRÍGUEZ

9

PLAZA
CAMPUZANO

ARIAS

MAXIMO

Campo de
San Mamés

LICENCIADO

ENSANCHE

11

POZA

12

ERCILLA

ELCANO

RECALDE

URQUIJO

CAPUCHINOS DE BASURTO

PLAZA
TORRES
QUEVEDO

M

PLAZA
VÍCTOR
CHÁVARRI

SIMÓN BOLÍVAR

MARÍA DÍAZ DE HARO

ALAMEDA DEL DR ARELIZA

PLAZA
INDAUTXU

ALAMEDA DE

INDAUTXU

P

Alhóndiga

BASURTO

San Mamés

T

Termibús
Station

LUIS BRIÑAS

AVENIDA SABINO ARANA

PÉREZ

GALDOS

PLAZA
ECHANIZ

SAN MAMÉS

FERNÁNDEZ DEL CAMPO

P

GUTURBAY

AVENIDA MONTEVIDEO

GENERAL EGUIA

EGAÑA

PLAZA DE
ZABÁLBURU

AUTOPISTA A8 SEGURA

PLAZA
ALTA
DONOSTI

AUTONOMÍA

PLAZA
GUARDIA
CIVIL

AUTONOMÍA

ZUGASTINOVIA

AMEZOLA

PLAZA
DE TOROS
VISTA
ALEGRE

MACHÍN

P

ESKIBEL

PABLO ALDU

ESCORONAO

PLAZA
GENERAL
LATORRE

PLAZA
AMEZOLA

PLAZA
GRAL. SALAZAR

RR. CAT

CAMINO UNZAR

CAMINO VILLABASO

JAÉN

ANDRÉS ISASI

AV BERGARA

0   300 m

Vitoria, San Sebastián & Madrid

municipal and provincial buses and Artxanda funicular – and offers discounts of
ten to fifty percent at various museums and shops. Alternatively, the **Creditrans**
farepass comes in denominations of €5, €10 and €15 (available at stations, tram
stops, kiosks and tobacconists' shops), which reduce in value as you use them, but
offer discounts on normal ticket prices (and have no time limit).

Accommodation

The best area to stay has to be the **Casco Viejo**, though that's largely the
reserve of budget hotels and *pensiones*. Staying in **Deusto** or **Castaños**, on
the north bank of the river, is a good alternative, handy for the art galleries and
main shopping districts, while Bilbao's luxury hotels tend to be scattered across
Ensanche, many featuring hip, contemporary architecture and award-winning
restaurants. For help with bookings, try the *turismo's* **central reservation service**

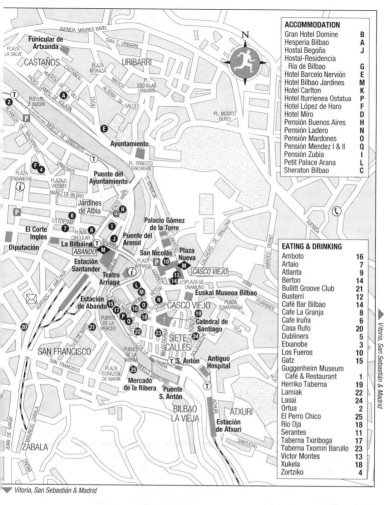

(☎902 877 298, ⓦwww.bilbaoreservas.com). Two year–round **campsites** are located near the beaches to the northeast, at Sopelana (*Sopelana*; ☎946 762 120, ⓦwww.campingsopelana.com), and Gorliz (*Arrien*; ☎946 771 911, ⓦwww .campingarrien.com), just beyond Plentzia.

Casco Viejo

Hotel Bilbao Jardines c/Jardines 9 ☎944 794 210, ⓦwww.hotelbilbaojardines.com. A rare midrange option in the heart of the Casco Viejo. Rooms are smart and functional, finished in pine and bright colours, with TV, modern bathrooms and free internet. ④

Hotel Iturrienea Ostatua c/Santa María 14 ☎944 161 500, ⓦwww.iturrieneaostatua.com. Clean,

informal two-star hotel, tucked away in the Casco Viejo, with restored antique furniture throughout and walls hung with original Basque paintings and moody photographs of the city's industrial past. Many rooms have plants trailing over balconies, and double-glazing to ensure guests are not disturbed by noise from the nearby bars. ④

Pensión Ladero c/Lotería 1, 4º ☎944 150 932, ⓦwww.pensionladero.es. Friendly management and clean, good-value rooms with modern furnishings and spotless, shared bathrooms. No lift. There is also a fifth-floor annexe reached by a narrow spiral staircase. **2**

Pensión Mardones c/Jardines 4, 2º & 4º ☎944 153 105, Ⓦwww.hostalmardones.com. Smart, clean rooms, with or without bath, and finished in dark wood; the fourth floor is preferable to the second-floor annexe. Entrance next to *Amboto* restaurant. **2**

Pensión Mendez I & II c/Santa María 13, 1º ☎944 160 364, Ⓦwww.pensionmendez.com. Comfortable and clean rooms, simply but adequately furnished. Those in *Mendez II* are slightly better, with en-suite bathrooms. *I* **2**, *II* **3**

Petit Palace Arana c/Bidebarrieta 2 ☎944 156 411, Ⓦwww.hthotels.com. Friendly, popular and conveniently located business hotel with smart, modern bathrooms, high-speed internet access and cable TV. **3**

Around Plaza Circular

Hostal Begoña c/Amistad 2, 1º ☎944 230 134, Ⓦwww.hostalbegona.com. Solid mid-range option very near the FEVE station and an easy walk from the Casco Viejo, with reasonable though view-less en-suite rooms and wi-fi. **2**

Pensión Buenos Aires Plaza Venezuela 1, 3º ☎944 458 800, Ⓔp.buenos.aires@hotmail.com. Comfortable and well-run *hostal* with a pleasant lounge and small bar. **2**

Pensión Zubia c/Amistad 5, 1º ☎944 248 566. Basic but clean *pensión*, handy for the station. **2**

Ensanche

Gran Hotel Domine Alameda de Mazarredo 61 ☎944 253 300, Ⓦwww.granhoteldomine bilbao.com. The work of designer Javier Mariscal, this is a wonderfully inspiring five-star hotel, appropriately close to the Guggenheim and sporting one of the most creative lobbies you'll ever see. Each floor has a unique design, while the luxurious rooms have bathrooms with transparent glass, and tubs designed by Philippe Starck. **5**

Hotel Carlton Plaza Moyúa 2 ☎944 162 200, Ⓦwww.hotelcarlton.es. The *grand dame* of Bilbao's

hotels, built in 1919 and still an atmospheric place to stay, though it's been superseded by the newer hotels in terms of comfort and facilities. The rooms are tastefully finished with stripey upholstery and fresh blues and pale yellows. **4**

Hotel López de Haro Obispo Orueta 2–4 ☎944 235 500, Ⓦwww.hotellopezdeharo.com. Luxury five-star hotel built in 1890, with comfortable, modern rooms and bathrooms, but retaining nineteenth-century touches. Great location, and extremely tranquil. **5**

Hotel Miro Alameda Mazarredo 77 ☎ 946 611 880, Ⓦwww.mirohotelbilbao.com. Attractive boutique hotel, with minimalist decor, bathrooms finished in black marble (separated from the chic, white-coloured rooms by a curtain), flat-screen TVs and a decent spa. **4**

Sheraton Bilbao c/Lehendakari Leizaola 29 ☎944 280 000, Ⓦwww.sheraton-bilbao .com. One of Bilbao's most distinctive buildings, a bold, creative design inspired by Eduardo Chillida, utilizing Iranian pink marble and rusty garnet tones for the exterior, and green and white marble in the bathrooms. The stylish rooms are luxuriously comfortable, with huge, incredibly comfy beds and 25″ TVs. Pool, free internet or wi-fi available. **5**

Castaños and Deusto

Hesperia Bilbao Campo Volantín 28 ☎944 051 100, Ⓦwww.hesperia-bilbao.com. Smart boutique hotel, opened in 2005 in a funky, contemporary building lined with multicoloured glass windows and overlooking the river. Rooms come with sleek, minimalist furnishings and plasma-screen TVs. Bike rental, free wi-fi and parking. **4**

Hostal-Residencia Ría de Bilbao Ribera de Deusto 32 ☎944 765 060, Ⓦwww.riabilbao.com. A quiet place overlooking the river, a 10-min walk from the Euskalduna. Garden and cooking facilities. Highly recommended. **3**

Hotel Barcelo Nervión Campo Volantín 11 ☎944 454 700, Ⓦwww.bchoteles.com. Plush chain hotel overlooking the Puente Zubizuri, with swish, designer rooms equipped with satellite TV and wi-fi, an open-plan bar in the lobby and a classy restaurant. Bike rental and weekend reductions. **3**

The City

Though Bilbao originally started out as a cluster of small fishing villages on the left bank of the Río Nervion, what's generally regarded as the old town – the **Casco Viejo**, which grew up between the fourteenth and nineteenth centuries – lies across the river on the east bank. Then, when Bilbao expanded hugely as it rose to industrial prominence during the nineteenth century, a much larger area on the left bank, all but encircled by a huge loop in the river, became home to the new town, or Ensanche. This remains the commercial heart of the city, a formally planned cityscape where the broad avenues that radiate from the central Plaza Moyúa afford direct views out to the mountains. Its main thoroughfare, the **Gran Vía Don Diego López de Haro**, runs from the Plaza Circular by Estación de Abando, to the Plaza Sagrado Corazón, situated between the **Euskalduna** and the huge **Campo de San Mamés**, home of Athletico Bilbao.

Casco Viejo and along the Río Nervion

The tight-knit maze of stone lanes that forms the **Casco Viejo** holds several major sights: the beautiful **Teatro Arriaga**, the elegantly arcaded **Plaza Nueva**, the Gothic **Catedral de Santiago** (Mon–Sat 10am–1pm & 5–7.30pm, Sun 10am–1pm) and the **Euskal Museoa Bilbao** at Plaza Miguel de Unamuno 4 (Tues–Sat 11am–5pm, Sun 11am–2pm; €3, free Thurs; ⓦ www.euskal-museoa .org). Housed in the former Colegio de San Andrés, where a beautiful cloister makes a lovely retreat from the city bustle, the museum is devoted to Basque archeology, ethnology and history. At the time of writing, it was due to expand into the old Lezama train station across the square, so it's hard to predict exactly what will be where when you visit, but the convent will probably continue to hold the ethnographic exhibits, which cover Basque traditions in costume, crafts and the like. Before leaving the old town, check out also the Art Nouveau **Mercado de la Ribera**, on c/de la Ribera along the riverbank (Mon–Fri 8am–2pm & 4.30–7pm, Sat 8am–2.30pm), which offers a vast array of fresh produce and seafood.

With pollution and decay very much a thing of the past, walking west from the Casco Viejo beside the Río Nervion is one of Bilbao's greatest pleasures – indeed, it's the favourite *paseo* for *bilbainos*. Not far beyond the **ayuntamiento**, the pedestrian-only **Puente Zubizuri**, designed by Santiago Calatrava, curves majestically across the river like a vast white sail filled by a fresh wind. Cross here if you're heading for the Guggenheim, or alternatively you can head three blocks north, to reach the Plaza Funicular, where the **Funicular de Artxanda** (daily Mon–Fri 7.15am–11pm, Sat & Sun 8.15am–11pm, Oct–May until 10pm; every 10min; €1), built in 1931, sweeps you 770m up the mountain for a panoramic view of the city. You can also see over into the next valley, with views of the Calatrava-designed airport and the ocean beyond. The top station is a nice spot for a picnic (with stone barbecues for public use), and you can stroll down the hill again (about 45min) through lush suburbs.

Museo Guggenheim

Frank O. Gehry's astounding **Museo Guggenheim** dominates the quayside, ten-minutes' walk west of the Casco Viejo (daily 10am–8pm, Sept–June Tues–Sun; €12.50, under-12s free; ⓦ www.guggenheim-bilbao.es). Cross the delicate arch of the Zubizuri footbridge to approach it from below, along the west bank, or take in the full panorama from across the river before crossing the Puente Pedro Arrupe in front of the University of Deusto; alternatively, for an aerial view, take the *ascensor* (or seven flights of steps) up to the Puente de la Salve.

The Guggenheim has been hailed by architect Philip Johnson as "the greatest building of our time". Completed in 1997, its construction on a derelict industrial site represented a colossal gamble by the Basque government, which pumped every peseta it could find into a high-risk bid that the showpiece project might stimulate the revitalization of Bilbao. Amazingly enough, it did. A gargantuan sculpture, whose sensual titanium curves glimmer like running water in the sun, it has inevitably overshadowed the artworks it contains.

While *Maman*, one of Louise Bourgeois's fearsome spiders, stands by the river, the Guggenheim's main entrance, on the city side of the building, is guarded by

Jeff Koons' altogether cuddlier giant flower sculpture, *Puppy*. Originally installed as a temporary exhibit for the opening ceremony, it became a permanent feature after *bilbainos* clamoured for it to stay. Once inside, visitors flow seamlessly through the various galleries, crisscrossing the vast, light-filled atrium on walkways. Gehry called the largest room on the ground floor his "fish gallery"; stretching away beneath the road bridge, it's permanently given over to Richard Serra's disorienting sculpture series, *The Matter of Time*, consisting of eight enormous shapes of rusted steel, coiled and labyrinthine. The rest of the museum hosts top-flight temporary exhibitions, and also displays a rotating selection from the Guggenheim Foundation's unparalleled collection of twentieth-century art, which features works by all the major modern and contemporary figures, including Kandinsky, Klee, Mondrian, Picasso, Cézanne, Chagall, Warhol, Calder and Rauschenberg, to name a few. One painting, though, is conspicuous by its absence: Picasso's *Guernica* – in the Centro de Arte Reina Sofía in Madrid (see p.102) – whose "return" the Basques have been demanding for years.

Tickets are valid for the whole day, so it's worth arriving early and taking a break for lunch – perhaps at the museum's classy, yet inexpensive, **restaurant** (see p.478). Free **guided tours** start at 11am, 12.30pm, 4pm and 6.30pm, though in practice English guides will only be provided if there's a big enough group – call ahead to make sure (☏944 359 090). English audioguides are included in the price.

West of the Guggenheim

The area of former docks and rail depots to the west (downriver) of the Guggenheim, known as **Abandoibarra**, is still under construction, though you can walk all the way along the riverbank to the Euskalduna, past the spanking-new **Zubiarte** shopping centre (daily 10am–10pm). Alternatively, head down Alameda de Mazarredo, west from the Guggenheim's main entrance, to reach the **Museo de Bellas Artes** (Tues–Sun 10am–8pm; Ⓦwww.museobilbao.com; €5.50, free on Wed), at the edge of a nice green park, the Parque de Doña Casilda de Iturriza. A conventional, reverential, old-fashioned art museum, this houses a diverse,

▲ Maman and the Museo Guggenheim

well-displayed collection, including works by El Greco, Goya and Van Dyck and some delightful Gothic altarpieces. Basque artists are much better represented than in the Guggenheim, with two rooms devoted to Juan de Echevarría, and one to Aurelio Arteta. Continuing through the park you come to the **Euskalduna**, another creative piece of architecture, blending rusty iron, glass, steel and concrete, and backed by the curved Puente Euskalduna. Built on the ruins of the city's last shipyard, which closed in the 1980s, it hosts conferences and classical perform-ances. It's a beautiful building to look around – particularly the tiled floors inside – but staff are rather snooty to the casual visitor. However, there are one-hour guided tours (Sat noon; €2), starting from door 4 on street level – call ☎944 035 000 or just turn up fifteen minutes early to get your ticket.

At quayside level, just past the Euskalduna, the **Museo Marítimo Ría de Bilbao** (Tues–Sun 10am–8pm; Ⓦwww.museomaritimobilbao.org; €5; ⓂSan Mamés) is a very fancy new museum that explains in intricate detail exactly how the *ría* between the city and the sea has been cleared over the centuries to deal with ever larger marine traffic. It's all very worthy, and you can clamber aboard assorted vessels in the old docks of the Euskalduna Shipyard outside; but sadly, hardly anyone seems to bother to visit.

Beaches

The city is well supplied with **beaches** along the mouth of the estuary and around both headlands. The metro means it's easier to reach the beaches on the east bank, such as those at **Sopelana** (ⓂLarrabasterra), including the nudist Playa de Arrietara. **Getxo** (ⓂAlgorta) has a pretty old quarter with white houses and green-painted doors, and an impressive waterfront promenade fringed with private mansions belonging to Bilbao's millionaire set. At the end of Metro Line 1, 15km north of the city, **Plentzia** (ⓂPlentzia) is generally cleaner and not quite so crowded as the beaches closer to town.

Eating, drinking and nightlife

Bilbao, like San Sebastián, is one of the culinary capitals of Spain. Innovative **restaurants** and Michelin-star winners knock out some of the most acclaimed cuisine in Europe, from traditional Basque fare to high-class *nueva cocina vasca* meals that can cost as much as a five-star hotel room, while the **tapas bars** are equally mouthwatering. Taking a high-speed *txikiteo* (tapas crawl) through the Casco Viejo is an essential part of any visit – the best targets tend to be clustered in the *siete calles* (seven streets), bordered by c/de la Ronda and c/Pelota, but there are also some good options on c/Diputacion in Ensanche.

Bilbao's most famous dish is undoubtedly **cod** (*bacalao*), traditionally served with *salsa vizcaina* (a sauce of red onions and peppers) or *al pil pil* (a garlic-based sauce). The city has a vibrant **nightlife**, especially at the weekends – and goes totally wild during the August **fiesta**, with scores of open-air bars, live music and impromptu dancing everywhere and a truly festive atmosphere.

Cafés

Cafe La Granja Plaza Circular. Founded in 1926, this spacious and elegant French-style café features iron columns and beautiful Art Nouveau lamps. Drinks and *pintxos* are served all day. Mon–Sat 5.30am–2am.

Cafe Iruña Jardines de Albia (on Colón de Larreategui). This historic café and bar was established in 1903, its elaborate murals and ornate

Mudéjar decor and tiling making it marvellously atmospheric. It's a great place for a drink or a few *pintxos* – the *pinchos morunos*, or mini-kebabs, are especially worth trying (€2).

Tapas bars

Artajo c/Ledesma 7; ⓂAbando. One of the best *pintxos* options outside the Casco Viejo, this venerable old bar, one of several on c/Ledesma, knocks out superb mussels in piquant anchovy and tomato sauce (*tigres*) from Yurre, a small village in Bizkaia. Tues–Sun 10am–11pm.

Atlanta c/Rodríguez Arias 28; ⓂMoyúa. A popular local bar celebrated for its *jamón serrano*, steak sandwiches and fried calamari; *menú* at €13. Daily 7am–2am.

Berton c/Jardínes 11. Friendly Casco Viejo bar, a warm inviting space with some outside tables and lots of drinking space inside. Fresh modern *pintxos* at €1.70, including quails' eggs with prawns and mushrooms, and lots of ham options, plus *raciones* of ham, anchovies and the like.

Busterri c/Licenciado Poza 43; ⓂIndautxu. The best *pintxos* bar in Ensanche: specialities include grilled anchovies and *jamón jabugo* (a rare cured ham from southwest Spain); *menú* at €13.50. Tues–Sun 10am–1am.

Café Bar Bilbao Plaza Nueva 6. Exceptional anchovy, ham and *bacalao al pil-pil* *pintxos*, served by *simpatico* staff, with everything labelled on the counter in the stylish old blue-tiled café, and some tables on the Casco Viejo's lovely main square. Daily 9.30am–11pm (closed Sun afternoons).

Los Fueros c/Fueros 6. If you fancy getting away from the crowds, nip behind the back of Plaza Nueva and try this small bar, specializing in grilled prawns (*gambas*) and barnacles (*percebes*). Mon, Tues & Thurs–Sat 11am–3pm & 6.30–10pm, Sun 10.30am–3pm.

Gatz c/Santa María 10. A cosy late-night tapas bar serving exquisite cod *pintxos* and a special Basque-style *ratatouille*. It's also a good place for a *tinto* or beer at night. Mon–Fri 1–3pm & 7–11pm (Fri till midnight), Sat 1pm–midnight, Sun 1–3pm.

Taberna Txiriboga c/Santa María 13. Lively little white-tiled tapas bar in the heart of the Casco Viejo, with a wide selection of *pintxos*. Mon–Sat 1–3pm & 7–11pm.

Xukela c/El Perro 2. With its red panelling and check tablecloths, this Casco Viejo tapas bar is oddly reminiscent of a French bistro, but it serves a wide range of snacks and a top-class wine list, with a lot of open space for drinkers who prefer to stand.

Restaurants

Amboto c/Jardines 2. This attractive, traditional Basque dining room sits above the *Amboto* tapas bar, with a huge menu, but *bacalao* (€14) is the speciality.

Casa Rufo c/Hurtado de Amézaga 5 ☎944 432 172. A deservedly popular *cocina*, with three cosy, themed dining rooms specializing in three main items: cod and two types of unbelievably succulent steak (*chuleton*), the main reason you'll need a reservation – it's priced by the kilo. Count on spending at least €50 for two people.

Etxanobe Euskalduna, Avda Abandoibarra 4 ☎944 421 071, ⓌAbandoibarra 4 ☎944 421 071, Ⓦen.etxanobe.com. The Euskalduna restaurant is another culinary star, run by yet another celebrated chef, Fernando Canales, who creates incredibly innovative, contemporary cuisine. Mains start from around €25, and there's a €57 tasting *menú*. Closed Sun.

Museo Guggenheim Café & Restaurant ☎944 239 333. Superb *nueva cocina* from the Martin Berasatagui stable at the restaurant (closed Tues eve, Mon & Sun), and a surprisingly inexpensive lunch *menú* (€13.50) at the café (Tues–Sun 9am–9pm). Be sure to reserve a table.

Ortua Alameda Mazarredo 18. Homely vegetarian restaurant doing an excellent *menú* for €9 – the servers will read you the choices. Convenient for a break from the Guggenheim. Mon–Fri 1–3.30pm.

El Perro Chico Aretxaga 2 ☎944 150 519. This traditional Basque *cocina*, overlooking the south bank of the river, became a big hit after Frank Gehry claimed it was his favourite – the seafood is particularly good. Closed Mon lunch & Sun.

Río Oja c/El Perro 6. Old-fashioned, inexpensive Casco Viejo restaurant with an unusual emphasis on hearty stews and sauces; sample some snails or mussels in a spicy red sauce, or get a full seafood *cazuela*.

Serantes c/Licenciado Poza 16 ☎944 212 129. A top-notch *marisquería*, where a meal comes to about €50 per head. Watch for specials on *langostino* and other crustacean delights. There's also an excellent tapas bar. Daily 10am–1am (closed Tues eve).

Victor Montes Plaza Nueva 8. This atmospheric bar and dining room, lined with a collection of over 1600 wines, offers traditional grills, special hams and fresh fish in its popular restaurant, or sumptuous *pintxos*; tables on the square in summer. Tues–Sun 10am–11pm.

Zortziko Alameda Manzarredo 17 ☎944 239 743, Ⓦwww.zortziko.es. An extremely fancy restaurant, with Parisian decor and some of the finest *nueva cocina* dishes concocted by acclaimed chef Daniel Garcia (€25 and up). Closed Sun & Mon.

Bars, clubs and live music

Bars (most serving tapas) can be found all through the **Casco Viejo**; c/Barrenkale is the heart of the madness, but the outdoor tables in the beautiful **Plaza Nueva** make a great place for a more relaxed drink in the early evening. **Ensanche** holds plenty of pubs and bars; lively areas with a slightly smarter atmosphere are the streets that stretch between the Plaza Circular and the Guggenheim, and farther east, around the junction of c/de Licenciado Poza and Gregorio de Revilla, a wealthy area known as **Pozas** (Ⓜ️Indautxu). The city also has a reasonably vibrant **club** scene, with the edgier San Francisco district south of the Casco Viejo, across the river and home to Bilbao's West African and Moroccan population, a hot area for dancing till dawn. Hard rock and punk fans tend to congregate in the grungy bars along c/Iturribide, northeast of the Casco Viejo.

Live music abounds in Bilbao; check the listings in the local newspaper *El Correo* (Ⓦwww.elcorreodigital.com). In addition to the popular music venues listed below, **Teatro Arriaga** (Ⓣ944 163 333, Ⓦwww.teatroarriaga.com) hosts dance and music events, as well as theatre. The **Euskalduna** (Ⓣ944 035 000, Ⓦwww.euskalduna.net), home of the Bilbao Symphony Orchestra, offers opera and classical music, and theatrical performances; you can pick up a bi-monthly programme from the box office (downstairs on the river level; Mon–Fri 9am–2pm & 4–7pm).

Bars

Bullitt Groove Club c/Dos de Mayo 3. Extremely hip bar-cum-club, with an eclectic clientele and mix of music, from the latest dance sounds to indie and rock. It usually opens at around 6pm at the weekends, and closes at around 6am.

Dubliners Plaza Moyúa 6. Bilbao is full of Irish pubs and this is one of the best, with pints of Guinness and Murphy's going for €5 and hearty *menús* for €15. Daily 8.30am–11pm (Fri & Sat till 3am).

Herriko Taberna c/de la Ronda 20. An excellent place for a straightforward, inexpensive meal and a drink, with wooden tables, a strong Basque nationalist atmosphere (this is the local Batasuna bar), and rock most nights. Mon–Sat 10am–3am, Sun 12.30pm–midnight.

Lamiak c/Pelota 8. A large café-bar with a cool gallery packed with tables upstairs, and a fashionable crowd at the weekends. Daily 4pm–midnight (2am weekends).

Lasai c/Ronda 2. A no-frills modern bar that tends to fill up with late-night drinkers at the weekends and is usually the last to close in the Casco Viejo. Daily 5pm–5/6am.

Taberna Txomin Barullo c/Barrencalle 40. A great laidback café-bar with nationalist murals and an alternative crowd. Daily noon–midnight.

Clubs and live-music venues

Azkena c/Ibanez de Bilbao 26, Ⓦwww.azkena.com; Ⓜ️Abando. Popular live-music space and bar, with simple, minimalist decor and dancefloor, that tends to get busy late in the evenings. Mon–Sat 5pm–2am (5am weekends).

BilboRock-La Merced Muelle de la Merced 1 Ⓦwww.bilbao.net/bilborock; Ⓜ️Abando.

This large, retro-styled converted church, just across the Puente La Merced from the Casco Viejo, is the city's best live venue for rock and alternative music.

Caos c/Simon Bolivar 10; Ⓜ️Indautxu. A lively *discoteca* in the southern half of the city, with a mix of dance and indie sounds. Mon–Thurs 4pm–12.30am, Fri & Sat 4pm–4.30am.

Congreso Muelle de Uribitarte 4; Ⓜ️Abando. An extremely chic *club du jour*, with plenty of house and a decent sound system – gets going well after midnight.

Cotton Club c/Gregorio de la Revilla 25 Ⓦwww.cottonclubbilbao.com; Ⓜ️Indautxu. Popular live-music and disco venue, entered on c/Simon Bolivar, featuring everything from jazz and blues to rock and house. Beer starts at €3, and there's no cover. Mon–Thurs 4.30pm–3am, Fri & Sat 6.30pm–6.30am, Sun 6.30pm–3am.

Conjunto Vacio Muelle de la Merced 3 Ⓦwww.conjuntovacio.net; Ⓜ️Abando. A popular nightclub on the south bank, with a Sun-morning session for hardcore clubbers. Fri & Sat midnight–4am, Sun 9am–1pm.

Hegoak c/Dos de Mayo 7 Ⓦwww.hegopop.com; Ⓜ️Abando. One of the best house clubs in the city, doubling as a live-music and alternative arts venue. Club nights are usually €10 – things get going from around midnight at the weekends.

Image Club c/Sabino Arana, Berango Ⓦtheimageclub.com; Ⓜ️Berango. The largest warehouse-type dance club in the region, 15min walk from Ⓜ️Berango, with two floors, balconies, and big-name DJs flown in to compete with the local stars.

Kafe Antzokia c/San Vicente 2 Ⓦwww.kafeantzokia.com; Ⓜ️Abando. This theatre-turned-nightclub has an emphasis on live shows, and attracts big names, from world music and reggae, to folk- and punk-influenced groups and Basque musicians. Resident DJs spin an eclectic mix Saturday nights, with plenty of local sounds. Open all day for drinks and light meals.

New High Club c/Naja 5; Ⓜ️Abando. The city's most visible gay club. In the main room, Spanish dance music is played, and in a small theatre upstairs XX-rated films are shown. There's a hyperactive "dark room" in the back. Open late.

Listings

Bookshops Tin-Tas, c/General Concha 10 (Ⓜ️Indautxu), is a large travel bookshop with a wide range of maps and guides (Mon–Fri 10am–8.30pm, Sat 10am–2.30pm & 5–8.30pm). FNAC, Alameda Urquijo 4 (Mon–Sat 10am–9pm), sells books, music and digital equipment. The best place to buy English and other foreign newspapers (one day late) is Librería Cámara (Mon–Fri 9am–1.30pm & 4–8pm) at Euskalduna 6 (Ⓜ️Abando). Librería de Bilbao on Alameda Mazaredo (opposite the Guggenheim) sells old postcards and books on the city (Mon–Sat 10.30am–2pm & 4–8.30pm).

Car rental Car-rental outlets can be found at the airport, or in the city at: Avis, Alameda Dr Areilza 34 ☎944 275 760; Europcar, Licenciado Poza 56 ☎944 422 849; Budget, Dr Nicolás Achúcarro 8 ☎944 150 870; all Ⓜ️Indautxu, while Hertz is at Dr Achúcarro 10 in Deusto ☎944 153 677.

Consulates The British consulate is at Alameda Urquijo 2 ☎944 157 722.

Football Athletico Bilbao (Ⓦwww.athletic-club.net), known as *Rojiblancos* because of their red-and-white striped shirts, and famous for only fielding Basque players or products of their own youth system, have never been relegated from the Primera División – though they've come very close in recent seasons. Watch them play or visit their exhibition centre at the Campo de San Mamés (the "cathedral of football", as *bilbainos* would have it).

Hospital Hospital de Basurto, Avda. de Montevideo 18 ☎944 418 700 (Ⓜ️San Mamés), or take the tram to the last stop. Call ambulances on ☎944 410 081 or 944 100 000 (24hr).

Internet access *San Mames Locutorio*, Luis Briñas 25 (daily 11am–11pm; Ⓜ️San Mamés) is opposite Termibus; *Laser Ciberlocal* at c/Sendeja 5 (daily 11am–3.30pm) and *Net-House* at c/Villarias 6 (daily 10.30am–10.30pm) are the most convenient for the Casco Viejo.

Post office Alameda Urquijo 19 (Mon–Fri 8am–9pm, Sat 9am–2pm; Ⓜ️Abando or Moyúa). There's another post office near the Guggenheim main entrance, Alameda Mazarredo 13 (same hours).

Shopping Basandere, c/Iparraguirre 4, near the Guggenheim, is touristy but a good place to pick up Basque souvenirs (Tues–Sat 10.30am–8.30pm, Sun noon–6pm). On the same street, La Carte des Vines at no. 7 sells quality wines.

Taxi TeleTaxi ☎944 102 121, Radio Taxi Bilbao ☎944 448 888.

Tours Bilbao Tour offers circular bus tours of the city from Plaza Ensanche: tickets are valid for 24hr (Jan, March, Nov & Dec Tues–Sun 11am & 12.30pm; April–June & July–Oct Tues–Sat 11am, 12.30pm & 4pm, July–Sept also 5.30pm, Sun 11am & 12.30pm; ☎944 795 760, Ⓦwww.busturistikoa .com; €12).

Inland Bizkaia

Inland Bizkaia is well off the beaten track, yet has much to offer, with spectacular walking and climbing country. The otherwise uninspiring factory town of **Durango**, 30km southeast of Bilbao (easily reached by train from Estación de Atxuri), is the gateway to the **Parque Natural de Urkiola**, incorporating the most accessible parts of the impressive Duranguesado Massif. To explore this area of rocky peaks, the best access point is the **Urkiola Pass** (on the Durango–Vitoria-Gasteiz road and bus route), where a trail leads behind the **Santuario de Urkiola** (and a couple of restaurants on the road) for about three hours to the highest peak, **Amboto** (1330m – the pass is 713m). This summit is a favourite with Basque walkers and climbers – the final scramble to the top can be a bit vertigo-inducing. A short walk up the lane on the other side of the main road takes you to a small **information centre** (daily 10am–2pm & 4–6pm).

Alternatively, head for the beautiful **Valle de Atxondo** off the Durango–Elorrio road on the other side of the park, where there are more walking possibilities. If you don't have your own transport, take the hourly buses as far as the signposted crossroads and then walk 2.5km to the pristine village of **AXPE**, nestling at the foot of Amboto – a good base for a couple of days' walking. The valley has become extremely chic, so things tend to be pricey: there's a good **agroturismo**, *Imitte-Etxebarria*, 500m before the village (☎946 231 659, ⓦwww.nekatur.net /imitte-etxebarria; ❸), and the 🏃 *Mendi Goikoa*, 400m up the hill (☎946 820 833, ⓦwww.mendigoikoa.com; ❺), two wonderfully restored old farmhouses with a smart restaurant (closed Mon–Thurs eve & Sun) on site. *Extebarri*, in the centre of the village (☎946 583 042, ⓦwww.asadoretxebarri.com; closed Sun eve & Aug), is another Basque gourmet paradise, with a €50 *menú* and €25 for mains.

Vitoria-Gasteiz and around

VITORIA-GASTEIZ, the capital of Araba (Alava) and the entire País Vasco autonomous region, crowns a slight rise in the heart of a fertile plain. Founded as **Vitoria** in 1181 by Sancho el Sabio, King of Navarre, on the site of the far older Basque village of **Gasteiz**, it was already a prosperous place by the time of its capture by the Castilian Alfonso VIII in 1200. Later, as the centre of a flourishing wool and iron trade, Vitoria became seriously rich, and the town still boasts an unusual concentration of Renaissance palaces and fine churches.

Vitoria-Gasteiz is a fascinating old city, all the better for lying off the tourist circuit. Its old core is full of rowdy bars and *tabernas*, not to mention an abundance of excellent Basque restaurants, making it a pleasant place to escape the crowds for a few days.

Arrival and information

The city's useful **turismo** is at Plaza del General Lomo 1 (Mon–Sat 10am–7pm, Sun 11am–2pm; ☎945 161 598, ⓦwww.vitoria-gasteiz.org/turismo), on the southern edge of the old town, or **Casco Medieval**. The RENFE **train station** is in the **Ensanche** district, the commercial centre south of here, at the southern end of pedestrianized c/Dato, while the **bus station** is on c/Los Herrán, ten-minutes' walk east of the old town. For **internet access**, head for the spacious *Ciber Queen* (daily 11am–2.30pm & 4.30–10pm; €1.50/hr) on c/Badaia.

Accommodation

There's surprisingly little **accommodation** within Vitoria's old town; the budget options are concentrated near the train and bus stations, while more expensive hotels, many aimed at business travellers, tend to be in Ensanche, south of the Casco Medieval. The only times you might have trouble locating a room are during the **jazz festival** in the third week of July (ⓦwww.jazzvitoria.com), or the **Virgen Blanca festival** (Aug 4–9).

🏃 **La Casa de los Arquillos** Paseo de los Arquillos 1 ☎945 151 259. Lovely little boutique hotel, which calls itself a B&B, in a superb central location in a medieval building converted to hold bright, stylish en-suite bedrooms. The one snag is this spot can get a little noisy. ❹

Hostal La Bilbaina c/Prudencio María de Verástegui 2 ☎945 254 400. Comfortable, modern rooms with bath above a large restaurant, all with satellite TV. ❸

Hotel Ciudad de Vitoria Portal de Castilla 8 ☎945 141 100, ⓦwww.hoteles-silken.com. Opulent *belle époque* hotel, beautifully restored,

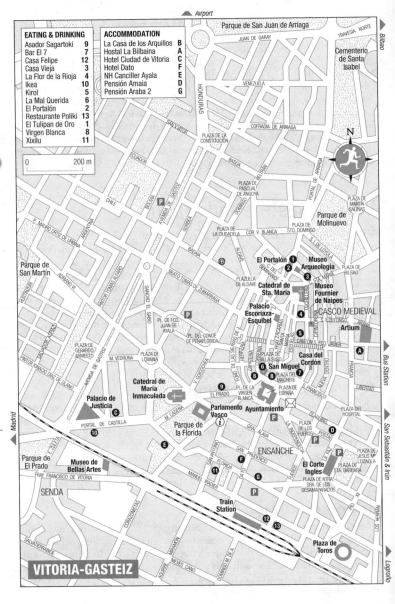

VITORIA-GASTEIZ

EATING & DRINKING

Asador Sagartoki	9
Bar El 7	7
Casa Felipe	12
Casa Vieja	3
La Flor de la Rioja	4
Ikea	10
Kirol	5
La Mal Querida	6
El Portalón	2
Restaurante Poliki	13
El Tulipan de Oro	1
Virgen Blanca	8
Xixilu	11

ACCOMMODATION

La Casa de los Arquillos	B
Hostal La Bilbaina	A
Hotel Ciudad de Vitoria	C
Hotel Dato	F
NH Canciller Ayala	E
Pensión Amaia	D
Pensión Araba 2	G

and offering comfortable lavishly appointed rooms with immaculate marble-clad bathrooms. Extras include fitness centre and parking on site. ④

Hotel Dato c/Dato 28 ☎ 945 147 230, ⓦ www .hoteldato.com. Beyond the gaudy mix of Egyptian statues and mirrors in the lobby, this cosy hotel has super-helpful staff and tastefully decorated rooms

with colourful batik bedspreads and free wi-fi. All rooms have baths; pay a little extra for one with an enclosed balcony. ②

NH Canciller Ayala c/Ramón y Cajal 5 ☎ 945 130 000, ⓦ www.nh-hotels.com. In a convenient and pleasant location on the edge of the Parque de la Florida, this is the modern counterpoint to the

Ciudad de Vitoria: the super-comfortable rooms come with polished wood floors and smart, contemporary furniture and fittings. ❹
Pensión Amaia c/La Paz 15 ☏945 255 497, Ⓦwww.pensionamaia.com. Friendly *pensión* with seven somewhat faded double rooms,

two triples and one single; all share modern bathrooms. ❷
Pensión Araba 2 c/Florida 25 ☏945 232 588. An excellent-value *pensión* in an immaculately kept family home, offering four clean rooms with or without bath. ❷

The City

The streets of the Romanesque **Casco Medieval** spread like a spider's web down the sides of the hill, surrounded on level ground by a neater grid of later development. You'll get the feel of the city simply by wandering through this old quarter. Although parts of it can be rather shabby, with very visible Batasuna and Basque independence support sprayed onto walls and posters, it is on the whole a harmonious place. All its graceful mansions and churches are built from the same greyish-gold stone, and many of the medieval buildings are amazingly well preserved. Among the finest is the **Palacio de Escoriaza-Esquibel** on c/Fray Zacarías, with its sixteenth-century Plateresque portal. On the southern edge of the old town, the porticoed **Plaza de España**, a popular location for early-evening strolling and drinking, is a gem, while the neighbouring **Plaza de la Virgen Blanca** is more elegant, with glassed-in balconies. If you find the hill itself a bit of a challenge, Vitoria offers a remarkable feature: **moving stairways** climb it from both the east (Cantón de San Francisco Javier) and west (Cantón de la Soledad) sides.

The heart of the old town is the venerable **Catedral de Santa María**, which is steadily undergoing a remarkable reconstruction process. You can tour the cathedral and witness the construction work up-close via guided tours (daily 11am–1pm & 5–7pm; €5; ☏945 255 135, Ⓦwww.catedralvitoria. com; booking essential). These start at the northern side of the cathedral, off Plaza de la Burullería, where there's also a small but informative exhibition, accessible without prior booking (daily 10.30am–2pm & 4.30–8pm; free). The **tour** takes you through the different periods of construction, beginning in the thirteenth century when the cathedral was an integral part of the town's defences, and explains how Renaissance attempts to remodel the heavy Gothic structure resulted in serious structural defects – one look at the severely twisted arches that hold the whole thing up may send you running for the exit. The fourteenth-century west doorway is superb, intricately and lovingly carved; seen from the level of the scaffolding, the faces of the saints appear distorted, since they were carved to be viewed from ground level. Behind the cathedral, down the hill on the left, **El Portalón**, now home to a fancy restaurant, is the most impressive of the surviving trading houses of Renaissance Vitoria-Gasteiz, its dusty red brick and wooden beams and balconies in marked contrast to the golden stone elsewhere. Over the road, at c/Correria 116, is the province's **Museo de Arqueología** (Tues–Fri 10am–2pm & 4–6.30pm, Sat 10am–2pm, Sun 11am–2pm; free), with well-presented displays of prehistoric, Roman and early medieval artefacts. Take time also to visit the fine medieval church of **San Miguel** (Mon–Sat 11am–noon & 6.30–8pm, Sun 10.30am–2.30pm), just above Plaza de España. Outside its door stands the fourteenth-century stone image of the Virgen Blanca, revered patron of the city.

East of the old town, not far from the bus station at c/Francia 24, is the **Artium** (Tues–Sun 11am–8pm; Ⓦwww.artium.org; €4.50, free Wed), the city's attractive museum of contemporary art, where a comprehensive collection of 1600 exhibits focuses on Basque and Spanish artists whose work is organized loosely in conceptual themes.

Fiesta de la Virgen Blanca

To experience the city's annual **Fiesta de la Virgen Blanca** (Aug 4–9) is to see the good-natured Vitorians at their finest. On the first day of the festival you need to be in the Plaza de la Virgen Blanca with a blue-and-white festival scarf, a bottle of champagne, a cigar and wearing old clothes. At 6pm, the umbrella-toting "Bajada del Celedón" – a life-size doll dressed in traditional costume – appears from the church tower and flies through the air over the plaza. This is the signal to spray champagne everywhere (hence the old clothes), light the cigar and put on your scarf – which the hard core don't take off until midnight on the 9th, when Celedón returns to his tower, signalling the end of the fiesta. In between, the town is engulfed in a continuous party.

Southwest of the centre, a magnificent mansion on the attractive, pedestrianized, tree-lined Paseo de Fray Francisco de Vitoria in Senda district holds the **Museo de Bellas Artes** (Tues–Fri 10am–2pm & 4–6.30pm, Sat 10am–2pm & 5–8pm, Sun 11am–2pm; free). Its fine collection centres on the period from 1700 to 1950; highlights include the *costumbrista* paintings, depicting Basque cultural and folk practices.

Eating and drinking

Vitoria-Gasteiz has a solid selection of quality **restaurants** and **cafés**, aimed principally at a no-nonsense local clientele – plazas de España and Virgen Blanca hold particularly appealing arrays of outdoor cafés – while **tapas bars** are spread throughout both Ensanche and the edges of the Casco Medieval. Look out for such regional specialities as potatoes with chorizo, *porrosalda* (leek soup) and *perretxikos* (wild mushrooms with egg). The city is also famous throughout Spain for its attachment to broad beans and, most of all, its **chocolates**; *trufas*, *bombones* and *vasquitos* can be purchased, along with cakes such as *chuchitos de Vitoria* (a bit like profiteroles) and other sugary delights, at Hueto e Hijos, c/Postas 4, or Goya, c/Dato 6, both in business since the nineteenth century.

The city's dynamic **nightlife** is primarily fuelled by its student population. The main areas are the streets off c/Dato in Ensanche, and the pubs on the eastern side of the Casco Medieval, particularly on c/Cuchillería, where places such as *Bar El 7* at no. 3 have a grungier, alternative feel. The *Cairo Stereo Club*, c/Aldave 9, is the liveliest club in town.

Tapas bars and restaurants

Asador Sagartoki c/Prado 18 ☎945 288 876, ⓦwww.sagartoki.es. Tucked away behind a tapas bar, this popular restaurant has rustic decor, exposed beams and succulent grilled meats such as *chuletillas* (steak) from €15–20 and a special cider-house *menú* (€38.50). Closed Sun pm & Mon.

Casa Felipe c/Fueros 28. A reasonably priced tapas bar with a local, no-frills atmosphere, specializing in excellent Basque dishes – try the *pimientos rellenos* and *chorizo a la sidra*. Closed Sun am & Mon.

Casa Vieja c/Chiquita 6 ☎945 146 565. A lovely old restaurant with exposed brick and a large open fireplace. Mains from €15, with a €28 special *menú* of traditional Basque food. Closed Sun eve & Mon.

La Flor de la Rioja c/Cuchillería s/n. Tiny, tumbledown old bar that seems like a relic from a bygone age.

Ikea Portal de Castilla 27 ☎945 144 747. Expensive, chic restaurant in a converted stone townhouse, serving good Basque food with a contemporary spin; mains from €20. The liver pâté is highly recommended. Closed Sun lunch & Mon.

Kirol c/Cuchillería 31. Dimly lit but friendly tapas bar in an old wood-beamed house, with a fine selection of *raciones*, including – for the brave – deep-fried pig's ear. Daily 12.30–3pm & 7pm–2am.

La Mal Querida c/Correría 10. Hip, modern tapas bar, serving innovative snacks and *raciones* both indoors and out, a few steps away from the Plaza de la Virgen Blanca.

El Portalón c/Correría 150 ☎945 142 755. Pricey restaurant specializing in traditional Basque cooking, set in beautiful sixteenth-century surroundings. There's a €25 lunch *menú*, but expect to pay twice that for dinner – and make a reservation. Closed Sun.

Restaurante Políki c/Manuel Iradier 48. A modern Basque restaurant with a superb *menú* for €25, and mains from €16. Closed Sun.

El Tulipán de Oro c/Correría 157. Cosy tapas bar in an aged wood-beamed house, serving *chorizo* flambéed at the bar over pig-shaped alcohol burners, with a €10 weekday *menú*.

Mon–Thurs & Sun 11.30am–11pm, Fri & Sat 11.30–midnight.

Virgen Blanca Plaza de la Virgen Blanca 2. Restaurant/bar with the feel of a British gastro-pub, in a great location overlooking the plaza, with an atmospheric dining room, exposed brick walls, wooden tables and a good €18.60 *menú*. Daily 9am–2am, closed Mon am.

Xixilu Plaza Amarika 2 ☎945 230 068. The restaurant beyond the bar is one of the best places to sample local Basque fare and is noted for its fish dishes such as *bacalao* (€12.50) and grilled meats such as *litiruelas* (lamb; €13.50).

Around Vitoria-Gasteiz

Attractive though the city is, a significant part of the charm of Vitoria-Gasteiz is the beauty of the surrounding countryside. Almost every hamlet in this once-rich farming territory has something of interest: an old stone mansion proudly displaying the family coat of arms, a lavishly decorated church, or a farmhouse raised on stilts.

A popular day-trip is to the village of **MENDOZA**, a few kilometres west of Vitoria-Gasteiz and dominated by a fortified tower-house now established as the **Museo de Heráldica Alavesa** (Tues–Sat 11am–3pm, Sun 10am–noon; free), which contains a fascinating collection of coats of arms of the Basque nobility through the ages and an exhibition of the history of the principal clans and their often bloody feuds.

Salvatierra and Zalduondo

To the east, on the **Llanada Alavesa** (Plain of Alava), lie some of the best-preserved villages of inland Euskal Herria. The main town on the plain is **SALVATIERRA**, situated on the Vitoria–Pamplona rail line. The old walled quarter rises above the countryside, offering splendid views, and the Gothic church of Santa María is visible from afar. At the other end of town, at c/Mayor 8, there's an extremely helpful **turismo** (☎945 312 535, ⓦwww.cuadrillasalvatierra.org), opposite which is an ageing *fonda* (☎945 300 052; ❷), attached to the *Bar Merino*.

To the northeast lies pretty **ZALDUONDO**, home to a simple bar-restaurant and the **Museo Comarcal** of local ethnography (Sun noon–2pm; free), which is housed in the sixteenth-century Palacio de los Lazárraga; look out for the heraldic crest over the main door, one of the most elaborate in the País Vasco. Zalduondo, although tiny, is famous for its traditional **carnaval** celebrations, where a Guy Fawkes-like figure, "Markitos", is ritually tried and then burned as a scapegoat for the misfortunes of the past year. A restored eighteenth-century house serves as a *casa rural*, *Eikolara* (☎945 304 332, ⓦwww.eikolara.com; ❹).

Rioja Alavesa

South of Vitoria-Gasteiz lies the wine-growing district of **Rioja Alavesa**, best combined with a tour, easiest done with your own transport, of the villages across the Ebro in La Rioja province (see p.415). In addition to a series of picturesque villages, the region's main attraction is its numerous **bodegas**, many featuring stunning contemporary architecture, not to mention fine wines – note that visits always require a phone call beforehand.

The main town of **LAGUARDIA**, served by regular buses from Vitoria-Gasteiz, makes a quieter alternative base to the more popular Rioja towns of

Logroño or Haro. If you're driving, don't miss the Balcon de la Rioja (1104m), a viewpoint 35km south of Vitoria-Gasteiz, with magnificent views over the plain. Laguardia is an interesting old walled town of cobbled streets and historic buildings, entered through the Puerta de San Juan. Its useful **turismo** on Plaza de San Juan (Mon–Sat 10am–2pm & 4–7pm, Sat from 5pm, Sun 10.45am–2pm; ℡945 600 845, Ⓦwww.laguardia-alava.com) has information on the many local *bodegas*, as well as the keys to the church of **Santa María de los Reyes**, with its ornately carved Gothic doorway. The elegant ⚒ *Castillo el Collado*, within the Bodegas Palacio, just outside town on the road to Elciego (℡945 621 200, Ⓦwww.jpmoser.com/castilloelcollado.html; ❺), is a fabulous **place to stay**. Alternatives include the luxurious *Hotel Villa de Laguardia*, outside the town wall at Paseo San Raimundo 15 (℡945 600 560, Ⓦwww.hotelvilladelaguardia .com; ❺), which also contains a good **restaurant**, and the good-value *Pachico Martínez*, c/Sancho Abarca 20 (℡945 600 009, Ⓦwww.pachico.com; ❸).

Two kilometres north of Laguardia, off the Vitoria-Gasteiz road and clearly visible from afar, the mesmerizing **Bodegas Ysios** (Mon–Fri 11am, 1pm & 4pm, Sat & Sun 11am & 1pm; €3; ℡945 600 640, Ⓦwww.bodegasysios.com) resembles some extraordinary ancient temple, with an undulating titanium roof designed by Santiago Calatrava (the architect of Bilbao airport). Another 5km south, in the appealing village of **ELCIEGO**, the **Bodegas Marques de Riscal** (€10; ℡945 606 590, Ⓦwww.marquesderiscal.com) surrounds a remarkable structure designed by Frank O. Gehry. A tangle of colossal multi-coloured titanium ribbons swaddles one of the most acclaimed new buildings in the world, the phenomenal *Hotel Marqués de Riscal* (℡945 180 880, Ⓦwww .luxurycollection.com/marquesderiscal.com; ❾), where room rates start at €450 and soar into the thousands.

On the road to Logroño, just 6km from the city, **Bodega Vina Real** offers tours of its vast, barrel-shaped facilities (Mon & Thurs–Sun 11.30am, 1pm & 4pm; ℡945 625 255), while, to the west, the attractive villages of **Samaniego** and **Labastida** offer more wine-touring opportunities.

Pamplona and around

PAMPLONA (Iruña) has been the capital of Navarra since the ninth century, and long before that was a powerful fortress town defending the northern approaches to Spain at the foothills of the Pyrenees – it takes its name from the Roman general Pompey. With a long history as capital of an often semi-autonomous state and an important stop on the Camino de Santiago, Pamplona is now a prosperous city of just under 200,000, with plenty to offer around its old centre, the **Casco Antiguo** – enticing churches, a beautiful park and the massive citadel. A robust, visceral place, with a rough-hewn edge and a strong streak of macho self-confidence, Pamplona makes an appealing year-round destination, but for anyone who has been here during the thrilling week of the **Fiestas de San Fermín** – described in all their glory in the box on p.490–491 – a visit at any other time can only be an anticlimax.

Arrival and information

Pamplona's helpful **turismo**, at c/Eslava 1 on the corner of Plaza San Francisco, is only accessible on foot (June Mon–Fri 10am–7pm, Sat 10am–2pm & 4–7pm, Sun 10am–2pm; July & Aug Mon–Fri 9am–8pm, Sat 10am–8pm, Sun 10am–2pm; San Fermín daily 8am–8pm; Sept–May Mon–Sat 10am–2pm & 4–7pm, Sun

10am–2pm; ℡848 420 420, ⓦwww.turismo.navarra.es).The central **post office** is on Paseo de Sarasate (Mon–Fri 8am–9pm, Sat 9am–7pm). For **internet** access, head for *Kuria Net*, c/Curia 15 (Mon–Sat 10am–10pm; €3/hr).

Drivers should leave their cars in the car parks either on c/Taconera or at the bull ring.The **bus station** is just in front of the citadel on c/Conde Oliveto, while the **train station** is 1.5km northwest on Avenida San Jorge, served by local bus #9.There's a handy central RENFE ticket office at c/Estella 8 (Mon–Fri 9am–1.30pm & 4.30–7.30pm, Sat 9.30am–1pm; ℡948 227 282), just north of the bus station. Pamplona's tiny **airport**, serving Barcelona and Madrid, is 6km south of the city centre.

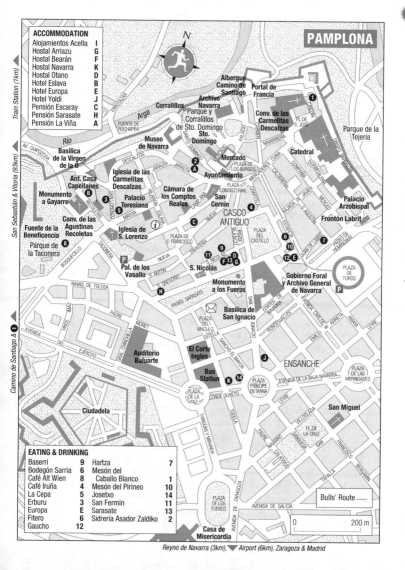

Pamplona's fiercely supported Primera División side, **Club Atletico Osasuna** (Ⓦ www.osasuna.es), play at the Reyno de Navarra 3km south of the city, while it's also worth checking out the **Frontón Labrit** opposite the Plaza de Toros, where *pelota* matches are held.

Accommodation

Much the most enjoyable area of Pamplona in which to stay is the Casco Antiguo, which holds a reasonable selection of **accommodation** in all price ranges. Note that the prices indicated below refer to the peak summer season but *not* San Fermín, when rates across the board double or even triple.

Casco Antiguo

Hostal Arriazu c/Comedías 14 ☎ 948 210 202, Ⓦ www.hostalarriazu.com. Conveniently central and surprisingly quiet *hostal*, with comfortable en-suite rooms. ❸

Hostal Bearán c/San Nicolás 25 ☎ 948 223 428. A clean and perfectly acceptable *hostal* in the heart of the old town. ❷

Hostal Otano c/San Nicolás 5 ☎ 948 227 036. Well-run *hostal* above a bar and restaurant that have been in the same family since 1929. Closed second half of July. ❸

Hotel Eslava Plaza Virgen de la O 7 ☎ 948 222 270, Ⓦ www.hotel-eslava.com. A cosy, welcoming hotel run by the Eslava family in a quiet corner of the old town – views from balconies overlook the plaza. Fifteen doubles and thirteen singles, with a bar in the basement. ❹

Hotel Europa c/Espoz y Mina 11 ☎ 948 221 800, Ⓦ www.hreuropa.com. The best of the upmarket hotels in the old town, just off Plaza del Castillo, with a marble-clad lobby and opulent rooms, and an excellent restaurant downstairs (see p.492). ❹

Pensión Escaray c/Nueva 24, 1° ☎ 948 227 825. Ageing but friendly place in a charming old building. Rooms are small but clean, with wooden floors and shared bathrooms. ❷

Pensión Sarasate Paseo Sarasate 30 ☎ 948 223 084. Simple but very nicely maintained little *pensión*, where all the rooms are en suite and some have balconies. ❷

Pensión La Viña c/Jarauta 8, 3° ☎ 948 213 250. One of the cheapest deals in town, a simple, clean *pensión* with shared bathrooms and great views over the old town. No lift. ❶

Ensanche

Alojamientos Acella Travesía de Acella 3 ☎ 948 261 000, Ⓦ www.hostalacella.com. A wide range of clean, modern but somewhat uninspiring double and single rooms, both en suite and sharing bathrooms, plus apartments for rent, overlooking Parque Yamaguchi 1km southwest of the Casco Antiguo. A refuge during San Fermín, though rates triple. ❷

Hostal Navarra c/Tudela 9, 2° ☎ 948 225 164, Ⓦ www.hostalnavarra.com. Well-established *hostal* going back more than forty years, near the bus station; all rooms have en-suite facilities and have been stylishly refurbished, and there's a laundry. ❸

Hotel Yoldi Avda. de San Ignacio 11 ☎ 948 224 800, Ⓦ www.hotelyoldi.com. An old hotel with smart, stylish rooms where the bullfighters stay during San Fermín. Garage parking. ❹

The City

Everything you're likely to want to see in Pamplona lies within its remarkably compact **Casco Antiguo**. Centering on the **Plaza del Castillo**, ringed with fashionable cafés, it's a glorious and very much lived-in jumble of buildings from all eras, where every twisting stone lane is worth exploring and intriguingly tatty old shops and bars lie concealed behind medieval shutters.

The **Catedral de Santa María** (mid-July to mid-Sept Mon–Fri 10am–7pm, Sat 10am–2.30pm; mid-Sept to mid-July Mon–Fri 10am–2pm & 4–7pm, Sat 10am–2pm; €4.40) is basically Gothic, built over a period of 130 years from the late fourteenth to the early sixteenth century but with an unattractive facade added in the eighteenth. It doesn't look promising, but the cloister and interior, containing the tomb of Carlos III and Eleanor in the centre of the nave and the ancient *Virgen de los Reyes* above the high altar, are magnificent: don't miss the many sculpted doorways, particularly the Puerta de la Preciosa, and the chapel with a lovely star vault, built by a fourteenth-century bishop to house his own tomb. You enter the cathedral from c/Dormitaleria, via the **Museo Diocesano**, a notable collection of Navarran sacred art, including some fabulous polychromed statues, housed in two superb buildings, the refectory and the kitchen.

Behind the cathedral, in one of the oldest parts of the city, you'll find the best remaining section of the **city walls**, where the Baluarte de Redín and Portal de Zumalacárregui (or de Francia) look down over a loop of the Río Arga. If you head out through the gate, you can take paths down to the river from where you get the full force of the impregnability of these defences. Follow the inside of the walls and you'll come to the impressive **Museo de Navarra** (Tues–Sat 9.30am–2pm & 5–7pm, Sun & public hols 11am–2pm; €2, free Sun) in the magnificent old hospital building on c/Santo Domingo. As well as interesting prehistoric and Roman archeological remains, including several vast mosaics, it holds an impressive art collection, among which are a portrait of the Marqués de San Adrián by Goya and a wide range of Navarrese painting. Heading back to the plaza via c/Santo Domingo and Plaza Consistorial you'll pass the **Mercado** and the fine Baroque **ayuntamiento**.

South of the old town, take time to wander the old **Ciudadela**, or Citadel (Mon–Sat 7.30am–9.30pm, Sun 9am–9.30pm; free), now a tranquil park and art-gallery venue, while opposite, on Avenida del Ejército, sit the sleek, dark-grey granite concert and exhibition halls of the **Auditorio Baluarte** (ⓦwww.baluarte .com), designed by local architect Patxi Mangado. Another vivid example of Spain's new architecture lies just north of the bus station, the bold metallic structure of the El Corte Inglés department store completed in 2005 by the same firm. Northwest of here is the **Parque de la Taconera**, a swathe of green at the end of the city walls, and a favourite spot with students and locals.

Eating and drinking

The greatest number of **restaurants** and raucous little **bars** are to be found on c/San Nicolás and its continuation, c/San Gregorio, and also along c/Estafeta on the *encierro* route. C/Jarauta is also thick with places to get a beer – you can join the locals watching *fútbol* on TV at the weekends. For good, inexpensive *menús*, and a wide range of **tapas** and *bocadillos*, head for the streets around c/Major, in particular c/San Lorenzo. Navarra is especially noted for its fine asparagus, red peppers and red wines, all readily available in the city – you can also sip a glass of *pacharán* (*patxaran* in Basque), a sweetish Navarran liquor flavoured with aniseed, coffee beans and vanilla.

Tapas bars

Baserri c/San Nicolás 32 ☎948 222 021. Highly acclaimed tapas bar, with a huge wine list and a varied, innovative array of snacks. A special *pintxos* menu features six award-winners, plus cheese, for €19, while the restaurant at the back offers conventional dinner *menús* from €24, with a gluten-free alternative for €18.
Bodegón Sarria c/Estafeta 50–52. Tapas bar and restaurant, where the *pintxos* taste as good as they look, hams hang from the beams, and the glossy brick walls are adorned with photos of Hemingway enjoying his favourite fiesta. *Menú* €11.50.

La Cepa c/San Lorenzo 2. Earthy, lively local bar with a fine selection of tapas and *bocadillos*. Mon–Sat 1pm–1am.
Erburu c/San Lorenzo 19–21. Excellent *menús* from €12 make this one of the best places to try traditional Navarran cuisine and wines, with a small dining area beyond the tapas bar. Tues–Sun 10am–11pm, Mon eve only, closed last two weeks of July.
Fitero c/Estafeta 58. Award-winning, bustling and very friendly tapas bar, just off the main square, where the counter is lined with unusual concoctions including cod crêpes and pepper stuffed with meat and béchamel.

Gaucho Traversa de Espoz y Mina 1. Popular tapas bar, going since the late 1960s, just off Plaza del Castillo, attracting a mixed crowd that tends to spill out across the street at weekends. Daily 8am–2am.

Mesón del Caballo Blanco c/Redín. The most atmospheric bar and restaurant in town, a converted medieval church with a tree-shaded terrace on top of the city walls and

Fiestas de San Fermín

Known in Spain as the **Fiestas de San Fermín**, or Sanfermines, and to the rest of the world as the **Running of the Bulls**, the city's legendary festival lasts from midday on July 6 until midnight on July 14. The daily, early morning bull-run, or **encierro**, is just one component of nine days of riotous nonstop celebration, which also features bands, parades and 24-hour dancing in the streets. Thanks to Ernest Hemingway's enthusiastic account of the run as "a damned fine show", in *The Sun Also Rises*, foreign tourists, and especially Americans, annually descend upon Pamplona in their thousands.

For the latest updates on the festivities, see ⓦ **www.sanfermin.com**.

Accommodation and security

To secure **accommodation** during the fiesta, it's essential to book well in advance – the town is packed to the gills, and hotels can triple their usual rates. If you do arrive without a reservation, check out the *turismo* opposite the bullring, which fills with women letting **rooms** at exorbitant prices, or just accept that you're going to sleep on the ramparts, in the park or plaza (along with hundreds of others), and deposit your valuables and luggage at the bus station (which also holds showers). To get a place at the **campsite**, *Ezcaba*, 7km east of town on the road to France (ⓣ948 330 315 or 948 331 665, ⓦwww.campingezcaba.com), you need to arrive a couple of days before the fiesta; in any case, it gets seriously overcrowded during San Fermín. The main bonus is that security is tight – admission is by pass only and there's a guard who patrols all night. During the fiesta, there's also a **free campsite**, just below *Ezcaba* by the river, but the security is poor. Irregular buses serve both. Some budget visitors choose to rent a room in some other city, such as Vitoria-Gasteiz or Estella, leave their luggage there, and then simply stay out on the streets in Pamplona for as long as they can.

Note that **ATMs** frequently run out of money during the festival, while local **banks** are closed over the weekend. And finally, the **petty crime** rate soars; cars and vans are broken into with alarming frequency, and people sleeping outdoors are often robbed, occasionally with violence.

El encierro

The **encierro**, or the Running of the Bulls, takes place each morning of the festival. Six bulls are released at 8am daily, to run from the Corralillos near Plaza Santo Domingo to the bullring, where they will fight that evening. They usually take around three minutes to race a fenced-off course of just over 800m, through Plaza Consistorial and along c/Estafeta; official *pastores* (shepherds) armed with big sticks make sure they keep going. A second batch of more placid animals follows in their wake to help round up stragglers. In front, around and occasionally beneath the bulls run the hundreds of locals and tourists who are foolish or drunk enough to test their daring against the horns.

Arrive early, by about 6am, if you want to **watch** the *encierro*. The best vantage points are near the starting point around the Plaza Santo Domingo or on the wall leading to the bullring. If possible, get a spot on the outer of the two barriers – don't worry when the one in front fills up and blocks your view, as all these people will be moved on by the police before the run. The event divides into two parts: first there's the actual running of the bulls, when the object is to run with the bull or whack it with a rolled-up newspaper. It can be difficult to see the bulls amid all the runners but you'll sense the sheer terror and excitement down on the ground; just occasionally, this spreads to the watching crowd if a bull manages to breach the wooden safety barriers. Then there's

fantastic views of Pamplona and mountains beyond. Mon–Sat eves only.

Mesón del Pirineo c/Estafeta 41. Alluring, intriguing and very narrow tapas bar, stretching deep into the recesses of a venerable old building, and attracting a somewhat older crowd than its neighbours.

a separate event after the bulls have been through the streets, when bullocks with padded horns are let loose on the crowd in the bullring. If you watch the actual running, the bullring will already be too crowded for you to get in there as well, so go on two separate mornings to see both things. For the bullring, you have to arrive at about 6am to get the free lower seats. If you want to pay for a seat higher up, buy from the ticket office outside, not from the touts inside. On Sunday, you have to pay.

We advise against it, but if you do decide to **run**, remember that although it's probably less dangerous than it looks, at least one person gets seriously injured (sometimes killed) every year. Find someone who knows the ropes to guide you through the first time, and don't try any heroics; bulls are weighed in tonnes and have very sharp horns. Don't get trapped hiding in a doorway, and don't get between a scared bull and the rest of the pack. Traditionally, women don't take part, though more and more are doing so; if you do, the officials may well try to remove you. Under-18s are barred.

The only official way in is at the **starting point**, Plaza Santo Domingo, entered via Plaza San Saturnino; shortly before the start, the rest of the course is cleared, and then at a few minutes before 8am you're allowed to make your way to your own preferred starting point (walk the course in advance to familiarize yourself with it). To mark the start, two rockets are fired, one when the bulls are released, a second when they are all out (it's best if these are close together, since the bulls are far safer if they're running as a herd rather than getting scared individually). As soon as the first goes, you can start to run, though if you do this you'll probably arrive in the ring well before the bulls and be booed for your trouble; if you wait a while, you're more likely to get close to the bulls, but you're not allowed to stop altogether. Although there are plenty of **escape points**, these are only for use in emergency – if you try to get out prematurely, you'll be shoved back. A third rocket is fired when all the bulls are in the bullring, and a fourth when they've all entered the corral within.

Other events

Pamplona offers plenty of other hazardous pursuits, especially once the atmosphere gets the better of a few people's judgement. Many visitors have fun hurling themselves from the **fountain** in the centre of town and from surrounding buildings (notably *La Mesillonera* – the mussel bar), hoping their friends will catch them below. Needless to say, several unfortunates each year aren't caught by their drunken pals. Other events include **music** from local bands nightly from midnight in the bars and at Plaza del Castillo, continuing until about 4am in the fairground on the Avenida de Bayona. **Fireworks** go off every evening in the Ciudadela (about 11pm), and there's a **funfair** on the open ground beside it. Competing **bands** stagger through the streets all day playing to anyone who'll listen.

Bullfights take place daily at 6.30pm. Tickets (€15–75) go on sale at the Plaza de Toros at 8am the day before. If you have no choice but to buy from the touts, wait until the fight has begun, as the price drops with each successive killing. At the end of the week (midnight July 14), the festivities are officially wound up for another year with a mournful candlelit procession, the **Pobre De**.

If you're hooked on danger, many **other Basque towns** have fiestas that involve some form of *encierro*. Among the best are Tudela (July 24–28), Estella (first weekend in August, and one of the few that has no official ban on women participants), Tafalla (mid-Aug), and Ampuero in Cantabria (Sept 7–8).

Cafés and restaurants

Café Alt Wien Parque de la Taconera. Known to the locals as *El Vienés*, this is a great place to eat a simple breakfast and read the paper in peaceful surroundings, though it can get crowded with families in the afternoon. Daily 9am–10pm. Closed Oct–April.

Café Iruña Plaza del Castillo 44. Elegant *belle époque* café and bar, with fine *pintxos*; there's seating on the plaza or inside the grand old nineteenth-century dining room, with its huge mirrors and decorative pillars. Daily 8am–10pm.

Europa c/Espoz y Mina 11 ☎948 221 800. Considered one of the best restaurants in Navarra, under the direction of local culinary star Pilar Idoate, who knocks out a carefully crafted seasonal menu featuring traditional and *nouvelle dishes*. Tasting *menús* €43 and €62. Closed Sun.

Hartza Juan de Labrit 19 ☎948 224 568. A superb restaurant in a beautiful old house with a garden near the bullring, featuring wooden beams and nineteenth-century sofas and decor. Contemporary Navarran cuisine from €22. Closed Sun eve, all Mon, and first three weeks in Aug.

Josetxo Plaza Príncipe de Viana ☎948 222 097, ⓦwww.restaurantejosetxo.com. The best restaurant in town, specializing in meat dishes such as *rabo de buey* (oxtail). Dinners from €48. Closed Sun.

San Fermin c/San Nicolás 44. Simple, first-floor dining room serving up classics such as *ajoarriero*, a tasty cod dish, seasonal vegetables and sumptuous desserts. Mains from €30. Daily except Mon 1–4pm, plus Fri–Sun 8.30–11pm.

Sarasate c/San Nicolás 19–21 ☎948 225 727. A great vegetarian restaurant established in the 1950s, with a *menú* for €10.50 and a list of organic wines. Closed Sun & Mon eves.

Sidrería Asador Zaldiko c/Santo Domingo 39. Close to the Museo Navarra, this typical Navarran grill and cider house knocks out excellent grilled steaks and lamb for just under €20, cooked over a wood-fired *parilla*. Closed Sun.

Around Pamplona: the Sierra de Aralar

The **Sierra de Aralar**, a two-hundred-square-kilometre plateau dominated by beech woods 30km northwest of Pamplona, is rich in legends of mythological creatures, dragons and demons. A good hiking destination, it holds paths of all grades, mostly well marked, crisscrossing the *sierra* and taking in prehistoric dolmens, waterfalls and caves. The *sierra* is also home to Navarra's oldest and most spectacularly situated church: the **Santuario de San Miguel in Excelsis**.

The village of **Lekunberri**, 25km from Pamplona on the Pamplona–San Sebastián motorway (A15), is the best place to find maps and information. Its old train station at c/Plazaola 21 has been converted into a helpful **turismo** (Mon–Fri 10am–2.30pm & 3–5pm, Sat & Sun 10am–2pm; ☎948 507 204, ⓔoit .lekunberri@navarra.es). From the doorstep you can set off along the former train tracks, now transformed into the picturesque Via Verde de Plazaola ("**Green Way**") leading south to Pamplona and north to Andoain in Gipuzkoa. The route is over 90km in all, mostly in poor condition, following the tracks all the way; the first 5km north from Lekunberri, however, are excellent, after which the track enters the 2.7-kilometre tunnel of Uitzi. Bring a torch (or follow the alternative path) to continue to the larger mountain village of **Leitza**, 8km farther north, which has an impressive assortment of Basque *caserios* (houses).

Santuario de San Miguel in Excelsis

From Lekunberri, a road heads 17km up the mountainside through beech and birch forest to the **Santuario de San Miguel in Excelsis**, passing on its way after 12km the *Casa Forestal* (*Guardetxea*), which offers hearty home-cooked meals (lunch from €10) and is a popular starting point for hikers. At the top (1237m), above a massive car park and a rather ugly bar, is the small, squat church of San Miguel (daily 10am–6pm), built mainly between 783 and 940, with some later additions. In its beautifully simple and austere interior, the only ornamentation is in the shape of eight carved capitals, six of them in the tiny twelfth-century central chapel. It also houses two wonderful medieval enamel works: the shrine of the archangel in the central chapel and the stunning twelfth-century gilt copper *retablo*, depicting a rosily smiling Madonna and Child flanked by Evangelists and Apostles. The sanctuary is an extremely popular pilgrimage destination – half the villages in Navarra have an annual *romería* to San Miguel, many centring around the saint's day of September 29.

Another route up to the church starts at the tiny village of **Arakil**, on the main train and bus routes between Vitoria and Pamplona. The single-track road is a tough but exhilarating climb whether on foot or by car, with breathtaking views across the valley and vultures circling overhead and below.

Practicalities

The Lekunberri area is not strong on **accommodation**: your best bet is the *Hostal Ayestarán I and II*, in the centre of Leukunberri at c/Aralar 22 (☎948 504 127; ❺), which also has a good-value restaurant, specializing in *alubias rojas* (kidney-bean stew). Nearby Aldatz, 2km away, holds an excellent *casa rural*, *Uhaldeko Borda* (☎948 396 013, ⓦwww.uhaldekoborda.com; ❸), while most of the other local villages have at least one *casa rural*, all of which can be booked from the *turismo* in Lekunberri.

Southern Navarra

South of Pamplona, the country changes rapidly; the mountains are left behind and the monotonous plains so characteristic of central Spain begin to open out. The people are different, too – more akin to their southern neighbours than to the Basques of the north. Regular buses and trains run south to **Tudela**, the second city of Navarra, passing through Tafalla and **Olite**, once known as the "Flowers of Navarra", while attractive smaller towns and villages dot the area.

Olite

OLITE, 42km south of Pamplona, is as gorgeous a small town as you could ever hope to stumble across, all the more unexpected a pleasure in that its larger neighbour Tafalla is quite unremarkable, and the town itself is surrounded by ugly modern developments. Reach its core, however, and you're confronted by the magnificent **Palacio Real de Olite** (daily 10am–2pm & 4–6/7pm; €2.80), a former residence of the kings of Navarra. A ramble of turrets, keeps and dungeons, the oldest part (Palacio Viejo) now houses a *parador*. Olite also holds two fine old churches, Romanesque **San Pedro** and Gothic **Santa María**, usually open during services only, the latter with a superb *retablo* and exterior portal – look out for the unusual figure of a man on an elephant.

Olite's central square, **Plaza Carlos III**, sits atop a series of impressive **medieval galleries** (Tues–Fri 11am–1pm, Sat & Sun 11am–2pm & 5–7pm; ☎948 741 885 for guided visits; €1.50), whose existence was a local legend for centuries before they were unearthed in the 1980s. Their original purpose is still a mystery, although it is thought they could have been a market or crypt, or even part of a secret tunnel linking Olite with Tafalla. Today, they house a somewhat random display on the town's history.

Olite's exuberant **Fiesta del Patronales** takes place on September 13–19, and there's a **medieval festival** the second weekend in August, leading up to the saint's day of Olite's patron, the "Virgin of the Cholera" on August 26, which commemorates the town's salvation from the cholera epidemic of 1885.

The **turismo** is at Plaza de los Teobaldos 10, opposite the *parador* (Mon–Sat 10am–2pm & 4–7pm, Sun 10am–2pm; ☎948 741 703, ⓦwww.olite.es), in the same building as the well-presented **Museo del Vino** (same hours; €3.50), emphasizing the town's central role in Navarra's wine industry, especially celebrated for its rosés. **Accommodation** in Olite includes the fabulous *Parador de Olite*, Plaza de los Teobaldos 2 (☏948 740 000, ⓦwww.parador.es; ⑥), and the atmospheric but frequently full *Casa Zanito*, c/Mayor 16 (☏948 740 002, ⓦwww .casazanito.com; ④). The cosy *Hotel Merindad de Olite*, Rúa de la Judería 11 (☏948 740 735, ⓦwww.hotel-merindaddeolite.com; ❸), offers medieval decor and modern comforts. If you want to **camp**, head for *Camping Ciudad de Olite*, 2km out of town on the Tafalla–Peralta road (☏948 741 014). The parador and other hotels have good **restaurants**, and there's a no-frills but fantastic-value *comedor* on the first floor of *Gambarte* at Rúa del Seco 15, with a €12 *menú* of Navarran specialities and jug of *tinto* guaranteed to fill you up for the rest of the day.

Ujué

Twenty kilometres east of Olite, a lonesome, winding road branches off to the east at San Martín de Unx, and after 8km brings you to tiny, hilltop **UJUÉ**. One of the true jewels of Navarra, this perfect medieval defensive village is perched high on the terraced hillside above the harsh, arid landscape; it's impossibly narrow to drive into, and all but impossible to park once you get all the way in.

Ujué is dominated by the thirteenth-century Romanesque church of **Santa María** (daily 8am–8pm), where the heart of King Carlos II of Navarra is supposedly preserved inside the altar. Views from the church's balconied exterior extend over the whole southern Navarra region of La Ribera. It's also the destination of a notable **romería** (pilgrimage), on the first Sunday after St Mark's Day (April 25), when half the populace of Tafalla, among others, walk through the night to celebrate Mass here in commemoration of their town's reconquest from the Moors in 1043.

From the main square by the church, a couple of pedestrianized cobbled streets plunge down to another beautiful little square, Plaza Mayor, which holds a ramshackle old bar with a balcony terrace, and a **casa rural**, *Casa Isolina Jurio* (☏948 739 037; ❷). There are two others in the village, *El Chófer I* and *II* (☏948 739 011; ❷), both comfortable places in a rustic style. The *Mesón Las Torres*, c/Santa María, just outside the church (Tues–Sun 1–4pm; ☏948 739 052), serves the local speciality of *migas de pastor* – fried breadcrumbs with *txistorro* sausage (€7.50) – and offers fantastic views of the snowcapped Pyrenees from its picture windows.

Tudela

TUDELA, on the banks of the Ebro 90km south of Pamplona, is the heart of La Ribera. While the outskirts are ugly and off-putting, the old town has an entirely different atmosphere. North of the richly decorated **Plaza de los Fueros** is a jumble of narrow, cobbled lanes apparently little changed since Alfonso I of Aragón ended the Moorish occupation of the city in 1114. The twelfth-century **Catedral** is a fine, strong, Gothic construction. It has a rose window above the intricately carved alabaster west doorway, which portrays a chilling vision of the Last Judgement. Inside there's an unusual *retablo* and some beautiful old tombs, while the Romanesque cloister has some deft primitive carvings, many badly damaged. Next door, the **Museo de Tudela** (Mon–Fri 10am–1.30pm & 4–7pm, Sat 10am–1.30pm; €3) is housed in the old dean's palace, with primarily ecclesiastical art and sculptures on display. On the edge of town, the bizarre thirteenth-century **Puente Sobre** over the Ebro looks as if it could never have carried the weight of an ox cart, let alone seven centuries of traffic on the main road to Zaragoza.

The local **turismo** is near the cathedral at c/Jucio 4 (Mon–Fri 9.30am–2pm & 4–8pm, Nov–Easter until 7pm, Sat 10am–2pm & 4–8pm, Nov–Easter until 7pm, Sun 10am–2pm; ☎948 848 058, ⓦwww.tudela.com). There's not all that much **accommodation** in the old town; the *AC Ciudad de Tudela* is in an eighteenth-century mansion on c/Misericordia (☎948 402 440, ⓦwww .ac-hoteles.com; ➎), but it's more of a business hotel really; otherwise, the best-value alternative is *Hostal Remigio* in the newer part, at c/Gaztambide 4 just off Plaza de los Fueros (☎948 820 850, ⓦwww.hostalremigio.com; ➌). You'll find many other places to **eat and drink** around Plaza de los Fueros; *Café Diamante* is a good spot to people-watch. Tudela's speciality is *menestra de verduras*, a sumptuous vegetable casserole, often served only in the spring.

The Pilgrim Route

The ancient pilgrimage route of the **Camino de Santiago** passes through Aragón and into Navarra just before Leyre, travelling through the province via **Sangüesa**, **Puente La Reina** (where it met an alternative route crossing the Pyrenees at Roncesvalles) and **Estella**, before crossing into Old Castile at Logroño. For more on the *camino*, see the box overleaf.

Monasterio de San Salvador de Leyre

The first stop on the pilgrim route in Navarra, the **Monasterio de San Salvador de Leyre**, stands amid mountainous country 4km from Yesa (on the main Pamplona–Jaca road) connected with both places by a daily bus in either direction. From **YESA** a good road leads up to Leyre, arriving at the east end of the monastery. Although the convent buildings are sixteenth to eighteenth century, the church is largely Romanesque; its tall, severe apses and belfry perched on the south apsidal roof are particularly impressive. After languishing in ruins for over a century, it was restored and reoccupied by the Benedictines in the 1950s and is now in immaculate condition. The crypt, with its sturdy little columns, is the highlight of the **guided tour** (Mon–Fri 10.15am–2pm & 3.30–7pm, Sat & Sun 10.15am–2pm & 4–7pm; Spanish-only guided tours, min fifteen people, every 45min; €2.10). The only other way to access the church – by coinciding with services (5 daily 6am–9.10pm) – is well worth doing, as the twenty or so white-habited monks employ Gregorian chant (except for the 6am Matins and 6pm weekend Mass).

The former hospice now holds a two-star **hotel**, the *Hospedería de Leyre* (☎948 884 100, ⓦwww.monasteriodeleyre.com; ➌), which has particularly good-value single rates. Even if you don't stay, the **restaurant** is well worth visiting for its carefully prepared three-course *menú* (€17).

Javier

From Yesa it's only 5km south to **JAVIER**, home to the fine **Castillo de Javier** (daily 9am–1pm & 4–7pm; €2), the birthplace of San Francisco Xavier in 1506. Javier had nothing to do with the Pilgrim Route, but it is a place of pilgrimage in its own right, as St Francis is the patron of Navarra and one of the most famous **Jesuits** – he travelled all over the Far East, dying in China in 1552, and is still remembered in Japan. The restored castle is primarily an absorbing **museum** dedicated to the saint's life; labels are in Spanish only.

The castle is a popular picnic spot with ample parking, and there's a tranquil, traditional **hotel** in the grounds, *Hotel Xavier* (☎948 884 006; ➍), which has a

The **Camino de Santiago** crosses into Navarra from France via the foothills of the Pyrenees, descending steeply to the historic abbey at **Orreaga-Roncesvalles** (see p.499). As the mountains peter out, the path passes alongside trout-filled rivers lined with beech trees and through traditional whitewashed Basque villages graced with Romanesque churches.

Navarra has invested considerably in this section of the route, and its twenty or so *albergues* – all with comfortable, if basic, facilities – are among the best along the *camino*. The path mainly follows dirt farm tracks, although some stretches have been paved, which makes the walking less messy but leaves pilgrims prone to blisters.

Traces of Charlemagne's tenth-century foray into Spain are everywhere in Navarra, from the pass before Roncesvalles by which he entered the country to a stone monument some 20km farther on that depicts the massive Stride of Roland, his favourite knight. The region also contains some of Hemingway's much-loved haunts; the *camino* passes through his trout-fishing base at **Auritz-Burguete**, just 3km from Roncesvalles, and lively **Pamplona**, another 40km into the walk.

There are a couple of stiff climbs, notably the 300m up to the **Alto de Perdón**, just outside Pamplona. Here, legend tells of an exhausted medieval pilgrim who stood firm against the Devil's offer of water in exchange for a renunciation of his Christian faith. The pilgrim was rewarded with the appearance of Santiago himself, who led him to a secret fountain.

Navarra boasts some of the finest Romanesque architecture in Spain, including the octagonal church at **Eunate**, 20km from Pamplona, thought to be the work of the Knights Templar, and the graceful bridge that gave its name to **Puente La Reina**, 4km farther on. The architectural highlight is undoubtedly the small town of **Estella**, where it's worth spending an afternoon exploring the Palacio de los Reyes de Navarra and the many lovely churches. The route from Estella is lined with vineyards, and Bodegas de Irache's free Fuente del Vino (wine fountain) just outside town is said to fortify pilgrims for the journey on through the Rioja region to Santiago de Compostela. For practicalities on the *camino*, see p.570.

good restaurant. Alternatively, try the slightly cheaper *Hotel El Mesón*, Plaza de Javier (⊕948 884 035, ⓦwww.hotelmeson.com; ❸), with a €15 *menú*.

Sangüesa

The Pilgrim Route proper next stops 8km away at **SANGÜESA**, a run-down little town that nonetheless holds a number of significant monuments, including several churches from the fourteenth century and earlier. Above all, don't miss the south facade of the church of **Santa María La Real**, at the far end of town beside the Río Aragón (Mon–Sat 10am–1.30pm & 4–6pm; €2), which has a richly carved doorway and sculpted buttresses: God, the Virgin and the Apostles are depicted amid a chaotic company of warriors, musicians, craftsmen, wrestlers and animals. Many of Sangüesa's streets can have changed little in centuries, and aside from the churches – Romanesque **Santiago** (open during daily 8pm service, Sun 10am–1pm) is also lovely – there are some handsome mansions, the remains of a royal palace and a medieval hospital, as well as the *ayuntamiento*, housed in the seventeenth-century Palacio de Ongay Vallesantoro. Sangüesa's helpful **turismo** is at c/Mayor 2, opposite Santa María (Mon–Sat 10am–2pm & 4–7pm, Sun 10am–2pm; ⊕948 871 411, ⓔoit.sanguesa@navarra.es). There's not much in the way of **accommodation**: the *Yamaguchi*, on the road to Javier (⊕948 870 127, ⓦwww.hotelyamaguchi .com; ❸), is the best option.

Puente La Reina

Few towns so perfectly evoke the days of the medieval pilgrimage as **PUENTE LA REINA** (Gares), 20km southwest of Pamplona. This is the meeting place of the two main Spanish routes: the Navarrese trail, via Roncesvalles and Pamplona, and the Aragonese one, via Jaca, Leyre and Sangüesa. From here on, all pilgrims followed the same path to Santiago.

At the eastern edge of town, the **Iglesia del Crucifijo** (open for services only) was founded in the twelfth century by the Knights Templar. Its porch, decorated with scallop shells (the badge of the Santiago pilgrims), contains an unusual Y-shaped crucifix. To one side is the former pilgrims' hospice, later in date, but still among the oldest extant. In town, the tall buildings along c/Mayor display their original coats of arms, and another pilgrim church, **Santiago** (daily 10am–1.30pm & 5–8pm), holds a notable statue of St James. The town's namesake **bridge** stands at the end of the street. The finest medieval bridge in Spain, it was built by royal command at the end of the eleventh century, and is still now used by pedestrians and animals only – vehicular traffic crosses an ugly modern bridge. The helpful **turismo** is at c/Mayor 105, near the bridge (June–Aug Tues–Sat 10am–2pm & 4–7pm, Sun 11am–2pm; ☎948 340 845, ⓦpuentelareina-gares.net). **Accommodation** is limited to the luxurious *Mesón del Peregrino*, Irunbidea s/n (☎948 340 075, ⓦwww.hotelelperegrino .com; ❼), a grand stone building with a modern pool, just out of town on the main road towards Pamplona; the sizeable *Hotel Jakue* next door (☎948 341 017, ⓦwww.jakue.com; ❹), which also has decent rooms; and the charming *Hotel Bidean* in the heart of town at c/Mayor 20 (☎948 341 156, ⓦwww.bidean .com; ❺). There's a good **campsite**, *El Molino*, at **Mendigorria**, 5km south (☎948 340 604, ⓦwww.campingelmolino.com), with a large swimming pool. The nicest **place to eat** in town is the *Joaquin*, c/Mayor 48.

Estella

Twenty kilometres west of Puente La Reina, **ESTELLA** (Lizarra) is another fine old town, rich in monuments but surrounded by unattractive sprawl. During the civil wars of the nineteenth century, this was the headquarters of the Carlists, and each May a pilgrimage up a nearby mountain still honours the dead.

The centre of town, in a loop of the river Ega, is bisected by Paseo de la Immaculada. Just north of the *paseo*, **Plaza de los Fueros** is at the heart of the old quarter, but most of the interesting buildings are situated across the river in Barrio San Pedro. Here on c/San Nicolás you'll find the twelfth-century **Palacio de los Reyes de Navarra**, Navarra's only large-scale Romanesque civil edifice, now open as an art gallery devoted to the Navarrese painter Gustave de Maeztu (Tues–Sat 11am–1pm & 5–7pm, Sun & public hols 11am–1.30pm; free).

Estella has a wealth of churches, the interiors of which may only be visited just before or just after Mass (normally Mon–Fri 7–8pm, Sun 11am–1pm), unless you're with a tour guide. Most are best seen from the outside, in any case. Particularly striking is the fortified pilgrimage church of **San Pedro de la Rúa**, just up the hill from the *turismo*, whose main doorway shows unmistakeable Moorish influence. From the former *ayuntamiento*, an elegant sixteenth-century building just opposite the Palacio, c/de la Rúa follows the *camino* route and leads past many old merchants' mansions. Farther along, you reach the abandoned church of **Santo Sepulcro**, sporting a carved fourteenth-century Gothic doorway. Retrace your steps and cross the hump-backed bridge, take the first left, then right up Los Pelares, and you come to the church of **San Miguel** – not a terribly inspiring building in itself, but with a north doorway that is one of the gems of the Pilgrim Route. Its delicate capitals are marvellous, as are the modelled reliefs of the *Three Marys at the Sepulchre* and *St Michael Fighting the Dragon*.

Practicalities

Estella's well-stocked **turismo** is next door to the Palacio de los Reyes de Navarra at c/San Nicolás 1 (April–Aug Mon–Sat 9am–8pm, Sun 10am–2pm; Sept Mon–Sat 10am–2pm & 4–7pm, Sun 10am–2pm; Oct–March Mon–Sat 10am–5pm, Sun 10am–2pm; ℡948 556 301, ⓦwww.estella-lizarra.com).

None of Estella's **accommodation** is particularly out of the ordinary, but there are some good-value budget places around the Plaza de los Fueros, including *Pensión San Andrés*, Plaza Santiago 58, 1° (℡948 554 158; ❷), and *Fonda Izarra*, c/Calderería 20 (℡948 550 678; ❷; closed Sept), which has a laidback bar. For a bit more comfort (and easier parking), head for the clean and modern *Hotel Yerri*, Avda. Yerri 35 (℡948 546 034; ❸).

Among several reasonable **restaurants**, the *Asador Astarriaga*, Plaza de los Fueros 12 (closed Sun eve), serves a well-priced *menú*, and *La Navarra*, c/Gustavo de Maeztú 16, is a little fancier. *La Moderna*, c/Mayor 54, is a bar that serves good *pintxos*.

Viana

VIANA, 40km southwest of Estella and the last stop before the La Rioja border, is an attractive town with many beautiful Renaissance and Baroque palatial houses. Cesare Borgia was killed here in 1507, at the age of thirty, as he laid siege to the town. Today, the main attraction is the Gothic church of **Santa María** (May–Sept 10am–1pm & 7–8.30pm, Sun 11.30am–1pm, other times with services only; €0.50 donation), with its outstanding Renaissance carved porch.

Viana's useful **turismo** is at Plaza de los Fueros 1 (Easter–Sept Mon–Sat 9am–2pm & 5–7pm, Sun 9am–2pm; Oct–Easter Mon–Sat 9am–2pm; ℡948 446 302, ⓦwww.viana.es). Logroño is only 10km away, but the *Hostal Casa Armendariz*, c/Navarro Villoslada 19 (℡948 645 078; ❸), has comfortable **rooms** with bath above a restaurant and *sidrería*, while the gorgeous *Palacio de Pujadas*, c/Navarro Villoslada 30 (℡948 646 464, ⓦwww.palaciodepujadas.com; ❺), is housed in a sixteenth-century palace, with opulent rooms and a fine **restaurant**.

The Navarran Pyrenees

The **Navarran Pyrenees** may not be as high as their neighbours to the east, but they're every bit as dramatic and far less developed. The historic **pass of Roncesvalles** provides the major route northeast through the mountains from Pamplona, as it has done for centuries – celebrated in the *Song of Roland* and, more recently, by Jan Morris, who called it "one of the classic passes of Europe and a properly sombre gateway into Spain". This was the route taken by countless pilgrims throughout the Middle Ages; Charlemagne's retreating army was decimated here by Basque guerrillas avenging the sacking of Pamplona; Napoleon's defeated armies fought a running battle along the pass as they fled Spain; and thousands of refugees from the Civil War made their escape into France along this narrow corridor.

Beautiful foothill valleys, particularly the **Valle de Baztán**, due north of Pamplona, and the **Valle de Salazar** to the east, make a perfect place to relax, with the largest concentration of good-value **casas rurales** in the province. The Pyrenees really start to get serious at the top of the **Valle de Roncal**, where there's challenging hiking up to and along the karst ridges nearby.

Auritz-Burguete

Northeast of Pamplona, the N135 winds upwards and across two valleys until it reaches the neighbouring villages of Auritz-Burguete and Orreaga-Roncesvalles, about half an hour's walk apart. The surrounding rolling country is superb for gentle riverside strolls, or simply to sit back and admire. **AURITZ-BURGUETE**, a typical Navarran Basque village straggling for 1km or so along its single street, has a pleasant atmosphere despite the through traffic. The best of its **hotels** is the *Hostal Burguete*, at the north end of the main street (℡948 760 005, ✆burguete@auritz-burguete.org; ❸), with its three echoing storeys of huge, spotless, squeaky-wood-floored rooms, most en suite. Hemingway stayed here in the early 1920s, and immortalized it in *Fiesta*; the room he favoured (no. 25, formerly no. 18) is still preserved much as he described it, save for discreetly placed photos of the great man. The *Loizu*, c/San Nicolás 13 (℡948 760 005, ⓦwww.hotelloizu.com; ❹), is also very pleasant, or for a more traditional feel, try the cosy *Casa Loperena*, a *casa rural* just off the through road (℡948 760 068; closed Dec–Easter; ❷). The *Loizu* has the best **restaurant** in town, with *menús* for €18 and game and regional specialities costing around €25 *a la carta*.

Orreaga-Roncesvalles

The few buildings on the gentle green slopes of tiny **ORREAGA-RONCES-VALLES**, 2.5km north of Auritz-Burgete, cluster around the Augustinian **Colegiata de Santa María** (daily 10am–8pm; free), its echoing church and beautiful Gothic cloister somewhat spoiled by the abbey's zinc roof. The Sala Capitular, to one side of the cloister and entered with the same ticket (daily 10am–2pm & 3.30–7pm, winter until 5.30pm, closed Wed in Jan; €1.10), houses a prostrate statue of Sancho VII el Fuerte (the Strong) atop his tomb; measuring 2.25m long, it is supposedly life-size. Here also is a fragment of the chains that Sancho broke in 1212 at the Battle of Navas de Tolosa against the Moors – a motif that found its way into the Navarrese coat of arms. A beautiful half-hour walk from behind the monastery (on the marked GR65 path, the Camino de Santiago) will bring you up to the **Puerto de Ibañeta**, said to be the very pass used by Charlemagne.

A small, decent **turismo** (Mon–Sat 10am–2pm & 4–7pm, Sun 10am–2pm; ℡948 760 301, ⓦwww.roncesvalles.es) is housed in an eighteenth-century millhouse behind the small *Hostal Casa Sabina*, next to the monastery (℡948 760 012; ❸). The much larger *La Posada* (℡948 760 225; ❸) is run by the monastery itself and offers some four-person rooms, and also has a decent dining room; bona fide pilgrims can stay here for a token donation, while the *Casa Sabina* offers a €9 pilgrim *menú* (7pm & 8.30pm).

Valle de Baztán

Due north of Pamplona, the heavily travelled N121a climbs over the Belate (Velate) pass before descending to the village of **ORONOZ-MUGAIRI** and the **Parque Natural Señorio de Bértiz** (daily: April–Sept 10am–8pm; Oct–March 10am–6pm; ⓦwww.parquedebertiz.es; €2), a combined botanical garden and recreational forest. Immediately beyond, at Oieregi, the N121a forks left to head up the scenic Valle de Bidasoa towards Irún and San Sebastián. Continuing along the right fork and the N121, you enter the **Valle de Baztán** with its succession of villages, beautiful landscapes and cave formations.

Elizondo and around

The "capital" of this most strongly Basque of Navarran valleys is **ELIZONDO**, 9km from Oronoz. What's visible from the through road leaves a poor impression, but, farther in, the town is full of typical Basque Pyrenean architecture, especially alongside the river. The local **turismo** is at San Nicolás 1 (Mon–Sat 10am–2pm & 4–6pm; ☏948 556 301, ⊛www.elizondo-baztan.com). Places to **stay** include two modern options: the three-star *Hotel Baztán* on the Pamplona road south of town (☏948 580 050, ⊛www.hotelbaztan.com; ❹), complete with garden and pool; and, back in town, the two-star *Hostal Saskaitz*, 200m east of the through road at c/María Azpilikueta 10 (☏948 580 488, ⊜hotelelizondo@biaizpe.net; ❹). The cheaper, central *Pensión Eskisaroi*, c/Jaime Urrutia 40 (☏948 580 013; closed Dec–Easter; ❷), offers en-suite rooms above a popular restaurant. You can also enjoy good food in the cosy, water-view *comedor* of the *Txokoto*, c/Braulio Iriarte 25 (closed Wed & Sept), while *Casa Galarza*, at the north end of town by the Río Baztán at c/Santiago 1 (closed Thurs in winter), is strong on seafood.

The last Spanish village before France, **ERRATZU**, 4km northeast, is another architectural jewel. It holds a few well-preserved **casas rurales**: *Casa Etxebeltzea*, a fourteenth-century seigneurial manor at the south edge of the medieval core (☏948 453 157, ⊛www.etxebeltzea-baztan.com; ❸); and the cheaper *Casa Kordoa* (☏948 453 222, ⊛www.kordoa.com; ❷).

Urdazubi-Urdax and Zugarramurdi

Northwest of Amaiur-Maya, the N121 climbs over the **Otxondo Pass** to the villages of Urdazubi-Urdax and Zugarramurdi, reached by separate side roads 16km and 20km respectively from Amaiur-Maya. Both make potential stopovers between Pamplona and the French Basque coastal towns of Biarritz and Bayonne.

URDAZUBI-URDAX, ringed by hills and guarded by a tiny castle overlooking the Río Olavidea, has three *hostales* and *pensiones*, the most central of which is the *Hostal Irigoiena* (☏948 599 267, ⊛www.irigoienea.com; closed Mon–Thurs in winter; ❹), in a renovated farmhouse. The more modest *Pensión Beotxea* is on the Zugarramurdi road (☏948 599 114; ❷). For **eating**, *Koska* at c/San Salvador 3 has reasonable *menús* (closed Sun eve & Mon). **ZUGARRAMURDI** is famous for its **caves**. The highlight of the **Cueva de las Brujas**, or Witches' Cave (daily: summer 9am–9pm; winter 9am–7.30pm; €3), is the giant natural arch through which the *regata de infierno* (Hell's stream) flows. *Akelarres*, or witches' sabbaths, were allegedly celebrated beneath it until the seventeenth century, and the area bore the brunt of persecution at the time of the Inquisition. That memory has passed into Basque legend – and into the content of the local **fiesta** – the "Witches' Festival" in July. The appealing village itself makes a good base for excursions into the surrounding countryside; one possibility is to walk 3km along the track beyond the caves into France to another set of caves, the **Grottes de Sare** (daily, by tour only: April–June & Sept 10am–6pm; July & Aug 10am–7pm; Oct 10am–5pm; Nov–March 2–5pm; ⊛www.grottesdesare.fr; €6.50). Zugarramurdi's few **casas rurales** are heavily subscribed at weekends: *Casa Teltxeguia* (☏948 599 167; ❷), or the larger, en-suite *Casa Sueldeguía* (☏948 599 088; ❷) are both in the village centre.

Valle de Salazar

East of Pamplona, 13km before Yesa, the N178 road leads northeast from Lumbier into the green, beautiful valley of the Río Salazar. One kilometre from Lumbier looms the entrance to the **Foz de Lumbier**, a major nesting place for

eagles, which can usually be spotted high up in the sides of the canyon or circling overhead. The most spectacular part of the lower valley, however, is the **Foz de Arbaiun-Arbayún**, a deep, six-kilometre gorge that can be descended by the intrepid, but is also visible from a roadside viewing platform. **Griffon vultures** scythe the skies above.

Ochagavía

Some 60km farther on, east of Pamplona the showcase Pyrenean village of **OCHAGAVÍA**, an attractive base for hiking, sits at the point where the Anduña and Zatoia rivers merge to form the Salazar. Its most alluring feature is the wide, tree-lined quays on either side of the river, crossed by a series of low stone bridges. Cobbled lanes wander off from here, winding past charming Pyrenean houses built with wood, stone and flat-tiled roofs.

Ochagavía has a central **turismo** on the west bank of the river (mid-June to mid-Sept Mon–Sat 10am–2pm & 4.30–8.30pm, Sun 10am–2pm; mid-Sept to mid-June Mon–Thurs & Sun 10am–2pm, Fri & Sat 10am–2pm & 4.30–7.30pm; ☏ 948 890 641; ⓦ www.ochagavia.com). The antique-furnished **rooms** of *Hostal Orialde* on the east bank (☏ 948 890 027; ❷), half of which are en suite, are better value than those of the nearby *Hostal Auñamendi* on Plaza Gúrpide (Plaza Blankoa; ☏ 948 890 189, ⓔ auniamendi@jet.es; ❸), though the decent **comedor** at the latter is one of the very few places to **eat** in town (closed Sat eve & Sun). More than a dozen **casas rurales** offer rooms in the traditional stone houses for which the town is famous; two worth singling out are *Casa Ñavarro* (☏ 948 890 335; ❷), with some en-suite rooms, and *Casa Osaba* (☏ 948 890 011, ⓦ www.casaosaba.com; ❶), both on the west bank.

The **Irati Forest** to the north is one of the most extensive pine and beech forests in Europe, and **Pico de Orhi** (2018m), the westernmost summit of over 2000m in the Pyrenees, offers excellent walking and climbing options with views every bit as spectacular as the highest peaks. For visitors relying on public transport, the forest is inaccessible, but there are some good walks in the hills surrounding Ochagavía.

Valle de Roncal

If you're really serious about exploring alpine mountains, the **Valle de Roncal**, the next major valley to the east, is considerably more rewarding, although it is very popular in July and August. **RONCAL**, the valley's "capital", holds a helpful regional **turismo** (daily 10am–2pm & 4.30–7.30pm; ☏ 948 475 256, ⓦ www.vallederoncal.es). As well as a *hostal*, the *Zaltua*, on the through road (☏ 948 475 008; ❷), there are also four **casas rurales**, the best of which, *Casa Villa Pepita* (☏ 948 475 133; ❷), serves *table d'hôte* meals at a very reasonable price. The local cheese, *queso del Roncal*, is considered a delicacy.

Isaba and around

ISABA, 7km north of Roncal, is a larger village where the network of streets loops around a giant fortified church. The local **turismo** is in the small, sterile modern district at its southern end (summer Tues–Sat 10am–2pm & 4.30–8.30pm, Sun 10am–2pm; winter Tues–Thurs 10am–2pm, Fri & Sat 10am–2pm & 4.30–7.30pm; ☏ 948 893 251, ⓦ www.isaba.es).

All eleven of the village's **casas rurales** (ⓦ www.roncal-salazar.com) tend to be booked at weekends, as the area is a major touring centre for the western Pyrenees, as well as a Nordic ski base in winter. *Casa Francisco Mayo* (☏ 948 893 166; ❷), where all rooms are en suite, and *Casa Garatxandi* (☏ 948 893 261; ❷), where two of the rooms share a bathroom, are recommended. The pick of the other **accommodation** options is the sleek and clean *Hostal Lola*, east of the busy through road at c/Mendigatxa 17 (Ⓣ948 893 012, Ⓦwww.hostal-lola.com; closed Nov; ❸), with a few precious parking spots and the best **restaurant** in town (€15 *menú*). The *Albergue Oxanea*, on c/Bormapéa, west of the main street (Ⓣ948 893 153; €12 per person for dorm bed), is a salubrious **hostel**, while Isaba's **campsite**, *Asolaze*, with large bungalows for rent (❹), is 6km upstream towards the border (Ⓣ948 893 034, Ⓦwww.campingasolaze.com; closed Nov & Dec). For magnificent scenery and the best walking, continue up the valley of the Río Belagoa. After around 17km you come to the area's most characterful local **restaurant**, the popular *Venta de Juan Pito* (Ⓣ948 893 080; closed weekends in summer). To **walk** from here in safety – the most obvious treks lead to peaks on the frontier ridge, but the landscape abounds in deep sinkholes – you'll need a proper **map** (such as Editorial Alpina's 1:40,000 *Ansó-Echo*), a compass and good conditions.

Travel details

Trains

For current timetables and ticket information, consult RENFE Ⓣ902 240 202, Ⓦwww.renfe.es or FEVE Ⓣ987 271 210, Ⓦwww.feve.es.
Bilbao Estación de Abando to: Alicante (5 daily; 16hr); Barcelona (2 daily; 9–11hr); Logroño (2 daily; 2hr 30min); Madrid (2 daily; 5–6hr); Salamanca (daily; 5hr 30min).
Bilbao Estación Atxuri to: Bermeo via Gernika (15–25 daily; 1hr 15min); Durango (10–12 daily; 40min); San Sebastián (9 daily; 2hr 30min–3hr).
Bilbao Estación de Santander to: Ambasaguas (3 daily; 1hr); Santander (3 daily; 3hr).
Irún to: Hendaye, France (every 30min 7.30am–9.30pm; 5min); San Sebastián (every 30min 5am–11pm; 30min).
Pamplona to: Madrid (3 daily; 3hr); San Sebastián (3 daily; 2hr); Tudela (daily; 1hr 15min); Vitoria (4 daily; 1hr); Zaragoza (4 daily; 2hr 30min).
San Sebastián to: Bilbao (9 daily; 2hr 30min–3hr); Burgos (5 daily; 3hr); Irún (every 30min; 30min); Madrid (3 daily; 5hr–6hr 30min); Salamanca (2 daily; 6hr); Vitoria (8 daily; 1hr 45min); Zaragoza (2 daily; 3hr 15min–4hr).
Vitoria to: Miranda del Ebro (14 daily; 30min).

Buses

Bilbao to: Barcelona (4 daily; 8hr); Bayonne (2 daily; 2hr 50min); Bermeo via Gernika and Mundaka (30 daily; 1hr 10min); Burgos (4 daily; 2hr); Durango (5 daily; 30min); Elantxobe (3 daily; 1hr 30min); Lekeitio (5 daily; 1hr 30min); León (2 daily; 7hr); Logroño (5 daily; 2hr 15min); Madrid (15 daily; 5hr 30min); Oñati (2 daily; 1hr 15min); Ondarroa via Markina (4 daily; 1hr 30min); Pamplona (6 daily; 4hr); San Sebastián (25–35 daily; 1hr 10min); Santander (30 daily; 1hr 30min); Vitoria (30 daily; 1hr); Zaragoza (10 daily; 4hr).
Irún to: Pamplona (3 daily; 2hr); San Sebastián (constantly; 30min).
Pamplona to: Burguete (daily; 1hr 30min); Elizondo (3 daily; 2hr); Estella (11 daily; 1hr); Irún (3 daily; 2hr); Isaba (daily; 2hr); Ochagavía (daily, except Sun; 2hr); Roncal (daily; 1hr 45min); San Sebastián (6 daily; 1–3hr); Yesa (1–2 daily; 1hr); Zaragoza (2–3 daily; 4hr).
San Sebastián to: Elizondo (2 daily; 2hr); Hondarribia (every 20min; 30min); Irún (constantly; 30min); Lekeitio (4 daily; 1hr 20min); Lesaka (2 daily; 1hr); Mutriku (4 daily; 50min); Bera (Vera) de Bidasoa (2 daily; 50min); Vitoria (7 daily; 2hr 30min); Zumaia (hourly; 1hr).
Vitoria-Gasteiz to: Araía via villages of Llanada Alavesa (2 daily; 1hr); Durango (4 daily; 1hr); Estella (4 daily; 1hr 15min); Laguardia (4 daily; 1hr 45 min); Logroño (8 daily; 2hr); Pamplona (10 daily, fewer on Sun; 1hr 30min).

Ferries

Bilbao to: Portsmouth (Ⓦwww.poferries.com; departs Bilbao & Portsmouth every 3 days Feb to mid-Dec, once in Jan; 28–34hr).

Cantabria and Asturias

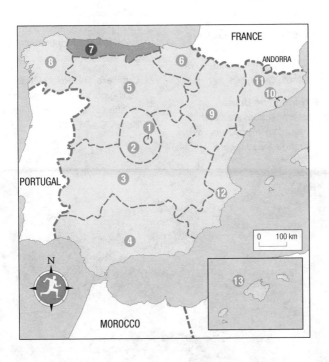

CHAPTER 7

Highlights

✳ **Playas** From El Sardinero to De Oyambre – with 202 beaches to choose from, you needn't worry about finding space for your towel. See pp.512 & 521

✳ **Santillana del Mar** Wander the narrow streets of this chocolate-box village, with its picturesque houses and stunning Romanesque church. See p.516

✳ **Cares Gorge** A horizontal walk through the vertical world of the Desfiladeso de Cares. See p.529

✳ **Naranjo de Bulnes** Looming above a ravishing mountain village, this vast, orange-tinted megalith is the icon of the Picos de Europa. See p.533

✳ **Avilés Carnaval** Experience Spain at its most vibrant during the Mardi Gras celebrations. See p.543

✳ **Santa María del Naranco, Oviedo** An enigmatic, jewel-like pre-Romanesque church. See p.547

✳ **Sidra** Asturias' national drink must be poured from a great height to attain optimum fizz. See p.548

✳ **Cudillero** This lovely little fishing port might have been air-lifted straight from a Greek island. See p.549

▲ Bulnes, Picos de Europa

Cantabria and

Asturias

W hile the northern provinces of Cantabria and Asturias are popular holiday terrain for Spaniards and the French, they remain hardly touched by the mass tourism of the Mediterranean coast, mostly because of the somewhat unreliable weather. But the sea is warm enough for swimming in the summer months, and the sun does shine, if not every day; it's the warm, moist climate, too, that's responsible for the forests and rich vegetation that give the region its name, *Costa Verde*, or the Green Coast. The provinces also boast old and elegant seaside towns, and a dramatic landscape that features tiny, isolated coves along the coast and, inland, the fabulous Picos de Europa, with peaks, sheer gorges and some of Europe's most spectacular montane wildlife.

Cantabria, centred on the city of Santander and formerly part of Old Castile, was long a conservative bastion amid the separatist leanings of its coastal neighbours. **Santander** itself, the modern capital, is an elegant, if highly conventional, resort, linked by ferry to Plymouth and Portsmouth in Britain. Either side lie attractive, lower-key resorts, crowded and expensive in August especially, but quieter during the rest of the year. The best are **Castro Urdiales**, to the east, and **Comillas** and **San Vicente de la Barquera** to the west. Perhaps the pick of the province's towns, though, is the beautiful **Santillana del Mar**, overloaded

The FEVE railway

Communications in Cantabria and Asturias are generally slow, with the one main road following the coast through the foothills to the north of the Picos de Europa. If you're not in a hurry, you may want to make use of the narrow-gauge **FEVE rail line** (ⓦ www .feve.es), which is unmarked on many maps and independent of the main RENFE system; note that rail passes are not valid on this service. The FEVE line can be broadly split into three routes: Bilbao in the Basque Country to Santander; Santander to Oviedo (where local services serve the triangle of Gijón, Avilés and Oviedo); and Oviedo to Ferrol in Galicia. The route is, on the whole, breathtakingly beautiful, skirting beaches, crossing *rías* and snaking through a succession of limestone gorges, but you will need several days to see it in its entirety. An expensive "train hotel" runs at night, but with the scenery the main attraction of the route, it's not the most practical way of getting about.

with honey-coloured mansions and, at times, with tourists, too. Inland lies a series of **prehistoric caves**: the most famous, **Altamira**, is no longer open to the public but is explained by a great museum, while another can be seen at **Puente Viesgo**, near Santander.

To the west are the harsh peaks and rugged coves of **Asturias**, a land with its own idiosyncratic traditions, which include status as a principality (the heir to the Spanish throne is known as the *Príncipe de Asturias*), and a distinctive culture that incorporates bagpipes and cider (*sidra* – served from above head height to add fizz). Asturias has a base of heavy industry, especially mining and steelworks – and a long-time radical and maverick workforce – but for the most part, the coastline is a delight, with wide, rolling meadows leading down to the sea. Tourism here is largely local, with a succession of old-fashioned and very enjoyable **seaside towns** such as **Ribadesella**, **Llanes** and **Cudillero**. Inland, everything is dominated by the **Picos de Europa**, though a quiet pleasure on the peripheries of the mountains, as in Cantabria, is the wealth of Romanesque, and even rare pre-Romanesque, churches found in odd corners of the hills. These reflect the history of the old Asturian kingdom – the embryonic kingdom of Christian Spain – which had its first stronghold in the mountain fortress of **Covadonga**, and spread slowly south with the Reconquest. To the north lie a trio of cities: **Oviedo**, a delightful regional capital, with a recently restored old centre; **Avilés**, at its best during the wild

Fiestas

January
22: Saint's day fiesta at San Vicente de la Barquera.

February/March
Start of Lent: Carnaval Week-long festivities in Avilés, Gijón, Oviedo, Mieres, Santoña – fireworks, fancy dress and live music.

March/April
Good Friday Over-the-top re-enactment of the Passion at Castro Urdiales.
Easter Sunday and Monday: Bollo Cake festival at Avilés.
First weekend after Easter: La Folía Torch-lit procession at San Vicente de la Barquera; a statue of the Virgin Mary is carried through town on a fishing boat.

June
29: La Amuravela Cudillero enacts an ironic review of the year – and then proceeds to obliterate memories.

July
Throughout July Weekly fiestas in Llanes, with Asturian dancers balancing pine trees on their shoulders and swerving through the streets. Also, tightrope walking and live bands down at the harbour.
First Friday: Coso Blanco Nocturnal parade at Castro Urdiales.
10: Fiesta at Aliva.
Mid-July: Festival de Folk Cultural fiesta at San Vicente de la Barquera.
15: Traditional festival at Comillas, with greased-pole climbs, goose chases and other such events.
16, 17 & 18: Fiestas in Tapia de Casariego.
25: Festival of St James Cangas de Onis.

Carnaval celebrations; and nearby **Gijón**, which enjoys a vibrant nightlife and cultural scene.

The Picos de Europa, in fact, take in parts of León, as well as Cantabria and Asturias, though for simplicity the whole national park is covered in this chapter.

Santander

Much the largest city in Cantabria, with a population approaching 200,000, **SANTANDER** is an elegant, refined resort with excellent transport connections. While its setting on the narrow Bahía de Santander is beautiful – from the heart of the city, you can enjoy clear views across the bay to rolling green hills and high mountains that seem to glow at sunset, and superb sandy **beaches** line much of the shorefront – the city centre lost most of its finest buildings to a massive fire in 1941. Nonetheless, the narrow lanes of the old town, running parallel to the waterfront, still abound in atmospheric bars and restaurants, and the beaches are broad and clean enough for Santander to rival Biarritz and San Sebastián as a favourite summer retreat for sophisticated holiday-makers from the interior. Santander may have a much more *bourgeois* identity than many of

August

Throughout August: Festival Internacional Music and cultural festival at Santander. This being one of the wealthiest cities of the north, you can usually depend on the festival featuring some prestigious acts.

First or second weekend: Descenso Internacional del Sella Mass canoe races from Arriondas to Ribadesella down the Río Sella, with fairs and festivities in both towns.

First Sunday: Asturias Day Celebrated above all at Gijón.

12: Fiesta at Llanes.

15: El Rosario The fishermen's fiesta at Luarca, when the Virgin is taken to the sea.

Last Friday: Battle of the Flowers At Laredo.

Last week: San Timoteo Fairly riotous festivities at Luarca: best on the final weekend of the month, with fireworks over the sea, people being thrown into the river and a Sunday *romería*.

September

7–9: Running of the bulls at Ampuero (Santander).

19: Americas Day in Asturias, celebrating the thousands of local emigrants in Latin America; at Oviedo, there are floats, bands and groups representing every Latin American country. The exact date for this can vary.

21: Fiesta de San Mateo at Oviedo, usually a continuation of the above festival.

Last Sunday: Campoo Day Held at Reinosa, and featuring a parade in traditional dress.

29: Romeria de San Miguel At Puente Viesgo.

November

First or second weekend: Orujo Local-liquor festival in Potes.

30: San Andrés Saint's day fiesta, celebrated with a small regatta at Castro Urdiales. The tradition is to sample sea bream and snails.

its earthier northern neighbours – and away from the beaches there's not all that much actually to see or do – but it's really not a bad place to while away a day or two.

In the summer, the city holds an **international university**, augmented by a **music and cultural festival** throughout August (Ⓦ www.festivalsantander .com).

Arrival and information

The **RENFE** and **FEVE** train stations stand side by side on the Plaza Estaciónes, just back from the waterside 500m west of the old town, and in the shadow of an escarpment that hides the main roads. A largely subterranean **bus station** (☎ 942 211 995; Ⓦ www.santandereabus.com) faces them directly across the square, while **ferries** from England dock nearby (Brittany Ferries; Ⓦ www.brittany-ferries.co.uk). An extensive network of **city buses** covers all areas; routes #1, #3, #4, #7 and #E shuttle between the centre and El Sardinero.

Ryanair **flights** from London and Dublin swoop across the bay to land in full view of the city at the **Aeropuerto de Santander** (☎ 942 202 100, Ⓦ www .aena.es), just 4km south at Parayas on the Bilbao road. Several car rental companies have outlets there; a taxi into town costs €15–18, and buses run nonstop to the bus station (6.30am–10.45pm; €1.60).

The municipal **turismo** stands in a park very near the ferry port, the **Jardines de Pereda** (mid-June to mid-Sept daily 9am–9pm; mid-Sept to Easter Mon– Fri 8.30am–7pm, Sat 10am–2pm; Easter to mid-June Mon–Fri 8.30am–7pm, Sat & Sun 10am–7pm; ☎ 942 203 000, Ⓦ www.ayto-santander.es). One block north, the **Cantabrian Regional Turismo** (daily 9am–9pm; ☎ 942 310 708, Ⓦ www.turismodecantabria.com) is housed in the appealing covered market

place of the Mercado del Este at 4 c/Hernán Cortés. The city's main **post office** is next to the Catedral on Avda. Alfonso XIII (Mon–Fri 8am–9pm, Sat 9am–2pm).

Accommodation

July and August aside, Santander usually has enough **accommodation** to go round – the fundamental choice lies in whether you want to stay in the **old town** or near **El Sardinero** beach; they're a little too far apart for a hotel in either district to make a good base for visiting the other.

Central Santander

Hostal Cabo Mayor c/Cádiz 1 ☎942 211 181, ⓦwww.hcabomayor.com. Six spotless little en-suite rooms, across from the train stations, with free wi-fi. ❸

Hotel Central Avda. General Mola 5 ☎942 222 400, ⓦwww.elcentral.com. Smart rooms, some with sea-view balconies, in an unbeatable location for the old-town atmosphere – and the ferry. ❻

Pensión Angelines c/Atilano Rodríguez 9, 1° 25 ☎942 312 584, ⓦwww.pensionangelines.com. Basic but scrupulously clean rooms, in a busy location very near the train, bus and ferry, and sharing all washing and WC facilities. ❷

Pensión La Corza c/Hernán Cortés 25 ☎942 212 950. Attractive, centrally located *pensión* with surprisingly modern, bright rooms. ❸

Pensión Plaza c/Cádiz 13 ☎942 212 967, ⓦwww.pension-plaza.com. Small, good-value modern *pensión* very near the train and bus stations. ❸

El Sardinero

Hostal Paris Avda. de los Hoteles 6 ☎942 272 350, ⓦwww.hparis.net. Upmarket *hostal*, ageing gracefully and very near the beach; some of its large, bright rooms have stylish balconies. ❺

Hotel Hoyuela Avda. de los Hoteles 7 ☎942 282 628, ⓦwww.gruposardinero.com. Traditional, upmarket and expensive hotel, perfect for the beach. Rates drop enormously out of season. ❼

Hotel Sardinero Plaza de Italia 1 ☎942 271 100, ⓦwww.gruposardinero.com. Smart and very large beachside hotel with style and character. ❺

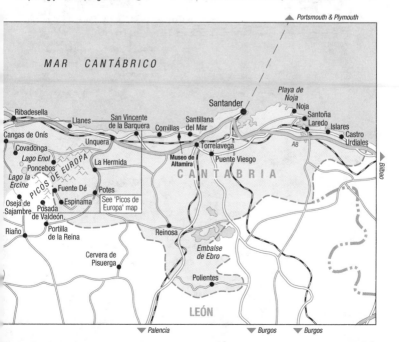

Pensión Coloma Avda. Maura 23 ☎942 270 636. The best budget option in Sardinero: clean, airy and right next to the beach. ❷

The rest of the city

Camping Cabo Mayor ☎942 391 542, ⓦwww.cabomayor.com. Well-equipped site with a swimming pool, 2km north of the casino on a bluff known as Cabo Mayor, 10min walk from Sardinero beach. Take bus #9 to Cueto from opposite the *ayuntamiento*. Closed mid-Oct to March.

Hostal Carlos III Avda. Reina Victoria 135 ☎942 271 616. Well-run *hostal* in a wonderful old mansion overlooking Playa de la Magdalena. Closed Nov–March. ❸

Hotel Real Paseo Pérez Galdós 28 ☎942 272 550, ⓦwww.hotelreal.es. Elegant, upmarket hotel, near Playa de la Magdalena, 10min walk from the centre, with good sea views and a seawater spa. ❼

San Glorio c/Ruiz Zorrilla 18 ☎942 312 962, ⓦwww.sanglorio.com. Cheap, clean and cheerful place 5min walk west of the stations, with a restaurant. ❸

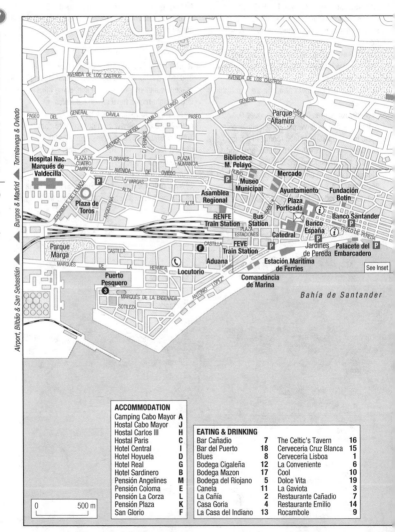

ACCOMMODATION

Camping Cabo Mayor	**A**
Hostal Cabo Mayor	**J**
Hostal Carlos III	**H**
Hostal Paris	**C**
Hotel Central	**I**
Hotel Hoyuela	**D**
Hotel Real	**G**
Hotel Sardinero	**B**
Pensión Angelines	**M**
Pensión Coloma	**E**
Pensión La Corza	**L**
Pensión Plaza	**K**
San Glorio	**F**

EATING & DRINKING

Bar Cañadio	7	The Celtic's Tavern	16
Bar del Puerto	18	Cervecería Cruz Blanca	15
Blues	8	Cervecería Lisboa	1
Bodega Cigaleña	12	La Conveniente	6
Bodega Mazon	17	Cool	10
Bodega del Riojano	5	Dolce Vita	19
Canela	11	La Gaviota	3
La Cañía	2	Restaurante Cañadio	7
Casa Goria	4	Restaurante Emilio	14
La Casa del Indiano	13	Rocambole	9

0   500 m

The Town

Santander is a large, sprawling city that focuses on two very distinct areas: the **old town**, a compact grid of streets that stretches along the shoreline of the bay, and the resort district that lines long, sandy **El Sardinero** beach, facing the open sea. As the crow flies, the two stand a couple of kilometres apart, but the coastal route between them is more than twice as long, as it leads around the wooded headland of **La Magdalena**.

Although the old town had to be entirely rebuilt after the fire of 1941 destroyed its medieval core, for the most part it doesn't look particularly modern, just slightly faded and dull. As you stroll around, the only area that holds any great appeal lies a block back from the waterfront, along the parallel

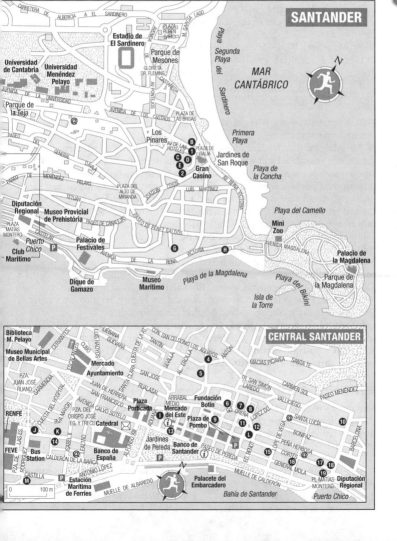

lanes that connect the colonnaded **Plaza Porticada** in the west to the **Plaza de Pombo** and the **Plaza Montero**. At the time of writing, the attractive Mercado del Este at c/Hernán Cortés 4 was being converted to re-house the city's **Museo Provincial de Prehistória**, whose displays on the province's prehistoric cave-dwellers are worth seeing if you plan to visit Altamira or Puente Viesgo.

There's nothing to see in the **Catedral**, a little further west toward the stations, part from the Gothic-Romanesque **crypt** down below (daily 8am–1pm & 4–8pm). Uphill to the northwest, at c/Rubio 6, the **Museo Municipal de Bellas Artes** (mid-June to mid-Sept Mon–Fri 11.15am–1pm & 5.30–9pm, Sat 10.30am–1pm; mid-Sept to mid-June Mon–Fri 10.15am–1pm & 5.30–9pm, Sat 10am–1pm; free) houses an eclectic mix of past and present, from Goya portraits to contemporary photos, including Philip-Lorca di Corcia's enigmatic and powerful *Head* portraits.

Ten-minutes' walk east of the old town, beyond the **Puerto Chico** where the pleasure boats dock, the up-to-the-minute **Museo Marítimo** (daily except Mon: May–Sept 10am–7.30pm; Oct–April 10am–6pm; €6) sets out to trace the history of Cantabria's involvement with the sea. If you don't read Spanish, enough captions are translated into English to provide a general overview, but you'll miss a lot of the detail, so only the aquarium that fills most of the basement is likely to hold your interest.

Peninsula de la Magdalena and the beaches

Perched on its eponymous headland at the eastern tip of the city, the **Palacio de la Magdalena** (bus #1 from Jardines del Pereda) affords magnificent views of the golden coastline. Built at the end of the nineteenth century by Alfonso XIII, whose residence was largely responsible for the town's fashionability, the grounds now make a popular retreat for families keen to escape the crowded beaches. A small, rather sad **zoo** now houses only a few penguins and some sea lions, but the real attraction is strolling around the gardens themselves. Should you find the hills hard work, a tourist train (€2) departs regularly from the park gates.

The first of Santander's beaches, **Playa de la Magdalena**, lies on the southern side of the headland. A beautiful yellow strand, sheltered by cliffs and flanked by a summer **windsurfing** school, it is deservedly popular. Around the headland to the north, two smaller and often slightly quieter beaches, **Camello** and **La Concha**, precede the main event, **El Sardinero**, which stretches for two magnificent kilometres, and is itself divided at high tide into two separate sections, Primera to the south and Segunda to the north.

If you find all the city beaches too crowded, catch a **taxi-ferry** across the bay (departs Puerto Chico every 20min; €4 return) to the long stretches of dunes at **Somo** – a major **surfing** destination where you'll find boards to rent and a summer **campsite** – and **Pedreña**.

Eating, drinking and nightlife

Santander's old town holds the largest selection of **cafés**, **bars** and **restaurants**, though plenty more lie close to El Sardinero. As both a university town and an upscale resort, Santander also offers lively **nightlife**, especially on summer weekends.

Tapas bars and restaurants

Bodega Cigaleña c/Daoiz y Velaverde. Atmospheric bar/museum decorated with old bottles. Closed Sun, last week in May & Nov and first week in June & Dec.

Bodega Mazon c/Hernán Cortés 57. *Bodega* serving tasty local food, such as *chipirones* and *tortilla*, plus wine and *sidra*, amid vast wine vats. Closed Sun.

Bodega del Riojano c/Río de la Pila 5. Traditional *bodega* serving good tapas, with a flagstone floor, beautifully painted casks and antique furniture. Popular with the thirty-plus crowd. Closed Sun eve & Mon.

La Cañía c/Joaquín Costa 45, Sardinero. Unpretentious restaurant with excellent seafood and a good €13 *menú*.

Casa Goria Travesía la Pila. Traditional tiled tapas bar, just off c/Río de la Pila, where the ceiling is adorned with hanging Cantabrian hams. Wonderful *empanadas* and *pinchos*, with a dining room at the back, should the popular bar be a little claustrophobic.

La Casa del Indiano Mercado del Este, c/Hernán Cortés 4. Very attractive South American-style sit-down bar inside the flagstone-floored market, open from breakfast onwards for drinks and snacks, with a fine spread of *pintxos*.

Cervecería Lisboa Plaza Italia, Sardinero. Of the clutch of restaurants in front of the casino, all with summer terrazas, this serves the best food, with a €22 *menú*.

La Conveniente c/Gómez Oreña 19. Very old-fashioned and very atmospheric nineteenth-century *bodega* with live music and fried fish, and other delicious, but pricey, snacks. From 7pm; closed Sun.

La Gaviota c/Marqués de la Ensanada, Barrio de Puerto Pesquero. The best of several similarly busy, unpretentious seafood restaurants down by the port, featuring a street barbecue of spectacular, freshly caught seafood. You can spend anything, from a few euros for a *menú* or plate of sardines, to a small fortune for fishy exotica.

Restaurante Cañadio and **Bar Cañadio** Plaza Cañadio ☏ 942 314 149. The *Cañadio* is the city's most famous restaurant, known far and wide for the sublime fish and regional cooking of Paco Quirós. Typical main dishes cost €18–24, or you can simply join the foodies at the more modest bar, snacking on delicious *raciones* (€9–13) or the even cheaper canapés.

Restaurante Emilio c/Cadiz 5. Handily placed near the bus station, with excellent fish soup and *fabada*, and friendly service.

Bars and clubs

Bar del Puerto c/Hernán Cortés 63. Swish bar and restaurant popular with the sailing crowd. Closed Sun night.

Blues Plaza Cañadio. Blues and jazz music bar, with an expensive restaurant attached. Closed Sun & Mon.

Canela Plaza Cañadio. Popular bar in a thronged plaza, always full at the start of the evening.

The Celtic's Tavern c/Gándara 3 esq c/General Mola. Live folk music, imported beers and English-speaking staff.

Cervecería Cruz Blanca c/Hernán Cortés 24. Another popular place to begin the evening, with a huge variety of international beers.

Cool c/San Emeterio 3, ⓦ www.coolsantander.com. Tiny, narrow and very hip bar, filled until late with a cool young crowd.

Dolce Vita c/General Mola 45. The biggest club in town, with two floors (dance/Latino) and a quieter bar area. Thurs–Sat; €6 entrance fee for men, women free.

Rocambole c/Hernán Cortés 35. Late-night club attracting a young and trendy crowd from 3am; Motown music and expensive drinks.

East to Castro Urdiales

Easily accessible by car but still appealingly rural, the coast east of Santander is becoming ever more developed for tourism. The best-known resort is **Laredo**, with its enormous beach, but lower-key alternatives include the villages of **Islares** and **Oriñon**, and the fishing ports of **Santoña** and **Castro Urdiales**.

Laredo and around

From its old core, sheltered behind a rocky promontory, **LAREDO**, poised 50km from Santander to the west and Bilbao to the east, has expanded westwards along the sandspit at the mouth of the Río Asón to become one of Cantabria's most popular resorts. In summer, the beaches and profusion of pubs, clubs and discos attract a young crowd keen to party, while there's enough of interest during the rest of the year to ensure that most of the hotels and restaurants remain open.

Laredo was Cantabria's provincial capital for a spell in the nineteenth century, and the village-like old town, the **Puebla Vieja**, stills retains the odd trace of its former walls and gates, climbing up towards a splendid thirteenth-century parish church, **Santa María de la Asunción** (daily 10am–1pm & 4–7.30pm). Beyond that, you can climb quickly out of town to the cliffs and to grand open countryside. A five-minute walk from the old town leads down to the best **beach** this side of San Sebastián, also known as the **Playa de Salvé**. A gently shelving crescent of sand, well protected from the wind, it stretches for a full 5km. **Boat trips** from the harbour's eastern end, nearest the old town, run west to Santoña, east to Castro Urdiales, or simply out into the sea (mid-June to mid-Sept; ☎608 392 666, ⓦwww.excursionesmaritimas.com).

Practicalities

Laredo's well-stocked **turismo** is housed in a former radio station at the west end of the old town, close to the **bus** terminal (daily: summer 9am–9pm; winter 9am–2pm & 5–7pm; ☎942 611 096, ⓦwww.laredo.es). The nearest FEVE **train** station is 5km inland, at **Treto**.

Most of Laredo's **accommodation** is near the beach, though you can find cheap rooms in the old town at *Pensión Cantabria*, c/Menéndez Pelayo 7 (☎942 605 073; ❷). Otherwise, *Hotel El Risco*, Blvd. Arenosa 2 (☎942 605 030, ⓦwww.hotelrisco.com; ❹), perched atop a hill with great views out to sea, is particularly good value, though if you want to be by the beach, you may prefer *Hotel Montecristo*, c/Calvo Sotelo 2 (☎942 605 700, Ⓔhotel_montecristo @hotmail.com; ❹), with its pleasant garden terrace. **Campsites** close to the beach include *Laredo* (☎942 605 035, ⓦwww.campinglaredo.com; closed mid-Sept to May).

The best area to look for **bars** and **restaurants** in the old town is c/Mayor, where several more options lie scattered uphill from *Guti* at no. 7, which specializes in mixed grills. There are also plenty of places to eat along the seafront, including *El Pescador*, Avda. de la Victoria 2 – their catch of the day is always excellent.

Finally, Laredo is the base of Mundo Submarino (☎942 611 861, ⓦwww .mundosubmarino.es), which runs PADI-affiliated **scuba diving** courses across the Cantabrian Sea.

Santoña

Just across the bay from the west end of Playa de Laredo lies the resort of **SANTOÑA**, shielded from the ocean by the mighty wooded hill of Monte Ganzo. Ferries run across the water to the small beach, or it's thirty minutes from Laredo by hourly bus. Santoña is still a working fishing port; you can watch the catch being unloaded before sampling it in the tiny bars grouped around the streets leading up from the port, particularly c/General Salinas.

Islares and Oriñon

If you're looking for somewhere more peaceful, the villages of **ISLARES** and **ORIÑON**, 8km east from Laredo on opposite sides of the Río Agüera, are pleasant and as yet little developed. Islares, on the east side of the river, is little more than a conglomeration of farming plots clustered around a tiny port and secluded beach, while Oriñon, down in the valley beside the main beach and sheltered by the mountains on either side, is an even better bet. Another, much wilder, beach is located 2km away around the headland below the village of

Sonabia. From here you can see the strange rock formation known as the *ojos del diablo* (devil's eyes) on the mountainside above.

Despite their size, the villages hold several **places to stay**. In Islares, *Hosteria Lantarón* (☎942 862 212, ⓦwww.aisiahoteles.com; ❸) boasts large, clean, modern rooms, many with beach terrazas, as well as an excellent restaurant, while the cheaper *Hostal Areníllas* (☎942 870 900; ❷) has its own campsite. In Oriñon, *El Conde* (☎942 878 624; ❷; open Easter & June–Sept) is a basic *pensión* with shared bathrooms, and there's also a nice beachfront **campsite** (☎942 878 630, ⓦwww.campingorinon.com).

Castro Urdiales

Twenty kilometres or so east of Laredo, **CASTRO URDIALES** is a congenial, handsome resort, somewhat less developed than Laredo. Rooms and space on the beaches are at a premium in high season and at weekends, when crowds descend from Santander and Bilbao. At such times, the main "town beach", **Playa del Brazomar**, a small strip of sand hemmed in by a cement esplanade, can be very busy. However, the crowds can be left behind by heading farther east to more secluded coves, or west to **Playa Ostende**, with its rough, dark sand. From this latter beach, there's an unusual walk back to town along the cliffs, with the sea pounding the rocks beneath you. In a tiny bay en route, the sea comes in under a spectacular overhang.

The town retains a considerable fishing fleet, gathered around a beautiful natural **harbour**. Above this looms a massively buttressed Gothic church, **Santa María**, and a lighthouse, built within the shell of a Knights Templar castle. These are linked to the remains of an old hermitage by a dramatic reconstructed **bridge**, medieval in age, but known locally as the Puente Romano, under which the sea roars at high tide. The old quarter, the **Mediavilla**, is relatively well preserved, with arcaded streets and tall, glass-balconied houses.

Practicalities

The **turismo** stands at the top end of Paseo Maritimo (Mon–Sat 9am–2pm & 5–7pm; ☎942 871 512, ⓦwww.castro-urdiales.net). **Parking** in town is appallingly difficult, while the **bus terminal** is a good half-hour walk east of the centre on c/Leonardo Rucabado, although town buses, and services to Bilbao, stop outside *Café-Bar Ronda* on Paseo Menendez Pelayo.

Castro Urdiales' best budget **accommodation** is scattered through the narrow, pedestrianized streets of the old town; reliable options include *Pensión La Sota*, beneath the seafront arches at c/La Correría 1 (☎942 871 188; ❷), which offers plain en-suite rooms, and the smarter, refurbished *Pensión La Mar*, c/La Mar 27 (☎942 870 524; ❷). Several more modern hotels lie closer to the beach in the newer part of town, including the imposing, classy, pastel-yellow *Hotel Las Rocas*, Avda. de la Playa (☎942 860 400, ⓦwww.lasrocashotel.com; ❺), where many of the comfortable upscale rooms enjoy sea views.

Places to **eat** clustered beneath the arches at the castle end of the harbour include *Mesón Marinero*, c/Correría 23 (☎942 860 005), a fish restaurant with a big arcaded terrace. Main courses cost upwards of €20, but you can dine very well and cheaply on *raciones* at the bar. The lively c/Ardigales, at the centre of the **nightlife** scene a block inland from the Paseo del Mar, is packed with *mesónes* and *tabernas*, including traditional *Sidrería Marcelo* at no. 10, which serves great snacks plus cider fresh from the barrel.

Santillana and the prehistoric caves

As you head west from Santander along the Cantabrian coast, the first major tourist destination is the outrageously picturesque village of **Santillana del Mar**. It can be unbearably overcrowded in summer, but it's still worth a visit, and even though the famous prehistoric cave paintings at nearby **Altamira** are no longer open to visitors, an excellent new museum explains the site in fascinating detail. A less impressive, though still very extensive, set of Altamira–epoch paintings can still be admired in another set of caves at **Punte Viesgo**.

Santillana del Mar

No less an authority than Jean-Paul Sartre, in *Nausea*, hailed **SANTILLANA DEL MAR**, 26km west of Santander, as "*le plus joli village d'Espagne*". While the crowds that flock here have unquestionably diminished its appeal, on a quiet day it remains as beautiful as ever, abounding in gorgeous sandstone churches and mansions. Its unusual name derives from a bastardization of "Santa Juliana", put to death by her husband for refusing to renounce her virginity, whose remains were brought here 1200 years ago. Referring to its literal translation, the locals jokily call it the "town of the three lies" – as it's neither very holy (*santi*) nor particularly flat (*llana*), and despite the *del Mar* actually stands a few kilometres back from the sea.

Arrival and information

Santillana's **turismo** is just off the main road at c/Jesús Otero 20, adjoining the village's largest car park (daily: June–Sept 9am–9pm; Oct–May 9.30am–1.30pm & 4.30–7.30pm; ☎942 818 812, ⓦwww.santillana-del-mar.com). Local **buses** stop nearby, while the nearest FEVE **train** station is in Torrelavega.

Accommodation

Santillana is not really a destination for budget travellers, even if there is a large **campsite**, *Camping Santillana* (☎942 818 250), with a pool and good facilities, 1km out along the Altamira road. If you're going to spend a night here, it's worth paying to stay in one of its many gorgeous upscale **hotels**, which uniquely include two **paradors**.

Casa del Marqués c/Canton 26 ☎942 818 888. Grand and very luxurious historic hotel, with tasteful, well-appointed rooms. ❺

Parador Gil Blas Plaza Mayor ☎942 028 028, ⓦwww.parador.es. Housed in a splendid mansion on the main square, this definitive *parador* features a delightful terrace restaurant. ❻

Parador Santillana Plaza Ramón Pelayo ☎942 818 000, ⓦwww.parador.es. Santilla's other luxury *parador* stands in a tasteful modern building that's set slightly back from the central square. ❻

Posada del Organista c/Los Hornos 4 ☎942 840 452, ⓦwww.casadelorganista.com. This beautiful eighteenth-century B&B, just up from the centre, serves great breakfasts. ❹

Santa Juliana c/Carrera 19 ☎942 840 106, ⓔsantajuliana@santillanadelmar.com. While ranking among Santillana's cheaper *posadas*, this still maintains high standards, and offers six attractive beamed rooms. ❸

The Town

Though Santillana consists of little more than two pedestrianized streets and a couple of plazas – Mayor and Las Arenas – it feels more like a sizeable medieval town that never grew beyond its original core than a village. The scale and elegance of its ochre-coloured stone buildings make strolling a delight, even if most now hold restaurants, hotels or souvenir shops, and the farms and fields that climb the adjacent hillsides give it a lovely rural atmosphere.

Many of the fifteenth- to eighteenth-century **mansions** clustered close to the Plaza Mayor still belong to the original families, but their noble owners have rarely visited in the last couple of centuries. Among the finest is the **Casa de los Hombrones**, on c/Cantón, which was named after the two moustached figures that flank its grandly sculpted escutcheon. Nearby, the **Museo de la Tortura** displays a macabre and disturbing collection of torture instruments,

▲ Casa de los Hombrones

with historical notes in English (daily 10am–8pm; €3.60). The elegantly proportioned village church, **La Colegiata** (daily 10am–1.30pm & 4–7.30pm), on Plaza Las Arenas, is dedicated to Santa Juliana, whose tomb it contains. Its most outstanding feature is its twelfth-century **Romanesque cloister** (€3), where the squat, paired columns and lively capitals are carved with images of animals and hunting, as well as religious scenes.

The seventeenth-century **Convento de Regina Coeli** (same hours and ticket), on the main road just across from the village entrance, houses an exceptional museum of painted wooden figures and other religious art: pieces brilliantly restored by the nuns and displayed with great imagination to show the stylistic development of certain images, particularly of San Roque, a healing saint always depicted with his companion, a dog who licks the plague sore on his thigh. There is supposedly a resident ghost, too, on the first floor.

Eating and drinking

Though it's disappointingly short on tapas bars, Santillana holds plenty of conventional **restaurants**. *Gran Duque,* c/Jesús Otero, serves a particularly good €26 *menú*, while two neighbouring places on Plaza La Gandara, close to the *turismo*, *La Villa* and *Los Blasones*, make good alternatives. You can also enjoy a pleasant meal outdoors, at the nice but expensive terrace restaurant of the *Parador Gil Blas*. The *Bar El Jardín*, on c/Canton across from the *Casa del Marqués*, has an appealing shady garden, whilst the terraza at *Café Concana*, on c/Hornos just off the Plaza Mayor, is a good spot for a quiet drink, or breakfast from €3.

The Caves of Altamira

The **Caves of Altamira** burrow into the hillside 2km west of Santillana. Dating from around 12,000 BC, they consist of an extraordinary series of caverns, adorned by prehistoric human inhabitants with paintings of bulls, bison, boars and other animals, etched in red and black with confident and impressionistic strokes. Sealed by a roof collapse thirteen thousand years ago, the murals were in near-perfect condition when rediscovered in the 1870s, their colours striking and vigorous; as Picasso put it, "After Altamira, everything is decadence". During the 1950s and 1960s, however, they seriously deteriorated due to the moisture released in the breath of visitors, and the caves are now **closed** to prevent further damage.

The remarkable **Museo de Altamira** alongside the site (Tues–Sat 9.30am–8pm, until 6pm Oct–May, Sun 9.30am–3pm; ℡942 818 815, ⓦmuseodealtamira.mcu.es; €2.40) centres on a "Neocave", a large and very convincing replica of a portion of the caverns that gives a spine-tingling sense of how the paintings look *in situ*. Comprehensive displays in the adjoining galleries trace human history all the way back to Africa, with three-dimensional replicas and authentic finds from Altamira and other Spanish sites, and plentiful captions in English. No one knows exactly why the Paleolithic art at Altamira was created, but according to archeologists it was not primarily related to hunting, in that the specific animals depicted were not eaten any more than other species.

Puente Viesgo

Genuine **prehistoric caves** can still be visited just outside the attractive village of **PUENTE VIESGO**, set in a river gorge amid magnificent forested escarpments on the N623 to Burgos, 15km southeast of Santillana or 24km southwest of Santander. Guided tours (in Spanish only) depart from an informative visitor centre located 1.5km up a winding mountain road from the village bus stop (served by SA Continental buses from the main station in Santander). Two of the four caves are open to the public, **Las Monedas** and the slightly better **El Castillo** (daily: April–Oct 9.30am–8pm; Nov–March 9am–3pm; ☏942 598 425; €3), but places are limited, and in summer it's best to book at least 24 hours in advance. The caves are magnificent, with weirdly shaped stalactites and stalagmites, and bizarre organ-like lithophones, natural features used by Paleolithic peoples to produce primitive music, while the astonishing paintings, depicting animals from mammoths to dogs, are clear precursors to the later developments at Altamira. Should you be unable to find a place on a tour, the visitor centre has an excellent digital exhibit enabling 360-degree views and interactive "tours".

The village has a luxurious four-star **hotel** on c/Manuel Pérez Mazo, the *Gran Hotel Balneario* (☏942 598 061, ⓦwww.balneariodepuenteviesgo.com; ❻), with its own spa, set in a glorious river valley. There's also a highly recommended *posada*, *La Anjana* (☏942 598 526, ⓦwww.posadalaanjana.es; ❹), with spacious, well-equipped rooms, where the price includes breakfast in the excellent restaurant. *Pensión La Terraza*, c/General 49 (☏942 598 102; closed Oct–June; ❸), with its simple rooms and shared bath, is typical of the cheaper alternatives that open in summer only.

South of Santander: Reinosa and the Ebro

South of Santander, a large area of quiet Cantabrian countryside is dominated by an extensive reservoir, the Pantano del Ebro. The N611 to Palencia brushes its shores en route to the pleasant old town of **Reinosa**. To the east, the **Río Ebro** trails a lovely valley, past a succession of unspoilt villages, Romanesque architecture and cave churches.

Reinosa

REINOSA is a pretty, characteristically Cantabrian town with glass-fronted balconies and *casonas* – seventeenth-century townhouses – displaying the coats of arms of their original owners. The **turismo** occupies one of these, midway down the main street, Avenida Puente Carlos III, near the distinctive Baroque church of **San Sebastián** (Mon–Fri 9.30am–2pm & 4–7pm, summer also Sat & Sun 10am–2pm; ☏942 755 215, ⓦturismoreinosa.es).

On the last Sunday in September – "**Campoo Day**" – the people of the Alto Campoo region, of which Reinosa is the capital, celebrate their unique folklore and traditions. Locals parade in distinctive alpine-style costume, complete with the unusual stilted clogs known as *albarcas*, and enjoy displays of traditional dance, typical foods and the usual late-night festivities.

Comfortable **accommodation** options include the little *Hotel Rubén*, c/Abrego 12 (☏942 754 914; ❷), close to the liveliest part of town, or the stylish *Posada San Roque*, further east at Avda. de Cantabria 3 (☏942 754 788; ❸).

For a small town, Reinosa holds a wide range of traditional **bodegas** and **mesónes**, concentrated around the central Plaza de la Constitución. *Pepe de los Vinos* is a good place for a glass of wine and a snack, while the restaurants *Avenida*, at Avda. Puente Carlos III 21, and *Tres Mares*, at Avda. de Cantabria 4, offer more substantial meals.

The western Cantabrian coast

The coast west of Santillana, as far as drab little **Unquera** on the border with Asturias, is dotted with a succession of small, low-key resorts. Both the main towns, **Comillas** and **San Vicente de la Barquera**, are worth a visit, having retained a traditional, earthy feel long since abandoned elsewhere in a flood of high-rise hotels and apartments. The **FEVE line** runs inland along this stretch, but the towns are linked by regular bus services.

Comillas

COMILLAS, 16km west of Santillana del Mar, is a curious rural town with pretty cobbled streets and squares, which in its centre seems almost oblivious of the proximity of the sea. It nonetheless boasts a pair of superb beaches: **Playa de Comillas**, the closest, has a little anchorage for pleasure boats and a few beach cafés, while the longer and less developed **Playa de Oyambre** is 4km west out of town towards the cape.

Oddly out of place in the otherwise provincial town is a trio of mansions, including a Gaudí-designed villa, **El Capricho**, an easy walk from the centre. With its whimsical tower, playful miniaturizations and futuristic use of colour, it has the incongruous air of a Hansel and Gretel gingerbread house. It now holds a restaurant (see below), but its gardens are open to visitors.

Next door to El Capricho is another nineteenth-century *modernista* flourish, the **Palácio de Sobrellano** (June–Aug daily 10am–9pm; Sept daily 10.30am–2pm & 4–7.30pm; Oct–May Wed–Sun 10.30am–2pm & 4–7.30pm; guided tour only, €4), designed by Gaudí's associate, Juan Martorell, and the former residence of the Marqués de Comillas, whose statue overlooks the beach, Rio-style, from a hillside. The Marqués, an industrialist friend of Alfonso XII, also commissioned the gargantuan **Universidad Pontífica**, on the hillside above, from Lluis Domenech i Montaner, another of the Barcelona *modernista* group; the gardens are open to the public.

Practicalities

Comillas' helpful central **turismo** is at c/La Aldea 2 (summer Mon–Sat 9am–9pm, Sun 11am–1pm & 5–8pm; winter Mon–Sat 11am–1pm & 4–7pm, Sun 11am–1pm; ☎942 720 768, ⓦwww.comillas.es). The FEVE line runs 10km inland at this point, but frequent **buses** use the main coast road. Market day is Friday.

If you're looking for **accommodation** with sea views, you can't beat *Hotel Josein* at c/Manuel Noriega 27 (☎942 720 225, ⓦwww.hoteljosein.com; ❻), where several rooms have galleries literally overhanging the Playa de Comillas. Alternatively, *Hostal Esmeralda*, c/Antonio López 7 (☎942 720 097, ⓦwww.hostalesmeralda.com; ❹), is a beautifully furnished place in the heart of town. Cheaper options include *Pensión Villa*, Cuesta Carlos Diaz de la Campa 21 (☎942 720 217, ⓦwww.pensionvilladecomillas.com; ❸), which comprises two buildings, one modern and comfortable above the main square and another more characterful house just off the Plaza de Ibañez, and *Pensión La Aldea*, c/La Aldea 5 (☎942 721 046; ❶), which has a superb restaurant downstairs. Both beaches have **campsites**, but the *Comillas* on the east side of town (☎942 720 074, ⓦwww.campingcomillas.com; closed Oct–May) is significantly better than *El Rodero* at Oyambre (☎942 722 040).

As for **food**, *El Capricho* (☎942 720 365) is a good Spanish *nouvelle cuisine* restaurant, with main courses starting around €20, while *Gurea*, c/Ignacio

Fernandez de Castro 12 (☏942 722 446), serves outstanding Basque cuisine, with a €30 *menú*; try their tasty *merluza pil pi* if you get a chance. Of the tapas bars around the main square, *Samovy* is especially recommended.

San Vicente de la Barquera

Twelve kilometres west of Comillas, the approach to **SAN VICENTE DE LA BARQUERA** is dramatic, with the town marooned on both sides by the sea and entered via a long causeway across the Río Escudo, the Puente de la Maza. Local lore maintains that if you manage to hold your breath all the way across the bridge, your wish will come true. Inland, dark green, forested hills rise towards the Picos de Europa, strikingly silhouetted as the sun goes down. Looking down from the hill that looms over the centre of town are an impressive Renaissance **ducal palace** (Tues–Sun 11am–2pm & 5–8pm; €1.20) and a Romanesque-Gothic church, **Santa María de los Ángeles**, the latter with a famous reclining statue of the Inquisitor Corro, born here in 1472; attached to the church are the ruins of a fourteenth-century pilgrims' hospital. The town itself, a thriving fishing port with a string of locally famed seafood restaurants, is functional rather than pretty, split by the main coast road with its thundering lorries, and with not all that much left of its historic core. If you're looking for a **beach**, there's a good sweep of sand fifteen-minutes' walk away, across the causeway on the east side of the river and flanked by a small forest.

Practicalities

The local **turismo** is on the main street in the heart of town, below the castle, at Avda. Generalísimo 20 (summer only Mon–Fri 10am–2pm & 4–8.30pm, Sat & Sun 10am–1.30pm & 4.30–7.30pm; ☏942 710 797, Ⓦwww.sanvicentedelabarquera.org). **Buses** stop 100m south of the old centre, at the bottom of Avenida Miramar near the west end of the causeway, while the nearest FEVE **train** station is 4km south at La Alcebasa.

   Accommodation is easy enough to find, with options to suit most budgets. The refined *Hotel Luzón* is on the seafront, alongside the main square at Avda. Miramar 1 (☏942 710 050, Ⓦwww.hotelluzon.net; ❹), while the modern *Hotel Boga Boga* is at Plaza José Antonio 9 (☏942 710 135, Ⓦwww.bogabogasvb.com; ❹). On the steps leading from the back of the main square, the homely *Pensión del Corro* (☏942 712 613, Ⓦwww.pensionelcorro.com; ❷) is the cheapest central option. There's also a pleasant **campsite**, *El Rosal* (☏942 710 165, Ⓦwww.campingelrosal.com; closed mid-Oct to mid-March), beside the beach.

   Though it's not immediately obvious when you peer into their cavernous interiors, the cluster of good seafood **restaurants** along Avenida Generalísimo also offer open-air tables on the quayside around the back. *Maruja* and *El Marinero* are relatively formal, but the pick of the bunch is 🏃 *El Pescador*, a big, rough-and-ready tapas bar serving a great array of seafood specialities. Back towards the causeway, the waterfront Avenida Miramar is awash with **bars** and **cafés**.

The Picos de Europa

The **PICOS DE EUROPA** may not be the highest mountains in Spain, but they're the favourite of many walkers, trekkers and climbers. Declared a national park in its entirety in 1995, the range is a miniature masterpiece: a mere 40km

PICOS DE EUROPA

▲ Torrelavega & Santander

MAR CANTÁBRICO

San Vicente de la Barquera

Unquera
Pimiango
Bustio
Colombres
Noriega
Villanueva

N 621

Puentenansa
Sobrelapeña

Panes

Santa María de Lebeña †

Cabezón de Liébana

Alevia
Llonín
Mier
Alles

Linares
Piñeres

La Hermida

Tama
Ojedo
Sotama

Potes

N 621

Deva

Llanés
Cué
San Roque
Peña Tú ▼
Vidiago

Desfiladero de la Hermida

CANTABRIA

Lon
Turieno

Monasterio de Santo Toribio de Liébana †

Brez
Camaleño

La Vega

Cosgaya

Parres
Posado
Caldueño

N 634 / E70

Ruenes
Trescares
Arangas

Cares

Tresviso

Sotres

P I C O S   D E   E U R O P A

Espinama

CA 185

Portilla de la Reina, Riaño & León

Carreña de Cabrales

Arenas de Cabrales

Poncebos

Tielve

Terenosa ▲

Río Duje

Refugio de Aliva

Portilla de la Reina ▼

Meré

Casañu

C 6312

Vega de Ario ▼

Camarmeña

Bulnes

Naranjo de Bulnes (2519m)

Peña Vieja (2613m)

Teleférico

Fuente Dé

Vega de Urriello

Cabaña Veronica ▲

Mirador del Cable

Portilla de la Reina ▼

Benia (Onís)
Con
Labra
Corao
La Riera

Cueva del Buxu

Lago de la Ercina

Caín

Torre de Cerredo (2648m) ▲

Collado Jermoso

LEÓN

Pto. de Pandetrave (1562m)

Riaño & León ▼

Cangas de Onís

Covadonga

Sames (Amieva)

Amieva

Lago de Enol

Vegarredonda

ASTURIAS

DESFILADERO DEL CARES

Vega Huerta

Vegabaño

Cordiñanes

Posada de Valdeón

Soto de Valdeón

Santa Marina de Valdeón

Cares

Pto. de Panderruedas (1540m)

DESFILADERO DE LOS BEYOS

Soto de Sajambre

Oseja de Sajambre

Sella

N 625

Puerto del Pontón ▼

Arriondas

◄ Ribadesella

La Tornín

Belello (Ponga)

Viego

N 634 / E70

Oviedo ▼

N

10 km

0

across in either direction, shoehorned in between three great **river gorges**, and straddling the provinces of Asturias, León and Cantabria. Asturians see the mountains as a symbol of their national identity, and celebrate a cave-shrine at **Covadonga** in the west as the birthplace of Christian Spain.

Walks in the Picos are amazingly diverse, with trails to suit all levels, from a casual morning's stroll to two- or three-day treks. The most spectacular and popular routes are along the twelve-kilometre Cares Gorge – which you can take in whole or part – and around the high peaks reached from the cable car at Fuente Dé and the subterranean funicular railway at Poncebos, though dozens of other paths and trails explore the river valleys or climb into the mountains. Take care if you go off the marked trails: the Picos can pose extreme challenges, with unstable weather and treacherous, unforgiving terrain, and what appears from a distance to be a slowly undulating plateau can too easily turn out to be a series of chasms and gorges.

Wildlife is also a major attraction. In the Cares Gorge, you may well see griffon vultures, black redstarts and ravens, though birdwatchers keep a special eye out for the red-winged, butterfly-like flight of the diminutive wallcreeper, named for the mouse-like way it creeps along the vertical cliff faces. Wild and domestic goats abound, with some unbelievably inaccessible high mountain pastures. Wolves are easy to imagine in the grey boulders of the passes, but bears, despite local gossip and their picturesque appearances on the tourist-board maps, are very seldom spotted. An inbred population of about a hundred specimens of *Ursus arctos pyrenaicus* (Cantabrian brown bear) remains in the southern Picos, most of them tagged with radio transmitters; another isolated group survives in western Asturias.

As road access has opened up the gorges and peaks, the Picos have been brought increasingly into the mainstream of tourism, and the most popular areas get very crowded in July and August. If you have the choice, and are content with lower-level walks, spring is best, when the valleys are gorgeous and the peaks still snowcapped, although the changing colours of the beech forests in autumn give some competition.

You can **approach** – and leave – the Picos along half a dozen roads: from León, to the south; from Santander and the coast, to the north and northeast; and from Oviedo and Cangas de Onis, to the northwest. Public transport serves much of the park, but services are generally infrequent, even in summer.

The east: the Cantabrian Picos

If you're driving along the coast and want to dip briefly into the Picos, the Asturian portion of the range, covered on p.531 onwards, is the most readily accessible. It takes little more effort, however, to reach the **Cantabrian** section of the mountains, where following the valley of the Río Deva from **Potes** to **Fuente Dé** takes you into the very heart of the Picos. Villages such as **Espinama** make superb overnight stops, and the opportunities for **hiking** are endless.

From the coast to Potes

The N621 heads inland from the coast at **Unquera**, at the mouth of the Deva on the Cantabria–Asturias border. Decision time comes 12km inland from there, at sleepy little **PANES**, where the C6312 forks west into Asturias, towards Arenas de Cabrales (see p.531) and Cangas de Onis (p.534), while the N621 continues south towards Potes.

Immediately south of Panes, you enter the eerily impressive gorge of the Río Deva, the **Desfiladero de La Hermida**, whose sheer sides are so high that

Accommodation

While options of all kinds abound in the more popular villages, it's always worth phoning ahead to book a room – especially in summer or at weekends, when whole towns can be booked solid. Up in the mountains, there are a number of alpine **refugios**, which range from organized hostels to free, unstaffed huts where you'll need to bring your own food. They provide blankets or hire out sleeping bags for around €1. In many places, guests have to leave their rucksacks outside the dorm, so bring a small padlock. **Camping** beside the *refugios* is accepted, and about half a dozen more campsites are scattered around the villages. Camping outside these sites is officially prohibited below 1600m, and subject to on-the-spot fines, but unofficially you won't be disturbed once away from populated areas.

Activity operators

Companies arranging activities of all kinds in the Picos, from canoeing and canyoneering to horseriding and mountain biking, include: **Cangas Aventura**, Ⓦwww.cangasaventura.com; offices at Avda. Covadonga 17, Cangas de Onís ☏985 848 887; Finca La Dehesa, Arriondas ☏985 841 699; and c/Posada Herrera s/n, Llanes ☏985 403 077; **Jaire Aventure**, Avda. Covadonga 14, Cangas de Onís ☏985 841 464, Ⓦwww.jairecanoas.com; **Montañas del Norte** ☏985 841 035, Ⓦwww.montanasdelnorte.com; offices at el Muelle 26, Ribadasella, and Plaza del Cañon 2, Arriondas; **Nakel Sportnature**, c/el Pico 9, Ribadasella ☏985 861 477, Ⓦwww.nakelsport.com; Picos Tour, c/San Roque 6, Potes ☏942 730 005, Ⓦwww.picostour.com; **Torretours**, Arenas de Cabrales ☏985 846 640, Ⓦwww.picosadventure.com; **Turaventura** ☏985 860 267, Ⓦwww.turaventura.com; offices at Caso de la Villa 50, Ribadasella, and Plaza del Cañon, Arriondas.

Banks

ATMs are located on the periphery of the region: at Panes, Potes, Arenas de Cabrales, Riaño and Cangas de Onis.

Climate

Good days for walking in the valleys occur even in the depths of winter, but at high altitudes the **walking season** lasts from late June to September, varying according to the preceding winter's snowfall. All year round, the weather is unstable, with brilliant sunshine rapidly turning to clouds, cold rain or dense mist; in summer, cloud often descends on the valleys, while higher up it remains bright and clear. Rain gear and a compass are highly advisable.

Equipment

Most trails in the Picos are stony, rugged and steep; **walking boots** are needed on all but the easiest routes. Safe, reliable water sources are sporadic, so carry a **bottle**. The routes given in this guide, unless mentioned otherwise, are straightforward and

---

they deny the village of **LA HERMIDA** any sunlight from November to April. The village consists of little more than a roadside cluster of **bars** and **hotels**, including the clean and modern *Pensión Marisa* (☏942 733 545; ❷), where the *Paquín* **restaurant** serves up fine traditional cooking, and the comfortable *Posada Campo* (☏942 733 510; ❷). From nearby **Urdón**, a path leads west to Sotres (see p.533); it's a pleasant few hours' walk, with mountains looming up around you.

Around 6km south of La Hermida, the village of **LEBEÑA** lies amid beautiful countryside just east of the main road. Its church of **Santa María**,

well marked; for walks at high altitude or off the marked trails, proper equipment and experience are essential, especially if you attempt any rock climbing.

Guided walks

Between July and mid-September, the national park service runs free daily **guided walks** of easy to moderate standard, leaving from various points around the park's perimeter. These are an excellent way for novice walkers to get to know the Picos, although guides don't necessarily speak any English. Call or visit the park offices for details. The national park offices also have lists of **guiding companies** operating in each province; contact details are given below.

Maps

Best are the **Adrados** editions, in two 1:25,000 sheets, one covering the western massif, the other the central and eastern massifs. Adrados also publish good walking and climbing guides. The Topografico Nacional de España 1:25,000 series, in four sheets, is neither as accurate nor as useful. Maps are available in Cangas de Onis, Caín, Potes, Sotres, Bulnes and Arenas de Cabrales.

Mountain federations

You can get further information on trekking and climbing in the Picos from these organizations: **Federacíon de Montañismo de Asturias**, c/Julian Clavería 11, Oviedo ☏985 252 362, @fempa1@hotmail.com; **Federacíon de Deportes de Montaña de Castilla y León**, Aptdo de Correos 3154, Valladolid ☏983 360 295, @www.fclm.com; and **Federacíon Cantabra de Deportes de Montaña**, Aptdo de Correos 64, Santander ☏942 755 294, @fcdme@navegalia.com.

National park offices

For **online information** on the Picos, see @reddeparquesnacionales.mma.es. The **main park office** is at c/Arquitecto Reguera 13 (☏985 241 412, @picos@mma.es) in Oviedo. Three **provincial offices** provide information on routes, activities and wildlife within the park, although each one tends to be short of information on the other two regions: Casa Dago, Avda Covadonga 43, Cangas de Onis, Asturias (☏985 848 614; see p.535); Sotama, Cantabria (☏942 730 555; see below); and Posada de Valdeón, León (☏987 740 549; see p.529). **Information centres** also operate in summer in Poncebos, Fuente Dé, Panes, Potes and Oseja de Sajambre.

Transport

No motorable **roads** cross the Picos (except the 4WD track from Espinama to Sotres), and circuits by road are long and slow; if you plan to trek across the range, make sure you allow sufficient time to get back to your starting point. **Bus** services along the main roads are limited to one or two a day, often at unsociable hours, and are very sketchy out of season. **Bikes** can be rented in Potes and other main towns.

built in the early tenth century by "Arabized" Christian craftsmen, is considered the supreme example of Mozarabic architecture, with its thoroughly Islamic geometric motifs and repetition of abstract forms.

Another half-dozen kilometres further south, with the mountains looming in all their glory to the west of the now-broad valley, you come to the huge **park visitor centre** at **SOTAMA** (daily: July–Sept 9am–8pm; Oct–June 9am–6pm; ☏942 738 109, @gcantabria@oapn.mma.es), which offers all the audio-visual displays and exhibitions, and information on guided walks, you could possibly need.

Potes

POTES, the main road junction and travellers' base on the east side of the Picos, is still just 500m above sea level, but it's beautifully situated, at the confluence of the Deva and Quiviesa rivers in the shadow of tall white peaks. A small market town, it gets very clogged with traffic in summer, but once you get away from the main road, the central lanes and riverbanks are truly attractive, and it's well worth taking a stroll along its cobbled alleyways, lined with little shops and bars. Several impressive timbered mansions stand hung with vines and geraniums. One, the Casa de Cultura at c/Sol 20, holds an interesting **map museum** (March–Dec daily except Mon 11am–2pm & 5–8pm; €5), while the thirteenth-century **Torre del Infanto** in the centre is now the *ayuntamiento*.

Potes' **turismo** is in the bus station at the west end of town, on the road to Fuente Dé (Mon & Thurs–Sat 10am–2pm & 4–7pm, Sun 10am–2pm; ☎942 730 787). In summer, daily Palomera **buses** run from Potes to Fuente Dé (Mon–Fri 3 daily, Sat & Sun daily). Services also run to Unquera, San Vicente and on to Santander three times a day, with two on Sunday.

Accommodation

Of Potes' abundant **accommodation** options, the best-value places are located on the banks of the Quiviesa in the heart of town.

Albergue El Portalón Vega de Liébana, 6km south of Potes ☎942 736 048, ⓦwww.albergue-el-portalon.com. Private hostel, with €15 dorm beds, where activities range from paragliding and mountain biking to climbing and trekking. ❶

Casa Cayo c/Cántabra 6 ☎942 730 150, ⓦwww.casacayo.com. Very friendly and welcoming little hotel in Potes' most atmospheric old street, enjoying lovely river views, with a lively bar and excellent restaurant downstairs. ❷

Casa Gustavo Guesthouse Aliezo, 3km east of Potes ☎942 732 010, ⓦwww.picos-accommodation.co.uk. English-owned farmhouse B&B, which arranges skiing and canoeing. A useful resource for visitors who don't speak Spanish to get help and advice on making the most of the Picos. ❷

Hostería Antigua c/Cántabra 9 ☎942 730 037. Fine and very central old inn, with nice wooden balconies, on a narrow medieval lane. ❸

Picos de Europa San Roque 6 ☎942 730 005, ⓦwww.hotelpicosdeeuropa.net. Large, somewhat anonymous hotel at the east end of town, offering comfortable en-suite rooms and guided tours. ❹

Eating

The best places to **eat** are once again near the rivers.

Bar Chente Plaza Capitan Palacios. Perched above the river, with a relaxing open-air terrace just below the main road, this bustling place serves good-value *menús*.

Café Llorente c/Cántabra 4. The wooden balcony of this busy bar, renowned for its good, cheap *raciones*, hangs high above the Quiviesa.

Casa Cayo c/Cántabra 6. Very nice hotel restaurant with a river-view dining room; prices are reasonable, and portions healthy. Closed Thurs.

Casa Susa c/Cántabra 5. Lively central *tapas* bar with a broad selection of tasty, well-priced *raciones*.

Taberna La Majada c/Independencia. Attractive little bar/restaurant, in an old cottage down by the river, serving snacks and inexpensive set meals.

Turieno to Cosgaya

A lovely little road, the CA185, heads west into the mountains from Potes, running beside the Río Deva below a grand sierra of peaks known as the Macizo Oriental. **TURIENO**, 3km along, is a quiet village where once you're off the main highway, you're as likely to share the road with a donkey as a car. Narrow mule tracks run to nearby hamlets that scarcely see a tourist from one year to the next; the walk to **Lon** and **Brez** is especially worthwhile, through a profusion of wild flowers and butterflies. Turieno has two good rural **hotels**, *Posada Javier* (☎942 732 122; ❸) and *Posada Laura* (☎942 730 854, ⓦwww .posadalaura.com; ❹), both in idyllic settings amongst forested fields, as well as the more functional but equally charming *Pensión Floranes* (☎942 732 104; ❷) at the opposite end of town. An attractive **campsite**, *La Isla* (☎942 730 896, ⓔcampicoseuropa@terra.es; closed Nov–March), is tucked behind an orchard in Turieno, with a swimming pool and **pony-trekking**. If that's full, the *San Pelayo* campsite in Baró (☎942 733 087, ⓦwww.campingsanpelayo .com; closed Nov to Easter), a little farther up the road towards Espinama, is good and has a pool.

Close by Turieno, above the main road from Potes, the eighth-century **Monasterio de Santo Toribio de Liébana** (daily 10am–1pm & 4–7pm; free) was one of the earliest and most influential monasteries in medieval Spain. Although much reconstructed, it preserves fine Romanesque and Gothic details, the largest claimed piece of the True Cross and some extraordinary Mozarabic paintings of the Visions of the Apocalypse (now replaced by reproductions).

The quiet and pretty village of **COSGAYA**, midway between Potes and Espinama, is another attractive potential base. Among several **hotels** in fine old houses on the main road, both the alpine-looking *del Oso* (☎942 733 018, ⓦwww.hoteldeloso.com; ❹), set in neat paddocks beside a tiny stream, and the *Hotel Cosgaya* (☎942 733 230; ❹) have outdoor swimming pools.

Espinama

Twenty kilometres from Potes – far enough to feel that you're finally deep into the heart of the mountains – **ESPINAMA** is a totally delightful little village, spilling down the hillside at the mouth of a slender gorge cut by the little Río Nevandi. Like Cosgaya, it straddles a busy road, but when the traffic dies down after dark it's a magical spot, and in the daytime there are plenty of walks in the nearby woods and meadows for those seeking rural tranquillity (see box, p.528).

Several great-value **accommodation** options in Espinama offer cosy en-suite rooms, mountain views, and good food year-round, including *Puente Deva* (☎942 736 658, ⓦwww.hostalpuentedeva.com; ❶), *Remoña* (☎942 736 605, ⓔhostalremona@eresmas.es; ❷), and the slightly more upmarket *Hostal Nevandi* (☎942 736 608, ⓦwww.apartamentosnevandi.com; ❸), which also has some well-priced self-catering apartments. The best of the restaurants is *Vicente Campo* at the *Puente Deva* (€11 *menú*), with its feel of a wayfarers' inn, and a crackling fire in winter. There's also a grocery store in the village.

Fuente Dé

The road comes to a halt 4km past Espinama, hemmed in on three sides by towering sheer-sided walls of rock. This is the source of the Río Deva; debate as to whether its name should be Fuente de Deva or Fuente de Eva has left it called simply **FUENTE DÉ**. Most visitors to this lonely spot are here to ride the **teleférico**, a cable car that climbs almost vertically up 900m of cliff (daily: summer 10am–8pm; shorter hours in winter; €8 one-way, €12 return; ☎942 736 610). It's an extremely popular excursion throughout the year, and though the cars set off every twenty minutes, you may well have a long wait to ascend, especially in the middle of the day. If that's the case, then you'll probably find yourself queuing again to come down, which in the mountain chill, 1900m above sea level, is not nearly so congenial.

The cable car provides easy access to an extraordinary mountainscape, well worth seeing even if you don't have time to hike any distance from the top.

7

Hiking in the eastern Picos: from Espinama and Fuente Dé

The best starting point for hikes into the mountains from the Picos' eastern side has to be **Espinama**, though if you're at all pressed for time, taking the cable car up from **Fuente Dé** and then hiking back down to Espinama (10km; 3–4hr) makes a quick and relatively pain-free alternative.

A superb trek (12.5km; 5hr) follows a dirt track (also passable in 4WD vehicles) from Espinama to the village of **Sotres**, 8km east of Poncebos. Setting off north from Espinama beneath an arching balcony alongside the *Peña Vieja* bar, the track climbs stiffly, winding past hand-cut hay fields and through groups of barns, until tall cliffs rise on either side to form a natural gateway. Through this you enter a different landscape of rocky summer pasture and small streams. As you near the highest point, 4.5km or perhaps two hours along, the track divides at a small barn; the left-hand path leads up to the *Refugio de Aliva* (see below) and the top of the cable car, but for Sotres you should continue straight ahead, past a chapel (visible from the junction), up to the ridge forming the pass.

Over the divide the scenery changes again, into a mass of crumbling limestone. In spring and winter, the downhill stretch of track here is slippery and treacherous to all but goats. From the foot of the hill, where a seasonal bar sells drinks, you'll have to climb slightly once again to the east to reach Sotres itself, which, when it appears, has a grim, almost fortified feel, clinging to a cliff edge above a stark green valley. Alternatively, a zigzag climb to the west marks the start of the five-kilometre route (around 2hr) to the more appealing village of **Bulnes**, as described on p.533.

Accommodation is available in both Sotres and Bulnes, but you can also stay higher up in the mountains in the hotel-like rooms of the remote *Refugio de Aliva* (☎942 730 999; closed Oct–April; ❷), which has a restaurant and its own fiesta, on July 2. That stands 4km northeast of the top of the Fuente Dé cable car, along the clearly signposted PR 24 trail, which then continues down another 2km to meet the track up from Espinama at the junction described above.

Many day-trippers simply wander around close to the upper station, known as **El Cable**, where they make an incongruous spectacle with their bathing suits and toddlers in tow. The views back down to the valley are amazing, while an enticing track immediately sets off higher into the wilderness – within a few minutes' walk there may not be another soul around. **Hikes** in this forbidding region are detailed in the box above.

Back down below, Fuente Dé itself holds only a tiny handful of buildings, the largest being a **parador** (☎942 736 651, ⓦwww.paradores.es; ❺), where the comfort inside belies the uninspiring exterior, there's a good restaurant, and bargain room rates are frequently available online. Across the road, *Hotel Rebeco* more conventionally resembles a mountain lodge (☎942 736 601, ⓔhotelrebeco@mundivia.es; ❹), and serves cheaper meals. There's also a **campsite**, *El Redondo*, hidden away above the road just before the *Rebeco* (☎942 736 699, ⓦwww.elredondopicosdeeuropa.com; closed Oct–May), and featuring a basic dormitory.

The south: the Leónese Picos

Although the southern flanks of the Picos de Europa lie in the region of **León** (otherwise covered in Chapter 5), visitors naturally experience the national park, and the mountains themselves, as a single unit. Exploring the southern side of the Picos from the north coast requires considerable time and effort, but those who do make the journey, or approach anywhere from the south, are rewarded with some of the mountains' most attractive little towns and villages, which also make a great approach to one of the finest hikes, along the **Cares Gorge**.

Posada de Valdeón

Whether you're literally coming from León, or simply touring the perimeter of the mountains, only one route leads into the heart of the Picos from the south. It starts from the pretty village of **POSADA DE VALDEÓN**, which stands at the junction of two minor roads. If you're approaching **from the east**, you'll get here by way of tiny **Portilla de la Reina**, a hamlet on the N621 that's served by León–Potes buses and lies 10km southeast of the high mountain pass known as the **Puerto de San Glorio**, a total of 38km southeast of Potes. The minor and quite enchanting LE243 runs 20km north from **Portilla de la Reina** to Posada, its last three ravishing kilometres as a narrow single-lane track. Coming **from the west**, LE244 leaves the N625 just south of another pass, the **Puerto del Pontón**, and a total of 45km south of Cangas de Onis; it remains broad and easy for its entire 23-kilometre run to Posada. Finally, it's also possible to reach the village **on foot** from Fuente Dé, in about four hours, over a mix of dirt tracks and footpaths.

The village itself is a lovely spot, surrounded by soaring mountain slopes, and makes an ideal base for any number of hikes – pick up full details, including a current programme of guided walks, from the **national park office**, tucked away up from the road across from the *Cumbrés Valdeón* hotel (Mon–Fri 8am–2.30pm, Sat & Sun 9am–2pm & 4–7pm; ☏987 740 549). **Accommodation** options are dotted all over Posada de Valdeón. The best value is the very friendly,

---

Hiking in the southern Picos: the Cares Gorge

Deservedly the most popular walk in the Picos takes hikers into the heart of the central massif, along the **Cares Gorge** (**Desfiladero de Cares**). Its most enclosed section, between Caín and Poncebos – a massive cleft more than 1000m deep and some 12km long – bores through some awesome terrain along an amazing footpath hacked out of the cliff face. Maintained in excellent condition by the water authorities, it's perfectly safe. Many day-trippers simply get a taste of it by walking as far as they choose to and from Caín, but with reasonable energy, it's perfectly possible to hike its full length – in both directions – in well under a day.

The **gorge** proper begins immediately north of Cain. Just beyond the end of the road, the valley briefly opens out, but then, as you follow the river downstream, it suddenly disappears – a solid mountain wall blocks all but a thin vertical cleft. In its early stages, the trail burrows dramatically through the rock, before emerging onto a broad, well-constructed and well-maintained footpath, which owes its existence to a long-established hydroelectric scheme. During busy periods, the first few kilometres of the trail tend to be thronged with day-trippers thrilling at the dripping tunnels and walkways. Once you get 4km or so from Caín, however, the crowds thin out, and the mountains command your total attention. They rise pale and jagged on either side, with griffon vultures and other birds of prey circling the crags. The river drops steeply, some 150m below you at the first bridge but closer to 300m by the end.

A little over halfway along, the canyon bends to the right and gradually widens along the **descent to Poncebos**. Roughly 7km and 9km into the gorge, enterprising individuals run makeshift, summer-only refreshments stands, handy as there are no springs. For its final 3km, the main route climbs a dry, exposed hillside; an alternative riverside path can be reached by a steep side-trail that zigzags down the precipice.

It is, of course, equally possible to walk all or part of the gorge from the north, starting at Poncebos (see p.532).

▲ The Cares Gorge

clean and homey ⅄ *Pensión Begoña* in the centre, where they serve delicious, inexpensive local food like wild boar stew and ultra-strong cheese (☎987 740 516; ❶), though if you prefer an en-suite room you'll have to opt for *Hostal Campo* next door, run by the same management (☎987 740 502 or *Begoña* number; ❷). At the slightly more upscale *Cumbrés Valdeón*, on the western edge of the village, several rooms have mountain-view balconies (☎987 742 701; closed mid-Dec to mid-Feb; ❸). It's also possible to get a dorm bed at the *Albergue Cuesta-Valdeón* (☎987 742 643, ⓦwww.alberguelacuesta.com; €7), on the northern outskirts, while there's a **campsite**, *El Valdeón* (☎987 742 605), 3km east at the hamlet of Soto de Valdeón.

Cordiñanes and Caín

The **Río Cares** runs through Posada del Valdeón, and its gorge begins just north of the village. Over its first section, as far as Caín, it remains relatively wide, running past brilliant green meadows at the base of the cliffs, and paralleled on its eastern side by a narrow paved road. The village of **CORDIÑANES**, 2km along – and also accessible on foot, via a dirt track on the western side of the river – makes for an especially peaceful night's stop, at either of two small **pensiones**: *El Tombo* (☎987 740 526; ❷) or *El Rojo* (☎987 740 523; ❷).

In summer, **CAÍN** itself, 6km further north, fills with hikers; a supermarket sells basic supplies. **Places to stay**, all with reasonable restaurants, include *La Ruta*, right at the opening of the gorge path (☎987 742 702, ⓦwww .hostallaruta.com; closed Nov–Feb; ❷), which has a pleasant covered terrace; *La Posada del Montañero* (☎985 742 711, ⓦwww.asturjoven.com /posada-montanero.html; ❸), which also has a terrace; and *Casa Cuevas* (☎987 742 720; ❷). Alternatively, you can **camp** in the meadow nearby for the princely sum of €3 (no amenities whatsoever).

The Sella valley

The road running along the western end of the Picos, the N625 between Riaño and Cangas de Onis, is arguably as spectacular as the Cares Gorge. Mountains rear to all sides and for much of the way the road traces the gorge of the

Río Sella. The central section of this, the **Desfiladero de los Beyos**, is said to be the narrowest motorable gorge in Europe – a feat of engineering rivalling anything in the Alps, and remarkable for the 1930s.

Not far south of the road's highest pass, the frequently foggy 1290-metre **Puerto del Pontón**, the exceptionally pretty village of **OSEJA DE SAJAMBRE** stands high on the steep slope of a broad and twisting valley. It currently lacks any facilities, but **SOTO DE SAJAMBRE**, 6km higher to the east, holds a lovely **hostal**, the *Peña Santa* (T 987 740 395; ❷), which also has dormitory beds (€26 in summer; €18 in winter) and a restaurant. An excellent base for walkers, Soto de Sajambre is a possible starting point for a south–north traverse of the western Picos massif to the lakes of Covadonga, as well as for treks in the valley of the Río Dobra. A summer-only *refugio*, *Vegabaño* (T 987 740 082), stands one hour above the village.

The north: the Asturian Picos

The most striking thing about the northern flanks of the Picos de Europa is just how near the mountains are to the sea. There's spectacular scenery to be enjoyed barely a dozen kilometres inland from resorts such as Ribadasella and Llanes. The AS 114 highway runs parallel to the coast through the foothill area known as **Cabrales**, providing easy access to the mountain fastnesses that lie to the south, beyond **Poncebos** and **Covadonga**.

Arenas de Cabrales

The main village of this region, **ARENAS DE CABRALES** (shown on some maps as Las Arenas), seems unremarkable if you simply scoot through, but stop for a while and you'll probably find it a cheerful, friendly little place. The area is famed for its exceptionally strong Cabrales cheese, and gastronomes will want to check out the **Cueva el Cares** (summer daily 10am–2pm & 4–8pm; winter Sat & Sun same hours; €4.50, guided tour in Spanish), a cheese-making museum a short way down the road towards Poncebos that has its own natural cave of fermenting cheese. On the last Sunday in August, Arenas hosts the **Asturian Cheese Festival**, an excuse for plenty of dancing and music but, oddly enough, not all that much cheese.

A helpful **turismo** booth on the main street near the bridge (summer Mon & Sun 9am–2pm & 4–9pm, Tues–Sat 9am–9pm; T 985 846 747, W www.cabrales.org) can fill you in on walking routes or transport schedules. Three daily **buses** run from outside the *turismo* towards Cangas del Onis and Oviedo.

Accommodation

Arenas is well blessed with **accommodation** options, including a number of charming *pensiones* that represent excellent value. Pricier options are all of a high standard, with little to choose between them. There's a **campsite**, *Camping Naranjo de Bulnes*, 1km east (T 985 846 578).

Casaño Barrio Casaño s/n T 985 846 798. Rustic yet well-equipped *hostal*, a short walk from the centre in a quieter setting just across the bridge. ❷

Covadonga El Castañedo T 985 846 566. Welcoming, homely, modern and comfortable rooms with shared bathroom, next door to the *turismo*. ❷

Picos de Europa c/Mayor s/n T 985 846 491, W www.hotelpicosdeeuropa.com. Large, central hotel, painted an unmissable shade of orange, and offering well-equipped en-suite rooms plus a pool and a pleasant mountain-view terraza. ❹

Torrecerredo Vega de Barrio s/n T 985 846 640, W www.picosadventure.com. Friendly hotel, enjoying great mountain views from its perch amid the fields on the hillside a few hundred metres along a narrow little lane from the west end of town. The English owners can arrange a wide range of mountain activities, including all-inclusive walking weeks. ❸

Villa de Cabrales c/Mayor s/n ☎985 846 719. Prices at this elegant hotel, at the west end of town, drop considerably out of season. En-suite rooms (no. 31 is the best), a good bar, and a garden terrace with mountain views. ❹

Restaurants and bars

Arenas is crammed with **restaurants** and speciality food shops. Wandering away from the main road, behind the *turismo*, swiftly brings you to the little square that holds the wonderful ⅄ *Sidrería Calluenga*, open on one side to a little stream, and serving fabulous local food, including clams with wild mushrooms for €12 and cod with potatoes for €9. Back on the highway, *Restaurante Cares* alongside the post office is a charming old bar that serves a decent €15 *menú*, *La Jueya* above the BBVA bank to the east is a good *sidrería*, and just up the hill behind it *Restaurante La Panera* has a terrace garden with nice views.

Poncebos

The dead-end AS264 branches south off AS114 at Arenas, climbing alongside the Cares river into the mountains. Most visitors simply go the first five, easy, kilometres to **PONCEBOS**, a gloomy little spot, too small to be considered even a village, that's home to an antiquated power plant and three unattractive and somewhat institutional **hotels**: *El Garganta del Cares* (☎985 846 463; ❹), *Hostal Poncebos* (☎985 846 447, ✉hostalponcebos@wanadoo.es; ❷) and the large *Mirador de Cabrales* (☎985 846 673, ⓦwww.arceahoteles.com; closed Oct–Feb; ❺). If you have your own transport, you're better off staying in Arenas or further afield, but for hikers Poncebos offers the twin advantages of lying at the northern end of the **Cares Gorge**, which as described on p.529 ranks among the Picos' very best trails, and at the foot of the steep, hour-and-a-half trek up the gorge of the Tejo stream to lovely little **Bulnes**.

Since 2001, Poncebos has also served as the base station for a bizarre **funicular railway** that takes around twelve minutes to burrow 2km upwards through the rock to a point 400m higher, just below Bulnes (daily: Easter & July–Sept 10am–8pm; rest of year 10am–12.30pm & 2–6pm; additional train Mon–Fri 8.30am; one-way €13.50, round-trip €17, cash only). You don't have to be a diehard mountaineer to feel there's something not quite right about an underground railway that tunnels through a beautiful mountain landscape without so much as a glimpse of light. For the casual visitor, however, it provides easy access to the inner recesses of the Picos massif, in a much less forbidding, and more picturesque, spot than the desolation encountered at the top of the Fuente Dé cable car (though that's exciting in its own way; see p.527).

Across from the foot of the funicular, a side path climbs the opposite side of the gorge to the cliffside village of **CAMARMEÑA**, where *La Fuentina* (☎985 846 625; ❷) is a bar with basic rooms and a tremendous view of the Naranjo de Bulnes peak.

Bulnes

BULNES itself is a tiny but delightful stone-built mountain village, nestled in the cleft cut by the Río Tejo between two high peaks. Long the exclusive preserve of hardy hikers, it's still coming to terms with the daily influx of nonchalant sightseers who now arrive on the funicular from Poncebos – when you emerge from the railway tunnel, it lies just a couple of hundred metres up and to the left, along an easy footpath. Many visitors now bring baby-buggies, and romping infants contrast strangely with exhausted trekkers in the two streamside cafés in the heart of the village.

Also alongside the stream, ⚲ *La Casa del Chiflon* (☏985 845 943, ⓦwww.casadelchiflon.com; ③) is a lovely little **B&B**, with a cosy bar and restaurant, that offers simple rooms for two, three or four guests. Another 200m uphill to the west, clearly visible from the village, *El Caleyon* (☏985 845 945, ⓦwww.caleyon.eu; ③) is very similar, and has a large mountain–view terrace.

Sotres

Although **SOTRES**, 9km east of Poncebos along the narrow CA-1, is among the less attractive of the Picos villages, as the trailhead for some superb hikes it's a well-established walkers' base. Both the *Pensión Casa Cipriano* (☏985 945 024, ⓦwww.casacipriano.com; ③) and the *Albergue Peña Castil* (☏985 945 070, ⓦwww.penacastil.com; ②) offer good-value **accommodation** and arrange hiking and 4WD expeditions. However, only *Casa Cipriano* has a restaurant, and in any case the food at the friendly **bar** at the north end of the village is better.

Hiking in the northern Picos: from Poncebos and Sotres

For visitors based on the northern flanks of the Picos, Poncebos and Sotres are the best spots from which to start hiking. As well as being the northern trailhead for the Cares Gorge, **Poncebos** also lies at the foot of the path up to Bulnes. Allow roughly 1hr 30min for that climb, which branches east from the Cares Gorge trail 1km south of Poncebos, across the photogenic medieval bridge of Jaya. While it's not a hard slog, if you have problems with vertigo, you're better off taking the funicular.

Sotres lies at the northern end of the ravishing 12.5-kilometre hike from Espinama (see above), and thus makes a good overnight halt for walkers heading right across the central Picos. A direct trail connects Sotres with Bulnes in just 5km, by way of the broad, windy pass of **Pandébano** (which, with care, can also be reached along primitive roads by car). The high meadows at the top are still used for summer pasture by villagers from Bulnes, some of whom spend the summer there in simple stone dwellings. An old, steep cobbled path leads down to Bulnes itself.

From both Bulnes village and the pass at Pandébano, well-used paths lead up to the **Vega de Urriello**, the high pasture at the base of the **Naranjo de Bulnes** (2519m). An immense slab of orange-hued rock, the Picos' trademark peak stands aloof from the jagged grey sierras around it. The approach from Pandébano is easier, a two- to three-hour hike along a track that passes the small *refugio* of **Terenosa** (☏985 252 362; no food; closed Oct–April). The direct path up from Bulnes is heavy going, and can take up to six hours in bad conditions, with a slippery scree surface that's very difficult, and dangerous when wet. Once up on the plateau, you'll find another *refugio*, the **Vega de Urriello**, at an altitude of 1953m (☏985 925 200), and a permanent spring, as well as large numbers of campers and rock climbers, for whom the Naranjo is a popular target.

Experienced trekkers can stay the night in the *Vega de Urriello refugio* and then continue across the central massif, through a roller-coaster landscape unforgiving of mistakes, to the **Cabaña Veronica** *refugio*, which is for emergency use only, and has just three bunks. An easy descent from there brings you to the top of the **Fuente Dé** cable car. Alternatively, you can continue west through further challenging terrain to another *refugio* at **Collado Jermoso** (☏987 283 232, ⓦwww.colladojermoso.com) before dropping down the ravine of Asotín takes you finally to Cordiñanes at the top of the **Cares Gorge**. The trek from Vega de Urriello should only be undertaken in a group equipped with proper maps and gear.

Covadonga

A separate spur road heads south into the Picos 4km east of Cangas de Onis, or 28km west of Arenas de Cabrales, following the Río Reinazo 5km upstream to reach **COVADONGA**. The **Reconquista of Spain** is said to have started, in 718, when the Visigothic King Pelayo and a small group of followers repulsed the Moorish armies – at odds, according to Christian chronicles, of 31 to 400,000. While the reality was slightly less dramatic, the Moors being little more than a weary and isolated expeditionary force, the symbolism of the event is at the heart of Asturian, and Spanish, national history, and the defeat allowed the Visigoths to regroup, slowly expanding Christian influence over the northern mountains of Spain and Portugal.

Although overwhelmed with tourists in summer, Covadonga remains a serious religious shrine. Daily Mass is celebrated in the **cave**, impressively sited on the side of a mountain above a waterfall and plunge pool, that contains Pelayo's sarcophagus (Mon–Fri 10am–6pm, Sat 9am–6pm; free). The grandiose nineteenth-century pink basilica across the road is more impressive from the outside than in, while the **Museo de Covadonga** nearby displays various religious treasures (daily except Tues 10.30am–2pm & 4–7pm; €3). There's also a small **turismo** (daily except Mon 10am–2pm & 3.30–6.30pm).

Of the half-dozen **accommodation** options in Covadonga, the *Gran Hotel Pelayo* right next to the caves (T 985 846 061, W www.granhotelpelayo.com; ●) is the fanciest, while the *Hospedería del Peregrino* is a cheap and cosy little **fonda** on the road into town (T 985 846 047, W www.picosdeeuropa.net/peregrino; ●), with an excellent restaurant specializing in *fabada asturiana*.

Lago de Enol and Lago de la Ercina

Beyond Covadonga, the road climbs sharply, to reach the placid **mountain lakes** of **Enol** and **La Ercina** after 12km. The **Mirador de la Reina**, a short way before the lakes, gives an inspiring view of the assembled peaks.

From the higher Lago de la Ercina, a good path leads east-southeast within three hours to the **Vega de Ario**, where there's a **refugio** (T 650 900 760; closed Nov–April), camping on the meadow, and unsurpassed **views** across the Cares Gorge to the highest peaks in the central Picos. Unless you have serious hiking experience for the steep descent to the Cares, this is something of a dead end, since to cross the bulk of the western peaks you'll need to backtrack at least to Lago Ercina to resume progress south.

Most walkers, however, trek south from the lakes to the **Vegarredonda** *refugio* (T 985 922 952). This popular route initially follows a dirt track but later becomes an actual path through a curious landscape of stunted oaks and turf. Vegarredonda, about three hours' walk, overlooks the very last patches of green on the Asturias side of the Cornión massif. From here the path continues west for another hour up to the viewing point, the **Mirador de Ordiales**.

Cangas de Onis

The busy market town of **CANGAS DE ONIS** stands at the junction of the main routes between the Picos and central Asturias. The surrounding peaks provide a magnificent if distant backdrop to its big sight – the so-called **Puente Romano** (Roman Bridge), splashed across the front of many Asturian tourist brochures. Although this high-arched bridge, with its cross dangling beneath, has been rebuilt many times, it retains a good deal of charm. The town's other attraction, less photogenic but perhaps more curious, is the little

Capilla de Santa Cruz (Mon–Fri 10am–2pm & 4–7pm, Sat 10am–2pm & 4–7.30pm; free). A fifteenth-century rebuilding of an eighth-century chapel that was founded over a Celtic dolmen, now visible through an opening in the floor, is one of the earliest Christian sites in Spain. To get there from the bridge, take the first left off the main road eastwards, the Avenida de Covadonga, and cross Río Güeña.

As an early residence of the fugitive Asturian-Visigothic kings, Cangas lays claim to the title of "First Capital of Christian Spain". Today, however, it belies such history: a somewhat scruffy, functional town, specializing in activity tourism, though good for a comfortable night, a drink in a nice little bar, and a solid meal after a spell in the mountains. It also abounds in souvenir stores selling local food and drink, such as cheese, cider and multi-coloured *fabadas* (beans).

Cangas' **turismo** is in the heart of town, on Plaza Ayuntamiento, on Avda. de Covadonga east of the bridge (July–Sept daily 10am–10pm; Oct–June Mon–Sat 10am–2pm & 4–7pm; ☎985 848 005, ⓦwww.cangasdeonis.com). Local **buses** stop right in front, while there's a **national park visitor centre** a short way east in Casa Dago, Avda. de Covadonga 43 (☎985 848 614, ⓦreddeparquesnacionales.mma.es). **Adventure tour operators** are dotted throughout town – see p.524.

Accommodation

Cangas being more of a convenient overnight stop than a long-term base, most of its **accommodation** options are unremarkable, but they're often over-subscribed in summer. The nearest **campsite** is 4km east in Soto de Cangas: *Covadonga* (☎985 940 097, ⓦwww.camping-covadonga.com; Easter & June–Sept).

Hotel Covadonga Avda. de Castilla 38 ☎985 848 135, ⓦwww.hotel-covadonga.com. Simple but friendly place, 5min walk south of the centre, offering good-value rooms with river views. ❸

Hotel Nochendi Constantino González 4 ☎985 849 513, ⓦwww.hotelnochendi.com. Very central and much more upscale modern hotel, with its own good restaurant. Closed Jan. ❺

Hotel Puente Romano Puente Romano 8 ☎985 849 339, ⓦwww.hotelimperion.com /puenteromano. Ochre-coloured villa in a great location across the bridge, holding 27 sizeable, comfortable rooms. ❸

Parador de Cangas de Onís Villanueva, Cangas de Onís ☎985 849 402, ⓦwww.parador.es. Spacious and very upscale *parador*, in the sumptuously restored monastery of La Vega, 2km north of town towards Arriondas. ❺

Pensión Labra Avda. de Castilla 1 ☎985 849 047. Closer to the bridge then the *Covadonga*, and a little cheaper, but not all its en-suite rooms have windows. ❷

Eating and drinking

Freshwater fish and *sidra* are the specialities in Cangas' **restaurants**. The *Sidrería/Mesón Puente Romano* on the west side of the bridge has a grand outdoor setting under plane trees, with good-value *menús* from €13; it's a good place to try *fabada*. Otherwise, head for ⚡ *La Sifonería* on c/San Pelayo, just off the southeast corner of the park on the south side of Avda. de Covadonga: a small tiled *sidrería* and tapas bar, kitted out with a great collection of antique soda siphons, and always packed with locals; the same owners run a fully-fledged restaurant, *A La Sombra de un Sifón*, nearby at c/San Pelayo 24. Also great for food and nightlife are the short alleyways immediately east of Plaza Ayuntamiento, where **bars** such as *El Corcho* and *Sidrería El Polesu*, both on c/Angel Tarano, serve delicious cider and snacks, with plenty of outdoor seating in summer. Finally, *La Golosa*, at Avda. de Covadonga 4 near the bridge, is an elegant breakfast option with a good array of pastries.

The Asturian coast: Llanes to Gijón

Once you get into Asturias, the coast becomes wilder and more rugged, as it parallels the **Picos de Europa** just 20km inland. The **FEVE line** hugs the shoreline as far as **Ribadesella**, an attractive little fishing port, before turning inland towards Oviedo. Beyond Ribadesella, towards Gijón, there are fewer appealing towns, though the fishing villages of **Lastres** and **Villaviciosa** are pleasant enough.

Llanes

Asturias's easternmost resort, **LLANES**, is a delightful seaside town, crammed between the foothills of the Picos and a particularly majestic stretch of the coast. To the east and west stretch sheer cliffs, little-known beaches and a series of beautiful coves, yours for the walking. The three town beaches are small but pleasant and very central, while the excellent **Playa Ballota** is only 3km to the east, with its own supply of spring water down on the sand (and a nudist stretch). A long *rambla*, the **Paseo de San Pedro**, runs along the top of the dramatic cliffs above the western town beach, the little **Playa del Sablón**.

In the centre of town, a tidal stream lined with cafés and seafood restaurants runs down into a small harbour. In the **old town** itself, a tangle of lanes twists around a small hill to the west and tall medieval walls shelter a number of impressive buildings in various stages of restoration or decay, which include the **Torre Medieval**, housing the *turismo*; the semi-ruined and overgrown Renaissance palaces of the **Duques de Estrada** and the **Casa del Cercau** (both closed to the public); and the **Basílica de Santa María**, built in the plain Gothic style imported from southern France.

Practicalities

There's a useful **turismo** in the Torre Medieval (mid-June to mid-Sept daily 10am–2pm & 5–9pm; mid-Sept to mid-June Mon–Sat 10am–2pm & 4–6.30pm, Sun 10am–2pm; ☎985 400 164, ⊛www.llanes.com). The FEVE **train** station is a short walk southwest of the centre, while the **bus** terminal is not far southeast of the stream, at the bottom end of c/Pidal.

Although sixty or more **hotels** are located in the vicinity of Llanes, there are surprisingly few options in the old town. The best rooms are in the beautiful, central *Posada del Rey*, c/Mayor 11 (☎985 401 332, ⊛laposadadelrey.iespana .es; ⑤), while the smart *Pensión La Guía* is just south of the old town at Plaza Parres Sobrino 1 (☎985 402 577, ⊛www.pensionlaguia.com; ③); *Sablón's Hotel* is just a short walk away, overlooking the Playa del Sablón (☎985 401 987, ⊛www .hotelsablon.com; ④). There's a large **campsite**, *Las Barcenas* (☎985 402 887; closed Oct–May), 2km east of town, although the slightly smaller *Entre Playas* (☎985 400 888; closed Oct–May except Easter), on the headland between the two town beaches to the east, is better situated.

For good **seafood** – and Asturian *sidra* – head for *La Marina*, a restaurant designed to resemble a boat at the end of the harbour, where you can sit outside and tuck into swordfish steaks and sardines. Alternatively, the simple open-air **café-restaurants** by the river, just inland from the bridge, serve up above-average seafood *raciones* for between €2.70 and €13 a dish; *Mesón del Riveru* is particularly good. Characterful 🍴 *El Bodegón*, spilling out onto benches in the tree-shaded Plaza de Siete Puertas near the harbour, is good for *sidra* and Asturian *raciones*, while for more formal meals and *menús*, try the restaurants on bustling c/Manuel Cué, including *El Pescador* and the neighbouring

Walking in Spain

Spain is one of the most mountainous countries in Europe, and as such is hugely popular with walkers of all levels. The classic long-distance walk is the ancient northern pilgrimage route, the Camino de Santiago; however, there are fantastic day hikes, climbs, circuits and longer trips possible almost everywhere, particularly among the high-altitude peaks of the Sierra Nevada in Andalucía, and in the north in the Pyrenees and the Picos de Europa.

On the GR11 near Setcases, the Pyrenees ▲

El Tajo gorge, Ronda ▼

PR and GR footpaths

The country's major footpaths are called **GR** (*Grande Recorrido*) or **PR** (*Pequeño Recorrido*), some of which make up part of the trans-European walking routes that extend across the entire continent. GR paths are the longest, and are marked by red-and-white stripes, while the smaller PR routes (yellow-and-white) can usually be done in a day. The best-known routes are the **GR11**, which crosses the Pyrenees from coast to coast, taking in Andorra along the way; the **GR65** and its variants, the Camino de Santiago; and the **GR7**, which starts from Tarifa in Andalucía, heads through the Sierra Nevada and up the Catalunya coast before veering up to the Pyrenees. Whatever route you're planning, a reliable **map** (see p.00 for details) and a compass (or GPS system) is essential, as is proper **equipment**.

Five easy walks

▶▶ **Montserrat** Catalunya's revered mountain can be seen on a day-trip from Barcelona, with a cog-wheel railway or cable car to the monastery, then funiculars to get you higher into the hills for easy path-walks. See p.706.

▶▶ **Parque Natural de Monfragüe** Easy-stroll trails for stork-, vulture- and eagle-spotting. See p.210.

▶▶ **Walks around Ronda** Rural wanders around Spain's "White Town" par excellence. See p.265.

▶▶ **La Mina to Acherito lake** A two-hour trail-hike from the top of the Valle de Echo brings you to the westernmost, and one of the more scenic, lakes of the Spanish Pyrenees. See p.647.

▶▶ **Congost de Mont-rebei** Spain is not short of gorges, but this one – at the boundary of Catalunya and Aragón – is among the most impressive and home to many raptors. See p.793.

In the mountains

In Andalucía, the **Sierra Nevada** mountain range and national park (see p.357) offers spectacular walking among the highest peaks in Europe after the Alps. It can be pretty hard going, but there are less challenging hikes available in the foothills, particularly in the lush valleys of **Las Alpujarras** (p.358) – familiar *Driving Over Lemons* territory, for those who have read the books. For the best trekking in central Spain, head for the **Sierra de Gredos** (p.169), just outside Madrid, where there are lots of excellent one- and two-day hikes in the shadow of the highest peak, Almanzor (2592m). To the north, in the Pyrenees, the largest concentration of peaks lies in the eastern half of the range, particularly in Catalunya's highly popular **Parc Nacional d'Aigüestortes i Estany de Sant Maurici** (p.800), where there are walks of all levels, from afternoon rambles to multi-day expeditions. Further challenges abound to the west, where the **Aragonese Pyrenees** (p.632) are home to the two highest peaks in the range, Aneto (3404m) and Posets (3375m). You need to be seriously committed and equipped to climb these, but in Aragón's **Parque Nacional de Ordesa** (p.647) there are both rewarding day-hikes and more intensive climbs. If asked to choose just one corner of Spain, though, many hikers would plump for the rugged **Picos de Europa** (p.521) in Cantabria and Asturias, since considering its relatively compact size – just 40km or so across – the range offers a surprising diversity of walks, from easy day treks to full-blown expeditions.

▲ Almond blossom, Las Alpujarras

▼ Camping in the Pyrenees

▼ Mountain goat, Picos de Europa

Hiker on the Camino de Santiago ▲

Cares Gorge ▼

Classic hikes

▶▶ **Camino de Santiago** Legendary, month-long trek – classified as a UNESCO World Heritage site since 1993 – running from the Pyrenees to Santiago de Compostela in Galicia. There's Romanesque architecture in Navarra, mighty Gothic cathedrals in Burgos and Léon, and some of the country's finest wines as you hike through La Rioja. The final stretch through Galicia is quite strenuous, with many climbs, but is rewarded with beautiful lush-green scenery. For practical details, see p.570; there are also features on the regional sections through Castilla y León (p.430), Navarra (p.496) and Galicia (p.568).

▶▶ **Circos de Laguna Grande and de las Cinco Lagunas** Scintillating one-day walk in the Sierra de Gredos, with lakes and the half-tame Gredos ibex to see. See p.170.

▶▶ **Parc Nacional d'Aigüestortes i Estany de Sant Maurici** The Carros de Foc circuit takes in the most scenic corners of the national park, with a challenging route linking the nine staffed refuges. See p.800.

▶▶ **Circo de Soaso** The best sampling of Aragón's Parque Nacional de Ordesa: upstream along the valley to a superb waterfall at the head of the *circo*, back via a spectacular corniche route called the Faja de Pelay. See p.651.

▶▶ **Cañon de Añisclo** Much less visited and wilder than its neighbour Ordesa, this river gorge is overlooked by wedding-cake palisades. See p.652.

▶▶ **Cares Gorge** The classic Picos de Europa hike, a spectacular twelve-kilometre route along a path hewn out of the cliff face. See p.529.

▶▶ **Baixa Garrotxa** A 28-kilometre loop walk through the spectacular Garrotxa volcanic region of northeastern Catalunya. See p.766.

▶▶ **Ascent of Pedraforca** One of the most revered peaks in Catalunya is an easy one to bag, with a variety of paths and technical routes up. See p.779.

La Covadonga. Viveros los Piratas del Sablón sells fresh seafood above a little cove immediately east of the Playa del Sablón. Old-fashioned *Confiteria Vega* on c/Mercaderes is the place for takeaway goodies.

Villahormes and Nueva

Following the coast (and FEVE line), the next tempting stop to the west of Llanes is **VILLAHORMES**. This is an unprepossessing-looking place: no more than a train station, a handful of houses, a café-bar and a very shabby-looking *hostal*. Follow the rusty signpost to **Playa de la Huelga**, however, and, after 1500m of driveable track, you reach one of the best swimming coves imaginable, with a rock arch in the bay and an enclosed sea pool for kids to splash around in safety. It is flanked by a pleasant bar-restaurant. The **Playa de Gulpiyuri**, 1km to the northeast, is an unusual beach set back from the shoreline but fed by an underground channel of seawater.

A thirty-minute walk west of Villahormes, or five minutes more on the train, will get you to another hamlet, **NUEVA**, tucked into a fold of the hills, and 3km inland from another gorgeous little cove. If you decide to **stay**, head for the *Ereba* at c/Triana 137 (℡985 410 139, ⊛www.orientedeasturias.com /ereba; ❸), a pleasant *casa rural*. There is also a good *pensión*, *San Jorge* (℡985 410 285; closed Nov–Feb; ❹), and a **campsite**, *Palacio de Garaña* (℡985 410 075, ⊛www.campingpalacio.com).

Ribadesella

RIBADESELLA, 18km west of Llanes, is an unaffected old port, split into two by the Sella river, and bridged by a long causeway. The entrancing **old town**, crammed up against the hillside to the east, consists of successive long stone alleyways, running parallel to the **fishing harbour** and bursting with great little bars and *comedores*. Freshly caught fish is still unloaded after midnight at the *lonja* and, although the catch is increasingly small, it's fun to hang out in the bars and watch it being hauled in. In the seafood joints lining the harbour you can sample delicacies such as *centolla* (spider crab) and *lubina* (sea bass), as well as Asturian specialities.

To the west, the excellent town **beach**, Playa Santa Marina, is lined with the impressive nineteenth-century mansions built by returning emigrants who'd prospered in the Americas. The seafront itself is a pleasant pedestrian promenade. Turn away from the sea at the west end of the bridge, along the riverbank, and in 200m you'll reach the **Cueva Tito Bustillo** (mid-March to mid-Sept Wed–Sun 10am–4.30pm; €4, no children under 7; ℡985 861 120). This Altamira-style cave is more impressive for its stalactites than its paintings, though it has a museum of prehistoric finds from the area. Only 350 visitors are allowed into the caves each day, so in summer you'll need to reserve far in advance.

Ribadesella's **turismo** is in the old town, at the east end of the causeway (May, June & mid-Sept to Oct Mon–Sat 10am–2pm & 5–8pm, Sun 11am–2pm; July to mid-Sept daily 10am–10pm; Nov–April closed Mon; ℡985 860 038, ⊛www.ribadesella.es). The **bus station** is just across the street, while the FEVE **train** station is on c/Santander at the top of the hill.

Accommodation

There are good **accommodation** options in both the old town and at the beach – several of the imposing mansions that line the latter now hold upscale hotels.

Albergue Ribadesella c/Ricardo Cangas 1 ⚊985 861 105, ⓦ www.albergueribadesella .com. Not surprisingly, this gorgeous hostel, set in a beachfront mansion facing the *Playa Santa Marina*, is often booked out by groups. Dorms €12.

Covadonga c/Manuel Caso de Villa 9 ⚊985 860 110. Atmospheric old building just inland from the fish market, where not all the rooms are en suite, but some have balconies overlooking the street; the *sidrería* downstairs has a boat-shaped bar. ❷

Gran Hotel del Sella c/Ricardo Cangas 17 ⚊985 860 150, ⓦ www.granhoteldelsella.com. One of the very grandest options beside the beach, set in a massive blue villa. ❺

Pensión Arbidel c/Escura 1 ⚊653 419 349. Inexpensive, cheerful little option, back from the sea at the south end of the old town. ❷

Puente del Pilar c/Puente del Pilar ⚊985 860 446, ⓦ www.desdeasturias.com/puentedelpilar. The best-value hotel on the beach as opposed to the town side of the river, this set is 200m back from the sea, and has a restaurant serving traditional Asturian food. Closed Oct–Easter. ❸

Villa Rosario c/Dionisio Ruisánchez 6 ⚊985 860 090, ⓦ www.hotelvillarosario.com. Located in a particularly impressive mansion, this modernized hotel has a fresher, hipper feel than its neighbours. ❻

Campsite

Camping Ribadesella Sebreño ⚊985 858 293, ⓦ www.camping-ribadesella.com. Ribadesella's best campsite is a few hundred metres from the sea, just south of the main road, beyond the west end of the beach, but has a good pool. Closed Oct–June except Easter.

Eating and drinking

When it comes to **food**, the old town holds almost infinite possibilities. The *Rompeolas*, c/Manuel Fernandez Juncos 9, is a classic old *sidrería*, with good grub and tables in the courtyard at the back, while both the cheerful *Sidrería La Marina* on c/Manuel Caso de la Villa and *Café Gaspar* on Plaza de Iglesia offer outdoor dining.

Lastres and Villaviciosa

Beyond Ribadesella, many tourists head inland, up to Cangas de Onis and the western flanks of the Picos de Europa. The route into the mountains – the N634 and N625 – is superb, following the valley and gorge of the Río Sella (see p.530). There are a few final temptations along the coast before Gijón, however, including the fishing villages of **Lastres** and **Villaviciosa**.

Lastres

LASTRES, 25km west of Ribadesella, off the Santander–Gijón highway below larger **Colunga**, is a tiny fishing village built dramatically on a steep cliffside with a new harbour and a couple of good beaches on its outskirts. It has largely escaped tourist attention so far, and if you've just come from a few strenuous days' trekking in the Picos, it's a good spot to recuperate.

Lastres only has a handful of **hotels**, but *Casa Eutimio*, near the port in Plaza San Antonio (⚊985 850 012, ⓦ www.casaeutimio.com; ❸) and with its own seafood restaurant, is a good bet. Some rooms at the more upscale *Miramar*, nearby at Bajada al Puerto (⚊985 850 120, ⓦ www.hotelmiramarlastres.com; ❹), have great sea views, while the *Palacio de los Vallados*, Pedro Villarta (⚊985 850 444, ⓦ www .palaciodevallados.com; ❹), is another appealing option. The excellent beach, Playa la Griega, 2km to the east, has a **campsite**, *Costa Verde* (⚊985 856 373; closed Oct–May except Easter). Two neighbouring **restaurants** on the road down to the port, *Sidrería El Escanu* and *Bar Bitacora*, serve good seafood, with terrace views.

Villaviciosa and around

VILLAVICIOSA, 30km east of Gijón, is set in beautiful Asturian countryside, on the shores of the Río Villaviciosa, with green rolling hills behind. There's a market on Wednesday and an atmospheric old town where you'll find the thirteenth-century **Iglesia de Santa María**. The town is famed as the "apple capital" of Spain, and visits to the **cider factory**, El Gaitero, 1.5km outside town on the Santander road, reveal how the country's most famous cider is manufactured (May–Sept Mon–Fri 10am–1.30pm & 4–6.30pm, Sat 10am–1.30pm; half-hour guided tours in Spanish, free). Nearby, there's a good **beach** for swimming – Playa Rodiles, visible from the main road.

The inconspicuous local **turismo** is tucked away next to Santa María church on Plaza de Obdulio Fernández (daily 10.30am–2pm & 4–7.30pm; ☏985 891 759, ⓦwww.villaviciosa.es). Two **hotels** on the central Plaza Carlos I, the grand but somewhat faded *Hotel Carlos I* (☏985 890 121; ❸) and the *Hotel Casa España* (☏985 892 030, ⓦwww.hcasaespana.com; ❸), offer smart, comfortable old-fashioned rooms, or you can stay more cheaply at the friendly *Pensión Sol*, nearby at c/Sol 27 (☏985 891 130, ⓔhostalcafedelsol @hotmail.com; ❷).

For **food**, there are several bar-restaurants around Parque Ballina, including the popular *sidrería El Roxu*, while *La Fabrica Chocolate*, at c/del Agua 11, serves a good *menú*.

Nine kilometres southwest of Villaviciosa, tucked away in the beautiful Puelles valley, lies the Cistercian monastery of **Valdedios** (Tues–Sun: May–Oct 11am–1pm & 4.30–6.30pm; Nov–April 11am–1pm; €1 per church). Abandoned for many years, the buildings are now being restored, and a small community of monks returned in 1992. It's worth a look around the grounds and impressive thirteenth-century monastery church, where you can attend one of the five offices sung daily, but the main sight is the wonderful **Iglesia de San Salvador**, built in the ninth century in the unique style known as Asturian, or pre-Romanesque; look out for the columns borrowed from a nearby Roman ruin and the beautiful geometric motifs in the stone windows.

Gijón and Avilés

After the tranquil Llanes coast or the isolation of the Picos, the hinterland of the Asturian steel and mining industries may come as a shock. Although the smoking factory chimneys and scarred hillsides in the general vicinity of **Gijón** and **Avilés** are not pretty, the cities themselves have plenty going for them: Gijón has surprisingly good beaches and legendary nightlife, while Avilés boasts a well-preserved old centre. In addition, both cities know how to party, especially during **Carnaval** and **Semana Santa**, when Avilés hosts some of the country's most spectacular parades.

Gijón

With 275,000 inhabitants, the port city of **GIJÓN** (Xixón) is the largest city in Asturias. Despite its industrial reputation, it remains largely surrounded by open green countryside, and it's a genuinely enjoyable place to visit, with its dynamic old core flanked either side by a huge curving beach and a vibrant pleasure port. Much of the city had to be rebuilt after the intensive bombardment it suffered during the Civil War, when miners armed with sticks of dynamite stormed the barracks of the Nationalist-declared army – the beleaguered colonel asked ships from his own side, anchored offshore, to bomb his men rather than let them be captured.

Arrival and information

Gijón's **turismo** is on a broad jetty in the middle of the marina (daily: mid-June to mid-Sept 9am–10pm; mid-Sept to mid-June 9am–8pm; ⓣ985 341 771, ⓦwww.gijon.info), with a café alongside. There's also a summer-only booth alongside the beach in the Jardines del Náutico. Both sell the **Gijón Card**, which gives free admission to the city's museums, free use of public transport, and many other discounts (€10/12/15 for 1/2/3 days).

FEVE and local RENFE **trains** use the station on Plaza El Humedal, 300m south of the **turismo**, while long-distance RENFE services arrive at a separate station on Avda. de Juan Carlos I, another 300m west. The **bus station** (a wonderful piece of Art Deco) is just south of the FEVE station, between c/Ribadesella and c/Llanes. The express bus from Asturias **airport** – costs €6 (6am–11pm; 35min).

GIJÓN

ACCOMMODATION

Hostal Don Pelayo	E
Hostal Manjón	C
Hotel Asturias	B
Hotel La Casona de Jovellanos	A
Hotel Pathos	D
Parador Molino Viejo	G
Pensión Gonzalez	F

EATING & DRINKING

La Botica Indiana	4
El Café de Moros	8
La Galana	3
La Gasolinera	7
Gavanna Playa	10
Heladería Islandia	5
La Iglesiona	9
El Jamonoar	9
El Lavaderu	2
La Perla del Norte	6
La Pondala	11
El Puerto	1

Accommodation

Gijón offers **accommodation** to suit all budgets, concentrated especially on the streets parallel to the Playa de San Lorenzo, such as c/San Bernardo. The pleasant municipal **campsite** is 1.5km east along the coast at Las Caserias (℡985 365 755; closed Oct–May except Easter).

Hostal Don Pelayo c/San Bernardo 22 ℡985 344 450, Ⓦwww.hostaldonpelayo.com. Very comfortable, central, refurbished *hostal*, with en-suite rooms, and equally well positioned for nightlife and beach. ❹

Hostal Manjón Plaza del Marqués 1 ℡985 352 378. Nicely located and reasonably priced *hostal*; ask for a room overlooking the harbour. ❸

Hotel Asturias Plaza Mayor 11 ℡985 350 600, Ⓦwww.hotelasturiasgijon.com. Friendly but pricey hotel on the attractive main square between the beach and port. ❹

Hotel La Casona de Jovellanos Plaza de Jovellanos 1 ℡985 342 024, Ⓦwww.lacasonade jovellanos.com. This atmospheric old building, in a peaceful setting on the neck of the peninsula, holds a dozen well-equipped en-suite rooms. ❹

Hotel Pathos c/Santa Elena 6 ℡985 176 400, Ⓦwww.celuisma.com. Very central, upscale hotel, where each of the crisp modern rooms is named in honor of a twentieth-century icon such as Che Guevara, and pop art adorns the public spaces. ❺

Parador Molino Viejo Parque de Isabel la Católica ℡985 370 511, Ⓦwww.parador.es. Luxury parador accommodation, set in an attractive park 500m inland from the east end of the beach. ❻

Pensión Gonzalez c/San Bernardo 30, 1° ℡985 355 863. Good *pensión* with large, airy rooms in a well-furnished old mansion house. A convenient location for Playa de San Lorenzo. ❷

The City

Gijón fans back along the coast in both directions from the stark rocky headland known as **Cimadevilla**, with the modern marina of the pretty **Puerto Deportivo** to the west (and the commercial port out of sight beyond that), and the town beach to the east. War damage has left little to see on **Cimadevilla** itself, though high up at the tip of the promontory a grassy park enjoys great views of the Cantabrian Sea, framed by Eduardo Chillida's sculpture *Elogio del Horizonte* (*Eulogy to the Horizon*).

The epicentre of today's city lies at the narrow "neck" of the peninsula, on the south side of Cimadevilla. To the west, the **Plaza del Marqués** holds a statue of Pelayo, the eighth-century king who began the Reconquest, but is dominated by the eighteenth-century **Palacio de Revillagigedo** (July & Aug Tues–Sat 11am–1.30pm & 4–9pm, Sun noon–2.30pm; rest of year Tues–Sat 10.30am–1.30pm & 4–8pm, Sun noon–2.30pm; free). Built in a splendid mix of neo-Baroque and neo-Renaissance styles, it houses a gallery of twentieth-century art and hosts music, theatre and other cultural events. Just behind it, the **Torre del Reloj** stands at c/Recoletas 5 (Jan to mid-June & Oct–Dec Tues–Sat 10am–2pm, Sun 11am–2pm; mid-June & Sept Tues–Sat 10am–2pm & 5–8pm, Sun 11am–2pm; July & Aug Tues–Sat 11am–2pm & 5–9pm, Sun 11am–2pm; free). A modern tower erected on the ruins of a sixteenth-century one, it holds interesting displays on local history, but is mainly worth climbing for the view across the city.

Immediately east from there, in the **Campo Valdés Roman Baths** alongside San Pedro, a subterranean museum displays the original baths from Roman Gigia (March–Sept Tues–Sat 10am–1pm & 5–8pm, Sun 11am–2pm & 5–7pm; Oct–Feb Tues–Sat 10am–1pm & 5–7pm, Sun 11am–2pm & 5–7pm; €2.40, free Sun). Though the attempt to bring the baths to life is impressive, with much audiovisual material (English and Spanish) and a walkway leading across the site, the remains themselves are sadly underwhelming.

The sands of the **Playa de San Lorenzo**, a lengthy golden beach reminiscent of the one at San Sebastián, curve 2km westwards from Campo Valdés. In the summer, the whole city seems to descend here on afternoons and weekends

▲ Palacio de Revillagigedo

– which makes things pretty crowded when the strand dwindles at high tide – while it's the focus of the evening *paseo* year-round, and even on the gloomiest winter day some hardy surfer is usually braving the waves.

At the far end of the beach, the tranquil **Parque Isabel La Católica** stretches back along the east bank of the Río Piles. Across the river, the **Museo del Pueblo de Asturias**, c/La Guelga off Paseo Dr Fleming, incorporates a bagpipe museum, with an amazing array of instruments from all over the Celtic world and beyond (July & Aug Tues–Sat 11am–1.30pm & 5–9pm, Sun 11am–2pm & 5–8pm; rest of year Tues–Sat 10am–1pm & 5–8pm, Sun 11am–2pm & 5–7pm; €2.40, free Sun).

Eating and drinking

The streets around the seafront and immediately behind contain a mass of little **café-restaurants**, all reasonably priced and most with a *menú*. If in doubt, head to any of the *sidrerías* (cider houses) around Plaza Mayor.

La Botica Indiana c/San Bernardo 2. Typical *sidrería* under the arches on the Plaza Mayor.

El Café de Moros c/de los Moros 13. This spacious, old-fashioned, wooden-floored café, with no outdoor seating, is good for breakfast and strong coffee.

La Galana Plaza Mayor 10. This large but very welcoming bar/restaurant on the central square is Gijón's best-known rendezvous for cider and food, from snacks to full meals.

Heladería Islandia c/San Antonio 4. Inventive ice-cream joint offering (among others) *sidra*, *fabada* and *cabrales* cheese flavours.

La Iglesiona c/Begoña 34. Among the larger of the enticing old tapas bars that line "La Ruta", with a fine array of hams hanging from the ceiling and a great line in tortillas, including tortilla de bacalao (cod).

El Jamonoar c/Begoña 38. Atmospheric old bar, serving *raciones* and good fish dishes, with a great-value three-course €8 *menú*.

La Pondala Avda. Dionisio Cifuentes 58, Somío ☎985 361 160. Upmarket restaurant, across the Río Piles in Somío, famous for its seafood and rice. Closed Thurs & Nov.

El Puerto Puerto Deportivo. Posh and pricey, but the seafood menu is interesting, even if your budget doesn't stretch to €60 for a taste of caviar. Closed Sun eve.

Nightlife

At the weekend, a lively **nightlife** scene kicks off around the area known as **La Ruta**, a grid enclosed by c/Santa Lucía, c/Buen Suceso and c/Santa Rosa, a few hundred yards east of Plaza del Carmen. Especially popular are *La Gasolinera*, on c/Santa Rosa, and *La Perla del Norte* next door. People then head to Cimadevilla, whose bars are crammed every day throughout the summer; try *El Lavaderu* on the wide, sidra-soaked Playa Periodista Arturo Arias.

All manner of **bars** line c/Rufo Rendueles and its extensions along the beach, including the stylish *Gavanna Playa*, but the main **club and disco** area is focused around **El Náutico** farther north, and along the streets nearby, especially lively c/Jacobo Olañeta and c/San Agustín.

In early July, the city hosts **Semana Negra**, officially an arts festival, but fast turning into another excuse for the locals to party. The hub of the action is around Gijón's El Molinón football stadium in Parque Isabel La Católica, and while there are a host of poetry recitals, art displays and culture groups dotted around, these days you are just as likely to experience loud music, candyfloss and fairground rides.

Avilés

AVILÉS, 23km west from Gijón, once ranked among the most polluted cities in Europe. It is ringed by line upon line of grim factories, so that even the hardiest of travellers may be put off by the approach, but the city has worked hard to clean up its act and its image, and those who press on to the arcaded centre of the old town will not be disappointed.

Carnaval in Asturias

Carnaval, the Mardi Gras week of drinking, dancing and excess, usually takes place over late February and early March. In Spain, the celebrations are reckoned to be at their wildest in Tenerife, Cadiz and Asturias – and, in particular, **Avilés**.

Events begin in Avilés on the **Saturday before Ash Wednesday**, when virtually the entire city dons fancy dress and takes to the streets. Many costumes are bizarre works of art ranging from toothbrushes to mattresses and packets of sweets. By nightfall, anyone without a costume is likely to be drenched in some form of liquid, as gangs of nuns, Red Indians and pirates roam the streets. Calle Galiana is central to the action, and the local fire brigade traditionally hoses down the street, and any passing revellers, with foam. A parade of floats also makes its way down this street, amid the frenzy.

The festivities, which include live music, fireworks and fancy-dress competitions, last till dawn. It's virtually impossible to find accommodation, but the celebrations continue throughout Asturias during the following week, so after a full night of revelling you can just head on to the next venue. Sunday is, in fact, a rest day before Carnaval continues in **Gijón** on the **Monday** night. Much the same ensues, and fancy dress is again essential; La Ruta is the place to be for the start of the night, with people and events shifting between Plaza Mayor and the harbour area till dawn. On **Tuesday** night, the scene shifts to **Oviedo**: the crowds are smaller here and events are less frantic, but a fair part of the city again dons costume. There's a parade along Calle Uria, a midnight fireworks display in the Plaza Escandelera, and live bands in the Plaza Mayor.

Finally, on the **Friday after Ash Wednesday**, **Mieres**, a mining town just southeast of Oviedo, plays host to Carnaval. Celebrations take place in an area known as Calle del Vicio, which locals claim contains the highest concentration of bars in the entire province.

Arrival and information

Avilés' excellent **turismo** is off Plaza de España, at c/Ruíz Gómez 21 (July to mid-Sept daily 10am–8pm; mid-Sept to June Mon–Fri 9am–2pm & 4.30–6.30pm, Sat & Sun 10am–2pm; ☏985 544 325, ⊛www.ayto-aviles.es). The local **FEVE**, **RENFE** and **bus stations** are all sited in the same terminus on Avenida Telares just down from Parque Muelle and the old town. Asturias **airport**, 14km west of Avilés and served by easyJet flights from London and Madrid, has all the usual car-rental outlets, and is connected to the city by express **buses** (6.30am–10.30pm; €1.20; 25min).

Accommodation

Accommodation in Avilés is surprisingly scarce, and the reasonably priced *hostales* fill quickly. A good place to start looking is c/Fruta, off Plaza España.

Hotel Don Pedro c/Fruta 22 ☏985 512 288, ⊛www.hdonpedro.com. Well-equipped rooms with beautiful stone walls. Its own little *pensión*, *La Fruta*, opposite, has a choice of rooms with or without bath. *Pensión* ❷, hotel ❹

Hotel Luzana c/Fruta 9 ☏985 565 840, ⊛www.hotel-luzana.com. This rather anonymous hotel has less character than the *Don Pedro*, but the rooms are fine, and its restaurant is good. ❹

Palacio de Marqués de Ferrera Plaza de España ☏985 129 080, ⊛www.nh-hotels.com. The most luxurious pad in town, offering weekend discounts. ❺

Pensión Puente Azud c/Acero 5 ☏985 550 177, ⊛www.hostalpuenteazud.com. Simple but good-value *pensión*, some way east of the centre, near the bridge. ❷

The City

Strewn with fourteenth- and fifteenth-century churches and palaces, Avilés' **old town** is extremely pleasant, and is home to most of the city's shops, bars and places to stay, as well as the pretty, walled **Parque de Ferrera**. Churches worth a closer look include the Romanesque **San Nicolás de Bari**, on c/San Francisco, and the thirteenth-century **Santo Tomás**. **La Iglesia de los Padres Franciscanos** contains the tomb of Don Pedro Menéndez de Avilés, the first governor of Spanish Florida, who founded the first European city in what is now the United States, St Augustine, in 1565. There are also some superb palaces, especially the Baroque **Camposagrado**, in Plaza Camposagrado, built in 1663, and the seventeenth-century **Palacio de Marqués de Ferrera** in Plaza de España, now an expensive hotel. Around the corner on c/San Francisco is the city's most distinctive monument, the seventeenth-century **Fuente de los Caños**, with its six grotesque heads spouting water.

Eating, drinking and nightlife

The area on and around plazas de España, Domingo Acebal and Carbayedo is full of promising **bars and restaurants**, especially along c/del Ferrería and c/Rivero. Both *Casa Tataguyo* at Plaza Carbayedo 6, a beautiful 1840s *mesón* (the oldest in town; closed mid-April to mid-May), and *La Fragata*, prettily sited near the church on Plaza Domingo Acebal, serve Asturian specialities and are moderately priced.

Assorted **bars** along c/de la Estación, diagonally across from the RENFE station, offer excellent lunchtime *menús* and *raciones*, especially *Tasca El Matú* at no. 17, with its secluded rear patio. Despite its unpromising setting near the train station, *Casa Lin*, Avda. Telares 3, is a fine *sidrería* with excellent seafood.

Oviedo

OVIEDO's bourgeois culture is a contrast to the working-class ethos of its neighbours. As the Asturian capital, it has long been fairly wealthy, a history that can be traced through its plethora of grand administrative and religious buildings, lovingly restored and rendering the city among the most attractive in the north. The old quarter, all the better for being completely pedestrianized, is a knot of squares and narrow streets built in warm yellow stone, while the newer part is redeemed by a huge public park right in its centre. Throughout the city are excellent bars and restaurants, many aimed at the lively student population.

Oviedo also boasts three small **churches** that rank among the most remarkable in Spain, built in a style unique to Asturias. All date from the first half of the ninth century, a period of almost total isolation for the Asturian kingdom, which was then just 65km by 50km in area and the only part of Spain under Christian rule. Oviedo became the centre of this outpost in 810, when it became the base for King Alfonso II, son of the victorious Pelayo.

Arrival and information

Oviedo's **turismo** is at Plaza de la Constitución 4 (daily: June 10am–7pm; July–Sept 9.30am–7.30pm; Oct–May 10am–2pm & 4.30–7pm; ☎ 985 086 060, ⊕ turismo.ayto-oviedo.es), while there's also a booth at Marqués de Santa Cruz 1 (daily: July–Sept 9.30am–2pm & 4–7.30pm; Oct–June 10am–2pm & 4.30–7pm; ☎ 985 227 586), and an office covering the whole of Asturias at c/Cimadevilla 4 (Mon–Fri 9am–2pm & 4.30–6.30pm, Sat & Sun 10am–2pm & 4.30–7.30pm; ☎ 985 213 385).

Both the RENFE and FEVE **train stations** are in the same building on Avenida de Santander, northeast of the city centre, while the **bus terminal** (☎ 985 222 422, ⊕ www.estaciondeautobusesdeoviedo.com) is just down the road to the northeast. Asturias **airport** is 50km northwest of the city; express buses to and from the airport cost €6 (7am–midnight; 40min).

Accommodation

Oviedo has a good supply of **accommodation**, with cheaper *hostales* concentrated along on c/Uría, opposite the train station, and along c/Nueve de Mayo and its continuation, c/de Caveda.

Gran Hotel España c/Jovellanos 2 ☎ 985 220 596, ⊕ www.granhotelespana.com. Grand hotel, more than a century old (though heavily restored), close by the cathedral. Reduced weekend rates. ❺

Hostal Arcos c/Magdalena 3, 2° ☎ 985 214 773, ⊕ www.hostal-arcos.com. Clean and welcoming, and in an unbeatable location in the heart of old Oviedo, just off Plaza Mayor. Rooms have sinks and TV. ❷

Hotel Cristal Naranco c/Carta Puebla 6 ☎ 985 220 012. Well-appointed, very modern little hotel with surprisingly large rooms, tucked down an alleyway at the south end of the old town. ❸

Hotel El Magistral c/Jovellanos 3 ☎ 985 204 242, ⊕ www.elmagistral.com. Comfortable, ultra-modern hotel near the cathedral. ❺

Hotel de la Reconquista Gil de Jaz 16 ☎ 985 241 100, ⊕ www.hoteldelareconquista.com. Luxurious and seriously decadent accommodation with a price tag to match, in a magnificent seventeenth-century palace near Parque de San Francisco. ❼

Hotel Santa Cruz c/Marqués de Santa Cruz 6 ☎ 985 223 711, ⊕ www.santacruzoviedo.com. Friendly place in a great location, with en-suite rooms overlooking Parque de San Francisco. ❸

Hotel Vetusta c/Covadonga 2 ☎ 985 222 229, ⊕ www.hotelvetusta.com. Stylish modern hotel on the edge of the old town, near the cider lanes, where half the rooms have mini-saunas. ❺

Pensión Riesgo c/Nueve de Mayo 16 ☎ 985 218 945. Small, good-value, family-run *pensión*, not too far from the bus station, with plain but spotless rooms. ❷

546

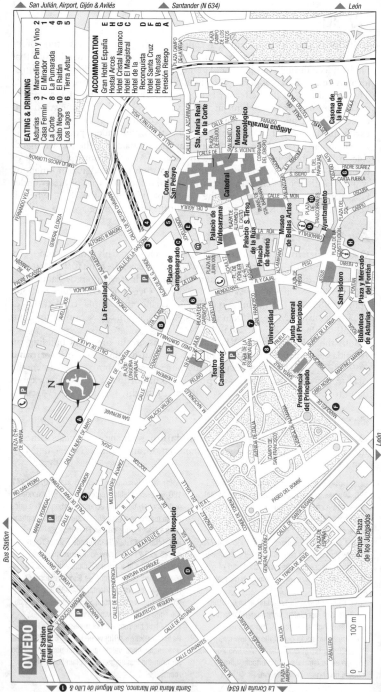

OVIEDO

Train Station
(RENFE/FEVE)

EATING & DRINKING

Asturias	3
Casa Fermín	7
La Corte	8
Gato Negro	10
Los Lagos	6
Marcelino Pan y Vino	2
El Mirador	1
La Pumarada	4
El Raitán	9
Tierra Astur	5

ACCOMMODATION

Gran Hotel España	E
Hostal Arcos	H
Hotel Cristal Naranco	G
Hotel El Magistral	C
Hotel de la Reconquista	D
Hotel Santa Cruz	F
Hotel Vetusta	B
Pensión Riesgo	A

Antigua muralla

Sta. María Real
de la Corte

Museo
Arqueológico

Conv. de
San Pelayo

Catedral

Casona de
la Regla

Palacio de
Valdecarzana

Palacio S. Tirso

Museo
de Bellas Artes

Palacio
de Toreno

San Isidoro

Plaza y Mercado
del Fontán

Palacio de
Camposagrado

La Foncalada

Ayuntamiento

Universidad

Junta General
del Principado

Biblioteca
de Asturias

Teatro
Campoamor

Presidencia
del Principado

Antiguo Hospicio

Parque Plaza
de los Juzgados

N

100 m

The Town

Around the cathedral, enclosed by scattered sections of the medieval town walls, a compact, attractive quarter preserves the remains of **Old Oviedo**. As at Gijón, much was destroyed in the Civil War when Republican Asturian miners laid siege to the Nationalist garrison; the defenders were relieved by a Gallego detachment when on the brink of surrender. The centre, nevertheless, preserves a plethora of medieval churches and squares, and some fine government buildings and townhouses financed by the industrial wealth of the area.

The cathedral and around

In the ninth century, King Alfonso II built a chapel, the **Cámara Santa** (Holy Chamber), to house the holy relics rescued from Toledo when it fell to the Moors. Remodelled in the twelfth century, it now forms the inner sanctuary of Oviedo's unusually uncluttered Gothic **Catedral** (Mon–Fri: March to mid-May & Oct 10am–1pm & 4–7pm; mid-May to June 10am–1pm & 4–8pm; July–Sept 10am–8pm; Nov–Feb 10am–1pm & 4–6pm; €3 for Cámara Santa & diocesan museum). With its primitive capitals, the innermost of the Cámara Santa's pair of interconnecting chapels is thought to be Alfonso's original building. The antechapel is a quiet little triumph of Spanish Romanesque; each of the six columns supporting the vault is sculpted with a pair of superbly humanized Apostles. Built around the attractive Gothic cloister, itself built on pre-Romanesque foundations, the **diocesan museum** holds a high-quality collection of devotional art and artefacts.

Assorted buildings nearby, including the eighteenth-century Palacio de Velarde on c/Santa Ana, house the **Museo de Bellas Artes** (July & Aug Tues–Sat 10.30am–2pm & 4.30–8pm, Sun 10.30am–2.30pm; Sept–June Tues–Fri 10.30am–2pm & 4.30–8.30pm, Sat 11.30am–2pm & 5–8pm, Sun 11.30am–2.30pm; free). The highlights of the bold collection of contemporary Spanish art are on the top floor: Picasso's *Mosquetero con Espada y Amorcillo* is a gleeful take on historical portraiture, while Dalí's lyrical *Metamorfosis de Angeles* has an unusually muted palette of browns and blues. The c/Santa Ana entrance brings you directly to another gem of the collection: El Greco's sombre portraits of the twelve Apostles (1585–90), which favour psychological depth over symbolism.

Currently closed for refurbishment, the **Museo Arqueológico**, behind the cathedral in the former convent of San Vicente, preserves sculpture from several "Asturian-Visigoth" churches. The nearest of these, **San Julian de los Prados**, or **Santullano** (May–Sept Tues–Fri 10am–12.30pm & 4–5.30pm, Sat 9.30–noon & 3.30–5pm; Oct–April Mon 10am–12.30pm, Tues–Sat 9.30–11.30am; €1.20 guided tour in Spanish), is ten-minutes' walk northeast along c/Gijón, right next to a highway. Built around 830, it is large and spacious, with an unusual "secret chamber" built into the outer wall. The original frescoes inside, still remarkably colourful, are executed in similar style to those of Roman villas – along with architectural motifs, you'll see two Latin crosses hung with the letters alpha and omega.

Santa María del Naranco and around

The greatest Asturian church, indeed the architectural gem of the principality, is **Santa María del Naranco** (April–Sept Mon & Sun 9.30am–1pm, Tues–Sat 9.30am–1.30pm & 3.30–7.30pm; Oct–March Mon 10am–12.30pm, Tues–Sat 10am–12.30pm & 3–4pm, Sun 10am–1pm; €3 guided tour in Spanish), majestically located on a wooded slope 3km above the city. It's 45-minutes' walk from the station through the quiet suburb of Ciudad Naranco, slowly climbing the slopes of the eponymously named Monte.

Asturian food and drink

Asturian food is not for the faint-hearted, and it's certainly not for vegetarians. The signature dish is **fabada**, a dense haricot-bean stew floating with pungent meats: black pudding, chorizo, ham and pork. It's served in a round terracotta dish, and you mop up the juice with the ubiquitous hunk of solid bread. **Seafood** is another feature, from sea urchins – particularly popular in Gijón – to sea bream and squid. The region produces a huge variety of **handmade cheeses**, most notably the veined and slightly spicy *cabrales*, which, in its purest form, is made with cow-, sheep- and goat-milk combined. Another variety is a small cone-shaped cheese, known as *afuega'l pitu*. It sometimes has a wrinkled exterior owing to its having been hung in cloth.

One sight you won't miss is waiters and punters pouring **sidra** (cider) – which you can only order by the bottle – from above their heads into wide-rimmed glasses, the idea being that you knock back the frothing brew in one go. Since it's a point of honour for the waiters to stare straight ahead rather than look at the glasses, and any residue that you don't drink within a minute or two is summarily discarded on the floor, it's hardly surprising the region seems to reek of stale cider.

The initial glimpses of the warm stone and simple bold outline, in perfect harmony with its surroundings, led Jan Morris to describe it as "formidable beyond its scale", but while it retains the ability to impress, the effect is somewhat lessened by the huge tour groups that descend upon it in summer. Originally designed as a palatial hunting lodge for Ramiro I (842–52), Alfonso's successor, it was converted into a church at the end of the ninth century. Architecturally, the open porticoes at both ends predate later innovations in Byzantine churches, while thirty or so distinctive decorative medallions skirt the roof.

A couple of hundred metres beyond Santa María is King Ramiro's palace chapel, **San Miguel de Lillo** (same hours and ticket as Santa María), built with soft golden sandstone and red tiles. Though generally assumed to be by the same architect as Santa María – Tiodo – its design is quite different. In fact, less than half of the original ninth-century church remains, the rest having been swept away by a landslide and clumsily rebuilt in the thirteenth century. The altar sits in Santa María del Naranco, and much of the interior sculpture has been removed to the Museo Arqueológico, but look for the window grilles carved from single slabs of limestone, and the superb Byzantine-style carved door frames depicting, incongruously enough, the investiture of a Roman consul, complete with circus-style festivities.

Farther up from the two little churches, a Rio-style **figure of Christ** looks out over the city, and is spectacularly illuminated at night. It was built by Republican prisoners of war, and, although ugly close up (it's constructed from concrete blocks), it affords wonderful views of the city below.

Eating, drinking and nightlife

Oviedo's most renowned area for **eating and drinking** lies immediately north of the cathedral, just outside the pedestrian district, where lively **c/Gascona** is festooned with a large neon sign proclaiming it "El Bulevard de la Sidra". Among its many spit-and-sawdust *sidrerías*, or **cider bars**, *Asturias* and *La Pumarada* are especially recommended. If you prefer a less raucous atmosphere, head instead for the graceful arcaded **Plaza de Fontán** near the old market, ringed by Asturian restaurants and excellent speciality food shops. Further cafés and bars are dotted throughout the old town, many with good-value *menús*, as well as pricier traditional *mesónes*.

Casa Fermín c/San Francisco 8 ☎ 985 216 497.
A classic, much-written-about restaurant, serving
imaginatively re-created Asturian dishes. You'll get
little for under €20, but it's worth it for a special
occasion. The *menú degustación* is €45. Closed Sun.

La Corte c/Fruela 21. This chic café-bar metamorphoses into a stylish restaurant at night. Try the
tasty *salmon a la naranja*.

Gato Negro Mon 5. Very popular, central *sidrería*
that serves a highly appetizing array of imaginative
raciones.

Los Lagos Plaza del Carbayón 4. Another branch
at c/Cervantes 7. Excellent *sidrería* filled with the
heady smell of strong Asturian foods, cider and
sawdust. Closed Sun.

Marcelino Pan y Vino c/Campoamor 17. Bustling,
basic sawdust-floored *sidrería*, jam-packed with

locals taking advantage of the generous portions.
Closed Sun.

El Mirador On the road to Naranco. One of
several decent restaurants with terraces that look
out over the whole city and the mountains
beyond.

El Raitán Plaza Trascorrales 6 ☎ 985 214 218.
Superb, atmospheric restaurant in a delightful
square off Plaza Mayor. There is a selection of
menús, ranging from €16 to the huge *menú
degustación de cocina Asturiana* for €32.
Closed Tues.

Tierra Astur c/Gascona 1. At the top of "El
Bulevard de la Sidra", this bustling place has a
wide wooden terrace and dishes up enormous
platters of local cheeses and meats, as well, of
course, as large quantities of cider.

West to Galicia

The coast west of Avilés, as far as the Río Navia, is rugged, with scarcely more
than a handful of resorts carved out from the cliffs. The most appealing are the
old port and resort of **Luarca**, and pretty little **Cudillero**. West again from the
Río Navia, the coast becomes marshy and, save for an honorable mention of
the attractive fishing village of **Tapia de Casariego**, unexceptional. Again, the
FEVE line trails the coast, with some spectacular sections, though a number of
the stations (including Cudillero and Luarca) are inconveniently sited some way
out of town.

Inland from Oviedo, the N634 and C630 offer a winding approach over the
hills to Lugo in Galicia. The old town of **Salas**, with its castle, is of passing
interest, but the main appeal of the route is the mountainous wildness, which
hardly sees a tourist from one year to the next.

Cudillero

CUDILLERO is a delightful, picturesque little fishing port, 25km west of
Avilés. The brightly coloured arcaded houses that rise, one above the other,
up the steep horseshoe of cliffs that surround the port give it the feel, and
appeal, of a Greek island, and it's usually thronged with visitors in summer.
There's no beach here, however – the nearest is **Playa Aguilar**, 3km east – so
the most obvious attractions are the **fish tavernas** in its cobbled, seaside
plaza.

Practicalities

The most direct route down into Cudillero is a precipitous and very narrow
road that twists its way down the cliffs from the **FEVE station**, a stiff 25–
minute walk or a hair-raising drive. **Motorists** would do better to follow the
longer road that leaves the N632 a couple of kilometres further west, and
approaches the village along the coast, passing the only sizeable car park. In
summer, there's a **turismo** in a modern building just before the harbour (daily
10am–9pm; ☎ 985 591 377, ⓦ www.cudillero.org).

Cudillero makes a lovely overnight stop, and is perfectly placed for passengers
using Asturias airport, 12km east. The nicest **hotel** in the village is the gorgeous

old 🎄 *La Casona de Pio*, by the harbour at c/Riofrio 3 (☎985 591 512, ⓦwww
.arrakis.es/~casonadepio; closed Jan; ④), with en-suite rooms, room service and
a great restaurant. Rates at the cosy seven-room *Pensión El Camarote*, further up
hill at c/García de la Concha 4 (☎985 591 202, ⓦwww.elcamarote.es; ③),
include breakfast, while the neighbouring *Pensión Alver*, c/García de la Concha
8 (☎985 590 005, ⓦwww.pensionalver.com; ②), is a pleasant and somewhat
cheaper alternative; both also offer large family rooms. The best of the local
campsites is *Camping Cudillero*, above Playa Aguilar (☎985 590 663, ⓦwww
.campingcudillero.com; closed Oct to mid-May except Easter).

Comparing menus at the many **restaurants** that squeeze into Cudillero's
focal square is a real joy; the *Isabel*, right by the water, is consistently excellent,
while the adjoining *La Paloma* serves delicious *raciones*.

Luarca

Beyond Cudillero, the N632 leaps over viaducts spanning deep, pine-wooded
gorges. About 50km west, the attractive port of **LUARCA** is accessed from the
N632 by a road that dips down steeply to the coast. A mellow place, it's built around
an S-shaped cove surrounded by sheer cliffs. Down below, the town is bisected by
a small, winding river, and knitted together by numerous narrow bridges.

Luarca is a seaside resort in a modest, faded sort of way, which has defiantly
retained its traditional character, including a few **chigres** – old-fashioned
Asturian taverns – where you can be initiated into the art of *sidra* drinking. The
fishing-harbour area is the heartbeat of the town: cross the bridge from the
plaza, and follow the river. You can watch the small fishing boats returning at
around midnight and see the catch auctioned off at the *lonja* at around 3pm the
following afternoon. The town **beach** is divided in two: the closer strip is
narrower but more protected; the broader one beyond the jetty is subject to
seaweed litter. From the *turismo*, c/de la Carril leads up to the cliffs overlooking
the port where you will find a decorative **cemetery** considered by many the
most distinctive in Asturias, a hermitage chapel and a lighthouse. Nearby, the
excellent **Aula del Mar** (summer daily 11am–1pm & 4–9pm; winter same
hours weekends only; €3), a marine zoology museum, contains the largest
collection of giant squid in Europe.

Practicalities

Luarca's **turismo** is at c/Caleros 11 (July–Sept Mon–Sat 10.30am–2pm &
4.30–8pm, Sun 11am–2pm & 5–7pm; Oct–June Tues–Fri 10.30am–2pm &
4.30–6.30pm, Sat 10.30am–2pm & 5–7pm, Sun noon–2pm; ☎985 640 083),
and there's also a summer kiosk on Plaza Alfonso X (daily 11am–3pm &
4–8pm). The **bus** station is just off c/del Crucero on the river, while the **FEVE
station** is 2km east.

The best central **hotel**, beside the river, is the *Gayoso*, Paseo Gómez 4 (☎985
640 050; ④); the *Villa La Argentina*, housed in a sumptuous belle époque
mansion, is a short walk east in the Villar district (☎985 640 102, ⓦwww
.villalaargentina.com; ④). Cheaper options in town include the modern, good-
value *Hotel Rico*, Plaza Alfonso 6 (☎985 470 559; ③), and the *Hotel Baltico*
(☎985 640 991; ③), which has nice views over the harbour and a good restaurant. There's also a year-round **campsite**, facing the lighthouse across a rocky
cove – *Los Cantiles*, which has facilities to match its superb setting (☎985 640
938, ⓦwww.campingloscantiles.com).

Villablanca, at Avda. de Galicia 27, is a great gourmet **restaurant** in the heart
of town, while another excellent place, *Casa Consuelo*, 5km west in Otur on the

main road, attracts diners from far around; try the *merluza con anguilas* (hake with eels). The port area holds several fine seafood places, endowed with the pick of the day's catch: *El Barometro* and *Casa del Mar* are both good, while portions at *Mesón El Ancre* are always large.

Tapia de Casariego

The best beach along the stretch of coast from Luarca to Ribadeo is almost the last in Asturias, the **Playa de Los Campos**, which flanks the fishing village of **TAPIA DE CASARIEGO**. This is a lively place, with an entertaining "alternative" Teatro Popular, and a very helpful **turismo** in a small kiosk in the plaza (mid-June to mid-Sept Mon–Sat 10.30am–2pm & 5–8.30pm; ☎985 472 968, ⓦwww.tapiadecasariego.com). It holds several reasonably priced **hotels**, including *La Ruta*, Avda. Primo de Rivera 38 (☎985 628 138; ❸), and *Puente de los Santos*, opposite at no. 45 (☎985 628 155, ⓦwww.hotelpuentedelossantos .com; ❸). Just outside town are two **campsites**, about 1km towards Ribadeo: *Playa de Tapia* (☎985 472 721; closed mid-Sept to May) and *El Carbayín* (☎&ⓕ985 623 709). Downhill from the main plaza, the port area is the place to **eat and drink**, though many bars only open evenings and at weekends. *Palermo*, on c/Bonifacio Amago 13, is an upmarket choice specializing in regional Asturian cuisine. For dessert, try the *helado de queso*.

Salas

Standing in the shadow of forested mountainsides, the winding, decorative stone streets of **SALAS**, 35km west of Oviedo, represent the last worthwhile stopover in Asturias. The town was once the home of the Marqués de Valdés-Salas, founder of Oviedo University and one of the prime movers of the Inquisition, and is chock-full of period buildings bearing the coats of arms of local noble families. The town **castle** is actually the Marqués's old palace; you can climb an adjoining tower from the *turismo* for fine views of the town and surrounding countryside. Among the other monuments are a sixteenth-century **Colegiata** and, in the main square, the tenth-century church of **San Martín**.

Salas' **turismo** is on Plaza de la Campa (mid-June to mid-Sept daily 11am–2pm & 4–8pm; mid-March to mid-June and mid-Sept to Oct Tues & Thurs–Sat 10am–2pm & 4–6.30pm, Wed & Sun 10am–2pm; Nov to mid-March Thurs & Sat 11am–2pm & 4–6pm, Sun 11am–2pm; ☎985 830 988, ⓦwww.ayto-salas .es). The town holds a couple of good **places to stay**: the elegant 🏃 *Hotel Castillo de Valdés Salas* (☎985 830 173, ⓦwww.castillovaldesalas; ❹), arranged around a lovely central courtyard in the castle, and featuring an out-of-the-ordinary restaurant; and the cheaper *Casa Soto*, c/Arzobispo Valdés 9 (☎985 830 037; ❷), which has big, clean rooms.

Travel details

Trains

RENFE

For current timetables and ticket information, consult RENFE ☎902 240 202, ⓦwww.renfe.es or FEVE ☎987 271 210, ⓦwww.feve.es.

Oviedo to: Barcelona (2 daily; 12hr–13hr 15min); León (7 daily; 2hr–2hr 30min); Madrid (3 daily; 5hr 50min–8hr 35min).

Santander to: Madrid (3 daily; 6hr 10min–8hr 35min), change at Palencia for east–west routes including León.

FEVE

This delightful independent service (🌐 www.feve
.es) runs along the north coast between Bilbao,
Santander, Oviedo and Ferrol. The narrow-gauge
railway is punctual and for the most part scenic,
but painfully slow for longer trips; the full journey
from Ferrol to Bilbao can't be done in one day. It's
best to think of the service divided between
through trains, which cover the longer distances
between the big cities, and local trains, which run
more frequently between the smaller towns. There
are also a few *cercanías*, or local branch lines,
most of which are centred around Gijón.

Through trains: Bilbao to Santander (3 daily; 3hr);
Santander to Oviedo (2 daily; 4hr 45min); Oviedo to
Ferrol (2 daily; 6hr 30min).

Local trains: Orejo to Santander (20 daily; 25min);
Santander to Puente de San Miguel (every 30min;
25min); Puente de San Miguel to Cabezon de la Sal
(hourly; 20min); Cabezon to Llanes (2 daily;
1hr 10min); Llanes to Ribadesella-Infiesto (7 daily
in summer, 4 daily in winter; 35min); Ribadesella to
Nava (7 daily; 1hr 8min); Nava to Oviedo (24 daily;
45min); Oviedo to Pravia (21 daily; 1hr); Pravia to
Cudillero (18 daily; 20–30min); Cudillero to Navia
(3 daily; 1hr 20min); Navia to Ribadeo (2 daily;
50min); Ribadeo to Ferrol (4 daily; 3hr).

Branch lines: Gijón to Avilés (30 daily; 40min);
Gijón to Pravia (for main line to Ferrol; 15 daily;
30min).

Buses

Most buses along the coast, and all those covering
longer distances, are run by Alsa (🌐 www.alsa.es).
Smaller companies connect coastal resorts with
inland destinations, with more frequent services in
July and Aug.

Castro Urdiales to: Bilbao (10 daily; 1hr);
Santander (13–18 daily; 1hr–1hr 50min); Vitoria
(3 daily; 1hr 15min–1hr 50min).

Comillas to: San Vicente (3 daily; 30min); Santander
(7 daily; 45min); Santillana (4 daily; 35min).

Gijón to: Bilbao via Oviedo (3 daily; 4–5hr); León via
Oviedo (10–11 daily; 2hr 30min); Madrid via Oviedo
(11–13 daily; 5hr 30min–6hr); Oviedo (every 15min;
1hr); Ribadeo via Luarca, Navia, Castropol and
Vegadeo (4 daily; 3hr–3hr 30min); Salamanca
(5 daily; 4hr 30min–5hr); Seville (3 daily; 12hr–12hr
45min); Villaviciosa (14–15 daily; 45min).

Llanes to: Oviedo via Ribadesella (7–9 daily;
1hr 30min–2hr 30min); San Vicente (6 daily;
30min); Santander (7 daily; 1hr 30min–2hr);
Unquera (4 daily; 20min).

Oviedo (full schedules on 🌐 www.estaciondeauto
busesdeoviedo.com) to: Avilés (every 30min; 1hr);
Cangas de Onis (10–14 daily; 1hr–1hr 30min);
A Coruña via Betanzos (3 daily; 3hr 45min–5hr
45min); Covadonga (5 daily; 1hr 20min–1hr
45min); Cudillero (1–2 daily; 1hr 10min); Gijón
(hourly; 1hr); León (10 daily; 1hr 30min–2hr); Lugo
(3 daily; 4hr 15min–5hr); Madrid (12 daily; 5hr
30min); Pontevedra (2 daily; 7hr 30min); Ribadeo
via Luarca (5 daily; 3hr); Ribadesella (7–10 daily;
1hr 20min–2hr); Santander (2–5 daily; 2hr 15min–
3hr 15min); Santiago (3 daily; 4hr 30min–6hr
45min); Valladolid (5 daily; 3hr 15min–4hr); Vigo
(2 daily; 6hr 45min–8hr); Villaviciosa (7 daily; 1hr).

Picos buses Arenas de Cabrales to Cangas de
Onis (4 daily; 45min); Bustio to Arenas via Panes
(2 daily; 50min); Cangas de Onis to Covadonga
(9 daily; 45min); Cangas de Onis to Posada de
Valdeón via Sajambre (daily in summer; 2hr
15min); Llanes to Madrid via Cangas, Sajambre and
Riaño (daily in summer; 3 weekly in winter; 6hr
15min); León to Posada de Valdeón via Riaño and
Portilla de la Reina (daily; 3hr); Potes to Espinama
to Fuente Dé (3 daily; 45min). Also Land Rover
service between Valdeón and Caín.

Ribadesella to: Lastres (7 daily; 35min); Llanes
(8–10 daily; 40min); Oviedo via Arriondas (change
at Arriondas for Cangas; 6–9 daily; 1hr–2hr); San
Vicente (daily; 1hr 10min); Villaviciosa (7 daily; 1hr).

San Vicente to: Llanes (5 daily; 35min);
Ribadesella (daily; 1hr); Santander (1–4 daily;
1hr–1hr 35min).

Santander (full schedules on 🌐 www
.santandereabus.com) to: Barcelona (2 daily; 8hr
30min); Bilbao (28 daily, 10 of which continue to
French border; 1hr 15min–2hr); Castro Urdiales
(9–13 daily; 1hr); Comillas (7 daily; 45min); Laredo
(18–23 daily; 40min); León (1–3 daily, 1 via Potes;
3hr 30min–5hr); Llanes (7 daily; 1hr 15min);
Logroño (1–2 daily; 3hr 20min–4hr 35min); Oviedo
(6 daily; 2hr 15min–3hr 15min); Potes via San
Vicente and Unquera (3 daily; 2hr 30min); Puente
Viesgo (7 daily; 30min); Santiago (2 daily; 9hr
45min); Santillana (7 daily in summer, 4 daily in
winter; 40min); San Vicente la Barquera (5 daily;
1hr); Vitoria via Castro Urdiales (5 daily; 2hr 30min);
Zaragoza (2–3 daily; 4hr 30min).

Ferries

Santander to: Plymouth (24hr); Portsmouth (22hr);
both 🌐 www.brittanny-ferries.co.uk.

Galicia

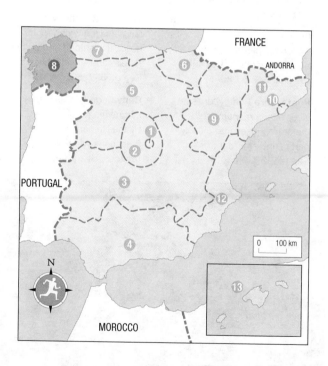

CHAPTER 8

Highlights

* **Santiago de Compostela** The goal of pilgrims for over a thousand years, this ravishing cathedral city is a labyrinth of ancient lanes and dramatic squares. See p.558

* **Sunset at Fisterra** Fantastic views over the Atlantic, from the very edge of the world. See p.582

* **Pimientos de Padrón** Randomly piquant green peppers fried in hot oil and sea salt. See p.585

* **Pontevedra** Pontevedra's sleepy *zona monumental* metamorphoses into a lively party zone after dark. See p.592

* **The Illas Cíes** The pristine sands of these three islets make for an irresistible day-trip. See p.596

* **The Parador at Baiona** Considering its unsurpassable setting, room rates at this fabulous hotel are surprisingly affordable. See p.597

* **Vieirasand white wine** Galicia is renowned for its delicious seafood and unique Ribeiro and Albariño wines. See p.555 & 587

* **Cañyon de Río Sil** A truly staggering gorge, carved by the Romans into still-functioning vine-growing terraces. See p.601

▲ Fisterra

Galicia

Passionately entangled with the Atlantic Ocean, at the northwest corner of the Iberian Peninsula, **Galicia** feels far removed from the rest of Spain. Everywhere is green, from the high forested hills to the rolling fields, a patchwork of tiny plots still farmed by hand; indeed, with its craggy coast and mild, wet climate, Galicia is more like Ireland than Andalucía. Its people take pride in their Celtic heritage – they even play the bagpipes (or *gaita galega*) – and in the fact that they still speak their own language, **Galego** (see p.982).

Galego food

Galegos boast that their **seafood** is the best in the world, and although the residents of Newfoundland may have a thing or two to say about it, there is no doubting the quality and sheer diversity of what is available. Local wonders to look out for include *vieiras* (the scallops whose shells became the symbol of St James), *mejillones* (the rich orange mussels from the *rías*), *cigallas* (Dublin Bay prawns, though often inadequately translated as shrimp), *anguilas* (little eels from the River Miño), *zamburiñas* (little scallops), *xoubas* (sardines), *navajas* (razor-shell clams), *percebes* (barnacles), *nécoras* (shore crabs) and *centollas* (spider crabs). *Pulpo* (octopus) is so much a part of Galego eating that there are special *pulperías* cooking it in the traditional copper pots, and it is a mainstay of local country fiestas. In the province of Pontevedra alone, Vilanova de Arousa has its own mussel festival (first Sun in Aug), Arcade has one devoted to oysters (first weekend in April), and O Grove goes all the way, with a generalized seafood fiesta. When eaten as tapas or *raciones*, seafood is not overly expensive, though you should always be wary of items like *navajas* and *percebes* that are sold by weight – a small plate-full can cost as much as €50. Throughout Galicia there are superb **markets**; the coastal towns have their rows of seafront stalls with supremely fresh fish, while cities such as Santiago have grand old arcaded market halls, piled high with farm produce from the surrounding countryside.

Another speciality, imported from the second Galego homeland of Argentina, is the **churrasquería** (grillhouse). Often unmarked and needing local assistance to find, these serve up immense *churrascos* – huge portions of boned steaks cooked on a traditional open grill (*parrilla*). The Galegos don't normally like their food highly spiced, but *churrascos* are usually served with a devastating garlic-based *salsa picante*. Other common dishes are *caldo galego*, a thick stew of cabbage and potatoes in a meat-based broth; *caldeirada*, a filling fish soup; *lacon con grelos*, ham boiled with turnip greens; and the ubiquitous *empanada*, a light-crusted pasty, often filled with tuna and tomato. Should you be around during the summer months, be sure to try *pimientos de Padrón*, sweet green peppers fried in oil, served as a kind of lucky dip with a few memorably spicy ones in each serving.

And yet Galicia is hardly off the beaten track. Its greatest city, **Santiago de Compostela**, ranked during the Middle Ages as the third city of Christendom, and pilgrims have been making their way here along the Camino de Santiago for well over a thousand years. Still focused around its unspoiled medieval core, a delightful labyrinth of ancient arcades and alleyways, Santiago remains an unmissable gem.

For modern visitors, however, Galicia has another irresistible attraction – its gorgeous **shoreline**, repeatedly indented with the long, narrow estuaries known here as *rías*. Above the slender sea-level strip, punctuated by tiny fishing villages, low-key resorts, and pretty, secluded sandy beaches, steep green slopes soar into the mysterious hills. Broadly speaking, the **Rías Altas** in the north are wilder and emptier, while the picturesque **Rías Baixas**, neighbouring Portugal, are warmer and more developed, and consequently attract many more visitors. In between the two lie the dunes and headlands of the **Costa do Morte**.

Apart from the modern ports of **A Coruña**, with its elegant glass-encased balconies, and **Vigo**, perched in splendour alongside its magnificent bay, the seaside towns are generally small. Sadly, however, in many areas of the Rías

Fiestas

January
1: Livestock fair at Betanzos.
6: Los Reyes Horseback procession of the Three Kings in Baiona.

March
1: San Rosendo Celanova's big festival, at the monastery.
Pre-Lent: *Carnavales* throughout the region.

April/May
Semana Santa (Holy Week) Celebrations include a symbolic *descendimiento* (descent from the Cross) at Viveiro on Good Friday and a Resurrection procession at Fisterra. On Palm Sunday, there are Stations of the Cross at Monte San Tecla, near A Guarda.
Sunday after Easter: Fiesta de Angula Elver festival at Tui.
Second Monday after Easter: Fiesta San Telmo At Tui.
Late April–early May (dates vary) Festival at Ribadavia celebrating and promoting Ribeiro wines.
May 1: *Romería* at Pontevedra marks the start of a month-long festival.
Last week: Vino de la Ribeira Sacra Festival at Monforte de Lemos.

July
First weekend: Rapa das Bestas The capture and breaking in of wild mountain horses at Viveiro.
11: Fiesta de San Benito At Pontevedra, with river processions, and folk groups, and a smaller *romería* at Cambados.
16: Virgen del Carmen Sea processions at Muros and Corcubión.
Second weekend: Medieval de Betanzos Three-day fair at Betanzos, reliving the town's time under Andrade rule.
Third weekend: International Festival of the Celtic World Galicia's most important music festival is held in Ortigueira (ⓦ www.festivaldeortigueira.com); pipe bands from all the Celtic lands perform, alongside musicians from around the world, and every event is free.

Baixas in particular, a lack of planning controls has resulted in the coastline becoming depressingly overbuilt, albeit with suburban villas and seaside apartments rather than high-rise hotels. With each town tending to merge into the next, those few resorts that still centre on sturdy little medieval harbours, such as **Cambados**, **Muros** and **Baiona**, are especially welcome.

Further inland, the settlements are more spread out, and the river valleys of the Miño and the Sil remain beautifully unspoiled, while the attractive provincial capitals of **Pontevedra**, **Ourense** and **Lugo** seem little changed since the Middle Ages.

Again like the Irish, the Galegos are renowned for having **emigrated** all over the world. Between 1836 and 1960, around two million Galegos, or roughly half the total population, left the region – largely due to the pressure on agricultural land, exacerbated by the custom that land was inherited in equal shares by all sons, and therefore fragmented and rendered less productive. Half of them ended up in Argentina, where Buenos Aires is often called the largest city in Galicia. An untranslatable Galego word, *morriña*, describes the exiles' particular sense of homesick, nostalgic longing. That Celtic melancholy has its counterpart in the exuberant devotion to the land, its culture and its produce that you'll

24–25: St James (San Yago) Two days of celebration in many places, with processions of bigheads and *gigantones* on the 24th and spectacular parades with fireworks and bands through the following evening.

25: Santiago Galicia's major fiesta, at its height in Santiago de Compostela. The evening before, there's a fireworks display and symbolic burning of a cardboard effigy of the mosque at Córdoba. The festival – also designated "Galicia Day" – has become a nationalist event with traditional separatist marches and an extensive programme of political and cultural events for about a week on either side.

August

First Sunday Albariño wine festival at Cambados; bagpipe festival at Ribadeo; *Virgen de la Roca* observances outside Baiona; pimiento festival at Padrón; *Navaja* (razor shell) festival at Fisterra.

16: Fiesta de San Roque Festivals at all churches that bear his name: at Betanzos, there's a Battle of the Flowers on the river and the launching of the *Fiesta del Globo*.

24: Fiesta (and bullfights) at Noia.

25: Fiesta de San Ginés At Sanxenxo.

Last Sunday: *Romería* sets out from Sanxenxo to the Praia de La Lanzada.

September

6–10: Fiestas del Portal At Ribadavia.

14: Fiesta do Marisco Seafood festival at O Grove.

October

13: Fiesta de la Exaltación del Marisco At O Grove – literally, "A Celebration in Praise of Shellfish".

November

11: Fiesta de San Martín At Bueu.

17: Magosto castaña Chestnut festival at Ourense.

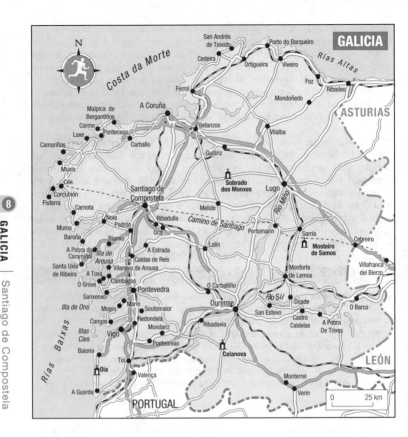

encounter in Galicia itself, as evinced in its music, literature and festivals. Above all, Galegos view their **food** and **wine** almost as sacraments; share in a feast of the fresh local seafood, washed down with a crisp white Albariño, and you may find the *morriña* gets a hold on you, too.

Santiago de Compostela

The ancient pilgrimage centre of **SANTIAGO DE COMPOSTELA** ranks among the most stunningly beautiful cities in all Spain. A superb ensemble of twisting stone lanes, majestic squares and ancient churches, interspersed with countless hidden nooks and crannies, its medieval core remains a remarkably integrated whole, all the better for being almost entirely pedestrianized. Little wonder it has been declared in its entirety to be both a national monument and a UNESCO World Heritage Site. Hewn from time-weathered granite, splashed with gold and silver lichen and sprouting vegetation from the unlikeliest crevices, the buildings and plazas, arcades and flagstones seem to blend imperceptibly each into the next. Warrens of honey-coloured streets wind their way past a succession of beautiful monasteries and convents, culminating in the approach to the immense Praza do Obradoiro, flanked by the magnificent Catedral, the supposed resting place of the remains of St James.

The **pilgrimage** to Santiago, which reached its peak during the eleventh and twelfth centuries, captured the imagination of Christian Europe on an unprecedented scale. People of all classes came to visit the supposed shrine of St James the Apostle (Santiago to the Spanish, Saint Jacques to the French), making this the third holiest site in Christendom, after Jerusalem and Rome.

Santiago still seems as busy as it must have been in the days of the first pilgrims. These days, tourists are as likely to be attracted by its art and history as by religion, but pilgrims still arrive in large numbers, sporting their *vieira* (scallop shell) symbol. Each year at the **Festival of St James** on July 25, a ceremony at his shrine re-dedicates the country and government to the saint. Those years in which the saint's day falls on a Sunday are designated "Holy Years", and the activity becomes even more intense. The next two will be in 2010 and 2021.

For all its fame, however, Santiago remains surprisingly small. Its total population is estimated at 116,000, of whom 33,000 are students at its venerable university. Almost everything of interest to visitors is contained within the densely packed historic core, known as the *zona monumental*, which takes roughly fifteen minutes to cross on foot but several days to explore thoroughly. Most of the commercial activities and infrastructure lie a short distance downhill to the south, in the less appealing modern quarter, which is also where the students tend to live. Wander away from the *zona monumental* in most other directions, however, and you can quickly reach wide-open countryside.

Locals and tourists alike flock to the old quarter for its round-the-clock sense of life and vibrancy, making it far more than a mere historical curiosity. Uniquely, it's also a city that's at its best in the rain; in fact, it's situated in the wettest fold of the Galego hills, and suffers brief but frequent showers. Water glistens on the facades, gushes from the innumerable gargoyles and flows down the streets.

Arrival and information

Santiago's **airport** (☎981 547 500), served by Ryanair flights from London Stansted, Liverpool, Barcelona and Valencia, is 13km east of town in **Labacolla**, on the road to Lugo. Ryanair offers its own connecting bus service (€3), and frequent buses also connect the airport with Santiago's **bus station** (1–2 hourly), 1km or so east of the old town; bus #5 (€0.90) will take you to the Praza de Galicia. From the **train station**, the *praza* is a ten-minute walk north.

Almost all the streets in the old quarter are pedestrianized, and very few hotels offer **parking** facilities, so **drivers** have little choice but to use one of the large car parks on the periphery. The closest to the cathedral is the huge Juan XXIII car park, a short distance north, which is also where all coach tours pull in. Local transport and car parks alike are operated by Tussa (ⓌÍwww.tussa.org).

The city's main **turismo** is in the old quarter at Rúa do Vilar 63 (daily: June–Sept 9am–9pm; Oct–May 9am–2pm & 4–7pm; ☎981 555 129, Ⓦwww .santiagoturismo.com), while a separate office nearby at Rúa do Vilar 43 (Mon–Fri 10am–8pm, Sat 11am–2pm & 5–7pm, Sun 11am–2pm; ☎981 584 081, Ⓦwww.turgalicia.es) provides information on Galicia as a whole. There are also smaller local offices at the Juan XXIII car park (summer Tues–Sat 9am–5pm), and at the airport (open to coincide with arrivals).

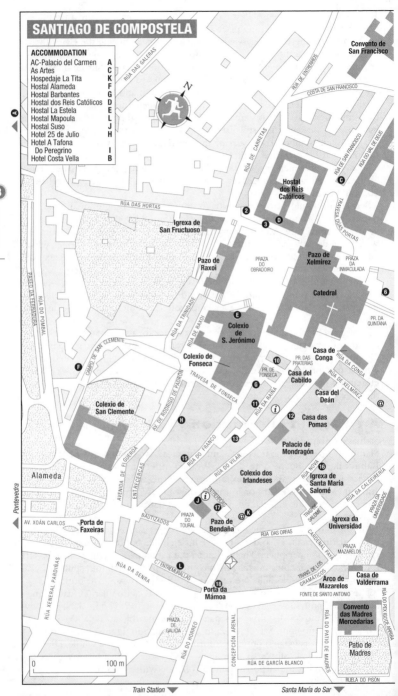

SANTIAGO DE COMPOSTELA

ACCOMMODATION
AC-Palacio del Carmen A
As Artes C
Hospedaje La Tita K
Hostal Alameda F
Hostal Barbantes G
Hostal dos Reis Católicos D
Hostal La Estela E
Hostal Mapoula L
Hostal Suso J
Hotel 25 de Julio H
Hotel A Tafona
  Do Peregrino I
Hotel Costa Vella B

GALICIA

8

Convento de San Francisco

RÚA DAS GALERAS

RÚA DE CARRETAS

COSTA DE SAN FRANCISCO

RÚA DE ENTERROS

RÚA DE SAN FRANCISCO

RÚA DO VAL DE DEUS

Hostal dos Reis Católicos

TRAVESA DUAS PORTAS

PRAZA DA INMACULADA

RÚA DAS HORTAS

Igrexa de San Fructuoso

Pazo de Raxoi

PRAZA DO OBRADOIRO

Pazo de Xelmírez

Catedral

PR. DA QUINTANA

PASEO DA FERRADURA

RÚA DO POMBAL

RÚA DE TRINIDADE

RÚA DE RAXOI

Colexio de S. Jerónimo

Colexio de Fonseca

PR. DAS PRATERÍAS

Casa de Conga

RÚA DA CONGA

CAMPO DE SAN CLEMENTE

TRAVESA DE FONSECA

PR. DE FONSECA

Casa del Cabildo

Casa del Deán

RÚA DE XELMÍREZ

Colexio de San Clemente

AV. DE RODRIGO DE PADRÓN

RÚA DA RAIÑA

Casa das Pomas

Palacio de Mondragón

Alameda

AVENIDA DE FIGUEROA

ENTRERRECEIRAS

RÚA DO FRANCO

RÚA DO VILAR

Colexio dos Irlandeses

Igrexa de Santa María Salomé

RÚA NOVA

RÚA DA CALDERERÍA

PRAZA DA UNIVERSIDADE

Pontevedra

AV. XOÁN CARLOS

Porta de Faxeiras

BAUTIZADOS

ENTRERRÍOS

PRAZA DO TOURAL

Pazo de Bendaña

TRASPE SALOMÉ

Igrexa da Universidade

RÚA DAS ORFAS

CARDENAL PAYA

PRAZA MAZARELOS

RÚA XENERAL PARDIÑAS

RÚA DA SENRA

C/ ENTREMURALLAS

Porta da Mámoa

TRANS. DE LOS GRAMÁTICOS

Arco de Mazarelos

FONTE DE SANTO ANTONIO

Casa de Valderrama

PRAZA DE GALICIA

RÚA DO HORREO

CONCEPCIÓN ARENAL

RÚA DE GARCÍA BLANCO

RÚA DO PATIO DE MADRES

RÚA DAS MADRES

Convento das Madres Mercedarias

Patio de Madres

RÚA DO REY ROCHE ARRIBA

RUELA DO PISÓN

0 — 100 m

560

Train Station ▼   Santa María do Sar ▼

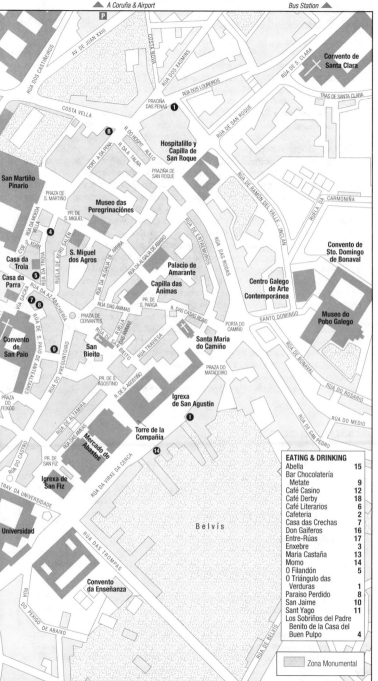

A Coruña & Airport

Bus Station

Convento de Santa Clara

RÚA DE S. CLARA

TRAS DE SANTA CLARA

RÚA DOS CASTIÑEIROS

AV. DE JUAN XXIII

COSTA NOVA

RÚA DOS XASMINS

RÚA DOS LOUREIROS

PRACIÑA DAS PENAS ❶

COSTA VELLA

RÚA DE SAN ROQUE

R. DO HOSPIT. ALILLO

PORT. A DA PEÑA

R. DA TAINA

B

Hospitalillo y Capilla de San Roque

PRAZIÑA DE SAN ROQUE

San Martiño Pinario

PRAZA DE S. MARTIÑO

Museo das Peregrinaciones

PR. DE S. MIGUEL

RÚA DE RAMÓN DEL VALLE - INCLÁN

RUELA DA CARMONIÑA

8 GALICIA

RÚA DA MOEDA VELLA

CDE. S. XOAN

Casa da Troia

❹

RÚA DA TROIA

S. Miguel dos Agros

RUELA DE XERUSALEN

RÚA DA ALGALIA DE ABAIXO

RÚA DE ENTREMUROS

RÚA DAS RODAS

Palacio de Amarante

Convento de Sto. Domingo de Bonaval

Casa da Parra

❺

❼ ❽

RÚA DA AZABACHERÍA

RÚA DA ALGALIA DE ARRIBA

Capilla das Ánimas

PR. DE S. PARGA

R. DAS CASAS REAIS

Centro Galego de Arte Contemporánea

Museo do Pobo Galego

VÍA SACRA

PRAZA DE CERVANTES

PR. DE S. MIGUEL

SANTO DOMINGO

Convento de San Paio

RÚA DE S. PAIO DE ANTEALTARES

❾

RÚA DO PREGUNTOIRO

RÚA DE SAN BIEITO

RÚA DAS ÁNIMAS

PORTA DO CAMIÑO

San Bieito

RÚA TRAVIESA

Santa María do Camiño

RÚA DE BONAVAL

RÚA DO ROSARIO

PRAZA DO FEIXOO

PR. DE S. AGOSTIÑO

R. DE S. AGOSTIÑO

PRAZA DO MATADOIRO

RÚA DO MEDIO

RÚA DE ALTAMIRA

Igrexa de San Agustín

❶

RÚA DE SAN PEDRO

RÚA DO CASTRO

RÚA DAS AMEAS

Mercado de Abastos

Torre de la Compañía

PR. DE SAN FIZ

⓮

Igrexa de San Fiz

RÚA DA VIRXE DA CERCA

TRAV. DA UNIVERSIDADE

Belvís

Universidade

RÚA DAS TROMPAS

RÚA DO PEXIGO DE ABAIXO

Convento da Enseñanza

RÚA DE BELVÍS

561

EATING & DRINKING

Abella	15
Bar Chocolatería Metate	9
Café Casino	12
Café Derby	18
Café Literarios	6
Cafeteria	2
Casa das Crechas	7
Don Gaiferos	16
Entre-Rúas	17
Enxebre	3
Maria Castaña	13
Momo	14
O Filandón	5
O Triángulo das Verduras	1
Paraiso Perdido	8
San Jaime	10
Sant Yago	11
Los Sobriños del Padre Benito de la Casa del Buen Pulpo	4

Zona Monumental

The history of the pilgrimage to Santiago

The great **pilgrimage to Santiago** was arguably Europe's first exercise in mass tourism. Following in the footsteps of Godescale of Puy, who reached Santiago in 951, an estimated half-million pilgrims per year arrived in the city during the eleventh and twelfth centuries. Although the shrine was visited by the great – Fernando and Isabel, Carlos V, Francis of Assisi – you didn't have to be rich to come. The various roads through France and northern Spain that led here, collectively known as **El Camino de Santiago** (The Way of St James, or the Pilgrim Route), were lined with monasteries and charitable hospices. Villages sprang up along the route, and an order of knights was founded for the pilgrims' protection. There was even a guidebook – the world's first – written by a French monk called Aymery Picaud, which recorded, along with water sources and places to stay, such facts as the bizarre sexual habits of the Navarrese Basques (said to expose themselves when excited, and protect their mules from their neighbours with chastity belts). It was an extraordinary phenomenon in an age when most people never ventured beyond their own town or village.

Why did they come? Some, like Chaucer's Wife of Bath, who had "been in Galicia at Seynt Jame", had their own private reasons: social fashion, adventure, the opportunities for marriage or even for crime. But for most pilgrims, it was a question of faith. Believing in the miraculous power of **St James**, they understood that the journey would guarantee a remission of half their time in Purgatory. Few doubted that the tomb beneath Santiago's high cathedral altar held the mortal remains of James, son of Zebedee and Salome and first cousin of Jesus Christ. It seems scarcely credible that the whole business was an immense **ecclesiastical fraud**.

Yet the legend, at each point of its development, bears this out. It begins with the claim, unsubstantiated by the Bible, that St James visited Spain after the Crucifixion, to spread the gospel. He is said, for example, to have had a vision of the Virgin in Zaragoza. He then returned to Jerusalem, where he was undoubtedly beheaded by Herod Agrippa. But the legend relates that two of James's followers removed his corpse to Jaffa, where a boat appeared, without sails or crew, and whisked them in just seven days to Padrón, 20km downstream from Santiago.

Accommodation

Santiago offers **accommodation** to suit all budgets, ranging from its gorgeous *parador* down to the many inexpensive *hostales* aimed at pilgrims and young travellers. As almost everyone, quite rightly, prefers to stay in the old quarter, that's where you'll find the biggest concentration of places, with cheaper options clustered especially on three parallel streets that lead south from the cathedral: Rúa Nova, Rúa do Vilar and Rúa do Franco (this last named after the French pilgrims, rather than the late dictator). Even during the July festival, there's rarely a problem, as half the bars in the city rent out rooms. **Compostur**, the city's official tourist agency, offers discount bookings and last-minute availability via a website and toll-free phone line (☎902 190 160 or ⓦwww.santiagoreservas.com).

AC-Palacio del Carmen Rúa das Oblatas s/n ☎981 552 444, ⓦwww.ac-hoteles.com. If you don't mind staying 10min walk west of the old quarter, this beautifully converted former convent offers Santiago's most affordable luxury, with very stylish modern rooms and an on-site restaurant. ⑤

As Artes Travesa Dúas Portas 2 ☎981 572 590, ⓦwww.asartes.com. Very attractive little hotel, close to the cathedral and boasting lots of character. Each of its seven en-suite rooms, of varying sizes, is named after a particular artist, and decorated in a distinctive but traditional and very cosy style. ④

The body was then buried, lost and forgotten for 750 years, before being rediscovered at Compostela in 813, at a time of great significance for the Spanish Church. Over the preceding century, the Moors had swept across the Iberian Peninsula, gaining control over all but the northern mountain kingdom of Asturias. They drew great strength from the inspiration of their champion, the Prophet Muhammad, whose death (in 632) still lay within popular memory, and a bone from whose arm was preserved in La Mesquita in Córdoba. Thus the discovery of the bones of St James, under a buried altar on a site traditionally linked with his name, was singularly opportune. It occurred after a hermit was attracted to a particular hillside by visions of stars; the hill was known thereafter as Compostela, from the Latin *campus stellae*, meaning "field of stars". Alfonso II, king of Asturias, came to pay his respects and built a chapel, and the saint was adopted as the champion of Christian Spain against the infidel.

Within decades, the saint had appeared on the battlefield. Ramiro I, Alfonso's successor, swore that James had fought alongside him at the Battle of Clavijo (844), and that the saint had personally slaughtered 60,000 Moors. Over the next six centuries *Santiago Matamoros* (Moor-killer) manifested himself at some forty battles, assisting, for example, in the massacre of the Inca's armies in Peru. That may seem an odd role for the fisherman-evangelist, but it presented no problems to the Christian propagandists who portrayed him most frequently as a knight on horseback in the act of dispatching whole clutches of swarthy, bearded Arabs with a single thrust of his long sword. (With consummate irony, when Franco brought his crack Moroccan troops to Compostela to dedicate themselves to the overthrow of the Spanish Republic, all such statues were discreetly hidden under sheets.)

The **cult of Santiago** was strongest during the age of the First Crusade (1085) and the Reconquest; people wanted to believe, and so it gained a kind of truth. In any case, as Richard Ford acidly observed, "If people can once believe that Santiago ever came to Spain at all, all the rest is plain sailing."

For more on the Camino de Santiago itself, see the boxes on pp.586 & 570.

Hospedaje La Tita Rúa Nova 46 ☎ 981 583 981. Five pleasant, bare-bones and very inexpensive rooms, sharing a bathroom and WC, above a bar in the old quarter. ❶

Hostal Alameda Rúa do San Clemente 32 ☎ 981 588 100. Smart, stylish rooms – some en suite – with polished floors, large windows and TV. Pleasantly located by the Alameda. ❸

Hostal Barbantes Rúa do Franco 3 ☎ 981 576 520, ⓦ www.libredonbarbantes.com. Clean and light en-suite rooms, all of which can be inspected online; some have balconies overlooking a pretty and very central little square. There's a good bar and restaurant below. ❸

Hostal dos Reis Católicos Praza do Obradoiro 1 ☎ 981 582 200, ⓦ www .parador.es. Santiago's magnificent *parador*, facing the cathedral, is one of the world's most famous – and possibly oldest – hotels. Its 136 irresistibly luxurious rooms are arranged around four separate tranquil courtyards, and there are also two restaurants and a plush bar. It's worth every penny, especially if you get a *paradores* multi-day discount. ❼

Hostal La Estela Avda. Raxoi 1 ☎ 981 582 796, ⓔ hostallaestela@yahoo.es. A good-value *hostal* on a pretty street just off the Praza do Obradoiro, offering both en-suite and shared-bath rooms, the best of which have views of the cathedral. ❷

Hostal Mapoula Rúa do Entremurallas 10 ☎ 981 580 124, ⓦ www.mapoula.com. Clean, friendly, third-floor *hostal*, with spacious, en-suite rooms, all with TV and phone; some sleep three or four guests. It's right in the heart of the action, and close to some good cafés and bars, so don't be put off by the somewhat dingy little alleyway. ❷

Hostal Suso Rúa do Vilar 65 ☎ 981 586 611. A neat, comfortable *hostal*, with a good bar-restaurant downstairs, alongside the *turismo* in a lively arcaded street. ❶

Hotel 25 de Julio Avda. De Rodrigo de Padrón 4 ☎ 981 582 295. This friendly, funky little B&B hotel,

just below the main pedestrian streets, holds six charming rooms – two have flowery balconies – and has a sunny café downstairs. Closed Jan. ❸
Hotel A Tafona Do Peregrino Rúa Virxe da Cerca 7 ☎981 568 923, ⓦwww.atafonadoperegrino .com. Hip modern hotel, immediately east of the old quarter – just across the road from the market place – stylishly converted from an old house and featuring lots of exposed stonework and gleaming tiles. Smart bedrooms, two lounges, and a bar-café downstairs. ❹

Hotel Costa Vella c/Porta de Peña 17 ☎981 569 530, ⓦwww.costavella.com. Welcoming, very comfortable and chi-chi hotel on the northern edge of the old quarter, with views over the rooftops. Rates include breakfast, served in the small flower-filled garden in summer. Paying a little extra gets you a larger room with a delightful balcony. ❹

As Cancelas Rúa de 25 de Julio 35 ☎981 580 266, ⓦwww.campingascancelas.com. Open all year and within possible walking distance of the town (2.5km northeast of the cathedral), with €6 tent pitches and some rental bungalows (❷). Served by buses #8 and #9, as well as the airport bus, it's reached via the road to A Coruña, branching off at the Avda. del Camino Francés.
As Sirenas ☎981 898 688, ⓦwww .comarcasantiago.com/sirenas.htm. A reasonable second choice if you have a car, this small and slightly cheaper (tents €3.50) campsite 11km northwest on the Santa Comba road has children's and adults' pools, and its own *pensión*. Open July to mid-Sept only.

The Catedral

All roads in Santiago lead to the **Catedral** (daily: summer 9am–8pm; winter 9am–7pm). You first appreciate the sheer grandeur of the cathedral upon venturing into the vast expanse of the Praza do Obradoiro. Directly ahead stands a fantastic Baroque pyramid of granite, flanked by immense bell towers and everywhere adorned with statues of St James in his familiar pilgrim guise with staff, broad hat and scallop-shell badge. This is the famous **Obradoiro facade**, built between 1738 and 1750 by an obscure Santiago-born architect, Fernando de Casas. No other work of Spanish Baroque can compare with it,

▲ Pilgrims in front of the Catedral

nor with what Edwin Mullins (in *The Road to Compostela*) sublimely called its "hat-in-the-air exuberance".

The main body of the cathedral is Romanesque, rebuilt in the eleventh and twelfth centuries after a devastating raid by the Muslim vizier of Córdoba, al-Mansur, in 977. Although, perhaps not surprisingly, he failed to find the body of the saint, he forced the citizens to carry the bells of the tower to the mosque at Córdoba – a coup that was later dramatically reversed (see p.325). The building's highlight – indeed, one of the great triumphs of medieval art – is the **Pórtico de Gloria**, the original west front, which now stands inside the cathedral, immediately behind the Obradoiro. Completed in 1188 under the supervision of Maestro Mateo, this represented both the culmination of all Romanesque sculpture and a precursor of the new Gothic realism, each of its host of figures being strikingly relaxed and quietly humanized.

The real mastery, however, is in the assured marshalling of the ensemble. Above the side doors are representations of Purgatory and the Last Judgement, while over the main door Christ presides in glory, flanked by his Apostles, and surrounded by the 24 Elders of the Apocalypse playing celestial music. St James sits on the central column, beneath Christ and just above eye level in the classic symbolic position of intercessor. To either side are the Prophets of the Old Testament. So many millions of pilgrims have given thanks at journey's end, by praying with the fingers of one hand pressed into the roots of the Tree of Jesse below the saint, that five deep and shiny holes have been worn into the solid marble. Finally, for wisdom, they would lower their heads to touch the brow of Maestro Mateo, the humble squatting figure on the other side.

The spiritual climax of each pilgrimage, however, comes when pilgrims climb steps behind the **High Altar** – a riot of eighteenth-century Churrigueresque – embrace the Most Sacred Image of Santiago, and kiss his bejewelled cape. The whole process is rounded off by the pilgrims making their confession and attending a High Mass.

The elaborate pulley system in front of the altar serves to move the immense "**Botafumeiro**" (incense burner), which, operated by eight priests (*tiraboleiros*), is swung in a vast thirty-metre ceiling-to-ceiling arc across the transept. Originally designed to fumigate bedraggled pilgrims, the Botafumeiro is now used only at certain services – ask whether there's one during your visit. The saint's bones, kept in a **crypt** beneath the altar, are also visited by a steady procession of pilgrims. They were lost for a second time in 1700, having been hidden before an English invasion, but were rediscovered during building work in 1879. In fact, they found three skeletons, which were naturally held to be those of St James and his two followers. The only problem was identifying which one

Las Cubiertas

A foray up to **Las Cubiertas**, the **cathedral roof**, is an experience not to be missed; the climb up leads through the upper floors of the cathedral interior (when no service is taking place), while the roof itself, which consists of shallow granite steps, offers superb views over the rest of the city, as well, of course, as the cathedral's own towers and embellishments. Every way you turn, it's crawling with pagodas, pawns, domes, obelisks, battlements, scallop shells and cornucopias.

Guided **tours** leave from the Pazo de Xelmírez (daily except Mon; hourly departures 10am–1pm & 4–7pm; €10; ☏981 552 985), but most feature a quick-fire Spanish commentary that may well leave you floundering; to arrange an English-language tour, at no extra charge, call five days in advance in summer, or two days in low season.

was the Apostle. This was fortuitously resolved as a church in Tuscany possessed a piece of Santiago's skull that exactly fitted a gap in one of those here.

To visit the **Treasury**, **Cloisters** and **Buchería** (Archeological Museum), to the right of the cathedral as you face it, and Mateo's beautiful **Crypt of the Portico**, which is accessed beneath the cathedral's main entry staircase (and is distinct from the crypt that holds James's relics), you need to buy a collective ticket (summer Mon–Sat 10am–2pm & 4–8pm, Sun 10am–2pm; winter Mon–Sat 10am–1.30pm & 4–6.30pm; Pazo de Xelmírez different hours, see below; €5). The late Gothic cloisters in particular are well worth seeing; from the plain, mosque-like courtyard you get a wonderful prospect of the riotous mixture of the exterior. The Buchería holds Mateo's original stone choir and the remains of the thirteenth-century cloister, while upstairs you'll find assorted relics of the cathedral's history, including the Botafumeiro itself when it's not in use.

Tickets to the cloisters and crypt also grant admission to the **Pazo de Xelmírez** (Palacio Arzobispal Gelmírez; Tues–Sun 10am–1.30pm & 4–7.30pm), adjoining the cathedral to the north and entered just to the left of the main stairs. Archbishop Xelmírez was a seminal figure in Santiago's development. He rebuilt the cathedral in the twelfth century, raised the see to an archbishopric and "discovered" a ninth-century deed that gave annual dues to St James's shrine of one bushel of corn from each acre of Spain reconquered from the Moors – a decree that was repealed only in 1834. His appropriately opulent palace features a vaulted twelfth-century kitchen and a thirteenth-century synodal hall, along with plenty of ancient statues.

The rest of the city

Historic Santiago, with its flagstone streets and arcades, is enchanting in its entirety. Each of the four squares that flank the cathedral has its own beauties, while the granite lanes to the south and east are filled with churches, convents and colleges, and several fascinating museums lie in the vicinity. To enjoy an overall impression of the whole architectural ensemble, take a walk along the promenade of the **Paseo da Ferradura** (Paseo de la Herradura), in the spacious **Alameda** just southwest of the old quarter, at the end of Rúa do Franco.

The cathedral squares

You could easily spend several hours exploring the squares around the cathedral. The **Praza do Obradoiro**, in front of the main facade, is the most formal and impressive of Santiago's public spaces. Its northern side is dominated by the elegant Renaissance **Hostal dos Reis Católicos** (Hostal de los Reyes Católicos). As late as the thirteenth century the cathedral was used to accommodate pilgrims, but slowly its place was taken by convents around the city. Fernando and Isabel, in gratitude for their conquest of Granada, added to these facilities by building this superb hostel for the poor and sick. Now a *parador*, it's very much *the* place to stay if you can afford it. Even if you're not staying here, stroll in for a look at its four lovely courtyards, the chapel with magnificent Gothic stone carvings or the vaulted crypt-bar (where the bodies of the dead were once stored).

In the equally large but somehow more intimate **Praza da Quintana**, a flight of broad steps joins the back of the cathedral to the high walls of the **Convento de San Paio**, and serves around the clock as an impromptu bench for students and backpackers. The "Porta Santa" doorway here is only opened during Holy Years, in which the feast of Santiago falls on a Sunday. To the south, the **Praza das Praterías**, the Silversmiths' Square, centres on an ornate fountain of four horses with webbed feet, and features the seventy-metre-high *Berenguela*, or

clock tower. On its west side, the extraordinarily narrow **Casa del Cabildo** was built in 1758 to fill the remaining gap and ornamentally complete the square – you'd never know to look at it, but it's a mere facade, with nothing behind it.

North of the cathedral, the grand Baroque frontage of the Benedictine monastery of **San Martiño Pinario** towers over the **Praza da Inmaculada**. At 20,000 square metres, this ranks among the largest religious buildings in Spain.

The museums

Santiago's most interesting museum relates the story of **pilgrimage** not only here but also to religious shrines the world over. The **Museo das Peregrinaciónes** (Tues–Fri 10am–8pm, Sat 10.30am–1.30pm & 5–8pm, Sun 10.30am–1.30pm; free) is housed in a sixteenth-century mansion, the Pazo de Don Pedro, a short way east of San Martiño Pinario monastery. Excellent models and displays cover the *camino*, the city and cathedral, and there's a comprehensive (and free) guide in English. Look out for the room that explores how depictions of St James himself have changed over the centuries, to reflect his changing image. The museum's real jewel, however, is an original copy of the twelfth-century *Codex Calixtinus*, a travel guide for pilgrims, which recommended routes and lodgings and pointed out the various dangers of the *camino*, such as the "malicious, swarthy, ugly, depraved, perverse, despicable, disloyal and corrupt" Navarrese. There's also a fascinating modern equivalent, drawn by Japanese artist Munehiro Ikeda in the 1980s.

A few minutes' walk farther east, just beyond the old quarter, the convent and church of **Santo Domingo** features a unique seventeenth-century triple stairway, each spiral of which leads to different storeys of a single tower. Set off up different flights, and you may lose each other for hours. The convent houses the fascinating **Museo do Pobo Galego** (Tues–Sat 10am–2pm & 4–8pm, Sun 11am–2pm; ⓦwww.museodopobo.es; free), which features a diverse overview of Galego crafts and traditions, with a moving account of Galicia's history of emigration. Many aspects of the way of life displayed haven't yet entirely disappeared, though you're today unlikely to see *corozas*, straw suits worn into the last century by mountain shepherds. The convent chapel now serves as the **Panteon de Galegos Ilustres**, home to the mortal remains of such local heroes as the poet Rosalia de Castro and the essayist and caricaturist Castelao. Gardens and orchards stretch up the hillside behind, offering a wonderful spot for a break from sightseeing.

Opposite the convent, the **Centro de Arte Contemporáneo de Galicia** (Tues–Sun 11am–8pm; free), a modern but beautiful addition to Santiago's heritage by the Portuguese architect Álvaro Siza, stages temporary exhibitions of contemporary art and sculpture.

Santa María do Sar

Outside the main circuit of the city, the most worthwhile visit is to the curious Romanesque church of **Santa María do Sar**. This lies about 1km down the Rúa de Sar, which begins at the Patio das Madres on the southern edge of the old city. Some attribute the remarkable fifteen-degree slant of its pillars to deficient foundations; to the faithful, it's proof of the mastery of its designers. It also has a wonderfully sculpted cloister, reputedly the work of Maestro Mateo.

Eating, drinking and nightlife

Galego food is plentiful and excellent in Santiago, with a plethora of great **places to eat**. The two main concentrations lie along the parallel rúas Franco and Raiña, which can get very busy in summer, and northeast of the cathedral on the

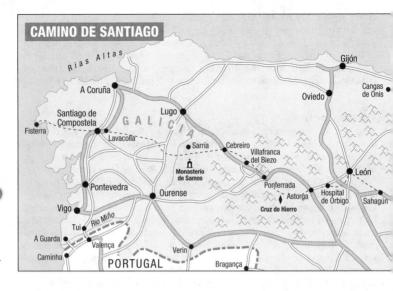

The Camino de Santiago

The **Camino de Santiago**, or Pilgrim Route, is the longest-established "tourist" route in Europe, and its final section through Galicia provides echoes of the medieval pilgrimage to the thousands who walk it every year, armed with the traditional staff and the scallop-shell emblem of St James. Today's pilgrims seldom walk from their homes to Santiago de Compostela and back; most follow one of the half a dozen or so standard pilgrimage routes through Spain and France. The most popular, the 750km **Camino Francés**, heads westward from the Roncesvalles (or Orreaga-Roncesvalles in Basque) in the Pyrenees across northern Spain. You don't have to be Christian, or even religious, to follow the route. For roughly half of all pilgrims, the journey to Santiago is prompted by their religious faith, while others want to experience their own spiritual quest, or simply to immerse themselves in Spanish history and culture. Whatever the reason for the journey, the *camino*'s popularity has exploded in recent decades; while only a handful of people walked to Santiago in the 1960s, the route now attracts over 100,000 pilgrims a year, half of whom are Spanish. In Holy Years, such as 2010, when St James's feast day (July 25) falls on a Sunday, the number of pilgrims more than doubles.

The Camino de Santiago in Galicia

The Camino de Santiago in Galicia passes few tourist sights, meandering instead through countless tiny villages. Pilgrims work a little harder on this last leg as the route clambers up and down steep hills and valleys, but the scenery is gorgeous compensation: green with oak forests and patchworked fields. Galicia is green for a reason, however; the region gets a lot of rain, and you can get caught in a storm even in summer.

The Galician government has made a huge effort to promote the *camino*, maintaining an extensive network of pilgrim hostels along the eight separate routes that converge on Santiago – all are listed on the website ⓦwww.xacobeo.es. The

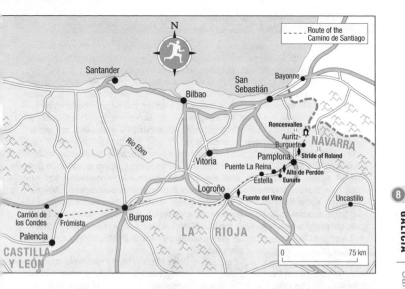

Camino Francés enters Galicia at the Pedrafita do Cebreiro pass, a desolate spot where hundreds of English soldiers froze or starved to death during Sir John Moore's retreat towards A Coruña in 1809. It's a fierce thirty-kilometre climb from Villafranca del Bierzo in León up cobbled paths often slick with mud and dung to the mountain village of **O Cebreiro**. There can be snow here in winter, and fog often obscures the spectacular views, but it's a magical place, with round, thatched-roof *pallozas* (stone huts) and intricate *horréos* (granaries).

The *camino* is naturally at its most more crowded in Galicia. The volume of pilgrims reaches a crescendo at **Sarría**, 115km from Santiago, which is the last major town where you can start walking and still earn a *compostela*; 12km southeast of here, the moss-covered **Monasterio de Samos** (daily 10.30am–1pm & 4.30–7pm; free), famous for its library in the Middle Ages, is one of the few surviving ancient buildings along the route.

The closer you get to Santiago, the more pilgrim rituals you'll encounter. Medieval pilgrims would wash themselves in the river at **Lavacolla**, 10km outside the city, to prepare for their arrival. During this ritual cleansing – often the first bath since leaving home – they'd pay extra attention to their private parts; *lavacolla* is said to mean scrotum-washing. From there, they'd race 5km to **Monte de Gozo** (Mount of Joy), where the first to cry "mon joie" on spotting Santiago's cathedral spires was declared the king of the group. Sadly, these days it's impossible to see the spires through the surrounding suburbs.

Although most people end their pilgrimage at **Santiago de Compostela**, some walk another 75km to Fisterra (Finisterra), a Celtic route towards the setting sun that predates the medieval pilgrimage by at least a millennium. The quiet, well-marked rural route ends at **Cabo Fisterra**, the westernmost point of mainland Europe. Below the lighthouse, at a small bronze sculpture of a pair of walking boots, pilgrims traditionally burn their clothes after a dip in the sea to celebrate the end of the journey.

Most pilgrims stay in hostels, called **albergues** or **refugios**, conveniently spaced anywhere from 10 to 20km apart. These provide simple accommodation in dormitories, are usually equipped with hot showers, sometimes have kitchen facilities and charge either a nominal fee of a few euros or ask for a donation. *Albergues* can get crowded in the summer months, and pilgrims sometimes have to sleep on mattresses on the floor. For those who crave a little more comfort, more upmarket choices are often available along the route. As a pilgrim, you'll also receive special treatment at restaurants – most will have a pilgrim *menú* for about €8 – and meals are served earlier than the Spanish norm, at about 8pm.

To prove your pilgrim status at the *albergues*, you'll need a **credencial** (pilgrim passport); it's best to get one in advance from your local pilgrim association (see below), although you can also pick one up at the *albergue* in Roncesvalles. You can then collect *sellos* (stamps, as proof of your pilgrimage) from *albergues*, churches and even some enterprising cafés, and finally show your stamped *credencial* in Santiago in order to get a *compostela* (certificate of pilgrimage). According to the official rules, you need only walk the final 100km of the route, or cycle the last 200km, to be entitled to a *compostela*. If your motives are other than strictly religious, apply for a *certificado* rather than a *compostela*.

It's difficult to lose your way. The *camino* sticks to good tracks and minor roads, is clearly marked with yellow arrows, and mostly passes through populated areas where locals can steer you in the direction of Santiago. Spring and autumn are the **best times to travel**, as the route is quieter than in the busy summer months; most *albergues* are open, and you'll miss the weather extremes of the *meseta* and the mountains. If you're fit and healthy, you can walk from Roncesvalles to Santiago de Compostela in about a month, covering around 25km a day. Nevertheless, it's a good idea to allow for extra time for rest days, unforeseen injuries or just a whimsical decision to linger in one of the lovely towns en route.

Pilgrim associations

Confraternity of St James ⊕020 7928 9988, ⊛www.csj.org.uk. The UK-based Confraternity is the most established and respected English-language pilgrims' association. It promotes research into the *camino*, publishes a newsletter, maintains a library and organizes meetings.

Friends of the Road to Santiago ⊛www.geocities.com/friends_usa_santiago. A US group that publishes a newsletter and produces a popular bulletin board.

Irish Society of the Friends of St James ⊛www.stjamesirl.com. Useful information for Irish pilgrims, including a discussion board.

Little Company of Pilgrims ⊛www.santiago.ca. Canadian organization that publishes a newsletter and offers helpful advice.

quieter rúas da Troia and Porta da Pena, where there's much more outdoor seating. As ever, the **tapas bars** are cheaper and more fun, and the food is often better, too, but there are also plenty of more formal **seafood restaurants**. Many of the tapas places are also busy **drinking** haunts, and with all those students to keep the city buzzing, you'll find further lively **bars** scattered all over the old quarter, as well as along Rúa Nova de Abaixo down in the new town. Locals have been up in arms recently at proposals that all bars should close at 5.30am.

If you're shopping for your own food, don't miss the large covered **Mercado de Abastos**, held daily until 3pm in the old halls of the Praza de Abastos, on the southeast edge of the old city. Thursday is the main market day, but it's also bustling on Saturdays. In addition, tiny delicatessens throughout town sell the traditional breast-shaped **cheese**, the rich *queso de tetilla*, and flat *tarta de Santiago* almond cakes, adorned with crosses in honour of the Apostle; the *tartas* at *El Coral* at Dr Texeiro 32 are particularly renowned.

Santiago is also the best place in Galicia to hear Celtic **music**, played either by solo performers on *gaitas* (bagpipes), or by student ensembles known as *tunas*, who stroll the streets in historic garb at night, especially in summer, playing assorted guitars, mandolins and fiddles.

Tapas bars and restaurants

Abella Rúa do Franco 30. One of this street's many seafood places, with generous portions and good service – try the *caldo gallego* (€2.80).

Don Gaiferos Rúa Nova 23 ☏ 981 583 984. Traditional restaurant, formal without being stuffy, in attractive cellar-like surroundings, where the speciality is superb seafood cuisine, with simple but delicious fish dishes from €21.

Entre-Rúas Callejon de Entre Rúas 2. Excellent seafood *raciones* at this small, unpretentious bar-restaurant, shoehorned into a tiny square up an even tinier alley between rúas Nova and Vilar.

Enxebre *Hostal dos Reis Católicos*, Praza do Obradoiro 1 ☏ 981 582 200. The less formal of the *parador's* two restaurants, housed in the attractive former cellars and with its own entrance just off the square, serves tasty variations on traditional Galego cuisine, with tapas-sized portions as well as daily specials for €17.

Maria Castaña Rúa da Raiña 19 ☏ 981 560 137. This delightful, cosy bar/restaurant, with rough-hewn tables and exposed stone, serves delicious food at reasonable rather than rock-bottom prices, from simple seafood tapas to paella-like fish *cazolos* for €27, and has bottles of fine Galego wine at very affordable prices.

Sant Yago Rúa da Raiña 12. Smoked hams and cheese are the speciality at this friendly, charming little tapas bar, but the tortillas and seafood are every bit as good, and very well priced, with almost nothing costing over €10, and a €13 *menú del día*. Aim to eat in the bar rather than the upstairs dining room.

Los Sobriños del Padre Benito de la Casa del Buen Pulpo Fonte de San Miguel 7. The long-winded name belies the simplicity, and quality, of the *pulpo* (octopus), *tortilla* and other tapas at this very plain little local restaurant, which has a few pavement tables, and serves white china jugs full of wine for just €4.

O Triángulo das Verduras Praciña das Penas 2 ☏ 981 576 212. Vegetarian restaurant with a creative flair, and an emphasis on organic ingredients.

Bars

Bar Chocolatería Metate Travesa de San Paio Antealteres. A must for chocolate fans; housed in a former chocolate factory, it offers a large menu of hot and cold alcohol- and non-alcohol-based chocolate drinks, in addition to more usual beverages.

Cafeteria *Hostal dos Reis Católicos*, Praza do Obradoiro 1. On a summer evening, the outdoor terrace at the *parador*, with views back towards the cathedral and out to the green hills, makes the perfect spot to linger over a sunset cocktail.

Café Casino Rúa do Vilar 35. With its deep sofas and wood panelling, plus outdoor seating on the old stone lane, this venerable café/tea room has a real old-world charm.

Café Derby Rúa das Orfas 29. This classic old café-bar between the old quarter and the Praza da Galicia and kitted out with dark-wood panelling, green leather barstools and bentwood chairs, has been a favourite local rendezvous for over eighty years.

Café Literarios Praza da Quintana. The terrace of this popular café, at the top of the broad stairs in the square behind the cathedral, makes a perfect venue for peaceful people-watching.

Casa das Crechas Via Sacra 5. Well-known folk bar just behind the Praza da Quintana, often with live Galego, Celtic or international folk music. Hanging *brujas* and a first-rate draught Kilkenny complete the effect.

O Filandón Rúa da Azabachería 6. Thread your way through the simple cheese and wine shop at the front to find a narrow, bustling bar in the cave-like space at the back, where students and wine-lovers enjoy cheap, high-quality local *vinos* and free morsels. Closed Sun.

Momo Virxen da Cerca 23. A popular hangout with wide-ranging appeal, full of students during term-time. Fantastic and varied decor includes Parisian-style mini café-bars, an outdoor terrace and a jungle dancefloor.

Paraiso Perdido Rúa Antealtares 3. Cavernous, mysterious bar that tunnels deeply away from a tiny square not far east of Praza da Quintana, with endless eclectically decorated subterranean nooks and crannies. The €4.50 *mojitos* are recommended.

San Jaime Rúa da Raiña 4. All the usual tapas are available inside this little bar, but the best reason to come is to nab one of the few tables on the pretty Praza de Fonseca, and enjoy the finest *chocolate con churros* in town.

Listings

Airlines Labacolla airport is served by a number of airlines, including Ryanair, Iberia, Air Europa and Spanair.

Bookshops Variable secondhand selection, including foreign-language titles, from Foas Veas, Rúa da Rosa 30, in the new town.

Bus information ☎ 981 542 416, ⊛ www.tussa.org.

Car rental Avis and Europcar have offices at the RENFE train station and the airport, Hertz at the airport only.

Internet cafés *Ciber Nova50* at the top end of Rúa Nova is very central, while *Mundonet*, Rúa Xelmírez 19, just off Plaza Praterías, will also look after backpacks.

Laundry Lavandería la Económica is a self-service launderette at Rúa Ramón Cabanillas 1, off Praza Roxa, a few blocks west of Praza de Galicia.

Post office Rúa das Orfas 17, pending the refurbishment of the main office on Rúa do Franco.

Trains RENFE information ☎ 902 240 202, ⊛ www.renfe.es; information and booking also available from travel agents in town.

The Rías Altas

Galicia's north coast has been ravaged by the ocean into a series of dramatic bays and estuaries known as the **Rías Altas** (High Estuaries). As you approach from Asturias, the coastline becomes noticeably more desolate, the road twisting around rocky inlets where wind-lashed villages cling to the shore, backed by eucalyptus forests and wild-looking hills. Driving is slow, though the final westward stretch of the **FEVE railway**, from Luarca to Ferrol, is perhaps the most picturesque of the entire route.

Ribadeo and around

RIBADEO, the easternmost Galego town and *ría*, has little to offer beyond a certain crumbling charm. Its finest architecture is concentrated around the Praza de España, site of the **turismo** (July & Aug Mon–Sat 10.30am–2pm & 4–8pm, Sun 10.30am–2pm; Sept–June Mon–Fri 10.30am–2pm & 4–7pm, Sat 10.30am–2pm & 4–8pm, Sun 10.30am–2pm; ☎ 982 128 689, ⊛ www.ribadeo .org). The **Palacio del Marquès de Sargadelos**, opposite, with its unusual decorative tower, is the town's main monument.

The pick of Ribadeo's **accommodation** has to be the modern *parador*, not far south at Rúa Amador Fernández 7 (☎ 982 128 825, ⊛ www.parador .es; ⑤), facing the green fields of Asturias across the Eo estuary. Its rooms spill down the riverbank in successive sunny tiers, each with its own glassed-in gallery. The *Mediante*, Praza de España 16 (☎ 982 130 453, ⊛ www .hotelmediante.com; ⑥), is a cheaper alternative. Immediately beneath the main road bridge across from Asturias, a short walk from Ribadeo's tiny and somewhat faded harbour, you'll find a quite superb seafood **restaurant**, the *San Miguel* (☎ 982 129 717).

Thanks to its succession of fine beaches, the coast immediately west of Ribadeo has been subject to almost continuous low-level strip development. It's well worth stopping at the **Praia As Catedrais**, however, 6km along, where low tide reveals a procession of extraordinary natural arches, towering from a stark sandscape. The waves are usually too strong for swimming, but it's an unforgettable spot for coastal hiking, along a network of boardwalks. There's a **campsite** another 6km west at Benquerencia (☎ 982 124 450, ⊛ www .campingbenquerencia.com).

Viveiro

VIVEIRO, 60km west of Ribadeo, has become more of a tourist centre than a port, with holiday homes spreading up the hillsides of the *ría* and along its many **beaches**. The old town, however, remains protected by the vestiges of its Renaissance walls. Largely closed to traffic, its narrow streets are lined with glass-fronted houses in delicate wooden frames.

The large **Praia de Covas** is a good ten-minutes' walk from town across a causeway, while the pick of several more peaceful beaches around the bay is the **Praia de Faro**, further up towards the open sea.

Viveiro's **turismo** is 100m north of the old town on the waterfront Avenida de la Marina (mid-June to mid-Sept Mon–Sat 11am–2pm & 5–8pm; ☎982 560 879). The **bus station** stands immediately opposite, while the **FEVE station** (3–4 trains daily in each direction to Ribadeo and Ferrol) is a ten-minute walk south.

Central places **to stay** include *Hotel Orfeo*, Rúa García Navia Castrillón 2 (☎982 562 101, ⓦwww.hotelorfeo.net; ❸), which has smart but characterless rooms overlooking the bay, and the cheaper *Hostal Vila*, Rúa Nicolás Montenegro 57 (☎982 561 331, ⓦwww.hotel-vila.net; ❸), in a drab street just outside the walls at the Porta del Vallado. There's also a **campsite** behind the Praia de Covas, *Viveiro* (☎982 560 004; closed Oct–May).

Places **to eat** are surprisingly hard to find: *Restaurante O Muro*, near the bus station on Avenida Cervantes, is a busy, functional *pulpería* and grill with a wide menu of fish and meats, while the more formal *Asador*, southwest of the square at Rua Melitòn Cortiñas 15, serves excellent but reasonably priced seafood.

Porto do Barqueiro and Ortigueira

West of Viveiro, shorefront development finally thins out, and the scenery grows ever more dramatic. The next two *ría* villages (and FEVE stops) are **PORTO DO BARQUEIRO**, 16km along, a tiny and very picturesque fishing port of slate-roofed houses near Spain's northernmost point, and the larger **ORTIGUEIRA**, 14km farther on, set amid a dark mass of pines and host to July's musical extravaganza, the International Festival of the Celtic World (see p.556).

Places to stay dotted around the tiny harbour at Porto do Barqueiro include the stylish and very comfortable *Hotel O Forno* (☎981 414 124; ❸). Ortigueira, too, has some decent hotels, including the *Perla*, Avda. de la Penela 105 (☎981 400 150; ❸), and the *Monterrey*, Avda. Franco 105 (☎981 400 135; ❷).

San Andrés de Teixido and Cedeira

While the FEVE heads inland after Ortigueira, drivers can make a worthwhile side-trip to the hermitage at **SAN ANDRÉS DE TEIXIDO**, the so-called Mecca of the Galegos. The tortuous road up here leaves the main AC862 at **Mera**, 9km west of Ortigueira, and climbs for a magnificent 12km farther, high above the coast, threading in and out of the pine forests into rolling clifftop meadows and bare heathland. The cliffs at **Vixia de Herbeira**, just short of the sanctuary, are said to be the tallest in Europe, at over 600m, while the church itself perches high above the ocean. Like so many of Galicia's sanctuaries, it is based on a pre-Christian religious site, but a monastery was already in place by the twelfth century. It now welcomes coachloads of *Galego* pilgrims, so the adjoining hamlet holds a café as well as plenty of souvenir stalls.

CEDEIRA, 12km southwest of San Andrés in its own attractive little *ría*, is a graceful port where elegant houses and pleasant tapas bars line the shaded, canalized mouth of a little stream, while a huge beach sweeps south. The best central **accommodation** is in the *Hostal Brisas*, Rúa Calvo Sotelo 19 (℡981 481 054; ❷), but the startling modern *Hotel Herbeira* commands great views of the beach and town from a hillside 1km to the south (℡981 492 167, ⓦwww .hotelherbeira.com; ❹), and has a large pool.

Ferrol

Historically one of Spain's principal naval bases and dockyards, the city of **FERROL** has struggled to survive the collapse of the shipbuilding industry. Unfortunately, the navy and dockyards have usurped the best of the coastline, leaving a provincial centre dominated by a status-conscious, navy-oriented community and a paint-spattered statue of El Caudillo (the Chief), **Francisco Franco**, who was born here in 1892. Although frequently considered a bastion of conservatism, Ferrol was also the birthplace of Pablo Iglesias, founder of the Spanish Socialist Party, whose government initially steered the country through the transitional years after the dictatorship.

Ferrol's **FEVE** and **RENFE** stations are in the same building, while the **bus station** is just outside. There's a seafront *parador*, housed in a fine Galego mansion at Rúa Almirante Fernández Martín (℡981 356 720, ⓦwww .parador.es; ❺), while the en-suite rooms at the central *Hostal Real*, Rúa Dolores 11–13 (℡981 369 255; ❷), are great value. For good **tapas**, simply stroll the length of Rúa Madalena, where *A Palloza* and *Bodega 147* are recommended pit stops.

Betanzos

Although Ferrol stands roughly opposite A Coruña, 20km across the mouth of the **Ría de Betanzos**, it's a seventy-kilometre trip by road or rail. The coast between the two is surprisingly rural, with the contours of the *ría* speckled with forests and secluded beaches. On the way, the ancient town of **BETANZOS**, 20km southeast of A Coruña, is built on a pre-Roman site so old that what was once a steep seafront hill is now located well inland at the confluence of the Mendo and Mandeo rivers. The base of the hill is surrounded by fragments of medieval walls, now largely built over.

You have to approach Betanzos via its dispiriting modern outskirts, but once you reach the attractive main square, **Praza dos Irmáns García Naveira**, you're just below its appealing hilltop old quarter. A short walk up from here brings you to the much smaller Praza da Constitución, home to the Gothic church of Santiago. Within the mass of twisting and tunnelling narrow streets immediately below stands the twelfth-century church of **Santa María do Azougue**, while the tomb of Conde Fernán Perez de Andrade "O Boo" (The Good), who commissioned its construction, lies in the Gothic **Igrexa de San Francisco** opposite.

Just behind the main square, in Rúa Emilio Romay, the excellent **Museo das Mariñas** (summer Mon–Fri 10am–2pm & 4–7pm, Sat 10.30am–1pm; €1.20) provides a fascinating insight into the history of Betanzos and neighbouring *mariñas* (sea-facing villages), including a colourful collection of period costumes.

Practicalities

Driving in central Betanzos is all but impossible; park down by the river, and walk up from there. The local **turismo** is on the main square (summer daily 10am–2pm & 5–8pm; winter Mon–Fri 10am–2pm & 4.30–7.30pm, Sat

10.30am–1pm; ℡981 776 666, ⓦwww.betanzos.net). **Buses** from A Coruña pull up just behind the square, while those from Ferrol arrive at the Betanzos Ciudad RENFE **train station**, ten-minutes' walk south, which is only used by the four daily trains between Ferrol and A Coruña. Other trains use the Betanzos Infesta station, 2.5km away at the top of a steep climb.

   Accommodation options are limited, but the central *Hotel Los Garelos*, Rúa Afonso IX 8 (℡981 775 922, ⓦwww.hotelgarelos.com; ❹), offers smart en-suite rooms. **Eating and drinking** possibilities largely centre on the row of attractive bars under the stone arcades of the main square, and the two tiny alleys that drop down between them. The popular *O Pote* on the first alley, the Travesía do Progreso, has a wide range of good tapas, or you can eat outdoors, under the arcades, at *Casa Carmen*, Rúa da Fonte de Unta 12, which specializes in *tortilla de Betanzos*, an omelette that sandwiches layers of spinach and tomato. *Café Versailles* on the square itself is a lovely Modernist café with decorative dark wood-panelling.

   If you're in Betanzos on August 16, don't miss the **Fiesta del Globo**, the highlight of which is the midnight launch from the Torre de Santo Domingo in the main square of the world's largest paper balloon, daubed with political slogans. There is also a medieval **festival** in the second weekend of July, when the town is transported back to the times of the Andrade lords.

A Coruña

The fine port of **A CORUÑA** centres on a narrow peninsula that juts from Galicia's northern coast, 64km north of Santiago. A broad headland curves in both directions from the end of that peninsula to create two large bays: one faces across to Ferrol, and shelters a large harbour, while the other lies open to the Atlantic, and is lined by a long sandy beach. In the dynamic city in between, a five-minute walk takes you from a bustling modern port to a relaxed resort, by way of old stone alleyways where tantalizing restaurants, tapas bars and night-spots jostle for attention.

Arrival and information

A Coruña's **bus** and **train** stations are on either side of Praza de Madrid. To reach the city centre, walk twenty minutes north, or take bus #1 or #1a to the Praza de María Pita (all city buses €1).

   Driving in A Coruña is extremely difficult and unrewarding; no map could do justice to the tangle of dead-end and one-way streets in the old quarter, and it's best to park as soon as possible, ideally in the central, underground **Los Cantones** car park.

   The **regional turismo** is at the Dársena de la Marina (Mon–Fri 10am–2pm & 4–7pm, Sat & Sun 11am–2pm; ℡981 221 822, ⓦwww.turgalicia.es), while a glass kiosk in the Praza de María Pita holds the **city turismo** (April–Sept Mon–Fri 9am–8.30pm, Sat 10am–2pm & 4–8pm, Sun 10am–3pm; Oct–March closed Mon–Fri 2.30–4pm; ℡618 790 665, ⓦwww.turismocoruna.com).

   A bright yellow **tourist tram** loops between the Dársena de la Marina, the Torre de Hercules and the beaches (July & Aug daily noon–9.20pm; every 20min; Sept–June Sat & Sun noon–7pm; hourly; €1). The **Coruña Card**, sold at the *turismo*, allows unlimited rides on the trams, free admission to the Torre de Hercules, and discounts on other attractions, for 48 hours; it costs €7 for one adult and one child, €15 for two adults and two children.

Casa das Ciencias

Arteixo, Fisterra & Carballo

CALVO SOTELO

PRAZA DE PORTUGAL

Casa de las Sciencias

Palacio de Congresos

ACCOMMODATION

Hostal Alborán	**F**
Hostal Centro Gallego	**A**
Hotel G. Hesperia Finisterre	**G**
Pensión El Parador	**C**
Hostal La Perla	**E**
Hostal Roma	**B**
Hostal Sol	**D**

AV. DE FISTERRA
ALFREDO VICENTI
AV. RUBINE
AV. 8. AIRES

DE LUGO

JUAN FLÓREZ

PRAZA DE VIGO

EL FERROL
BETANZOS
FONSECA
COMPOSTELA

PRAZA DE PONTEVEDRA

AV. LINARES RIVAS

PRAZA DE OURENSE

PIERAO UNIFICADO SANTA LUCÍA Y LINARES RIVAS

SÁNCHEZ BREGUA

C. JUANA DE VEGA

DURÁN LORIGA

Praia do Riazor

La Coraza

Enseada do Orzán

Casa Museo Picasso

Rosaleda

PIERAO DE LA BATERÍA

La Terraza

Estación Marítima

PIERAO DE CALVO SOTELO

Praia do Orzán

LOS CANTONES
ESTRELLA
RÚA NUEVA
RÚA ALTA
BARRE DE LA MAZA
JUAN CANALEJO

@

A
B
1

Xardins de Méndez Núñez

C

Kiosko Alfonso

OLMOS
GALERA
REAL
DE SAN ANDRÉS

2

Igrexa de S. Andrés

SOL
DE ORZÁN
CORREÓN

ROTONDA DO MATADERO

C. DEL HOSPITAL

Gobierno Civil

3
4

E

D

DE ZALAETA

Conv. de las Capuchinas

C. PANADERAS
SAN ROQUE

PIERAO DE TRANSATLÁNTICOS

Porto da Coruña

Dársena da Marina

AV. DA MARINA
RIEGO DE AGUA
FRANJA

S. NICOLÁS

San Nicolás

PL. DE S. AGUSTÍN

Mercado

MERCADO

5

F
6

Puerta Real

S. Jorge

PR. DE ESPAÑA

i

PRAZA MARÍA PITA

AV. DE LA MARINA

Galerías Coruñesas

Palacio Municipal

M. ASTRAY

PASEO MARÍTIMO
PASEO MARÍTIMO
VERAMAR

P. DE LA DÁRSENA
SANTIAGO
TABERNAS

Igrexa de Santiago

G

Colegiata de Santa María del Campo

NTRA SRA DEL ROSARIO
HERRERÍAS
ZAPATERÍA
MAESTRANZA

OLD TOWN

P. DEL PARROTE

Casa de la Cultura

CORTADURÍA

PASEO MARÍTIMO

Enseada de San Amaro

S. FRANCISCO

Xardín de San Carlos

Hospital Militar

Museo Militar

Convento de Santo Domingo

Xardíns da Maestranza

Museo Arqueolóxico e Histórico

PASEO SIR JOHN MOORE

Casino
Club Náutico

EATING & DRINKING

Bar Suso	**3**
Mesón do Pulpo	**6**
Otros Tiempos	**2**
Coral	**5**
El Serrano	**4**
Taberna Los Olmos	**1**

Z

0   100 m

Accommodation

Whatever your budget, the pedestrian streets that approach Praza María Pita and the old town are the best hunting grounds for **accommodation**, though if you're driving you won't be able to park nearby.

Hostal Alborán Rúa Riego de Agua 14 ☎981 226 579, ⓦwww.hostalalboran.com. Excellent location near Praza María Pita, with thirty comfortable rooms, all with bath and TV, and some with balconies overlooking the attractive pedestrianized street. ❷

Hostal Centro Gallego Rúa Estrella 2 ☎981 222 236. The simple rooms at this budget hotel, above a bar, are great value for such a central location. ❷

Hostal La Perla Rúa Torreiro 11 ☎981 226 700. Friendly, spacious rooms with TV and bathroom, a short way from Praza María Pita and the best tapas bars. ❷

Hostal Sol Rúa Sol 10 ☎981 210 362. Behind the unprepossessing modern exterior, with its bordello-style flashing sign, the rooms are stylish and comfortable. ❸

Hotel G. Hesperia Finisterre Paseo del Parrote 2 ☎981 205 400, ⓦwww.hesperia-finisterre.com. The top option in town, this vast orange waterfront five-star comes complete with tennis courts, Olympic-size swimming pool and every conceivable luxury. ❻

Pensión El Parador Rúa Los Olmos 15 ☎981 222 121. Very clean, spruce en-suite rooms, with floor-to-ceiling windows, above a small bar in a pedestrian street that can get noisy at night. ❷

Pensión Roma Rúa Nueva 3 ☎981 228 075, ⓦwww.pensionroma.com. Good-value, clean, modern rooms with TV and bathroom, plus internet access. Closed Oct–June. ❸

The City

A Coruña is known as the "City of Glass", thanks to the distinctive glass-fronted galleries of its sea-facing houses. Originally designed so local residents, whose lives were so intertwined with the ocean, could watch the activity of the harbour in shelter, these form a magnificent ensemble. Rising to six or more storeys, they stretch along the Avenida da Marina in front of the port.

The heart of the city, just inland, is the colonnaded **Praza de María Pita**. A Coruña's role as the departure point for the Spanish Armada in 1588 earned it a retaliatory visit from Sir Francis Drake the following year. His attack was only repelled when a humble local heroine, María Pita, killed the English standard-bearer; her spear-waving statue now dominates the square.

To the east, the narrow and atmospheric streets of the **old town** wind around the Romanesque churches of **Santiago** and **Santa María del Campo**, and are shielded from the sea by a high wall. A small walled garden, the **Xardín de San Carlos**, holds the tomb of English general Sir John Moore, who died in battle near A Coruña in 1809 during the British retreat from the French during the Peninsular Wars. A wall nearby holds poet Charles Wolfe's contemporary lines describing his original hasty battlefield burial – "Not a drum was heard, not a funeral note" – along with a similarly melancholic offering by Galicia's most famous poet, Rosalía de Castro.

Beyond here, on a former island at the port entrance, the restored Castelo San Antón was once a garrison and, until the 1960s, a military and political prison. Today it houses the **Museo Arqueolóxico e Histórico** (July & Aug Tues–Sat 10am–9pm, Sun 10am–3pm; Sept–June Tues–Sat 10am–7pm, Sun 10am–2.30pm; €2). As well as fascinating ancient finds, including pre-Christian gold jewellery, it holds an unusual full-size replica of an Iron Age wicker and leather boat.

Although the site of A Coruña was home to the Iron Age Artabri tribe, one of whose hillforts can still be seen at nearby Elviña, it was the Romans who built the landmark **Torre de Hercules** (April–June & Sept daily 10am–7pm; July & Aug Mon–Thurs & Sun 10am–9pm, Fri & Sat 10am–midnight; Oct–March daily 10am–6pm; €2). Said to be the world's only still-functioning Roman lighthouse, it dominates the northern tip of the headland, amid a

▲ Glass-fronted houses, Avenida da Marina

sweeping expanse of grass and heather. It's an impressive spectacle, though it was rebuilt in the eighteenth century and only a few foundation stones from the Roman era remain on show. The views from the top, out over the Atlantic and back to the city, are superb.

A state-of-the-art **Aquarium** (July & Aug daily 10am–9pm; Sept–June Mon–Fri 10am–7pm, Sat & Sun 10am–8pm; €10) stands on the next headland along. Far more than just a series of fish tanks, it offers a vast array of interactive displays that will delight adults and children alike, as well as the 4.5-million-litre *Nautilus* tank, which submerges you into a world filled with the marine life of the Atlantic coast. Follow the Paseo Marítimo around to reach the superbly designed **Museo Domus** (Museum of Mankind; daily: July & Aug 11am–9pm; Sept–June 10am–7pm; ⓦ www.casaciencias.org; €2), which takes visitors on an educational trip around the workings of the human body. At the other end of the peninsula, in a tower atop a hill in the lovely little Parque Santa Margarita, the **Casa das Ciencias** (House of Science; same hours and admission fee) is an enjoyable interactive science museum, intended mainly for kids, and filled with gadgets to play with.

South of the Museo Domus, on the opposite side of the peninsula from the Dársena, lies the sweeping golden arc of the city's main beaches, **Praia do Orzán** and the contiguous **Praia de Riazor**. They're surprisingly clean and unpolluted, and you need to arrive early in summer to grab a prime spot.

Pablo Picasso lived in A Coruña from the ages of 9 to 13, and produced his first oil paintings here. The **Casa Museo Picasso**, his former home at Payó Gomez 14, can be visited by appointment (closed Sun & Mon; ☎981 184 278; free); it's of interest mainly for its authentic (but not original) period furnishings rather than the few reproduced paintings by both Pablo and his father.

Eating, drinking and nightlife

The small streets leading west from Praza de María Pita, from Rúa da Franxa, through to Rúa La Galera, Rúa Los Olmos and Rúa Estrella, are crowded with bars that offer some of Spain's tastiest **seafood**. The cluster of *marisquerías* on

Rúa da Franxa includes the popular *Mesón do Pulpo* at no. 9; further on lie plenty of seafood tapas bars – try *Bar Suso* at Rúa La Galera 31 or *Taberna Los Olmos* at Rúa Los Olmos 22 – and good *jamonerías*, such as *Otros Tiempos* at Rúa La Galera 56 and *El Serrano* at no. 23. If you prefer to dine more formally, the pick of the waterfront **restaurants** along the Avenida da Marina nearby is the *Coral*, set slightly back in a tiny square at Rúa da Estacada 9 (☎981 200 569).

In summer, the beachfront **bars** across the peninsula do a roaring trade. Another good place to start the evening is Rúa Orillamar, where bars such as *Nectar* and *A Repichoca* are always full at weekends. For **late-night** action, *A Cova Folk* and *A Cova Celtica* on Rúa do Orzan have live *Galego* music, while the perennial *Pirámide* on the same street is a Latin nightclub.

Listings

Bookshops Librería Colón, Rúa Riego de Agua 24, has possibly Galicia's best selection of English-language books, plus a wide range of foreign newspapers.

Football A Coruña's football team, Deportivo (⊛www .canaldeportivo.com), which consistently finishes in the top half of La Liga, plays its home matches, usually on a Sun evening, at the Estadio del Riazor, just metres from the beach west of the city centre.

Internet Access at Comunicopy, Rúa Angel 19 (July & Aug Mon–Fri 10am–4pm; Sept–June Mon–Fri 10am–8pm, Sat 10am–2pm).

Laundry Laundromats are located on Avda. Conchiñas, Avda. Fisterra and at Rúa Juan Florez 63.

Post Office Main post office is on Avda. da Marina.

The Costa da Morte

Wild, windy and occasionally desolate, the **Costa da Morte**, west of A Coruña, is often passed over by tourists heading south to the beaches of the Rías Baixas. But while the Costa da Morte lacks both the climate and the infrastructure for large-scale tourism, it boasts equally beautiful coves, tiny fishing villages huddled against the headlands, and forested mountain slopes aplenty.

Its fearsome name, which means Coast of Death, stems from the constant buffeting the shoreline receives from the Atlantic waves. The most notorious of the countless **shipwrecks** that litter the seabed is the oil tanker *Prestige*, which snapped in two following a ferocious storm in 2002. The release of its 77,000 tonnes of crude oil had disastrous consequences for marine life, as well as Galicia's fishing and tourism. Over 16,000 fishermen and 6500 fishing boats were grounded for months, and 662 of Spain's 1064 beaches (437 in Galicia alone) were affected by oil, which travelled as far east as southwestern France. Thanks to the extraordinary efforts of thousands of volunteers and troops, however, barely a trace of oil remained just twelve months later.

The coast from **Camariñas to Fisterra** is the most exposed and westerly stretch of all. Ever since a Roman expedition under Lucius Florus Brutus was brought up short by what seemed to be an endless sea, it has been known as *finis terrae* (the end of the world), and it is not hard to see why. This is prime territory, however, for hunting *percebes* (barnacles), one of Galicia's most popular and expensive seafood delicacies, which have to be scooped up from the very waterline. Collectors are commonly swept away by the dreaded "seventh wave", which can appear out of nowhere from a calm sea.

While it's well worth following the coastal road right the way to Fisterra, you'll need to allow plenty of time. **Driving** is slow, and, with no train lines,

buses (predominantly operated by Monbus; ⓦwww.monbus.es) are the only public transport option.

You should also be warned that even where the isolated coves do shelter fine beaches, you will rarely find resort facilities. While the beaches may look splendid, braving the water is recommended for only the strongest of swimmers, and the climate is significantly wetter and windier here than it is a mere 100km or so further south.

Malpica de Bergantiños

Few potential stopping points lie immediately west of A Coruña. If you're driving, take the toll motorway to its end at the busy inland road junction of **Carballo**. Heading north from there for 15km brings you to **MALPICA DE BERGANTIÑOS**, the first of a succession of tiny seaside ports. Crammed onto the neck of a narrow peninsula, Malpica consists of a harbour on one side and a marvellous – though exposed – beach hardly 100m away on the other. *Hostal Panchito*, overlooking the fishing boats at Praza Villar Amigo 6 (☎981 720 307; ❸), has smart **rooms** with private bath, while *San Francisco*, Rúa Eduardo Pondal, is a good seafood **restaurant**, where you can choose your dinner from a tankful of live sea creatures.

The best local beach, the sheltered **Praia de Niñons**, is roughly 6km west. Follow signs for **Corme**, then turn right at the village of Niñons, from where narrow lanes thread through fields of maize to the sea. A granite church with a *fuente* (fountain) stands guard just above the beach itself, a crescent of thick sand that stretches out to either side of a little stream. Young Spaniards set up fireside campsites here in summer, but the solitary bar isn't open at night.

Laxe and Traba

Some 24km southwest from Malpica, having crossed the River Anllóns via an ancient bridge at **Ponteceso**, the coast road reaches **LAXE** (pronounced "la-shay"), which offers the area's safest swimming. A formidable seawall protects a small harbour, while the long sweep of fine, clean sand is backed by café-lined streets. The most appealing **place to stay** is the *Hostal Bahía*, above a burger bar at Avda. Generalísimo 24 (☎981 728 304; ❸), where all rooms are en suite and some have seaview balconies. Housed in an ancient archway that leads off the attractive little seafront square not far north, Praza Rámon Juega, the *Casa do Arco* is the best local **restaurant**, though there are cheaper tapas bars nearby.

Just outside Laxe are two beaches, the deserted **Praia de Soesto**, which, though exposed, more than rivals the town beach, and a perfect cove, the **Praia de Arnado**. **TRABA**, 6km south, has its own massively long beach, the **Praia de Traba**, remote as anything, and backed by sand dunes and a jigsaw of mini-fields.

Camariñas and Muxía

Another 25km on from Laxe, picturesque **CAMARIÑAS** marks the start of Galicia's wild west, at the region's westernmost extremity. Its seafront buildings are almost entirely modern, curled around an attractive harbour that holds a fishing fleet as well as the yachts of well-heeled visitors. **Accommodation** prices are surprisingly low. The nicest rooms at the lovely little flower-bedecked ⚘ *Hotel Puerto Arnela*, facing the sea at Praza del Carmen 20 (☎981 705 477; ❸), have their own balconies, while *Pension Gaviota*, set slightly back on Rúa do Rio (☎981 736 030, ⓔhostalgaviota@hotmail.com; ❷), is a good

▲ The rocks at Muxía

cheaper option. The *Café Bar Playa*, in the centre of the harbour, serves great-value tapas and *raciones*.

A five-kilometre trek from Camariñas leads to the lighthouse at **Cabo Vilán**, guarding the treacherous shore on a rocky outcrop; climb the adjacent rocks for a stunning sea view. Winds whip viciously around the cape, and the huge, sci-fi propellers of the adjacent wind farm spin eerily, lit by the searchlight beam of the lighthouse once darkness falls.

On the tip of a rocky promontory across the *ría* from Camariñas, the small port of **MUXÍA** itself is nothing special. Make your way up to the Romanesque church on the hill above, though, and there's a fabulous view to either side of the headland. Paths lead down to the eighteenth-century **Santuario da Virxe da Barca**, where a massive sea-level church marks what was once an important site of Galicia's pre-Christian animist cult. The cult was centred around the strange granite rocks at the farthest point of the headland, some of which are precariously balanced and said to make wonderful sounds when struck correctly; others supposedly have healing power. In later times, the rocks were reinterpreted as being the remains of the stone ship that brought the Virgin to the aid of Santiago, an obvious echo of the saint's own landing at Padrón. There's great **seafood** at the tiny, tumbledown *Casa Marujita*, up left from the far end of the seafront road.

Corcubión and Estorde

Twenty kilometres south of Muxía, or 100km from A Coruña along the direct inland road (C552), the port of **CORCUBIÓN** serves as the gateway to Fisterra. Though ribbon-strip development now joins it to its industrialized neighbour **Cée**, it retains a certain elegance. The best place to stay near here is the delightful if somewhat isolated **hostal**, the *Praia de Estorde* (☎981 745 585; ❸), which commands a fine white-sand beach that nestles in a small cove at **ESTORDE**, 7km west and 1km short of the larger village of **Sardiñeiro**.

Just across the road, there's a small wooded **campsite**, *Ruta de Finisterre* (☎981 746 302; closed mid-Sept to mid-June).

Fisterra

The town of **FISTERRA** (**Finisterre**) still looks like it's about to drop off the end of the earth. On a misty, out-of-season day, it can feel no more than a grey clump of houses wedged into the rocks, but it puts on a cheerier face in the summer sunshine. Just beyond the western end of its long harbour wall, a tiny bay cradles a pretty little beach, overlooked by an ancient chapel. The *Casa Velay* here is the cheapest **hostal** around (☎981 740 127; ❶), while the *Rivas*, Estrada de Faro (☎981 740 027; ❷), is also excellent value; the *Finisterre*, Rúa Federico Ávila 8 (☎981 740 000; ❸), is a larger, more upscale alternative. For **food**, bypass the fancier restaurants with giant lobster tanks and head for the south side of the harbour, where you'll find a cluster of places with *sardiñadas* (open-air sardine grills) and fresh *mariscos*. *Bar Galeria*, Rúa Real 25, is a lively bar with good music.

The actual tip of the **headland** lies 4km beyond, first along a heathered mountainside, then through a pine-forest plantation. Stop on the way out of town at **Santa María das Areas**, a small but atmospheric church with a beautiful carved altar, which, like the strange weathered tombs left of the main door, is considerably older than the rest of the building. At the cape itself, a squat, square lighthouse perches high above the waves. When, as so often, the whole place is shrouded in thick mist and the mournful foghorn wails across the sea, it's an eerie spot. Traditionally, this is where pilgrims would burn their clothes, signalling the end of the pilgrimage, and also collect their scallop shell; the wearing of a scallop throughout the journey is a relatively recent phenomenon. *O Semaforo*, right at the lighthouse, offers five upscale guest rooms and serves a €20 lunch *menú* (☎981 725 869, ⓦwww.finisterrae.com/semaforo; closed Nov; ❺), or you can get tapas at *O Refuxio*, the bar below.

Ezaro, O Pindo and Carnota

Around **EZARO**, where the Río Xallas meets the sea, the scenery is marvellous. The rocks of the sheer escarpments above the road are so rich in minerals that they are multicoloured, and glisten beneath innumerable tiny waterfalls. Upstream there are warm, natural lagoons and more cascades. Continue another couple of kilometres to the little, far from picturesque port of **O PINDO**, beneath a stony but thickly wooded hill dotted with old houses. As well as a small beach, this holds a handful of pleasant **places to stay**, including *A Revolta* (☎981 764 864; ❷), which has a recommended *marisquería*, and the sea-view *Pensión Sol E Mar* (☎981 760 298; ❷).

Towards Carnota, the series of short beaches finally joins together into one long, unbroken line of dunes, swept by the Atlantic winds. The village of **CARNOTA** is a couple of kilometres from the shore, but its palm trees and old church are still thoroughly caked in salt. Reaching the beach requires you to follow a long wooden boardwalk across the marshes.

Ría de Muros e Noia

The **Rías Baixas**, much the most touristed portion of Galicia's coastline, starts in the north with the **Ría de Muros e Noia**. In truth, it's so close to the Costa da Morte that there's little difference in climate or appearance, and it remains relatively underdeveloped, but unspoiled little **Muros** is well worth visiting.

Muros

Some of the best traditional Galego architecture outside Pontevedra can be found in the old town of **MUROS**, enhanced by a marvellous natural setting at the widest point of the Ría de Muros, just before it meets the sea. The town rises in tiers of narrow streets from the curving waterfront, where fishing boats unload their catch, to the Romanesque Iglesia de San Pedro. Everywhere you look are squat granite columns and arches, flights of wide steps, and benches and stone porches built into the house fronts. There's also a nice – though small – **beach** on the edge of town next to the road to Fisterra.

A seasonal **turismo** (July to mid-Sept Mon–Fri 10am–2pm & 4–7pm, Sat 10.30am–3pm, Sun 11am–2pm & 4–9pm; ☎981 826 050, ⓦwww.muros.es) is located in the central square, where the coast road bends. The pick of the seafront **hostales** has to be the lovely *Hostal Ría de Muros* at Rúa Castelao 53 (☎981 826 056; ❸), where two of the spacious and tastefully furnished double rooms on the top storey have balconies and great sea views. Another *hostales* stretches back from the road nearby: *J Lago*, Rúa Castelao 3 (☎981 827 503; ❷). Commanding a majestic panorama of the bay from the hillside above town, and reached via a ferociously steep narrow road, ⚘ *Jallambau Rural*, Lugar de Milla-flores (☎981 826 056, ⓦwww.jallambaurural.com; ❹), is a superbly equipped and positioned four-room **B&B** that can also be rented in its entirety as a holiday home.

As for **places to eat**, *Pulpería Pachanga*, Rúa Castelao 29, has a stone-vaulted interior, fresh seafood and grilled meats, while the Praza da Pescadería, a block back from the seafront behind the *Ría de Muros*, holds several good café-restaurants, including the *Xamonería O Varadoiro*, a cheap ham, cheese and tapas place. Monbus **bus** services stop across from the *Ría de Muros*.

Noia

NOIA (Noya), 25km east of Muros near the head of the *ría*, is, according to a legend fanciful even by Galego standards, named after Noah, whose Ark is supposed to have struck land nearby. Scarcely less absurd is Noia's claim to be a "Little Florence", on the strength of a couple of nice churches and an arcaded street. *Hospedería Valadares*, Rúa Egás Móniz 1 (☎981 820 436, ⓦwww.hospederiavaladares.com; ❷), offers simple **rooms** a short walk from the old core.

Castro de Baroña

From Noia the AC301 heads inland through deep, lush gorges towards Padrón. To trace the southern side of the Ría da Noia, sometimes called the "Cockle Coast", follow the C550 as it winds past dunes that serve in good weather as excellent beaches.

From the roadside *Castro de Baroña* restaurant, just outside **BAROÑA** (Basonas) 18km along, a fifteen-minute walk down through the woods leads to a lovely little beach. Built on top of a rocky outcrop that juts from the sand into the sea, and somehow spared by the mighty Atlantic waves for the last two millennia, are the remains of the **Castro de Baroña** itself. This once-impregnable pre-Roman settlement consists of the circular stone foundations of several thatched dwellings, as also seen at A Guarda farther south, which were in turn enclosed behind a fortified wall.

Ría de Arousa

Tourism on a significant scale starts to make its presence felt in the next *ría* south, the **Ría de Arousa**. The most popular destination is the old port of **O Grove** – linked by bridge to the island of **A Toxa**, which holds a very upscale enclave of luxury hotels – while much the nicest of the old towns hereabouts is **Cambados**,

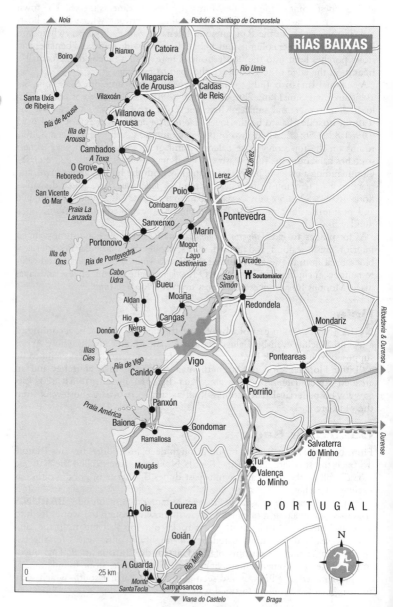

renowned for its beautiful central plaza. Sadly, both are bypassed by the rail line south from Santiago, which swings inland at **Vilagarcía de Arousa**.

While strip development mars much of the coast, just inland the hillsides are a patchwork of tiny fields, primarily planted with the grapes that go into the delicious local **Albariño wine**. Gourmets will want to sample authentic *pimientos* in the village of **Padrón**.

Santa Uxía de Ribeira

The thriving fishing port of **SANTA UXÍA DE RIBEIRA** is the main town on the north side of the Ría de Arousa. In itself, it's not an attractive place, but many families use it as a base for such superb nearby beaches as the **Praia da Lombiña**, a few kilometres east. **Accommodation** options include the *Hostal Las Carolinas*, facing the port at Paseo das Carolinas 28 (℡981 870 075; ❸), or you can **camp** at the small *Coroso* site, on the Praia de Coroso that curves away immediately east of the port (℡981 838 002, ⓦwww.campingcoroso.com; closed Oct–March). Fine tapas bars along the harbourside Paseo del Malecón include *La Parra*, which has outdoor seating, while there's more formal dining at *Penín*, Diego Delicado 5.

A long, winding eight-kilometre drive up the bare hillside northeast of town leads to the **Mirador de la Curota**, 498m above sea level, which commands stunning views all the way down the coast to the Illas Cíes.

Padrón

According to legend, St James completed his miraculous posthumous voyage to Galicia by sailing up the Ría de Arousa as far as **PADRÓN**. Accumulating silt from the Río Ulla having left it stranded a dozen kilometres inland, Padrón is no longer even on the sea, and the old town now consists of a handful of narrow pedestrian lanes squeezed between two busy roads. There's surprisingly little to show for the years of pilgrimage, except an imposing seventeenth-century church of Santiago, where the *padrón* (mooring post) to which the vessel was tied supposedly resides under the high altar.

Not far east of the old quarter, just across the tracks from the pink-painted RENFE station, the house of nineteenth-century Galego poet **Rosalía de Castro** is now a **museum** (June–Sept Tues–Sat 10am–2pm & 4–8pm, Sun 10am–1.30pm; Oct–May Tues–Sat 10am–1.30pm & 4–7pm, Sun 10am–1.30pm; €2). Unless you're a devotee of her work, the jumble of texts, photographs and bric-a-brac may not hold much interest, but the low-ceilinged rooms furnished in period style have character, and the gardens are pleasant.

Padrón's small **turismo** is on the main Avenida de Compostela close by, beside a pretty little park (July–Sept daily 10am–1.30pm & 4–8pm; Oct–June Mon–Fri 10am–1.30pm & 4–7pm; ℡627 210 777). The best-value place to **stay** is the *Pension Jardín*, Rúa Salgado Araújo 3 (℡981 810 950; ❷), a beautiful eighteenth-century house overlooking the park.

Padrón is best known as the source of the small green peppers known as *pimientos de Padrón*. Available in summer only, they're served whole, shallow-fried in oil and liberally sprinkled with sea salt. Most are sweet, but around one in ten is memorably hot. Try them at *O Pementeiro*, Praza do Castro 3; there's also a top-quality octopus **restaurant**, the *Pulpería Rial*, on the tiny Plazuela de Traviesa.

Illa de Arousa

The first two towns on the southern shore of the Ría de Arousa, **Vilagarcía de Arousa** and **Vilaxoán**, just over 20km southwest of Padrón, are a bit too

Smugglers

Smuggling is a long-established tradition in Galicia. Not all the boats that sail into its picturesque fishing harbours are carrying fish; not all the lobster pots sunk offshore hold crustaceans; not all those huts on the mussel rafts are occupied by shellfish-growers. All along the coast lie beaches known locally as the "Praia de Winston", notorious for the late-night arrivals of shipments of foreign cigarettes.

It's no longer possible to laugh off the smugglers as latter-day Robin Hoods, however. Taking advantage of the infrastructure developed over the years by small-time tobacco smugglers, and of the endlessly corrugated coastline, the big boys have moved in. First came stories of large nocturnal deliveries of hashish; then the Medellín cartel of Colombia began to use Galicia as the European entrance point for large consignments of **cocaine**. Sixty percent of all cocaine seized in Europe is detected in Spain, while the Spaniards themselves are the world's largest users of the drug. There's much talk of certain segments of the population suddenly acquiring inexplicable riches, and Cambados has seen several gruesome drug-related murders. A series of police crackdowns has yet to reverse the trend that has locals worrying that Galicia is becoming "another Sicily".

industrialized to make worthwhile stops. A little further south, however, a two-kilometre road bridge leads out to the wooded **ILLA DE AROUSA**, which holds some great beaches. Effectively part of the mainland, the island holds a sizeable permanent population, concentrated in the eponymous fishing port at its northern end. Turn south as soon as you cross the bridge to reach a small "natural park", the **Parque Carreirón**. If you're driving, you'll have to leave your car at the point where the island narrows to a mere 50m wide, but you can walk on from here to reach half a dozen fine, isolated beaches, backed by trees and saltwater marshes much loved by migratory water birds. The nicest of the **campsites** just before the end of the road, *El Edén* (☎986 527 378, ⓦwww .eledencampingplaya.com), has its own tapas bar. There's also a *hostal* in the town, *Benalua*, Rúa Méndez Núñez (☎986 551 335; ❷), which offers simple but comfortable en-suite double rooms.

Cambados

By contrast with most of its neighbours, the village of **CAMBADOS**, 5km south of the Illa de Arousa bridge, is exquisite. The paved stone **Praza de Fefiñáns** at its core is an idyllic little spot, lined on all sides with beautiful buildings, including a seventeenth-century church. As the vines crammed into its every spare square centimetre testify, Cambados is the main production centre for Galicia's excellent **Albariño wines** (see box opposite). The seafront itself, 200m west, is unremarkable, though a small island at its southern end holds the vestiges of a watchtower originally erected to look out for Viking raiders, while the vast seaweed-strewn flats exposed at each low tide play host to legions of redoubtable freelance clam- and cockle-pickers known as *mariscadoras*.

Cambados's helpful **turismo** is close to the ocean, on the Praza do Concello (summer Mon–Fri 10am–2pm & 4.30–8.30pm, Sat & Sun 10.30am–2pm & 4.30–7.30pm; winter Mon–Fri 10am–2pm & 4.30–7.30pm, Sat & Sun 10.30am–2pm & 4.30–7.30pm; ☎986 520 786, ⓦwww.cambados.es). There's a fine **parador** nearby, housed in a modern approximation of a traditional *pazo*, or manor house – the *Albariño*, Paseo Cervantes (☎986 542 250, ⓦwww .parador.es; ❺) – as well as several more ordinary but perfectly comfortable

hotels, such as *Os Pasos*, Rúa Eduardo Pondal 1 (☎986 542 020; ❷). A *bodega* on the Praza de Fefiñáns, *Bar Laya*, makes a great place to stop for a liquid lunch, while the attractive *Raxeria Martinez*, a few metres away at Rúa Real 16, has good *menús*.

O Grove and A Toxa

O GROVE, at the northern tip of the peninsula and across the bay from Cambados, exists primarily as a family resort. It is packed with places to stay, while inexpensive bars and restaurants compete for the attention of the summer influx of visitors. Across the bridge, the pine-covered islet of **A TOXA** (La Toja) caters for a completely different clientele. It's very explicitly a playground for the wealthy, with expensive hotels and luxury holiday homes set in the forest clearings, and a nine-hole golf course so guests can practise their swing.

Just before the village of **Reboredo**, 3km west of O Grove, the **Acquarium-galicia** is among the largest aquariums in Spain (June to mid-Oct daily 10am–9pm; mid-Oct to May Fri–Sun 10am–8pm; ⓦwww.acquariumgalicia.com; €9). As well as displaying a huge selection of Atlantic marine life, it arranges ninety-minute trips on the *ría* in glass-bottomed boats (April–June & Oct 2–4 daily; July–Sept every half-hour 10.30am–7.30pm; €15).

The wines of Galicia

Thanks largely to the international success of its crisp, dry **Albariño**, which has become the best known of all Spanish white wines, Galicia is now recognized as a premium wine-producing region. The Romans first introduced vines two thousand years ago, growing them on high terraces sculpted by slaves into the banks of rivers like the Miño and Sil. With its mild climate and high rainfall, Galicia is more akin to Portugal than to the rest of Spain – Galego wines, and especially Ribeiro, were much exported to Britain during the seventeenth and eighteenth centuries, before declining relations between Britain and Spain led the Portuguese to develop their own wineries, which produce similar wines to this day.

Technically, "Albariño" is the name of a grape variety, introduced to Galicia by monks who followed the Camino de Santiago all the way from the Rhine during the twelfth century – it literally translates as "white wine from the Rhine". Albariño cultivation centres around the **Rías Baixas** (ⓦwww.doriasbaixas.com), where around five thousand farmers grow grapes on tiny, scattered plots, often banding together to form co-operatives to bottle and market their wine. The largest co-operative winery, Condes de Albarei, 2km south of Cambados, is open for guided tours and visits (☎986 543 535, ⓦwww.condesdealbarei.com).

The best-selling wine in Galicia itself is **Ribeiro**, produced in the region around **Ribadavia** on the river Miño. It comes in both white and red, from such grape varieties as Treixadura, Torrontés and Loureira. The recent success of Albariño having spurred greater quality control, white Ribeiro has lost its previous trademark cloudiness, and is seen as the closest Spanish approximation to the dry Muscadet of France. Ribadavia's tourist office (ⓦwww.ribadavia.net) organizes guided tours, and can also provide maps and listings for free, self-guided winery visits.

Only the **Ribeira Sacra** region, concentrated along the stunning canyon of the Río Sil (see p.601), produces more red than white wine. That it's not better known is largely because two thirds of it never reaches the market but is drunk by the producers themselves. There are no large wineries or even co-operatives, but the three thousand or so farmers who create it have instigated a tourist route through the region and its vineyards (ⓦwww.ribeirasacrata.com).

Practicalities

A small seasonal **turismo** kiosk stands by the port of O Grove (June Mon–Sat 10am–2pm & 4–7pm, Sun 11am–2pm; July & Aug Mon–Sat 10am–8pm, Sun 10am–2pm; Sept–May Tues–Sat 10am–2pm & 5–7pm, Sun 11am–2pm; ☎986 731 415, ⓦwww.turismogrove.com). Among dozens of **places to stay** along the waterfront Rúa Teniente Dominguez and its continuation, Rúa Castelao, are *Hotel Puente de la Toja*, facing the bridge to the island at Rúa Castelao 206 (☎986 730 761, ⓦwww.hotelpuentedelatoja.com; ❹), *Hotel Tamanaco*, nearby at Rúa Castelao 164 (☎986 730 446; ❸), and the cheaper *Hotel Isolino*, Avda. Castelao 30 (☎986 730 236; ❷).

The most luxurious **accommodation** is on A Toxa, which holds three very opulent hotels indeed, including the outstanding *Gran Hotel Hesperia La Toja* (☎986 730 025, ⓦwww.granhotelhesperia-latoja.com; ❽). The *Gran Hotel's* **spa** facilities include a dazzling turquoise indoor pool with a cascading waterfall, while treatments on offer involve liberal use of mineral salts and mud. For a particularly decadent massage, you can even have yourself rubbed with chocolate oil, then given a chocolate body mask.

Among the best of the many beachfront **campsites** along the coast west of O Grove are *Moreiras* (☎986 731 691, ⓦwww.campingmoreiras.com), 3km out, and *Paisaxe II*, just outside the pretty village of **San Vicente do Mar** 4km further on (☎986 738 331, ⓦwww.campingplayapaisaxe.com; closed Nov–March). Both have rental bungalows and *cafeterías*.

For **eating**, the waterfront by the port is chock solid with the inevitable *marisquerías*, but holds disappointingly few tapas places. *O Lavandeiro* here, at Rúa Hospital 2, is a cheap but dependable restaurant. If you're here in the autumn, try to catch O Grove's Fiesta do Marisco festival on September 14.

Ría de Pontevedra

Of all the Rías Baixas, the long, narrow **Ría de Pontevedra** is the archetype, closely resembling a Scandinavian fjord with its steep and forested sides. **Pontevedra** itself is a lovely old city, set slightly back from the sea at the point where the Río Lérez begins to widen out into the bay. Though it lacks a beach of its own, it makes a good base for expeditions along either shore of its *ría*. The **north coast** is the more popular with tourists, with **Sanxenxo** (Sanjenjo) as its best-known resort, but if you want to avoid the crowds, head for the **south coast**, which stretches out past secluded beaches towards the rugged headland, ideal for camping in privacy.

Praia La Lanzada and the north-shore beaches

The southern side of the narrow neck of the peninsula that holds O Grove is adorned with the region's largest beach, the vast golden arc of **PRAIA LA LANZADA**. Packed with sun worshippers in summer and a favourite of windsurfers in winter, it has a tiny chapel at its southern end. The terrace of the **restaurant** *La Lanzada*, perched on the peninsula at its western end, provides a good vantage point to admire the whole strand, while there are plenty of **campsites** down at sea level, such as the recommended *Muiñeira* (☎986 738 404, ⓦwww.campingmuineira.com; closed mid-Sept to Easter), or *O Espiño* (☎986 738 048).

To the east are several more excellent **beaches**, often far less crowded than La Lanzada and most with a nearby campsite, should you wish to stay. Praia Montalvo is backed by pines and has great views of the Illas Cíes and Ons (camping ☎986 724 087; closed Oct–May), and the larger Praia Canelas complex, adjacent to the village of the same name, is also good (camping ☎986 691 025, ⓦwww.campingplayacanelas.com; closed mid-Oct to March).

Sanxenxo

The coastal strip between La Lanzada and **SANXENXO** (Sanjenjo), 16km southeast – which also includes the barely distinguishable resort of **Portonovo**, 3km west of Sanxenxo – is the epicentre for Galicia's one real exercise in mass tourism. Well over a hundred largely seasonal **hotels** line the route, most of them relatively small affairs set near little beaches. Individually they tend to be nice enough, but cumulatively they're overwhelming, especially as the major attraction is the serious summer **nightlife**, so they're interspersed with bars and clubs that keep going from 10pm until 8am nightly.

At the east end of the main beach, the **Praia de Silgar**, a modern marina, holds Sanxenxo's **turismo** (summer daily 10am–2pm & 4–9pm; winter Tues–Sat 10.30am–2pm & 4–7.30pm, Sun 10.30am–2.30pm; ☎986 720 825, ⓦwww.sanxenxo.org). Reasonable, inexpensive **accommodation** options along Ruá Carlos Casas in the heart of Sanxenxo include *Hotel Casa Román* at no. 2 (☎986 720 031; ❸) and *Hostal Venezuela* at no. 6 (☎986 720 086; closed Oct–May; ❷). For a change of pace, *Antiga Casa de Reis* is a lovely seven-room **B&B** in a restored farmhouse, up in the hills 2km northeast (☎986 690 550, ⓦwww.antigacasadereis.com; ❺).

Illa de Ons

In the ocean at the mouth of the Ría de Pontevedra lies the beautiful **ILLA DE ONS**, wilder and more windswept than the nearby Illas Cíes, and home to a community of fishermen and some interesting birdlife. There are good walking tracks here with terrific views of coast and sea; you can hike round the entire island in about three hours, or climb to the lighthouse and back in just over an hour.

While you arrive at the pretty Praia das Dornas, the eastern shore is indented with half a dozen small but very sandy **beaches**, so it's easy enough to escape the crowds and find your own patch of paradise. The best of the lot is the **Praia de Melide**, a gorgeous stretch of white sand near the northern tip. If you want to stay, you can **camp** for free in the specified *zona de acampada*.

Ferries run to Illa de Ons daily between mid-July and mid-September, and weekends only between May and September, costing €12.50 return. Naviera Mar de Ons sail from Sanxenxo, Portonovo and Marín (☎986 225 272, ⓦwww.mardeons.com), as do Cruceiros Rías Baixas (☎986 731 343), while Vio Viajes depart from Portonovo and Bueu (☎986 441 678, ⓦwww.isladeons.net).

Combarro and Poio

The fishing village of **COMBARRO**, 7km west of Pontevedra, boasts the largest collection of **hórreos** (stone granaries) in Galicia, lining the waterfront and looking out across the ría to Marín. A path cut into the rocks leads from the main square behind the *hórreos*, littered with souvenir shops and poky but atmospheric bars and tavernas, several of which have outdoor tables; during Combarro's **sardine festival**, on June 23, the fish are grilled in the open air on the shore. Inland, the tight streets are lined with little houses, each with Baroque stone balconies and galleries, winding claustrophobically towards the chapel of San Roque at the heart of town.

Two kilometres east of Combarro, above the modern town of **POIO**, the seventeenth-century Benedictine **MONASTERIO DE POIO** is a haven of calm (Mon–Sat 10.30am–1.30pm & 4.30–8pm, Sun 4.30–8pm; €1.50. Its cloister features a million-piece mosaic mural of the Camino de Santiago, created between 1989 and 1992 by Czech artist Anton Machourek, and there's also an eccentric little museum of tiny books. The monastery also contains a wonderful *hospedaría* (℡986 770 000; ❸), modern and efficient despite the age and beauty of its setting. On the main road through Poio, *Casa Solla*, Avda. Sineiro 7 (℡986 872 884; closed Mon, plus Thurs & Sun eves), is a very fancy, expensive modern **restaurant**, with delicious gourmet food and good views over the fields.

Pontevedra

Compact, charming and very tourist-friendly, **PONTEVEDRA** is the quintessential old Galego town. Located just short of its namesake *ría*, at the last bend in the Río Lérez, it was supposedly founded by a Greek hero returning from the Trojan War, and later became a prosperous medieval fishing port. Although it has lost its ancient walls, it still centres on an attractive *zona monumental*. A maze of pedestrianized flagstoned alleyways, interspersed with colonnaded squares, granite crosses and squat stone houses with floral balconies, the old quarter is always lively, making it perfect for a night out enjoying the local food and drink.

Arrival and information

Both the **bus** and **train** stations are about 1km southeast of the centre, side by side, and connected to the central Praza de España by half-hourly buses (from platform 14 of the bus station; €1). If you're **driving**, you won't be able to penetrate the historic core; it's best to park on the fringes, in the big car parks under Rúa Santa Clara and Praza de España. The main **turismo** is at Calle Xeneral Gutierrez Mellado 1 (summer Mon–Sat 10am–2pm & 4.30–7.30pm, Sun 10am–2pm; winter Mon–Fri 10am–2pm & 4–6pm, Sat 10am–12.30pm; ℡986 850 814), but a pair of seasonal kiosks (July–Sept Mon–Sat 10am–2pm & 5–9pm) are better located on Praza de España and Praza Orense. **Internet** access is at *Ciber Ruinas* (daily until early hours of the morning; €1/hr) on Rúa Riestra, next to the ruins of Santo Domingo church.

Accommodation

Finding good **accommodation** in Pontevedra is a little challenging. While it's definitely preferable to stay in the winding streets of the **zona monumental**, where there is at least a good *parador*, that area holds very few mid-range options, so you may well have to settle for a plain, simple budget alternative. Hotels in the new town, largely congregated on and around **Avenida de Vigo**, tend to be characterless and overpriced.

Casa Alicia Avda. de Santa María 5 ℡986 857 079. Good-value, well-kept rooms, all en suite, in a pleasant house on the edge of the old quarter. ❷
Casa Maruja Rúa Alta ℡639 252 773. Very plain but clean and perfectly acceptable en-suite rooms, opposite *Casa Alicia*. ❷

Hospedaje Penelas Rúa Alta 17 ℡986 855 705. An atmospherically located *hospedaje* in the old quarter, offering simple but spotlessly clean rooms with wafer-thin walls and shared bathrooms. ❷
Hotel Madrid Rúa Andrés Mellado 5 ℡986 865 180, ⓦwww.hotelmadrid.org. A somewhat

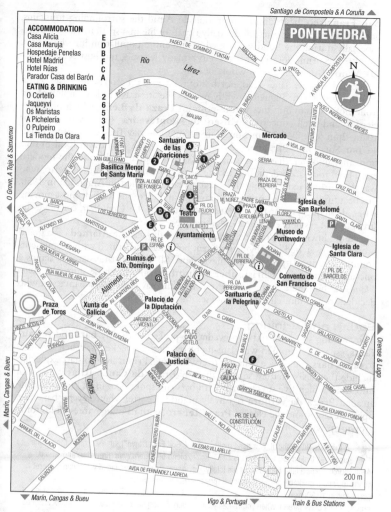

PONTEVEDRA

ACCOMMODATION
Casa Alicia   E
Casa Maruja   D
Hospedaje Penelas   B
Hotel Madrid   F
Hotel Rúas   C
Parador Casa del Barón   A

EATING & DRINKING
O Cortello   2
Jaqueyvi   6
Os Maristas   5
A Pichelería   3
O Pulpeiro   1
La Tienda Da Clara   4

O Grove, A Toja & Sanxenxo ◀

Marín, Cangas & Bueu ◀

▼ *Marín, Cangas & Bueu*

Vigo & Portugal ▼

Train & Bus Stations ▼

Orense & Lugo ▶

0   200 m

anonymous hotel, with standard modern rooms, in the new town, a short walk south of La Peregrina. ❷

Hotel Rúas Rúa Padre Sarmiento 20 ☏ 986 846 416, ✉ hotelruas@terra.es. This handsome building is in an excellent location, very near the Museo de Pontevedra; the rooms are modern and

en suite, but a little small, and it can get very noisy at night. ❹

Parador Casa del Barón Rúa del Barón 19 ☏ 986 855 800, 🌐 www.parador.es. Elegant but delightfully cosy *parador*, housed in a historic stone mansion that's tucked into a tiny square in the heart of the old quarter, with a little off-street parking. ❻

The Town

The boundary between Pontevedra's old and new quarters is marked by the **Praza da Peregrina** – site of a pilgrim chapel, the **Santuario de la Peregrina**, a tall, eye-catching Baroque structure with a floor plan in the shape of a scallop shell – and the **Praza da Ferrería**, a paved square lined by arcades on one side and rose trees on the other. To the east is the town's main church,

San Francisco, best admired from outside. Amid the surrounding fountains, gardens, and open-air cafés, all the daily rituals of life in a small town take place, especially during the Sunday *paseo*, when the entire population hits the streets. It's also the prime location for the city's many festivals, the busiest of which, **Os Maios**, lasts through the whole of May.

Assorted narrow lanes lead north from Praza da Ferrería into the **zona monumental**. Rúa Figueroa swiftly reaches the attractive little complex of old stone houses adjoining the picture-postcard **Praza da Leña**, which holds the elegant and well-conceived **Museo de Pontevedra** (June–Sept Tues–Sat 10am–2pm & 4.30–8.30pm, Sun 11am–2pm; Oct–May Tues–Sat 10am–2pm & 4–7pm, Sun 11am–2pm; free; ⓦ www.museo.depo.es). This traces local history from megaliths and hand axes, via pre-Roman gold and silver, to the modern era. Three rooms are dedicated to the artist and writer Alfonso Castelao, who was driven into exile during the Franco years, and died in Argentina in 1950. His beautifully observed paintings, drawings and cartoons, at their most moving when depicting prewar poverty and the horror of the Civil War, celebrate the strength and resilience of the Galego people.

Leading down from Praza de España towards the sea, the **Alameda** is a grand promenade watched over by magnificent buildings and dotted with monuments commemorating largely naval achievements. Slightly off the Alameda stands a one-armed **statue** of **Christopher Columbus**, one of whose ships, the *Santa María*, was built here. Some locals even claim the navigator was a native son who decided to pass himself off as Genoese.

Eating and drinking

The twisting streets of old Pontevedra are packed with tiny **bars** and **restaurants**, especially jammed with late-night revellers at weekends. When it comes to **tapas bars**, the choice is almost overwhelming. Prime areas to start exploring include the *zona*'s prettiest squares: the tiny **Praza da Cinco Rúas** is a central hub, from which five streets lined with bars run spoke-like in all directions; the arcaded **Praza da Verdura** is a lively nightlife centre, where several bars have open-air tables; and the elegant **Praza Teucro**, with its orange trees, holds some grown-up wine bars.

🏃 **O Cortello** Rúa Isabel II. This dark, rustic tapas bar, tucked just behind the Santa María church, takes a little finding – but it's totally wonderful, and remarkably cheap. It closes surprisingly early, at 10.30pm.

Jaqueyvi Rúa Dona Tareixa. When you've had your fill of seafood, come to this smart tapas bar, in front of the Teátro Municipal, for traditional Galician hams and cheeses.

🏃 **Os Maristas** Praza da Verdura s/n. Busy bar, open late, with a lot of outdoor seating, that serves a full menu of *raciones* but is renowned for the astonishing liqueur, Tumba Dios

("God Falls Down"), an esoteric but fearsome blend of *aguardiente* (firewater) and *vino de pasas* (raisin wine), laced with sundry secret herbs and spices.

A Pichelería Rúa Princesa s/n. Sophisticated but very atmospheric wine bar, just south of Praza da Cinco Rúas.

O Pulpeiro Rúa San Nicolás 7. Central, simple tapas bar, just off the Praza da Cinco Rúas, which serves great fresh octopus and seafood.

La Tienda da Clara Rúa Princesa s/n. Upscale tapas as well as fine wines, with some outdoor tables on the attractive Praza de Teucro.

The southern shore

Though the first stretch of the southern side of the Ría de Pontevedra is extremely ugly, those who press on beyond the military town of **Marín**, 7km southwest of Pontevedra, will be amply rewarded with a series of gorgeous and largely deserted little bays. **Buses** from Pontevedra's Praza de Galicia run right around the headland and along the southern shore of the *ría*.

Praia de Mogor, Bueu and beyond

Beyond Marín the bay broadens into a series of breathtaking sandy coves. A narrow side road drops away from the main coast road immediately beyond the naval academy outside Marín, leading to three beaches. The second of these, the **Praia de Mogor**, is perfect, with fields of green corn as the backdrop to a crescent of fine, clean sand, one end of which is shielded by a thick headland of dark green pines. There are a couple of seasonal bar-cum-restaurants overgrown with vines, and the villagers' rowing boats are pulled up in the shade of the trees.

BUEU (pronounced *bwayo*), a quiet market town 19km from Pontevedra, offers pleasant strips of **beach** stretching away from its rambling waterfront; the quieter spots are round the headland to the west. **Accommodation** options include the *Incamar*, Rúa Montero Ríos 147 (℡986 390 026, ⓔincamar @terra.es; ➌). Ferry trips to the Illa de Ons are detailed on p.589.

A smaller road turns away from the sea at Bueu, towards Cangas, but if you continue along the coast, towards the pretty little village of **ALDÁN** and the cape of **Hío**, it's possible to find unspoilt expanses of pine trees and empty beaches. This is an ideal area to **camp**, with a campsite that also offers rental bungalows (℡986 329 468, ⓦwww.campingaldan.com; bungalows ➍). Particularly worth following is the minor road to the huge boulders at **Cabo Udra**, where the waves come crashing down in deserted coves and wild horses roam the hillside.

Ría de Vigo

Following the main road south from Bueu, you cross the steep ridge of the Morrazo peninsula to astonishing views on the far side over the **Ría de Vigo**, one of the most sublime natural harbours in the world. The *ría*'s narrowest point is spanned by a vast suspension bridge that carries the Vigo–Pontevedra highway; you'll see its twin towers from all around the bay. On the inland side is what amounts to a saltwater lake, the inlet of **San Simón**. The road and railway from Pontevedra run beside it to **Redondela**, separated from the sea by just a thin strip of green fields, and pass close to the tiny San Martín islands, once a leper colony and used during the Civil War as an internment centre for Republicans. Beneath these waters lies a fleet of Spanish bullion galleons, sunk by a combined Anglo-Dutch force at the Battle of Rande in 1703.

The city of **Vigo** looks very appealing, spread along the waterfront, but although it makes a good base for trips along the south shore to **Baiona**, across the bay to **Cangas**, and, especially, out to the wonderful **Illas Cíes**, it has few attractions of its own.

Cangas

Thanks to recent road construction, the resort of **CANGAS** is rapidly expanding. It's worth visiting simply for the superb, twenty-minute **ferry** trip across the *ría* from Vigo (Mon–Fri every 30min 6.30am–10.30pm; Sat hourly 6.30am–10.30pm; Sun hourly 8.30am–9.30pm; €3.70 return, €2.40 if the outbound trip is before 8am), but there's an excellent beach, too. The **Praia de Rodeira** is a beautiful five-hundred-metre stretch of sand with majestic views across the water – alight from the ferry, turn right and walk along the seafront for ten minutes to reach it. Cangas is at its most lively during the Friday **market**, when the seafront gardens are filled with stalls.

The beaches and hills west of Cangas are stunning and all but deserted. The best target is the **Praia de Melide**, at the tip of the peninsula 2km beyond **Donón**. An isolated cove backed by woods and a lighthouse, it offers superb walks along the cape.

Practicalities

Cangas's **turismo** is right where the ferries dock (daily 10am–2pm & 4–8pm; ℡986 300 875, ⓦwww.cangas.org). Ferry services to the Illas Cíes also leave from here in summer (July & Aug; 4–5 daily; 1hr), and there's a **bus** station alongside. You can find pleasant sea-view **rooms** in town at the modern *Hotel Airiños*, at Avda. Eugenio Sequeiros 30 (℡986 304 000, ⓦwww.airinos.com; ❹), and the *Playa*, at the start of the Praia de Rodeira, at Avda. Ourense 78 (℡986 303 674, ⓦwww.hotel-playa.com; ❹).

The main cluster of **bars and restaurants** is around the port. Up some steps, slightly to the left of the jetty as you face the town, the *Bar Celta*, looking out over the bay at Rúa Alfredo Saralegui 28, is an excellent old-fashioned tapas bar; *Casa Macillos*, next door, is similar. *Taberna O Arco*, on the central Praza do Arco, and *O Porrón*, just beyond the covered market at Eugenio Sequeiros 15, are two good bars specializing in seafood.

Moaña

Hourly boats from Vigo (same hours and prices as to Cangas) also leave for **MOAÑA**, 5km along the coast from Cangas, and similar to it in feel. Again, much of the appeal of a trip here is the ferry ride, which takes you right alongside the local *mejilloneiras* – ramshackle rafts, perched on the river like water-spiders and sometimes topped by little wooden huts, which are used for cultivating mussels. Moaña itself boasts a fine, long **beach**, but relatively few facilities for visitors. Places **to stay** include the pleasant *Hostal Prado Viejo*, Rúa Ramón Cabanillas 16 (℡986 311 634, ⓦwww.pradoviejo.com; ❸), which has en-suite rooms and private parking.

Soutomaior

On the N550 north of Vigo, on the old road from Pontevedra, a worthwhile detour 2km east of the village of Arcade leads to the twelfth-century hilltop **castle of Soutomaior** (daily except Mon: summer 11am–2pm & 5–9pm; winter 11am–2pm & 4–7pm; €1.50; ⓦwww.cameliagalicia.com). The rambling halls and towers of the castle itself are used for temporary exhibitions, while its superb landscaped grounds are planted with mighty sequoias and other exotic species. One former inhabitant travelled to Samarkand early in the fifteenth century, as ambassador to the court of Tamerlane the Great.

The castle grounds also hold a lovely rural **hotel**, the *Pousada del Castillo de Soutomaior* (℡986 705 105, ⓦwww.hotelpousadadelcastillo.com; ❹), a gorgeous place to stay even though very few rooms have the views you'd expect of such a location.

Vigo

Few cities enjoy such a magnificent natural setting as **VIGO**. Arrayed along the sloping southern shoreline of its namesake estuary, it enjoys superb views not only of the bay itself, surrounded by green forest ridges, but also out towards the ocean. While it's undeniably magnificent when seen from a ship entering the harbour, however, it has to be said that once ashore it fails to live up to that initial promise, and few visitors use it as anything more than an overnight stop.

Although Vigo is now the largest city in Galicia, home to some 300,000 people, Baiona, closer to the mouth of the *ría*, was the principal port hereabouts until the nineteenth century. Then the railways arrived, and Vigo became the first Galego town to industrialize, with the opening of several large sardine canneries. It's now Spain's chief fishing port, with wharves and quays that stretch almost 5km along the shore.

Arrival and information

Vigo's **turismo** is just up from the port at Avda. Cánovas del Castillo 22 (July & Aug Mon–Fri 9.30am–2pm & 4.30–7.30pm, Sat & Sun 10am–2pm & 4.30–7.30pm; Sept–June Mon–Fri 9.30am–2pm & 4.30–6.30pm, Sat 10am–1.30pm; ☎986 430 577, ⓦwww.turismodevigo.org). The most convenient central **car parks** are on the seafront at Rúa das Avenidas, and beneath the Porta do Sol, while local **bus** routes #12, #12B and #C4C (all €1) connect the Porta do Sol with the **RENFE station**, 500m southeast, and the **bus station**, another 500m beyond that to the south. Vigo's **airport**, 9km east on bus route #9A, is served by Clickair flights from London Gatwick and Barcelona (ⓦwww.clickair.com).

Accommodation

Vigo's **hotels** are concentrated in two main areas: around the old town, down by the port, which is close to the best restaurants and bars; and in the less atmospheric streets up by the train station.

Hostal Ancla Dorada Rúa Irmandiños 2 ☎986 223 403, ⓦwww.ancladorada.com. Welcoming family hotel, 200m west from the train station towards the old town, with clean, simple rooms, some with shared bathrooms and some sleeping up to four, with free wi-fi. ❷

Hostal Nueva Colegiata Praza da Igrexa 3 ☎986 220 952. Well-kept and good-value *hostal* on a lovely central square. All rooms are en suite, and there's a cheap café downstairs. ❷

Hotel Águila Rúa Victoria 6 ☎986 431 398, ⓦwww.hotelaguila.com. Old-fashioned but well-equipped hotel near the Porta do Sol, with bags of charm. All rooms are en suite and with cable TV, though some are a bit small. ❸

Hotel Husa Bahía de Vigo Rúa Canovas del Castillo 24 ☎986 226 700, ⓦwww.hotelbahiadevigo.com. This seventeen-storey high-rise, facing the port, is the city's chief luxury option, with whirlpool baths in all rooms. Its café is decorated like an ocean liner, while the restaurant, *Marisquería Bahía*, is huge. Check online for bargain weekend rates. ❺

Hotel Lino Vigo Rúa Lepanto 26 ☎986 439 311, ⓦwww.hotel-lino.com. Close to the train station, with a range of rooms, all en suite. Breakfast is included. ❹

Hotel Puerta del Sol Rúa Porta do Sol 14 ☎986 222 364, ⓦwww.alojamientosvigo.com. Clean, very central hotel that offers small but pleasant en-suite rooms, with TV and wi-fi, plus a couple of five-person apartments. ❺

The City

While Vigo's passenger port has long passed its heyday, it retains the prime spot in the middle of this stretch of shore. Here, generations of Galego emigrants have embarked for and returned from the Americas, and Caribbean immigrants have had their first glimpse of Europe. These days, cruise passengers mingle with tourists arriving at the **Estación Marítima de Ría** off the ferries from Cangas and Moaña, and set off to explore the steep, cobbled streets that climb up into the old city, known as **O Berbés** and crammed with shops, bars and restaurants.

Along the seafront early in the morning, kiosks revive fishermen with strong coffee, while there and in the lively daily market hall nearby, the **Mercado da Pedra**, their catch is sold. Immediately below, women set out plates of fresh oysters on permanent granite tables to tempt passers-by on the aptly named **Rúa da Pescadería**. On **Rúa Carral**, shops sell kitsch marine souvenirs.

A stiff but enjoyable climb up from the old town, mostly along stone staircases, brings you to the top of the **Castro** hill. So named for the circular ancient ruins still visible on one side, and also the site of a seventeenth-century castle, the hill enjoys comprehensive views. The much larger **Parque de Castrelos**, 2km southwest, holds one of Galicia's best museums in Galicia, as well as extensive formal gardens and woodlands. Set in an attractive old manor house, the **Museo Quiñones de Leon** (Tues, Thurs & Fri 10am–1.30pm & 5–8pm; Wed 10am–8pm; Sat 5–8pm; Sun 10am–1.30pm; free; Ⓦwww .museodevigo.org) focuses both on the archeology and history of Vigo and its region, and on a fine collection of Galego art.

Most of the **beaches** near Vigo are crowded and unappealing. Farther south, however, the beach at **Samil** is better, while those at **Vao** and **Canido**, further on, are also quite reasonable, and equipped with campsites – including *Canido* (Ⓣ986 462 072, Ⓦwww.campingsonline.com/canido).

Eating and drinking

Rúa da Pescadería is the liveliest place for **lunch**, at an outdoor table amongst the oyster sellers. Most of one side of the street is taken up by the *Marisquería Bahía*, allegedly the largest seafood restaurant in Spain, decorated with an odd mixture of underwater scenes and antelope heads. The seafood is predictably excellent and prices aren't too steep, starting at around €15. Climbing the nearby stairs to Praza A Pedra, you'll find the understated *El Emigrante*, a good place for *raciones*. Virtually all of the **bars** in the old streets serve great tapas; good options on Rúa dos Cesteiros, off Praza de Constitución, include the deliberately rustic *Taberna da Curuxa* and the no-frills *Taberna A Pedra*.

The Illas Cíes

The most irresistible sands of the Ría de Vigo must be those on the three islands of the **Illas Cíes**, which can be reached by boat from Vigo, and (less regularly) from Baiona and Cangas. Sprawling across the entrance to the *ría*, battered by the open Atlantic on one side but sheltering delightful sandy beaches where they face the mainland, the islands were long used by raiders such as Sir Francis Drake as hide-outs from which to ambush Spanish shipping, but are now a nature reserve. The most southerly, **Illa de San Martiño**, is an off-limits bird sanctuary; the other two, **Illa do Monte Ayudo** and **Illa do Faro**, are joined by a narrow causeway of sand, which cradles a placid lagoon on its inland side. Most visitors stay on the sands, with their sprinkling of bars and a campsite in the trees, so if you want to escape the crowds, it's easy to find a deserted spot – particularly on the Atlantic side. From the beach, a long climb up a winding rocky path across desolate country leads to a lighthouse with a commanding ocean view.

The **campsite** (Ⓣ986 438 358, Ⓦwww.campingislascies.com; closed Oct–May) is the only legal accommodation on the islands, so if you want to stay in mid-season, book ahead to make sure there's space. There is a small shop, as well as a couple of decent restaurants, but as they're free to charge what they choose, if you're on a budget you might prefer to take your own supplies.

Ferries to the islands (40min; €18.50 return) run from Estación Marítima in Vigo in June (4 daily; first leaves Vigo at 11am, last leaves Cíes at 9pm) and from July until the first week of September (8 daily; first leaves Vigo at 9.45am, last leaves Cíes at 9pm). From Cangas and Baiona, they run only between July and the first week of September (4 daily from each; first leaves Cangas at 10.15am, last return leaves Cíes at 7pm; first leaves Baiona at 10.45am, last return leaves Cíes at 7.30pm). Only a certain number of visitors are allowed to visit the Cíes on any one day, so aim for an early boat to make sure.

Baiona and Praia de América

BAIONA (Bayona), 21km south of Vigo, is situated just before the open sea at the head of a miniature *ría*, the smallest and southernmost in Galicia. This small and colourful port, which nowadays makes a very healthy living from its upscale tourist trade, was the first place in Europe to hear of the discovery of the New World, when Columbus's *Pinta* appeared on March 1, 1493, an event commemorated by numerous sculptures scattered around the town. An exact replica of the *Pinta* sits in the harbour (daily 10am–8.30pm; €2), which these days contains pleasure yachts rather than fishing boats.

The **medieval walls** that surround the wooded promontory adjoining Baiona enclose an idyllic *parador* (see below). It's definitely worth paying the €1 fee to walk around the parapet, which provides a series of changing, unobstructed views across the *ría* to the chain of rocky islets that leads to the Illas Cíes. Another hugely enjoyable footpath circles beneath the walls at sea level, and provides access to several diminutive beaches. These are not visible from the town proper, which despite its fine esplanade has only a small, if attractive, patch of sand.

Galicia's best-known **beach** lies a couple of kilometres east of Baiona, across the mouth of the bay. The **Praia de América** is a superb, long curve of clean sand that remains surprisingly underdeveloped considering its reputation, lined at a discreet distance by imposing suburban villas, only a few of which hold hotels or other businesses. To reach it, head north from the main highway from Vigo to Baiona at the village of **Ramallosa**, where a splendid little Roman bridge crosses the Río Miñor. A coastal footpath leads 2km from there to the beach, but you can also drive.

Practicalities

Baiona's seasonal **turismo** is on the seafront, by the gate that leads up to the *parador* (April, May & Sept–Dec Mon–Fri 10am–2pm & 3–7pm, Sun 11am–2pm & 4–7pm; June Mon–Sat 10am–2pm & 4–8pm, Sun 11am–2pm & 4–8pm; July & Aug daily 10am–3pm & 4–9pm; ☎986 687 067, ⓦwww.baiona.org). **Buses** between Vigo and A Guarda stop nearby.

By far the nicest **accommodation** in Baiona – in fact, it's hard to imagine a better location anywhere in the world – is the gorgeous ⚜ *Parador Conde de Gondomar* (☎986 355 000, ⓦwww.parador.es; ❼), which, though totally surrounded on the headland by genuine medieval walls, is actually a modern version of a traditional Galego manor house. The rooms are spacious and comfortable, with superb views, and, as well as two restaurants, it has a couple of bars, both open to non-residents, one of which stands alone in the grounds. Otherwise, you can find hotels along either the seafront esplanade or Rúa Ventura Misa, the narrow pedestrianized street that runs just behind it. The most appealing is the twelve-room *Pazo de Mendoza*, a converted manor house with sea views on the corner of Praza Pedro de Castro (☎986 385 014, ⓦwww.pazodemendoza.es; ❹). The *Hotel Tres Carabelas*, Rúa Ventura Misa 61 (☎986 355 441, ⓦwww.hoteltrescarabelas.com; ❸), is a mid-range option one block inland.

There's a huge, year-round **campsite** at *Playa América*, with lots of rental bungalows (☎986 365 404, ⓦwww.campingplayaamerica.com; bungalows ❹), and another, *Bayona Playa,* nearer town on a long spit of land at **Praia Ladeira**, 1km east (☎986 350 035, ⓦwww.campingbayona.com).

Seafood restaurants abound on Praza Pedro de Castro and along Rúa Ventura Misa, most with tanks stuffed full of doomed marine creatures. Among the best are *El Túnel*, at no. 21, and *Plaza*, a little farther along, both of which have outdoor seating on a pleasant, sheltered square. *Jaqueyvi* on Rúa de Reloxo is a smart little restaurant that specializes in rice with fish, and another *Jaqueyvi*, a block along Rúa

Ventura Misa, serves great ham. Ventura Misa is also the hub of the town's **nightlife**, with several bars and pubs, such as *O Refuxio d'Anton*, staying open late.

Oia

The C550 highway continues due south for 30km from Baiona to the mouth of the Río Miño, which marks the frontier with **Portugal**. Once a windswept wilderness, this straight stretch of coastline is now scattered with *hostales* and hotels. There are no beaches, but the sight of the ocean foaming through the rocks is mightily impressive.

Immediately around the first curve from Baiona, a massive granite statue known as the **Virgen de la Roca** towers above the sea; on appropriately solemn religious occasions, devotees climb up inside it and onto the boat she holds in her right hand. Halfway between Baiona and A Guarda, beneath the town of **OIA** – itself little more than a very tight bend in the road – nestles a remarkable Baroque **monastery**, with its sheer stone facade surviving the constant battering of the ocean.

Nearby, facing dramatically out to sea from the hillside, the *Talaso Atlantico* (T 986 385 090, W www.talasoatlantico.com; ⑤) is a **spa-hotel** specializing in thalassotherapy, or seawater treatment. Between relaxing in the large, heated indoor seawater pool, with its huge picture windows and assorted high-pressure jets, guests can sample a wide range of seaweed wraps and beauty treatments.

A Guarda

Just short of the mouth of the Miño, the workaday port of **A GUARDA** (La Guardia) is largely the modern creation of emigrants returned from Puerto Rico. The extensive remains of a **celta** – a pre-Roman fortified hill settlement – stand just above the town in the thick pine woods of **Monte Santa Tecla**, reached by a stiff thirty-minute climb or an easy drive. Occupied between roughly 600 and 200 BC, the *celta* was abandoned when the Romans established control over the north. The site consists of the foundations of well over a hundred circular dwellings, crammed tightly inside an encircling wall. A couple of them have been restored as full-size thatched huts; most are excavated to a metre or so, though some are still buried. On the north slope of the mountain there is also a large **cromlech**, or stone circle, while continuing upwards you pass along an avenue of much more recent construction, lined with the Stations of the Cross, and best seen looming out of a mountain mist. Five minutes farther on, at the top, are a church, a small **archeological museum** (March–Nov daily 9.30am–11pm; €1) of Celtic finds from the mountain, two restaurants and a hotel (see below).

A Guarda itself has a couple of small **beaches**, but there's a better stretch of sand at the village of **Camposancos** about 4km south, facing Portugal and a small islet capped by the ruins of a fortified Franciscan monastery. A **ferry** (daily: every 30min summer 9.30am–10.30pm, winter until 7.30pm; pedestrians €1, car & driver €3 one way) links Camposancos with Caminha in Portugal.

Practicalities

There's a seasonal **turismo** at Rúa do Porto 48 (June–Sept daily 9am–3pm & 7–9pm; T 986 614 546, W www.concellodaguarda.com). ATSA **buses** (every 30min from Tui; 3 daily from Baiona) arrive at the small Praza Avelino Vicente, well above the port.

Much the best **hotel** in A Guarda is the beautiful *Hotel Convento de San Benito*, right by the port, at Praza San Benito (T 986 611 166; ④), housed in an old Benedictine convent. Alternatively, the one-star *Hotel Pazo Santa Tecla*

(☎986 610 002; ❸), above the *celta* at the top of Monte Santa Tecla, boasts glorious views along the coast and the Río Miño; all rooms are en suite. There's **camping** out towards the river at *Camping Santa Tecla*, 1km or so from town (☎986 613 011). Low-key but excellent seafood **restaurants** line the waterfront in town, including the friendly *Anduriña* at no. 58.

Tui

TUI (Tuy, pronounced *twee*), 24km northeast up the Miño from A Guarda and roughly the same distance south of Vigo, is the principal Galego frontier town on the river, staring across to the neat ramparts of Portuguese **Valença do Minho**. In truth, Valença is a much more compelling destination – its old quarter is positively delightful – but Tui has its moments, too. The old town stands back from the river, tiered amid trees and stretches of ancient walls above the fertile riverbank. Sloping lanes, paved with huge slabs of granite, climb to the imposing fortress-like **Catedral** dedicated to San Telmo, patron saint of fishermen, while a pair of enticing little river beaches lie on the far side of the old town from the main street.

Practicalities

Tui's **turismo** is located in a huge church-like building on Rúa Colón (Mon–Fri 9.30am–2pm & 4.30–6.30pm; ☎986 601 789). If you're coming by **train** from Ribadavia or Ourense, it's much quicker to go to Guillarei station, a three-kilometre taxi ride east of town, than to wait for a connection to Tui itself.

As for **accommodation**, *Hostal La Generosa*, at no. 37 on old Tui's main street, the acacia-lined Paseo Calvo Sotelo (☎986 600 055; ❶), is ageing gracefully and excellent value, and is opposite the **bus** stop for Vigo and A Guarda. The more modern *Hotel Colón*, Rúa Colón 11 (☎986 600 223, ⓦwww.hotelcolontuy .com; ❹), has large comfortable rooms, a pool and great views across to Valença. Best of the lot, though, if your budget will stretch, is the imposing *Parador San Telmo* (☎986 600 300, ⓦwww.parador.es; ❻), out near the border and featuring extensive landscaped grounds with a good swimming pool and tennis courts.

The best of the remarkably few **restaurants** in old Tui are the expensive but excellent *O Nuevo Cabalo Furado*, on Praza de Generalísimo next to the cathedral, and its much more affordable but equally good sister, *O Vello Cabalo Furado*, on the street below.

Crossing the border

A fifteen-minute walk leads from Tui to the Portuguese border, across an iron bridge designed by Eiffel; the ravishing little town of **VALENÇA DO MINHO**, dwarfed behind its mighty ramparts, lies a similar distance beyond. There's no border control at the bridge: just stroll (or drive) across and head up the hill to the centre.

Inland Galicia

While most visitors to Galicia concentrate their attentions on Santiago and the coast, the interior of the region holds some significant points of interest. In particular, the **Romans** were always more interested in mining gold from inland Galicia than they were in its coastline, and some remarkable vestiges of their ancient occupation still survive, including the terraced vineyards along the stupendous **canyon of the Río Sil**, and the intact walls of unspoiled **Lugo**. The obvious route for exploring the region is the one used by the Romans, following the beautiful **Río Míño** upstream, via towns such as **Ribadavia** and **Ourense**, and through the wine regions of **Ribeiro** and **Ribeira Sacra**.

Ribadavia

Roughly 60km east of either Vigo or Tui along the A52 motorway, but more pleasantly approached by following the N120 highway or the train line up the lovely valley of the Miño – which tends to fill with mist every morning – the riverside town of **RIBADAVIA** is a good deal grander than its size might promise. Centre for a thousand years of the Ribeiro wine industry, as well as several fine churches and a sprawling **Dominican monastery**, it holds an interesting **Barrio Xudeo** (Jewish Quarter), dating from the eleventh century when Ribadavia received its first Jewish immigrants. By the fourteenth century, Jews had become half the town's population, and formed one of the most important and prosperous Jewish communities in Spain, although many were forced to convert to Catholicism during the Inquisition. Head for the tiny square behind the Iglesia de la Magdalena for a wonderful view of the hillside terraces. Look out, too, for the remains of the small but quaint **Castillo de los Condes de Ribadavia**, immediately above the Praza Maior.

Ribadavia's **turismo** is in a Baroque former palace on the central Praza Maior (July–Sept daily 10am–3pm & 5–8pm; Oct–June Mon–Fri 9.30am–2.30pm & 4–6.30pm, Sat 10.30am–2.30pm & 4–6.30pm, Sun 10.30am–2.30pm; ☎988 471 275, ⓦwww.ribadavia.com).

The only **hostal** in the old town is also on the Praza Maior – the *Hostal Plaza* (☎988 470 576; ➋), which has good en-suite rooms and a restaurant – as are several other bar-restaurants, including *La Huella del Gato*.

Celanova

The high and winding road along the south bank of the Miño through Cortegada to the border at São Gregorio makes a good excursion, and can also be used as part of the route to **CELANOVA**, 35km southeast of Ribadavia. This is hardly more than a village, consisting of a long, narrow main square that's appealingly overshadowed by a vast and palatial **Benedictine monastery**. Felipe V retired into monastic life here, having spent much of his reign securing the throne in the War of the Spanish Succession (1701–13). The monastery is now a school, but you can explore its two superb cloisters – one Renaissance, the other Baroque – and the cathedral-sized church. Most beautiful of all is the tiny, tenth-century Mozarabic chapel of **San Miguel** in the garden.

Celanova's **turismo** is in the monastery complex, reached by a doorway off the main square, and offers **guided tours** (office daily 9am–2pm & 4–7pm; tours hourly; €1.20; ☎988 432 201). The **hotel** *Betanzos* on Castor Elices 12 (☎988 451 036; ➋) is excellent value for money, with some en-suite rooms.

Ourense

Set slightly back from the Miño atop a low hill, the old quarter of **OURENSE** (Orense), one of Galicia's four provincial capitals, is more attractive and person-able than you might expect from the dispiriting urban sprawl that surrounds it. While not a place to spend more than one night – or even break a train or bus journey, as both stations are a considerable way out, across the river – the old quarter does at least offer a handsome and lovingly restored tangle of stepped streets, patrician mansions with escutcheoned doorways, and grand little churches squeezed into miniature arcaded squares. At its heart is the dark **Catedral**, an imitation of Santiago's, with a painted (but greatly inferior) copy of the Pórtico de Gloria, and a museum of religious clutter in the cloisters (daily except Sun: July & Aug 10am–1pm & 4–7pm; Sept–June noon–1pm & 4–7pm; €1).

A bewildering number of bridges cross the River Miño as it curves extravagantly through Ourense. The oldest is the thirteenth-century **Ponte Romana**, but the most visually impressive is the new **Ponte Milenio**, a futuristic road bridge with an undulating pedestrian loop that provides great views. A kilometre or so west, the **Termas Chavasqueira** (Tues–Thurs 10am–3pm & 5–11pm, Fri 10am–3pm & 5pm–3am, Sat 10am–3am, Sun 10am–11pm; €5) boast indoor and outdoor spa pools and are a great way to wind down after a hard day on the road.

Practicalities

Ourense has two **turismos**: a provincial one at the city end of the Ponte Romana (summer Mon–Fri 9am–2pm & 4–8pm, Sat 10am–2pm & 4–8pm, Sun 10am–2pm & 5–7pm; winter Mon–Fri 9am–2pm & 4.30–6.30pm; ☎988 372 020), and a local one in the old quarter, at Rúa das Burgas 12 (Mon–Fri 10am–2pm & 3–8pm, Sat & Sun 11am–2pm; ☎988 366 064, ⓦwww.ourense.es).

Hostales on Rúa Hermanos Villar near the cathedral include *Hostal Candido* at no. 15 (☎988 229 607; ❶), which offers nine basic en-suite rooms above a lovely old-fashioned *chocolatería*, and the upmarket *Hotel Zarampallo* at no. 19 (☎988 230 008, ⓦwww.zarampallo.com; ❸). Most luxurious of all is *Gran Hotel San Martín*, overlooking Parque San Lázaro, at Rúa Curras Enriquez 1 (☎988 371 811, ⓦwww.ghhoteles.com; ❻).

Among the many good **restaurants** in the old quarter, *Casa de María* at Rúa San Miguel 7 serves a great-value €10 *menú* and has some balcony seating above a pretty little square, while sleepy Praza Maior holds appealing options, including *Mundial* at no. 8.

Cañon de Río Sil

Inland Galicia's most spectacular scenery can be admired not far northeast of Ourense, though it's only practicable to explore this area by car, and you can expect the driving to be slow. Follow the N120 out of the city, alongside the Río Miño, and after 20km you'll reach the confluence of the Miño with the lesser **Río Sil**. For roughly 50km east from here, the final stretch of the Sil is quite extraordinarily picturesque and dramatic, flowing through a stunning canyon known as the **Gargantas del Sil**.

This magnificent gorge is the heartland of the **Ribeira Sacra wine** region – the only place in Galicia that produces more red than white wine – and even where they're all but vertical, the river cliffs are almost always terraced with grape vines. A high mountain road climbs east from the N120 just before the confluence, then winds along the topmost ridge of the canyon's southern flank, passing through a succession of lovely villages. After just under 50km, just before the village of **CASTRO CALDELAS**, a side road drops back down to the river, where a small jetty is the base for **boat trips** on the Sil (daily in summer; prices and schedules vary; ☎902 100 403, ⓦwww.hemisferios.es). Head up the northern bank from here, to enjoy the most impressive vistas of all from the spot shortly before the village of **DOADE**, where a statue of a woman grape harvester commemorates nine centuries of viniculture.

Places to stay are scattered along the south side of the river, none finer than the tenth-century monastery of **San Estevo**, 8km up from the N120, which has been converted into a superb ⚘ *parador* (☎988 010 110, ⓦwww.parador.es; ❻). Its ancient cloisters remain intact, but it also boasts ultra-modern **spa** facilities,

▲ Río Sil

including a whirlpool bath set on an outdoor terrace, and a beautifully styled contemporary **restaurant**. Cheaper but still attractive alternative hotels include *A Forxa* in nearby Luintra, 4km west (☎988 201 025, ⓦwww.hotelaforxa .com; ❸), and the *Caldelas Sacra* at Rúa Grande 17 in Castro Caldelas (☎988 203 423, ⓦwww.caldelas-sacra.com; ❷). For details of **outdoor activities** such as rafting, canoeing, canyoneering and horseriding in the canyon, contact Galitur Sports (☎988 269 544, ⓦwww.galitursport.com).

Monforte de Lemos

A dozen kilometres north of Doade, or 66km south of Lugo along the C546, the rail junction of **MONFORTE DE LEMOS** makes a satisfyingly unspoilt and ancient overnight stop. The town proper, which is home to an incongruously gigantic yet elegant Renaissance **Colegio**, encircles a hill of largely tumbledown old houses. Right at the top of the hill, a rambling ensemble that includes the **Torre de Homenaxe** and a four-hundred-year-old monastery houses the imposing *Parador de Monforte de Lemos* (☎982 418 484, ⓦwww .parador.es; ❻), while a short way down the slope, ⚲ *O Grelo* is a fabulous **restaurant** with an inventive if expensive take on traditional Galego cuisine (☎982 404 701; closed Sun pm).

Monforte's **turismo**, way down below alongside the Colegio (daily 10am–2pm & 4–7pm; ☎982 404 715, ⓦwww.concellodemonforte.com), can advise on tours of the Ribeira Sacra wine region and its Romanesque monuments. **Accommodation** in the town itself includes the riverside *Hostal Puente Romano* at Praza Dr Goyanes 6 (☎982 403 551, ⓦwww.hpuenteromano.com; ❷), while restaurants and tapas bars line the pedestrian Rúa Cardenal.

Lugo

The oldest city in Galicia, and as "Lucus Augusti" the first regional capital two thousand years ago, **LUGO** is, these days, a small town that's chiefly remarkable for its stout **Roman walls**. Rated as the finest late Roman military fortifications to survive anywhere, the walls with which the Romans enclosed this hilltop, overlooking the Miño river, still form a complete loop around the old town. Few traces remain of the 71 semi-circular towers that once punctuated the perimeter; instead, a broad footpath now runs atop the full 2.5-kilometre length of the ramparts, so a thirty-minute walk takes you all the way around, to admire the city core from every angle. Though repeatedly conquered by Moors, Vikings and Visigoths, Lugo was never destroyed, and remains a provincial capital. It has always been bypassed, however, by the Camino de Santiago.

Sadly, insensitive building and a busy loop road make it impossible to appreciate the walls from any distance outside, but the road does at least keep traffic out of the centre, which maintains an enjoyable if slightly neglected medley of medieval and eighteenth-century buildings. The most dramatic of the old city gates, the **Porta de Santiago**, in the southwest, offers access to an especially impressive stretch of wall, leading past the large, mossy **Catedral**. Originally Romanesque when built in the twelfth century, it has been repeatedly rebuilt since then, with flamboyant Churrigueresque flourishes still conspicuous despite the more recent Neoclassical facade.

Walk down Rúa Nova and you'll come to the excellent **Museo Provincial** (July & Aug Mon–Fri 11am–2pm & 5–8pm, Sat 10am–2pm; Sept–June Mon–Fri 10.30am–2pm & 4.30–8.30pm, Sat 10.30am–2pm & 4.30–8pm, Sun 11am–2pm; free), partly housed in the old Convento de San Francisco. This is a well-displayed collection of Galego art, contemporary Spanish work swiped from the Prado, and an early collection of Galicia's Sargadelos china, alongside the more predictable Roman remains and ecclesiastical knick-knacks.

Practicalities

Lugo's **turismo** is hidden away in a small shopping arcade off the south side of the Praza Maior (July & Aug daily 10am–2pm & 4–8pm; Sept–June Mon–Sat 10am–2pm & 4–7pm; ℡982 231 361, ⓦwww.concellodelugo.org). Both the **train station** (to the north) and **bus terminal** (to the east) are immediately outside the walls, roughly 600m apart.

Hotels in all price ranges are scattered through the walled town, especially around the central Praza Maior; the upscale *Méndez Núñez* is just north at Rúa Raíña 1 (℡982 230 711, ⓦwww.hotelmendeznunez.com; ❸). Budget **hostales** outside the walls include the pleasant *Hostal Mar de Plata*, next to the bus station at Ronda de Muralla 5 (℡982 228 910; ❶).

As ever, the lively old lanes hold countless **bars** and **restaurants**, with the densest concentration along the long, straight Rúa Nova – both *Méson O Castelo*, no. 23, and *Os Tres Pes*, no. 17, offer good, cheap *menús*. Nearby Rúa da Cruz holds swankier **restaurants**, including *Verruga* at no. 12, and the equally posh *Alberto* at no. 4.

Sobrado dos Monxes

The twelfth-century Cistercian monastery of **Sobrado dos Monxes** (Mon–Sat 10.15am–1pm & 4.30–7pm, Sun 12.15–1pm & 4.30–7pm; €0.60) makes a highly worthwhile detour en route between Lugo and Santiago. The range of the abbey buildings proclaims past royal patronage, their scale emphasized by the tiny village below, while the huge church itself sprouts flowers and foliage from every niche and crevice, its honey-coloured stone blossoming with lichens and mosses. Within, all is immensely grand – long, uncluttered vistas, mannerist Baroque, and romantic gloom; there are superb, worm-endangered choirstalls (once in Santiago's cathedral) and, through an arch in the north transept, a tiny, ruined Romanesque chapel. A community of monks maintains the monastery and operates a small shop.

Travel details

Trains

Besides the FEVE line along the north coast from Asturias to Ferrol (see p.000), two **main lines** lead to and from Galicia: one from Madrid via Ávila, Medina del Campo and Zamora to Ourense; the other from León to Monforte de Lemos, the junction between Lugo and Ourense. Many trains continue to Santiago de Compostela and A Coruña, but you can usually get about more easily using the *regionales*. Galicia has two **regional lines**: the first runs from A Coruña to Vigo via Santiago; the second from Vigo to Ourense and on to Monforte. Two further **minor lines** connect Ferrol with A Coruña, and A Coruña with Lugo and Monforte.

A Coruña to: Barcelona (2 daily; 17hr); Betanzos (2 daily; 30min); Bilbao (daily; 12hr); Burgos (3 daily; 8–9hr); Ferrol (daily; 1hr); León (3 daily; 5–6hr); Lugo (2 daily; 2hr); Madrid (2 daily; 8hr 30min–10hr 30min); Ourense (4 daily; 2hr 15min–3hr); Santiago de Compostela (14 daily; 45min); Vigo (9 daily; 2hr 10min); Zaragoza (2 daily; 12hr).

Ourense to: A Coruña (4 daily; 2hr 15min–3hr); Burgos (2 daily; 4–6hr); León (2 daily; 4hr); Madrid (2 daily; 5hr 30min–7hr); Medina del Campo (2 daily; 3hr 30min–4hr 30min); Monforte de Lemos (3 daily; 40min); Ponferrada (3 daily; 2hr 30min); Pontevedra (2 daily; 2hr 30min); Ribadavia (daily; 20min); Santiago de Compostela (4 daily; 1hr 30min–2hr); Vigo (4 daily; 2hr).

Santiago de Compostela to: A Coruña (14 daily; 45min); Bilbao (daily; 10hr 45min); Burgos (daily; 8hr); Irún (daily; 11hr 30min); León (daily; 6hr); Madrid (2 daily; 8–9hr); Medina del Campo (2 daily; 5hr 20min); Ourense (4 daily; 1hr 30min–2hr); Pontevedra (10 daily; 1hr); Vigo (10 daily; 1hr 30min).

Vigo to: Barcelona (1–2 daily; 15hr–16hr 30min); Burgos (2–3 daily; 8hr); Irún (daily; 11hr 30min); León (3 daily; 6hr); Madrid (2 daily; 7hr 30min–10hr); Medina del Campo (2 daily; 6hr 30min); Ponferrada (3 daily; 4–5hr); Pontevedra (15–18 daily; 30min); Ribadavia (daily; 1hr 30min); Santiago de Compostela (10 daily; 1hr 30min); Tui (2 daily; 45min); Zaragoza (1–2 daily; 9–12hr).

Buses

A Coruña to: Betanzos (every 30min, hourly at weekends; 45min); Camariñas (3–5 daily; 1hr 45min); Carnota (1–2 daily; 2hr 40min); Cée (2–7 daily; 2hr 15min); Corme (2–7 daily; 1hr 30min); Ferrol (hourly; 1hr); Fisterra (2–7 daily; 2hr 30min); Laxe (2–6 daily; 1hr); Lugo (8–14 daily; 2hr); Madrid (8 daily; 7hr); Malpica (5–7 daily; 1hr 15min); Ourense (6 daily; 3hr 30min); Oviedo (4 daily; 3hr 45min–6hr); Pontevedra (10 daily; 1hr 45min); Santiago de Compostela (hourly; 1hr 30min); Ribadeo (5 daily; 4hr); Vigo (9 daily; 2hr 15min); Viveiro (6 daily; 3hr 30min).

Costa da Morte to: Camariñas–Muxía–Cée (3 daily; 30min/1hr 30min); Fisterra–Corcubión–Muxía–Camariñas (3 daily; 15min/1hr 15min/2hr); Fisterra–Muros (3 daily; 1hr); Laxe–Muxía (daily; 1hr 30min); Muros–Cée (9 daily; 1hr); Muxía–Camariñas (3 daily; 30min).

Lugo to: A Coruña (hourly; 2hr); Foz (5 daily; 2hr); Ourense (5 daily; 2hr); Pontevedra (5 daily; 2hr); Santiago de Compostela (9 daily; 2hr); Vigo (5 daily; 3hr); Viveiro (4 daily; 2–3hr).

Ourense to: Celanova (8 daily; 1hr 30min); A Coruña (6 daily; 3hr 30min); Lugo (5 daily; 2hr); Santiago de Compostela (6 daily; 2hr 30min); Vigo (12 daily; 2hr).

Pontevedra to: Bueu (14 daily; 30min); Cambados (11 daily; 1hr); Cangas (14 daily; 1hr); A Coruña (9 daily; 2hr); O Grove (10 daily; 1hr); Isla de Arousa (5 daily; 1hr 30min); Lugo (5 daily; 3hr); Noia (daily; 1hr 30min); Ourense (7 daily; 2hr); Padrón (14 daily; 1hr); Santiago de Compostela (every 30min; 1hr); Tui (4 daily; 1hr); Vigo (every 30min; 30min–1hr); Vilagarcía (15 daily; 45min).

Santiago de Compostela to: Betanzos (7 daily; 1hr 30min); Camariñas (4 daily; 3hr); Cambados (5 daily; 2hr); Cée (3–7 daily; 2hr); A Coruña (hourly; 1hr 30min); Ferrol (6–8 daily; 2hr 30min); Fisterra (3–7 daily; 2hr 30min); Lugo (9 daily; 2hr); Madrid (3–6 daily; 9hr 30min); Malpica (3 daily; 2hr); Muros (hourly; 2hr 30min); Noia (hourly; 1hr 30min); Ourense (9 daily; 2hr 30min); Padrón (every 30min; 45min); Pontevedra (hourly; 1hr); Vigo (hourly; 1hr 30min–2hr); Vilagarcía (9 daily; 1hr).

Vigo to: Baiona (every 15min; 1hr); Barcelona (1 or 2 daily; 14hr); Cangas (20 daily; 1hr); A Coruña (7–9 daily; 3hr); O Grove (9 daily; 1hr 15min); Lugo (5–6 daily; 3hr); Madrid (3 daily; 8hr); Noia (daily; 3hr); Oporto and Lisbon (3 weekly; 3hr 30min/6hr); Ourense (13 daily; 2hr); Oviedo (daily; 6hr 15min); Padrón (12 daily; 2hr); Pontevedra (every 30min; 30min–1hr); Ribadavia (13 daily; 1hr 30min); Santiago de Compostela (every 30min; 2hr 30min); Tui (every 30min; 45min).

Aragón

Highlights

* **Basilica de Nuestra Señora del Pilar, Zaragoza** The majestic shrine of one of the most revered patron saints of Spain. See p.614

* **Aljafería, Zaragoza** Explore the most spectacular Moorish monument outside Andalucía. See p.615

* **Teruel** Historic provincial capital brimming with superb Mudéjar architecture. See p.623

* **Albarracín** Wander along medieval lanes past balconied houses in this picturesque town. See p.627

* **El Maestrazgo** Head off the beaten track to roam atmospheric medieval villages in this wild, mountainous region. See p.628

* **Castillo de Loarre** A fairy-tale castle in the Pyrenean foothills, with sweeping views. See p.636

* **Parque Nacional de Ordesa** Dramatic, canyon-slashed landscape for fine high-altitude hiking. See p.647

▲ Basilica de Nuestra Señora del Pilar, Zaragoza

9

Aragón

Politically and historically Aragón has close links with Catalunya, with which it formed a powerful alliance in medieval times, exerting influence over the Mediterranean as far away as Athens. Locked in on all sides by mountains, it has always had its own identity, with traditional *fueros* like the Basques and a written Aragonese language existing alongside Castilian. The modern *autonomía* – containing the provinces of Zaragoza, Teruel and Huesca – is well out of the Spanish political mainstream, especially in the rural south, where Teruel is the least populated region in Spain. Coming from Catalunya or the Basque Country, you'll find the Aragonese pace, in general, noticeably slower.

It is the **Pyrenees** that draw most visitors to Aragón, with their sculpted valleys, stone-built farming villages and excellent trekking. Some valleys are getting noticeably developed with *urbanizaciones* serving expensive ski resorts, but they still have stunning foci in the **Parque Nacional de Ordesa** and the **Parque Natural de Posets–Maladeta**, with their panoply of canyons, waterfalls and peaks. Aragón's Pyrenean towns are also renowned for their sacred architecture; **Jaca** has the country's oldest **Romanesque** cathedral.

The most interesting monuments of central and southern Aragón are, by contrast, **Mudéjar**: a series of churches, towers and mansions built by Muslim workers in the early decades of Christian rule, justly added to UNESCO's World Heritage list in 2001. In addition to its absorbing Roman remains, **Zaragoza**, the Aragonese capital and the only place of any real size, sets the tone with its remarkable **Aljafería Palace**. Other examples are to be found in a string of smaller towns, in particular **Tarazona**, **Calatayud** and – above all – the southern provincial capital of **Teruel**. In southern Aragón, the captivating walled village of **Albarracín** is incredibly picturesque, while to the east lies the isolated region encompassing the **Sierra de Gúdar** and **El Maestrazgo**, a wild countryside stamped with dark peaks and gorges.

Zaragoza, Teruel and southern Aragón

The city of Zaragoza houses nearly half of Aragón's 1.5 million population, and most of its industry. It's a big but enjoyable place, with a lively zone of bars and restaurants tucked in among remarkable monuments, and it's a handy transport nexus, too, both for Aragón and beyond. Its province includes the Mudéjar towns of **Tarazona**, **Calatayud** and **Daroca**, and, along the border with Navarra, the old **Cinco Villas**, really just ennobled villages, of which the most interesting is **Sos del Rey Católico**. Wine enthusiasts may also want to follow the **Ruta de los Vinos**, south from Zaragoza through Cariñena to Daroca.

Teruel province is a lot more remote, and even the capital doesn't see too many passing visitors. It is unjustly neglected, considering its superb Mudéjar monuments, and if you have transport of your own, there are some wonderful rural routes to explore: especially west, through **Albarracín** to Cuenca, or south to Valencia. The valleys and villages of the **Sierra de Gúdar** and **El Maestrazgo**, which borders Valencia province, are the most remote of the lot: a region completely untouched by tourism, foreign or Spanish, and where transport of your own is a big help.

Zaragoza

ZARAGOZA is an inviting city that has managed to absorb its rapid growth with a rare grace, and its centre, at least, reflects an air of prosperity in its wide, modern boulevards, and stylish shops and bars. Highlights include the spectacular Moorish **Aljafería**, an impressive collection of **Roman ruins** and an awesome basilica, devoted to one of Spain's most famous incarnations of the Virgin Mary, **Nuestra Señora del Pilar**.

The city's **fiestas** in honour of the revered saint – which take place throughout the second week of October – are well worth planning a trip around, so long as you can find accommodation. In addition to the religious processions (which focus on the 12th), the local council lays on a brilliant programme of cultural events, featuring top rock, jazz and folk bands, floats, bullfights and traditional *jota* dancing.

In 2008, Zaragoza hosted the splashy **Expo Zaragoza** (ⓦwww .expozaragoza2008.es), which celebrated the theme of water and sustainable development. The gleaming Expo site, sprawled along the river just west of the city centre, featured plenty of intriguing architecture, including the iconic **Water Tower**, which loomed at nearly 76m tall, with a sheet of water at the entrance, spiral ramps and a top-floor bar with sweeping views of the city; and a sleek bridge pavilion designed by Zaha Hadid. The Expo site is to be transformed into a high-end business centre, and a number of the key edifices will likely remain to host exhibits and the like. Thanks to the Expo, Zaragoza's centre was also spruced up, including general restoration work on many of its historic buildings. Check with the tourist office about what parts of the Expo are open to the public; several city buses head near the site, including #23, which departs from the Plaza de la Independencia.

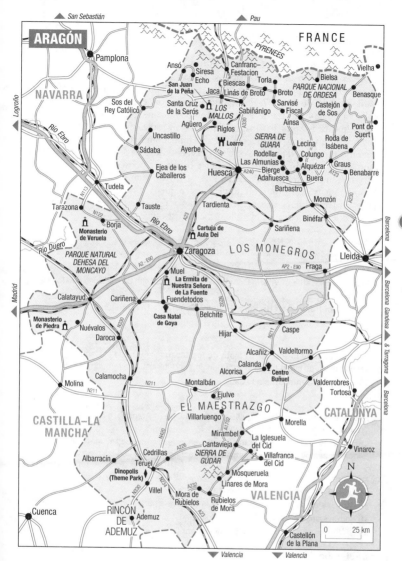

Arrival and information

Zaragoza's **airport**, serving domestic flights and Ryanair services from London Stansted and Milan, is 10km northwest of the city centre; an airport bus plies back and forth in conjunction with flights (Mon–Sat, every half hour 6am to 10.30pm; on Sun, hourly 6am–10pm; €1.50). Taxis should cost €20. **Trains** use the Estación Delicias, just over 3km from the centre. From here, catch bus #51 right outside the station to the Paseo Constitución, a ten-minute walk from El Tubo, or bus #25 on Avenida Navarra which will take you to Avenida César Augusto, just west of Plaza del Pilar. If you decide to walk, a small **turismo** booth (daily 10am–8pm) at the station can supply you with a map. **Buses** also arrive at the train station, including Agreda and Alsa services for Asturias, Barcelona, Bilbao, Galicia, León, Madrid and several destinations in Old Castile; La Oscense/Agreda services to Huesca and Jaca; and Eurolines buses and services south to Daroca, Cariñena and Muel.

For departures to other destinations, it's best to check with the main **turismo** opposite the basilica on Plaza del Pilar (Easter–Sept daily 9am–9pm; Oct–Easter 10am–8pm; ☎ 976 393 537, ⓦ www.turismozaragoza.com). This caters for the city, while an office on Plaza de España (Mon–Fri 10am–2pm & 5–8pm, Sat & Sun 10am–2pm & 5–8pm) has maps on places and routes throughout the Zaragoza province. From July to October you'll also find about two dozen tourist information officers – dressed in white or blue jackets – at various points around the centre (most speak English), and special **tourist buses** ply between all the main sights every fifteen minutes from Plaza del Pilar at c/Don Jaime (€6). The tourist office also offers a walking tour (in English, by request) through the old town (€5; approximately 2 hours) that departs Saturdays at 6pm in summer (4pm in winter); reserve one day in advance by calling the tourist office.

Fiestas

May
First Friday: Battle of Vitoria Commemorated in Jaca with processions and folkloric events.
Monday of Pentecost: Romería Nuestra Señora de Calentuñana At Sos del Rey Católico.

June
Nearest Sunday to the 19th: Fiesta de los Mozos Celebrated in Cantavieja with a serious religious event but also with dancing and the usual fairground activities.
25: Fiesta de Santa Orosia In Jaca.

July
First and second week: Vaquilla del Ángel One of Aragón's major festivals sees Teruel burst into ten days of festivities.
Last two weeks: Pireneos Sur World music festival at Sallent de Gallego, with performances by international artists on a floating stage in Lanuza reservoir.

August
Early August: Fiesta de San Lorenzo In Huesca.
14–15: Fiestas del Barrio Street markets and mass parties in Jaca.
16 Patron saint's festival at Biescas – "bigheads" and eats.
27–28 *Encierros* – crazy local bull-running – at Cantavieja.

September
Early September: Feria de Teruel Annual town fair.
4–8 Fiesta at Barbastro includes *jota* dancing, bullfights and sports competitions (such as pigeon-shooting contests).
8 Virgin's birthday prompts fairs at Echo and Calatayud.
8–14 Bull-running and general celebrations at Albarracín.

October
Second week Aragón's most important festival in honour of the *Virgen del Pilar*. Much of the province closes down around the 12th, and at Zaragoza there are floats, bullfights and *jota* dancing.

Accommodation

The central, atmospheric **Casco Viejo** has upwards of a dozen *pensiones*, both around Plaza del Pilar and the small streets off c/Méndez Núñez, although they can be noisy at night. Alternatively, there are a number of decent options dotted around to the east of Plaza de España.

Casco Viejo

Albergue Juvenil Baltázar Gracián c/Franco y López 4, off Avda. de Valencia ☏ 976 306 692, to reserve a bed, ☏ 902 088 905 Mon–Fri 8am–8pm, ✉ balta@aragon.es. Basic but clean rooms sleeping two, four or eight people on bunk beds with bedding and breakfast included. Check-in is noon–9pm, and there's a midnight curfew. Under 26s €13, over 26s €17.

Catalonia Zaragoza Plaza Manifestacion 16 ☏ 976 205 858, ⓦ www.hoteles-catalonia.es. Inside a gorgeous *modernista* building on the edge of the old town, this hotel blends contemporary design with traditional features such as a wrought-iron lift. Rooms feature designer furnishings and a simple, understated colour scheme. ❺

Hostal Plaza Plaza del Pilar 14, 1º ☏ 976 294 830, ⓦ www.hostalplaza-santiago.com. The rooms are adequate, if a little musty and dated, with faded bedspreads, but they have TV and bathroom, and the location is unbeatable. ❷–❸

Hotel Palafox Casa Jiménez s/n ☏ 976 237 700, ⓦ www.palafoxhoteles.com. The closest five-star to the Casco Viejo, sporting a blend of contemporary, Aragonese and Mudéjar design by Pascua Ortega. Excellent facilities, including parking, a fine restaurant, internet access and an outdoor pool. ❼

Hotel Reino de Aragón c/Coso 80 ☏ 976 468 200, ⓦ www.hotelreinodearagon.com. Smart Silken chain hotel with a boutique feel. Rooms combine classical and contemporary style, with satellite TV and marble-clad bathrooms. Sometimes offers good online deals in low season. ❼

Hotel Sauce c/Espoz y Mina 33 ☏ 976 205 050, ⓦ www.hotelsauce.com. Along with its great name, this hotel boasts attractively furnished, a/c rooms with bathrooms and satellite TV. ❸

Hotel Vía Romana c/Don Jaime I 54 ☏ 976 398 215, ⓦ www.husa.es. Smart mid-range option just off the Plaza del Pilar, beautifully restored, with neat, comfortable rooms and cheap weekend deals. ❹

Hotel Zentro Zaragoza c/Coso 86 ☏ 976 703 300, ⓦ www.hotelzentrozaragoza.com. The city's latest upscale hotel, also from Silken, reveals a *modernista* facade and an elegant, cool-toned lobby (peer down through plexiglass at the underground Roman remains) that gives way to handsome rooms, with wi-fi and satellite TV. Check the website for good last-minute or low-season offers. ❼

Pensión Descanso San Lorenzo 2 ☏ 976 291 741. Light, clean, cheap rooms with plenty of character and friendly owners, next to a pleasant, tree-shaded square. TV but shared bathrooms. ❷

Pensión La Peña c/Cinegio 3, 1º ☏ 976 299 089. Comfortable, clean and inexpensive rooms with shared bathrooms at this family-run *pensión* – the ongoing construction work nearby makes it noisy during the day. The *comedor* here, open to all and usually frequented by elderly locals, dishes up particularly vast quantities of simple home-cooked food. ❶

Posada de las Almas c/San Pablo 22 ☏ 976 439 700. This atmospheric hotel has worn but functional rooms, and boasts the oldest restaurant in town (1705), which has a certain faded charm and does wonderfully inexpensive *menús* (€10, weekend *menú* €15) of hearty local fare. Restaurant closed Sun dinner & Mon. ❸

Zaragoza Hostel c/Predicadores 70 ☏ 976 282 043, ⓦ www.alberguezaragoza.com. New, central, spacious hostel built in a solid, medieval building near the banks of the Ebro. Doubles and dorm rooms, free internet, kitchen use and breakfast included. €25 per bed.

Camping

Camping Casablanca Valdefierro, 2km from the centre along the Avda. de Madrid ☏ 976 753 870. A rather barren-looking site, but large and well equipped, with a swimming pool. Bus #36 from Plaza del Pilar or Plaza de España runs past. Closed mid-Oct to March.

The City

The **Plaza del Pilar** is the obvious point to start exploring Zaragoza. The square, paved in a brilliant, pale stone, was remodelled in 1991, creating a vast, airy expanse from **La Seo**, past the great **Basilica de Nuestra Señora del Pilar**, and over to Avenida César Augusto. The *plaza* spans the city's entire history: Roman ruins at both ends; between the churches, a Renaissance exchange house, the **Lonja**; and

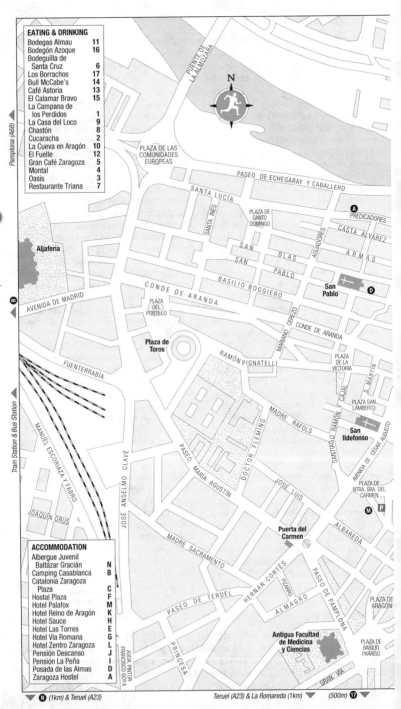

EATING & DRINKING

Bodegas Almau	11
Bodegón Azoque	16
Bodeguilla de Santa Cruz	6
Los Borrachos	17
Bull McCabe's	14
Café Astoria	13
El Calamar Bravo	15
La Campana de los Perdidos	1
La Casa del Loco	9
Chastón	8
Cucaracha	2
La Cueva en Aragón	10
El Fuelle	12
Gran Café Zaragoza	5
Montal	4
Oasis	3
Restaurante Triana	7

ACCOMMODATION

Albergue Juvenil Baltazar Gracián	N
Camping Casablanca	B
Catalonia Zaragoza Plaza	C
Hostal Plaza	F
Hotel Palafox	M
Hotel Reino de Aragón	K
Hotel Sauce	H
Hotel Las Torres	E
Hotel Vía Romana	G
Hotel Zentro Zaragoza	L
Pensión Descanso	J
Pensión La Peña	I
Posada de las Almas	D
Zaragoza Hostel	A

N

9 ARAGÓN

Pamplona (A68)

Aljafería

PLAZA DE LAS COMUNIDADES EUROPEAS

PASEO DE ECHEGARAY Y CABALLERO

SANTA LUCÍA

SANTA INÉS

PLAZA DE SANTO DOMINGO

PREDICADORES

A

CASTA ÁLVAREZ

AGUADORES

ARMAS

SAN BLAS

SAN PABLO

BASILIO BOGGIERO

San Pablo

D

AVENIDA DE MADRID

CONDE DE ARANDA

PLAZA DEL PORTILLO

MARIANO CEREZO

CONDE DE ARANDA

PLAZA DE LA VICTORIA

Plaza de Toros

RAMÓN PIGNATELLI

S. MARTÍN

PLAZA SAN LAMBERTO

FUENTERRABÍA

MADRE RÁFOLS

SANTIAGO RAMÓN Y CAJAL

San Ildefonso

AVENIDA DE CÉSAR AUGUSTO

Train Station & Bus Station

MANUEL ESCORIAZA Y FABRO

JOSÉ ANSELMO CLAVÉ

PASEO MARÍA AGUSTÍN

DOCTOR FLEMING

JOSÉ LUIS

PLAZA DE NTRA. SRA. DEL CARMEN

M

P

ALBAREDA

JOAQUÍN ORÚS

Puerta del Carmen

MADRE SACRAMENTO

HERNÁN CORTÉS

PIZARRO

ALMAGRO

PASEO DE PAMPLONA

PLAZA DE ARAGÓN

PASEO DE TERUEL

PRINCESA

AVDA. PINTOR FRANCISCO GOYA

Antigua Facultad de Medicina y Ciencias

GRAN VÍA

PLAZA DE BASILIO PARAÍSO

N (1km) & Teruel (A23)

Teruel (A23) & La Romareda (1km)

(500m) 17

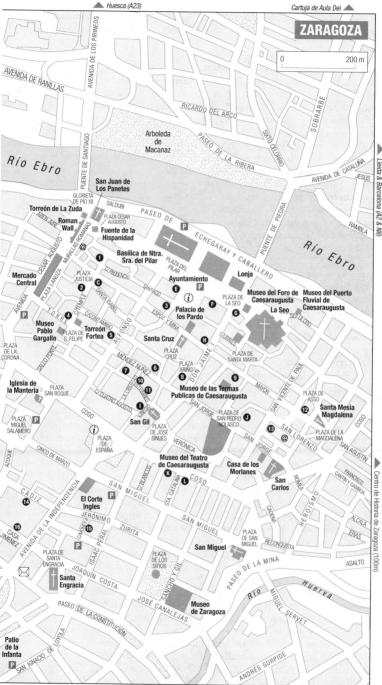

ZARAGOZA

0   200 m

AVENIDA DE LOS PIRINEOS

AVENIDA DE RANILLAS

RICARDO DEL ARCO

SOBRARBE

Arboleda de Macanaz

PASEO DE LA RIBERA

SIXTO CELORRIO

Río Ebro

AVENIDA DE CATALUÑA

JESÚS

PUENTE DE SANTIAGO

GLORIETA DE PÍO XII

San Juan de Los Panetes

SALDUBI

PASEO DE ECHEGARAY Y CABALLERO

RAMBLA

Torreón de La Zuda

ABEN-AIRE

Roman Wall

PLAZA CÉSAR AUGUSTO

Fuente de la Hispanidad

PUENTE DE PIEDRA

Río Ebro

MURALLAS ROMANAS

CÉSAR AUGUSTO

@

C/ PRUDENCIO

Basílica de Ntra. Sra. del Pilar

PLAZA DEL PILAR

Lonja

AVENIDA

PLAZA LANUZA

PLAZA JUSTICIA

SANTIAGO

Ayuntamiento

Museo del Foro de Caesaraugusta

Museo del Puerto Fluvial de Caesaraugusta

Mercado Central

TORRE

SANTA ISABEL

ESPOZ Y MINA

PLAZA DE LA SEO

La Seo

TEMPLE

Palacio de los Pardo

SEPULCRO

Museo Pablo Gargallo

TORRELLAS

CONTAMINA

PLAZA DE S. FELIPE

Torreón Fortea

ALONSO

Santa Cruz

C/UBIERES

PLAZA DE LAS CORONA

GRILLO PONTE

PLAZA CRUZ

PLAZA DE SANTA MARTA

PLAZA DE LA CORONA

MÉNDEZ NÚÑEZ

PLAZA ARIÑO

DON JAIME I

Iglesia de la Mantería

PLAZA SAN ROQUE

LA LIBERTAD

Museo de las Termas Publicas de Caesaraugusta

SAN JORGE

MAYOR

SAN VICENTE DE PAÚL

PLAZA DE ASSO

Santa Mesía Magdalena

PLAZA MIGUEL SALAMERO

C/ CUATRO AGOSTO

COSO

ESPOZ

San Gil

PLAZA DE JOSÉ SINUES

PLAZA DE SAN PEDRO NOLASCO

SAN JORGE

SAN LORENZO

@

PLAZA DE LA MAGDALENA

SAN AGUSTÍN

COSO

PLAZA DE ESPAÑA

CINCO DE MARZO

VERÓNICA

Museo del Teatro de Caesaraugusta

Casa de los Morlanes

San Carlos

HEROÍSMO

ROMEA

CANTÍN Y GAMBOA

FRANCISCO

AZOQUE

CÁDIZ

SAN MIGUEL

STA. CATALINA

COSO

ALCALÁ

ERAS

El Corte Ingles

AVENIDA DE LA INDEPENDENCIA

JERÓNIMO

COMPROMISO

ISAAC PERAL

ZURITA

SAN MIGUEL

PLAZA DE SAN MIGUEL

RECONQUISTA

ASALTO

CASA JIMENEZ

PLAZA DE SANTA ENGRACIA

JOAQUIN COSTA

SANCHO Y GIL

PLAZA DE LOS SITIOS

San Miguel

PASEO DE LA MINA

Río HUERVA

MIGUEL SERVET

Santa Engracia

PASEO DE LA CONSTITUCIÓN

JOSÉ CANALEJAS

Museo de Zaragoza

Patio de la Infanta

SAN IGNACIO DE LOYOLA

ANDRÉS GURPIDE

at the centre, some modern statuary and the **Fuente de la Hispanidad**, a giant waterfall shaped like a section of Central America and the Caribbean to commemorate 1492.

Basilica de Nuestra Señora del Pilar

Majestically fronting the Río Ebro, the **Basilica de Nuestra Señora del Pilar** (daily 5.45am–9.30pm, until 8.30pm in winter; free) is one of Spain's greatest and most revered religious buildings. It takes its name from a pillar – the centrepiece of the church – on which the Virgin Mary is said to have descended from heaven in an apparition before St James the Apostle. The structure around this shrine is truly monumental, with great corner towers and a central dome flanked by ten brightly tiled cupolas; it was designed in the late seventeenth century by Francisco Herrera el Mozo and built by Ventura Rodríguez in the 1750s and 60s.

The **pillar**, topped by a diminutive image of the Virgin, is constantly surrounded by pilgrims, who line up to touch an exposed (and thoroughly worn) section, encased in a marble surround. The main artistic treasure of the cathedral is a magnificent alabaster reredos on the high altar, a masterpiece sculpted by Damián Forment in the first decades of the sixteenth century.

Off the north aisle is the **Museo Pilarista** (Tues–Sun 9am–1.30pm & 4–5.30pm; €2), where you can inspect at close quarters the original sketches for the decoration of the domes by Francisco de Goya, González Velázquez and Francisco and Ramón Bayeu. Your ticket also admits you to the **Sacristía Mayor**, off the opposite aisle, with a collection of religious paintings and tapestries. You'll have to pay extra, however, if you want to enjoy the panoramic views from the **Torre**, the tower at the northwest corner of the church (Mon–Thurs & Sat 9.30am–2pm & 4–6pm; €2).

Around Plaza del Pilar

The old cathedral, **Catedral de San Salvador**, known as **La Seo** (Tues–Fri 10am–1.30pm & 4–6pm, Sat 10am–noon & 4–6pm, Sun 10–11.30am & 4–6pm; €2.50), stands at the far end of Plaza del Pilar. The gleaming exterior is essentially Gothic-Mudéjar with minor Baroque and Plateresque additions, while to the left of the mian entrance is a Mudéjar wall with elaborate geometric patterns. Inside, the superb *retablo mayor* contains some recognizably Teutonic figures executed by the German Renaissance sculptor, Hans of Swabia.

Just outside the cathedral, marked by a striking entrance portal lined with onyx, is the **Museo del Foro de Caesaraugusta** (Tues–Sat 10am–1.30pm & 5–7.30pm, Sun 10am–1.30pm; €2), one of four absorbing museums in the Caso Viejo dedicated to Zaragoza's Roman heritage (a ticket covering all four costs €6) – the city's name derives from that of Caesar Augustus (César Augusto in the Spanish form). This one comprises the ruins (primarily foundations) of the old Roman forum, located in an impressive underground chamber beneath the *plaza*, as well as a small exhibition including displays of artefacts found on site. A short walk to the other side of La Seo is the **Museo del Puerto Fluvial de Caesaraugusta** (Tues–Sat 10am–1.30pm & 5–7.30pm, Sun 10am–1.30pm; €2), which preserves the remains of Roman river-port buildings.

Midway between the two cathedrals stands the sixteenth-century **Lonja** (Tues–Sat 10am–2pm & 5–9pm, Sun 10am–2pm; free), the old exchange building, a Florentine-influenced structure, with an interior of elegant Ionic columns, open periodically for art exhibitions. On the other side of the basilica are the remains of **Roman walls** and the **Torreón de la Zuda** (July to mid-Oct daily 10am–8pm; rest of year Mon–Sat 10am–2pm & 4.30–8pm, Sun 10am–2pm; free), part of Zaragoza's medieval fortifications.

South of Plaza del Pilar

A block south of the square, in the impeccably restored Palacio de los Pardo at c/Espoz y Mina 23, the **Museo Ibercaja Camón Aznar** (Tues–Fri 9am–2pm & 6–9pm, Sat 10am–2pm & 6–9pm, Sun 11am–2pm; free with photo ID) houses the private collections of José Camón Aznar, one of the most distinguished scholars of Spanish art. Highlights include a permanent display of most of Goya's prints (the artist was born at nearby Fuendetodos; see p.618). At the far end of the street, which becomes c/Mayor, the church of **Santa María Magdalena** has the finest of Zaragoza's several Mudéjar towers (currently being restored). Keep walking east along c/San Augustín and you'll reach the **Centro de Historia de Zaragoza** (Tues–Sat 10am–2pm & 5–9pm, Sun 10am–2pm; free), with innovative galleries on Zaragoza's history, organized thematically; it's also often used for contemporary art exhibitions (Spanish text only).

Farther south on Plaza de San Pedro Nolasco, a vast modern canopy covers the ruins of the Roman theatre, part of the **Museo del Teatro de Caesaraugusta** (Tues–Sat 10am–8.30pm, Sun 10am–1.30pm; €3). Buy tickets here for the smaller **Museo de las Termas Públicas de Caesaraugusta** at c/San Juan and San Pedro 3–7 (Tues–Sat 10am–1.30pm & 5–7.30pm, Sun 10–1.30pm; €2), which displays what's left of the Roman baths. You can see more works by Goya at the **Museo de Zaragoza** (Tues–Sat 10am–2pm & 5–8pm, Sun 10am–2pm; free), in the Plaza de los Sitios, while other exhibits often span the city's Iberian, Roman and Moorish past. Close by is a pair of interesting churches: **San Miguel**, with a minor *retablo* by Forment and a Mudéjar tower, and **Santa Engracia**, with a splendid Plateresque portal and paleo-Christian sarcophagi in its crypt. Two further Mudéjar towers can be seen at **San Pablo** (under ongoing restoration), over to the west of Plaza del Pilar, with another *retablo* by Damián Forment, and **San Gil**, near Plaza de España. On the western side of the Casco Viejo, the **Museo Pablo Gargallo** (Tues–Sat 10am–2pm & 5–9pm, Sun 10am–2pm; free), in the attractive Renaissance Palacio Argillo at Plaza San Felipe 3, houses the work of the celebrated Aragonese sculptor.

The Aljafería

Moorish Spain was never very unified, and from the tenth to the eleventh century, Zaragoza was the centre of an independent dynasty, the Beni Kasim. Their palace, the **Aljafería** (April–Oct daily 10am–2pm & 4.30–8pm; Nov–March daily 10am–2pm & 4–6.30pm; closed Thurs & Fri mornings Feb–June & Sept–Dec when the *Cortes* is in session; €3; ☎976 289 683), was built in the heyday of their rule in the mid-eleventh century, and as such predates the Alhambra in Granada and Seville's Alcázar. Much, however, was added later, under twelfth- to fifteenth-century Christian rule, when the palace was adapted and used by the *reconquista* kings of Aragón. Since 1987, the Aragonese parliament has met here.

The foremost relics from the original design are a tiny and beautiful **mosque**, adjacent to the entrance, and farther on an intricately decorated court, the **Patio de Santa Isabella**. From here, the **Grand Staircase** (added in 1492) leads to a succession of mainly fourteenth-century rooms, remarkable for their carved *artesonado* ceilings; the most beautiful is in the Throne Room. Free guided **tours** run at 10.30am, 11.30am, 12.30pm, 4.30pm, 5.30pm and 6.30pm.

Eating, drinking and nightlife

Most of Zaragoza's **bars** are concentrated in the Casco Viejo, along with an array of economic **restaurants** and *comedores*. As you'd expect in a place of this size, you'll also find upmarket restaurants scattered throughout the rest of the city. For **tapas** – and plenty of late-night drinking – head to **El Tubo**, the series of narrow streets near Plaza de España, particularly Estébanes, Cuatro de Agosto and La Libertad; also try the areas around Plaza de Santa Marta or Plaza de San Pedro Nolasco.

Tapas bars, cafés and restaurants

Bodegas Almau Estébanes 9. Spirited tapas bar established in 1870, with a handsome, tiled interior that gives way to a bustling outdoor area strewn with pebbles and barrel-tables. A range of tasty tapas, including their speciality anchovies. Mon–Sat 11am–2pm & 7pm–midnight.

Bodegón Azoque Casa Jiménez 6. Upscale tapas bar, with a smart business crowd weekdays sipping quality wine at the rustic, wood-encased bar. Barrels of wine stand at the door, while diners graze on sardines and the celebrated *jamón de Jabugo*. Daily 11.30am–midnight.

La Bodeguilla de Santa Cruz c/Santa Cruz 3. A characterful bar that looks like a cross between Aladdin's cave and an old apothecary, serving a creative selection of beautifully presented tapas and *raciones*. Mon–Fri 8pm–midnight, Sat 1–3.30pm & 8pm–midnight.

Los Borrachos Paseo Sagasta 64 ☎976 275 036. This is a bit of a trek south of the old town, but worth it for the unique blend of old-world charm and special game dishes such as venison, boar and pheasant. Reckon on €45 and up for a meal with wine. Closed Sun eve & Mon lunch.

Café Astoria c/San Vicente de Paúl 20. Stylish eatery with modern art on the walls, a great salad selection, an unusual variety of reasonably priced, French-influenced dishes and lavish tapas. Mon–Sat 8.30am–11pm (until 1am weekends).

El Calamar Bravo c/Moneva 5. A hugely popular and inexpensive stand-up tapas bar with outstanding *calamares* sandwiches (€2.50) and *patatas bravas* (€1.50), all smothered in mayonnaise and *piquante* salsa. The bar is due to change location to the nearby Cinco de Marzo. Daily till 11pm.

La Cueva en Aragón c/Libertad. Lively tapas joint that's also known as "El Champi", for its signature tapa – succulent mushrooms topped with a powerful garlic sauce.

El Fuelle c/Mayor 57. Earthy local *cocina*, specializing in no-frills Aragonese cuisine, especially meat dishes. Great atmosphere and value for money. Closed Sun eve & Mon.

Gran Café Zaragoza c/Alfonsin I 25. Historic, genteel café, with a nineteenth-century interior of dark-wood ceilings and a burnished wooden bar, with large windows that overlook the street. Daily 8.30am–10pm.

Montal Torre Nueva 29 ☎976 298 998. An old shop dating from 1919 that becomes an alluring restaurant at night, with a tapas bar on ground level and a Renaissance balcony for an elegant dinner of regional fare – reservations are essential, and prices hover around €35 per person.

Restaurant Triana Estébanes 7 ☎976 293 082. No-nonsense, bi-level, family-run restaurant with aged photos of Zaragoza, and antique radios. On weekdays, locals gather round the tightly packed tables for the generous €10 *menú* and other hot and filling Aragonese eats. Closed Sun eve.

Bars and clubs

The Casco Viejo has several hopping *zonas* of **music and tapas bars** and **nightclubs**, including the area around c/Cantamina and c/Temple, which hits its stride at the weekends after midnight.

Bull McCabe's c/Cadiz. One of the most popular of Zaragoza's Irish bars, with two floors and reasonably priced pints of the black stuff. Mon–Fri 9.30am–1/2am, Sat 2pm–2.30am, Sun 5pm–2am.

La Campana de los Perdidos c/Prudencio 7. Traditional bar with great atmosphere and regular local performers; jazz and folk music (Thurs, Fri & Sun from 9pm) in the cave-like cellar.

La Casa del Loco c/Mayor 10. Rock pub with plenty of live acts, and a mix of the latest English and Spanish sounds otherwise. Cover €7–10 for live shows. Thurs–Sat 9.30pm–6am.

Chastón c/Plaza Ariño 4. Pleasant city-centre bar with jazz and blues sounds, a mellow, woody interior with lots of comfy cushions and a summer terraza. Starts getting busy after 11pm. Daily 6.30pm–1am or later.

Cucaracha c/Temple 25. Raucous place in the heart of Casco Viejo's bar district, especially popular for its range of mind-numbing shots. Tends to get busy well after midnight. Wed–Sat from 9pm.

Da Luxe Plaza de la Pilar 12. Plush *discoteca*, home of the late-night party crowd, just behind the main *turismo*. Mon–Wed & Sun noon–3am, Thurs–Sat noon–6am.

Oasis c/Boggiero 28. A grand old concert hall a glitzy disco and pub, with live shows that sometimes include drag acts. Fri & Sat from 9pm.

Listings

Banks Barclays has numerous branches in the city: Paseo María Augustin 3; c/San Vincente Martir 18; Avda. Goya 58; Avda. de Madrid 141–143. Citibank is at Paseo de Sagasta 9.

Car rental Atesa, Avda. Valencia 6 ☏ 976 350 408; Avis, Passeo Fernando el Católico 9 ☏ 976 489 236; Hertz, Avda. de Goya 61–63 ☏ 976 320 400.

Cinema Filmoteca de Zaragoza, Plaza de San Carlos 4, has an arts programme, including original-language movies (€2). ⊛ www.zaragozafilmo.tk.

Flea market El Rastro usually takes place near La Romareda (Wed & Sun am) for clothes, accessories and household objects, but check at the *turismo*. The more eclectic Mercadillo (Sun am) is held outside the bullring and near Plaza San Francisco. An art market (oil paintings and the like) also takes place in Plaza Santa Cruz (Sun am).

Football Real Zaragoza (⊛ www.realzaragoza .com), the local *Primera Division* side, play at La Romareda stadium in the south of the city.

Hospital Miguel Servet, Plaza Isabel la Católica 1 ☏ 976 765 500.

Internet access *Locutorio San Lorenzo*, c/San Lorenzo 26 (daily 10am–3pm & 4.30–11.30pm); *Conecta-T* at Muralles Romanas 4 (Mon–Fri 10am–11pm, Sat & Sun 11am–11pm).

Post office The main *correos* is at Paseo de la Independencia 33 (Mon–Fri 8.30am–8.30pm, Sat 8.30am–2pm).

Shops The big shopping street is Paseo de la Independencia, south of Plaza de España, lined with chain shops including a branch of El Corte Inglés, and the Caracol shopping centre. Northwest of the city lies the Grancasa, Zaragoza's largest shopping centre, with the usual range of shops, including Spanish brands Zara and Mango.

Skiing If you plan to go skiing in the Pyrenees, you're probably best off buying a package deal from a travel agent in Zaragoza. Try Marsans: there's a branch at Avda. de la Independencia 18 ☏ 976 236 965, ⊛ www.marsans.es, and others on Paseo María Agustín.

Taxis Radio-Taxi Aragón ☏ 976 383 838; Radio-Taxi Zaragoza ☏ 976 424 242.

Around Zaragoza

Few tourists spend much time exploring the sights and towns around Zaragoza, and with the Pyrenees just a step to the north, it is perhaps no wonder. However, wine buffs heading south might want to follow the **Ruta de los Vinos** through **Cariñena**, while Goya enthusiasts will be more interested in **Muel**, and his birthplace in **Fuendetodos**. Nearby lies **Belchite**, one of Spain's most poignant reminders of the Civil War.

Northwest of the capital, the **Cinco Villas** stretch for some 90km along the border with Navarra. These are really little more than villages, set in delightful, scarcely visited countryside; their title is owed to Felipe V, who awarded it for their services in the War of the Spanish Succession (1701–14). The most absorbing of the five is the northernmost "town", **Sos del Rey Católico**, on the A127 to Pamplona.

The wine route and Goya trail

There are **vineyards** dotted all over Aragón, but the best wines – strong, throaty reds and good whites – come from the region to the south of Zaragoza, whose towns and villages are best explored with your own transport. The tourist authorities have marked out a **Ruta del Vino** through the area; an alternative route could take you on a brief **Goya trail**, to see frescoes and his birthplace.

Muel and Fuendetodos

MUEL marks the northernmost point of the region and was once a renowned pottery centre. It has seen much better days, however, and few trains stop any more. The town's interest lies in a Roman fountain and a hermitage, **La Ermita de Nuestra Señora de la Fuente** (Mon–Sat 10am–2pm & 4–7pm,

The enduring legacy of Belchite

Of all the reminders of the Spanish Civil War, the war-torn town of **Belchite** (20km east of Fuendetodos and 50km southeast of Zaragoza) is perhaps the most haunting. It's also the most unforgettable, which is why this casualty of war was left untouched after it was bombed by Franco's forces. Residents built up a new Belchite 1km away from its ravaged sibling.

The sign at the entrance for the bombed-out Belchite reads simply "*Belchite, Pueblo Viejo*". Dusty streets are lined with abandoned houses, their twisted wrought-iron balconies dangling askew. Peeling shutters creak in the wind, while crumbling walls bear bullet holes. The church is especially affecting, with jagged holes in the ceiling gaping at the sky, and crushed rocks in place of where the pews used to be. The only signs of life are the occasional shepherd and his flock, weaving through the silent ruins to the green fields beyond. Autobuses ABASA (℡976 229 886 or 976 554 588, ⓦwww.abasa.es) run from Zaragoza (3–4 daily).

Sun 10am–2pm; free), which has some early frescoes of saints by Goya painted in 1772. It's signposted on the edge of town, with a small car park nearby.

The famous artist, who became court painter to Carlos IV, spent his early childhood in the village of **FUENDETODOS**, 24km southeast. Here you can visit the **Casa Natal de Goya** (Tues–Sun: summer 10am–2pm and 4–8pm, winter 11am–2pm & 4–7pm), the eighteenth-century labourer's house where Goya was born in 1746; it has been faithfully restored, complete with rustic, period decor. The house is clearly signposted in the heart of the old part of the village, along c/Zuloaga – it's best to park on the outskirts and walk in. Entry is included with tickets to the **Museo del Grabado de Goya** (same times; €3), 100m farther along c/Zuloaga at no. 3, which exhibits four of the artist's print series: *Caprichos* (Caprices), *Desastres* (Disastres), *Tauromaquia* (Bullfighting) and *Disparates* (Absurdities).

Cariñena

Twenty-four kilometres west of Fuendetodos, just off the main A23 highway, **CARIÑENA** is a larger, rather unattractive town, with a clutch of **wine bodegas**. There's a small **Museo del Vino**, at Camino de la Platero 1 (Tues–Fri 10am–2pm & 4–7pm, Sat 11am–2pm & 5–8pm, Sun 11am–2pm; €1.50), which can supply information about touring the local vineyards. A good place to taste and buy wine is the *tienda* at **Grandes Vinos y Viñedos**, the largest *bodega* in Aragón (shop open Mon–Fri 8am–2pm & 4–6pm; ⓦwww.grandesvinos.com). Call ahead to tour the facilities (℡976 621 261; €10 including wine-tasting); times will be fixed when ten or more people sign up. To get there, follow the N330 north towards Zaragoza and after 3km turn left at the sign for Santuario de Ntra. Sra. de Lagunas.

Sos del Rey Católico and the Cinco Villas

North of Zaragoza, the **Cinco Villas** comprise **Tauste**, **Ejea de los Caballeros**, **Sádaba**, **Uncastillo** and **Sos del Rey Católico**. Sos, the most interesting of the five, attracts the most visitors, while remote, tranquil Uncastillo, and Sádaba, with its handsome castle, are also very rewarding. Only one **bus** a day makes it up from Zaragoza to Sos, so you'll need your own transport if you want to explore farther. For those en route to the Pyrenees (the road past Sos continues to Roncal in Navarra) or to Pamplona, the Cinco Villas make a pleasant stopoff.

Zaragoza to Sos

TAUSTE, closest of the "towns" to Zaragoza, has an interesting parish church built in the Mudéjar style – and **accommodation** at the central *Casa Pepe*, c/Santa Clara 7 (☎976 855 832; ❸). Nearby **EJEA DE LOS CABALLEROS** retains elements of Romanesque architecture in its churches and has a handful of **places to stay**, including *Hostal Aragón*, c/Media Villa 21 (☎976 660 630; ❷), which offers simple rooms, some with shared bathrooms. Twenty kilometres northwest, **SÁDABA** boasts an impressive thirteenth-century castle, as well as the remains of an early synagogue, and a comfortable **hotel**, *Hospedería de Sádaba*, c/Mayor 18 (☎976 675 377, ⓦwww.lahospederiadesadaba.com; ❹), built in a stone-walled thirteenth-century manor. The decent restaurant serves up hearty Aragonese dishes; look for the old wine press in the bar. **UNCASTILLO**, northwest of Sadaba, also has a castle, as its name suggests, this time dating from the twelfth century, and the remains of an aqueduct. In the castle is the small **Museo de la Torre** (July to mid-Sept daily 11am–2pm & 5–8pm; rest of the year Wed–Fri 11am–2pm, Sat–Sun 11am–2pm & 4–6pm; ☎976 679 121), with simple exhibits on the castle and Uncastillo's history. **Accommodation** is fairly limited, but there are some good choices, including the charmingly renovated, excellent-value *Posada la Pastora* (☎976 679 499; ❹).

Sos del Rey Católico

SOS DEL REY CATÓLICO, 120km from Zaragoza, derives its name from Fernando II, El Rey Católico, born here in 1452 and as powerful a local-boy-made-good as any Aragonese town could hope for. The narrow cobbled streets of the Centro Histórico, like so many in Aragón, are packed with marvellously grand mansions, including the **Casa Palacio de Sada** (June–Sept daily 10am–2pm & 4–8pm; Oct–May Wed–Sun 10am–1pm & 4–7pm; €2.60, €4 including guided walk through the village) at its heart, where Fernando is reputed to have been born. The nearby eleventh-century Romanesque parish church of **San Esteban**

▲ Sos del Rey Católico

(Mon–Sat 10.30am–1pm & 3.30–5.30pm, Sun 10am–noon & 4–6pm) has an unusual lower chapel, dedicated to Santa María del Perdón. Above the town, the ruined **Castillo de la Peña Felizana** offers magnificent views over the village's terracotta rooftops and surrounding countryside.

The small **turismo** is in the Palacio de Sada (same times as Casa Palacio de Sada; ℡948 888 524). The cheapest **accommodation** in town is the handsome, well-maintained *Albergue de Sos* in a medieval *torre* on c/Meca (℡948 888 480, Ⓦwww.alberguedesos.com; under 26s €15, over 26s €17.50), with stone walls, brightly patterned furnishings and spacious, clean public areas. Otherwise, it's well worth splurging at the superb ⚑ *Parador Sos del Rey Católico* (℡948 888 011, Ⓦwww.parador.es; closed mid-Jan to Feb; ❼), a modern building whose rooms offer spectacular panoramic views across the hills. The elegant restaurant features Aragonese specialities, such as *ternasco*, or young lamb, and wine from the Campo de Borja region. The comfortable, though otherwise characterless, *Hotel Triskel*, c/de las Afueras 9 (℡948 888 570; ❹), overlooks the old town, with a lovely view – get one with a balcony.

Tarazona and around

The Aragonese plains are dotted with reminders of the Moorish occupation, and nowhere more so than at **TARAZONA**, a wonderfully atmospheric old town loaded with Mudéjar architecture. If you're en route to Soria or Burgos, it's an ideal place to break the journey. Don't miss out, either, on the tranquil Cistercian monastery of **Veruela**, 15km southeast, off the N122 to Zaragoza.

Tarazona

Tarazona's most absorbing sights lie in the old upper town, incorporating the **Judería** and **Morería** (Jewish and Moorish quarters, respectively), which stands on a hill overlooking the river, with medieval houses and mansions lining the *callejas* and *pasadizos* – the lanes and alleyways.

At the heart of the old town is Plaza de España, flanked by a truly magnificent sixteenth-century **ayuntamiento**, with a facade of coats of arms, sculpted heads and figures in high relief. A frieze, representing the triumphal procession of Carlos V after his coronation as Holy Roman Emperor in Bologna, runs the length of the building, while the large figures underneath represent Hercules and other classical heroes performing feats of mythological proportions. From here, a *ruta turística* directs you up to the church of **Santa María Magdalena** (open for services only), the Mudéjar tower of which dominates the town. Within the church, look for the interesting fifteenth-century wooden lectern, carved in a geometric pattern. From the entrance there are especially good views of the eighteenth-century **Plaza de Toros** below – an octagonal terrace of houses, with balconies from which spectators could view the *corrida*. From the church you can continue uphill to the sixteenth-century convent church of **La Concepción**, again with a slender brick tower, or head down Rúa Baja, past the imposing Palacio Episcopal, to Plaza Arcedianos and the **Centro Moshé de Portella** (generally summer Sat & Sun 11am–2pm & 5–7pm; winter Sat & Sun 11.30am–1.30pm & 6–8pm; free). The centre highlights Tarazona's rich Jewish heritage pre-1492 through various multimedia displays and exhibits, and includes a small reconstruction of a synagogue.

In the lower town, the principal sight is the **Catedral**, built mainly in the fourteenth and fifteenth centuries. It's a typical example of the decorative use of brick in the Gothic-Mudéjar style, with a dome built to the same design as that of the old cathedral in Zaragoza. The interior, with its Mudéjar cloisters, has been closed for restoration for over ten years, but is expected to open (perhaps optimistically) in mid-2009.

If you're around for the **fiesta** on August 27, watch out for "El Cipotegato", a luckless character dressed in jester-like red, green and yellow stripy pyjamas who runs through the streets while everyone pelts him with tomatoes. He kicks off the town's annual week-long festivities, during which there are street parties, live music and bullfights.

Practicalities

The **turismo** is on Plaza de San Francisco, the main square below the cathedral (Mon–Fri 9am–1.30pm & 4.30–7pm, Sat & Sun 10am–1.30pm & 4.30–7pm; ☏976 640 074, ⓦwww.tarazona.org).

There are several **accommodation** choices in the centre: one of the better spots in town is *Condes de Visconti* at c/Visconti 15 (☏976 644 908, ⓦwww .condesdevisconti.com; ❹), a lovely sixteenth-century *palacete* with fifteen individually decorated rooms. Cheaper options include the *Hostal Palacete de los Arcedianos*, Plaza Arcedianos 1 (☏976 642 303, ⓦwww.palacetearcedianos .com; ❸), near the *ayuntamiento*, with decent en-suite rooms. On Plaza la Merced sits the new ⚲ *La Merced de la Concordia* (☏976 199 344, ⓦwww .lamerced.info; ❹), in a 1501 *palacete* with modern flourishes that juxtapose nicely with the historic interior: pale-wood floors, recessed lights and sleek furnishings meet stone walls and restored wood-beam ceilings. Enjoy creatively prepared regional fare in the elegant, soft-toned restaurant.

The *El Galeón*, in the lower town at Avda. La Paz 1, is a mid-priced **restaurant**, with good traditional food, including grilled *ternasco* (lamb). *El Caserón 2*, on Reino Aragón 2, just north of the old town, has haunches of ham dangling over the bar, and serves up traditional cuisine. For drinks, try *S'ha Feito* in the old bullring, or the cluster of bars on Plaza de Nuestra Señora and around c/Cañuelo behind Plaza de San Francisco.

Monasterio de Veruela

The **Monasterio de Veruela** (Mon & Wed–Sun 10.30am–8.30pm, Oct–March until 6.30pm; €2), isolated in a fold of the hills 15km to the southeast of Tarazona, and standing within a massively fortified perimeter, is one of Spain's great religious houses. The monastery is uninhabited now, but the magnificent church, built in the severe twelfth-century transitional style of the Carthusians, is kept open. The monastery admission ticket also gives access to the fourteenth-century cloisters and convent buildings, plus a well-run **Museo del Vino** (same hours as the monastery; ⓦwww.campodeborja.com), which sits in the monastic grounds. The museum offers several floors of snazzy, child-friendly exhibits that trace Campo de Borja wine from vineyard to glass; and adults will enjoy the €1 tastings of wine served at high tables overlooking the ancient monastery.

Calatayud, Piedra and Daroca

Like Tarazona, **Calatayud** is a town of Moorish foundation, with some stunning Mudéjar towers. It also offers access to a Cistercian monastery, **Piedra**, set in lush parkland. To the southeast lies **Daroca**, a pretty town surrounded by ruined but impressive old walls.

Calatayud

If you're passing, it's worth climbing up to the old upper town of **CALATAYUD** (Ⓦ www.calatayud.com), where, amid a maze of alleys, stand the church of **San Andrés** and the **Colegiata de Santa María**, both of which have ornate Mudéjar towers (Sun & services at 6.30pm). Santa María, the collegiate church, also has a beautifully decorative Plateresque doorway, while towards the river, at c/Valentín Gomez 3, **San Juan el Real** (daily 8am–1pm & 4–8pm; free) has frescoes attributed to the young Goya. Ruins of the Moorish **castle** survive, too, on high ground at the opposite end of town from the train station. The views from here are outstanding, though for a closer view of the towers, you'd do better to climb the hill to the hermitage in the centre of the old town. The **turismo** is on Plaza del Fuerte (Tues–Sun 10am–1pm & 4–7pm; Ⓣ 976 886 322). If you're going to stay in town, try the *Hospedería Mesón la Dolores*, at Plaza Mesones 4 (Ⓣ 976 889 055, Ⓦ www.mesonladolores.com; ❹), in a rustic eighteenth-century building with stone arches, tiled floors and dark wood ceilings.

Monasterio de Piedra

The **Monasterio de Piedra** – "The Stone Monastery" – lies 20km south of Calatayud, 4km from the village of **NUÉVALOS**. The monastic buildings, once part of a grand Cistercian complex, are a ruin, but they stand amid park-like gardens (daily 9am–8pm, until 6pm in winter; €12), which seem all the more verdant in this otherwise harsh, dry landscape. The whopping entrance fee includes a guided tour of the monastery's cloisters, church, wine cellar, refectory and kitchens. Red arrows mark out a **route** through the park and take you past a series of waterfalls, grottoes and lakes. If there are crowds, it will be easy enough to escape them, though be warned that you're not allowed to take food into the park.

There are two **places to stay** up here: the luxurious *Hotel Monasterio de Piedra*, near the park entrance (Ⓣ 976 849 011, Ⓦ www.monasteriopiedra .com; ❾), and, a little further down the road, the well-equipped and reasonably priced *Hotel Las Truchas* (Ⓣ 976 849 040, Ⓦ www.hotellastruchas.com; ❹), with its own pool, tennis courts, gym and free bike rental. Down in the village, the *Hotel Río Piedra*, at the foot of the road up to the monastery (Ⓣ 976 849 007, Ⓦ www.hotelriopiedra.com; B&B ❸), has a range of rooms, some with terraces. Alternatively, there's a **campsite**, *Lago Park Camping*, 1km from Nuévalos (in the other direction from the monastery) on a promontory by a reservoir (Ⓣ 976 849 038; closed Oct–March).

Just one **bus** daily runs from Zaragoza (from c/Almagro 18) to Nuévalos, leaving at 9am and returning at 5pm; note that from October to June, the bus only runs on Tuesdays and Thursdays and at weekends.

Daroca

DAROCA, 38km southeast of Calatayud, is a charming old town, set within an impressive run of **walls** that include no fewer than 114 towers and enclose an area far greater than that needed by the present population of around 2200. The last major restoration of the walls was in the fifteenth century, but though largely in ruins today, they are still magnificent.

You enter the town through its original gates, the **Puerta Alta** or stout **Puerta Baja**, the latter endowed with a gallery of arches and decorated with the coat of arms of Carlos I. Within, Calle Mayor runs between the two gates, past ancient streets dotted with Romanesque, Gothic and Mudéjar churches. The appeal of Daroca lies more in the whole ensemble rather than any specific monuments, though the principal church, the Renaissance **Colegial de Santa**

María (summer daily 10.30am–2pm & 5–8pm; winter Tues–Sun 11.30am–1pm & 5–7pm), off c/Mayor on Plaza de Espana, does have a small museum of religious artefacts, including robes, silverwork, *retablos* and paintings. The small **turismo** in front of the *Colegial* (Mon 10.30am–2pm, Tues–Sun 10am–2pm & 4–7.30pm; ☎976 800 129) has pamphlets describing a walking tour.

One of the nicer spots **to stay** is *La Posada del Almudí*, c/Grajera 7, near Plaza Santiago, off c/Mayor (☎976 800 606, ⓦwww.posadadelalmudi.com; ❸), with gorgeously furnished rooms in an artfully restored mansion house, plus a bar and good restaurant. The new *Hotel Cien Balcones*, c/Mayor 88 (☎976 545 071, ⓦwww.cienbalcones.com; ❹), has, as the name suggests, balconies galore, many fronted by wrought-iron handiwork, and overlooking a breezy patio. The comfortable, white-walled rooms feature crisp linens and gleaming bathrooms. On the outskirts of town on the Carretera Sagunto-Burgos, near the Puerta Alta, is *Hostal Legido* (☎976 800 190; ❷) with a tapas bar patronized by locals; call ahead to confirm they're open, as they're sometimes closed in low season. Daroca is connected to Calatayud, Teruel and Cariñena/Zaragoza by a couple of daily **bus** services; buses pull in on the c/Mayor close to the Puerta Baja.

Teruel

The little provincial capital of **TERUEL** is basically a market town, catering for its rugged and sparsely populated rural hinterlands. This is a true backwater corner of Aragón: one survey found that it was the only part of Spain where deaths outnumbered births. This prompted the oft-overlooked region to come up with the playful slogan "*Teruel existe*" ("Teruel exists"), which has helped, slowly but surely, in drawing some curious visitors. That said, it's still one of the least-trammelled parts of Spain: if you're looking for remote, you're in the right region, with its back-of-beyond villages and medieval sights that haven't been prettified. The land, too, is high and harsh, with the coldest winters in the country.

Arrival and information

Teruel doesn't feel quite like a city, despite its capital status, and the separation of the Centro Histórico, the old town, from the new reinforces this by making it feel small and provincial. **Trains** run from Zaragoza and Valencia, **buses** from most destinations in the province, as well as Barcelona and Madrid – their respective stations are located on the fringes of the Centro Histórico, with Plaza del Torico at its heart. From the train station, walk up La Escalinata and c/Nueva; from the bus station, walk north a short way up the ring road, taking the first left to Plaza Judería.

There are numerous bus companies in Teruel, so check the timetables in the windows before buying a ticket on departure, as some buses are considerably slower than others. The **turismo** is located just to the left of La Escalinata, a short walk from the train station on c/San Francisco (Mon–Sat 9am–2pm & 4.30–7/8pm, Sun 10am–2pm & 4.30–7/8pm; ☎978 602 279, ⓦwww.teruel.org). **Parking** in the old town can be a challenge, and it's best to aim for one of the official car parks located on the edges (€9–11/day).

Accommodation

Accommodation is rarely a problem, though you'll need to book if you're here for the raucous **Fiesta Vaquilla del Ángel** (early July).

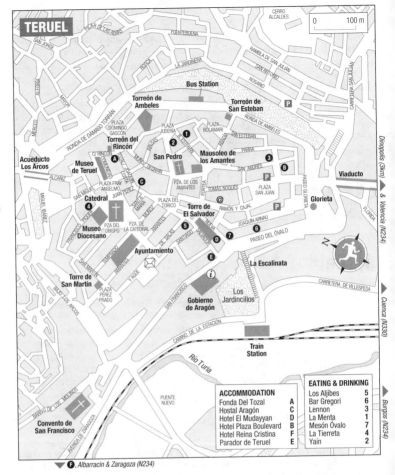

TERUEL

ACCOMMODATION
Fonda Del Tozal	A
Hostal Aragón	C
Hotel El Mudayyan	D
Hotel Plaza Boulevard	B
Hotel Reina Cristina	F
Parador de Teruel	E

EATING & DRINKING
Los Aljibes	5
Bar Gregori	6
Lennon	3
La Menta	1
Mesón Óvalo	7
La Tierreta	4
Yaín	2

▼ Ⓕ, Albarracín & Zaragoza (N234)

Fonda del Tozal c/Rincón 5 ☏ 978 601 022. A characterful *hostal* in an ancient building, offering simple rooms with bath (though it can get chilly in winter). The large bar downstairs is an atmospheric place for a drink. ②

Hostal Aragón c/Santa María 4 ☏ 978 611 877. Small but comfortable rooms equipped with TV and bathroom – it's best to book in advance. Note, though, that the thin walls mean it can get noisy in the evenings. ①

Hotel El Mudayyan c/Nueva 18 ☏ 976 623 042, ⓦ www.elmudayyan.com. Lovely, petite hotel where you can – quite literally – explore underground Teruel. Medieval tunnels, once used by priests to travel to and from the sacristy, extend below the hotel, and intrepid guests can venture into them (as far as they dare), led by the

owners who can expound on Teruel's history. Mudayyan's eight rooms are snug but individually decorated with Mudéjar touches, while a small Moroccan-style tearoom makes for a relaxing afternoon. ④

Hotel Plaza Boulevard Plaza Tremedal 3 ☏ 978 608 817, ⓦ www.bacohoteles.com. Smart hotel near Plaza San Juan. Rooms have modern decor, wooden floors and king-size beds. ③

Hotel Reina Cristina Paseo del Óvalo 1 ☏ 978 606 860, ⓦ www.gargallohoteles.es. Attractive hotel with an excellent restaurant, located by the Torre del Salvador. Rooms come with modern bathrooms, TVs and a/c, with fairly standard but comfortable decor. ④

Parador de Teruel 2km out on the Zaragoza road ☏ 978 601 800, ⓦ www.parador.es. This modern building, in an inspired position on a wooded hillside overlooking the town and towers, has a swimming pool and tennis courts but not much in the way of character. ⑥

The Town

Teruel is a likeable and impressively monumental place, with some of the finest **Mudéjar** work in Spain. Like Zaragoza, it was an important Moorish city and retained significant Muslim and Jewish communities after its Reconquest by Alfonso II in 1171. As you approach town, the Mudéjar towers, built by Moorish craftsmen over the next three centuries, are immediately apparent. These – and the fabulous Mudéjar ceiling in the cathedral – should not be missed. The Centro Histórico, on a hill above the Río Turia, has a confusing layout, enclosed by the odd patch of wall, and with a viaduct linking it to the modern quarter to the south. Leading off to the north is a sixteenth-century aqueduct, **Los Arcos**, a slender and elegant piece of monumental engineering.

Arriving by train, you'll see straight ahead of you **La Escalinata**, a flight of steps decorated with bricks, tiles and turrets that is pure civic Mudéjar in style – note the iron gap in the wall to the left, where lifts shoot up to the *paseo*, part of the extensive redevelopment of the site in 2004 by British architect David Chipperfield. From the top of the steps c/El Salvador leads to the **Torre de El Salvador** (daily 11am–2pm & 4.30–7.30pm; €2.50), the finest of the town's four Mudéjar towers. It's covered with intricately patterned and proportioned coloured tiles, to stunning effect, echoed closely in its more modest sister tower, **Torre de San Martín** (exterior only), best reached via c/de los Amantes. A common feature of all the towers is that they stand separate from the main body of the church, a design most probably influenced by the freestanding minarets of the Muslim world.

The **Catedral de Santa María de Mediavilla** (daily 11am–2pm & 4–8pm, until 7pm in winter, last entry 30min before closing; €3), built in the twelfth century but gracefully adapted over subsequent years, boasts another fine Mudéjar tower, incorporating Romanesque windows and a lantern that combines Renaissance and Mudéjar features. The interior follows a more standard Gothic-Mudéjar pattern and at first sight seems unremarkable, save for its brilliant Renaissance *retablo*. Climb the stairs by the door, however, and put money in the illuminations box, and the fabulous **artesonado ceiling** is revealed. This was completed between 1260 and 1314 by Moorish craftsmen, in a gorgeous and fascinating mix of geometric Islamic motifs and medieval painting of courtly life.

Standing next to the cathedral, the sixteenth-century Palacio Episcopal houses the **Museo Diocesano** (same hours; €3 joint ticket with cathedral). Inside, look out for the *Calvario*, a beautiful woodcarving of Jesus (whose arms are missing), St John and the Virgin Mary, carved in the fifteenth century but for many years hidden behind a wall in a church in Sarrón, where it was discovered in 1946. Another highlight is the *Arbol de la Vida*, a striking seventeenth-century ivory carving of Christ.

A couple of blocks from the museum is Plaza del Torico, flanked by a trio of *modernista* houses. Just beyond here, in another attractive square, is the church of **San Pedro** (daily 10am–2pm & 4–8pm, 10am–8pm in Aug; €2), once again endowed with a Mudéjar tower. Its fame, however, relates to the adjacent **Mausoleo de los Amantes** (same hours; €4), a chapel containing the alabaster tomb of the Lovers of Teruel, Isabel de Segura and Juan Diego Martínez de Marcilla. This pair's thirteenth-century tale of thwarted love is a legend throughout Spain. The story goes that Diego, ordered by his lover's family to go away and prove himself worthy, left Teruel for five years, returning only to find that Isabel was to be married that same day. He asked for a last kiss, was refused

ARAGÓN | Teruel

and expired, heartbroken; Isabel, not to be outdone, arranged his funeral at San Pedro, kissed the corpse and died in its arms. The lovers' (reputed) bodies were exhumed in 1955 and now lie illuminated for all to see; it is a macabre and popular pilgrimage for newlyweds. You can buy a combined ticket for both sites, and the **Mudéjar tower** (€4 with just San Pedro), for €7.

The well-run **Museo de Teruel** (Tues–Fri 10am–2pm & 4–7pm, Sat & Sun 10am–2pm; free), on Plaza Fray Anselmo, is also worthwhile for its range of exhibits on local folklore and traditional rural life, including pottery, silverwork and a reconstructed interior of an eighteenth-century chemist shop. The museum also showcases interesting temporary exhibits. Lastly, travellers with children might want to check out **Dinopolis** (daily 10am–8pm; €22, under-12s €14; Ⓦ www.dinopolis.com), a lavish theme park on the outskirts of town, replete with rides, guides dressed (and acting) like mad professors, and dinosaur exhibits.

Eating and drinking

Jamón de Teruel is the town's most celebrated gastronomic creation – the region's dry but cold winds create an ideal climate for curing. You'll find the tasty, fat-streaked *jamón* in shops and served up in tapas bars and restaurants all over the Centro Histórico. The main areas for **food** are on the eastern side of the old town, principally Plaza Judería, c/Bartolomé Esteban, c/Abadía and c/San Esteban (the first street into the old town from the bus station), though there are several lively cafés on Plaza del Torico. For **bars**, check out the streets around Plaza Judería and Plaza Bolamar.

Los Aljíbes c/Yagüe de Salas 3. A buzzing café and *bodega* specializing in Aragonese and Navarran cuisine such as *migas a la Pastora* and juicy lamb (entrees €12–15), with a well-stocked tapas counter and an extensive wine list featuring local vintages. Daily 8am–11pm. Closed Sun in Aug & Sept plus last 2 weeks of July.

Bar Gregori Paseo del Óvalo 6. This friendly tapas bar is the locals' choice, complete with the famous *jamón* and pigs' ears. Outside tables plus good, keenly priced wine and *sangría* make for a chill place to pass the evening. The *Gregori Plus* next door is a little more upmarket and just as popular (closed Tues). Daily until 12.30am.

Lennon c/San Andrés 23. A vast, laid-back bar with several rooms, comfy chairs and sofas, occasional live music and a pool table. Tues–Sun 3pm–midnight, or as late as 4am depending on customers.

El Rincón de Ademuz

El Rincón de Ademuz (Ⓦ www.rincondeademuz.com), 30km due south of Teruel, is a strange little region: a Valencian province enclosed within Aragonese territory. It's a very remote corner of Spain, with a bleak kind of grandeur, and scarcely a tourist from one year to the next.

The place to head for – and if you're bussing it, the only realistic place to get to from Teruel – is **ADEMUZ** itself, without doubt Spain's tiniest and least significant provincial capital. Strung along a craggy hill at the confluence of two long rivers, this could make a beautiful base for walking, and there's a fascination just in wandering the streets with their dark stone cottages and occasional Baroque towers. If you want to stay, try the decent *hostal, Casa Domingo* at Avda. Valencia 1 (☏ 978 782 030; ❷), with bath and TV, which also serves basic meals.

For energetic **trekking**, Torre Baja lies to the north along the Río Turia, and beyond it the beautiful village of Castielfabib. The most interesting of these little Ademuz hamlets, Puebla de San Miguel, is to the east, in the Sierra Tortajada, easily accessible by road from Valencia, but also from a small route just out of Ademuz in the Teruel direction, east over the Río Turia bridge and signposted to Sabina, Sesga and Mas del Olmo.

La Menta c/Bartolomé Esteban 10. The city's top restaurant, with a carefully constructed menu that changes weekly, and sumptuous dishes of Aragonese classics for €18 and up. Closed Mon & middle two weeks of Jan & July.

Mesón Óvalo Paseo del Óvalo 2. A very popular *mesón* with warm, tangerine-coloured walls, quality cooking (the trout dishes are excellent) and a range of Maestrazgo specialities from €14.

La Tierreta Francisco Piquer. Tucked away behind the cathedral sits this elegant restaurant, with pale-wood walls and white curtains. The innovative dishes (€14–20) are rooted in regional produce, such as monkfish flavored with saffron culled from the nearby Monreal de Campo, wild sea bass with seasonal mushrooms, and a gazpacho of watermelon and tomato.

Yaín Plaza de la Judería 9. Proof that creative, gourmet fare has a place in Teruel. The sleek restaurant (named after the Hebrew word for "wine", because of its location on Plaza de la Judería) reveals gleaming dark wood, alabaster lamps and an impressive wine cellar. Regional dishes (€13–19) with a twist include *pimiento del piquillo* (bright-red peppers shaped like a piquillo, or "little beak") stuffed with cod and quail drizzled in chocolate sauce and a garbanzo puree. The tasting *menú* (€39.50) makes for a memorable splurge.

Albarracín

ALBARRACÍN, 37km west of Teruel, is one of the more accessible targets in rural southern Aragón – and one of the most picturesque towns in the province, poised above the Río Guadalaviar and retaining, virtually intact, its medieval streets and tall, balconied houses. There's a historical curiosity here, too, in that from 1165 to 1333, the town formed the centre of a small independent state, the kingdom of the Azagras.

Despite its growing appeal as a tourist destination, Albarracín's dark, enclosed lanes and those buildings that remain unrestored, with their splendid coats of arms, still make for an intriguing wander – reminders of lost and now inexplicably prosperous eras. Approaching from Teruel, you may imagine that you're about to come upon a large town, for the **medieval walls** swoop back over the hillside – protecting, with the loop of the river, a far greater area than the extent of the town, past or present.

Take c/de Santiago from near the main bridge up towards the walls, and you reach Santiago church and a gateway, the Portal del Molina. If instead you take c/de la Catedral, you reach a small square (cars can access this from the other side) with the **Catedral** (Mon–Sat 10.30am–2pm & 4.30–6.30pm, until 6pm in winter, Sun 10.30am–2pm; free), a medieval building remodelled in the sixteenth and eighteenth centuries, a bit farther along. Keep walking and you'll reach the **Museo de Albarracín** (Mon–Sat 10.30am–2pm & 4.30–6.30pm, Sun 10.30am–2pm; €2), with exhibits on local history and where you can buy tickets to tour the crumbling but atmospheric **Castillo** nearby (daily 11am, noon, 1pm, 4.30pm & 5.30pm; in winter, afternoon tours at 4pm & 5pm €2). On the other side of the town, the **Torre Blanca** (same times as Museo de Albarracín; €2) provides a spectacular panorama of the whole area. Combined tickets to all four main sites are €5.50.

Practicalities

The **turismo**, on c/San Antonio, next to the main bridge (daily 10am–2pm & 4–8pm, Oct–May until 7pm; ☏978 710 251 or 978 710 262, ⓦwww.comarcadelasierradealbarracin.es), has information on both the town and the surrounding region. **Accommodation** is generally housed in attractive converted mansions. If you want to stay – and you'll have to if you arrive on the daily **bus** from Teruel – try the good-value *Hostal Los Palacios*, beyond the Portal de Molina (☏978 700 327, ⓦwww.montepalacios.com; ❷), with a

▲ Albarracín

terrace bar offering lovely views; or the inviting, family-run *Casa Santiago*, at the top of a stone staircase near the Plaza Mayor (☎978 700 316, ⓦwww .casadesantiago.net; ❸), a restored country house of nine cozy, individually decorated rooms – with colourful quilts and wood-beamed ceilings – and sunlit sitting rooms where you can gaze over the brightly tiled roofs of Albarracín. There's also an exceptionally cheap **youth hostel**, the *Albergue Juventud Rosa Bríos*, in a medieval mansion just past the cathedral at c/Santa María 5 (☎902 088 905; ❶). Albarracín's local **fiesta** takes place from September 8 to 17.

Moving on from Albarracín, if you have transport, you could take a fabulous route west to Cuenca through beautiful country, by way of **Frías de Albarracín** and the **source of the Río Tajo** (see p.195). **Parking** is plentiful on the roads in and out of the town.

Sierra de Gúdar and El Maestrazgo

The mountains of the **Sierra de Gúdar** and **El Maestrazgo**, to the east and northeast of Teruel, are an area of great variety and striking, often wild, beauty, with their severe peaks, deep gorges and lush meadows. One hundred years ago, this now impoverished region had four times the number of inhabitants that it does today. Defeated in their attempts to make a living from agriculture, many left to seek their fortunes in the cities, leaving behind the crumbling remains of once grand, honey-hued farmhouses that dot the landscape and stone-walled terraces etched into the steep-sided hills.

Inevitably, **buses** are infrequent, but most villages are connected with each other and/or Teruel once a day. A bus (Mon–Fri) leaves Teruel in the afternoon for Mosqueruela via Mora de Rubielos, Rubielos de Mora and Linares Mora, returning in the early morning. The main approaches to El Maestrazgo are also from Teruel (daily bus to Cantavieja and La Iglesuela del Cid in the mid-afternoon, returning early morning), or from Morella in the province of Castellón (see p.857). Note that bus schedules can vary, so confirm with the *turismo* in Teruel. For more **information** on the Maestrazgo, check out ⓦwww.elmaestrazgo.com.

Sierra de Gúdar

A landscape of sharp, rocky crags, the **Sierra de Gúdar** is easy to access by following the N234 southeast from Teruel and then heading northeast into the mountains along the A232. This will bring you to the lovely medieval village of **Mora de Rubielos**, 42km from Teruel, and then onto its even more stunning twin, **Rubielos de Mora**. Head north from here for **Linares de Mora**, turn-off point for the Valdelinares ski resort, and **Mosqueruela**, another charming and remote mountain village.

Mora de Rubielos and Rubielos de Mora

These confusingly named villages have fine collections of medieval houses, with small, wrought-iron balconies, often bedecked with flowers. For such a small place, **MORA DE RUBIELOS** has an extremely grand **castle** (Tues–Fri 10am–2pm & 5–7.30pm, Sat & Sun 10am–2pm & 5–8pm; €2), built in a luminous pinkish gold stone, which, during the Middle Ages, served as both defensive fort and noble residence, and was the heart of town life. Inside, several fairly nondescript rooms squeezed between the castle's outer and inner walls are set around a courtyard of pointed arches. One room hosts a small **Museo Etnológico** – a motley collection of rustic antiquities. If it's open, it's worth having a peek inside the bulky, Gothic **Ex Colegiata de Santa María** below the castle.

If you're **driving**, take the road to Virgen de la Vega (A228), off the Teruel road, which skirts the old town, right past the castle (there's parking on site). There's a small **turismo** at c/Hispanoamericano 5 (Tues–Fri 10am–2pm & 5–7.30pm, Sat & Sun 5–8pm; ☎978 806 132). The attractively restored *Hotel Jaime I*, in an old mansion on Plaza de la Villa near the *ayuntamiento* (☎978 800 092, ⓦwww .hoteljaime.com; ❺), is a comfortable place to stay and has a decent **restaurant**.

RUBIELOS DE MORA, 14km from Mora, is a gem of a village and a great place to while away a couple of hours wandering the narrow streets, admiring the handsome *palacios* with their finely carved wooden eaves. The **Ex Colegiata de Santa María la Mayor**, on Plaza de Marques de Tosos, has an ostentatious tiered bell tower. If you want to see inside, ask at the **turismo** in the *ayuntamiento* on Plaza de Hispano América (July & Aug Tues–Fri 10am–2pm & 5–7.30pm, Sat & Sun 10am–2pm & 5–8pm; Sept–June Tues–Fri 10am–2pm & 4.30–7pm, Sat & Sun 10am–2pm & 4–7pm; ☎978 804 001, ⓔrubimora@teleline.es). The *Los Leones* **hotel**, at Plaza Igual y Gil 3 (☎978 804 477, ⓦwww.losleones .info; ❹), near the church, is a beautifully restored seventeenth-century palace complete with antique bedsteads and heavy wooden doors, and also has a smart **restaurant** with an excellent array of regional specialities. The handsome *Hotel de la Villa*, on Plaza del Carmen (☎978 804 640, ⓦwww.hotel-de-la-villa.com; ❹), also makes for a memorable stay, with a restored sixteenth-century facade, a stone-arch entrance, beamed ceilings and a fine restaurant.

Northeastern Sierra

The vegetation becomes scrubbier and the views more dramatic as the A1701 climbs north 23km from Rubielos to **LINARES DE MORA**, a beguiling place, with houses piled higgledy-piggledy up the mountainside and glorious views. Its ruined castle is situated, rather precariously, on a jutting rock above the village, while another promontory hosts a church. There are two reasonable options for **accommodation**: the *Hostal La Venta* (☎978 802 018; ❸), on the edge of the village just off the main road, has a decent **restaurant**, while *El Portalico* (☎978 802 110; ❷), a bit farther ahead on the edge of the old quarter, is set in a historic mansion house with pleasant en-suite rooms with TV.

A couple of kilometres beyond the village, the superbly positioned **Mirador del Puerto de Linares** (1555m) affords hair-raising views down an almost vertical slope to the village below. Continuing northeast along the A1701, you'll come to **MOSQUERUELA**. With its ramshackle streets and back-of-beyond charm, this sleepy village feels as if it hasn't changed much since its foundation in 1262, and it's not uncommon to see flocks of sheep being herded through the centre. The village boasts an attractive, porticoed **Plaza Mayor** and a couple of pretty churches, but there's not much more to detain you. If you want to stay, there's a good modern **hotel**, the *Montenieve* (☎978 805 123; ❸), with comfortable if rather plain rooms, a five-minute walk from the Plaza Mayor. Beyond here the road narrows and becomes rougher as it leads another 24km to Villafranca and La Iglesuela del Cid.

Southern Maestrazgo

Approaching the Maestrazgo from Teruel on the A226, you pass nearby **Cedrillas** with its conspicuous, ridge-top castle ruin. From here the road starts climbing into the hills, scaling high mountain passes and affording tantalizing views of the valleys. The first village of any size is **Cantavieja**, while to the southeast lies the fairly well-preserved **La Iglesuela del Cid**.

Cantavieja and El Cid country

CANTAVIEJA, dramatically situated by the edge of an escarpment, at an altitude of 1300m, is a little livelier and larger than most Maestrazgo villages, though its population is still under a thousand. The beautiful, porticoed **Plaza de Cristo Rey** is typical of the region, and the escutcheoned *ayuntamiento* bears a Latin inscription with suitably lofty sentiments: "This House hates wrongdoing, loves peace, punishes crimes, upholds the laws and honours the upright." The *plaza* is halfway up c/Mayor from Plaza de España: the latter is on the main road, and has limited parking. The village makes a useful base for exploring – or walking in – the region, with a **turismo** on c/Mayor (mid-July to mid-Sept daily 10am–2pm & 4–7pm; rest of the year usually weekends only; ☎964 185 414, ⓦwww.cantavieja .es). In the same building is the relatively new **Museo de las Guerras Carlistas de Cantavieja** (summer daily 10am–2pm & 4–8pm; rest of year Wed 4–7pm, Thurs–Sat 10am–2pm & 4–7pm, Sun 10am–2pm; €1.50), a small museum that documents the nineteenth-century Carlist Wars in Cantavieja via panels, scale models, old uniforms, newspaper clippings and weapons. Cantavieja is also home to a stylish and modern **hotel**, the 🍴 *Balfagón*, on the main road at the southern edge of town (☎964 185 076, ⓦwww.hotelbalfagon.com; ❹), and the reasonable *Pensión Julián* (☎964 185 005; ❶), a bit farther on. There's also an unexpectedly chic **restaurant**, *Buj*, specializing in refined Aragonese cuisine, a few doors down from the hotel (☎964 185 033; lunchtimes only; closed Feb). The food at the *Balfagón* is also excellent (closed Sun dinner except in Aug), and it does a €14 *menú*. The area is famous for its truffles, which, unusually, are rooted out by dogs rather than pigs.

The best views of Cantavieja can be found on the rough and narrow road to **MIRAMBEL**, 15km to the northeast and walkable in about four hours. The village has a population of a mere 144 and preserves a very ancient atmosphere, with its walls, gateways and stone houses. It was temporarily thrown into a whirl of excitement when Ken Loach filmed *Land and Freedom* (1995) here, but these days it's back to its usual, sleepy self. There's an excellent little **fonda**, the *Guimera*, on the main street, c/Agustín Pastor 28 (☎964 178 269; ❶) with en-suite rooms and a good-quality, popular **restaurant** serving a hearty €12 *menú* of home-cooked dishes.

LA IGLESUELA DEL CID is 11km to the southeast of Cantavieja, and another fine walk along a rough country road. The village's name bears witness to the exploits of El Cid Campeador, who came charging through the Maestrazgo in his fight against the infidel, though other than the El Cid *romería*, a fiesta organized by the village, forty days after Easter (usually in May), there's nothing else to commemorate the legendary hero. Its ochre-red, dry-stone walls, ubiquitous coats of arms and stream, now little more than a trickle cutting through the village, are picturesque enough in this remote countryside, but there's not much else to see. The central, compact Plaza de la Iglesia is enclosed by the old *ayuntamiento*, the attractive **Iglesia Parroquial de la Purificacíon** and a restored eighteenth-century *palacio*, now home to a stunning luxury **hotel**, ⚲ *Hospedería La Iglesuela del Cid* (☎964 443 476, ⓦ www.laiglesueladelcidhospederia.com; ❺), with an expensive restaurant. There is also a decent *hostal*, *Casa Amada*, on the main road through the village, c/Fuente Nueva (☎964 443 373; ❷), which offers substantial country cooking.

Northwest from Cantavieja

Another dramatic, almost alpine, route is in store if you head 30km northwest from Cantavieja, past Cañada de Benatanduz to **VILLARLUENGO**, an enchanting village of ancient houses stacked on a terraced hillside. Two budget options lie within the village: the friendly *Fonda Villarluengo*, at Plaza Castel 1 (☎978 773 014; ❶), with centrally heated, en-suite double rooms above a bar and *comedor*, and *Fonda Josefina*, at c/La Fuente 1 (☎978 773 151; ❶), with decent en-suite rooms.

Continue 6km farther north, over the Villarluengo Pass (1132m), and you'll come to the wonderfully atmospheric ⚲ *Hostal de la Trucha*, situated in an old farmhouse along the banks of the tranquil Río Pitarque (☎978 773 008, ⓦ www.gargallo-hotels.com; ❹), with a **restaurant** that serves trout caught a few metres away. A further 19km, over another pass and past the striking jagged limestone ridges known as **Los Órganos de Montoro**, the road drops down to the small village of **Ejulve**, and then 11km north to the N211 between Montalbán and Alcañiz.

Northern Maestrazgo

The northern limits of the Maestrazgo edge into Tarragona province in Catalunya, and can be approached from Tarragona/Gandesa, or from Zaragoza via Alcañiz, where the N232 forks: east to the lovely town of **Valderrobres**, with its a superb castle and elegant Gothic church, and south to **Calanda** and a new centre dedicated to film-maker Luis Buñuel.

Calanda

Just 15km beyond Alcorisa on the N211, **CALANDA** is home to the **Centro Buñuel** (Tues–Sun 10.30am–1.30pm & 4–8pm; €3.50; ⓦ www.cbcvirtual.com) at c/Mayor 48, on the edge of town. The centre is dedicated to surrealist film-maker Luis Buñuel, who was born here in 1900. Buñuel left Spain in the 1930s, spending his most creative periods in France and then Mexico, where he died in 1983, but remained fond of his hometown throughout his life. The centre houses a series of innovative displays on the man and his movies, and also has an extensive film library.

Valderrobres

VALDERROBRES is one of the Maestrazgo's most attractive towns. It stands 53km from Calanda, near the border with Catalunya and astride the Río Matarraña, whose crystal waters, flanked by lush valleys, teem with trout.

The old quarter sits north of the river, connected to the new town by Avenida Hispanidad and the Puente de Piedra, with the unassuming seventeenth-century **ayuntamiento** on Plaza España just over the bridge – this was considered so characteristic of the region that it was reproduced in Barcelona's Poble Espanyol (see p.692) in 1929. A short walk from here and dominating the town are the **Castillo-Palacio** (generally closed Mon; confirm hours with *turismo*; €3), once owned by the archbishops of Zaragoza, and a Gothic parish church – **Santa María** – which has a fine rose window (open during services only).

The **turismo** is at Avda. Cortes de Aragón 7, near the iron bridge (July & Aug daily 9am–2pm & 4–7pm; Sept–June Wed–Sat 10am–2pm & 4–6pm, Sun 10am–2pm; ☎978 890 886, Ⓦwww.comarcamatarranya.es). The only **place to stay** in the old quarter is the venerable *Fonda La Plaza*, opposite the *ayuntamiento* (☎978 850 106, Ⓦwww.posadalaplaza.com; ❸), which has atmospheric, en-suite rooms in a medieval mansion. In the new town, the most comfortable option is *El Salt* at Elvira Hildalgo 14 (☎978 890 865, Ⓦwww.hotelelsalt.com; ❸), not far from the river, with parking, while just up Avenida Hispanidad from the bridge is plain but adequate *Hostal Querol* (☎978 850 192, Ⓦwww.hostalquerol.com; ❸), which has a **bar** and excellent *comedor*.

The Aragonese Pyrenees

Aragón has the highest and best stretch of the **Pyrenees** on the Spanish side, offering everything from casual day-walks in the high valleys to long-distance treks across the mountains. There are numerous trails, marked as either **GR** (*Grande Recorrido* – long-haul, red-and-white blazes) or **PR** (*Pequeño Recorrido* – short-haul, blue-and-white- or yellow-and-white-marked) trails.

The most popular jumping-off point for the mountains is **Jaca**, an attractive town in its own right, with an important cathedral. From here, most walkers head northeast to the spectacular alpine landscape of the **Parque Nacional de Ordesa**, with its canyons and waterfall valleys. Northwest of Jaca, the valleys of **Ansó** and **Echo** offer less rigorous hiking, while southeast of the park, **Aínsa**, with its picturesque old town, makes another pleasant gateway to the mountains. Still farther east, **Benasque** provides access to the two loftiest Pyrenean peaks, Aneto (3404m) and Posets (3371m), protected by a *parque natural*, as well as to the bluff-top cathedral-village of **Roda de Isábena**. In winter, there's **skiing** at the well-equipped resorts of Candanchú, Astún, Formigal, Panticosa and Cerler.

There are several possible **routes into the region**. For Jaca and Ordesa, the most obvious way is via **Huesca**, the provincial capital, no great shakes in itself but convenient for visiting the great castle of **Loarre**, **Los Mallos** sugarloaf mountains or the increasingly popular sub-range **Sierra de Guara**, whose gorges rank among the country's most labyrinthine landscapes. You can travel by rail through Huesca, Jaca and up to Canfranc just before the Spanish border – though there, sadly, the trains stop. Rail-buses, however, continue **into France** through the **Somport tunnel**, while drivers can also cross over the **Puerto del Portalet** to the east or, east of Ordesa, go through

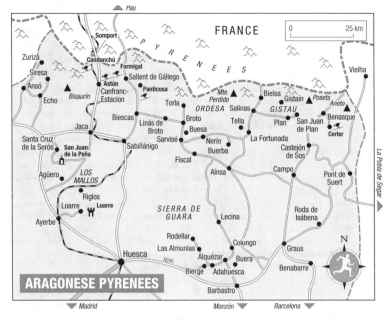

the **Bielsa tunnel**. All of these are open year-round, except during periods of exceptionally heavy snow.

From the east: Monzón and Barbastro

From Catalunya, you're likely to approach the Pyrenees via Lleida (Lérida), especially by public transport. If you have your own transport, you could follow a little-used minor route along the Río Cinca valley from Fraga, just west of Lleida. Most travellers access either Huesca or Benasque via **Monzón** and **Barbastro**; both have regular bus connections with Lleida, though their appeal lies strictly in a handful of sights.

Monzón

The grim, mostly modern town of **MONZÓN**, 75km from Lleida, stands in a triangle between the rivers Cinca and Sosa (the latter usually dry), a strategic position that explains its Templar castle on the crumbling rock above. Originally a ninth-century Moorish fort, it was later made over to the Templars by Ramón Berenguer IV and was home to Jaime I (king of Aragón 1213–76) in his youth. The **castle ruins** (summer Tues–Sat 10am–1pm & 5–8pm, Sun 10am–2pm; winter Tues–Sat 11.30am–1pm & 3–5pm, Sun 10am–2pm; €3) include a tenth-century Moorish tower and a group of Romanesque buildings.

The **bus station** is northwest of the castle, between the old and new towns. There's comfortable **accommodation** at two-star *Hotel Vianetto*, Avda. Lérida 25 (℡974 401 900; ❸), with a garage and a decent, if slightly expensive, restaurant. Most travellers, though, will just stop for a **meal**: try *Asador Marisquería Jairo*, south of the Río Sosa at c/Santa Barbara 10 (closed Mon), or *Piscis*

(Ⓦ www.piscismonzon.com), close to the bus station at Plaza de Aragón 1; despite the fishy name, the latter's a plush all-rounder with a more affordable €25 *menú de degustación*.

Barbastro

BARBASTRO, 20km from Monzón, straddling the Río Vero before it joins the Cinca, is historically of signal importance. The union of Aragón and Catalunya was sealed here in 1137 by the betrothal of Petronila, infant daughter of Ramiro of Aragón, to Count Ramón Berenguer IV of Barcelona.

Although it's now just a slightly shabby provincial market town, Barbastro retains an air of past dignity in its old quarter. Just a few steps from the bus station, south of the river, the Gothic **Catedral** (daily 10am–1.30pm, until noon on Sun & 4.30–7.30pm; optional guided visit to Museo Diocesano €2) has a *retablo* begun under the authority of Damián Forment. When he died in 1540 only part of the alabaster relief had been completed, and the remainder was finished by his pupil Liceire in 1560. The broad, austere nave, staked out by six fluted columns sprouting palmate ribbing into the vault, contrasts sharply with the Rococo carved dome of the chapel of San Victorián, on the left as you enter. Just northeast of the cathedral on the Plaza de la Constitución, the facade of the restored fifteenth-century **ayuntamiento**, designed by the Moorish chief architect to Fernando el Católico, is also worth a look. Elsewhere, narrow, pedestrianized shopping streets radiating out from the arcaded, central **Plaza del Mercado** are lined by faded-pastel houses piled up with their backs towards the river; tree-lined **Paseo del Coso** at the southwest edge of the old quarter sprouts outdoor tables for many of the town's bars and cafés.

Babastro is best known for its **wine** – both Hemingway and Orwell tippled here during the 1920s and 1930s – and the town lies at the centre of the Somontano *denominación de origen* vintage district, one of the top dozen in Spain; the industry is documented in a wine **museum** next door to the *turismo* (Mon–Fri 9am–8pm, Sat 11am–8pm; free). Over twenty wineries cluster within a fifteen-kilometre radius of town, and tours can be arranged (with advance notice) to many – details from the *turismo* or Ⓦ www.dosomontano.com – though most also have shops with tasting areas.

Practicalities

From the **bus station** at the southwest end of Paseo del Coso, there are regular departures for Benasque, Huesca and Lleida. The helpful English-speaking **turismo** is 200m uphill and south from the station, inside the restored Conjunto de San Julián y Santa Lucía (July & Aug Mon–Sat 10am–8pm, Sun 10am–2pm & 4–7pm; Sept–June Tues–Sat 10am–2pm & 4.30–8pm; ☎974 308 350, Ⓦ www.barbastro-ayto.es).

Appealing budget **accommodation** is scarce, so it's best to plump for one of two mid-range establishments at the northeast edge of the Casco Viejo: *Hostal Pirineos* at c/General Ricardos 13 (☎974 310 000, Ⓦ www.hostalpirineos.com; ❷), and the *Hotel Clemente* closer to the river at c/Corona de Aragón 5 (☎974 310 186, Ⓔ clemente.3066@cajarural.com; ❸). Besides the respected *comedors* of these two *hostales*, several independent **restaurants** take advantage of the wine trade. The most central is *La Viña de San Julián* (closed Sun pm & Mon), just beside the *turismo* in a round, brick-walled *comedor*, considered one of the town's best. Off in the new quarter over the Avenida Pirineos bridge, *Flor*, at c/Goya 3 (☎974 311 056, Ⓦ www.restauranteflor.com), serves *nouvelle cuisine* in updated surroundings; allow over €40 *a la carta*, more if you crack into the stratospheric wine list.

Huesca and around

HUESCA is the least memorable of the three Aragonese provincial capitals, and you might bypass it altogether. However, it does provide a base for exploring the emphatically memorable **Los Mallos** pinnacles and the striking castle at **Loarre**, northwest of town, as well as the **Sierra de Guara** just northeast.

Huesca

Huesca's **Casco Viejo**, tucked into a loop of *paseos* and the Río Isuela, is a bit over-modernized with its neo-Iberian brickwork. Dead centre stands a late Gothic **Catedral**, whose unusual facade combines the thirteenth-century portal of an earlier church with a brick Mudéjar gallery, and a pinnacled, Isabelline uppermost section. The great treasure inside (visitable only via the Museo Diocesano except when services are on) is the *retablo* by Damián Forment, a Renaissance masterpiece depicting the Calvary, the Crucifixion and the Deposition. Next door, the **Museo Diocesano** (Mon–Sat 10.30am–1.30pm & 4–6pm, until 7.30pm in summer, 3.30–5.30pm spring/autumn; €3; ⓦ www.museo.diocesisdehuesca.org) contains a rather mixed collection, gathered from churches in the surrounding countryside. On Plaza Universidad 1, the **Museo de Huesca** (Tues–Sat 10am–2pm & 5–8pm, Sun 10am–2pm; free) features an assortment of archeological items from across the province, as well as Goya lithographs.

Practicalities

Huesca's **estación intermodal** (joint train and bus terminals) lies southwest of the centre off c/Zaragoza, a main thoroughfare. The understocked **turismo** is on Plaza Luís López Allué (daily 9am–2pm & 4–8pm; ⓣ 974 292 100, ⓦ www.huescaturismo.com).

In mid-summer and during skiing season, when more montane lodgings fill and the overflow is forced down to Huesca, it's worth booking **accommodation** in advance. *Hostal El Centro*, c/Sancho Ramírez 3 (ⓣ 974 226 823, ⓦ www.hostalelcentro.com; ❸), offers well-renovated en-suite rooms, many with a balcony, in a grand old building with a lift. More comfortable choices on the central Plaza Lizana, just downhill from the cathedral, include the *Hostal Lizana/Lizana 2* at nos. 6–8, the latter a slightly plusher annexe of the former (ⓣ 974 220 776, ⓦ www.hostal-lizana.com; ❸–❹), and the adjacent three-star *Husa Sancho Abarca* at no. 13–15 (ⓣ 974 220 650; ❺), where most modern rooms have all expected amenities including internet access. The local **campsite**, *San Jorge*, lies at the end of c/Ricardo del Arco (ⓣ 974 227 416; closed Nov–April).

Restaurants offer solid mountain fare, including lamb and freshwater fish specialities. *Restaurante Cafetería Navas*, at c/Vicente Campo Palacio 3 (closed Sun pm & Mon), is considered Huesca's top eatery by virtue of its delicious fish and game dishes and home-made desserts; the chef's full works will cost you around €40 with house wine, but there are €18 and €30 *menús de degustación*. A more affordable, trendy choice is 🔾 *La Bodeguita del Centro* (closed Mon), under the eponymous *hostal*, with a basement restaurant (*menú* €13) and a street-level bar doing *cazuelas*, *raciones* and wines by the glass. For other excellent **tapas bars** and **nightlife**, head for the *zona* around c/San Lorenzo and c/Padre Huesca, between the Coso Bajo and the Plaza de Santa Clara, while for *horchata*, cakes, crepes and real *gelato*, there's *Los Italianos* at Coso Bajo 18 (daily 7.30am–10pm).

Castillo de Loarre and Ayerbe

Castillo de Loarre (March–Oct 10am–2pm & 4–7pm, until 8pm June 15–Sept 15; rest of year 11am–1.30pm & 3–5.30pm; closed Mon except July & Aug; €2) is Aragón's most spectacular fortress – indeed, there are few that can rival it anywhere in Spain. As you approach, the castle seems to blend into the hillside, but up close assumes a breathtaking grandeur: compact but intricate, its south ramparts rooted in a sheer palisade, commanding the surrounding landscape.

Its builder was Sancho Ramírez, king of Aragón and Navarra (ruled 1063–94), who used it as a base for his resistance to the Moorish occupation. Inside the curtain walls is a delicately proportioned Romanesque church, with individually carved capitals in the apse and around the windows. Of a pair of towers, the **Torre de la Reina** has ornate windows, while the taller **Torre del Homenaje** – climbable to the penultimate storey – is dominated by a massive hooded fireplace.

The castle stands some 30km northwest of Huesca, on the most direct route via the village of Bolea, and 4km beyond the village of **Loarre**. By **public transport**, it's an awkward journey, as bus timetables in particular conspire against a day-trip. **LOARRE** village has two daily buses (Mon–Sat) from Huesca in the afternoon, but there's adequate **accommodation** in both Loarre and **AYERBE**, 7km southwest, with the nearest train station. The closest choice to the castle is the three-star *Hospedería de Loarre*, a restored seventeenth-century mansion on Loarre's central Plaza Miguel Moya (☎974 382 706, ⓦwww.hospederiadeloarre.com; ❹); the rooms were redecorated in 2006, with wi-fi and air conditioning, and the **restaurant** is well respected (€18 *menú* or €30–35 *a la carta*; closed Sun). Failing this, Loarre has two *casas rurales*, and Ayerbe three, the most characterful being *Antigua Posada del Pilar* at Ayerbe's Plaza Aragón 38 (☎974 380 052; ❶), with good suppers offered. There's also a quiet **campsite**, 1.5km out of Ayerbe on the road to Loarre, *La Banera* (☎974 380 242; closed Nov–April). **Restaurant** options in Ayerbe include the sustaining *Floresta*, at the start of the Loarre road (*menú* €12, *carta* €22), and the fancier *Rincón del Palacio*, next to a medieval manor house on the main Plaza de Ramón y Cajal, where the €25 *menú* gives you access to the best of the *carta*. At no. 11 on the same *plaza*, *Bar El Pozo de Sherea* acquits itself well for tapas and drinks.

Los Mallos

The rail and A132 road northwest out of Huesca give views of the fantastic, russet-tinged sugarloaf formations known as **Los Mallos** – "The Ninepins", beloved of abseilers and divided into two separate groups at Riglos and Agüero. Their majesty, however, may not protect them from being lapped by a proposed new dam at Biscuarés on the Río Gállego.

If you're travelling **by train** and want a closer look, get off at Riglos station (an unattended platform; ask the conductor to stop) and walk about 700m up the access drive to **Riglos** village, tucked high up underneath the most impressive stretch of the peaks. There's **accommodation** above the *Bar Restaurante El Puro* at *Casa Toño* (☎974 383 176; ❷), or at the new activity-orientated FAM **refugio** at the village entrance (☎974 383 051, ⓦwww.refugioderiglos.es; 6- to 8-bed dorms), offering meals, too.

More *mallos* loom behind **Agüero**, an isolated village 5km off the main Huesca–Pamplona road at Murillo de Gállego or a seven-kilometre walk from **Concilio** rail station (again, ask to be set down). Agüero itself is characterful, unspoilt and graced by two **Romanesque churches**: central San Salvador (June 15–Sept 30 Tues–Sun 4–6pm) and remote Santiago (June 15–Sept 30 Tues–Sun 11am–1pm) 700m east of town, both with superb, always-viewable portal carvings by the Master of San Juan de la Peña (see p.000).You may **stay** at *Hostal La Costera* at the top of the village (☏974 380 330, ⓔs.geocities.com/hostalacostera; ②–③), with basic, prefab rooms (some with shared bathrooms) but lovely grounds, a pool and restaurant. Murillo de Gállego is less impressive but serves as the local base for **river-rafting**, with several outfitters along the highway; Grupo Explora (☏974 383 022, ⓦwww.evasiongrupoexplora.com) is about the most established.

Sierra de Guara

North of the N240 road from Huesca to Barbastro sprawls the **Sierra de Guara**, a thinly inhabited region protected as a *parque natural* since 1990.The *sierra* has no dramatic peaks – the highest point is 2078-metre Puntón de Guara – and the low-altitude vegetation often looks distinctly scrubby, but its allure lies lower down, in an unrivalled array of sculpted gorges, painted prehistoric caves and appealing villages.This is the main centre for **canyoning** in Spain, and indeed Europe; **hiking** is best in spring or autumn, though walking opportunities are relatively limited and trail marking often poor.

The eastern half of the Guara is far more popular, and covered by the Alpina 1:40,000 **map** *Sierra de Guara II*, a must for touring. Due to massive depopulation, there's **no public transport** anywhere in the region, except for a single daily service (July & Aug only), run for the benefit of canyoners, from Alquézar to Fuente de Lecina; similarly, the only petrol and bank (with an ATM) is at Alquézar.

Alquézar and around

At the far southeastern corner of the range and *parque*, 22km from Barbastro, **ALQUÉZAR** ("Alquezra" in Aragonese) is the Guara's main gateway and most (over)developed tourist centre. Amphitheatrically tiered above the Río Vero, it's an atmospheric yet tidy village, though packed to the gills most weekends and all summer. Arcaded lanes culminate in the eighth-century Moorish **citadel** on a pinnacle overlooking the river; the Christians took it in 1064, and by the start of the twelfth century had built the **Colegiata de Santa María la Mayor** (daily 11am–2pm & 4–6pm; €2) within its fortifications. Only the cloister, its column capitals carved with biblical scenes, remains from the Romanesque era; the Gothic-Renaissance church, dating from the sixteenth and seventeenth centuries, is crammed with a miscellany of Baroque art, mostly polychrome wood except for an unpainted pine organ, and a masterful thirteenth-century wooden Crucifixion in the side chapel. From near the citadel a path leads for 45 minutes down to the river and the **Puente de Villacantal**, one of several ancient bridges in the *sierra*, while from Plaza Mayor another recognized route takes in the **Puente de Fuentebaños** and views of the river from a metal catwalk.

There's a **turismo** at the edge of town on c/Arrabal (Easter & July & Aug daily 9am–2pm & 4.30–8pm; Sept–June weekends only, same hours), which sells the recommended Alpina map, several **canyoning outfitters**, and an attractive **pool** up by the mandatorily used **car park**. There's plenty of **accommodation**, including *Albergue Rural de Guara*, on c/Pilaseras, above the main car park (☏974 318 956, ⓦwww.alburgueruraldeguara.com; closed Nov–March); friendly *Casa Jabonero* at c/Pedro Arnal 8 (☏974 318 908; ①); *Villa de Alquézar* at c/Pedro Arnal 12 (☏974 318 416, ⓦwww.villadealquezar.com; B&B ③), whose larger doubles have castle-view balconies (though some rooms are cell-like); and ⚸ *Hostal Narbona* at c/Baja 19 (☏974 318 078, ⓦwww.hostalnarbona.com; ②), with cheery, pastel-decor rooms.There's also the nearby *Alquézar* **campsite**, 1km downhill by the petrol pump (☏974 318 300). Many **bars and restaurants** lining Plaza Nueva at the southwest edge of the village are generally mediocre and overpriced, banking on their views of the castle; two of the more tolerable here are cheap-and-cheerful *Mesón del Vero*, and *La Cocineta*, with *menús* at €22 and courteous if "relaxed" service. *Hostal Narbona*'s *comedor* is probably a better choice, with *menús* (€13–32) featuring duck and lamb.

With your own transport, you can head 5km southwest for slightly precious but imaginative *nouvelle* Spanish cuisine at *El Puntillo* (T 974 318 168, W www .elpuntillo.com; €28 *menú degustación*), in **ADAHUESCA**; they also offer three rooms, one suitable for families (❹). Finally, the village of **BUERA**, 6km southeast across the river, has another worthy lodging and eating option in ⚘ *La Posada de Lalola* (T 974 318 347, W www.laposadadelalola.com; ❹), which has exquisite designer rooms opening onto a garden and serves respectable *table d'hôte* fare (reservations necessary; allow €30).

North: the road to Lecina

The district road from below Alquézar heads northeast to **COLUNGO**, 5km distant – attractive in a low-key way with arched doorways and massive buttressed church. **Accommodation** includes friendly, 2006-renovated *Hostal Mesón de Colungo* (T 974 318 195, W www.mesondecolungo.com; ❷), offering meals; you can sample the locally made *aguardiente de anís* at *A'Olla* bar-restaurant opposite.

The road continues past two of the four prehistoric **painted caves** of the Vero valley, which have protective grilles and can only be entered on escorted tours arranged through local *turismos*. However, a visit to Colungo's **Centro del Arte Rupestre** (July to mid-Sept Tues–Sun 10am–2pm & 4.30–8pm; €2) should give you enough background to appreciate the cave paintings, as most can be seen through the grilles. Signposted lay-bys indicate the start of the forty-minute trail for the **Covacho de Arpán**, with its striking image of a stag, and, shortly afterwards, the half-hour track to the **Tozal de Mallata** (painted with abstract figures); the **Covacho de Barfaluy** is accessed by a forty-minute trail from Lecina. Visits to the remote **Abrigo de Chimiachas** involve a long 4WD journey, beginning from near Alquézar.

LECINA, 16km from Colungo, has some imposing houses – it was one of the wealthier Guara villages – and good views northeast to the high peaks. There's a superb **place to stay** here: ⚘ *La Choca* (T 974 343 070; closed Nov–March except weekends; ❷), a restored mansion opposite the church with some of the best food in the Guara (lunch Sat & Sun; *table d'hôte* supper Easter & July & Aug, otherwise weekends only; guests have preference); reckon on €16 a head plus drink. There's also a **campsite** down by the river, *Lecina* (T 974 318 386, W www.campinglecina .com; closed Oct–May), which doubles as the local canyoning outfitter.

The area around Lecina is one of the few places in the Guara where **walkers** are actively catered for. The local municipality has waymarked sixteen PR trails, indicated on a sketch map available from *La Choca*; a good outing is the three-hour loop out of Lecina via Almazorre and Betorz.

Northwest: the road to Rodellar

West from Alquézar and Adahuesca, the next significant habitation is **BIERGE**, with the most important religious monument in the Guara: the **Ermita de San Fructuoso**, at the north end of the village (late June to Sept daily except Tues noon–1pm & 5–6pm, €1.50; summon warden on T 660 701 997 off season). The twelfth-century building was adorned with frescoes in two stages during the latter half of the thirteenth century, depicting a Crucifixion, the trial and martyrdom of Fructuoso (an early bishop of Tarragona), the trial of John the Evangelist (complete with a demon whispering disinformation to the judging king's ear), and – tucked inside the arch – two angels blowing the last trump.

Bierge **accommodation** ranges from the impeccably appointed ⚘ *Hotel Era Conte* just northeast of town (☎ 974 343 410, ⓦ www.eraconte.com; ❸, suites ❹), which does evening meals, to *Casa Barbara* (☎ 974 318 060, ⓦ www .casabarbara.net; 8-bed dorms; closed Nov–Easter; half-board obligatory), a welcoming canyoners' *albergue* on the west outskirts, with good food – including own-baked breads and fruit turnovers – served out in the garden. Otherwise, the most reliable local **restaurant** is *Alcanadre* 700m along the Rodellar road (Easter & June–Sept), where *platos combinados* are better value than the somewhat anemic *menú*.

North along the ridgetop HU341, the scenery gets grander after about 5km, with canyons yawning to either side. Soon you descend through woods past *Expediciones*, the shadiest **campsite** of three in the Alcanadre river valley (☎ 974 318 600, ⓦ www.expediciones-sc.es; closed Oct–Easter), home also to the most established canyoning operator hereabouts, and 2km farther, **LAS ALMUNIAS**, the first proper village, with the newly refurbished *Casa Tejedor* (☎ 974 318 686, ⓦ www.casatejedor.com; 2- to 8-person apts; closed Nov–April); simple meals are served downstairs, and there's an *albergue* annexe (3- or 4-bed rooms) across the way.

RODELLAR, some 4km beyond and 18km from Bierge at road's end, looks achingly photogenic draped along a ridge above the Río Mascún, though the reality close up in peak season is likely to be cars parked nose-to-tail on the approaches (they're banned in the village) and overstretched **accommodation**, limited to *Casa Arilla* (☎ 974 318 343; ❷; closed Dec–March) and apartments at adjacent *Casa Javier* (☎ 974 318 613; ❹; closed Oct–March). *El Puente*, 1500m south by the river and the medieval Pedruel bridge (☎ 974 318 312; closed Dec–March), is the more alluringly set of two **campsites**; there's also the interesting *Refugio Kalandraka* beyond Rodellar's church (☎ 639 447 727, ⓦ www.refugio-kalandraka .es), complete with sound-stage for live events. **Eating and drinking** options are similarly restricted to cheap-and-cheerful *Florentino* and a nearby snack-bar. If you're not a member of the canyoning fraternity, you can just do the **hike** north to the abandoned hamlet of **Otín** (2hr 30min one way).

Jaca and around

Jaca is approached through nondescript, traffic-choked suburbs of ever-expanding apartment blocks and ski chalets: an unpromising introduction to this early Aragonese capital and stronghold, from which the kingdom was recaptured from the Moors. The old centre, however, is a lot more characterful, flanked by a huge star-shaped citadel, and endowed with a landmark Romanesque cathedral. This, and the monastery of **San Juan de la Peña**, 20km southwest, are the major local sights, though in winter there's a bonus in the proximity of **Candanchú** and Astún, Aragón's most established ski resorts. Rail enthusiasts may be tempted by the trip to **Canfranc**, almost at the French border.

Jaca

After a spell in the mountains, **JACA**'s relatively "big town" feel and facilities may be an equal attraction to any monuments. It's enlivened by the cadets of the mountain-warfare battalion based here, as well as a summer English-language university. The battle of **Las Tiendas** in 758, when Moorish armies were repulsed in large part by women, is still commemorated on the first Friday in May, in a mock all-women battle between "Christians" and "Muslims".

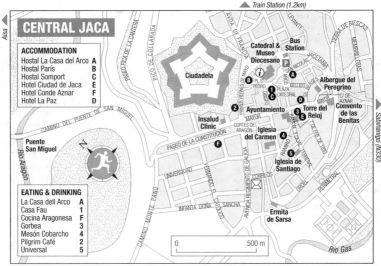

▲ Train Station (1.2km)

CENTRAL JACA

ACCOMMODATION
Hostal La Casa del Arco	A
Hostal París	B
Hostal Somport	C
Hotel Ciudad de Jaca	E
Hotel Conde Aznar	F
Hotel La Paz	D

EATING & DRINKING
La Casa dell Arco	A
Casa Fau	1
Cocina Aragonesa	F
Gorbea	3
Mesón Cobarcho	4
Pilgrim Café	2
Universal	5

▼ Huesca (C125) & Puente la Reina de Jaca (N240)

Orientation, arrival and information

The northeast side of Jaca's old quarter, beyond the cathedral and south of the bus station, is a little frowsy, and shelters most of the budget accommodation and rowdier bars; the southwestern district, abutting either side of Avenida Regimiento de Galicia, is smarter, with sidewalk cafés, more touristy restaurants and banks.

The **train station** is a fair walk from the centre; take a bus from the stop outside to the **bus station** on Avenida Jacetania, around the back of the cathedral. Useful long-distance buses include those for Pamplona, Biescas via Sabiñánigo, and Echo/Ansó, as well as more frequent services to Zaragoza and Huesca. **Drivers** will find parking easiest in the less congested southwestern quarter, especially around the far end and side streets off the Paseo de la Constitución, though look out for pay-and-display zones; a large underground car park is next to the bus station.

The helpful **turismo** at Plaza de San Pedro (summer Mon–Sat 9am–9pm, Sun 9am–3pm; winter Mon–Fri 9am–1.30pm & 4.30–7pm, Sat 10am–1pm & 5–7pm; ☏974 360 098, ⓦwww.jaca.es) stocks a range of free leaflets.

Accommodation

Just one **campsite** survives nearby: *Camping Victoria*, 1.5km out of town on the Pamplona road (☏974 360 323), is basic but shady and with a bar-restaurant on site.

Hostal La Casa del Arco c/San Nicolás 4 ☏974 364 448, ⓦwww.lacasadelarco.net. Just five well-restored, stone-walled rooms (doubles and triples), in a medieval building above the handy eponymous bar and restaurant. ❷–❸
Hostal París Plaza de San Pedro 5 ☏974 361 020. Best budget *hostal* in town, across from the cathedral and offering clean, spacious rooms with washbasin (some en-suite singles). ❷

Hostal Somport c/Echegaray 11 ☏&ⓕ974 363 410. Jaca's most affordable en-suite digs, in another renovated old building; there's also a salubrious ground-floor bar-restaurant. ❷
Hotel Ciudad de Jaca c/Siete de Febrero 8 ☏974 364 311. Centrally located but quiet place with good en-suite rooms in a modern building. ❸
Hotel Conde Aznar Paseo de la Constitución 3 ☏974 361 050, ⓦwww.condeaznar.com.

Attractive family-run hotel, now in its third generation of management, with well-renovated rooms in pale soft furnishings and off-street parking. ⑤

Hotel La Paz c/Mayor 41 ⓣ 974 360 700, ⓦ www .alojamientosaran.com/f_lapaz.htm. Large, somewhat airless en-suite rooms with heating in winter. Closed Nov. ③

The Town

Jaca is an ancient town, founded by the Romans and occupied continuously since. It had a very brief period of Moorish rule after being captured around 716, but the Christians soon reconquered the town and held it, save for a few years, from then on. Jaca's greatest period, however, came after 1035, when **Ramiro I**, son of Sancho of Navarre, established a court here and presided over the first parliament on record.

The Catedral

The **Catedral** (daily 8am–2pm & 4–8pm; free) is the main legacy of Jaca's years as the seat of the young Aragonese kingdom, and ranks as one of Spain's most architecturally important monuments. Rebuilt on previous foundations during Ramiro I's reign, it was the first Spanish cathedral with French Romanesque traits and, as such, exerted considerable stylistic influence on other churches along the Camino de Santiago.

Ramiro's endowment of the cathedral was undoubtedly intended to confirm Jaca's role as a Christian capital, in what was still an overwhelmingly Moorish Iberian peninsula. Its design introduced the classic three-aisled basilica, though unhappily the original Romanesque simplicity has been much obscured since by florid Renaissance decoration. The building retains some original sculpture, however, including realistic carving on the capitals and doorway – a sixteenth-century statue of Santiago looks down from the portal. Inside, the main treasure is the silver-clad **shrine of Santa Orosía**, Jaca's patron saint; a Bohemian noble, married into the Aragonese royal family, Orosía was martyred by the Moors in around 870 for refusing to renounce her faith and marry a Muslim chieftain.

The unusually good **Museo Diocesano** in the cloisters is closed indefinitely for renovations. If and when it reopens, highlights are an eerily modern Pantocrator fresco from a church in Ruesta, a walnut crucified Christ, and the *Flight into Egypt* and *Adoration of the Magi* from Navasa, all of twelfth-century vintage.

The Ciudadela and Puente San Miguel

The **Ciudadela** (aka Castillo de San Pedro), a redoubtable sixteenth-century fort built in the French pentagonal-stellar plan then prevalent, is still part-occupied by the military. You can visit a section of the interior by guided tour only (Tues–Sun: April–June, Sept & Oct 11am–noon & 5–6pm; July & Aug 11am–2pm & 5–9pm; Nov–March 11am–noon & 4–5pm; €10). Its walls offer good views of the surrounding peaks, and of the wooded countryside around.

Below the citadel, reached along a steep dirt road from the end of the Paseo de la Constitución, is a remarkable fifteenth-century bridge, the three-arched **Puente San Miguel**. Across this bridge over the Río Aragón, pilgrims on the Camino Aragonés – a branch of the **Camino de Santiago** – entered Jaca. It must have been a welcome sight, marking the end of the arduous Pyrenean stage into Spain over the Puerto de Somport. From Jaca, the pilgrims headed westwards, through Puente la Reina de Jaca, towards Navarra, where they joined up with the more popular route from Roncesvalles. This section of the Camino de Santiago – like other branches of the route – has experienced quite a revival since the early 1990s, though it's constantly threatened with either inundation by dams or covering over by building projects. In town, there's a well-run

Albergue del Peregrino (pilgrims' hostel), installed partly in the medieval hospital on c/Conde Aznar (reception daily 3–10.15pm; €9 per pilgrim, bedding extra fee), while route maps and pilgrimage-related souvenirs are widely available.

Eating and drinking

Jaca has an inviting selection of reasonably priced **restaurants** and **bars**, and there's a lively after-dark atmosphere during summer and the ski season. July and August see **concerts** in the university gardens or the castle grounds.

La Casa del Arco c/San Nicolás 4. That rare Spanish breed: a vegetarian, no-smoking restaurant (though wine is served). Filling international dishes from a *carta* (allow €17), with fresh-squeezed juices, teas and alcohol in the adjoining bar under the arcade. Closed Sun in winter.

Casa Fau Plaza de la Catedral 4. Classic tapas bar, with a few tables under the arches, more inside, and notoriously rude staff. All the usual platters, plus *ciervo* (venison) sausage, *boletus* (wild mushrooms) and quiche.

Cocina Aragonesa Paseo de la Constitución 3. The *comedor* of the *Conde Aznar* hotel features game, fish and original desserts in its *cocina del mercado*. There's a choice of unusually interesting *menús* for about €16, while *a la carta* won't much exceed €26, plus wine. Closed part Nov.

Gorbea c/Mayor, corner c/Ramón y Cajal. Excellent Basque-style *pintxos* at this small bar opposite the *ayuntamiento*, redone in 2007

with wood trim. A *media caña* plus *changurro* (crab) *pintxo* won't much top €3.

Mesón Cobarcho c/Ramiro Primero 2. Don't let the decor – part Gaudí, part Flintstones – distract you from the excellent cooking; the €15 *menú* features both seafood and meat, though *a la carta* is pricey at €27–33.

Pilgrim Café Avda. del Primer Viernes de Mayo 7. Inevitably a bit touristy, and the fare (burgers, *pintxos*, *platos combinados*, *bocadillos*, coffees) is nothing exceptional, but this occupies a fine wood-floored *modernista* building with outdoor tables facing the Ciudadela's lawn.

Universal c/Campoy Irigoyen 11. Very popular, self-described "brasa-bar" specializing in *cochinillo* (suckling pig), *caracoles* (snails) and other wood-fired, country-style grills (€11–13), as well as cheaper platters. Homestyle desserts, courteous service and a skylit *comedor* are other pluses. Closed Mon & Oct.

Listings

Adventure activities Alcorce Aventura upstairs at Avda. Regimiento Galicia 1 (☎974 356 781) organize a variety of expeditions; English-speaking staff.

Hospital Besides the main one on c/Rapitan, beyond the train station, there's the very central, public Insalud clinic on Paseo de la Constitución, good for minor ailments.

Maps La Unión at c/Mayor 34 and El Siglo at c/Mayor 17 sell all the maps and guides required for the region.

Outdoor gear In the centre, Charli at Avda. Regimiento de Galicia 3, and Intersport-Piedrafita, at Avda. de Francia 4, have a limited stock, as does the ground-floor premises of Alcorce Aventura.

South to Santa Cruz de la Serós and San Juan de la Peña

San Juan de la Peña, up in the hills southwest of Jaca, is the best-known monastery in Aragón. In medieval times, San Juan was an important detour on the pilgrim route from Jaca to Pamplona, since it reputedly held the Holy Grail – actually a Roman-era chalice that later turned up in Valencia cathedral. These days, most tourists – and there are many, including school parties – visit mainly for the Romanesque cloister.

The most direct **route to the monastery** begins from the Jaca–Pamplona (N240) highway. A side road, 11km west of Jaca, leads south 4km to the village of **Santa Cruz de la Serós**, and from here it's a further 7km uphill to San Juan. There's no public transport, although you could take a Puente La Reina/Pamplona bus from Jaca to the turning – assuming an overnight stay in Santa Cruz. From there, walkers can take the **old path** up to San Juan in about an hour. The path, waymarked as Variant 2 of the GR65.3.2, is signposted from near the church (where there is also a map-placard). The road takes a more circuitous route around the mountainside, giving wonderful views of the Pyrenean peaks to the north and distinctive Peña de Oroel to the east.

Santa Cruz de la Serós

The picturesque village of **SANTA CRUZ DE LA SERÓS**, which comes to life in summer, is dominated by its thick-set but nonetheless stylish Romanesque **church of Santa María** (daily 10am–2pm & 3–8pm; €2 or included in San Juan de la Peña admission), once part of a large Benedictine monastery that flourished until the sixteenth century. Places to **eat and drink** at the village outskirts include *O'Fogaril*, featuring cheapish Aragonese platters such as *pucherico de alubias* (bean hotpot) and *chistorra* sausage, best enjoyed in the bar area, and the *Hostelería Santa Cruz* near the church, with a dull *menú* but better *a carta*, including *boliches* and local beans. In addition, the latter has high-standard **rooms** (℡974 361 975, Ⓦ www.santacruzdelaseros.com; ❸), four with balconies.

San Juan de la Peña

SAN JUAN DE LA PEÑA actually comprises two monasteries, 2km apart, both run as ruthlessly efficient money-spinners by a private foundation; coming from Santa Cruz, you reach the lower, older one first. Built into a hollow under a rocky escarpment, from which seep various springs, the lower **Monasterio Viejo** (spring & autumn Tues–Sun 10am–2pm & 4–7pm; summer Tues–Sun 10am–2.30pm & 3.30–8pm; winter Wed–Sun 11am–2pm; €6) is an unusual and evocative complex, even in its partial state of survival. Here, in 1071, the Latin Mass was first introduced to the Iberian peninsula by Cluniac monks, replacing the older Mozarabic one. Visits begin at the **Sala de Concilios** – once the refectory – and the adjacent, double-naved, ninth-century **Mozarabic chapel**. These were

▲ Monasterio Viejo, San Juan de la Peña

adapted as the crypt of the main Romanesque **church**, built two centuries later, and both retain fragments of Romanesque frescoes. Upstairs, alongside the main church, is an open-air **pantheon** for Aragonese and Navarrese nobles; reliefs on the Gothic tombs depict events from the early history of Aragón. An adjacent enclosed pantheon for the kings of Aragón was remodelled in a cold, Neoclassical style during the eighteenth century and later sacked by Napoleon's troops.

All these are just appetizers, however, for the twelfth-century Romanesque **cloisters**. Only two of the bays survive intact, but the capitals – depicting scenes from the Old Testament and the life of Christ – rank among the greatest examples of Romanesque carving in Spain. They were the artistry of an anonymous, idiosyncratic craftsman who left his mark on a number of churches in the region. He is now known as the **Master of San Juan de la Peña**, his work easily recognizable by the unnaturally large eyes on the figures.

The seventeenth-century **Monasterio Nuevo** with its a flamboyant Baroque facade was mostly converted in 2007 into two fairly fatuous *centros de interpretación* (€5–10 admission depending on how many, along with the church, you visit). The rear-left (south) wing of the monastery has become a similarly overpriced four-star *hospedaría*. Facing the complex is a picnic-ground in a forest-enclosed meadow; arriving by car, you must park under the trees during high season – a shuttle bus (€2) takes you down to the Monasterio Viejo. In low season, you're allowed to park in the bus bays at the lower monastery.

Canfranc-Estación

When the French railways discontinued their part of the local trans-Pyrenean line, the enormous train station at **CANFRANC-ESTACIÓN**, 23km north of Jaca, slowly but surely became a vandalized white elephant. It was a sad fate for an elegant spot that saw the French and Spanish heads of state attend its inauguration in 1928, and which served as a location for the film *Doctor Zhivago*. A train derailed on the French side in March 1970, destroying a critical bridge and cutting the rail line, though Spanish undercutting of French ski-resort prices ensured its continued closure (ironically, the Spanish slopes are now pricier). However, following the opening of the Somport car tunnel (free) in early 2003, EU funding for the rehabilitation of the rail line between Oloron-Ste-Marie and Canfranc has been approved, and the first step was the still-ongoing conversion of Canfranc station as a luxury hotel and conference centre.

The village – replacing Canfranc-Pueblo down the valley, mostly destroyed by fire in 1944 – exists primarily to catch the passing tourist trade, with a few souvenir shops and lodgings. It's just about worth the day's trip from Jaca, even if you don't continue into France, for the train ride up the valley and the cool mountain air on arrival. **Accommodation**, all on or just off the through highway, includes the high-quality *Albergue Pepito Grillo* (☎974 373 123, ⊛www.pepitogrillo.com; 6-bunk rooms; open most of year) and the neighbouring, chalet-style *Hotel Villa Anayet* (☎974 373 146; ❸), with a pool. Near *Villa Anayet*, Casa Rural Marieta (☎974 373 365; B&B ❸), has been upgraded to *hostal* status, with wi-fi and a cozy *comedor* (€19 for Aragonese specialities). Cheaper (€12) **meals** are offered at the *Hotel Villa Anayet's comedor*, though cooking is more careful and a €14 *menú* wider ranging at *Borda l'Anglassé*, in the southern sector of town.

Though there's no proper train (yet), you can travel on into France several times daily through the tunnel on **buses** run by the French SNCF. Consult Canfranc's **turismo** in the Casa de la Villa (mid-June to mid-Sept Mon–Sat 9am–1.30pm & 5–8pm; rest of year Tues–Sat 9am–1.30pm & 4–7pm, closed Nov 1–15; ☎974 373 141, ⊛www.canfranc.es) for current details of trains, skiing and the local summer **classical-music festival**.

Echo and Ansó

Echo and **Ansó** are two of the most attractive valleys in Aragón, their rivers – Aragón Subordan and Veral – joining the Río Aragón west of Jaca. Until the 1960s, both valleys felt extremely remote, with villagers wearing traditional dress and speaking a dialect, *Cheso*, derived from medieval Aragonese. These days, they're very much on the map for Spanish weekenders and foreign visitors, and the last rural activity seriously engaged in is timber-cutting.

There's only one daily **bus** (Mon–Sat), calling first at Echo and Siresa before continuing 11km west on a broad, improved road to Ansó; it leaves Jaca at 6.30pm, arriving in Ansó at 8.10pm, and begins the journey back from Ansó at 6am the next day. For **trekking** in the region, the 1:40,000 Editorial Alpina booklet *Valles de Ansó y Echo* is useful. This shows the very enjoyable two-and-a-half-hour hiking **trail from Siresa to Ansó**, waymarked as the PR18 and signposted as "*Fuen d'a Cruz*" by the stream below Siresa.

Skiing in Aragón

There are five **ski resorts** in the Aragonese Pyrenees, and all of them – following Jaca's unsuccessful bids to host the 2010 and 2014 Winter Olympics – are well equipped. You may find that package deals, bought from any travel agent in northern Spain, work out cheapest, but there are also often mini-packages arrangeable through the *turismos* and hotels of each valley. Take advantage of slow, midweek periods and avoid the busiest weekends and major holidays, when all accommodation within a forty-kilometre radius is booked a month in advance.

The westernmost centres are **CANDANCHÚ** (Ⓦwww.candanchu.com) and **ASTÚN** (Ⓦwww.astun.com), north of Canfranc (5 daily buses from Jaca). The resorts – smaller Astún dating from 1975, and slightly higher Candanchú, the first established in these mountains – are just 4km apart, but do not have a link or shared lift passes. Astún's chairlifts are prone to closure from high winds; also, liaisons between the sectors can be obscure, and you really need to be of intermediate ability to enjoy this resort (beginners are probably better off at Candanchú). There's just a single, monolithic chalet-style **hotel** at Astún, the *Europa* (Ⓣ974 373 312, Ⓔhoteleuropa@astun.com; ④). Three other hotels are available (amongst many apartments) at Candanchú, the most attractive being the *Candanchú* (Ⓣ974 373 025, Ⓦwww.hotelcandanchu.com; ⑤), though there's also a slightly-pricier-than-usual *albergue*, *El Águila* (Ⓣ974 373 291, Ⓦwww.infobide.com/elaguila; open ski season, July & Aug).

Among the other ski centres, **FORMIGAL** (closest reasonable lodgings at Sallent de Gállego; recommended is characterful and clean *Balaitus* – Ⓣ974 488 959, Ⓦwww.hotelbalaitus.com; ③) and **PANTICOSA** (try the *Vicente*, Ⓣ974 487 022; ③, just above the eponymous village) are both served by daily buses from Jaca via Biescas. Formigal and its 137km of pistes matches or exceeds Candanchú/Astún for interest and challenge, with packages offered from the UK in conjunction with charters to Huesca's new airport (see Ⓦwww.aramon.co.uk), but Panticosa – despite massive investment since 1994 – remains too low and too limited in its piste plan for expert skiers, though families love it for its many chairlifts and conveyor belts. The remotest and highest Aragonese resort is **CERLER**, close to Benasque; it, too, has undergone a huge face-lift, with snow cannons, well-coordinated high-speed chairlifts and fifty runs (totalling 60km) finishing through forest, making it an excellent intermediate centre. Much the best accommodation choice here is ⚑ *Casa Cornel*, a converted twelfth-century manor house in the old village at c/Obispo 11 (Ⓣ974 551 102, Ⓦwww.casacornel.com; *hostal* wing B&B ③, hotel wing B&B ⑤).

Valle de Echo

ECHO (ex-Hecho), "capital" of its eponymous valley, is a splendid old village, where whitewash outlines the windows and doors of the massive stone houses. It figures in Aragonese history as the seat of the embryonic Aragonese kingdom under Conde Aznar Galíndez in the ninth century, and as the birthplace of "warrior king" Alfonso I. Although it seems ancient, Echo as you see it is barely two centuries old – like so many villages in these hills, it was burnt and sacked during the Napoleonic Wars.

An annual arts festival, which ran from 1975 to 1984, has left a permanent legacy in the open-air **gallery of sculpture** on the hillside just west of the village. Created by a group of artists, the 46 pieces are not individually stunning but, taken as a whole, quite compelling. Near the enormous central church, the more conventional **Museo Etnológico/Casa Mazo** (Easter, July & Aug daily except Mon pm 10.30am–1.30pm & 6–9pm; €1.50) has interesting collections on Pyrenean rural life and folklore.

The **turismo** occupies premises amidst the sculpture garden (daily except Sun eve & Mon am June–Sept 10am–1.30pm & 5.30–8pm; ☎974 375 329). Of Echo's several **places to stay**, the clear first choices are *Casa Blasquico*, barely marked at Plaza Palacio de la Fuente 1 (☎974 375 007, ⓦwww.casablasquico .com; ➋), with five tastefully converted en-suite rooms, and the *Casa Chuanet*, on the hillside opposite (☎974 375 033; ➋), with appealingly decorated en-suite rooms above the *Bar Danubio*. A **campsite**, *Valle de Echo* (☎974 375 361), lies just south of the village, though *Borda Bisáltico* (☎974 375 388), 6km north with great views, offers a higher standard, with sloping lawn pitches, an *albergue* and good if pricey food at its *asador*.

Don't miss the chance to **eat** at ⌘ *Casa Blasquico* (reservations mandatory ☎974 375 007; closed part Sept), where the emphasis is on game, lamb, duck and mushroom crêpes, definitely worth a €30 or so splurge *a la carta*, including dessert and house wine – if money's tight, there's a cheaper *menú*. Owner-chef Gaby Coarasa was among the first stars of Pyrenean *nouvelle cuisine* in the 1980s, and the walls of the tiny *comedor* sport awards to prove it. If you can't get in, friendly ⌘ *Bar Subordán* next door will feed you with superb, inexpensive *raciones* of *longaniza* and *chipirrones*, as well as good salads and desserts.

Siresa and beyond

Two kilometres north of Echo stands the small, quiet village of **SIRESA**. Keeping watch over riverside pastures is a remarkable ninth-century monastic church, the massive, austere **San Pedro** (daily 11am–1pm & 5–8pm; €1.50). The owners of the pleasant local **hotel**, the *Castillo d'Acher* (☎974 375 313, ⓦwww.castillodacher.com; ➋), also have apartments suitable for families, and operate a competent **restaurant**.

Walkers may be tempted to continue up the valley from Siresa, along the GR65.3.3, a minor variant of the Camino de Santiago; much of the paved road can be missed out by following the "Vía Romana", not Roman but certainly early medieval, signposted 3km above Siresa. Once through the **Boca de Infierno** gorge (a popular canyoning venue), you emerge at **Selva de Oza**, where there's a pleasant bar (but no campsite). Selva is the jumping-off point for climbing **Castillo de Acher** (2390m); the other limestone peaks, including **Bisaurín** (2669m) and **Agüerri** (2449m), are best tackled from the excellent *Refugio de Gabardito* (☎974 375 387 or Patchi on 676 198 197, ⓔinfo@gabardito.com; 48 bunks), farther along the track serving the *Borda Bisáltico* campsite. The *refugio* is affiliated to Val d'Echo Activa (☎974 375 421, ⓦwww.valdechoactiva.com), an activity centre on the village bypass road (summer daily except Mon am 11am–1.45pm & 6–8.30pm);

their main programme is **La Senda de Camille** (Ⓦwww.lasendadecamille.com), a spectacular, six-stage, refuge-to-refuge circular trek taking in some of the French side, too, for which they make guaranteed hut reservations.

North of Selva de Oza, the paved road ends near **La Mina**, trailhead for the two-hour hike up to the **Acherito lake**, one of the local beauty spots. **Laraille/Laraya** peak (2147m) just overhead is another popular target, as is the nearby frontier peak of **Lariste** (2168m). The GR11 long-distance footpath also passes through La Mina, on its way west from Canfranc, heading towards Zuriza in the Valle de Ansó, a short day's hike distant; at **Zuriza**, there's the shady if rather regimented *Camping Zuriza* (Ⓣ974 370 196), with an *albergue* (6- or 8-bunk rooms), and bar-restaurant. Some may prefer 5km of track-tramping up-valley to the more laidback, enchantingly situated *Refugio de Linza* (Ⓣ974 348 289, Ⓦwww.refugiodelinza.com; 90 bunks), with 7km of nordic pistes and ski/snowshoe rental in winter.

Valle de Ansó

Once a prosperous, large village, **ANSÓ** fell upon hard times during the 1950s depopulation of rural Aragón. Since then, however, there's been a modest revival, with Jaca and Pamplona professionals keeping second residences here, and a seasonal traffic of tourists catered to by a central-*plaza* **turismo** (daily summer 10am–2pm & 4–6pm) and two **ATMs**. It's certainly an attractive weekend base, with a little river beach down by the Río Veral. There are few specific sights besides a photo- and video-enhanced **Museo Etnológico** (summer daily 10.30am–1.30pm & 3.30–8pm; €2), housed in sixteenth-century San Pedro church with its huge gilt *retablo*.

Among **accommodation**, top spot is ⚘ *Posada Magoría*, in palatial quarters by the church (Ⓣ974 370 049, Ⓔposadamagoria@gmail; ❸), with a garden and views from wood-floored rooms; they serve excellent communal vegetarian meals (preference given to guests). The best alternative is *Casa Baretón* at c/Pascual Altemir 16 (Ⓣ974 370 138, Ⓦwww.casabareton.com; ❷), a well-restored eighteenth-century mansion, again with meal service. A **campsite** (Ⓣ665 926 149) operates beside the municipal **swimming pool** at the south end of the village.

Among very few **restaurant** options, *Kimboa* at the north end of town is easily the best, their own-reared meat served under the terrace canopy in summer (lunch only out of season). Many visitors head 6.5km up the valley to cheap-and-cheerful *Borda Arracona*, a converted farmstead with wood-fired grills served in two *comedores*, or continue another 1.5km to *Borda Chiquín*, with summer seating outside under a walnut tree, where €16 nets you three courses, including grilled chops and house wine.

Parque Nacional de Ordesa and around

PARQUE NACIONAL DE ORDESA Y MONTE PERDIDO (Ⓦwww .ordesa.net) was one of Spain's first protected national parks, and is perhaps its most dramatic, with beech and poplar forests, mountain streams, dozens of spring-to-summer waterfalls and a startling backdrop of limestone palisades. Impressive **wildlife** includes golden eagles, lammergeiers, griffon and Egyptian vultures and Pyrenean chamois – the last so great in number that at certain times hunters are allowed to cull the surplus. The park is an enduringly popular destination for walkers, and its foothill villages are predictably commercialized.

In midsummer, you'll need to book accommodation well in advance, even at campsites. Nevertheless, this is the Aragonese Pyrenees at their most spectacular, and well worth a few days of anyone's time.

The route to Ordesa

The closest, and thus most popular, gateway village is **Torla**, from where the GR15.2 leads into the park. Coming **from the southwest**, a daily **bus** service from Sabiñánigo (departs 11am) to Aínsa stops at Torla (arrives noon) and all villages en route, including Biescas, Linás de Broto, Broto, Sarvisé and Fiscal. In July and August, there's an additional weekday service between Sabiñánigo (departs 7pm) and Sarvisé via Torla. Sabiñánigo receives several daily buses from Jaca, the 10.15am and 6.15pm departures connecting directly with the onward services cited above.

Coming **from the southeast**, there's a year-round service from Barbastro (Mon–Sat 7.45pm) as far as Boltaña, though from mid-July to September 1 there's an additional departure at 11am, which dovetails nicely with the bus leaving Aínsa at 2.30pm, arriving in Torla at 3.30pm. For the valleys on the eastern side of the park, there's just a single daily bus (July & Aug Mon–Sat; rest of year 3 weekly; 8.45pm), as far as Bielsa.

Sabiñánigo, Biescas and Linás de Broto

There's not much joy in industrial **SABIÑÁNIGO** and you'll probably want to push straight on; it is, however, an almost unavoidable transport hub, especially coming from Huesca – the **bus terminal** is right outside the **train station**.

If you miss the year-round bus to Torla, best take the 6.30pm Sallent de Gállego service that passes pleasant **BIESCAS**, 17km north, with several **places to stay**. Among these, *Pensión Las Herras* offers both en-suite and sink-only rooms in an old stone house in a quiet cul-de-sac across the river from the *ayuntamiento* (ⓣ974 485 027; ❶), while *Casa Ruba*, just off the Plaza del Ayuntamiento (ⓣ&ⓕ974 485 001; ❸), has been in the same family since 1884 and has a lively bar and respected *comedor*. There's a **turismo** by the bridge (most of year Mon–Sat 10am–2pm & 6–8pm, Sun 10am–2pm; ⓣ974 485 002). Stone-built **LINÁS DE BROTO**, enviably set 17km east on the way to Torla, also makes a reasonable (and relatively calm) base: on the through road, choose between the co-managed *Hostal Cazcarro* (❷), where the *comedor* is, and fancier, wood-floored *Hotel Las Nieves* (ⓣ974 486 109, ⓦwww.hotellasnieves.net; ❸), and a family-friendly *albergue* with lovely communal areas, ⚑ *El Último Bucardo* (ⓣ974 486 323, ⓦwww.elultimobucardo.com; ❷, family quads ❸, also dorms).

Torla

The old stone village of **TORLA**, just 8km short of Ordesa, is well encased in ranks of modern hotels, and awash with souvenir stalls. It exists very much as a walkers' base, and almost everything is geared to park visitors. The **bus** from Sabiñánigo and Aínsa stops at the southern edge of town, by the huge, free car park where all visitors to the canyon must leave their vehicles in high season (see p.650 for details of shuttle-bus service). The **turismo** is on Plaza Nueva (late June to mid-Sept Mon–Sat 9.30am–1.30pm & 5–9pm; ⓣ974 229 804); the village also has an **ATM**, **post office** and **shops** – the highest in the valley – stocking basic foods and mountain gear. The closest of three **campsites** along the road out to Ordesa is riverside *Río Ara*, 2km from Torla on the far side of the stream (ⓣ974 486 248; closed Nov–Easter).

Top mid-range **accommodation** choices are the *Hostal Alto Aragón/Hotel Ballarín*, uphill from the main drag, opposite each other (ⓣ&ⓕ974 486 155;

❷–❸); the *Ballarin's comedor* offers sustaining *menús*. Among several fancier hotels, well-kept ⚹ *Villa de Torla* on Plaza Nueva (☎974 486 156, ⓦwww .hotelvilladetorla.com; closed Jan 6–March 15; ❸) is professionally run, with a pool and a decent restaurant (*menú* €14); third-floor rooms are best. For budget lodgings, try *Casa Borruel* on c/Fatás (☎974 486 067; ❶), near the *turismo*, or the friendly, high-standard *Albergue Lucien Briet* (☎974 486 221; mostly 7-bunk rooms), and an excellent ground-floor restaurant (*Bar Brecha*). Note that from October to Easter, most accommodation shuts from Monday to Thursday. Independent **restaurants** don't offer much value, except for *A'Borda Samper*, just off the high street, also a tapas bar.

Broto, Buesa and Sarvisé

If Torla's full or just too commercialized for your liking, you can try one of the villages just southeast along the road to Aínsa. **BROTO**, 4km south of Torla, is a noisy, teeming place, its old quarter hemmed in by traffic and new construction. Upriver, just beside the village's collapsed Romanesque bridge, is the quietest **accommodation**, and one of the last to fill, *Casa O'Puente* (☎974 486 072; ❷); you could also try *Hotel Mirador* up the road towards Oto (☎974 486 177, ⓦwww .ordesa.net/hotel-elmirador; ❸), with airy modern rooms, a decent **restaurant** and off-street parking. There's a **turismo** (June–Sept Mon–Sat 9am–1pm & 5–9pm; ☎974 486 413) plus a bank ATM. If you're walking, you can follow a well-trodden *camino* to Torla in 45 minutes; part of the GR15.2, it begins near the ruined bridge.

Some 2km south of Broto, a side road leads up and east to **BUESA**, one of the most unspoiled villages in the region, its two *barrios* flanking a wooded vale; seven of the nine remaining families still live from livestock-breeding. One of the exceptions runs aptly named ⚹ *El Balcón del Pirineo*, with sweeping views from the **bar-restaurant** terrace, fair-priced grills and ambitious desserts considering the locale. The same welcoming bunch have tiered, state-of-the-art **apartments** just uphill (☎974 486 175, ⓦwww.balcondelpirineo.com; 2- to 8-person; ❸), plus doubles and quads in a restored *casa rural* (❷) by the church.

Some 2km south of the Buesa turning is **SARVISÉ**, the lowest and least distinctive village of the Valle de Broto – it was mostly burned during the Civil War – but with more high-quality **accommodation**. Top picks are the secluded *Casa Puyuelo* (☎974 486 140, ⓔcasapuyuelo@staragon.com; ❸), with small but comfortable rooms; *Hotel Viña Oliván* at the start of the Fanlo road (☎974 486 358, ⓦwww.vinaolivan.com), with large if bland modern rooms in the main wing (❷), and cottage-apartments opposite fitting up to four (❹); and – among the best in the Aragonese Pyrenees – ⚹ *Hotel Casa Frauca* on the main road (☎974 486 182, ⓦwww.casafrauca.com; closed Jan 6–March; ❷), with cosy, custom-furnished, wood-floored rooms in three formats, occupying a 1904 mansion that survived the fire. Their famous ground-floor *comedor* draws crowds from near and far for daily-changing gourmet fare (€30–35 *a la carta*; reservations required).

Fiscal and Aínsa

Below Sarvisé, the Ara river valley turns east and widens markedly, with evidence of drastic depopulation; villages just off the road are largely deserted, their fields gone to seed. Aragón has the highest proportion of abandoned settlements in Spain, but here the impetus was a never-executed dam at Jánovas. In 1959, local property was expropriated for a pittance by the hydro company, and by 1964 many villagers had been forced to move, their houses dynamited by the Guardia Civil to get the point across.

One village that's recovered a bit through tourism is **FISCAL**, its older houses scattered agreeably on the far bank of the river from the highway. **Accommodation** here includes *Saltamontes* (☏974 503 113; 6- or 8-bunk rooms), an *albergue* opposite the church; and the comfortable *Hostal Casa Cadena*, near the top of the village (☏974 503 077; ③), with an evening-only wine, ham and cheese bar. The next decent place of any size is **AÍNSA**, its hilltop **old quarter** prettified with stone-paved walkways and boutiques to cash in on some of the cross-border trade pouring through the nearby Bielsa tunnel. Yet the *casco viejo* remains attractive, centred on an exceptional Romanesque church with a primitive crypt, triangular cloister and a climbable belfry, plus a vast, arcaded Plaza Mayor. **Accommodation** in the medieval *barrio* includes *Casa El Hospital*, an old stone house right next to the church (☏974 500 750, ⓦwww .casadelhospital.com; ③), or for a splurge, the two-star, slightly kitsch *Posada Real* at Plaza Mayor 6 (☏974 500 977, ⓦwww.posadareal.com; ⑤). Old-town **eating** options are more plentiful, if expensive; *Bar Restaurante Fes* at c/Mayor 22 offers reasonable value, while *Bar Bodega L'Alfil*, c/Travesera s/n, is the place for somewhat pricey *raciones*, cider and herbal liqueurs.

Cañon de Ordesa and central park treks

An asphalt road from Torla leads 4km to the Puente de los Navarros, and from here continues another 4km to the entrance to the **Cañon de Ordesa**, heart of the *parque nacional*. At peak times (Easter, July & Aug, parts of Sept & Oct), all private cars are banned beyond Puente de los Navarros, and you're encouraged to use the regular **shuttle bus** (daily 6/7am–8.30/10pm; every 15min July & Aug; €3 one way, €4.50 return) from the car park at the village outskirts. On-foot access from Torla means the well-marked **GR15.2 path**, which starts beside the *Hotel Bella Vista*, crossing to the east bank of the river; at Puente de la Ereta, it links up with the GR11 – the left fork leads to Bujaruelo, while the right fork takes you directly to **Pradera de Ordesa**, at the entrance to the

▲ Parque Nacional de Ordesa

Cañon de Ordesa, some two hours' walk out of Torla and the start of most of the hikes set out below. With a car, the closest you can get is the small parking area just before the San Antón campsite, at the start of the **PR134** (not shown on Alpina maps), which crosses the river on a new wooden bridge to link up with the GR15.2 well above Torla.

Locally, you can buy a range of **maps** of the park; clearest is the 1:50,000 IGN sheet (also covering Gavarnie, across the French border), though cheaper ones are adequate if you're going to stick to the popular, signed paths. All maps mark the park's network of very basic stone **refugios**, where you might stay on longer treks, as **camping** is prohibited in the park except for one-night bivouacs at elevations varying from 1800m (Añisclo/Escuaín zones) to 2500m (Balcón de Pineta).

Cascade and cirque walks

Most day-trippers to the Cañon de Ordesa aim no farther than an easy loop to the *mirador* at the **Cascada del Abánico**, with a return path on the opposite bank of the Río Arazas. However, there are dozens of other trails from La Pradera de Ordesa (where there's a **park information office**; daily 9am–2pm & 4–7pm), encompassing most levels of enthusiasm and expertise.

The **Circo de Soaso** is one of the most popular and rewarding, but not too difficult, day-hike destinations. A steep, signposted path brings you out at the **Cola de Caballo** (Horsetail Waterfall) in three to four hours (6–7hr round trip). The trail begins through beech forest and then climbs past a *mirador*, to emerge at the upper reaches of a startling gorge. For more solitude in summer, an alternative approach involves climbing the steep **Senda de los Cazadores** (Hunters' Path), which emerges at the Mirador de Calcilarruego; from here the path levels out along the **Faja de Pelay**, which merges with the Circo de Soaso.

Visits to the impressive **Cascada de Cotatuero** begin steeply but easily through woods to a vantage point below the waterfall. An exciting onward route beckons here, if you have a head for heights. With the help of iron pegs, climb above the falls to reach the Brecha de Rolando and trek onwards to Gavarnie (see below) – an all-day undertaking.

Another route signposted towards the **Cascada de Carriata** heads into the trees and then leaves the contour trail to begin a steep zigzag up to the cascade, most impressive in late spring when melted snow keeps it flowing. At a fork on the open mountainside, the left-hand option ascends to the top of the gorge wall via a series of thirteen iron pegs, not so intimidating as those near Cotatuero and feasible for any reasonably fit walker. The right-hand fork contours spectacularly along the canyon's north wall to meet up with the path up to Cotatuero.

Refugio Góriz and Monte Perdido

A path climbs within an hour from the top of Circo de Soaso to the **Refugio Góriz** (2169m; ☎974 341 201). More elaborate than many refuges with its proper beds and overpriced restaurant, it's packed to the gills during summer, but you can camp alongside, provided you dismount your tent each morning.

Góriz is a classic starting point for the ascent of **Monte Perdido** (3355m). This is a scramble rather than a climb but a serious expedition nonetheless, requiring proper equipment. It takes around five hours to get to the summit, which is reached via an almost permanently frozen lake, Lago Helado.

Torla to Gavarnie

Ordesa adjoins the French **Parc National des Pyrénées**, and it's common to traverse to the French village of **Gavarnie**. This is a fair haul, best apportioned over two days, and more easily done (following the old pilgrimage route) from Torla; routes out of the canyon proper are longer and harder.

Leaving Torla, you follow the GR15.2 as far as the fork for the Puente de los Navarros, then climb down to the river and follow the GR11 markers up the valley. There's a **campsite**, *Camping Valle de Bujaruelo*, after another 3.5km (☎974 486 348; closed Oct 21–Easter), with a decent **restaurant**, and, 3km farther, the ruined shrine and medieval bridge of **San Nicolás**. Here the *Mesón de Bujaruelo* (☎974 486 412, ⓦwww.mesondebujaruelo.com; doubles, quads, dorm) is an **albergue** that also keeps a basic, shadeless campsite outside and offers meals. From the old bridge, the path heads over the mountains and down to Gavarnie – six to eight hours' walk, partly on broad track.

Escuaín and Añisclo

In the southeast corner of Ordesa yawns a pair of **canyons** – **Escuaín** and **Añisclo** – every bit the equal of the Cañon de Ordesa but with far fewer visitors. The lack of transport to the trailheads, tricky parking and limited local accommodation contribute to this, but the extra effort is amply rewarded.

Cañon de Añisclo

The **Cañon de Añisclo** is the more spectacular of the two canyons, and more frequented. If you have your own transport, you can reach it on a minor but paved road from Sarvisé to Escalona (10km north of Aínsa) – though a one-way system forces you to park 1.6km above the canyon. Westbound traffic from Escalona runs through the narrow **Desfiladero de las Cambras**, at the far end of which knots of parked cars announce the mouth of the canyon. From here, two broad paths – each as good as the other – lead north across two rivers into this wild gorge; it's a five-hour round trip through the most impressive section to **La Ripareta**. Long-haul trekkers also use the canyon as an alternative approach to the *Refugio Goriz* (see p.651), exiting the main gorge via the Fon Blanca ravine.

If you're doing a day walk, good **places to stay** locally include **NERÍN**, 45-minutes' walk west of the canyon along the GR15 trail, via the deserted hamlet of Sercué. Nerín has a fine Romanesque **church** – typical of these settlements – and an *albergue* (☎974 489 010; 6-bunk rooms), which serves meals to residents only. Alternatively, there's *Pensión El Turista* (☎974 489 016; ❷) and plush, chalet-style *Hotel Palazio* (☎974 489 002; ⓦwww.hotelpalazio.com; ❸), both with **restaurants**. Attractive **BUERBA**, just south of the canyon, is the closest habitation and offers the relaxed, en-suite ☀ *Casa Marina* (☎608 714 450, ⓔsoniadecea@yahoo.es; ❷), with young, English/French-speaking management and evening meals (vegetarian on request).

Garganta de Escuaín

Garganta de Escuaín, more properly the Río Yaga valley, is reached most easily from **LAFORTUNADA**, 17km northeast of Aínsa, where *Hotel Badaín* (☎974 504 006, ⓦwww.hotelbadain.com; ❸) has a restaurant (dull *menú* €17 with wine), though in **ESCALONA**, 6km south, ☀ *Hotel Arnal* (☎974 505 206, ⓦwww.hotelarnal.com; ❸) is newer and much better value, with tasteful wood-floored rooms, wi-fi, off-street parking and *comedor menús* (€15 & €20), plus appetizing *platos combinados*.

From Lafortunada, the quickest way into canyon country without transport is along the **GR15 trail**; it's a two-hour climb to the picturesque village of **Tella**, with a clutch of Romanesque churches to walk to outside the village and a

park information office (April–Nov daily 9am–2pm & 4–7pm). Beyond, the trail drops to the river at **Estaroniello** hamlet before climbing through thick woods to **Escuaín**, an abandoned settlement taken over in summer by enthusiasts exploring the gorge just upstream. There's another park information office here (same hours) but no other amenities, so bring enough food to sustain you farther into the water-sculpted ravine. The GR15 continues west, then south to handsome **Bestué** village, the only habitation en route to Nerín or Buerba (all 4–5hr distant) – but again there are no facilities here, so take all you need for a traverse.

Day-hikers, however, should cross the gorge east on a non-GR trail to **Revilla**, a similarly desolate hamlet on the opposite bank. From there you can backtrack to Tella or follow the lovely and little-trodden **PR39** path through Estaroniello to **HOSPITAL DE TELLA**, 3km west of Lafortunada, which has a roadside *restaurante*, the *Casa Quino* (℡974 504 055; ❶), with two *habitaciones*. You can complete this itinerary in a single, long summer's day, taking in the best this limestone Shangri-la has to offer. If you have transport, leave it at Tella or Hospital de Tella – the PR39 links them.

The Valle de Gistau

The **Valle de Gistau**, long beloved of Spaniards, but still attracting relatively few foreign guests, is the next valley up from Escuaín, draining east to west. A delightfully secluded area, it's also the easiest jump-off point for the *Viadós refugio* (see p.655) and thence to the peak of Posets. A web of PR and GR trails links several villages here – just as well, since bus services are down to just three a week.

PLAN is the valley's "capital", with shops, and an exceptionally nice **swimming pool** at the start of the track to Chia, and **accommodation**, including the *Hotel Mediodía* (℡974 506 006, ⓦwww.hotelmediodia.com; ❷), with recently redone, stone-and-wood-trimmed rooms, and a *comedor*, the best independent **restaurant** is *Casa Ruche*, on the bypass road, flanked by two ATMs. **SAN JUAN DE PLAN**, 2km north, offers perhaps the best-value place to **stay and eat** in the valley: the central ⚘ *Hostal Casa la Plaza* (℡&℻974 506 052; ❷), with tasteful, wood-decor rooms and an excellent, mountain-style *menú* downstairs – though they only serve dinner. For lunch, repair to nearby *Casa Sanches* on the same *plaza*, with a good-value *menú*, tucked into by passing tourists and local construction crews alike; the *comedor* is smoky but there's a small summer terrace out front.

Casas rurales abound in **GISTAÍN** some 3km west, including the ebulliently friendly *Casa Zueras* (℡974 506 038; ❶ with shared bathrooms), or the nearby *Casa Palacín* (℡974 506 295; ❸), with en-suite rooms in a converted medieval mansion – both are in the village centre. Conventional lodging is limited to *Pensión Casa Alvira*, opposite the church (℡974 506 078; ❶); en-suite rooms are spartan but adequate, with TV and some valley views. Downstairs is the only independent **restaurant** in the village – good value for fare such as *acielgas* (chard) and *trucha a la navarra*, especially if taken on half-board basis.

Heading west from Gistaín, the GR19 trail leads through **Sin** en route to **SALINAS** – where *Caserío San Marcial* (℡974 504 010), on the west side of the highway, has a single quad apartment (€90) and **camping** terraces – and eventually to Lafortunada. The spectacular **Senda Colgada del Canal del Cinca** (PR137) peels off a half-hour or so west of Salinas to reach (within 2hr) **Bielsa**, the northeasterly gateway to Ordesa, with a daily evening bus service from Aínsa. Much of this trail is a spectacular corniche with occasional galleries, hacked out with hand tools in the early twentieth century to service a hydro-electric canal linking the Pineta valley and Lafortunada.

Bielsa

BIELSA, 8km north of Salinas by road, was all but destroyed during the Civil War – it was one of the last Republican strongholds, aerial photos from late 1938 showing it roofless and burnt like a mini-Berlin – and today, its character is further distorted by the needs of Spanish and (especially) French day-trippers. That said, it becomes more congenial by night, with good-value **accommodation** near the Plaza Mayor including the *Hostal Pirineos Meliz*, west uphill (☎974 501 015; ❷), old-fashioned but en suite and with a ground-floor restaurant, and the much plusher *Hotel Valle de Pineta*, off the southeast corner (☎974 501 010, ⓦwww .hotelvalledepineta.com; ❸), with spacious, wood-floored rooms and balconies on the south side of the building, plus a good-value *comedor*. After dark, make for *La Terrazeta* nearby for cheap *menús*, or the idiosyncratic ☘ *Bar El Chinchecle*, one block downhill northeast from the *plaza*, where you can cobble together tapas, washed down by home-made liqueurs or sherry and attended by a danceable folk-music soundtrack from across the globe. A **museum** (mid-June to mid-Oct Tues–Sun, guided visits 5pm, 6.15pm & 7.30pm; €3) in the *ayuntamiento* on Plaza Mayor chronicles both Bielsa's wartime experience, and its outrageous winter **carnival**.

Benasque and around

Serious climbers and trekkers gravitate to **Benasque** in the Ésera river valley, for overhead, just out of sight, loom the two highest peaks in the Pyrenees: **Aneto** (3404m) and **Posets** (3371m). The town can be reached most easily from Huesca or Barbastro on regular buses. Southeast of Benasque, near the Catalunya border, the cathedral village of **Roda de Isábena** stands in glorious isolation on its bluff.

Benasque

Though now surrounded by apartment blocks, **BENASQUE** remains an agreeable place occupying a wide stretch of the Ésera river valley, good for a rest before or after the rigours of trekking. It combines modern amenities with old stone houses, some of them built by the Aragonese nobility of the seventeenth century and now being assiduously renovated by weekenders.

The **turismo** at the southeast edge of town (daily: summer 9am–2pm & 4.30–9pm; winter 10am–2pm & 5–9pm; ☎974 551 275, ⓦwww.turismobenasque .com) documents current activity outfitters and has a single coin-op **internet** terminal. Acceptable **accommodation** begins with mountaineer-friendly ☘ *Hotel Avenida* at Avda. de los Tilos 3 (☎974 551 126, ⓦwww.h-avenida.com; ❸); plush, wood-interior, wi-fi-equipped *Hotel Aragüells* next door at no. 1 (☎974 551 619, ⓦwww.hotelaraguells.com; ❹), also with apartments in the old quarter; or, with transport, roadside *Hostal Casa Rosita* 3km south in **ERISTE** (☎974 551 307, ⓦwww.casarosita.com; ❸), with easy parking and reservoir views.

In terms of **restaurants**, carnivores should head for *Asador Restaurante Bardanca* at c/Las Plazas 6 (reserve on ☎974 551 360), with good house wine and meat platters by weight – up to a kilo if you wish. Further afield, *Casa Rosita* in Eriste has good-value *menús* and *platos* in its *comedor* or on the view terrace. *La Parilla* on Ctra. Francia (the bypass road) purveys *nouvelle* Aragonese cooking at around €30 *a la carta* (or €16 *menú*). Among **bars**, *Sayó* at c/Mayor 13 also has a decent *menú* but is best for tapas and an affordable tipple; *Bar Plaza*, predictably enough on Plaza Mayor, is a tad cheaper for the same items, its outdoor tables a favourite sundown rendezvous point. In these economically straitened times, **take-away**

Benasque attracts committed climbers and trekkers, and if you're one of them you'll be intent on bagging the **peaks of Aneto and/or Posets**. These ascents require crampons, ice-axe and a rope, and a helmet to guard against falling rocks; the inexperienced should go with one of the local activity outfitters, all found on or just off Avenida de los Tilos. For casual walkers, however, there are plenty of possibilities. The Aragonese mountain club has marked out various **PR paths**, documented in a locally available guide. The trails, to surrounding villages and also to all three local *refugios*, are routed so that you avoid roads as much as possible – some, though, are even more rigorous than the average GR path.

Benasque is a major halt on the **GR11 trail** and its variants, hereabouts at their most spectacular. The easiest and most popular **traverse** is northwest, just upstream from town, along the Estós valley and over the Puerto de Gistaín to the *Refugio de Viadós* (℡974 506 163; open Easter week, weekends thereafter and then daily late June to late Sept), an eight- to nine-hour hike. Seasoned trekkers may prefer the path that heads northwest up the Eriste valley, 4km southwest of Benasque, and then over the high Collado de Eriste on the shoulder of Posets peak, before dropping down to Viadós. This longer route is best broken partway at the *Refugio Ángel Órus* (℡974 344 044).

Heading east past Maladeta, use the public **shuttle bus** (6 daily 5.15am–5.15pm, €8.90 one way, €14.70 return) from the Plan de Senarta camping area (4km upstream from Benasque) up the Vallivierna valley, which cuts out a lot of dreary track-tramping; from the unstaffed Coronas hut here at track's end (from which the last bus returns at 6pm), the GR11 climbs, then descends east through lonely, lake-spangled country to the *Hospitau Refugi Sant Nicolau* (see p.804) on the Viella road – the better part of two days' hiking from Coronas, with a tent advisable. Another bus from Benasque (6 daily 4.30am–6pm; €6.80 one way, €10.50 return) brings you to **La Besurta**, near the top of the Ésera valley and just below the *Refugio Renclusa* (℡974 552 106; open Easter week & late June to late Sept). From here the HRP heads southeast over the high Molières pass (crampons always required), giving eye-to-eye views of Aneto, before dropping down another empty valley to the *Sant Nicolau* refuge – again, tents are recommended.

9

ARAGÓN | Benasque and around

food is increasingly popular: try *El Puchero*, near La Parilla, and the *Posets* deli on Avda. de los Tilos.

Roda de Isábena

Attractive hill villages are ten a penny in Aragón, but **RODA DE ISÁBENA**, in the middle of nowhere on a minor road between El Pont de Suert and Graus (just 80km from Benasque via Campo by paved, if initially narrow, roads), is unique for its superb Romanesque **cathedral** at the heart of town. Originally a monastic church, it's a three-aisled affair with Lombard apses and an eighteenth-century, octagonal belfry notable from afar, but there ends any conformity to pattern. The ornate entrance portal, with six series of capitalled columns inside a Renaissance portico, breaches the south wall, because the west end of the nave is occupied by a carved choir and a fine organ, claimed to be one of the best in Europe. Mass is celebrated on the purported **sarcophagus of San Ramón**, squirming with twelfth-century carvings showing the Nativity and the Flight into Egypt. Immediately below the raised altar area is a vast triple crypt, the central section with worn column capitals but the northerly one graced by brilliant Romanesque frescoes (currently closed for restoration), thought to be painted by the unknown **Master of Taüll**. Admission to the cathedral is by guided visit only (6 daily 11.15am–6.30pm; €2.50), though you can see the cloister and its colonnade (eroded like the crypt's) by patronizing the excellent restaurant installed in the former refectory. When you've finished admiring the cathedral, it's enjoyable just to wander the attractive streets and gawp at the views, literally 360-degree from the *mirador*, which make it understandable why the medieval counts of Ribagorça chose Roda as a stronghold.

A single daily Graus–El Pont de Suert **bus** passes along the valley-floor road 1.5km below, but most people come with their own transport. It's a popular weekend retreat, so you need to book **accommodation** year-round at good-value *Hospedería de Aragón Roda de Isábena*, right on the terraced central *plaza* (℡974 544 554, Ⓦwww.hospederia-rdi.com; ❸), offering rooms with a view and all mod cons, For food, *Bar Mesón de Roda* does decent meals and breakfasts with a ringside seat on the *plaza*, but the best ✴**restaurant** here is the one attached to the *hospedería* (reserve on ℡974 544 545) with the *a la carta* dishes so reasonable (€20–25 for three hearty courses) that there's little point in taking the €16 *menú* unless you're on half-board at the hospedería.

Travel details

Trains

Huesca to: Canfranc (2 daily; 2hr 45min); Jaca (3 daily; 2hr 15min); Sabiñánigo (3 daily; 1hr 55min); Zaragoza (4–7 daily; 50min–1hr).

Zaragoza to: Barcelona (16 daily; 4–5hr; AVE 2hr); Bilbao (4 daily; 5hr); Burgos (5 daily; 4hr); Cáceres (daily; 7hr); Cádiz (daily; 9hr); Córdoba (2 daily; 6–8hr); Gijón (2 daily; 9hr); Girona (daily; 6hr 30min); Huesca (4–7 daily; 50min–1hr); Irún (4 daily; 4hr–5hr 30min); Jaca (3 daily; 3hr 20min); León (3 daily; 6hr); Lleida (10–12 daily; 1hr 40min); Logroño (9 daily; 2hr); Lugo (2 daily; 8–9hr); Madrid (12 daily; 3hr); Málaga (daily; 11hr); Medina del Campo (1–3 daily; 3hr 30min–6hr); Orense (2 daily; 10hr); Oviedo (2 daily; 8hr); Palencia (3 daily; 4–5hr); Pamplona (7 daily; 2–3hr); Sabiñánigo (3 daily; 3hr); Salamanca (3 daily; 4hr 30min–8hr); San Sebastián (4 daily; 4hr); Seville (daily; 7hr); Tarragona (5–10 daily; 3hr; AVE to Tarragona Camps 1.5hr); Teruel (3 daily; 3hr); Valladolid (3 daily; 5–6hr); Vigo (2 daily; 11hr); Vitoria-Gasteiz (daily; 3hr).

Buses

Aínsa to: Bielsa (daily 8.45pm, returns 6am next day; 40min); Plan (July & Aug Mon–Sat, otherwise Mon, Wed & Fri only 8.45pm, returns 5.45am next day; 1hr); Sabiñánigo (daily 2.30pm; 2hr).
Barbastro to: Benasque (Mon–Sat 11.30am & 5.20pm; 2hr); Boltaña via Aínsa (Mon–Sat 7.45pm, returns next day 6.45am; July 15–Aug 31 also 11am, returning 3pm; Huesca–Barbastro 10am/6.30pm services link with this); Lleida (6–7 daily; 1hr 15min).
Huesca to: Barbastro (4–7 daily; 50min); Barcelona (2–4 daily; 4hr 20min); Fraga (daily; 2hr

15min); Jaca (4–5 daily; 1hr); Lleida (4–7 daily; 2hr 15min); Loarre (2 daily; 45min); Monzón (5–9 daily; 1hr 15min); Pamplona (3 daily; 2hr 50min); Sabiñánigo (4–5 Mon–Sat, 3–4 Sun & public hols; 55min); Zaragoza (18 Mon–Fri, 10 Sat, Sun & public hols; 1hr).
Jaca to: Ansó via Echo and Siresa (daily; 1hr 40min); Astún/Candanchú (5 daily; 45min); Biescas (1–2 daily; 55min); Canfranc-Estación (5 daily; 30min); Huesca (4–5 daily; 1hr); Pamplona (1–2 daily; 1hr 35min); Sabiñánigo (2 daily; 20min); Zaragoza (3–5 daily; 2hr 15min).
Roda de Isábena to: El Pont de Suert (daily Mon–Fri 4.37pm, returns next day at 6.15am; 1hr); Graus (daily 7.18am, returns 4pm; 40min).
Sabiñánigo to: Aínsa (daily 11am via Torla/Fiscal); Sarvisé (Fri 7pm & Sun 5pm, returns immediately, July & Aug daily 7pm, returns immediately).
Teruel to: Albarracín (daily; 2hr); Barcelona (daily; 5hr); Cantavieja/La Iglesuela del Cid (daily; 2hr 30min–3hr); Cuenca (daily; 2hr 30min); Valencia (5 daily; 2hr); Zaragoza (7 daily; 2hr). All services reduce dramatically on Sun.
Zaragoza to: Astorga (daily; 7hr 30min); Barcelona (hourly; 3hr 45min); Bilbao (9 daily; 4hr); Burgos (3 daily; 4hr 15min); Cariñena (2 daily; 45min); A Coruña (daily; 12hr); Huesca (every half-hour; 1hr); Jaca (6 daily; 2hr 15min); León (3 daily; 7hr); Lleida (5 daily; 2hr 30min); Logroño (3 daily; 2hr 15min); Lugo (2 daily; 11hr); Madrid (hourly; 3hr 45min); Palencia (daily; 5hr 45min); Ponferrada (2 daily; 9hr); Salamanca (2 daily; 7hr); Santiago de Compostela (daily; 13hr); Soria (2 daily; 3hr); Sos del Rey Católico (daily; 2hr 15min); Tarragona (7 daily; 2hr 45min); Valladolid (5 daily; 5hr); Zamora (2 daily; 7hr).

Barcelona

CHAPTER 10 **Highlights**

＊ **Las Golondrinas** Sightseeing boats make harbour and coastal trips all year round. See p.668

＊ **La Boqueria** The city's – some say Spain's – greatest market. See p.677

＊ **Gran Teatre del Liceu** Tour the city's famous opera house, and then drop in for a coffee at the Café de l'Opera. See p.677

＊ **Plaça del Rei, Barri Gòtic** The most concentrated grouping of historic monuments in the old town. See p.680

＊ **MNAC** A thousand years of Catalan art contained within the superbly restored Museu Nacional, on the slopes of Montjuïc. See p.690

＊ **La Pedrera** The *modernista* works of architect Antoni Gaudí define the city – his sinuous apartment block is a virtuoso work. See p.698

＊ **Parc Güell** If you visit only one city park, make it this one – an extraordinary flight of fancy. See p.702

＊ **Bar hopping, El Raval** Barcelona's funkiest neighbourhood is the best place for a night on the tiles. See p.715

▲ La Pedrera

Barcelona

Barcelona, the self-confident and progressive capital of Catalunya, vibrates with life. A thriving port and prosperous commercial centre of three million people, the city is almost impossible to exhaust, and even in a lengthy visit you will likely only scrape the surface. It boasts some superb **museums** – including the world-class Museu Nacional d'Art de Catalunya (MNAC), and individual art museums dedicated to Pablo Picasso, Joan Miró and Antoni Tàpies – as well as outstanding *modernista* **architecture**, most perfectly expressed in Antoni Gaudí's extraordinary church of the Sagrada Família. The winding alleys and ageing mansions and churches of the picture-postcard **Barri Gòtic** (Gothic Quarter) suck in a good proportion of the daily sightseeing traffic, while from early morning to long after midnight the world-famous boulevard that is the **Ramblas** is choked with people shopping, chatting in cafés, listening to buskers or watching the street performers. On sunny afternoons, the city's **beaches** and Passeig Marítim promenade beckon thousands of sunbathers, strollers, cyclists and diners.

Barcelona has long had the reputation of being the avant-garde capital of Spain, especially in design and architecture, while the legacy of hosting the **1992 Olympics** was an outstanding set of cultural and sports facilities on the hill of **Montjuïc**. In **El Raval**, new bars, restaurants, boutiques and galleries have mushroomed in the wake of the striking contemporary art museum, MACBA, while beyond the Port Olímpic the old industrial quarter of **Poble Nou** is the latest to be regenerated as the **Diagonal Mar** development of five-star hotels, convention centres and public plazas. Beyond the city limits, the one day-trip everyone should make is to the mountain-top monastery of **Montserrat**, 40km northwest, not least for the extraordinary ride up to the monastic eyrie.

Although you'll be constantly warned of **petty crime** in the city, don't be unduly paranoid. Barcelona is rarely any more dangerous than any other big city and it would be a shame to stick solely to the tourist boulevards, since you'll miss so much. Tapas bars hidden down alleys little changed for a century or two; designer boutiques in gentrified old-town quarters; bargain lunches in workers' taverns; unmarked gourmet restaurants; craft outlets and workshops; *fin-de-siècle* cafés; restored medieval palaces; neighbourhood markets and specialist galleries – all are just as much Barcelona as the Ramblas or Gaudí's Sagrada Família.

Festivals in Barcelona

February

12: Festes de Santa Eulàlia (ⓦ www.bcn.cat/santaeulalia) A week's worth of music, dances, parades of *gegants* (giants), *castellers* (human castle-builders) and fireworks in honour of one of Barcelona's patron saints.

Easter

Semana Santa (Holy Week) There's a procession from the church of Sant Agustí on c/de l'Hospital (El Raval) to La Seu, starting at 4pm on Good Friday, while Palm Sunday sees the blessing of the palms at La Seu.

April

23: Dia de Sant Jordi (ⓦ www.bcn.cat/stjordi) Celebrated as a nationalist holiday in Catalunya, the city fills with roses and books, exchanged by sweethearts as gifts.

May

Festival de Música Antiga Attracts medieval and Baroque groups from around the world, based at L'Auditori concert hall but with some free shows in old-town squares.

11: Dia de Sant Ponç Celebrated with a street market on c/de l'Hospital (El Raval).

Last week: Primavera Sound (ⓦ www.primaverasound.com) Attracts top names in the rock, indie and electronica world.

Last week: Festival de Flamenco de Ciutat Vella (ⓦ www.flamencociutatvella.com) Annual old-town flamenco bash.

June/July

Sónar (ⓦ www.sonar.es; buy tickets well in advance) Europe's most cutting-edge electronic music and multimedia festival – more formally known as the International Festival of Advanced Music and Multimedia Art – attracts up to 100,000 visitors. By day, the focus is on events at MACBA/CCCB; by night, the action shifts to out-of-town L'Hospitalet, with all-night buses running from the city to the *Sónar* bars and clubs.

21: Festa de la Musica (ⓦ www.bcn.cat/festadelamusica) Scores of free concerts in squares, parks, civic centres and museums across the city.

Arrival

Barcelona's **airport** is 18km southwest of the city at El Prat de Llobregat, and linked to the city by regular train and bus services. The city's main Barcelona Sants **train station**, the **ferry terminal** and the Barcelona Nord **bus station** are all more central, with convenient metro stations for onward travel. In most cases, you can be off the plane, train, bus or ferry and in your hotel room within the hour. **Driving** into Barcelona is also reasonably straightforward, with traffic only slow in the morning and evening rush hours (Mon–Fri 7.30–9.30am & 6–8.30pm).

By air

Barcelona's **airport** (general information ☎ 902 404 704, ⓦ www.aena.es) has three adjacent terminals (A, B and C), with taxis and airport buses found immediately outside each terminal and the airport train station a short distance away.

23/24: Verbena/Dia de Sant Joan The eve and day of St John is the city's wildest annual celebration, with bonfires and fireworks (particularly on Montjuïc), drinking and dancing, and watching the sun come up on the beach. The day itself (24th) is a public holiday.

End June to August: Festival de Barcelona Grec (ⓦ www.barcelonafestival.com) Major performing-arts festival incorporating theatre, music and dance.

August
Festa Major de Gràcia (ⓦ www.festamajordegracia.cat) Music, dancing, fireworks and *castellers* in the neighbourhood's streets and squares.

September
24: La Mercè The city's biggest traditional festival lasts for a week around the 24th – the 24th itself is a public holiday (and there's free entry that day to city museums). Highlights include costumed giants, breathtaking firework displays and competing teams of *castellers*.

24: BAM (ⓦ www.bcn.cat/bam) Alternative music festival, concurrent with La Mercè, with free rock, world and fusion gigs around the old town and at Diagonal Mar Fòrum during Mercè week.

October/November
Third week: Festival de Tardor Ribermúsica (ⓦ www.ribermusica.org) Wide-ranging four-day music festival held in the Born, with free concerts in historic and picturesque locations.

End October to November: Festival de Jazz (ⓦ www.the-project.cat) This respected annual festival highlights big-name solo artists and bands.

December
1–22: Fira de Santa Llúcia A Christmas market and crafts fair outside La Seu.
25 & 26 Nadal (Christmas Day) and **Sant Esteve** (St Stephen's Day) are public holidays.
31: Cap d'Any (New Year's Eve) Street and club parties, and mass gatherings in Plaça de Catalunya and other main squares. You're supposed to eat twelve grapes in the last twelve seconds of the year for twelve months of good luck.

The direct **airport train service** (daily 6am–11.44pm; journey time 20min; €2.60) runs every thirty minutes to Barcelona Sants (the main train station), and continues on to Passeig de Gràcia (best stop for Eixample, Plaça de Catalunya and the Ramblas) and Estació de França (for La Ribera). City travel passes (*targetes*) and the Barcelona Card are valid on the airport train. Otherwise, the **Aerobus** (Mon–Sat 6am–1am; €3.90) leaves every six to fifteen minutes, stopping in the city at Plaça d'Espanya, Gran Via de les Corts Catalanes, Plaça Universitat, Plaça de Catalunya (in front of El Corte Inglés) and Passeig de Gràcia. It takes around thirty minutes to reach Plaça de Catalunya, longer in the rush hour. A **taxi** from the airport to the centre costs €20–25, including the airport surcharge.

Note that some "Barcelona" flights are no such thing: for Ryanair arrivals at **Girona** airport, 90km north of Barcelona, there's a connecting Barcelona Bus service to Barcelona Nord bus station, and there are also connecting buses from **Reus** airport (near Tarragona) to Barcelona Sants.

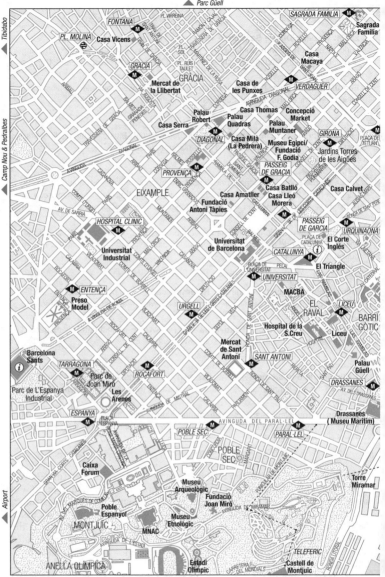

▲ Parc Güell

By train

The main station for national and international arrivals is **Barcelona Sants** (ⓂSants Estació), 3km west of the centre, which has a tourist office (with an accommodation booking service), as well as car-rental outlets, and left-luggage facilities. From Sants, metro line 3 runs direct to Drassanes and Liceu (for the Ramblas) and Catalunya (for Plaça de Catalunya).

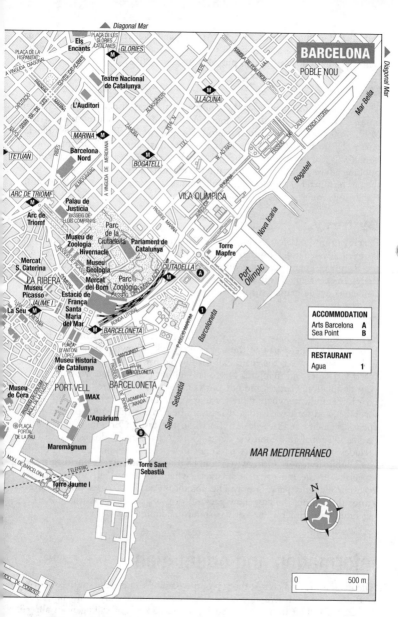

Some Spanish inter-city services and international trains also stop at **Estació de França**, 1km east of the Ramblas and close to ⓂBarceloneta. Other possible arrival points by train are **Plaça de Catalunya**, at the top of the Ramblas (for trains from coastal towns north of the city, and towns on the Puigcerdà–Vic line), and **Passeig de Gràcia** (Catalunya provincial destinations).

The high-speed **AVE** line between Barcelona and Madrid (via Tarragona and Zaragoza) has cut journey times in half between the two cities (2hr 45min–3hr

25min, depending on the service). Arrivals and departures are at Barcelona Sants, though a second high-speed station is planned at La Sagrera, east of the centre beyond Glòries (though probably not until 2013).

By bus

The main bus terminal, used by international, long-distance and provincial buses, is **Barcelona Nord** on Avinguda Vilanova (main entrance on c/Ali-Bei; ℡902 260 606, Ⓦwww.barcelonanord.com; ⓂArc de Triomf), three blocks north of Parc de la Ciutadella. There's a bus information desk on the ground floor (daily 7am–9pm), with the ticket offices above at street level (advanced booking advised). Some inter-city and international services also make a stop at the bus terminal behind Barcelona Sants station on c/de Viriat (ⓂSants Estació). Either way, you're only a short metro ride from the city centre.

By ferry

Ferries from the Balearics dock at the **Estació Marítima**, Moll de Barcelona, Port Vell, located at the bottom of Avinguda Paral.lel (ⓂDrassanes), not far from the Ramblas. There are ticket offices inside the terminal. Ferries from Genoa (Italy) dock at the **Moll de Sant Bertran**, just along from the Moll de Barcelona, while **cruise ships** tie up at several points in the inner harbour.

By car

Driving into Barcelona along any one of the *autopistes*, head for the Ronda Litoral, the southern half of the city's ring road. Following signs for Port Vell will take you towards the main exit for the old town; exits for Gran Via de les Corts Catalanes and Avinguda Diagonal will suit better if uptown Barcelona is your destination. Garages and **car parks** in the city centre are linked to display boards that indicate where there are free spaces. These are expensive (up to €25 for 24hr), and for day visitors, at least, it's best to use the **Metropark**, a park-and-ride facility at Plaça de les Glòries in the eastern Eixample (junction of Avgda. Diagonal and Gran Via de les Corts Catalanes; ⓂGlories). The €7 fee includes up to eighteen hours' parking and a ticket for unlimited travel on the city's public transport. Otherwise, it can be tough to find **street parking** spaces, especially in the old town and Gràcia, where it's nearly all either restricted access or residents' parking only. The ubiquitous residents' **Área Verda meterzones** throughout the city allow pay-and-display parking for visitors, for €2.80 per hour, with either a one- or two-hour maximum stay.

Information and orientation

The main tourist office is at the top of the Ramblas, under the southeast corner of **Plaça de Catalunya**, down the steps (ⓂCatalunya; daily 9am–9pm; ℡807 117 222 if calling from within Spain, ℡932 853 834 if calling from abroad, Ⓦwww.barcelonaturisme.com). There are also tourist offices at the **airport** (daily 9am–9pm); at **Barcelona Sants** (April–Sept daily 8am–8pm; Oct–March Mon–Fri 8am–8pm, Sat, Sun & public hols 8am–2pm); and at **Plaça de Sant Jaume** in the Barri Gòtic, entrance at c/Ciutat 2 (Mon–Fri 9am–8pm, Sat 10am–8pm, Sun & public hols 10am–2pm). At all of them, you can book accommodation, buy discount cards and reserve space on guided tours. There are also staffed kiosks in main tourist areas, such as outside the Sagrada Família

Discount cards

If you're going to do a lot of sightseeing, you can save yourself money by buying one of the widely available discount cards.

Barcelona Card (2 days €25, 3 days €30, 4 days €34 or 5 days €40; full details on Ⓦwww.barcelonaturisme.com). Free public transport, plus big discounts at museums, venues, shops, theatres and restaurants. It's available at tourist offices, points of arrival and other outlets, though there's a ten-percent discount if you buy online.

Articket (€20; valid 6 months; Ⓦwww.articketbcn.org). Free admission to seven major art centres and galleries (MNAC, MACBA, CCCB, Museu Picasso, Fundació Antoni Tàpies, Fundació Joan Miró, and the Centre Cultural Caixa Catalunya at La Pedrera). Buy at participating galleries or at tourist offices.

Ruta del Modernisme (€12; valid one year; Ⓦwww.rutadelmodernisme.com). An excellent English-language guidebook, map and discount-voucher package that covers 115 *modernista* buildings in Barcelona and other Catalan towns, offering discounts of up to fifty percent on admission fees, tours and purchases. It's also packaged with *Let's Go Out*, a guide to *modernista* bars and restaurants (total package €18), with both available from the Centre del Modernisme desk at the main Plaça de Catalunya tourist office.

and on the Ramblas. The city tourist offices charge €1 for their **maps** – you can pick up a good free one instead from the information desk on the ground floor of El Corte Inglés department store, outside the main tourist office. *Barcelona: The Rough Guide Map* is also a good investment.

The **Institut de Cultura**, Palau de la Virreina, Ramblas 99 (ⓂLiceu; Mon–Sat 10am–8pm, Sun 11am–3pm; ☎933 161 000, Ⓦwww.bcn.cat/cultura), provides information on what's happening in the city, as well as ticket sales. The City Council (*Ajuntament*) has a website with an English-language version (Ⓦwww.bcn.cat) for tracking down everything from sports centres to festival dates. There is also the city's **Informació Metropolitana** line (Mon–Sat 8am–10pm; ☎010; English spoken), which can help with information about transport and other public services. For information about **travelling in Catalunya**, go to Palau Robert, Pg. de Gràcia 107, Eixample (ⓂDiagonal; Mon–Sat 10am–7pm, Sun & public hols 10am–2.30pm; ☎932 388 091, Ⓦwww.gencat.cat/palaurobert).

City transport and tours

Much of what you'll want to see in the city centre – La Seu, Museu Picasso, markets, Gaudí buildings, history museums and art galleries – can all be reached on foot in under twenty minutes from Plaça de Catalunya. But Barcelona also has an excellent integrated **public-transport system**, which comprises the metro, buses, trams, local trains and a network of funicular railways and cable cars. The local transport authority, **Transports Metropolitans de Barcelona** (TMB; Ⓦwww.tmb.net), has full timetable and ticket information on its website, and route and ticket information is posted at major bus stops and all metro and tram stations.

A transit plan divides the province into six zones, but as the entire metropolitan area of Barcelona (including the airport) falls within Zone 1, that's the only one you'll normally need to worry about. On all the city's public transport there's a **flat fare** of €1.30 per journey, but it's cheaper to buy a **targeta** (discount ticket-strip), which is available at metro, train, tram and funicular stations, but not on

BARCELONA TRANSPORT

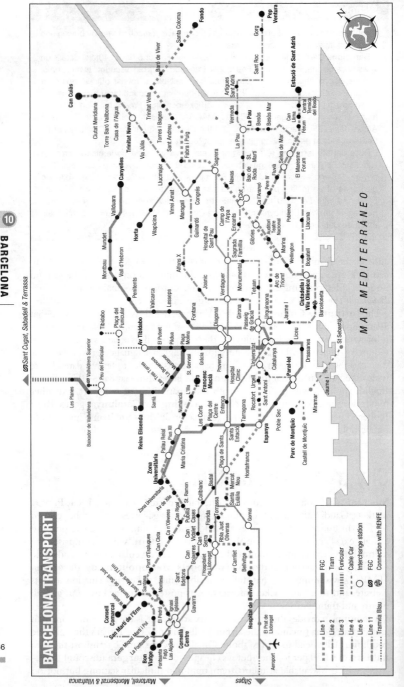

MAR MEDITERRÁNEO

Line 1
Line 2
Line 3
Line 4
Line 5
Line 11
Tramvia Blau

FGC
Tram
Funicular
Cable Car
Interchange station
FGC
Connection with RENFE

the buses. The **T-10** ("tay day-oo" in Catalan) gives you ten journeys for €7.20, and can be used by more than one person at a time – just feed it through the barrier for each person travelling. Changing transport within 1hr 15min counts as one journey with the T-10 (you'll have to re-punch the ticket but it only registers once). There's also a single-person, one-day **T-Dia** at €5.50 for unlimited travel within Zone 1, plus combinations up to the 5-Dies (5 days; €21.70). Heading for Sitges, Montserrat and other **out-of-town destinations**, you'll need to buy a specific ticket or relevant zoned *targeta*.

Metro, buses, trams and trains

The efficient **metro** runs on six lines, though two more are currently under construction. Entrances are marked with a red diamond sign. Its hours of operation are Monday until Thursday, plus Sunday and public holidays 5am to midnight; Friday 5am to 2am; Saturday and the day before a public holiday 24hr. **Bus routes** operate daily, roughly from 4/5am until 10.30pm, though some lines stop earlier and some run on until after midnight. The night buses fill in the gaps on all the main routes, with services every twenty minutes to an hour from around 10pm to 4am.

The **tram system** has departures every eight to twenty minutes throughout the day from 5am to midnight. **Lines T1**, **T2** and **T3** depart from Plaça Francesc Macià and run along the uptown part of Avinguda Diagonal to suburban destinations in the northwest – useful tourist stops are at L'Illa shopping centre and the Maria Cristina and Palau Reial metro stations. Line **T4** operates from Ciutadella-Vila Olímpica (where there's also a metro station) and runs up past the zoo and Teatre Nacional to Glòries before trundling down the lower part of Avinguda Diagonal to Diagonal Mar and the Forùm site.

The city has a commuter train line run by the **Ferrocarrils de la General- itat de Catalunya** (FGC; ☎932 051 515, ⓦwww.fgc.cat), with its main stations at Plaça de Catalunya and Plaça d'Espanya. You'll need this for Montserrat and Tibidabo. The national rail service, operated by RENFE (☎902 240 202, ⓦwww.renfe.es), runs all the other services out of Barcelona, with local lines – north to the Costa Maresme and south to Sitges – designated as **Rodiales/Cercanías**. The hub is Barcelona Sants, with services also passing through Plaça de Catalunya (heading north) and Passeig de Gràcia (south).

Taxis

Black-and-yellow **taxis** have a green roof light on when available for hire. There's a minimum charge of €1.80 (€1.90 after 8pm Sat, Sun & public hols), and after that it's €0.82/1.04 per kilometre. Taxis charge extra for baggage, for trips to the airport and for a multitude of other things, but they have meters, so prices are generally transparent; asking for a receipt (*rebut*) should clear up any confusion. They can be called on the following numbers (though English is unlikely to be spoken): ☎933 577 755; ☎933 001 100; ☎933 033 033; ☎933 300 300; ☎934 208 088.

City tours

Taking a tour is a good way to orientate yourself on arrival. The **Bus Turístic** (tour bus) can drop you outside virtually every attraction in the city. Alterna- tively, Barcelona has some particularly good **walking tours**, showing you parts of the old town you might not find otherwise, while **bike tours** and **sight- seeing boats** offer a different view of the city.

Barcelona Walks ⊤ 932 853 832, Ⓦ www
.barcelonaturisme.com. Advance booking advised
(at Pl. de Catalunya tourist office) for the
1hr 30min Barri Gòtic walking tour (daily 10am in
English; €11). Also Picasso tours (Tues–Sun
10.30am in English; €13.50, includes entry to
Museu Picasso), a Modernisme tour (Sat & Sun
4pm in English; €11), and a Gourmet and Cuisine
tour (Fri & Sat 11am, English available; €15
includes tastings).

Bus Turístic Ⓦ www.tmb.net, Ⓦ www
.barcelonaturisme.com. Sightseeing service (departures every 5–25min) linking all the main sights.
Northern and southern routes depart from Plaça de
Catalunya (daily: April–Sept 9am–8pm; Oct–March
until 7pm), while the Fòrum route (April–Sept daily
9.30am–8pm) runs from Port Olímpic to Diagonal
Mar and back, via the beaches. Tickets (valid for all
routes) cost €20 for one day or €26 for two days,
and also give discounts at various attractions,
shops and restaurants. Buy on board the bus or at
any tourist office.

Catamaran Orsom ⊤ 934 410 537, Ⓦ www
.barcelona-orsom.com. Afternoon catamaran trips
around the port (Easter week & June–Sept daily;
May & Oct daily except Tues & Thurs; €12.50) and
summer-evening jazz cruises (June–Sept; €14.90).
Ticket kiosk at the quayside opposite the Mirador

de Colon, at the bottom of the Ramblas
(Ⓜ Drassanes).

Fat Tire Bike Tours ⊤ 933 013 612, Ⓦ www
.fattirebiketoursbarcelona.com. Four-hour bike
tours (€22) to the Old Town, Sagrada Família, port
area and beach. Tours meet at the c/de Ferran side
of Plaça de Sant Jaume, Barri Gòtic; Ⓜ Jaume I
(twice daily mid-April to mid-Sept; daily rest of the
year; no tours mid-Dec to end of Feb). Reservations
not required, but you can check details at the
rental shop at c/Escudellers 48.

Las Golondrinas ⊤ 934 423 106, Ⓦ www
.lasgolondrinas.com. Daily sightseeing boats
depart from Pl. Portal de la Pau, behind the
Mirador de Colon, at the bottom of the Ramblas
(Ⓜ Drassanes) – trips are either around the port
(35min; €5.50), or port and coast including the
Port Olímpic and Diagonal Mar (1hr 30min;
€11.50). Departures June–Sept at least hourly;
Oct–May daily.

My Favourite Things ⊤ 637 265 405, Ⓦ www
.myft.net. Highly individual tours, whether it's
bohemian Barcelona, where and what the locals
eat, or the signature tour, My Favourite Fusion,
which gives an insider's view of the city. Tours
(in English) cost €26 per person and last 4hr.
Departures are flexible, so call or email for
information.

Accommodation

Hotel rooms in Barcelona are among the most expensive in Spain and finding
a vacancy can be very difficult, especially at Easter, in summer and during
festivals or trade fairs. You're advised to book in advance – several weeks at peak
times – especially if you want to stay at a particular place. The absolute cheapest
double/twin room in a simple family-run **pension**, sharing a bathroom, costs
around €50 (singles from €30), though it's more realistic to budget on a
minimum of €70 a night. If you want air-conditioning, a TV, soundproofing and
an elevator to your room, there's a fair amount of choice around the €100 mark,
while up to €200 gets you the run of decent **hotels** in most city areas. For
Barcelona's most fashionable and exclusive hotels, room rates are set at European
capital norms – from €250 to €400 a night. Right at the other end of the scale
is the burgeoning number of city **youth hostels**, where a dorm bed goes for
€20–30 depending on the season.

You can book accommodation (no commission) at the tourist offices, but only
in person on the day – they do not make advance reservations, nor do they have
a telephone reservation service. However, you can **book online** through the
tourist office website (Ⓦ www.barcelonaturisme.com), or with Barcelona On-
Line (Ⓦ www.barcelona-on-line.es; phone reservations on ⊤ 902 887 017), who
also offer self-catering **apartments** in the city (from €110 per night). Or
contact My Favourite Things (see above), who can help you find apartments
and B&B accommodation.

Hotels and hostales

First things first: if you hanker after a **Ramblas** view, you're going to pay heavily for the privilege – generally, there are much better deals to be had either side of the famous boulevard, often just a minute's walk away. Alongside some classy boutique choices, most of the very cheapest city accommodation is found in the **Barri Gòtic** old-town area, where there are loads of options, from basic *pensiones* to three-star hotels. The other main location for budget accommodation is on the west side of the Ramblas in **El Raval**, which still has its rough edges but is changing fast as the whole neighbourhood undergoes a massive face-lift. East of the Barri Gòtic, in **Sant Pere** and **La Ribera**, there are a number of safely sited budget, mid-range and boutique options, handy for the Museu Picasso and Born nightlife area. North of Plaça de Catalunya, the central spine of the **Eixample** is the Passeig de Gràcia, which has some of the city's most fashionable and luxurious hotels, often housed in converted palaces and mansions. For **waterfront** views, look at hotels in **Port Vell**, at the end of the Ramblas, and at the **Port Olímpic**, southeast of the old town – while new four- and five-stars abound much further out on the metro at the rather soulless **Diagonal Mar** conference and events site. If you don't mind being a metro ride from the museums and buildings, then the northern district of **Gràcia** is probably the best base, as you're only ever a short walk away from excellent bars, restaurants and clubs.

The Ramblas

The listings below are marked on the map on pp.674–675.

Benidorm Ramblas 37 ☎ 933 022 054, ⓦ www.hostalbenidorm.com; Ⓜ Drassanes. Refurbished place opposite Plaça Reial that offers real value for money. Rooms available for one to five people, with bathtubs, showers, and a Ramblas view if you're lucky. ⓪

H1898 Ramblas 109 ☎ 935 529 552, ⓦ www.nnhotels.es; Ⓜ Catalunya. The former HQ of the Philippines Tobacco Company has been given a boutique refit, adding five grades of rooms in deep red, green or black. Public areas reflect the period – 1898 – and there's the fanciest *Starbucks* in town on the premises. ⓿, Ramblas views ⓽

Lloret Ramblas 125 ☎ 933 173 366, ⓦ www.hlloret.com; Ⓜ Catalunya. Gilt mirrors, old paintings, and wrinkled leather sofas in the lounge speak of a faded glory for this one-star hotel. But the rooms all have upgraded bathrooms, TV, heating and a/c, and many have Ramblas-facing balconies. ⓸

Mare Nostrum Ramblas 67, entrance on c/Sant Pau ☎ 933 185 340, ⓦ www.hostalmarenostrum.com; Ⓜ Liceu. Cheery two-star *hostal* with comfortable double or triple/family rooms, some with balconies and street views, others internal, and a simple breakfast included. Their new one-star hotel, *Hotel Curious* (ⓦ www.hotelcurious.com), offers funkier rooms nearby, a couple of

blocks up in El Raval on c/del Carme. ⓸, *Curious* ⓹

Barri Gòtic

The listings below are marked on the map on pp.674–675.

Alamar c/Comtessa de Sobradiel 1 ☎ 933 025 012, ⓦ www.pensioalamar.com; Ⓜ Drassanes. If you don't mind sharing a bathroom, then this simply furnished *pensión* makes a convenient base. Twelve rooms (including 5 singles) have basin and double-glazing; most also have little balconies. Also laundry service and use of a small kitchen. ⓶

Cantón c/Nou de Sant Francesc 40 ☎ 933 173 019, ⓦ www.hotelcanton-bcn.com; Ⓜ Drassanes. Refurbished one-star hotel that's only two blocks off the Ramblas and close to the harbour and Port Vell. Forty rooms feature uniform blue-and-white trim curtains and bedspreads, central heating and a/c, fridge and wardrobe. ⓸

Fernando c/Ferran 31 ☎ 933 017 993, ⓦ www.hfernando.com; Ⓜ Liceu. A mix of rooms with sinks and TV, with or without en-suite shower. Dorm accommodation also available (€25) in four- to eight-bed rooms; some have attached bathroom, and all have lockers. All accommodation is cheaper outside July & Aug. ⓸

El Jardí Pl. Sant Josep Oriol 1 ☎ 933 015 900, ⓦ www.hoteljardi-barcelona.com; Ⓜ Liceu. The location sells this small hotel – overlooking the very attractive Pl. del Pi – which explains the steep prices for rooms that can be a bit bare and poky. Some rooms (the top ones have terraces) look directly onto the square. ④ , balcony/terrace ⑤

Levante Bxda. de Sant Miquel 2 ☎933 179 565, ⓦwww.hostallevante.com; Ⓜ Jaume I. A backpackers' favourite with singles, doubles, twins and triples on two rambling floors. Communal bathrooms get pretty busy, and the rather noisy comings and goings aren't to everyone's liking. Six apartments with kitchen (from €30 per person per day) also available, sleeping five to seven people. ③

Mari-Luz c/de la Palau 4, 2º ☎933 173 463, ⓦwww.pensionmariluz.com; ⓂLiceu/ Jaume I. A splendid budget place, with contemporary-art prints on the walls, central heating, laundry facilities and a small kitchen. It can be a tight squeeze when full, as there are five dorm rooms (sleeping 4–6), two of these en suite, plus six inexpensive doubles and a triple, all with shared bathrooms. A dozen attractive apartments (ⓦwww .apartaments-unio.com; sleeping 2–6; €70–100 per night) a few minutes' walk away in El Raval offer more privacy. Dorms €15–22, rooms ② – ③

Neri c/de Sant Sever 5 ☎933 040 655, ⓦwww .hotelneri.com; ⓂLiceu/Jaume I. Delightful eighteenth-century palace that's been given the boutique treatment – swags of flowing material, rescued timber, subdued colours, granite-toned bathrooms and lofty proportions provide a common theme. A beamed library and stylish roof terrace provide a tranquil escape, while breakfast is served either out in the courtyard in summer or in chef Jordi Ruiz's fine contemporary Mediterranean restaurant. ⑧

Rembrandt c/Portaferrissa 23 ☎933 181 011, ⓦwww.hostalrembrandt.com; ⓂLiceu. A clean, safe, old-town budget *pensión* with friendly English-speaking owners, who request "pin-drop silence" after 11pm. Simple tile-floored rooms (with or without private bathroom) have a street-side balcony or little patio, while larger rooms are more versatile and can sleep up to four. Apartments also available nearby (c/ Canudua 13, ⓦwww.apartrembrandt.com) offering en-suite single and double rooms. ③ , apartment rooms ④

Port Vell

The listings below are marked on the map on pp.674–675.

Duquesa de Cardona Pg. de Colom 12, Port Vell ☎932 689 090, ⓦwww.hduquesadecardona .com; ⓂDrassanes. Step off the busy harbourfront highway into this soothing four-star haven, remodelled from a sixteenth-century mansion. Not all the "classic" (ie standard) rooms

have views, but everyone has access to the stylish roof-deck overlooking the harbour, which boasts (if that's the word) probably the city's smallest outdoor pool. ⑥

Marina View B&B Pg. de Colom, Port Vell ☎609 206 493, ⓦwww.marinaviewbcn.com; ⓂDrassanes. A classy, personally run place in a great location – the two front rooms have terrific harbour views. There's far more of a hotel feel here than simple B&B – then again, these aren't exactly run-of-the-mill B&B prices. Breakfast is included (served in the room). Advance reservations essential (contact for directions), two-night minimum stay usually required. ⑥

Sant Pere and La Ribera

The listings below are marked on the map on pp.674–675.

Banys Orientals c/Argenteria 37 ☎932 688 460, ⓦwww.hotelbanysorientals.com; ⓂJaume I. Funky boutique hotel offering stylish rooms at decent prices. Hardwood floors, crisp white sheets and urban-chic decor make it a hugely popular choice. ⑤

Chic & Basic c/de la Princesa 50 ☎932 954 652, ⓦwww.chicandbasic.com; ⓂJaume I. Punchy, in-your-face boutique hotel with 31 decent-sized rooms mixing glamour and comfort. Chic, certainly; basic, not at all, though the concept eschews room service, mini-bars and tons of staff at your beck and call, so it won't suit everyone. There's a more budget *Chic & Basic* on c/Tallers (near Pl. Universitat, El Raval) and Barri Gòtic apartments, too (details on the website). ⑤

Nuevo Colón Avgda. Marquès de l'Argentera 19, 1º ☎933 195 077, ⓦwww.hostalnuevocolon .com; ⓂBarceloneta. A really pleasant *hostal* – in the hands of the same friendly family for over seventy years, offering spacious, hotel-quality rooms, some en suite – and three self-catering apartments available by the night, which sleep up to six (€155). ③

Pensió 2000 c/Sant Pere Més Alt 6, 1º ☎933 107 466, ⓦwww.pensio2000.com; ⓂUrquinaona. As close to a family-run B&B as Barcelona gets – seven huge rooms in a welcoming mansion apartment strewn with books, plants and pictures. A third person could easily share most rooms (€23 supplement). ③ , en suite ④

El Raval

The listings below (except the *Market*) are marked on the map on pp.674–675.

Gat Raval c/Joaquín Costa 44, 2º ☎934 816 670, ⓦwww.gataccommodation.com; ⓂUniversitat. At the boutique end of the budget market, with a lime-green theme. Each room sports folding chair, sink, TV, fan/heating, and signature back-lit street photographs/artwork. Only six of the 24 rooms have en-suite showers, but communal facilities are good. ❹

Gat Xino c/Hospital 149–155 ☏ 933 248 833, ⓦ www.gataccommodation.com; Ⓜ Sant Antoni. The sister hotel to the *Gat Raval* shares the same signature style, facilities and colour scheme, but all 35 rooms here are en suite, while four suites have much more space and bigger bathrooms (and one has a terrace). You also get a breakfast of coffee, cereal and toast. ❺

🏃 **Grau** c/Ramelleres 27 ☏ 933 018 135, ⓦ www.hostalgrau.com; Ⓜ Catalunya. A really friendly *pensión*, with attractive rooms on several floors; renovated superior rooms also have balconies, a/c, new bathrooms and a touch of modern Catalan style. Six small private apartments in the same building (sleeping 2–5; available by the night; from €95) offer a bit more independence. ❹

🏃 **Market** c/Comte Borrell 68, at Ptge. Sant Antoni Abat ☏ 933 251 205, ⓦ www.markethotel.com.es; Ⓜ Sant Antoni. See map p.689. A stone's throw from Sant Antoni market and El Raval (half a block north of c/Tamarit), the designer-budget *Market* hotel makes a definite splash with its part-Japanese, part neo-colonial look. It's a feel that flows through the building and down into the impressive restaurant, where the food is exceptionally good value. ❺

Peninsular c/de Sant Pau 34 ☏ 933 023 138, ⓦ www.hotelpeninsular.net; Ⓜ Liceu. An interesting old building originally belonging to a priestly order, which explains the slightly cell-like quality of the hotel rooms. There's an attractive inner courtyard, while breakfast is served in the arcaded dining room. ❹

Sant Agustí Pl. Sant Agustí 3 ☏ 933 181 658, ⓦ www.hotelsa.com; Ⓜ Liceu. Barcelona's oldest hotel is housed in a former seventeenth-century convent building on a restored square. The best rooms are located in the attic, from where there are rooftop views. Breakfast included. ❻

La Terrassa c/Junta del Comerç 11 ☏ 933 025 174, ⓦ www.laterrassa-barcelona.com; Ⓜ Liceu. Popular budget choice, where all 45 rooms on various floors (there's an elevator) have built-in closets, shower rooms, effective double-glazing, ceiling fans and heaters. They are fairly plain, and "basic-interior" rooms don't have much natural light, but other rooms either face the street or the sunny courtyard. ❸

Port Olímpic

Arts Barcelona c/Marina 19–21, Port Olímpic ☏ 932 211 000, ⓦ www.ritzcarlton.com/hotels/barcelona; Ⓜ Ciutadella-Vila Olímpica. See map pp.662–663. Thirty-three floors of five-star-plus designer luxury, with fabulous views of the port and sea. Service and standards are first-rate, and the rooms feature floor-to-ceiling windows and enormous marble bathrooms. Seafront gardens encompass an open-air pool and hot tub, and there's a 43rd-floor spa. Special rates start at around €200; otherwise, from €300. ❾

Eixample

The listings below are marked on the map on pp.696–697.

🏃 **Australia** Ronda Universitat 11, 4° ☏ 933 174 177, ⓦ www.residenciaustralia.com; Ⓜ Universitat. A very welcoming budget *pensión*. Three of the four rooms have basins and balconies, and share two bathrooms; the other is classed as a suite with private bathroom, a/c, TV, fridge, and kettle for tea and coffee. Just down the street in another building are some more tidy suites, also with full facilities. ❸, suites ❹

Axel c/d'Aribau 33 ☏ 933 239 393, ⓦ www.axelhotels.com; Ⓜ Universitat. A snazzy "hetero-friendly" hotel set in the Gaixample, with stylishly appointed rooms in which designer fabrics, complimentary beauty products and flat-screen TVs come as standard. Also a restaurant and bar, chillout area, terrace pool, sauna and fitness centre. ❻

Casa Fuster Pg. de Gràcia 132 ☏ 932 553 000, ⓦ www.hotelcasafuster.com; Ⓜ Diagonal. *Modernista* architect Lluís Domènech i Montaner's magnificent Casa Fuster (1908) is the backdrop for five-star-plus luxury. Rooms are in earth tones, with high-spec bathrooms, flat-screen TVs and remote-controlled light and heat, while public areas make full use of the architectural heritage – from the magnificent pillared lobby bar to the panoramic roof terrace and pool. ❽

Condes de Barcelona Pg. de Gràcia 73–75 ☏ 934 450 000, ⓦ www.condesdebarcelona.com; Ⓜ Passeig de Gràcia. Straddling two sides of c/Mallorca, the *Condes* is fashioned from two former palaces – rooms are classily styled, some with jacuzzi and balcony, and some with views of Gaudí's La Pedrera. There's also a pretty roof terrace and plunge pool, while Michelin-starred Basque chef Martín Berasategui is at the helm in the acclaimed *Lasarte* restaurant. ❽

Confort Trav. de Gràcia 72 ☏ 932 386 828, ⓦ www.mediumhoteles.com; FGC Gràcia/ Ⓜ Fontana. Handy for uptown shopping or Gràcia nightlife, this modern two-star has far more character than most, with chic little rooms and an attractive terrace. ⑤

D'Uxelles Gran Via de les Corts Catalanes 688 ☏ 932 652 560, ⓦ www.hotelduxelles .com; Ⓜ Girona/Tetuan. Elegant nineteenth-century townhouse rooms featuring high ceilings, wrought-iron bedsteads, antique mirrors, tiled floors and country-decor bathrooms – some also have balconies and little private patios. ⑤

Eurostars Gaudí c/Consell de Cent 498–500 ☏ 932 320 288, ⓦ www.eurostarshotels.com; Ⓜ Monumental. An excellent four-star choice within walking distance of the Sagrada Família. The comfortable rooms have contemporary furniture, marble bathrooms, black-out curtains and flat-screen TV. Buffet breakfast included. ⑤

Expo Barcelona c/Mallorca 1–23 ☏ 936 003 020, ⓦ www.expogrupo.com; Ⓜ Sants-Estació. The bright, spacious rooms at this four-star hotel (just a minute from Sants station) have a sliding window onto a capacious terrace, and the best have views across to Montjuïc. There's also a rooftop pool, a good buffet breakfast and the metro right on your doorstep. ⑤

Girona c/Girona 24 ☏ 932 650 259, ⓦ www .hostalgirona.com; Ⓜ Urquinaona. Rug-laid corridors, polished wooden doors, paintings and restored furniture announce a family *pensión* kept with care. A fair choice of rooms, either with shower and loo or just shower, and some bathroom-less singles, too. ③

Goya c/de Pau Claris 74, 1° ☏ 933 022 565, ⓦ www.hostalgoya.com; Ⓜ Urquinaona. Boutique-style *pensión* offering a dozen fabulous rooms in *Hostal Goya* and seven more on the floor below in *Goya Principal*, all stylishly decorated and with excellent bathrooms. There's a decent range of options, with the best rooms opening directly onto a balcony or terrace. ④, balcony/terrace rooms ⑤

HMB c/Bonavista 21 ☏ 933 682 013, ⓦ www.hostalhmb.com; Ⓜ Diagonal. Tucked away at the bottom of Gràcia, this great little budget *pensión*, with just a dozen rooms with flat-screen TVs, co-ordinated furnishings and decent bathrooms, is a safe, well-run choice and good value for money. ⑤

Inglaterra c/Pelai 14 ☏ 935 051 100, ⓦ www .hotel-inglaterra.com; Ⓜ Universitat. Boutique hotel with harmoniously toned rooms with snazzy bathrooms. Some rooms have cute private terraces, others street-side balconies. Best of all is the romantic roof-terrace. ⑤

Omm c/Rosselló 265 ☏ 934 454 000, ⓦ www .hotelomm.es; Ⓜ Diagonal. The black-and-grey designer experience that is *Omm* isn't to every-one's taste and can seem a bit oppressive, but matters improve inside the immaculate, minimalist, open-plan rooms – everyone gets a balcony, with the quietest rooms sited at the rear. ⑧

Prestige Pg. de Gràcia 62 ☏ 932 724 180, ⓦ www.prestigepaseodegracia.com; Ⓜ Passeig de Gràcia. It's almost a parody of itself it's so cool – minimalist rooms, an oriental-style patio garden, and the Zeroom lounge with style library – but the staff keep things real and pride themselves on their city know-how.

San Remo c/Ausias Marc 19, 2° ☏ 933 021 989, ⓦ www.hostalsanremo.com; Ⓜ Urquinaona. The doubles aren't a bad size for the money, and the small, tiled bathrooms are pretty good for this price range. ③

the5Rooms c/Pau Claris 72, 2° ☏ 933 427 880, ⓦ www.thefiverooms.com; Ⓜ Urquinaona. The impeccably tasteful "five rooms" set the standard for luxury city B&B. Despite the high-spec surroundings, the feel is house-party rather than hotel – breakfast is served whenever you like, drinks are always available, and the owner Jessica is happy to sit down and talk you through her favourite bars, restaurants and galleries. ⑥

Torre Catalunya Avgda. de Roma 2–4 ☏ 936 006 999, ⓦ www.expogrupo.com; Ⓜ Sants-Estació. Landmark four-star-deluxe hotel outside Sants station. Rooms above the twelfth floor are superior in terms of views and services, but all are elegantly turned out and boast huge beds, flat-screen TVs and very good bathrooms. An extensive buffet breakfast is served on the 23rd floor, accompanied by panoramic views. The website has the best rates, often remarkably low for this class of hotel. ⑤

Youth and backpacker hostels

Some traditional backpacker dives survive here and there, but they have largely been superseded by purpose-built modern **hostels** with en-suite dorm rooms as well as private rooms. They compare well in price with budget rooms in the very cheapest *pensiones*, and internet access, self-catering kitchens, common rooms and laundry facilities are standard. Rates at most places drop a few euros in the winter. **Security** is pretty good at most hostels, with staffed reception desks and 24hr access commonplace, but you should still always use the lockers or safes provided.

Albergue Verge de Montserrat Pg. de la Mare de Déu del Coll 41–51, Horta ☎ 932 105 151, ⓦ www .xanascat.cat; Ⓜ Vallcarca (follow Avgda. República d'Argentina, c/Viaducte de Vallcarca and then signs), or bus #28 from Plaça de Catalunya stops just across the street. Converted mansion close to Parc Güell, with gardens, terrace and city views. Dorms sleep four, six, eight or twelve, and there's a local restaurant just around the corner or meals provided. €17–25, non-HI members €2 extra, includes breakfast.

Alternative Creative Youth Home Ronda Universitat, Eixample ☎ 635 669 021, ⓦ www.alternative -barcelona.com; Ⓜ Catalunya. See map on pp.696–697. A self-selecting art and counter-culture crowd makes its way to this highly individual hostel – you don't even find out the exact address until you book, and once there you can expect a stylishly refurbished space with wi-fi, projection lounge and cool music. Takes a maximum of 24 people spread over three small dorms, with walk-in kitchen, lockers and laundry. €20–32.

Barcelona Mar c/de Sant Pau 80, El Raval ☎ 933 248 530, ⓦ www.youthostel-barcelona.com; Ⓜ Parallel/Drassanes. See map on pp.674–675. Large, rather clinically furnished hostel with lots of beds, on the fringe of the Rambla de Raval. Dorms – in six-, eight-, ten-, fourteen- or sixteen-bed rooms – are mixed, and beds are ship's-bunk-style, with a little curtain for privacy. €18–27, includes continental breakfast.

Center Ramblas c/Hospital 63, El Raval ☎ 934 124 069, ⓦ www.center-ramblas.com; Ⓜ Liceu. See map on pp.674–675. Very popular two-hundred-bed hostel, 100m from the Ramblas. Dorms (sleeping 3–10) have stone-flagged floors and individual lockers, and there's 24hr access. No credit cards. Under-25s €17–21, over-25s €21–25, non-HI members €2 extra, includes breakfast.

Centric Point Pg. de Gràcia 33 ☎ 932 156 538, ⓦ www.equity-point-com; Ⓜ Passeig de Gràcia. See map on pp.696–697. Around 450 beds spread across several floors of a refurbished *modernista* building. Good-quality private twins, doubles, triples and quads, all with shower room, balcony and views, while dorms (also all en suite) sleep up to fourteen. A roof terrace has spectacular views of Gaudí's Casa Batlló. Prices include continental breakfast and free internet; dorms €17–24, private rooms ❹–❺

🏃 Itaca c/Ripoll 21, Barri Gòtic ☎ 933 019 751, ⓦ www.itacahostel.com; Ⓜ Jaume I. See map on pp.674–675. Bright and breezy house close to La Seu, with spacious dorms (sleeping 8 or 12) with lockers and balconies. Dorms are mixed, though there's also a private room and apartment (sleeps up to 6; from €100 per night), and with a hostel capacity of only thirty it doesn't feel at all institutional. Dorms €18–26, private rooms ❸

Sea Point Pl. del Mar 1–4, Barceloneta, book online at ⓦ www.equity-point.com. See map on pp.662–663. Neat little bunk rooms sleeping six or seven, with an integral shower-bathroom and big lockers. The attached café, where you have breakfast, looks right out onto the boardwalk and palm trees. Open 24hr. Dorms €18–23, includes breakfast and free internet.

The City

Everyone starts with **the Ramblas**, the kilometre-long tree-lined avenue that splits the old town in two, Barri Gòtic to its east and El Raval to the west. The **Barri Gòtic** (Gothic Quarter) is the medieval nucleus of the city – around five hundred square metres of narrow streets, mansions, museums and historic buildings including the mighty Gothic cathedral, **La Seu**. Further east across Via Laietana lie the traditional *barri* (neighbourhood) of **Sant Pere**, with its terrific market, and **La Ribera**, the latter being a noted nightlife centre and also home to the celebrated **Museu Picasso**. West of the Ramblas is **El Raval**, traditionally the sleaziest part of the old town, though recent regeneration has made this one of the funkiest places in the city to eat, drink and shop – its cultural attractions are focused on **MACBA**, Barcelona's contemporary art museum, and Gaudí's **Palau Güell**. Beyond El Raval, above the old working-class *barri* of Poble Sec, rises the fortress-topped hill of **Montjuïc**, which contains some of the city's best museums, galleries and gardens, as well as the main Olympic stadium.

At the bottom of the Ramblas is the harbour area known as **Port Vell** (Old Port), where a swing bridge skips across the harbour to the **Maremàgnum**

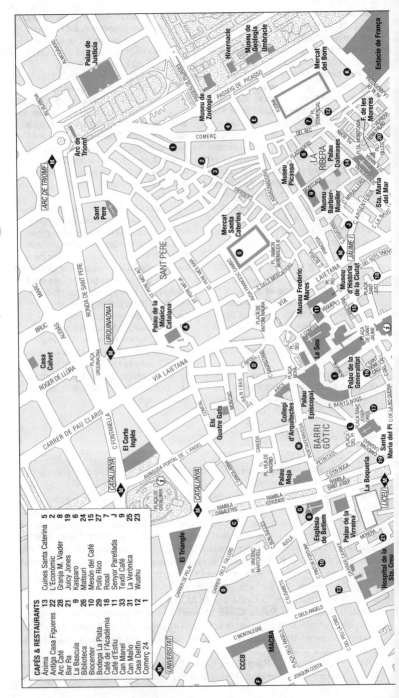

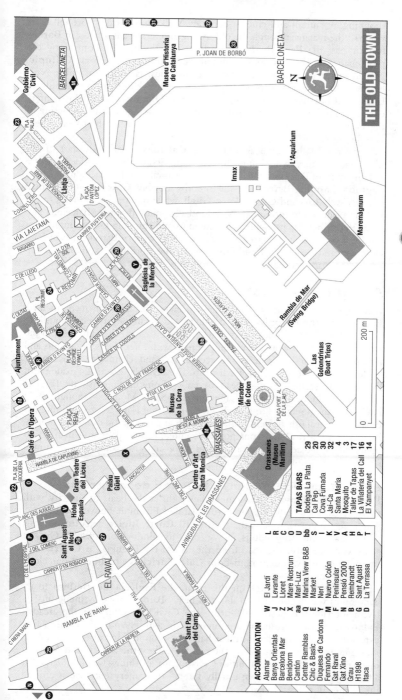

THE OLD TOWN

BARCELONETA

Gobierno Civil

Museu d'Història de Catalunya

P. JOAN DE BORBÓ

PLA PALAU

Llotja

VÍA LAIETANA

Església de la Mercè

L'Aquàrium

Imax

Maremàgnum

Ajuntament

Café de l'Opera

Museu de la Cera

Rambla de Mar (Swing Bridge)

Las Golondrinas (Boat Trips)

0   200 m

PLA DE LA BOQUERIA

Mirador de Colón

Gran Teatre del Liceu

Palau Güell

Centre d'Art Santa Mònica

DRASSANES

Hotel España

Sant Agustí el Nou

Drassanes (Museu Marítim)

EL RAVAL

RAMBLA DE RAVAL

Sant Pau del Camp

BARCELONA

N

TAPAS BARS

Bodega La Plata	29
Cal Pep	20
Cova Fumada	30
Jai-Ca	32
Santa Maria	4
Mosquito	3
Taller de Tapas	17
La Vinateria del Call	16
El Xampanyet	14

ACCOMMODATION

Alamar		L	El Jardí	W
Banys Orientals		J	Levante	J
Barcelona Mar		Z	Lloret	Z
Benidorm		C	Mare Nostrum	X
Cantón		O	Mar-Luz	aa
Center Ramblas		U	Marina View B&B	bb
Chic & Basic		E	Market	S
Duquesa de Cardona		Y	Neri	I
Fernando		M	Nuevo Colón	K
Gat Raval		F	Peninsular	V
Gat Xino		N	Pensió 2000	A
Grau		B	Rembrandt	H
H1898		G	Sant Agustí	P
Itaca		D	La Terrassa	T

675

shopping, restaurant and cinema complex. Walking east from Port Vell takes you past the marina, through the old fishing and restaurant quarter of **Barceloneta**, past the **Parc de la Ciutadella** and the zoo, and out along the promenade to the bar-and-restaurant zone that is the **Port Olímpic**. Northeast along the coast from here, the old industrial suburb of **Poble Nou** has been transformed in recent years, with a five-kilometre promenade of landscaped beaches now running up as far as **Diagonal Mar**. This conference and exhibition district expands upon the buildings and infrastructure of the Universal Forum of Cultures, the diversity and sustainability expo held here in 2004.

At the top of the Ramblas, **Plaça de Catalunya** marks the start of the nineteenth-century extension of the city – the **Eixample** – a gridded expanse holding most of Barcelona's celebrated architectural wonders, including Gaudí's **Sagrada Família**. Beyond lie the suburbs, notably **Gràcia**, with its small squares, lively bars and Gaudí's **Parc Güell**, while other suburban trips might include a ride out to the **Camp Nou** football stadium (home of Barcelona FC) or to **Pedralbes** for its applied art museums and stunning Gothic monastery. Finally, if you're saving yourself for just one aerial view of Barcelona, wait for a clear day and head for **Tibidabo**, way to the northwest, a mountain-top amusement park backed by the Collserola hills.

Along the Ramblas

It is a telling comment on Barcelona's character that one can recommend a single street – **the Ramblas** – as a highlight. No day in the city seems complete without a stroll down at least part of what, for Lorca, was "the only street in the world which I wish would never end". Lined with cafés, shops, restaurants and newspaper stalls, it's at the heart of Barcelona's life and self-image – a focal point for locals every bit as much as for tourists. The Ramblas is actually made up of five separate sections strung head to tail – from north to south: Rambla Canaletes, Estudis, Sant Josep, Caputxins and Santa Mònica – though you'll rarely hear them referred to as such. Here, under the plane trees, you'll find pet canaries, tropical fish, flowers, plants, postcards and books. You can buy jewellery, have your palm read and your portrait painted, play cards with a man on an upturned cardboard box (not a good idea) or enjoy the antics of the human statues and performance artists.

From Plaça de Catalunya to Palau de la Virreina
Plaça de Catalunya (Ⓜ Catalunya) lies right at the heart of the city, with the old town and port below it, the planned Eixample above and beyond. The main landmark here is the massive **El Corte Inglés** department store, which has some stupendous views from its ninth-floor *cafetería*. On the southwest side, over the road from the top of the Ramblas, is **El Triangle** shopping centre, whose ground-floor **Café Zurich** is a traditional Barcelona meeting place.

Down the Ramblas, over on the right, the **Església de Betlem** (daily 8am–6pm) was begun in 1681, built in heavy Baroque style by the Jesuits; its lavish interior was destroyed during the Civil War. Opposite, the arcaded **Palau Moja** dates from the late eighteenth century and still retains a fine exterior staircase and elegant great hall. The ground floor of the building is now a cultural bookshop, while the palace's gallery, the **Sala Palau Moja**, is open for art and other exhibitions relating to all things Catalan (Tues–Sat 11am–8pm, Sun 11am–3pm; usually free) – the gallery entrance is around the corner in c/Portaferrissa.

Farther along the Ramblas, on the corner of c/Carme, sits the imposing eighteenth-century **Palau de la Virreina** (ⓂLiceu). The palace is used by the city council's culture department, with a walk-in information centre and ticket office, and two galleries for changing exhibitions of contemporary art and photography (Tues–Fri 11am–2pm & 4–8.30pm, Sat 11am–8.30pm, Sun 11am–3pm; admission usually charged; Ⓦwww.bcn.cat/virreinacentredelaimatge). Duck into the courtyard to see the city's two official **carnival giants** (*gegants vells*), representing the celebrated thirteenth-century Catalan king, Jaume I, and his wife Violant.

La Boqueria and Gran Teatre del Liceu

Beyond the Palau de la Virreina lies the city's most famous market, known locally as **La Boqueria**, though officially the Mercat Sant Josep (Mon–Sat 8am–8pm; Ⓦwww.boqueria.info; ⓂLiceu). Built between 1836 and 1840, it's a riot of noise and colour, with great piles of fruit and vegetables, dried herbs, exotic mushrooms, cured meats and an amazing variety of fish and seafood. If you're going to buy, do some browsing first, as the flagship fruit and veg stalls by the entrance tend to have higher prices than those farther inside. There are some excellent stand-up snack bars in here, open from dawn onwards for the traders – the *Pinotxo* near the Ramblas entrance (Mon–Sat 6am–5pm; closed Aug) is the most famous.

Past the market is the part of the Ramblas known as **Plaça de la Boqueria**, marked (in the middle of the pavement) by a large round mosaic by Joan Miró. A little way beyond is the **Gran Teatre del Liceu**, Barcelona's celebrated opera house, which burned down for the third time in 1994 but has been rebuilt in its former neo-Baroque style. Tours of the lavishly gilded auditorium and interior depart from the modern extension, the Espai Liceu (tours daily 10am, 11.30am, 12.30pm & 1pm; €4/8.50, Ⓦwww.liceubarcelona.com). You'll learn most on the more expensive hour-long 10am guided tour; the other,

▲ La Boqueria

cheaper tours are self-guided and last only twenty minutes. Offered as an option only on the 10am tour is the chance to visit the private rooms of the **Cercle del Liceu** (€3 extra), the opera house's members' club. Across the way, at Ramblas 74, is the famous **Café de l'Opera**, traditional favourite of opera performers and *cognoscenti* for over a century – you'll be charged a premium for sitting at the Ramblas tables.

Plaça Reial to Mirador de Colón

A hundred metres or so farther down the Ramblas, the elegant nineteenth-century **Plaça Reial** (Ⓜ Liceu), hidden behind an archway on the left, is easy to miss. Laid out in around 1850, the Italianate square is studded with tall palm trees and decorated iron lamps (by the young Gaudí), bordered by arcaded buildings and centred on a fountain depicting the Three Graces.

Off the Ramblas at the southern end of the square, **Carrer dels Escudellers** was once a thriving red-light street, but it has gradually hauled itself up by its bootlaces and teeters on the edge of respectability. Bars and restaurants around here attract a youthful crowd on the whole, nowhere more so than those flanking **Plaça George Orwell**, at the eastern end of c/dels Escudellers. The wedge-shaped square was created by levelling an old-town block – a favoured tactic in Barcelona to let in a bit of light – and it's quickly become a hangout for the grunge crowd.

A little farther down the Ramblas on the right, the Augustinian convent of Santa Mònica dates originally from 1626, making it the oldest building on the Ramblas. It was entirely remodelled in the 1980s and now houses the **Centre d'Art Santa Mònica** (Tues–Sat 11am–8pm, Sun 11am–3pm; free; Ⓦ www .centredartsantamonica.net), which displays temporary exhibitions of contemporary art.

The city's wax museum, the **Museu de la Cera** (July–Sept daily 10am–10pm; Oct–June Mon–Fri 10am–1.30pm & 4–7.30pm, Sat & Sun 11am–2pm & 4.30–8.30pm; €6.65; Ⓦ www.museocerabcn.com; Ⓜ Drassanes), is located on the opposite side of the Ramblas, at nos. 4–6, in an impressive nineteenth-century bank building; the entrance is down Passatge de Banca. Needless to say, it's extremely ropey and enormously amusing, culminating in cheesy underwater and space capsules and an unpleasant "Terror" room. You also won't want to miss the museum's extraordinary grotto-bar, the *Bosc de les Fades* ("Forest of the Fairies"), festooned with gnarled plaster tree trunks, hanging branches, fountains and stalactites.

At the foot of the Ramblas is Plaça Portal de la Pau (Ⓜ Drassanes) and the harbourside, dominated by a slender iron column topped by a statue of Columbus, who was received in Barcelona by Fernando and Isabel on his triumphant return from the New World in 1493. You can ride the elevator inside the **Mirador de Colón** (daily: June–Sept 9am–8.30pm; Oct–May 10am–6.30pm; €2.50) for some stunning aerial views of the city.

The Drassanes: Museu Marítim

Opposite Columbus, set back from the road on the western side of the Ramblas, are the **Drassanes**, medieval shipyards dating from the thirteenth century. Originally used as a dry dock to fit and arm Catalunya's war fleet in the days when the Catalan-Aragonese crown was vying with Venice and Genoa for control of the Mediterranean, the shipyards were in continuous use until well into the eighteenth century. Nowadays, the huge, stone-vaulted buildings make a fitting home for the excellent **Museu Marítim** (daily 10am–8pm; €6.50, afternoon of first Sat of month free; Ⓦ www.museumaritimbarcelona.com;

Ⓜ Drassanes), whose centrepiece is a copy of the sixteenth-century *Royal Galley*, a soaring red-and-gold barge rowed by enormous oars. Pick up the audio-guide (included in the entrance fee) and home in on some of the more illuminating digressions: on steam navigation, fishing methods, life at sea, or the growth of the port of Barcelona, for example. Combination tickets offer discounted trips on the harbour sightseeing boats or up the Mirador del Colón, while there's also a good café-restaurant (Mon–Sat lunch, plus Thurs–Sat dinner), which puts out tables in the pleasant courtyard – on summer evenings, this becomes a popular patio lounge-bar.

The Barri Gòtic

The **Barri Gòtic**, or Gothic Quarter (Ⓜ Jaume I), forms the very heart of the old town, spreading out from the east side of the Ramblas. It's a remarkable concentration of medieval buildings principally dating from the fourteenth and fifteenth centuries, when Barcelona reached the height of its commercial prosperity before being absorbed into the burgeoning kingdom of Castile. It takes the best part of a day to see everything here, with the cathedral – La Seu – a particular highlight, and you certainly won't want to miss the archeological remains at the Museu d'Història de la Ciutat or the eclectic collections of the Museu Frederic Marès. That said, sauntering through the atmospheric alleys or simply sitting at a café table in one of the lovely squares is just as much an attraction.

The picture-postcard images of the Barri Gòtic are largely based on the streets north of c/de Ferran and c/de Jaume I, where tourists throng the boutiques, bars, restaurants, museums and galleries. South of here – from Plaça Reial and c/d'Avinyo to the harbour – the Barri Gòtic is rather more traditional (or sometimes just plain run-down).

Plaça de Sant Jaume

The quarter is centred on **Plaça de Sant Jaume**, a spacious square at the end of the main c/de Ferran. On the south side stands the city hall, the **Ajuntament**, parts of which date from as early as 1373, though the Neoclassical facade is nineteenth century. You get a much better idea of the grandeur of the original structure by nipping around the corner, down c/de la Ciutat, for a view of the former main entrance. On Sundays (10am–2pm; free; entrance on c/Font de Sant Miquel), you're allowed into the building for a self-guided tour around the splendid marble halls and galleries, with the highlight being the magnificent restored fourteenth-century council chamber, known as the **Saló de Cent**.

Right across the square rises the **Palau de la Generalitat**, traditional home of the Catalan government, from where the short-lived Catalan Republic was proclaimed in April 1931. There's a beautiful cloister on the first floor, while opening off this are the intricately worked chapel and salon of Sant Jordi (St George, patron saint of Catalunya as well as England), and an upper courtyard planted with orange trees, overhung by gargoyles and peppered with presidential busts. You can visit the interior on a **guided tour** on the second and fourth Sunday of each month (10am–2pm; every 30min–1hr; free; entrance on c/Sant Honorat, passport/ID required); these last an hour, and include an introductory video about the Catalan state and its history, though only one or two of the tours each day are conducted in English. The Generalitat is also traditionally open to the public on April 23 (expect a 2hr wait) – **Dia de Sant Jordi** (St George's Day) – when the whole square is festooned with bookstalls and rose sellers. It's also usually open for visits on two other public holidays: September 11 and September 24.

La Seu

Barcelona's cathedral, **La Seu** (daily 8am–12.45pm & 5.15–7.30pm, cathedral and cloister free; otherwise, 1–5pm; €5, includes entrance to all sections; Ⓦ www.catedralbcn.org), is one of the great Gothic buildings of Spain. Located on a site previously occupied by a Roman temple and then an early Christian basilica, it was begun in 1298 and finished in 1448, save for the principal facade, which wasn't finally completed until the 1880s (and is currently obscured by scaffolding). The cathedral is dedicated to the city's co-patroness, **Santa Eulàlia**, martyred by the Romans for daring to prefer Christianity, and her tomb rests in a crypt beneath the high altar. The rest of the interior is typically ornate, with no fewer than 29 side chapels, but the most magnificent part of the cathedral is its fourteenth-century **cloister**, which looks over a lush garden complete with soaring palm trees and – more unusually – a gaggle of honking geese. White geese have been kept here for over five hundred years, either (depending on which story you believe) to reflect the virginity of Santa Eulàlia or as a reminder of the erstwhile Roman splendour of Barcelona (geese having been kept on the Capitoline Hill in Rome). Finally, don't leave the cathedral without ascending to the **roof** (Mon–Fri 10.30am–12.30pm & 5.15–6.30pm, Sat 10.30am–12.30pm; €2.20), which provides intimate views of the cathedral towers and surrounding Gothic buildings and spires.

Plaça del Rei and around

The most concentrated batch of historic monuments in the Barri Gòtic is the grouping around **Plaça del Rei**, behind the cathedral apse. The square was once the courtyard of the Palau Reial Major, the palace of the counts of Barcelona, and stairs climb to the great fourteenth-century **Saló del Tinell**, the palace's main hall, which nowadays hosts various exhibitions and concerts.

The palace buildings also include the romantic Renaissance **Torre del Rei Martí** as well as the beautiful fourteenth-century **Capella de Santa Agata**. There's currently no public access to the tower, but the interiors of hall and chapel can be seen during a visit to the **Museu d'Història de la Ciutat** (MHCB; April–Sept Tues–Sat 10am–8pm, Sun & public hols 10am–3pm; Oct–March Tues–Sat 10am–2pm & 4–8pm, Sun & public hols 10am–3pm; €6, includes entry to other MHCB sites; Ⓦ www.museuhistoria.bcn.cat), housed in the building that closes off the rest of Plaça del Rei. The museum's crucial draw is its underground archeological section – nothing less than the extensive remains of the Roman city of Barcino, stretching under Plaça del Rei and the surrounding streets as far as the cathedral. The remains date from the first to the sixth centuries AD and reflect the transition from Roman to Visigothic rule.

Boho Barcelona and the Four Cats

There's not much to see in the shopping zone north of the cathedral, but a century or so ago a tavern called **Els Quatre Gats** (The Four Cats; c/Montsió 3, Ⓦ www.4gats .com) burned brightly as the epi-centre of Barcelona's bohemian in-crowd. It was opened in 1897 as a gathering place for artists and literary types, with the building gloriously decorated in exuberant Catalan Art Nouveau style. *Els Quatre Gats* soon thrived as the scene of poetry readings and the venue for cultural debate, while a young Picasso designed the menu. Today, a modern restoration displays something of its former glory, with the bar-restaurant overseen by a copy of Ramon Casas' famous wall-painting of himself and café founder Pere Romeu on a tandem bicycle (the original is in MNAC).

Not much survives above chest height, but explanatory diagrams show the extent of the streets, walls and buildings, while models, mosaics, murals and displays of excavated goods help flesh out the reality of daily life in Barcino. Note that your ticket is also valid for the monastery at Pedralbes and the interpretation centre at Parc Güell.

Another extraordinary display greets visitors in the **Museu Frederic Marès** (Tues–Sat 10am–7pm, Sun 10am–3pm; €4.20, Wed afternoon & first Sun of month free; ⓦ www.museumares.bcn.cat), which occupies a further wing of the old royal palace; the entrance is through Plaça de Sant Iu, off c/dels Comtes. Frederic Marès (1893–1991) was a sculptor, artist and restorer who more or less singlehandedly restored Catalunya's decaying medieval treasures in the early twentieth century. The ground and basement floors of the museum consist of his personal collection of medieval sculpture, but it's the upper two floors, housing Marès' personal collectibles, which tend to make jaws drop. These present an incredible retrospective jumble gathered during fifty years of travel, with entire rooms devoted to keys and locks, cigarette cards and snuff boxes, fans, gloves and brooches, playing cards, walking sticks, dolls' houses, toy theatres and archaic bicycles, to name just a sample of what's on show.

Santa María del Pi and around

The fourteenth-century **Església de Santa María del Pi** (Mon–Sat 8.30am–1pm & 4.30–9pm, Sun 9am–2pm & 5–9pm) stands at the heart of three delightful little squares, five-minutes' walk from the cathedral or just two minutes from ⓜ Liceu on the Ramblas. The church boasts a Romanesque door but is mainly Catalan-Gothic in style, whose rather plain interior only serves to set off some marvellous stained glass, the most impressive of which is contained within a huge rose window. The church stands on the middle square, **Plaça Sant Josep Oriol**, the prettiest of the three, overhung with balconies and scattered with seats from the *Bar del Pi*. This whole area becomes an **artists' market** at the weekend (Sat 11am–8pm, Sun 11am–2pm), while buskers and street performers often appear here, too. A **farmers' market** spills across Plaça del Pi on the first and third Friday and Saturday of the month, selling honey, cheese, cakes and other produce, while the cafés of **Carrer de Petritxol** (off Plaça del Pi) are the place to come for a hot chocolate – *Dulcinea* at no. 2 is the traditional choice.

El Call Major and the Antiga Sinagoga

South of Plaça Sant Felip Neri you enter what was once the medieval Jewish quarter of Barcelona, centred on c/Sant Domènec del Call. After decades of neglect, the city authorities have signposted some of the surrounding streets and points of interest in what's known as **El Call Major** (*Call* is the Catalan word for a narrow passage), most notably the site of the main synagogue, the **Antiga Sinagoga** at c/Marlet 5, on the corner with c/Sant Domènec del Call (Mon–Fri 11am–6pm, Sat & Sun 11am–3pm, sometimes closed Sat for ceremonies; ⓦ www.calldebarcelona.org; €2). Not many people stop by the synagogue – if you do, you'll get a personalized tour of the small room by a member of the local Jewish community.

Most other local Jewish buildings were destroyed, though a plaque further down c/Marlet (junction with c/Arc Sant Ramon del Call) marks the site of the former rabbi's house, while up in Plaçeta Manuel Ribé another house originally belonging to a veil-maker now serves as a small museum, the **Centre d'Interpretació del Call** (Wed–Fri 10am–2pm, Sat 11am–6pm, Sun & public hols 11am–3pm; free; ⓦwww.museuhistoria.bcn.cat). You can ask here about guided tours, open days and activities that aim to shed more light on Barcelona's Jewish heritage.

El Raval

The old-town area west of the Ramblas is known as **El Raval** (from the Arabic word for "suburb"). In medieval times, it was the site of hospitals, churches and monasteries and, later, of trades and industries that had no place in the Gothic Quarter. Many of the street names still tell the story, like c/de l'Hospital or c/dels Tallers (named for the district's slaughterhouses). By the twentieth century, the area south of c/de l'Hospital had acquired a reputation as the city's main red-light district, known to all as the Barrio Chino, or Barri Xinès in Catalan – China Town. Even today in the backstreets around c/de Sant Pau and c/Nou de la Rambla are found pockets of sleaze, while a handful of old bars trade on their former reputations as bohemian hangouts. However, El Raval is transforming rapidly. The main engine of change was the building of the contemporary art museum, MACBA, around which entire city blocks were demolished, open spaces created and old buildings cleaned up. To the south, between c/de l'Hospital and c/de Sant Pau, a new boulevard – the Rambla de Raval – has been gouged through the former tenements and alleys, providing a huge pedestrianized area. Bars, restaurants, galleries and boutiques have followed in the wake of this development, although you'd still hesitate to call El Raval gentrified, as it clearly still has its rough edges.

MACBA and CCCB

Anchoring the northern reaches of El Raval is the huge, white, almost luminous **Museu d'Art Contemporani de Barcelona** or **MACBA** in Plaça dels Àngels (mid-June to mid-Sept Mon & Wed 11am–8pm, Thurs & Fri 11am–midnight, Sat 10am–8pm, Sun & public hols 10am–3pm; rest of the year closes weekdays at 7.30pm; closed Tues all year; €4 or €7.50 depending on exhibitions visited, Wed €3; ⓦwww.macba.es; ⓜCatalunya/Universitat). Once inside, you go from the ground to the fourth floor up a series of swooping ramps that afford continuous views of the plaça below – usually full of careering skateboarders – and the sixteenth-century Convent dels Àngels. The collection represents the main movements in contemporary art since 1945, mainly in Catalunya and Spain but with a good smattering of foreign artists as well. The pieces are shown in rotating exhibitions, so you may catch works by Joan Miró, Antoni Tàpies, Eduardo Chillida, Alexander Calder, Robert Rauschenberg or Paul Klee. Joan Brossa, leading light of the Catalan avant-garde "Dau al Set" group, has work here, too, as do contemporary Catalan conceptual and abstract artists.

Adjoining the MACBA building, up c/Montalegre, is the **Centre de Cultura Contemporània de Barcelona** or **CCCB** (Tues–Sun 11am–8pm, Thurs until 10pm; €4.50 or €6 depending on exhibitions visited, first Wed of month free; ⓦwww.cccb.org), which hosts temporary art and city-related exhibitions as well as supporting a cinema and a varied concert and festival programme. At the back of the building, the *C3* café-bar has a sunny *terraza* on the modern square joining the CCCB to MACBA.

Hospital de la Santa Creu and around

The district's most substantial relic is the **Hospital de la Santa Creu** (ⓜLiceu), which occupies a large site between c/del Carme and c/de l'Hospital. The attractive complex of Gothic buildings was founded as the city's main hospital in 1402, a role that it retained until 1930. Today, it has been converted to cultural and educational use, and its spacious cloistered **garden** (daily 10am–dusk), punctuated by orange trees, provides airy respite from El Raval's dark streets. Just inside the c/del Carme entrance (on the right) are some superb seventeenth-century *azulejos* and a tiled Renaissance courtyard; there's also a rather nice café-*terraza* in the garden at the c/de l'Hospital side.

Walking west along c/de l'Hospital, it's 100m or so to the bottom of **c/de la Riera Baixa**, a narrow street that's at the centre of the city's secondhand/vintage clothing scene. Just a few steps beyond, you can consider the merits of the latest boulevard to be driven through the old town, the **Rambla de Raval**. In many ways, it's still finding its feet – the ongoing Illa Robabdor construction site halfway down will eventually house a hotel and film institute, while the juvenile trees are yet to throw much shade on the *rambla*'s benches. But the local inhabitants – many of Asian origin – have been quick to appreciate the open space of the *rambla*, while an increasing number of fashionable bars are interspersed amongst the video stores, kebab shops, *halal* butchers and grocery stores. A Saturday **street market** (selling everything from samosas to hammocks) adds a bit more character.

Palau Güell

El Raval's outstanding building is the **Palau Güell**, at c/Nou de la Rambla 3 (Tues–Sat 10am–2.30pm; free; ⓂDrassanes/Liceu), an extraordinary townhouse designed by the young Antoni Gaudí for wealthy shipowner and industrialist Eusebi Güell i Bacigalupi. At a time when architects sought to conceal the iron supports within buildings, Gaudí turned them to his advantage, displaying them as attractive decorative features. The roof terrace, too, makes a virtue of its functionalism, since the chimneys and other outlets are decorated with glazed tiles, while inside, columns, arches and ceilings are all shaped and twisted in an elaborate style that was to become the hallmark of Gaudí's later works.

The building is under long-term restoration, which isn't expected to be completed until 2010. At the time of writing, there was free access to view the facade, ground floor and part of the basement, but with limited hours and limited numbers allowed in at any one time, you can expect to have to queue or be given a specific time-slot.

Sant Pau del Camp

Carrer de Sant Pau cuts west through El Raval to the church of **Sant Pau del Camp** (St Paul of the Field; Mon 5–8pm, Tues–Fri 10am–1.30pm & 5–8pm, Sat 10am–1.30pm; admission to cloister €2; ⓂParal.lel), its name a reminder that it once stood in open fields beyond the city walls. One of the most interesting churches in Barcelona, Sant Pau is laid out in the cruciform Greek style, with a main entrance decorated with faded Romanesque carvings of fish, birds and faces, and a tranquil twelfth-century cloister.

Sant Pere

The Barri Gòtic is bordered on its eastern side by Via Laietana, which was cut through the old town at the beginning of the twentieth century. Across it to the east stretches the quiet neighbourhood of **Sant Pere**, home to two remarkable buildings, the Palau de la Música Catalana concert hall and the restored neighbourhood market, Mercat Santa Caterina.

Lluis Domènech i Montaner's stupendous **Palau de la Música Catalana** (ⓂUrquinaona) doesn't seem to have enough breathing space in the tiny c/Sant Pere Més Alt. Built in 1908 for the Orfeó Català choral group, its bare brick structure is lined with tiles and mosaics, the highly elaborate facade resting on three great columns, like an elephant's legs. The stunning interior, meanwhile, incorporates a bulbous stained-glass skylight capping the second-storey auditorium – which contemporary critics claimed to be an engineering impossibility. Successive extensions and interior remodelling have opened up the original site – the **Petit Palau** offers a smaller auditorium space, while to the side an enveloping glass facade provides the main public access to the box office, terrace restaurant and foyer bar. This is where you come to buy tickets for the fifty-minute-long **guided tours** of the original interior (daily 10am–3.30pm, Easter week & Aug until 6pm, in English on the hour; €10; Ⓦwww.palaumusica.org). You can also reserve tickets online, but as visitor numbers are limited you'll almost certainly have to book a day or two in advance.

At the very heart of Sant Pere is the **Mercat Santa Caterina** (Mon 8am–2pm, Tues, Wed & Sat 8am–3.30pm, Thurs & Fri 8am–8.30pm; ☎933 195 740, Ⓦwww.mercatsantacaterina.net; ⓂJaume I), whose splendid restoration has retained its nineteenth-century balustraded walls and added a dramatic multi-coloured wave roof. During the renovation work, the foundations of a major medieval convent were discovered on the site – parts of the walls are visible behind glass at the rear of the market. Santa Caterina is one of the best places in the city to come and shop for food, and its market restaurant and bar, *Cuines Santa Caterina*, is definitely worth a special visit in any case.

La Ribera

South of Sant Pere, **La Ribera** sports Barcelona's biggest single tourist attraction, the Museu Picasso. The sheer number of visitors in this neighbourhood rivals the busiest streets of the Barri Gòtic, and this has had a knock-on effect in terms of the bars, shops and restaurants found here. La Ribera is at its most hip, and most enjoyable, in the area around the **Passeig del Born**, the elongated square leading from Santa María church to the old Born market. This – widely known as the Born – is one of the city's premier nightlife centres.

Museu Picasso

The **Museu Picasso**, c/de Montcada 15–19 (Tues–Sun & public hols 10am–8pm; €9, exhibitions €5.80, first Sun of month free; ☎932 563 000, Ⓦwww .museupicasso.bcn.cat; ⓂJaume I), is housed in a series of medieval palaces converted specifically for the museum. It's one of the most important collections of Picasso's work in the world, but even so, some visitors are disappointed: the museum contains none of his best-known works, and few in the Cubist style. But what is here provides a unique opportunity to trace Picasso's development from his early paintings as a young boy to the major works of later years. There are free **guided tours** in English (Thurs 6pm & Sat noon), but you'll need to book in advance (by phone or by email through the website).

Particularly fascinating are the **early drawings**, in which Picasso – still signing with his full name, Pablo Ruíz Picasso – attempted to copy the nature paintings in which his father specialized. Paintings from his art-school days in **Barcelona** (1895–97) show tantalizing glimpses of the city that the young Picasso was beginning to know well – the Gothic old town, the cloisters of Sant Pau del Camp, Barceloneta beach – and even at the ages of 15 and 16 he was producing serious work. Later, there are paintings from the famous **Blue Period** (1901–04), the Pink Period (1904–06) and from his Cubist (1907–20) and Neoclassical (1920–25) stages. The large gaps in the main collection (for example, nothing from 1905 until the celebrated *Harlequin* of 1917) only underline Picasso's extraordinary changes of style and mood. This is best illustrated by the large jump after 1917 – to 1957, a year represented by his 44 interpretations of Velázquez's masterpiece **Las Meninas**, in which Picasso brilliantly deconstructed the individual portraits and compositions that make up Velázquez's work.

Along Carrer de Montcada

The street that the Museu Picasso is on – **Carrer de Montcada** – is one of the best-looking in the city. It was laid out in the fourteenth century and, until the Eixample was planned almost five hundred years later, was home to most of the city's leading citizens. Spacious mansions were built around central courtyards, from which external staircases climbed to the living rooms on the first floor. Today, almost all the mansions and palaces along La Ribera's showpiece street serve instead as art and applied art museums, private galleries, and craft and gift shops, sucking up the trade from Picasso-bound visitors.

The **Museu Barbier-Mueller**, c/de Montcada 14 (Tues–Fri 11am–7pm, Sat 10am–7pm, Sun 10am–3pm; €3, first Sun of month free), is a terrific collection of pre-Columbian art housed in the renovated sixteenth-century Palau Nadal. Temporary exhibitions highlight wide-ranging themes, and draw on a peerless collection of sculpture, pottery, jewellery, textiles and everyday items, with some

---

Picasso in Barcelona

Although born in Málaga, **Pablo Picasso** (1881–1973) spent much of his youth – from the age of 14 to 23 – in Barcelona, and there are echoes of the great artist at various sites throughout the old town. Not too far from the museum, you can still see many of the buildings in which Picasso lived and worked, notably the **Escola de Belles Arts de Llotja** (c/Consolat del Mar, near Estació de França), where his father taught drawing and where Picasso himself absorbed an academic training. The apartments where the family lived when they first arrived in Barcelona – Pg. d'Isabel II 4 and c/ Cristina 3, both opposite the Escola – can also be seen, though only from the outside. Less tangible is to take a walk down c/d'Avinyo, which cuts south from c/de Ferran to c/Ample. Large houses along here were converted into brothels at the turn of the twentieth century, and Picasso used to haunt the street, sketching what he saw – women at one of the brothels inspired his seminal Cubist work, **Les Demoiselles d'Avignon**.

pieces dating back as far as the third century BC. The shop is worth a browse, too, with a wide range of ethnic artefacts for sale.

Santa María del Mar and the Born

At the bottom of c/de Montcada sits the glorious church of **Santa María del Mar** (daily 9am–1.30pm & 4.30–8pm; Sun choral Mass at 1pm; ⓂJaume I/Barceloneta), begun under orders of King Jaume II in 1324, and built in only five years, an exquisite example of Catalan-Gothic architecture. The church was at the heart of the medieval city's maritime and trading district, and it came to embody the supremacy of the Crown of Aragon (of which Barcelona was capital) in Mediterranean commerce.

Fronting the church is the fashionable **Passeig del Born**, lined with classy boutiques, bars and cafés, and capped at the far end by the hulking skeleton of the **Mercat del Born**, which served as the city's main wholesale fruit and veg market until 1971. The former market stands directly on top of the remains of part of the eighteenth-century city, and the massive cast-iron frame now protects the surviving metre-high walls of period shops, factories, houses and taverns. Work is still ongoing, but the eventual plan is to retain the archeological remains within a cultural and interpretation centre.

Parc de la Ciutadella

East of La Ribera, across Passeig de Picasso, the **Parc de la Ciutadella** is the largest green space in the city centre. It's also the meeting place of the Catalan parliament (no public access), occupying part of a fortress-like structure right at the centre of the park, the surviving portion of the star-shaped Bourbon citadel from which the park takes its name. The main gates are on Passeig de Picasso (ⓂBarceloneta), and there's also an entrance on Passeig de Pujades (ⓂArc de Triomf); only use ⓂCiutadella-Vila Olímpica if you're going directly to the zoo, as there's no access to the park itself from that side.

In 1888, the park was chosen as the site of the **Universal Exhibition**, and the city's *modernista* architects left their mark here in a series of eye-catching buildings and monuments. Just inside the main entrance, Domènech i Montaner designed a castle-like building intended for use as the exhibition's café-restaurant. Dubbed the Castell dels Tres Dragons, and once a centre for *modernista* arts and crafts, it's now used by the zoological section of the city's Museu de Ciències Naturals, but it's fair to say that the decorated red-brick exterior of the **Museu de Zoologia** (Tues–Sun 10am–2.30pm, Thurs & Sat until 6.30pm; combined ticket with Museu de Geologia €3.70, first Sun of month free, separate charge for special exhibitions; ⓦwww.bcn.es/museuciencies) knocks spots off the rather dry displays of stuffed birds, insects and animals. The sister museum is the nearby **Museu de Geologia** (same hours, price and website as Museu de Zoologia), another restored period piece, with nineteenth-century cases of exhibits housed in a classical, pedimented building. However, the two real unsung glories of Ciutadella are its plant houses, the **Umbracle** (Palmhouse) and **Hivernacle** (Conservatory), arranged either side of the Museu de Geologia (both daily 8am–dusk; free).

Ciutadella's most popular attraction by far is the city's zoo, the **Parc Zoològic** (daily: Jan, Feb, Nov & Dec 10am–5pm; March–May & Oct 10am–6pm; June–Sept 10am–7pm; €16; ⓦwww.zoobarcelona.com), taking up most of the southeast of the park. There's an entrance on c/de Wellington, as well as one inside the park. It boasts seven thousand animals representing four hundred different species – simply too many for a zoo that is still essentially nineteenth century in character, confined to the formal grounds of a public park and devoted to entertainment rather than education. However, the zoo's days here in its current form are numbered – there are advanced plans to move the marine animals to a new coastal zoo and wetlands area (possibly by 2010) at the Diagonal Mar seashore, though the mammals are likely to stay at Ciutadella.

Port Vell

Perhaps the greatest transformation in the city has been along the waterfront, where harbour and Mediterranean have once again been placed at the heart of Barcelona. At the inner harbour, known as **Port Vell** (ⓂDrassanes), the old wharves and warehouses have been replaced by an entertainment zone that is reached by the wooden **Rambla de Mar** swing bridge. This strides across the harbour to **Maremàgnum** (daily 11am–11pm), two floors of gift shops and boutiques, plus a range of bars and restaurants with harbourside seating and high prices.

Next door, **L'Aquàrium** (daily: July & Aug 9.30am–11pm; Sept–June 9.30am–9pm, until 9.30pm at weekends; €16; Ⓦwww.aquariumbcn.com) drags in families and school parties to see fish and sea creatures in 21 themed tanks representing underwater caves, tidal areas, tropical reefs, the planet's oceans and other maritime habitats. It's vastly overpriced, and despite the claims of excellence it offers few new experiences, save perhaps the eighty-metre-long walk-through underwater tunnel, which brings you face to face with rays and sharks. **IMAX Port Vell** next to the aquarium has three screens showing films in 3D or in giant format (Ⓦwww.imaxportvell.com; €8–12 depending on the film).

The only surviving warehouse on the harbourside is known as the Palau de Mar, home to the **Museu d'Història de Catalunya** (Tues & Thurs–Sat 10am–7pm, Wed 10am–8pm, Sun 10am–2.30pm; €4, first Sun of month & public holidays free; Ⓦwww.mhcat.net; ⓂBarceloneta), which entertainingly traces the history of Catalunya from the Stone Age to the twentieth century. On the fourth floor, the café-bar boasts a glorious view from its huge terrace.

Barceloneta

There's no finer place for lunch on a sunny day than the **Barceloneta** neighbourhood (ⓂBarceloneta), bound by the harbour on one side and the Mediterranean on the other. It was laid out in 1755 – a classic eighteenth-century grid of streets where previously there had been mudflats – to replace part of La Ribera that was destroyed to make way for the Ciutadella fortress to the north. The long, narrow streets are still very much as they were planned, broken at

---

The cross-harbour cable car

The most thrilling ride in the city centre is across the inner harbour on the cable car, the **Trasbordador Aeri**, which sweeps from the **Torre Sant Sebastià**, at the foot of Barceloneta, to the **Torre Miramar** in Montjuïc, with a stop in the middle at **Torre de Jaume I**. The views are stunning, approaching either Montjuïc or Barceloneta, and you can pick out with ease the towers of La Seu and Sagrada Família, while the trees lining the Ramblas look like the forked tongue of a serpent.

Departures are every fifteen minutes (daily 10.30am–7pm, June–Sept until 8pm), though in summer and at weekends you may have to wait for a while at the top of the towers for a ride, as the cars only carry about twenty people at a time. **Tickets** cost €9 one-way or €12.50 return.

intervals by small squares and lined with multi-windowed houses. The neighbourhood **Mercat de la Barceloneta** (Mon 7am–3pm, Tues–Thurs 7am–3pm & 4.30–8.30pm, Fri 7am–8.30pm, Sat 7am–4pm), beautifully refurbished in 2007, boasts a couple of classy restaurants. Barceloneta's many other seafood restaurants are found scattered right across the tight grid of streets but most characteristically lined along the harbourside **Passeig Joan de Borbó**, where for most of the year you can sit outside and enjoy your meal.

On the seaward side of Barceloneta, what was once a scrappy fishermen's strand is now furnished with boardwalks, outdoor cafés, showers, benches, climbing frames, water fountains and public art. **Platja de Sant Sebastià** is the first in a series of beaches that stretches north along the coast as far as the River Besòs. A double row of palms backs the **Passeig Marítim**, a sweeping stone esplanade that runs as far as the Port Olímpic, a fifteen-minute walk away.

Port Olímpic to Diagonal Mar

From any point along the Passeig Marítim, the soaring twin towers of the Olympic port impose themselves upon the skyline, while a shimmering golden mirage above the promenade slowly reveals itself to be a huge copper fish (courtesy of Frank O. Gehry, architect of the Guggenheim in Bilbao). These are the showpiece manifestations of the huge seafront development constructed for the 1992 Olympics. The **Port Olímpic** (ⓂCiutadella-Vila Olímpica), site of the Olympic marina and many of the watersports events, is backed by the city's two tallest buildings – the **Torre Mapfre** and the steel-framed **Hotel Arts Barcelona** – while the surrounding area has filled up with restaurants, bars, shops and nightspots.

Beyond here, on the far side of the port, **Nova Icària** and **Bogatell** beaches stretch up to the **Poble Nou** (New Village) neighbourhood, a largely nineteenth-century industrial area now undergoing major redevelopment (tagged **22@** by the city authorities). This has already had a significant effect, as some of Barcelona's hottest clubs, galleries and art spaces are now found in Poble Nou. It's fifteen-minutes' walk from Port Olímpic to the end of Bogatell beach, while crossing the main highway backing the beach puts you at the bottom of the pretty, tree-lined **Rambla Poble Nou** – drop by *El Tio Che*, Rambla Poble Nou 46 (daily 10am–midnight), a famous old café where you can get an orange or lemon *granissat* or *orxata* to drink.

The waterfront north of Poble Nou – known as **Diagonal Mar** – is anchored by the huge Diagonal Mar shopping mall at the foot of Avinguda Diagonal (ⓂEl Maresme Forùm, or tram T4), with several new five-star hotels, convention centres and exhibition halls grouped nearby. The dazzling **Edifici Forùm** building, hovering – seemingly unsupported – above the ground, is the work of Jacques Herzog, architect of London's Tate Modern, while the main open space is the second-largest square in the world (150,000 square metres) after Beijing's Tiananmen Square. In summer, temporary bars, dancefloors, open-air cinema and chill-out zones are established at the **Parc del Forùm**, and the city authorities have shifted many of the bigger annual music festivals and events down here to inject a bit of life outside conventions.

Montjuïc

Rising over the city to the southwest, the steep hill of **Montjuïc** took its name from the Jewish community that once settled on its slopes, and there's been a castle on the heights since the mid-seventeenth century, which says much about the hill's obvious historical defensive role. Since the erection of buildings for the

International Exhibition of 1929, however, Montjuïc's prime role has been cultural, and you could easily spend a day or two at its varied attractions, which include six museums and galleries, various landscaped gardens and the famous Poble Espanyol, quite apart from the buildings and stadiums associated with the 1992 Olympics. For those short on time, the Museu Nacional d'Art de Catalunya (MNAC) is undoubtedly the highlight, though Miró fans will not want to miss the Fundació Joan Miró.

Plaça d'Espanya and around

From **Plaça d'Espanya**, past the square's 47-metre-high twin towers, you can either make the stiff climb on foot, or take the long outdoor escalators. On either side of the avenue and terraces are various exhibition buildings from 1929, still in use as venues for the city's trade fairs, while the central position in front of the Palau Nacional is given over to the illuminated fountains, the **Font Mágica**, which form part of a spectacular sound and light show on selected evenings (May–Sept Thurs–Sun 8–11.30pm, music starts 9.30pm; Oct–April Fri & Sat 7pm, 7.30pm, 8pm & 8.30pm; free).

To the right of the fountain (before climbing the steps/escalators), and hidden from view until you turn the corner around Avinguda del Marquès de Comillas, is **Caixa Forum** (Mon–Fri & Sun 10am–8pm, Sat 10am–10pm; free; ⓦ www.fundacio.lacaixa.es), a terrific arts and cultural centre set within

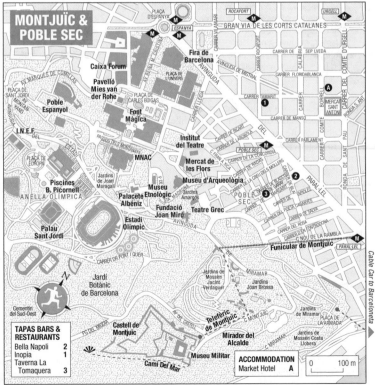

Getting there

- The **metro** (ⓂEspanya) deposits you at the foot of Avinguda de la Reina Maria Cristina, for easy access to Caixa Forum, Poble Espanyol and MNAC. The Olympic area can then be reached by escalators behind MNAC.
- The **Funicular de Montjuïc** (April–Sept Mon–Fri 7.30am–8/10pm, Sat, Sun & public hols from 9am; every 10min; normal city transport tickets and passes valid) departs from inside the station at ⓂParal.lel. At the upper station on Avinguda de Miramar you can switch to the Telefèric de Montjuïc or bus services (see below), or you're only a few minutes' walk from the Fundació Joan Miró.
- The **cross-harbour cable car** (see box, p.687) from Barceloneta drops you outside the Jardins de Miramar, on the far southeastern slopes. From here, it's a ten-minute walk to the Telefèric de Montjuïc and funicular station and another five to the Fundació Joan Miró.

Getting around

- **Bus Montjuïc Turístic** (open-top bus service; daily Easter week & last week June to first week Sept, otherwise weekends and holidays only; departures every 40min, 10am–9.20pm; €3). There are two routes, one starting at Pl. d'Espanya (ⓂEspanya), the other at the foot of the Ramblas at Pl. Portal de la Pau (ⓂDrassanes). The service covers every major sight on the hill, with several connecting stops, so you can switch routes, and the ticket lets you get on and off at will. The other bus service is the city bus designated "**PM**" (ie Parc de Montjuïc; city transport tickets and passes valid), covering much the same route. There are bus stops outside the upper station of the Funicular de Montjuïc.
- **Telefèric de Montjuïc** The Montjuïc cable car (daily service: April, May & Oct 10am–7pm, June–Sept 10am–9pm, Nov–March 10am–6pm; €5.70 one way, €7.90 return; ⓦwww.tmb.net), from Avinguda de Miramar, whisks you up to the castle and back in automated eight-seater gondolas.

the old Casamarona textile factory (1911). The centre houses the Fundació La Caixa's celebrated contemporary art collection, focusing on the period from the 1980s to the present, with hundreds of artists represented, from Antoni Abad to Rachel Whiteread. Works are shown in partial rotation, along with temporary exhibitions. The café is a pleasant spot in an airy converted space within the old factory walls.

Immediately across from the Caixa Forum, set back from the road, the 1986 reconstruction by Catalan architects of the iconic **Pavelló Mies van der Rohe** (daily 10am–8pm; guided visits Wed & Fri 5–7pm; €4; ⓦwww.miesbcn.com) recalls part of the German contribution to the 1929 exhibition. Originally designed by Mies van der Rohe, the pavilion has a startlingly beautiful conjunction of hard straight lines with watery surfaces, its dark-green polished onyx alternating with shining glass.

Museu Nacional d'Art de Catalunya (MNAC)

The towering Palau Nacional, centrepiece of Barcelona's 1929 International Exhibition, was due to be demolished once the exhibition was over, but gained a reprieve and five years later became home to one of Spain's great museums, the **Museu Nacional d'Art de Catalunya** (MNAC; Tues–Sat 10am–7pm, Sun & public hols 10am–2.30pm; €8.50, ticket valid 48hr, first Sun of the month free; combined ticket with Poble Espanyol €12; ⓦwww.mnac.cat). This is by far the best art museum in Barcelona, showcasing a thousand years of

Catalan art in stupendous surroundings. The collection of Romanesque frescoes in particular is the museum's pride and joy, while MNAC also has impressive holdings of European Renaissance and Baroque art, as well as an unsurpassed collection of "modern" (ie nineteenth- and twentieth-century) Catalan art up until the 1940s – everything from the 1950s and later is covered by MACBA. In addition, temporary blockbuster exhibitions (separate admission charge) change every two to four months.

The **Romanesque** collection is the best of its kind in the world. From the eleventh century, the Catalan villagers of the high Pyrenees built sturdy stone churches, which were then lavishly painted in vibrantly coloured frescoes. To save them from robbery and degradation, these were painstakingly removed early in the twentieth century and remounted in mock church interiors within the museum. The frescoes, still luminescent after eight hundred years, have a vibrant, raw quality, best exemplified by those taken from churches in the Boí valley in the Catalan Pyrenees – such as the work of the anonymous "Master of Taüll" on the churches of Sant Climent and Santa Maria; look out for details such as the leper, to the left of the Sant Climent altar, patiently suffering a dog to lick his sores.

The **Gothic** collection is also extensive, ranging over the whole of Spain – particularly good on Catalunya, Valencia and Aragón – and again, laid out chronologically, from the thirteenth to the fifteenth century. The evolution from the Romanesque to the Gothic period was marked by a move from mural painting to painting on wood, and by the depiction of more naturalistic figures showing the lives (and rather gruesome deaths) of the saints and, later, portraits of kings and patrons of the arts.

In the **Renaissance** and **Baroque** sections, major European artists from the fifteenth to eighteenth centuries are represented. There are works by (among others) Peter Paul Rubens, Jean Honoré Fragonard, Francisco de Goya, El Greco, Francisco de Zurbarán and Diego Velázquez, though the museum is, of course, keen to play up Catalan artists of the period, who largely absorbed the prevailing European influences – thus Barcelona artist Antoni Viladomat (1678–1755), whose twenty paintings of St Francis, executed for a monastery, are shown here in their entirety.

MNAC ends on a high note with its **modern Catalan art** collection, which is particularly good on *modernista* and *noucentista* painting and sculpture, the two dominant schools of the nineteenth and early twentieth centuries. Rooms highlight individual artists and genres, shedding light on the development of art in an exciting period of Catalunya's history, while there are fascinating diversions into *modernista* interior design (with some pieces by Gaudí), avant-garde sculpture and historical photography.

Museu Etnològic and Museu d'Arqueològia de Catalunya

Downhill from MNAC, the **Museu Etnològic** (June–Sept Tues–Sat noon–8pm, Sun 11am–3pm; Oct–May Tues & Thurs 10am–7pm, Wed & Fri–Sun 10am–2pm; €3.50, first Sun of month free; @www.museuetnologic.bcn.cat) boasts extensive cultural collections from across the globe. The museum concentrates on rotating exhibitions, which usually last for a year or two and focus on a particular subject or geographical area. Refreshingly, Spain and its regions aren't neglected, which means that there's usually also a focus on the minutiae of rural Spanish life and work, or an examination of subjects such as medieval carving or early industrialization.

Lower down the hill is the important **Museu d'Arqueològia de Catalunya** (Tues–Sat 9.30am–7pm, Sun & public hols 10am–2.30pm; €3;

@www.mac.cat), whose collection spans the centuries from the Stone Age to the Visigoths. The Second Punic War (218–201 BC) saw the Carthaginians expelled from Iberia by the Romans, who made their provincial capital at Tarragona (Tarraco), with a secondary outpost at Barcelona (Barcino). An upper floor interprets life in Barcino itself through a collection of tombstones, statues, inscriptions and friezes. Some of the stonework is remarkably vivid, depicting the faces of some of Barcino's inhabitants as clearly as the day they were carved.

Poble Espanyol

A five-minute walk over to the western side of MNAC brings you to the **Poble Espanyol**, or "Spanish Village" (Mon 9am–8pm, Tues–Thurs 9am–2am, Fri 9am–4am, Sat 9am–5am, Sun 9am–midnight; €8, night ticket €5, combined ticket with MNAC €12; @www.poble-espanyol.com). This was designed for the International Exhibition, and its streets and squares consist of famous or characteristic buildings from all over the country. "Get to know Spain in one hour" is what's promised – and it's nowhere near as cheesy as you might think. As a crash-course introduction to Spanish architecture it's not at all bad: everything is well labelled and at least reasonably accurate. The echoing main square is lined with cafés, while the streets, alleys and buildings off here contain around forty workshops where you can see engraving, weaving, pottery and other crafts. Get to the Village as it opens if you want to enjoy it in relatively crowd-free circumstances – once the tour groups arrive, it becomes a bit of a scrum.

Fundació Joan Miró

Montjuïc's highlight for many is the **Fundació Joan Miró** (Tues–Sat 10am–7pm, July–Sept until 8pm, Thurs until 9.30pm, Sun & public hols 10am–2.30pm; €8, exhibitions €4, price includes audio-guide; @www.fundaciomiro-bcn.org), possibly Barcelona's most adventurous art museum, opened in 1975 and set among gardens overlooking the city. Joan Miró (1893–1983) was one of the greatest of Catalan artists, establishing an international reputation while never severing his links with his homeland. He had his first exhibition in 1918, and after

---

The Olympics on Montjuïc

The main road through Montjuïc climbs around the hill and up to the city's principal Olympic area, centred on the **Estadi Olímpic**. Built originally for the 1929 exhibition, the stadium was completely refitted to accommodate the 1992 opening and closing ceremonies, while to one side a vast *terraza* provides one of the finest vantage points in the city. Long water-fed troughs break the concrete and marble expanse, while the confident, space-age curve of Santiago Calatrava's **communications tower** dominates the skyline. Around the other side, just across the road from the stadium, the history of the Games themselves – and Barcelona's successful hosting – are covered in the **Museu Olímpic i de l'Esport**, Avgda. de l'Estadi 21 (Mon & Wed–Sat 10am–6pm, Sun & public hols 10am–2.30pm; €4; @www.fundaciobarcelonaolimpica.es).

The 1992 Olympics were the second planned for Montjuïc's stadium. The first, in 1936 – the so-called "**People's Olympics**" – were organized as an alternative to the Nazis' infamous Berlin Games of that year, but the day before the official opening Franco's army revolt triggered the Civil War and scuppered the Barcelona Games. Some of the 25,000 athletes and spectators who had turned up stayed on to join the Republican forces.

▲ Fundació Joan Miró

that spent his summers in Catalunya (and the rest of the time in France) before moving to Mallorca in 1956, where he died. His friend, the architect Josep-Luís Sert, designed the beautiful building that now houses the museum, a permanent collection of paintings, graphics, tapestries and sculptures donated by Miró himself and covering the period from 1914 to 1978.

The paintings and drawings, regarded as one of the chief links between Surrealism and abstract art, are instantly recognizable. For a rapid appraisal of Miró's entire *oeuvre*, look in on the museum's **Sala K**, whose 23 works are on long-term loan from a Japanese collector. Here, in a kind of potted retrospective, you can trace Miró's development as an artist, from his early Impressionist landscapes (1914) to the minimal renderings of the 1970s. Other exhibits include his enormous bright tapestries (he donated nine to the museum), pencil drawings and sculpture outside in the gardens. Young experimental artists have their own space in the **Espai 13** gallery. There's also a bookshop selling posters, and a café-restaurant (lunch 1.30–3pm, otherwise drinks, pastries and sandwiches) with outdoor tables on a sunny patio – you don't have to pay to get into the museum to use this.

Castell de Montjuïc and around

A few minutes' walk east of the Fundació Joan Miró, the Telefèric de Montjuïc tacks up the hillside, offering magnificent views on the way, before depositing you within the walls of the eighteenth-century **Castell de Montjuïc**. The fort served as a military base and prison for many years after the Civil War, and it was here that the last president of the prewar Generalitat, Lluís Companys, was executed on Franco's orders on October 15, 1940.

You are free to take a walk along the ramparts, and there's a little outdoor café within the walls. You have to pay to go inside the inner keep, where there's a splendid *mirador* and rather more dull **Museu Militar** (April–Oct Tues–Sun 9.30am–8pm; Nov–March Tues–Fri 9.30am–5/6pm, Sat & Sun until 7/8pm; €3, mirador only €1; ⓦwww.museomilitarmontjuic.es), which presents endless swords, guns, medals, uniforms, armour and model castles in a series of rooms around the parade ground and down on the lower level of the bastion. The fortress is army (and therefore state) property and its museum has long been considered an anachronism by the city. However, the Spanish government recently decided to hand the fortress over to the city and it will eventually be converted into a Peace Museum.

Below the castle walls, a panoramic pathway – the **Camí del Mar** – has been cut from the cliff edge, providing scintillating views. The path is just over 1km long and ends at the back of the castle battlements near the **Mirador del Migdia**, where there's a great open-air chill-out bar, *La Caseta del Migdia* (weekends all year from 10 or 11am, plus summer weekend DJ nights; Ⓦwww.lacaseta.org).

Montjuïc's main gardens are scattered across the southern and eastern reaches of the hill, below the castle. Principal among them is the **Jardí Botànic de Barcelona**, on c/Dr Font i Quer, on the slopes behind the Olympic stadium (daily: Feb, March & Oct 10am–6pm; April, May & Sept 10am–7pm; June–Aug 10am–8pm; Nov–Jan 10am–5pm; €3.50, free last Sun of month; Ⓦwww .jardibotanic.bcn.cat) – the Montjuïc buses run here directly, or the entrance is just a five-minute walk around the back of the Estadi Olympic.

The Eixample

As Barcelona grew more prosperous throughout the nineteenth century, it was clear that the city had to expand beyond the Barri Gòtic. A contest was held to design the city's new quarters and the winning plan was that of the engineer Ildefons Cerdà i Sunyer, who drew up a grid-shaped new town marching off to the north, intersected by long, straight streets and cut by broad, angled avenues. Work started in 1859 on what became known as the *Ensanche* in Spanish – in Catalan, the **Eixample**, or "Extension". It immediately became the fashionable area in which to live, and the moneyed classes moved from their cramped quarters by the old port to luxurious apartments on the wide new avenues. As the money in the city moved north, so did a new class of *modernista* architects who began to pepper the Eixample with ever more striking examples of their work. The buildings – most notably the work of **Antoni Gaudí**, **Lluís Domènech i Montaner** and **Josep Puig i Cadafalch**, but others, too (see box opposite) – have effectively turned the Eixample into a huge urban museum around which it's a pleasure to wander.

The Eixample is still the city's main shopping and business district, spreading out on either side of the two principal (and parallel) thoroughfares, **Passeig de Gràcia** and **Rambla de Catalunya**. The best-known *modernista* buildings are those in the famous block known as the **Mansana de la Discòrdia** and Gaudí's **La Pedrera** apartment building, found on Passeig de Gràcia. Almost everything else you're likely to want to see is found to the east of here, in the area known as **Dreta de l'Eixample** (the right-hand side), including Gaudí's extraordinary **Sagrada Família** church – the one building in the city to which a visit is virtually obligatory. Other museums in the *Dreta* are devoted to Egyptian antiquities, and Catalan art and ceramics, with a special draw provided by the gallery dedicated to the works of Catalan artist **Antoni Tàpies**. A few blocks southeast of the Sagrada Família, Barcelona's major avenues all meet at the swirling roundabout of **Glòries**, where a further set of cultural and archi-tectural attractions awaits. There's less to get excited about on the left-hand side of Rambla de Catalunya – the so-called **Esquerra de l'Eixample**. This was intended by its nineteenth-century planners for public buildings, institutions and industrial concerns, many of which still stand, though it's the few contem-porary urban parks between Sants station and Plaça d'Espanya that are the only appeal for tourists.

Modernisme

Modernisme, the Catalan offshoot of Art Nouveau, was the expression of a renewed upsurge in Catalan nationalism in the 1870s. The early nineteenth-century economic recovery in Catalunya had provided the initial impetus, and the ensuing cultural renaissance in the region – the Renaixença – led to the fresh stirrings of a new Catalan awareness and identity.

Lluís Domènech i Montaner (1850–1923) – perhaps the greatest *modernista* architect – was responsible for giving Catalan aspirations a definite direction with his appeal, in 1878, for a national style of architecture, drawing particularly on the rich Catalan Romanesque and Gothic traditions. The timing was perfect, since Barcelona was undergoing a huge expansion, with plenty of new space to work in. By 1874, **Antoni Gaudí i Cornet** (1852–1926) had begun his architectural career. He was born in Reus (near Tarragona; see p.820) to a family of artisans, and his work was never strictly *modernista* in style, but the imaginative impetus he gave the movement was incalculable. Fourteen years later, the young **Josep Puig i Cadafalch** (1867–1957) would be inspired to become an architect as he watched the spectacularly rapid round-the-clock construction of Domènech's *Grand Hotel* on the Passeig de Colom. It was in another building by Domènech (the café-restaurant of the Parc de la Ciutadella) that a craft workshop was set up after the exhibition of 1888, giving Barcelona's *modernista* architects the opportunity to experiment with traditional crafts such as ceramic tiles, ironwork, stained glass and decorative stone carving. This combination of traditional crafts with modern technology was to become the hallmark of *modernisme* – a combination that produced some of the most fantastic and exciting architecture to be found anywhere in the world.

The three architects mentioned above provide the bulk of the most extraordinary buildings that Barcelona has to offer. But keep an eye out for lesser-known architects who also worked in the Eixample, such as **Josep María Jujol i Gilbert** (1879–1949), renowned as Gaudí's collaborator on several of his most famous projects (including the mosaics at Parc Güell), the hard-working **Jeroni Granell i Barrera** (1867–1931), and **Josep Vilaseca i Casanoves** (1848–1910), who was responsible for the brick Arc de Triomf outside the Parc de la Ciutadella. **Josep Domènech i Estapa** (1858–1917) became Barcelona's main institutional architect, providing buildings as diverse as the prison and observatory.

It's **Gaudí**, though, of whom most have heard – by training, a metalworker; by inclination, a fervent Catalan nationalist and devout Catholic. His buildings are the most daring creations of all Art Nouveau, apparently lunatic flights of fantasy that, at the same time, are perfectly functional. His architectural influences were Moorish and Gothic, while he embellished his work with elements from the natural world. Yet Gaudí rarely wrote a word about the theory of his art, preferring its products to speak for themselves.

Mansana de la Discòrdia

The most famous grouping of buildings, the so-called **Mansana de la Discòrdia** or Block of Discord, is just four blocks up from Plaça de Catalunya (ⓂPasseig de Gràcia). It gets its name because the adjacent buildings – built by three different architects – are completely different in style and feel.

On the corner of c/de Consell de Cent, at Pg. de Gràcia 35, the six-storey **Casa Lleó Morera** is by Domènech i Montaner, completed in 1906. It's the least extravagant of the buildings in the block, and far more striking is Puig i Cadafalch's **Casa Amatller** (1900), a few doors up at no. 41. The facade is studded with coloured ceramic decoration, while inside the hallway, twisted stone columns are interspersed by dragon lamps, all further illuminated by fine stained-glass doors and an interior glass roof. It was built for Antoni

EIXAMPLE

Camp Nou Stadium

TRAVESSERA DE LES CORTS
AVINGUDA DE SARRIA
PLAÇA FRANCESC MACIA
TRAVESSERA
AVINGUDA DIAGONAL
CARRER DEL MARQUES DE SENTMENAT
CARRER DE LLEUDIADOR
CARRER D'ENTENÇA
CARRER DE BUENOS AIRES
CARRER DEL VALLESPIR
CARRER DE NUMANCIA
CARRER DE JOSEP TARRADELLAS
CARRER DE LONDRES
CARRER COMTE D'URGELL
Museu Centre de l'Esport
CARRER DE BERLIN
PLAÇA DEL CENTRE
Casa Sayrach
CARRER   DE PARIS
C DE ROBRENYO
C DE MELCIOR DE PALAU
CARRER DE VILADOMAT
CARRER CASANOVA
CARRER DE MUNTANER
CARRER D'ARIBAU
CARRER DE ENRIC GRANADOS
CARRER DE CORSEGA
ENTENÇA
HOSPITAL CLINIC
Barcelona Sants
SANTS-ESTACIO
CARRER DEL ROSSELLO
Escola Industrial
PLAÇA PAÏSOS CATALANS
CARRER DE PROVENÇA
CARRER DE MALLORCA
Hospital Clinic
CARRER DE PROVENÇA
Parc de l'Espanya Industrial
C DE MALLORCA
C DE L'ELISI
TARRAGONA
C DE LLANÇA
CARRER D'ENTENÇA
CARRER DE ROCAFORT
CARRER DE CALABRIA
CARRER DE MALLORCA
ESQUERRA DE L'EIXAMPLE
CARRER DE VALENCIA
C DE VALENCIA
AVINGUDA DE ROMA
C DEL RECTOR TRIADO
C DE SANT NICOLAU
HOSTAFRANCS
C DE C. CENT
CARRER D'ARAGO
PLAÇA DE DOCTOR LEFAMEND
Parc Joan Miró
CARRER DE CONSELL DE CENT
CARRER DE LA DIPUTACIO
CARRER COMTE D'URGELL
CARRER DE VILLARROEL
CARRER CASANOVA
CARRER DE MUNTANER
CARRER D'ARIBAU
CREU COBERTA
Les Arenes
PLAÇA D'ESPANYA
ROCAFORT
GRAN VIA DE   LES CORTS CATALANES
URGELL
Universitat de Barcelona
PLAÇA DE LA UNIVERSITAT
ESPANYA
AVINGUDA DE LA REINA MARIA CRISTINA
AVINGUDA PARAL·LEL
CARRER D'ENTENÇA
CARRER DE ROCAFORT
CARRER DE CALABRIA
CARRER DE VILADOMAT
CARRER DEL COMTE BORRELL
CARRER DE SUPULVEDA
UNIVERSITAT
CARRER DE FLORIDABLANCA
RONDA SANT ANTONI
CARRER VALLDONZELLA

Amatller, a Catalan chocolate manufacturer, art collector, photographer and traveller, and there are **guided tours** of the house (Mon–Fri at 11am, noon, 5pm & 6pm, plus Sun at noon; €8; reservations at the house or call ☎934 877 217, ⓦwww.amatller.org), which include a visit to Amatller's photographic studio and chocolate-tasting in the original kitchen.

Perhaps the most extraordinary creation on the Block of Discord is next door, at no. 43, the **Casa Batlló** (daily 9am–8pm, access occasionally restricted; €16.50; ⓦwww.casabatllo.cat; advance sales also from TelEntrada ☎902 101 212, ⓦwww.telentrada.com) – designed for the industrialist Josep Batlló – whose original construction was considered dull by contemporaries. Antoni Gaudí was hired to give it a face-lift and contrived to create a facade that Dalí later compared to "the tranquil waters of a lake". **Self-guided audio tours** show you the main floor, the patio and rear facade, the ribbed attic and the celebrated mosaic roof-top chimneys. It's best to reserve a ticket in advance, as – despite the steep entrance fee – this is a very popular attraction.

ACCOMMODATION

Alternative Creative Youth Home	N	Expo Barcelona	G
Australia	M	Girona	O
Axel	I	Goya	P
Casa Fuster	B	HMB	C
Centric Point	J	Inglaterra	R
Condes de Barcelona	E	Omm	D
Confort	A	Prestige	H
D'Uxelles	L	San Remo	Q
Eurostars Gaudí	K	the5Rooms	P
		Torre Catalunya	F

TAPAS BARS & RESTAURANTS

Alkimia	1	Gaig	4
Cerveseria Catalana	3	TapaÇ24	6
Ciudad Condal	7	Tragaluz	2
La Flauta	5		

Fundació Antoni Tàpies

Turn the corner onto c/d'Aragó and at no. 255 you'll find Domènech i Montaner's first important building, the Casa Montaner i Simon (1880). The building originally served the publishing firm after which it was named, but was converted in 1990 to house the **Fundació Antoni Tàpies** (Tues–Sun 10am–8pm; €6; Ⓦ www.fundaciotapies.org; Ⓜ Passeig de Gràcia).

It's a beautiful building dedicated to all aspects of the life and work of Catalunya's most eminent postwar artist. Tàpies was born in the city in 1923 and was a founding member (1948) of the influential Dau al Set ("Die at Seven"), an avant-garde grouping of seven artists. He was interested in collage (using newspaper, cardboard, silver wrapping, string and wire) and engraving techniques from an early age, and later developed an abstract style that matured during the 1950s. His large works are deceptively simple, though underlying messages and themes are signalled by the inclusion of everyday objects, unusual materials and symbols on the canvas. Tàpies' work is not immediately accessible (in the way of, say, Miró), and you're either going to love or hate the gallery:

697

temporary exhibitions focus on selections of his work from every period, while three or four exhibitions a year highlight works and installations by other contemporary artists.

Museu Egipci de Barcelona

Half a block east of Passeig de Gràcia, the **Museu Egipci de Barcelona** at c/de València 284 (Mon–Sat 10am–8pm, Sun 10am–2pm; €7; Ⓦwww .museuegipci.com; ⓂPasseig de Gràcia) is an exceptional collection of artefacts from ancient Egypt, ranging from the earliest kingdoms to the era of Cleopatra. The emphasis is on the shape and character of Egyptian society, and a serendipitous wander is a real pleasure, turning up items such as a wood and leather bed of the First and Second Dynasties (2920–2649 BC), some examples of cat mummies of the Late Period (715–332 BC) or a rare figurine of a spoonbill (ibis) representing an Egyptian god (though archeologists aren't yet sure which).

La Pedrera

Gaudí's weird apartment block at Passeig de Gràcia 92 (ⓂDiagonal) is simply not to be missed – though you can expect queues whenever you visit. Constructed as the Casa Milà between 1905 and 1911, and popularly known as **La Pedrera**, or the Stone Quarry, it was declared a UNESCO World Heritage Site in 1984. Its rippling facade, which curves around the street corner in one smooth sweep, is said to have been inspired by the mountain of Montserrat, and the apartments themselves, whose balconies of tangled metal drip over the facade, resemble eroded cave dwellings.

The **self-guided visit** (entrance on c/Provença; daily: March–Oct 9am–8pm; Nov–Feb 9am–6.30pm, closed 1 week Jan; Ⓦwww.lapedreraeducacio.org; €8) includes a trip up to the extraordinary roof terrace to see at close quarters the enigmatic chimneys, as well as an informative exhibition about Gaudí's work installed under the 270 curved brick arches of the attic. El Pis ("The Apartment") on the building's fourth floor recreates the design and style of a *modernista*-era bourgeois apartment in a series of rooms that flow seamlessly from one to another. Perhaps the best experience of all, however, is **La Pedrera de Nit** when you can enjoy the rooftop and night-time cityscape with a complimentary *cava* and music (late June & July Fri & Sat 9–11.30pm; €13) – advance booking is essential, either on the day in person at the ticket office or from TelEntrada (Ⓣ902 101 212, Ⓦwww.telentrada.com).

Casa Milà is still split into private apartments and is administered by the Fundació Caixa de Catalunya. Through the grand main entrance of the building you can access the Fundació's first-floor **exhibition hall** (daily 10am–8pm; free; also free guided visits Mon–Fri 6pm), which hosts temporary shows by major international artists.

Sagrada Família

The Eixample's most famous monument is, without question, Gaudí's great **Temple Expiatori de la Sagrada Família** (daily: April–Sept 9am–8pm; Oct–March 9am–6pm; €8, €11.50 including guided tour, audio guide €3.50; Ⓦwww.sagradafamilia.org; ⓂSagrada Família). It's an essential stop on any visit to Barcelona, for more than any building in the city it speaks volumes about the Catalan urge to glorify uniqueness and endeavour.

Begun in 1882 by public subscription, the Sagrada Família was originally intended as a modest, expiatory building that would atone for the city's increasingly revolutionary ideas. When Gaudí took charge, he changed the direction and scale of the project almost immediately, seeing in the Sagrada Família an opportunity to reflect his own deepening spiritual and nationalist feelings. Indeed, after he finished Parc Güell in 1911, Gaudí vowed to devote himself solely to the Sagrada Família, and he was adapting the plans ceaselessly right up to his death. He was run over by a tram on the Gran Vía in June 1926 and died in hospital two days later. His death was treated as a Catalan national disaster, and all of Barcelona turned out for his funeral procession.

Although the church survived the Civil War, Gaudí's plans and models were destroyed in 1936 by the anarchists. Nonetheless, work restarted in the late 1950s amid great controversy, and has continued ever since – as have the arguments. On balance, it's probably safe enough to assume that Gaudí saw the struggle to finish the building as at least as important as the method and style. However, the current work has attracted criticism for infringing Gaudí's original spirit, while tunnelling under the temple for the high-speed AVE train line has kicked up a huge stink among critics who claim that the church will be put at risk (not so, say the tunnel engineers). All in all, though the project might be drawing inexorably towards realization, no one is yet prepared to put forward a definite completion date, leaving plenty more time for argument.

The size alone is startling – Gaudí's original plan was to build a church capable of seating over 10,000 people. In particular, twelve extraordinary **spires** rise to over 100m. They have been likened to everything from perforated cigars to celestial billiard cues, but for Gaudí they symbolized the twelve Apostles. A precise symbolism also pervades the facades, each of which is divided into three porches devoted to Faith, Hope and Charity, and each uniquely sculpted. The eastern **Nativity facade** (facing c/de la Marina) was the first to be completed and is alive with fecund detail, its very columns resting on the backs of giant tortoises. Contrast this with the Cubist austerity of the western **Passion facade** (c/de Sardenya), where the brutal story of the Crucifixion is played out across the harsh mountain stone. Gaudí meant the south facade, the **Gloria**, to be the culmination of the Temple – designed (he said) to show "the religious realities of present and future life … man's origin, his end."

The reality is that the place is still a giant building site. However, for the first time a recognizable church interior is starting to take shape and the whole church will be roofed in due course. Extraordinary columns branch towards the spreading stone leaves of the roof, a favourite Gaudí motif inspired by the city's plane trees. **Elevators** (same hours as the church; €2) run up the towers of the Passion and Nativity facades, from where you'll be rewarded by partial views of the city through an extraordinary jumble of latticed stonework, ceramic decoration, carved buttresses and sculpture. Your entrance ticket also gives you access to the crypt, where a **museum** (same hours) traces the career of the architect and the history of the church. The 45-minute **guided tours** run hourly in season (May–Oct, in English at 11am, 1pm, 3pm & 5pm), mornings only the rest of the year, and you can book a place on the next one when you turn up.

Hospital de la Santa Creu i de Sant Pau

While you're in the neighbourhood, it would be a shame not to stroll the four blocks from the Sagrada Família to Lluís Domènech i Montaner's innovative **Hospital de la Santa Creu i de Sant Pau** (Ⓜ Hospital de Sant Pau), possibly the one building that can rival the church for size and invention. You are free to walk into the landscaped grounds, past the whimsical **pavilions** that make up the hospital interior. Craftsmen adorned every centimetre with sculpture, mosaics, stained glass and ironwork, while much of the actual business of running a hospital was hidden away in a series of underground corridors that connects the buildings together. Naturally, the *modernista* hospital buildings are now deemed to have served their purpose; behind them spreads the high-tech central block of the new hospital. The pavilions have instead been turned over to educational and cultural use (a Museum of Medicine is mooted), and include the **Centre del Modernisme** (daily 10am–2pm; Ⓦwww.rutadelmodernisme.com), where you can find out about and buy the city's Ruta del Modernisme sightseeing package. You can also sign up here for informative **guided tours** of the complex (daily at 10.15am & 12.15pm in English, plus others in Spanish/Catalan; €5), which can tell you more about the six-hundred-year history of the hospital.

Plaça de les Glòries Catalanes and around

Barcelona's major arterial routes all meet at the **Plaça de les Glòries Catalanes** (ⓂGlòries). For years, it's been no more than a swirling traffic roundabout, though current plans put Glòries at the heart of the city's latest wave of regeneration. By 2012, the roundabout traffic is to be tunnelled underground, thus opening up a grand pedestrianized park, which will contain a cultural and design centre. Glòries is already positioned as a gateway to the Diagonal Mar district, with trams running down Avinguda Diagonal to the Diagonal Mar shopping centre and Forùm site. Meanwhile, the signature building on the roundabout is Jean Nouvel's cigar-shaped **Torre Agbar** (142m), a highly distinctive aluminium and glass tower with no fewer than four thousand windows, housing the headquarters of the local water company. Nouvel also designed the new **Parc del Centre del Poble Nou** further down the Diagonal, an eye-catching contemporary park of giant ferns, herb gardens, sculptures and play areas set between carrers Bilbao, Bac de Roda and Marroc.

On the north side of Glòries, on c/Dos de Maig, the **Els Encants** flea market takes up the entire block below c/Consell de Cent (Mon, Wed, Fri & Sat 9am–6pm, plus Dec 1–Jan 5 Sun 9am–3pm; ⓂEncants/Glòries). Go in the morning to see it at its best – haggling is *de rigueur*, but you're up against experts.

Off to the southwest of Glòries lie the twin cultural pillars of the **Teatre Nacional de Catalunya** (see p.720) and **L'Auditori** (see p.718) contemporary city concert hall, the latter also housing the **Museu de la Música** (Mon & Wed–Fri 11am–9pm, Sat, Sun & public hols 10am–7pm; €4, first Sun of month free; Ⓦwww.museumusica.bcn.cat; ⓂGlòries/Marina), which displays a remarkable collection of instruments and musical devices, from seventeenth-century serpent horns to reel-to-reel cassette decks.

Meanwhile, the city's only surviving bullring, the **Plaza de Toros Monumental**, stands three blocks west of Glòries, at Gran Via de les Corts Catalanes 749 (ⓂMonumental). The city authorities are minded to ban bullfighting altogether, so its days are numbered – one possible future use may be as a new site for the flea market, which will be forced to move once reconstruction work at Glòries is in full swing.

Esquerra de l'Eixample

The most eye-catching parts of the Esquerra de l'Eixample lie just a short distance from the city's main train station, Barcelona Sants. Basque architect Luis Peña Ganchegui's **Parc de l'Espanya Industrial** (ⓂSants Estació) lies just two-minutes' walk away, around the southern side of the station. Built on the site of an old textile factory, it has a line of red and yellow-striped lighthouses at the top of glaring white steps, with an incongruously classical Neptune in the water below.

To the south, down c/de Tarragona, **Parc Joan Miró** (ⓂTarragona) was laid out on the site of the nineteenth-century municipal slaughterhouse. It features a raised piazza whose main feature is Joan Miró's gigantic mosaic sculpture *Dona i Ocell* (*Woman and Bird*), towering above a shallow reflecting pool. The rear of the park is given over to games areas and landscaped sections of palms and firs, with a kiosk café and some outdoor tables found in amongst the trees.

The former **Les Arenes** bullring (ⓂEspanya) backing on to Parc Joan Miró is undergoing a massive Richard Rogers-inspired refit, to convert it into a leisure and retail complex with enormous roof terrace, while retaining the Moorish facade of 1900. Also spared the wrecker's ball is the six-storey *modernista* **Casa Papallona** (1912), on the eastern side of Les Arenes on c/de Llança. It's one of the city's favourite house facades, crowned by a huge ceramic butterfly.

Gràcia

Beginning at the top of the Passeig de Gràcia, and bordered roughly by c/de Balmes to the west and the streets above the Sagrada Família to the east, **Gràcia** was once a separate village but has been a fully fledged suburb of the city since the late nineteenth century. Actual sights are few, but wander the narrow,

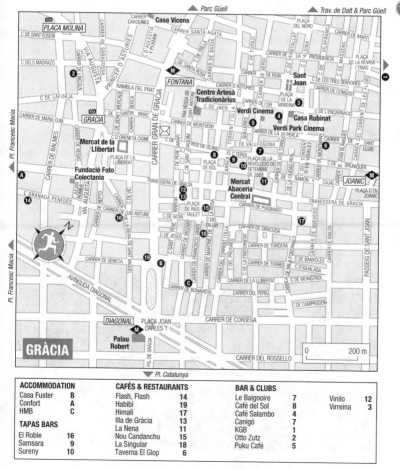

gridded streets, catch a film or hit one of the excellent local bars or restaurants, and you'll soon get the feel of a neighbourhood that – unlike some in Barcelona – still has a soul. **Getting there** by public transport means taking the FGC train from Plaça de Catalunya to Gràcia station, or the metro to either Diagonal, to the south, or Fontana, to the north.

Pretty **Plaça de la Virreina**, backed by its much-restored parish church of Sant Joan, is one of Gràcia's favourite squares, with the *Virreina Bar* and others providing drinks and a place to rest. In the streets around here, between carrers Torrijos and Verdi, are most of the neighbourhood's boutiques, galleries, cinemas and cafés, with c/Verdi in particular always worth a stroll. A short walk to the southwest, **Plaça del Sol** is the beating heart of much of the district's nightlife, while **Plaça Rius i Taulet**, the "clock-tower square", a couple of minutes to the south across Travessera de Gràcia, is another popular place to meet for brunch. Also, don't miss the market, the **Mercat de la Libertat**, Plaça de la Libertat, a block west of c/Gran de Gràcia, its food stalls sheltered by a *modernista* wrought-iron roof. It's been under restoration, but is due to have reopened by 2009.

Parc Güell

From 1900 to 1914, Gaudí worked for Eusebio Güell – patron of his Palau Güell, off the Ramblas – on the **Parc Güell**, on the outskirts of Gràcia (daily: May–Aug 10am–9pm; Sept & April 10am–8pm; Oct & March 10am–7pm; Nov–Feb 10am–6pm; free). This was Gaudí's most ambitious project after the Sagrada Família, commissioned as a private housing estate of sixty dwellings and furnished with paths, recreational areas and decorative monuments. In the end, only two houses were actually built, and the park was opened to the public instead in 1922.

Laid out on a hill, which provides fabulous views back across the city, the park is an almost hallucinatory expression of the imagination. Pavilions of contorted stone, giant decorative lizards, a vast Hall of Columns (intended to be the estate's

▲ Parc Güell

market), the meanderings of a huge ceramic bench – all combine in one manic swirl of ideas and excesses.

At the main entrance on c/Olot, the former porter's lodge is now the **Centre d'Interpretació** (Tues–Sun 11am–3pm; €2.30, combined ticket with Museu d'Història de la Ciutat €6; Ⓦwww.museuhistoria.bcn.cat), offering a rather perfunctory introduction to the park's history, design and building methods used. Far better is the **Casa Museu Gaudí** (daily: April–Sept 10am–8pm; Oct–March 10am–6pm; €4; Ⓦwww.casamuseugaudi.org), which maintains Gaudí's ascetic study and bedroom much as they were in his day, while other rooms display a diverting collection of furniture he designed, as well as plans and objects relating to the park and to Gaudí's life.

To get to the park, take **bus** #24 from Plaça de Catalunya to the eastern side gate, by the car park; or the **metro** to Vallcarca, from where you walk down Avinguda de l'Hospital until you see the escalators on your left, then follow these (and the short sections of path in between) to the western park entrance (15min). **Walking from Gràcia** (and ⓂLesseps), turn right onto the Travessera de Dalt and follow the signs up steep c/Larrard, which leads straight to the main entrance of the park on c/Olot (10min).

Camp Nou and FC Barcelona

Northwest of the centre, within the city's Les Corts area (behind the university buildings), the magnificent **Camp Nou** football stadium of **FC Barcelona** will be high on the visiting list of any sports fan. "More than just a club" is the proud boast, and certainly during the dictatorship years the club stood as a Catalan symbol around which people could rally – arch-rivals, Real Madrid, on the other hand, were always seen as Franco's club. The stadium was built in 1957, and enlarged to accommodate the 1982 World Cup semi-final, and now seats a staggering 98,000 people in steep tiers that provide one of the best football-watching experiences in the world. However, recent seasons have been testing for the fans, to say the least. Having finally wrestled the initiative back from the "Galacticos" of Real Madrid, winning La Liga in 2005 and 2006, and the European Champions League in 2006, Barça imploded. The team lost ground again to Real, who won the league in both 2007 and 2008, and Barça have turned to former player and all-Catalan hero, Pep Guardiola, to turn the tide as their new coach.

The Camp Nou is only really full for big games against the top Spanish teams and for major European ties. For all other games, some **tickets** are put on general sale a week before each match (and may be available at ticket booths on the day, Ⓣ934 963 600, Ⓦwww.fcbarcelona.com, or from other ticket agencies). For a typical league game at Barcelona, you're likely to pay €30–50 (and be seated *very* high up). If you can't get to a game, a visit to the stadium's **Museu del Futbol** (April–Oct Mon–Sat 10am–8pm, rest of year until 6.30pm, Sun 10am–3pm; museum only €8.50, including tour €13) is hardly second best, since it's a splendid celebration of Spain's national sport. The entrance is on Avinguda Arístides Maillol, through Gates (*Accés*) 7 and 9 (ⓂCollblanc/Maria Cristina, then 10min walk). The all-inclusive ticket allows you on the **self-guided tour**, winding through the bowels of the stadium, through the changing rooms, out onto the pitchside and up to the press gallery and directors' box for stunning views. The **museum** is jammed full of silverware and memorabilia, while photograph displays trace the history of the club back to 1901. Finally, you're directed into the **FC Botiga Megastore**, where you can buy anything from a replica shirt down to a branded bottle of wine.

Palau Reial de Pedralbes and the Pavellons Güell

Opposite the university on Avinguda Diagonal, the **Palau Reial de Pedralbes** (ⓂPalau Reial) is an Italianate palace set in formal grounds. Since 1990, the city has used its rooms to show off its applied art collections, and until the projected Centre del Disseny (Design Centre) at Glòries is completed – which means for the foreseeable future – the palace contains separate **museums** of ceramics (ⓦwww.museuceramica.bcn.cat), decorative arts (ⓦwww.museuartsdecoratives.bcn.cat) and textiles and clothing (ⓦwww .museutextil.bcn.cat) – the latter collection moved here in 2008 from its long-time home in La Ribera. All the museums can be visited on the same ticket (all open Tues–Sat 10am–6pm, Sun & public hols 10am–3pm; combined ticket €4.20, free on first Sun of the month). The **gardens** (10am–dusk; free), meanwhile, are a calm oasis, where – hidden in a bamboo thicket, to the left-centre of the palace facade – is the "*Hercules fountain*" (1884), an early work by Gaudí.

From the palace, it's a fifteen-minute walk up Avinguda Pedralbes to the Monestir de Santa María de Pedralbes. Just a couple of minutes along the way, you'll pass the **Pavellons Güell** on your left. Built as a summer residence for the family of Gaudí's patron, Eusebi Güell, the gatehouse, gardens and entrance were designed by Gaudí at the same time as he was working on the family's Palau Güell in the old town. An extraordinary dragon-gate made of twisted iron snarls at passers-by, its razor-toothed jaws spread wide in a fearsome roar. During the week, you can't go any further than the gate, but it's well worth coinciding with the **guided visits** (Mon, Fri, Sat & Sun 10.15am & 12.15pm in English, plus 11.15am & 1.15pm in Spanish/Catalan; €5; ⓦwww.rutadelmodernisme.com), especially to see inside Gaudí's innovative stables, now used as a library by the university's historical architecture department.

Monestir de Santa María de Pedralbes

At the end of Avinguda Pedralbes, the Gothic **Monestir de Santa María de Pedralbes** (Tues–Sat 10am–2pm, June–Sept 10am–5pm, Sun & public hols 10am–3pm; combined ticket with Museu d'Història de la Ciutat €6, first Sun of the month free; ⓦwww.museuhistoria.bcn.cat) is reached up a cobbled street that passes through a small archway set back from the road. It's a twenty-minute walk from Palau Reial metro station, or ten minutes from FGC Reina Elisenda (frequent trains from Plaça de Catalunya). Alternatively, bus #22 from Plaça de Catalunya stops outside (30min ride).

Founded in 1326 for the nuns of the Order of St Clare, this is in effect a self-contained religious community, preserved on the outskirts of the city. Access is allowed to the historic parts of the complex, including the harmonious **cloisters**, which are built on three levels and adorned by the slenderest of columns. The preserved rooms opening off here give the clearest impression of early monastic life you're likely to see in Catalunya: there's a large refectory, chapterhouse, fully equipped kitchen and infirmary, while in the nuns' former dormitory is shown a selection of the rarer treasures. The adjacent **church** (usually 11am–1pm & 5–8pm) retains some of its original stained glass, while in the chancel, to the right of the altar, the foundation's sponsor, Elisenda de Montcada, wife of Jaume II, lies in a superb, carved marble tomb.

CosmoCaixa

A dramatic refurbishment in 2005 transformed the city's science museum into a must-see attraction – it's an easy place to spend a couple of hours, and can be seen on your way to or from Tibidabo. Partly housed in a converted *modernista* hospice, **CosmoCaixa** (Tues–Sun 10am–8pm; €3, first Sun of month free, children's activities €2, planetarium €2; ⓦ www.fundacio.lacaixa.es) retains the original building but has added a light-filled public concourse and a huge underground extension with four subterranean levels. The main exhibits are all down on the bottom floor, centred on the enormous open-plan Sala de la Matèria (Matter Room), where hands-on experiments and displays investigate life, the universe and everything, "from bacteria to Shakespeare". The two big draws here are the one hundred tonnes of "sliced" rock in the **Mur Geològic** (Geological Wall) and, best of all, the **Bosc Inundat** – nothing less than a thousand square metres of real Amazonian rainforest, complete with croc-filled mangroves, anacondas and giant catfish. There are also daily shows in the **planetarium** (Spanish and Catalan only, but worth experiencing), and a café-restaurant with outdoor seating beneath the restored hospital facade.

CosmoCaixa is at c/Teodor Roviralta 47–51, just below the city ring road, the Ronda del Dalt. The easiest way **to get there** is by FGC train from Plaça de Catalunya to Avinguda del Tibidabo station, and then walk up the avenue, turning left just before the ring road (10min) – or the Tramvia Blau (see p.706) or Bus Turístic can drop you close by.

Tibidabo

If the views from the Castell de Montjuïc are good, those from the 550-metre heights of **Mount Tibidabo** – which forms the northwestern boundary of the city – are legendary. On one of those mythical clear days you can see across to Montserrat and the Pyrenees. The very name is based on this view, taken from the Temptations of Christ in the wilderness, when Satan led him to a high place and offered him everything that could be seen: *Haec omnia tibi dabo si cadens adoraberis me* ("All these things will I give thee, if thou wilt fall down and worship me").

The views aside, many people make the trip for the rather wonderful **Parc d'Atraccions** (days and hours vary, but basically June–Sept & public hols Wed–Sun; rest of year weekends only; closed Jan & Feb; noon until 7–11pm depending on season; Skywalk ticket €11, full admission €24; ⓦ www .tibidabo.es), Barcelona's funfair, which has been thrilling the citizens for over a century. The self-styled "magic mountain" is a mix of traditional rides and a few more hi-tech attractions, laid out around several levels of the mountaintop. Some of the more famous attractions are grouped under the "Skywalk Promenade" ticket, including the aeroplane ride, a Barcelona institution that's been spinning since 1928. There are more amazing views if you climb the steps of the neighbouring church, the **Templo Expiatorio de España**, inside which a lift (daily 10am–2pm & 3–7pm; €2) deposits you just under the feet of Christ, from where the city, surrounding hills and sea shimmer in the distance.

Follow the road from the Tibidabo car park and it's only a few minutes' walk to Norman Foster's **Torre de Collserola** (Wed–Sun 11am–2.30pm & 3.30–7pm; July–Sept until 8pm; €5; ☎ 934 069 354, ⓦ www.torredecollserola.com), a soaring communications tower high above the tree line, with a glass lift that whisks you up ten floors (115m) for yet more stunning views – 70km, they claim, on a good day.

To get to Tibidabo, first take the **FGC train** (Tibidabo line 7) from the station at Plaça de Catalunya to Avinguda Tibidabo (the last stop). An antique tram service, the **Tramvia Blau** (mid-June to mid-Sept daily 10am–8pm; rest of year weekends & public hols, plus Christmas and Easter weeks 10am–6pm; departures every 15–30min; €2.60 one way, €3.90 return), then runs you up the hill to Plaça Doctor Andreu; out of season, there's a bus service instead during the week. By the tram and bus stop on Plaça Doctor Andreu there are several café-bars and restaurants, where you change to the **Funicular del Tibidabo**, with connections (every 15min) to Tibidabo at the top (operates when the Parc d'Attraccions is open; €3 return, reimbursed with park admission ticket). Alternatively, the **Tibibus** runs direct to Tibidabo from Plaça de Catalunya, outside El Corte Inglés (from 10.30am, every day the park is open; €2.50, reimbursed with park admission ticket).

Out of the city: Montserrat

The **mountain of Montserrat**, with its strangely shaped crags of rock, its monastery and ruined hermitage caves, stands just 40km northwest of Barcelona, off the road to Lleida. It's the most popular day-trip from the city, reached in around ninety minutes by train and then cable car or rack railway for a thrilling ride up to the monastery. Once there, you can visit the basilica and monastery buildings, and complete your day with a walk around the woods and crags, using the two funicular railways that depart from the monastery complex. Inevitably, monastery and mountain are ruthlessly exploited as a tourist trip from the city or the Costa Brava, while the main **pilgrimages** take place on April 27 and September 8, but don't be put off – the place itself is still magical and well worth a visit.

Monastery and mountain

Legends hang easily upon Montserrat. Fifty years after the birth of Christ, St Peter is said to have deposited an image of the Virgin carved by St Luke in one of the mountain caves. The so-called Black Virgin (*La Moreneta*) icon was subsequently lost in the early eighth century, after being hidden during the Muslim invasion, but reappeared in 880, accompanied by the customary visions and celestial music. A chapel was built to house it, superseded in 976 by a Benedictine monastery, set at an altitude of nearly 1000m. Miracles abounded and the Virgin of Montserrat soon became the chief cult image of Catalunya and a pilgrimage centre second in Spain only to Santiago de Compostela. Its fortunes declined in the nineteenth century, though in recent decades Montserrat's popularity has again become established; today, in addition to the tourists, tens of thousands of newly married couples come here to seek *La Moreneta's* blessing on their union.

Only the Renaissance **Basilica** (daily 7.30am–8pm; free) is open to the public. **La Moreneta** (access 8–10.30am & noon–6.30pm), blackened by the smoke of countless candles, stands above the high altar. The best time to visit the basilica is when Montserrat's world-famous **boys' choir** sings (Mon–Fri 1pm & 6.45pm, Sun noon & 6.45pm, though *not* during school holidays at Christmas/New Year and from late June to mid-Aug). Near the entrance to the basilica, the **Museu de Montserrat** (Mon–Fri 10am–5.45pm, Sat & Sun 9am–7pm; €6.50) presents a few archeological finds, as well as an art collection that boasts paintings by Caravaggio, El Greco, Tiepolo, Degas, Monet, Picasso and others. There's also the **Espai Audiovisual** (Mon–Fri 10am–5.45pm, Sat & Sun 9am–7pm; €2), which tells you something of the life of a Benedictine community.

Two separate **funiculars** run from points close to the cable-car station (daily 10am–6pm; weekends only in winter; departures every 20min). One drops to the path for **Santa Cova** (€2.70 return), a seventeenth-century chapel built where the icon is said to have been found originally. It's an easy walk there and back that takes less than an hour. The other funicular rises steeply to the hermitage of **Sant Joan** (€6.60 return, joint ticket for both funiculars €7.50), from where it's a tougher 45-minutes' walk to the **Sant Jeroni** hermitage, and another fifteen minutes to the Sant Jeroni summit (1236m).

Practicalities

To reach the Montserrat cable-car and rack-railway stations, take the **FGC train** (line R5, direction Manresa), which leaves from Plaça d'Espanya (ⓂEspanya) daily at hourly intervals from 8.36am. Get off at Montserrat Aeri (52min) for the connecting cable car, the **Aeri de Montserrat** (☎938 350 005, ⓦwww.aeridemontserrat.com) – you may have to queue for fifteen minutes or so, but then it's an exhilarating five-minute swoop up the sheer mountainside. The alternative approach is by cog-wheel mountain railway, the **Cremallera de Montserrat** (☎902 312 020, ⓦwww.cremalleradmontserrat.com), which departs from Monistrol de Montserrat (the next stop after Montserrat Aeri, another 4min); again, services connect with train arrivals from Barcelona, and take about twenty minutes to climb to the monastery.

A desk and information board at Plaça d'Espanya station details all the fare options. A **return ticket** from Barcelona costs €15 (either for train and cable car or train and *cremallera*), and there are also two combined tickets: the **Trans Montserrat** (€21), which includes the metro, train, cable car/*cremallera*, use of the two funiculars and entry to the audiovisual exhibit; and the **Tot Montserrat** (€35), which includes the same plus museum entry and a self-service cafeteria lunch. Both tickets are also available at the Plaça de Catalunya tourist office in Barcelona.

There's a **visitor centre** at Montserrat (daily 9am–5.45pm, July–Sept until 7pm; ☎938 777 701, ⓦwww.montserratvisita.com), where you can pick up maps of the complex and mountain. They can also advise you about the **accommodation** options, from camping to staying at the three-star hotel, but these are all overpriced, as are the **cafés and restaurants**; they are also all very busy at peak times. Best views are from the *Restaurant de Montserrat* (meals €25) in the cliff-edge building near the car park, though here and in the self-service restaurant (included in the Tot Montserrat ticket), one floor up, there's no *à la carte* choice – that is, you have to order a full meal – and the food can at best be described as adequate. There's also a self-service cafeteria near the upper cable-car station, a bar in the square further up, plus a patisserie and a supermarket – and there's a lot to be said for taking your own picnic and striking off up the mountainside.

Cafés, tapas bars and restaurants

Good cafés, tapas bars and restaurants are easily found all over the city, though you'll probably do most of your eating where you do most of your sightseeing. However, if you venture no farther than **the Ramblas**, or the streets around La Seu, you are not going to experience the best of the city's cuisine – in the main tourist areas, food and service can be indifferent and prices high. You need to be a bit more adventurous, and explore the backstreets of neighbourhoods such as **Sant Pere**, **La Ribera**, **El Raval** and **Poble Sec**, where you'll find excellent restaurants, some little more than hole-in-the-wall cafés or traditional taverns, others surprisingly funky and chic. In the **Eixample**, prices tend to be higher, though you'll find plenty of lunchtime bargains around; **Gràcia**, further out, is a pleasant place to spend the evening, with plenty of good mid-range restaurants. For fish and seafood, you're best off in the harbourside **Barceloneta** district or at the **Port Olímpic**.

Cafés, snacks and fast food

Many establishments are classics of their kind – century-old cafés or unique neighbourhood haunts – while others specialize in certain types of food and drink. A **forn** is a bakery, a **pastisseria** a cake and pastry shop, both often with cafés attached. A **xocolateria** specializes in chocolate, including the drinking kind. In a **granja** or **orxateria**, more like milk bars than regular cafés, you'll be able to sample traditional delights such as *orxata* (*horchata*, tiger-nut drink), ice cream, and *granissat* (*granizado*, a crushed ice drink flavoured with orange, lemon or coffee). Pizza, burger, felafel/kebab and cappuccino joints are ubiquitous, especially on the Ramblas and on the main streets in the Eixample.

All the places below are marked on the map on pp.674–675.

Antiga Casa Figueres Ramblas 83, El Raval; Ⓜ Liceu. Wonderful *modernista* pastry shop with a few tables outside. Mon–Sat 9am–3pm & 5–8.30pm.

Café d'Estiu Pl. de Sant Iu 5–6, Barri Gòtic; Ⓜ Jaume I. A summer-only café housed on the delightful interior terrace of the Museu Frederic Marès. April–Oct Tues–Sun 10am–10pm.

Granja M. Viader c/Xuclà 4–6, El Raval; Ⓜ Liceu. A traditional *granja* bar, tucked away down a narrow alley just off c/del Carmé. Mon 5–8.45pm, Tues–Sat 9am–1.45pm & 5–8.45pm; closed two weeks in Aug.

🏃 **Kasparo** Pl. Vicenç Martorell 4, El Raval; Ⓜ Catalunya. Sited in the arcaded corner of a quiet square off c/Bonsuccés. Sandwiches, tapas and assorted *platos del dia* are on offer – and there's also muesli, Greek yoghurt and toast and jam for early birds. Daily 9am–10pm, until midnight in summer; closed Jan.

Mesón del Café c/Llibreteria 16, Barri Gòtic; Ⓜ Jaume I. Tiny, offbeat bar where you'll probably have to stand to sample the pastries and the excellent coffee, including a cappuccino laden with fresh cream. Mon–Sat 7am–11pm.

Rosal Pg. del Born 27, La Ribera; Ⓜ Jaume I. The *terraza* at the end of the Born gets the sun all day, making it a popular meeting place, and it's also packed on summer nights. Daily 9am–2am.

🏃 **Textil Café** c/de Montcada 12–14, La Ribera; Ⓜ Jaume I. Set inside a shady, cobbled medieval courtyard, and serving hummus, tzatziki, quiche, salads, chilli, lasagne and big sandwiches, while a *menú* offers a more substantial meal. Tues & Wed 10am–8.30pm, Thurs 10am–midnight, Fri & Sat 10am–1am, Sun 10am–midnight; in winter, Tues–Thurs daytime only.

Tapas bars

"Creative tapas" is the current Barcelona buzzword – you're as likely to get a samosa or a yucca chip as a garlic mushroom these days – and you can eat really well just dining on tapas, especially in some of the new-wave places that are deadly serious about their food. However, tapas are not a particularly Catalan phenomenon, and most old-style city **tapas bars** tend to concentrate on specialities from other Spanish regions, especially Galicia and the Basque Country. The most famous concentration of traditional places is down by the port in the Barri Gòtic, along c/Ample, c/de la Mercè, c/del Regomir and their offshoots. Jumping from bar to bar for dinner is going to cost you at least as much as eating in a medium-priced restaurant, say €25 a head, and twice as much in the really good places.

Barri Gòtic

The tapas bars below are marked on the map on pp.674–675.

Bodega La Plata c/de la Mercè 28; ⓂDrassanes. An old-town classic, with a marble counter open to the street, and dirt-cheap wine straight from the barrel. Anchovies are the speciality. Daily 10am–4pm & 8–11pm.

Taller de Tapas Pl. Sant Josep Oriol 9; ⓂLiceu. More restaurant than bar, the "Tapas Workshop" boasts a year-round outdoor terrace in a pretty location by the church of Santa Maria del Pi. Prices are high (dishes €5–15), but the food's reliable – fish is the speciality. There's another branch in the Born at c/Argenteria 51, and a rather less atmospheric beer-house-style outlet in the upper Barri Gòtic at c/Comtal 28. Mon–Sat 9.30am–midnight, Sun noon–midnight.

La Viñatería del Call c/Sant Domènec del Call 9; ⓂJaume I. This wood-table tavern is principally an eating place – with a menu of *pa amb tomàquet*, cheese, ham, *escalivada*, fish, fried peppers and the like – but it's also a great late-night bar, with a serious wine list and jazz and flamenco sounds. Mon–Sat 6pm–1am.

Sant Pere

The tapas bars below are marked on the map on pp.674–675.

Mosquito c/dels Carders 46; ⓂJaume 1. Delicious pan-Asian tapas, including fragrant noodle salads, potato chaat, chicken tikka skewers and crispy pakoras, each around €3–5. Tues–Sun 5pm–1am, Fri & Sat until 2.30am.

Santa Maria c/Comerç 17; ⓂJaume I. Paco Guzmán's new-wave tapas bar has a glass-fronted kitchen turning out taste sensations – such as Catalan sushi, octopus confit, yucca chips or quail with salsa. Around €40 for a great meal. Tues–Sat 1.30–3.30pm & 8.30pm–12.30am; closed two weeks in Aug.

La Ribera

The tapas bars below are marked on the map on pp.674–675.

Cal Pep Pl. de les Olles 8; ⓂBarceloneta. There's no equal in town for fresh-off-the-boat and out-of-the-market tapas, and though prices can be high (a meal will cost €40 a head, including drinks), it's definitely worth it. If you don't want to queue, get there on opening for a seat at the bar. Mon 8–11.45pm, Tues–Fri 1.15–4pm & 8–11.45pm, Sat 1.30–4pm; closed Aug.

El Xampanyet c/de Montcada 22; ⓂJaume I. Bustling, blue-tiled bar with seafood tapas, sweet sparkling wine by the glass or bottle, and local *sidra*. As is often the way, the drinks are cheap and the tapas rather pricey, but there's always a good atmosphere. Tues–Sat noon–4pm & 6.30–11pm, Sun noon–4pm; closed Aug.

Barceloneta

The tapas bars below are marked on the map on pp.674–675.

Cova Fumada c/Baluard 56; ⓂBarceloneta. This busy, old-style bar is behind the brown wooden doors on Barceloneta's market square (there's no sign). The seafood is straight from the market's fish stalls, though the house speciality is the *bomba* (spicy potato-meat-ball). Mon–Fri 9am–3pm & 6–8pm, Sat 9am–3pm; closed Aug.

Jai-Ca c/Ginebra 13; ⓂBarceloneta. Always a great choice, with seafood platters piled on the bar, from bundles of razor clams to plump anchovies. Meanwhile, the fryers in the kitchen work overtime, turning out crisp baby squid, fried shrimp and pimientos del Padrón. Daily 10am–11pm.

Poble Sec

The tapas bar below is marked on the map on p.689.

Inopia c/Tamarit 104; ⓂPoble Sec. You'll have to make a special journey to this sleek, in-the-know tapas bar, stuck in sightseer's no-man's-land, but it's unquestionably worth it. It's the brainchild of Albert Adrià, brother of Ferran Adrià (of best-restaurant-in-the-world fame, *El Bulli*), and it's always standing-room-only for the best "classic tapas" in town. You can eat and drink for around €25. Tues–Fri 7–11pm, Sat 1.30–3.30pm & 7–11pm.

Eixample

The tapas bars below are marked on the map on pp.696–697.

Cerveseria Catalana c/de Mallorca 236; ⓂPasseig de Gràcia. This place is serious about its tapas and its beer – the counters are stacked high, supplemented by a blackboard list of daily specials, while the walls are lined with bottled brews from around the world. Daily 9am–1am.

Ciudad Condal Rambla de Catalunya 18; ⓂPasseig de Gràcia. A really handy city-centre pit stop that caters for all needs, from breakfast onwards, and the best of the large uptown tapas-hall-style places. Daily 7.30am–1.30am.

Tapaç24 c/Diputació 269; ⓂPasseig de Gràcia. Carles Abellan, king of pared-down designer cuisine at his famed restaurant *Comerç 24*, offers a simpler tapas menu (most dishes €6–14) at this retro basement bar-diner. There's always a rush and a bustle at meal times, and you might well have to queue. Daily 8am–midnight.

Sarrià

Bar Tomás c/Major de Sarrià 49; FGC Sarrià. It requires a dedicated trip to the 'burbs (12min on the train from Pl. Catalunya FGC station) to taste the *patatas bravas* of the gods – spicy fried potatoes with garlic mayo and *salsa picante* for a couple of euros. They fry between noon and 3pm and between 6pm and closing, so if it's only *bravas* you want, note the hours. Daily except Wed 8am–10pm; closed Aug.

Restaurants

Most **restaurants** in Barcelona serve a mixture of local Catalan and more mainstream Spanish food, with the best concentrating on seasonal market produce. Regional Spanish and colonial Spanish cuisine is fairly well represented, too, from Basque and Galician to Cuban and Filipino, while traditionally the fancier local restaurants tended towards a refined Catalan-French style of dining. This has been superseded recently by the two dominant trends in **contemporary Spanish cooking**, namely the food-as-chemistry approach pioneered by Catalan superchef Ferran Adrià and the more accessible tendency towards so-called **fusion** cuisine (basically Mediterranean flavours with exotic touches). Nearly all restaurants offer a weekday (ie Mon–Fri) three-course **menú del dia** at lunchtime, with the cheapest starting at about €9, rising to €12–15 in fancier places. At night, the set menus aren't generally available, but you'll still be able to dine in a huge variety of restaurants for around €25 a head – though you can, of course, pay

---

Barcelona's vegetarian restaurants

Vegetarians will find themselves pleasantly surprised by the choice available in Barcelona if they've spent any time in other areas of Spain. The restaurants listed below are the pick of the specifically vegetarian places in the city, but you'll also be able to do pretty well for yourself in tapas bars and modern Catalan brasseries and restaurants.

La Bascula c/Flassaders 30, La Ribera ℡933 199 866; Ⓜ Jaume I. See map pp.674–675. An old chocolate factory in the backstreets has been given a hippy-chic makeover and serves up speciality pastas, gourmet sandwiches, crepes and salads. Their original café, *La Cereria* (Bxda. Sant Miquel 3–5 ℡933 018 510; Wed–Sat 7pm–midnight), is also now open again for more of the same in the Barri Gòtic. No credit cards. Wed–Fri 7pm–midnight, Sat 1pm–midnight.

Biocenter c/Pintor Fortuny 25, El Raval ℡933 014 583, reservations ℡667 042 313; Ⓜ Liceu. See map pp.674–675. The fixed-price *menú* starts at 1pm, with soup and a trawl through the salad bar for a first course, followed by market-fresh mains. For dinner, they dim the lights, add candles and sounds, and turn out a few more exotic dishes, from red veg curry to ginger tofu (mains €7–10). Daily 1–4pm, plus dinner Thurs–Sat 8–11.15pm.

Illa de Gràcia c/Sant Domènec 19, Gràcia ℡932 380 229; Ⓜ Diagonal. See map p.701. Sleek, inexpensive vegetarian dining room where the food is a cut above – think grilled tofu, stuffed aubergine gratin or wholewheat spaghetti carbonara. Tues–Fri 1–4pm & 9pm–midnight, Sat & Sun 2–4pm & 9pm–midnight; closed mid-Aug to mid-Sept.

Juicy Jones c/Cardenal Casañas 7, Barri Gòtic ℡933 024 330; Ⓜ Liceu. See map pp.674–675. Veggie and vegan restaurant and juice bar with a *menú* that touches all corners of the world – cashew, carrot and coriander soup could be followed by pumpkin-stuffed gnocchi. Another outlet in El Raval (c/de l'Hospital 74) offers more space, a similar menu and the same young, funky vibe. No credit cards. Daily 10am–midnight.

a lot more. If your main criteria are price and quantity, look for a **buffet restaurant** (*Fresc Co* has several outlets, and there are many others), where €9 or €10 gets you unlimited access to the hot and cold *buffet lliure* (free buffet).

Barri Gòtic

Ⓜ Liceu/Jaume I. The restaurants below are marked on the map on pp.674–675.

Arc Café c/Carabassa 19 ☎ 933 025 204. Setting the standard for the chilled-out bistro-bars seemingly now on every corner, the *Arc*'s seasonally changing menu is great value, and the kitchen is open all day. There are Greek salads, spring rolls, home-made burgers and Thai curries, with main dishes around €10. Mon–Thurs 10am–1am, Fri 10am–3am, Sat 11am–3am, Sun 11am–1am.

Café de l'Acadèmia c/Lledó 1 ☎ 933 198 253. Creative Catalan cooking served in a romantic, stone-flagged old-town restaurant or on a lovely summer *terraza* in the medieval square outside. The prices are pretty reasonable (mains €11–18) and it's always busy, so reservations are essential. Mon–Fri 1.30–4pm & 8.45–11.30pm; closed 2 weeks in Aug.

Matsuri Pl. Regomir 1 ☎ 932 681 535. Good Southeast Asian cuisine in an attractive restaurant, concentrating on Thai-style noodles, soups, curries and salads, plus sushi and sashimi. Around €25 a head. Mon–Thurs 1.30–3.30pm & 8.30–11.30pm, Fri 1.30–3.30pm & 8.30pm–midnight, Sat 8.30pm–midnight.

Sant Pere

Ⓜ Jaume I. The restaurants below are marked on the map on pp.674–675.

Comerç 24 c/Comerc 24 ☎ 933 192 102. Chef Carles Abellan presents "glocal" cooking (ie "global" and "local"), dishes from around the world served in an oh-so-cool stripped-down warehouse interior. The meal comes tapas-style, and prices are high (around €80 a head), but this is sheer invention dressed up as contemporary dining. Tues–Sat 1.30–3.30pm & 8.30pm–12.30am; closed 2 weeks in Aug.

Cuines Santa Caterina Mercat Santa Caterina, Avgda. Francesc Cambó s/n ☎ 932 689 918. The neighbourhood market has a ravishing open-plan restaurant, with refectory tables set under soaring wooden rafters. The food ranges from pasta to sushi, Catalan rice dishes to Thai curries (most things cost €9–12), or you can just drink and munch superior tapas at the horseshoe bar. Bar daily 8am–midnight; restaurant daily 1–4pm & 8–11.30pm, Thurs–Sat until 12.30am.

L'Econòmic Pl. de Sant Agusti Vell 13 ☎ 933 196 494. The beautifully tiled dining room makes the perfect surroundings for a hearty three-course *menú*, costing around €10. It's nearly always full, but you can wait outside under the arcades until a table is free. No credit cards. Mon–Fri 12.30–4.30pm; closed Aug.

La Ribera

Ⓜ Jaume I/Barceloneta. The restaurants below are marked on the map on pp.674–675.

Casa Delfin Pg. del Born 36 ☎ 933 195 088. Old-school paper-tablecloth bar-restaurant that packs in the locals for a cheap and cheerful *menú*. The whole blowout shouldn't top €12. Mon–Sat 8am–5pm; closed Aug.

Senyor Parellada c/Argenteria 37 ☎ 933 105 094. Utterly gorgeous renovation of an eighteenth-century building. Food is traditional Catalan through and through (dishes €8–15), while more than a dozen puds await those who struggle through. Daily 1–4pm & 8.30pm–midnight.

Wushu Avgda. del Marquès de l'Argentera 1 ☎ 933 107 313. Aussie-chef Bradley's cool Asian wok bar turns out super-authentic *pad Thais*, Malaysian *laksas*, Vietnamese rice-paper rolls, red and green curries, Chinese *lo mein* noodles and the like. You can eat really well for around €25 or so, and the kitchen serves continuously from opening to close. Tues–Sat 1pm–midnight, Sun 1–4pm.

El Raval

Ⓜ Liceu/Catalunya. The restaurants below are marked on the map on pp.674–675.

Ànima c/dels Angels 6 ☎ 933 424 912. Arty neighbourhood restaurant where the seasonally influenced fusion food comes immaculately presented. Most mains cost around €14, though there's an especially good lunchtime deal. Mon–Sat 1–4pm & 9pm–midnight.

Bar Ra Pl. de la Garduña 3 ☎ 615 959 872. Extremely hip restaurant-bar behind La Boqueria, serving up eclectic world cuisine for breakfast, lunch and dinner, on a sunny patio. Daily 9am–2am.

Biblioteca c/Junta del Comerç 28 ☎ 934 126 221. One of the most agreeable places to sample what Barcelona calls "creative cuisine", where the market-led, seasonally changing menu never fails to impress. Fish might be cooked Japanese- or

Basque-style, and the signature dish is venison pie served with a market-fresh veg purée. Meals cost around €40. Mon–Fri 8pm–midnight, Sat 1–3.30pm & 8pm–midnight; closed two weeks in Aug.

Pollo Rico c/de Sant Pau 31 ☏ 934 413 184. It's been here forever and, while it's not to everyone's taste, if you're in the market for spit-roast chicken, fries and a beer, served quick-smart at the bar, this is the place. You'll be hard pushed to spend €15. Daily except Wed 10am–midnight.

Poble Sec

Ⓜ Paral.lel/Poble Sec. The restaurants below are marked on the map on p.689.

Bella Napoli c/Margarit 14 ☏ 934 425 056. The pizzas – the best in the city – come straight from the depths of a beehive-shaped oven, or there's a big range of *antipasti*, pasta, *risotti* and veal *scaloppine*, with almost everything priced between €8 and €12. Tues 8.30pm–midnight, Wed–Sun 1.30–4.30pm & 8.30pm–midnight.

Taverna La Tomaquera c/Margarit 58. A chatter-filled tavern where the grilled chicken will be the best you've ever had. The entrecôtes are enormous, while the locals limber up with an appetizer of pan-fried snails with chorizo and tomato. Most main dishes cost €7–11. No credit cards. Tues–Sat 1.30–3.45pm & 8.30–10.45pm; closed Aug.

Barceloneta

Ⓜ Barceloneta. The restaurants below are marked on the map on p.pp.674–675.

Can Manel Pg. Joan de Borbó 60 ☏ 932 215 013. An institution since 1870. If you want lunch outside on the shaded terrace, get here by 1.30pm. Paella, *fideuà* and *arròs a banda* are staples – from around €13 per person – while the catch of the day ranges from cuttlefish to sole, bream or hake (up to €22). Daily 1–4pm & 8pm–midnight.

Can Maño c/Baluard 12 ☏ 933 193 082. There's rarely a tourist in sight in this old-fashioned locals' diner. It's an authentic experience, which is likely to cost you less than €12 a head. No credit cards. Mon–Fri 8am–5.30pm & 8–11pm, Sat noon–5pm; closed Aug.

Port Olímpic

Ⓜ Ciutadella-Vila Olímpica. The restaurant below is marked on the map on pp.662–663.

Agua Pg. Marítim 30 ☏ 932 251 272. Much the nicest boardwalk restaurant on the beachfront strip, perfect for brunch, though if the weather's iffy you can opt for the sleek, split-level dining room. The menu is seasonal, contemporary Mediterra-nean – grills, *risotti*, pasta, salads and tapas – and

the prices are pretty fair (meals up to €30), so it's usually busy. Daily 1–4pm & 8–11.30pm, Fri & Sat until 12.30am.

Eixample

The restaurants below are marked on the map on pp.696–697.

Alkimia c/Indústria 79 ☏ 932 076 115; Ⓜ Sagrada Família. "Alchemy" is what's promised by the name, and that's what chef Jordi Vilà delivers in bitingly minimalist style – think *pa amb tomàquet* (Catalan bread rubbed with tomato and olive oil), only liquidised and served in a shot glass. It's a Michelin-starred operation, so reservations are vital and the bill might reach €100 a head. Mon–Fri 1.30–3.30pm & 8.30–11pm; closed Easter & 2 weeks in Aug.

La Flauta c/d'Aribau 23 ☏ 933 237 038; Ⓜ Universitat. One of the city's best-value lunch menus (around €12) sees potential diners queuing for tables daily – get there before 2pm. Mon–Sat 8am–1am.

Gaig c/Aragó 214 ☏ 934 291 017; Ⓜ Passeig de Gràcia/Universitat. The Gaig family restaurant was first founded in 1869 out in the Horta neighbourhood, but under fourth-generation family member, Carles Gaig, it has now found a sleek downtown home at the *Hotel Cram*. It has a towering reputation for quality reinterpretations of traditional Catalan dishes, but when starters can cost €35, and the *menú degustación* is €100 or so, you're talking about a true special-occasion place. Mon 9–11pm, Tues–Sat 1–3.30pm & 9–11pm; closed 3 weeks in Aug.

Tragaluz Ptge. de la Concepció 5 ☏ 934 870 621; Ⓜ Diagonal. A designer space, where the classy Mediterranean-with-knobs-on cooking doesn't disappoint, though mains run €16–25. Cheaper eats come courtesy of the *Tragarapid* menu, which offers club sandwiches and the like. Daily 1.30–4pm & 8.30pm–midnight, Thurs–Sat until 1pm.

Gràcia

The restaurants below are marked on the map on p.701.

Flash, Flash c/de la Granada del Penedès 25 ☏ 932 370 990; Ⓜ Diagonal. Classic 1970s survivor, with Pop Art photography and tortillas (most €5–8) served any way you like, from plain and simple to elaborately stuffed or doused in *salsa*, with sweet ones for dessert. Bar daily 11am–2am; restaurant daily 1pm–1.30am.

🏃 **Samsara** c/Terol 6 ☏ 932 853 688; Ⓜ Fontana. Laid-back place offering contemporary tapas and "platillos" (little plates), including brochettes of asparagus tempura, mini hamburgers and inventive salads, most costing

€5–6. It's totally Gràcia – yes, that's a chill-out soundtrack and yes, there's a projection screen above the bar. Mon–Thurs & Sun 8.30pm–1.30am, Fri & Sat 8.30pm–3am.

🏃 **La Singular** c/Francesc Giner 50 ☎ 932 375 098; Ⓜ Diagonal. The tiniest of kitchens turns out refined Mediterranean dishes at moderate prices (€8–14). There's always something appealing on the menu for veggies, too. There are only nine tables, so go early or reserve. Mon–Thurs 1.30–4pm & 9pm–midnight, Fri 1.30–4pm & 9pm–1am, Sat 9pm–1am.

Taverna El Glop c/Sant Lluís 24 ☎ 932 137 058; Ⓜ Joanic. The rusticity stops just the right side of parody and the lunch *menú* is one of the city's best deals; otherwise, €15–25 a head for grills and other tavern specials, prepared in front of you on the open kitchen range. Daily 1–4pm & 8pm–1am.

Nightlife

There's often little difference between a **bar** and café (indeed, many places incorporate both words in their name), but some of the other names you'll see do actually mean something: a *bodega* specializes in wine; a *cervesería* in beer; and a *xampanyería* in champagne and *cava*. Barcelona also has a range of **designer bars** geared towards late-night drinking, and there's a **club** nightlife that is one of Europe's most enjoyable. Local **listings magazines** (*Guia del Ocio*, Ⓦ www.guiadelociobcn.es; and *Time Out Barcelona*, Ⓦ www .timeout.cat) cover current opening hours and club nights, and most bars, cafés, boutiques and music stores carry flyers and free magazines containing news and reviews. It's worth noting that – unlike restaurants – most bars stay open throughout August.

Bars

Generally, the bars in the old town are a mixture of traditional tourist haunts, local drinking places or fashionista hangouts. **La Ribera** is still one of the hottest destinations, with Passeig del Born (the square at the end of c/de Montcada behind Santa María del Mar) the main focus. In the **Barri Gòtic**, it's the streets around c/d'Avinyó and c/Escudellers that have their share of the action; over in upper **El Raval**, the most fashionable places are opening up near MACBA. The **Port Olímpic** and the **Port Vell** Maremàgnum complex are more mainstream summer night-time playgrounds for locals and tourists alike. There are scores of bars in both these areas, all either themed or otherwise fairly mundane, but with the advantage that you can simply hop from one to another if you don't like your first choice. Other stylish designer bars or DJ-led music bars are concentrated mainly in the **Eixample** and the streets to the west of **Gràcia**, particularly on c/Santaló and c/Marià Cubí in **Sant Gervasi**. Local bars are usually licensed to stay open till 11pm, although some keep going till 3am. Music bars usually stay open till 2 or 3am, after which it's time to hit the clubs.

Barri Gòtic

Ⓜ Catalunya/Liceu/Jaume I

L'Ascensor c/Bellafila 3 (bottom of c/de la Ciutat). Antique wooden elevator doors signal the entrance to this popular local bar. Untouristy, and with a comfortable feel. Daily 6.30pm–3am.

🏃 **Bar del Pi** Pl. Sant Josep Oriol 1. Best known for its terrace tables in one of Barcelona's prettiest squares – a prime people-watching spot. Mon–Sat 9am–11pm, Sun 10am–10pm; closed 2 weeks in Jan & all Aug.

Glaciar Pl. Reial 3. Traditional Barcelona meeting point and the first and best of the *terrazas* on Pl. Reial. Packs out at weekends. Mon–Thurs 4pm–2am, Fri & Sat 4pm–3am, Sun 9am–2am.

🏃 **Milk** c/Gignàs 21. Irish-owned bar and bistro that's quickly carved out a niche as a welcoming neighbourhood hangout, backed by a funky soundtrack. Mon–Sat 6.30pm–3am, Sun 11am–3am.

There's a vibrant local gay and lesbian crowd in Barcelona, not to mention the lure of nearby Sitges, mainland Spain's biggest gay resort. There's a particular concentration of bars, restaurants and clubs in the so-called **Gaixample**, the "Gay Eixample", an area of a few square blocks just northwest of the main university in the Esquerra de l'Eixample. The biggest event of the year is Carnival in Sitges (see p.811), while there's the **Barcelona International Gay and Lesbian Film Festival** every October (ⓦwww.cinemalambda.com). The city's annual **lesbian and gay pride march** is on the nearest Saturday to June 28, starting in the evening at Plaça Universitat.

There's a **lesbian and gay city telephone hotline** on ℡900 601 601 (daily 6–10pm). Aside from the weekly bar and club listings in *Guia del Ocio* and *Time Out Barcelona*, there's also a good free **magazine** called *Nois* (ⓦwww.revistanois.com), which carries an up-to-date review of the scene. Cómplices, c/Cervantes 2 (ⓂLiceu; ⓦwww.libreriacomplices.com), and Antinous, c/Josep Anselm Clavé 6 (ⓂDrassanes; ⓦwww.antinouslibros.com), are recommended **gay bookshops** – the latter has a café at the back.

Gay bars and clubs

As well as the clubs reviewed below, the biggest gay club night in the city is **Gay Day** (Sun, at *Space Barcelona*, ⓦwww.gaydaybcn.com).

Aire c/Valencia 236, Eixample; ⓂPasseig de Gràcia. The hottest, most stylish lesbian bar in town. Thurs–Sat 11pm–3am, July & Aug also Tues & Wed.

Arena Madre c/Balmes 32, Esquerra de l'Eixample ⓦwww.arenadisco.com; ⓂPasseig de Gràcia. The "Mother" club sits at the helm of the Arena empire, all within a city block (pay for one, get in to all) – frenetic house and chart at *Arena Madre* (Mon–Sat 12.30–5am, Sun 7pm–5am), high disco antics at *Arena Classic* (c/de la Diputació 233; Fri & Sat 12.30–6am), more of the same plus dance, r 'n' b, pop and rock at the more mixed *Arena VIP* (Grand Via de les Corts Catalanes 593; Fri & Sat 1–6am), and the best in house at *Arena Dandy* (Grand Via de les Corts Catalanes 593; Fri & Sat 1–6am).

Café Dietrich c/Consell de Cent 255, Eixample; ⓂUniversitat. Well-known music-bar, with drag shows punctuating the DJ sets. Daily 6pm–2.30am.

Metro c/Sepúlveda 158, Eixample ⓦwww.metrodiscobcn.com; ⓂUniversitat/Urgell. A gay institution, playing either current dance and techno or retro disco. Daily midnight–5am.

Punto BCN c/Muntaner 63–65, Eixample; ⓂUniversitat. A Gaixample classic that attracts an uptown crowd for drinks, chat and music. Daily 6pm–2.30am.

Salvation Ronda de Sant Pere 19–21, Eixample ⓦwww.matineegroup.com; ⓂUrquinaona. Huge Ibiza-scene gay club playing the best in European house. Fri–Sun midnight–5am.

Zeltas c/Casanova 75, Eixample ⓦwww.zeltas.net; ⓂUrgell. Pumped-up house-music bar for the pre-club crowd (Wed–Sun 11pm–3am). They also operate *Kiut* (c/Consell de Cent 280, Eixample, ⓦwww.kiutdisco.com; ⓂUniversitat/Passeig de Gràcia), a new "cute" lesbian dance space (Thurs–Sun 11.30pm–5am).

Oviso c/Arai 5, Pl. George Orwell; ⓂDrassanes. Holding a mirror up to the neighbourhood, the *Oviso* fits right in with the scruffy urban square outside – a shabby-chic mural-clad café-bar, popular with a hip young crowd. Daily 10am–2.30am, Fri & Sat until 3am.

Travel Bar c/Boqueria 27. Backpacking Catalans have brought their experiences home to provide a bar where travellers can hang out and meet like-minded souls, sign up for walking/biking/drinking tours, practise their Spanish and generally chill out. Mon–Thurs & Sun 9am–2am, Fri & Sat 9am–3am.

Sant Pere

 Casa Paco c/d'Allada Vermell 10; ⓂJaume I. The *barri*'s signature bar is this cool-but-casual music joint that's a hit on the weekend DJ scene – the tag line "not a disco, just a bar with good music" says it all. Mon–Thurs & Sun 9am–2am, Fri & Sat noon–3am; Oct–March opens 6pm.

La Ribera

Ⓜ Jaume I/Barceloneta

La Fianna c/Banys Vells 19. Flickering candelabras, parchment lampshades, rough plaster walls and deep colours set the Gothic mood in this stylish lounge-bar that's "putting the beat in the Born". Daily 6pm–1.30am, Thurs–Sat until 2.30am.

El Nus c/Mirallers 5. Still has the feel of the shop it once was, down to the antique cash register, though it's now a kind of jazz-bar-cum-gallery – a quiet, faintly old-fashioned, late-night place. Daily except Wed 7.30pm–2.30am.

La Vinya del Senyor Pl. Santa Maria 5. Nook-and-cranny wine bar with tables right outside the lovely church of Santa Maria del Mar. Tues–Thurs noon–1am, Fri & Sat noon–2am, Sun noon–midnight.

El Raval

Ⓜ Catalunya/Liceu/Universitat

Almirall c/Joaquim Costa 33. Dating from 1860, Barcelona's oldest bar – a venerated leftist hangout – is a great place to chat or to kick off an evening of more intense bar-hopping. Daily 7pm–3am.

Café de les Delícies Rambla de Raval 47. One of the first off the blocks in this revamped neighbourhood, and still the best – cute and cosy, mellow and arty, with a summer terrace and food for sharing. Daily except Wed 6pm–2am, Fri & Sat until 3am; closed 2 weeks in Aug.

London Bar c/Nou de la Rambla 34. Opened in 1910, this well-known bar attracts a mostly tourist clientele these days, but it's still worth looking in at least once for the exuberant *modernista* decor (while trying to ignore the authentic old-town sleaze just up the street). Tues–Sat 7pm–4am; closed 2 weeks in Aug.

Marsella c/de Sant Pau 65. Authentic, atmospheric 1930s bar where absinthe is the drink of choice. It's frequented by a spirited mix of local characters and young trendies, all looking for a slice of the old Barri Xines. Mon–Sat 10pm–3am; closed 2 weeks in Aug.

Muy Buenas c/del Carme 63. Arguably El Raval's nicest watering hole, with a hip, eager-to-please staff making things go with a swing. It's got a restored *modernista* interior, a long marble trough functioning as the bar, and beer pulled from antique beer taps. Tues–Sat 9am–3am.

🏃 **Resolis** c/Riera Baixa 22. A once decayed, century-old bar has been turned into a cool

hangout with decent tapas – if you only come to one bar in El Raval, come here. Mon–Sat 11am–1am.

Zelig c/del Carme 116. The photo-frieze on granite walls and a fully stocked cocktail bar make it very much of its *barri* but *Zelig* stands out from the crowd – two Dutch owners offer a chatty welcome, a tendency towards 1980s sounds and a slight whiff of camp. Tues–Sun 7pm–2am, Fri & Sat until 3am.

Poble Sec

🏃 **Bar Seco** Pg. Montjuïc 74; Ⓜ Paral.lel. It's just a bit out of the way in Poble Sec, but the "*Dry Bar*" is a local hit, especially for its quality veggie-friendly food and organic beers and wines. Mon noon–2am, Tues–Sat 9am–2am, Sun 9am–midnight.

Tinta Roja c/Creu dels Molers 17; Ⓜ Poble Sec. Highly theatrical tango bar with a succession of crimson rooms leading through to a stage at the back. There's cabaret and live music (tango, rumba and Cuban) a couple of nights a week. Wed, Thurs & Sun 8pm–1.30am, Fri & Sat 8pm–3am; closed 2 weeks in Aug.

Eixample

Belchica c/Villaroel 60; Ⓜ Urgell. Barcelona's first Belgian beer bar, which guarantees a range of decent brews. It's not a theme bar, just an enjoyable local bar playing electronica, new jazz, lounge, reggae and other left-field sounds. Mon & Sun 7pm–1am, Tues–Sat 6pm–3am.

Dry Martini c/Aribau 166; Ⓜ Hospital Clinic. White-jacketed bar tenders, dark wood and brass, cigar smoke heavy in the air, middle-aged paunches – it could only be the city's legendary uptown cocktail bar. Mon–Thurs 1pm–2.30am, Fri & Sat 1pm–3am, Sun 6.30pm–2.30am.

Quilombo c/d'Aribau 149; Ⓜ Diagonal. Unpretentious music bar – just a bare box of a room really – that's rolled with the years since 1971, featuring live guitarists, Latin American bands and a clientele that joins in enthusiastically. Mon–Thurs & Sun 9pm–3am, Fri & Sat 7.30pm–3.30am.

Sante Café c/Comte d'Urgell 171; Ⓜ Hospital Clinic. A minimalist-style place that's more of a café during the day but chills out at night, with DJs guesting at the weekend. Mon–Fri 9am–3am, Sat & Sun 5pm–3am; closed Aug.

Gràcia

🏃 **Café del Sol** Pl. del Sol 16; Ⓜ Fontana. The grandaddy of the Plaça del Sol scene sees action day and night, and on summer evenings, when the square is packed, there's not an outdoor table to be had. Daily 1pm–2.30am.

El Canigó Plaça de la Revolucio 10; ⓂFontana/
Joanic. Family-run neighbourhood bar now entering
its third generation. Weekend evenings it packs out
with a young, hip and largely local crowd. Tues–
Sun 11am–midnight.

Puku Café c/Guilleries 10; ⓂFontana. Come early
and it's a relaxed place for a bite to eat and a drink.
At weekends, it morphs into an equally chilled
electro-lounge as "indietronica" DJs take the helm.
Mon–Thurs & Sun 7pm–1am, Fri & Sat 7pm–3am.

 Vinilo c/Matilde 2; ⓂDiagonal/Fontana. A
very cosy dive bar, with the lighting set at a
perpetual dusk – time easily slips away in here.
Daily 7pm–2am, Fri & Sat until 3am.

Virreina Pl. de la Virreina 1; ⓂFontana. Popular
bar with seats outside in one of Gràcia's loveliest
squares. Mon–Thurs & Sun 10am–1am, Fri & Sat
10am–2am.

Sant Gervasi

Gimlet c/Santaló 46; FGC Muntaner. This favoured
cocktail joint is especially popular in summertime,
when the streetside tables offer a great vantage-
point for watching the party unfold. Daily
7.30pm–3am.

Universal c/Marià Cubí 182; FGC Muntaner. A
classic designer bar that's been at the cutting edge
of Barcelona style since 1985. Be warned: they
operate a strict door policy here, and if your face
doesn't fit you won't get in. Mon–Thurs 11pm–
3.30am, Fri & Sat 11pm–5am.

Clubs

The main city-centre **neighbourhoods** for clubbing are the Barri Gòtic, El Raval,
Eixample and Gràcia, though it's actually the peripheral areas where you'll find the
bulk of the big-name warehouse and designer venues. Poble Nou, for example,
might not attract you during the day, but will be high on the list of any seasoned
clubber, as will the otherwise tourist fantasy village of Poble Espanyol in Montjuïc.
Admission prices are difficult to predict: some places are free before a certain
time, others charge a few euros entry, a few only charge if there's live music, while
in several entry depends on what you look like rather than how much is in your
pocket. Those that do charge tend to fall into the €10–20 range, though this usually
includes your first drink. If there is free entry, don't be surprised to find that there's
a minimum drinks charge of anything up to €10. Note that the distinction
between a music-bar and a club is between a **closing time** of 2am or 3am and at
least 5am. Many of those listed below stay open until 6am or 7am at weekends –
fair enough, as they've usually barely got started by 3am.

Barri Gòtic

Fantastico Ptge. dels Escudellers 3 ⓦwww
.fantasticoclub.com; ⓂDrassanes. A cheery dive
for the pop, indie and electro crowd who want to
listen to the Kaiser Chiefs, The Killers, The Pigeon
Detectives and the like. Wed–Sun 11pm–3am.

Fonfone c/dels Escudellers 24 ⓦwww.fonfone
.com; ⓂDrassanes. Cunningly designed, beautifully
lit bar attracting a young crowd into fast, hard
music, though it changes mood with satin soul,
disco and Best-of-Eighties nights. Daily 10pm–3am.

Karma Pl. Reial 10 ⓦwww.karmadisco.com;
ⓂLiceu. A stalwart of the scene, this old-school
studenty basement place can get claustrophobic at
times. Sounds are indie, Britpop and US college,
while a lively local crowd gathers at the square-
side bar and *terraza*, which is open from 6pm.
Tues–Sun midnight–5.30am.

La Macarena c/Nou de Sant Francesc 5
ⓦwww.macarenaclub.com; ⓂDrassanes. A
heaving, funky, electronic temple with a tolerant
crowd – they have to be, as there's not much
space. Daily midnight–4am, Fri & Sat until 5am.

El Raval

La Concha c/Guardia 14; ⓂDrassanes.
The Arab–flamenco fusion throws up a great
atmosphere, worth braving the slightly dodgy area
for. It's a rather kitsch, gay-friendly joint, with
some uninhibited dancing to flamenco and *rai* by
tourists and locals alike. Daily 5pm–3am.

Moog c/Arc del Teatre 3 ⓦwww.masimas.com;
ⓂDrassanes. Influential club with a minimalist look
playing techno, electro, drum 'n' bass, house, funk
and soul to an up-for-it crowd. Daily
midnight–5am.

La Paloma c/Tigre 27 ⓦwww.lapaloma-bcn.com;
ⓂUniversitat. At the time of writing, the best-
known casualty of the City Hall's current crusade
against late-night noise. If and when it does
reopen, it's unmissable – a fabulous 1903-era
ballroom and concert venue where old and young

This year's model

Barcelona always has another fad up its sleeve, and now it's upscale dining-and-dancing in extravagant gastro-clubs. The clientele is A-list celeb, footy player and WAG, well-heeled tourist and local rich kid, with the trend exemplified by the beautiful-people hangouts **CDLC** (Pg. Marítim 32, Port Olímpic ☎932 240 470, ⓦwww.cdlcbarcelona.com; ⓂCiutadella-Vila Olímpica) and **Shôko** (Pg. Marítim 36, Port Olímpic ☎932 259 200, ⓦwww.shoko.biz; ⓂCiutadella-Vila Olímpica), while uptown venues include the glam **Danzarama** (Gran Via de les Corts Catalanes 604, Esquerra de l'Eixample ☎933 425 070, ⓦwww.danzarama.com; ⓂUniversitat) and the **Buda Restaurante** (c/Pau Claris 92, Dreta de l'Eixample ☎933 184 252, ⓦwww.budarestaurante.com; ⓂCatalunya).

alike are put through their rumba and cha-cha-cha steps, with DJs kicking in after midnight on an assorted roster of club nights.

Poble Nou

Razzmatazz c/dels Almogavers 122 & c/Pamplona 88 ⓦwww.salarazzmatazz.com; ⓂBogatell/ Marina. *Razzmatazz* hosts the biggest in-town rock gigs (the concert hall capacity is 3000), while at weekends the former warehouse turns into "five clubs in one", spinning indie, rock, pop, techno, electro-retro and more in variously named bars such as "*The Loft*", "*Pop Bar*" or "*Lolita*". One price gets you entrance to all the bars. Fri & Sat 1–6am.

Poble Sec

Mau Mau c/Fontrodona 33 ⓦwww.maumauunderground.com; ⓂParal.lel. Great underground lounge-club, cultural centre and chillout space with a roster of guest DJs playing deep, soulful grooves. Strictly speaking, it's a private club, but membership is only €5. Thurs 11pm–2.30am, Fri & Sat 11pm–3.30am.
Sala Apolo c/Nou de la Rambla 113 ⓦwww.sala-apolo.com; ⓂParal.lel. This old-time ballroom is now a hip concert venue with regular live gigs on two stages and an eclectic series of club nights, foremost of which is the weekends' long-running techno/electro Nitsa Club (ⓦwww.nitsa.com). Wed midnight–5am, Thurs–Sat 12.30–5am.

Montjuïc

La Terrrazza Avgda. Marquès de Comillas, Poble Espanyol ⓦwww.laterrrazza.com; ⓂEspanya. Open-air summer club that's *the* place to be in Barcelona. Nonstop dance, house and techno, though don't get there until at least 3am, and be prepared for the style police. May–Oct Thurs–Sat midnight–7am.

Eixample

Antilla BCN c/Aragó 141–143 ⓦwww.antillasalsa.com; ⓂHospital Clinic/Urgell. Latin and Caribbean

tunes galore for out-and-out good-time dancing. Daily 10.30pm–5am, weekends until 6am.
Barcelona City Hall Rambla de Catalunya 2–4 ⓦwww.ottozutz.com; ⓂCatalunya. Very popular dance joint – the handy location helps – which hosts some of the most varied club nights around, from 80s' revival to electro. Daily midnight–6am.
Space Barcelona c/Tarragona 141–147 ⓦwww.spacebarcelona.com; ⓂTarragona. This was the first *Space* launched outside Ibiza, and it's a thumpingly young, extremely posey joint. Fri & Sat midnight–6am, Sun 9pm–3am.
Velvet c/Balmes 161; ⓂDiagonal. One of the few survivors of the first wave of stylish dance-bars in the 1980s, this lavish creation of designer Alfredo Arribas was inspired by the velveteen excesses of film-maker David Lynch. Daily 10.30pm–4.30am.

Gràcia

KGB c/Alegre de Dalt 55; ⓂJoanic. This warehouse bar and club was the first with the industrial look back in the 1980s. It was a well-known techno haunt, though current gigs and music policy aren't so rigid now, ranging from rumba to hip-hop. Thurs 1–4.30am, Fri & Sat 1–6am.
Otto Zutz c/de Lincoln 15 ⓦwww.ottozutz.com; FGC Gràcia. It first opened in 1985 and has since lost some of its glam cachet, but this three-storey former textile factory still has a shed-load of pretensions. The sounds are basically hip-hop, r 'n' b and house, and with the right clothes and face, you're in. Tues–Sat midnight–6am.

Les Corts

Bikini c/Deu i Mata 105, off Avgda. Diagonal ⓦwww.bikinibcn.com; ⓂLes Corts/María Cristina. This traditional landmark of Barcelona nightlife (behind the L'Illa shopping centre) offers a regular diet of great gigs followed by club sounds, from house to Brazilian. Wed–Sun midnight–5am; closed Aug.

Entertainment, music and the arts

As you would expect from a city of its size, Barcelona has a busy entertainment calendar – throughout the year there'll be something worth catching, whether it's a gig, cabaret show or night at the opera. The **music** scene is particularly strong, with jazz, rock and **flamenco** to the fore, and Catalans like their **cinema** and **theatre**.

A useful first stop for **tickets and information** is the Palau de la Virreina, Ramblas 99 (Mon–Sat 10am–8pm, Sun 11am–3pm; ⊕933 161 000; Ⓜ Liceu; ServiCaixa (⊕902 332 211, ⓦ www.servicaixa.com) and TelEntrada (⊕902 101 212, ⓦ www.telentrada.com) are the main booking agencies for music, theatre, cinema and exhibition tickets. There's also a ticket desk on the ground floor of **FNAC** (Mon–Sat 10am–10pm), the books and music megastore in El Triangle shopping centre, Plaça de Catalunya.

The main clubs, concert halls and venues are listed below, but for up-to-date information, the city council's Institute of Culture website, ⓦ **www.bcn.cat /cultura**, covers every aspect of art and culture in the city. Otherwise, the best **listings magazines** are the weekly *Guía del Ocio* (ⓦ www.guiadelociobcn.com, in Spanish) and *Time Out Barcelona* (ⓦ www.timeout.cat, in Catalan), online or from any newspaper stand. There's also a free monthly "*Cultural Agenda*" guide in English available from tourist offices and the Palau de la Virreina.

Classical music and opera

Most of Barcelona's **classical-music concerts** take place in the extravagantly decorated Palau de la Música Catalana or at the purpose-built, contemporary L'Auditori, while **opera** is performed at its traditional home, the Gran Teatre del Liceu on the Ramblas. Other interesting concert venues include the Barri Gòtic's Saló del Tinell, FNAC at El Triangle (the shopping centre) at Plaça de Catalunya, and the CCCB and Fundació Joan Miró (the last two particularly for contemporary music). There are also free concerts in Barcelona's parks each July, the so-called **Clàssics als Parcs**.

L'Auditori c/Lepant 150, Eixample ⊕932 479 300, ⓦ www.auditori.org; Ⓜ Marina/Monumental. Concerts by the Orquestra Simfònica de Barcelona i Nacional de Catalunya (season runs Sept–May), plus other orchestral and chamber works, jazz and world gigs. L'Auditori is the main venue for Nous Sons (New Sounds), the annual contemporary music festival (March & April).

Gran Teatre de Liceu Ramblas 51–59, Raval ⊕934 859 900, ⓦ www.liceubarcelona.com; Ⓜ Liceu. Full programme (Sept–June) of opera and recitals, plus late-night concerts (*sessions golfes*). Check the website, and make bookings well in advance.

Palau de la Música Catalana c/Sant Francesc de Paula 2, off c/Sant Pere Més Alt, Sant Pere ⊕932 957 200, ⓦ www.palaumusica.org; Ⓜ Urquinaona. Home of the Orfeó Català choral group, and venue for the Orquestra Ciutat de Barcelona among others, though over a season (Sept–June) you can catch anything here, from *sardanes* to pop concerts.

Dance

Barcelona is very much a **contemporary dance** city, with regular performances at theatre venues such as the Mercat de les Flors, TNC, Teatre Lliure and Institut del Teatre. For most visitors, however, dance in Barcelona means either the Catalan national dance, the **sardana** (see box opposite), or catching a **flamenco** show. Although its home is indisputably Andalucía, flamenco also has deep roots in and around Barcelona, courtesy of its *andaluz* immigrants – if you're here at the end of April, don't miss the wild flamenco shows and parties of the **Feria de Abril de Catalunya**, a ten-day festival held down at the Fòrum site.

Celebrating Catalan-style

Catalunya's national folk dance, the **sardana**, is danced every week in front of La Seu, in Plaça de la Seu (Easter to end Oct Sat 6pm). Mocked in the rest of Spain, the Catalans claim theirs is a very democratic dance. Participants (there's no limit on numbers) all hold hands in a circle, each puts something in the middle as a sign of community and sharing, and since it is not overly energetic (hence the jibes), old and young can join in equally.

The main event in a traditional Catalan festival is usually a **parade**, either promenading behind a revered holy image (as on saints' days or at Easter) or a more celebratory costumed affair that's the centrepiece of a neighbourhood festival. At the main Eulàlia (Feb), Gràcia (Aug) and Mercè (Sept) festivals, and others, you'll encounter parades of **gegants**, five-metre-high giants with papier-mâché heads based on historical or traditional figures. Also typically Catalan is the **correfoc** ("fire-running"), where brigades of drummers, dragons and devils with spark-shooting flares fitted to pitchforks cavort in the streets. Perhaps most peculiar of all are the **castellers**, the human tower-builders who draw crowds at every traditional festival, piling person upon person, feet on shoulders, to see who can construct the highest, most aesthetically pleasing tower (ten human storeys is the record).

Mercat de les Flors c/de Lleida 59, Poble Sec ⊤934 261 875, ⓦwww.mercatflors.org; Ⓜ Poble Sec. The city's old flower market serves as the "national centre for movement arts", with dance the focus of its very varied programme – from Asian performance art to European contemporary dance.
El Tablao de Carmen Poble Espanyol, Montjuïc ⊤933 256 895, ⓦwww.tablaodecarmen.com; Ⓜ Espanya. The long-standing *tablao* in the Poble Espanyol at least looks the real deal, sited in a replica Andalucian street. Prices start at around €35 for the show and a drink, rising to €70 and upwards for show plus dinner. Tues–Sun, shows at 7.45pm & 10pm.
Tarantos Pl. Reial 17, Barri Gòtic ⊤933 191 789, ⓦwww.masimas.com; Ⓜ Liceu. For a cheap flamenco taster, you can't beat this small bar in front of a stage where young singers, dancers and guitarists perform nightly at 8.30pm, 9.30pm & 10.30pm. Entry is just €6.

Film

All the latest films reach Barcelona fairly quickly, though at most of the larger cinemas and multiplexes (including the Maremàgnum screens at Port Vell) they're usually shown dubbed into Spanish or Catalan. However, several cinemas do screen mostly **original-language** ("V.O.") foreign films; the best are listed below. Tickets cost around €7, and most cinemas have one night (usually Mon or Wed) – *el dia del espectador* – when entry is **discounted**, usually to around €5. Many cinemas also feature **late-night** screenings (*madrugadas*) on Friday and Saturday nights, which begin at 12.30am or 1am. Every July, there's a giant-screen **open-air cinema** at the Castell de Montjuïc (Mon, Wed & Fri night; €4; ⓦwww.salamontjuic.com), with live music from 9pm, and the film at 10.15pm – bring a picnic.

Cine Maldà c/del Pi 5, Barri Gòtic ⊤934 813 704; Ⓜ Liceu. Hidden away in a little shopping centre, just up from Plaça del Pi, the Maldà is a great place for independent movies and festival winners, all in V.O.
FilmoTeca Avgda. de Sarrià 33, Esquerra de l'Eixample ⊤934 107 590, ⓦwww.gencat.cat /cultura/icic/filmoteca; Ⓜ Hospital Clinic. Run by the Generalitat, the FilmoTeca shows three or four different films (often foreign-language, and usually in V.O.) every day – themed programming and retrospectives are its stock-in-trade. Tickets are just €2.70 per film, or there's an €18 pass allowing entry to ten films.
Verdi c/Verdi 32, and **Verdi Park** c/Torrijos 49, Gràcia ⊤932 387 990, ⓦwww.cines-verdi.com /barcelona; Ⓜ Fontana. Sister cinemas in adjacent streets showing independent, art-house and V.O. movies.

Live music

Many major bands include Barcelona on their tours, playing either at sports stadium venues or big clubs such as *Razzmatazz*, *Sala Apolo* and *Bikini* (see "Clubs" in the previous section). Tickets run from €20 to €50, depending on the act, though there are cheaper gigs (€5–20) almost every night of the year at a variety of smaller clubs and bars. The two main annual **music festivals** are Primavera Sound (May; indie and rock) and Sónar (June; electronica).

There's a distinct **"Barcelona sound"** among local bands, known as *mestiza* – a cross-cultural fusion of rock, reggae, rap, hip-hop, rai, son, flamenco, rumba and electronica. It's typified by Parisian-born, Barcelona-resident Manu Chao, who's the biggest name around, and its heartland is the immigrant melting pot of El Raval, whose postcode – 08001 – lends a name to the sound's hippest flagbearers. Also worth checking out are fusion bands such as Cheb Balowski, Macaco and Ojos de Brujo, while street and hip-hop freestyle names to watch out for include Payo Malo and LA Kinky Beat.

Espacio Movistar c/Pascual i Vila s/n, Les Corts ⓦ www.espacio.movistar.es; Ⓜ Palau Reial/ Collblanc. A huge multi-entertainment space in the university campus zone that puts on major gigs, DJ sessions, film shows and festivals; there's also a bar and internet lounge and plenty of student action, from Playstation booths to chill-out zones.

Harlem Jazz Club c/Comtessa de Sobradiel 8, Barri Gòtic ☎ 933 100 755; Ⓜ Jaume I. Small venue for mixed jazz styles, from African and gypsy to flamenco and fusion; live music nightly at 11pm and 12.30am (weekends 11.30pm & 1am). Usually free midweek, otherwise cover charge up to €10; closed Aug.

Jamboree Pl. Reial 17, Barri Gòtic ☎ 933 191 789, ⓦ www.masimas.com; Ⓜ Liceu. There's a really good range of jazz gigs here, with sessions at 9pm & 11pm (from €10), with an additional Mon-night jam session (€4). Best of all, every night you can stay on for the club, playing funk, swing, hip-hop and r 'n' b from around midnight until 5am.

Jazz Sí Club c/Requesens 2, El Raval ☎ 933 290 020, ⓦ www.tallerdemusics.com; Ⓜ Sant Antoni. Every night from 8 or 9pm there's something different: rock, blues and jam sessions, plus jazz, *mestizo*, son cubano and flamenco.

🏃 **Sidecar** Pl. Reial 7, Barri Gòtic ☎ 933 021 586, ⓦ www.sidecarfactoryclub.com; Ⓜ Liceu. Hip bar – pronounced "See-day-car" – that's a good place to catch local rock, indie, roots and fusion acts. Admission for most gigs around €7–10, though some up to €20. Tues–Sun 8pm–4.30am, gigs usually at 10.30pm.

Theatre and cabaret

The **Teatre Nacional** (National Theatre) was specifically conceived as a venue to promote Catalan productions, and features a repertory programme of translated classics (such as Shakespeare in Catalan), original works, and productions by guest companies from elsewhere in Europe. The other big local theatrical project is the **Ciutat del Teatre** (Theatre City) on Montjuïc, which incorporates the progressive Teatre Lliure and the Insitut del Teatre theatre and dance school. Some theatres draw on the city's strong **cabaret** tradition – more music-hall entertainment than stand-up comedy, and thus a little more accessible to non-Catalan/Spanish speakers. Same-day **half-price tickets** (Tiquet-3) for some shows can be bought at the Caixa de Catalunya desk (Mon–Sat 11am–9.30pm) in the Plaça de Catalunya tourist office.

🏃 **Café Teatre Llantiol** c/Riereta 7, El Raval ☎ 933 299 009, ⓦ www.llantiol.com; Ⓜ Paral.lel/Sant Antoni. Idiosyncratic cabaret café-theatre whose varied shows feature a mix of mime, song, poetry, clowns, magic and dance; performances usually at 9pm & 11pm, with an additional late-night Sat special. Also the venue of the once-a-month Giggling Guiri (ⓦ www.comedyinspain.com) comedy night (in English). Closed Mon.

Teatre Lliure Pl. Margarida Xirgu, Poble Sec ☎ 932 289 747, ⓦ www.teatrelliure.cat; Ⓜ Poble Sec. The "Free Theatre" performs the work of contemporary Catalan and Spanish playwrights, as well as reworkings of the classics, from Shakespeare to David Mamet.

Teatre Nacional de Catalunya (TNC) Pl. de les Arts 1, Glòries ☎ 933 065 700, ⓦ www.tnc.cat; Ⓜ Glòries. Features major productions by Catalan, Spanish and

European companies, as well as smaller-scale plays, experimental works and dance productions.
Teatre Poliorama Ramblas 115, El Raval ⓣ933 177 599, ⓦwww.teatrepoliorama.com;

ⓜCatalunya. Specializes in modern drama (Catalan and translation) and musicals, often featuring the talents of offbeat Catalan companies such as Tricicle and Dagoll Dagom.

Shopping

While not on a par with Paris or the world's other style capitals, Barcelona still leads the way in Spain when it comes to **shopping**. It's the country's fashion and publishing capital, and there's a long tradition of innovative design, in both designer clothes and household accoutrements. The **annual sales** (*rebaixes, rebajas* in Castilian) follow the main fashion seasons – mid-January until the end of February, and throughout July and August. Shop **opening hours** are typically Monday to Saturday 10am to 1.30/2pm and 4.30 to 7.30/8pm, though all the bigger shops stay open over lunchtime, while smaller shops close on Saturday afternoons or may vary their hours in other ways. Major **department stores and shopping malls** open Monday to Saturday 10am–10pm. Barcelona's **daily food markets**, all in covered halls, are open Monday–Saturday 8am–3pm and 5–8pm, though the most famous, La Boqueria on the Ramblas, opens right through the day.

Antiques, arts, crafts and design

The best area for browsing is around c/de Palla, between La Seu and Plaça del Pí, combined with the antique market on Thursdays in front of La Seu. The **Tallers Oberts**, or Open Workshops (ⓦwww.tallersoberts.org), are usually held over the last two weekends of May, when there are art- and craft-studio visits, exhibitions, guided tours and other events.

Almacenes del Pilar c/Boqueria 43, Barri Gòtic; ⓜLiceu. A world of frills, lace, cloth and materials used in the making of Spain's traditional regional costumes.

Artesania Catalunya c/Banys Nous 11, Barri Gòtic; ⓜLiceu. The local government's arts and crafts promotion board has an old-town showroom, where it's always worth looking in on the current exhibitions.

Cereria Subirà Bxda. Llibreteria 7, Barri Gòtic; ⓜJaume I. Barcelona's oldest shop (since 1760), selling handcrafted candles.

Fantastik c/de la Mercè 31, Barri Gòtic;

ⓜDrassanes/Barceloneta. At the "bizarre bazaar" (the shop with the bicycle outside) there are beguiling gifts, crafts and objects from four continents.

La Manual Alpargatera c/Avinyó 7, Barri Gòtic; ⓜLiceu. Workshop making and selling *alpargatas* (espadrilles) to order, as well as other straw and rope work.

Vinçon Pg. de Gràcia 96, Eixample; ⓜPasseig de Gràcia. This palace of design houses stylish and original items, pioneered since the 1960s by Fernando Amat. Temporary art and design exhibitions are held here, too.

Books

You'll find English-language books, newspapers and magazines at the stalls along the Ramblas, and a good selection of English-language books (novels and general, unless otherwise stated) at the following shops:

Altair Gran Via de les Corts Catalanes 616, Eixample; ⓜUniversitat. Travel superstore with a huge selection of books, guides, maps and world music.

Casa del Llibre Pg. de Gràcia 62, Eixample; ⓜPasseig de Gràcia. Barcelona's biggest book emporium.

Elephant c/Creu dels Molers 12, Poble Sec; ⓜPoble Sec. Only stocks English-language books, with cheap prices for current novels, classics, children's books and secondhand.

Hibernian Books c/Montseny 17, Gràcia; ⓜFontana. Barcelona's best secondhand English bookstore.

Laie c/Pau Claris 85, Eixample; Ⓜ Passeig de Gràcia. This has been Barcelona's favourite

bookshop for years, though probably just as much for its good café-restaurant.

Clothes, shoes and accessories

New **designers** can be found in the medieval streets and alleys of La Ribera, around Passeig del Born, but also down c/d'Avinyó in the Barri Gòtic, between c/del Carme and MACBA in El Raval, and along c/Verdi in Gràcia. For **secondhand and vintage clothing**, stores line the whole of c/de la Riera Baixa (El Raval), with others nearby on c/del Carme and c/de l'Hospital, and on Saturdays there's a street market there.

Antonio Miró c/Consell de Cent 349, Eixample; Ⓜ Passeig de Gràcia. The showcase for Barcelona's most innovative designer, Antonio Miró, especially good for classy men's suits, though now also branding jeans, accessories, fragrances and household design.

Camper c/Pelai 13–37, El Triangle, Eixample; Ⓜ Catalunya, and Rambla de Catalunya 122, Eixample; Ⓜ Diagonal; plus others. Spain's favourite shoe store opened its first shop in Barcelona in 1981. Hip, well-made, casual city footwear.

Custo Barcelona Pl. de les Olles 7, La Ribera; Ⓜ Barceloneta, and c/Ferran 36; Barri Gòtic; Ⓜ Liceu. Hugely colourful and highly priced designer tops, sweaters and casual wear for men and women.

Czar Pg. del Born 20, La Ribera; Ⓜ Jaume I. A galaxy of running shoes, pumps, sneakers, bowling shoes and baseball boots.

Giménez & Zuazo c/Elisabets 20, El Raval; Ⓜ Catalunya/Jaume I. Cutting-edge women's fashion – funky and informal.

Jean-Pierre Bua Avgda. Diagonal 469, Eixample; Ⓜ Diagonal. The city's temple for fashion victims: a

postmodern shrine for Yamamoto, Gaultier, Miyake, Westwood, Miró and other international stars.

Lailo c/Riera Baixa 20, El Raval; Ⓜ Liceu. Secondhand and vintage clothes shop that's usually worth a look, with a massively wide-ranging stock.

Mango Pg. de Gràcia 8–10, Eixample; Ⓜ Passeig de Gràcia, and Pg. de Gràcia 65, Eixample; Ⓜ Passeig de Gràcia; plus others. Barcelona is where Mango began, and prices here are cheaper than in North America and other European countries. At Mango Outlet (c/Girona 37, Eixample; Ⓜ Girona), you'll find last season's gear, starting at just a few euros.

Muxart c/Rosselló 230, Eixample; Ⓜ Diagonal, and Rambla Catalunya 47, Eixample; Ⓜ Catalunya. Barcelona's top-class shoe designer.

Naifa c/Doctor Joaquim Dou 11, El Raval; Ⓜ Liceu. Original, colourful, informal, very reasonably priced men's and women's clothing.

U-Casas c/Espaseria 4, La Ribera; Ⓜ Jaume I; plus others. Never mind the funky shoes, the stores are pretty spectacular, especially the branch in the Born, where an enormous shoe-shaped bench-cum-sofa takes centre stage.

Department stores and malls

The Tomb Bus shopping line service connects Plaça de Catalunya with the Diagonal (Pl. Pius XII), an easy way to reach the uptown L'Illa and El Corte Inglés stores. Departures are every seven minutes or so (Mon–Fri 7am–9.38pm, Sat 9.10am–9.20pm); tickets (available on the bus) are €1.65 one way, €6.25 for one day's unlimited travel.

El Corte Inglés Pl. de Catalunya 14, Eixample; Ⓜ Catalunya, and Avgda. del Portal de l'Angel 19–21, Barri Gòtic; Ⓜ Catalunya, plus uptown branches at Avgda. Diagonal 471, 545 & 617, Eixample; Ⓜ María Cristina. Visit Pl. de Catalunya for nine floors of clothes, accessories, cosmetics, household goods, toys and top-floor café; while for music, books, computers and sports gear, head for Portal de l'Angel.

L'Illa Avgda. Diagonal 545–559, Eixample; Ⓜ María Cristina. Landmark uptown mall stuffed full of designer fashion, plus FNAC (music and books),

Decathlon (sports) and El Corte Inglés (department store).

El Mercadillo c/Portaferrissa 17, Barri Gòtic; Ⓜ Liceu. Double-decker complex of shops selling skate-, club- and beachwear and shoes.

El Triangle Pl. de Catalunya 4, Eixample; Ⓜ Catalunya. Shopping centre at the top of the Ramblas, dominated by the flagship FNAC store, which specializes in books (good English-language selection), music CDs and computer software.

Food and drink

Bubó c/Caputxes 10, La Ribera; ⓂJaume I. There are chocolates and then there are Bubó chocolates – extraordinary creations by pastry and choc maestro Carles Mampel, with an associated minimalist new-wave tapas place, *Bubobar*, next door at no. 6.

Casa Gispert c/Sombrerers 23, La Ribera; ⓂJaume I. Roasters of nuts, coffee and spices for over 150 years – a truly delectable store.

Formatgeria La Seu c/Dagueria 16, Barri Gòtic; ⓂJaume I. The best farmhouse

cheeses from all over Spain. Catherine, who's Scottish, will introduce you to the world of cheese at one of the regular cheese-and-wine tastings, or you can simply try before you buy. Closed Mon & Aug.

Papabubble c/Ample 28, Barri Gòtic; ⓂDrassanes. Groovy young things rolling out home-made candy to a chillout soundtrack. Closed Mon & Aug.

Vila Viniteca c/Agullers 7–9, La Ribera; ⓂBarceloneta. Very knowledgeable specialist in Catalan and Spanish wines.

Music

Independent **music** and CD stores are concentrated on and around c/dels Tallers (El Raval), just off the top of the Ramblas.

Discos Castelló c/Tallers 3, 7, 9 & 79, El Raval; ⓂCatalunya. Major local music retailer with separate stores for classical (no. 3), general (no. 7), hip-hop, rock, pop and merchandise (no. 9) and jazz and 70s pop/rock (no. 79).

Etnomusic c/del Bonsuccés 6, El Raval; ⓂCatalunya. World-music specialist, especially

good for reggae, Latin and all types of South American music.

Wah Wah Discos c/Riera Baixa 14, El Raval; ⓂLiceu. Vinyl heaven for record collectors – rock, indie, electronica, blues, folk, prog, jazz, soul and rarities of all kinds.

Listings

Banks and exchange There are ATMs all over the city, including at the airport, Barcelona Sants station and Barcelona Nord bus station. For out-of-hours exchange offices, look down the Ramblas, or go to Barcelona Sants (daily 8am–8pm); El Corte Inglés, Pl. de Catalunya (Mon–Sat 10am–9.30pm); or Turisme de Catalunya tourist office, Pl. de Catalunya 17 (Mon–Sat 9am–9pm, Sun 9am–2pm).

Bike rental Rental costs around €15–20 a day with the following companies: Biciclot, Pg. Marítim 33–35, Port Olímpic (ⓂCiutadella-Vila Olímpica), ☎932 219 778, ⓦwww.biciclot.net; Fat Tire Bikes, c/Escudellers 48, Barri Gòtic (ⓂLiceu/Drassanes), ☎933 013 612, ⓦwww.fattirebiketoursbarcelona.com; Un Coxte Menys/Bicicleta Barcelona, c/Esparteria 3, La Ribera (ⓂBarceloneta), ☎932 682 105, ⓦwww.bicicletabarcelona.com.

Consulates Australia, Pl. Gala Placidia 1–3, Gràcia (ⓂDiagonal/FGC Gràcia), ☎934 909 013, ⓦwww.embaustralia.es; Britain, Avgda. Diagonal 477, Eixample (ⓂHospital Clínic), ☎933 666 200, ⓦwww.ukinspain.com; Canada, c/Elisenda de Pinós 10, Sarrià (FGC Reina Elisenda), ☎932 042 700, ⓦwww.canada-es.org; Republic of Ireland, Gran Via Carles III 94, Les Corts (ⓂMaría Cristina/Les Corts), ☎934 915 021; New Zealand, Trav. de Gràcia 64, Gràcia (FGC Gràcia), ☎932 090 399;

US, Pg. de la Reina Elisenda 23, Sarrià (FGC Reina Elisenda), ☎932 802 227, ⓦwww.embusa.es.

Emergency services ☎112; ☎061 ambulance; ☎080 fire service; ☎091 police.

Ferries Buy tickets for services to the Balearics (July & Aug are very busy) inside the terminal from: Trasmediterranea (☎902 454 645, ⓦwww.trasmediterranea.es) to Palma de Mallorca, Mahón and Ibiza; Iscomar (☎902 119 128, ⓦwww.iscomar.com) to Palma de Mallorca, Mahón and Ibiza; or Balearia (☎902 160 180, ⓦwww.balearia.net) to Palma de Mallorca. Navi Grandi Veloci (☎934 439 898, ⓦwww1.gnv.it) has a year-round service to Genoa, Italy.

Hospitals The following have 24hr accident and emergency services: Centre Perecamps, Avgda. Drassanes 13–15, El Raval (ⓂDrassanes), ☎934 410 600; Hospital Clínic i Provincial, c/Villaroel 170, Eixample (ⓂHospital Clínic), ☎932 275 400; Hospital del Mar, Pg. Marítim 25–29, Vila Olímpica (ⓂCiutadella-Vila Olímpica), ☎932 483 000; Hospital de la Santa Creu i Sant Pau, c/Sant Antoni Maria Claret, Eixample (ⓂHospital de Sant Pau), ☎932 910 000.

Internet access A stroll down the Ramblas, or through the Barri Gòtic, La Ribera, El Raval and Gràcia, will reveal a host of possibilities (€1 per hr).

There's also wi-fi in an increasing number of bars, *pensiones*, hotels and public places.

Laundries Lavomatic, a self-service laundry, has two old-town branches (both Mon–Sat 9am–9pm): at Pl. Joaquim Xirau 1, Barri Gòtic (ⓂDrassanes), and at c/Consolat del Mar 43–45, Pl. del Palau, La Ribera (ⓂBarceloneta). At La Lavanderia de Ana, c/Carme 63, El Raval (ⓂUniversitat; Mon–Sat 9am–8pm), you can leave your laundry for a standard wash-and-dry (from around €7–8).

Left-luggage Barcelona Sants (daily 7am–11pm; €3–4.50 per day). There are lockers at the Estació de França, Passeig de Gràcia station and Barcelona Nord (all 6am–11.30pm; €3–4.50).

Pharmacies Usual hours are weekdays 9am to 1pm and 4pm to 8pm. At least one in each neighbourhood is open daily 24hr (and marked as such) – *Farmacia Clapiés*, Ramblas 98 (Ⓣ933 012 843; ⓂLiceu) is a convenient 24hr pharmacy. A list of out-of-hours pharmacies can be found in the window of each pharmacy.

Police The easiest place to report a crime is at the Guàrdia Urbana station at Ramblas 43, opposite Pl. Reial (Ⓣ932 562 430; ⓂLiceu (24hr; English spoken). To get a police report for your insurance, you need to go to the Mossos d'Esquadra station at c/Nou de la Rambla 76–80, El Raval (ⓂParal.lel), Ⓣ933 062 300 (take your passport). Otherwise, contact the police on: Mossos d'Esquadra Ⓣ088, Policía Nacional Ⓣ091, Guàrdia Urbana Ⓣ092.

Post offices The main post office (*correus*) is on Pl. d'Antoni López, Barri Gòtic (ⓂBarceloneta/Jaume I), Ⓣ934 868 050, ⓦwww.correos.es (Mon–Fri 8.30am–9.30pm, Sat 8.30am–2pm). There's a poste restante/general delivery service here (*llista de correus*), plus express post, fax service, mobile top-ups and phonecard sales.

Swimming pools The city's most spectacular pool is the summer-only open-air Piscina Municipal de Montjuïc, Avgda. Miramar 31, Montjuïc (mid-June to early Sept daily 11am–6.30pm; €4.90). Otherwise, there are indoor and outdoor beachside pools at Club Natació Atlètic Barceloneta, Pl. del Mar, Barceloneta (Mon–Fri 6.30am–11pm, Sat 7am–11pm, Sun 8am–5pm, until 8pm mid-May to Sept; €10).

Telephone offices The cheapest way to make an international call is to go to one of the ubiquitous phone centres, or *locutorios*, which specialize in discounted overseas connections – you'll find them scattered through the old city, particularly in El Raval.

Ticket agencies You can buy concert, sporting and exhibition tickets with a credit card using the ServiCaixa (Ⓣ902 332 211, ⓦwww.servicaixa .com) automatic dispensing machines in branches of La Caixa savings bank. It's also possible to order tickets by phone or online through ServiCaixa or TelEntrada (Ⓣ902 101 212, ⓦwww.telentrada .com). For advance tickets for all *ajuntament*-sponsored concerts and events, visit the Palau de la Virreina, Ramblas 99.

Travel details

Trains

Barcelona to: Cerbère, France (18 daily; 2hr 55min); Figueres (hourly; 1hr 40min); Girona (at least hourly; 1hr 15min); Lleida (9 daily; 2hr 30min–3hr); Madrid (AVE up to 20 daily, every 30–60min at peak times, 2hr 45min–3hr 25min; other services 8 daily, 5–9hr); Portbou (hourly; 2hr 20min); Puigcerdà (7 daily; 3hr 20min); Ripoll (hourly; 2hr); Sitges (every 30min; 25–40min); Tarragona (AVE up to 14 daily, 35min; other services every 15–30min, 1hr); Valencia (16 daily; 4–5hr); Vic (hourly; 1hr 15min); Zaragoza (AVE 14 daily, 1hr 30min–1hr 50min; other services up to 8 daily, 3hr 45min–5hr 30min).

Buses

Barcelona to: Alicante (4 daily; 9hr); Andorra (2 daily; 4hr 30min); Banyoles (2–3 daily; 1hr 30min);

Besalú (2–3 daily; 1hr 45min); Cadaqués (2–5 daily; 2hr 20min); Girona (Mon–Sat 6–9 daily, Sun 3 daily; 1hr 30min); Lleida (Mon–Sat 12 daily, Sun 4 daily; 2hr 15min); Lloret de Mar (July to mid-Sept 10 daily; 1hr 15min); Madrid (15 daily; 8hr); Olot (2–3 daily; 2hr 10min); Palafrugell (8 daily; 2hr); La Pobla de Segur (daily; 3hr 30min); La Seu d'Urgell (2 daily; 4hr); Tarragona (18 daily; 1hr 30min); Torroella (3 daily; 4hr 30min); Tossa de Mar (July to mid-Sept 12 daily; 1hr 35min); Valencia (10 daily; 5hr 30min); Vall d'Aran (daily; 7hr); Viella (June–Nov daily; 7hr); Zaragoza (11 daily; 4hr 30min).

Ferries

Barcelona to: Genoa, Italy (3 weekly; 18hr); Palma, Mallorca (June–Sept up to 4 daily, less frequent in winter; 4–9hr); Ibiza (June–Sept daily, rest of the year 2–4 weekly; 9hr); Mahón (daily; 7hr 30min).

11

Catalunya

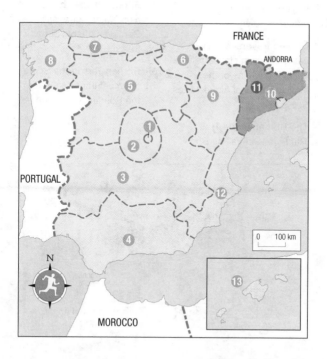

CHAPTER 11

Highlights

✳ **The Dalí Triangle** Gain a glimpse into the life and work of this flamboyant artist. See p.750

✳ **Girona** The labyrinthine "City of a thousand sieges" boasts a two-thousand-year-old history. See p.751

✳ **Wet and wild** The Noguera Pallaresa offers the best rafting in Spain. See p.794

✳ **Classic traverses** Follow paths between staffed refuges in the mountains of the Parque Nacional Aigüestortes. See p.804

✳ **The Romanesque Trail** The Pyrenean Vall de Boí features many of the finest Romanesque churches in Spain. See p.806

✳ **Cava country** Enjoy a glass of Spain's magnificent bubbly at one of the *modernista* vineyards around Sant Sadurní d'Anoia. See p.809

✳ **Sitges** Sample the frenetic nightlife or, better still, the Carnaval, of chic Sitges. See p.810

✳ **Roman Tarragona** Some of the most important remains of the Roman occupation. See p.817

▲ Girona

Catalunya

Y ou can't think of visiting Barcelona without seeing something of its surroundings. Although the city has long been one of Spain's more international centres, the wider area of **Catalunya** (Cataluña in Castilian Spanish, Catalonia in English) retains a distinct – and proud – regional identity that borrows little from the rest of Spain, let alone from the world at large. Out of the city – and especially in rural areas – you'll hear Catalan spoken more often and be confronted with better Catalan food, which is often highly specialized, varying even from village to village. Towns and villages are surprisingly prosperous, a relic of the early industrial era, when Catalunya developed far more rapidly than most of Spain, and the people are enterprising and open, celebrating a unique range of festivals in almost obsessive fashion. There's a confidence in being Catalan that dates back to the fourteenth-century Golden Age, when what was then a kingdom ruled the Balearics, Valencia, the French border regions, Sardinia and even parts of Greece and Corsica. Today, Catalunya is officially a semi-autonomous *comunidad*, but it can still feel like a separate country – cross the borders into Valencia or Aragón and you can sense the difference.

Catalunya is also a very satisfying region to tour, since two or three hours in any direction puts you in the midst of varying landscapes of great beauty, from rocky coastlines to long, flat beaches, from the mountains to the plain and from marshlands to forest. On the whole everything is easily reached from Barcelona; the city is linked to most main centres by excellent bus and train services. The obvious targets are the **coasts** north and south of the city, and the various **provincial capitals** (Girona, Tarragona and Lleida), destinations that make a series of comfortable day-trips.

The best of the beach towns lie on the famous **Costa Brava**, which runs up to the French border. This was one of the first stretches of Spanish coast to be developed for mass tourism, and though that's no great recommendation, the large, brash resorts are tempered by some more isolated beaches and lower-key holiday and fishing villages, such as **Cadaqués**. Just inland from the coast, the small town of **Figueres** contains the Teatre-Museu Dalí, Catalunya's biggest tourist attraction. South of Barcelona, the **Costa Daurada** is less enticing, though it has at least one fine beach at **Sitges** and the attractive coastal town of **Tarragona**; inland, the appealing cava **vineyards** around Sant Sadurní d'Anoia or the romantic monastery of **Poblet** figure as approaches to the enjoyable provincial capital of **Lleida**.

Even on a short trip, you can take in the medieval city of **Girona** and the surrounding area, which includes the isolated **Montseny hills** and the extraordinary volcanic **Garrotxa** region. With more time, you can head for the

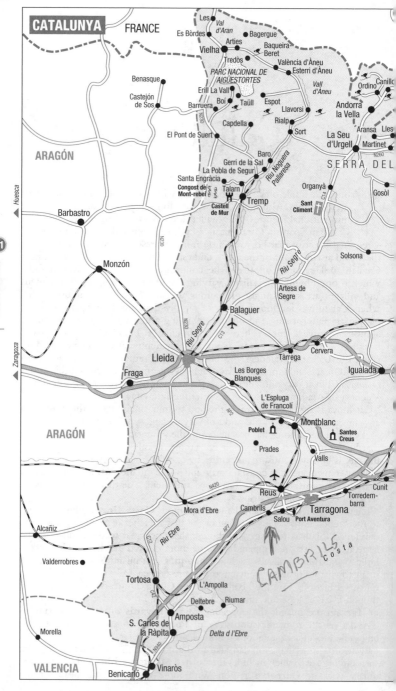

FRANCE

Les
Val d'Aran
Es Bòrdes
Bagergue
Arties
Vielha
Baqueira-
Beret
Tredòs
València d'Àneu
PARC NACIONAL DE
AIGÜESTORTES
Esterri d'Àneu
Benasque
Erill La Vall
Espot
Castejón
de Sos
Boi
Taüll
Llavorsí
Vall
d'Àneu
Ordino
Canillo
Barruera
Andorra
la Vella
Capdella
Rialp
El Pont de Suert
Sort
Aransa
Lles
La Seu
d'Urgell
Martinet
Baró
SERRA DEL
Gerri de la Sal
Riu Noguera Pallaresa
La Pobla de Segur
Santa Engràcia
Organyà
Congost de
Mont-rebei
Talarn
Sant
Climent
Gosòl
Castell
de Mur
Tremp

ARAGÓN

Barbastro

Monzón

Riu Segre
Solsona

Artesa de
Segre

Balaguer

Lleida

Fraga

Les Borges
Blanques
Tàrrega
Cervera
A2
Igualada

L'Espluga
de Francolí

Montblanc
Poblet
Santes
Creus
Prades
Valls

Reus
Cunit
Torredem-
barra
Mora d'Ebre
Cambrils
Tarragona
Salou
Port Aventura

Alcañiz

Valderrobres

Riu Ebre

CAMBRILS
Costa

Tortosa
L'Ampolla

Deltebre
Riumar
Amposta
Morella
S. Carles de
la Ràpita
Delta de l'Ebre

VALENCIA
Benicarló
Vinaròs

Huesca

Zaragoza

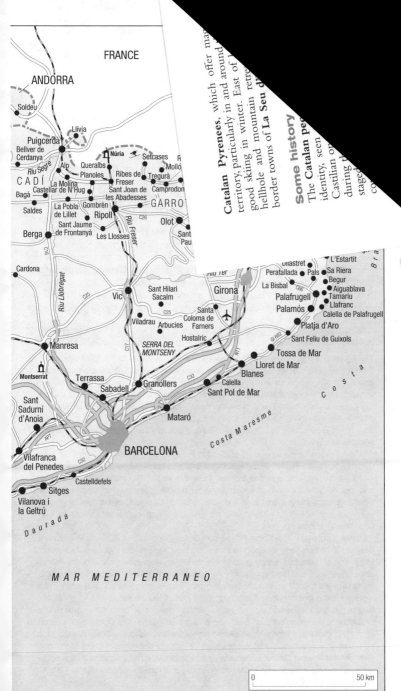

FRANCE

ANDORRA

Soldeu

Llívia

Puigcerdà

Bellver de
Cerdanya

Riu Segre

Alp   Queralbs   Setcases
La Molina Planoles Ribes de Tregurà Molló
CADÍ   Freser
Castellar de N'Hug Sant Joan de Camprodon
Bagà   les Abadesses
       Gombrèn   GARRO
Saldes La Pobla Ripoll
        de Lillet
        Sant Jaume   Riu Freser Olot
Berga   de Frontanyà Les Llosses   Sant
                                          Pau
Cardona   C26

Núria

Riu Ter

Ollastret   L'Estartit
Peratallada Pals Sa Riera
                         Begur
La Bisbal   C66   Aiguablava
        Palafrugell   Tamariu
        Palamós   Llafranc
              Calella de Palafrugell

Sant Hilari   Girona
Sacalm

Vic   Santa
           Coloma de
Viladrau   Arbucies Farners
                 Hostalric   Platja d'Aro
                          Sant Feliu de Guixols
SERRA DEL
MONTSENY   Tossa de Mar
Manresa
                     Lloret de Mar
Montserrat   Blanes
Terrassa   Calella
     Sabadell Granollers
                 Sant Pol de Mar   Costa
Sant
Sadurní   Mataró
d'Anoia   Costa Maresme
Vilafranca
del Penedes
              BARCELONA
        Castelldefels
Sitges
Vilanova i
la Geltrú
   Daurada

MAR MEDITERRANEO

0 ——————— 50 km

Catalan Pyrenees, which offer mag...
territory, particularly in and around...
good skiing in winter. East of...
hellhole and mountain retreat...
border towns of La Seu d...

Some history

The Catalan peo...
identity, seen...
Castilian op...
during th...
stage...

gnificent and relatively isolated hiking ... he **Parc Nacional de Aigüestortes**, and ... ere is **Andorra**, a combination of tax-free ... t set beyond the quieter, generally neglected ... Urgell and **Puigcerdà**.

... ple have an individual and deeply felt historical and cultural ... most clearly in the language, which takes precedence over ... street names and signs. Despite being banned for over thirty years ... he Franco dictatorship, Catalan survived behind closed doors and has ... a dramatic comeback since the Generalísimo's death. As in the Basque ... untry, though, regionalism goes back much farther than this. On the expulsion of the Moors in 874, Guifré el Pelós (Wilfred the Hairy) established himself as the first independent **Count of Barcelona**; his kingdom flourished and the region became famous for its seafaring, mercantile and commercial skills, characteristics that to some extent still set the region apart. In the twelfth century came union with Aragón, though the Catalans kept many of their traditional, hard-won rights (*usatges*). From then until the fourteenth century marked Catalunya's **Golden Age**, and in 1359 the Catalan Generalitat – Europe's first parliamentary government – was established.

In 1469, through the marriage of Fernando V (of Aragón) to Isabel I (of Castile), the region was added on to the rest of the emergent Spanish state.

Català

The traveller's main problem throughout Catalunya is likely to be the **language** – *Català* (Catalan). *Català* has more or less taken over from Castilian, a phenomenon known as the *venganza* (revenge), though few visitors realize how ingrained and widespread the language is and sometimes commit the error of calling it a dialect. On paper, *Català* looks like a cross between French and Spanish and is generally easy to understand if you know those two but, spoken, it has a distinct, rounded sound and is far harder to come to grips with, especially away from Barcelona, where accents are stronger.

When Franco came to power, publishing houses, bookshops and libraries were raided and *Català* books destroyed. While this was followed by a let-up in the mid-1940s, the language was still banned from the radio, TV, daily press and, most importantly, schools, which is why many older people today cannot necessarily write *Català* (even if they speak it all the time). As for Castilian, in Barcelona virtually everyone can speak it, while in country areas, many people can sometimes only understand, not speak, it.

Català is spoken in Catalunya proper, part of Aragón, much of Valencia, the Balearic Islands, the Principality of Andorra and in parts of the French Pyrenees, albeit with variations of dialect (it is thus much more widely spoken than several better-known languages such as Danish, Finnish and Norwegian). It is a Romance language, stemming from Latin and, more directly, from medieval Provençal and *lemosí*, the literary French of Occitania. Spaniards in the rest of the country belittle it by saying that to get a *Català* word you just cut a Castilian one in half. In fact, the grammar is much more complicated than Castilian, and the language has eight vowel sounds (including three diphthongs). In the text we've tried to keep to *Català* names (with Castilian in parentheses where necessary) – not least because street signs and *turisme* maps are in *Català*. Either way, you're unlikely to get confused as the difference is usually only slight: ie Girona (Gerona) and Lleida (Lérida). For a Catalan glossary, see p.980.

February/March/April

Lent: Carnaval Sitges has Catalunya's best celebrations. Celebrations also at Solsona, Sort, Rialp and La Molina.

Easter: Semana Santa (Holy Week) Celebrations at Besalú, Girona and La Pobla de Segur.

April 23: Semana Medieval de Sant Jordi A week of exhibitions, games, dances and medieval music in Montblanc, to celebrate the legend of St George (ⓦwww.setmanamedieval.org).

May/June

May 11–12: Festa Major Annual festival in Lleida.

First fortnight: Festa de la Lana Annual wool fair in Ripoll.

Third week of May: Fires i Festes de la Santa Creu Processions and music in Figueres.

Corpus Christi (variable): Festa de Corpus Christi Big processions in Sitges – and streets decorated with flowers.

Patum Festival in Berga.

June 21–23: Festa de Sant Patllari In Camprodon.

June 24: Dia de Sant Joan Celebrated everywhere; watch out for things shutting down for a day on either side.

July

10: Sant Cristòfol Traditional dances and processions in Olot.

Third week: Festa de Santa Cristina At Lloret de Mar.

August

First weekend: Festa Major At Andorra la Vella.

19: Festa de Sant Magi In Tarragona.

September

8: The Virgin's Birth celebrated in Cadaqués, Núria, L'Escala and Queralbs. Processions of gigantes at Solsona. Festivals at Sort and Esterri d'Àneu.

22: Sant Maurici At his *ermita* in the national park above Espot.

23: Festa de Santa Tecla Processions of *gigantes* and human castles in Tarragona.

Nearest weekend to 24: Festa de Sant Primus and Felician At Besalú.

October

8: Feria de Vielha Annual fair.

Last week: Fires i Festes de Sant Narcis In Girona.

November

1: Sant Ermengol Celebrations in La Seu d'Urgell.

December

18: Festival de Nuestra Senyora de Esperança At Cadaqués.

Throughout the following centuries the Catalans made various attempts to secede from the stifling grasp of central bureaucracy, which saw the Catalan enterprise as merely another means of filling the state coffers. Early industrialization, which was centred here and in the Basque country, only intensified political disaffection, and in the 1920s and 1930s anarchist, communist and socialist parties all established major power bases in Catalunya. In 1931, after the fall of the dictator General Primo de Rivera, a **Catalan Republic** was proclaimed and its autonomous powers guaranteed by the new Republican government. Any incipient separatism collapsed, however, with the outbreak of the Civil War, during which Catalunya was a bastion of the Republican cause, Barcelona holding out until January 1939.

In revenge, Franco pursued a policy of harsh suppression, attempting to wipe out all evidence of Catalan cultural and economic primacy. Among his more subtle methods was the encouragement of immigration from other parts of Spain in order to dilute regional identity. Even so, Catalunya remained obstinate, the scene of protests and demonstrations throughout the dictatorship, and after Franco's death a **Catalan government** was formally reinstated in 1979. This, the semi-autonomous **Generalitat**, enjoys a high profile and is gradually extending its power. It controls education, health and social security, with a budget based on taxes collected by central government and then returned proportionally – as well, the local police, or *Mossos d'Esquadra*, continue to replace the national forces. For 23 years, the region elected centre-right governments led by nationalist leader **Jordi Pujol**, but in 2003 a leftist coalition won power for the first time, making former Barcelona mayor **Pasqual Maragall i Mira** president. In 2006, he was succeeded by Andalucía native José Montilla Aguilera, the first president of the Generalitat in modern history to have been born outside of Catalunya.

The Costa Brava

Stretching from Blanes, 60km north of Barcelona, to the French border, the unfairly maligned **Costa Brava** (Rugged Coast) boasts wooded coves, high cliffs, pretty beaches and deep blue water. Struggling under its image as the first developed package-tour coast in Spain, it is very determinedly shifting away from mass tourism. It is undeniable that the unharnessed tourist boom wreaked damage in some areas, but the old *sangría*-and-chips image, which was never as widespread as press reports would suggest, is giving way to greater prominence for the area's undoubted natural beauty and fascinating cultural heritage.

Broadly, the coast is split into three areas: **La Selva** at the southern tip, clustered around brash **Lloret de Mar**, which most closely resembles the area's once-popular image, and the medieval walled town of **Tossa de Mar**; the stylish central area of **Baix Empordà** between Sant Feliu de Guíxols and Pals, popular with the chic Barcelona crowd, which boasts some wonderfully scenic stretches of rolling coastline around Palamós and the beaches and villages of inland Palafrugell and hilltop Begur; and the more rugged **Alt Empordà** in the north, marked by the broad sweep of the Golf de Roses, site of a nature reserve, the Parc Natural dels Aiguamolls de l'Empordà, and the alluring peace of the ancient Greek and Roman settlement of Empúries, before giving way to the spectacular Cap de Creus headland and park, home to the bohemian **Cadaqués**, which attracts an arty crowd paying tribute to Salvador Dalí; the artist lived

Driving is the easiest way to get around and gives you access to some of the more remote parts of the coast, though expect the smaller coastal roads to be very busy in summer and parking to be tricky in the major towns. **Buses** in the region are almost all operated by Sarfa, which has an office in every town and offers an efficient service along the length of the coast. You could consider using Girona or Figueres as a base for lateral trips to the coast, as both are big bus termini and within an hour of the beach. The **train** from Barcelona to the French border runs inland most of the time, serving Girona and Figueres, but emerging on the coast itself only at Llançà. There are also daily **boat services** (*cruceros*), which operate along the coast between Easter and September (see Travel details at the end of the chapter). Finally, you can access some of the lovelier coves by walking all or just parts of the fabulous **Camí de Ronda** necklace of footpaths that runs along almost all of the coastline.

most of his life in the labyrinthine warren of converted fishermen's huts in a neighbouring cove – now a fabulous museum.

Lloret de Mar

Sixty-six kilometres northeast of Barcelona, tourist-central **LLORET DE MAR** is everything you've ever heard about it and a lot more besides. Yet underneath its undeniably brash commercialism and gaudy nightlife is a centuries-old town trying to make itself known; the result is one of Europe's highest concentrations of clubs clustered around a delightful fifteenth-century church, high-rise monstrosities alongside genteel mansions and a packed main beach that belies some splendid rocky coves tucked away either side of town.

Arrival and information

Cruceros and other coastal **boats** dock at the beach, which is where the ticket offices are too; in the summer there are around a dozen daily services up and down the coast. The **bus station** is north of the town centre, on Carretera de Blanes. As well as regular services from nearby Tossa, there are several daily buses from Barcelona and Girona. The most central **turisme** is on the seafront at Pg. Camprodon i Arrieta 1 (June–Sept Mon–Sat 9am–8pm, Sun 9am–1pm & 4–7pm; Oct–May Mon–Sat 9am–1pm & 4–7pm, Sun 10am–1pm; ☎972 364 735, ⊛www.lloretdemar.org), with a smaller one at the bus station (Mon–Fri 9.30am–1pm & 4–8pm, Nov–April until 7pm; ☎972 372 943).

Accommodation

Most **hotels** in Lloret are block-booked by agents, so you must book in advance, especially in the summer. As you'd expect, there are a lot of high-rise hotels, but there are also some very good places in the old part of town not far from the beach.

Hostal La Habana c/Les Taronges 11 ☎972 367 707, ⊛www.lahabanalloret.com. Smart, family-run *pensió* on a narrow street leading from the beach to the old town. The bright, larger rooms have small kitchens and living room, TV and tiled bathrooms. ❷

Hotel Guitart Rosa c/St Pere 67 ☎972 365 100, ⊛www.guitarthotels.com. Sheer indulgence at this pink-coloured colonial mansion on the edge of the old town, a 5min walk from the sea, with lovely *modernista* touches and comfortable, modern rooms. ❹

Hotel Miramar Pg. Jacint Verdaguer 6 ☎972 364 762, ⓦwww.hotelmiramarlloret.com. Well-maintained hotel near the town hall, with spacious rooms equipped with satellite TV and a/c, overlooking the beach. Prices dip in low season. ❻

Hotel Santi Marta Platja de Santa Cristina ☎972 364 904, ⓦwww.hstamarta.com. A tranquil escape, this luxurious hotel sits above a quiet beach and the Ermita de Santa Cristina, between Lloret and Blanes, with elegant rooms and spell-binding views of the sea. ❽

The Town

Any sightseeing in Lloret is centred on the warren of streets in the **old town**, amid the sometimes overwhelming hustle of T-shirt shops and tourist paraphernalia. Holding court over all this is the colourful church of **Sant Romá** (services only), originally built in Gothic style in 1522. A spectacular *modernista* renovation was begun in 1914, but much of this work was destroyed in the Civil War; only the adjacent **Capella del Santíssim**, with its Byzantine cupolas, Mudéjar and Renaissance influences (daily 10am–2pm & 5–8pm), remains. You can explore Lloret's maritime legacy – illustrated by ship models and a replica of an 1848 figurehead – and other aspects of the town's history in a new museum, the **Museu del Mar** (same hours as *turisme*; €4), sharing space (and phone number) with the town's *turisme* in one of Lloret's few remaining nineteenth-century mansions, on the town's stately promenade, Can Garriga.

The beaches

Lloret's main **beach** and neighbouring Fenals beach, where many of the hotels are grouped, get packed and noisy; the south end of Fenals, backed by a pine wood, is much less crowded. Farther afield are a number of tiny **coves** favoured by local bathers. Of the more accessible by road and public transport, Cala Santa Cristina and the adjacent Cala Treumal are the best, while the lovely Cala Boadella is popular with nudists; all are off the Blanes road.

On a headland above the last beach are the surprisingly tranquil **Jardins de Santa Clotilde** (May–Oct Tues–Sun 10am–1pm & 4–8pm; €4), ornamental gardens laid out in *modernista* style in 1919 and offering fabulous views over the Mediterranean; visitor numbers are limited to fifty at a time, but you're most likely to find yourself alone, even in August. In April and May, you can often catch live jazz (Sun at noon) in the gardens; ask at the tourist office for details.

Eating and drinking

Although you're never going to be far from a fast-food joint, there's still a reasonably good choice of places to **eat** in the old town. All types and qualities of cuisine abound, including Italian, Greek and Mexican. **Clubs** are mainly centred around Avinguda Just Marlés, the main road into town running perpendicular to the seafront, while the liveliest **bars** dot the streets around Plaça d'Espanya and Plaça del Carme, just behind the beach.

Calamic Carnisseria Velle 5. Robust seafood dishes – such as *merluza*, or hake, with clams – and a weekday *menú* for €13.25. Closed Mon.

Can Tarrades Plaça d'Espanya 7 ☎972 366 121. The best Catalan choice, where you'll pay around €25 (on weekends at lunch, they offer a decent €16 *menú*, which includes paella *mixta*, with meat and fish).

La Lonja c/St Cristòfol 2. Mid-priced dishes made with fresh fish from the restaurant's own *parada*, or stall, in the local market.

Soda c/Grau 2, just north of the old town. For tasty cocktails with a local Lloret crowd, head for this stylish "cockteleria" and café, where you can also enjoy light bites, such as *bocadillos* and the like.

Tossa de Mar

Arriving by boat at **TOSSA DE MAR**, 13km north of Lloret, is one of La Selva's highlights, the medieval walls and turrets of the Vila Vella rising pale and shimmering on the hill above the modern town. Caught on the brink of becoming a full-blown tourist trap, Tossa is still very attractive and makes a much more restful base than Lloret.

Arrival and information

Tossa is an easy day-trip from Barcelona (1hr 30min by **bus**) or Lloret (linked by half-hourly buses); the bus station is at Avgda. del Pelegrí 25, behind the efficient **turisme** (June–Sept Mon–Sat 9am–9pm, Sun 10am–2pm & 5–8pm; June & Sept closed Sun afternoon; Oct & April–May Mon–Sat 10am–2pm & 4–8pm; Nov–March Mon–Sat 10am–2pm & 4–7pm; ☎972 340 108, ⓦwww.infotossa.com). To reach the centre, and the beaches, head straight down the road opposite the bus station and turn right along Avinguda Costa Brava. *Crucero* **boats** stop right at the centre of the beach, with the ticket offices nearby.

Accommodation

There's plenty of **accommodation** in the warren of tiny streets around Sant Vicenç church and below the old city walls. There are five local **campsites**, all within 2–4km of the centre; the better ones are *Cala Llevadó*, 3km out, off the road to Lloret (☎972 340 314, ⓦwww.calallevado.com; closed Oct–April), and the plush *Pola*, in a pretty cove 4km north off the corniche road to Sant Feliu (☎972 341 050; closed Oct–May).

Can Lluna c/Roqueta 20 ☎972 340 365, ⓦwww .fondalluna.com. Basic, tidy *pensió* – white-walled rooms and tiled floors – run by an amiable family, and tucked away in the old town. Some rooms have views of the stone turrets and the sea beyond, while the roof also offers lovely vistas. B&B ②

Gran Hotel Reymar Platja de Mar Menuda s/n ☎972 340 312, ⓦwww.ghreymar.com. Sumptuous beachfront hotel across the bay from the Vila Vella, managed by the Best Western chain. Modern rooms come with marble-clad bathrooms and terraces overlooking the sea. It has its own car park. Closed Nov–April. ⑧

Hotel Cap d'Or Pg. del Mar 1 ☎972 340 081, ⓦwww.capdor.spain.com. Very friendly ivy-clad *pensió* nestling under the walls of the old town and on the seafront, with eleven rooms equipped with TV, bathroom and a/c. Closed Nov to mid-March. B&B ④

Hotel Capri Pg. del Mar 17 ☎972 340 358, ⓦwww.hotelcapritossa.com. The plain rooms of this comfortable, seafront hotel come with bathrooms, TV and a/c. Most have terraces and buffet breakfast is included. Closed Dec–Feb. ④

Hotel Diana Plaça d'Espanya 6 ☎972 341 886, ⓦwww.hotelesdante.com. Nicely located hotel in a *modernista* mansion on an attractive square, and with a bar on the seafront behind. Large rooms have sea or *plaça* (cheaper) views, tiled floors and lots of character. Closed Dec–Feb. ⑥

Hotel Tonet Plaça de l'Església 1 ☎972 340 237, ⓦwww.hoteltonet.com. Pleasant family-run hotel with comfortable, good-value rooms equipped with TV. One of the few places in town open all year. ③

The Town

Founded originally by the Romans, Tossa has twelfth-century walls surrounding an old quarter, the **Vila Vella**, a maze of cobbled streets, whitewashed houses and flower boxes, slowly climbing the headland and offering terrific views over beach and bay. At the top you'll find the nineteenth-century **Far de Tossa** (summer daily 10am–10pm; winter Tues–Sun 10am–6pm; €3), now home to an innovative exhibition on Mediterranean lighthouses. Just below here, not far from the ruins of the town's fifteenth-century Gothic church, stands a **statue of Ava Gardner**, who made the town famous in the 1950 film, *Pandora and the Flying Dutchman*. Back in the old quarter, the **Museu Municipal**, at Plaça Roig i Soler 1 (June–Sept Mon–Sat 10am–2pm & 4–8pm; Oct–May Tues–Sat 10am–2pm & 4–6pm, Sun 10am–2pm; €3), features some Chagall paintings, a Roman mosaic and remnants, including ceramic vases, from a nearby excavated Roman villa.

The beaches

Tossa's best **beach** (there are four) is the Platja de la Mar Menuda, around the headland away from the old town, and is very popular with divers; look for a natural pink cross in the granite, supposedly marking where Sant Ramon de Penyafort gave a dying man his absolution in 1235. The central Platja Gran, though pleasant, gets crowded; if you have your own transport, the tiny coves north and south of the town are much more rewarding. Booths on the main beach sell tickets for **boat trips** (which operate from Easter to October) around the surrounding coastline; the trip to Sant Feliu is especially good.

Eating and drinking

Tossa offers a range of restaurants, from top-notch seafood spots to simple *sangría*-and-tapas joints. Passeig del Mar and the road behind it, c/Portal, are brimming with alfresco options. Come evening, Carrer de Sant Josep gets lively with revellers hitting the bars.

Bahía Pg. del Mar 19 ☎ 972 340 322. A swish interior and breezy terrace is the comfortable setting for tasty seafood meals (*menús* from €16 weekdays).

Bar Vila Vella on the main path up to the lighthouse. The outdoor stone terrace, featuring superb views of the town and beach, fills with a lively crowd of visitors and locals, especially when the

▲ Platja Gran, Tossa de Mar

vats of *sangría* (€8 per jug) come tumbling out. Daily 11am–9pm.

Castell Vell c/Pintor Roig i Soler s/n ☎972 341 030. In a tranquil corner of the old town, serves excellent fish and seafood on a terrace shaded with vines (*menú* from €23). Closed Nov–Feb.

🏃 **La Cuina de Can Simon** c/Portal 24 ☎972 341 269. This venerable joint turns out classic regional dishes with a twist, such as Catalan broad beans with sea cucumber (mains €25–35) in an elegant dining room of linen-topped tables, stone walls and oil paintings. Closed Tues & mid-Oct to March.

Tahiti c/Sant Josep 28 ☎972 341 402. Head to this hopping spot for live music, generally traditional Spanish, from rumba to guitar.

Baix Empordà

North from La Selva, while there are still one or two touristy places, the feel of the **Baix Empordà** marks a change from one of package holiday hotspots to a more stylish type of town with a greater local flavour. Known as the Triangle d'Or (Golden Triangle), as the rising property prices and burgeoning number of four- and five-star hotels will bear out, it is much favoured by chic Catalans and foreign visitors seeking less mass-tourism-oriented delights. The first part includes a smarter version of Lloret in **Platja d'Aro** – with a particularly lively nightlife, popular with weekenders from Barcelona – and the more family-friendly Sant Antoni de Calonge, bookended by the working fishing ports of **Sant Feliu de Guíxols** and **Palamós**, both of which remain largely aloof from their boisterous neighbours. Farther north, the area around **Palafrugell** boasts some fabulous cove towns, while hilltop **Begur** stands over a string of lovely little coves. **Inland** lures include the medieval towns of Pals and Peratallada, atmospheric Iberian ruins at Ullastret and the pottery industry of La Bisbal.

Sant Feliu de Guíxols and around

Separated from Tossa by 22km and, reputedly, 365 curves of stunning corniche, **SANT FELIU DE GUÍXOLS** is a bustling town with a decent beach and a cluster of handsome *modernista* buildings, evidence of its prosperous nineteenth-century cork industry. Its origins go back as far as the tenth century, when a settlement grew up around a Benedictine **monastery**, whose ruins, including the arched Porta Ferrada, still stand in Plaça Monestir. The church of Sant Feliu es la Mare de Déu dels Àngels has a Romanesque facade and beautifully crafted crucifix dating from the same period, though it was rebuilt in Gothic style in the fourteenth century. The church is open for services only, while the rest of the complex is part of the **Museu d'Història de la Ciutat** (Tues–Sat 10am–1pm & 5–8pm, Sun 10am–1pm; free), which contains absorbing exhibitions on the history of the town.

Sant Feliu's old-world style is at its most apparent in the *modernista* **Casa Patxot** (built in 1917 and now home to the Chamber of Commerce) at Pg. del Mar 40, on the corner of Rambla Portalet, and the curious Moorish-style **Nou Casino La Constància** nearby, at Pg. dels Guíxols 1–3; begun in 1851 and later adorned with *modernista* touches and brightly coloured swooping arches, the casino makes an atmospheric place for an afternoon coffee. The *passeig* follows the sweep of the coarse sand **beach** and yachting marina, while the streets back from the sea are great for a stroll past the shops and bars and the eighteenth-century **Plaça del Mercat**, with its lively daily market.

Practicalities

Cruceros **boats** dock on the main beach, where you'll also find the various ticket offices. Teisa **bus** services to and from Girona stop opposite the monastery, while the SARFA bus station (for buses to and from Palafrugell, Girona and Barcelona) is five-minutes' walk north of the centre on the main Carretera de Girona, at the junction with c/Llibertat. The **turisme** is at Plaça del Mercat 28, behind the main promenade (June–Sept daily 10am–2pm & 4–8pm; Oct–May Mon–Sat 10am–1pm & 4–7pm, Sun 10am–2pm; ℡972 820 051, ⓦwww.guixols.cat).

A score of family-run **pensiones** and **hotels** in the old town streets are all within a five-minute walk of each other and the sea: a favourite budget choice is the central *Hostal Casa Buxó*, c/Major 18 (℡972 320 187; Easter–Oct; ❸), while one back from the seafront in the market square is the friendly, family-run *Hotel Plaça*, Plaça del Mercat 22 (℡972 325 155, ⓦwww.hotelplaza.org; ❺).

The town is known locally for its fish **restaurants**, with most serving a reasonable *menú*. The atmospheric *Cau del Pescador*, c/Sant Domènec 11, has a huge choice of seafood and weekday *menú* for €19. The stylish *Eldorado* (closed Tues) at Rambla Vidal 23 does a weekday €17 *menú*, while next door at Rambla Vidal 19 is their tapas establishment, *Eldorado Pintxos*, with a range of well-priced, fresh tapas that you can enjoy on the breezy terrace. For fresh fish and hearty meat dishes (€15–18 mains), try the amiable *La Cava* at c/Joan Maragall 11.

S'Agaró

On a headland north of Sant Feliu is the curious village of **S'Agaró**, created in the 1920s and where every house was built in the *modernista* style by Rafael Masó, a student of Antoni Gaudí; the short Camí de Ronda leading to the fabulous **Platja Sa Conca** is the best way to explore and take in a swim. Also in S'Agaró, located in tranquil grounds overlooking Platja Sant Pol at the southern end of the village, is the Costa Brava's first five-star hotel, ⚑ *Hostal de La Gavina* (℡972 321 100, ⓦwww.lagavina.com; ❾), its palatial, marble-floored rooms adorned with elegant hand-carved furniture and exquisite antique rugs and lamps; the luxury continues with wood-panelled dining rooms, bars, terraces, a saltwater pool and spa.

Platja d'Aro and around

A few kilometres to the north, **PLATJA D'ARO** is a neon strip of bars and shops running parallel to, but hidden from, a long sandy beach. It's by no means picturesque, but it does offer excellent **nightlife**, a great **beach** and some stylish **shopping**. The cheapest **restaurants** line the main road through town, but for a view of the beach try the laid-back *Friends* at Pg. Marítim 62, with a mid-range menu of Spanish and international favourites. *Big Rock* (℡972 818 012; ❻), on a hilltop 3km northeast at Avinguda Fanals s/n, is a luxurious farmhouse doubling as a rustic hotel with a couple of rooms and a restaurant, serving traditional Catalan fare; call ahead to confirm that it's open. The **turisme** (June 22–Sept 11 daily 10am–2pm & 4–8pm; rest of year Mon–Sat 10am–1pm & 4–7pm, Sun 10am–2pm; ℡972 817 179, ⓦwww.platjadaro.com) is at Cinto Verdaguer 4, on the junction with central Avinguda S'Agaró.

Beyond Platja d'Aro, the road leads to the more family-oriented but not terribly pretty town of **SANT ANTONI DE CALONGE**; more enticing are the **coves** and beaches strung out between the two towns, all of which can be reached on foot by the serpentine and sometimes tricky **Camí de Ronda** or by a number of footpaths descending from the main road.

Palamós and around

Immediately northeast of Sant Antoni de Calonge, **PALAMÓS** was founded in 1277 and sacked by Barbarossa in 1543, its old quarter set apart from the new on a promontory at the eastern end of the bay. If you're arriving by car, aim for the marina at this end of town, and park on the seafront. The working fishing port here is home to the mildly interesting **Museu de la Pesca** (mid-June to mid-Sept Tues–Sun 10am–9pm; mid-Sept to mid-June Tues–Sat 10am–1.30pm & 3–7pm, Sun 10am–2pm & 4–7pm; €3), chronicling the town's fishing and maritime history. The museum also organizes a variety of trips on the *Rafael* sailing boat, built in 1915 (June–Sept; 4 different excursions from €12 to €25).

Even if the museum doesn't grab you, the old town is a great place for an afternoon wander and an evening at one of the fantastic **restaurants**, such as the traditional *El Rabal de Mar* at c/Pagès Ortiz 53 (closed Tues), or the locally renowned *Maria de Cadaqués* (closed Sun eve & Mon), just off the marina at c/Tauler i Servià 6, which was founded in 1936 as a fishermen's tavern serving excellent shellfish and *calamares*. The **nightlife** makes no concessions to foreign tastes, and is consequently a much more fun and spontaneous affair; the best places are between the old town and the port in the La Planassa area (towards the end of the promontory), most notably *La Plata* (usually open from 8 or 9pm), in a ruined building at Plaça San Pere 11, with a lively downstairs bar and leafy terrace upstairs. Later, revellers decamp to the string of vivacious bars at the marina, a short walk east.

Accessible from Palamós by road or along the Camí de Ronda are two fabulous **beaches**. The first, the idyllic **Cala S'Alguer**, is framed by nineteenth-century fishermen's huts, while the larger **Platja de Castell** was rescued from the clutches of property developers, thanks to a local referendum. Perched on the headland at the northern tip of Platja de Castell are the tranquil ruins of an Iberian settlement, visited by surprisingly few people.

Palafrugell and around

Seven kilometres north of Palamós, and 4km inland from a delightful coastline, lies the old town of **PALAFRUGELL**, comprised of a cluster of streets and shops around a sixteenth-century church, and at its liveliest during the morning market. The surrounding area boasts tranquil, pine-covered slopes, which back three of the most alluring villages on the Costa Brava – Calella, Llafranc and Tamariu – each with a distinct character and all with scintillatingly turquoise waters. With no true coastal road, the beach development here has been generally mild – low-rise, whitewashed apartments and hotels – and although a fair number of foreign visitors come in season, it's also where many of the better-off Barcelonans have a villa for weekend and August escapes. All this makes for one of the most appealing (though hardly undiscovered) stretches of the Costa Brava.

Practicalities

Between June and September, **buses** run from Palafrugell to Calella and then on to Llafranc (7.40am–8.30pm: July & Aug every 30min, June & Sept roughly hourly). These services reduce to four times daily from October to May. A less frequent service runs to the more distant beach at Tamariu (June–Sept, 3–4 daily). Buses arrive at Palafrugell's SARFA **bus terminal** at c/Luís Companys 2, a ten-minute walk from the town centre. There's a **turisme** near the terminal, c/Carrilet 2 (May & Sept Mon–Sat 10am–1pm & 5–8pm; July & Aug Mon–Sat 9am–9pm, Sun 10am–1pm; Oct–April Mon–Sat 10am–1pm & 4–7pm, Sun 10am–1pm; ☎972 300 228, ⓦwww.visitpalafrugell.cat). You'll also find tourist information at c/Santa Margarida 1 (Mon–Sat 10am–1pm & 5–8pm, Oct–March till 7pm, Sun 10am–1pm).

There are **places to stay** at any of the nearby beaches, though rooms are expensive and zealously sought-after. In the summer, it's easier and cheaper to stay in Palafrugell itself and get the bus to the beach: it's still wise to try and book ahead. The best budget choice is *Fonda L'Estrella*, c/de les Quatre Cases 13 (℡972 300 005, ⓦwww.fondalestrella.com; ❸), on a little street near the main Plaça Nova. The simple, cool rooms are arranged around a cloistered courtyard dating from 1605. On the other side of the square, the *Hostal Plaja* at c/Sant Sebastià 34 (℡972 610 828, ⓦwww.hostalplaja.com; ❹) is slightly pricier, with plain but comfortable rooms and a secure garage.

If you stay in Palafrugell, you'll have to **eat** there as well, since the last bus back from the beaches is at around 8.30pm. The friendly *La Taverna* (closed Mon), just off c/de la Verge Maria on the narrow c/de Giralt i Subirós, has a decent *menú*, and delicious local seafood, including sea bream and monkfish. Pricier are *La Xicra*, c/de Sant Antoni 17, a pleasant Catalan restaurant, where a meal will run to €35 a head, and the similarly priced and highly praised *Mas Oliver* (℡972 301 041; closed Tues & mid-Dec to mid-Feb) on Avinguda d'Espanya (outside town on the ring road). The **market** runs from Tuesday to Sunday (7am–1pm); it's on c/Pi i Margall, leading north from Plaça Nova.

Calella de Palafrugell

One of the most captivating towns on the Costa Brava, **CALELLA DE PALAFRUGELL** possesses a gloriously rocky coastline punctuated by several tiny sand and rocky **beaches** strung out along a backdrop of whitewashed arches and *fin-de-siècle* villas. From the thoroughly charming area around the minuscule main beaches, the town stretches southwards along a winding Camí de Ronda to the hidden **El Golfet** beach. Above this cove, the Cap Roig headland is home to the **Jardí Botanic de Cap Roig** (daily: June–Sept 9am–8pm; Oct–May 9am–6pm; €6), a cliff-top botanical garden and castle begun in 1927 by an exiled colonel from the tsar's army and his aristocrat English wife; the grounds also host open-air jazz concerts in July and August.

Accommodation is not cheap here; the best bets are the *Hotel Sant Roc* at Plaça Atlàntic 2 (℡972 614 250, ⓦwww.santroc.com; ❼), a plush hotel with superb views over the coves, and the friendly *Mediterrani*, c/Francesc Estrabau 40 (℡972 614 500, ⓦwww.hotelmediterrani.com; closed Oct–April; ❹), with views that are almost as good. There are several **restaurants** worth seeking out: *La Gavina* (Fri–Sun lunch, plus Sat dinner), c/Gravina 7, where you can enjoy excellent traditional Catalan cooking and a wide selection of fish and seafood for around €12–15; and *Tragamar* (Mon–Thurs lunch only, closed Tues), Platja del Canadell, offering a more modern take on local cuisine, including gorgonzola-scented rice and grilled salmon, in a lovely setting below the promenade (at beach level), with seafood dishes for €15–20. While you're in Calella or neighbouring Llafranc, try *cremat*, a typical drink of the fishing villages in this region, reputedly brought over by sailors from the Antilles. The concoction contains rum, sugar, lemon peel, coffee grounds and sometimes a cinnamon stick; it will be brought out in an earthenware bowl and you have to set fire to it, occasionally stirring until (after a few minutes) it's ready to drink.

Llafranc

A gentle, hilly, twenty-minute walk high above the rocks along the Camí de Ronda brings you to **LLAFRANC**, tucked into the next bay, with a good, if packed, stretch of **beach** and a glittering **marina**. A little more upmarket than Calella, it's a self-consciously opulent place with expensive beachside restaurants and hillside villas glinting in the sun. Steps lead up from the port for the winding climb through residential streets to the **Far de Sant Sebastia**, where you'll be rewarded with some terrific views; you'll also find the sumptuous *Hotel El Far* (℡972 301 639, ⓦwww.elfar.net; ❻), with an alluring restaurant, and eight charming rooms and a suite, each with a panoramic balcony.

Back in Llafranc there are further attractive **hotels**, most with great restaurants. Perched halfway up a flight of steps, the *Hotel Casamar*, c/del Nero 3 (℡972 300 104, ⓦwww.hotelcasamar.net; ❹), has lovely views of the bay from its rooms with balconies. On the seafront, the *Hotel Terramar*, Pg. Cipsela 1 (℡972 300 200, ⓦwww.hterramar.com; ❺), is a comfortable option, and has rooms overlooking the beach. For a **meal** try *Llevant*, inside the hotel at c/Francesc Blanes 5, famed for its seafood (€24 *menú*), or *La Llagosta* in the *hostal* at c/Francesc Blanes 24 (on the seafront), which serves a decent *menú* for around €12. The cheapest option is *León*, behind the seafront at c/de Pere Pascuet 30, serving a hearty lunchtime *menú*.

Tamariu to Begur

TAMARIU, 4km north of Llafranc, is quieter still and a great favourite with well-heeled Catalan families. The town's action is focused on the small seafront, and the **promenade** – lined with tamarind trees, the source of the town's name – has a hushed allure, with small shops, pavement restaurants and elderly people sitting on their front porches. Geared more towards second-homers, the town boasts few **hotels**, but most are good: the seafront *Tamariu*, Pg. del Mar 2 (℡972 620 031, ⓦwww.tamariu.com; ❻), originally a fishermen's tavern in the 1920s, has simple but comfortable rooms with terrace. **Eating** places scatter the promenade, although there is little to set them apart from one another.

It's a pleasant drive along the coast from here to Begur, passing **PLATJA D'AIGUABLAVA**, with the lovely *Parador de Aiguablava* (℡972 622 162, ⓦwww.parador.es; ❻), set on a craggy headland jutting out into the sea. It's a modern hotel, the rooms lacking the character of historic *paradores*, but with superb facilities and large windows throughout to show off the magnificent views. The restaurant serves up a range of local dishes, including those rooted in Catalunya's *mar i muntanya* cuisine, such as delicious chicken with lobster. Just 1km north is the tiny and exclusive cove of **FORNELLS**, 3km from Begur.

Begur and around

In the lee of a ruined hilltop castle, chic **BEGUR**, about 7km from Palafrugell and slightly inland, stands at the centre of a web of winding roads leading down to its tranquil and equally stylish **beaches** (connected to the town by summer minibus services). Narrow streets lead to the simple exterior and surprisingly ornate Gothic interior of the **Església Parroquial de Sant Pere**; most remarkable is the odd contrast between statuary and architecture, especially the simplicity of the alabaster Madonna and Child compared with the busy altarpiece. Watching over it all, the thrice-destroyed **Castell de Begur** offers fabulous perspectives of the rocky coves to the south and the curving swathe of the Golf de Roses to the north.

From here roads lead east to the **Cap de Begur**, with its spectacular *mirador*, the coves of **SA TUNA** and **AIGUAFREDA**, linked by a scenic footpath (1km), and the pretty hamlet of **SA RIERA**, where you can walk to **Platja del Raco** and **Platja Illa Roja**, some of the best beaches on the coast.

The **turisme** at Avdga. Onze de Setembre 7 (Mon–Fri 9am–2pm & 4–7pm, Sat 10am–2pm & 4–7pm, Sun 10am–2pm; ℡972 624 520, ⓦwww.visitbegur .cat), just south of Begur's main square, Plaça de la Vila, can help with maps. There are a few fairly expensive **hotels** at the beaches, while in Begur itself is the charming family-owned *Hotel Rosa*, c/Pi i Ralló 19 (℡972 623 015,

@www.hotel-rosa.com; ④). The same owners also run the nearby, inviting restaurant *Fonda Caner*, at no. 10, with tiled floors and partially exposed stone walls, and savoury *comida Catalana*, including a *menú* for €20. Further options for a **meal** or a **drink**, besides the beachside spots, are around the Plaça del la Villa; try *Can Torrades* at c/Pi i Tató 5 for traditional Catalan fare.

Inland: Palafrugell to Torroella de Montgrí

Inland from Palafrugell there are several towns and villages that make for a peaceful afternoon's escape from the beach or even as quiet bases from which to explore the region.

Pals

The journey north to Torroella de Montgrí can be broken at **PALS**, 7km from Palafrugell and Begur. This fortified medieval village was long neglected until it was painstakingly restored by a local doctor after the Civil War, which has earned it the rather unfortunate side effect of being invaded by scores of day-trippers. Even so, its fourteenth-century streets and hilltop setting make it an enjoyable place for a stroll amid the golden-brown buildings clustering around a stark tower, all that remains of the town's Romanesque **castle**; below is the beautifully vaulted Gothic **Església de Sant Pere** and Romanesque **Torre de les Hores**. You could also look into the **Museu Casa de Cultura Ca La Pruna**, c/La Mina (June–Sept Tues–Sat 10am–1.30pm & 4–8pm; Oct–May Tues–Sun 10am–1.30pm; €1.50), with exhibits including odds and ends retrieved from an English warship sunk in the siege of Roses in 1808. There's a good **turisme** in the old town at Plaça Major 7 (daily: April–May 10am–2pm & 4–7pm; June–Aug 10am–2pm & 5–8pm; Sept–March 10am–5pm; ☎972 637 380, @www.pals.es), and also on the edge of the new town at c/Aniceta Figueres 6 (June–Aug same hours; ☎972 667 857).

La Bisbal and around

LA BISBAL, 12km northwest of Palafrugell and on the main road to Girona, is a medieval market town in an attractive river setting. Since the seventeenth century, La Bisbal has specialized in the production of **ceramics**, and pottery shops line the main road through town (c/de L'Aigüeta), great for browsing and picking up some terrific local pieces; if the industry grabs you, the **Terracota Museu** (June–Sept Mon–Sat 11am–2pm & 4.30–8.30pm, Sun 11am–2pm; €3) at c/Sis d'Octubre de 1869 99 (the main road into town from Palafrugell) makes for an interesting diversion. Ceramics apart, La Bisbal is a pleasant stop anyway, as its handsome old centre retains many impressive mansions, the architectural remnants of a once thriving Jewish quarter and the fortified medieval **Castell Palau** (Tues–Sat 11am–2pm & 5–8pm, Sun 11am–2pm; €2, guided tour €3), built for the bishops of Girona.

If you fancy a luxurious **stay** or **meal** locally, *Hotel Castell d'Empordà*, perched on top of a hill 3km north of the town in an eight-hundred-year-old castle that once belonged to one of Columbus's captains (☎972 646 254, @www.castelldemporda .com; ⑦), is a most rewarding detour. The *Arcs de Monells*, 3km northwest at c/Vilanova 1 in Monells, is an equally lavish base (☎972 630 304, @www .hotelarcsmonells.com; ⑧), a lovely hotel in a fourteenth-century hospital.

Peratallada and Ullastret

Five kilometres northeast of La Bisbal, the medieval walled town of **PERATAL-LADA** has preserved a rustic feel, with the help of its tiny cobbled streets, stone arches and shaded squares. An influx of small hotels and restaurants has proved to be surprisingly in keeping with their thirteenth-century Romanesque setting, making it both an alluring place for a meal and a stroll or a fabulous base away from the beach. The focal point is the **Castell de Peratallada** (closed to visitors), whose origins have been dated to pre-Roman times. As for **hotels**, the *Hostal La Riera*, Plaça les Voltes 3 (☎972 634 142, ⓦwww.lariera.com; ❹), in a seventeenth-century building, is the most economical option; more expensive are the tiny *Hostal Miralluna*, Plaça de l'Oli 2 (☎972 634 304, ⓦwww .hostalmiralluna.com; ❼), housed in an eighteenth-century lodging set back from the street, and the bougainvillea-strewn *El Pati*, c/Hospital 13 (☎972 634 069, ⓦwww.hotelelpati.net; ❼), which also does a decent *menú*.

Six kilometres northeast lie the remains of the Iberian settlement of **Puig de Sant Andreu d'Ullastret** (Tues–Sun: Easter & June–Sept 10am–8pm; Oct–May 10am–2pm & 3–6pm; €1.80), a lovely, peaceful ruin with a fascinating museum. The site is just north of the friendly, historic village of **Ullastret**, signposted off the main road.

Torroella de Montgrí and L'Estartit

TORROELLA DE MONTGRÍ, 8km from Ullastret and 9km beyond Pals, was once an important medieval port, but today has been left high and dry by the receding Mediterranean. It now stands 5km inland, beneath the shell of the huge, crenellated **Castell de Montgrí** (at 302m, a stiff thirty-minute walk away), built by King Jaume II between 1294 and 1301, but never completed. The town itself remains distinctly medieval in appearance with its narrow streets, fine mansions and fourteenth-century parish church of **Sant Genís** (Mon–Fri 10.30am–12.30pm & 3.30–5.30pm, Sat 10.30am–12.30pm & 3–9pm, Sun 8.30am–noon & 7–9pm, closed Wed am). The **Centre Cultural de la Mediter-rània** (July & Aug Mon–Sat 10am–2pm & 6–9pm, Sun 10am–2pm; Sept–June Mon–Sat 10am–2pm & 5–8pm, Sun 10am–2pm; ☎972 755 180, ⓦwww .museudelamediterrania.org; free), in the Can Quintana at c/d'Ullà 31, a few minutes from arcaded Plaça de la Vila, has interesting displays on local history and culture. The **turisme** is in the Centre Cultural (same hours).

If you decide to **stay**, try the *Fonda Mitja*, at c/Església 14 (☎972 758 003, ⓦwww.fondamitja.com, closed Sept; ❸), just off Plaça de la Vila, which has comfortable en-suite singles and doubles with TV and a homely restaurant providing breakfast or full-board. For a more luxurious stay, book into the fabulous ninth-century *Palau Lo Mirador*, Pg. de l'Església 1 (☎972 758 063, ⓦwww.palaulomirador.com; ❺), the former palace of the counts of Torroella. In summer, a **turisme** booth operates in the free car park on the L'Estartit road (mid-June to mid-Sept Mon 10am–2pm, Tues–Sat 10am–1pm & 5–8pm; ☎972 755 180). The town is probably best known for its **Festival Internacional de Música**, held each July and August in the main square and church.

The nearest beach is 6km to the east at **L'ESTARTIT**, an otherwise unexceptional resort town with a small **turisme** at the northern end of Passeig Marítim (generally Mon–Fri 9.30am–2pm & 4–7pm, Sat & Sun 10am–2pm & 4–7pm; ☎972 751 910, ⓦwww.visitestartit.com), which runs along the seafront. Call in here for information about the nearby **Illes Medes**, Catalunya's only offshore islands – kiosks in the area sell boat trips in the summer. The tiny islands form a protected nature reserve, hosting the most important colony of herring gulls in the Mediterranean, numbering some eight thousand pairs, and offer some of the best **diving** and snorkelling on the coast. *Hotel Les Illes* (☎972 751 239, ⓦwww.hotellesilles.com; ❸), at c/Illes 55, is a great place **to stay**, and organizes its own popular diving excursions. There are plenty of **bars** and **restaurants** along the seafront, and hourly **buses** from Torroella de Montgrí.

Alt Empordà

Beyond Torroella de Montgrí, the scenery changes quite abruptly as you move into the fertile plains and wetlands of the southern part of the **Alt Empordà**, dominated by the broad swathe of the Golf de Roses. Coves give way to long stretches of sand as far north as **Roses**, which nestles in its own closed-in bay and is the closest town to *El Bulli*, one of Spain's most celebrated restaurants.

On the way, the landscape passes through low-key developments such as the pleasant old fishing port of **L'Escala**, made more remarkable by the presence of **Empúries**, a ruined Greek and Roman settlement and one of Spain's most important archeological sites. Beyond Roses, the familiar crashing rocks and deeply indented coves return with a vengeance in the wild Cap de Creus headland. The jewel in the crown here is **Cadaqués**, eternally linked to **Salvador Dalí**, who lived for years in the neighbouring fishermen's village of **Portlligat**, now home to an absorbing museum in his former bizarre residence. For the final run to the French border, the road swoops along the coast through quieter villages such as whitewashed **El Port de la Selva**.

L'Escala and Empúries

At the southernmost end of the sweeping billhook of the Golf de Roses, **L'ESCALA** is split between its shabby but picturesque *nucli antic*, or **old town**, favoured by local holidaymakers, and the more commercial **Riells** quarter (which has a beach), the haunt of foreign visitors. Infinitely more appealing, the narrow pedestrianized streets of the old town huddle around the ancient port, where you'll find medieval mooring posts and a cannonball embedded in the wall of the house at c/Joan Massanet 2 (close to the seafront at the end of c/Pintor de Massanet), fired from a ship in May 1809. A further enticement is L'Escala's proximity to the archeological site of **Empúries**, which lies just a couple of kilometres out of town. Empúries has immense historical significance, being the first entry point of classical Mediterranean culture into Iberian Spain – its fascination derives from its distinct Greek and Roman quarters as one culture steadily usurped the other. You can see the ruins in a leisurely afternoon, spending the rest of your time on the pleasant duned stretch of sand in front of the ruins. L'Escala is also widely known for its canning factories where Catalunya's best **anchovies** (*anxoves*) are packaged. You can sample them in any bar or restaurant, or buy small jars to take home from shops around town.

Practicalities

Buses stop on Avinguda Girona, just down the road from the **turisme** at Plaça de las Escoles 1 (mid-June to mid-Sept Mon–Sat 9am–8pm, Sun 10am–1pm; mid-Sept to mid-June Mon–Fri 9am–1pm & 4–7pm, Sat 10am–1pm & 4–7pm, Sun 10am–1pm; ☎972 770 603, ⓦwww.lescala.cat), on the edge of the old town. **Parking** is tricky, although there are a number of small car parks around the centre or meters along the promenade between the old port and Riells.

Accommodation options include *Hotel Voramar*, Pg. Lluis Albert 2 (☎972 770 108, ⓦwww.hotelvoramar.com; B&B ❺), with a saltwater pool and bar above the waves (prices reduce by fifty percent in winter). There's also a good **hostel**, *Alberg Empúries*, behind the beach near Empúries at c/Les Coves 41 (☎972 771 200; €21.60 dorm bed plus breakfast in high season), and a smart hotel, *Hostal Empúries* (☎972 770 207, ⓦwww.hostalempuries.com; ❺), with newly refurbished rooms, near the main entrance to the site.

Freshly caught fish and seafood are the speciality of the town's **restaurants**, with a good choice in the port and the old town; for tapas, try *La Cava del Port* at c/del Port 33, near the seafront. For a **drink**, you're also better off staying in the *nucli antic*, where you'll find a range from fishermen's taverns to trendy bars.

Empúries: the site

Empúries was the ancient Greek Emporion (literally "trading station"), founded in the early sixth century BC by merchants who, for three centuries, conducted a vigorous trade throughout the Mediterranean. In 218 BC, their settlement was taken by Scipio, and a Roman city – more splendid than the Greek, with an amphitheatre, fine villas and a broad marketplace – grew up above the old Greek town. The Romans were replaced in turn by the Visigoths, who built several basilicas, and Emporion disappears from the records only in the ninth century when, it is assumed, it was wrecked by either Saracen or Norman pirates.

The **site** (daily: Easter & June–Sept 10am–8pm; rest of year 10am–6pm; €3; audioguides €3.60; audiovisual show €1.80) lies behind a sandy bay about 2km north of L'Escala: you can enter via the beach in summer, but at other times the main entrance and car park lie on the road farther inland. The remains of the original **Greek colony**, destroyed by a Frankish raid in the third century AD – at which stage all inhabitants moved to the Roman city – occupy the lower part of the site. Among the ruins of several temples, to the south on raised ground is one dedicated to Asklepios, the Greek healing god whose cult was centred on Epidauros and the island of Kos. The temple is marked by a replica of a fine third-century BC statue of the god, the original of which (along with many finds from the site) is in the Museu Arqueològic in Barcelona. Nearby are several large water filters: Emporion had no aqueduct so water was stored here to be filtered and purified and then supplied to the town by means of long pipes, one of which has been reconstructed. Remains of the town gate, the **agora** (or central marketplace) and several streets can easily be made out, along with a mass of house foundations, some with mosaics, and the ruins of Visigoth basilicas. A small **museum** stands above, with helpful models and diagrams of the excavations, as well as some of the lesser finds, and an excellent audiovisual display giving a brief history of the settlement. Beyond this stretches the vast but only partially excavated **Roman town**. Here, two luxurious villas have been uncovered, and you can see their entrance halls, porticoed gardens and magnificent mosaic floors. Farther on are the remains of the **forum**, **amphitheatre** and outer walls.

The Golf de Roses

The **Golf de Roses** stretches between L'Escala and Roses, a wide bay backed for the most part by flat, rural land, well watered by the Muga and Fluvià rivers. Left to its own quiet devices for centuries, this coast is distinct from the otherwise rocky and touristy Costa Brava, and has really only suffered the attentions of the developers in towns at either end of the bay, most notably in the few kilometres between the giant marina-cum-resort of Empuriabrava and Roses.

Parc Natural dels Aiguamolls de l'Empordà

Halfway around the bay, in two parcels of land on either side of Empuriabrava, is one of Spain's more accessible nature reserves. The **Parc Natural Dels Aiguamolls de l'empordà** (open daily; free) is an important wetland reserve created by the Catalan government in 1983 to save what remained of the Empordà marshland, once covering the entire plain here but gradually reduced over the centuries as a result of agricultural developments and cattle-raising. The park attracts a wonderful selection of birds to both its coastal terrain and the paddy fields typical of the area.

From Empúries, it's 7km to Sant Pere Pescador and 14km to the **visitors' centre** at El Cortalet (daily: April–Sept 9.30am–2pm & 4.30–7pm; Oct–March 9.30am–2pm & 3.30–6pm; ☎972 454 222, ⓦwww.parcsdecatalunya .net), where you can pick up a brochure marking the recommended routes in the park. The visitors' centre also provides free **parking**. There are two main paths around the lagoons and marshes: the first takes around two hours, while a second five-hour trek crosses more open land and can be cycled. Hides have been created along the way; morning and early evening are the best times for birdwatching and you'll spy the largest number of species during the migration periods (March–May & Aug–Oct). You'll almost certainly see marsh harriers and various waterfowl, and might spot bee-eaters and the rare glossy ibis.

Without your own transport, access is by one of the several daily **buses** of the SARFA company plying the Figueres–Roses road; get off the bus at Castelló d'Empúries and take the turning south in the direction of Sant Pere Pescador. After about 4km, you'll see a sign on the left pointing the way to the centre. Best **campsites** for the park include the massive *Nàutic Almatà* (☎972 454 477, ⓦwww.campingparks.com; closed Oct to mid-May). The nearest village to the visitors' centre is **SANT PERE PESCADOR**, 3km south, pleasant enough but surrounded by a glut of sprawling, extremely busy campsites. You can rent bikes here, handy given the flat countryside, but the hordes of tourists make Castelló d'Empúries, 8km farther on, a more attractive base. If you need to stay in Sant Pere, the eighteenth-century farmhouse *Can Ceret*, c/Mar 1 (☎972 530 433, ⓦwww.canceret.com; ❹), offers comfortable rooms and excellent meals.

Castelló d'Empúries

The delightful small town of **CASTELLÓ D'EMPÚRIES**, halfway between the beach at Roses (only fifteen minutes by bus) and Figueres, is also midway between the two halves of the *parc natural*. A five-minute walk from the outskirts where the bus halts (and where cars should be parked) takes you into a small medieval conglomeration that's lost little of its genteel charm. Formerly the capital of the counts of Empúries, the town's narrow alleys and streets conceal some fine preserved buildings, a medieval bridge and a towering thirteenth-century church, **Santa María** (daily 9am–8pm; free) whose ornate doorway and alabaster altarpiece alone are reward enough for the trip; known as the Cathedral of the Empordà, it was intended to be the centre of an episcopal see, but opposition from the bishopric of Girona meant this was never to be, thus leaving Castelló with a church out of proportion to the town. The church's **Museu Parroquial de Santa María** (daily 10am–1pm & 4–8pm; €2) contains a mildly interesting collection of silver and gold religious artefacts.

The **turisme** (summer daily 10am–2pm & 3–7pm; winter Mon–Sat 10am–2pm & 4–6pm, Sun 10am–1pm; ☎972 156 233, ⓦwww.castellodempuries.org) occupies the same premises as the **Presó i Cúria**, or medieval prison (same times; €1) on Plaça Jaume I, which has a curiosity value in the graffiti scratched by prisoners on the walls. The best **places to stay** include the *Hotel Canet* (☎972 250 340, ⓦwww.hotelcanet.com; ❹), Plaça Joc de la Pilota 2, which has a good terrace restaurant, and the same owners' lavish seventeenth-century mansion at *Hotel de la Moneda*, Plaça de la Moneda 8–10 (☎972 158 602, Ⓦwww.hoteldelamoneda.com; ❺).You'll also find several *cases rurales* in the area, including the lovely *El Molí* (☎972 525 139, Ⓦwww.elmolidesiurana.com; ❹), set among vast gardens with oaks and laurel trees, near the village of **Siurana d'Empordà**, between Figueres and Sant Pere Pescador.

Roses

ROSES, 9km from Castello, enjoys a brilliant situation beneath medieval fortress walls at the head of the grand, sweeping bay. It's a site that's been inhabited for over three thousand years – the Greeks called the place *Rhoda*, when they set up a trading colony around the excellent natural harbour in the ninth century BC – but apart from the ruined **Castell de la Tinitat** and the citadel, now part of the absorbing **Museu de la Ciutadella** (Tues–Sun: April–Sept 10am–8/9pm; Oct–March 10am–6pm; €2.50), there's little in present-day Roses to hint at its long history. Instead, Roses is a full-blown package resort that trades exclusively on its 4km of sandy beach, which has fostered a large and popular watersports industry. If you're staying, don't skip a day-trip to Cadaqués, which you can reach via a short bus ride over the hill.

The **bus station** is on the corner of c/Gran Vía Pau Casals and Rambla Ginjolers. If you feel like staying, the **turisme** (Mon–Fri 9am–7pm, Sat 10am–6pm, Sun 10am–1pm; ☎972 257 331, Ⓦwww.roses.es), on the seafront promenade near the citadel, has an extensive **accommodation** list. Serious fans of Spain's new cuisine should make a pilgrimage to 🍴 *El Bulli* (April–Sept, generally dinner only; ☎972 150 457, Ⓦwww.elbulli.com), the showcase of celebrated chef Ferran Adrià: creative, mind-boggling dishes of the highest quality are served in tranquil, stylish premises 7km from Roses, on the winding road to Montjoi. Expect to pay up to €200 and up, and you'll have to make a reservation at least a year months in advance to land a coveted seating.

Cadaqués and around

CADAQUÉS is by far the most pleasant place to stay on the northern Costa Brava, reached only by the winding road over the hills from either Roses (16km) or Port de la Selva (12km) and consequently retaining an air of isolation. With whitewashed and bougainvillea-festooned houses lining narrow, hilly streets, a tree-lined promenade and craggy headlands on either side of a working fishing port, it's genuinely picturesque.Already by the 1920s and 1930s the place had begun to attract the likes of Picasso, Man Ray, Lorca, Buñuel, Thomas Mann and Einstein, but Cadaqués really "arrived" as an **artistic-literary colony** after World War II when Surrealist painter **Salvador Dalí** and his wife Gala settled at nearby Portlligat, attracting for some years a floating bohemian community. Today, a seafront statue of Dalí, haughtily gazing on the artists, well-heeled Barcelonans and art-seeking foreigners who have rolled up in his wake, provides the town's physical and spiritual focal point.

Arrival and information

Buses arrive at the little SARFA bus office on c/Sant Vicenç, on the edge of town, next to a large pay **car park**. From here, you can walk along c/Unió and c/Vigilant to the seafront or climb up through the old streets to reach it. Just back from Plaça Frederic Rahola on the promenade, the **turisme** is at c/des Cotxe 2 (late-June to mid-Sept Mon–Sat 9am–9pm, Sun 10am–1pm & 5–8pm; mid-Sept to late-June Mon–Sat 9am–1pm & 3–6pm; ☎972 258 315, Ⓦwww.cadaques.cat).

Accommodation

Cadaqués can get very busy in the peak season, and it's a good idea to book in advance if possible. There's a noisy though well-equipped **campsite** (☏972 258 126, ⓦ www.campingcadaques.com; closed Oct–March) on the road to Portlligat, 1km out of town.

Hostal Cristina Riera Sant Vicenç 1 ☏972 258 138. Just about as central as you can get, with simple, white-walled rooms, some of which overlook the main plaza. Internet access (for a fee). ❸

Hostal La Residència c/Caritat Serinyana 1 ☏972 258 312, ⓦ www.laresidencia.net. Magnificent building, built in 1904 (the year that Dalí was born) and loaded with character, though the rooms are relatively ordinary – the suites are elaborately decorated with Dalí in mind, however, and the balconies have stunning views. ❹

Hostal Vehí c/Església 6 ☏972 258 470. Friendly and family-owned, this excellent-value *pensió* has a lovely central location near the church, and is consequently very popular. Choice of simple rooms with or without bathroom. Closed Dec & Jan. ❶–❷

L'Hostalet de Cadaqués c/Miquel Rosset 13 ☏972 258 206, ⓦ www.hostaletcadaques.com. Pleasant, small hotel with a stone-and-iron facade

that gives way to eight stylish, immaculate rooms (with wi-fi), each named after a different *cala*, or cove; a glossy, commissioned photo of each cove hangs over the bed. ❸

Llané Petit c/Dr Bartomeus 37 ☏972 251 020, ⓦ www.llanepetit.com. Friendly, relaxing hotel at the southern end of the town. All rooms have cable TV and a/c, and most have terraces with sea views. Closed Jan & Feb. ❺

Misty Ctra. Portlligat ☏972 258 962, ⓦ www .hotel-misty.com. Hacienda-style hotel set around a garden and swimming pool on the road to Portlligat, on the edge of town. Extras include small pool, tennis court and tranquil garden. Closed Jan & Feb. ❹

Playa Sol Platja Pianc 3 ☏972 258 100, ⓦ www .playasol.com. Set in a curve of the seafront, this quiet hotel offers simply furnished but comfortable rooms with TV, a/c and balconies affording superb views of the town or over tranquil gardens. Closed Nov–March. ❺

The Town

With its art galleries and studios, smart restaurants and trendy clothes shops, Cadaqués makes for an interesting stroll. At the top of the hill is the austere-looking sixteenth-century **Església de Santa Maria** (Mon–Sat 10.30am–12.45pm & 4–6.30pm, Sun 10.30am–noon), containing an ornate eighteenth-century

▲ Cadaqués

altarpiece and a side chapel on the left painted by Dalí. Below the church, the **Museu de Cadaqués** on c/Narcis Monturiol 15 (10.30am–1.30pm & 4–7pm, closed Sun; €4) features temporary exhibitions by local artists and intriguing displays relating to aspects of Dalí's work. Local **beaches** are all tiny and pebbly, but there are some enjoyable walks around the harbour and nearby coves; the helpful tourist office has further information and maps.

Eating and drinking

Moderately priced seafood **restaurants** are strung along the seafront, any of which are worth trying, while dotted about the old town and along c/Miquel Rosset are places to suit a wide range of tastes and budgets. **Nightlife** is a pleasurable blend of laid-back idling at the beachside terraces and stylish hobnobbing around the bars and restaurants on c/Miguel Rosset, including at the lively *La Frontera*, at no. 22. One place not to miss is Dalí's favourite haunt, *L'Hostal* (open from 8pm daily), at Pg. del Mar 8, which features live bands and still retains a slightly surreal air.

Can Tito c/Vigilant s/n ☎972 259 070. Managed by part of the same family that runs *Casa Anita*, *Can Tito* specializes in Catalan cuisine, with many dishes featuring seafood, including grilled anchovies and a robust shellfish paella.

Casa Anita c/Miquel Rosset 16 ☎972 258 471. Traditional Catalan food that makes this place an institution in town; be prepared to queue.

Casa Nun Portitxó 6 ☎972 258 856. This lovely restaurant offers top-notch regional fish and meat dishes, and an €18 *menú*, which you can enjoy on the small, sunny terrace perched above the Plaça des Portitxó. Closed lunch Tues–Thurs.

La Sirena c/Es Call s/n ☎972 258 974. Tucked away in the old town, this appropriately named restaurant – "*sirena*" means "mermaid" – serves some of the best seafood in town.

Casa-Museu Salvador Dalí

A well-signposted twenty-minute walk north of Cadaqués and 3km by road is the tiny harbour of **PORTLLIGAT**, former home of Salvador Dalí. The artist had spent much of his childhood and youth in Cadaqués, and later, with his wife and muse, Gala, he converted a series of waterside fishermen's cottages in Portlligat into a sumptuous home that has all the quirks you would expect of the couple, such as speckled rooftop eggs and a giant fish painted on the ground outside. The house is now open to the public as the **Casa-Museu Salvador Dalí** (mid-June to mid-Sept daily 9.30am–9pm; rest of year Tues–Sun 10am–6pm; closed Jan 6 to mid-March; last entry 50min before closing; ☎972 251 015, ⓦwww.dali-estate.org; €8), and although there's not much to see in the way of art, it's worth the visit to see first-hand how the bizarre couple lived until Gala's death in 1982, after which Dalí moved to Figueres. Visitor numbers are strictly controlled and you have to **book a visit** by ringing the museum beforehand; you can also book a ticket on the website.

Tours take in most of the house, and include Dalí's studio, the exotically draped model's room, the couple's master bedroom and bathroom and, perhaps best of all, the oval-shaped sitting room that Dalí designed for Gala, which, apparently by accident, boasts stunning acoustics. Upstairs you can see the garden and swimming pool where the couple entertained guests – they didn't like too many strangers trooping through their living quarters. The phallic swimming pool and its various decorative features, including a giant snake and a stuffed lion, are a treat.

Cap de Creus

A road winds 8km from Dalí's house past glimpses of wave-plundered coves to the wind-buffeted **Cap de Creus** headland, the easternmost tip of the Iberian peninsula, providing breathtaking views of the coast and topped by a lighthouse built in 1853. It's now occupied by the **Museu Espai Cap de Creus** (daily 9am–1pm & 2.30–5.30pm; €1), with a small exhibition on the surrounding *parc natural,* and the incongruously hip *Bar Sa Freu* next door. The weather-beaten old building on the clifftop behind is the *Cap de Creus* bar and **restaurant** (Mon–Thurs noon–8pm, Fri–Sun 11am–midnight), which occasionally hosts live music. Note that it's not possible to continue north beyond this point – you'll have to double back to Cadaqués. If you fancy viewing the Cap de Creus from the sea, you'll find a few boats along the seafront that do hour-long excursions, including the *Creuers Cadaques* (℡972 159 462; €12.50 per person; daily noon, 4pm & 6pm in summer, depending on weather).

El Port de la Selva and around

Thirteen kilometres northwest of Cadaqués, **EL PORT DE LA SELVA** is centred on its fishing and pleasure **ports**, while either side is a ribbon of lovely **coves** with some of the cleanest water in the Mediterranean: those to the north are far more rugged and reached on foot or by sea, while the ones to the west are easier to get to and, therefore, more popular.

The few places to **stay** are generally of a high standard: the *Hostal La Tina*, c/Mayor 15 (℡972 387 149, ⓦwww.hostallatina.com; ❹), is comfortable and central; or there's the more expensive *Hotel Porto Cristo*, c/Major 59 (℡972 387 062, ⓦwww.hotelportocristo.com; ❺), with sumptuously decorated rooms. Choice of **restaurants** is limited basically to the above hotels and *pensiones*. There are also a few **campsites** within 2km of the beach, the best being *Port de la Vall*, Ctra. de Llanca km 6 (℡972 387 186, ⓦwww.campingportdelavall .com; closed Oct–Easter).

It's 8km up the paved **road** from here, via Selva de Mar, to the Benedictine monastery of **Sant Pere de Rodes** (Tues–Sun: June–Sept 10am–7.30pm; Oct–May 10am–5pm; €3.60; Tues free), just below the 670-metre-high summit of the Serra de Roda; approaching **by foot**, use the marked trail (1hr 30min) through the Vall de Santa Creu, which begins at Molí de la Vall. The first written record of the monastery dates back to 879, and in 934 it became independent, answerable only to Rome: in these early years, and thanks especially to the Roman connection, the monks became tremendously rich and powerful. As the monastery was enlarged it was also fortified against attack, starting a period of splendour that lasted four hundred years before terminal decline set in. Many fine treasures were looted when it was finally abandoned in 1789, and it was also pillaged by the French during the Peninsular War; some of the rescued silver can be seen in Girona's Museu d'Art. Once one of the most romantic ruins in all of Catalunya, its central church universally recognized to be the precursor of the Catalan Romanesque style, it is being robbed of a great deal of its charm by overzealous restoration. No original columns or capitals remain in the cloister and some of the work looks too clinical. The redeeming feature, apart from the view, is the **cathedral**, which retains its original stonework from the tenth to fourteenth centuries, including eleventh-century column capitals carved with wolves' and dogs' heads.

Nearby is the peaceful pre-Romanesque church of **Santa Elena**, all that remains of the small rural community that grew up around the monastery. Above the monastery (and contemporary with it) stands the much more atmospheric ruined **Castell de Sant Salvador**, a thirty-minute scramble up a steep, narrow path. This provided the perfect lookout site for the frequent invasions (French or Moorish), which normally came from the sea; in the event of attack, fires were lit on the hill to warn the whole surrounding area.

Girona and around

Under an hour inland from the coast, the city of **Girona** with its medieval core provides a startling and likeable break from sand and sea. It's an easy day-trip from the Costa Brava, or Barcelona (frequent train and bus connections), but it really warrants more time – two or three nights will show you the best of the city and let you enjoy some of the surrounding countryside. North of Girona, **Figueres** holds one of the most visited museums in Spain: the **Teatre-Museu Dalí**, created by Salvador Dalí, an enthralling glimpse of the artist's genius.

To see more of the province of which Girona is capital, head for beautiful **Besalú** – one of the oldest and most attractive of Catalan towns – and **Olot**, at the heart of the **Garrotxa** region. Much of this is an ancient volcanic area, now designated the **Parc Natural de la Zona Volcànica**, whose rolling, fertile countryside is pitted with spent craters. Some of these are within Olot's city limits, but the best such scenery is around **Santa Pau** just east. Northeast of Olot, several good excursions take you into the foothills of the nearby Pyrenees. Southwest, between Girona and Barcelona, visitors with a little more time can explore the **Serra del Montseny**, whose spa towns make a restful diversion.

Girona

Sited on a hillside overlooking the Riu Onyar, the ancient, walled city of **GIRONA** has been fought over in almost every century since it was founded as the Roman fortress of Gerunda on the Vía Augusta. Following the Moorish conquest of Spain, Girona was an Islamic town for over two hundred years, a fact apparent in the web of narrow central lanes, and there was also a continuous Jewish presence here for six hundred years. By the eighteenth century, Girona had been besieged on 21 occasions, and during the nineteenth earned the nickname "Immortal" by surviving five attacks, of which the longest was a seven-month assault by the French in 1809.

Not surprisingly, all this attention has left Girona a hotchpotch of architectural styles, from Romanesque to *modernisme*, yet the overall impression is of an overwhelmingly beautiful medieval city, whose attraction is heightened by its river setting. There are several excellent museums and a cathedral equalling any in the region. Even if these leave you unmoved, it's hard to resist the lure of simply wandering the superbly preserved streets, fetching up now and again at the river, above which tall, pastel-coloured houses lean precipitously.

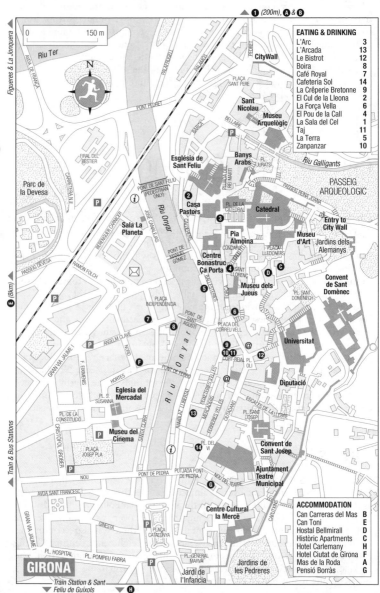

▲ ❶ (200m), Ⓐ & Ⓑ

EATING & DRINKING

L'Arc	3
L'Arcada	13
Le Bistrot	12
Boira	8
Café Royal	7
Cafeteria Sol	14
La Crêperie Bretonne	9
El Cul de la Lleona	2
La Força Vella	6
El Pou de la Call	4
La Sala del Cel	1
Taj	11
La Terra	5
Zanpanzar	10

ACCOMMODATION

Can Carreras del Mas	B
Can Toni	E
Hostal Bellmirall	D
Històric Apartments	C
Hotel Carlemany	H
Hotel Ciutat de Girona	F
Mas de la Roda	A
Pensió Borràs	G

GIRONA

Arrival and information

Girona's **airport** (ⓦ www.barcelona-girona-airport.com), 13km south of the city, has daily scheduled service by budget airlines from across Europe. The arrivals hall has several **car rental** booths, as well as a ticket booth for the hourly **bus service** to both Girona train/bus stations (4.30am–12.30am; €2.05) and even more frequently to Barcelona's Estació del Nord (8.30am–12.15am; €12); a taxi into Girona costs around €22. Sarfa buses (ⓦ www.sarfa.com) serve most resorts along the Costa Brava.

The **train station** is off Crta Barcelona in the modern, western part of the city; the **bus station** – also serving international arrivals – is behind the same building on Plaça d'Espanya. Both are a fifteen-minute walk southwest from the Barri Vell. You're more likely to use a **taxi** – the handiest ranks are at the train station, Plaça Catalunya and the old-town end of Pont de Pedra – than the city bus lines.

Girona is sandwiched by the toll *autopista* A7 (west of town) and the free N-II highway (east). If you **drive** in, you'll find **parking** generally nightmarish: the Barri Vell especially is a controlled-access zone for residents only, so you'll be fined or towed unless your lodgings provide parking. Use the fee car park at Plaça Catalunya, or compete for free spaces in the lot by Pont Pedret or up on Passeig Fora Muralla, just outside the medieval walls near the university campus (difficult during term time).

The main provincial **turisme** is at Rambla de la Llibertat 1, the tree-lined promenade one block behind the river (April–Sept Mon–Fri 8am–8pm, Sat 8am–2pm & 4–8pm, Sun 9am–2pm; Oct–March Mon–Sat 9am–5pm, Sun 9am–2pm; ☎ 972 226 575, ⓦ www.en.costabrava.org); this has English-speaking staff and stocks useful maps and brochures, accommodation lists and local-transport timetables. There's also a **municipal office** at the river end of c/Berenguer Carnicer (July 1–Sept 15 Mon–Sat 9am–8pm, Sun 9am–2pm; rest of year Mon–Sat 9am–2pm & 3–5pm; ⓦ www.ajuntament.gi).

Accommodation

There are over thirty officially classified *pensiones*, *hostals*, hotels and self-catering apartments on both sides of the river, so with few exceptions (indicated below) you shouldn't need to book ahead. With transport, consider some excellent **cases de pagès** slightly out of town. The nearest **campsite** is *Can Toni*, 8km south at Fornells de la Selva (☎ 972 476 117), with excellent amenities.

Can Carreras del Mas c/Creu 34, Bordils ☎ 972 490 276, ⓦ www.cancarrerasdelmas.com. Just three rooms and an apartment at this stone-farm conversion in a more "contemporary" style, with plenty of exposed stone and brick; a small swimming pool is a bonus. In July & Aug, must rent entire house; rest of year ④

Històric Apartments c/Bellmirall 4/A ☎ 972 223 583, ⓦ www.hotelhistoric.com. In a restored building, superb two- or four-person flats (④) with fully equipped kitchens (though there's an on-site restaurant). The same management has a luxury hotel next door (⑤), its eight state-of-the-art units (including two suites) boasting double glazing, designer baths, satellite TV, a/c and internet access. Private parking for both.

Hostal Bellmirall c/Bellmirall 3 ☎ 972 204 009. Beautifully refurbished fifteenth-century building with artily exposed pointing in the stone walls and welcoming female management purveying an excellent, filling breakfast. There are only seven rooms (two without bath), so it's wise to book ahead. Closed Jan–Feb. ③

Hotel Carlemany Plaça Miquel Santal ☎ 972 211 212, ⓦ www.carlemany.es. Comfortable if standard four-star rooms in the modern part of the city, about 20min walk from the old town and convenient if you're driving. The hotel restaurant, *El Pati Verd*, is famous locally, offering traditional and innovative cooking at €40 a head (closed Sun). ⑤

Hotel Ciutat de Girona Nord 2 ☎ 972 483 038, ⓦ www.hotel-ciutatdegirona.com. Girona's smartest hotel, with a minimalist-boutique feel and chic, comfortable rooms and bathrooms. Free extras include wi-fi, music systems and minibar; frequent web-only specials. ❻

🏃 **Mas de la Roda** c/Creu 31, Bordils, 10km northeast on the C255, then through village to old quarter ☎972 490 052, ⓦwww.masdelaroda .com. Four sizeable, en-suite, non-smoking rooms

(doubles to quads) at this well-restored stone house with two lounges and pleasant breakfast room; organic dinners prepared by French-Swiss co-proprietor. Ample off-street parking. ❹

Pensió Borràs Travesia Auriga 6, but enquiries Plaça Bell-lloc 4 ☎972 224 008. Friendly cheapie redolent of Spain in the 1980s; about half the rooms have both en-suite bath and balcony. ❷

The City

Although most of the modern city, including the attractive nineteenth-century **Mercadal** district, sprawls west of the Riu Onyar, points of interest are concentrated in the compact medieval quarter, or **Barri Vell**, on the east bank of the river, where most visitors spend nearly all their time. This thin wedge of hillside, still partially enclosed by medieval walls, contains all the sights and monuments, and as it takes only twenty minutes or so to walk from end to end, it's easy to explore thoroughly.

From the lively, café-lined **Rambla**, a favourite place for the evening stroll, streets rise through **El Call**, the beautifully preserved Jewish quarter, to the **cathedral**, which dominates old Girona. Restoration and gentrification have not completely banished workaday shops and bars, with Girona's student contingent providing a further balance to chi-chi galleries and high-end outlets for designer clothing and furniture that reflect the fact that Girona and its province have the highest per-capita income in Spain.

The Catedral

Balanced on a steep slope scaled by a majestic Baroque staircase, the **Catedral** (April–Oct Mon–Fri 8am–8pm; Nov–March Mon–Fri 10am–7pm, Sat 10am–4.30pm, Sun 2–7/8pm; €5 includes cloister & treasury, free Sun) is an outstanding example of Catalan Gothic. There has been a place of worship here since Roman times, and a mosque stood on the site before the foundation of the cathedral in 1038. Most of the building dates from the fifteenth century, though parts are four hundred years older, notably the five-storey **Torre de Carlemany** and the Romanesque cloister.

The main Rococo **facade**, remodelled in the eighteenth century, writhes with exuberant ornamentation: floral motifs, coats of arms, and niche statues (mostly 1960s copies) in three tiers. The aisle-less interior overwhelms with its single **nave** spanning 22.5m, the second-widest Gothic vault in the world after St Peter's in Rome. Contemporary sceptics deemed the proposed design unsafe, and the vault was raised in 1417 only after an appeal by the architect, Guillermo Bofill, to an independent panel of experts. The walls rise past stained-glass windows, the only objects interrupting the sweep of space being freestanding piers at the apsidal end forming an ambulatory around the choir.

From the main body of the cathedral, there's access to the irregularly shaped, late twelfth-century **cloister** (same hours as cathedral; €4 excludes cathedral, includes treasury, free Sun), which features minutely carved figures and scenes on double column capitals. Finally, the tour route leads to the **Tresor Capitular** (Chapter

Treasury), four overstuffed rooms of religious art whose highlights include (in the third room) Beatus' *Commentary on the Apocalypse*, illuminated in 975 by Mozarabic miniaturists, and (in the last room) a magnificent twelfth-century Italian tapestry, the *Creation*, the finest surviving specimen of Romanesque textile, depicting in strong colours the forces of light and darkness, Adam naming the animals and the creation of Eve, plus seasonal rural activities.

Museu d'Art and Església de Sant Feliu

Girona's **Museu d'Art** (Tues–Sat 10am–7pm, Oct–Feb until 6pm, Sun 10am–2pm; €2), in the well-restored episcopal palace next door to the cathedral, has galleries arranged chronologically as you climb through five floors (the top for temporary exhibits). Lower wings highlight Romanesque and Gothic art, particularly rare manuscripts, such as an amazing martyrology from the monastery of Poblet, and impressive *majestats* (wooden images of Christ garbed in a tunic). Other striking objects rescued from country churches include the tenth-century portable altar from Sant Pere de Rodes, one of the few still preserved in Europe, and an intricately detailed twelfth-century crossbeam from Cruïlles. You then progress through Renaissance works – fifteenth-century *retablos*, polychrome saints and the wonderfully expressive *Virgin of Palera*, fine tiles and ceramics – to nineteenth- and twentieth-century Catalan art on the upper floors, encompassing works by the so-called Olot School of artists, plus some entertaining *modernista* sculpture.

One of Girona's best-known landmarks is the blunt tower of the **Església de Sant Feliu** (Mon–Sat 10am–2.30pm & 4–6pm, Sun 10–11am; free), nicely framed as you descend the cathedral steps. Shortened by a lightning strike in 1581, the belfry tops a hemmed-in church that happily combines Romanesque, Gothic and Baroque styles. The north transept contains the **tomb of Sant Narcís**, patron of the city, while some elegantly sculpted Roman and early Christian **sarcophagi** are embedded in the wall either side of the high altar.

Banys Àrabs

Very near the cathedral, reached by going through the **Portal de Sobreportas** (fourteenth century but built on visible Roman foundations), and then turning right, stand the **Banys Arabs** (Mon–Sat 10am–7pm, July & Aug until 8pm, Oct–March until 2pm, Sun & public hols 10am–2pm; €1.80), probably designed by Moorish craftsmen around 1194 and rebuilt a century later. Closed down in the fifteenth century, supposedly to protect public morals, the building was appropriated by a Capuchin convent in 1617. After years of dereliction, the baths were restored by local architects Rafael Masó and Emili Blanc in 1929, and subsequently opened to the public as a museum. The finest of their type in Spain outside of Granada, they have the usual underfloor heating system in the *caldarium* (steam room) and the Roman-derived layout of four principal rooms. The *apodyterium* (changing room) is the most interesting; there are niches for clothes and a stone bench for relaxation after bathing, while the room is unusually lit by a central vaulted skylight supported by an octagon of columns.

Museu Arqueològic and Passeig de la Muralla

From the Banys Arabs it's a short downhill stroll, over the usually dry Riu Galligants, to the **Museu Arqueològic** (Tues–Sat 10am–2pm & 4–7pm, Oct–May until 6pm, Sun 10am–2pm; €2.30), housed in the former Benedictine monastery of **Sant Pere Galligants**. The twelfth-century **church** itself contains Roman artefacts, including a vivid mosaic showing a chariot race, unearthed in 1876 at a nearby Roman villa. Galleries above the cloister methodically outline the region's history from Paleolithic to Roman times, but unless you read Catalan or Spanish, or pay €2 for the English-language guidebook, you'll get little out of the exhibits.

Near the museum you can gain access to the **Passeig de la Muralla**, with steps through landscaped grounds beside the Banys Arabs leading up onto the **city walls** (daily 8am–10pm; free), from where there are fine views over Girona and the Ter valley. Once onto the ramparts, you can walk right round their perimeter, with intermediate exits near the Museu d'Art, behind the Convent de Sant Domènec and at the gate of the university, before the final descent to Plaça Catalunya, at the south end of the old town. Detours worth taking include the steps down to the shaded gardens of the **Jardins dels Alemanys**, with ruined seventeenth-century barracks where German mercenaries were billeted, and, further on, the rubble-strewn site of the **Torre Gironella**, where Jewish citizens were locked up for their protection during anti-Semitic riots in 1391 and which was finally destroyed by Napoleon's troops during the 1809 siege.

Carrer de la Força and the Jewish Quarter

Heading south instead of north from the Portal de Sobreportas, **Carrer de la Força** leads past what's considered the best-preserved **Jewish quarter** in Western Europe. A Jewish community of 25 families was well established in Girona by the late ninth century, with an initial settlement near the cathedral later shifting up to **Carrer de la Força**, which follows the course of the Roman Via Augusta. With a population of over three hundred at its peak, the new quarter became known as the **Call** or the **Aljama**, forming an autonomous municipality within Girona, under royal protection in exchange for payment of tribute. Cabbalistic scholarship thrived here under the leadership of **Rabbi Moisés Ben Nahman** (born 1194; Nahmánides or Bonastruc ça Porta in Catalan), and members of the community excelled in the professions – commerce, property speculation and banking – reserved for them. But from the thirteenth century onwards, Gironan Jews suffered systematic and escalating persecution; in 1391, a mob stormed the Call and killed forty of its residents, after which the neighbourhood became a restrictive ghetto like those of northern Europe, until the expulsion of the Jews from Spain in 1492.

The Aljama wasn't allowed to open windows, or more than one door, onto c/de la Força, so the inmates created a maze-like, multi-level complex of rooms, stairways and all-important courtyards, which in the final century of Jewish life here contained the synagogue, kosher slaughterhouse and communal baths. The **Centre Bonastruc ça Porta** at no. 8 comprises much of this, plus a café, small bookshop, and the **Museu d'Història dels Jueus** (Mon–Sat 10am–8pm, Nov–April until 6pm, Sun 10am–3pm; €2). This, disappointingly, is long on speculative archeology and short on substantive exhibits, these being principally a room full of enormous **grave steles** from the Bou d'Or cemetery on Montjuïc hill northeast of town, their fervent Hebrew inscriptions the most definitive legacy of Jewish life here. Temporary expositions are apt to be more rewarding.

Museu d'Historia de la Ciutat

Housed in the eighteenth-century Capuchin monastery of Sant Antoni at c/de la Força 27, the **Museu d'Historia de la Ciutat** (Tues–Sat 10am–2pm & 5–7pm, Sun 10am–2pm; €3) completes the Barri Vell's complement of museums, and, despite Catalan-only labelling, is likely to prove the most rewarding one – and certainly the most eclectic. A portion of the monastic catacombs is on the right as you enter, with niches for the (vanished) deceased. The entire ground floor is devoted to the development of local industry and technology, with an antique dealer's bonanza (salvaged from around the province) of ancient phones, typewriters, printing presses, dynamos and even an arc-lamp cine projector. The first floor covers the history of broadcasting in Catalunya – complete with some magnificent old radio sets – and Roman Gerunda, featuring a rather crude mosaic from a villa on the surrounding plain. On the top floor, you'll find coverage of the city's walls and their various besiegings, a modern-art exhibition, plus material on the evolution of the *sardana*.

Museu del Cinema

Tucked away on the west bank of the Onyar at c/Sèquia 1, the **Museu del Cinema** (May–Sept Tues–Sun 10am–8pm; Oct–April Tues–Fri 10am–6pm, Sat 10am–8pm, Sun 11am–3pm; €4) is a fascinating and fun museum detailing the history of cinema from the first moving images to the present day. Based on the private collection of award-winning local director Tomàs Mallol, the museum has a good mix of interactive exhibits and informative displays to please kids and adults alike. It's especially good on surprisingly sophisticated attempts – shadow theatre, magic lanterns, early 3D photography – by diverse cultures to create animated images prior to the Lumière brothers' first true cinema in 1895; the ground-floor shop stocks a full complement of movie memorabilia.

Eating, drinking and nightlife

Most of Girona's more adventurous **restaurants** and **bars** (plus some obvious tourist-traps) are grouped along and just off c/de la Força, or on c/Ballesteries, while daytime **cafés** cluster on or around the Rambla de la Llibertat, and on the parallel Plaça del Vi. **Nightlife** is varied, with venues scattered across the Barri Vell, Mercadal and the former tradesmen's quarter of Pedret, about 700m north of the old town, between the rail line and the riverbank, where the most long-lived outfit is *La Sala del Cel* at no. 116, a vast, multi-level club (Fri/Sat only) with visiting and resident DJs. In summer, pricey open-air bars – collectively known as *Les Carpes* – operate in the Parc de la Devesa, with live music or dancing from Wednesday to Saturday.

From late September into October are the back-to-back, well-established jazz and film **festivals**. Formal events and **concerts** by foreign guest artists tend to take place in the Teatre Municipal, the Teatre de Sant Domènec, the Centre Cultural la Mercé, or Sala la Planeta (Ⓦ www.laplaneta.net) at Passeig Canalejas 3. Watch for flyers at the *turisme* or at *La Terra* for these and more ephemeral venues.

Restaurants

Le Bistrot Pujada de Sant Domènec 4. Stylish, belle-époque decor inside, massively popular tables on steps outside. Evening meals, however, don't quite live up to the surroundings; best stick to the better-value lunchtime *menú* or just a drink.

Boira Plaça de la Independencia 17. The best food on the square, very popular with locals and visitors alike, with *plaça* tables or a river-view salon inside. Very good quality if not terribly generous tapas, and wine by the glass (under €20 for two), or push the boat out at the *a la carta*-only restaurant, with *plats del dia* for €7–15.

La Crêperie Bretonne c/Cort Reial 14. Savoury and sweet crêpes, prepared by a French expat, plus salads and Breton cider, form the basis of good-value *menús*. Narrow street frontage belies the vast, striking interior, which is dominated by a converted minibus (part of the pantry). Summer tables in the street. Closed Sun, & Wed lunchtime in winter.

El Cul de la Lleona Calderers 8. Cosy if potentially pricey bistro specializing in Moroccan dishes; three courses (including house wine and lovely Catalan or North African sweets) can run to €30. Also a much cheaper "local" *menú* at lunchtime, plus summer tables on the nearby fountain-*plaça*. Closed Mon & Sun.

La Força Vella c/de la Força 4. Cheap-and-cheerful old-quarter option, with quantity (generous) often taking precedence over quality. *Menús* (€15) served in the stone-clad area in front of the bar, or at tables outside; rich fare encompasses snails, sausage, rabbit and kidneys. Until 4pm for lunch, 11pm for dinner.

El Pou de la Call c/de la Força 14. More-elaborate-than-usual dishes served in exceptionally pleasant surroundings right next to the Call; *menús* comprise three courses such as vegetarian *terrina*, squid rings with parsley and garlic, plus baked apple with custard, but *a la carta* (allow €30) is more varied. No outdoor seating, but a/c premises.

Taj c/Cort Reial 6 ☎972 222 655. All the North Indian/Bengali standards, with a stress on tandoori dishes, at this hole-in-the-wall, though purists will be outraged by such things as artichokes in the balti. But it's cheapish, friendly and very popular – bookings mandatory.

Cafés and bars

L'Arc Plaça Catedral 9. The only café in Girona with a cathedral on the terrace. During the day, it's a pleasant spot for coffee or *orxata*, while at night its vaulted, wood-beamed interior becomes a secluded hideaway.

L'Arcada Rambla Llibertat 38. Bar-café tucked under the arcades, with designer-minimalist interior and sought-after outdoor tables, serving good breakfast pastries, pasta and pizza. Daily 7.30am–12.30am.

Cafeteria Sol Plaça del Vi. No-nonsense place that's good for breakfast or *plats combinats* under the arcade.

La Terra c/Ballesteries 23 (tiny sign on door). Popular student hangout that's wonderfully cavernous space, with glazed tiles everywhere and river-view windows. Juices, foreign beers, coffees, cakes, quiches, teas in a pot. Daily 4.30pm–2am.

Zanpanzar c/Cort Reial 10–12. Started life to great acclaim as a tapas bar doing Basque-style *pintxos* such as *bacalao* and Gernika *pimientos* (€5 & up); there's now an attached full-on restaurant (*menú* €10; allow €25 *a la carta*). Closed Mon.

Listings

Books and maps Ulyssus, c/Ballesteries 29, is an excellent travel-book specialist with lots of Spanish- and Catalan-language guides to Catalunya, plus all Editorial Alpina and Catalan government ICC maps.

Buses Sarfa (⊛www.sarfa.com) serves Figueres and Costa Brava villages; Teisa (⊛www.teisa-bus.com) handles all services northeast through the Garrotxa to Olot; and Barcelona Bus (⊛www.barcelonabus.com) does express services to Barcelona and Figueres.

Car rental Most agencies are in or near the train station, including Avis (☎972 224 664) and Hertz (☎972 210 108). Local companies, such as Cabeza, c/Barcelona 30 (☎972 218 208, ⊛www.miescaparate.com/cabeza), are cheaper, though cars have to be returned to Girona.

Hospital Dr Josep Trueta, Avgda. França 60 (☎972 202 700), at the northern outskirts of town, is best for emergencies; urban bus #2 gets you there.

Internet access *Communica-T Net*, c/Peralta 4 (Mon–Sat 10.30am–10.30pm, Sun 4–10.30pm); *La Lli-Breria*, c/Ferreries Velles 16 (Mon–Sat 9am–1am, Sun 9am–10.30pm).

Police Policia Municipal at c/Bacià 4 ☎972 419 092; Mossos d'Esquadra (☎972 213 450).

Púbol

If you've been to, or plan to visit, the other two Dalí museums in Alt Empordà, you'll want to make the journey (easiest with your own transport) 22km from Girona to attractive **PÚBOL** village, site of the small medieval castle that Dalí bought and restored for his wife Gala in 1970. Now open to the public as the **Casa-Museu Castell Gala Dalí** (March 15–June 14 & Sept 16–Nov 1 Tues–Sun 10am–6pm; June 15–Sept 15 daily 10am–8pm; Nov 2–Dec 31 Tues–Sun 10am–5pm; closed Jan–March 15; last admission 45min before closing; €7), it contains a lurid mix of precious artworks and Baroque kitsch that the pair bought or made, including a suitably surreal bronze chess set Dalí created in honour of Marcel Duchamp. The castle itself, while perhaps not as wacky as the dwelling at Portlligat, has its quirks as well, such as the womb-shaped fireplace off the kitchen, and the crypt (formerly a tithe warehouse for grain) where Gala is entombed. There's plenty of biographical material on display, in particular photos of Dalí in his 1930s–40s prime, and a fascinating album devoted to Gala (1894–1982), née Elena Dimitrievna Diakonova. Her collection of *haute couture* dresses is on the top floor, while her Cadillac is still parked in the garage.

Dalí's innate snobbery was stoked considerably when, in 1982 (the year of Gala's death), he was awarded the title of Marqués de Dalí de Púbol by King Juan Carlos. He lived permanently at the castle thereafter, writing extensively and painting his last authenticated work (*Kite's Tale and Guitar*) until a fire broke out in 1984, severely injuring Dalí and obliging him to move to Figueres.

Figueres and around

Lying some 37km north of Girona, **FIGUERES** is irrevocably linked to Salvador Dalí. The town is all but overshadowed by the **Teatre-Museu Dalí**, installed by the artist in a building as surreal as the exhibits within, and the only reason most people come here. Stay longer, though, and you'll find a pleasant county town with a lively *rambla* and a few other worthwhile sights.

Arrival and information

Arriving at the **train or bus stations**, you reach the town centre (600m distant) by simply following "Museu Dalí" signs. **Parking** a car is nearly impossible in the centre; either pay to use designated car parks or resign yourself to walking in from the outskirts.

There's a small **turisme booth** just outside the bus station (July 1–Sept 15 Mon–Sat 9.30am–1.30pm & 4.30–7pm), while the main **turisme** is on Plaça

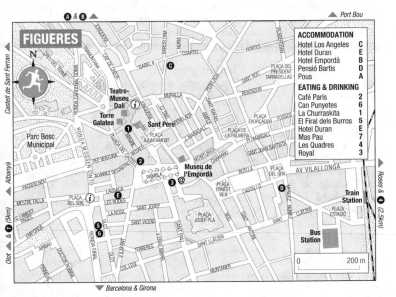

del Sol (Easter–June & Oct Mon–Fri 8.30am–3pm & 4.30–8pm, Sat 9.30am–
1.30pm & 3.30–6.30pm; July & Aug Mon–Fri 8.30am–9.30pm, Sat 9am–
9pm, Sun 9am–3pm; Sept Mon–Fri 8.30am–8pm, Sat 9am–8pm; Nov–Easter
Mon–Fri 10am–2pm, Sat 10am–2pm & 3–6pm; ☎972 503 155, ⓦwww
.figueresciutat.com).

Accommodation

Accommodation options range from basic to upmarket, with several adequate
central choices, though many of the better hotels (with ample parking) lie on
main roads out of town. There's a smallish, shady **campsite**, *Pous*, 3km out on
the N-II to France (☎972 675 496; closed Nov–March).

Hotel Duran c/Lasauca 5 ☎972 501 250, ⓦwww
.hotelduran.com. Comfortable, old-style lodgings
redone in 2006 as a minimalist boutique hotel. ❺
Hotel Empordà edge of town on the N-II road
northwest ☎972 500 562, ⓦwww.hotelemporda
.com. Renovated in 2005 as a boutique hotel, with
Japanese-style balcony doors plus state-of-the-art
baths, and perhaps best for drivers. Noted locally
for its excellent restaurant. ❻

Hotel Los Ángeles c/Barceloneta 10 ☎972 510
661, ⓦwww.hotelangeles.com. Two-star standard,
quiet but slightly overpriced, with bathrooms the
same size as the smallish bedrooms, done up in
vulgar-Spanish-Modern. Wi-fi and off-street parking
costs extra. ❸
Pensió Bartis c/Mendez Nunyez 2 ☎972 501
473. The best-value budget accommodation, above
a bar on a busy street. ❷

Teatre-Museu Dalí

Figueres' **Teatre-Museu Dalí** (March–May & Oct Tues–Sun 9.30am–5.15pm;
June daily 9.30am–5.15pm; July–Sept daily 9am–7.15pm; Nov–Feb daily
10.30am–5.15pm; €11; ⓦwww.salvador-dali.org) is Spain's most visited
museum after Madrid's Prado and Bilbao's Guggenheim, but it's as much
absurdist theatrical fantasy as conventional art collection. Appropriately enough,
before destruction at the end of the Civil War, the building *was* the municipal
theatre, and venue for Dalí's first painting exhibition in 1918 (when he was 14).
Upon reconstruction in 1974, the artist set about fashioning it into a repository
for some of his most bizarre works. Having moved to the adjacent **Torre
Galatea** in 1984, Dalí died there on January 23, 1989; his body, against his
express wishes, now lies behind a simple granite slab in a basement gallery of
the museum.

The copiously signposted **building** on Plaça Gala i Salvador Dalí was
designed as an exhibit itself. Three-cornered imitation bread rolls speckle the
exterior walls, one of which is painted terracotta pink; topped by a huge
metallic-glass dome, the roof line is studded with giant eggs and faceless
bronze mannequins preparing to dive from the heights. In the courtyard, the
"**Rainy Cadillac**" contains three more vine- and snail-infested mannequins,
with a statue of a buxom biblical queen on the bonnet, while overhead a
totem pole of tyres supports Gala's rowboat, from which hang pendulous
blobs of resin, made using condoms as moulds. Inside, steps from the stage
area under the dome lead to the **Mae West Room**, where a carefully
manipulated viewing of some draperies and a labial red sofa converge into a
portrait of the actress. The **Palau de Vent** on the first floor is dominated by
the ceiling painting of Gala and Dalí ascending to heaven, their grubby feet
dangling in the viewer's face.

All the pranks and optical illusions can distract from the reality that there's
far more "serious" art here than generally credited, both by Dalí and other
artists of his choosing. Lesser-known "conventional" canvases from the 1920s

⑪

▲ Teatre-Museu Dalí

(*Portrait of His Sister*) are juxtaposed with more stereotypically surreal later material such as *Soft Self-Portrait with Bacon* and *Portrait of Picasso*, while *The Spectre of Sex Appeal* is the epitome of Dalí's shame-ridden pathology. Gala as *Atomic Leda* and *Galatea of the Spheres* are two of many portraits of his muse, culminating in the Portlligat-set *Dalí from the Back Painting Gala from the Back* (1972–73), though there are some of friends, too, such as Laurence Olivier as Richard III.

The rest of town

The **Museu de l'Empordà** at Rambla 1 (Tues–Sat 11am–9pm, Oct–June until 7pm, Sun & public holidays 11am–2pm; €3 or same ticket as Teatre-Museu Dalí) hosts a serious collection, albeit labelled in Catalan only, bolstered by donations from the Prado and wealthy Figuerans. The first floor combines Greek and Roman ceramics with medieval polychrome wood Virgins, while upstairs there's a gallery of Empordan sculptors and painters, of which the "modern" division of local landscapes and portraits is best. The third floor is enlivened with works by Dalí, Joan Miró, Ramon Reig and Antoni Tàpies among others, though these holdings are occasionally removed for temporary exhibits.

The only other sight is the huge **Castell de Sant Ferran** (daily: July–Sept 10.30am–7pm; Oct–June 10.30am–2pm; €5.50), 1km northwest of town – follow Pujada del Castell from just beyond the Teatre-Museu Dalí. Built in 1753 to defend against French invasion – and failing signally to do so during the Napoleonic Wars – it remains one of the vastest citadels in Europe. During the Civil War, it was used as a barracks for newly arrived members of the International Brigade before they moved on to the front, and also served as the Republicans' last bastion, when Figueres became their capital for a week in February 1939 after the fall of Barcelona. More recently, it was used as a prison for Colonel Tejero after his failed coup attempt in 1981. The outer circuit of star-shaped **walls** exceeds 3km, so consider shelling out another €10 for a two-hour tour that includes a jeep ride around the perimeter, and then a dinghy trip through the cathedral-like **water cisterns** under the parade ground, engineering marvels sufficient to outlast a year's siege.

Eating and drinking

The gaggle of touristy **restaurants** flanking the narrow streets around the Teatre-Museu Dalí is generally worth avoiding in favour of less obvious prospects, outlined below. If you have a car, you could make for one of the atmospheric places to eat in the **villages outside Figueres**. Five-hundred-year-old *Les Quadres* (closed Wed), in the hamlet of El Far d'Empordà, 2.5km southeast (off the road to Roses), specializes in duck (mains €11–16), while 5km southwest, on the road to Besalú near the turning for Avinyonet de Puigventós, *Mas Pau* (℡972 546 154, ⓦwww.maspau.com) occupies a tastefully refurbished sixteenth-century farmhouse surrounded by gardens and offers exquisite contemporary Catalan cuisine (€70 minimum for seasonal *menú* plus dessert; closed Mon & Tues lunch); it's also an alluring place to spend the night (❼).

Classic, locally patronized **cafés** on the *rambla*, which doubles as a busy traffic circle, include *Café Paris* at no. 10, with mix-and-match decor, tapas, sandwiches and teas, or the *Royal* opposite at no. 28, with *modernista* tiled walls and *orxata* served as it should be. Figueres used to be fairly comatose **at night**, with local youth making a beeline for the coast, but a string of frequently changing **bars** on Plaça del Sol is doing a bit to change that.

Restaurants

Can Punyetes Ronda Firal 92. Decidedly meaty fare served in a rustic-decor environment.

La Churraskita c/Magre 5. An exception to the baleful pattern around the Teatre-Museu Dalí, this purveys Argentine-style grills, pizzas and pasta for about €20 a head.

El Firal dels Burros Ronda Firal 100. Late-serving, economical *bodega* where cheese and pâté accompanies wine.

Hotel Duran c/Lasauca 5.The *menjador* here is widely reckoned the best eatery in town – it was a regular Dalí haunt – and does regional dishes with a modern flair (€17 *menú*, €40-plus *a la carta*).

La Garrotxa

The *comarca* of **La Garrotxa** (ⓦwww.turismegarrotxa.com), west of Girona and Figueres, is one of the most absorbing parts of inland Catalunya. **Olot**, with its attractive old centre and museums, is the county capital and a potential base, though the tranquil historic town of **Besalú** on the east serves as another gateway to the mountainous, upper part of the county, **Alta Garrotxa**, which extends north of the Riu Fluvià and Olot to the limestone peaks along the French border. To the south, the **Baixa Garrotxa** is littered with dormant volcanoes incorporated within the **Parc Natural de la Zona Volcànica**, at the heart of which is the pretty medieval village of **Santa Pau**, perhaps the best base with your own transport.

Besalú

From the road, the imposing eleventh-century bridge by the confluence of the Fluvià and Capellada rivers is the only sign that there is anything remarkable about **BESALÚ**, 27km west of Figueres. But once over the pedestrian-only span, you'll encounter steep narrow streets, sunbaked squares and cave-like arcaded shops bearing silent witness to an illustrious history out of proportion to its current humble status. Besalú was an important town before the medieval period – Roman, Visigothic, Frankish and Muslim rulers came and went – but all the surviving monuments date from the tenth to twelfth centuries, when it briefly became the seat of a small, independent principality under the dynasty of Guillem el Pilós. Despite having a total population of just eight hundred, it prospered and remained a place of importance well into the fourteenth century.

The most striking legacy of Besalú's grandeur is the splendid **Pont Fortificat** over the Riu Fluvià, with a fortified gatehouse complete with portcullis in the middle. Like Girona, Besalú had a **Jewish community** from at least the ninth century onwards, royally protected as of 1264; Christian intolerance finally drove the Jews from Besalú in 1436. Originally attached to a synagogue, now excavated above, their **Miqvé** (ritual bathhouse – the only one in Spain) hides inconspicuously down by the river, at the end of signposted Baixada de Mikwè (may be open, otherwise 5 daily visits Mon–Fri, 2 Sat & Sun; €2.35; enquire at the *turisme*). It proves to be a high, single-vaulted chamber, with steps leading down into the former plunge pool.

Continuing in the same direction, you'll reach the porticoed **Plaça de la Llibertat**, site of the Tuesday market and enveloped by medieval buildings such as the thirteenth-century Casa de la Vila, now home to the *ajuntament*. Arcaded at its start, c/Tallaferro leads up from here to the **Castell** and the half-repaired shell of **Santa María**, which for just two years (1018–20) was the cathedral of the Besalú bishopric; political union with Barcelona ended this short-lived episcopal independence.

Further west, a vast, fan-shaped *plaça*, the Prat de Sant Pere, is dominated by the Benedictine monastic **Església de Sant Pere**, founded in 977. The barrel-vaulted interior is impressive enough, with a fine colonnaded ambulatory preserving four carved column capitals with monsters and human figures, but the church's most distinctive feature is the arched Gothic window of the west facade, flanked by a pair of grotesque stone lions. Working your way up c/Ganganell brings you to extensively rebuilt twelfth- to fourteenth-century **Sant Vicenç**, whose Gothic side-entrance arches and capitals bear intricately carved mythical monsters; this church, too, has a thirteenth-century rose window, high up on its southwest facade. Sant Pere (Mon–Fri 7.30pm/8pm, Sun noon) and Sant Vicenç (weekdays same times, Sun 9am) are usually open only for services; the *turisme* runs guided tours at 12.30pm to both (€2.10).

Practicalities

The **bus** stop is on the main Olot–Girona road, from where it's a short walk south to the useful **turisme** on Plaça de la Llibertat (daily 10am–2pm & 4–7pm; ☎972 591 240, ⓦwww.besalu.net).

The best budget **accommodation** choice is atmospheric *Residencia María*, partly occupying a palace on Plaça de la Llibertat (☎972 590 106; ❸). A bit west, the excellent-value 🎋 *Hotel Comte Tallaferro* at c/Ganganell 2 (☎972 591 609, ⓦwww.grupcalparent.com; B&B ❸) enjoys an ideal setting just off Plaça de Sant Pere, its sixteen beautifully furnished, wood-floored rooms and suites with big windows and exposed stone pointing. Possibly the best location has been bagged by *Els Jardins de la Martana*, a converted, antique-tiled belle époque mansion set in tranquil gardens across the old bridge (☎972 590 009, ⓦwww.lamartana.com; B&B ❺). The nearest **campsite** is grassy, tent-friendly *Can Coromines*, just off the N-260, 5km towards Figueres (☎972 591 108, ⓦwww.cancoromines.com; closed Nov–March), also with apartments to rent, a pool, lively bar and pizzeria.

For **meals**, *Cal Parent* (closed Mon Nov–Easter), inside the *Fonda Siqués* up on the main road, is generally reckoned the town's best interpreter of regional cuisine; allow €30–35 per head *a la carta* only. In the same budget bracket, *Pont Vell*, c/Pont Vell 24, is more alluringly situated, with outdoor tables more or less under the bridge. *Can Quei* (closed Wed) at Plaça Sant Vicenç is more basic, with weekday *menús* (€14–20) and summer tables outside by the church.

Oix, Beget and Rocabruna

From Castellfollit de la Roca, 14km west of Besalú, a paved one-lane road leads 10km northwest to the attractive village of **OIX**, flanked by a small medieval bridge. You can **stay** at the *Hostal de la Rovira*, a well-restored mansion with a ground-floor **restaurant**, opposite the Romanesque church of Sant Llorenç on Plaça Major (☎972 294 347, ⊛www.hostaldelarovira.es; B&B ❹).

Eighteen kilometres northwest, a wide paved road leads to the showcase village of **BEGET**, done up by lowlanders as a weekend retreat and now veering perilously close to tweeness. The graceful twelfth-century church of **Sant Cristòfor**, standing on the west side of the village, is celebrated for its particularly solemn and serene *Majestat*. All but a dozen or so of these Catalan wooden images of a fully dressed Christ were destroyed in 1936; this example is one of the very few that can be seen in its intended context (sporadic hours; €1; keys may be at house no. 7 opposite). Of Beget's three **restaurants**, the most accomplished and best value is *Can Jeroni* (€20-plus *a la carta*), with seating by an old bridge and views of the church. The two **accommodation** options are affiliated, and with the same rather shocking colour scheme: *Can Feliça*, apartments by the church (☎972 130 764; ❸), and *Hostal El Forn*, near the top of the village (☎972 741 230; ❸).

Some 7km farther west, **ROCABRUNA** stands just below the watershed dividing La Garrotxa from the county of El Ripollès (though the official border is at Beget), and boasts a ruined castle and a handsome Romanesque church. The only place to **stay**, 2km west on the main road and then 1km down a dirt track, is friendly, English-speaking *Casa Etxalde* (☎972 130 317, ⊛www .geocities.com/etxaldeberri; ❹); self-catering kitchens make it ideal for trekkers and cyclists. Surprisingly for such a tiny place, Rocabruna itself has two good **restaurants**, which draw crowds on weekend nights from far afield: *Can Po*, on the main road past the church, is the more ambitious (reckon on €30–50; weekend reservations mandatory ☎972 741 045), while *Can Plujà* (opposite the turn-off to the church; ☎972 741 064) offers honest mountain food such as goat chops and blackberry sorbet for €24–28 *a la carta*.

Olot

OLOT, capital of La Garrotxa, makes a feasible regional base, more rewarding than its sprawling, anonymous outskirts suggest; narrow lanes north from the busy through-road lead to the *barri vell* with its intimate squares, elegant shops, pleasant *rambla* and convivial cafés. Most of the centre consists of eighteenth- and nineteenth-century buildings, a consequence of devastating earthquakes (1427–28) that levelled the medieval town. Olot lies between three small, dormant volcanic cones, **Volcà de Montsacopa** with its picturesque summit chapel being the closest.

Arrival and information

The **bus station** is at the east end of c/Bisbe Lorenzana, the main through-road. **Drivers** can usually **park** (both fee and for free) near the post office 200m southwest; otherwise, use two central enclosed car parks. The **turisme** is just inside the Museu Comarcal at c/Hospici 8 (Mon–Fri 9am–2pm & 5–7pm, Sat 10am–2pm & 5–7pm, Sun 11am–2pm; ☎972 260 141, ⊛www.olot.org), keeping local accommodation lists, maps and transport timetables. There's **internet** access at *Café 1900* on c/San Rafel.

Accommodation

Olot town has a range of **accommodation**, and with transport you could stay at one of the good *turismes rurals* in neighbouring hamlets.

Hostal Sant Bernat Ctra. de les Feixes 31 ☎972 261 919, ⊛www.hostalsantbernat.com. Although a bit out of the way towards the northeast end of town, these en-suite, 2005-refurbished lodgings are quiet and friendly, offering a long-hours on-site café/bar with woodstove, and a garage handy for those with a car or bike. ❸

Mas La Garganta La Pinya hamlet (follow signs 2km west out of Olot toward Riudaura) ☎972 271 289, ⊛www.masgarganta.com. *Casa de pagès* set in a rambling restored farmhouse looking southwest over the fertile Vall d'en Bas towards Puigsacalm volcano. Rooms are tasteful and en suite, and excellent meals are served on a view terrace, though there's also a self-catering kitchen.

Two-night minimum stay. Half-board only (no dinner Sun) ❹

🏃 **Mas El Guitart** Above Sant Andreu de Socarrats village ☎972 292 140, ⊛www .guitartrural.com. Perched just above the Romanesque *ermita* of Santa Margarida in the Vall de Bianya, northwest of Olot off the C26, this *casa de pagès* has four mock-antique-furnished wood-floor rooms and an on-site spa with alternative therapies, as well as an apartment for six. Two-night minimum stay. Weekdays ❸, weekends ❺

La Vila c/Sant Roc 1 ☎972 269 807, ⊛www .pensiolavila.com. Centrally located *pensió*, with simple but en-suite, comfortable rooms, plus a lift. Breakfast (extra) served at the *menjador*. ❸

The Town

The narrow *barri vell* lanes around Plaça Major run the gamut from down-at-heel to swish, the smarter shops and patisseries evidence of historical prosperity based on the production of textiles and religious statuary. **Sant Esteve church** marks the heart of town, its tower a useful landmark; just northwest, the central *rambla*, **Passeig d'en Blay**, is lined with pavement cafés, busiest in the early evening, and adorned by *modernista* monuments including the **Teatre Principal**.

The local late eighteenth-century cotton-milling industry operated in tandem with workshops printing patterned textiles; the latter were instrumental in the formation of the Escola Pública de Dibuix (Public School of Drawing) in 1783. Joaquim Vayreda i Vila (1843–94), one of the leading lights of the so-called **Olot School** of painters, was a pupil at the school, but an 1871 trip to Paris brought him under the spell of Millet's rural painting and exposed him to the Impressionists. From these influences, and the Garrotxa scenery, sprang the distinctive style of the Olot artists.

Some of the Olot School's best work can be seen in the town's excellent **Museu Comarcal de la Garrotxa** (Mon & Wed–Sun 11am–2pm & 4–7pm, closed Sun pm; €3), installed in a converted eighteenth-century hospital at c/Hospici 8, a side street off the main road. Part of the museum traces the development of Olot through photos, while extensive exhibits also document rural and town crafts, in particular numerous late nineteenth-century workshops for the production of *barretinas* or *gores* – the typical Catalan men's cap. The bulk of the collection, though, is work by local artists and sculptors; canvases include Joaquim Vayreda's *Les Falgueres*, typical in its rendering of the Garrotxa light, and Ramon Casas' famous *La Càrrega*, long thought to depict the suppression of a 1902 Barcelona demonstration, but actually painted in 1899. Among sculpture, the work of Miquel Blay i Fabrega – a notional disciple of Rodin – and Josep

Clarà i Ayals predominates; other pieces by them can be seen outside in the eponymous Plaça Clarà, and Passeig d'en Blay. Besides the saints' images from religious workshops, the secular figures of Ramon Amadeu are outstandingly vivid and, on occasion, humorous.

A twenty-minute walk from the centre is **Parc Nou** with its landscaped **Jardí Botànic** (daily: April–Sept 9am–9pm: Oct–March 9am–7pm; free) and the **Casal dels Volcans**, a Palladian building housing the **Centro d'Informacio del Parc Natural de la Zona Volcànica** (July to mid-Sept Mon–Fri 9am–2pm & 5–7pm, Sat 10am–2pm & 5–7pm, Sun 10am–2pm; mid-Sept to June Mon–Fri 10am–2pm & 4–6pm, Sun 10am–2pm), covering the region's natural history, as well as the **Museu dels Volcans** (Tues–Sun: July–Sept 11am–2pm & 4–7pm; Sept–June 10am–2pm & 3–6pm; €3, or free with Museu Comarcal ticket). Even if you can't read the Catalan/Castilian labelling, photos and maps of the local craters, rock samples and even a floor-shaking simulation of an earthquake are accessible to all.

Eating, drinking and nightlife

Olot, and the Garrotxa in general, is home to the **Cuina Volcànica** group, whose restaurateur members use eleven core local ingredients – including beans, boar and truffles – in their recipes. That said, notable in-town choices are few, so with transport and a fuller wallet, you'll do better on the outskirts.

About a dozen **bars and cafés** are scattered between Passeig d'en Blay and Plaça Carmé just east of the old town, many grouped in the slightly shabby streets northeast of Plaça Mayor. Two evergreens to pick out are genteel *Cocodrilo* at c/Sant Roc 3–5, just off Plaça Mayor (Mon–Sat 6pm–2.30am) and galleried *Café 1900* at c/San Rafel 18 near Sant Esteve (8am–midnight). More youthful, alternative choices include *Bruixes i Maduixes*, c/Bonaire 11, with quality German beers on tap; or Senegalese-run *Bar Malem*, c/Pare Antoni Soler 6, a spacious converted clothing factory decorated with original artwork.

Les Cols northern outskirts of town on Crta de la Canya, towards the C153 ☎972 269 209. The typical *masia* exterior belies an ultra-modern interior where excellent *cuina de mercat* (seasonal ingredients) prevails. Budget €40 minimum; possible to take meals here weekdays on half-board basis if staying at *Mas La Garganta*. Lunch until 3.30pm, dinner until 11pm. Reservations advised. Closed Mon, Tues & Sun eves & mid-July to mid-Aug.

La Garrotxa c/Serra i Ginesta 14. Don't be put off by the institutional decor of this self-service Cuina Volcànica restaurant near the museum. Good house red wine and a changing list of specials (€9.50 *menú* or slightly pricier *a la carta*) – fish soup, pork cheek, grilled quails, rabbit stew, pigfoot brawn

with Santa Pau beans – represents excellent value, if not always flawless execution. Open daily for lunch, also Sat pm April–Sept.

Can Guix c/Mulleras 3. Cheap and basic locals' order-and-pay-at-the-bar spot where *raciones* (they're big; *mitja* – half – *raciones* possible) run €2–5 each, and wine is served by the *porrón* (a traditional glass pitcher). Closed Tues eve, Wed & Sun.

L'Hostalet in Les Hostalets d'en Bas, 10km from Olot on the C152 ☎972 690 006. The best of three restaurants in this attractive village with seating in a vaulted cellar, this Cuina Volcànica affiliate offers three courses for around €24 *a la carta*, including own-made desserts. Closed Sun pm, Tues & a random month in summer.

Parc Natural de la Zona Volcànica

Most of the **Baixa Garrotxa** region – easiest accessible on the minor GI524 that runs between Banyoles and Olot – is volcanic in origin, incorporated within the **Parc Natural de la Zona Volcànica de la Garrotxa**, covering almost 120 square kilometres. It's not, however, a zone of belching steam and boiling mud; the last eruption was almost 12,000 years ago, since which the ash and lava have weathered into a fertile soil whose luxuriant vegetation masks the contours of the dormant volcanoes. There are forty cones in the park, the largest some 160m high and 1500m across the base.

The best way to appreciate the park is by hiking (maps from information centres in Olot and Santa Pau). Alternatively, you can drive to clearly signposted car parks off the GI524, where there are shorter walks to the main volcanoes: the Area de Can Serra, 4km from Olot, gives access to the beech forest of **Fageda d'en Jordà**, while the Area de Santa Margarida, 3km farther on, towards Banyoles, has trails to the **Volcà del Croscat** (1.4km), the largest and youngest cone in the park, and **Volcà de Santa Margarida** (1km), near Santa Pau. Without your own transport, **access** is problematic, since the only bus is the weekly Olot–Banyoles service (Wed 7.15am from Olot, 1.30pm from Banyoles) via Santa Pau. If you're feeling adventurous, you could book a hot-air balloon ride over the volcanoes, setting off from between Croscat and Santa Margarida (daily 7/8am; 1hr; ☎972 680 255, ⓦwww.voldecoloms.com; €160), with *cava* and a hearty breakfast thrown in.

Santa Pau

The central village of the volcanic zone, medieval **SANTA PAU**, 9km southeast of Olot, makes another great base; slightly less discovered than Besalú, it's even more atmospheric, presenting a defensive perimeter of continuous and almost windowless house walls. Santa Pau's outer archways open onto dark, ancient buildings, many sympathetically converted into business premises and homes. The core of the village is the engagingly sloping thirteenth-century **Firal dels Bous** (Cattle Market, alias Plaça Major), with arcaded shops; the badly restored Gothic church of **Santa Maria**; and the **turisme** (Mon & Wed–Sat noon–6pm, Sun noon–3pm; ☎972 680 349).

At no. 6 of the adjacent **Plaçeta dels Balls**, you'll find expensive but tasty **meals** at *Cal Sastre* (closed Sun eve & Mon, open Fri & Sat only in winter), though several other better-priced restaurants – including *modernista*-decor *Cal Fesol* – have sprung up on the approaches to the old quarter. The best-value **accommodation** is 🍴 *Can Menció* at Plaça Major 17 (☎972 680 014 or 616 669 6880, ⓦwww.garrotxa.com/canmencio; closed Mon & Sept 15–30; ❷), seven very sweet en-suite wood-trimmed rooms, some with balcony and all with designer baths; there's a rear-facing lounge with self-service bar, and up front the village's liveliest café-bar, with ringside seats on the *plaça*. For **self-catering**, *Can Marfany*, Plaça Major 4 (☎972 680 518, ⓦwww.canmarfany.com; min one-week stay), offers three small but comfortable apartments; for a less restrictive policy and units fitting up to six people, try *Can Pere Petit* at c/Pont 9 (☎616 657 529). Of two local **campsites**, *Ecològic Lava*, 3km away near two volcanic cones (☎972 680 358), is large and well equipped.

Serra del Montseny and around

Southwest of Girona, the train line and main road to Barcelona both give a wide berth to the province's other great natural attraction, the **Serra del Montseny**, mountains rising in parts to 1700m. It's a well-forested region, and from here comes the bulk of Catalunya's mineral water, bottled in small spa villages. You can approach from either Girona or Barcelona, though if you're using public transport (generally La Hispano Hilariense) you'll have to stay the night in whichever village you aim for, since infrequent services – from the bus station in Girona or from Barcelona's Pla de Palau – rarely allow for day-trips. On the westward side of the mountains, the road swoops down through wooded slopes to the pleasant market and university town of **Vic**, standing at the crossroads of the Girona–Lleida and Barcelona–Pyrenees roads.

Sant Hilari Sacalm and Viladrau

Located some 40km from Girona, **SANT HILARI SACALM** is a pleasant spa town that makes an enjoyable base for a couple of days. It's famous for its *Via Crucis Vivent*, or Easter-time Passion stagings, the most full-blown of several such in Catalunya. Much of its **accommodation** caters for people taking the curative local waters, and consequently open only from late June to early September; one option that seems to operate most of the year is the central, modern *Hostal Torras*, Plaça del Doctor Gravalosa 13 (T972 868 096; ❸; closed Jan), which also serves good food. A **turisme** in the Edifici Can Rovira (Mon–Sat 11am–2pm & 4–7pm, Sun 11am–2pm; T972 869 686, Wwww .santhilari.org) has details of bus connections in the area.

It's a splendid, winding seventeen-kilometre drive southwest to **VILADRAU**, another mountain spa town, though not as large as Sant Hilari. By public transport, you have to approach from the other side of the range, by taking the train from Barcelona to Vic, and connecting with the local bus from there (daily 1pm; 45min). The bus returns at 8.45am the following morning. Being more difficult to reach, Viladrau preserves a very tranquil feel within its old streets. There are plenty of local wooded walks through attractive surrounding countryside – ask at the sporadically functioning *turisme* on Plaça Major – and two atmospherically old-fashioned places to **stay**: *Hotel La Coromina*, on the main road into town (T938 849 264, Wwww.xaletcoromina.com; ❺), a romantic ivy-clad hideaway among trees, with the excellent attached *Salvador Casaseca* **restaurant** (half-board available); or the cheaper *Hostal Bofill* at c/Sant Marçal 2 near Plaça Major (T938 849 012, Wwww.hostalbofill.com; half-board only ❺), a vast *belle époque* period piece. The **Parc Natural de Montseny information centre** (Mon–Sat 11am–2.30pm & 4.30–6pm, Sun 10am–2.30pm) is clearly signposted on the outskirts of town, with informative displays and maps of the region.

Vic

The quickest approach to Serra del Montseny from Barcelona is by train north towards Ripoll. About an hour out of the city, the route reaches handsome **VIC**, whose few well-preserved monuments are just about worth stopping to see. Capital of an ancient Iberian tribe, Vic was later a Roman settlement (part of a second-century temple survives in town) and then a wealthy medieval market centre. A twice-weekly (Tues & Sat) **market** continues to thrive in the enormous arcaded main square; the town is also renowned for excellent **sausages**, sold in the market and in the cluster of specialist stores around the northeast corner of Plaça Major.

Vic's Centre Històric is dominated by a rather dull, Neoclassical **Catedral** (daily 10am–1pm & 4–7pm; free), containing some impressive murals by Josep María Sert. Next door, in Plaça del Bisbe Oliba, the more interesting **Museu Episcopal** (April–Sept Tues–Sat 10am–7pm, Sun 10am–2pm; Oct–March Tues–Fri 10am–1pm & 3–6pm, Sat 10am–7pm, Sun 10am–2pm; €4) houses a wealth of eleventh- and twelfth-century frescoes and wooden sculptures rescued from local Pyrenean churches – the most important collection of Romanesque art outside Barcelona's Museu d'Art de Catalunya.

The best reason to come to Vic, however, is for one of its two annual **music festivals**: the *Mercat de Música Viva* (Live Music Market; Wwww.mmvv.net), four days of live events in mid-September spanning genres from marching bands to Catalan *cançó*; and the mid-May *Festival de Jazz*, mostly centred on the club *Vic Bang Jazz Cava* on Rambla dels Montcada (ⓦwww.jazzcava.com).

Practicalities

From the **train station**, walk east straight along the road opposite (c/Jacint Verdaguer) to reach Plaça Major. **Drivers** will need to park on the outskirts, as traffic is highly restricted (and parking virtually impossible) in the centre. The **turisme** is just off the square (Mon–Sat 10am–2pm & 4–8pm, Sat until 7pm, Sun 10.30am–1.30pm; ⓣ938 862 091, ⓦwww.victurisme.net); the plushest **accommodation** is resolutely modern *Hotel J Balmes Vic*, at c/Francesc Pla "El Vigatà" 6 (ⓣ938 891 272, ⓦwww.hoteljbalmes.com; B&B ❺), northeast of the Centre Històric. Vic overflows with good **restaurants**, and Barcelona foodies reckon it worth a special trip; the renowned *La Taula*, Plaça Don Miquel de Clariana 4 (ⓣ938 863 229; closed Sun eve, Mon, part Feb & part Aug), in an old mansion east of Plaça Major, does fine seasonal and *del mercat* fare at around €30 a head.

The Catalan Pyrenees

You don't have to travel far from the coast nor Catalunya's three largest cities before you reach the foothills of the **Catalan Pyrenees**, the easternmost stretch of the mountain chain that divides Spain and France. From Barcelona, you can reach **Ripoll** by train in under three hours. The area northwest of here has been extensively developed with **skiing stations**; during summer, it's also quite busy, particularly in the valleys leading to **Camprodon**. Following the Freser valley north from Ripoll brings you to **Ribes de Freser**, start of the private train line up to **Núria** (a combination of shrine and recreation centre), one of the most stunning rides in Catalunya. Farther north, by the French border, **Puigcerdà** has the only surviving train link with France over the Pyrenees, while nearby the peculiar Spanish enclave of **Llívia** lies wholly enclosed within France.

For serious Pyrenean walking – and a wider range of scenery, flora and fauna – you need to head farther west, beyond **La Seu d'Urgell** and the adjacent duty-free principality of **Andorra**, which approximately mark the middle of the Catalan Pyrenees. Although more tampered with (by hydroelectric projects in particular) than the Aragonese peaks to the west, the mountains here offer some of the best trekking in the whole range. The **Noguera Pallaresa** valley, the **Val d'Aran** and the superbly scenic **Parc Nacional d'Aigüestortes i Estany de Sant Maurici** are all reasonably accessible, offering easy hiking as well as more specialist routes. A farther lure is the **Vall de Boí** on the western edge of the national park, with its concentration of magnificent **Romanesque churches**.

A complication for anyone intent upon seeing more than a small part of the Catalan Pyrenees in one go, even with their own transport, is the **geographical layout** of the region. The Val d'Aran, in the northwestern corner of Catalunya, has an east–west orientation, as do the Cerdanya uplands, but most of the other valleys run north–south, with few lateral roads, which means that connecting between them on two or four wheels is not always easy. Determined hikers can

Skiing in the Catalan Pyrenees

If you want to **ski** in the Catalan Pyrenees, it's usually cheapest to buy an inclusive **package** – prices are a bit more than in the French Pyrenees, but around 25 percent less than in the Alps. The main destination promoted overseas is Andorra, though some agents and websites offer Baqueira-Beret in Spain, too. If you're already in Spain, you'll get most choice through a travel agency in Barcelona or any of the larger Catalan towns, though an increasing number of resorts are offering on-the-spot "mini-packages". The local *turisme* usually has information about valley hotels offering such all-in deals of half-board and lift pass, which save a good 25 percent compared to doing it independently, even more if you show up on weekdays. Full **kit** (skis, boots, poles) typically costs €14–19 per day, less for multi-day periods, while **lift passes** bought on their own cost €26–44 daily (again, proportionately less for longer periods), depending on day of the week and complexity or quality of the lift system.

Pyrenean skiing tends to cost a bit less than elsewhere because the range lacks international cachet and (until recently) convenient airports; Barcelona and Toulouse are the busiest choices, but Perpignan, Reus and Girona also have year-round flights, and Lleida's airport (actually some way north at Balaguer) should open in 2009. The **clientele** is family-oriented and almost totally Spanish, with a smattering of French and Portuguese. There's little of the snootiness or (except in Andorra) nocturnal excess often found in the Alps, and as a foreigner you'll be the object of benign curiosity or outright friendliness – though outside of Andorra you may have trouble finding English-speaking instruction. **Infrastructure** is improving as large sums are periodically spent on snow cannons or new lifts. The downside is that, cannons or not, snow can be thin and/or mushy, since Catalunya gets its weather from the Mediterranean rather than the damper Atlantic; don't set out for a week's holiday without checking **conditions** first, especially after March 1. The best Spanish Catalan **downhill** resorts for beginners or families are Port del Comte, west of Berga; Port-Ainé, above the Noguera Palleresa; La Molina at the southern edge of the Cerdanya; and Espot Esquí at the eastern edge of the Parc Nacional de Aigüestortes i Estany de Sant Maurici. Intermediate and advanced skiers might prefer La Masella, adjacent to La Molina; Boí-Taüll at the western edge of Aigüestortes; and Baqueira-Beret at the head of the Val d'Aran. For **cross-country skiing**, the northern margin of the Cerdanya (see p.781) has a cluster of excellent centres at Aransa, Guils Fontanera and Lles, while the western Cadí has well-regarded pistes at Lavansa.

follow various passes between the valleys; otherwise, you'll need to backtrack a bit out of the mountains before venturing up a new valley.

Ripoll

RIPOLL occupies so prominent a place in Catalan history that it's impossible not to be initially disappointed by this rather shabby spot, buzzing with traffic and divided by the polluted Riu Ter. The inhabitants seem to agree, resigned to working here but deserting it in droves on Saturday afternoons, when Ripoll assumes the air of a ghost town until Monday.

Yet just ten-minutes' walk from the southeast corner of town – where trains and buses stop – lies one of the most remarkable monuments in the Catalan Pyrenees, the **Monestir de Santa María**, founded in 888 by Guifré el Pelós (Wilfred the Hairy) to spur Christian resettlement of the surrounding valleys following the expulsion of the Moors. Sadly, the old Benedictine monastery was destroyed in an 1835 fire; today's barrel-vaulted **nave** (daily 10am–1pm & 3–7pm, until 6pm in winter; €3) is a copy of the original structure erected over Guifré's tomb by Abbot Oliba, a cousin of the Besalú counts, in the early eleventh century. The magnificent, twelfth-century Romanesque **west portal**, however, survived the fire, and is now protected against the elements by a glass conservatory – and from the over-curious by a low iron barrier. The portal squirms with carvings of religious and astrological subjects: the Apocalypse (across the top), the Book of Kings (to the left), Exodus (to the right), scenes from the lives of David, St Peter and St Paul (at the bottom), and the months of the year (around the inner side of the pillars).

The adjacent, twin-columned **cloister** (daily 10am–1pm & 3–7pm, until 6pm in winter; same ticket as nave) was far less damaged in the succession of earthquakes, sackings and fires visited on the monastery, and is particularly beautiful. The **capitals** on the lower of two colonnades, dating from the twelfth-century Romanesque "Golden Age", portray monks and nuns, beasts mundane and

▲ Monestir de Santa María

mythical, plus secular characters of the period. Across the Plaça Abat Oliba from Santa María, the fourteenth-century church of **Sant Pere** is only open when it serves as a a venue for Ripoll's **music festival**, staged on successive weekends during July and August.

Besides the monastery there's little to detain you, though down in the modern district, two *modernista* specimens may claim your attention: the spouting stone flourishes and battlements of **Can Bonada**, c/del Progrés 14, on the way to the bus and train stations, and the tiny church of **Sant Miquel de la Roqueta** (1912), a couple of blocks up the hill, looking like a pixie's house with a witch's cap on top – and designed by Antoni Gaudí's contemporary Joan Rubió.

Practicalities

The **train and bus stations** stand within sight of each other, a ten-minute walk from the heart of town, over the Pont d'Olot to Plaça de l'Ajuntament. The **turisme**, on the adjacent Plaça d'Abat Oliba, near the monastery (Easter, June, July & Sept daily 9.30am–1.30pm & 4–7pm; Aug daily 10am–2pm & 4–8pm; Oct–May Mon–Sat 9.30am–1.30pm & 4–7pm, Sun 10am–2pm; ☎972 702 351), stocks plenty of maps, pamphlets and local-transport timetables.

Accommodation tends to be uninspiring – you're better off basing yourself nearby and making a flying visit. *Mas La Riba* (☎972 198 092, ⓦwww .maslariba.es; B&B ❸), a **casa de pagès** in the hamlet of **Les Llosses**, 18km away on the road to Berga, then 6km farther on its own dirt track, is a good alternative to Ripoll's overpriced *hostales* and hotels. Simple en-suite doubles and triples occupy a rambling, sixteenth-century manor with ample common areas, including a pool; in such a remote locale, it's best to take half-board (❺). **Eating and drinking** options in Ripoll itself are far from plentiful. The only notable full-service restaurants in the centre are *Pizzeria Piazetta*, under the *Hostal del Ripollès* on Plaça Nova, and *Canaules* next door – both are reasonable (€21 *a la carta*) and appetizing.

Northeast: the Riu Ter valley

From Ripoll, the **Riu Ter valley**, dotted with beautiful Romanesque churches and monasteries, leads northeast into the mountains. To follow the whole route by public transport you'll have to be prepared to wait (sometimes overnight) for buses, which get scarcer the higher you go. The first two towns, **Sant Joan de les Abadesses** and **Camprodon**, are easy to reach on day-trips from Ripoll or Olot. Other, more distant villages take more time and effort, but are correspondingly less developed, except in the vicinity of the **Vallter 2000** ski resort.

Sant Joan de les Abadesses and around

The small town of **SANT JOAN DE LES ABADESSES**, 11km northeast of Ripoll, owes its existence to the eponymous **monastery** (daily: March, April & Oct 10am–2pm & 4–6pm; May, June & Sept 10am–2pm & 4–7pm; July & Aug 10am–7pm; Nov–Feb 10am–2pm, also 4–6pm weekends; €3), founded in 887 by Guifré el Pelós, apparently for the benefit of his daughter Emma, the first abbess. However, the institution was closed temporarily in 1017 by Pope Benedict III after politically motivated accusations of immorality by Count Bernat Tallaferro, to whom devolved – not coincidentally – all the feudal privileges of the convent. The present church, consecrated in 1150, is a single-nave structure of impressive austerity, built to a Latin-cross plan with five apses, housing in the central one a curious thirteenth-century wooden sculpture depicting Christ's Deposition, the *Santíssim Misteri*, in its main chapel. Admission to the church also includes entry to the Gothic **cloister** and the **Museu del Monestir**, whose well-presented exhibits include superb choirstall partitions with (for example) a fox carrying off a hen and a wild boar playing the bagpipes, as well as a fine series of late medieval altarpieces.

Elsewhere in town, there are few specific sights other than the old quarter, a fair-sized grid of ancient houses along streets almost shorter than their names, all leading to a small but appealingly arcaded **Plaça Major**. The slender twelfth-century bridge down in the well-tilled valley was only restored in 1976, after being destroyed in fierce fighting in February 1939, during the final Republican retreat of the Civil War.

Practicalities

Buses arrive at a shelter behind the monastery church apse; the well-stocked **turisme** occupies the cloistered, fifteenth-century Palau de l'Abadia, just left from the Museu del Monestir's entrance (May–Oct daily 10am–2pm & 4–7pm; Nov–April Mon–Sat same hours; ☎972 720 599, ⓦwww.santjoandelesabadesses.cat).

In theory, Sant Joan would make a far more pleasant base than Ripoll; in practice, there's just one **accommodation** option in the newer district near the bus stop: *Pensió Can Janpere* at c/del Mestre Josep Andreu 3 (☎972 720 077; ❸), with comfortable en-suite rooms with heating and TV. Preferable, however, if you have a car is a *turisme rural*, 🛏 *Mas Mitjavila*, 10.5km northwest of Sant Joan in the hamlet of **SANT MARTÍ D'OGASSA** (☎972 722 020, ⓦwww .casesrurals.com/rural/masmitjavila; B&B ❹). From the north side of the new bridge, follow the asphalt road 4.2km to the ex-mining village of Ogassa Surroca, then continue the remaining distance on a cement driveway. Along with the adjacent tenth-century church of Sant Martí, *Mas Mitjavila* was once a dependency of the monastery of Sant Joan; it enjoys a superb eyrie setting 1.3km up, overlooking the valleys of Ripoll. Rooms (more like suites) accommodate four, or five at a pinch; they're rustic but have all mod cons, plus kitchens. Meals are available in the dinner-only restaurant, in the old sheep barn. Back in town, the only full-service **restaurant** is *Can Janpere*, with a €12 *menú*; it's closed for lunch in low season, when the alternative is *Brasseria Gil* at c/Major 6.

Camprodon

As you climb gradually along the lively Riu Ter from Sant Joan, the first place with any mountain-town character is **CAMPRODON** (950m), a fact exploited in the nineteenth century by the Catalan gentry who arrived by a (now defunct) rail line to spend summer in the hills – the tracks' former course is now a marked cycling route, **La Ruta del Ferro**. The town still retains the prosperous air of those times, with shops full of leather goods, outdoor gear, cheese and sausages. Ornate villas front a *rambla* clogged with towering trees, and some of the other townhouses are embellished with *modernista* flourishes.

Like Ripoll, Camprodon straddles the confluence of two rivers, here the Ter and the Ritort, and is knit together by little bridges. The principal one, sixteenth-century **Pont Nou**, still has a defensive tower (follow "Pujada al Pont" signs to climb it). From here you can follow the narrow main commercial street to the restored Romanesque monastic church of **Sant Pere** (consecrated in 904), near the northeast end of town next to the larger parish church of Santa María. There is also a small **castle** overhead, most easily reached by crossing the Pont Nou and then climbing the narrow lanes on the far side.

Camprodon was the birthplace of the composer **Isaac Albéniz** (1860–1909), a fact that neither the town nor the region made much of until recently – probably because there's little distinctively Catalan in the music he produced during his wanderings through Spain, France and England. However, the great man now has a street named after him, a bust near Sant Pere, an eponymous July **music festival** and a less worthwhile commemorative **museum** (daily except Tues 11am–2pm & 4–7pm; €3), near the bridge.

Practicalities

Buses from Ripoll stop at a shelter at the southeast edge of town on the bypass road, 300m south of the main Plaça d'Espanya, where you'll find the **turisme** in the *ajuntament* building (Tues–Sat 10am–2pm & 4–7pm, Sun 10am–2pm; ☎972 740 010).

Accommodation tends to be expensive, given the town's role as a minor ski resort, and advance reservations are advisable at peak season. On often noisy c/Josep Morer there's *Can Ganansi* at no. 9 (☎972 740 134; ❸); quieter *Pensió La Placeta* overlooks Plaça del Carmé (☎972 740 807; ❹), just east of c/Josep Morer and the first square you reach as you come into town from Sant Joan. For a splurge, try *Hotel de Camprodon* on Plaça Dr. Robert 3, by the Casal Cinema (☎972 740 013; ❹), a *modernista* building with elegant common areas.

Can Ganansi's **restaurant** offers two different *menús* plus local dishes such as duck and stuffed *pebrots*. Alternatively, *Bar-Restaurant Núria* at Plaça d'Espanya 11 is a characterful place better for *a la carta* dinners featuring frogs' legs, snails and partridge than the basic lunch *menú*. Best in show, and best sited, is ⚘ *El Pont 9* (☎972 740 521; closed Mon low season), with views to the bridge and *nouvelle* Catalan cuisine such as oxtail stew or duck livers with artichokes (*menú* €16, *a la carta* €25–30).

Beyond Camprodon: the Ter valley

Beyond Camprodon you're increasingly dependent on your own transport and, ultimately, your own legs. Most people venturing this way are either hikers, or skiers driving northwest up the **Ter valley** to the pistes of Vallter 2000, with comparatively little traffic moving northeast up the **Ritort valley** that isn't bound for France. The construction of holiday flats for lowlanders, and of short-term tourist facilities, now reigns supreme, but you can still glimpse the area's former agricultural economy in the herds of cattle ambling home at dusk.

The first settlement that might prompt a stop is **VILALLONGA DE TER**, 5km from Camprodon. Opposite the standard-issue Romanesque church of **Sant Martí** on the main *plaça* are two **accommodation** possibilities: *Hostal Pastoret* at Constitució 9 (☎972 740 319; half-board ❸), and *Hostal Cal Mestre* around the corner at c/del Pou 1 (reception at c/Major 3; ☎972 740 407; B&B ❸).

Alternatively, bear left 1km past Vilallonga for the steep, five-kilometre detour to **TREGURÀ DE DALT**, perched on a sunny hillside, with sweeping views east over the valley. There's excellent food and **accommodation** (including family apartments) at welcoming ⚘ *Fonda Rigà* (☎972 136 000, ⓦwww.fondariga.com; half-board ❹), its rooms redone in 2007 to hotel standards with orthopedic beds, plus good savoury Catalan breakfasts and three-course *table d'hôte* dinners with own-label wine in the **restaurant**.

Setcases and Vallter 2000

SETCASES, 6km northwest of Vilallonga in the Ter valley, has been completely gentrified since the 1980s. Once an important agricultural village, it was almost totally abandoned until the nearby ski station began to attract hoteliers, chalet developers and second-home owners.

The ski trade ensures that short-term beds and food are relatively pricey, with half-board often required in season; affordable **accommodation** in the village centre, away from the riverside bypass road, is at *Hostal El Molí* (☎972 136 049, ⓦ www.elmoli.net; closed weekdays off-season; half-board ④), with just a handful of cozy, rustic attic rooms, a big lounge and stone-walled *menjador*. The more impersonal *Hotel La Coma* at the entrance to the village (☎972 136 073, ⓦ www.hotellacoma.com; half-board ⑤) represents the top standard here, with big balconied rooms. Locals flock to Setcases **to eat** at weekends, most notably at 🏃 *Can Jepet* (reserve on ☎972 136 104, ⓦ www.restaurantcanjepet.com; closed Thurs Oct–June). The food – well-presented salads, grilled quail with artichoke and roast peppers, home-made *flan* – is excellent value at under €23 a head.

Situated at the head of the valley, below the frontier summits of Bastiments (2874m) and Pic de la Dona (2702m), compact **VALLTER 2000** (no public transport) is the easternmost downhill ski resort in the Pyrenees. While south-facing, the glacial bowl here has a chilly microclimate that lets snow linger into April most years – though runs remain heavily dependent on cannons. The range of pistes is enough to keep you interested for a weekend, when Barcelonans flood the place.

The Upper Freser valley and Núria

From Ripoll, the **Freser valley** rises to Ribes de Freser (912m) and then climbs steeply to Queralbs, where it swings eastwards through a gorge of awesome beauty. Just above Queralbs, to the north, the Riu Núria has scoured out a second gorge, beyond which lie the ski station and valley sanctuary of **Núria**. You can take the **train** all the way from Barcelona on this route, one of Catalunya's most extraordinary rides. The first stretch is to Ribes de Freser, a two-and-a-half-hour ride (or just 20min from Ripoll). From there, the **Cremallera** (Zipper) rack-and-pinion railway takes over; the small carriages of this private line take another 45 minutes to reach Núria.

Ribes de Freser

The unavoidable start-point for trips to Núria, **RIBES DE FRESER** offers more plentiful and better-value **accommodation** then Ripoll. Pick of this, very close to the *Cremallera* station, is *Hotel Caçadors*, c/Balandrau 24–26 (☎972 727 006, ⓦ www.hotelsderibes.com), with four grades (②–④) of en-suite rooms in two separate premises. If you're still stuck, ask at the helpful **turisme** at Plaça de l'Ajuntament 3 (Mon–Sat 10am–2pm & 5–8pm, Sun 10am–1pm; ☎972 727 728, ⓦ www.vallderibes.cat). For **eating** out, the restaurant at the *Caçadors* offers all the Catalan standards with a nouvelle twist, better value taken on half-board basis. The main alternative, at no. 14 of the through-road, is *Can Sart*, offering grills and salads.

Along the Cremallera Line

The *Cremallera* makes a fabulous introduction to the mountains. After a leisurely start through the lower valley, the tiny, blue-and-white, two-car train lurches up between great crags before starting to climb high above both river and forests.

Occasionally, it slows down, leaving you poised between a sheer drop into the valley and an equally precipitous rock-face soaring overhead.

The only intermediate stop on the *Cremallera* is at **QUERALBS** (1220m), an attractive stone-built village now being dwarfed by newer apartment complexes on its outskirts. Near the highest point, beside the GR11 trail that passes Queralbs, stands the tenth-century church of **Sant Jaume**, adorned by a fine colonnaded porch with sculpted column capitals; inside, there's a painted wooden altar with scenes from the Life of Christ. En-suite **accommodation** in small, wood-trimmed rooms is provided by *Hostal L'Avet*, on the main street (☎ 972 727 377; open daily June 24 to mid-Oct, weekends only at other times; half-board only ❹). The *table d'hôte* fare at the attached *Ca La Mary* restaurant is very good (allow €23 each), though opening hours can be idiosyncratic. More reliable is *El Restaurant de la Plaça* (closed Tues), where a similar amount gives you the run of a *carta* with delights such as *cèpe* soup and sausages.

For year-round board and lodging, head 3km out of Queralbs to the well-signposted 🏶 *Mas La Casanova* on the opposite side of the valley (☎ 972 198 077, Ⓦ www.maslacasanova.com; B&B ❸), in **FUSTANYÀ** hamlet. This good-value **casa de pagès** is set in a superbly restored farmhouse; the outgoing owners provide reasonable *table d'hôte* evening meals, with large family suites also available. The only drawback is that the wood architecture amplifies any sound.

Núria

Beyond Queralbs, the *Cremallera* hauls itself up the precipitous valley to **NÚRIA**, twenty minutes farther on. Once the train passes the mouth of the Gorges del Freser, seen tantalizingly to the right, and enters the Gorges de Núria, the views are dramatic. Once through a final tunnel, you emerge into a south-facing bowl, with a small lake at the bottom and – at the far end – the hideously monolithic, *café au lait*-coloured **Santuari de Nostra Senyora de Núria** (1964m), founded in the eleventh century on the spot where an image of the Virgin was supposedly discovered. This avatar is believed to bestow fertility on female pilgrims, and many Catalan girls – presumably the result of successful supernatural intervention – are named after her.

The sanctuary combines a dull church, tourist office (which posts weather reports), bar, restaurants, ski centre and **hotel**. Rates at the *Hotel Vall de Núria* (☏972 732 030, ⊕www.valdenuria.cat; two-night minimum stay; closed a month after Easter; half-board only ❺–❻) and a dozen self-catering apartments vary wildly by season, and its **restaurant** is also pricey. The only budget lodging is the youth hostel *Pic de L'Àliga* (☏972 732 048), marvellously poised at the top of the ski centre's cable-car line (though this often doesn't run in summer). **Camping** is permitted only at a designated site behind the sanctuary complex.

Besides the hotel, **eating** options include *La Cabana dels Pastors*, behind the complex, offering expensive bistro fare at lunchtime only; the *Bar Finestrelles*, downstairs in the sanctuary building, with typical bar snacks; and, best value of all, the lunchtime-only *Autoservei* self-service restaurant in the west wing, where you can eat reasonably well for significantly under €20.

Berguedà

An alternative initial approach to the eastern Catalan Pyrenees is via the *comarca* of **Berguedà**, west of Ripoll. It's easiest with your own transport: from Barcelona, the fast, improved C1411 road runs through Manresa and then heads due north to Puigcerdà, via the **Túnel del Cadí**, Spain's longest (and at €10.50, most expensive) toll-tunnel. You can arrive by bus, too – heading first for **Berga**, the region's main town, from Barcelona – though this approach can be slower than the train trip to Puigcerdà via Ripoll.

There's nothing as immediately spectacular in this region as the Núria train journey, though northeast of Berga, villages and hamlets such as **Gombrèn**, **Sant Jaume de Frontanyà** and **Castellar de N'Hug** lend architectural interest. To the northwest, the vast Serra del Cadí offers the best local walking, including treks around (and a possible ascent of) the twin peaks of that most recognizable of Catalan mountains, **Pedraforca**.

Berga

The Pyrenees seem to arrive with startling abruptness at **BERGA**, the capital of Berguedà *comarca*. The town itself is fairly dull, bearing ample traces of its long

---

Walking and skiing at Núria

Despite the day-trippers and hordes of kids engaged in pony-riding and boating on the lake, solitude is easily found amidst the bleak, treeless scenery at Núria. Fit **trekkers** can move on to the rounded summit of **Puigmal** (2909m), a four- to five-hour hike; the 1:25,000 *Puigmal-Núria* Editorial Alpina contoured map/guide booklet is recommended. Most people, however, aren't this committed, so the **return to Queralbs** along the river gorge (2hr 30min) ranks as the most popular hike out of Núria. The GR11 threads the gorge on a high-quality, well-marked path, but you'll still need good shoes and a water bottle. With an early start, you can make the long day's walk through the **Gorges de Freser**, following the GR11.7 (the "Camí del Enginyers") to a lunch stop at the *Refugi Coma de Vaca* (☏972 198 082, ⊕www.comadevaca.com; staffed Easter & mid-June to mid-Sept, or by arrangement on ☏649 229 012), then doubling back on another marked trail down the other side of the gorge to just below Queralbs.

Downhill **skiing** at Núria – best for beginners and weak intermediates – is surprisingly popular, given that the piste plan is very limited, the chair-lift only reaches 2262m, and the maximum altitude difference is a paltry 288m.

history as an industrial centre, but it does have a ruined castle, a well-preserved, part-pedestrianized medieval core and onward bus connections to higher settlements in the county, provided by ATSA at the top of Passeig de la Pau. It's also served by twice-daily buses from Barcelona (2hr).

The other main season and reason to come to Berga is at Corpus Christi week, when the town hosts the **Festa de la Patum**, one of Catalunya's most famous festivals. For five days (Wed–Sun), medievally garbed *gegants* process to brass-band music along streets packed with dancing, jostling, chanting Catalans intent on a good time. A *guita* (dragon) attacks onlookers in the course of a symbolic battle between good and evil, fireworks blazing from its mouth, while the climax comes on the Saturday night, with a dance performed by masked men covered in grass.

The helpful **turisme** is in the heart of the old town at c/dels Àngels 7 (☎938 211 384, ⓦwww.ajberga.cat). **Accommodation** is impossible to find during Patum unless you've booked weeks in advance. Among seven places to stay, try the small but well-appointed *Hotel Passasserres*, Passeig Abeuradors (☎938 210 645; ❹), with sauna, gym and off-street parking; or *Pensió del Guiu* on Ctra de Queralt, en route to the eponymous shrine (☎938 210 315; ❸). The most famous **restaurant** in town is *Sala* at Pg. de la Pau 27 (closed Sun eve & Mon) – count on well over €60 for a full gourmet meal, including mushrooms in autumn. If your budget doesn't stretch to that, the *menjador* of the *del Guiu* offers regional specialities, while *Bar La Barana* at the heart of the old town on Plaça Sant Pere does economical *menús*.

The Serra del Cadí

For equipped and experienced trekkers, the **Serra del Cadí** northwest of Berga offers three or four days' trekking through often wild, lonely areas. Various paths and tracks cross the range, though the favourite excursion remains the ascent of Pedraforca. The summer heat is intense and finding fresh water can be problematic, so peak **visitors' seasons** are May–June and September (mushroom-collecting time). In recognition of its unique landscape, the Cadí was declared a *parc natural* years ago, and it maintains a few fairly well-placed, staffed refuges, accessible from a number of foothill villages, themselves served poorly, if at all, by bus – you may have to drive, walk or hitch to them from larger towns down-valley. For extended explorations, you'll need the Editorial Alpina 1:25,000 *Serra del Cadí/Pedraforca* and *Moixeró* maps and guide, or the Catalunya IGN *Mapa Excursionista* for the same area.

From the Llobregat valley extending north of Berga two main routes forge west into the Cadí. **From Bagà**, a partly paved road follows the Riu Bastareny to the hamlet of **Gisclareny**. A busier paved highway beginning just south of **Guardiola de Berguedà** runs parallel to the Saldes river to **Gòsol** village, via **Saldes** village, closest habitation to Pedraforca.

Bagà, Saldes and Gósol

BAGÀ, the second town in the *comarca* after Berga, has something going for it in the form of a tiny old quarter with an arcaded plaça (La Porxada), a hybrid Romanesque-Gothic church and two **accommodation** options: old-fashioned *Hotel La Pineda*, c/Raval 50 (☎938 244 515; half-board only ❹), at the eastern end of the main shopping street, and 🏕 *Hotel Ca L'Amagat*, quietly placed in the heart of the old quarter at c/Clota 4 (☎938 244 032, ⓦwww.hotelcalamagat .com; half-board only ❹), and meticulously refurbished along with its barn-like *menjador*. If you plan to enter the *parc natural* from here, it's worth stopping off at Bagà's **park information office** at c/la Vinya 1 (daily 9am–1.30pm, also Mon–Fri 3.30–7pm, Sat 4–6.30pm) for maps and the like.

Strung out grimly along the old course of the C1411 (a newer bypass skirts the town), **Guardiola de Berguedà** lies on the bus routes from Berga (21km south) and Ripoll, and only 1.5km north of the turning for Saldes and Gòsol. It's not a place to get stuck, as there's no longer any accommodation, or any bus service west.

The first significant village, after 18km, is diminutive **SALDES**, set dramatically at the foot of Pedraforca and the usual starting point for explorations of the peak. Here you'll find a *turisme* with haphazard hours (often weekends only), a shop or two with trekking provisions, and not much else – accommodation is restricted to *Cal Xic*, a *casa de pagès* 1.5km west of the village in Cardina hamlet, at the start of the road up towards Pedraforca (☎938 258 081; ❸). Although a somewhat sterile building, en-suite rooms are heated, clean and cheerful, the *desayuno salado* with charcuterie and wine hearty. The only other reliably open facility in the area (except mid-Dec and Feb, when it closes), 5.5km east back towards Guardiola, is *Hostal Pedraforca* (☎938 258 021, ⓦwww .pedraforca.com; ❹), again no architectural marvel but friendly, and enviably set in a wood with unbeatable views of the peak.

The old stone-built village of **GÓSOL**, 10km beyond Saldes, is a far more substantial place, spilling appealingly off a castellated hill. Pablo Picasso came here from Paris during the summer of 1906 and stayed some weeks in fairly primitive conditions, inspired to paint by the striking countryside; one of the streets off Plaça Major is named after him. Gósol makes a good alternative base to Saldes for explorations of the entire Cadí, with well-trodden trails up towards the less spectacular back flank of Pedraforca. There are two somewhat basic **hostales**, both with decent attached **restaurants**: *Cal Franciscó*, on the little roundabout as you enter town (☎&ⓕ973 370 075; ❷), and the smaller, central *Can Triuet*, Plaça Major 4 (☎973 370 072; ❷). There's also a **campsite**, *Cadí*, southwest of the village, off the lower road to Tuixén (☎973 370 134).

Pedraforca and beyond

Most people tackle **Pedraforca** ("Stone Pitchfork") from Saldes; a good ninety-minute path (marked as the PR124) short-cuts the road up, which passes fifteen-minutes' walk below the **Refugi Lluís Estasen** (1647m; reserve in season on ☎938 220 079). The ascent of the 2491-metre peak is a popular outing from here, steep but not technically demanding if you **approach clockwise** via the scree-clogged *couloir* heading up the "fork"; at the divide between the two summits you'll meet the proper PR123 path coming up from Gòsol. The **anticlockwise climb** from the refuge via the Canal de Verdet is harder, and descending that way almost impossible. However you do it, count on a round trip of five to six hours.

From the *Estasen* refuge, a day's walk separates you from either the *Refugi Sant Jordi* to the east, or the Segre valley to the north. The easiest traverse route north, on a mixture of 4WD tracks and paths marked as the PR124's continuation, goes through the **Pas dels Gosolans**, a notch in the imposing, steeply dropping north face of the Cadí watershed. An hour's steep descent below, *Refugi Cesar Torres* at **PRAT D'AGUILÓ** (2037m; ☎973 250 135; staffed summer & weekends) is well situated near one of the few springs in the Cadí. From the refuge the PR124 continues down to a point just southwest of Bellver de Cerdanya (see p.785); alternatively, arrange a ride along the 15km of track north via Montellà to Martinet, on the main valley road linking La Seu d'Urgell with Puigcerdà.

Northeast of Berga

From Berga, a bus service heads northeast to **LA POBLA DE LILLET**, an hour away; you can also get here by the afternoon (Mon–Sat) bus from Ripoll, 28km to the east, via Gombrèn. Here two ancient bridges arch over the infant Riu Llobregat, with a well-stocked **turisme** beside the smaller one (daily summer and Easter 10am–2pm & 5–8pm); the old districts either side of the stream make for a brief, pleasant stroll, but the main local attractions lie just outside of town: the *carrilet*, or **narrow-gauge railway**, from here up to Castellar de N'Hug, which makes a stop 2km along at the **Jardins Artigas** (July–Sept daily 10am–7pm; Oct–June Sat & Sun 10am–5pm, guided visits only weekdays; €3), designed by Antoni Gaudí in 1901 for local industrialist Joan Artigas. Straddling the Llobregat near a pungent-smelling paper mill, the gardens constitute an enjoyable ensemble of walkways, bridges, sculpted planter boxes and railings and belvederes.

From La Pobla there's a steady eleven-kilometre ascent by road northeast towards Castellar de N'Hug, a distance covered by evening **bus** (Mon–Sat) up from Berga via La Pobla. Alternatively, take the **carrilet** (daily summer, weekends only spring/autumn). Three kilometres out of La Pobla on the left stands **El Clot del Moro**, a flamboyant *modernista* building designed by Rafael Guastavino in 1901 as a cement factory; it's now the **Museu del Ciment Asland** (July to mid-Sept daily 10am–2pm & 4–7pm; rest of year weekends only 10am–3pm; €3). Just below Castellar are the **Fonts del Llobregat**, source of the river that divides Catalunya in two. Catalans come here as if on a pilgrimage – summer droughts cause many local rivers to dwindle to nothing, so there's great pride in any durable water source, and this one has never stopped in living memory.

Castellar de N'Hug and around

Heaped up against the ridge of the Serra de Montgrony at an altitude of 1400m, **CASTELLAR DE N'HUG** makes a good if slightly touristy base for the Moixeró section of the *parc natural*, or (in winter) for snow sports at Alp 2500 (see p.782). Peak times here are September and October – mushroom-hunting season in the surrounding forests – and the skiing season of January and February. Among ample **accommodation**, first choices are the friendly *Hostal Fonda La Muntanya* at Plaça Major 4 (☎938 257 065; B&B ❸), with excellent, copious dinners, refurbished rooms, and apartments, or *Pensió Fanxicó*, across the way (☎938 257 015; ❹).

North of Castellar, the bleakly scenic BV4031 road, sporadically snowploughed during winter, continues over the range to La Molina and the Collada de Toses via the 1880-metre **Coll de la Creueta**. From the southeast edge of the village, another road leads 11km to the medieval **Santuari de Montgrony** (Mon–Fri 9am–6pm, Sat & Sun 9am–8pm), magnificently perched on a cliff-face and incorporating a simple *hostal* and well-regarded restaurant (☎972 198 022, ⓦ www.montgrony.net; closed Tues Oct–June; B&B ❹).

East to Sant Jaume de Frontanyà

The eleventh-century church at **SANT JAUME DE FRONTANYÀ**, the most imposing Romanesque church in the region, lies 12km southeast of La Pobla de Lillet, easily accessible by a paved road not yet shown on many commercial or tourist-office maps; the turning south from the B402, 2km east of La Pobla, is well marked. Set at the foot of a naturally terraced cliff, the church is built in the shape of a Latin cross with three apses and a twelve-sided lantern. The town – for thus it is offficially, despite a population of seven – offers two excellent, characterful **restaurants**: *Cal l'Eloi* (closed Mon), with a hearty three-course *menú* including wine (€17), and *Fonda Cal Marxandó* (closed Tues & July 1–15), with *a la carta* meals for about €24; the latter also has inexpensive, shared-bath **rooms** (☎938 239 002; B&B ❷) above its beam-ceilinged *menjador*.

To the French border: the Cerdanya

The train from Barcelona ends its run on the Spanish side of the frontier at Puigcerdà, having cut through the Spanish portion of the **Cerdanya**. This wide agricultural plain, flanked by mountains to the north and south, shares a past and a culture with French Cerdagne over the border. The division of the area followed the 1659 Treaty of the Pyrenees, which also gave France control of neighbouring Roussillon, but left Llívia as a Spanish enclave just inside France. Spanish Cerdanya remains marginally more rural and traditional than the French side, though it began to be a popular summer holiday area for wealthy Barcelonans during the nineteenth century, a trend that has accelerated since the 1990s, with blocks of second-home flats dwarfing nearly every village. Besides skiing – the main impetus for all this construction – golf, horseriding, glider piloting and even hot-air ballooning are popular, with the gently rolling countryside ideal for such activities.

A **train service** continues into France at Latour de Carol (4–5 daily, with a change of trains), with quick connections for Toulouse (2hr 30min–3hr). This is the only surviving trans-Pyrenean rail route and provides a good alternative method of leaving or entering Spain – for the former, reserve a seat in advance in Barcelona, or you may find yourself turfed out at Latour de Carol to fight for space with French holiday-makers on their way home. **Drivers** enter France via the small town of Bourg-Madame, 2km from Puigcerdà; it's also a simple matter to walk there across the no-longer-controlled border.

Ripoll to Puigcerdà

All routes **from Ripoll** initially follow the Freser river north to Ribes de Freser (see p.775), and then veer west, climbing steadily up the Rigart river valley. The train line to Puigcerdà sticks to the bottom of the valley, while the N152 road takes a higher course, allowing a good look south over the Serra de Montgrony. Beyond the Collada de Toses, technically in the Cerdanya, the ski resort of **Alp 2500** is one of the more serious wintersports areas in the Catalan Pyrenees.

Planoles, Fornells de la Muntanya and Toses

PLANOLES, 7km from Ribes, is nothing extraordinary as a village but makes a good base for the nearby ski slopes. There's an outstanding **casa de pagès**, ☩ *Cal Sadurní*, set in a superbly restored farmhouse on a natural terrace just uphill from the train station (☎972 736 135; half-board only ❺). This is packed out most weekends, when the pricey *a la carta* restaurant is open to non-residents, and offers a mix of doubles and family-size quads, with breakfast served in a separate refectory and *menú*-format dinners for guests.

The nearby hamlet of **FORNELLS DE LA MUNTANYA**, 8.5km beyond Planoles, also has a popular restaurant, *Can Casanova* (closed Tues & dinner except Fri & Sat; reserve on ☎972 736 075), with large if basically presented portions of hearty mountain cuisine from a limited menu. It's good value at under €23 per person, including a strong house wine; lunch is served until 5pm, savoury breakfast 9–11am.

TOSES, 3.5km beyond Fornells, is the last village in the Rigart valley and, at 1450m, one of the highest permanently inhabited settlements in Spain. The only **accommodation**, 100m from the train station, is *Cal Santpare* (☎972 736 226; B&B ❸), with comfortable en-suite rooms. The glory of Toses is its tenth-to twelfth-century church of **San Cristòfol**, at the southeast end of the village, with a simple barrel-vaulted nave and a so-called Lombard belfry, rectangular and gable-roofed. The ancient, hard-to-work key (obtainable from *Cal Pep* on the square – their nearby affiliate *Les Forques d'en Pep* is a good **restaurant**) allows you inside to see the **frescoes** (skilful copies of originals in the MNAC in Barcelona). The main theme, Christ's Ascension, is half-obliterated, but there's a well-preserved image around the lancet window of a lad hefting a sheep – highly apt for this pastoral community.

Beyond Toses, road and rail line enter Cerdanya respectively over and under the Collada de Toses – the train by the **Cargol** ("Snail") **tunnel**, where the line executes a complete spiral to gain altitude. The pass affords excellent views west, the bare rolling mountains of the Montgrony range relieved by swathes of deep green forest.

Alp 2500 and Alp village

The broad meadows of Tosa d'Alp (2537m) and Puigllançada (2406m) form the pistes of **LA MOLINA** (ⓦwww.lamolina.cat) and **MASELLA**, adjacent ski resorts linked via lifts, runs and a good-value joint pass, marketed together as "**ALP 2500**" and claimed to be the largest ski area in the Spanish Pyrenees. By Spanish Pyrenean standards, the skiing is impressive – publicly run La Molina is more suitable for beginners and has more *après* activity; more extensive, private Masella is better managed, with more scenic runs.

Getting to the slopes, it's really best to have your own car, though during winter an infrequent "Bus Blanc" is provided, with one early-morning departure up from the flatlands, and two returns in the afternoon. With the exception of the wood-and-stone chalet *Niu dels Falcons*, c/Font Moreu 10 in La Molina (☎972 892 073, ⓦwww.niudelsfalcons-xalet.com; half-board only ❺), **accommodation** at the foot of the slopes is overpriced and sterile; you're far better off staying in the villages of the Cerdanya to the north. Closest is **ALP**, 6km northwest, where the friendliest **accommodation** is *Ca l'Eudald*, Pg. Agnès Fabra 4 (☎972 890 033, ⓦwww.caleudald.com; B&B ❹), famous for its gourmet ⚴**restaurant** in the basement (*menú* from €15, *carta* around €30).

Puigcerdà

Although founded by King Alfonso I of Aragón in 1177 as a new capital for then-unified Cerdanya, **PUIGCERDÀ** (pronounced "Poocherdah") retains no compelling medieval monuments, partly owing to heavy bombing during the Civil War. The church of Santa María was among wartime casualties, but its forty-metre-high **belltower** still stands in the namesake *plaça*. The east end of town, down the pleasant, tree-lined Passeig Deu d'Abril, escaped more lightly; the gloomy parish church of **Sant Domènec** retains medieval murals in its third, left-hand chapel, where surviving fragments show the Dominican friar Peter of Verona's head being split by a sabre. The town's greatest attraction, however, is its atmosphere – if you've just arrived from France, the attractive streets and squares of the old quarter, busy pavement cafés on the merged *plaças* of Santa María and dels Herois and well-stocked shops (curiously, open Sun am but shut Sun pm and Mon), present a marked contrast to moribund Bourg-Madame just over the border.

Practicalities

From the **train station** (outside which buses also stop) in Plaça de l'Estació, a free **funicular-plus-lift** (daily 5.30am–midnight) as well as steep steps lead up to Plaça de l'Ajuntament in the heart of town, with reviving views far west over the Cerdanya. To one side stands the Casa de la Vila, with the **municipal turisme** alongside at c/Querol 1 (June to mid-Sept daily 9am–2pm & 3–8pm; mid-Sept to May Mon–Sat 9am–1pm & 4–7pm, Sun 9am–1pm; ☎972 880 542). The giant **regional turisme**, 1.5km southwest of town near the *Puigcerdà Park Hotel* (same hours as town *turisme* except mid-Sept to May Sun 10am–1pm; ☎972 140 665, ⓦwww.cerdanya.org), is particularly well stocked with leaflets and is more convenient with your own transport.

There's not a great selection of **accommodation** in Puigcerdà, and you might consider staying in one of the nearby villages instead. Acceptable budget options in town include *Hostal Residència Rita Belvedere* at c/Carmelites 6–8 (☎972 880 356 or 608 088 085; ❸), which offers excellent views, private parking and a variety of rooms, but works only limited periods (July 25–Sept 30 daily; winter holidays; Christmas–Easter Fri & Sat; & public hols); or *Fonda Cerdanya* at c/Ramon Cosp 7 (☎972 880 010; B&B ❷), with half-board (❹) usually obligatory at the ground-floor restaurant (open to all). For a splurge, you can't do better than the *Hotel del Lago*, Avgda. Dr Piguillém (☎972 881 000, ⓦwww.hotellago .com; ❺), set in a garden just off Plaça Barcelona towards the recreational lake, some units having beamed ceilings and fireplaces.

Passing French tourists are responsible for the relatively high prices and bland *menús* in Puigcerdà, but there are still some quality, good-value **restaurants**. At the budget end of the scale, *Sant Remo* at c/Ramon Cosp 9 has a pleasant upstairs *menjador* (copious *menús* €12–14). For a jump in standards and (slightly) prices, try *El Caliu* at c/Alfons Primer 1 (*menús* €12–16) or *La Maison de Foie Gras* at c/Escoles Pies 3, specializing in foie gras (of course), duck and cheese. The obvious, touristy outdoor **cafés** should be shunned in favour of *Granja Major* on c/Major 15 (closed Tues eve & Wed), with crêpes, waffles, juices and hot drinks. The most distinctive **bar** is *Cerveseria Claude*, on arcaded Plaça Cabrinetty, you can sit indoors or out, tippling your way around the world's breweries.

Villages around Puigcerdà

You'll find better-value accommodation, and often food, in the hamlets and villages immediately south of Puigcerdà, which are home to some distinguished *turismes rurals*. Top billing goes to *Residència Sant Marc*, 1.5km south of town on the road to **LES PERERES** (☎972 880 007, ⓦwww.santmarc.es; B&B ❺). Set on a 150-hectare stud farm, this elegant *belle époque* mansion with on-site restaurant has huge, varied common areas and wood-floored rooms with antique furniture; reservations are recommended in summer.

Two kilometres east of Puigcerdà in **AGE**, the *Cal Marrufès/Cal Senaire* is a tasteful restoration of an old stone-built farm in the village centre (☎972 141 174, ⓦwww.calmarrufes.com), offering both rooms (B&B ❹) and quad apartments (€130–170). In sleepy **URTX**, 5km south of Puigcerdà, friendly *Cal Mateu* (☎972 890 495; B&B ❸) is part of a working dairy farm; the good-value en-suite rooms are bland modern rather than rustic and the breakfasts are nothing special, but self-catering is available. Urtx hasn't any other facilities; the closest good **eats** are 1.5km downhill inside the decommissioned Queixans RENFE station, where *L'Estació* (closed Wed; book on ☎972 882 400) proves massively popular for its plain but plentiful pork, lamb, mushroom and *escalivada* platters (€16 three-course *a la carta* plus drinkable house wine).

Finally, another luxurious choice, a bit beyond Sanavastre on the outskirts of **ISÒVOL**, is ✻ *Ermitatge de Quadres* (☎972 197 285, ⓦ www.ermitatgedequadres .es; B&B ⑤), five state-of-the-art apartments (fitting up to six for €170) and a *nouvelle cuisine* restaurant built next to the eponymous thirteenth-century *ermita* on a minor branch of the Camino de Santiago.

Llívia

The Spanish town of **LLÍVIA**, 6km from Puigcerdà but totally surrounded by French territory, is a curious place indeed, worth visiting not least so you can say you've been there. There are several **buses** daily from Puigcerdà RENFE station; under your own power, bear left at the unmarked roundabout by the *Hotel Prado* 1km outside town, just before the border at Bourg-Madame, and keep to the main road.

French **history** books claim that Llívia's anomalous position is the result of an oversight. According to the traditional version of events, in discussions following the Treaty of the Pyrenees, French delegates insisted on possession of the 33 Cerdan villages between the Ariège and newly acquired Roussillon. The Spanish agreed, and then pointed out that Llívia was technically a town rather than a village, and was thus excluded from the terms of the handover. Llívia had in fact been capital of the valley until the foundation of Puigcerdà, and Spain had every intention of retaining it at the negotiations, which were held in Llívia itself.

Despite a manic, ongoing chalet-building programme at the outskirts, there's a deceptively large central old town with shops focused on the fifteenth-century fortified **church** (June–Sept daily 10am–1pm & 3–7pm; Oct–May Tues–Sun 10am–1pm & 3–6pm), which boasts fine carved-wood sacred art in the northerly side-chapels. Since 1982, a popular **music festival** has been held in and around the church on August weekends. Opposite the church, the unusual **Museu Municipal** (closed for works until 2010) contains the interior of the oldest pharmacy in Europe, functioning from 1594 until 1918. Displays that should weather the renovation feature apothecarial pots, hand-painted boxes of herbs, local Bronze Age relics and even the eighteenth-century bell mechanism from the church.

Practicalities

With its cap set for the ski trade, Llívia has ample if often pricey **accommodation**. More reasonable choices are limited to stone-built *Hostal Ruso* near the church (☎972 146 264; B&B ③), *Fonda Mercé* at the east edge of the old town (☎972 897 001, ⓦ www.fondamerce.com; B&B ④), and *Hotel L'Esquirol* on the bypass road (☎972 146 363, ⓦ www.hotelesquirol.net; B&B ④). Besides the respected *menjador* of the *Mercé* (*menú* €15, *a la carta* allow €30; closed Sun eve), recommendable **restaurants** include *Les Brases de Llívia* (Thurs–Sun; daily in Aug) at Font Citrana 8–10, a designer-converted barn specializing in good-value grilled meat, and *Cal Cofa* just off Plaça Major at c/Frederic Bernades 1, where €23–28 *a la carta* nets hearty country fare.

Bellver de Cerdanya and Martinet

The second-largest village in the Cerdanya – almost a town – and a possible halting point on the road between Puigcerdà and La Seu d'Urgell, **BELLVER DE CERDANYA** stands on a low hill on the left bank of the trout-laden Segre, 18km west of Puigcerdà. Its semi-fortified hilltop old town, with an arcaded Plaça Major and a massive summit church, is visually polluted by a hideous telecoms antenna, but still merits a stop. Romanesque **Santa María de**

Talló lies 2km southeast of the town. Known locally as the "Cathedral of Cerdanya", this is a rather plain church, but has a few nice decorative touches in the nave and apse, and retains a wooden statue of the Virgin as old as the building itself.

The **turisme** occupies an old chapel at Plaça Sant Roc 9 (Easter, mid-June to mid-Sept & Christmas Mon–Sat 11am–1pm & 6–8pm, Sun 11am–1pm; ⓣ973 510 229). The best place to **stay** is *Fonda Biayna*, c/Sant Roc 11 (ⓣ973 510 475; B&B ❹), an atmospheric, rambling old mansion of creaky wood-floored rooms with small bathrooms, wall art and antique furnishings. It also has wi-fi and a lively downstairs bar, much patronized by locals, while the adjacent *menjador* is the best **restaurant** in town, with €10.50 *menú* and more adventurous *a la carta* choices such as Cerdanyan *trinxat* and duck with beans.

Continuing downstream along the Segre on the N260, you're next likely to stop at **MARTINET**; the road from the refuge at Prat d'Aguilo, in the Cadí foothills just south (see p.779), also emerges here. Martinet is mostly strung uninspiringly along the through-road, c/El Segre, but there's quieter accommodation at *Fonda Miravet*, north of the highway on c/de les Arenes 2 (ⓣ973 515 016; ❸), with views across a little stream. For **meals**, try the *Fonda Pluvinet* (closed Wed, also Mon & Tues eves low season) at c/El Segre 13, which does quality *a la carta* at €22–28 per head.

The road to Andorra

The semi-autonomous principality of Andorra is not much of a summertime goal in itself, and you'll get significantly better trekking (if that's what you're after) in the Pyrenees to either side. However, if you're curious – or in transit towards France – the route there is a reasonably interesting one, covered regularly by buses **from Barcelona** (from Ronda Universitat 4). These end their run in La Seu d'Urgell (4hr), the last Spanish town before Andorra. You can also approach La Seu d'Urgell **from Puigcerdà**, by moving west along the N260.

Whether travelling by public transport or driving yourself, the most interesting route is via **Cardona** and **Solsona** on the C26; this eventually joins the C14 for the final run up the often dramatic **Segre valley** to La Seu.

Cardona and Solsona

CARDONA, about halfway between Barcelona and Andorra, is dominated by a medieval hillside castle, whose eleventh-century chapel contains the tombs of the counts of Cardona. The castle has been converted into a four-star **hotel** (ⓣ938 691 275, ⓦwww.paradores.es; ❻), which as a luxurious overnight stop is hard to beat, particularly since it also contains an excellent Catalan restaurant, where *table d'hôte* dinner runs to a relatively reasonable €30 per head (plus drink). Another remarkable Cardona feature is its salt "mountain", the **Salina**, close to the river – a massive saline deposit exploited since ancient times.

Twenty kilometres further on amidst a forested upland, the *comarca* capital of **SOLSONA** with its small, walled and gated *barri vell* has considerable charm. The **Catedral** here, just up through the Portal del Pont from the through-road, is gloomy and mysterious in the best tradition of Catalan Gothic, with fine stained glass and a diminutive twelfth-century image of the Virgin, reminiscent of the Montserrat icon, in its own chapel at the end of the south transept. An adjacent seventeenth-century bishop's palace houses the **Museu Diocesà**

(Tues–Sat 10am–1pm & 4.30–7pm, Oct–April 4–6pm, Sun 10am–2pm; €3), featuring Romanesque frescoes, altar panels and sculpture taken from local churches.

Buses use a terminal at the northwest edge of town; there's a **turisme** down the main through-road in the *comarcal* building (Mon–Sat 9am–1pm & 4–7pm, Sun 10am–1pm). High-quality **accommodation** comprises the five-room ⚑ *Hostal La Freixera* at c/de Sant Llorenç 46B in the old town (☎ 973 723 757, ⓦ www.lafreixera.com; B&B ❻), a restored fourteenth-century mansion; or *Hotel Sant Roc*, Plaça de Sant Roc 2, off the through-road (☎ 973 480 006, ⓦ www .hotelsantroc.com; ❺), a 1929-vintage *modernista* mansion tastefully converted – without being too harshly minimalist – into a luxury hotel with wi-fi, basement spa, full-service restaurant, breakfast buffet and after-hours bar. Independent **restaurants** are thin on the ground; try *La Criolla* in the centre of the old town, or salubrious and airy *Sant Antoni* (closed Wed), diagonally opposite the Portal del Pont at Avgda. del Pont 11, with an €11 *menú* in the *menjador* but also very good *plats combinats* and tapas in the bar area at odd hours.

La Seu d'Urgell

The capital of Alt Urgell *comarca*, **LA SEU D'URGELL** lies beside the Riu Segre 23km upstream from Organyà. For years a rather sleepy place with a neglected medieval core, La Seu underwent a mild transformation after the 1992 Olympic canoeing competitions were held adjacent. There are now some fancy hotels, as well as the purpose-built canoe and kayaking facilities by the Segre, and of late La Seu has become a popular dormitory community for Andorran workers priced out of their principality by its stratospheric housing costs.

Arrival, information and accommodation

The **bus station** is on c/Joan Garriga Massó, just north of the old town; buses leave here for Puigcerdà and Andorra (see box on p.788 for details). The friendly, well-stocked **turisme** is on Avgda. de les Valls d'Andorra, (Mon–Sat 10am–2pm & 5–8pm, 4–6pm in winter; ☎ 973 351 511, ⓦ www.turismeseu.com), the main road into town from the north. Drivers should use the handy free **parking** area signposted about 200m east of the cathedral.

Best placed and most characterful of the proper new town **hotels** is the ⚑ *Andria*, Pg. Joan Brudieu 24 (☎ 973 350 300, ⓦ www.hotelandria.com; B&B ❺), an elegant, historic establishment with antique-furnished rooms, terracotta floors and huge bathrooms. Top of the heap is exclusive *El Castell de Ciutat* (☎ 973 350 000, ⓦ www.hotelelcastell.com; ❼), now reinvented as a "wellness and anti-stress" spa, 500m west of La Seu, at the foot of Castellciutat citadel as the name implies. Also in Castellciutat, perched above the river and access road, with a pool and restaurant, *Hostal La Glorieta* (☎ 973 351 045; ❸) gets nearly the same views without the expense.

The Town

Named after the imposing cathedral at the north end of c/Major, La Seu has always had a dual function as episcopal seat and commercial centre – there's still a street farmers' **market** each Tuesday and Saturday, attracting vendors from across the county. A bishopric had been established here by 820, and it was squabbling between the bishops of La Seu d'Urgell and the counts of Foix over land rights that led to Andorra's independence late in the thirteenth century.

The original cathedral and city, on the hill just west where **Castellciutat** village now stands, was destroyed during the eighth century by Moorish invaders. The present **cathedral** (June–Sept Mon–Sat 10am–1pm & 4–7pm, Sun 10am–1pm; Oct–May Mon–Sat 11am–1pm & 4–6pm, Sun 11am–1pm) was consecrated in 839 but completely rebuilt in 1175, and restored several times since. Nonetheless, it retains some graceful interior decoration and a fine **cloister** with droll carved capitals; you can see this by buying an inclusive ticket at the cloister portal (same hours as cathedral; €3), which also admits to the adjacent eleventh-century church of Sant Miquel and the **Museu Diocesà** with its brilliantly coloured tenth-century Mozarabic manuscript with miniatures, the *Beatus*.

Other than these few sights, time is most agreeably spent strolling the dark, cobbled and arcaded streets west of the cathedral. A strong medieval feel is accentuated by the fine buildings lining c/dels Canonges (parallel to c/Major); the town's fourteenth-century stone corn-measures still stand under the arcade on c/Major. For a completely different kind of colonnade, head west from the old town along c/de Joaquim Viola Lafuerza, across Avgda. de Pau Claris, to the riverside **Parc de Valira** and its modern cloister made of pink stone, with satirical carved capitals of twentieth-century figures and events.

Eating and drinking

After a millennium nadir, traditional **tapas bars** in La Seu's old town are staging a diffident comeback: *Bar Eugenio* at c/Major 20 is one reliable survivor, while *Ca La Lluisa* at Plaça d'Espanya showcases good if expensive tapas such as pickled mushrooms, and also has a *menjador* (*menú* €12). *Cal Pacho* (closed Sun), in a quiet corner on c/la Font (at the southern end of c/Major, then east), is a more accomplished **restaurant**, with a bargain lunch *menú* and *a la carta* dinner dishes (Fri & Sat pm only) – salmon-stuffed endive and roast goat will set you back around €26, dessert and drink extra. Outside the old quarter, the *Andria's menjador* has *menús* at €22–30, featuring home-reared chicken and mushrooms in season.

Andorra

After seven centuries of feudalism, modernity finally forced itself upon the **PRINCIPALITY OF ANDORRA**, 450 square kilometres of precipitously mountainous land between France and Spain. A referendum held on March 14, 1993 (henceforth the big national holiday) produced an overwhelming vote in favour of a democratic constitution, replacing a system in effect since 1278, when the Spanish bishops of La Seu d'Urgell and the French counts of Foix settled a long-standing quarrel by granting Andorra semi-autonomous status under joint sovereignty.

Despite the counts' sovereignty passing successively to the French king and then the French president, the principality managed largely to maintain its independence over the centuries. The Spanish and French co-seigneurs appointed regents who took little interest in Andorra's day-to-day life. The country was run instead by the *Consell General de les Valls* (General Council of the Valleys), made up of appointed representatives from Andorra's seven valley communes, who ensured that the principality remained well out of the

European mainstream – it even managed to remain neutral during the Spanish Civil War and World War II.

It was during these conflicts that Andorra began its economic mushrooming, as locals smuggled goods from France into Spain during the Civil War and, a few years later, goods from Spain into France under German occupation. After World War II, this trade was replaced by duty-free alcohol, tobacco and electronics, and by the demand for winter skiing. Much of the principality became little more than an unsightly, drive-in megastore, clogged with French and Spanish visitors. Seasoned Spain-watcher John Hooper has called Andorra "a kind of cross between Shangri-la and Heathrow Duty-Free",

Andorra practicalities

Getting there

From Spain, there are numerous daily buses from **Barcelona**, plus many services (and 5 daily minibuses) from the airport. There are also services from **Lleida** (4–6 daily), **Girona** town and airport (2 daily), and **Reus** airport (every evening). Most frequent are services from **La Seu d'Urgell** (Mon–Sat hourly 7am–8pm, Sun 5 daily 7.45am–6.30pm), taking forty minutes to reach Andorra la Vella, and another five minutes to Escaldes.

From France, daily buses leave **L'Hospitalet** at 7.35am and 7.45pm, arriving at Pas de la Casa 25 minutes later; from Pas de la Casa, the onward bus journey to Andorra la Vella takes an hour.

Even if you're **driving**, consider leaving the car behind and taking the bus – in high season (summer or winter) the traffic is so bad that the bus isn't much slower, and **parking** in Andorra la Vella is an expensive ordeal. On the plus side, **petrol** is famously cheap – about 12–15 percent less than in Spain – so fill up before leaving.

Leaving Andorra

Buses back to **La Seu d'Urgell** from Andorra la Vella (Mon–Sat 14 daily 8.05am–9.05pm; Sun 5 daily 8.20am–7.20pm) leave from Plaça de Guillemó; buses may originate in Escaldes. **To France**, there are at least two buses daily from Andorra la Vella to L'Hospitalet (1hr) at 5.45am and 5pm.

Getting around

Internal **bus services**, arranged in six lines, are cheap and frequent. The following routes run between about 7am and 9pm: Escaldes–Sant Julià de Lòria; Andorra la Vella–Escaldes–La Massana–Ordino; Andorra la Vella–Escaldes–Encamp. Slightly less frequent lines run, from roughly 8am to 8pm, Andorra la Vella–Canillo (continuing to Soldeu and Pas de la Casa in winter), and Andorra la Vella–La Massana–Arinsal. Buses leave from Avgda. Princip Benlloch. In winter, there's a supplemental "**Ski Bus**" service (free, show your lift pass) between La Massana, Ordino, Arinsal and Arcalis.

Currency, mail and phones

Andorra never had its own **money**, and the euro is now the currency. There's a shared, "foreign" postal system, with both a French and Spanish **post office** in Andorra la Vella and Canillo, for example. Andorra has its own **phone system** and phone code – ⓣ376 – applicable to the whole republic. A single mobile network, MobileAnd/STA, provides surprisingly good coverage even in the deepest valleys, but roamers beware – charges for both incoming and outgoing calls are exorbitant, as the network is not subject to EU tariff caps.

Language

Andorra is the only nation where Catalan is the official **language**, but Spanish and – to a much lesser extent – French are widely understood.

while the Spanish daily *El País* once dismissed it as a "high-altitude Kuwait".

Ironically, though, this **tax-free status** held the seeds of Andorra's belated conversion to democracy. Although the inhabitants enjoyed one of Europe's highest standards of living, up to twelve million visitors a year began to cause serious logistical problems; the country's infrastructure was overstretched and the valleys increasingly blighted by speculators' building sites, while the budget deficit grew alarmingly since little revenue went towards the public sector. Spain's 1986 entry to the EU exacerbated the situation, diminishing the difference in price of imported goods between Spain and Andorra (which now typically measures about twenty percent). The 1993 referendum was an attempt to come to terms with these economic realities – or rather some of them, since nobody seriously suggested that the solution would be to introduce direct taxation: there is still no income tax in Andorra, and barely any indirect taxes either (VAT is a paltry 4 percent). Instead, the strategy has been to transform Andorra into an "**offshore**" **banking centre** to rival the likes of Gibraltar, Liechtenstein and the Caymans, with the faint whiff of unsavouriness that attaches to such places.

Following the referendum, the state's first **constitutional election** was held in December 1993, to elect the 28-seat Consell General or parliament (4 MPs from each parish). Only the nine-thousand-plus native Andorrans were entitled to vote (out of a then-population of 60,000, now up to 78,000, most foreigners being Spanish, Portuguese or French). Since 1993, Andorran citizens (those born there, or who have lived there for over twenty years) have been able to join trade unions or political parties as well as vote, while the various ministers appointed by the Consell General run the government and determine independent foreign policy; Andorra is a member of the United Nations and the Council of Europe, but not the EU.

Given all this, it's useful to remember that as recently as 1950 Andorra was virtually cut off from the rest of the world – an archaic region that, romantically, happened also to be a separate country. There are still no planes or trains, but otherwise **development** has been all-encompassing. Despite new bypass roads and bus lanes, it can take an hour in bumper-to-bumper traffic to drive the few kilometres from La Seu d'Urgell to Andorra la Vella, the main town. Most of the principality – even the steeper slopes – is a perpetual chalet-building site; mega ski resorts monopolize many attractive corners, with enlargements of existing ones and laying out of new ones planned. If you're not a ski fanatic (Ⓦwww.skiandorra.ad), you might still spend a day or so on cheap shopping or spa-dipping, and it's worth getting well clear of the capital to see some of the scenery that entranced early visitors. Don't expect to find an unspoilt spot anywhere, though, unless you're prepared to head up the mountains on foot – and if you are, there are more rewarding places either side of Andorra to shoulder a rucksack.

Andorra la Vella

Set at an altitude of over 1000m, **ANDORRA LA VELLA** – with its stone church, river and enclosing hills – must once have been an attractive little town. Today, the main street is a seething mass of bad restaurants (specializing in six-language menus), tacky bars and garish shops crammed with everything from booze, perfumes and watches to cars and appliances. There's partial respite in the **Barri Antic**, on the heights above the river Valira south of the main through-road, Avgda. Princep Benlloch. But even here, the sole monument is the sixteenth-century **Casa de la Vall**, which used to house the Consell General before a mammoth new "parliament" was built adjacent.

Practicalities

Buses from La Seu leave passengers on Avgda. Princep Benlloch, near the church of Sant Esteve, though other services use the big terminal down by the river. There are various public **car parks** scattered around town; the huge open-air Parc Central is the cheapest and usually has spaces. The **turisme**, on c/Dr Vilanova 13 (summer Mon–Sat 10am–1pm & 3–7pm, Sun 10am-1pm; winter Mon–Sat 10am–1.30pm & 3–7pm; ☎376 820 214), below the Barri Antic, has lists of local accommodation and bus timetables.

Some of the scant reasonably priced **accommodation** is at 2004-renovated, three-star *Hotel Florida* at c/La Llacuna 13 (☎376 820 105, ⓦwww.hotelflorida .ad; ❹), with balconied rooms, sauna and small gym, and 1940-vintage *Hotel Pyrénées* at Avgda. Princep Benlloch 20 (☎376 878 879, ⓦwww.hotelpyrenees .com; ❹), with an elegant *menjador* and wi-fi; rear rooms are quieter and have better views. Quality **restaurants** are thin on the ground in town; *Papanico* at Avgda. Princep Benlloch 4 does acceptable tapas and *plats combinats*, while in the Barri Antic *Minim's* on tiny Placeta de la Consrocia is a small, stylish place doing Spanish/Catalan food (€12 *plat del dia*, €35 dinner *carta*). If you do stay the night, you could check out the "live and dance" **club**, *Àngel Blau*, in c/de la Borda (ⓦwww.angelblauclub.com), where live jazz alternates with DJ events, or the two **cinemas** (Avgda. Meritxell 26 & 44).

Up the Valira d'Ordino

It's hard to believe that not all of Andorra is like the capital (sadly, much of it is), but you can effect a partial escape by heading up the **Valira d'Ordino**. At **LA MASSANA**, 7km out of Andorra la Vella, the road splits, the left-hand fork climbing up to the ski resorts of **ARINSAL** and **PAL**. The former is the most developed – with eight daily buses from Andorra la Vella, 23 runs, a bubble-lift and lively nightlife – while the latter is a pretty, stone-built village with a fine belfried Romanesque church. Pal ski centre (also reached by bubble-lift from La Massana) is 5km beyond the village, a good, scenic beginners-to-intermediate centre but with limited piste plan if the Setúria sector is shut or the link with Arinsal is cut – as it may be in late spring. Arinsal and Pal are marketed together with Ordino-Arcalis as "Vallnord" (ⓦwww.vallnord.com), with a common lift-pass scheme and free shuttle bus between them, though only Arinsal and Pal have a physical link. About the only Arinsal **accommodation** not monopolized by ski packages is basic but friendly and helpful *Hotel Poblado* opposite the bubble-lift (☎376 835 122; ❸), with good-value half-board; independent **restaurants** aren't a strong point, except for Aragonese-style grill specialist *L'Hort de Casa* opposite the turning for Pal (dull *menú*, allow €27 for *a la carta*), or *Borda Raubert*, just above La Massana on the road (budget €35; closed Tues).

A right fork at La Massana leads to **ORDINO**, a relatively agreeable but increasingly built-up place with a handful of old stone edifices surrounded by new chalets and apartment buildings. The only free **car park** is just downhill from the edge-of-town **turisme** (Mon–Sat 8.30am–1pm & 3–6.30pm, Sun 9am–1pm; ⓦwww .ordino.ad). Carrer Major, threading through the tiny old quarter towards the church, takes you past stone-built *Hotel Santa Barbara* on a small *plaça* (☎376 837 100; ❹), an agreeable place to **stay**. The same lane passes three **restaurants**, the best of which is 🍴 *Armengol* (*Casa Leon*) at no. 12, with an excellent four-course lunch *menú* containing thick soup, salad, entrée and home-made dessert. Some 2km beyond Ordino, at **SORNÀS** hamlet, there's a more basic, late-opening **grill**, *Les Fargues*, where the *menú*, including rabbit, runs to under €14.

There's more choice of food and lodgings in the little villages of the valley proper, along the 8km north of Ordino; the landscape becomes more appealing here, with fewer tower-cranes and high-rises. There's also the partly Romanesque church of **Sant Martí de Cortinada** (daily 10am–1pm & 3–7pm) to visit, with original frescoes, located in La Cortinada hamlet, 2.5km north of Ordino. The most reasonable **accommodation** en route is *Pensió Vilaró*, slightly isolated just below the village of **LLORTS**, some 5km from Ordino (☎376 850 225; B&B ❷ shared bathrooms), popular with hikers on the nearby GR11. Llorts also offers the best rural **restaurant** in this valley, *L'Era del Jaume* (☎376 850 667; closed Sun eve), which specializes in grills (€35 *a la carta*, though there's a cheaper lunchtime *menú*).

El Serrat and Ordino-Arcalis

Eighteen kilometres (and 3 daily buses) from Andorra la Vella, **EL SERRAT** stands at the head of the valley, graced by some tumbling waterfalls. Here you'll find four hotels, the last **accommodation** before the ski centre of Ordino-Arcalis, including the *Hotel Tristaina* (☎376 850 081; ❸).

From El Serrat the road climbs steeply 5km more to the ski resort of **ORDINO-ARCALIS**, which, owing to its height, retains snow well into April and is probably the most pleasant place to ski at intermediate level in Andorra, with a mostly local clientele, and views north over the Tristaina lakes to the border ridge beyond. In summer, the area around the base of **La Coma** lift sees steady traffic for the sake of the half-hour walk north to the cirque containing the **Tristaina lakes**; after your exertions, the good-value **restaurant** complex here is worth a visit (average €10–13 self-service, €24 upstairs at the full-service; open for lunch year-round except May & Nov).

The road to France: the Valira del Orient

It's around 35km from Andorra la Vella to the French border at Pas de la Casa by the overground route (4km less by the tunnel, €5.70 toll well worth paying in misty or blizzard conditions), served as far as Soldeu by hourly buses from the capital. Just 2km northeast of Andorra La Vella, **ESCALDES** is little more than a continuation of the capital – cars, coaches, hotels and restaurants – though it does have an excellent **spa complex** to unwind at, **Caldea** (daily 9am–11pm, until midnight Sat & high season; Ⓦwww.caldea.com; admission fee to "thermoludic" area, massages extra).

Some 9km upvalley from Escaldes, a side road climbs to **MERITXELL** village, built around the **Santuari de Meritxell**, the principality's spiritual heart. The starkly hideous shrine of the Virgin was designed by Ricardo Bofill to replace a Romanesque one burnt down in 1972. Of much more interest is the excellent-value ⚘ *Hotel l'Ermita* just below (☎376 751 050, Ⓦwww.hotelermita .com; closed Nov & part June; B&B ❹), with very high-standard units and a **restaurant** (one of two in the village).

Canillo

CANILLO, 14km from Andorra la Vella and 3km from Meritxell, makes another good skiing base: along the main road (and bus route) between Andorra la Vella and Soldeu, but far enough away from both to retain some character. On the east edge of town, most of the belfried Romanesque church of **Sant Joan de Caselles** (daily 10am–1pm & 3–7pm) is originally eleventh century, with a unique stucco-relief Crucifixion complete with sun, moon and lance-wielding Romans. Back in the centre, a warren of old streets north of the highway leads to **Sant Sadurní**, nearly as ancient. When snow levels permit, a bubble-lift rises south up to **El Forn**, part of El Tarter ski centre (this, along with Soldeu, Grau Roig and Pas de la Casa sectors, is marketed – and lift-passed – as "Grand Valira", Ⓦwww.grandvalira.com).

Hotels line the main through-road, with only one budget choice: the basic *Comerç* (☎376 851 020; ❷), whose **restaurant** offers French-style *table d'hôte*. Alternatively, *Molí del Peano* has fondue, *cassoulet* and grills.

Soldeu-El Tarter

Development at **SOLDEU-EL TARTER**, 6–8km beyond, is surprisingly restrained considering they lie at the base of the largest ski domain in Andorra – or indeed, as is claimed, the Pyrenees – with ample skiing for all ability levels. It's the best resort in Andorra for beginners, a fact appreciated by the British and Spanish families in attendance. Two **hotels** in Soldeu not completely dominated by packages are welcoming *Roc de Sant Miquel* at the west approaches (☎376 346 791, ⓦwww.hotel-roc.com; ❺), a youth-orientated spot with Anglo-Andorran management, a cozy bar and wi-fi; or the more comfortable *Soldeu Maistre* facing a little square above the road (☎376 801 963; B&B ❹). Independent **restaurants** are apt to be better in El Tarter, where *La Soldanella* on the through-road has solid if not wildly exciting fare (*menú* €16), while ⫶ *Borda de l'Horto* 1.5km west excels at *nouvelle* Catalan dishes in a converted barn, with polished service; allow €30 for three courses, plus expensive wine.

The Noguera Pallaresa valley

The **Noguera Pallaresa**, the most powerful river in the Pyrenees, was once used to float logs down from the mountains to the sawmills at La Pobla de Segur, a job now done by truck. These days, the river is known for its **river-rafting** opportunities, while the valley also provides an efficient way of getting to the Val d'Aran and the east flank of the Parc Nacional d'Aigüestortes i Estany de Sant Maurici. Transport hub of the valley is **La Pobla de Segur**, which can be reached directly from Barcelona or Lleida. Approaching from the east, there's a road from La Seu d'Urgell to **Sort** (2 minibuses daily), in the middle of the valley, through 53km of gorgeous scenery. **Buses** leave Barcelona (from Plaça de la Universitat) for La Pobla de Segur (3hr), via dismal Artesa de Segre; it's better to take the **train** from Lleida to La Pobla – a spectacular ride with glimpses of cliff and reservoir water between spells in the many tunnels.

Talarn, Santa Engràcia and Congost de Mont-rebei

However you approach, the first interesting stop in the Noguera Pallaresa valley, 2km northwest of Tremp, is the large, fortified hill town of **TALARN**, 2km northwest of Tremp, where ⫶ *Casa Lola*, c/Soldevila 2 (ⓦwww.casalola.info; closed Sun pm), shines as a beacon of country cuisine including *girella* (a sort of lamb-and-rice haggis), duck-ham-and-quince-jelly salad, or oxtails stewed with mushroom and fruits (meals €23–26 *a la carta*, plus drink), attracting clientele from near and far. Proprietress "Lola" (Florita) is a character, giving free *pa amb tomàquet*-making lessons to the uninitiated; she also has several state-of-the-art, self-catering studios upstairs (☎973 650 814; ❸).

Alternatively, if you have your own transport, you can head out from just below Talarn along a narrow but paved ten-kilometre road west to **SANTA ENGRÀCIA**, perhaps the most spectacularly located village in Catalunya, tumbling off the south flank of a rock monolith. Here, ⫶ *Casa Guilla* (☎973 252 080, ⓦwww.casaguilla.com; closed Dec–Feb; half-board only ❻), a restored rambling farmhouse with sweeping views, offers rustic, en-suite rooms – including a family quad – plus a mineral-water pool, dinnertime refectory, wi-fi and bar; reservations are strongly advised all season.

If you're based at either of these spots, a highly recommended outing is to the **Congost (Desfiladero) de Mont-rebei**, which marks the boundary between Catalunya and Aragón and forms the heart of a natural reserve. Here the Noguera Ribagorçana has carved out a gorge through the Serra de Montsec, where sheer rock walls rise to 500m above water level; the narrows are visited by a spectacular but perfectly safe path carved out of the left-bank palisade in 1982, replacing an older (1924) one inundated by a dam project. The most straightforward **access** involves heading west from Tremp on the C1311 county road, signposted "Pont de Montanyana"; after about 25km, just before entering Pont, bear left onto a marked track for the *congost/desfiladero*. After another 6km, bearing right when given the choice, you arrive at a parking area and seasonally staffed **information booth**. From here, you can see the mouth of the gorge on the far side of the river's flood plain; after about fifteen minutes' progress along a steadily narrowing track, you cross the Barranco de la Maçana on a metal suspension bridge. Track now becomes path as you climb slightly to enter the narrows proper, about forty minutes from the car park; after traversing the canyon for up to another half-hour, you go back the way you came – or continue to Àger village on what's part of the GR1. The gorge walls are home to large numbers of raptors, some of which you're likely to glimpse, while the river itself shelters otters – which you're most unlikely to see.

Once back at the car park, you can vary the return to Tremp by taking a more southerly, minor road via La Torre de Amargós, beyond which villages are studded with unheralded **castles** left from the age when this ridge was the frontier against the Moors. The most intact of these are at **Alsamora** (turn right just before Sant Esteve de la Sarga) and **Mur**, accessed by turning left just before Guàrdia de Noguera and proceeding 5km to the eleventh-century fort (guided visits only Sat 11am–1pm & 5–7pm, Sun 11am–1pm). This, with an intact, silo-like tower inside and tapered round west end, resembles nothing so much as a sailing ship. From Guàrdia, you've 10km north back to Talarn.

La Pobla de Segur

Thirteen kilometres north of Tremp, **LA POBLA DE SEGUR** is a lively enough town if you want to break your journey, although most people only come here for onward connections. Train and bus services from Lleida terminate here, in time to catch a midday bus continuing up the Noguera Pallaresa through Sort and Llavorsí, passing within 7km of Espot, a major entry point to Parque Nacional Aigüestortes. Local services also journey west to El Pont de Suert, Boí and Capdella for the southwestern margins of the Aigüestortes region, and to Vielha through its namesake tunnel.

The **RENFE** station is in the new town, from where you walk up the road, cross the bridge and head along the main street 200m towards the kiosk-shelter, which serves as the **bus** terminal. There's little to recommend for **refreshment** other than *Bar Restaurant El Raier*, at Avgda. Madrid 3, at the west edge of town past the post office. A well-stocked **turisme** at the north end of town (Mon–Sat 9am–2pm) stands by the *ajuntament*.

Gerri de la Sal and around

From La Pobla de Segur the C13 road threads through the **Barranc de l'Infern** and the **Congost de Collegats**, impressive, consecutive gorges hewn by the Noguera Pallaresa through three-hundred-metre-high cliffs. Unfortunately, since a series of tunnels was blasted through much of the defile, drivers see little of the spectacular valley unless they detour towards Pujol and an observation point, though the narrow, abandoned old road is still open to cyclists and

Rafting on the Noguera Pallaresa

The main **rafting season** on the Noguera Pallaresa lasts from April until September, though some organizations offer programmes from March to October if snowmelt (and the power company controlling dam sluices) are amenable. The original rafts – used for the journey downstream to the sawmills of La Pobla de Segur – were logs lashed together ten-wide. Today's watersport versions are reinforced **inflatables**, up to 6.5m long. If you sign on for a trip – which guarantees a soaking and about as much excitement as any well-balanced person would want – you'll usually share a boat with seven others, including your guide/pilot, who sits in the rear.

The 14km between Llavorsí and Rialp is the easiest and thus most commonly rafted sector of the river, while the 18km from Sort to Desfiladero de Collegats is advanced and even more scenic. Daily **departures** are typically at 11am and noon; in the former, you'll be in the water by 11.20am, and clambering into the return-shuttle van at Rialp by 12.40pm. **Prices** range from €35 for a two-hour rafting trip (Llavorsí to Rialp or Sort) to €85 for the entire 38-kilometre stretch from Llavorsí to Collegats (a full afternoon's outing; lunch extra).

pedestrians. The Catalan intelligentsia began coming here to admire the formations during the 1880s, and the section of the canyon known as **L'Argenteria**, with its sculpted, papier-mâché-like rock-face streaked with rivulets, was apparently the inspiration for Antoni Gaudí's La Pedrera apartment building in Barcelona.

As the gorge opens out, you emerge at the rickety village of **GERRI DE LA SAL** – "de la Sal" because of the local salt-making industry. You'll see still-functioning salt pans by the riverside as you pass by, but the most obvious landmark is the Benedictine monastery of **Santa María** (Easter & June–Sept daily 11am–1pm & 4.30–7.30pm; otherwise by appointment on ☎973 662 068; €1.50), facing the village on the far side of a beautiful old bridge. The monastery was originally founded in 807, though the present structure, with its huge and dilapidated bell-wall, dates from the twelfth century.

With a vehicle, you can break the journey locally; Gerri can muster a lone **restaurant** on the through-road, but there are more facilities 4km north at tiny **BARÓ**, including *Bar Restaurant Cal Mariano* (☎973 662 077; ❷), one of two lodgings and four eateries here, always open as it's the main bar. On the east bank of the river at *El Carro* (summer daily; otherwise weekends; ☎973 662 148), a mother-and-son team do wood-roasted meat meals (allow €30) with an ingenious funnel rotisserie.

Sort, Rialp and Port-Ainé

SORT, 30km north of La Pobla, retains an old centre of tall, narrow houses, though it's now hemmed in by apartment buildings. This development is owed partly to the fact that Sort and neighbouring villages have, since the late 1980s, ranked among the premier **river-running spots** in Europe. Every year during late June and early July, valley communities stage the **Raiers (Rafters) festival**, re-enacting the exploits of the old-time timber pilots.

Because of the upmarket rafting (and ski) clientele it attracts, Sort has priced itself out of any casual trade, and in any case it's not a place to linger unless you're here for the action. Its main street is almost exclusively devoted to rafting and adventure shops – among these, Rubber River (☎973 620 220, ◍www .rubber-river.com) is reputable, and maintains its own hotel. The **turisme** is on the main street (summer Mon–Fri 9am–2pm & 5–9pm, Sat 10am–1pm &

5–8pm; ☎973 621 002); **buses** stop at an obvious shelter at the north end of town where the two through-roads join up.

RIALP, 3km north, is a more appealing and manageable mix of old houses and new boutiques or chalets, and still supports a sawmill; the updated *Hotel Victor* (☎973 620 379, ⓦ www.hvictor.com; B&B ❹), with a decent **restaurant**, is also the bus stop and ticket office. Sixteen kilometres northeast, **PORT-AINÉ** (ⓦ www.port-aine.com) offers some of the best beginners' and intermediates' **skiing** in the Catalan Pyrenees on its thirty-odd longish runs, which got a redesign and lift upgrade in 2004. Snow conditions are generally good, even in spring. You can stay at the base of the lifts at *Hotel Port Ainé 2000* (☎973 627 627; ❻), with 180-degree views; the closest budget **accommodation** is at pretty hillside **Roní** 11km below, with *Pensió Restaurant Ravetllat* at the south entrance to the village (☎973 621 363; ❹).

Llavorsí

Probably the most attractive base along this stretch of the valley is **LLAVORSÍ**, 10km above Rialp at the meeting of the Noguera Pallaresa and Cardós rivers. Despite extensive renovation and a mammoth power substation across the way, this tight huddle of stone-built houses and slate roofs still retains character. There are two good riverside **campsites**, both with pools and bars: the *Aigües Braves*, 1km north of town (☎973 622 153; closed Oct–April), and the smaller and basic but tent-friendly *Riberies* just east of the centre (☎973 622 151; closed mid-Sept to mid-June). There's ample **accommodation** (reserve in advance in rafting season): try the *Hotel de Rei* on the riverfront (☎973 622 011; ❹), or the welcoming *Hostal Noguera* on the opposite bank (☎973 622 012, ✉ noguerahostal@wanadoo.es; ❸), with many balconied rooms overlooking the water. Their **restaurant** also has river-view seating and a decent three-course *menú* with wine for €16.

Established local **adventure operators** offering rafting, canyoning, hydrospeed, mountain biking and rock-climbing include Roc Roi at Plaça Nostra Senyora de Biuse (☎973 622 035, ⓦ www.rocroi.com); Yeti Emotions (☎902 322 201, ⓦ www.yetiemotions.com), some 500m south of Llavorsí, on the west bank of the river; and the central, most consistently open Rafting Llavorsí (☎973 622 158, ⓦ www.raftingllavorsi.com).

The Vall d'Àneu

From Llavorsí the road continues upstream along the Noguera Pallaresa, past the turning for Espot and the placid, artificial lake of Pantà de la Torrasa, to La Guingueta d'Àneu at the head of the reservoir. This is the first of three villages incorporating the name of the local valley, the **Vall d'Àneu**. By 2009, an ambitious series of viaducts and bridges should allow you to bypass the upper two villages and head directly for the Port de la Bonaigua.

ESTERRI D'ÀNEU, 4km farther beyond the lake – and from late September to June, the end of the line for the bus from Barcelona – was transformed overnight during the early 1990s from somnolent farming community to chic resort. The old quarter's few houses huddled between the road and the river, an arched bridge and slender-towered Sant Vicenç church still form a graceful ensemble, but the new apartment buildings and fancy hotels to the south are another matter. The expansion of the Baqueira-Beret ski domain to a point accessible all year from the Vall d'Àneu has set off another spasm of construction.

Still, there are worse spots to end up of an evening. The cheapest **place to stay and eat** is at friendly *Fonda Agustí* (☎973 626 034; B&B ❸), in a quiet location behind the church at Plaça de l'Església 6, with an old-fashioned, popular *menjador*; there's only a four-course *menú* on offer, plainly presented to the point of austerity, but for the price you can't really complain. Alternatively, try tidy, cheerful *Pensió La Creu* at c/Major 3 (☎973 626 437, ⓦwww .pensiolacreu.com; B&B ❸), some of its rooms with river view.

València d'Àneu to Port de la Bonaigua

Three kilometres farther up the main road, now the C28, **VALÈNCIA D'ÀNEU**'s core of traditional stone houses and small Romanesque church is well enveloped by modern chalet development spurred by the expansion of Baqueira-Beret onto this side of the Bonaigua pass. València was once far more important than its current sleepy profile suggests; an ongoing archeological dig on the outskirts has brought to light the remains of a tenth-century **castle**, apparently the power base of counts who ruled over many of the surrounding valleys.

The best choice for **accommodation** here – don't be put off by the odd Spanish coach tour – is good-value 🍴 *Hotel La Morera* (☎973 626 124, ⓦwww .hotel-lamorera.com; closed April & mid-Oct to Christmas; B&B ❺), with balconied rooms, a valley-side pool and wonderful breakfasts; dinner is also excellent as long as you dine *a la carta* and shun the relatively dull half-board *table d'hôte*. Honourable mention goes to the smaller *Hotel Lo Paller* on c/Major, in the village centre off the highway (☎973 626 129; ❸), its harsh exterior belying a pleasant rear garden and interior rustic decor. Another worthwhile spot to **eat** – certainly the chalet-construction crews favour it – a few doors down on the same street is *Felip*, with *menú* or an ample *carta*.

Beyond València, the ascending road, soon joining the new bypass, quits the Noguera Pallaresa and the quilt of green and brown fields around Esterri; the Riu de la Bonaigua takes over as the roadside stream, amidst forests of silver birch, pine and fir. The views get ever more impressive as you approach the tree line, above which sits the **restaurant-bar** *Les Ares* (daily except Tues), beside the Ermita de la Mare de Déu de les Ares, with a good-value lunch (1–4pm) *menú*. Three hairpin bends above the *ermita* is the car park for the start of a fine if somewhat strenuous full-day **hiking circuit** south from here via Estany Gerber through the Circ de Saborèdo, with its half-dozen lakes and staffed **refuge** (2310m; ☎973 253 015), then back to the pass; drive or arrange a ride to or from the starting point, as bus timings are unhelpful. Farther on, near the top of the bleak **Port de la Bonaigua** (2072m; usually kept open in winter for the ski trade), snow patches persist year-round, half-wild horses graze and you get simultaneous panoramas of the valleys you've just left and the Val d'Aran to come.

The Val d'Aran

The **Val d'Aran**, its legendary greenness derived from streams rather than especially high rainfall, is completely encircled by the main Pyrenean watershed and its various spur-ridges. Although it has belonged to Aragón or Catalunya – and later unified Spain – since 1192, the valley, with the Garona River cleaving down the middle, eventually opens to the north, and is actually much more accessible from France. Like Andorra, it was effectively independent for much of its history, and for centuries was sealed off from the rest of Spain by snow for seven months of the year; the Vielha tunnel (completed between 1948 and 1953 using slave labour furnished by Republican POWs) now provides a year-round link with the provincial capital of Lleida along the N230 highway.

Since the early 1980s, life in the valley has changed beyond recognition. Summertime scythe-wielding hay-reapers have been replaced by Massey Ferguson balers, overlooked by holiday chalets that have sprouted at the edge of each and every village. Although the development is relatively sympathetic – the new stone-clad buildings blend in with the Aranese originals – vast numbers of chi-chi restaurants and sports shops don't quite fit with the little medieval villages they surround. By leaving the perennially congested main valley road it's still possible to get some idea of the region as it was fifty years ago, but even there don't expect virgin rural expanses. Aran is best regarded as a comfortable, brief stop en route to more spectacular destinations, and overall the valley is one of the most expensive, overdeveloped and (unless you're skiing) overrated corners of alpine Catalunya. Among themselves the inhabitants speak Aranés, a **language** (not a dialect, as a glance at the bizarre road signs, and official tourist literature, will tell you) based on elements of medieval Gascon and Catalan, with a generous sprinkling of Basque vocabulary. *Aran*, in this language, means "valley": Nautaran (High Valley) is the most scenic eastern portion. The Aranese spelling of local place names, when different from Catalan, is given in parentheses.

Baqueira-Beret

The ride down from Port de la Bonaigua isn't for the acrophobic or those with dodgy brakes, with its hairpins and sharp drop into the Ruda valley on one side. The first place you meet coming down from the pass is **BAQUEIRA-BERET** (Ⓦ www.baqueira.es), a mammoth skiing development that has served as the biggest engine of change in the region. The resort core itself is modern, posey (the Spanish royal family and government ministers frequent it) and has little to offer other than multi-star hotels, but it's no trouble to stay nearby and show up for the skiing, some of the best in these mountains – at least until March, when the snow can get mushy and/or thin. Day lift-passes are the priciest in the Pyrenees, but you are being pampered with numerous chair-lifts; groomed, wide pistes; a first-class accident recovery service; and an interlinked domain of over seventy runs. The Bonaigua sector, added in 2003–04, is, with its mostly south- and east-facing slopes, less reliable.

Salardú and around

SALARDÚ, a few kilometres farther west, is in effect the capital of **Nautaran**, the highest of the three divisions of the Val d'Aran. It's also the most logical base: large enough to offer a reasonable choice of accommodation and food, but small enough to feel pleasantly isolated (except in Aug, or peak ski season). With steeply pitched roofs clustered around the church, it retains some traditional character, though the main attraction in staying is its **surrounding villages**, all centred on beautiful Romanesque churches. Salardú's is the roomy, thirteenth-century church of **Sant Andreu**, set in its own pleasant grounds. The doors are flanked by the most ornate portal in the valley, whose carved column capitals feature birds feeding their young and four eerie little human faces peeping out; inside, some fine sixteenth-century fresco patches, restored in 1994, include Christ Enthroned, the Assumption, various saints, and smudged panels of the Four Virtues personified.

Practicalities

There's an unreliable, summer-only wooden **turisme** hut, just off the main road at the central car park (theoretically June–Sept daily 10am–1.30pm & 4.30–8pm).

The one **bank** in the village has an ATM; there's also a **swimming pool** (mid-June to Aug daily 11am–7pm).

Except at the height of the summer, you should be able to find a **bed** (if not a room) easily enough. Trekker-friendly **refuges** include *Rosta*, Plaça Major 1, in a three-hundred-year-old building on the main square (☏973 645 308, Ⓦwww.refugirosta.com; closed May, June, Oct & Nov; half-board in non-en-suite doubles ❹), and *Juli Soler Santaló*, 200m east of the car park next to the pool (☏973 645 016, Ⓦwww.refugisalardu.com; closed April to mid-June & mid-Sept to early Dec; dorms or four-bunk en suites). For conventional **accommodation**, try *Pensió Casat* at c/Major 6 (☏973 645 056; ❸), the more upmarket *Hotel deth Pais* in Plaça dera Pica (☏973 645 836; closed May & Nov; B&B ❹), with underfloor heating and a few balconies; and, top of the heap for Salardú, *Hotel Colomers* near the bank (☏973 644 556; B&B ❺), with designer rooms and a few luxury suites.

Most Salardú lodgings serve good-value **meals**: non-guests can eat excellent *menús* at *Refugi Juli Soler Santaló* or *a la carta* (allow €26) at *Prat Aloy*, an affiliate of the *Hotel deth Pais* across the river. While the *Refugi Rosta's* restaurant is decent enough (€19 *menú*), its main appeal is the nicest **bar** in town: *Delicatesen*.

Surrounding villages

Nautaran houses are traditionally built of stone, with slate roofs, and there's surprisingly little to distinguish a four-hundred-year-old home from a four-year-old one. Many display dates on their lintels – not of the same vintage as the churches but respectable enough, with some going back as far as the sixteenth century.

UNYA (Unha), 700m up the hill into the Unyola valley, has a church as old as the one in Salardú, though you're more likely to be interested in several **restaurants** and *vinacotecas* (wine-bars) here, the most economical and consistently open being *Es de Don Joan*, serving game and Aranese cuisine, and *Casa Perez*.

BAGERGUE, 2km higher up the road (or reached via the GR211 path from Unya) remains the most countrified of the Nautaran settlements. The most famous of several **restaurants** is 🍴 *Casa Peru* (Mon, Tues, Thurs & Fri eves, Sat & Sun lunch; closed Wed, May–June & Oct–Nov weekdays; reserve on ☏973 645 437), which deserves the plaudits adorning its entrance thanks to offerings including an *olha aranesa* (hotpot) to die for, venison meatballs in wild mushroom sauce, wild-fruit flan with meringue plus good house wine, all for just €30. Bagergue also has excellent-value **accommodation** at 🍴 *Hotel Seixes* (☏973 645 406, Ⓦwww.seixes.com), which fills quickly; it's at the village entrance, with relatively easy parking. Choose between wood-trimmed rooms in the original *hostal* wing (B&B ❹), or the much newer hotel wing (B&B ❺).

Across the river from Salardú, and about twenty-minutes' walk upstream along the country lane signposted as the *Camin Reaiu* (King's Rd), **TREDÒS** was once the prettiest Nautaran village, but has had its old core – including a massive church with freestanding belfry – overwhelmed by a rash of new ski chalets. The central *Restaurante Saburedo* is a find, with a hearty four-course *menú* for €14 (*a la carta* at weekends €20–23). They also have en-suite and shared-bath **rooms** (☏973 645 089; ❸), as does *Casa Micalot* (☏973 645 326; ❸) on the same lane. Much the smartest **place to stay** here, though, is the *Hotel de Tredòs*, on the outskirts of the village (☏973 644 014, Ⓦwww.hoteldetredos.com; B&B ❺), with a small pool and chalet-style rooms.

Arties

ARTIES, 3km west of Salardú, features the usual complement of recent holiday homes, with more a-building. Nevertheless, it has considerable appeal, particularly in its old village core straddling the Garona, and its two **churches**: Santa María, with Templar fortifications, and deconsecrated Sant Joan on the main road, home to a sporadically open museum.

The best budget **accommodation** is quiet, good-value *Pensió Barrie*, alias *Casa Portolá* (☎973 640 828; ❸), at c/Mayor 21 – three floors of wood-and-tile en-suite rooms. For more comfort, try stylish *Hotel Besiberri*, by the stream at c/Deth Fòrt 4 (☎973 640 829, ⓦwww.hotelbesiberri.com; closed May–June & Oct 15–Nov 15; B&B ❹), with smallish but well-appointed rooms, bigger suites and lovely common areas.

Tried and tested **restaurant** options, more numerous than Salardú's, include *Tofanetti* (closed Thurs) up on the highway, purveying Italian/Spanish fusion fare (*menú* €14, *carta* €22); and adjacent, Zimbabwean-run *El Pollo Loco* (all year), which offers four *menús* under €25 (including a vegetarian one), most featuring the chicken of the name, washed down by organic cider. For something slightly more upmarket, try *Asador Iñaki* (closed Mon) across the road for Basque-style grills and a few regional dishes (*menús* €16–30).

Vielha

From Nautaran, you move west into **Mijaran** (Mid-Aran), whose major town is **VIELHA**, administrative centre for the whole valley and end of the line for the bus from Barcelona and La Pobla de Segur in summer (arrives 2.30pm, departs 11.40am). You may also reach Vielha from Lleida, via El Pont de Suert, a spectacular route in its final stages that culminates in the newly rebored **Túnel de Vielha**, nearly 6km long.

In truth, the ride to Vielha from either direction is more attractive than the intensely (over-) developed town itself, and there's little reason to stay, particularly if you have your own wheels or can make a bus connection onwards. If you have time to kill, pop into the parish church of **Sant Miquèu**, right in the centre on the east bank of the Riu Nere; its twelfth-century wooden bust, the *Crist de Mijaran* – probably part of a *Descent from the Cross* – is reckoned the finest specimen of Romanesque art in this part of the Pyrenees. The **Museu dera Val d'Aran** (Tues–Sat 10am–1pm & 5–8pm, Sun 11am–2pm; €1.50), at c/Major 26, west of the church and across the Nere, is also worth a look for its coverage of Aranese history and folklore.

Practicalities

Buses stop 100m downhill from the major roundabout at the west end of town. The **turisme** beside the **post office** at c/Sarriulera 6, on the church square (daily 9am–9pm; ☎973 640 110, ⓦwww.torismearan.org), offers maps and complete valley accommodation lists. There's an **internet** café, imaginatively named *Cyber Café*, at Plaza Coto Marzo, behind the church. **Accommodation** in Vielha is mostly aimed at a skiing clientele – coming from the church, you'll find the best of the inexpensive places by turning left along the main street and then right down the lane just across the bridge towards the main **car park**. At Plaça Sant Orenç 3, there's *Hotel El Ciervo* (☎973 640 165, ⓦwww.hotelelciervo.net; closed June & Nov; ❹), and comfortable *Hotel Turrull* at no. 7 (☎973 640 058; ❹).

Least expensive and most central of Vielha's **restaurants** is the *Basteret*, c/Major 6b, whose *carta* includes ham-stuffed trout and blueberry cheesecake (budget €24); they've a tapas bar, *Petit Basteret*, next door. For something a bit more upmarket, head for *Deth Gorman* (closed Tues & June) above the church, strong on game and freshwater fish (€24–30 for 3 courses), or make the two-kilometre detour east to Escunhau hamlet, where *Casa Turnay* in the centre (closed May, June, Oct & Nov weekdays) features Aranese-style game, fish and elaborate vegetable dishes for a similar amount.

Baixaran

Downvalley from Vielha lie **Arròs** (6km) and **Es Bòrdes** (Era Bordeta; 9km), two places that play a key role in Aranese domestic architecture. Es Bòrdes supplies the granite for the walls and Arròs the slates for the slightly concave roofs generally demanded in Nautaran and Mijaran. **ARRÒS** is effectively in the lower **Baixaran** (Low Aran) region, and the balconied houses here, around the octagonal belltower, have rendered white walls and red-tiled roofs. Among **restaurants**, *Boixetes de Cal Manel* at the outskirts is massively popular (€20–30 *carta*; closed Mon, part May & part Nov), while four-table, cult eatery *El Raconet* at c/de Crestalhèra 3 (☎973 641 730; closed Nov and low-season weekdays) has creative local cuisine for €30–35 a head.

Much of Baixaran is afflicted with rows of mega-stores selling cheap booze, fags, clothing and sportsgear to the French. **LES**, 20km from Vielha, with a small **spa** and less expensive **accommodation** and **meals**, proves more pleasant. Best old-town option, on the far side of the stream bridge, is ⚑ *Hostal Talabart* (☎973 648 011, ⓦwww.hoteltalabart.com; closed Nov; half-board only ❹) with a rear pool garden and the best rooms in the attic; French-tripper patronage hasn't dented the quality of the sustaining four-course *menú* (€17) at the friendly *menjador*. From Les it's 5km to the **French border** at Eth Pònt de Rei; 8km to Fos, the first village with bus service and accommodation; and 16km to the first significant French town, Saint-Béat.

Parc Nacional d'Aigüestortes i Estany de Sant Maurici

Deservedly the most popular target for trekkers in the Catalan Pyrenees is the **Parc Nacional d'Aigüestortes i Estany de Sant Maurici**, an extensive mountainous area constituting Catalunya's only national park (albeit not recognized as such by international bodies owing to intrusive hydroelectric works). Established in 1955, and considerably enlarged between 1986 and 1996 to over 140 square kilometres, it's a harshly beautiful rock-, pasture- and forest-strewn landscape containing spectacular snow-splashed peaks of up to 3000m, nearly four hundred lakes and dramatic glacial valleys. For the less adventurous, there are various mid-altitude rambles through bucolic scenery. The **Sant Nicolau valley** and its tributaries (in the west) have many glacial lakes and cirques, as well as the water-meadows of **Aigüestortes** (Twisted Waters) themselves. In the eastern sector, highlights include the **Circ de Saborèdo** and the **Peguera valley**, as well as the **Estany de Sant Maurici**, at the head of the Escrita valley. Just outside the park, in the "peripheral protective zone" of 270 square kilometres, are even more lake-spangled cirques.

The most common **trees** are fir and Scots pine, along with silver birch and beech, especially on north-facing slopes; numerous wildflowers appear in spring and early summer. As for **fauna**, wild boar, fox and hare roam here, and at the

- **Entry** to the park is free, but private cars are completely excluded. The only means of vehicle access is via 4WD taxis, which ply from designated ranks in both Espot and Boí. Driving yourself, the closest you can get are the car parks 4km west of Espot, at the east boundary, or the smaller car park at La Farga, north of Boí in the west, by the edge of the peripheral zone.

- **Accommodation in the park** is limited to five mountain refuges (staffed with wardens during summer – you'll need sleeping bags at all of them), but there are six more in nearly as impressive alpine areas in the peripheral zone. Each refuge has bunk beds, meal service and a telephone or emergency transmitter. FEEC-managed places (all those outside the park boundaries) allow you to self-cater inside; CEC-managed ones (inside the park) do not. Most refuges are booked solid during July and August, and on most weekends from late June to early September, so you'll need to reserve far in advance (best through ⓦwww.lacentralderefugis.com).

- **Camping** in the park is officially forbidden, and technically restricted within the peripheral zone – for which you're supposed to secure a permit from the nearest village – but as long as you pitch your tent well away from refuges and paths, and dismount it during daylight hours, nobody will bother you. There are managed campsites at Taüll in the west, and at Espot in the east.

- The region is covered by several Editorial Alpina **map-booklets** (ⓦwww.editorialalpina.com): the two you'll need for walking any of the routes described below are Sant Maurici for the east, and Vall de Boí for the west, both 1:25,000 and widely available. You can also buy the 1:40,000 Parc Nacional d'Aigüestortes I Estany de Sant Maurici, without the booklet. If you intend to approach from the north, you'll need the 1:40,000 Val d'Aran Alpina map. Sketch-maps provided by the park information offices are insufficient for route-finding – get a proper commercial map if you intend to leave the most popular paths.

- Be aware of, and prepared for, **bad weather**, which in the Pyrenees can arrive almost without warning. In midsummer, many rivers are passable that would otherwise not be, but temperature contrasts between day and night are still very marked. Local climatic patterns in recent years have alternated between daily rain showers throughout July and August, or prolonged drought, with a general trend towards hotter, drier summers. The best times to see the wonderful colour contrasts here are autumn and early summer. Many passes, even those mapped with a pedestrian trail over them, will be difficult or impossible without special equipment after a harsh winter owing to lingering snow. If you're going to do a less common traverse, tell the warden of the refuge you'll be leaving, who should be able to give current **route pointers** and, if there's any cause for concern, phone or radio ahead to your destination to give an estimated time of arrival – and perhaps make you a reservation.

- In **winter**, the park is excellent for cross-country and high-mountain **skiing**, though there are as yet no marked routes. The refuges usually open around Christmas and Easter, as well as on selected weekends and school holidays in between. Two ski **resorts** abut the fringes of the park – Boí-Taüll to the west and Espot Esquí to the east – with another under construction on the slopes of the Pic de Llena southwest of Capdella.

⑪

CATALUNYA | Parc Nacional d'Aigüestortes i Estany de Sant Maurici

very least you should see *isards* (chamois); otters are considerably more elusive. Endemic **birds** include the golden eagle, kestrel, ptarmigan and black woodpecker.

Which **approach** to the park you use rather depends upon which zone you intend to explore and how strenuous you want your walking to be. Access to the Sant Maurici sector is via the village of **Espot**, just beyond the eastern fringes of the park and within 7km of the main highway from La Pobla de Segur to València d'Àneu. The quickest access to the high and remote peaks is via **Capdella**, south of the park at the head of the Flamisell river – this is the next valley west from Noguera Pallaresa, served by sporadic bus from La Pobla de Segur. For the westerly Aigüestortes, the usual approach is from **Boí** via **El Pont de Suert**, which has regular bus service from La Pobla de Segur and Vielha. Finally, from the Val d'Aran, narrow roads, then tracks, and finally trails lead up from **Tredòs** to the *Restanca* and *Colomers* refuges respectively, on the north flank of the peripheral zone. It's somewhat boring hiking up this way, but at least you're not at the mercy of sparse bus schedules.

If you can afford only a day or two, and are strictly reliant on **public transport**, then Boí is probably the best target. It's easy to reach, just off the bus line to Caldes de Boí, and you can catch the public bus past the La Farga trailhead or a 4WD taxi up to Aigüestortes.

Map: Parc Nacional d'Aigüestortes i Estany de Sant Maurici

Arties — Tredòs & Salardú

AIGUAMÒTX VALLEY

0 — 3 km

Lac Redon
GR11
Lac de Rius
Port de Rius
Lac Tort de Rius
Lac de Mar
GR11
Ref. de la Restanca (2010m)
Montardo (2830m)
Ref. Colomèrs (2130m)
Port d'Oelhacrestada (2474m)
Estany Obaga
Estany de Besiberri
Estany Monges
GR11
Port de Caldes (2567m)
Port de Colomèrs
Circ de Colomrs
Estany Travessani
Besiberri Nord (3015m)
2760 m
Ref. Joan Ventosa i Calvell (2200m)
Besiberri Sud (3017m)
Estany Negre
Port de Colomrs (2604m)
Coll de Contraig (2748m)
Pico de Coma lo Forno (3033m)
Estany de Cavallers
Estany de Contraig
Estanys Gémena
Punta Alta (3015m)
Pic de Contraig (2957m)
COMA LES BIENES
Ref. d'Estany Llong (2000m)
Pala Alta de Sarradé (2982m)
Caldes de Boí
Estany Sarradé
Riu de Noguera de Tor
LA FARGA
P
P
Estany Llebreta
Aigüestortes
Collado de Dellui (2576m)
Erill la Vall
Boí
Taüll
GR11.20
Barruera
Durro
Collado de Morrano (2632m)
Cardet
Sant Quirç
GR11.20
Estanys del Pessó
Collado del Pessó (2680m)

El Pont de Suert — El Pont de Suert — Boí-Taüll Ski Station — Capdella & Port de Rus

Capdella

There are weekday evening **buses** from La Pobla de Segur to **CAPDELLA**, 30km upstream. The village, the highest of half a dozen in the little-visited Vall Fosca, is in two quite distinct parts. The upper part harbours the dorm-style *Refugi Tacita* (☎973 663 121, ⓦwww.tacitahostel.com; open daily July–Sept, otherwise by arrangement), run by a welcoming couple who offer excellent meals. The lower quarter, 2km below – where the bus stops – is based around the oldest hydroelectric power plant in these parts, dating back to 1914. Here, volubly friendly *Hotel Monseny*, 800m south and officially in Espui village (☎973 663 079; closed Dec–Easter; half-board only ④), has a pool and a well-regarded restaurant.

Into the park

From Capdella it's a half-day trek, past the Sallente dam, to the wonderful **Refugi Colomina**, an old wooden chalet set among superb high mountain

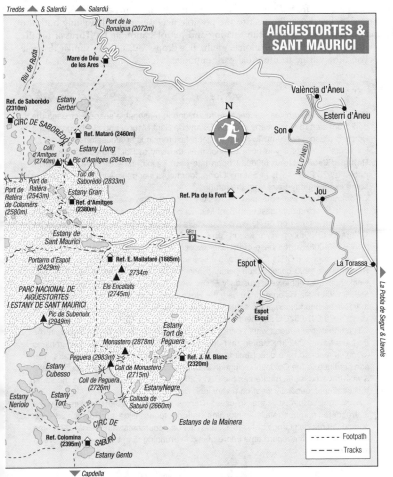

lakes on the southern perimeter of the park (2395m; part open year-round, but staffed only early Feb, mid-March to mid-April & mid-June to mid-Sept; ☏ 973 252 000). You can cut out much of the trek by taking the *teléferic* (cable car) from the back of the Sallente reservoir to within 45-minutes' walk of the refuge (July–Sept daily upward departures 9am & 3pm, down-ward 1pm & 6pm).

The refuge's immediate surroundings have several short outings suitable for any remaining daylight. The more adventurous will set out the following day to **Estany Llong** and its refuge, via Estany Tort and the Collada de Dellui (2576m). Alternatively, there's the classic (if difficult) traverse due north into the national park via the Coll de Peguera (2726m), taking six hours. You end up near the base of the Sant Maurici dam at **Refugi Ernest Mallafré** (1885m; open mid-June to late Sept; ☏ 973 250 118), poised for further walks. If it's full, the comfortable **Refugi d'Amitges** is just ninety minutes away (2380m; open late Feb, Easter & mid-June to late Sept; ☏ 973 250 109).

Espot and Espot Esquí

The approach from Espot is less strenuous, though purists (and people with heavy backpacks) will object to the possible necessity of road-walking both the very steep 7km up from the turning and petrol station at **La Torassa** on the main road where the Barcelona–Vielha bus drops you, and the similar distance beyond the village to the usual park entrance.

Classic traverses

One of *the* classic hikes – accessible to anyone in reasonable shape – crosses the park from east to west, starting at the Estany de Sant Maurici and climbing over the Portarró d'Espot (2429m). To reach the jeep-taxi terminus at Aigüestortes, it's about six hours' walking; if you have to hoof it all the way to Boí, allow ten hours. The **Refugi d'Estany Llong** (2000m; open late Feb, Easter, June to mid-Oct; satellite phone ☏ 973 299 545) is at **Estany Llong**, four hours along this wide track; there are some excellent day-treks from the refuge.

Committed and well-equipped trekkers will find better traverses from the east side of the park. Heading northeast from Sant Maurici on the GR11 path, you can, within five to six hours via the Port de Ratèra de Colomèrs (2580m), reach 2006-rebuilt **Refugi de Colomèrs** (2130m; open weekends Feb & March, daily Easter & mid-June to late Sept; ☏ 973 253 008), at the base of its lake-swollen cirque. From Colomèrs, most hikers continue along the GR11 for an easy but scenic day, partly in the park, to **Refugi de la Restanca**, a 1990 construction perched near its namesake reservoir (2010m; open weekends most of the year, plus daily Easter week & mid-June to late Sept; ☏ 608 036 559, ⓦ www.restanca.com); from here the **Hospitau Refugi Sant Nicolau** right by the main Vielha-bound road at the southern mouth of the tunnel (1630m; open most of the year; ☏ 973 697 052), is another four hours away along the GR11.

The fifth of the refuges within park boundaries, **Refugi Josep Mariá Blanc**, in the Peguera valley (2320m; staffed mid-June to Sept; ☏ 973 250 108, ⓦ www.jmblanc .com), is reached by a direct trail from Espot in around three and a half hours. You can continue to the Colomina refuge in another three and a half to four hours: this is a well-travelled route, marked as the GR11.20 variant trail. From Colomina the same trail continues generally west on a very long day to Taüll.

A recognized circuit – the so-called **Carros de Foc** (Chariots of Fire; ⓦ www .carrosdefoc.com for details) – links nine staffed refuges inside, and just outside, the park; each refuge stamps trekkers' Carros de Foc documents with the date and time of your arrival – the record time (more manic fell-running than trekking) is just over a single day.

ESPOT (1320m), long showing signs of its decades as a tourist centre, is now in the grip of a chalet-building boom occasioned by **Espot Esquí** (ⓦwww .espotesqui.com), 2km above, sharing a lift pass with co-managed Port-Ainé. Despite a northeast orientation, it hasn't got a snow record to match most neighbouring resorts; many runs may be closed by mid-March, and the whole place can shut for the day at 3pm.

The **Casa del Parc** information office at the edge of Espot (June–Sept daily 9am–1pm & 3.30–6.45pm; Oct–May Mon–Sat 9am–2pm & 3.30–5.45pm, Sun 9am–2pm; ☎973 624 036) has **maps** of the park, weather reports, and snow-shoe rental in winter. Nearby is the **jeep-taxi** terminal (€4.85 to Sant Maurici; ☎973 624 105). The best-value **accommodation** in Espot village is *Casa Felip* (☎973 624 093; B&B ❷), simple but spotless with most rooms en suite, plus laundry service and a small front garden. Other possibilities include the plain-roomed, balcony-less *Pensió La Palmira* (☎973 624 072; B&B ❸, half-board only in summer ❹), in the village centre, and the comfortable, well-managed 🏨 *Hotel Roya*, next to *Casa Felip* (☎973 624 040, ⓦwww.hotelroya.net; open most of year; B&B ❹), with a lift, limited private parking, a fancy *menjador* and some of the large rooms with renewed baths. Among nearby **campsites**, *De La Mola*, 2.5km downhill (☎973 624 024; open Easter & July–Sept), has a pool, while at the far (upstream) edge of Espot, beyond the old bridge, tiny but grassy *Solau* (☎973 624 068), in the eponymous *barrio,* also rents out rooms (❷) – useful if the village centre is full.

Quality **eating** opportunies include vine-shrouded *Ju Quim* (closed Mon & 3 weeks after Easter) in the centre, packed at lunchtime thanks to its good-value *menú*; and the *menjador* of the *Pensió La Palmira* (three-course *menú* €12.50).

Into the park

From Espot, another road leads 3.5km to the park boundary, and from there a farther 3.5km to the end of the tarmac at the **Estany de Sant Maurici**. The GR11 trail avoids most of the road, or alternatively take a 4WD taxi – €5.50 per passenger each way is money well spent to miss out some fairly dull road-trudging. Once you're at the lake, the classic postcard view is south, dominated by the 2700-metre-plus spires of **Els Encatats** ("The Enchanted Ones"), in legend two men and their dog, who snuck off to go hunting instead of to church on the day of the patron saint's festival, were lured heavenward by a spectral stag, and then forthwith turned to stone by a divine lightning bolt.

El Pont de Suert and the route to Boí

The westerly approach to Aigüestortes begins just past **EL PONT DE SUERT**, a small town 41km northwest of La Pobla de Segur; all buses stop at a terminal by the southeast edge of town. The centre is dominated by an unmissably hideous modern church, erected in 1955 in perverse homage to the Romanesque churches farther up the valley. The backwards-orientated interior, with the altar on the west, "works" better, with sunlight filtering in through strips of glass brick. Otherwise, El Pont de Suert is tolerable enough if you have to overnight before catching the bus north to Boí the next day (June–Sept daily 11.15am), though you shouldn't need to, as the morning buses from Vielha, Lleida and La Pobla all dovetail with the Boí service. If you miss the bus or it's out of season, a marked riverside trail – **El Camí de l'Aigua** – takes you up the Vall de Boí in under a day. The only **accommodation** in the old town is *Hotel Can Mestre* at Plaça Major 8 (☎973 690 306; ❸), or *Hostal Cotori* on adjacent Plaça del Mercadel (☎973 690 096; ❷), with a pleasant river-view **restaurant**. Both *plaças* have arcaded porticos sheltering **café** tables.

Up the Vall de Boí

Some 2km northwest of El Pont de Suert, a good side road – the L-500 – forges north along the **Vall de Boí**, following the Noguera de Tor towards Caldes de Boí, passing the turn-offs for several villages on the way. It's an area crammed with **Romanesque churches**, the finest such in Catalunya. The catch is that most of their frescoes are reproductions, the originals having long since been whisked away to the MNAC in Barcelona. The most-visited churches all have the same admission price (€1.20) and opening hours (summer daily 10am–2pm & 4–8pm; winter Mon–Sat 10.30am–2pm & 4–7pm, Sun 10.30am–2pm).

BARRUERA, 13km along and the valley "capital", has several places to **stay**, least expensive, most characterful and best for groups being *Casa Coll*, an echoing old mansion near the top of c/Major in the old town (☎973 694 005, Ⓦwww.casacoll.info; ❷), with a mix of en-suite rooms and not, and common areas crammed with antiques. For more comfort, repair to the resolutely modern *Hotel Farré d'Avall*, also in the old quarter (☎973 694 029, Ⓔhotel @farredavall.com; ❸). Barruera supports the valley's main, well-stocked **turisme**, right opposite the petrol station (summer daily 9am–2pm & 5–7pm, winter same hours except Sun 10am–2pm; ☎973 694 000, Ⓦwww.vallboi .com). Just across the way from the cramped campsite stands Barruera's Romanesque **church**, the riverside **Sant Feliu**, with its engaging thirteenth-century portal and creaky-floored interior.

Farther on, just before the turn-off for Boí, a one-kilometre side road leads west to **ERILL LA VALL**, whose twelfth-century church of **Santa Eulàlia** sports an unusual arcaded porch, and a six-storey belfry rivalling Sant Climent's in Taüll (see p.808); the interior is now done up as a gallery of sacred art, with a replica of a carved-wood twelfth-century *Deposition* given pride of place. In high season, Erill is a relatively quiet base, more likely to have a vacancy than either Boí or Taüll, and thus far blessedly free of chalets at the outskirts. Top **accommodation** choices are adjacent in the centre: the well-appointed 🍴 *Hostal La Plaça*, opposite the belfry (☎973 696 026, Ⓦwww.hostal-laplaza .com; ❹), with a few galleried family suites and posh, very accomplished *a la carta* **restaurant** (allow €30); and the simpler *Hostal L'Aüt* (☎973 696 048, Ⓔlauteril@wanadoo.es; ❸), with a popular *menjador* serving a tasty if not especially copious *menú* with good house wine for €17 (*carta* €22 and up). At the village entrance opposite the car park, *La Granja d'Erill* is your other eating choice, with good-value *a la carta* (from €20).

Boí

BOÍ stands 1km above the main road, which continues up to Caldes de Boí. On arrival, the village proves something of an anticlimax: a minuscule medieval core swamped by a mess of car parks, modern buildings (with more under construction) and old houses defaced with new brick repairs. Twelfth-century **Sant Joan** church has been extensively renovated, the only original parts being the squat belfry and part of the apse; reproduction frescoes on the spandrels of the north aisle feature vivid animals symbolic of Christian virtues, such as the camel of submission and humility.

One compensation for being based in Boí is that you're well poised to visit other local villages and their churches **on foot**. The non-GR path to Erill la Vall from Boí, across the valley, takes half an hour; the hiking route to Durro is the well-signposted GR11.20 path, which you can pick up behind Boí village – it starts just over the little bridge and takes around an hour to follow. In the other direction, the GR11.20 up to Taüll takes about forty minutes, greatly shortcutting the steep three-kilometre road.

Practicalities

Although Boí is the least prepossessing of local villages, you may need to **stay** at the beginning of (or conclusion to) a visit to the park. Despite being out of the way, one good choice is *Hostal Pascual*, down by the junction and bridge, equidistant from Erill (☎973 696 014, ⓦwww.hostalpascual.com; B&B ❸; open Easter week, June–Sept, Christmas & New Year), with helpful owners, wood-trimmed, tile-floor rooms and a pleasant terrace atop one of the two *menjadors*. In the village itself, central *Hotel Pey* (☎973 696 036, ⓦwww.hotelpey.com; B&B ❸) is more comfortable, with a lift and both a *hostal* and hotel wing. There are also some clean, partly en-suite **rooms** in *Casa Tenda* (☎973 696 034; ❶), just through the stone archway in the old quarter – follow the "*habitacions*" sign.

Eating out, you'll not do better than at the *Casa Higinio*, 200m up the road to Taüll, above the village centre, featuring excellent meat grills, fine *escudella* (minestrone soup) and trout – the lunch *menú* with house wine runs to about €14, though dinner is *a la carta* only (around €24).

The **Casa del Parc information office** is tucked under an archway in the old quarter (June–Sept daily 9am–1pm & 3.30–6.45pm; Oct–May Mon–Sat 9am–2pm & 3.30–5.45pm, Sun 9am–2pm; ☎973 696 189); maps are sold at a slight mark-up. The **4WD taxis** have a rank, and ticket office, on central Plaça del Treio (book space on ☎973 696 314 or 629 205 489; €4.85 each way). There are bank **ATMs** on the main through-road – the only ones beyond Barruera.

Into the park – and Caldes de Boí

It's 3.5km from Boí to the **national park entrance**, and another 3.5km to the scenic waterfalls of **Aigüestortes**, tumbling from their eponymous water meadows into Estany Llebreta. A final kilometre above the falls – passed closely by both road and trail (see below) – there's another **park information booth** (July–Sept daily 9.30am–2pm & 4–7pm), next to which is a map-placard with various suggested **day-hikes**; the most popular leads east to Estany Llong (1hr).

From Boí's square, **4WD taxis** make the trip as far as the information booth, waiting to depart until they're full (July 1–Sept 15 8am–7pm, spring/autumn 9am–6pm). The closest you can get to the park boundary in your **own vehicle** is the La Farga car park, or another, much smaller one 1.5km east, and right at the boundary. If you leave your car at either, and arrange for a 4WD taxi to meet you and take you farther uphill, at day's end you can follow the trail from the infomation booth (signposted "*Aparcament*"), which shortcuts the road by a good 45 minutes.

Alternatively, you can flag down the one midday bus from the junction of the Boí side road up to **Caldes de Boí**, 5km upstream, where the bus line ends. Considered the best **spa** (ⓦwww.caldesdeboi.com) in the Spanish Pyrenees, this offers a menu of every conceivable treatment (May 30–Oct 12) and **accommodation** in two hotels, the marginally more affordable being the rustic *Caldes* (☎973 696 230; B&B ❺).

Nearby, the conspicuously high dam at the south end of Estany de Cavallers marks the trailhead for walks towards the beautiful natural lakes northwest of the park, just below Besiberri and Montarto peaks; the closest refuge is **Joan Ventosa i Calvell**, at Estany Negre (2220m; open mid-June to late Sept & some winter weekends; ☎973 297 090, ⓦwww.refugiventosa.com), just over an hour away and itself within easy reach of the *Colomers* or *Restanca* huts.

Taüll and Boí-Taüll

TAÜLL has been altered considerably by the ski resort of Boí-Taüll on the mountainside a few kilometres to the southeast. There's an enormous holiday complex 1.5km beyond the village at Pla de l'Ermita, en route to the ski station, and all summer Taüll is targeted by tour coaches and family cars seeking out panoramic picnic spots. But away from the peripheral ski chalets, the village centre preserves considerable character, and is certainly preferable to Boí as a base.

Moreover, two of the best local Romanesque churches stand in the village. **Sant Climent de Taüll** is the more immediately impressive by virtue of its famous six-storey belfry and triple apse with intricate brickwork. Inside, some original fresco fragments survive along with a respectable collection of religious art. The admission ticket entitles you to climb the rickety wooden steps to the top of the belltower for sweeping views through the delicately arched windows. At the heart of Taüll, **Santa María** (daily 10am–8pm; free) is very similar in design, though after a millennium of subsidence, there's not one right angle remaining in the building, with the four-storey belfry in particular at an engaging list.

Some 11km southeast of Taüll, the ski centre at **Boí-Taüll** (Ⓦwww .boitaullresort.es) is the newest in the Catalan Pyrenees and the only rival to Baqueira-Beret or Massella for really serious skiing, with 49 pistes, well over half of them red-rated; accordingly, it's not the best resort for beginners or weak intermediates.

Practicalities

Budget **accommodation** options include *Casa Plano Minguero,* well located in the upper part of the village (Ⓣ973 696 117; ❶), with simple balconied doubles and its own parking (a problem in the village). *Ca de Corral*, run by the sister of the *Bar Mallador* management (see below), offers well-refurbished rooms, with especially good bathrooms, in an old house well sited in the lower part of the village (Ⓣ973 696 176, Ⓦwww.cadecorral.com; ❷); there's a lounge with woodstove, and breakfast can be arranged at co-managed *Bar La Plaça* by Santa María church. For something smarter, try ⚔ *Pensió Santa María* (Ⓣ973 696 170, Ⓦwww.taull.com/santamaria; closed Nov & part May; B&B ❸), a lovingly restored old house featuring self-catering garden studios, tastefully rustic upstairs rooms and a courtyard restaurant with Ana's excellent cooking, or welcoming ⚔ *El Xalet de Taüll* (Ⓣ973 696 095, Ⓦwww .elxaletdetaull.com; B&B ❺), whose big strength is the attic breakfast room and library (wi-fi) with fireplace and panoramic plate-glass windows – the easiest way of recognizing the building from below. A **campsite** (Ⓣ973 696 174), also offering wooden bungalows, spreads attractively on the grassy slope below Sant Climent church.

The **restaurant** of *Pensió Sant Climent* is justly popular for filling, no-nonsense meals (*menús* with drink at €10 & €15) – reserve in season on Ⓣ973 696 052. *El Caliu*, at the top of Taüll, is well regarded for more careful, consistently good cooking (€15 weekday *menú*; €30 *a la carta*). At the start of the road up to the ski resort, on the ground floor of an apartment, *El Fai* matches *El Caliu* for quality in snail, mushroom and rabbit dishes (€15 *menú*, €25 *carta*). Last but not least, just beside Sant Climent church, ⚔ *Bar Mallador* (closed May to early June & mid-Oct to Nov) is run by nice folk with good taste in music, and serves as the most popular village **bar** (garden seating in summer), also offering bistro-style snacks (including grills) and **internet** access.

The South

The great triangle of land **south** of Barcelona is not the first place most people think of going to when they visit Catalunya. It's made up of the province of Tarragona and part of the province of Lleida (the rest of which takes in the western Pyrenees) and, with the exception of the obvious attractions of the coast and a trinity of medieval monasteries, almost all the interest lies in the provincial capitals themselves.

Just forty minutes south of Barcelona, vibrant **Sitges** is one of the few exceptions, boasting some fine *modernista* architecture and bolstered by its reputation as a major gay summer destination. Beyond this is the **Costa Daurada** – the coastline that stretches from just north of Tarragona to the Delta de l'Ebre – which suffered less exploitation than the Costa Brava, and it's easy enough to see why it was so neglected. All too often the shoreline is drab, with beaches that are narrow and characterless, backed by sparse villages overwhelmed by pockets of villas. There are exceptions, though, and if all you want to do is relax by a beach for a while, there are several down-to-earth and perfectly functional possibilities, including **Cambrils**.

The Costa Daurada really begins to pay dividends, however, if you can forget about the beaches temporarily and plan to spend a couple of days in **Tarragona**, the provincial capital. It's a city with a solid Roman past – reflected in an array of impressive ruins and monuments – and it makes a handy springboard for trips inland into Lleida Province. South of Tarragona, Catalunya peters out in the lagoons and marshes of the **Delta de l'Ebre**, a riverine wetland that's rich in bird life – perfect for slow boat trips, fishing and sampling the local seafood.

Inland attractions are fewer, and many travelling this way are inclined to head on out of Catalunya altogether, not stopping until they reach Zaragoza. It's true that much of the region is flat, rural and dull, but nonetheless it would be a mistake to miss the outstanding monastery at **Poblet**, only an hour or so inland

Cava country

Catalunya is the home of **cava**, Spain's eminently drinkable, and very affordable, sparkling wine (EU regulations mean it's illegal to call it "champagne"). Cava is usually defined by its sugar content: *seco* (literally "dry") has around half the sugar of a *semi-seco* ("very sweet"). In addition to selling cheap bottles of bubbly, the region's famous *bodegas* often offer informative tours and tastings, and are located in stunning properties, attractions in themselves. Most can be found in the Penedés region near the town of **Sant Sadurní d'Anoia**, 36km northeast of Sitges, and a little farther from Barcelona, but easily accessible via the AP7/E15 highway that zips right past it. You'll see one of the most celebrated producers from the road: *Freixenet* (Mon–Thurs 10am–1pm & 3–4.30pm, Fri–Sun 10am–1pm; ☎938 917 096, ⊛www .freixenet.com) offers tours, but you need to call in advance. There's also a shop (Mon–Thurs 10am–2.30pm & 4–7pm, Fri–Sun 10am–2.30pm). *Bodegas Codorníu* (☎938 913 342, ⊛www.codorniu.com) is about 2km from the highway, just outside town, with incredibly beautiful premises designed by *modernista* Josep Maria Puig I Cadafalch; it's also credited with bringing champagne production to Spain in 1872. Tours run Mon–Fri 9am–5pm, and weekends 9am–1pm; reservations are essential – you can call or book online. There are regular trains to Sant Sadurní from Estació-Sants Barcelona (40min).

from Tarragona, and the wonderful cava **bodegas** around Sant Sadurní d'Anoia. A couple of other nearby towns and monasteries – notably medieval **Montblanc** and **Santa Creus** – add a bit more interest to the region, while by the time you've rattled across the huge plain that encircles the provincial capital of **Lleida** you've earned a night's rest. Pretty much off the tourist trail, Lleida makes a pleasant overnight stop, from here, it's only two and a half hours to Zaragoza, or you're at the start of dramatic road and train routes into the western foothills of the Catalan Pyrenees.

Sitges

SITGES, 40km from Barcelona, is definitely the highlight of the coast south of the city. Established in the 1960s as a holiday town, whose liberal attitudes openly challenged the rigidity of Franco's Spain, it has now become the great weekend escape for young Barcelonans, who have created a resort very much in their own image. It's also a noted **gay** holiday destination, with a nightlife to match: indeed, if you don't like vigorous action of all kinds, you'd be wise to avoid Sitges in the summer – staid it isn't. As well as a certain style, the Barcelona trippers have brought with them the high prices from the Catalan capital – the bars, particularly, can empty the deepest wallets – while finding a place to stay in peak season can be a problem unless you arrive early in the day or book well

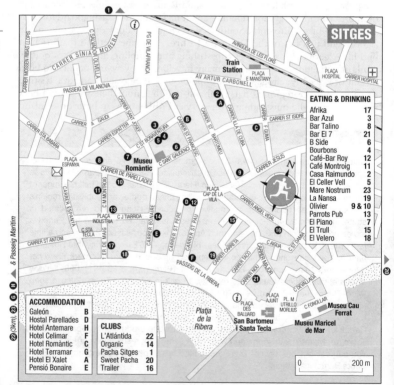

in advance. None of this deters the varied and generally well-heeled visitors, however – nor should it, since Sitges as a sort of Barcelona-on-Sea is definitely worth experiencing for at least one night.

The town itself is reasonably attractive: a former fishing village whose pleasing houses and narrow streets have attracted artists and opted-out intellectuals for a century or so. The beaches, though crowded, are far from oppressive, and the town has a smattering of cultural interest.

Arrival and information

Trains to Sitges leave Barcelona's Estació-Sants every ten to twenty minutes throughout the day; the station is about ten-minutes' walk from the town centre and seafront. **Buses** stop in front of the train station, except those to and from Barcelona, which stop outside the main *turisme*. If you're driving, it's probably best to pay for a **car park** rather than leave your vehicle on the street: car parks are marked on the map.

On arrival, the main **turisme** (mid-June to mid-Sept Mon–Sat 9am–8pm; rest of year Mon–Fri 9am–2pm & 4–6.30pm; ☎938 945 004, ⓦwww.sitgestur .com), at c/Sínia Morera 1, is worth a visit for the useful map with local listings on the back, and all sorts of English-language information about the town. There's a smaller office in the old town on Passeig de la Ribera (mid-June to mid-Sept daily 10am–2pm & 4–8pm; rest of year Sun–Thurs 10am–2pm, Fri–Sat 10am–2pm & 4–7pm).

Accommodation

There are dozens of **hotels** of all types and prices in Sitges, but it's a good idea to reserve in high season as they fill up quickly. If you arrive without a reservation, a short walk through the central streets and along the front (particularly Passeig de la Ribera) reveals most of the possibilities – the places near the station are not exactly glamorous, but are more likely to have space. Come out of season (after Oct and before May) and the high prices tend to soften a little, though in midwinter you may have real difficulty finding anywhere open, especially at the budget end of the scale. The nearest local **campsite** is *El Rocà* (☎938 940 150; closed Nov to late March), well signposted north of the *turisme* under the railway bridge.

Hotel Antemare c/Mare de Déu del Montserrat 50 ☎938 947 000, ⓦwww.antemare.com. One street back from the sea, but a long walk from the central part of town, this classy hotel has very stylish rooms at reasonable rates. Also offers thalasso-therapy (seawater spa). ❼

Pensió Bonaire c/Bonaire 31 ☎938 945 326. Just back from the sea, this tiny *pensió* is one of

the least expensive around. Closed Oct–March. ❸

Hotel Celimar Pg. de la Ribera 20 ☎938 110 170, ⓦwww.hotelcelimar.com. Pleasant seafront hotel, worth trying for a balconied room with a view. Prices fall a category outside high season. ❼

Galeón c/Sant Francesc 46–48 ☎938 940 612, ⓦwww.hotelsitges.com. Decent mid-range option, with simple, clean rooms equipped with satellite TV and a/c – there's a small garden and pool at the back. ⑤

Hostal Parellades c/de les Parellades 11 ☎938 940 891, ✉ hostalparellades@hotmail .com. The large, airy rooms and decent location make this a good first choice. Closed Oct–March. ③

Hotel Romàntic c/Sant Isidre 33 ☎938 948 375, ⓦ www.hotelromantic.com. Attractive, converted nineteenth-century villa in the quiet streets away from the front, not far from the train station, with lots of ornate, *modernista* touches and rooms with heaps of character; some have a terrace

overlooking the palm-shaded gardens. It's a favourite with gay visitors. Closed end Oct to Easter. ⑤

Hotel Terramar Pg. Marítim 80 ☎938 940 050, ⓦ www.hotelterramar.com. Superb position at the end of the long promenade, and splendid views from its large, balconied rooms. Extras include satellite TV and internet access, though it's a long trudge back from the best bars. ⑥

Hotel El Xalet c/Illa de Cuba 35 ☎938 110 070, ⓦ www.elxalet.com. Charming, discreet hotel in a beautiful *modernista* house near the train station. There are only ten rooms – booking ahead is essential in summer. B&B ⑤

The Town

It's the **beach** that brings most people to Sitges, and it's not hard to find, with two strands right in town, to the west of the church. From here, a succession of *platjas* of varying quality and crowdedness stretches west as far as the *Hotel Terramar*, a couple of kilometres down the coast. A long seafront promenade, the **Passeig Marítim**, runs all the way there, and all along there are beach bars, restaurants, showers and watersports facilities. Beyond the hotel, following the train line, you eventually reach the more notorious nudist beaches, a couple of which are exclusively gay.

Back in town, it's worth climbing up the knoll overlooking the beaches, topped by the Baroque parish church – known as *La Punta* – and a street of old whitewashed mansions, known locally as the Corner of Calm. One contains the **Museu Cau Ferrat**; home and workshop to the artist and writer Santiago Rusiñol (1861–1931), its two floors contain a massive jumble of his own paintings, as well as sculpture, painted tiles, ceramic, glasswork, drawings and various collected odds and ends, such as the decorative ironwork (over 800 pieces) Rusiñol brought back in bulk from throughout Catalunya. Two of his better buys were the minor El Grecos at the top of the stairs on either side of a crucifix. The museum also contains works by the artist's friends (including Picasso) who used to meet in the *Els Quatre Gats* bar in Barcelona.

Two other museums are worth giving a whirl on a rainy day. The **Museu Maricel de Mar**, next door to the Museu Cau Ferrat, has more minor artworks, medieval to modern, and maintains an impressive collection of Catalan ceramics and sculpture. More entertaining is the **Museu Romàntic** (guided tour every hour), located right in the centre of town, at c/Sant Gaudenci 1, off c/Bonaire. The museum aims to show the lifestyle of a rich Sitges family in the eighteenth and nineteenth centuries by displaying some of their furniture and possessions. It's full of nineteenth-century knick-knacks, including a set of working music boxes and a collection of antique dolls.

A date worth noting in your diary is the **International Film Festival** (ⓦ www.cinemasitges.com), held in a number of venues around the town,

All **museums** in Sitges have the same opening hours and prices: Tues–Sat 9.30am–2pm & 4–7pm, mid-June to mid-Oct 3.30–6.30pm, Sun 10am–3pm; €3.50 each (free first Wed of month) or €6.40 for a **combined ticket** for all the museums, valid for a month; you can purchase tickets at the museums.

which runs for about ten days in October or November (exact dates change, information and venues from the *turisme*) every year. Originally a horror and fantasy film extravaganza, it has grown to embrace a wide range of genres and attracts some big-name actors and directors.

Eating and drinking

International tourism has left its mark on Sitges: multilingual and "international" menus, a euphemism for burgers, are everywhere. Fortunately, there are also some good **restaurants**, with a fairly wide range of cuisines and quality, and some reasonable *menús*. Good areas to explore are the side streets around the church, or the beachfront for more expensive seafood restaurants. You can get picnic supplies at the town's **market**, the Mercat Nou, very close to the train station, on Avinguda Artur Carbonell. For **ice cream**, check out *Olivier*, a chain with branches at c/Parellades 43 and c/Jesus 11.

Late-opening **bars** centre on pedestrianized c/1er (Primer) de Maig (popularly known as *Calle del Pecado*, or Street of Sin) and its continuation, c/Marqués de Montroig, while c/de les Parellades and c/Bonaire complete the block. In summer, this is basically one long run of disco-bars, pumping music out into the late evening, interspersed with the odd restaurant or fancier cocktail bar, all with outdoor tables vying for your custom. If you're looking for more **genteel nightspots**, try those on the seafront.

Restaurants

Casa Raimundo c/Illa de Cuba 39. A classy restaurant, with paintings on the yellow walls and a good range of fish and seafood dishes. Tues–Fri 9am–midnight, Sat noon–midnight, Sun noon–5pm.

El Celler Vell c/Sant Bonaventura 21. Excellent Catalan food served in rural-chic surroundings. Around €25 a head. Mon, Tues & Thurs 8.30–11.30pm, Fri–Sun 1–3.30pm & 8.30–11.30pm.

Mare Nostrum Pg. de Ribeira 60. Long-established fish restaurant situated on the seafront, with a menu that changes according to the catch and season. Around €25 a head, unless you stick to the *platos del día*.

La Nansa c/Carreta 24. A small *nansa* (fishing net) hangs outside this amiable, family-run restaurant, which has wood-panelled walls, brass lanterns, and coastal paintings. The top-notch seafood- and fish-focused menu (mains €14–23) includes the regional favourite, *arroz a la Sitgetana*, rice with meat, prawns, clams, and a generous splash of Sitges Malvasia wine. Closed Wed lunch, Tues & Jan.

El Trull c/Mossèn Félix Clarà 3, off c/Major. Fairly pricey French-style restaurant in the old town, with exceptional foie gras (€15) and sumptuous "Trull style" fish casserole (€20). There's a handy English menu. 7.30pm–midnight, closed Wed.

El Velero Pg. de la Ribera 38 ☏ 938 942 051. One of the town's most celebrated restaurants, right on the promenade with a glass terrace at the front and a plush interior. Huge menu offers plenty of seafood and classics such as paella, with a grand tasting

menú for €48. Closed Sun eve (except July to mid-Sept), Mon all day & Tues lunch.

Cafés, bars and clubs

L'Atlántida Platja de les Coves, Sector Terramar, 3km out of town ⊛ www.latlantidasitges.com. The town's favourite club, with a huge open-air dance-floor big enough for 1500. The cliff-top *discoteca* can be reached on regular buses, which run there and back all night from the bottom of c/1er de Maig.

Bar Talino c/de les Parellades 72. A friendly tapas bar, where you can fill up on traditional favourites, including hot, ham-flecked croquettes.

Cafes Afrika c/1er de Maig 7. One of the best of the music bars despite an unprepossessing entrance, popular with a house crowd.

Café-Bar Roy c/de les Parellades 9. An old-fashioned café with dressed-up waiters and marble tables. Watch the world go by from its prime street-side perch, over a glass of *cava* or a fancy snack. Open daily noon till late.

Montroig Café c/Marqués de Montroig 11. Large, two-level, buzzy café with a shady courtyard out back, where you can sip *cerveza* or *café con leche* while soaking up sun and the social scene.

Pacha Sitges c/San Dídac s/n, Urb Valpineda ⊛ www.pachasitges.com. Mother of all *Pachas*, opening in 1967 and spawning a global dynasty of mega clubs; fans won't be disappointed – two massive dancefloors, a huge sound system and big-name residents and visiting DJs.

Parrots Pub Plaça de la Indústria. Stylish bar at the top of c/1er de Maig that's a required stop at some point in the day; it's just one place you can pick up the free gay map of Sitges. Cocktails from €4.50. You can also check out *Parrot's Restaurant* at c/Joan Tarrida 18.

Sweet Pacha Port Esportiu d'Aiguadolç ⓦwww .pachasitges.com. One of the latest outposts in the Pacha empire is *Sweet Pacha*, which opened for the 40th anniversary in 2007, and aims for a more chic-lounge experience, with plenty of white leather and a back-lit bar.

Tarragona

Sited on a rocky hill, sheer above the sea, **TARRAGONA** is an ancient place. Settled originally by Iberians and then Carthaginians, it was later used as the base for the Roman conquest of the peninsula, which began in 218 BC with Scipio's march south against Hannibal. The fortified city became an imperial resort and, under Augustus, Tarraco was named capital of Rome's eastern Iberian province – the most elegant and cultured city of Roman Spain, boasting at its peak a quarter of a million inhabitants. Temples and monuments were built in and around the city and, despite a history of seemingly constant sacking and looting since Roman times, it's this distinguished past which still asserts itself throughout modern Tarragona.

Time spent in the handsome upper town quickly shows what attracted the emperors to the city: strategically – and beautifully – placed, it's a fine setting for some splendid Roman remains and a few excellent museums. There's an attractive medieval section, too, while the rocky coastline below conceals a couple of reasonable beaches. If there's a downside, it's that Tarragona is today the second-largest port in Catalunya, so the views aren't always unencumbered – though the fish in the Serrallo fishing quarter is consistently good and fresh. Furthermore, the city's ugly outskirts to the south have been steadily degraded by new industries which do little for Tarragona's character as a resort: chemical and oil refineries and a nuclear power station.

The city divides clearly into two parts: a predominantly medieval, walled upper town (where you'll spend most of your time) known as **La Part Alta**, and the prosperous modern centre below, referred to as **Eixample**, or the Centre Urbà. Between the two cuts is the **Rambla Nova**, a sturdy provincial rival to Barcelona's, lined with fashionable cafés and restaurants, culminating at its southern end with the lovely **Balcó del Mediterràni**, overlooking the sea. Parallel, and to the east, lies the **Rambla Vella**, marking – as its name suggests

– the start of the old town. To either side of the *rambles* are scattered a profusion of relics from Tarragona's Roman past, including various temples and parts of the forum, theatre and amphitheatre.

Arrival and information

The **train station** is in Eixample: when you arrive, turn right and climb the steps ahead of you and you'll emerge at the top of the Rambla Nova, from where everything is a short walk away. In addition to the regular trains, there are now hourly high-speed AVE trains from Barcelona Sants, which have cut journey times to Tarragona to thirty-five minutes. However, tickets are pricey and the Camp de Tarragona AVE station is ten minutes out of town, which involves as taxi ride into the centre. The **bus terminal** is at the other end of the Rambla Nova, at Plaça Imperial Tarraco.

The **turisme** is at c/Major 39 (July–Sept Mon–Sat 9am–9pm, Sun 10am–2pm; Oct–June Mon–Sat 10am–2pm & 4–7pm, Sun 10am–2pm; ☎977 250 795,

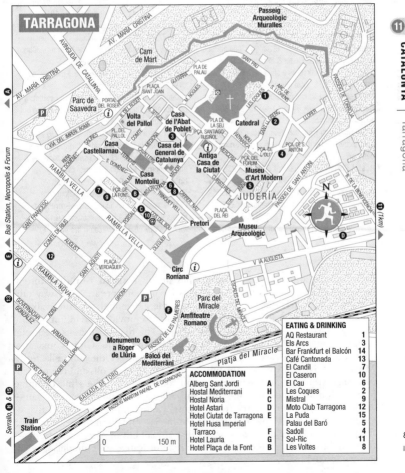

TARRAGONA

ACCOMMODATION
Alberg Sant Jordi	A
Hostal Mediterrani	H
Hostal Noria	C
Hotel Astari	D
Hotel Ciutat de Tarragona	E
Hotel Husa Imperial Tarraco	F
Hotel Lauria	G
Hotel Plaça de la Font	B

EATING & DRINKING
AQ Restaurant	1
Els Arcs	3
Bar Frankfurt el Balcón	14
Café Cantonada	13
El Candil	7
El Caseron	10
El Cau	6
Les Coques	2
Mistral	9
Moto Club Tarragona	12
La Puda	15
Palau del Baró	5
Sadoll	4
Sol-Ric	11
Les Voltes	8

0   150 m

@ www.tarragonaturisme.cat), and there are also information booths (weekends, Easter & summer, same hours) at Plaça Imperial Tarraco, Portal del Roser, Rambla Nova and at the junction of the Via Augusta and Rambla Vella. If you're travelling farther afield you might find the **regional tourist office** handy – it's just south of Rambla Nova at c/Fortuny 4 (Mon–Fri 9.15am–2pm & 4–6.30pm, Sat 9.15am–2pm; T977 233 415, @www.gencat.net).

Accommodation

Tarragona makes a great stopover, and is certainly less exhausting than Sitges. A prime, central spot in town is along the pedestrianized Plaça de la Font, off Rambla Vella; if you're driving, you could park in the underground car park under the plaça. The cheapest lodgings are at the *Alberg Sant Jordi*, while there are a number of campsites east of town, including the well-maintained *Camping Las Palmeras* (T977 208 081, @www.laspalmeras.com; €21–23 a pitch) at **Platja Llarga**, 3km northeast along the coast.

Alberg Sant Jordi Avgda. President Companys 5 T977 240 195, @www.xanascat.cat and @www.resa.es. An IYHF hostel (in the summer) with basic doubles and singles 5min from the bus terminal; breakfast included in the price. Reservations advised in July & Aug (closed Easter & Christmas). During the school year, it functions as a student residence, with preference given to local students. Double €47 (under-26s pay a couple of euros less).

Hostal Mediterrani Orosi 11 T977 249 353, @www.hostalmediterrani.com. Comfy, simple rooms just 50m from the train station, so a good spot to bed down if arriving late or departing early. ❷

Hostal Noria Plaça de la Font 53 T977 238 717, @info@hostalnoria.com. Decent *pensión* above a no-frills bar popular with locals, with small but clean singles and doubles with bathroom. ❷

Hotel Astari Via Augusta 95–97 T977 236 900, @www.hotelastari.com. Friendly three-star hotel

on the road to the beaches, with decent swimming pool; there's a daily parking fee of €7.10. ❹

Hotel Ciutat de Tarragona Plaça Imperial Tarraco 5 T977 250 999, @www.sbhotels.es. Impersonal but very comfortable hotel on the main roundabout at the entrance to Rambla Nova. ❻

Hotel Husa Imperial Tarraco Pg. Palmeras s/n T977 233 040, @www.husa.es. The city's best and most expensive hotel, modern but beautifully positioned, sitting on top of the cliff and facing out to sea, but next to a tacky casino. ❻

Hotel Lauria Rambla Nova 20 T977 236 712, @www.hlauria.es. Well-located three-star hotel just off the main *rambla*, with small outdoor pool and modern, if functional, rooms. ❹

Hotel Plaça de la Font Plaça de la Font 26, T977 246 134, @www.hotelpdelafont.com. Central, cosy hotel with simple, well-scrubbed rooms with TV, and a small restaurant (€13.50 *menú*) with a cheery terrace on the *plaça*. ❸

The City

Much of the attraction of Tarragona lies in the **Roman remains** dotted around the city. Some of the most impressive monuments are a fair way out (see "Around Tarragona" on p.820), but there's enough within walking distance to occupy a good day's sightseeing and to provide a vivid impression of life in Tarragona in imperial Roman times. The five main sights – Passeig Arqueològic Muralles, Forum de la Colonia, Amfiteatre, Circ Roma and Casa Castellarnau –have been grouped together under the umbrella term **Museu d'Historia de Tarragona** (excludes the Necropolis and the Museu Nacional Arqueològic; @www.museutgn.com) and have the same opening hours (summer Tues–Sat 9am–9pm, Sun 9am–3pm; winter Tues–Sat 9am–7pm, Sun 10am–3pm). Entry to each costs €2.45, and a ticket to all five is €9.25. Start at the **Volta del Pallol** (Mon–Sat 9am–9pm, Sun 9am–3pm; free), near the Portal del Roser, which has a small but informative introductory exhibition on the Roman town, and an evocative scale model of what it once looked like.

Passeig Arqueològic Muralles

After a quick look in the *volta*, you can walk through the Portal del Roser and enter the **Passeig Arqueològic Muralles**, a promenade which encircles the northernmost half of the old town. From the entrance at the Portal del Roser, a path runs between **Roman walls** of the third century BC and the sloping, **outer fortifications** erected by the British in 1709 to secure the city during the War of the Spanish Succession. Megalithic walls built by the Iberians are excellently preserved in places, too, particularly two awesome gateways; the huge blocks used in their construction are quite distinct from the more refined Roman additions. Vantage points (and occasional telescopes) give views across the plain behind the city and around to the sea, while various objects are displayed within the *passeig*: several Roman columns, a fine bronze statue of Augustus and eighteenth-century cannons still defending the city's heights. Just beyond the entrance on the right, a small doorway leads up to the battlements where you get fine views of the old city.

Roman Tarragona

The most interesting remains in town are those of the ancient **Necropolis**, a twenty-minute walk out of the centre down Avinguda Ramón i Cajal, which runs west off Rambla Nova. Here, both pagan and Christian tombs have been uncovered, spanning a period from the third to the sixth century AD. The Necropolis is undergoing renovations and is closed, but may reopen in 2009 or 2010; you can, though, visit the small **Museu i Necropolis Paleocristians**, at c/Ramon i Cajal 80 (June–Sept Tues–Sat 10am–1.30pm & 4–8pm, Sun 10am–2pm; Oct–May Tues–Sat 9.30am–1.30pm & 3–5.30pm, Sun 10am–2pm; €2.40 joint ticket with the Museu Nacional Arqueològic). The museum contains a few sarcophagi and some of the most fascinating finds, such as an ivory doll with moveable arms and legs, and you can peek at the main burial grounds through the fence. Most of the relics attest to Tarragona's importance as a centre of Christianity: St Paul preached here, and the city became an important Visigothic bishopric after the break-up of Roman power.

Back in the centre of town, the Roman forum, or rather forums, have also survived, since – as provincial capital – Tarragona sustained both a ceremonial **Forum Provincial** (the scant remnants of which are displayed on Plaça del Forum) and a **Forum de la Colonia** on c/Lleida, whose more substantial remains are on the western side of Rambla Nova, near the Mercat Central. Located on the flat land near the port, this was the commercial centre of imperial Tarraco and the main meeting place for locals for three centuries. The site, which contained temples and small shops ranged around a porticoed square, has been split by a main road: a footbridge now connects the two halves where you can see a water cistern, house foundations, fragments of stone inscriptions and four elegant columns.

Tarragona's other tangible Roman remains lie close to each other at the seaward end of the Rambla Vella. Most rewarding is the **Amfiteatre**, built into the green slopes of the hill beneath the *Imperial Tarraco* hotel. The tiered seats backing onto the sea are original, and from the top you can look north, up the coast, to the headland; the rest of the seating was reconstructed in 1969–70, along with the surviving tunnels and structural buildings.

Above here, on the Rambla Vella itself, are the visible remains of the Roman circus, the **Circ Roma**, whose vaults disappear back from the street into the gloom and under many of the surrounding buildings. You can exit through the Roman **Pretori** tower on Plaça del Rei.

The old town

Roman fragments are incorporated into many of the towering mansions in the medieval **Part Alta**, the heart of Tarragona, spreading northeast of the Rambla Vella. The central c/Major climbs to the quarter's focal point, the **Catedral** (mid-March to May Mon–Sat 10am–1pm & 4–7pm; June to mid-Oct Mon–Sat 10am–7pm; mid-Oct to mid-Nov Mon–Sat 10am–5pm; rest of year 10am–2pm; €3.50), which sits at the top of a broad flight of steps. This, quite apart from its own grand beauty, is a perfect example of the transition from Romanesque to Gothic forms. You'll see the change highlighted in the main facade, where a soaring Gothic portal is framed by Romanesque doors, surmounted by a cross and an elaborate rose window. Except for services, entrance to the cathedral is through the **cloisters** (*claustre*; signposted up a street to the left of the facade), themselves superbly executed with pointed Gothic arches softened by smaller round divisions. The cloister also has several oddly sculpted capitals, one of which represents a cat's funeral being directed by rats. The ticket also gives access to the **Museu Diocesà**, piled high with ecclesiastical treasures.

Strolling the old town's streets will also enable you to track down one of Tarragona's finest medieval mansions and lesser-known museums, the **Casa Castellarnau** on c/Cavallers 14. The interior courtyard alone rewards a visit, with its arches and stone coats of arms built over Roman vaults. Otherwise, the small-scale collections are largely archeological and historical (Roman jars and the like), rescued from banality by some rich eighteenth-century Catalan furniture and furnishings on the upper floor.

Museu Nacional Arqueològic

The most stimulating exhibitions in town are in adjacent buildings off Plaça del Rei, opposite the entrance to the Pretori and Circ Roma. The splendid **Museu Nacional Arqueològic** (June–Sept Tues–Sat 10am–8pm, Sun 10am–2pm; Oct–May Tues–Sat 10am–1.30pm & 4–7pm, Sun 10am–2pm; €2.40) is a marvellous reflection of the richness of imperial Tarraco. Its huge collection is well laid out, starting in the basement with a section of the old Roman wall preserved *in situ*. On other floors are thematic displays on the various remains and buildings around the city, accompanied by pictures, text and relics, as well as whole rooms devoted to inscriptions, sculpture, ceramics, jewellery – even a series of anchors retrieved from the sea. More importantly, there's an unusually complete collection of mosaics, exemplifying the stages of development from the plain black and white patterns of the first century AD to the elaborate polychrome pictures of the second and third centuries.

Serrallo

A fifteen-minute walk west along the industrial harbour front from the train station (or the same distance south from the Necropolis) takes you to the working port of **SERRALLO**, Tarragona's so-called "fishermen's quarter". Built a century ago, the harbour here isn't particularly attractive, but authentic enough – fishing smacks tied up, nets laid out on the ground for mending – and the real interest for visitors is the line of **fish and seafood restaurants** which fronts the main Moll dels Pescadors. The warehouses nearby, back towards town, have been given a face-lift, as has the *Estació Marítima* (cruise-ship terminal) and there's also the mildly interesting **Museu Porte de Tarragona** (June–Sept 10am–2pm & 5–8pm, Sun 11am–2pm; Oct–May Tues–Sat 10am–2pm & 4–7pm, Sun 11am–2pm; €1.80), with exhibits on the port's history.

Eating and drinking

There are plenty of good **restaurants** in the centre of Tarragona; many – particularly in and around Plaça de la Font – have outdoor seating in the summer and English-language menus. Alternatively, you could try the fish and seafood places down in Serrallo; not cheap, but the food is as fresh as can be and you can find some *menús* for around €15 in the narrow street behind the main Moll dels Pescadors. *Pescado romesco* is the regional **speciality** and you'll find it on several *menús* around town: romesco sauce has a base of dry pepper, almonds and/or hazelnuts, olive oil, garlic and a glass of Priorat wine. Beyond this there are many variations, as cooks tend to add their own secret ingredients. You'll find the best **bars** around the cathedral and in the streets between the train station and Rambla Nova.

Restaurants

AQ Restaurant c/Les Coques 7 ☎977 215 954. Glossy, innovative restaurant – the sky-lit dining room sports honey-hued walls and sleek furnishings – with impressive cuisine to match (main dishes €18–20). Husband-and-wife team Quintín and Ana (after whom the restaurant is named) serve up seasonal fare with flair including a tuna tartare topped with cherry chutney and *mero*, or grouper, with shitake mushrooms. Closed Sun & Mon.

Els Arcs Misser Sitges 13 ☎977 218 040. Ancient, graceful stone arches – hence the name – preside over a cosy dining room. Fresh Mediterranean dishes include turbot with toasted pine nuts; a tasty weekday *menú* goes for €23. Closed Sun & Mon.

El Caseron c/de Cos del Bou 9. Small restaurant just off Plaça de la Font, with a decent menu of staples – rabbit, paella, grills and fries – and a good *menú* for €14–16. Closed Mon eve.

Les Coques c/Sant Llorenç 15 ☎977 228 300. Top-notch Catalan fare, including a cod carpaccio and pig's trotters with wild mushrooms, in a comfortable restaurant near the cathedral. €13–15 for mains. Closed Wed eve & Sun.

Mistral Plaça de la Font 19. Pizzas for around €7–8, plus a decent *menú*. Other tasty offerings include paella, served out on the tables on the square in summer. Closed Sun.

Palau del Baró c/Santa Anna 3 ☎977 241 464. Lovely courtyard area and dining rooms set in an eighteenth-century mansion. Well-prepared regional fare includes shellfish in romesco sauce, *arroz negro* and *fideuà* (Catalan noodles) with clams and monkfish. Good-value €15 weekday lunch *menú*, and €18 dinner *menú*. Closed Mon & Sun eve.

La Puda Moll dels Pescadors 25. In the Serrallo quarter, this popular fish restaurant has tables overlooking the harbour inside and out. There's a short selection of seafood tapas, and *menús* that don't come cheap at €27–35, but are excellent.

Sadoll c/Mare de Déu de la Mercè 1. Inviting restaurant tucked away in a quiet corner near the cathedral, and featuring an elegant Art Nouveau dining room. Fresh, creative dishes include duck with a pineapple chutney. Weekday *menús* are €14. Closed Sun.

Sol-Ric Vía Augusta 227, east of the city ☎977 232 032. Try the exceptional seafood, or specialities (€15–18), such as veal with Roquefort cheese, at this amiable restaurant set in an old house with antique furniture and wooden beams.

Les Voltes c/Trinquet Vell 12 ☎977 230 651. Atmospheric restaurant, with a fabulous location within a Roman *volta*, recommended for its hearty seafood and grilled meats. *Menú* for €15. Closed Sun eve & Mon.

Bars and cafés

Bar Frankfurt el Balcón Rambla Nova 3. Outdoor tables in the best spot on the *rambla*, on the balcony overlooking the sea next to the statue of Roger de Lluria. Great for coffee, beer, tasty *platos combinados* and *bocadillos*, with Frankfurter sausages (€6.20), not surprisingly, also on the menu. Daily 9am–10pm.

Café Cantonada c/Fortuny 21. Civilized café-bar whose roomy interior and pool table encourage extended visits. Good tapas and internet access. Sometimes closed Mon.

El Candil Plaça de la Font 13. Fashionable, friendly café by day, which transforms into a cellar bar with exposed stone arches and tapas at night, with a wide selection of herbal teas, hot chocolate and coffees as well as beer and *cava*. Daily 11am–3pm & 5pm–midnight.

El Cau c/Trinquet Vell 2. Situated in an underground Roman vault in the old town, this dark venue has live indie-pop or rock every Sat night. Daily 10pm–4am.

Moto Club Tarragona Rambla Nova 53. Busy and ever-popular *rambla* bar since 1953, with seating outside and a range of tapas and snacks to accompany the *tinto*, *cava* or Spanish beers. Daily from 7am–midnight or 2am, depending on the crowd.

Around Tarragona

The coast between Tarragona and the historic town of **Altafulla**, 11km north, is littered with additional Roman remains, well worth checking out, though for all but the Roman **aqueduct** you'll need your own transport.

Aqüeducte de les Ferreres and other Roman remains

Perhaps the most remarkable (and least visited) of Tarragona's monuments stands 4km outside the original city walls, reached via a small, signposted road off the main Lleida highway. This is the Roman **Aqüeducte de les Ferreres** (free; parking on site), which brought water from the Riu Gayo, some 32km distant. The most impressive extant section, nearly 220m long and 27m high, lies in an overgrown valley in the middle of nowhere: the utilitarian beauty of the aqueduct is surpassed only by the one at Segovia and the Pont du Gard, in the south of France. Popularly, it is known as El Pont del Diable (Devil's Bridge) because, remarked Richard Ford, of the Spanish habit of "giving all praise to 'the Devil', as Pontifex Maximus". Take bus #75, marked "Sant Salvador" (every 20min; last bus back at around 10.45pm), from the stop outside Avgda. Prat de la Riba 11, off Avinguda Ramón i Cajal, a ten-minute ride.

Other local Roman monuments of similar grandeur line the main road north towards Barcelona (N340) – keep an eye out for signs as they can be easy to miss. The square, three-storeyed **Torre dels Escipions**, a funerary monument built in the second century AD and nearly 10m high, stands just off the N340, 6km northeast of Tarragona. A couple of kilometres farther north, at the Altafulla junction, you'll see signs to the **Pedrera Romana del Medol** (June–Sept Tues–Sat 9am–8pm, Sun 9am–3pm; Oct–May Tues–Sat 10am–4pm, Sun 10am–2pm; free), an excavated quarry that provided much of the stone used in Tarragona's constructions. Keep heading towards Barcelona, and 20km from Tarragona, near the town of Creixell, rears the triumphal **Arc de Berà**, built over the great Via Maxima in the second century AD.

Reus – Gaudí's birthplace

Gaudí aficionados (and particularly those with children in tow) might want to take a spin through the small, handsome city of **REUS** (14km west of Tarragona), where the *Moderniste* master, Gaudí, was born in 1852. The sleek **Gaudí Centre** (Mon–Sat 10am–2pm & 4–8pm, July–Sept 10am–8pm, Sun 10am–2pm; €6; ⓦwww .gaudicentrereus.com), in Plaça del Mercadal, offers a thoroughly engaging overview of the great artist via three gleaming floors of tactile and sensory exhibits. While Reus has no Gaudí buildings – he left at the age of 16 – it does feature a smattering of other *Moderniste* buildings, all of which form part of the town's **Ruta del Modernisme**. You can pick up a map at the helpful tourist office (mid-June to mid-Sept Mon–Sat 9.30am–8pm, Sun 10am–2pm; mid-Sept to mid-June Mon–Sat 9.30am–2pm & 4–8pm, Sun 9.30am–2pm; ☎977 010 670, ⓦwww.reus.cat /turismece), which is inside the Gaudí Centre.

Besides Gaudí, Reus is popular for its good shopping, especially clothing, thanks in part to the town's once-thriving textile industry. The city has some decent **accommodation**, including the comfortable, mid-range *Hotel Gaudí*, Raval de Robuster 49 (☎977 345 545, ⓦwww.gargallohotels.es; ❹), and the central *Hostal Santa Teresa*, Santa Teresa 1 (☎977 316 297, ⓦwww.hostalsantateresa.com; ❶), with basic, clean rooms. As for **food**, one of the finer dining options is on the top floor of the centre: *GaudiR* (☎977 127 702; closed Sun, Mon eve), with a breezy terrace overlooking Reus' rooftops, serves up splendid regional fare, including fragrant fish and rice specialities.

Altafulla

ALTAFULLA makes a reasonable stop for a wander about the old town, with its 400-year-old castle (privately owned), the Baroque **Església Parroquial de Sant Marti** (services only), completed in 1705 with its distinctive octagonal dome, and a pair of gateways left standing from the original medieval walls. Nearer the beach and surrounded by a sleepy estate of holiday homes, the **Villa Romana dels Munts** (May–Sept Tues–Sat 10am–1.30pm & 4–8pm, Sun 10am–1.30pm; Oct–April Tues–Sat 10am–1.30pm & 3–6pm, Sun 10am–2pm; ☎977 652 806; €1.80) is one of the most important finds in the region, primarily because of the exceptional mosaics and paintings that decorated its rooms and thermal baths, indicating an owner of high standing – the mosaics are preserved in the Museu Nacional Arqueològic in Tarragona and today the villa is worth a look chiefly for the ruins of its thermal baths, which include a remarkably well-preserved arch and water tank.

The helpful **turisme**, Calle Marqués de Tamarit 16 (summer: Mon–Fri 10am–2pm & 6–9pm, Sat 10am–12.30pm & 6–9pm, Sun 10am–2pm; winter: Mon–Sat 10am–1pm & 5–8pm; ☎977 651 426) offers guided visits through town, (summer: Mon 7pm; winter Sat 11am; call first to confirm). **Accommodation** includes *Casa Gran* (☎977 650 779, ⓦwww.xanascat.cat; under-26s €17.90, over-26s €21.90, with breakfast), which is tucked away in a charming, sixteenth-century house at Placeta 12, just inside the old town, while farther up, near the castle, the *Hotel Gran Claustre* (☎977 651 557, ⓦwww.granclaustre.com; ⓞ), at c/del Cup 2, offers twenty luxurious rooms combining contemporary style with historical elegance, all within an enchanting mansion built in 1746; there's also an extremely swish pool facing the castle walls and a roof-top jacuzzi.

Costa Daurada

The coast south of Tarragona is an uninspiring prospect. The occasional beaches are not easily reached by public transport, and few of them have anything to encourage a stop. This part of the Costa Daurada, however, does boast the gigantic Port Aventura theme park, and the pretty harbour-town of **Cambrils**.

PortAventura and around

Just outside the resort of Salou lies **PortAventura** (daily: mid-June to mid-Sept 10am–midnight; mid-Sept to mid-June 10am–8pm; ☎902 202 220, ⓦwww .portaventura.es), which comprises PortAventura Park (€42 per day; €63 for two days; €73 for three days, which includes Caribe Aquatic Park), an amusement park that boasts five themed "lands" including China and the Wild West, each offering death-defying rides, garish restaurants and live entertainment; Caribe Aquatic Park, a water park (€21.50 per day); and several smart hotels. With its own RENFE station, it's one of the largest theme parks in Europe.

Cambrils

CAMBRILS, set back from a large harbour, still has working boats and fishing nets interspersed among its restaurants and hotels. In summer, it's as full as anywhere along the Catalan coast, and is probably better seen as a day-trip from Tarragona, only fifteen minutes to the north. Out of season, though, it's more

Around 35km west of Tarragona lies one of Spain's up-and-coming wine regions, the **Priorat**, awarded its DOC in 2001. The red wine produced here, and in the adjacent Montsany DOC, is highly sought-after, and the *cellers* have started to follow their more established competitors in La Rioja by cashing in with wine tours and tastings. The *turisme* in Tarragona has up-to-date information, or you can try the local office in Falset (Mon–Fri 9am–3pm & 4–7pm, Sat 10am–2pm, Sun 11am–2pm; ☎977 831 023, ⓦwww.priorat.com). Most tours cost €4–6, and many have English-speaking guides – reservations are essential. Good choices include the *Cellers de Scala Dei* (☎977 827 027) in the village of Scala Dei, which offers free daily tours in English, and the celebrated *Costers Del Siurana* in Gratallops (Mon–Fri 8.30am–1pm & 3–6.30pm; ☎977 839 276, ⓦwww.costersdelsiurana.com). You'll also find a number of good restaurants that offer tasting menus and Priorat wines, including *Mas Trucafort* (☎977 830 160, ⓦwww.mastrucafort.com), set in a nineteenth-century farmhouse on the outskirts of Falset, on the road to Bellmunt del Priorat.

relaxed, and while inexpensive accommodation isn't easy to come by, it might be worth persevering for a night to eat in the good fish restaurants and amble around the harbour and nearby beaches. There's a **market** in town every Wednesday (9am–2pm). Worth a visit if only for the views is the **Museu Torre del Port**, at Pg. Miramar 31 (Tues–Sat 11am–2pm & 4–8pm, Sun 11am–2pm; €1), a seventeenth-century circular watchtower in the harbour, which has been converted into a maritime museum.

Practicalities

Arriving by bus from Tarragona, you'll pass through Salou and can ask to be dropped in Cambrils on the harbourfront. By **train**, you're faced with a fifteen-minute walk from the inland part of town down to Cambrils–Port and the harbour: from the station, turn right and then right again at the main road, heading for the sea. Across the bridge on your left is the main **turisme** (Mon–Fri 9am–2pm & 5–8.30pm, Sat & Sun 10am–1.30pm & 6–9pm; winter, generally not open weekend afternoons; ☎902 154 741, ⓦwww.cambrils-tourism.com), at Pg. de les Palmeres 1, which has free maps, local bus and train timetables posted on the door, and may be able to help find a room. From here, Cambrils–Port is straight ahead, down any of the roads in front of you.

There are plenty of **hotels** in town, but as with all places on the coast, you'll need to reserve in high season, especially if you want to be on the harbour. One street in from the sea is *Hotel Princep*, at c/Narcís Monturiol 2 (☎977 361 127, ⓦwww.hotelprincep.com; ❹), which is not very pretty from the outside but comfortable and clean within; the *Hotel-Restaurant Miramar*, Pg. Miramar 30 (☎977 360 063; ❹), is nicely positioned overlooking the sea. There are also nine **campsites** in and around Cambrils, and the *turisme* has a free map showing where they all are. Closest to the centre is *Don Camilo* (☎977 361 490, ⓦwww.playacambrils.com; closed Nov–April) at Avgda. Diputació 42; the others are spread up and down the coast in both directions.

For a meal, there's plenty of choice and some splendid fish **restaurants** along the harbour. Expect to pay around €15 for a good *menú*, though *a la carta* seafood at one of the harbour-front restaurants comes in at considerably more than that, such as at the elegant – and Michelin-starred – *Rincón de Diego* (closed Sun eve & Mon), c/Drassanes 7, which serves up exquisite dishes featuring fruits from the sea. You'll find less pricey fare along c/Pau Casals.

Tortosa

The only town of any size in Catalunya's deep south is **TORTOSA**, slightly inland astride the Riu Ebre. In the Civil War the front was outside Tortosa for several months until the Nationalists eventually took the town in April 1938. The battle cost 35,000 lives, and is commemorated by a gaunt metal monument on a huge stone plinth in the middle of the river in town. The fighting took its toll in other ways, too: there's little left of the medieval quarter, the *barri antic*, which lies on the east bank of the Ebro, north of the modern commercial district. The **Catedral de Santa Maria** (Tues–Sat 10am–1pm & 4.30–7pm, Sun hours vary, but generally 12.30–2pm) is worth a look, however; founded originally in the twelfth century on the site of an earlier mosque, it was rebuilt in the fourteenth century, and its Gothic interior and quiet cloister – although much worn – are very fine.

Tortosa's brightest point is also its highest. **La Suda**, the old castle, sits perched above the cathedral, glowering from behind its battlements at the Ebre valley below and the mountains beyond. Like so many in Spain, the castle has been converted into a luxury *parador* (see below), but there's nothing to stop you climbing up for a magnificent view from the walls, or from going into the plush bar and having a drink. From the cathedral, c/de la Suda takes you straight there. On the other side of La Suda, the **Jardins del Príncep** beneath the castle houses a collection of **sculptures** of the human figure by Santiago de Santiago (April to mid-Sept Tues–Sat 10am–1.30pm & 4.30–7.30pm, Sun 10am–1.30pm; mid-Sept to March Tues–Sat 10am–1pm & 3.30–6.30pm, Sun 11am–1.30pm; €3).

Practicalities

Moving on from Catalunya, regular **buses** run from Tortosa to Vinaròs (in Castellón Province to the south), from where you can reach the wonderful inland mountain town of Morella. **Trains** head south, passing through Vinaròs, on their way to Valencia. The main **turisme** (May to mid-Sept Tues–Sat 10am–1.30pm & 4.30–7.30pm, Sun 10am–1.30pm; mid-Sept to April 10am–1.30pm & 3.30–6.30pm; ☎977 449 648, ⓦwww.turismetortosa.com) is in the central Plaza del Carrilet, near the Parque Municipal. You'll also find a small, helpful *turisme* in the Jardins del Príncep (generally same hours as the main *turisme*, see above; ☎977 442 005).

For budget **beds**, try the amiable *Hotel Virginia*, at Avgda. de la Generalitat 139 (☎977 444 186; ❷). For a splurge, though, it's well worth opting for the splendid *Parador Nacional Castell de la Suda* (☎977 444 450, ⓦwww.parador.es; ❻). The *parador* also has one of the better **restaurants** in town, open daily to non-guests and specializing in fish from the Ebro delta. In town, for robust regional dishes – including fresh fish and shellfish – try *Paiolet* (☎977 446 653), on Rambla Felip Pedrell 56, perched near the cathedral. Just west of the old town is the elegant Rosa Pinyol, Hernan Cortés 17 (☎977 502 001; closed Sun, Mon eve), serving up excellent local seasonal fare (mains €12–18), such as *suquet de anguilla*, a Catalan stew made with eels.

The Delta de l'Ebre

In the bottom corner of Catalunya is the **Delta de l'Ebre** (Ebro Delta), 320 square kilometres of sandy delta constituting the biggest wetland in Catalunya and one of the most important aquatic habitats in the western Mediterranean.

Designated a natural park, its brackish lagoons, marshes, dunes and reed beds are home to thousands of wintering birds and provide excellent fishing; around fifteen percent of the total Catalan catch comes from this area. The scenery is unique in Catalunya, with low roads running through field after field of rice paddies, punctuated by solitary houses and small villages, before emerging onto dune-lined beaches. Since much of the area of the **Parc Natural de Delta de l'Ebre** is a protected zone, access is limited, and it's best to visit with your own transport.

Deltebre and around

The best place to head to first to get an idea of the area is **DELTEBRE**, at the centre of the delta, 30km from Tortosa. The **park information centre** is on the main highway, on the edge of town at Martí Buera 22 and well signposted (Mon–Fri 10am–2pm & 3–6pm, Sat 10am–1pm & 3–6pm, till 7pm in summer, Sun 10am–2pm; ☎977 489 679, ⓦwww.deltebre.net). The centre can provide you with a map of the delta and has information about tours and local walks. There's also an interesting **Ecomuseum** (same timings; €1.20), with an aquarium displaying species found in the delta. Deltebre has three or four places to stay, all reasonably priced, as well as a youth hostel, *Mossèn Antoni Batlle* (☎977 480 136; €18–21 per dorm bed), at Avinguda de les Goles del Ebre, close to the information office.

A **river cruise** is one of the best ways to experience the delta. A boat leaves daily at 11.30am (1hr 20min; €7) from the dock (Transbordador Garriga) just south of the information centre. Ferries also ply back and forth from here (daily 6am–10pm; €1.80) to **Sant Jaume d'Enveja**, which gives access to **Platja dels Eucaliptus**, 8km away, where there's a modern hotel and restaurant, *Mediterrani Blau* (☎977 479 079, ⓦwww.mediterraniblau.com; ❹), and a **campsite**, *Eucaliptus* (☎977 479 046, ⓦwww.campingeucaliptus.com). If you do camp, bring plenty of mosquito repellent, as the insects are a pest, especially in the evening.

Alternatively, head 10km east from the information centre towards **RIUMAR**: just before you reach the village take the right turn to the wharf area next to the *Casa Nuri* restaurant. Contrary to what the road signs might say, the **Illa de Buda**, the largest of the islands in the delta, is a protected reserve and now off limits to tourists – the cruises that leave from here (around 5 times daily; €6.50) follow a similar route to those from Deltebre, taking you to the river mouth and back. The *Casa Nuri* (daily 10am–10pm) is a good place to try the local speciality, *arròs a banda*, which is similar to *paella* except that the rice is brought before the seafood. Riumar itself offers good, if windy, bathing on a sandy beach, connected to the road by duckboards winding through the dunes, and more remote beaches accessible to the north.

Inland: the route to Lleida

The train line from Barcelona forks at Tarragona, and the choice is either south towards Tortosa or **inland** for the fairly monotonous ride northwest across the flat lands to Lleida. The Tarragona–Lleida bus is a slightly more attractive proposition than the train, if only because it climbs the odd bluff and ridge on the way for good views over the plain. The bus also takes you directly to the region's only major attraction, the monastery of Poblet, which you could see in half a day and then move on to Lleida. Access to the monastery by train is possible, but means walking some of the way along a signposted footpath through

Wines of Spain

**One of the great pleasures of eating out in Spain is the
chance to sample some of the country's excellent wines. Over
fifty percent of the European Union's vineyards lie in Spain
and *vino* (wine), either *tinto* (red), *blanco* (white) or *rosado*
(rosé), is the invariable accompaniment to every meal.**

La Rioja DOC ▲

Jerez's Tio Pepe sherry ▼

Crianza or reserva?

One thing worth knowing about Spanish wine is the terms related to the ageing process that defines the best wines; *crianza* wines must have a minimum of two years' ageing before sale, including at least six months in oak casks; red reserva wines at least three years (of which one must be in oak); red gran *reserva* at least two years in oak and three in the bottle. White *gran reserva* guarantees five years' ageing (of which six months must be in oak). Another thing to look for is a **Denominación de Origen** (DO, the Designation of Origin) label on the back of the bottle, denoting that the wine has satisfied the demanding quality assessment carried out by the relevant regional wine control board. A slightly superior category, **Denominación de Origen Calificada** (DOC), also exists.

Sherry

The classic Andalucian wine is **sherry** – *vino de Jerez* – and is produced in the area west of the town of **Jerez de la Frontera**. Served chilled, it is a perfect drink to wash down tapas. The main distinctions are between *fino* or *jerez seco* (dry sherry), *amontillado* (medium dry), and *oloroso* or *jerez dulce* (sweet), and these are the terms you should use to order. *Manzanilla* is another member of the sherry family produced in the seaside town of **Sanlúcar de Barrameda**; the vineyard's proximity to the sea gives it a delicate, briny tang. Similar is *montilla*, an excellent dry sherry-like wine from the province of **Córdoba**. The main distinction between this and the other *finos* is that no alcohol is added at the production stage, prompting the *cordobeses* to claim that theirs is the more natural.

Top wine bodegas

Many *bodegas* (wineries) welcome visitors and offer informative guided tours and tastings, for which you usually have to book in advance.

▶▶ **Bodegas Alejandro Fernández** Ribera del Duero. Producers of the superb Tinto Pesquera. See p.408.

▶▶ **Bodegas Bilbaínas** La Rioja Alta. One of the oldest *bodegas*, established in 1901. See p.419.

▶▶ **Condes de Albarei** Galicia. Co-operative *bodega* turning out excellent Albariño wines. See p.587.

▶▶ **Bodegas Codorníu** Penedès. Spain's first producers of cava, located in outstanding premises designed by *modernista* architect Josep Maria Puig i Cadafalch. See p.809.

▶▶ **Bodegas Marques de Riscal** La Rioja Alavesa. Designed by Guggenheim architect Frank O. Gehry and incorporating a luxury hotel. See p.486.

▶▶ **Bodegas Muga** La Rioja Alta. Renowned for its painstaking traditional methods, such as using egg whites to clean the wine of impurities. See p.419.

▶▶ **Bodegas Ysios** La Rioja Alavesa. Located in a stunning building with titanium-clad roof, designed by Santiago Calatrava. See p.486.

▶▶ **Cellers de Scala Dei** Priorat. Well-established winery attractively set in old monastery buildings. See p.822.

▶▶ **González Byass** Jerez. One of the biggest sherry producers, and makers of the Tio Pepe brand. See p.311.

▲ Bodegas Marques de Riscal

▼ Bodegas Ysios

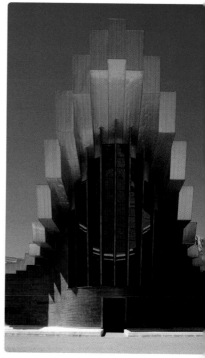

▼ Cava

Catalan "champers"

Cava is Spain's answer to champagne, grown mostly in the Penedès region in Catalunya. "Cava" simply means "cellar" and was the word chosen when the French objected to the use of "champagne". The wine is usually defined by its sugar content: *seco* ("dry") has around half the sugar of a *semi-seco* ("very-sweet").

Vineyard, Castilla-La Mancha ▲

Muga bodega, La Rioja ▼

Top wine regions

CASTILLA-LA MANCHA

The dry central plains yield Spain's most common bottled wine, Valdepeñas, a good standard red, full bodied and juicy and usually blended with white grapes. Recommended labels include Los Llanos, Viña Albali and Señorio de Guadianeja.

CATALUNYA

Catalunya produces scores of excellent wines, such as Bach, Raimat, Torres and the new and pricey Priorat-zone reds that have taken the wine world by storm – the ones to look out for are Clos Mogador and Alvaro Palacios.

GALICIA

Galicia's fragrant white wines have long been widely drunk in Spain and are increasingly gaining inter-national recognition. The two main grape varieties are the Ribeiro, which produces a crisp, dry wine, and the intense, aromatic Albariño, considered superior in body and character, and fetching a higher price. Both wines perfectly complement the region's limitless supply of seafood. The best labels include Fefiñanes, Fin de Siglo and San Trocado.

RIBERA DEL DUERO

Ribera del Duero in Castilla y León is another top-drawer, and currently fashionable, region, which produces Spain's most expensive wine reminis-cent of Portuguese Vinho Verdes, Vega Sicilia, made through a lengthy maturing process. Other outstanding reds from the region include Pesquera, Viña Pedrosa, Protos and Señorío de Nava, while the white Belondrade y Lurtón is also well worth sampling.

LA RIOJA

La Rioja, in the north, produces one of Spain's classic wines. Some of the best names are Cune, Faustino I & V, Berberana, Beronia, Marqués de Cáceres, Montecillo, Muga, Viña Ardanza, Palacio and Izadi.

farmland – a pleasant experience if the weather's fine, since the surroundings are lovely.

Montblanc

The walled medieval town of **MONTBLANC**, 8km before the turning to the monastery at Poblet, is also on the train line to Lleida, so it's easy enough to see both on the same trip. It's a surprisingly beautiful place to discover in the middle of nowhere, and the evening *passeig* around the picturesque Plaça Major is lively. There are many fine little Romanesque and Gothic monuments contained within a tight circle of old streets; all are marked on a map in front of the town's medieval gateway, the **Torre-portal de Bové**, which is just 100m or so up from the train station. On the southern side of the walls, the **Torre-portal de Sant Jordi** marks the spot where San Jordi, or St George (patron saint of Catalunya as well as England), slew the dragon, an event commemorated with a fiesta on April 23.

Just above the central square, Plaça Major, stands the grand Gothic parish church of **Santa María la Major**; its elaborate facade has lions' faces on either side of the main doorway and cherubs swarming up the pillars. There's a fine view from the once-fortified mound that rises behind the church (known as the Pla de Santa Bàrbara) – over the rooftops, defensive towers and walls, and away across the plain. Farther east along c/Major, another church to track down is **Sant Miquel** (Tues–Sat 11am–1pm & 4–6.30pm) on Plaça St Miquel, built in the fourteenth century, with Romanesque and Gothic elements and an impressive coffered ceiling. Montblanc also has a fine local history museum, the **Museu Comarcal de la Conca de Barberà** (Tues–Sat 10am–2pm & 4–7pm, Sun 10am–2pm; €2.90), just off Plaça Major below the church, which is bright and informative, although all annotated in Catalan.

Practicalities

There's a very helpful **turisme** (Mon–Sat 10am–1.30pm & 3–6.30pm, Sun 10am–2pm; ☎977 861 733, ⓦwww.montblancmedieval.org) in the old church of Sant Francesc, just outside the walls at the eastern end of c/Major. Montblanc makes a fine base for visiting Poblet – even on foot, it's only 8km to the monastery. The friendliest place to stay is the *Fonda Cal Blasi*, c/Alenyà 11–13 (☎977 861 336, ⓦwww.fondacalblasi.com; B&B ❸), a restored nineteenth-century stone townhouse a short walk from Plaça Major; it also serves meals.

The Monestir de Poblet

There are few ruins more stirring than the **Monestir de Poblet** (daily 10am–12.45pm & 3–6pm, closes half an hour earlier in the winter and Sundays; closed Christmas, Jan 1 & 6, and a few days in Easter; ☎977 870 254, ⓦwww.larutadelcister.info; €5; 1hr guided tour obligatory, departs roughly half hourly), lying in glorious open country, vast and sprawling within massive battlemented walls and towered gateways. Once *the* great monastery of Catalunya, it was in effect a complete manorial village and enjoyed scarcely credible rights, powers and wealth. Founded in 1151 by Ramón Berenguer IV, who united the kingdoms of Catalunya and Aragón, it was planned from the beginning on an immensely grand scale. The kings of Aragón-Catalunya chose to be buried in its chapel and for three centuries diverted huge sums for its endowment, a munificence that was inevitably corrupting. By the late Middle Ages Poblet had become a byword for decadence – there are lewder stories about this than any

If you plan on visiting all three monasteries in the area – Poblet, Reial Monestir de Santes Creus and Monestir de Vallbona de les Monges – you can purchase a **joint ticket**, at each of the monasteries, for €9. For more information, head to Poblet's *turisme* at Pg. Abat Conill 9 (Tues–Sat 10am–1.30pm & 3–6pm, Sun 10am–2pm; in winter until 5pm; ℡977 871 247).

other Cistercian monastery – and so it continued, hated by the local peasantry, until the Carlist revolution of 1835 when a mob burned and tore it apart.

The monastery was repopulated by Italian Cistercians in 1940 and over the decades since then it's been subject to a superb job of restoration. Much remains delightfully ruined, but, inside the main gates, you are now proudly escorted around the principal complex of buildings. As so often, the **cloisters**, focus of monastic life, are the most evocative and beautiful part. Late Romanesque, and sporting a pavilion and fountain, they open onto a series of rooms: a splendid Gothic **chapterhouse** (with the former abbots' tombs set in the floor), wine cellars, a parlour, a **kitchen** equipped with ranges and copper pots and a sombre, wood-panelled **refectory**.

Beyond, you enter the **chapel** in which the twelfth- and thirteenth-century tombs of the kings of Aragón have been meticulously restored by Frederico Marès, the manic collector of Barcelona. They lie in marble sarcophagi on either side of the nave, focusing attention on the central sixteenth-century altarpiece. You'll also be shown the vast old **dormitory**, to which there's direct access from the chapel choir, a poignant reminder of Cistercian discipline. From the dormitory (half of which is sealed off since it's still in use), a door leads out onto the cloister roof for views down into the cloister itself and up the chapel towers.

Getting there by bus

Two three **buses** a day (Mon–Sat only) run to Poblet from Tarragona or Lleida, passing right by the monastery. It's an easy day-trip from either city, or can be seen on the way between the two – the gap between buses is roughly three hours, which is enough time to get around the complex. You could also **stay overnight** at Poblet, an even more attractive proposition if you have your own transport, since there are several pleasant excursion targets in the surrounding countryside. The solitary *Hostal Fonoll* (℡977 870 333, ⊛www.hostalfonoll.com) outside the main gate of the monastery has decent rooms (❸), and a restaurant and cafeteria (daily 9am–3.30pm; €15 weekday *menú*, from 1–3.30pm); 1km up the road, around the walls, the hamlet of **LES MASIES** has a couple of hotels and restaurants, including the *Villa Engràcia* (℡977 870 308; B&B ❹), an attractive former spa built in 1888, which has a pool, tennis courts and parking.

Getting there by train

The approach by **train** is much more atmospheric than by bus. You get off at the ruined station of **L'ESPLUGA DE FRANCOLÍ**, from where it's a beautiful three-kilometre walk to the monastery, much of it along a signposted country track. L'Espluga has a few places **to stay**, including the *Hostal del Senglar* (℡977 870 121, ⊛www.hostaldelsenglar.com; ❸), in the middle of town on Plaça Montserrat Canals. In an attempt to benefit from the busloads of tourists heading to Poblet, L'Espluga has developed several attractions in recent years, the most interesting of which is **Cova de la Font Major** (summer Tues–Sun 10.30am–1.30pm & 4.30–7.30pm; Aug open Mon; winter Tues–Sun 10.30am–1.30pm & 4–6pm; €5), a large cavern inhabited in prehistoric times, and now a museum and activity centre.

Around Poblet: excursions

If you have time and transport, a couple of excursions into the countryside surrounding Poblet are well worth making. The red-stone walled village of **PRADES**, in the Serra de Prades, 20km from the monastery, is a beautifully sited and tranquil place that needs no other excuse for a visit. The *Fonda Espasa*, c/Sant Roc 1 (℡977 868 023; ❸), just outside the old quarter on the main road, offers simple **accommodation** if you decide you like it enough to stay on. Prades is also the place to be during the second weekend of July, when they replace the water in the fountain with *cava*, and you can join in and help yourself – or, order a bottle of bubbly at a terrace bar in the porticoed plaza and enjoy the scene.

The other option is to take in two more twelfth-century Cistercian monasteries. The **Reial Monestir de Santes Creus** (Tues–Sun 10am–1.30pm & 3–6pm; €4.50; in the summer, open until 7pm; ℡977 638 329) is the easier to reach, 7km north of the Barcelona–Lleida highway, clearly signposted on minor road TP2002. It's built in Transitional style, with a grand Gothic cloister and some Romanesque traces, and you can explore the dormitory, chapterhouse and main church. Trickier to find, though worth the drive, is the **Monestir de Vallbona de les Monges** (Tues–Sat 10.30am–1.30pm & 4.30–6.45pm, Sun noon–1.30pm & 4.30–6.45pm; Nov–Feb closes 6pm; Aug open Mon; ℡973 330 266; €3), north of Poblet, reached via the C14 from Montblanc. This has been occupied continuously for over 800 years, and the church is particularly fine.

Lleida

LLEIDA (Lérida), at the heart of a fertile plain near the Aragonese border, has a rich history. First a *municipium* under the Roman empire and later the centre of a small Arab kingdom, it was reconquered by the Catalans and became the seat of a bishopric in 1149. Little of those periods survives in today's city but there is one building of outstanding interest, the old cathedral, which is sufficient justification in itself to find the time for a visit. If you have to spend the night in Lleida – and you will if you're heading north to the Pyrenees by train or bus – there are a couple of museums and a steep set of old-town streets to occupy any remaining time. Rooms are easy to come by, and the students at the local university fill the streets and bars on weekend evenings in good-natured throngs.

Arrival and information

Plaça de Sant Joan is a fifteen- to twenty-minute walk east of the **train station**, with the **bus station** a similar distance in the other direction, down Avinguda de Blondel. The very informative **turisme** (Mon–Sat 10am–2pm & 4–7pm, Sun 10am–1.30pm; ℡973 700 402, Ⓦwww.turismedelleida.com) is at c/Mayor 31.

Accommodation

There are a couple of **places to stay** right outside the train station, and more along the road straight ahead – Rambla Ferran – which leads into the centre. Otherwise, press on to the central Plaça Sant Joan, around which there are several possibilities. There's a **campsite**, *Les Basses* (℡973 235 954; closed Oct to mid-May), a couple of kilometres out of town on the Huesca road. Take the bus labelled "BS" or "Les Basses" (every 45min from Rambla Ferran).

Alberg Sant Anastasi Rambla d'Aragó 11 ☎973 266 099. Lleida's youth hostel, smartly renovated and centrally located. €15.80 for a dorm bed (under 25s), and €18.90 for everyone else (€3 cheaper in low season).

Hostal Mundial Plaça de Sant Joan 4 ☎973 242 700. About as central as you can get, with basic but clean rooms, both with bath (❷) and without (❶).

Hotel Principal Plaça de la Paeria 7 ☎973 230 800, ⓦwww.hotelprincipal.net. Starting to show its

age, but this is still one of the more comfortable options around Plaça de Sant Joan. ❸

Hotel Real Avgda. Blondel 22 ☎973 239 405, ⓦwww.hotelrealleida.com. The most comfortable hotel in the old town, in a great location facing the river, and rooms featuring simple, modern design and tiled bathrooms. ❹

Hotel Sansi Lleida c/Alcade Porqueras 4–6 ☎973 244 000, ⓦwww.sansihotels.com. A smart, modern hotel on the north side of the old town with hassle-free parking and plenty of bars nearby. ❺–❻

The City

The **Seu Vella** (Tues–Sun 10am–1.30pm & 4–7.30pm, 3–5.30pm in winter; €3), or old cathedral, is entirely enclosed within the walls of the ruined castle (La Suda), high above the Riu Segre, a twenty-minute climb from the centre of town – or you can take the lift from the hill behind Plaça de Sant Joan (generally daily 7am–midnight; €0.20). It's a peculiar fortified building, which in 1707 was deconsecrated and taken over by the military, remaining in their hands until 1940. Enormous damage was inflicted over the years (documented by photos in a side chapel) but the church remains a notable example of the Transitional style, similar in many respects to the cathedral of Tarragona. Once again the Gothic cloisters are masterly, each walk comprising arches different in size and shape but sharing delicate stone tracery. They served the military as a canteen and kitchen. Outside, the views from the walls, away over the plain, are stupendous.

You can climb back down towards the river by way of the new cathedral, **La Seu Nova** (Mon–Fri 9.30am–12.30pm & 5.30–7pm, Sat & Sun 9.30am–1pm & 5.30–8.30pm; free), a grimy eighteenth-century building only enlivened inside by a series of minuscule, high stained-glass windows.

Nearby, the new, spacious **Museu de Lleida**, c/Sant Crist 1 (June–Sept Tues–Sun 10am–8pm; Oct–May Tues–Sun 10am–7pm; €3), is the city's flagship museum, merging collections that were previously in the Archeological and Diocesan museums. Two floors show off ancient finds from throughout Lleida and Catalunya, including Romanesque altarpieces, a Visigoth baptismal font and stone sculptures from the Seu Vella.

Also worth a look is the **Museu d'Art Jaume Morera** (Tues–Sat 11am–2pm & 5–8pm, Sun 11am–2pm; free), a permanent display of twentieth-century Catalan art housed in the same building as the tourist office on c/Mayor 31. The museum is due to be moved; check with the tourist office for more information. For top-notch exhibits of contemporary art, check out the **Centre d'Art La Panera**, Plaça de la Panera 2 (Tues–Sat 11am–2pm & 5–8pm, Sun 11am–2pm; free). The building's history is as interesting as the art inside: it dates back to the twelfth century, when it was Lleida's trading exchange and market, and you can still see evidence of its medieval roots in the original colonnade made up of a line of 21 stone columns. In the early 1600s, the building was acquired by the canonry of the cathedral, who used it to store and sell food products, and hence its official name, *La Panera dels Canonges*, or The Canons' Pantry.

Once you've visited the cathedral and museums, you've just about seen all that Lleida has to offer, though its central pedestrianized shopping streets are good for a browse, and you can wind up in **Plaça de Sant Joan** for a drink in one of the outdoor cafés.

Eating and drinking

Lleida is famous for its **snails**, roasted over a wood fire with peppers and garlic (*caragols a la llauna*), and served up in restaurants in both the old and new parts of town. The block of streets north of the church of Sant Marti also holds a variety of restaurants; the university is close by, and this is where the students come to eat and, as night falls, to hang out at the loud **music-bars** along the block formed by c/Sant Marti, c/Camp de Mart, c/Balmes and Avinguda Prat de la Riba. For more **nightlife**, there are a few clubs on c/Comtes d'Urgell: *Rumbavana* with a Latin theme and salsa classes at no. 31, and *L'Antic*, across the rail tracks at no. 40, a more conventional house club. If you fancy something a little mellower, try *Antares*, c/Ballesters 15 (open from 7pm daily), which has live jazz on Fridays and a wide selection of alcoholic drinks as well as herbal teas.

El Celler del Roser c/Cavallers 24. One of the better spots to sample the celebrated snails is at this friendly place, with wood tables and exposed brick.

Gardeny at c/Salmerón 10 ☎973 234 510. A more expensive option specializing in modern Lleida cuisine, with a weekday *menú* for around €15. Closed Mon & Tues.

La Huerta Avgda. Tortosa 7 ☎973 245 040. Located out of the centre of town, near the river and east of the train station. If you'd like to try market-fresh regional cuisine, don't miss this established restaurant; the name means "garden", and specialities celebrate Lleida's fertile fields, and include the savoury *escalivada*, made with grilled peppers, onions and aubergine.

Trastevere c/Camp de Mart 27. Traditional Italian restaurant with smart decor serving up pricey pizzas.

Zeke Avgda. Prat de la Riba 42. Popular and lively tapas bar, with a range of reasonably priced robust small dishes, such as the traditional Catalan *pan amb tomaquet*, bread rubbed with tomato and drizzled in olive oil.

Travel details

For services from Barcelona to destinations in Catalunya, see p.724.

Trains

For current timetables and ticket information, consult RENFE ☎ 902 240 202, ✉www.renfe.es. NB By 2010, a high-speed rail service should be operating, linking Girona, Figueres, La Jonquera and Perpignan but not calling at any Costa Brava resorts.

Figueres to: Barcelona (27 daily; 1hr 30min–2hr); Colera (9 daily; 25min); Girona (27 daily; 25–35min).

Girona to: Barcelona (29 daily; 1hr 10min–1hr 30min); Figueres (27 daily; 35min).

Lleida to: Barcelona via Valls or Reus/Tarragona (17 daily; 2hr–4hr 15min, AVE 1hr); La Pobla de Segur (3 daily; 2hr 10min); Tarragona (8 daily; 1hr 30min–2hr); Zaragoza (20 daily; 1hr 50min).

Ribes de Freser to: Núria (9–13 daily in summer; 35min); Queralbs (9–13 daily; 15min).

Ripoll to: Barcelona (12 daily; 2hr 30min); Puigcerdà (5–6 daily; 1hr 20min; 4 continue to the first French station, Latour de Carol).

Sitges to: Barcelona (every 30min; 25–40min);

Cunit (12 daily; 15min); Tarragona (every 30min; 1hr).

Tarragona to: Barcelona (every 30min; 1hr); Cambrils (12 daily; 20min); Cunit (10 daily; 50min); Lleida (12 daily; 2hr, *talgo* 1hr, AVE 30min); Sitges (direct every 30min; 1hr); Tortosa (13 daily; 1hr); Valencia (16 daily; 4hr, *talgo* 2hr 15min); Vilanova i la Geltrú (20 daily; 50min); Zaragoza (12 daily; 3hr 30min).

Buses

Cadaqués to: Barcelona (2 daily; 2hr 20min); Castelló d'Empúries (4 daily; 1hr); Figueres (3 daily; 1hr 5min); Roses (4 daily; 30min).

Camprodon to: Molló (Mon–Sat 1 daily; 15min); Setcases (2 daily; 30min).

L'Escala to: Barcelona (July–Sept 3 daily; 2hr 40min); Figueres (4 daily; 45min); Girona (2 daily; 1hr); Palafrugell (4 daily; 45min); Pals (4 daily; 35min); Sant Pere Pescador (4 daily; 20min); Torroella de Montgrí (4 daily; 20min).

Figueres to: Barcelona (3–8 daily; 1hr 30min); Cadaqués (3 daily; 1hr 5min); Castelló d'Empúries

(5 daily; 15min); El Port de la Selva (2 daily; 40min); L'Escala (4 daily; 45min); Espolla (daily; 35min); Girona (Mon–Sat 4–8 daily, Sun 3; 1hr); Olot (2–3 daily; 1hr 30min); Palafrugell (5 daily; 1hr 30min); Pals (3 daily; 1hr 20min); Roses (5 daily; 30min); Sant Pere Pescador (4 daily; 35min); Torroella de Montgrí (3 daily; 1hr 10min).

Girona to: Barcelona (Mon–Fri 7 daily, Sat & Sun 3; 1hr 30min); Besalú (Mon–Sat 8 daily, Sun 4; 45min); L'Escala (Mon–Sat 2 daily; 1hr); Figueres (Mon–Sat 8 daily, Sun 3; 1hr); Olot (Mon–Sat 14 daily, Sun 9; 1hr 15min); Palafrugell (hourly; 1hr 15min); Palamós (23 daily; 1hr); Platja d'Oro (23 daily; 45min); Sant Feliu (Mon–Sat 13 daily, Sun 5; 45min); Sant Hilari Sacalm (Mon–Fri 3 daily, Sat daily; 1hr 15min); Tossa de Mar (July–Sept 2 daily; 1hr).

Les to: Baquiera-Beret via Vielha & Salardú (ski season up to 10 daily; summer 5 daily; 45–50min)

Lleida to: Artesa de Segre (5 daily; 1hr); Barcelona (Mon–Sat 10 daily, Sun 4; 2hr 15min); Huesca (5 daily; 2hr 30min); La Seu d'Urgell (daily; 3hr); Montblanc (6 daily; 1hr 30min); Pobla de Segur (daily; 2hr); Poblet (Mon–Sat 3 daily; 1hr 15min); Tarragona (3 daily; 2hr); Vielha, via Túnel de Vielha (2 daily; 3hr); Zaragoza (Mon–Sat 6 daily, Sun 2; 2hr 30min).

Lloret de Mar to: Barcelona (July–mid-Sept 10 daily; 1hr 15min); Girona (5 daily; 1hr 20min); Palafrugell (2 daily; 1hr 30min); Palamós (2–4 daily; 1hr); Platja d'Aro (2–4 daily; 50min); Sant Feliu (2–4 daily; 40min); Tossa de Mar (every 30min; 15min).

Olot to: Barcelona (Mon–Sat 7–8 daily, Sun 4; 2hr 15min); Besalú (Mon–Sat 8 daily, Sun 6; 30min); Camprodon (1–2 daily; 45min); Figueres (2–3 daily; 1hr); Girona (11 daily Mon–Sat, Sun 4; 1hr 15min); Ripoll (5 daily; 50min–1hr); Santa Pau (Wed am; 15min); Sant Joan de les Abadesses (2–3 daily; 50min).

Palafrugell to: Barcelona (8 daily; 2hr); L'Escala (4 daily; 35min); Figueres (5 daily; 1hr 30min); Girona (19 daily; 1hr); Lloret de Mar (1hr 30min); Palamós (20 daily; 15min); Pals (4 daily; 10min); Sant Feliu (17 daily; 45min); Sant Pere Pescador (3 daily; 1hr); Torroella de Montgrí (4 daily; 25min).

La Pobla de Segur to: Barcelona (2 daily; 3hr 30min); Capdella (June–Sept Mon, Wed, Fri at

6.55pm, Oct–May Mon–Fri daily at 6pm; 1hr); Esterri d'Aneu (2 daily Mon–Sat; 1hr 15min); Lleida (daily; 2hr); El Pont de Suert (Mon–Sat 1 daily at 9.30am; 1hr 30min); Vielha (June–Sept 15 Mon–Sat 1 daily midday; 3hr).

El Port de la Selva to: Figueres (4 daily; 40min).

Puigcerdà to: Alp (2 daily; 10min); Bagà/Berga (2 daily; 35min–1hr); Llívia (3–4 daily; 20min); La Molina (daily; 30min); La Seu d'Urgell (3 daily; 1hr).

Ripoll to: Camprodon (6–8 daily; 45min); Gombrèn (Mon–Fri 1 daily; 20min); Guardiola de Berguedà (Mon–Fri 1 daily; 2hr); La Pobla de Lillet (Mon–Fri 1 daily; 1hr 45min); Olot (3–4 daily; 50min); Sant Joan de les Abadesses (6–8 daily; 20min).

Sant Feliu to: Barcelona (8 daily; 1hr 30min); Girona (July–Sept 11 daily; 2hr); Lloret de Mar (July & Aug 2 daily; 40min); Palafrugell (16 daily; 45min); Palamós (19 daily; 30min); Platja d'Aro (19 daily; 15min).

La Seu d'Urgell to: Andorra la Vella (Mon–Sat 14 daily, Sun 5; 40min); Barcelona (4 daily; 3hr 40min); Lleida (4 daily; 2hr 30min); Puigcerdà (3 daily; 1hr); Sort (2 daily minibuses; 1hr 15min).

Tarragona to: Barcelona (18 daily; 1hr 30min); Berga (July & Aug 1 daily, rest of year Sat & Sun only; 3hr 10min); L'Espluga (3 daily; 1hr); La Pobla de Lillet (July & Aug daily, rest of year Sat & Sun only; 4hr 15min); La Seu d'Urgell (daily at 8am; 3hr 45min); Lleida (6 daily; 1hr 45min); Montblanc (3 daily; 50min); Poblet (Mon–Sat 3 daily; 1hr 5min); Salou-Cambrils (every 30min; 20min); Tortosa (Mon–Fri 1 daily; 1hr 30min); Valencia (7 daily; 3hr 30min); Valls (12 daily; 20min); Zaragoza (4 daily; 4hr).

Tortosa to: Deltebre (Mon–Fri 5 daily, Sat 2; 1hr); Tarragona (Mon–Fri daily; 1hr 30min).

Tossa de Mar to: Barcelona (July–Sept 12 daily; 1hr 35min); Girona (July–Sept 2 daily, Oct–June daily; 1hr); Lloret de Mar (every 30min; 15min).

Vielha to: Lleida (2 daily; 3hr); La Pobla de Segur (June–Sept 15 1 daily; 3hr).

Cruceros boats

Tossa de Mar to: Sant Feliu (June–Sept 5 daily; 45min); Platja d'Aro/Sant Antoni de Calonge/Palamós (June–Sept 4 daily; 1hr 15min/1hr 25min/1hr 45min).

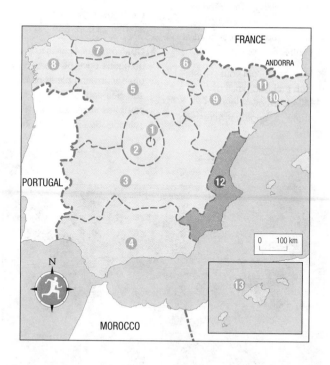

Valencia and Murcia

FRANCE

ANDORRA

PORTUGAL

MOROCCO

N

0   100 km

✳ **Las Fallas** One of the country's most famous festivals – an explosive week-long celebration of fireworks and bonfires in March. See p.834 & *Fiestas colour section*

✳ **La Ciudad de las Artes y Ciencias, Valencia** Breathtaking, cutting-edge contemporary architecture, and Europe's largest cultural centre. See p.844

✳ **Horchata** Cool your throat with a chilled glass of Valencia's own tiger-nut shake; strange but refreshing. See p.846

✳ **Paella** Try Spain's most famous dish in its home setting. See p.851

✳ **Sagunto** Visit the imposing Moorish fortress and Sagunto's historic medieval centre. See p.852

✳ **F/18 Benicàssim** Huge annual music festival featuring the biggest names in alternative pop. See p.855

✳ **Cuatro calas** Águilas's gorgeous cove beaches offer an inviting blend of sun, sea and, on some stretches in low season, solitude. See p.881

▲ La Ciudad de las Artes y Ciencias

Valencia and Murcia

The area known as the **Levante** (the East), combining the provinces of Valencia and Murcia, is an incongruous mix of the ancient and modern, of beauty and beastliness. The rich *huerta* of **Valencia** is one of the most fertile regions of Europe: crowded with orange and lemon groves, date-palm plantations, and rice fields still irrigated by systems devised by the Moors. Evidence of the lengthy Moorish occupation can be seen throughout the province, in the castles, crops and place names – Benidorm, Alicante, Alcoy are all derived from Arabic. The growing self-assurance of the region is evident in the increasing presence of *Valenciano* – a dialect of Catalan – which challenges Castilian as the main language of education and broadcasting in the area. There's even an extreme nationalist group that denies the dialect's Catalan origins, but it hasn't managed to convince anyone else.

Murcia is quite distinct, a *comunidad autónoma* in its own right, and there could hardly be a more severe contrast with the richness of the Valencian *huerta*. This

Valencian cuisine

Gastronomy is of great cultural importance to the Valencians. Rice is the dominant ingredient in dishes of the region, grown locally in paddy fields still irrigated by the Moorish canal system (*acequias*). Gourmets tend to agree that the best **paellas** are to be found around (but not *in*) Valencia, the city where the dish originated. The genuine version doesn't mix fish and meat – it typically contains chicken, rabbit, green beans, *garrofón* (large butter beans), snails, artichokes and saffron – and should be prepared fresh and cooked over wood (*leña*), not scooped from some vast, sticky vat; most places will make it for a minimum of two people, with advance notice.

Other **rice-based dishes** vary around the region: *arroz negro* is rice cooked with squid complete with ink, which gives the dish its colour, and served with *all i oli*, a powerful garlic mayonnaise. *Arroz al horno* is drier, baked with chickpeas. *Fideuá* is seafood and noodles cooked paella-style. The most famous, *arroz a banda*, is found on the south coast around Denia – it's rice cooked with seafood, served as two separate dishes: soup, then rice. Around Alicante, you can try *arroz con costra*, which is a meat-based paella topped with a baked egg crust. Apart from rice, **vegetables** (best *a la plancha*, brushed with olive oil and garlic) are always fresh and plentiful.

The sweet-toothed should try **turrón**; made of nuts and honey, it traditionally comes in a soft, flaky variety or very hard, like nougat (the *turrón* from Jijona is the finest). You could follow it with an **horchata** (or *orxata*), a rich drink made from tiger nuts (*chufas*) or almonds (*almendras*), and sometimes served in ice-form.

southeastern corner of Spain is virtually a desert and is some of the driest territory in Europe. It was fought over for centuries by Phoenicians, Greeks, Carthaginians and Romans, but there survives almost no physical evidence of their presence – or of five hundred years of Moorish rule, beyond an Arabic feel to some of the small towns and the odd date palm here and there. The province's capital city of **Murcia**, with its lovely cathedral and terrace tapas bars, makes for a comfortable base for exploring the region.

Much of the **coast** is marred by heavy overdevelopment, with concrete apartment blocks and sprawling holiday complexes looming over many of the best beaches. However, away from the big resorts, particularly around **Denia** and **Xàbia** (Jávea) in Valencia, there are some attractive isolated coves, while the historic hilltop settlements of **Altea** and **Peñíscola** are undeniably picturesque, if touristy. In Murcia, the resorts of the **Mar Menor** are reasonably attractive and very popular with Spanish families in high season; the best

Fiestas

February

Week before Lent: Carnaval Águilas' *carnaval* is one of the wildest in the country. Good carnival celebrations also in Vinaròs.

March/April

12–19 March: Las Fallas de San José Valencia's *Las Fallas* is by far the biggest of the bonfire festivals, and indeed one of the most important fiestas in all Spain. The whole thing costs over €1 million, most of which goes up in smoke (literally) on the final *Nit de Foc* when the grotesque caricatures, fashioned from papier-mâché and wood, are burned. Throughout, there are bullfights, music and stupendous fireworks; see the *Fiestas* colour section.

19 March: Día de San José Smaller *fallas* festivals in Xàtiva, Benidorm and Denia.

Third Sun of Lent: Fiesta de la Magdalena Castellón de la Plana celebrates the end of Moorish rule with pilgrimages and processions of huge floats.

Semana Santa (Holy Week) In Elche, there are, naturally, big Palm Sunday celebrations making use of the local palms, while throughout the week there are also religious processions in Cartagena, Lorca, Orihuela and Valencia. The **Easter processions** in Murcia are particularly famous, and they continue into the following week with, on the Tuesday, the *Bando de la Huerta*, a huge parade of floats celebrating local agriculture, and, on the Saturday evening, the riotous "Burial of the Sardine" which marks the end of these spring festivals.

April 22–24: Moros y Cristianos After a colourful procession in Alcoy, a huge battle commences between the two sides in the main square.

May

1–5: Fiestas de los Mayos Fiesta in Alhama de Murcia, and *Moros y Cristianos* in Caravaca de la Cruz.

Second Sun: La Virgen de los Desamparados The climax of this celebration in Valencia is when the statue of the Virgin is transferred from her basilica to the cathedral.

Third Sun: Moros y Cristianos In Altea.

June

23–24: Noche de San Juan Magnificent *hogueras* festival in Alicante (and San Juan de Alicante) with processions and fireworks, culminating as huge effigies and bonfires are burnt in the streets at midnight. Celebrated on a smaller scale on the beaches of Valencia (Malvarossa, Cabanyal and Aloboraya) with bonfire-jumping.

beaches are in the extreme south, around **Águilas**, where you'll find some dazzling unspoilt coves. The increasingly vibrant cities of **Valencia** and **Alicante** are the major urban centres, and there are several delightful historic small towns and villages a short way inland, such as **Morella**, **Xàtiva** and **Lorca**.

The Valencia area has a powerful tradition of **fiestas**, and there are a couple of elements unique to this part of the country. Above all, throughout the year and more or less wherever you go, there are mock battles between Muslims and Christians (*Moros y Cristianos*). Recalling the Christian Reconquest of the country – whether through symbolic processions or recreations of specific battles – they're some of the most elaborate and colourful festivities to be seen anywhere, above all in Alcoy (see box, p.689). The other recurring feature is the *fallas* (bonfires) in which giant carnival floats and figures are paraded through the streets before being ceremoniously burned.

Altea also celebrates with a popular tree-bearing procession and a bonfire in the old town.

July

Early July: Fiestas de la Santísima Sangre Dancing in the streets of Denia, plus music and mock battles.

15–20: Moros y Cristianos In Orihuela.

Second week: Feria de Julio In Valencia, with music, bullfights and above all fireworks, ending with the Battle of the Flowers in the Alameda.

Penultimate weekend: FIB Benicàssim's international music festival, a massive party bringing together the major names in alternative and electronic music.

25–31: Moros y Cristianos Villajoyosa sees battles by both land and sea.

August

4: Festa del Cristo de la Salut Festival in El Palmar with processions by boat into the lake.

First week Local fiesta in Segorbe.

Mid-Aug: Misteri d'Eix Elche presents a mystery play, based on a drama dating back to medieval times.

14–20: Feria de Agosto Xàtiva's fair has a very extensive cultural dimension including concerts, plays and exhibitions, plus bullfights and barrages of fireworks.

15 Local festivities in Denia.

Last week: La Tomatina A riotous free-for-all of tomato-throwing takes place in Buñol on the last Wednesday of the month). Morella hosts a music festival.

Last Wed Local fiesta in Sagunto and at the same time the great *Moros y Cristianos* festival and a mystery play in Elche.

September

4–9: Moros y Cristianos In Villena.

Second week: Bull-running through Segorbe's streets.

8–9: Les Danses Celebrations in Peñíscola's old quarter include a human tower construction.

22: Fiesta de Santo Tomás in Benicàssim with bands and a "blazing bull".

October

Second Sun: La Virgen de Suffrage Benidorm celebrates its patron saint's day.

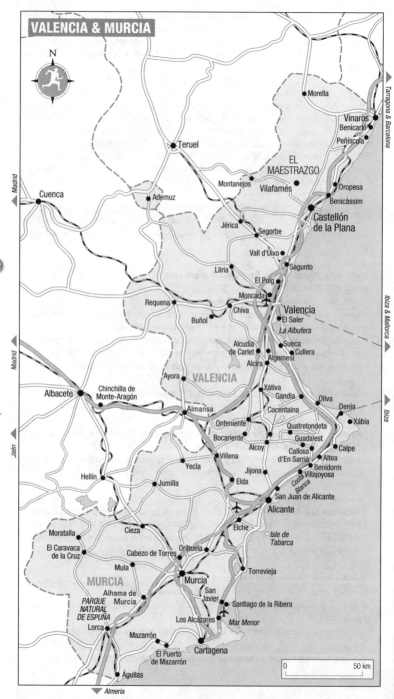

N

Tarragona & Barcelona

Ibiza & Mallorca

Ibiza

Madrid

Madrid

Jaén

Almería

Morella

Vinaròs
Benicarló
Peñíscola

Teruel

EL
MAESTRAZGO

Cuenca

Ademuz

Montanejos
Vilafamés

Oropesa
Benicàssim

Jérica
Segorbe

Castellón
de la Plana

Vall d'Uixo

Lliria

Sagunto
El Puig
Moncada

Requena
Chiva

Valencia
El Saler
La Albufera

Buñol

Alcudia
de Carlet
Algemesi

Sueca
Cullera

Alcira

VALENCIA

Ayora

Xàtiva
Gandia

Albacete

Chinchilla de
Monte-Aragón

Cocentaina

Oliva

Denia

Almansa

Onteniente

Quatretondeta

Xàbia

Bocariente

Guadalest

Alcoy
Callosa
d'En Sarrià

Calpe
Altea

Villena

Benidorm

Hellín

Yecla

Jijona

Villajoyosa
Costa
Blanca

Elda

San Juan de Alicante

Jumilla

Alicante

Cieza

Elche

Isle de
Tabarca

Moratalla

El Caravaca
de la Cruz

Cabezo de Torres
Orihuela

Mula

Torrevieja

MURCIA

Murcia

Alhama de
Murcia

San
Javier

PARQUE
NATURAL
DE ESPAÑA

Santiago de la Ribera

Lorca

Los Alcázares

Mar Menor

Mazarrón

Cartagena

El Puerto
de Mazarrón

Águilas

0   50 km

Getting around by public transport is relatively straightforward with frequent train and bus services, though you'll need your own transport to really explore the area. The motorway network is excellent, but tolls are quite pricey.

Valencia

Valencia is emerging as one of the nation's most progressive cities. Spain's third largest, it continues to reinvent itself at a heady pace. Well on the way to equalling the cosmopolitan vitality of Barcelona and the cultural variety of Madrid, the city has finally shaken off a slightly provincial reputation. In the last decade or so, a vast, iconic new cultural complex – **La Ciudad de las Artes y Ciencias** – has emerged, a state-of-the-art metro has opened and dozens of hip new bars, restaurants and boutiques have injected new life into the historic centre. Also emblematic of the fact that the times-they-are-a-rapidly changing is the redevelopment of the beach and port area, powered by the hosting of the prestigious yachting jamboree, The America's Cup. Nevertheless, despite its size and *stylista* cachet, Valencia retains an unpretentious if tangibly charged air. With low-cost airlines bussing in visitors by the planeload, tourism has also hit the city in a big way, and the ubiquitous English breakfast has become a fixture on the blackboards of Plaza de la Reina.

Always an important city, Valencia was fought over for the agricultural wealth of its surrounding *huerta*. After Romans and Visigoths, it was occupied by the Moors for over four centuries with only a brief interruption (1094–1101) when **El Cid** recaptured it. He died here in 1099, but his body, propped on a horse and led out through the gates, was still enough to cause the Moorish armies – previously encouraged by news of his death – to flee in terror. It wasn't until 1238 that Jaime I of Aragón permanently wrested Valencia back. It has remained one of Spain's largest and richest cities ever since.

The city has long boasted some of the best **nightlife** to be found in mainland Spain. *Vivir Sin Dormir* (Live Without Sleep) is the name of one of its bars, and it could be taken as a Valencian mantra. The city is alive with noise and colour throughout the year, with explosions of gunpowder, fireworks and festivities punctuating the calendar. Valencia's **fiestas** are some of the most riotous in Spain and the best is *Las Fallas*, March 12–19 (see *Fiestas* colour section), which culminates in a massive bonfire where all the processional floats are burned.

Arrival and information

Arriving by train at Valencia's beautifully tiled **Estación del Nord**, you're close to the town centre; walk north along Avenida Marqués de Sotelo to the Plaza del Ayuntamiento, the central square. The **bus station** is some way out on the north side of the river; take local bus #8 or #79 or the metro to Turia, or allow a half hour if you decide to walk. The **airport** is 8km out of town, and served by metro lines #1 & #3; the most convenient stop for the centre is Colón. Alternatively, a taxi will set you back around €14. The **Balearic ferry terminal** connects with Plaza del Ayuntamiento via bus #4 and with the train station via the #19.

Most of Valencia's sights are centrally located and can be reached on foot, while there are efficient **public transport** links to the outlying sights (including the Ciudad de las Artes y Ciencias) and the beaches. Buses cost €1.20 per journey (a ten-journey Bono-Bus pass costs €5.20), trams and the metro €1.30 (for inner zone A; more info on the metro system at ⓦ www.metrovalencia.com). If you

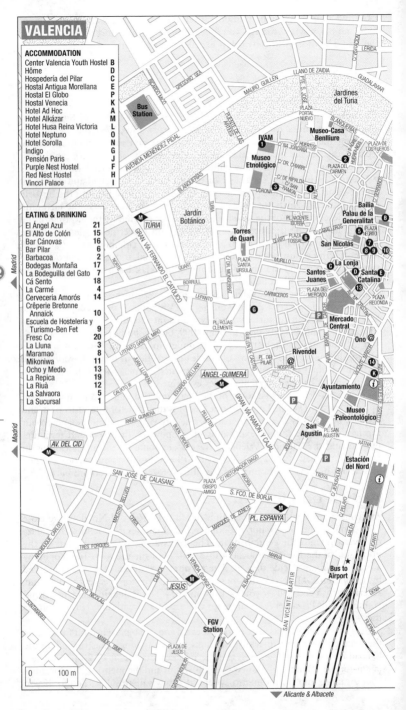

VALENCIA

ACCOMMODATION

Center Valencia Youth Hostel	B
Hôme	D
Hospedería del Pilar	C
Hostal Antigua Morellana	E
Hostal El Globo	P
Hostal Venecia	K
Hotel Ad Hoc	A
Hotel Alkázar	M
Hotel Husa Reina Victoria	L
Hotel Neptuno	O
Hotel Sorolla	N
Indigo	G
Pensión Paris	J
Purple Nest Hostel	F
Red Nest Hostel	H
Vincci Palace	I

EATING & DRINKING

El Ángel Azul	21
El Alto de Colón	15
Bar Cánovas	16
Bar Pilar	6
Barbacoa	2
Bodegas Montaña	17
La Bodeguilla del Gato	7
Cá Sento	18
La Carmé	4
Cerveceria Amorós	14
Crêperie Bretonne Annaick	10
Escuela de Hostelería y Turismo-Ben Fet	9
Fresc Co	20
La Lluna	3
Maramao	8
Mikoniwa	11
Ocho y Medio	13
La Repica	19
La Riuà	12
La Salvaora	5
La Sucursal	1

Madrid

Madrid

Alicante & Albacete

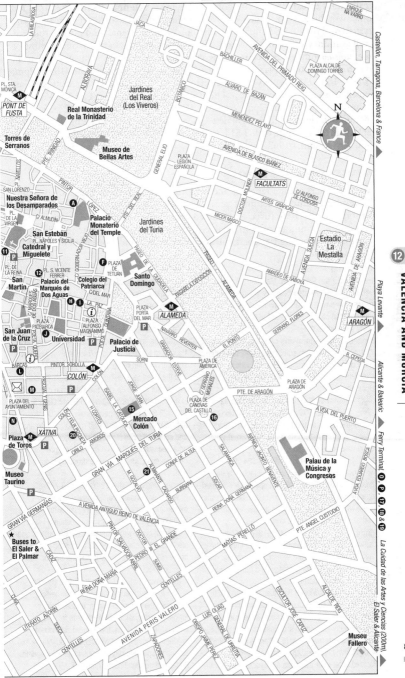

N

LA MILAGROSA

PL. STA MÓNICA

PONT DE FUSTA

ALBORAYA

JACA

BACHILLER

AVENIDA DEL PRIMADO REIG

PLAZA ALCALDÉ DOMINGO TORRES

ENRIQUE NA VARRO

Jardines del Real (Los Viveros)

BOTÁNICO

ÁLVARO DE BAZÁN

MENÉNDEZ PELAYO

Real Monasterio de la Trinidad

Torres de Serranos

PTE. TRINIDAD

GENERAL ELIO

Museo de Bellas Artes

PINTOR

AVENIDA DE BLASCO IBÁÑEZ

PLAZA LEGIÓN ESPAÑOLA

PL. SAN LORENZO

LÓPEZ

C/ ALMUDIN

PTE. DEL REAL

FACULTATS

C/ALFONSO DE CÓRDOBA

ARTES GRÁFICAS

DOCTOR MOLINER

Nuestra Señora de los Desamparados

PL. DE LA VIRGEN

Palacio Monaterio del Temple

Jardines del Turia

MICER MASCÓ

San Esteban

PL. NÁPOLES Y SICILIA

Catedral y Miguelete

GOBERNADOR VIEJO

PASEO DE LA CIUDADELA

PLAZA DE TETUÁN

Estadio La Mestalla

PL. DE LA REINA

PL. S. VICENTE FERRER

Santo Domingo

PASARELA EXPOSICIÓN

AVENIDA SUECA

AMADEO DE SABOYA

AVENIDA DE ARAGÓN

San Martín

Palacio del Marqués de Dos Aguas

Colegio del Patriarca

C/DEL MAR

LA PAZ

PLAZA PORTA DEL MAR

ALAMEDA

PASEO DE LA ALAMEDA

SERRANO FLORES

ARAGÓN

San Juan de la Cruz

PLAZA PATRIARCA

Universidad

PLAZA ALFONSO MAGNÁNIMO

Palacio de Justicia

NAVARRO REVERTER

EL PONTÓ

R. CEPEDA

BARCAS

PINTOR SOROLLA

COLÓN

SORNI

GRABADOR ESTEVE

PLAZA DE AMÉRICA

PLAZA DE ARAGÓN

PASTOR Y FORNS

COLÓN

PLAZA DEL AYUNTAMIENTO

JORGE JUAN

C/ SERRANO MORALES

PLAZA DE CÁNOVAS DEL CASTILLO

PTE. DE ARAGÓN

AVDA. DEL PUERTO

XATIVA

ISABEL LA CATÓLICA

Mercado Colón

Plaza de Toros

FÉLIX VICENTE

AMOROS

CIRILO

TORRES

SALAMANCA

Museo Taurino

GRAN VÍA MARQUÉS DEL TURIA

M. GODÍA

ALMIRANTE CADARSO

CONDE DE ALTEA

BURRIANA

ÓSCAR

REINA DOÑA GERMANA

Palau de la Música y Congresos

A VENIDA ANTIGUO REINO DE VALENCIA

GRAN VÍA GERMANÍAS

PINTOR SALVADOR ABRIL

DOCTOR PEDRO III EL GRANDE

SUECA

MATIAS PERELLÓ

PTE. ÁNGEL CUSTODIO

AVDA. JACINTO BENAVENTE

CADIZ

★ **Buses to El Saler & El Palmar**

REINA DOÑA MARÍA

CIBA

LITERATO AZORÍN

SUECA

CENTELLES

CENTELLES

AVENIDA PERIS VALERO

ZAPADORES

LUIS OLIAG

OBISPO JAIME PÉREZ

ESCULTOR JOSÉ CAPUZ

AV. GENERAL URRUTIA

ALCALDE REIG

ESCULTOR JOSÉ CAPUZ

Museu Fallero

Alicante & Cartagena

Castellón, Tarragona, Barcelona & France   Playa Levante   Alicante & Balearic   Ferry Terminal, ⓞ ⓟ ⑰ ⑱ & ⑲   La Cuidad de las Artes y Ciencias (200m), El Saler & Alicante

12   VALENCIA AND MURCIA

839

really want to explore the city, consider buying a **Valencia Card** (€8/14/18 for one/two/three days), which gives you unlimited access to the entire transport system and discounted entry to many museums, bike rental and guided tours, as well as money off your bill at bars and restaurants – you can buy one at most of the *turismo* offices, at major hotels and newspaper kiosks. The city's hi-tech, flagship **turismo**, at Plaza de la Reina 19 (Mon–Sat 9am–7pm, Sun 10am–2pm; ☎963 153 931, ⓦwww.turisvalencia.es), has English-speaking staff and an excellent stock of information. There are also branches at c/Paz 48 (Mon–Fri 9am–7pm, Sat 10am–2pm & Sun 11am–2pm; ☎963 986 422, ⓦwww .comunitatvalenciana.com), c/Poeta Querol (Mon–Fri 9.30am–7pm, Sat 10am–2pm, Sun 11am–2pm; ☎963 514 907) and the train station (Mon–Sat 9am–7pm, Sun 10am–2pm; ☎963 528 573).

Accommodation

Valencia offers a huge range of **accommodation**, from historical hotels to hip hostels and sunny beachfront properties. The city centre, between the train station and the Río Turia, is sprinkled with budget hotels and hostels, while you'll find a number of comfortable spots overlooking the beaches. There are **campsites** all along the coast, but none less than 18km from the city.

Hotels

Hospedería del Pilar Plaza Mercado 19 ☎963 916 600. A well-located *hostal* with large, airy rooms, some with private shower, and some more modern than others. Rooms at the front can be noisy. ❶, with bath ❷

Hostal Antigua Morellana c/En Bou 2 ☎963 915 773, ⓦwww.hostalam.com. A tastefully renovated hotel close to the Barrio del Carmen, whose quiet, excellent-value rooms exude a country-living air. Book ahead. ❸

🏃 **Hostal El Globo** Paseo de Neptuno 42–44 ☎963 727 777, ⓦwww.hostalelglobo.com. One of the freshest and friendliest beach options. Rooms are funkily furnished and have great views. Good value in low season. ❹–❺

Hostal Venecia c/En Llop 5 ☎963 524 267, ⓦwww.hotelvenecia.com. Don't be fooled by the *hostal* tag; this is an upmarket, impeccably managed operation in the running for three stars. Some rooms come with views over the Plaza del Ayuntamiento, and all are calm, clean and comfy. Wi-fi. ❹–❺

Hotel Ad Hoc c/Boix 4 ☎963 919 140, ⓦwww .adhochoteles.com. Valencia's first boutique hotel is suitably comfortable and stylish, with exposed brick walls and textile wall-hangings, in a building with plenty of period character. ❺

Hotel Alkázar c/Mosén Femades 11 ☎963 529 575, ⓦwww.hotel-alkazar.es. It doesn't have the most modern decor, but this hotel is dependable and centrally located on a pedestrianized street. ❹

Hotel Husa Reina Victoria c/Barcas 4 ☎963 520 487, ⓦwww.husa.es. An upmarket, centrally located hotel near the Plaza del Ayuntamiento with faux-Victorian decor and period furniture. Off-season and weekend discounts available according to occupancy levels. ❻–❼

Hotel Neptuno Paseo de Neptuno 2 ☎963 567 777, ⓦwww.hotelneptunovalencia.com. Lovely, light-flooded hotel with a spare, modern look: white furnishings, a glass elevator, gleaming hardwood floors and a beach-facing terrace strewn with low sofas and plump red pillows – a prime spot to ease into the Valencia evening. The top-notch *Tridente Restaurant* serves up creative Valencian cuisine. ❺

Hotel Sorolla Centro Convento Santa Clara 5 ☎963 523 392, ⓦwww.hotelsorolla.com. Comfortable, slightly Asian-influenced rooms (all with a/c and some with sun terraces) and a good location on a pedestrianized street make this a great deal on weekends, when the price drops by more than half. ❹–❺

Pensión Paris c/Salvá 12 ☎963 526 766, ⓦwww.pensionparis.com. Welcoming, family-owned place where the rooms (some with en-suite bathrooms, some with shower and shared bathroom) come with vintage ceilings, shutters and plenty of character, as well as tightly focused views of the old university. ❶, with shower and/or bathroom ❷

🏃 **Vincci Palace** La Paz 42 ☎962 062 377, ⓦwww.vinccihoteles.com. Well-heeled hotel with the history to match: housed in a former *palacete*, with a lovely facade fronted by wrought-iron balconies, that offered safe lodging to intellectuals during the Civil War. Comfortable rooms, soft beds, sparkling bathrooms and all the amenities. Prices can dip significantly midweek. ❻

Hostels

Center Valencia Youth Hostel c/Samaniego 18 ☎963 914 915, ⓦwww.center-valencia.com. Just about as central as you can get, this amiable, clean, pale-yellow hostel sits in bustling Barrio del Carmen, just a stumble away from a slew of bars and cafés. Roof terrace and free wi-fi/internet; breakfast included. Dorm €18.50–22, over 25 €20.50–22.

Hôme Youth Hostel & Hôme Backpackers c/La Lonja 4 ☎963 916 229 & Plaza Vicente Iborra ☎963 913 797, ⓦwww.likeathome.net. These stylish backpacker hostels are located in the heart of the historic quarter and feature retro-chic furnishings and clean dorms, plus private rooms. Full kitchen, laundry and internet facilities, bike rental and a friendly atmosphere. Dorm €24 (€14–22 at Plaza Vicente Iborra branch), doubles ❸

Indigo c/Guillem de Castro 64 ☎963 153 988, ⓦwww.indigohostel.com. Funky and vivacious, this *hostal* has lime-green walls and minimalist dorms,

as well as all the usual facilities. Price includes free breakfast and internet. Dorm €16–19, doubles ❷

Red Nest & Purple Nest hostels c/de la Paz 36 ☎963 427 168 & Plaza Tetuan 5 ☎963 532 561, ⓦwww.nesthostelsvalencia.com. Bright, cheery, sister backpacker hostels with well-maintained dorms and doubles, and a youthful energy – pub-crawls with new-found friends seem to be a nightly norm. Free wi-fi with your own computer; otherwise, internet €1/hr. *Purple Nest* has its own bar, which makes for a particularly social atmosphere. Dorm €15–21 (weekend €18–23), doubles ❸

Campsite

Devesa Gardens Nazaret-Oliva ☎961 611 136, ⓦwww.devesagardens.com. Eighteen kilometres out, near El Saler beach and La Albufera; take the hourly bus from the junction of Gran Vía and c/Sueca to El Saler-Perelló. Spacious grounds surrounded by pine forest, and with great amenities, including a swimming pool and tennis courts.

The City

The most atmospheric area to explore is undoubtedly the maze-like streets of the **Barrio del Carmen** (in Valenciano "de Carmé"), roughly the area north of the Mercado Central to the Río Turia, extending up to the Torres de Serranos and west to the Torres de Quart. This once-neglected quarter of the city continues to undergo regeneration, as buildings are renovated and stylish cafés open up next to crumbling townhouses, all of which makes for an incredibly vibrant, alternative neighbourhood. The **city walls**, which, judging from the two surviving gates, must have been magnificent, were pulled down in 1871 to make way for a ring road, and the beautiful church of **Santo Domingo**, in Plaza de Tetuan, has been converted into a barracks – it was from here that General Milans del Bosch ordered his tanks onto the streets during the abortive coup of 1981. This incident, however, isn't representative of the city's political inclination, which has traditionally been to the left – Valencia was the seat of the Republican government during the Civil War after it fled Madrid, and was the last city to fall to Franco.

The oldest part of the city is almost entirely encircled by a great loop of the **Río Turia**, which is now a landscaped **riverbed park**. In 1956, after serious flooding damaged much of the old town, the river was diverted. The ancient stone bridges remain, but the riverbed now houses cycle ways, footpaths and football pitches, as well as the astonishing **Ciudad de las Artes y Ciencias**, Europe's largest cultural complex and the most ambitious construction project the city has ever undertaken.

Valencia's main beach is the **Playa de la Malvarrosa** (see p.849) to the east of the city centre, which becomes Playa de las Arenas at its southern end.

Plaza del Ayuntamiento and around

Within the **Plaza del Ayuntamiento** is a central square lined with flower stalls, and an impressive floodlit fountain. The *ayuntamiento* houses the **Museo Histórico Municipal** (Mon–Fri 9am–2pm; €2), whose library has an impressive eighteenth-century map of Valencia showing the city walls intact.

The distinctive feature of Valencian architecture is its wealth of elaborate Baroque facades – you'll see them on almost every old building in town, but none so extraordinary or rich as the **Palacio del Marqués de Dos Aguas**. Hipólito Rovira, who designed its amazing alabaster doorway, died insane in 1740, which should come as no surprise to anyone who sees it. Inside is the **Museo Nacional de Cerámica** (Tues–Sat 10am–2pm & 4–8pm, Sun 10am–2pm; €2.40, free Sat pm & Sun), with a vast collection of ceramics from all over Spain, and particularly Valencia, itself a major ceramics centre, largely owing to the size of its *morisco* population. Apart from an impressive display of *azulejos*, the collection contains some stunning plates with gold and copper varnishes (*reflejos*) and a trio of evocatively ornate eighteenth-century carriages. In the same decorative vein as the *palacio* is the church of **San Juan de la Cruz** (or San Andrés) next door, whose facade is currently being restored.

Nearby to the northeast, in the Plaza Patriarca, is the Neoclassical former **Universidad**, with lovely cloisters where free classical concerts are held throughout July, and the beautiful Renaissance **Colegio del Patriarca**, where the small **art museum** (daily 11am–1.30pm; €1.20) includes excellent works by El Greco, Morales and Ribalta. Another Ribalta, *The Last Supper*, hangs above the altar in the college's **chapel**; in the middle of the *Miserere* service (Fri 10am), it's whisked aside to reveal a series of curtains. The last of these, drawn at the climactic moment, conceals a giant illuminated crucifix. The whole performance is amazingly dramatic, and typical of the aura of miracle and mystery that the Spanish Church still cultivates. The university **library** contains the first book printed in Spain, *Les Trobes*, in 1474.

The Catedral and around

Northwest from the university is the café-rich **Plaza de la Reina**, which is overlooked by the florid spire of the church of Santa Catalina and octagonal tower of Valencia's **Catedral** (Mon–Fri 10am–6.30pm, Sat 10am–5.30pm, Sun 2–5.30pm; €3). The fee covers the museum (see below) and an audioguide in a language of your choice, but if you'd rather not pay, you still have the option of attending Mass outside tourist hours. The cathedral, founded in the thirteenth century, embraces an eclectic combination of architectural styles, with the lavishly ornate Baroque main entrance leading to a largely Gothic-built interior. It's an exhausting climb up the cathedral tower, known as the **Miguelete** (daily 10am–7.30pm; €2), but the spectacular views of the city and its many blue-domed churches more than compensate.

An increasing number of visitors, however, come for the cathedral's most celebrated religious icon: a gold and agate chalice (the Santo Cáliz), said to be the one used by Christ at the Last Supper – the **Holy Grail** itself, and no mean asset in an era of post-*Da Vinci Code* fever. It's certainly old and, hidden away throughout the Dark Ages in a monastery in northern Aragón, it really did inspire many of the legends associated with the Grail. Other treasures include the two Goya paintings of the San Francisco chapel, one of which depicts an exorcism (the corpse was originally naked, but after Goya's death a sheet was painted over it). The cathedral's **museum** contains more paintings and also a 2300-kilo tabernacle made from gold, silver and jewels donated by the Valencian people. Above the structure's crossing, the cathedral's fourteenth-century lantern is another fine feature, as are its soaring windows glazed with thin sheets of alabaster to let in the Valencian light.

Leaving the cathedral through the Puerta de los Apóstoles, you enter the **Plaza de la Virgen**. Here, close to the doorway, the Tribunal de las Aguas, the black-clad regulatory body of Valencia's water users, meets at noon every

▲ Plaza de la Virgen

Thursday to judge grievances about the irrigation system of the *huertas*. The practice dates back to Moorish times, and Blasco Ibáñez (1867–1928) describes their workings in detail in his novel *La Barraca*, which is about peasant life in the Valencian *huerta* and remains the best guide to the life of the region at that time.

Two footbridges allow the clergy (only) to go straight from the cathedral into the archbishop's palace and on to the domed basilica of **Nuestra Señora de los Desamparados** (daily 7am–2pm & 4.30–9pm; free), also on the Plaza de la Virgen, where thousands of candles constantly burn in front of the image of the Virgin, patron of Valencia.

From the plaza, c/Caballeros leads to the **Palau de la Generalitat**, which dates from the fifteenth century and today is the seat of the Valencian autonomous government. Security is understandably tight, however, and to see inside you'll need to make an appointment (☎963 863 461; English-speaking guide available). It's worth the effort to see the beautifully painted ceilings and frescoes depicting a meeting of the assembly (1592) in the Salón Dorado, and the tiled Salón de Cortes.

La Lonja and the markets

If you tire of Baroque excesses, you could head for the wonderfully sombre interior of the Gothic **La Lonja** (also known as Lonja de la Seda, or the Silk Exchange; Tues–Sat 10am–2pm & 4.30–8.30pm, Sun 10am–3pm; free; at weekends, free hourly guided tours in English), in the Plaza del Mercado. The main focus of this UNESCO-listed building is its superb main hall, with an elegant rib-vaulted ceiling supported by slender, spiralling columns; the wooden trading tables are now used on Sundays by coin and stamp collectors.

Opposite is the enormous **Mercado Central**, a *modernista* iron, girder and glass structure built in 1928, embellished with a collage of tiles and mosaics, and crowned with swordfish and parrot weather vanes. It's one of the biggest markets in Europe – fitting for *huerta* country – with almost a thousand stalls selling fruit and vegetables, meat and seafood, hard-to-find herbs and health foods. It winds down by around 2pm, and is closed all day on Sundays.

About 1km to the southeast, Valencia's other market, the renovated **Mercado Colón** on c/Cirilo Amoros, is an even more impressive *modernista* building. Its open-sided rectangular design loosely resembles a church, with slim wrought-iron columns supporting a steep pitched roof, and monumental arched facades at either end. However, it's the building's detail that's really outstanding, combining two-tone brickwork with broken tile mosaic chimneys, features that reveal the influence of *modernista* architect Antoni Gaudí – indeed, the market's architect, Francisco Mora, was a close personal friend of the Catalan genius. The Mercado Colón now houses colourful flower stalls, a bookstore, upmarket cafés and the lovely restaurant *El Alto de Colón*, with a vaulted ceiling of a Valencian mosaic, and large windows that offer glimpses of the market's eye-catching *modernista* ironwork.

Along the Jardínes del Turia

The **Museu de Belles Artes** (Tues–Sun 10am–8pm; free), on the far side of the river, has one of the best general collections in Spain, with works by Bosch, El Greco, Goya, Velázquez, Ribera and Ribalta, as well as quantities of modern Valencian art. The museum takes up the southwest corner of the **Jardines del Real** (also called Los Viveros). The gardens – the largest of Valencia's parks – host various events during the summer: a book fair in May and a music fair in July with open-air concerts.

As you head back into town, don't miss the fourteenth-century **Torres Serranos** (Tues–Sat 10am–2pm & 4.30–8.30pm, Sun 10am–3pm; €2, free Sun), an impressive gateway defending the entrance to town across the Río Turia, with panoramic views from the top. The other gateway, guarding the western approach, is the **Torres de Quart**, a simpler structure but equally awesome in scale, that was once a women's prison.

A couple of minutes' walk east of here is the **Instituto Valenciano de Arte Moderno** or **IVAM** (Tues–Sun 10am–8pm; €2, free Sun), whose main gallery at c/Guillém de Castro 118 has a permanent display of works by sculptor Julio González, as well as many excellent temporary exhibitions by mainly Spanish contemporary artists. It also has a smaller gallery near Plaza del Carmen at c/Museu 2 (opening dependent on exhibition; free), currently devoted to temporary shows. In keeping with other known modern-art museums, IVAM also features an excellent restaurant *La Sucursal* (see p.847).

To gain some insight into Valencia's Fiesta de las Fallas (see *Fiestas* colour section), head for the **Museu Fallero**, Plaza de Monteolivete (Tues–Sat 10am–2pm & 4.30–8.30pm, Sun 10am–3pm; €2), near the riverbed park (bus #95 from Torres de Serrano). Here you'll find a fascinating array of *ninots* that have been voted the best of their year, and consequently saved from the flames. If you can't get enough of these giants, the **Museo del Gremio de Artistas Falleros**, Avda. San José Artesano 17 (Mon–Fri 10am–2pm & 4–7pm, Sat 10am–1.30pm; €1.80), houses the ones-that-got-away by permission of the Guild of Fallas Artists, as well as a photographic exhibition. Take bus #12 from c/Cerdan de Tallada, near the Palacio de Justicia.

La Ciudad de las Artes y las Ciencias

More than any other project, the breathtaking **Ciudad de las Artes y las Ciencias** (City of Arts and Sciences; ☎902 100 031, ⊛www.cac.es), still rising from the riverbed, symbolizes the autonomous government's vision for Valencia and its quest to establish the city as a prime tourist destination. The giant complex consisting of four futuristic edifices designed mainly by Valencian architect Santiago Calatrava, and the recent completion of the iconic pistachio-nut-shaped **Palacio de las Artes** has confirmed it as Europe's largest cultural centre.

The architecture itself is simply stunning. Even if you only have a day or two in the city, it's well worth the effort getting here to take in the eye-catching buildings surrounded by huge, shallow pools. Calatrava's designs adopt an organic form, his technical and engineering brilliance providing the basis for his pioneering concrete, steel and glass creations. However, despite near universal acclaim for its architecture, the complex has not completely escaped criticism. Some feel that the vast cost of constructing the complex should have been used to tackle the city's pressing social issues, while others have been less than overwhelmed by some of the content inside the Ciudad's startling structures.

To decide for yourself, start in the **Hemisfèric** (normally 10am–7pm; €7.50), arguably the most astonishing building of the lot: a striking eye-shaped concrete structure – complete with lashes, and an eyeball that forms a huge concave screen used to project IMAX movies. Unfortunately, the documentary films are pretty disappointing, and spoiled by gimmicky laser effects. Next door, the colossal **Museo de las Ciencias** (Science Museum; daily 10am–7pm, July to mid-Sept until 9pm; €7.50), whose protruding supports make the building resemble a giant sun-bleached carcass, is crammed with interactive exhibits about science, sport and the human body that are sure to appeal to children. Parallel to these two buildings unfolds the **Umbracle**, a series of eighteen-metre-high arches towering over a landscaped walkway shaded with vegetation from throughout the region, including palms, honeysuckle, bougainvillea and, of course, orange trees.

Some 500m to the south, the **Parque Oceanográfico** (mid-June to mid-July & Sept 1–15 daily 10am–8pm; mid-July to Aug daily 10am–midnight; rest of year Mon–Fri & Sun 10am–6pm, Sat 10am–8pm; €23.30), designed by Félix Candela, is one of the world's largest aquariums. It's divided into ten zones, with beluga whales in the arctic area, Japanese spider crabs in the temperate zone, and a kaleidoscopic collection of reef fish, sharks and turtles in the seventy-metre tunnel that forms the tropical zone. If you're looking to dine in style while touring the complex, here's the place to do it: eat with the fishes at *Submarino* (reservations required: ℡961/975 565; mains €25–35), which offers eclectic fusion fare – think garlic foam atop the finest *fruit de la mer* – in a sleek, under-water space with fish darting past your table.

The final section of the centre is the majestic **Palacio de las Artes** (box office Mon–Fri 10am–6pm; closed Aug 4–24, but phone lines open all year; ℡902 202 383, ⓦwww.lesarts.com), a high-tech performing arts palace, with renowned musical director Lorin Maazel at the helm. Stages and halls of varying sizes – all with splendid acoustics – host ballet, opera and classical-music concerts, among others. There are performances throughout the year, and it's well worth snagging a ticket to see one.

There are several discounted ticket options – a combined **entrance** to all three attractions is €30.60. While this is valid for one, two or three (not necessarily consecutive) days, you'll need at least one full day to see everything. The main transport link to the Ciudad is by **bus**; take #35 (a special tourist route) from Avenida Marqués de Sotelo, just south of the Plaza del Ayuntamiento. If you're coming straight from the bus station, take #95 (20min). You can also catch #95 at the Torres de Serrano. The closest **metro** stop is Alameda (20min walk).

Bioparc

If you're travelling with kids, the city's new **Bioparc** (daily: summer 10am–9pm; rest of year until 6/9pm; €20, under-12 €15; ☎902 250 340, ⓦwww.bioparcvalencia.es), an "immersion" open-air zoo west of the city centre, on Avenida Pío Baroja, might entice. As far as zoos go, the well-maintained Bioparc tries to be a different sort of animal. The creators have made serious attempts to be as eco-aware and animal-friendly as possible, with recreated African savanna and Malagasy landscapes that are home to roaming rhinos, giraffes, antelopes, gorillas, leopards, elephants and lions. To get there, you can take **metro** lines #3 and #5 to Nou d'Octubre (10min walk), or various **buses** from different points in the city, including #7, #17, #29 and #95.

Eating

As befits Spain's third-largest city, the cuisine scene is wonderfully varied and suits all budgets. For **tapas** and cheap eats, head to the area around the Mercado Central, where there are plenty of places offering set meals for under €15; Barrio del Carmen is also sprinkled with lively tapas bars. The multi-ethnic Ruzafa neighbourhood, just south of the centre, is becoming increasingly popular for inexpensive international fare. While Valencia is the home of **paella**, the finest places to eat it are, in fact, out of town, in Perellonet or El Palmar (see p.851), or along the city beach – Paseo Neptuno is lined with small hotels, all with their own paella and *marisco* restaurants.

El Alto de Colón Inside Mercado Colón ☎963 530 900. Elegant, vaulted restaurant with a menu that skews high-end Mediterranean with innovative flourishes, such as sticky rice heaped with fresh shellfish.

El Ángel Azul c/Conde Altea 33 ☎963 745 656. A favourite haunt of the city's chattering classes, *The Blue Angel* excels in Spanish and Mediterranean cuisine with gourmet twists. Mains come in at around €15–19, and include everything from fresh fish and hearty meats to an aromatic Arabic *pastela*, made with moist chicken with cinnamon, pine nuts, almonds and honey; the wine list is also a talking point. Closed Mon eve, Sun & part of Aug.

Bar Pilar On the corner of c/Moro Zeit 13, just off Plaza del Esparto ☎963 910 497. This boisterous joint, which has been around since 1917, gets packed on most nights, with the beer-happy crowd spilling out onto the pavement. The speciality is *clochinas* (mussels), which you can slurp at the bar, then toss the shells into buckets on the floor.

Barbacoa Plaza del Carmen 6 ☎963 922 448. Veteran meatery in the heart of Barrio del Carmen. The steaks are sizzled where you sit, and demand is usually such that reservation is recommended at weekends.

Bodegas Montaña c/José Benlliure 69 ☎963 672 314. In the old fishermen's quarter of Cabañal

Horchata

Valencia is known for its **horchata** – a drink made from *chufas* (tiger nuts) served either liquid or *granizada* (slightly frozen). It is accompanied by *fartons* (long, thin cakes). Legend has it that the name "horchata" was coined by Jaume I, shortly after he conquered Valencia. He was admiring the *huerta* one hot afternoon, and an Arab girl offered him a drink so refreshing that he exclaimed, "*Aixó es or, xata*" (this is gold, girl).

There are **horchaterías** all over the city: the two oldest are *El Siglo* and *Santa Catalina*, on the southwest corner of Plaza de la Reina; the most centrally located are on Plaza San Lorenzo, just in from the Torres de Serranos, while the most renowned is *Daniel*, Avda. de la Horchata 41 (☎961 858 866; ⓜPalmaret; closed mid-Dec to Feb), where you can sit on the terrace and escape from the summer heat of the city. Traditionally, however, the best *horchata* comes from **Alboraya**, formerly a village in the Valencian suburbs, now absorbed into the city – take bus #70 or metro line #3.

sits this vintage, cheery tapas bar – one of the oldest (and best) in the city. Bodegas Montaña used to supply wine to the merchant ships, and still features one of the most impressive wine cellars in the city. Graze on a wonderful array of tapas from anchovies and *michirones* (cooked fava beans) to cod croquettes, which get a nutty kick from pinenuts. Closed Sun dinner & second half of Aug.

La Bodeguilla del Gato c/Catalans 10, ☏ 963 918 235. Lively tapas bar with exposed brick-and-mustard walls hung with bullfighting posters. Munch on *pulpo a la Gallega*, octopus dusted with paprika, and crisp flamen-quines, croquettes of pork, ham and cheese.

Ca' Sento c/Méndez Núñez 17, west of the centre, near the port ☏ 963 301 775. Tucked away in a low-key, portside neighbourhood, *Ca' Sento*'s petite, discreet appearance – just nine tables – belies the creative prowess going on in the kitchen. The menu hinges on the freshest *frutas del mar*, which innovative chef Raúl Aleixandre, a protégé of Catalan Ferrán Adrià, wisely allows to shine on their own merit, teasing out their natural, sea-soaked flavours with unique accompaniments: raw oysters arrive with a dollop of lime foam, while tuna belly quivers under a spray of soy sauce. Mains around €25–30. ⓂMarítim-Serrería, then 15min walk. Closed Mon, Sun & part of Aug. Reservations essential.

La Carmé c/Sogueros 2 ☏ 963 922 532. Chande-liers sparkle, an old piano sits in the corner and mosaic tiles adorn the bar at this atmospheric restaurant, with a cosmopolitan menu that ranges from succulent duck to Hungarian goulash. Closed Sun & part of Aug. Usually open for dinner only.

Crêperie Bretonne Annaick c/Bordadores 4 ☏ 963 153 524. At least one old London bus is still doing the rounds, (literally) propping up the bar in this humorously conceived Catalan chain. Fun interior design, professional crepes and *cañas* with genuine fizz makes this perfect for an after-cathedral lunch. Closed Mon.

Fresc Co c/Félix Pizcueta 6, also at c/Salamanca 6. It may have a groaning pun for a name but this place packs in a true cross section of city society. They come for the all-you-can-eat, all-day buffet (€8.50 weekday lunch, €9.95 after 6pm and at weekends) filling up on fresh, healthy Valencian produce.

La Lluna c/San Ramón 23 ☏ 963 922 146. Inexpensive, friendly and unpretentious vegetarian restaurant right in the heart of the Barrio del Carmen with a bargain-priced *menú*. Closed Sun, Aug & Easter.

Maramao c/Correjería 37 ☏ 963 923 174. Basement restaurant with a modish, gallery feel, original stonework and a tile-topped zinc bar. Staff, and most of the ingredients, are passionately Italian, the pasta's home-made and the lunch *menú* only €10.5.

Ocho y Medio Plaza Lope de Vega 5 ☏ 963 922 022. Named after the Fellini film, this bi-level restaurant, with dusky peach walls, blonde-wood floors and views of the Santa Catalina church, excels at innovative French-tinged Mediterranean fare, from their speciality, rich foie gras, to grilled squid with black risotto. Closed Sat lunch & Sun.

La Pepica Paseo Neptuno 6 ☏ 963 710 366. Founded in 1898, this inviting, spacious paella restaurant has hosted plenty of rich and famous, from Hemingway and Orson Welles to swaggering bullfighters and the Spanish royal family. Settle in on the sun-speckled terrace and tuck into fresh fish and seafood and aromatic paellas. Closed Sun dinner & second half of Nov.

La Salvaora c/Calatrava 19 ☏ 963 921 484. This slender Andalucian restaurant, with high, dark-wood tables and white-marble floors, pays homage to flamenco singers and stars via black-and-white photos along the walls; creative fare from around Spain includes tripe tossed with red peppers and steak with a port reduction. Closed Mon. The owners also run *La Bulería* (c/Obispo Jaime Pérez 24, west of the Ciudad de las Artes y las Ciencias) where you can watch full-fledged flamenco shows over dinner (Thurs–Sun); inquire at *La Salvaora* for more information.

La Sucursal c/Guillém de Castro 118 ☏ 963 746 665. Valencia's IVAM features a superb restaurant that matches (if not sometimes trumps) the art within. The elegant, spare *La Sucursal* features artisanal cuisine with a twist, from saffron-scented rice studded with lobster to a cauliflower mousse. Mains are €21–35. Closed Sat lunch, Sun, part of Aug & Easter.

Bars and clubs

The heady days of *La Ruta del Bacalao* (when people drove hundreds of kilome-tres to party in Valencia's out-of-town warehouses) may be long gone, but Valencia still takes its **nightlife** seriously. The **Barrio del Carmen** is one of the liveliest areas at night, especially around c/Caballeros, with scores of small cafés, music-bars and restaurants. The whole area between Plaza de la Reina,

Plaza Santa Ursula and Plaza Portal Nueva is heaving at the weekend. Calle Juan Llorenç, west of the city centre, is another popular area to bar- and club-hop, with lively Latin and salsa-style clubs. Across the River Turia, near the **university**, particularly on and around c/Blasco Ibáñez, and just north, around Plaza Benicamlet, you'll find a more studenty, alternative-music-style nightlife, especially during the school year. In **summer**, the bars lining the **Malvarrosa beach** are the places to be.

To get a grip on what's going on, pick up *24–7 Valencia* or *Hello Valencia*, free monthly English-language listings guides, which you can find at various city-centre bars, including *Finnegan's* on Plaza de la Reina. The websites Ⓦ www.thisisvalencia.com and Ⓦ www.valenciavalencia.com both offer updated overviews of Valencia nightlife and restaurants. For a local, Spanish-language lowdown on the club scene, check out *A Little Beat* magazine (Ⓦ www.alittlebeat.com) available free in boutiques and trendier bars. Note that the big nightclubs are generally open Thursday to Saturday, and usually get going after midnight.

Barrio del Carmen

Bolsería Café Bolsería 41. Sleek nightspot that can sometimes take itself too seriously. That said, it's a comfortably swish way to enjoy the Valencia night, with potent cocktails, a cool house and pop soundtrack, and a more mature crowd.

Cafe de Madrid c/de la Abadía de San Martín 10. This two-floor Valencian haunt is considered the birthplace of *Agua de Valencia* – the classic Valencian *combinado* (cocktail), made with orange juice, cava and vodka and served by the jug – and, as you might expect, the bartenders are true connoisseurs at making the fruity cocktail. The welcoming bar has managed to maintain a wonderfully old-fashioned air – dark wood, burgundy walls, antique mirrors – while still drawing a buzzy, stylish set until the small hours.

Café de las Horas Conde de Almodóvar 1. Baroque-tinged, gay-friendly bar with a gurgling fountain, tiled floors and a marble bar. Drop in early evening for a romantic glass of wine, or join the crowds later in the night getting tipsy on chilled jugs of *Agua de Valencia*.

Café del Duende c/Túria 62. For an intimate flamenco experience, this tiny, unpretentious bar hosts compelling live performances on Thurs, and occasionally Fri.

🏃 **Cafe del Negrito** and **Cava del Negret** Plaza del Negrito 1 & c/Calatrava 15. These sociable bars sit on one of Valencia's loveliest plazas for an outdoor cocktail. Come evening, a bohemian crowd gathers for conversation and *cervezas al aire libre*.

Café Infanta Plaza Tossal 3. Head inside this amiable spot for moody lighting, dusty chandeliers and yesteryear movie posters; or, park yourself at one of the breezy outdoor tables, and soak up potent cocktails whilst enjoying the *barrio*'s noctural parade of people.

Fox Congo c/Caballeros 35 ☎ 963 925 527. On the Barrio's main strip, this dimly lit, funky club reveals a sexy interior – copper pillars, black banquettes, glowing onyx bar – along with potent cocktails and dance tunes. Gets hopping after 11pm.

Jimmy Glass Jazz Bar c/Baja 28. Authentically smoky, shoebox-shaped jazz club putting on quality live acts for a studenty audience.

Radio City c/Santa Teresa 19. This veteran drinking den hosts poetry, films and live music, with full-on flamenco on Tues.

🏃 **Sant Jaume** c/Caballeros 51. Of the many bars on this main drag, the characterful *Sant Jaume*, set in a small converted pharmacy with aged mirrors and tiles, is one of the most popular, with a great terrace that swells with a nightly crowd.

Across the Río Turia

Black Note Polo y Peirolón 15. Funky club with live soul, reggae and jazz-influenced sounds.

Murray Club Blasco Ibañez 111. Loud, alternative, student-jammed club, with tunes ranging from hip-hop to indie rock to electronica. Thurs–Sun.

El Tornillo Campoamor 42. Bohemian student hangout spinning indie, alternative and left-field electronica. Look for the *tornillo* (screw) that marks the spot outside.

Around town and the beach

Dub Club c/Jesus 91. Slightly out on a southern limb, but if you're looking for more of a funk ambience, this hip, chilled dance spot usually delivers. Thurs–Sun.

The city has a robust **gay scene**, with plenty of bars clustered in the Barrio del Carmen, and especially along c/Quart. In general, though, much of Carmen nightlife is gay-friendly, including amiable cafe-bars such as *Cafe de las Horas* (see opposite). Listings of gay Valencian venues are produced by the **Col·lectiu Lambada de lesbianes, gais, transsexuals i bisexuals**, c/Sant Dionís 8 (℡963 342 191, ⓦwww.lambdavalencia .net), available free at most venues or any of the city's tourist offices. One of the most popular late-night venues is **Venial**, c/Quart 26 (ⓦwww.venialvalencia.com), which has given itself the apt moniker of "The Queen of the Night" – with disco balls, laser shows and pounding music. In summer, it's usually open daily; the rest of the year, it's open weekends, and sometimes during the week – check the website to confirm. The lively club **Deseo 54**, c/Pepita, north of the centre (ⓦwww.deseo54.com; Fri & Sat), sees plenty of revellers decked out in wild outfits (or lack thereof) – think sequins on some nights, shirtless on others.

Latex Dr Montoro 6, just north of Barrio del Carmen, near Avda. Constitución. This hotspot is where the crowds go when the *barrio* bars have closed. Two dance floors, one dominated by electro and house, the other tending towards more eclectic tunes, including hip-hop and reggae. Thurs–Sat, though sometimes longer in summer.

Pacha c/San Vicente 305, south of the city centre. The Valencian branch of the Spanish superclub features booming house tunes and two floors of writhing dancers in party gear. Thurs–Sat.

Vivir Sin Dormir Paseo Neptuno 42. Once a legend, and now a lively pub-club with a long bar and an outdoor terrace, particularly popular with travellers.

Listings

Airlines Iberia c/de la Paz 14 ℡963 520 500, or their telephone information line ℡902 400 500.

Banks Main branches of most banks are around the Plaza del Ayuntamiento or along c/Las Barcas.

Beaches Malvarrosa is pretty clean for a city beach and has an elegant promenade. Catch the tram from Pont de Fusta, or bus #32 runs from the Plaza del Ayuntamiento, supplemented during the summer by buses from various points in the centre; ask at the tourist office. You can also catch the tram to Playa Las Arenas, and then stroll north along the beach to Malvarrosa. Pick up the #5 metro at the central Colón station to Marítim Serrería, and switch to the #6 line to Neptú. El Saler, 10km south of the city, is a more pleasant beach: a long, wide stretch of sand with pine trees behind and a nudist area at its northern end. A bus leaves from the corner of Gran Vía Germanías 27 and c/Sueca and also Plaza Cánovas (May–Sept every 30min; Oct–April hourly; 30min).

Bookstores English-language books are available from the abc International Bookshop on c/Ruzafa or upstairs at FNAC, c/San Vicente.

Car rental Best value is Cuñauto, c/Burriana 51 ℡963 748 561. Otherwise, there's Avis (airport & c/Isabel la Católica 17 ℡963 510 734, ⓦwww .avis.com); Hertz (airport & c/Segorbe 7 ℡963 415 036, ⓦwww.hertz.com); Atesa (airport & Estación

del Nord ℡963 517 145, ⓦwww.atesa.es).

Cinema Original-language films are shown regularly at the subsidized municipal Filmoteca, Plaza del Ayuntamiento, and sometimes also at Albatros Mini-Cines, Plaza Fray Luís Colomer, and Babel, c/Vincente Sancho Tello 10, both of which offer cut-price tickets on Mon nights.

Consulates UK c/Colón 22, 5-H ℡963 520 710; USA c/Dr Romagosa 1, 2-J ℡963 516 973.

Cycling Cycle paths are marked in green. Orange Bikes, c/Santa Teresa 8 ℡963 917 551, ⓦwww .orangebikes.net rents bicycles (€10–15 per day) and also does repairs.

Ferries Information and tickets from Trasmediter-ránea, Muelle de Poniente (℡902 454 645, ⓦwww.trasmediterranea.es), or from any of the half-dozen travel agents on Plaza del Ayuntami-ento. Note that if you are going to the Balearics outside of the summer months, it's cheaper and quicker to go from Denia (see p.862).

Hospital Hospital General, Avda. del Cid, at the Tres Cruces junction ℡961 972 00; Ⓜ Avda. del Cid.

Internet access Most hostels and hotels offer internet access, whether wi-fi or an internet centre. You'll also find plenty of *locutorios* (phone centres) around town, most of which have internet access (€2–5 per hr). *Workcenter*, Xativa 19, next to the Xativa metro (24hr, except Fri

7am–11pm, Sat 10am–2pm & 5–9pm, Sun 10am–2pm & 5–11pm; ☎961 120 830, ⑨www. workcenter .es) charges €12 for first half hour, and €11 for each following half hour.

Markets Check out the crowded Sun morning flea market, next to the football stadium on c/Sucia. Otherwise, there are markets selling clothes and general goods in a different location daily – ask at the tourist office for details. For food, the Mercado Central is a treat.

Police c/Los Mestres 2 ☎963 920 607.

Post office Plaza del Ayuntamiento 24 (Mon–Fri 8.30am–8.30pm, Sat 9.30am–2pm).

Telephones Plaza de la Reina 2 (Mon–Sat 10am–8.30pm, Sun noon–8pm).

Taxis Radio Taxi ☎963 703 333; Tele Taxi ☎963 571 313; Valencia Taxi ☎963 740 202.

Tours Valencia Guias, Paseo de la Pechina 32 (☎963 850 827, ⑨www.valenciaguias.com) offers a range of excellent tours in many languages, including by bike. They also rent bicycles.

Trekking Treks through various mountain areas in the region are organized year-round. You can either join a guided group or, if you want to go it alone, the Centro Excursionista de Valencia, Plaza Tabernes de Valldigna 4 ☎963 911 643, provides route maps and info.

Around Valencia

There are a number of good **day-trips** to be made from Valencia, including a visit to the monastery at El Puig or a meal at some of the region's very best paella restaurants at El Palmar, El Perelló or Perellonet.

Real Monasterio del Puig de Santa María

Eighteen kilometres north of Valencia on the road to Sagunto is the small town of **El Puig** (pronounced "pooch"), where it's well worth spending a couple of hours visiting the impressive **Real Monasterio del Puig de Santa María** (Tues–Sat 10am–1pm & 4–7pm, in winter closes at 6pm; free), a huge fort-like structure flanked by four towers that dominates the town and surrounding countryside. The Orden de la Merced – the order that acts as guardians of the sanctuary – was founded by Pedro Nalaso in 1237 after he'd seen a vision of the Virgin Mary on the nearby hill. It is a favourite pilgrimage destination for Valencians and royalty alike, from Jaime I to the present monarchs Juan Carlos I and Doña Sofia, although in Franco's time it was put to a rather different use – as a prison.

In the lower cloister, the **Museum of Print and Graphics** (one of the most important in Europe) contains a wealth of artefacts, including the smallest book in the world – the size of a thumbnail. Looking at it through a magnifying glass reveals the Padre Nuestro (Lord's Prayer) in half a dozen languages. Other star exhibits include a copy of the Gutenberg Bible and a wonderful pictorial atlas of natural history, both from the sixteenth century. In the upper cloister, the **ceramics room** houses various Roman pieces, but its real treasures are the fourteenth-century plates, bowls and jars recovered from the seabed close to El Puig. Keep an eye out, too, throughout the monastery for the neck manacles that the monks use as candle holders.

El Puig is served by **train** (every 30min; 20min) and **bus** (hourly; 30min) from Valencia.

La Albufera and the paella villages

La Albufera, just 12km south from Valencia, is a vast lagoon separated from the sea by a sandbank and surrounded by rice fields. Being one of the largest bodies of fresh water in Spain, it constitutes an important wetland, and attracts tens of thousands of migratory birds – a throng composed of 250 species, of which ninety breed here regularly. In the Middle Ages, it was ten times its present size but the surrounding paddies have gradually reduced it. After growing contamination by industrial waste, domestic sewage and insecticide, the area was turned

La Tomatina – the tomato-throwing festival of Buñol – is about as wild and excessive as Spanish fiestas get. Picture this: 30,000 people descend on a small provincial town, at the same time as a fleet of municipal trucks, carrying 120,000 tonnes of tomatoes. Tension builds. "To-ma-te, to-ma-te" yell the crowds. And then the truckers let them have it, hurling the ripe, pulpy fruit at everyone present. And everyone goes crazy, hurling the pulp back at the trucks, at each other, in the air … for an hour. It's a fantasy battle made flesh: exhausting, not pretty and not to everyone's taste. But it is Buñol's contribution to fiesta culture, and most participants will tell you that it is just about as much fun as it is possible to have with your clothes on. Not that you should wear a great deal.

La Tomatina has been going since 1944 but has got a lot bigger in recent years, following a string of articles in the press in Spain and abroad. The novelist Louis de Bernières was one of the first foreign writers to cover the event: he wrote a superb account that is reprinted in *Spain: Travelers' Tales*, and concluded that, if he planned his life well and kept his health, he could attend another nineteen Tomatinas, before he would be too enfeebled for the occasion.

If the idea appeals, then you'll need to visit Buñol on the **last Wednesday of August** (but call the Valencia tourist office just to check, as some years it takes place a week early). You can get there by train or bus in around an hour, but if you're not staying overnight try to arrive early, with a spare set of clothing that you should leave at a bar. The tomato trucks appear on the central Plaza del Ayuntamiento at around noon, and then the battle commences: this is no spectator sport – everyone is considered fair game. At 1pm, an explosion signals the end of the battle and nobody hurls another speck of tomato for the next twelve months. Instead, the local fire brigade arrives to hose down the combatants, buildings and streets, and a lull comes over the town. And then, miraculously, within the hour, everyone arrives back on the street, perfectly turned out, to enjoy the rest of the fiesta, which, oddly enough, includes such refined pursuits as orchestral concerts in the town's open-air auditorium. For more information, check out the festival website Ⓦ www.latomatina.es, or try the town's own website Ⓦ www.bunyol.es.

As Buñol's **accommodation** options are limited – and with no reason to visit outside Tomatina time – most people take in the fiesta as a day-trip from Valencia, but if you want to stay, try either *Pensión Venta Pilar*, Avda. Perez Galdos 5 (Ⓣ 962 500 923, Ⓦ www.posadaventapilar.com; ❷–❸), or the more upmarket *Hotel Condes de Buñol*, Avda. Blasco Ibañez 13 (Ⓣ 962 504 852, Ⓦ www.condesdebunol.com; ❹).

into a natural park. Whether you're into birdwatching or not, the lagoon area makes a relaxing change from the city. By far the easiest way to explore La Albufera is to jump aboard a *bus turistic* (summer Mon–Sat 9 daily; winter Thurs–Sun 3–4 daily; €14; Ⓣ 963 414 400, Ⓦ www.valenciabusturistic.com); they leave from the Plaza de la Reina in Valencia, and the trip includes a boat trip on the lake and a guided tour.

It's possible to "hop on, hop off" the *bus turistic*, and tuck into some **paella**, or eels with *all i pebre* (piquant sauce) for lunch in the lakeside village of **EL PALMAR**, which is packed with restaurants. One of the better restaurants is *Mateu*, on the main street, c/Vincente Baldovi, at no. 17 (Ⓣ 961 620 270; closed Wed in winter). On August 4, El Palmar celebrates its **fiesta**; the image of Christ on the Cross is taken out onto the lake in a procession of boats to the *illuent*, or centre, of the lake, where hymns are sung. Another 2km farther along the road to El Perelló is the small – and otherwise unexceptional – village of **PEREL-LONET**, where you can eat some of the better paella around. Try *Blayet*, Avda. Gaviotas 17 (Ⓣ 961 777 184; closed Sun dinner & Mon; book for weekend meals).

It is also a comfortable **hostal** (☎961 777 454, ⓦ www.blayet.com; ❸). *Gaviotas*, next door (☎961 777 575; closed Tues; booking required), also does good *mariscos* and *all i pebre*. Also worth a visit is *Vert i Blau*, farther down Avda. Gaviotas at no. 72, for *patatas Amparín* – a potato tapa with a kick. The nearest **campsite** is *Devesa Gardens* (☎961 611 136), 2km out on the Carretera El Saler, near the golf course of the same name. Regular hourly **buses** run from the Gran Vía Germanías in Valencia via El Saler and on to the lagoon, El Palmar and El Perelló.

North of Valencia: the Costa del Alzahar

Most of the Costa del Alzahar north of Valencia is dotted with **beach resorts**, with some of the best sands around **Benicàssim**, north of the provincial capital, **Castellón de la Plana**. Farther north still, the historic walled city of **Peñíscola** commands a spectacular cliff-top location, while **Vinaròs** is more port than resort. Apart from the appeal of the coastline, there are fine Roman ruins at **Sagunto**, sweeping mountain scenery and good hiking around **Segorbe** and **Montanejos**, while the fortified town of **Morella** is definitely worth a visit for its castle and Gothic architecture.

Sagunto and Vall d'Uixo

Twenty-four kilometres north of Valencia are the fine Roman remains of **SAGUNTO** (Sagunt). This town passed into Spanish legend when, in 219 BC, it was attacked by Hannibal in one of the first acts of the war waged by Carthage on the Roman empire. Its citizens withstood a nine-month siege before burning the city and themselves rather than surrendering. When belated help from Rome arrived, the city was recaptured and rebuilding eventually got under way. Chief among the ruins is the second-century Roman amphitheatre, the **Teatro Romano** (Tues–Sat 10am–8pm, Oct–April until 6pm, Sun 10am–2pm; free; contact the tourist office for programme information), the basic shape of which survives intact. After years of renovation (occasionally controversial), it's now functional and you can take in plays and concerts, from *Hamlet* to classical music and ballet, during the summer (usually Aug). The views from its seats are wonderful, encompassing a vast span of history – Roman stones all around, a ramshackle Moorish castle on the hill behind, medieval churches in the town below and, across the plain towards the sea, the black smoke of modern industry. Further Roman remains are being excavated within the walls of the huge **acropolis–castle** (same hours). Also worth a look is Sagunto's well-preserved Jewish quarter, where you'll find medieval houses among the cobbled alleyways. The well-run **Museu Històric de Sagunt**, c/Castillo (summer Tues–Sat 11am–8pm, Sun 10am–2pm; winter Tues–Sat 11am–6pm, Sun 11am–3pm; ☎962 664 096; free), which occupies two floors of a fourteenth-century medieval house, features archeological finds from Sagunto and around, including Latin and Hebrew inscriptions and sculptures.

Twenty-eight kilometres north of Sagunto, at **Vall d'Uixo**, is the underground river of San José, featuring caves with wonderful stalactites. Along with boat trips through the caves (March daily 11am–1.15pm & 3.30–5.45pm; April to mid-July & mid-Sept to Oct daily 11am–1.15pm & 3.30–6.30pm; mid-July to mid-Sept daily 10.30am–1.15pm & 3.30–8pm; Nov–Feb Tues–Sun 11am–1.15pm & 3.30–5pm; €6.50; ⓦ www.riosubterraneo.com), the attendant tourist complex also has a swimming pool, restaurant and auditorium, which holds summer concerts.

Practicalities

The theatre and castle complex is a twenty-minute walk from the train station. The route is signposted and passes the **tourist office** on Plaza Cronista Chabret (summer Mon–Fri 8am–3pm & 4.30–7.30pm, Sat 10.30am–2pm & 4–6.30pm; Sun 10am–2pm; winter 8am–3pm & 4.30–6.30pm, Sat 9am–2pm & 4–6.30pm, Sun 9am–2pm; ☏962 655 859, ⊛www.aytosagunto.es), and the Jewish quarter.

There are half-hourly **trains** and very frequent **buses** to Sagunto from Valencia; ten to twelve daily buses from Sagunto pass through Vall d'Uixo. For **accommodation** near Sagunto, try the leisure complex *La Pinada*, 3km out of town on the CN234, the road to Teruel (☏962 660 850, ⊛www .complejoturisticolapinada.com; ❹), which has swimming pools and saunas B&B. Alternatively, *Hostal Carlos*, near the station on the busy Avda. País Valencia at no. 43 (☏962 660 902; ❷), is half the price and conveniently located.

Segorbe and Montanejos

About 30km inland from Sagunto is **SEGORBE**, the Roman Segóbriga, which is worth a visit more for its tranquillity and surrounding scenery than its sights, though part of the old city wall remains. It lies in the valley of the Río Palancia, among medlar and lemon orchards.

Segorbe's **cathedral** was begun in the thirteenth century, but suffered in the Neoclassical reforms, and only the cloister is original. Its **museum** (Tues–Sat 11am–1.30pm & 5–7pm, Sun 11am–1.30pm & 4.30–6pm; €3) contains a few pieces of Gothic Valencian art, with a *retablo* by Vicente Maçip. One kilometre outside town on the road to Jérica, you'll find the "fountain of the provinces" which has fifty spouts, one for each province of Spain, each labelled with the coat of arms.

There are daily **trains** and **buses** between Valencia and Segorbe. If you want **to stay**, the renovated *Hospedería el Palen* at c/Franco Ricart 9 (☏964 710 740, ⊛www.elpalen.com; B&B ❸), set in a historic building in the centre of town, is very comfortable. Segorbe has its **fiestas** at the beginning of September, when *La Entrada* takes place, and bulls are run through the town by horses.

From Segorbe, it's 38km to **MONTANEJOS** (not to be mistaken for Montan, the village just before). Turn off at Jérica for the road to Montanejos, or catch the bus from Segorbe. This tiny village is popular with visitors for the hot springs, **Fuente de Baños**, where the water emerges at 25°C and has medicinal properties. Walks around the village join up with the nationwide network of paths, the *Gran Recorrido*. If you want to **stay** here, there's the *Refugio de Escaladores* (☏964 131 317), a good budget place with camping, dorms and wood cabins (❷); the inexpensive *Hostal Gíl*, at Avda. Fuente de Baños 28 (☏964 131 380, ⊛www.hotelgil.com; B&B ❹); or the comfortable *Hotel Rosaleda del Mijares*, Carretera de Tales 28 (☏964 131 079, ⊛www .hotelesrosaleda.com; ❹), right next to the spa.

Castellón de la Plana

Farther north along the coast, **CASTELLÓN DE LA PLANA** is the main city in the north of the Valencia region, and a provincial capital. It's a prosperous enough place, with a sight or two, but there's no real reason to linger long here, except perhaps for the nearby beaches. In the centre of town, there's a fine seventeenth-century **ayuntamiento**. Nearby rises the sixteenth-century belltower **El Fadrí** (viewing by appointment: ☏964 227 556; guided visits

Mon–Fri noon), and the neo-Gothic **Concatedral de Santa María** (Mon–Sat 8.30am–1pm & 6–8.30pm, Sun 9am–1pm & 6–8pm; guided visits Mon–Fri 10am & 6pm; free) – the original eleventh-century building was destroyed in the Civil War. The impressive contemporary premises of the **Museo de Bellas Artes** on Avda. Hermanos Bou 28, some six blocks west of Plaza Santa Clara (Tues–Sat 10am–8pm, Sun 10am–2pm; free), are also worth a visit, with some valuable works by Francisco Zurbarán and Sorolla, and ceramics and sculptures.

There are **beaches** at Castellón's *grau* (port), 5km east of the centre, but you'll find the best stretches along the coastal road north to Benicàssim. **Buses** for the former leave regularly from Plaza Borrull, while for the latter, departures are from nearby Plaza Farrell.

Practicalities

Arriving by **bus** or **train**, you'll find yourself at the combined station on Avenida Pintor Oliet (regular services to destinations north and south, as well as two daily except Sun to Morella). To get to the centre, either walk the twenty minutes or so down Paseo Morella, or catch the frequent bus #9, which also stops at Plaza María Agustina. Here, there's the regional **turismo** (summer Mon–Fri 9am–7pm, Sat 10am–2pm; winter Mon–Fri 9am–2pm & 4–7pm, Sat 10am–2pm; ☎964 358 688, ⓦwww.comunitatvalenciana.com), which has a wealth of information about the city and the whole province. If you do decide to **stay the night**, the family-run, friendly *Hostal La Esperanza*, c/Trinidad 37 (☎964 222 031; ❶), has clean rooms, though none with private bathrooms. Alternatively, 2km from the beach sits the *Pensión Los Herreros*, Avda. del Puerto 28 (☎964 284 264, ⓦwww.hotelherreros.com; ❷).

There are plenty of **places to eat**, especially in the streets just south of Plaza Santa Cruz. By the *grau*, *Rafael*, c/Churruca 28 (☎964 282 185; closed Sun), offers an excellent, if somewhat pricey, selection of seafood, hauled in fresh daily.

Vilafamés

VILAFAMÉS, 24km inland from Castellón, is an attractive hill town that successfully mixes the medieval, Renaissance and modern. In the highest part of town, there's an ancient ruined castle, conquered by Jaime I in 1233. The fifteenth-century Palau del Batlle houses the **Museo de Arte Contemporáneo** (summer Tues–Fri 10am–1.30pm & 5–8pm, Sat & Sun 10.30am–2pm & 5–8pm; winter Tues–Fri 10am–1.30pm & 4–7pm, Sat & Sun 10.30am–2pm & 4–7pm; ☎964 329 152; €2), a collection of over five hundred sculptures and paintings including works by Miró, Lozano and Mompó. There are clean, wooden-beamed **rooms** at *El Rullo*, c/de la Fuente 2 (☎964 329 384; ❷–❸), which also has a restaurant, with a weekday *menú* for €10. The welcoming *casa rural El Jardin Vertical*, c/Nou 15 (☎964 329 938, ⓦwww.eljardinvertical.com; ❺), in a seventeenth-century stone-walled house, reveals views of the rolling countryside and six lovely, rustic rooms. The restaurant serves up a tasting dinner *menú* for €35.

Benicàssim and around

BENICÀSSIM, a few kilometres north of Castellón, is famed for its Moscatel wine, and was once well known as a wine-producing area, although today the town is much more of a tourist resort, and better known for its annual music festival. Very few vineyards remain, but you can take a

The annual **Festival Internacional de Benicàssim** (FIB; ⓦwww.fiberfib.com) in late July draws tens of thousands to hear the world's biggest names in alternative pop and rock. The dance tents are generally just as buzzing as the live-music stages, with DJs playing right through till 7am. There's a massive campsite, and a festival ticket (3 days; €180) entitles you to free camping for nine days around the event.

wine-tasting tour at *Bodegas Carmelitano* on c/Bodolz 10, just off Avda. Castellón (summer 9am–1.30pm & 4–8pm; winter 9am–1.30pm & 3.30–6.30pm; ⓣ964 30 08 49; €2).

Although Benicàssim is heavily developed for package tourism, budget accommodation is easy to come by in the streets around the **turismo**, c/Santo Tomás 74–76 (summer Mon–Fri 9am–2pm & 5.30–8.30pm, Sat & Sun 10.30am–1.30pm & 5.30–8.30pm; winter daily 9am–2pm & 5–8pm; ⓣ964 300 102, ⓦwww.benicassim.org). *Hotel Residencia Canada*, c/La Pau 1 (ⓣ964 304 611, ⓦwww.hotelcanadabenicassim.com; ❷), has sunny, en-suite rooms, especially good value for single travellers. From the same owners is the more upmarket *Hotel Montreal*, by Terrers beach at c/Les Barraques 5 (ⓣ964 300 681, ⓦwww.hotelmontreal.es; ❹), with comfy, polished-floor rooms, swimming pool and sun-dappled garden terrace, and a buffet-style restaurant open in the summer. For the utmost in pampering (and prices) try *El Palasiet*, Pontazgo 11 (ⓣ964 300 250, ⓦwww.palasiet.com; ❼), a spa-hotel overlooking Playa Voramar, about 3km from town. In addition to elegant, pale-toned rooms, the luxe hotel features a thermal centre with thalassotherapy treatments – think whirlpools with algae – along with sweet-chocolate facial peels and onyx-stone massages. You'll find a slew of **campsites** in the area; *Camping Florida*, Sigalero 34 (ⓣ964 392 385), is close to the beach, with a pool and tennis courts. In the centre of town, there are plenty of **restaurants** along c/Santo Tomás, including delicious Spanish and Italian cuisine at *Manduca*, c/Santo Tomás 69 (ⓣ964 301 718).

Six kilometres inland from Benicàssim is the **Desierto de las Palmas**, a nature reserve with a scattering of ruins (including the atmospheric *monasterio antiguo*, abandoned in the late eighteenth century) and walking circuits. The name was coined by Carmelite monks whose presence in the area dates back to 1697.

There's a regular **bus** service from Castellón to Benicàssim: buses leave from the bus stop on Avenida Pintor Oliet roughly every fifteen minutes in summer, every thirty minutes in winter. There are also five daily buses to Vinaròs, two of which stop at Peñíscola en route. There are also fairly regular **trains** for both Vinarós and Castellón, leaving from the small, usually deserted station, ten-minutes' walk north of the *turismo*.

Peñíscola

There's not much else along the stretch of coast north of Benicàssim until you reach **PEÑÍSCOLA**, 60km away. The setting is one of Spain's most stunning: a heavily fortified promontory jutting out into the Mediterranean, zealously shielding its warren of alleys and lanes with perfectly preserved medieval walls. Yet it's also one of the starkest – immediately below the old walls, the requisite line of eyesore high-rises snakes out along the seafront like a besieging army. There was once a Phoenician settlement here, and later it saw Greek,

Carthaginian, Roman and Moorish rulers, but the present castle was built by the Knights Templar, with alterations by Pedro de la Luna. Pope Benedict XIII (Papa Luna) lived here for six years after he had been deposed from the papacy during the fifteenth-century Church schisms. The **castle** today (daily: summer 9.30am–9.30pm; winter 10.30am–5.30pm; €3.50), where part of *El Cid* was filmed, is well worth a visit to admire the colossal vaulted guards' quarters, basilica and the views from its roof. The resort's slender **beach** has recently been beefed up with several thousand tonnes of Saharan sand; the farther north you get from the castle, the quieter it becomes. There's also a smaller cove beach, Playa Sur, 200m west of the old town.

Practicalities

You'll find the **turismo** is on Paseo Marítimo (summer Mon–Fri 9am–8pm, Sat & Sun 10am–1pm & 4.30–8pm; winter Mon–Fri 9.30am–1.30pm & 4–7pm, Sat 10am–1pm & 4–7pm, Sun 10am–1pm; ☎964 480 208, ⓦwww.peniscola.org), and a kiosk just below the entrance to the walled city – both provide a decent map that marks all the town's **accommodation**, including the eleven campsites, and an informative leaflet about the castle. The most atmospheric lodgings are to be had inside the walled city: there are rooms above the *Chiki Bar* at Mayor 3 (☎964 480 284; ❷), and they also serve an €11 *menú*. The more comfortable *Hostal Aranda*, c/General Aranda 3 (☎964 480 816, ⓦwww.hostalaranda.com; ❹), has clean rooms with pastel walls and tiled floors. If you'd rather be within striking distance of the beach, *Simó*, in the shadow of the walls at c/Porteta 5 (☎964 480 620, ⓦwww.restaurantesimo.es; B&B ❸), has bright rooms with sea views. The area just below the old town is thick with **restaurants**, many serving local dishes such as *suquet de peix* (fish stew), and *all i pebre de polp* (small octopus with garlic and pepper sauce). For dinner, the rustic, long-established *El Peñón*, c/Santos Mártires 22 (☎964 480 716; Nov–March Fri–Sun only), serves quality seafood. The lively restaurant-lounge *Mandarina*, Avda. Papa Luna 1, has a breezy terrace that fills with locals and visitors throughout the day and night: enjoy a meal – salads, seafood, pasta – and then ease into the warm evening over cocktails. **Buses** shuttle between Peñíscola and Vinaròs every half-hour between 7.30am and 11pm, stopping at various points along Avenida Papa Luna. For points south, you'll have to change bus at Benicarló (c/San Francisco).

Vinaròs

The **beaches** of the scruffy port-cum-resort **VINARÒS**, next along the coast, are small but rarely packed, and in town there's an elaborate Baroque church, with an excellent local produce market nearby. Near the seafront, the **turismo** (summer daily 10am–1.30pm & 5.30–8pm; winter Mon–Sat 10am–1.30pm & 5.30–6.45pm, Sun 10.30am–1.30pm; ☎964 453 334, ⓦwww.vinaros.org) has a decent map and will help to locate **accommodation**: one good option is *Casablanca*, a *pensión*-cum-hotel located within smelling distance of the sea at c/Sant Pasqual 8 (☎964 450 425). The older rooms (❷) have character aplenty, the newer ones (B&B ❸) are tastefully finished and some come with excellent disabled facilities. Antique tiles and furniture adorn the reception and stairs, there's a flower-festooned roof terrace, and the old couple who run it couldn't be nicer. In low season, single travellers can stay in a double room at half-price. Alternatively, *Habitaciones Vinaròs* at c/Pintor Puig Roda 8 (☎964 452 475; ❶) is clean and cheap.

In the early evening, it's worth going down to the dockside **market** to watch the day's catch being auctioned and packed off to restaurants all over the region. Locally caught fish is excellent, with the *langostinos* reputedly the best in Spain. Almost overlooking the portside action, *Bar Puerto* on c/Costa y Borràs is a fine spot for a bite to eat or a drink. Opposite is *El Faro* (☏964 456 362), a converted lighthouse with an open design facilitating disabled access; they also serve up some of the more creative cuisine in town. Locals fill up on fresh fish at the simple *La Isla*, Passeig de Sant Pere 5 (☏964 452 358; closed Mon).

There are two **buses** on to Morella (8am & 4pm weekdays only), leaving Plaza de Sant Esteve. Both the half-hourly service to Peñíscola, and the six daily buses to Castellón (three of which stop at Benicàssim) leave from the corner of Avenida de Leopold Querol and Passeig del 29 de Setembre. The town's **train station**, over 2km west of the centre, has eight daily services to Valencia (via Castellón) and nine to Barcelona (via Tarragona).

Morella

MORELLA, 62km inland on the road from the coast to Zaragoza, is the most attractive – and possibly most friendly – town in the province of Castellón and one of the most remarkable in the area. A medieval fortress town, it rises from the plain around a small hill crowned by a tall, rocky spur and a virtually impregnable **castle** that dominates the surrounding countryside. A perfectly preserved ring of ancient walls defends its lower reaches. The city was recovered from the Moors in the thirteenth century by the steward of Jaime I. He was reluctant to hand it over to the crown, and it is said that the king came to blows with him over the possession of the city.

Arrival and information

Buses run to Morella from Vinaròs (Mon–Fri 2 daily) and Castellón (Mon–Fri 2 daily, Sat daily). Morella is one possible approach to the Maestrazgo region of southern Aragón (see p.628) – buses leave for Alcañiz (Mon & Fri 10am) and Cantavieja/Villafranca del Cid (Mon–Fri daily, early evening departure). Be prepared for lower temperatures here than elsewhere in the province, and for snow in winter. The **turismo** is located in Plaza de San Miguel (summer daily 10am–2pm & 4–7pm; winter Tues–Sat 10am–2pm & 4–6pm, Sun 10am–2pm; ☏964 173 032, ⬤www.morella.net), just inside the impressive stone portal of the same name, which the bus sometimes stops at. The principal stop, however, is opposite Beneito Tower, inside the town's southernmost stretch of wall. There's also **internet** access in the cramped but friendly *Ciberlocutori Nou*, c/Sant Julià 2.

Accommodation

You can find inexpensive **accommodation** at *Hostal La Muralla*, c/Muralla 12 (☏964 160 243; B&B ❷), and at the slightly more modern and comfortable *Hotel El Cid*, Puerta San Mateo 3 (☏964 160 125, ⬤www .hotelelcidmorella.com; ❸), both of which are located within minutes of the bus stop (handy for the brutally early timetable), and offer inspirational views of the hills (*El Cid* also has balconies). Otherwise, ⚲ *Hotel Cardenal Ram* at c/Cuesta Suñer 1, a converted medieval cardinal's palace (☏964 173 085, ⬤www.cardenalram.com; ❹), is an atmospheric place to bed down, and has a good restaurant. *La Fonda Moreno*, c/Sant Nicolau 12 (☏964 160 105, ⬤www .lafondamoreno.com), has nine pleasant, bright rooms, along with an inviting restaurant. During fiestas and national holidays, you should book rooms in advance, as Morella is very popular with Spanish holidaymakers.

The Town

Chief among the town's monuments is the church of **Santa María la Mayor** (*Iglesia Arciprestal*; Tues–Sun: summer 10am–2pm & 4–7pm; winter 11am–2pm & 4–6pm; also Mon in Aug; free), a fourteenth-century Gothic construction with beautifully carved doorways and an unusual raised *coro* reached by a marble spiral stairway. A few minutes' walk to the left, at the foot of the castle, is the restored **Convento de San Francisco** (daily: summer 11am–7pm; winter 11am–5pm; €2), worth visiting for its elegant Gothic cloister and chapterhouse. The **fortress** itself (same hours) is in ruins, but still impressive. It's a tiring climb, but there are tremendous views in every direction from the crumbling courtyard at the top – down over the monastery, bullring and town walls to the plains. In the distance are the remains of the peculiar Gothic **aqueduct** that once supplied the town's water.

Not far from the monastery is the curious **Museo Tiempo de los Dinosaurios** (Tues–Sun 11am–2pm & 4–7pm, Oct–April until 6pm; €2), containing fossils of dinosaurs found in the area. Also of interest is the house on c/de la Virgen de Villavana where San Vicente Ferrer performed the prodigious miracle of resurrecting a child who had been chopped up and stewed by its mother – she could find nothing else fit for a saint to eat. Annually, Morella hosts a **festival of classical music** in the first two weeks of August.

Eating and drinking

Morella's main porticoed street, Els Porxos, bisected by steep steps leading down to the lower walls, is the place for **food**, with its bars, bakeries (head to *Gorreta 2* for breakfast, with good coffee and delicious *flaons*, a local speciality made

▲ Morella

from cinnamon, cheese and almonds) and cafés – the hundred-plus-year-old *Rourera* is excellent for tapas. Morella is also prime **truffle** country – to sample the local *trufa negra* and other gourmet-rustic delicacies, head to the *Casa Roque*, Cuesta San Juan 1 (☏ 964 160 336; closed Sun eve & Mon).

The Costa Blanca

South of Valencia stretches a long strip, the **Costa Blanca** (White Coast), with some of the **best beaches** on this coast, especially between Gandía and Benidorm. Much of it, though, suffers from the worst excesses of **package tourism**, with concrete building projects looming over much of the coast, and more on the way. It pays to book ahead in summer, particularly in August. Campers have it somewhat easier – there are hundreds of campsites – but driving can be a nightmare unless you stick to the toll roads.

If you're taking the inland route as far as **Gandía**, you'll get the opportunity to see the historic town of **Xátiva**.

Xàtiva and around

The ancient town of **XÀTIVA** (Játiva), 50km south of Valencia, was probably founded by the Phoenicians and certainly inhabited by the Romans. Today, it's a scenic, tranquil place and makes a good day-trip. Medieval Xàtiva was the birthplace of Alfonso de Borja, who became Pope Calixtus III, and his nephew Rodrigo, father of the infamous Lucrezia and Cesare Borgia. When Rodrigo became Pope Alexander VI, the family moved to Italy.

Xàtiva has a fine collection of mansions scattered around town, but most are private and cannot be entered. Many of the churches have been recently renovated, and the **old town** is a pleasant place to wander. From here, it's a long and tiring walk up a steep hill (there's the option of a tourist train for €4) to the plain but sturdy **castle** (Tues–Sun 10am–7pm; Nov–Feb until 6pm; €2.10) – follow signposts from the main square, Plaza del Españoleto, or take a taxi from outside the *turismo*. On the way, you'll pass the thirteenth-century **Iglesia de San Feliu** (Tues–Sat 10am–1pm & 4–7pm, Nov–March 3–6pm, Sun 10am–1pm; if the church is closed during listed hours, the house next door can let you in), a hermitage built in transitional Romanesque-Gothic style; ancient pillars, fine capitals and a magnificent Gothic *retablo* are the chief attractions of the interior.

Back in the centre of town, the **Museo del Almudín** (mid-June to mid-Sept Tues–Fri 9.30am–2.30pm, Sat & Sun 10am–2pm; mid-Sept to mid-June Tues–Fri 10am–2pm & 4–6pm, Sat & Sun 10am–2pm; €2.20) consists of two separate sections, one an archeological collection, the other an art museum. The latter includes several pictures by José Ribera (who was born here in 1591) and engravings by Goya – *Caprichos* and *Los Proverbios*. A portrait of Felipe V is hung upside down in retribution for his having set fire to the city in the War of the Spanish Succession and for changing its name (temporarily) to San Felipe.

Fiestas are held during Semana Santa and in the second half of August, when the *Feria de Agosto* is celebrated with bullfights and livestock fairs.

Practicalities

Xàtiva is served by **buses** and **trains** from Valencia; the train (1hr) is cheaper, and leaves every half-hour. There are also connections to Gandía (bus) and Alicante (train). Arriving in town by train, follow c/Baixada Estación up towards the central tree-lined c/Alameda Jaume I, where you'll find the **turismo** at no. 50 (summer Tues–Fri 10am–2.30pm & 5–7.30pm, Sat & Sun 10am–2pm; winter Tues–Fri 10am–1.30pm & 4–6pm, Sat & Sun 10am–2pm, ☏962 273 346, ⓦwww.comunitatvalenciana.com). If you're enjoying Xàtiva's peace and quiet and want to **stay**, options are fairly limited. The quiet, comfortable *Hotel Murta* at c/Ángel Lacalle s/n (☏962 276 611; ❸) is a good budget find; if you'd like to go the luxe route, try the wonderful *Hostería de Mont Sant* on the way up to the castle (☏962 275 081, ⓦwww.mont-sant.com; ❺–❻), which has stunning gardens and a pool.

Keep an eye open for **arnadí** in the bakeries – it's a local speciality of Moorish origin, a rich (and expensive) sweet made with pumpkin, cinnamon, almonds, eggs, sugar and pine nuts. For a good **restaurant**, head for the mid-priced *Casa La Abuela*, c/Reina 17 (☏962 281 085; closed Sun); many Valencians drive out here to savour its traditional fare, from robust rices to stews, and a €15 *menú*. For something less expensive, try the ageing, *azulejo*-rich charm of *Casa Floro*, Plaza Mercat 46 (closed Sun), with traditional fish and meat dishes.

Gandía

There's not much along the coast until you get to **GANDÍA**, 65km south of Valencia and the first of the main resorts, which attracts mainly Spanish visitors. A few kilometres inland from the modern seafront development, the old town is quiet and provincial, with one sight that's well worth seeing, and some good, inexpensive accommodation.

Gandía was once important enough to have its own university, but the only real testimony to its heyday is the **Palacio Ducal de los Borja**, built in the fourteenth century, with Renaissance and Baroque additions and modifications. There are regular guided tours throughout the year (Mon–Sat 10am–2pm & 4.30–8.30pm, Sun 10am–2pm; ☏962 871 4 65; €5). Tours are in Spanish, but photocopied translations are available at the reception. Duke Francisco de Borja was much responsible for the golden age of the town (late fifteenth to early sixteenth century) in terms of urban and cultural development. Learned and pious, the duke opened colleges all over Spain and Europe, and was eventually canonized. The palace contains his paintings, tapestries and books, but parts of the building itself are of equal interest, such as the *artesonado* ceilings and the pine window shutters, so perfectly preserved by prolonged burial in soil and manure that resin still oozes from them when the hot sun beats down. There are also several beautiful sets of *azulejos*, but these are outshone by the fourteenth-century Arabesque wall tiles, whose brilliant lustre is unreproducible as it was derived from pigments of plants that became extinct soon after the Muslims left.

Practicalities

Both **buses** and **trains** arrive on Avenida Marqués de Campo. The **turismo** is opposite the station (Mon–Fri 9.30am–1.30pm & 4–8pm; in summer 3.30pm–7.30pm; Sat 9.30am–1.30pm; ☏962 877 788, ⓦwww.gandiaturismo.com). There's a handful of **places to stay**; good bets include *Hotel Los Naranjos*, c/Avda. del Grau 67 (☏962 873 143, ⓦwww.losnaranjoshotel.com; B&B ❸), and, closer to the beach, the comfortable *Hostal-Residencia Clibomar* at c/Alcoy 24 by the Playa de Gandía (☏962 840 237; closed Nov–Easter; ❸). The exceptionally pleasant *Albergue Mar i Vent* is on the beachfront at **Playa de Piles**, 5km down the coast (☏962 831 748; €7.45 under 26, €10.60 over 26). In summer, about six daily buses run there from outside the train station; in winter, there are three to four.

The upmarket *L'Ullal*, on c/Benicanena 12, just west of the old town (☎962 877 382; closed Sat eve & Sun), is famed for its inspiring use of local ingredients. The inviting *Menjars Lucio*, c/Cavanilles 10, behind Plaza Prado (☎ 962 041 797 or 695 229 535; closed Mon & Sun), serves up a lively mix of traditional and creative cuisine, from tasty tapas to grilled meats and fish.

Gandía beach

Buses run every fifteen to twenty minutes (6am–11.30pm) from the *turismo* down to the enormous **beach**, Gandía Playa, 4km to the east. The beach is packed in summer and lined with apartment blocks, where remarkably good-value rooms are available out of season. You'll find the town's second **turismo** here at Paseo Neptuno 45 (summer Mon–Sat 9.30am–8.30pm, Sun 10am–1.30pm; winter Mon–Fri 9.30am–2pm & 4–7.30pm, Sat & Sun 10am–1.30pm; in winter, office may close additional days; ☎962 842 407). The beach zone is a good place for **seafood** and paellas; don't miss *fideuà*, a local speciality with a strong seafood flavour, cooked with vermicelli instead of rice, and freshly made *cocques* (similar to pizzas) from Taro bakery on Passeig de los Germaines. *La Gamba*, on Carretera Nazaret-Oliva, a few blocks back from the sea (☎962 841 310; lunch only, except Thurs–Sat in summer, when also open for dinner; closed Mon), serves up fresh seafood, with mains €15–20. *Marítim*, c/Ermita 2 (☎962 965 994), offers similar freshly caught produce and prices, including tasty *fideuà* and *la pescadilla*, a small type of hake. The real deal, though, is their weekday *menú* for €10. For **nightlife**, head farther up the beach and inland to Plaça del Castell, where elaborately named bars such as *La Sonrida Del Pelicano* and *Por Que Doblan Las Campanas* stay open until 4am, at which time the action moves on to Gandía's **clubs**: *Bacarrá* has house DJs, *CocoLoco* mainly salsa and Latin sounds, while at *Falkata*, music varies night by night and includes techno and house.

Around the cape: Gandía to Altea

A string of attractive little towns and beaches stretches from **Gandía** to **Altea** before you reach the developments of Benidorm and Alicante, but your own transport is essential to enjoy the best of them, and accommodation can be pricey. The most inexpensive option along this coast is to camp – there are scores of decent **campsites**, and a useful booklet listing them is available from local *turismos*. Try *La Merced*, 12km northwest of Altea in Calpe, Urb La Merced 32 (☎965 830 097), or *El Naranjal*, 1.5km out of Xàbia on the Carretera de Cabo (☎965 792 989, ⊛www.campingelnaranjal.com).

Denia and Xàbia

DENIA, at the foot of Parque Natural Montgó, is a sizeable, sprawling town even without its summer visitors. Beneath the wooded capes beyond, bypassed by the main road, stretch probably the most beautiful **beaches** on this coastline – it's easier if you have a car to get to most of them, though there are a couple of buses that make the trip from the port.

At the heart of this area, very near the easternmost Cabo de la Nao, is **XÀBIA** (Jávea), an attractive, prosperous town surrounded by hillside villas, with a fine beach and a very pleasant old town. In summer, both Denia and Xàbia are lively in the evenings, especially at weekends, as they're popular with *valencianos*. There are plenty of idyllic cove beaches close to Xàbia; one of the best is **Cala Portitxol** (also known as Playa la Barraca), a wonderful sand-and-pebble bay, backed by high cliffs, 5km east of the main beach, where you'll find a tremendous seafood restaurant, *La Barraca* (☎965 770 919), that's renowned for its paella; book well ahead on Sundays.

An FGV **tram** service travels from Denia to Alicante throughout the day, departing from the train station at the port, near the *Hotel Costa Blanca*. **Buses** also run hourly to Alicante, departing from Plaza Archiduque Carlos. There are also daily **ferry services** to Mallorca and Ibiza: for information, contact Baleària (☎902 191 068, Ⓦwww.balearia.com), or Iscomar (☎902 119 108, Ⓦwww.iscomarferrys.com), which usually has the cheapest fares. If you want to **stay** in Denia, *Hostal Residencia Cristina*, Avda. del Cid 5 (☎966 423 158, Ⓦwww.hostal-cristina.com; ❸), has bright, sparse but comfortable rooms, all with TV and some with private bath; they offer discounts if you stay longer than one night. *Hostal Residencia Loreto*, c/Loreto 12 (☎966 435 419, Ⓦwww.hostalloreto.com; ❸–❹), has good-value rooms kitted out rustic-style. The *Hotel Costa Blanca*, Pintor Llorens 3 (☎965 780 336, Ⓦwww.hotelcostablanca.com; ❹), is more upmarket and handy for the train station and port.

In Xàbia, *Hotel Xàbia*, by the port at Pío X 5 (☎965 795 461, Ⓦwww.hotel-javea.com; ❺), has balmy sea views. You can enjoy even more exclusive maritime views at the modern *Parador de Jávea* on Avenida del Mediterráneo (☎965 790 200, Ⓦwww.parador.es; ❻–❼). **Nightlife** is centred round the beach bars. Later in the evening, the crowds move to the out-of-town clubs on the road to Cabo de San Antonio.

Altea

Heading southeast, you pass the dramatic rocky outcrop known as the **Peñón de Ifach**, its natural beauty now irretrievably besmirched by the encroaching concrete towers of the neighbouring package resort of **Calpe** (Calp). Just 11km to the south, though, **ALTEA** is a much more attractive proposition: a small resort set below a historic hilltop village, with views overlooking the whole stretch of coastline. Restrained tourist development is centred on the seafront, where there's a pebble beach and attractive promenade of low-rise apartment buildings interspersed with tottering old fishermen's houses. There are plenty of cafés and restaurants along the seafront, as well as the **turismo** (summer usually Mon–Fri 10am–2pm & 5–8pm, Sat 10am–1pm; rest of year reduced hours; ☎965 844 114).

The old village, or *poble antic*, up the hill is even more picturesque, with its steep lanes, white houses, blue-domed church and profuse blossoms. In summer, the entire quarter is packed with pavement diners and boutique browsers. **Accommodation** can be tricky in high season, but *Hostal El Fornet*, c/Beniards 1 (☎965 843 005, Ⓦwww.albir21-hostalfornet.com; ❷ with bath; €10 less without) high up on the northern edge of the old village, is a good choice. The swanky *Hotel Altaya* on the seafront at c/San Pedro 28 (☎965 840 800, Ⓦwww.hotelaltaya.com; ❹) has prime sea views from balustraded balconies. It's a treat **to eat** in the old town, with most of the alfresco dining centred on Plaza de la Iglesia. If you're feeling flush, *Oustau*, c/Mayor 5 (☎965 842 078; closed Mon in winter), is one of the better-known old-town open-air options, with French-influenced cuisine, while the good-value *Mr X*, Partida El Planet 136 (☎965 842 881; closed Tues), serves cosmopolitan fare – from duck with oranges to grilled fish – in a converted farmhouse; mains are €16–18. By the seafront, the similarly priced *Sant Pere 24*, at c/Sant Pere 24 (☎965 844 972; winter closed Sun eve & Tues), serves up delicious seafood and rice combinations. The best places to **drink** are to be found around the main square of the old village: *Tribú* on Plaza Tónico Ferrer is a hip bar with great electro, funk and lounge sounds.

Benidorm

Hugely high-rise, vaguely Vegas and definitely dodgy, **BENIDORM** is king when it comes to package tourism. Sixty years ago, Rose Macaulay described Benidorm as a small village "crowded very beautifully round its domed and tiled church on a rocky peninsula". The old part's still here, but it's so overshadowed by the kilometres of towering concrete that you'll be hard-pressed to find it. If you want hordes of British and Scandinavian sunseekers, scores of "English" pubs, almost two hundred discos and club-bars, and bacon and eggs for breakfast, then this is the place to come. The **Playa de la Levante**, Benidorm's biggest highlight, with its 2km of golden sand, is undeniably pleasant when you can see it through the hordes of roasting bodies. A little farther from the centre is the slightly more relaxed and less exposed **Playa de Ponienete**, which has slightly more Spanish flavour.

Arrival and information

Trains arrive at the top of town, off Avenida de Beniarda, while the main **bus stop** is at the junction of Avenida de Europa and c/Gerona, with the ticket offices in the shopping centre there. You'll find Benidorm's helpful **turismo** in the old town, at Avda. Martínez Alejos 16 (Mon–Fri 9am–9pm, mid-Sept to mid-June until 8pm, Sat 10am–1pm; ☏965 851 311, ⓦwww .benidorm.org). There's also a small kiosk on Avenida de Europa. Getting to Alicante, you can either take the **FGV tram** or a **bus**, but the tram is quicker and more convenient. There's also a night-train service that runs along the coast to Alicante in July and August. For Valencia, there are no trains, but a regular bus service.

Accommodation

With over 40,000 hotel beds and hundreds of apartments, finding a **place to stay** isn't a problem (except perhaps in Aug). Budget places are clustered around the old town, and out of season many of the giant hotels slash their prices drastically, making Benidorm a cheap base from which to explore the surrounding area.

Gran Hotel Bali c/Luís Prendes ☏966 815 200, ⓦwww.granhotelbali.com. For a real splurge, check in to the 52-storey, 776-room *Gran Hotel Bali*, Europe's highest hotel (and the preferred choice of visiting rock royalty), where prices can plummet by half in the low season. B&B ❻

Hostal Santa Faç c/Santa Faç 18 ☏965 854 063, ⓦwww.santafazhotel.com. Comfortable and friendly, this is one of the better *hostales* in town. ❹

Hotel Rocamar c/Cuatro Esquinas 18 ☏965 850 552. Smack in the heart of the old town, with basic but clean rooms. ❹

Pensión Orozca Avda. Ruzafa 37 ☏965 850 525.

This longtime *pensión* may have a ubiquitous (read: dismal) concrete exterior, but rooms are decent, and it's an easy stroll through the old town to the sea. ❸

Poseiden Hotels c/Esperanto 9 ☏965 850 200, ⓦwww.hotelesposeidon.es. Offers the kind of bland comfort that Benidorm excels in, along with the usual conveniences, such as swimming pools and terrace bars. Prices dip considerably in low season. ❺

Campsite

Camping Raco Avda. Doctor Ochoa 19 ☏965 868 552, ⓦwww.campingraco.com. One of the best – and greenest – of Benidorm's myriad campsites.

Eating

Fish and chips dominate, and if you're after a fry-up, you'll be spoilt for choice. For **tapas**, follow the natives to *La Tasca del Pueblo*, c/Marques de Comillas, a checked tablecloth'n'antlers joint that nevertheless serves quality, reasonably priced *platos*. Usually crammed to the gills (no pun intended), *Posada del Mar*,

Paseo Colón, is a lively **seafood** spot, where you can tuck into freshly caught fish, prawns and the like. For a departure from the Benidorm crowds and cacophony, amble down to the quiet restaurant in the *Club Náutico Benidorm*, south of the teeming centre, on the waterfront on Paseo Colón (T965 853 067), where you can sample fresh seafood on a breezy terrace with just the sounds of water slapping against the sides of nearby docked boats.

Inland from Benidorm

In total contrast to the coastal strip, the remote mountainous terrain inland from Benidorm harbours some of the most traditional and isolated villages in the Valencia region – tourist-swamped Guadalest excepted. Better roads and local government grants (which encourage the conversion of rural properties into guesthouses) are slowly opening up this area to tourism, but for now the austere *pueblos* retain an untouched character, Castilian is very much a second language, and the main visitors are hikers. The area is rich in birdlife, with golden eagles, and, in autumn, griffon vultures, often spotted soaring over the limestone ridges. There's no bus or train service, other than links to Alcoy and Guadalest (generally only once daily to and from Benidorm), so you'll need your own wheels to get around.

West from Benidorm, an excellent new highway heads 21km to **GUADALEST**, justifiably one of the most popular tourist attractions in Valencia. The sixteenth-century Moorish castle town is built into the surrounding rock, and you enter the town through a gateway tunnelled into the mountain. If you can put up with the hordes of tourists and gift shops, it's worth visiting for the view down to the reservoir (accessible via the village of Beniarda just to the west) and across the valley. In the main street, you'll find the **Casa Típica**, an eighteenth-century house-museum (Mon–Fri & Sun: summer 10am–7pm; winter 10am–6pm; donation), with exhibitions of antique tools and agricultural methods. The **turismo**, c/Avenida de Alicante (generally Tues–Thurs 10.30am–2pm & 3–7.30pm, winter until 6pm, Sat 11am–1.30pm; T965 885 298, Wwww.guadalest.es), is helpful and has maps of the town, along with updated info on local accommodation.

If the landscape around Guadalest appeals, you could take the wonderfully scenic CV70 road that continues on westwards up the valley, passing the village of **CONFRIDES** after 10km, where *El Pirineo* (T965 885 858; ❷) has basic rooms with views, and then follows a serpentine route towards the town of Alcoy (see box, p.869). The best base for exploring the villages of this region and the craggy peaks of the Serra d'Aitana is the hamlet of **QUATRETONDETA**, 4km northeast of the village of Gorga. Here you'll find the welcoming, British-run *Hotel Els Frares* at Avda. Pais Valencia 20 (T965 511 234, Wwww.elsfrares.com; B&B ❹), with pleasant en-suite rooms, a couple of log fires and good food (including a daily veggie dish). They also offer a self-catering cottage, and the owners lead brisk walking tours around the region

All the villages in the area are well signposted, and most, including Quatretondeta, have wonderful municipal **swimming pools** (July & Aug only). At **Balones**, 10km west of Quatretondeta, the bar-café *El Mirador* (closed Mon) offers friendly service, good valley views and a €8 *menú*. Tiny **Facheca**, 7km east of Balones, also has a good bar-restaurant and a beautiful pool. It's possible to loop back to the coast from here via a highly scenic route that passes through **CASTELL DE CASTELLS**, an isolated village 10km to the east, where there are several good places to stay: *Casa Pilar* (T965 518 157, Wwww.casapilar.com; ❹), an amiable small guesthouse with attractive rooms and fine home-cooking served in an atmospheric cellar, and *Hotel Rural Serrella*, c/Alcoy 2 (☎965 518 138, ⓦwww.hotel-serrella.com; B&B ❷), which is less attractive, if blessed with more than enough chandeliers and wooden beams for the price.

Continuing eastwards from Castell de Castells, it's another 15km to the village of **Tàrbena**, and then a further 12km to **Callosa d'En Sarrià**; just 3km away from here you'll find the **Fuentes del Algar**, a series of very pretty waterfalls in a secluded spot, which makes a perfect place for a dip. From here it's just 15km to Benidorm, or the coastal highway south to Alicante.

Alicante (Alacant)

There is little to see anywhere along the coast south of Benidorm before you reach **ALICANTE (ALACANT)**. This thoroughly Spanish city has a decidedly Mediterranean air: its wide esplanades, such as the Rambla Méndez Núñez, and its seafront *paseos*, full of terrace cafés, are perfect for people-watching. Founded by the Romans, who named it Lucentum (City of Light), and dominated by the Arabs in the second half of the eighth century, the city was finally reconquered by Alfonso X in 1246 for the Castilian crown. In 1308, Jaime III incorporated Alicante into the kingdom of Valencia.

Today, Alicante is Valencia's second-largest city, and receives millions of visitors through its airport each year. With its long sandy beaches, mild and pleasant climate, renovated old town and lively nocturnal offerings, this is definitely a city to spend at least one night in. The main **fiesta**, *Las Hogueras*, is at the end of June, and ignites a series of cracking celebrations second only to *Las Fallas* in Valencia.

Arrival and information

The main **train station**, Estación de Madrid, on Avenida Salamanca, has direct connections to Madrid, Albacete, Murcia and Valencia. Travel to Benidorm and Denia is now facilitated by the FGV **tram**. From Mercado Central, the red #1 line offers a direct journey to Benidorm/Denia; from Puerta del Mar, you'll need to change at La Isleta. Check out the FGV website – ⓦwww.fgvalicante .com – for updates (the tram is being expanded to eventually have stops at Plaza Luceros, the train station and the airport), maps and information; fares start at €1.05. The **bus station** for local and long-distance services is on c/Portugal 13. The **airport** is 12km south of the centre, in El Altet. The #C-6 bus service into town (6.55am–11.10pm, every 40min; €1.50) stops outside the bus station and on the central Rambla Méndez Núñez. Going the other way, the bus leaves from Plaza Puerta del Mar (6.30am–10.20pm).

Alicante's helpful **turismo** is at Avda. Rambla Méndez Núñez 23 (Mon–Fri 9am–8pm, Sat 10am–8pm, Sun 10am–2pm; ☎965 200 000, ⓦwww .alicanteturismo.com). There are also branches on Explanada de España (Mon–Fri 10am–7pm, Sat 10am–2pm) and at the bus and train stations (Mon–Fri 9am–2pm & 4–6pm).

Accommodation

The bulk of Alicante's **accommodation** is concentrated at the lower end of the old town, above the Explanada de España (an attractively tiled seafront walk seen on all local postcards), on c/San Fernando and c/San Francisco. Among

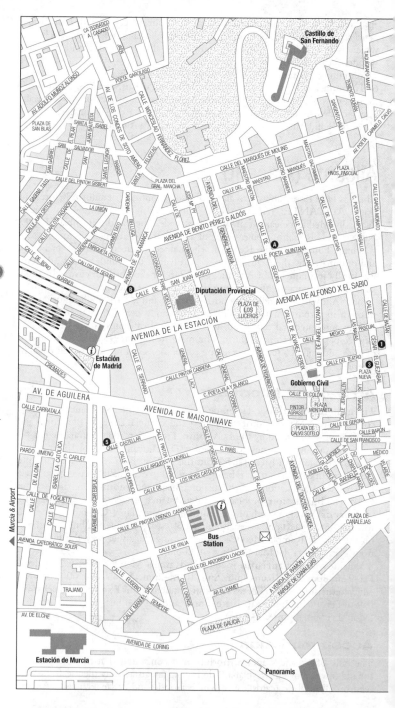

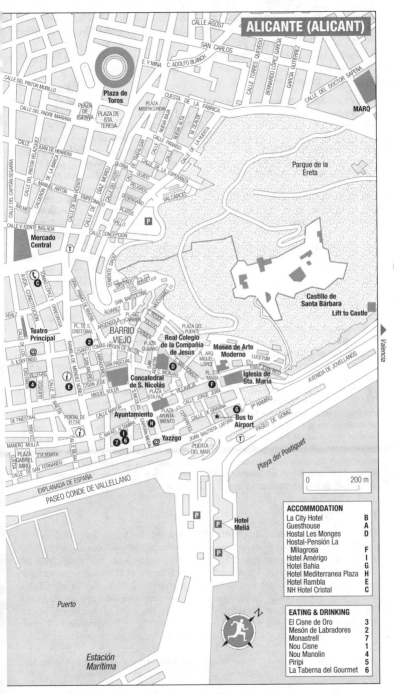

ALICANTE (ALICANT)

Plaza de Toros

MARQ

Parque de la Ereta

Castillo de Santa Bárbara

Lift to Castle

▶ Valencia

Mercado Central

Teatro Principal

BARRIO VIEJO

Real Colegio de la Compañía de Jesús

Museo de Arte Moderno

Concatedral de S. Nicolás

Iglesia de Sta. María

Ayuntamiento

★ **Bus to Airport**

Yazzgo

Playa del Postiguet

Hotel Meliá

Puerto

Estación Marítima

0	200 m

ACCOMMODATION

La City Hotel	B
Guesthouse	A
Hostal Les Monges	D
Hostal-Pensión La Milagrosa	F
Hotel Amérigo	I
Hotel Bahia	G
Hotel Mediterranea Plaza	H
Hotel Rambla	E
NH Hotel Cristal	C

EATING & DRINKING

El Cisne de Oro	3
Mesón de Labradores	2
Monastrell	7
Nou Cisne	1
Nou Manolin	4
Piripi	5
La Taberna del Gourmet	6

several **campsites** along the coast, the leafy *Costa Blanca* in El Campello is one of the nearest, located 500m from the beach and accessible by hourly tram (℡ 965 630 670, Ⓦ www.campingcostablanca.com). Otherwise, *Internacional La Marina*, 29km out on the Ctra. Alicante–Cartagena and served by Costa Azul buses, is pleasantly located in some woods, near a good beach (℡ 965 419 200, Ⓦ www.campinglamarina.com).

La City Hotel Avda. de Salamanca 16 ℡ 965 131 973, Ⓦ www.lacityhotel.com. Bright, modern hotel near the train station, with a cool-toned lobby that gives way to comfortable rooms with crisp bedspreads and blonde-wood furnishings. Excellent value for the price – and ideal for those with an early-morning train to catch. ❸–❹

Guesthouse c/Segura 20 ℡ 650 718 353, Ⓦ www.guesthousealicante.com. Inviting, cheery guesthouse that's lovingly cared for by the amiable owner Antonio. Individually decorated, spic-and-span rooms and apartments reveal personal touches, such as complimentary coffee and tea, along with free wi-fi. ❷

Hostal-Pensión La Milagrosa c/Villavieja 8 ℡ 965 216 918, Ⓦ www.hostallamilagrosa.com. Run with impressive efficiency and always busy. The great-value rooms (apartments holding up to eight people are also available; €60 for two, €20 for each extra person) are simple, spotless and inviting, and come with or without bath. A wonderful roof terrace seals the deal. ❷ with shared bath, ❸

🏃 **Hostal Les Monges** c/San Agustín 4 ℡ 965 215 046, Ⓦ www.lesmonges.net. Named after the convent of cloistered nuns (*monges*) that sits across the street, this is one of the better – and more original – deals in Alicante, with lovely, strikingly styled rooms. Some are antique-chic, while others are Japanese-influenced, and are accessed from corridors lined with vibrant *azulejos*, oddball curios and unlikely paintings – a true

labour of love. Ask for an upstairs rooms if you're a light sleeper. ❸

🏃 **Hotel Amérigo** Rafael Altamira 7 ℡ 965-146 570, Ⓦ www.hospes.es. Past meets present in the city's choicest hotel, housed in a magnificently restored seventeenth-century convent. Sleek rooms reveal gleaming hardwood floors and delicate white curtains, while the breezy rooftop deck has a pool, sauna and spa, and a "chill-out" zone where you can relax under the night sky. The tapas bar and restaurant, *Senzone*, is as design savvy as the hotel, with creatively prepared regional cuisine. ❺–❻

Hotel Bahia c/Juan Bautista Lafora 8 ℡ 965 206 522, Ⓦ www.hotelbahia.es. This friendly, unpretentious hotel on the seafront has a bright reception and unassuming, coolly comfortable rooms, some with sea views. ❸

Hotel Mediterranea Plaza Plaza del Ayuntamiento 6 ℡ 965 210 188, Ⓦ www.eurostarshotels.com. Tasteful four-star hotel, accessed by an arch in the plaza. Large, soberly furnished rooms come with all mod cons and benfit from a location in the heart of town. ❹–❺

Hotel Rambla Rambla Méndez Núñez 9 ℡ 965 144 580. Refurbished hotel with bright, pleasant rooms, all neutrally furnished and tiled. ❹

NH Hotel Cristal c/Thomás López Torregrosa 11 ℡ 965 143 659, Ⓦ www.nh-hotels.com. Svelte addition to the NH chain, with lots of glass, minimalist straight lines and shiny, parquet-floored rooms. ❹, with discounts generally at weekends.

The Town

The rambling **Castillo de Santa Bárbara** (daily: April–Sept 10am–8pm; Oct–March 9am–7pm; free), an imposing medieval fortress located on the bare rocky hill above the town beach, is Alicante's main historical sight. It's best approached from the seaward side where a 205-metre shaft has been cut straight up through the hill to get you to the top; the **lift** (daily 10am–6.45pm; €2.40) entrance is on Avenida de Jovellanos. Almost opposite are the Iberian and Roman remains that have been found on the site, but most of the present layout dates from the sixteenth century. The castle grounds, or **Parque de la Ereta**, are attractively landscaped, with olive groves, pathways, a café and tremendous views of the city.

One of Alicante's other main attractions, the **Museo de Arte Moderno**, north of the impressive *ayuntamiento*, is currently closed (due to reopen in 2010).

It houses a remarkably good collection of works by Picasso, Tàpies, Miró and Dalí. Otherwise, you could do a lot worse than visit the impressive, very stylish **Museo Arqueológico** or **MARQ** (Tues–Sat 10am–7pm, Sun 10am–2pm; €3; ⓦwww.marqalicante.com), on Plaza Dr Gómez Ulla, featuring locally found relics from the Iberian to medieval periods; bus #2 from Rambla Méndez Núñez will get you there. You can also get off at the MARQ tram stop, from where it's a ten-minute walk.

Beaches

The city's beach – **Playa del Postiguet** – gets very crowded in summer, and the **beaches** at **San Juan de Alicante**, about 6km out, are very built-up, but reached either by bus #21 or #22 from the Plaza del Mar or via the FGV tram (get off at the Costa Blanca stop). **Playa Arenales**, backed by sand dunes, is more pleasant; it's 12km south of the city and reachable by the hourly Baile bus from the main bus station. You can also take a day-trip to **Isle de Tabarca** (a marine reserve), to the south – boats leave, weather permitting, from the Explanada de España (June–Sept 6 daily; Oct–May daily; phone to clarify sailing and fare on ☏965 216 396) – but the rock tends to get very cramped and crowded during the summer.

Eating, drinking and nightlife

The most pleasant lunch location is at one of the many **restaurants** clustered around the *ayuntamiento* and c/Mayor, most of which do decent *menús* (and the ubiquitous paella) for around €10. For sheer cosmopolitan choice, however, c/San Fernando is fast becoming the city's most interesting place to eat. If you want to buy your own food, visit the enormous **Mercado Central**, housed in a wonderful old *modernista* building on Avenida Alfonso X el Sabio. Near here there are plenty of good places to buy Alicante's famous nougat-like **turrón**, with many shops on c/Capital Serralla, and in the centre on c/Mayor – Turrón 1880 is the best. Another market (a major outdoor event) is held by the Plaza de Toros (Thurs & Sat 9am–2pm).

El Cisne de Oro c/César Elguezabal 23. Locals crowd the curved bar at this lively, petite tapas bar to munch on the justly loved signature grilled pork loin, mushrooms, pepper and mayonnaise. Also on the menu is the regional speciality of *mojama*, salted, cured tuna. *Nou Cisne*, around the corner, offers similar tasty tapas in a slightly bigger and brighter space.

Mesón de Labradores c/Labradores 19. For tapas, try the buzzing bar (dinner only; closed Mon).

Monastrell c/San Fernando 10 ☎965 200 363; closed Mon & Sun. Minimalist, upscale restaurant run by the same owners as *La Taberna*, and serving up delicious Spanish cuisine with a twist, such as squid sandwich with ink alioli.

Nou Manolín c/Villegas 3 ☎965 200 368. Serves up market-fresh regional fare. There's also an atmospheric tapas bar.

Piripi Av Oscar Esplá 30 ☎965 227 940. Elegant place with excellent rice dishes prepared using fresh seasonal produce.

La Taberna del Gourmet c/San Fernando 10, next door to *Monastrell* ☎965 204 233. With its sea-defence style frontage, it's hard to miss this stylish haunt featuring some of the more creative, exclusively sourced tapas and organic wines in Alicante – everything from lamb sweetbreads to scrambled eggs with chorizo; tapas start at €10, mains €17–30.

Bars and nightlife

For **drinking** and the best **nightlife**, the old town, or Barrio Santa Cruz (around the cathedral and Plaza del Carmen), still rules: most of the small, smoky bars have a 4am curfew. In El Barrio, as it's known, you could start out at *Desdén*, c/Labradores 22, which plays jazz in the afternoon and house, dance and funk through the night. *Desafinado*, Santo Tomás 6, has great jazz, while *Celestial Copas* on c/San Pascual draws an arty crowd. When it comes to **clubs**, *Sala Stereo*, c/Pintor Velázquez 5, plays alternative and indie with frequent live acts, while *Jamboree!*, c/San José 10, specializes in rocksteady, ska, jazz and roots. Over towards the west end, *Tribeca*, c/San Fernando, is an American-style bar that does gourmet burgers round the clock, while farther west along the same street (no. 46), on Plaza Gabriel Miró, the stylish *Z Klub* starts spinning its laidback club sounds at 4am.

Alicante's **gay scene** is centred on the veteran *Byblos* on c/San Fernando. Also wildly popular is *El Forat*, on Plaza Santa Faz (Fri & Sat from 11pm), with an over-the-top decor of twinkling lights, huge bunches of fake flowers and caricatures of divas on the walls. For those who prefer a more chilled evening, there's the gay café-bar *Or i Ferro*, c/Belando 12 (daily 4pm–11.30pm, until 2am Fri & Sat), in the upper part of town, within walking distance of the Mercado Central.

Listings

Airlines Both Iberia (☎965 919 188) and British Airways (☎966 919 472) have offices at the airport.
Banks Along Avda. Rambla Méndez Núñez, and the Explanada – where you'll also find *bureaux de change* offices.
Cinema Cine Astoria, Plaza del Carmen, sometimes has original-language films; or the Panoramis complex in the port for Hollywood movies.
Consulates UK, Plaza Calvo Sotelo 1–2 ☎965 216 022.

Police The *Comisaría* is at c/Médico Pascual Pérez 27 ☎965 148 888.
Post office Near the bus station at the junction of c/Alemania with c/Arzobispo Loaces (Mon–Fri 8am–8.30pm, Sat 9.30am–1pm).
Internet *Locutorios* (phone centres) are scattered around the city, particularly along c/San Francisco and c/San Fernando, and many have internet access (€1–2 per hr).

Inland: Elche and Orihuela

ELCHE (ELX), 20km inland and south from Alicante, is famed throughout Spain for its exotic **palm forest** and for the ancient stone bust known as La Dama de Elche discovered here in 1897 (and now in the Museo Arqueológico in Madrid). The palm trees, originally planted by the Moors, are still the town's chief industry – not only do they attract tourists, but the female trees produce dates, and the fronds from the males are in demand all over the country for use in Palm Sunday processions and as charms against lightning. You can see the forest, unique in Europe, almost anywhere around the outskirts of the city; the finest trees are those in the famous, specially cultivated **Huerto del Cura** at Porta de la Morera 49 (daily: April–Sept 9am–8pm; Oct–March 10am–6pm; €5).

Elche is also the home of a remarkable **fiesta** in the first two weeks of August, which culminates in a centuries-old mystery play – *Misteri*, held in the eighteenth-century **Basílica Menor de Santa María** over August 14–15. Additional celebrations include one of the best examples of the Moros y Cristianos mock battles. Over several days, the elaborately costumed warriors fight it out before the Moors are eventually driven from the city and the Christian king enters in triumph.

There are **trains** and **buses** more or less hourly from Alicante to Elche. There are limited **accommodation** options: try *Pensión Juan*, c/Pont dels Ortissos 15 (☎965 458 609; ❶), for basic rooms with shared bathroom. Elche's smartest place is *Hotel Huerto del Cura*, located just south of the Huerto del Cura at Porta de la Morera 14 (☎966 612 050, Ⓦwww.hotelhuertodelcura.com; ❺), with ground-level, wood-beamed rooms leading onto stunning gardens. The *Bar Águila*, on c/Dr Caro 31, is a convivial **drinking** and **tapas** spot, while the **restaurant** in the park, *Parque Municipal* (☎965 453 415), serves delicious *arroz con costra*, the local rice dish. For a more upmarket version of the same dish and other Levantine/Andalucian delicacies, head to the acclaimed *El Granaino*, 300m west of the Punete d'Altamira at c/José María Buck 40 (☎966 664 080; closed Sun & mid-Aug).

Orihuela

Just over 50km southwest of Alicante lies the capital of the Vega Baja district, **ORIHUELA**, where in 1488 Los Reyes Católicos held court. The town's aristocratic past is reflected in the restored old quarter, and the impressive renovation of the **Teatro Circo**. Despite its proximity to the coast, Orihuela retains its provincial charm and is worth a wander. It also has a natural attraction in **El Palmeral**, the second-largest palm forest in Spain – walk out beyond Colegio de Santo Domingo or take the Alicante bus (from the centre) and ask to be dropped off. Many of the town's seventeenth- and eighteenth-century mansions are closed to the public; however, you can roam around the Palacio Rubalcana occupied by the *turismo* and parts of the **Palacio Marqués de Arneva**, which now houses the *ayuntamiento*.

Opposite the *turismo* is the **Iglesia de Santiago** (Tues–Fri 10am–2pm & 4–7pm, Sat 10am–2pm; free), one of the town's three medieval churches – all of which are Catalan Gothic (subsequently altered), a style you won't find any farther south. The oldest part of the church is the front portal, the Puerta de Santiago, a spectacular example of late fifteenth-century Isabelline style. Inside, the furniture is Baroque, and there's a *retablo* by Francisco Salzillo. Heading back down towards the town centre, just past the *ayuntamiento*, you'll see the second medieval church, the **Iglesia de Santas Justa y Rufina** (same hours as Santiago) – its tower is the oldest construction in the parish and has excellent gargoyle sculptures.

Just round the corner, on c/Salesas Marques Arneva, is one of Orihuela's hidden treasures, the Baroque **Monastario de la Visitación Salesas**; it's currently closed for renovations, so check with the *turismo* about opening hours. The cloisters contain several paintings by the nineteenth-century artist Vincente López – a monk will show you around.

Right in the centre of the old town is the medieval **Catedral** (Mon–Fri 10am–2pm & 4–6.30pm, Sat 10am–2pm; free), no bigger than the average parish church, built with spiralling, twisted pillars and vaulting. A painting by Velázquez, *The Temptation of St Thomas*, hangs in a small museum in the nave – and don't overlook the Mudéjar-influenced, fourteenth-century Puerta de las Cadenas. The **Museo Diocesano de Arte Sacro** (same hours as cathedral; if not open, ask cathedral staff), above the cloister, contains an unexpectedly rich collection of art and religious treasures (including a painting by Ribera), many of which are brought out during Semana Santa, the town's most important fiesta. The **Museo de Semana Santa**, Plaza de la Merced 1 (Tues–Sat 10am–2pm & 5–8pm, in winter 4–7pm, Sun 10am–2pm; ☎966 744 089; €2), explores the history and elaborate costumes and rituals of the Semana Santa celebrations.

Orihuela's other main sight is the Baroque **Colegio de Santo Domingo** (Tues–Fri 10am–1.30pm & 4–7pm, Sat 10am–2pm & 4–7pm, Sun 10am–2pm; free), out towards the palm forest. Originally a Dominican monastery, it was converted into a university in 1569 by Pope Pius V, then closed down by Fernando VII in 1824. The two cloisters are well worth seeing, along with the fine eighteenth-century Valencian tiles in the refectory. For a view of the town and surrounding plains, walk up to the seminary on top of the hill. From Plaza Caturla in the centre of town, take the road leading up on the right; not far from the top, there are a couple of steeper shortcuts to the right.

Practicalities

Arriving by **bus** or **train**, you'll find yourself at the combined station at the bottom of Avenida de Teodomiro, where there's a helpful (but seldom open) tourist information desk. Otherwise, the main **turismo** is located in the impressive Palacio Rubalcara, c/Francisco Die 25 (Tues–Sat 10am–2pm & 5–8pm, in winter 4–7pm, Sun 10am–2pm; ☎965 302 747). For **accommodation**, *Hostal Rey Teodomiro*, five blocks straight up from the train station at Avda. Teodomiro 10 (☎966 743 348; ❸), has clean, bright, unpretentious rooms, all with bath; otherwise, the refurbished four-star *Hotel Meliá Palacio de Tudemir* (☎966 738 010, ⓦwww.hotelpalaciodetudemir.com; ❹–❺) is suitably palatial, with wall-mounted excavations inscribed in ancient Arabic, and calming rooms and corridors; the restaurant offers a €17 *menú*; on weekends it's €20.

If you cross over the road from the *Hostal Rey Teodomiro* and take the first right, you'll find *Mesón Don Pepe* at c/Valencia 3, which has **tapas** and a good weekday lunch *menú*, as well as *arroz con costra*, a local speciality (literally "rice and crust", made with rice, eggs, *embutidos*, chicken and rabbit). Another popular spot is *Bar Manolo*, c/Rio 16 (☎965 302 093; closed Tues), with tasty traditional tapas. For excellent regional fare, including *arroz con costra*, do as the locals and head to *Casa Corro*, Palmeral de San Antón, out of town on the Carretera Nacional in the direction of Alicante (☎965 302 963; sometimes closed for part of the year, so call ahead).

Murcia

MURCIA, according to the nineteenth-century writer Augustus Hare, would "from the stagnation of its long existence, be the only place Adam would recognize if he returned to Earth". Things have certainly changed – today, the city of over 350,000 boasts a modern, spruced-up centre and a healthy cultural life. Founded in the ninth century on the banks of the Río Segura (no more than a trickle now) by the Moors, the city soon became an important trading centre and, four centuries later, the regional capital. It was extensively rebuilt in the eighteenth century, and the buildings in the old quarter are still mostly of this era.

Today, it's the commercial centre of the region, and most of the industry is connected with the surrounding agriculture. An increasing number of tourists are taking advantage of budget-airline flights here, while a substantial student population ensures that there's a thriving bar and club scene.

Arrival and information

Both bus and train stations are on the edge of town. If you're arriving by **bus**, either walk southeast via plazas Pedro Pou and San Pedro towards the cathedral, or get there by bus #15. The **train station** is across the river at the southern edge of town – you can take bus #9 or #39 to the centre. The town's **airport** is 45km away in San Javier (see "Listings" p.877). You'll find two helpful **municipal offices**; the main one is close to the cathedral on Plaza Cardenal Belluga (April–Oct Mon–Sat 10am–2pm & 5–9pm, Sun 10am–2pm; Oct–March Mon–Sat 10am–2pm & 4.30–8.30pm, Sun 10am–2pm; ☎968 358 749, ⓦwww .murciaciudad.com for city info, ⓦwww.murciaturistica.es for regional info), while another is near the theatre on c/Santa Clara (same hours; ☎968 220 659).

Accommodation

Murcia has a decent, if rather basic, range of **accommodation**, particularly in the mid-range bracket. You'll find most hotels and *pensiones* conveniently located, in and around the city centre.

Hotel Arco De San Juan Plaza de Ceballos 10 ☎968 210 455, ⓦwww.arcosanjuan.com. Engagingly frumpish floral drapes dominate the rooms in this Neoclassical palace turned hotel. The facade is probably worth the price alone. ❸

Hotel Hispano II c/Radio Murcia 3 ☎968 216 152. A welcoming mid-range hotel, with a highly regarded restaurant and private garage. They also run the adjoining *Pensión Hispano I* (c/Trapería 8 ☎968 216 152; ❶–❷), which has been undergoing extensive renovations; check with the hotel. ❸–❹ B&B.

Hotel Rincón de Pepe c/Apóstoles 34 ☎968 212 239, ⓦwww.nh-hotels.com. One of the best hotels in Murcia, paved with pink Portuguese marble and featuring a famous downstairs restaurant and bar. Discounted weekend rates. ❺–❻

Hotel Zenit Murcia Plaza San Pedro 5–6 ☎968 214 742, ⓦwww.zenithoteles.com. Comfortable, three-star hotel (part of the Zenit chain) that sits in the thick of things, paces from lively Plaza de las Flores. A cool-toned lobby, tidy rooms and all the amenities. ❹

Pensión Campoy c/Diego Hernández 32 ☎968 254 591. Recently refurbished with clean, spartan rooms, this is perfectly situated for the train station. ❶

Pensión Murcia c/Vinadel 6, Entresuelo ☎968 219 963. Central *hostal* that operates on a floor of a residential building; simple rooms, some a bit musty, with or without bath. ❷

The City

The **Catedral** (daily: summer 7am–1pm & 6–8pm; winter 7am–1pm & 5–8.30pm; winter hours vary, so check with the nearby *turismo*) towers over the

MURCIA

0   150 m

▲ Albacete & Madrid

▲ Post Office

▲ Albacete & Madrid

▲ Cartagena, Airport & Almería

▼ Cartagena, Train Station & G

ACCOMMODATION

Hotel Arco De San Juan	F
Hotel Hispano II	C
Hotel Rincón de Pepe	E
Hotel Zenit Murcia	D
Pensión Campoy	G
Pensión Hispano I	B
Pensión Murcia	A

EATING & DRINKING

El Grumete	3
Mesón del Corral de	
José Luis	1
Las Mulas	4
La Muralla	6
Hotel Rincón de Pepe	E
La Tapa	5
Los Ventanales	2

Jardín de la Constitución

Museo de Bellas Artes

Plaza de Toros

ESTADIO
LA CONDOMINA

Jardín de la Fama

Universidad

La Merced

Santa Ana

Santo Domingo

Santa Clara

Casino

Catedral

Palacio Episcopal

Museo Arqueológico

El Corte Inglés

Teatro Romea

Jardín de San Esteban

San Esteban

Santa Catalina

Ayuntamiento

Museo Hidráulico

Palacio Almudí

Jardín de la Pólvora

San Nicolás

San Pedro

Las Verónicas

Iglesia del Pilar

Jardines del Malecón

Bus Station

Museo Salzillo

Palacio de Justicia

mansions and plazas of the centre. Begun in the fourteenth century and finally completed in the eighteenth, it's a strange mix of styles, dubbed "Mediterranean Gothic". The outside is more interesting architecturally, particularly the west side with its Baroque facade, and the tower rising on the north, which you can climb for great views of the city. Inside, the most remarkable aspect is the florid Plateresque decoration of the chapels – particularly the **Capilla de los Vélez** (1491–1505). Originally designed as a funeral area, but never completed, it's one of the finest examples of medieval art in Murcia and one of the most interesting pieces of Hispanic Gothic; an urn in the niche of the main altar contains the heart of Alfonso the Wise. The **museum** has some fine primitive sculptures and, above all, a giant processional monstrance – 600kg of gold and silver twirling like a musical box on its revolving stand.

Across the Plaza Cardenal Belluga stands the newest addition to Murcia's architectural heritage. Rafael Moneo's extension to the **ayuntamiento** closes the square with a strict regular building that faces the cathedral facade with a rhythmic twentieth-century version of the Baroque *retablo*.

The **Museo Salzillo**, west of the centre in Plaza San Agustín, near the bus station (July & Aug Tues–Fri 10am–2pm & 5–8pm, Sat 10am–2pm; Sept–June Tues–Sat 10am–2pm & 5–8pm, Sun 11am–2pm; ☎968/291 893, ⓦwww .museosalzillo.es; €3), has an extraordinary collection of the figures carried in Murcia's renowned Semana Santa procession. They were carved in the eighteenth century by Francisco Salzillo and display all the cloying sentimentality and delight in the "rustic" of that age. Other museums include the **Museo de Bellas Artes** at c/Obispo Frutos 12 (Tues–Sat 10am–9pm, Oct–April until 8.30pm, Sun 10am–2pm; free), with a representative collection of Renaissance and Golden Age art, contemporary sculpture and even an esoterically carved door said to have belonged to a Portuguese witch; and the **Museo Arqueológico**, Gran Vía Alfonso X 5 (closed for renovation at the time of writing; projected hours July & Aug Tues–Sun 10am–9pm; Sept–June Tues–Sat 10am–8.30pm, Sun 10am–2pm; free), which has an extensive collection of ceramics and potsherds (broken fragments of pottery).

The **casino** (closed for renovation at the time of writing), at c/Trapería 22, is a quirky delight and well worth a visit. The building dates from 1847 and combines an Arabic-style patio and vestibule, an English-style library reading room, a Pompeiian patio with Ionic columns, a billiard room and French ballroom. Most extraordinary of all, perhaps, is the neo-Baroque ladies' powder room (open to all), the ceiling of which depicts angelic ladies among the clouds, powdering their noses and tidying their hair.

Eating, drinking and nightlife

Murcia is known as *la huerta de Europa* (the orchard of Europe), and although this might be a slight exaggeration, you'll find local produce on most restaurant menus: vegetable soups, grills and paellas are the main specialities. It's also an important rice-growing region, and the local variety, Calasparra, which ripens very slowly, is the variety used to make paella.

Restaurants and tapas bars

When talk turns to **tapas**, Murcia doesn't often come up; it should. Come evening, do as the locals and *ir de tapeo* in and around Plaza de las Flores, Plaza Santa Catalina and along Gran Vía Alfonso X. For well-priced traditional Spanish, it's also worth checking out the *mesones* in the Plaza de Julián Romea (beside the theatre) and on and around Plaza San Juan.

▲ Murcia's Catedral

El Grumete c/Vara de Rey 6 & Plaza San Nicolas 3. If you're in the mood for seafood, this is the spot for tasty, fresh *mariscos* served by weight. Both branches closed Mon.

Hotel Rincón de Pepe c/Apósteles 34 ☏ 968 212 239. The ultimate – and priciest – Murcian gastronomic experience. Expect to pay around €55 a head for a meal, which will invariably include some inspired combinations of Murcia's famous fruit and veg – be sure to leave room for the *leche frita flambeada* for dessert. Restaurant closed Sun dinner & Mon.

Mesón del Corral de José Luís Plaza de Santo Domingo 23 ☏ 968 214 597. Locals flock to this long-time spot for the quality Murcian cuisine.

Las Mulas c/Ruiperez 5. An earthy tapas experience, with a delicious *patatas real murcia* (a scrambled egg and potato concoction named after the local football team).

La Tapa Plaza de las Flores 13. For outdoor tapas, settle in at one of the tables scattered near the plaza fountain, and graze on tasty bites including young eel tossed with potatoes, and grilled *pulpo*, or octopus.

Los Ventanales c/Alejandro Seiquer. This popular tapas eatery has various branches around the city (the most central on c/Alejandro Seiquer) and peddles in five different strains of *patatas a lo pobre*.

Bars and clubs

As a university town, Murcia has a disarmingly vibrant and diverse **nightlife** during term time, with a scene that hasn't yet succumbed to style-bar uniformity – to get a grip on what's hot, pick up a copy of the free listings magazines, such as *Guía de Ocio*. One of the liveliest areas for **bars** is around the university, near the Museo de Bellas Artes, in particular c/Dr Fleming, c/de Saavedra Fajardo and the side streets off them. A good place to start the evening is on the terrace of *El Refugio* on the nearby Plaza de Bolsas, which is more or less at the centre of the action. At 3am, the action disperses to the **clubs**, which are located all over the city: *Mundaka*, at Ctra. Catalina 26, is the premier house and techno venue with national and international DJs; *Super 8*, out at Avda. Ciclista Mariano Rojas, spins alternative sounds; while *El Garaje de la Tia Maria*, Avda. Miguel de Cervantes, mashes up everything from electrodisco to Nirvana and Vivaldi.

There is also a sizeable **gay scene** in Murcia: *Piscis*, Plaza Santo Domingo 6, is a popular bar, with the crowd moving on later to the *Metropol* club, off Ctra. Puente Tocinos.

El Ahorcado Feliz c/Cánovas del Castillo. A hopping theme bar that could best be described as Maghrebi Gothic.

Atomic Bar c/Simón García. Low leather seats and velvet drapes, and live music, from blues to rock.

B12 c/Trinidade 17. For a departure from pop-Español, try this cool club with funk, hip-hop and reggae.

El Bosque Animado Plaza Cristo del Rescate. This central, aptly named "Animated Forest" has outdoor tables for evening cocktails on the breezy plaza, and inside, artificial trees twinkling with lights.

Kennedy Bar Callejón Burruezo, just west of Jardín San Esteban. Irish-style pubs may be ubiquitous in Spain, but some are worth seeking out, such as this amiable spot. Original stone arches grace the spacious interior, and a long bar invites conversation between the lively crowd of locals and visitors; check out, too, the elevated church pulpit brought over from England, which makes for a romantic drinking nook. They also host comedy shows – ask at the bar for dates – which sometimes include well-known humorists.

La Muralla Below Hotel Rincón de Pepe. Certainly one of Murcia's most memorable bars is this underground, low-lit bar where you can sip cocktails in the shadow of the original Moorish city walls. They also host regular jazz sessions.

Listings

Airport Located 45km away at San Javier on the Mar Menor (☎968 172 000). Ryanair, easyJet and some charters fly to the UK, and there are limited internal flights to Almería, Barcelona and Madrid. To get to the airport, bus #73 goes daily from the bus station at 1pm & 5.30pm, and also at 3.15pm on Mon, Fri & Sun. Coming the other way, buses run daily at 5.45pm, 7.15pm & 10.45pm. Alternatively, bus #70 runs pretty much hourly to San Javier, from where it's a 3km walk or taxi ride.

Banks All the big ones, with foreign exchange desks, are on the Gran Vías.

Car rental Europcar, Avda. Miguel de Cervantes 7 ☎968 283 086, ⓦwww.europcar.es; Sol Mar, Avda. Juan de Borbón 36 ☎968 239 387, ⓦwww .solmar.es; Atesa, c/Azarbe del Papel 16 ☎968 200 337, ⓦwww.atesa.es.

Hospitals Hospital General Universitario "Reina Sofia", Avda. Intendente Jorge Palacios ☎968 359 000; Red Cross ☎968 355 339.

Internet Locutorios (phone centres) are scattered around the city, particularly around the centre and the bus station, and most have internet access (€1–2 per hr).

Market The Mercado Municipal, c/Verónicas (Mon–Sat 8am–2pm), has stacks of wonderful local produce including fresh fruit.

Police Avda. San Juan de la Cruz ☎968 358 750.

Post office Plaza Circular (Mon–Fri 8.30am–8.30pm, Sat 9.30am–2pm).

Shopping El Corte Inglés has two buildings either side of Gran Vía Salzillo. The main shopping area is around the Gran Vías.

The coast south of Torrevieja

The stretch of coast around the south of **Torrevieja** has been developed at an alarming rate, and is now home to a mix of Europeans, Russians and locals. Just to the south is a series of pleasant beaches, known collectively as **Las Playas de Orihuela** (as they come within Orihuela's provincial boundary). Both Playa La Zenía and Playa Cabo Roig are good, clean options with car parks and cafés (the restaurant at Cabo Roig is also exceptionally good and enjoys wide views over the harbour).

The Murcian Costa Cálida starts at **Mar Menor** (Lesser Sea), a broad lagoon whose shallow waters (ideal for kids) warm up early in the year, making this a good out-of-season destination. With its high-rise hotels, the "sleeve" (la manga) looks like a diminutive Benidorm; the resort of **SANTIAGO DE LA RIBERA** on the land side of the lagoon is a more appealing place to spend a day or two by the coast, and is popular with murciaños. There's a good sandy beach, an attractive promenade and an important sailing club here – the calm sea is perfect for novices. The **turismo** is located 300m back from the seafront on c/Padre Juan (summer Mon–Fri 10am–2pm & 5.30–8.30pm, Sat & Sun 10.30am–1.30pm;

winter Mon–Fri 10am–2pm & 5–7pm Sat & Sun 10am–1.30pm; ℡968 571 704). For **accommodation**, homely rooms with good sea views can be had at the family-owned, nautical-themed *Hotel El Marino*, Explanada Barnuevo 13 (℡968 572 121, ✉elmarino@terra.es; ❸). If you're looking for seafood, you'll get the best in town at *Lonja Mar Menor* on the beach at Paseo Colón (℡968 573 657); a plate of *fritura*, or small fried fish, goes for €12, while a generous *mariscada*, with shrimp, clam and prawns, is €38. Also on Paseo Colón is *Pescadería de Miguel*, with an array of seafood at slightly lower prices. There are two **campsites** in the area: *Pueblo De San Javier* in San Javier (℡968 181 080), and *Mar Menor* on the Alicante–Cartagena road (℡968 570 133).

The nearest **train station** is Balsicas (connected with Murcia, San Pedro and Santiago by hourly buses). Trains run direct from here to Barcelona, Valencia and Madrid. **Buses** also run every two hours to Cartagena.

Cartagena

Whether you're approaching **CARTAGENA** from one of the numerous resorts along Mar Menor, inland from Murcia, or from Almería to the south, it's not a pretty sight, even if the rusting mineworks that scar the landscape have their own austere appeal. It's only when you reach the old part of town down by the port, with its narrow medieval streets, packed with bars and restaurants, that the city's real character emerges.

Cartagena was Hannibal's capital city on the Iberian peninsula, named after his Carthage in North Africa, and a strategic port and administrative centre for the Romans. International Nautical Week is celebrated here in June. In July, the Mar de Músicas festival presents some of the best in world music, and in November the city hosts both a nationally famous jazz festival and an International Festival of Nautical Cinema. The **fiestas** of Semana Santa are some of the most elaborate in Spain, with processions leaving from the church of Santa María de Gracia in the early hours of Good Friday morning.

Arrival, information and accommodation

Cartagena's **bus station** is on c/Trovero Marín, with the FEVE **train station** (trains running to Los Nietos on the Mar Menor) almost next door and the RENFE station nearby at the end of Avenida América. The city's **turismo** is on Plaza del Almirante Basterreche (summer Mon–Fri 10am–2pm & 5–7pm, Sat 10am–1pm; winter Mon–Fri 10am–2pm & 4–6pm, Sat 10am–1pm; ℡968 506 483, ⦿www.cartagena.es). There's also a smaller office on Plaza del Ayuntamiento, which maintains similar hours (closes a half-hour earlier – at 1.30pm – during day hours) but also opens all year round on Sundays (10.30am–1.30pm).

Places to stay are quite thin on the ground, with the lower-end options somewhat underwhelming. *Pensión Oriente*, c/Jara 27 (℡968 502 469; ❶), offers very basic, wooden-shuttered rooms in an old house with communal bath. The comfortable *Hotel Los Habaneros*, c/San Diego 60 (℡968 505 250, ⦿www.hotelhabaneros.com; ❹), is nicely convenient, being round the corner from the bus and train stations, while the sleek *NH Cartagena*, Real 2, Plaza Héroes de Cavite (℡968 120 908, ⦿www.nh-hotels.com; ❹), flaunts plenty of fashionably elongated design inside a pagoda-style exterior, along with the hotel chain's signature Ferran Adrià-inspired "nhube" restaurants and lounge spaces, where you can munch on a bocadillo or heartier traditional fare.

The City

Cartagena does not have an excess of sights and much of what it does have is in ruins. The vast military **Arsenal** that dominates the old part of the city dates from the mid-eighteenth century and, like the Captaincy General building, is still in use and heavily guarded, although guided tours are in the offing (ask at the *turismo* for details, as well as for the museum hours below). However, you can visit the **Naval Museum**, c/Menéndez Pelayo 6 (generally Tues–Sun 10am–1.30pm; free), set in the walls of the Arsenal, with a room dedicated to Cartagena-born Isaac Peral, the inventor of the submarine; and the **National Museum for Underwater Archeology** (same hours), which is a long walk round the outer walls of the Arsenal on the way to the lighthouse, and has a reconstructed Roman galley and a lot of interesting exhibits salvaged from shipwrecks. The **Museo Arqueológico**, c/Ramón y Cajal 45 (Tues–Fri 10am–2pm & 5–8pm, Sat & Sun 11am–2pm; free), in the new part of town, is built on a Roman burial ground and has an excellent collection of Roman artefacts and a good introduction to the ancient history of the city.

The best of Cartagena's churches is **Santa María de Gracia** on c/San Miguel, which contains various works by Salzillo, including the figures on the high altar. There are more works by Salzillo and a fine art collection in the Neoclassical church **La Caridad** on c/la Caridad. You'll see a large number of *modernista* buildings around the city. Most of these are the work of former Cartagenian and disciple of Gaudí, Victor Beltri (1865–1935). In particular, have a look at **Casa Maestre** in Plaza San Francisco; **Casa Cervantes**, c/Mayor 15; and the old **Hotel Zapata**, Plaza de España.

To get a feel of the city's distinguished past, wander along the sea wall towards the old **military hospital**. It's a huge, empty, but evocative building, now falling into disrepair, and no one will mind you having a poke around. From the lighthouse there are great views of the harbour and city, but perhaps the best **city views** are from Torres Park, reached along c/Gisbert. Past the ruins of the old cathedral, the road winds down back into Plaza del Ayuntamiento.

Eating and drinking

There are plenty of local **bars** and **restaurants** in the old town with Spanish-only menus and uninflated prices. Many of the most characterful places are strung out along c/Mayor, just off the Plaza del Ayuntamiento. *El Mejillonera*, c/Mayor 4, does fine Gallego-style *pulpo*. For more upmarket food, head to the chic *Azafrán*, c/Palma 3 (℡968 523 172; closed Mon dinner & Sun), within striking distance of Plaza de España and serving pricey, gourmet variations on local specialities, including aromatic *arroces*. *Mare Nostrum*, down by the port (℡968 522 131), also offers excellent seafood dishes (€16–20), including *mero marinera*, grouper with clams and crayfish.

The Golfo de Mazarrón

South of Cartagena, much of the scenic coastline down to the border with Andalucía is undeveloped, with a succession of fine coves lying beneath a backdrop of arid, serrated hills. The region's main resorts, **El Puerto de Mazarrón** and **Águilas**, are both fairly small scale and easy-going, mainly attracting Spanish families. Public transport is limited, however, so you'll need your own vehicle to get to the better beaches.

El Puerto de Mazarrón

Despite a fair amount of development, **EL PUERTO DE MAZARRÓN** is pretty quiet even in season, and, with five **buses** a day from Cartagena, fairly accessible. Much of the **accommodation** is in expensive resort hotels, although there are cheaper alternatives. *Pensión Los Cisnes*, c/Sierra de Cazorla (T968 153 122, Wwww.pensionloscisnes.com; ❷), is convenient for the bus station, with clean if somewhat faded rooms. For more comfort, head for *Hotel Bahía*, Playa de la Reya (T968 594 000, Wwww.hotelbahia.net; ❹), or *Hotel Playa Grande*, Avda. Castellar 19 (T968 155 715, Wwww.grupolameseguera .com; ❹–❺), both right on the beach itself. The massive **campsite**, *Playa de Mazarrón*, on Ctra. Bolnuevo (T968 150 660, Wwww.playamazarron.com), is open year round. You'll find a useful **turismo** at Plaza Toneleros 1 (Mon–Fri 9am–2pm & 5–8pm, Sat 9.30am–1.30pm & 4.30–7pm; summer also Sun 9.30am–1.30pm; T968 594 426, Wwww.mazarron.es).

There are great **beaches** within easy reach of El Puerto de Mazarrón. Buses head 6km southwest along the coast to Bolnuevo, where there's a superb stretch of sand. West of Bolnuevo, the route becomes a dirt track, with access to several coves popular with nudists, until you reach the headland of Punta Calnegre, 15km from El Puerto de Mazarrón, where there are more good stretches of sand. Alternatively, if you head northeast from El Puerto de Mazarrón the best beaches are around Cabo Tiñoso, 13km away. If you get tired of sunbathing, the nature reserve at **La Rambla de Moreras**, 2km north of Bolnuevo, has a lagoon that attracts a variety of migratory birds.

The best bet for **seafood** is *El Puerto*, out on a limb at the far end of Paseo de la Sal (T968 594 805). Alternatively, at the canteen-style *Beldamar*, Avenida Costa Cálida (T968 594 826; reduced hours in winter), you can buy fresh fish and have it cooked for you on the spot. For tasty local **tapas**, try the popular bar below *Pensión La Línea*. *Los Cazadores*, 5km along the road to Águilas (T968 158 943; closed Sun dinner), has hearty meat and fish dishes, and a *menú* for €10. In summer, the terraces along the Paseo Marítimo are good for an evening **cocktail**.

Águilas

ÁGUILAS, 47km from Mazarrón, and almost on the border with Andalucía, is surrounded by plastic-sheeted fields of tomatoes – one of the few things that can grow in this arid region – and hemmed in by the parched hills of the Sierra del Contar. Along with the cultivation of tomatoes, fishing is the mainstay of the economy here, and a fish auction is held at around 5pm every day in the port's large warehouse. **Carnaval** is especially wild in Águilas, and for three days and nights in February, the entire population lets its hair down with processions, floats and general fancy-dress mayhem.

Arrival and information

You'll find the **turismo** on Plaza de Antonio Cortijos, near the port (summer Mon–Fri 9am–2pm & 5–10pm, Sat 10am–2pm & 5–10pm, Sun 10am–2pm; winter generally Mon–Fri 9am–2pm & 5–7pm, Sat 10am–2pm; T968 493 285, Wwww.aguilas.org). **Buses** arrive at the station, itself adjacent to the **train** station at the end of c/Espalda Cuña. Services run to Murcia (Mon–Fri 6 daily, Sat & Sun 3 daily). Almería, Cartagena (both 2 daily) and Lorca (Mon–Fri 13 daily, Sat & Sun 4 daily). There are also more **trains** daily to both Murcia and Lorca (5 in July & Aug). If you plan on exploring the surrounding beaches, renting a car or bike is a good idea; **car rental** is available from Auriga, c/Iberia 65 (T968 414 582), while **mountain bikes** can be rented from along c/Barcelona (around €15 per day).

Accommodation

Aguilas features a decent selection of **hotels** – though some are a bit dated – and budget beds. You'll generally have no problem finding available rooms, except during Carnaval in February, when it's best to book ahead.

Albergue Juvenil 3km out of town at Calarreona along the Carretera Almería ☎ 968 413 029. Basic and clean; in summer, when the hostel is busy, they also offer a simple *menú* for €5.75. Under 25s €7.45, over 25s €10.60.

Hotel Calareal Near the beach at c/Aire 99 ☎ 968 414 562, ⓦ www.hotel-calareal.com. In the luxury bracket, this friendly hotel offers smart, parquet-floored rooms with good views of the Cabeza del Caballo, a mini-Gibraltar-style rock jutting into the bay. ❺

Hotel Carlos III c/Rey Carlos III 22 ☎ 968 411 650, ⓦ www.hotelcarlosiii.com. Several blocks nearer the seafront and several decades back in time is this dowdy and overpriced hotel, but the 1970s vintage sofas, mirrored bar and ceiling fans lend an air of august decay. ❸–❹

Hotel Madrid Plaza de Robles Vives 4 ☎ 968 411 109. Period charm, with chequered marble, a wicker-furnished lounge and some good deals in low season. ❸

Pensión La Huerta c/Barcelona 2 ☎ 968 411 400, ⓦ www.pensionlahuerta.com. Among the budget options, this is probably the best bet, with clean rooms. ❷

Campsite

Águilas 1km out of town along the Carretera Cope-Calabardina ☎ 968 419 205. Pleasant site situated among pine trees in the Urbanización Los Geráneo.

The town and its beaches

Águilas is a popular spot, as the beaches are plentiful (some served by public transport) and the area has a superb year-round climate. The town itself has managed to escape the worst excesses of tourism, and retains much of its rural charm and character.

You'll find fine **beaches**, and over thirty small *calas* (coves) in the vicinity – those to the north are rockier and more often backed by low cliffs, while the best are the wonderful, fairly undeveloped **cuatro calas** south of town. You'll need your own wheels to reach these beaches, which get better the farther you get away from Águilas, but all are signposted. The first two, **Calarreona** and **La Higuérica** have fine sands and are backed by dunes and the odd villa, but 6km south of Águilas where the coast is completely wild, the ravishing back-to-back sandy coves of **Cala Carolina** and **Cala Cocedores** are simply superb.

If you don't have your own transport, there is a chain of beaches north of Águilas served by regular buses (generally mid-July to end-Aug only). **Playa Hornillo**, is a nice beach with a couple of bars (and you could actually reach it by walking from the train station), while **Playa Amarillo** is decent but in a built-up area. The bus also passes *playas* Arroz, La Cola and finally Calabardina (7km from town), where the bus service ends. If you feel energetic, you could head across **Cabo Cope** to yet another chain of beaches beginning at Ruinas Torre Cope.

Eating and drinking

For a fine selection of fresh fish, grilled octopus or *arroz a la piedra* (a tasty rice dish with fish, shrimps and tomato), head for either *El Puerto*, right by the port on Plaza Robles 18 (☎ 968 447 065; closed Tues), or *Las Brisas*, in the shadow of the *faro* on Explanada de Puerto (☎ 968 448 288; closed Mon), where salty fishing types hog the bar, and a wooden terrace overlooks the bay. Locals also swear by *La Veleta*, a bit of a hike westwards on c/Blas Rosique 6 (☎ 968 411 798; closed Sun). There's also a good covered **market**, three blocks inland from the port, with plenty of locally grown fresh fruit and vegetables.

Lorca

Many of the historic villages of inland Murcia are accessible only with your own transport, but one place you can reach easily is **LORCA**, an attractive former frontier town whose historic centre still has a distinct aura of the past. For a time, it was part of the Córdoba caliphate, but it was retaken by the Christians in 1243, after which Muslim raids were a feature of life until the fall of Granada, the last Muslim stronghold. Most of the town's notable buildings – churches and ancestral homes – date from the sixteenth century onwards.

Lorca is famed for its **Semana Santa** celebrations, which outdo those of both Murcia and Cartagena, the next best in the region. There's a distinctly operatic splendour about the dramatization of the triumph of Christianity, with characters such as Cleopatra, Julius Caesar and the royalty of Persia and Babylon attired in embroidered costumes of velvet and silk. The high point is the afternoon and evening of Good Friday.

Arrival, information and accommodation

Hourly trains and buses connect Lorca with Murcia, although the train is cheaper and a little quicker. Arriving by **train**, get off at Lorca Sutullera; **buses** arrive at the adjacent station. Heading south to Granada there are four daily buses. The **turismo**, on c/Lópe Gisbert (daily: summer Mon–Sat 9.30am–2pm & 5–8pm, Sun 10am–2.30pm; winter Mon–Sat 9.30am–2pm & 5.30–7.30pm, Sun 10am–2pm; ☎968 441 914, ⓦwww.ayuntalorca.es), can provide a good map, an excellent hour-long guided architectural walk around the town and plenty of glossy material.

Even though it really only takes an hour or two to look around Lorca, it's still a reasonable place to stop overnight, with inexpensive **rooms** all along the highway. Although a bit of a hike from the centre, the friendly, tastefully renovated *Hotel Félix* (Lorca's oldest) on Avda. Fuerzas Armadas 146 (☎968 467 654, ⓦwww.hotelfelix.com; ❷) has rustic, cool-toned rooms with balconies, and a restaurant that serves up an economical Murcian *menú* for €10. Despite an unpromising exterior, the *Hotel Alameda* has decent rooms, in the centre of town at c/Musso Valiente 8 (☎968 406 600, ⓦwww.hotel-alameda.com; ❸). Rooms have a bird's-eye view of the Semana Santa parades. *Jardines de Lorca*, on Alameda Rafael Méndez (☎968 470 599, ⓦwww.hotelesdemurcia.com; B&B ❺; prices dip to nearly half in low season), sits in a restful residential zone, near a leafy park after which it's named. Note that if you're coming at Easter you'll have to book at least three months in advance (for any accommodation), or stay in Murcia or Águilas.

The Town

Before heading up to the old town, it's worth popping into the **Centro de Artesanía**, next door to the *turismo*, which displays and sells work combining traditional crafts with avant-garde design (Mon–Sat 10am–2pm & 5.30–7.30pm; free).

The old part of town lies up the hill from c/López Gisbert. The **Casa de los Guevara** (summer Tues–Sat 10am–2pm & 5–7.30pm, Sun 10am–2pm; winter Tues–Sat 10am–2pm & 4.30–7pm; €3), next to the *turismo*, is an excellent example of civic eighteenth-century Baroque architecture and is the best mansion in town. On the corner of Plaza San Vicente and c/Corredera, the main shopping artery, is the **Columna Milenaria**, a Roman column dating from around 10 BC: it marked the distance between Lorca and Cartagena on the *via*

Heraclea, the Roman road from the Pyrenees to Cádiz. The Gothic **Porche de San Antonio**, the only gate remaining from the old city walls, lies at the far end of c/Corredera. On Plaza de España, the focal point of the town, and seemingly out of proportion with the rest, you'll find the imposing **Colegiata de San Patricio** (daily 11am–1pm & 4.30–6.30pm, Sat & Sun until 8pm; free), with its enormous proto-Baroque facade, built between the sixteenth and eighteenth centuries – there's a marked contrast between the outside and the sober, refined interior, which is largely Renaissance. Nearby is the **ayuntamiento**, with its seventeenth- to eighteenth-century facade. An equally impressive front is presented by the sixteenth-century **Posito**, down a nearby side street – originally an old grain storehouse, it's now the municipal archive.

Somewhat unfortunately, the brooding thirteenth- to fourteenth-century **Castillo** (Easter & mid-July to Sept Tues–Sun 10.30am–6.30pm; reduced hours rest of the year; €10, €12 including toy-town train and *Centro de Visitantes*, see below), overlooking the town, has been turned into an expensive, medieval-themed tourist attraction. Note that though there's the toy-town train-bus ride up to the castle, it's perfectly possible to walk (or drive) up via the impoverished *barrio antiguo* above the Colegiata de San Patricio, too. To be fair, the castle complex does reveal some well-presented exhibits about its history, plus re-enacted scenes of warfare using wooden stone-throwers and knights – but it all seems a bit contrived nonetheless. In August, the castle offers nocturnal visits (Tues–Sat 8.30pm–1am, last entry 11.30pm), which are a draw among locals, it seems, more because you can tour the place without the midday sun beating down than for anything else. In town, a flashy visitor centre, **Centro de Visitantes**, Antiguo Convento de la Merced s/n (Tues–Sun 9.30am–2pm & 4–7pm; ☎902 400 047, ⓦwww.lorcatallerdeltiempo.com; €3.50), has exhibits on Lorca, along with plenty of tourist info, though it's only worth going in if you've already bought the castle ticket.

Eating and drinking

Restaurante Barcas Casa Cándido, c/Santo Domingo 13 (☎968 466 907; closed Mon), is the grandaddy of the Lorcan eating scene, but you'll find a fine assortment of other **restaurants** such as *Juan de Toledo*, c/Juan de Toledo 14 (☎968 470 215; closed Mon, also closed Sun in Aug). The accommodating, colourful *El Hornero*, with guacamole-green walls and blue-beamed ceilings, on Plaza San Vicente 4 (☎ 968 471 287), offers robust international fare (including veggie dishes). For **tapas**, it's worth skirting the lower reaches of the old town to where the handsome, *azulejo*-fronted *Meson El Camino*, c/Alfonso X El Sabio, draws an animated local crowd.

El Caravaca de la Cruz

EL CARAVACA DE LA CRUZ, 60km from Lorca and an important border town, is best approached from Murcia (hourly buses; 1hr 30min), though there is one daily service from Lorca. The town is dominated by the **Castillo**, which contains a beautiful marble and sandstone church, **El Santuario de Vera Cruz** (Mon–Fri 8am–2pm & 4–7pm, Sat 8am–2.30pm & 4–7pm, Sun 10am–2.30pm & 4–7pm). The church houses the cross used in the Semana Santa celebrations; on May 3, it's "bathed" in the temple at the bottom of town to commemorate the apparition of a cross to the Moorish king of Valencia, Zayd Abu Zayd, in 1231. There's also an adjacent **museum** (daily 10am–2pm & 4–8pm, in winter until

7pm; €4), which concentrates on religious art and history, and also boasts a basement with archeological remains from the original medieval castle walls and towers. The churches that tower over the rest of the town, **La Iglesia del Salvador** and **La Iglesia de la Concepción**, are also worth a visit; the latter contains some excellent examples of carved Mudéjar wood. For **accommodation**, there are comfortable, upmarket en-suites at *Hotel Central*, Gran Vía 18 (☎968 707 055, ⓦwww.hotelcentralcaravaca.com; ❹). As for **food** and **drink**, the cafés clustered around Plaza del Arco are good for an alfresco refreshment after a hike up to the castle, while *Los Viñales*, Avda. Juan Carlos I 41 (☎968 708 458; closed Mon dinner & Tues), is a good *comida casera* restaurant, with attached **tapas** bar.

Travel details

Trains

For current timetables and ticket information, consult RENFE ☎902 240 202, ⓦwww.renfe.es or FEVE ☎987 271 210, ⓦwww.feve.es.

Alicante to: Albacete (9 daily; 1hr 30min); Benidorm (half-hourly to hourly; 1hr 10min); Denia (half-hourly to hourly; 2hr 15min); Madrid (9 daily; 3hr 45min); Murcia (14–23 daily; 1hr 15min); Valencia (10 daily; 1hr 30min–2hr 15min); Xàtiva (5 daily; 1hr 20min).

Murcia to: Águilas (3–5 daily; 2hr); Alicante (14–23 daily; 1hr 30min); Barcelona (4 daily; 7hr); Cartagena (8 daily; 1hr); Lorca (12–18 daily; 1hr); Madrid (5 daily; 4hr 30min); Orihuela (14–23 daily; 20min).

Valencia to: Alicante (12 daily; 1hr 30min–2hr 15min); Barcelona (14 daily; 2hr 50min–4hr 45min); Benicàssim (8 daily; 1hr 10min); Castellón de la Plana (every 30min; 45min–1hr); Gandía (every 30min; 50min); Madrid (10–14 daily; 3hr 30min–4hr 30min); Málaga (6 daily; 9hr); Murcia (12 daily; 3hr 25min); Orihuela (12 daily; 3hr); Peñíscola (9 daily; 1hr 30min); El Puig (every 20min; 20min); Sagunto (every 30min; 30min); Segorbe (3 daily; 1hr); Teruel (3 daily; 2hr 25min); Xàtiva (every 30min; 1hr); Zaragoza (2 daily; 5hr–6hr 45min).

Buses

Alicante to: Albacete (9 daily; 2hr 30min); Almería (5 daily; 5hr 30min); Barcelona (11 daily; 8hr); Cartagena (8 daily; 2hr); Granada (6 daily; 5hr); Madrid (8 daily; 6hr); Málaga (6 daily; 8hr); Murcia (8 daily; 1hr 45min); Orihuela (10 daily; 1hr 20min); Torrevieja (15 daily; 1hr).

Murcia to: Águilas (3–6 daily; 2hr); Albacete (11 daily; 2hr 30min); Alicante (8 daily; 1hr 45min); Almería (4–6 daily; 3hr 30min); Barcelona (9 daily; 8hr); Cartagena (17–26 daily; 1hr); Granada (6 daily; 6hr); Lorca (6–17 daily; 1hr 15min); Madrid (12 daily; 6hr 30min); Málaga (5 daily; 7hr); El Puerto de Mazarrón (3–4 daily; 1hr 30min); Orihuela (5–16 daily; 1hr); Valencia (4–7 daily; 4hr 45min).

Valencia to: Alicante (15–21 daily; 2hr 30min–3hr 30min); Barcelona (17–19 daily; 4hr 15min–5hr); Benidorm (15–20 daily; 2hr 30min); Bilbao (3 daily; 9hr); Castellón de la Plana (4–9 daily; 1hr 30min–2hr); Cuenca (3 daily; 4hr); Denia (10–11 daily; 1hr 45min); Gandía (11–14 daily; 1hr); Madrid (16–19 daily; 4hr); Murcia (11–14 daily; 3hr 15min); Orihuela (2 daily; 3hr); El Puig (14 daily; 30min); Sagunto (25 daily; 45min); Segorbe (4–7 daily; 1hr 15min); Seville (3 daily; 11hr).

Balearic connections

From **Alicante** Iberia 1–2 daily flights to Ibiza.

From **Denia** Baleària ferry service to Sant Antoni, Ibiza (2 daily; 2hr 15min & 4hr); Ibiza Town (3 daily; 2hr); Palma (4 daily; 5hr) and Formentera (daily; 3hr 45min). Iscomar also sails to Ibiza Town (1–2 daily except Sat; 4hr 30min).

From **Valencia** Trasmediterránea sails to: Palma de Mallorca (June–Sept 2 daily; 5hr 45min & 7hr 15min; Oct–May weekly; 9hr); Ibiza (June–Sept daily; 2hr 45min; Oct–May weekly; 4hr 45min); Mao, Menorca (Sat; 14hr). Iscomar also sails to Palma (5 weekly; 9hr 30min) and Baleària runs daily services to both Palma (6hr 45min) and Ibiza (3hr 45min). Both Air Europa (2–3 daily; 40min) and Air Berlin (daily; 45min) operate flights to Palma, while Vueling flies daily to Ibiza (40min).

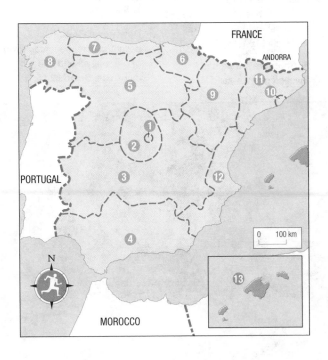

13

The Balearic Islands

CHAPTER 13

Highlights

* **Dalt Vila** Explore Ibiza Town's souk-like walled city, a UNESCO World Heritage Site. See p.891

* **Ibiza's clubs** The mother of all dance scenes fired by the globe's leading turntablists. See p.894

* **Ibiza's calas** Dozens of exquisite, bite-shaped cove beaches, including Benirràs and Cala Mastella. See p.895

* **Formentera's beaches** Sweeping white-sand beaches and pellucid waters. See p.898

* **Palma's old town** Charming Renaissance mansions cluster this delightful part of Mallorca's capital city. See p.904

* **Deià, Mallorca** One of Mallorca's prettiest villages, perched high above the ocean. See p.909

* **Downtown Ciutadella** A delightful little Menorcan town of mazy lanes and fine old mansions. See p.924

▲ Benirràs, Ibiza

The Balearic Islands

E ast of the Spanish mainland, the four chief Balearic islands – Ibiza, Formentera, Mallorca and Menorca – maintain a character distinct from the rest of Spain and from each other. Ibiza is wholly unique, its capital Ibiza Town loaded with historic interest and a Mecca for thousands of clubbers and gay visitors, while the north of the island has a distinctly bohemian character. Tiny **Formentera** has even better beaches than its neighbour – if nowhere near the same cultural interest. Mallorca, the largest and best-known Balearic, also battles with its image, popularly reckoned as little more than sun, booze and high-rise hotels. In reality, you'll find all the clichés, most of them crammed into the mega-resorts of the Bay of Palma and the east coast, but there's lots more besides: mountains, lovely old towns, some beautiful coves, and the Balearics' one real city, Palma. Mallorca is, in fact, the one island in the group you might come to other than for beaches and nightlife, with scope for plenty of hiking. And finally, to the east, there's Menorca – more subdued in its clientele, and here, at least, the booming modern resorts are kept at a safe distance from the two main towns, the capital Maó, and the charming, pocket-sized port of Ciutadella.

Access to the islands is easy from Britain and mainland Spain, with plenty of **flights** in summer, though in winter only Mallorca is really well connected. In addition, **ferries** and **catamarans** link Barcelona, Valencia, Alicante and Dénia with the islands, and there are plenty of inter-island ferries, too, though these can be pricey and fully booked in summer. For fuller details on **routes**, see "Travel details" on p.925-926.

The main fly in the ointment is cost: as prime "holiday islands", the Balearics charge considerably above mainland prices for **rooms** – from mid-June to mid-September rates can double, and rooms can be in very short supply. Rental **cars** can also be hard to come by at this time. Travelling around by **bus**, **moped**, **scooter and bicycle** are all perfectly feasible, but note that car-rental companies do not allow their vehicles to be taken from one island to another.

Catalan is spoken throughout the Balearics, and each of the three main islands has a different dialect, though locals all speak Castilian (Spanish). For the visitor, confusion arises from the difference between the islands' road signs and street names – which are almost exclusively in Catalan – and many of the maps on sale, which are in Castilian. In particular, note that Menorca now calls its capital Maó rather than Mahón, while both the island and town of Ibiza are usually referred to as Eivissa. In this chapter we give the Catalan name for towns, beaches and streets, except for Ibiza and Ibiza Town which are not widely known by their Catalan names outside Spain.

THE BALEARICS

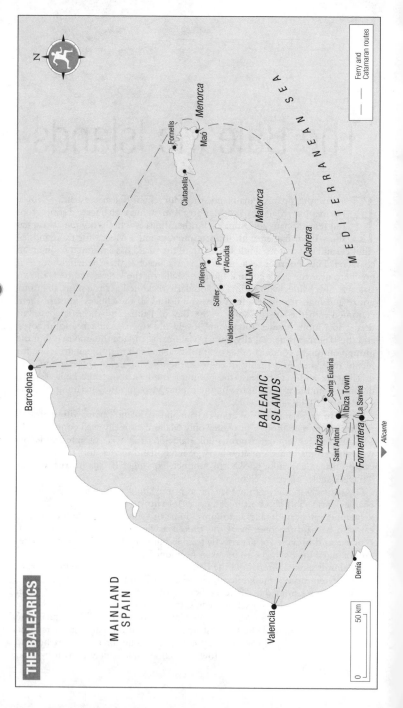

MAINLAND
SPAIN

Barcelona

Menorca
Fornells
Maó
Ciutadella

Mallorca

Pollença
Port
d'Alcúdia
PALMA
Sóller
Valldemossa

Cabrera

M E D I T E R R A N E A N   S E A

*BALEARIC
ISLANDS*

Santa Eulària
Ibiza
Sant Antoni
Ibiza Town
La Savina
Formentera

▼ *Alicante*

Denia

Valencia

N

Ferry and
Catamaran routes

0   50 km

Ibiza

IBIZA, or **Eivissa** in Catalan, is an island of excess – beautiful, and blessed with scores of stunning cove beaches and dense pine forests. Nevertheless, it's the islanders (*eivissencs*) and their visitors who make it special. Ibiza has long attracted hedonistic characters and wealthy bohemians, and the locals remain determinedly blasé about the mullet-haired fashionistas and celebrities who flock to the island today.

For years, Ibiza was *the* European hippie escape, but nowadays it's the extraordinary clubbing scene that most people come here to experience. The island can lay a strong claim to being the globe's **clubbing capital**, with virtually all of the world's top house DJs and many more minor players performing here during the summer season. However, visit between October and May, and you'll find a much more peaceful island – just one club (*Pacha*) and a few funky bars remain open through the winter. **Ibiza Town**, the capital, is the obvious place to base yourself: only a short bus ride from two great beaches – **Ses Salines** and **Es Cavallet** – and crammed with bars, restaurants and boutiques. The other main towns – **Sant Antoni** and Santa Eulària – are far less cosmopolitan and interesting. Around the entire shoreline, you'll find dozens of exquisite **cove beaches** (*calas*), many all but deserted even in high season, though you'll need your own transport to reach the best spots. **Inland**, the scenery is hilly and thickly wooded, dotted with a series of tiny hamlets, each boasting a stunning whitewashed village church and an atmospheric local bar or two.

Salt attracted the Greeks, and after them the Phoenicians and **Carthaginians**, for whom Ibiza was a prime burial site. Under Roman rule, the island continued to prosper, but thereafter a gradual decline set in, and from medieval times until the early twentieth century Ibiza was an impoverished backwater. Beatniks discovered the island in the 1950s, and Ibiza began to reinvent itself as one of the most chic locations in the Mediterranean.

Today, Ibiza's tourism-driven prosperity has seen more and more coastline consumed by rampant development. Property prices are astronomical, and a massive new road-building programme has besmirched the southern half of the island. Yet despite these pressures, Ibiza's natural allure still remains compelling, and it's not hard to find a pristine cove beach or a lonely forested trail to explore if you make the effort.

Ibiza practicalities

There's a good **bus service** between Ibiza Town, Sant Antoni, Santa Eulària, Portinatx, the airport and a few of the larger beaches. In summer, **boats** from the three main towns serve various destinations along the coast. However, renting a car or moped (see p.894) will widen your options no end. The excellent website Ⓦ www.ibiza-spotlight.com is highly informative.

Ibiza Town and around

IBIZA TOWN (Ciutat d'Eivissa) is easily the most attractive settlement on the island. Colossal medieval walls guard the old quarter of Dalt Vila, which is topped by a sturdy cathedral and a tottering castle and contains a couple of museums.

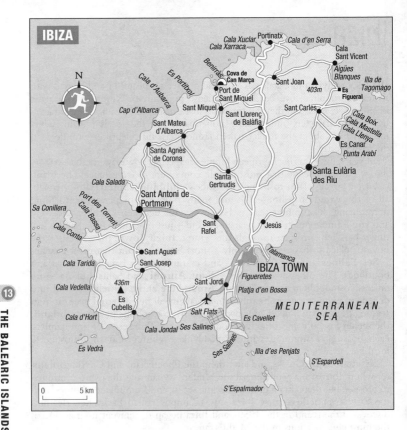

During summer nights, the whitewashed streets of the neighbouring port area are packed with people darting between chic boutiques and hip bars. In winter, things are much more peaceful, and the focus of activity shifts to the area around the graceful boulevard Passeig Vara de Rey.

Arrival and information

Ibiza's international **airport** is situated 6km southwest of Ibiza Town; buses leave for Ibiza Town (May–Oct every 30min 6.50am–11.50pm, plus hourly nightbuses July & Aug; Nov–May hourly 7am–10.30pm; €1.70) and also for Sant Antoni and Santa Eulària (both mid-June to mid-Sept only, every 1hr 30min, 7.45am–11.30pm). There are two **ferry terminals**: one on Avgda. Sta Eulària (for Formentera), and the other on Passeig des Moll (mainland and Mallorca).

The port areas of La Marina and Sa Penya face the waterfront, while **Dalt Vila**, literally "High Town", is a short walk uphill to the south. Ibiza Town's **bus station** is about 1.5km northwest of the centre, just off the inner ring road; regular buses run from here to the port area. You'll find the main **turisme** on Passeig Vara de Rey (June–Sept Mon–Fri 8.30am–7.30pm, Sat 9am–2pm; Oct–May Mon–Fri 8.30am–1.30pm & 4.30–7pm; ☎971 301 900).

Accommodation

Most of the **budget accommodation** is in the port area, particularly around Passeig de Vara de Rey. In the height of the tourist season, last-minute vacancies are very hard to come by.

Apartamentos Roselló c/General Juli Cirer i Vela ☎971 302 790, ☏www .apartamentosrosello.com. These apartments enjoy a wonderful tranquil location right above the Med, with panoramic views towards Formentera. Virtually all have superb south-facing sun terraces, and spacious living areas with kitchen facilities. A bit tricky to find, but best reached through the tunnel (*el túnel*) behind Dalt Vila. ❹

Casa de Huéspedes Vara de Rey Passeig de Vara de Rey 7 ☎971 301 376, ☏www.hibiza.com. Offering style on a budget, the *Vara del Rey* has light, shabby-chic rooms with fans and washbasins, though bathrooms are shared. ❹

Hostal Bimbi c/Ramón Muntaner 55, Figueretes ☎971 305 396, ☏www.hostalbimbi.com. A friendly little place, popular with backpackers, that's very close to Figueretes beach and a 10min walk from the centre. Rooms – singles, doubles and triples – are well kept, some have private bathrooms. Prices rise steeply in July & Aug. Closed Nov–Easter. ❸

Hostal Residencia Juanito & Hostal Residencia Las Nieves c/Joan d'Austria 18 ☎971 315 822. Two simple *hostales* run by the same management, with plain, clean rooms, some en suite. ❸

Hostal Residencia Parque Caieta Soler s/n ☎971 301 358, ☏www.hostalparque.com. Stylish, recently remodelled place, in an excellent central location, with gorgeous if smallish rooms. All have modish bathrooms and a/c. ❺

Hostal Residencia Sol y Brisa Avgda. Bartomeu Vicente Ramón 15 ☎971 310 818. A family-run *hostal* with small, tidy rooms in a very handy central location. Bathrooms are shared. ❸

Hostal Residencia La Ventana Sa Carrossa 13 ☎971 390 857, ☏www.laventanaibiza.com. Classy hotel inside Dalt Vila, with elegant but diminutive rooms, all with four-poster beds. There's a great restaurant and roof terrace. ❽

El Hotel Passeig Marítim ☎971 315 963, ☏www .elhotelpacha.com. The most stylish address in Ibiza Town, this very hip hotel successfully combines modernist design with Ibiza rustic chic. All the rooms are supremely spacious and scattered with modish artefacts, though the pool is tiny. ❾

Hotel Lux Isla c/Josep Pla 1, Talamanca ☎971 313 469, ☏www.luxisla.com. Just off the beach in Talamanca, 1.5km from Ibiza Town's marina, this is a well-run, excellent-value modern hotel with bright, comfortable rooms, most with sea-view balconies and a/c. B&B ❹

The Town

The city's stone walls reach a dramatic climax at the imposing **Portal de ses Taules**, a triple gateway designed to withstand the heaviest artillery barrage. Inside this monumental entrance lies the historic, UNESCO-listed enclave of **Dalt Vila**. Just beyond the main gate, elegant **Plaça de Vila** is lined with restaurants and cafés and makes a delightful setting for some tapas or a meal.

Heading east uphill along Sa Carrossa, it's a steep climb past the pretty church of **Sant Domingo** and along c/Santa María to Plaça de la Catedral. Some 90m above sea level, this lofty perch has been a place of worship for over two thousand years, originally occupied by a Carthaginian temple, then a Roman replacement and later a mosque. Today's thirteenth-century **Catedral** (daily: June–Oct 9.30am–1.30pm & 4–7pm; Nov–May 10am–2pm; free) is pleasingly austere, its sombre, sturdy Gothic lines supported by giant buttresses, though inside the decor contains somewhat trite Baroque embellishments.

Opposite the catedral, the **Museu Arqueològic d'Eivissa i Formentera** (April–Sept Tues–Sat 10am–2pm & 5–7.30pm, Sun 10am–2pm; Oct–March Tues–Sat 10am–1pm & 4–6pm, Sun 10am–2pm; €2.80) has some interesting Phoenician and Carthaginian exhibits, including images of the fertility goddess Tanit. Ibiza's Moorish period is dealt with inside the neighbouring **La Cúria** (same hours), a converted courthouse that has some flashy video displays and fine ceramics.

IBIZA TOWN

MEDITERRANEAN SEA

Port d'Eivissa   N

Estació
Marítim

◄ Bus Station (1.5km) & Airport (6km)

Mallorca, Menorca & ► The Mainland

DIPUTAT JOSEP RIBAS
CARLES III
JOSEP MARIA
FELIP II
ANTON JAUME
CARLES V
AVDA STA. EULALIA

PEDRO
FRANCES
GASPAR PUIG
QUADRADO

PASSEIG DES MOLL
PLAÇA
ANTONI RIQUER
PLAÇA DE
SA TERTULIA

BARTOLOMEU DE ROSELLÓ

AVDA IGNASI W. ALLS
C. D'ASTURIA
RAMON
RAMON.
C/ CAJAL

LA MARINA
CRUE
RIAMBAU
BISTORIERS
BISBE DE MONTER

PASSEIG DES MOLL
BARCELONA
EMILI POU

V. SOLER
C/ GARIJO

SA PENYA
C/ D'EMNITT
C/ DE LA VERGE
FOSC
C/ DEL RETIR

PEDRO
JOAN
VICENTE
ICERTE
C. DE MADRID
BARTOLOMEI
PASSEIG DE VARA DE REY

D'AZARA
C/ DE BARCELONA
C/ CONTE ROSSELLO
ABEL
MATUTE

C/ CASTELAR
C/ DE LA MAR
BISBE SA FONTANI
PLAÇA
SA FONTANI
PALAU

C. BISBE ISM ELM
PLAÇA DE LA
CONSTITUCIO

MANEL
C/ SANT PERE
DES PASSADIS
SANTA
LLÚCIA

VISTA ALEGRE
ALTA
C/ PEDRERA

Teatro
Pereira
SALA 2
AVICENA
CAETA
JAUME I

Mercat

Baluard de
Sant Joan

Portal de
ses Taules
Museu
d'Art
Contemporani

Baluard de
Santa Llúcia

Baluard de
Santa Llúcia

EATING & DRINKING

Bar JJ	3
Bar Zuka	2
Bon Profit	11
La Brasa	10
C'an Alfredo	6
Comidas Bar San Juan	5
Madagascar	8
Los Pasajeros	1
La Plaza	12
Rock Bar	4
Sunrise	7
Sunset	9

PLAÇA
DES PARC

PLAÇA
DE VILA
SANTA CREU
SANT
SANT

Seminari

DALT VILA

Baluard des
Portal Nou

SANTA
SOL
SANTA
SANT FRU
C/ SANT LLUIS
SANT CARLES
JOAN ROMAN
C/ SANTA MARIA

SAGRADA
FAMILIA
PONENT
GEN RIQUER
IGNASI

Museu
d'Arqueològic

SAGRADA FAMILIA

Sant
Domingo

GEN BALANZAT

La Cúria
Catedral
Ajuntament

ACCOMMODATION

Apartamentos Roselló	I
Casa de Huéspedes Vara de Rey	F
Hostal Bimbi	J
Hostal Residencia Juanito	C
Hostal Residencia Las Nieves	D
Hostal Residencia Parque	G
Hostal Residencia Sol y Brisa	E
Hostal Residencia La Ventana	H
El Hotel	A
Hotel Lux Isla	B

CONQUISTA
C/ MAJOR
C/ CIRIAC
PL. DE LA
CATEDRAL

PLAÇA
DE
ESPANYA

Baluard de
Sant Jaume

Castle

Baluard de
Santa Tecla

Baluard de
Sant Jordi

Baluard de
Sant Bernat

ES SOTO

0   100 m

13

THE BALEARIC ISLANDS | Ibiza Town and around

Outside the walls

The port areas of **Sa Penya** and **La Marina** snuggle between the harbour and
the ramparts, a maze of raked passages and narrow lanes crimped by balconied,
whitewashed houses. This highly atmospheric quarter is packed with boutiques,
bars and restaurants. Farther to the west, the **new town** is generally of less interest,
but the boulevard-like Passeig de Vara de Rey and the leafy, pedestrianized Plaça
des Parc just to the south both host some fine cafés.

Set on a rocky hillside off Via Romana are the remains of a huge **Punic
necropolis** (Tues–Sat 10am–2pm & 6–8pm, Sun 10am–2pm; free). There's not
that much to see today – though you can descend into some of the tombs – but
thousands of terracotta pieces, amphorae and amulets have been uncovered here.
Ibiza, the sacred island of the goddess Tanit, functioned as an A-list burial site,
with wealthy Carthaginians paying by special minted currency for the shipment
of their bodies to the island upon death.

Eating

Ibiza Town has a glut of **cafés** and **restaurants**. Many of the pricier places are up in Dalt Vila, while less expensive establishments are dotted round the lower town. For a good **breakfast**, head for *Madagascar* on Plaça des Parc, or the *Croissant Show* on Plaça de sa Constitució.

Self-caterers should check out the **market** on Plaça de sa Constitució for organic fruit and vegetables, or the Spar on Plaça des Parc.

Restaurants

Bon Profit Plaça des Parc 5. Excellent canteen-style place with a bargain-priced menu and really hearty, flavoursome food. No reservations taken, and be prepared to share a table.

La Brasa c/Pere Sala 3 ☎971 301 202. Classy restaurant with a delightful garden terrace shaded by palms. The menu concentrates on Mediterranean fish and grilled meat, and there's always a daily special.

C'an Alfredo Passeig de Vara de Rey ☎971 311 274. Caters to any wallet, with main courses from €8 to €20 and a menu of Spanish, local and international dishes.

Comidas Bar San Juan c/G. de Montgri 8. Tiny, atmospheric, family-owned place with moderate prices and a menu featuring many local dishes.

Los Pasajeros c/Vicent Soler s/n. Bustling, very inexpensive first-floor restaurant that's a kind of staff canteen for the hardcore club crowd. Spanish food and cheap wine. May–Oct only, open until 2am.

La Plaza Plaça de Vila 18 ☎971 307 617. For a memorable meal in historic surrounds, this Dalt Vila restaurant is a good choice. There's a great terrace and fine southern Mediterranean cuisine.

Drinking and nightlife

Ibiza's **bar and club scene** is nothing short of incendiary. Start in Plaça des Parc in *Sunset* or *Madagascar*, where drinks prices are reasonable, and then head for the stylish bars of Sa Penya – *Bar Zuka* on c/de la Verge and *Rock Bar* at the eastern end of c/Garijo are two good choices. In winter, there's far less going on, but the bars on Plaza des Parc can get quite lively.

▲ Dancer at Amnesia

Some of the globe's most spectacular **clubs** are spread across the southern half of Ibiza. Each club employs costumed PR teams who parade through Ibiza Town in a competitive frenzy of night hype. Processions of horned devils, gold-painted angels and leather-thonged Muscle Marys strut through the streets bearing club banners to drum up custom. Clubs cost €25–55 to get in, are open between midnight and 6am, and charge stratospheric prices for drinks – try to blag a guest pass from one of the bars mentioned on p.893.

Clubs

Amnesia Ibiza Town–Sant Antoni road, km 6 ☏971 198 041, Ⓦwww.amnesia-ibiza .com. Historically Ibiza's most innovative club, and the setting for the acid-house revolution. The atmosphere can be explosive; the best nights are hosted by Cream, Cocoon and Manumission. Daily June–Sept.

Anfora c/Sant Carles 7, Dalt Vila ☏971 302 893, Ⓦwww.disco-anfora.com. Intimate gay club located in a cave in Dalt Vila. Unpretentious, and the drinks prices are moderate. Daily May–Oct.

El Divino Port d'Eivissa ☏971 190 176, Ⓦwww.eldivino-ibiza.com. On the north side of Ibiza Town's harbour, with superb views of Dalt Vila from its luxuriant outdoor terrace. Musically, it's mainly soulful house. Daily June–Sept.

Pacha Avgda. 8 d'Agost ☏971 313 600, Ⓦwww.pacha.com. The grande dame of the scene, and the locals' favourite club. There's house music in the main room, a Global Zone with alternative sounds, a Funky Room, a salsa salon, plus a beautiful outdoor terrace. DJs including Deep Dish and Erick Morillo spin tunes here. Daily April–Sept; Oct–March weekends only.

Privilege Ibiza Town–Sant Antoni road, km 7 ☏971 198 160, Ⓦwww.privilegeibiza .com. Gargantuan club with a hangar-like main room, fourteen bars, a garden terrace, pool, chill-out dome and café. Rarely busy though. Daily June–Sept.

Space Platja d'en Bossa ☏971 396 793, Ⓦwww.space-ibiza.es. Ibiza's most modern club has a vast main room, two huge terraces and a plethora of other chill-out zones and alternative rooms. Its Sunday session and gay night (La Troya) are legendary.

The **gay scene** is centred on c/de la Verge, where dozens of bars cater for an almost exclusively (male) gay crowd – try *Bar JJ* – the one exception being *Sunrise*, which also draws a lesbian clientele. Check out the excellent **websites** Ⓦwww.ibizaboy.net and Ⓦwww.gayibiza.net for up-to-date information.

For **live music**, check out *Teatro Pereira*, c/Comte de Rosselló 3 (daily 8pm–4am; free), which showcases blues, reggae, rock and jazz acts.

Listings

Car rental Avis (☏971 809 176) and Hertz (☏971 809 178) are at the airport. Class Rent-a-Car, Cala Llonga ☏971 196 285 is a good local agency.
Consulates UK, Avgda. d'Isidor Macabich 45 ☏971 301 818 (Mon–Fri 8.30am–1.30pm).
Ferries There are sailings to the mainland and Mallorca with Trasmediterránea, Baleària and Iscomar. Boats to Formentera are operated by several companies, including Transmapi (☏971 310 711, Ⓦwww.trasmapi.com) and Umafisa (☏971 314 513).

Hospital Hospital Can Misses, 2km west of the port ☏971 397 000.
Internet access *Chill*, Via Púnica 49 (Mon–Sat 9.30am–11.30pm, Sun 5–9pm).
Laundry Wash & Dry, Avgda. d'Espanya 53.
Moped rental Motos Valentín, Bartomeu Vicent Ramón 19 ☏971 310 822.
Post office Avgda. d'Isidor Macabich 45–1 (Mon–Fri 8.30am–2pm).

Around Ibiza Town: the beaches

There's sea and sand close to Ibiza Town at **Figueretes**, **Platja d'en Bossa** and **Talamanca**, but the first two of these are built-up continuations of the capital, and only at the third is there any peace and quiet. All are accessible by short and inexpensive ferry rides from the terminal near the foot of Avgda. Santa Eulària.

Ses Salines and Es Cavallet

To the **south of Ibiza Town**, stretching from the airport to the sea, are thousands of acres of **salt flats**. For two thousand years, Ibiza's prosperity was dependent on these salt fields (*salines*), a trade that was vital to the Carthaginians. Even today, some salt production continues. Buses from Ibiza Town leave regularly for the gorgeous beach of **SES SALINES**, whose fine white sand arcs around a bay, the crystal-clear waters fringed by pines and dunes. The beach also has a handful of superb beach bars, including *Sa Trinxa*. From Ses Salines, it's a brief walk through the dunes to **ES CAVALLET**, another fine sandy beach that's a favourite of gay visitors.

The east coast

Heading northeast from Ibiza Town, it's just 15km to **SANTA EULÀRIA DES RIU**, a slightly mundane little town that does at least boast an attractive hilltop **church** – a fortified whitewashed sixteenth-century construction with a beautifully shady, arched entrance porch. **SANT CARLES**, 7km to the north, is an agreeable one-horse village where you can refuel at the legendary *Anita's* bar, which attracts farmers and resident bohemians in roughly equal proportion.

East of Sant Carles the road passes through burnt-red fields of olive, almond and carob trees to several almost untouched beaches. **CALA LLENYA**, a broad sandy cove with sparkling waters, is the nearest, and is popular with families. Tiny **CALA MASTELLA**, 2km farther north, is a supremely peaceful spot, with a diminutive sandy beach, crystal-clear sheltered water and two simple fish restaurants, *Sa Seni* and *El Bigotes*. Just north of Cala Mastella, **CALA BOIX** is another stunning sandy cove, a little larger and more exposed, where you'll find fine, moderately priced seafood at the *Restaurant La Noria* (T971 335 397) and spacious rooms with air conditioning at the *Hostal Cala Boix* (T971 335 224; ❸). Continuing north from Cala Boix, the coastal road follows an exhilarating, serpentine route above the shore, through thick pine forests and past the lonely nudist beach of **AIGÜES BLANQUES**.

The north

Twenty kilometres from Ibiza Town, **SANT JOAN** is a pretty hilltop village home to a typically minimalist, whitewashed Ibizan church, a sprinkling of café-bars and the *Hostal Can Pla Roig* (T&F971 333 012; ❸), which has clean, if spartan, rooms. North of the village are some wonderful beaches, especially remote **CALA D'EN SERRA**, a tiny, exquisite sandy cove, with turquoise waters perfect for snorkelling and a snack bar. **BENIRRÀS**, 9km northwest of Sant Joan, is another beautiful bay, backed by high, wooded cliffs with three simple café-restaurants. This is one of Ibiza's prime hippie-centric beaches – dozens gather here to burn herbs and pound drums to the setting sun on Sundays.

The next village to the west is **SANT MIQUEL**, where there's an imposing fortified church, and a number of simple tapas bars – try *Es Pi Ver* for an inexpensive meal. The once astonishingly beautiful inlet at **PORT DE SANT MIQUEL**, 3km north of the village, has been badly mauled by the developers, but outside high season it's not too packed here, and the sheltered bay is great for children.

Sant Antoni de Portmany and around

For years unchallenged at the top of Europe's *costa hooligania* league table, the package resort of **SANT ANTONI DE PORTMANY** is trying hard to shake off its tarnished image. The high-rise concrete skyline and British pubs of the "West End" aren't at all enticing, but the Sunset Strip on the western side of town is an appealing place for a drink: *Café Mambo* is one of a dozen options. For a different vibe, drop by *Bar M* on Avgda. Dr. Fleming or the *Ibiza Rocks* hotel on c/Cervantes, which both host some terrific gigs featuring emerging rock bands. San An's **clubs** attract legions of young British clubbers but few locals. *Eden* on Avgda. Dr. Fleming (ⓦwww.edenibiza.com; May-Sept), which looks like a psychedelic mosque, has the best reputation, and resident summer DJs here include Pete Tong.

Very regular buses leave for Ibiza Town, and there are frequent departures to the *calas* Vedella, Conta and Tarida (May–Oct).

Beaches near Sant Antoni

Heading south of Sant Antoni, it's just a few kilometres to some exquisite coves. Sheltered **CALA BASSA** gets packed with holidaying families in high season, but it does have a campsite (Ⓣ971 344 599, ⓦwww.campingcalabassa .com; closed Oct–March), while the more exposed beach of **CALA CONTA** is less crowded, with restaurants above the shore including the bohemian *Sunset Ashram*, which often has live music. The most beguiling beach in the Balearics, **CALA D'HORT**, is in the extreme southwest of the island, with a lovely quiet sand-and-pebble shoreline plus three good, moderately priced seafood restaurants. From the shore there are mesmeric vistas of **Es Vedrà**, an incisor-shaped 378-metre-high islet that's revered by islanders and island hippies alike, and is the subject of various myths and legends – including a claim to be Homer's island of the sirens.

The Sant Josep road

Taking the scenic southern road to Ibiza Town you pass via **SANT JOSEP**, a pretty village with a selection of café-restaurants including *El Destino* (closed Sun) for tasty, reasonably priced veggie dishes, and *Racó Verd* (ⓦwww .racoverd.es), which has healthy food and often hosts gigs and cultural events. Some 7km southwest of Sant Josep, **CALA JONDAL**, is a popular pebble beach where you can get delicious juices and food at *Tropicana*, and lounge around on sumptuous sunbeds at the upmarket *Blue Marlin*, which also has a fine, pricey menu.

Formentera

Just eleven nautical miles south of Ibiza Town, **FORMENTERA** (population 8212) is the smallest of the four main Balearic islands, measuring just 20km from east to west. Formentera's history more or less parallels that of Ibiza, though between 1348 and 1697 it was left uninhabited for fear of pirate raids. Like Ibiza, it was a key part of the 1960s hippie trail (Pink Floyd made an album here), and the island retains a distinctly bohemian character.

Formentera is very arid, and mainly covered in rosemary, which grows wild everywhere; it also crawls with thousands of brilliant-green **Ibiza wall lizards** (*Podarcis pityusensis*), which flourish in parched scrubland. The economy is tourism-based, taking advantage of some of Spain's longest, whitest and least-crowded beaches. Development has been limited, and visitors come here seeking escape rather than sophistication, though the island does attract plenty of day-trippers from Ibiza in high season. Nude sunbathing is the norm just about everywhere, except in Es Pujols.

Arrival and information

Regular **ferries** (return €32–41) make the crossing from Ibiza. There's a basic **bus** service from the port of arrival, **La Savina**, to the main settlements. Getting about by **bicycle** is very popular, since apart from the hill of La Mola, the island is extremely flat; there are several rental places by the ferry dock, and in Es Pujols (€8–12 per day). **Scooters** and **cars** are also available.

The island's only **turisme**, by the port in La Savina (Mon–Fri 10am–2pm & 5–7pm, Sat 10am–2pm; ☏971 322 057, ⊛www.formentera.es), can help with accommodation and cycle routes, and provide maps.

Accommodation

It's almost essential to make an **advance reservation** between late June and September, as the bulk of the island's limited supply of beds is snapped up early. No camping is permitted in Formentera.

Las Banderas Platja de Migjorn ☏604 644 832. A quirky, bohemian B&B, liberally scattered with Moroccan artefacts and enjoying a relaxed vibe. Rooms are functional but not that comfortable. It's right on the beach, next to the *Blue Bar* (see p.898). Closed Nov–March. ❹

Hostal Residencia Illes Pitiüses Sant Ferran ☏971 328 189, ⊛www.illespitiuses.com. Its location – right on the main cross-island road – isn't pretty, but the modern rooms offer comfort, and all have satellite TV and a/c. Café downstairs. ❹

Hostal Residencia Mar Blau Caló de Sant Agustí ☏&ℱ971 327 030. Small, attractive hotel next to a tiny fishing harbour. Offers bright, inviting rooms with sea views, and also some good apartments. Closed Nov–March. ❺

Formentera: useful numbers

Car rental Autos Ca Marí ☏971 322 921; Isla Blanca ☏971 322 559.
Emergencies For the police, fire brigade or ambulance, call ☏112.
Ferries Umafisa ☏971 323 007; Transmapi ☏971 322 703, ⊛www.trasmapi.com; Trasmediterrànea ☏971 315 050, ⊛www.trasmediterranea.es.
Taxis La Savina ☏971 328 016; Sant Francesc ☏971 322 243; Es Pujols ☏971 322 016.

Hostal Residencia Mayans Es Pujols ☎&℉971
328 724. Well-priced hotel with modern rooms,
each with either island or sea views, and a
swimming pool. Closed Nov–March. ④

Pensión Bon Sol Sant Ferran ☎971 328 882.
Cheap, simple place above a bar, with clean and
fairly spacious rooms. Bathrooms are shared.
Closed Nov–March. ②

Around the island

There's nothing much to **LA SAVINA**, Formentera's only port, apart from a
taxi rank, rows of rental mopeds – all racked up for a quick getaway – and a few
places to stay. The island capital, **SANT FRANCESC XAVIER**, is 4km inland
and serves as Formentera's commercial and shopping centre with a handful of
restaurants, cafés and a supermarket, plus the island's main post office, at Plaça de
sa Constitució 1. The only real sight here is the mighty fortified **church**, now
stripped of its defensive cannons, that sits in the large central square.

Heading east from here, it's a short hop to the village of **SANT FERRAN**,
home to *Pepe*, a long-established and laidback bohemian bar-cum-restaurant,
which is something of an island institution. From Sant Ferran, a side road leads
to **ES PUJOLS**, Formentera's main resort development – though it's tiny, and
tame by mainland standards. Here you'll find two fine sandy beaches and clear,
shallow waters, plenty of good seafood restaurants, some late-night bars and the
only club on the island.

Northwest of Es Pujols are the absolutely spectacular sands of **Platja de Ses
Illetes**, and, across a narrow channel, the uninhabited island of **Espalmador**,
where there's another great beach, and water turquoise enough to trump any
Caribbean brochure. It's possible to wade across most of the year, or you can
get to Espalmador on one of the regular boats from La Savina (May–Oct only;
€10 return).

Taking up most of Formentera's southern coastline, **Platja de Migjorn** is a
sweeping bay with 5km of pale sands and crystalline waters. Head for the central
part of the beach, which is virtually untouched and home to the legendary *Blue
Bar*, one of the finest *chiringuitos* in the Balearics.

East of here, the main road leaves the flatlands to snake up through pine forests
as it skirts the northern flanks of **La Mola**, at 192m the island's highest point.
En route you'll pass the enjoyable *El Mirador* restaurant (☎971 327 037), with
exceptional views across the island, before reaching the drowsy little town of
El Pilar. Beyond here, the road straightens for the final two-kilometre dash to
the **Far de La Mola** (lighthouse), which stands on cliffs high above the blue
ocean. It was here that Jules Verne was inspired to write his *Journey Round the
Solar System* as he gazed into the clear night sky.

Eating and drinking

Es Pujols, the principal resort, has a plethora of **bars and restaurants**, with
menus to suit most budgets – though few places really stand out, *Cafetería
Espardell* on the promenade is popular. Formentera's limited **nightlife** is
centred in Pujols; there's a strip of late bars and one hip club, *Xueño* (🖱 www
.xueno.com), which features DJs from Ibiza and Italy.

Elsewhere on the island, *Restaurant Rafalet* in Caló de Sant Agustí (☎971 327
077) is great for seafood, or you can eat *pa amb coses* ("bread and things") in the
adjacent bar area for a lot less. Over on Platja de Migjorn, *Lucky* (10am–sunset)
has excellent salads and Italian food, while at the neighbouring *Blue Bar* (☎971
187 011) you can dine under the stars, listening to inspirational ambient music.

Sant Ferran has several good bars around its plaza, including the atmospheric
Fonda Plate, which has a vine-shaded terrace. Most of Formentera's *hostales*

serve meals, or you can get your own supplies from the SYP supermarket in Sant Francesc Xavier.

Mallorca

Few Mediterranean holiday spots are as often and as unfairly maligned as **MALLORCA**. The island is commonly perceived as little more than sun, sex, booze and high-rise hotels – so much so that there's a long-standing Spanish joke about a mythical fifth Balearic island called *Majorca* (the English spelling), inhabited by several million tourists every year. However, this image, spawned by the helter-skelter development of the 1960s, takes no account of Mallorca's beguiling diversity. It's true that there are sections of coast where high-rise hotels and shopping centres are continuous, wedged beside and upon one another and broken only by a dual carriageway to more of the same. But the spread of development, even after fifty years, is surprisingly limited, essentially confined to the Badia de Palma (Bay of Palma), a thirty-kilometre strip flanking the island capital, and a handful of mega-resorts notching the east coast.

Elsewhere, things are very different. **Palma** itself, the Balearics' one real city, is a bustling, historic place whose grand mansions and magnificent Gothic cathedral defy the expectations of many visitors. And so does the northwest coast, where the rearing peaks of the rugged **Serra de Tramuntana** cosset beautiful cove beaches, a pair of intriguing monasteries at Valldemossa and Lluc, and a string of delightful old towns and villages – Deià, Sóller and Pollença, to name but three. There's a startling variety and physical beauty to the land, too, which, along with the warmth of the climate, has drawn tourists to visit and well-heeled expatriates to settle here since the nineteenth century, including artists and writers of many descriptions, from Robert Graves to Roger McGough.

Mallorca practicalities

Palma lies at the hub of an extensive **public transport** system, with **bus** services linking the capital to all Mallorca's principal settlements and even a couple of **train** lines – one, a beautiful ride up through the mountains to Sóller (see box, p.909), is an attraction in itself. And with your own transport, Palma is within two hours' drive of anywhere on the island. The main constraint for travellers is **accommodation**, or lack of it, though out of season things ease up and you can idle round, staying pretty much where you want. Bear in mind also that several of Mallorca's former **monasteries** rent out renovated cells at exceptionally inexpensive rates – reckon on €25–50 per double room per night. The Monastir de Nostra Senyora at Lluc (see p.912) and the Ermita de Nostra Senyora del Puig outside Pollença (see p.913) are both reachable via public transport.

Palma and around

In 1983, **PALMA** became the capital of the newly established Balearic Islands autonomous region, since when it has developed into a go-ahead and cosmopolitan commercial hub of over 300,000 people. The new self-confidence is plain to see in the city centre, a vibrant and urbane place, which is akin to the big cities of the Spanish mainland – and a world away from the heaving tourist enclaves of the surrounding bay. There's still a long way to go – much of suburban Palma remains obdurately dull and somewhat dilapidated – but the centre now presents a splendid ensemble of lively shopping areas, mazy lanes and refurbished old buildings, all enclosed by what remains of the old city walls and their replacement boulevards.

Arrival and information

Mallorca's whopping international **airport** is 11km east of Palma. It has **car rental** outlets, 24-hour **ATMs** and **currency exchange** facilities, as well as a **provincial tourist office** (Mon–Sat 9am–6pm, Sun 9am–1pm), which will supply public transport timetables, maps and accommodation lists. If you need help finding **accommodation**, try the helpful Prima Travel in the main arrivals hall (☎971 260 143, ⓦwww.prima-travel.com), which has English-speaking staff and a good selection of hotels, apartments and villas.

The airport is linked to the city and the Bay of Palma resorts by a busy highway, which shadows the shoreline from S'Arenal in the east to the resort of Magaluf in the west. **Bus** #1 leaves for Palma every fifteen minutes from the main entrance of the terminal building, just behind the taxi rank (6am–2.30am; €1.85), and goes to Plaça Espanya, on the north side of the city centre. A **taxi** from the airport to the city centre will set you back around €25.

Palma **ferry terminal** is about 4km west of the city centre. **Bus** #1 leaves every fifteen minutes from outside Terminal 2 (6am–2.30am; €1.85) bound for the Plaça Espanya. The **taxi** fare for the same journey is about €10.

In the city centre, there's another **provincial tourist office** just off the Passeig d'es Born at Plaça de la Reina 2 (Mon–Fri 9am–8pm, Sat 9am–2pm; ☎971 712 216), while the main **municipal office** is on the north edge of Plaça Espanya not far from the main bus station (Mon–Fri 9am–7pm, Sat 9am–2pm). Both provide island-wide information, dispensing free maps, accommodation lists, bus and ferry schedules, lists of car-rental firms, boat-trip details and all sorts of special-interest leaflets.

Accommodation

The bulk of Palma's **accommodation** is dotted around the city centre – fortunately enough, as this is by far the most engaging part of the city; the immediate suburbs are quite unprepossessing. Note that in high season some places insist on a minimum stay of two or three nights.

Hostal Brondo c/Ca'n Brondo 1 ☎971 719 043, ⓦwww.hostalbrondo.net. A stylish little place in a central but quiet location, with Mallorcan antiques and newly done-up rooms. Both en-suite and shared-facility doubles. ❷

Hostal Ritzi c/Apuntadors 6 ☎971 714 610, ⓦwww.hostalritzi.com. Basic, one-star rooms in an ancient but well-maintained five-storey house off the Passeig d'es Born; can get noisy at night. ❷

Hotel Araxa c/Alférez Cerdá 22 ☎971 731 640, ⓦwww.hotelaraxa.com. Attractive four-storey modern hotel with pleasant gardens and an outdoor swimming pool. Most rooms have balconies. It's in a quiet residential area about 2km west of the centre. To get there by public transport, take EMT bus #6 and get off at c/Marquès de la Sènia, just before the start of Avgda. Joan Miró; it's a 5- to 10min walk from the bus stop. ❺

Hotel Born c/Sant Jaume 3 ☎971 712 942, ⓦwww.hotelborn.com. Comfortable and justifiably popular hotel in an excellent downtown location. Set in an old, refurbished mansion with its own courtyard café. ❺

Hotel Dalt Murada c/Almudaina 6 ☎971 425 300, ⓦwww.daltmurada.com. Set in a magnificent sixteenth-century mansion with period architecture and all modern comforts and conveniences. Great central location, too – just behind the town hall. ❻

Hotel Palau Sa Font c/Apuntadors 38 ☎971 712 277, ⓦwww.palausafont.com. This smooth and polished four-star hotel, decorated in earthy Italian colours and graced by sculptures and other modern works of art, manages to be both stylish and welcoming. There's a small pool on the roof terrace, and some rooms enjoy inspiring views of the cathedral. B&B ❻

Hotel Saratoga Passeig Mallorca 6 ☎971 727 240, ⓦwww.hotelsaratoga.es. An excellent modern hotel with swimming pool. Most rooms have balconies overlooking either the boulevard (a bit noisy) or the interior courtyard and pool (quieter). ❺

The City

Finding your way around Palma is fairly straightforward once you're in the city centre. The obvious landmark is the **Catedral**, which dominates the waterfront and backs onto the oldest part of the city, a cluster of alleys and narrow lanes whose northern and eastern limits are marked by the zigzag of avenues built beside – or in place of – the city walls. On the west side of the Catedral, Avgda. d'Antoni Maura/Passeig d'es Born cuts up from the seafront to intersect with Avgda. Jaume III/Unio at Plaça Rei Joan Carles I. These busy thoroughfares form the core of the modern town.

The Catedral

Five hundred years in the making, Palma's **Catedral** (April, May & Oct Mon–Fri 10am–5.15pm, Sat 10am–2.15pm; June–Sept Mon–Fri 10am–6.15pm, Sat 10am–2.15pm; Nov–March Mon–Fri 10am–3.15pm, Sat 10am–2.15pm; €4.50) is a

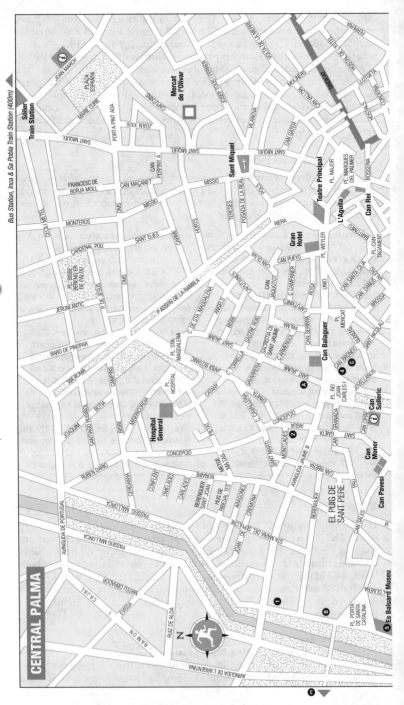

CENTRAL PALMA

Bus Station, Inca & Sa Pobla Train Station (400m)

Sóller
Train Station

THE BALEARIC ISLANDS

13

PLAÇA
ESPANYA

JOAN MARCH

MARIE CURIE

SANT MIQUEL

PORTA PINTADA

JOAN XXIII

FRANCESC DE
BORJA MOLL

CAN MAÇANET

CAN PERPINYÀ

MONTEROS

OMS

MISSIO

MISSIO

SANT ELIES

CARME

HORTS

TERESES

POSADA DE LA REAL

PUIG

SANT MIQUEL

SANT MIQUEL

CAPUTXINS

Mercat
de l'Olivar

VILANOVA

CAN GATER

JOSEP TOUS I FERRER

MOLINERS

CAN FULLON

Sant Miquel

RIERA

VOLTA DE LA MERE

HOSTAL DE L'ESTEL

LLOTGETA

CORDERIA

FERRERIA

RESTALS

CECILI METEL

CARDENAL POU

PL. BISBE
BERENGER
DE PALOU

JERONI ANTIC

BARÓ DE PINOPAR

VIA ROMA

CAMPINS

BOTIA

SANTIAGO RUSIÑOL

JOAQUIM

BISBE

PASSEIG DE LA RAMBLA

C. DE STA. MAGDALENA

ANGELS

BISBE

SASTRE RING

SACRISTIA DE
SANT JAUME

SANT JAUME

C. TORRELLA

GABARRERA

ERMITA

C. CAVALLERIA

CANYELLES

CONCEPCIO

P. DE JESUS

PL. STA.
MAGDALENA

JARDÍ BOTÀNIC

PL.
HOSPITAL

CATANY

PL. REI
JOAN
CARLES I

CAN OLIVA

CAN PUEYO

Gran
Hotel

PL. WEYLER

CAN JAQUOTOT

C. CAMPANER

CAPUTXINS

RIOSA

UNIO

PALMA

CARMENGEK

CAN SERINA

Can Balaguer

PL.
MERCAT

CAN BRONDO

SANT MIQUEL

Teatre Principal

L'Aguila

Can Rei

PL.
MAJOR

PL. MARQUES
DEL PALMER

BOSSERIA

BARTOMEU

PL. CAN
TAGAMENT

CAN SANTA CILIA

OLLETTA

CAN DANUS

BROSSA

CAN MORLAU

JOVELLANOS

Can
Solleric

Can
Moner

SANT CRIST

CAN OFRE

GRANADA

GAIETA

AIGUA

MONTCADES

SANT MARTÍ

METGE MATAS

BONAIRE

HUG DE
BERGA TES

ARAGONES

CREMONA

STA MARIA DEL SEPULCRE

JOAN

Hospital
General

IMMERCORDIA

CONFLENT

TOMELOSES

CARDADES

BERENGUER
SANT JOAN

RUBEN DARIO

CERDANYA

CAN RIBERA

AVINGUDA JAUME II

BERENGER

PAU

EL PUIG DE
SANT PERE

CAN SALES

VI

Can Pavesi

L'OLIVERA

Es Baluard Museu

PL. PORTA
DE SANTA
CATALINA

PASSEIG DE PORTUGAL

AVINGUDA DE PORTUGAL

PASSEIG MALLORCA

AVINGUDA MALLORCA

CAJAL

MATEU OBRADOR

PISSA

I

RUIZ DE ALDA

RAMON

AVINGUDA DE L'ARGENTINA

N

1

B

2

4

A

3

5

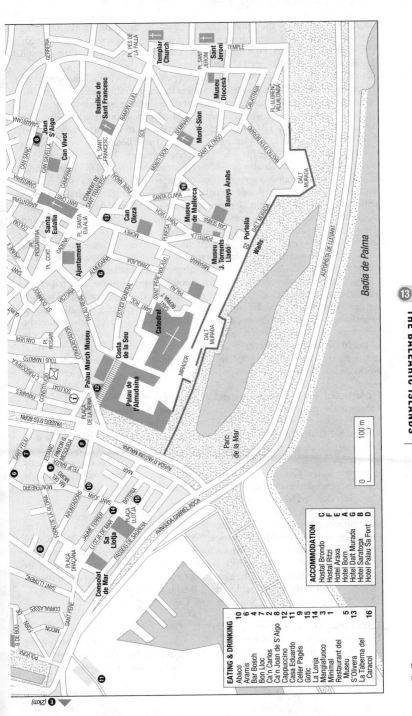

THE BALEARIC ISLANDS

Badia de Palma

Parc de la Mar

| 0 | 100 m |

EATING & DRINKING

Abaco	10
Aramis	6
Bar Bosch	4
Bon Lloc	7
Ca'n Carlos	2
Ca'n Joan de S'Aigo	8
Cappuccino	12
Casa Eduardo	11
Celler Pagès	9
Gòtic	15
La Lonja	14
Mangiafuoco	3
Minimal	1
Restaurant del Museu	5
S'Olivera	13
La Taberna del Caracol	16

ACCOMMODATION

Hostal Brondo	C
Hostal Ritzi	F
Hotel Araxa	E
Hotel Born	A
Hotel Dalt Murada	G
Hotel Saratoga	B
Hotel Palau Sa Font	D

Templar Church

Sant Jeroni

Basílica de Sant Francesc

Museu Diocesà

Joan S'Aigo

Can Vivot

Monti-Sion

Santa Eulalia

Ajuntament

Can Oleza

Banys Àrabs

Museu de Mallorca

Portella

Museu J. Torrents Lladó

Palau March Museu

Costa de la Seu

Catedral

Palau de l'Almudaina

Consolat de Mar

Sa Llotja

➤ ❸ (2km)

magnificent building – the equal of almost any on the mainland – and a surprising one, too, with its interior featuring *modernista* touches designed by Antoni Gaudí. The original church was built following the Christian Reconquest of the city, and the site taken, in fulfilment of a vow by Jaume I, was that of the Moorish Great Mosque. Essentially Gothic, with massive exterior buttresses to take the weight off the pillars within, the church derives its effect through its sheer height, impressive from any angle but startling when glimpsed from the waterside esplanade.

In the central nave, fourteen beautifully aligned, pencil-thin pillars rise to 21m before their ribs branch out – like fronded palm trees – to support the single-span, vaulted roof. The **nave**, at 44m high, is one of the tallest Gothic structures in Europe, and its length – 121m – is of matching grandeur. This open, hangar-like construction, typical of Catalan Gothic architecture, was designed to make the high altar visible to the entire congregation, and to express the mystery of the Christian faith, with kaleidoscopic floods of light filtering in through the **stained-glass windows**. For once, the light isn't trapped by the central *coro* (choir) that normally blocks the centre of Spanish cathedrals. The innovative sidelining of the *coro*, and the fantastic forms of the lighting system above the altar, were Gaudí's work, undertaken between 1904 and 1914. At the time, these measures were deeply controversial; no *coro* had ever before been removed in Spain, but the artistic success of the project was undeniable, and it was immediately popular.

On the way into the church, you pass through three rooms of assorted ecclesiastical bric-a-brac, which comprise the **Museu de la Catedral**. The first room's most valuable exhibit, in the glass case in the middle, is a gilded silver monstrance of extraordinary delicacy, its fairy-tale decoration dating from the late sixteenth century. The second room is mainly devoted to the Gothic works of the **Mallorcan Primitives**, a school of painters who flourished on the island in the fourteenth and fifteenth centuries, producing strikingly naive devotional works of bold colours and cartoon-like detail.

Palau de l'Almudaina and Palau March Museu

Opposite the cathedral entrance stands the **Palau de l'Almudaina** (April–Sept Mon–Fri 10am–5.45pm, Sat 10am–1pm; Oct–March Mon–Fri 10am–1pm & 4–5pm, Sat 10am–1pm; €3.20, plus €0.80 for audioguide; free entry on Wed to EU citizens showing their passport), originally the palace of the Moorish *walis* (governors) and later of the Mallorcan kings. The interior has been painstakingly restored, but its rabbit warren of rooms and corridors has been left comparatively bare, the main decorative highlight being a handful of admirable Flemish tapestries, each devoted to classical themes.

Just to the north along c/Palau Reial stands the opulent 1930s townhouse of the Mallorcan magnate and speculator Joan March (1880–1962), now opened to the public as the **Palau March Museu** (Mon–Fri 10am–6pm, Nov–March until 5pm, Sat 10am–2pm; €3.60; ⓦwww.fundbmarch.es). The highlight here is the splendid Italianate courtyard, which is used to display a potpourri of modern art drawn from the March collection. Amongst the twenty or so pieces on display, there are two Henry Moore sculptures, a Rodin torso and a fetchingly eccentric *Orgue del Mar* (*Organ of the Sea*) by Xavier Corbero.

The rest of the city

The most engaging part of the city is the medina-like maze of **old-town** streets at the back of the cathedral, and here, at c/Portella 5, the **Museu de Mallorca** (Tues–Sat 10am–7pm, Sun 10am–2pm; €3) occupies one of the many fifteenth- and sixteenth-century patrician mansions that dot this section of town. It holds an extensive collection of Mallorcan archeological finds as well as some exceptionally fine medieval religious paintings, including further examples of the work of the Mallorcan Primitives.

A five-minute walk away along Pont i Vich and Pare Nadal, and occupying, oddly enough, the site of the old Moorish soap factory, the **Basílica de Sant Francesc** (daily 9.30am–12.30pm & 3.30–6pm, but closed Sun afternoon; €1) is the finest among the city's bevy of medieval churches. It's a substantial building, founded towards the end of the thirteenth century, and the main facade displays a stunning severity of style, with a great sheet of dressed sandstone stretching up to an arcaded balcony and pierced by a gigantic rose window. Entered via a fine trapezoidal Gothic cloister, the cavernous interior is a little disappointing, but you can't miss the monumental **high altar**, a gaudy affair illustrative of High Baroque. The odd-looking statue outside the church – of a Franciscan monk and a Native American – celebrates the missionary work of **Junipero Serra**, a Mallorcan priest dispatched to California in 1768, who subsequently founded San Diego, Los Angeles and San Francisco.

From the basilica, it's a couple of minutes' walk west to **Santa Eulàlia** (Mon–Fri 7am–12.30pm & 5.45–8.30pm, Sat 7am–1pm & 4.30–8.45pm, Sun 8am–1pm & 6.30–8.30pm; free), the first church to be built after King Jaume's arrival, a typically Gothic construction with a yawning nave originally designed – as in the cathedral – to give the entire congregation a view of the high altar. Close by, the **Ajuntament** (town hall) is a debonair example of the late Renaissance style, with a grand and self-assured foyer.

On the west side of the city centre, the **Passeig Mallorca** is bisected by the deep, walled watercourse that once served as the city moat and is now an especially handsome feature of the city. One of the old bastions overlooking the watercourse, on Plaça Porta Santa Catalina, has recently been turned into the **Es Baluard Museu d'Art Modern i Contemporani** (Modern & Contemporary Art Museum; Tues–Sun 10am–11pm, Oct–May until 8pm; €6; ⓦ www.esbaluard .org), where pride of place goes to a rare and unusual sample of Picasso ceramics, most memorably a striking, white, ochre and black vase-like piece entitled *Big Bird Corrida*.

Eating

Eating in Palma is less pricey – or can be – than anywhere else in the Balearics. Inexpensive **cafés** and **tapas bars** are liberally distributed around the city centre, with a particular concentration in the side streets off the Passeig d'es Born and Avgda. Antoni Maura. In central Palma, especially along the harbourfront and around Plaça Llotja, many **restaurants** are unashamedly geared to the tourist trade, with menus in a babble of Euro-tongues. Most serve perfectly reasonable food, mainly grilled meats and fish, but away from these enclaves you'll find that prices are a little lower and menus more exclusively Catalan and Spanish. At all but the most expensive of places, €25–30 will cover the cost of a starter, main course and half a bottle of wine.

Cafés and tapas bars

Bar Bosch Plaça Rei Joan Carles I. One of the most popular and inexpensive tapas bars in town, the traditional haunt of intellectuals and usually humming with conversation. At peak times, you'll need to be assertive to get served.

Bon Lloc c/Sant Feliu 7. One of the few vegetarian café-restaurants on the island, centrally situated off the Passeig d'es Born, with an informal atmosphere and good food at low prices. Mon–Sat 1–4pm.

Ca'n Joan de S'Aigo c/Can Sanç 10. In a tiny alley near Plaça Santa Eulàlia, this long-established coffee house has wonderful, freshly baked *ensaimadas* (cinnamon-flavoured spiral pastry buns). Charmingly formal, period-piece decor. Daily except Tues 8am–9pm.

Cappuccino c/Conqustador. Enjoyable terrace café occupying the lower level of the Palau March Museu. Serves inventive salads and sandwiches, as well as various coffee combinations.

Minimal Passeig Mallorca 10. Slick, modern café in a pleasant setting in the stone arcade bordering (an almost traffic-free part of) the *passeig*. Illy coffee, and a delicious range of salads from €8–12. Mon–Sat 11am–11pm.

La Taberna del Caracol c/Sant Alonso 2 ☎971 714 908. Deep in the depths of the old town, this smashing tapas bar occupies charming old premises – all wooden beams and ancient arches. A first-rate range of tapas begins at just €6. Mon–Sat 1–3.30pm & 7.30–11.30pm. Reservations advised at peak times.

Restaurants

Aramis c/Montenegro 1 ☎971 725 232. Set in a sympathetically refurbished old stone mansion on a side street off Passeig d'es Born, this superb restaurant has an imaginative menu with an international range of dishes – ravioli and pumpkin, wild mushrooms en croute, for example – and there's an unbeatable *menú* (€14) plus a wonderful house red. Reservations recommended. Mon–Fri 1–3.30pm & 8–11pm, Sat 8–11pm.

Ca'n Carlos c/Aigua 5 ☎971 713 869. Charming, family-run restaurant featuring first-class Mallorcan cuisine that takes in such delights as cuttlefish and snails. Good dishes to sample are *fava parada* (dried bean stew) and *caragols de la mallorquina* (snails). Main courses around €15. Mon–Sat 1–4pm & 8–11pm.

Casa Eduardo c/Contramoll Mollet 4 ☎971 716 574. Spick-and-span restaurant located upstairs in one of the plain modern buildings beside the fish dock. There's an enjoyable view of the harbour, but the real treat is the fresh fish – a wonderful range, all simply prepared, though grilled is best. It's located just across from – and east of – the foot of Avgda. Argentina. Main courses average €16. Tues–Sat 1–3.30pm & 8–11pm.

Celler Pagès Off c/Apuntadors at c/Felip Bauza 2 ☎971 726 036. Tiny, inexpensive restaurant with an easy-going family atmosphere serving traditional Mallorcan food – try the stuffed marrows with home-made mayonnaise. Reserve at weekends. Mon–Sat 1–3.30pm & 8–11pm.

Mangiafuoco Plaça Vapor 4, Santa Catalina ☎971 451 072. Tuscan-owned restaurant-cum-wine bar offering top-notch Italian food and specializing in dishes featuring truffles. Try the *pappardelle al tartuffo* and prepare to be wowed, especially when it's washed down with one of the superb house wines. Attractive setting, too – metres from the top of the low ridge that overlooks the harbourfront. Daily except Tues 1.30–3.30pm & 8–11pm.

Restaurant del Museu Es Baluard Museu, Plaça Porta Santa Catalina s/n ☎971 908 199. Adjacent to the Es Baluard gallery, this excellent restaurant occupies two modernist glass cubes with views out across the bay. The menu is based on Mallorcan cuisine, but there are all sorts of international flourishes – try the lamb. Main courses cost around €16 in the evening, slightly less during the day. Tues–Sun noon–3.30pm & 8–11pm.

S'Olivera c/Morey 5 ☎971 729 581. Appealing restaurant, with antique bric-a-brac and paintings dotted round the walls. Food includes a first-rate range of tapas (around €6 per portion), plus a good-value lunchtime *menú* (€10). Mon–Sat 1.30–3.30pm & 8–11pm.

Drinking and nightlife

There's a cluster of lively **late-night bars** – mostly with music as the backdrop rather than the main event – amongst the narrow side streets backing onto Plaça Llotja. A second concentration of slightly more upmarket bars embellishes the bayside Avgda. Gabriel Roca, about 3km west of the city centre.

The **club scene** in Palma is small but worth investigating after around midnight; entry charges cost between €6 and €24, depending on the night and what's happening.

Late-night bars and clubs

Abaco c/Sant Joan 1 ☎971 714 939. Set in a charming old mansion, this is easily Palma's most unusual bar, with an interior straight out of a Busby Berkeley musical: fruits cascading down its stairway, caged birds hidden amid patio foliage, elegant music and a daily flower bill you could live on for a month. Drinks, as you might imagine, are extremely expensive (cocktails cost as much as €15), but you're never hurried into buying one. It is, however, rather too sedate to be much fun if you're on the razzle. Daily 9pm–2am, closed most of Jan.

Gotic Plaça Llotja 2. Tiny bar and café with a candlelit patio and pavement tables that nudge out across the square, adding a touch of romance.

La Lonja c/Llotja de Mar 2. A popular, well-established haunt, with revolving doors and pleasantly old-fashioned decor; the background music caters for (almost) all tastes. Tapas, too.

Tito's Plaça Gomila 3 ☎971 730 017, ⓦwww .titosmallorca.com. With its stainless steel and glass exterior, this long-established nightspot looks a bit like something from a sci-fi film. Outdoor lifts carry you up from Avgda. Gabriel Roca (the back entrance) to the dance floor, which pulls in huge crowds from many countries – or you can go in through the front entrance on Plaça Gomila. The music (anything from house to mainstream pop) lacks conviction, but it's certainly loud. June to early Sept daily 11pm–5am, Oct–May Fri–Sun 11pm–5am; €20.

Around Palma

Anywhere in the west or centre of the island is readily accessible as a **day-trip** from Palma. If you're after a quick **swim** the most convenient option is to stick to the resorts strung along the neighbouring **Badia de Palma** (Bay of Palma). Locals tend to go east on the #15 bus (every 10min; 30min) from Plaça Espanya to **S'Arenal**, where there's an enormously long, albeit very crowded, sandy beach.

A second appealing option, though there are no buses to it, is the **Castell de Bellver** (April–Sept Mon–Sat 8.30am–8.30pm, Sun 10am–6.30pm; Oct–March Mon–Sat 8.30am–7pm, Sun 10am–5pm; €2, free on Sun), a strikingly well-preserved fortress of canny circular design built for Jaume II at the beginning of the fourteenth century. The castle perches on a wooded hilltop some 3km west of the city centre and offers superb views of Palma and its harbour.

Andratx, Sant Elm and Sa Dragonera

Inland from the Bay of Palma, you could spend an hour or two exploring **ANDRATX**, a small, undeveloped town huddled among the hills to the west of the city – there are hourly buses. From here, it's another short bus ride through a pretty, orchard-covered landscape to low-key **SANT ELM**. Plans are afoot to expand the resort, but at present it's a quiet spot where there's a reasonable chance of a **room** in high season – try either the *Hostal Dragonera* (☎971 239 086, ⓦwww.hostaldragonera.net; closed Nov–April; ❸), a simple, modern building with clean and neat rooms, most of which offer sea views. For such a small place, there's also a surprisingly wide choice of **cafés and restaurants**, one of the best being *Vista Mar*, at c/Jaime I 46, which specializes in seafood and has a charming terrace and ocean views – reckon on €40 for a complete meal, including house wine.

With more time to spare, you catch a **boat** across from Sant Elm's minuscule harbour to the austere offshore islet of **Sa Dragonera**, an uninhabited chunk of rock some 4km long and 700m wide, with an imposing ridge of sea cliffs dominating its northwestern shore; the main pull here – apart from hiking on this traffic-free islet – is the birdlife; the ferry trip takes fifteen minutes each way and the return fare is €10.

Northern Mallorca

Mallorca is at its scenic best in the gnarled ridge of the **Serra de Tramuntana**, the imposing mountain range that stretches the length of the island's western shore, its soaring peaks and plunging sea cliffs intermittently intercepted by valleys of olive and citrus groves and dotted with some of the island's most beguiling towns and villages. There are several possible routes through the region, but perhaps the most straightforward – especially if you're reliant on public transport – is to travel

The Serra de Tramuntana provides the best walking on Mallorca, with scores of **hiking trails** latticing the mountains. Generally speaking, paths are well marked, though apt to be clogged with thorn bushes. There are trails to suit all levels of fitness, from the easiest of strolls to the most gruelling of long-distance treks, but in all cases you should come properly equipped – certainly with an appropriate hiking **map** (available in Palma and at Sóller tourist office), and, for the more difficult routes, a **compass**. Spring and autumn are the best times to embark on the longer trails; in midsummer, the heat can be enervating and water is scarce. Bear in mind also that the mountains are prone to mists, though they usually lift at some point in the day. For obvious safety reasons, lone mountain walking is not recommended.

up from Palma to Sóller, in the middle of the coast, and use this town as a base, making selected forays along the coastal road, the **Ma-10**. Sóller is within easy striking distance of the mountain village of **Deià** and the monastery of **Valldemossa** to the southwest, or it's a short haul northeast to the monastery of **Lluc**, the quaint town of **Pollença** and the relaxing resort of **Port de Pollença**.

As far as **beaches** are concerned, most of the region's coastal villages have a tiny, shingly strip, and only around the bays of Pollença and Alcúdia are there more substantial offerings. The resorts edging these bays have the greatest number of hotel and *hostal* rooms, but elsewhere **accommodation** requires some forethought. To compensate, distances are small, the roads are good and the **bus** network is perfectly adequate for most destinations – one of the most useful services is the run along the Ma-10 from Port de Sóller to Port de Pollença and on to Port d'Alcúdia (April–Oct Mon–Sat 2 daily). **Taxis** can work out a reasonable deal, too, if you're travelling in a group – the fare for the thirty-kilometre trip from Palma to Sóller is about €45, for instance.

Sóller

If you're arriving by train at **SÓLLER**, the obvious option is to take the **tram** (7am–9pm, every 30min–1hr; 15min; €3 each way) from outside the station down to the seashore at **Port de Sóller**, just 5km away. If you do pass straight through, however, you'll miss one of the most laid-back and enjoyable towns on Mallorca, though it's the general flavour of the place that appeals rather than any specific sight: the town's narrow, sloping lanes are cramped by eighteenth- and nineteenth-century stone houses, whose fancy grilles and big wooden doors once housed the region's well-heeled fruit merchants. All streets lead to the main square, **Plaça Constitució**, an informal, pint-sized affair of crowded cafés just down the hill from the train station. The square is dominated by the hulking mass of the church of **Sant Bartomeu**, a crude but still somehow rather engaging neo-Gothic remodelling of the medieval original, its main saving grace being the enormous rose window cut high in the main facade. Inside, the cavernous nave is suitably dark and gloomy, the penitential home of a string of gaudy Baroque altarpieces.

There's also a reasonably good chance of finding a vacant **room** in Sóller during the high season. Options include the *Hotel El Guía*, c/Castanyer 2 (☎971 630 227, 🖳www.sollernet.com/elguia; closed Dec–April; ❹), a lovely, old-fashioned one-star place metres from the train station; and the much more upmarket *Ca'l Bisbe*, in an immaculately restored old mansion, also a short stroll from the station at c/Bisbe Nadal 10 (☎971 631 228, 🖳www.hotelcalbisbe .com; ❺). Easily the best place to **eat** in town is 🍴 *Don Capriani*, Gran Via 43

(☎971 633 049; closed Mon), where the speciality is home-made pasta, and main courses average around €16.

Port de Sóller

PORT DE SÓLLER is one of the most popular resorts on the west coast, and its horseshoe-shaped bay must be the most photographed spot on the island after the package resorts around Palma. The high jinks of the Badia de Palma are, however, about the last thing imaginable at this relatively staid, family-oriented resort. The best **swimming** is along the pedestrianized area of **Platja den Repic**, where the water is clear and the beach clean and well maintained. Also good fun is the fifty-minute stroll out to the **lighthouse**, which guards the cliffs above the entrance to Port de Sóller's harbour. From here, the views out over the wild and rocky coast are spectacular, especially at sunset. Directions couldn't be easier, as there's a tarmac road all the way: from the centre of the resort, walk round the southern side of the bay past the Platja den Repic beach and keep going.

Trams from Sóller clank to a halt beside the waterfront, bang in the centre of town and a couple of minutes' walk from the **turisme**, which is located beside the church on c/Canonge Oliver (March–Oct Mon–Fri 9am–1pm & 3–6pm, Sat 10am–1pm; ☎971 633 042, @www.sollernet.com). They will provide a full list of local hotels and *hostales*. Outside peak season, there's a good chance of a reasonably priced room at the attractive ⚓ *Hotel Es Port*, c/Antonio Montis s/n (☎971 631 650, @www.hotelesport.com; ❺), which occupies an old mansion with lovely gardens set back from the main part of the port. Alternatively, there's a string of modern waterfront hotels, the pick of which is is the noticeably spick-and-span *Hotel Marina* (☎971 631 461, @www.hotelmarinasoller.com; ❺), flanking the Platja den Repic.

Port de Sóller heaves with **cafés** and **restaurants**, but standards are very variable: the more authentic places tend to be found along the side streets surrounding the waterfront. One appealing option is *Es Faro*, which perches high up on the cliffs at the entrance to the harbour (☎971 633 752), offering spectacular views and great food – reservations are strongly recommended.

Deià

It's a dramatic, ten-kilometre journey southwest from Sóller along the Ma-10 to the beautiful village of **DEIÀ**, where the mighty Puig des Teix mountain ramps down to the coast. Doubling as the coastal highway, Deià's main street skirts the base of the Teix, showing off most of the village's hotels and restaurants. At times, this thoroughfare is too congested to be much fun, but the tiny heart of the village, tumbling over a high and narrow ridge on the seaward side of the road, still preserves a surprising tranquillity. Here, labyrinthine alleys of old peasant houses curl up to a pretty country **church**, in the precincts of which stands the

THE BALEARIC ISLANDS | Northern Mallorca

grave of **Robert Graves**, the village's most famous resident – marked simply "Robert Graves: Poeta, E.P.D." (*En Paz Descanse*: "Rest In Peace"). From the graveyard, the views out over the coast are truly memorable.

Graves put Deià on the international map, and his old home, **Ca N'Alluny** (Tues–Sun 10am–5pm; €5; timed visits by advance reservation on ☎971 636 185, Ⓦwww.fundaciorobertgraves.com), a substantial stone building beside the main road about 500m east of the village, was opened to the public in 2006. For the most part, the house has been returned to its 1940s appearance, and its rooms are decorated with Graves's own furnishings and fittings. The study, where Graves produced much of his finest work, is of particular interest.

Cala de Deià, the nearest thing the village has to a beach, comprises some 200m of shingle at the back of a handsome rocky cove of jagged cliffs, boulders and white-crested surf. It's a great place for a swim, the water clean, deep and cool, and there's a ramshackle beach bar. It takes about thirty minutes to walk from the village to the *cala*, a delightful stroll down a wooded ravine – or a five-minute drive.

Practicalities

The Palma–Port de Sóller **bus** scoots through Deià five times daily in each direction, dropping passengers in the centre of the village on the main street. There's no tourist office as such, but all of Deià's hotels and *hostales* have – or at least should have – copies of a locally produced village guide to pretty much everything, and it's free. You can also check out the **website** Ⓦwww.deia -mallorca.com.

Of the handful of places where there's a chance of finding a reasonably priced **room** in high season, the best option is the unassuming ⚑ *Pensión Miramar*, a short, steep walk above the main road at c/Ca'n Oliver s/n (☎971 639 084; Ⓦwww.pensionmiramar.com; closed Dec–April; ❹); this *pensión* is in a traditional house, and although the rooms are unadventurous, they are perfectly adequate, and there are smashing views over the village from the terrace. Deià also possesses one of the most agreeable hotels on Mallorca, the ⚑ *Es Moli*, a supremely comfortable establishment in an immaculately maintained building with superb gardens overlooking the main road at the west end of the village (☎971 639 000, Ⓦwww.esmoli.com; closed Nov–March; ❼).

▲ Deià

Robert Graves first lived in Deià during the 1930s, returning after the end of World War II to remain in the village until his death in 1985. During his first stay, he shared a house at the edge of the village with Laura Riding, an American poet and dabbler in the mystical. Riding had come to England in 1926 and, after she became Graves' secretary and literary collaborator, the two of them had an affair. The tumultuous course of their relationship created sufficient furore for them to decide to leave England, and they chose Mallorca on the advice of Gertrude Stein. Graves and Riding were forced to leave Mallorca in 1936 at the onset of the Spanish Civil War, and back in England Riding ditched Graves, who subsequently took up with a mutual friend, Beryl Hodge. Graves returned to Mallorca in 1946, Hodge joined him and they were married in Palma in 1950. They were not, however, to live happily ever after. Graves had a predilection for young women, claiming he needed female muses for poetic inspiration, and although his wife outwardly accepted this waywardness, she did so without much enthusiasm. Furthermore, while Graves' novels (*Goodbye to All That*; *I, Claudius* and *Claudius the God*) became increasingly well known and profitable, his romantic poetry – of which he was particularly proud – fell out of fashion, and his last anthology, *Poems 1965–1968*, was widely ignored.

As for **eating** in Deià, you're spoilt for choice. There's a concentration of cafés and restaurants along the main street towards the west end of the village, including *Sa Font Fresca* (closed Sun), which offers reasonably priced tapas and *bocadillos*, and, further up the price scale, the *Restaurant Jaime* (☎971 639 029; closed Mon), which offers mouthwatering Mallorcan cuisine.

Valldemossa

Some 10km **southwest of Deià** along the Ma-10 lies the ancient and intriguing hill town of **VALLDEMOSSA**, a sloping jumble of rusticated houses and monastic buildings set in a lovely valley and backclothed by mountains. The origins of Valldemossa date to the early fourteenth century, when the asthmatic King Sancho built a royal palace here in the hills, where the air was easier to breathe. Later, in 1399, the palace was given to Carthusian monks from Tarragona, who converted and extended the original buildings into a **monastery**, now the island's most visited building after Palma Catedral.

Remodelled on several occasions, most of the present complex, the **Real Cartuja de Jesús de Nazaret** (Mon–Sat 9.30am–5.30pm, June–Sept until 6.30pm, Nov–Feb until 4pm, Sun 10am–1pm; €7.50), as it's formally named, is of seventeenth- and eighteenth-century construction, its square and heavy church leading to the shadowy corridors of the cloisters beyond. The monastery owes its present fame almost entirely to the novelist and republican polemicist **George Sand**, who, with her companion, the composer **Frédéric Chopin**, lived here for four months during 1838–39 in a commodious set of vacant cells – the last monks had been evicted during the liberal-inspired suppression of the monasteries three years earlier. Their stay is commemorated in Sand's *A Winter in Majorca*, a stodgy, self-important book that is considerably overplayed hereabouts, being available in just about every European language.

A visit begins in the gloomy, aisleless **church**, which is distinguished by its fanciful bishop's throne, and then continues in the adjoining cloisters, where the **prior's cell** is, despite its name, a comfortable suite of bright, sizeable rooms with splendid views down the valley. Farther along the corridor, **cell no. 2** exhibits miscellaneous curios relating to Chopin and Sand, from portraits and a lock of hair to musical scores and letters (it was in this cell that the composer wrote the *"Raindrop" Prelude*). There's more of the same in **cell no. 4**, plus Chopin's favourite piano, which, after three months of unbelievable complications, arrived just three weeks before the couple left for Paris. Considering the hype, these incidental mementoes are something of an anticlimax, but persevere: upstairs, there's a small but outstanding collection of **modern art**, including work by Miró, Picasso, Francis Bacon and Henry Moore. And be sure also to take the doorway beside the prior's cell that leads outside the cloisters to the enjoyable **Palace of King Sancho**. It's not the original palace at all – that disappeared long ago – but it is the oldest part of the complex, and its fortified walls, mostly dating from the sixteenth century, accommodate a string of handsome period rooms.

Practicalities

Valldemossa is easily reached by **bus** from Deià, Sóller and Palma. Buses stop beside the bypass at the west end of town; from here, it's just a couple of minutes' walk to the monastery – cross the bypass and keep straight.

For **accommodation**, there are two appealing options, beginning with *Hostal Ca'n Mario*, c/Uetam 8 (☎971 612 122, ⓦwww.hostalcanmario.net; ❸), an attractive *hostal* with an elegant, curio-cluttered foyer and comfortably old-fashioned rooms; it's situated just a couple of minutes' walk from the monastery. Alternatively, the more upmarket ⚐ *Es Petit Hotel*, just along the same street at c/Uetam 1 (☎971 612 479, ⓦwww.espetithotel-valldemossa.com; ❻), occupies a tastefully refurbished old house and has fifteen rooms, most with excellent views.

The centre of Valldemossa is packed with **restaurants and cafés**, mostly geared up for day-trippers – and many offer dire fast food at inflated prices. Nonetheless, there are one or two quality places amongst the dross, the best being the low-key, family-run restaurant at the *Hostal Ca'n Mario* (closed Sun eve).

Sóller to Lluc

Without doubt, the most interesting approach to the northernmost tip of the island is the continuation of the **Ma-10** northeast from Sóller, with the road slipping through the highest and harshest section of the **Serra de Tramuntana**. For the most part, the mountains drop straight into the sea, comprising precipitous and largely unapproachable cliffs with barely a cove in sight – the accessible exceptions are the shingly beach at **Cala Tuent** and the horribly commercial hamlet of **Sa Calobra** next door. Easily the best place to break your journey is at **LLUC**, tucked away in a remote mountain valley about 35km from Sóller. Mallorca's most important place of pilgrimage since the middle of the thirteenth century, supposedly after a shepherd boy named Lluc (Luke) stumbled across a tiny, brightly painted statue of the Madonna here in the woods, Lluc is dominated by the austere, high-sided dormitories of the **Monestir de Nostra Senyora** (daily 10am–11pm, until 8pm in winter; free). At the centre of the monastery is the main shrine and architectural highlight, the **Basílica de la Mare de Déu de Lluc**, a dark and gaudily decorated church, whose heaviness is partly relieved by a dome over the central crossing. On either side of the nave, stone steps extend the aisles round the back of the Baroque high altar to a little chapel. This is the holy of holies, built to display the much-venerated statue of the Virgin, commonly known as **La Moreneta** ("The Little Dark-Skinned One") ever since the original paintwork peeled off in the fifteenth century to reveal brown stone underneath.

Allow time, too, for a visit to the monastery museum, the **Museu de Lluc** (daily 10am–1.30pm & 2.30–5pm; €3), and for a stroll along the **Camí dels Misteris del Rosari** (Way of the Mysteries of the Rosary), a broad pilgrims' footpath that winds its way up the rocky hillside behind the monastery.

Practicalities

Buses to Lluc, which is situated about 700m off the Ma-10, stop right outside the monastery. **Accommodation** at the monastery (☎971 871 525, ⒲www .lluc.net) is either in simple rooms with private bath (❶) or in two-room apartments (❸); rooms (but not apartments) are subject to an 11pm curfew. In summer, phone ahead if you want to be sure of space; at other times, simply book at the monastery's information office on arrival. There are two **restaurants** beside the monastery car park, plus a café-bar, but far preferable is the appealing *Sa Fonda*, in the monks' former refectory, where you can get tasty Spanish dishes – but note that the meat dishes are more satisfactory than the fish.

Pollença

Heading northeast from Lluc, the Ma-10 twists through the mountains to travel the 20km on to **POLLENÇA**, a pretty and ancient little town that nestles among a trio of hillocks where the Serra de Tramuntana fades into the coastal flatlands. Following standard Mallorcan practice, the town was established a few kilometres from the seashore to protect it against sudden pirate attack, with its harbour, Port de Pollença (see p.914), left as an unprotected outpost. For once, the stratagem worked. Unlike most of Mallorca's old towns, Pollença avoided destruction, and the austere stone houses that cramp the twisting lanes of the centre mostly date from the eighteenth century. In the middle, **Plaça Major**, the main square, accommodates a cluster of laid-back cafés and the dour facade of the church of **Nostra Senyora dels Àngels**, a sheer cliff-face of sun-bleached stone pierced by a rose window. Pollença's pride and joy is, however, its **Via Crucis** (Way of the Cross), a long, steep and beautiful stone stairway, graced by ancient cypress trees, which ascends **El Calvari** (Calvary Hill) directly north of the principal square. At the top, a much-revered statue of the **Mare de Déu del Peu de la Creu** (Mother of God at the Foot of the Cross) is lodged in a simple, courtyarded **Oratori** (Chapel), whose whitewashed walls sport some of the worst religious paintings imaginable. However, the views out over coast and town are sumptuous. On Good Friday, a figure of Jesus is slowly carried by torchlight down from the Oratori to the church of Nostra Senyora dels Àngels, in the **Davallament** (Lowering), one of the most moving religious celebrations on the island.

There are further magnificent views from the **Ermita de Nostra Senyora del Puig**, a rambling, mostly eighteenth-century monastery that occupies a serene and beautiful spot on top of the Puig de Maria, a 320-metre-high hump facing the south end of town. The Benedictines now own the place, but the monks are gone and today a custodian supplements the order's income by renting out cells to tourists. To get to the monastery, take the signposted turning left off the main Pollença–Inca road just south of town, then head up this steep, 1.5-kilometre lane until it fizzles out, to be replaced by a cobbled footpath that winds up to the monastery entrance. It's possible to drive to the top of the lane, but unless you've got nerves of steel, you're better off leaving your vehicle by the turning near the foot of the hill. Allow just over an hour each way if you're walking from the centre of town.

Practicalities

Buses to Pollença halt immediately to the south of Plaça Major, metres from the **turisme** (Mon–Fri 9am–2pm & 2.30–4pm, Sat 9am–1pm). The most central place to **stay** is the *Hotel Juma*, Plaça Major 9 (☎971 535 002, ⒲www .hoteljuma.com; ❺), a medium-sized hotel with comfortable, air-conditioned modern bedrooms above a café. Also in the centre, at c/Roser Vell 11, is the very welcoming *La Posada de Lluc* (☎971 535 220, ⓦwww.posadalluc.com; ❺), which occupies an intelligently revamped old mansion where the Lluc monks once used to stay when they were in town. There are also much cheaper lodgings at the Ermita de Nostra Senyora del Puig (☎971 184 132; ❶), where the old monks' cells have been renovated to provide simple accommodation. Be warned, though, that it can get cold and windy at night, and the refectory food is mediocre.

Pollença does well for **cafés** and **restaurants**: on Plaça Major, the *Café Espanyol* offers snacks and a good strong cup of coffee, the *Juma* serves up first-rate tapas, and the ☀ *Restaurante Il Giardino* provides superb Italian-style cuisine with mains from €15 (daily from 7pm, closed Nov to mid-March).

Port de Pollença

Over at **PORT DE POLLENÇA** things are a little more touristy, though still pleasantly low-key. With the mountains as a backdrop, the resort arches through the flatlands behind the Badia de Pollença, a deeply indented bay whose sheltered waters are ideal for swimming. The **beach** is the focus of attention, a narrow, elongated sliver of sand that's easily long enough to accommodate the crowds. A rash of apartment buildings and hotels blights the edge of town, and the noisy main road to Alcúdia runs close to most of the seashore, but all in all the place is very appealing, especially along the pedestrianized seashore **Passeig Anglada Camarasa**.

For a change of scene, passenger **ferries** shuttle between the marina and the Platja de Formentor (April–Oct 5 daily; 30min), one of Mallorca's most attractive beaches, while **boat trips** cruise the bay (June to mid-Oct Mon–Sat daily; 2hr 30min) or work their way along to Cap de Formentor (Mon–Wed & Fri daily; 1hr). There's also a delightful three-kilometre (each way) **hike** across the neck of the Península de Formentor to the remote shingle beach of **Cala Boquer**.

Practicalities

Buses to Port de Pollença stop by the marina right in the centre of town – and metres from the seafront **turisme** (Mon–Fri 8am–3pm & Sat 9am–1pm; ☎971 865 467). The flatlands edging the Badia de Pollença make for easy, scenic cycling, and **mountain bikes** can be rented from *March* at c/Joan XXIII 89 (☎971 864 784).

There are lots of reasonably priced and convenient **accommodation** options. One first-rate choice is the unassuming *Hostal Bahía*, Passeig Voramar 31 (☎971 866 562, ⓦwww.hoposa.es; closed Nov–March; ❹), in a lovely location a few minutes' walk north of the marina along the pedestrianized part of the seafront and offering thirty rooms in one of the port's older villas. Much pricier is the *Hotel Can Llenaire*, Carretera Llenaire (☎971 535 251, ⓦwww.hotelllenaire.com; ❼), which occupies an imposing Mallorcan manor house on the brow of a hill with wide views over the Badia de Pollença. There are just eleven rooms, each decked out in period style, and the hotel is clearly signposted down a country lane from the main coastal road just east of the centre of the resort.

Among a plethora of **restaurants**, the most obvious choice is the recently remodelled ☀ *Restaurant Stay*, out on the marina's Moll Nou jetty (☎971 864 013), a chic place that features the freshest of seafood; it's a popular (and romantic) spot, so reservations are advised – count on around €25 for a main course. Another possibility is *Café La Balada del Agua del Mar*, Passeig Voramar 5, one of the prettiest cafés along the promenade, with mains averaging €15.

Península de Formentor

Travelling northeast out of Port de Pollença, the road soon weaves up into the craggy hills of the twenty-kilometre-long **Península de Formentor**, the final spur of the Serra de Tramuntana. At first, the road (which suffers a surfeit of tourists from mid-morning to mid-afternoon) travels inland, out of sight of the true grandeur of the scenery, but after about 4km the **Mirador de Mal Pas** rectifies matters with a string of lookout points perched on the edge of plunging, north-facing sea cliffs. From here, it's another couple of kilometres to the woods backing onto the **Platja de Formentor**, a pine-clad beach of golden sand in a pretty cove. It's a beautiful spot, with exquisite views over to the mountains on the far side of the bay. **Buses** run to the beach from Port de Pollença (May–Oct Mon–Sat 4 daily).

Beyond the turn-off for the beach, the main peninsula road runs along a wooded ridge, before tunnelling through Mont Fumat to emerge on the rocky mass of **Cap de Formentor**, a tapered promontory of bleak sea cliffs and scrub-covered hills that offers spectacular views out along the coast from the environs of its lighthouse.

Alcúdia

It's just 10km round the bay from Port de Pollença to the pint-sized town of **ALCÚDIA**, whose main claim to fame is its impeccably restored medieval walls and incredibly popular open-air market (Tues & Sun), with everything from souvenir trinkets to fruit and veg. Situated on a neck of land separating two large, sheltered bays, the site's strategic value was first recognized by the Phoenicians, and later by the Romans, who built their island capital, Pollentia, here in the first century AD.

It only takes an hour or so to walk around the antique lanes of Alcúdia's compact centre, and to explore the town walls and their fortified gates. This pleasant stroll can be extended by a visit to the meagre remains of Roman **Pollentia**, whose broken pillars and mashed foundations lie just outside the town walls (Tues–Fri 10am–3pm, Nov–June until 4pm, Sat & Sun 10.30am–1pm; €2). The entrance ticket includes admission to the small but excellent **Museu Monogràfic** nearby – just inside the walls.

Buses to Alcúdia stop beside – and immediately to the south of – the town walls on Avgda.dels Princeps d'Espanya. For **food**, there are several good cafés on Plaça Constitució, including *Restaurant Sa Plaça*, a smart little place featuring Mallorcan cuisine, with main courses at around €21.

Port d'Alcúdia

PORT D'ALCÚDIA, 3km south of Alcúdia, is easily the biggest and busiest of the resorts on the Badia d'Alcúdia, its raft of restaurants and café-bars attracting crowds from a seemingly interminable string of high-rise hotels and apartment buildings. The tower blocks are, however, relatively well distributed and the streets neat and tidy. Predictably, the daytime focus is the **beach**, a superb arc of pine-studded golden sand, which stretches south for 10km from the combined marina and fishing harbour.

Port d'Alcúdia acts as northern Mallorca's summertime transport hub, with frequent **bus** services to and from all the neighbouring towns and resorts, plus Palma. The main **turisme** is situated on Carretera d'Artà, about 2km south round the bay from the marina (Easter to Oct Mon–Sat 9am–7pm; ☎971 892 615). It can supply all sorts of information, most usefully free maps marked with all the resort's hotels and apartments, but bear in mind that in winter almost everywhere is closed. In addition, there's a superabundance of **car, moped and bicycle rental** companies strung out along Carretera d'Artà.

Parc Natural de S'Albufera

Heading south around the bay from Port d'Alcúdia, it's about 6km to the **Parc Natural de S'Albufera** (daily: April–Sept 9am–6pm; Oct–March 9am–5pm; free), a slice of protected wetland, which is all that remains of the marshes that once extended round most of the bay. The signposted entrance to the park is on the Ma-12, but access is only on foot or cycle – so if you're driving, you'll need to use the small car park near the entrance. About 1km from the entrance, you come to the park's **reception centre**, from where footpaths radiate out into the reedy, watery tract beyond. It's a superb habitat, with ten well-appointed hides allowing excellent **birdwatching**. Over two hundred species have been spotted: resident wetland-loving birds, autumn and/or springtime migrants, and wintering species and birds of prey in their scores. There's no problem getting here by public transport – **buses** from Port d'Alcúdia to Ca'n Picafort stop beside the entrance.

Menorca

The second largest of the Balearic Islands, boomerang-shaped **MENORCA** is often and unfairly maligned as an overdeveloped, package-tourist ghetto. Contrary to its reputation, however, Menorca remains the least developed of the Balearics, an essentially rural island with rolling fields, wooded ravines and humpy hills filling out the interior in between its two main – but still notably small – towns of **Maó** and **Ciutadella**. Much of this landscape looks pretty much as it did at the turn of the twentieth century, and only around the edges of the island, and then only in parts, have its rocky coves been colonized by sprawling villa complexes. Neither is the development likely to spread: determined to protect their island from the worst excesses of the tourist industry, the Menorcans have clearly demarcated development areas and are also pushing ahead with a variety of environmental schemes – the island was declared a UNESCO Biosphere Reserve in 1993, and over forty percent of it now enjoys official protection.

Furthermore, Menorca is dotted with **prehistoric monuments**, weather-worn stone remains that are evidence of a sophisticated culture. Little is known of the island's prehistory, but the monuments are thought to be linked to those of Sardinia and are classified as examples of the **Talayotic culture**, which is usually considered to have ended with arrival of the Romans in 123 BC. **Talayots** are the rock mounds found all over the island – popular belief has it that they functioned as watchtowers, but it's a theory few experts accept: they have no interior stairway, and only a few are found on the coast. The megalithic **taulas** – huge stones topped with another to form a T, around 4m high and unique to Menorca – are even more puzzling. They have no obvious function, and they are almost always found alongside a *talayot*. Some of the best-preserved *talayot* and *taula* remains are on the edge of Maó at the **Talatí de Dalt** site. The third prehistoric structure of note is the **naveta** (dating from 1400 to 800 BC),

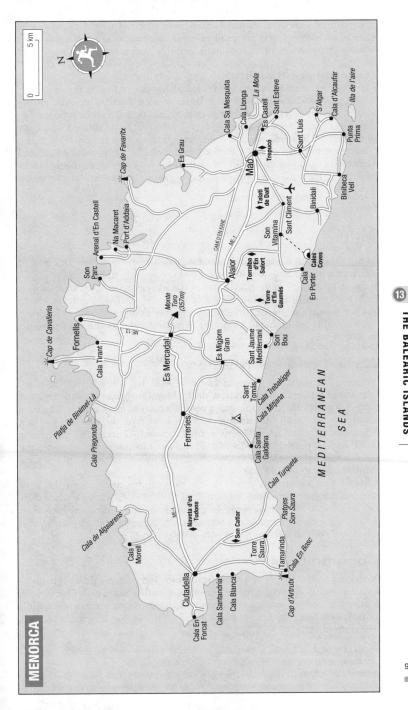

MENORCA

stone-slab constructions shaped like an inverted bread tin. Many have false ceilings, and although you can stand up inside, they were clearly not living spaces – communal pantries, perhaps, or more probably ossuaries.

Menorca practicalities

Menorca stretches from the enormous natural harbour of Maó in the east to the smaller port of Ciutadella in the west. **Bus** routes are distinctly limited, adhering mostly to the main central road between these two, occasionally branching off to the larger coastal resorts. Consequently, you'll need your own **vehicle** to reach any of the emptier **beaches**, which are sometimes down a track fit only for 4WD.

Accommodation is at a premium, with limited options outside Maó and Ciutadella – and you can count on all the beds in all the resorts being block-booked by the tour operators from the beginning to the end of the season (May–Oct).

Maó

MAÓ (Mahón in Castilian), the island capital, is likely to be your first port of call. It's a respectable, almost dull little town, the people restrained and polite. So is the architecture – an unusual hybrid of classical Georgian townhouses, which reflect a strong British connection, and tall, severe Spanish apartment blocks shading the narrow streets. Port it may be, but there's no seamy side to Maó, and the harbour is now home to a string of restaurants and cafés that attract tourists in their droves.

Arrival and information

Menorca's **airport**, just 5km southwest of Maó, has a handful of car-rental outlets and a **tourist information desk** (May–Oct Mon–Fri 8am–9pm, Sat 9am–1.30pm; ☏971 157 115) with a good selection of free literature. There are hourly buses to **Maó bus station**, which is located on the west side of Plaça S'Esplanada; the taxi fare will set you back about €10. **Ferries** from Barcelona and Palma sail right up the inlet to Maó harbour, mooring directly beneath the town centre. From behind the ferry dock, it's a five-minute walk up the wide stone stairway to the old part of town.

Maó's main **turisme** is down on the harbourfront, metres from the ferry terminal (Mon–Fri 8am–8pm, Sat 8am–1pm; ☏971 355 952). It can provide maps of the island and free leaflets giving the lowdown on almost everything from archeological sites and beaches to bus timetables, car rental and accommodation. The island's official **website** is ⓦwww.e-menorca.org.

Accommodation

Maó has a limited supply of **accommodation**, and excessive demand tends to inflate prices at the height of the season. Despite this, along with Ciutadella it remains the best Menorcan bet for bargain lodgings, with a small concentration of **hostales**. None of these places is inspiring, but they're reasonable enough, and convenient.

Hostal La Isla c/Santa Caterina 4 ☏971 366 492. Rooms at this amenable *hostal* may be on the small side, but they are reasonably attractive and comfortable, and all have private bathroom

and TV. There's a popular bar and restaurant downstairs, too. ❷

Hotel Port-Mahón Avgda. Fort de l'Eau 13 ☏971 362 600, ⓦwww.sethotels.com. An elegant

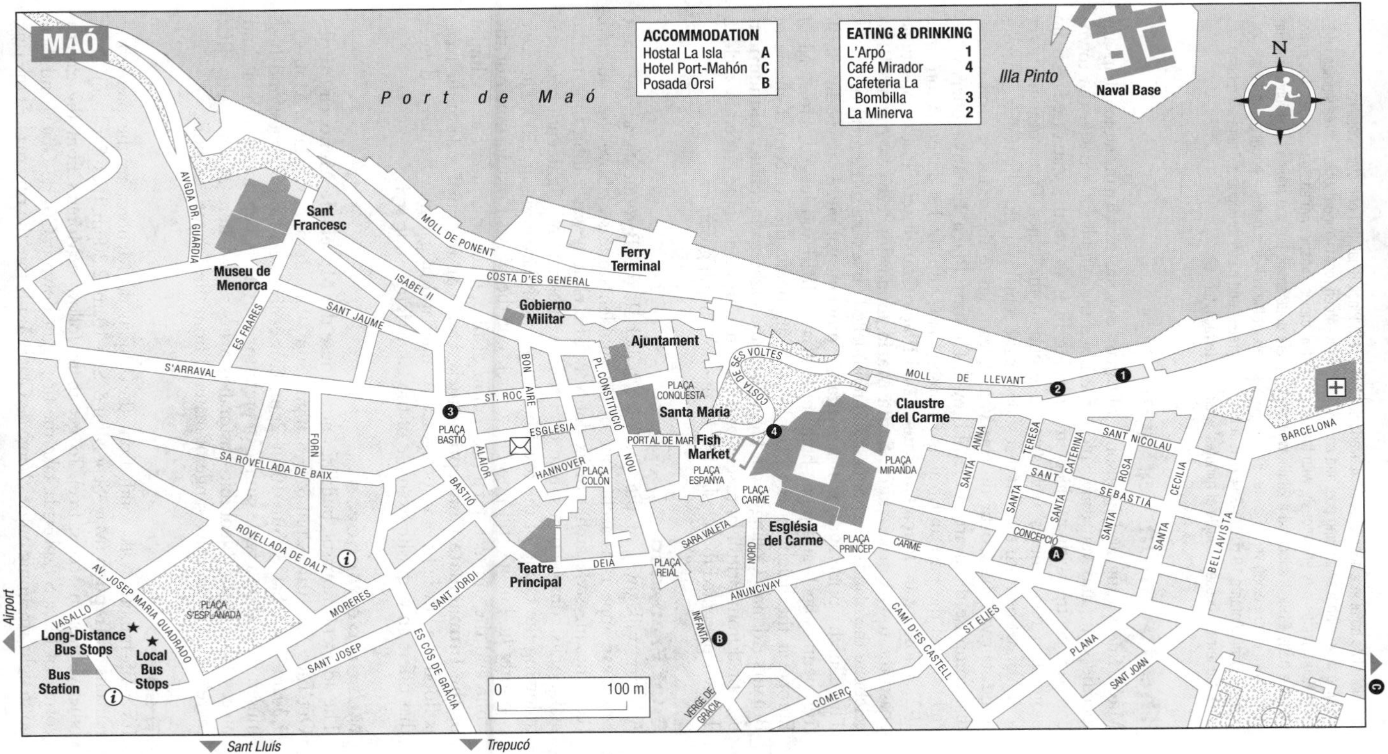

MAÓ
ACCOMMODATION
Hostal La Isla A
Hotel Port-Mahón C
Posada Orsi B
EATING & DRINKING
L'Arpó 1
Café Mirador 4
Cafeteria La Bombilla 3
La Minerva 2
Port de Maó
Illa Pinto
Naval Base
N
Sant Francesc
Museu de Menorca
Ferry Terminal
Gobierno Militar
Ajuntament
Santa Maria
Fish Market
Claustre del Carme
Església del Carme
Teatre Principal
Long-Distance Bus Stops
Local Bus Stops
Bus Station
AVGDA DR. GUARDIA
MOLL DE PONENT
COSTA D'ES GENERAL
ISABEL II
SANT JAUME
ES FRARES
S'ARRAVAL
FORN
SA ROVELLADA DE BAIX
ROVELLADA DE DALT
AV. JOSEP MARIA QUADRADO
VASALLO
PLAÇA S'ESPLANADA
MORERES
SANT JOSEP
ES CÒS DE GRÀCIA
SANT JORDI
BASTIÓ
PLAÇA BASTIÓ
ST. ROC
BON AIRE
ESGLÉSIA
ALAIOR
HANNOVER
PLAÇA COLÓN
PL. CONSTITUCIÓ
NOU
PORTAL DE MAR
PLAÇA CONQUESTA
PLAÇA ESPANYA
COSTA DE SES VOLTES
MOLL DE LLEVANT
PLAÇA CARME
PLAÇA MIRANDA
PLAÇA PRINCEP
CARME
DEIÀ
PLAÇA REIAL
SARA VALETA
NORD
ANUNCIVAY
INFANTA
VERGE DE GRÀCIA
COMERÇ
CAMÍ D'ES CASTELL
ST ELIES
PLANA
SANT JOAN
BELLAVISTA
SANTA ANNA
SANTA TERESA
SANT CATERINA
SANTA CONCEPCIÓ
SANT NICOLAU
SANTA ROSA
SANT SEBASTIÀ
SANTA CECILIA
BARCELONA
0 100 m
Airport
Sant Lluís
Trepucó
C

colonial-style hotel in a superb location overlooking the Maó inlet, with a swimming pool and all mod cons. Room prices vary enormously, with the top whack a hefty €192. It's located a 20min walk east of the town centre along via c/Carme. ⑥

Posada Orsi c/Infanta 19 ⓉＴ971 364 751. In a large, old terrace house a couple of minutes' walk from Plaça Reial, this one-star *hostal* has seventeen rooms, nine doubles, three singles and five triples, mostly with shared facilities. The rooms are quite small, but you couldn't possibly complain about the colour scheme – bright pinks, reds, greens and blues throughout. There's a rooftop terrace, too. ②

The town and aournd

Maó's fine setting and handsome old mansions are its charm, rather than any specific sight, and you can explore the place thoroughly in a day – the town's compact centre, with its deep streets rising high above the water's edge, is no more than ten-minutes' walk from one end to the other. From near the ferry terminal, set beneath the cliff that supports the remains of the city wall, a generous stone stairway, the **Costa de Ses Voltes**, leads up to the series of small squares that comprise the heart of the old town. The first, **Plaça Espanya**, offers views right across the port and bay, and houses Maó's fish market, in operation since 1927. Close by are **Plaça Conquesta** and **Plaça Constitució**. Plaça Constitució boasts the town's main church, **Santa María**, founded in 1287 by Alfonso III to celebrate the island's Reconquest and remodelled on several subsequent occasions. The church's pride and joy is its **organ**, a monumental piece of woodwork, all trumpeting angels and pipes, built in Austria in 1810 and lugged across half of Europe at the height of the Napoleonic Wars under the concerned charge of Britain's Admiral Collingwood. Next door, the eighteenth-century **ajuntament** benefited from British largesse, too, its attractive arcaded facade graced by a clock that was presented to the islanders by the first British governor.

Sant Francesc

A short walk away, at the end of c/Isabel II, the Baroque facade of **Sant Francesc** appears as a cliff-face of pale golden stone set above the rounded, Romanesque-style arches of its doorway. The church was a long time in the making, its construction spread over the seventeenth and eighteenth centuries following the razing of the town by the piratical Barbarossa in 1535. The nave is poorly lit, but it's still possible to pick out the pinkish tint in much of the stone and the unusual spiral decoration of the pillars. In contrast, the **Chapel of the Immaculate Conception**, tucked away off the north side of the nave, is flooded with light – an octagonal wonderland of garlanded vines and roses that offers an exquisite example of the Churrigueresque style.

Museu de Menorca

The adjacent monastic buildings now house the **Museu de Menorca** (April–Oct Tues–Sat 10am–2pm & 6–8.30pm, Sun 10am–2pm; Nov–March Mon–Fri 9.30am–2pm, Sat & Sun 10am–2pm; €3), easily the island's biggest and best museum, holding a wide sample of prehistoric artefacts, beginning with bits and pieces left by the Neolithic pastoralists who settled here around 4000 BC; there's also an extensive range of material from the Talayotic period.

Trepucó

It's a 35-minute walk south from the Museu de Menorca to the prehistoric remains of **Trepucó** (May–Sept Mon & Sun 10am–2.30pm, Tues–Sat 10am–8pm; otherwise, open access; free). To get there, follow c/Moreres from the eastern corner of Plaça S'Esplanada, take the first right down c/Cós de Gràcia and then go straight, streaming onto c/Verge de Gràcia just before the ring road. At the ring road, go straight over the roundabout and follow the twisting lane dead ahead, past the cemetery, and thereafter follow the signs.

Surrounded by olive trees and dry-stone walls, the tiny site's focal point is a 4.2-metre-high and 2.75-metre-wide **taula**, one of the largest and best preserved of these T-shaped monoliths on the island. The *taula* stands inside a circular compound that is edged by the remains of several broadly circular buildings. These were thoroughly excavated by a team of archeologists from Cambridge University in the late 1920s, but even they couldn't work out how the complex was structured. There are two cone-shaped **talayots** close by, the larger one accessible, the other not.

Eating and drinking

Maó has a place in culinary history as the eighteenth-century birthplace of **mayonnaise** (*mahonesa*). Various legends, all of them involving the French, claim to identify its inventor: take your pick from the chef of the French commander besieging Maó; a peasant woman dressing a salad for another French general; or a housekeeper disguising rancid meat from the taste buds of a French officer. The French also changed the way the Menorcans bake their bread, while the British started the dairy industry and encouraged the roasting of meat. Unfortunately, traditional Balearic food is not very much in evidence these days, as most of Maó's **restaurants** specialize in Spanish, Catalan or Italian dishes. These tourist-oriented establishments are mainly spread out along the harbourside – the Moll de Ponent west of the main stairway, the Moll de Llevant to the east. There's also a smattering of cheaper restaurants and **coffee bars** in the centre of town, though surprisingly few **tapas bars**.

Nightlife is not Maó's forte, though there are some fairly lively **bars** along the harbourfront that stay open until around 2am on summer weekends.

Cafés and restaurants

L'Arpó Moll de Llevant 124 ☏ 971 369 844. Well-established seafood specialist with a prime selection of fish dishes from €15. Try the paella or the *caldereta de llagosta* (lobster stew).

Café Mirador Plaça Espanya 2. Located a few steps from the fish market, this appealing café-bar offers a good range of snacks and tapas, and has great views over the harbour from its terrace. Jazz is the favoured background music.

Cafeteria La Bombilla c/Sant Roc 31. Pleasant little café, in the town centre on Plaça Bastió, offering a tasty range of tapas, averaging about €3 per portion. Has a relaxing outside terrace, too.

La Minerva Moll de Llevant 87 ☏ 971 351 995. One of the more polished restaurants in town, with a menu focused on seafood. The paella is outstanding, and so is the *menú*, a relative snip at €16. Reservations well-nigh essential at the height of the season.

Across the island

The road from Maó to Ciutadella, the **Me-1**, forms the backbone of Menorca, and what little industry the island enjoys – a few shoe factories and cheese plants – is strung along it. Here also is the island's highest peak, **Monte Toro**, from the top of which there are wondrous views.

Talatí de Dalt

Just 4km out of Maó on the Me-1, you pass the short and clearly signposted country lane that leads to **Talatí de Dalt** (May–Sept daily 10am–sunset, €3; Oct–April open access, free), another illuminating Talayotic remnant. Much larger than

Trepucó, the site is enclosed by a Cyclopean wall and features an imposing *taula*, which is adjacent to the heaped stones of the main *talayot*. All around are the scant remains of prehistoric dwellings. The exact functions of these are not known, but there's no doubt that the *taula* was the village centrepiece, and probably the focus of religious ceremonies. The rustic setting is charming – olive and carob trees abound and a tribe of semi-wild boar roots around the undergrowth.

Es Mercadal and Monte Toro

The old market town of **ES MERCADAL** squats amongst the hills at the very centre of the island about 20km west of Maó. It's an amiable little place of whitewashed houses and trim allotments whose antique centre straddles a quaint watercourse. From Es Mercadal, you can set off on the ascent of **Monte Toro**, a steep 3.2-kilometre climb along a serpentine road. At 357m, the summit is the island's highest point and offers wonderful vistas. From this lofty vantage point, Menorca's geological division becomes apparent: to the north, Devonian rock (mostly reddish sandstone) supports a rolling, sparsely populated landscape edged by a ragged coastline; to the south, limestone predominates in a rippling plain that boasts both the island's best farmland and, as it approaches the south coast, its deepest valleys.

Monte Toro has been a place of pilgrimage since medieval times, and the Augustinians plonked a monastery on the summit in the seventeenth century. Bits of this original construction survive in today's **convent**, which shares the site with a monumentally ugly statue of Christ. Much of the convent is out of bounds, but the public part, approached across a pretty courtyard, encompasses a couple of gift shops, a delightful terrace café and a cosy church.

Ferreries and beyond

Heading on from Es Mercadal, the Me-1 swings past the village of **FERRERIES** before sliding across the agricultural flatlands of the western part of the island. There are prehistoric remains to either side of the road, but easily the most interesting is the **Naveta d'es Tudons** (May–Sept daily 10am–sunset, €3; Oct–April open access, free), Menorca's best example of a *naveta*, located just 6km short of Ciutadella. Seven metres high and fourteen long, the structure is made of massive stone blocks slotted together in a sophisticated dry-stone technique. The narrow entrance leads into a small antechamber, which was once sealed off by a stone slab; beyond lies the main chamber where the bones of the dead were stashed away after the flesh had been removed.

Ciutadella and around

Like Maó, **CIUTADELLA** sits high above its harbour, though navigation is far more difficult here, up a narrow channel too slender for anything but the smallest of cargo ships. Despite this nautical inconvenience, Ciutadella has been the island's capital for most of its history, the narrow, cobbled streets of its compact, fortified centre brimming with fine old palaces, hidden away behind high walls, and a set of Baroque and Gothic churches very much in the Spanish tradition.

Essentially, it's the whole architectural ensemble that gives Ciutadella its appeal, which, together with some excellent restaurants and an adequate supply of *hostales* and hotels, makes this a lovely place to stay. Allow at least a couple of days, more if you seek out one of the charming cove beaches within easy striking distance of town: **Cala Turqueta** is the pick of the bunch.

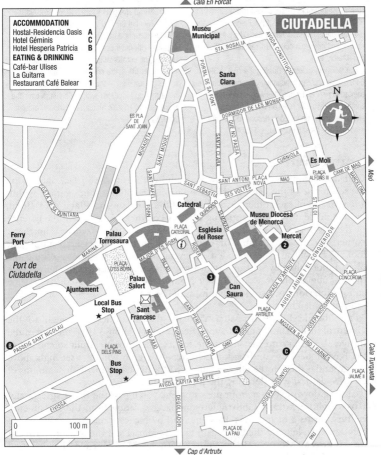

ACCOMMODATION
Hostal-Residencia Oasis A
Hotel Géminis C
Hotel Hesperia Patricia B

EATING & DRINKING
Café-bar Ulises 2
La Guitarra 3
Restaurant Café Balear 1

CIUTADELLA

Arrival and information

Buses from Maó and points east pull in on the south side of Plaça dels Pins, west of the town centre metres from the main square, Plaça d'es Born. **Local buses** shuttle up and down the west coast from the north side of Plaça dels Pins. **Car ferries** dock on the north side of the harbour, about five-minutes' walk from the centre.

The **turisme**, opposite the cathedral on Plaça Catedral, bang in the middle of the old town (May–Oct Mon–Fri 9.30am–8.30pm, Sat 9am–1pm; Nov–April Mon–Fri 9am–1pm & 5–7pm, Sat 9am–1pm; ☎971 382 693), has buckets of information on Menorca as a whole and Ciutadella in particular.

Accommodation

There's hardly a plethora of **accommodation** in Ciutadella, but the town does have a handful of fairly comfortable and reasonably priced *hostales* dotted in and around the centre.

Hostal-Residencia Oasis c/Sant Isidre 33 ☎ 971 382 197. Just a few metres from Plaça Artrutx, this old-fashioned, one-star *hostal* has nine simple rooms next door to a courtyard-restaurant. Closed Oct–March. ❷

Hotel Géminis c/Josepa Rossinyol 4 ☎ 971 384 644, ⓦ www.hotelgeminismenorca.com. Distinctively painted in pink and white, this well-tended, very comfortable two-star hotel on a quiet residential street has thirty rooms, each decorated in bright modern style. Closed mid-Dec to Feb. ❸

Hotel Hesperia Patricia Passeig Sant Nicolau 90 ☎ 971 385 511, ⓦ www .hoteles-hesperia.es. The smartest hotel in town, popular with business folk and handy for the centre. The comfortable, modern rooms come with all facilities, the only downer being the lack of a sea view – though the best rooms have rooftop balconies with wide vistas over the town centre. There's also an outside swimming pool. ❹

The Town

Ciutadella's compact **centre** crowds around the fortified cliff face shadowing the south side of the harbour. The main plazas and points of interest are within a few strides of each other, on and around the main square, **Plaça d'es Born**, in the middle of which is a soaring **obelisk** commemorating the futile defence of the town against the marauding Turks in 1558. In the square's northeast corner, the massive **Palau Torresaura**, built in the nineteenth century but looking far older, is the grandest of several aristocratic mansions edging the plaza. Embellished by self-important *loggias*, its frontage displays the family coat of arms above a large wooden door giving onto an expansive courtyard. The antique interior, however, is off limits, as the house is still owner-occupied – like most of its neighbours.

From beside Palau Torresaura, c/Major d'es Born leads through to the **Catedral** (daily 9am–1pm & 6–9pm; free), built by Alfonso III at the end of the thirteenth century on the site of the town's chief mosque. Built so soon after the Reconquest, its construction is fortress-like, with windows set high above the ground – though the effect is somewhat disturbed by the flashy columns of the Neoclassical west doorway, the principal entrance.

Cutting down c/Roser from the cathedral, you'll pass the tiny **Església del Roser**, whose striking Churrigueresque facade, dating from the seventeenth century, boasts a quartet of pillars engulfed by intricate tracery. At the end of c/Roser, turn left and then left again for c/Seminari and the **Museu Diocesà de Menorca** (Mon–Sat 10am–2pm; €2.50), housed in an old and dignified convent. Inside, the museum's collection comprises a hotchpotch of Talayotic and early Classical archeological finds, notably a superbly crafted miniature bull and a similarly exquisite little mermaid, both Greek bronzes dating from the fifth century BC.

Behind the museum, on Plaça Llibertat, lies the **mercat** (market), another delightful corner of the old town, where fresh fruit, vegetable and fish stalls mingle with lively and inexpensive cafés selling the freshest of *ensaimadas*. Alternatively, **c/Seminari** proceeds north to intersect with the narrow, pedestrianized main street running through the old town – here **c/J.M. Quadrado**, though it goes under various names along its route. To the east of this intersection is a parade of whitewashed, vaulted arches, **Ses Voltes**, distinctly Moorish in inspiration and a suitable setting for several attractive shops and busy cafés. C/J.M. Quadrado then leads into **Plaça Nova**, a minuscule square edged by some of the most popular pavement cafés in town. Continuing east along c/Maó, you leave the cramped alleys of the old town at Plaça Alfons III.

Eating and drinking

For an early **breakfast**, make your way to the **market** on Plaça Llibertat, where a couple of simple cafés serve coffee and fresh pastries. Later in the day, around **lunchtime**, aim for c/J.M. Quadrado, Plaça Nova or Plaça Alfons III, which together hold a good selection of inexpensive café-bars, offering tapas and light meals. In the **evening**, more ambitious and expensive food is available at a string of excellent restaurants down by the harbourside, or at a couple of good places tucked away near Plaça d'es Born. Almost all the harbourside places have the advantage of an outside terrace, but note that – unlike those restaurants near the Plaça d'es Born – they usually close down in winter.

Café-bar Ulises Plaça Llibertat. This amenable, low-key café-bar next to the market is a locals' favourite. Their *ensaimadas*, a snip at €1.50 each, are the best in town. Mon–Sat from 8am.

La Guitarra c/Nostra Senyora dels Dolors 1 ☏ 971 381 355. Located a short walk from the cathedral, this is arguably the best restaurant in town, a family-run affair featuring the very best of Menorcan cuisine, with main courses – anything from seafood to lamb – averaging a very reasonable €12–18. They also do a particularly delicious

lobster stew for €35 per person. The restaurant occupies an old cellar.

Restaurant Café Balear Es Pla de Sant Joan 15 ☏ 971 380 005. Justifiably popular, this attractively decorated restaurant sits at the back of the harbour by the bridge. The terrace is the best place to eat, but there are tables inside, too. The food is first-rate, with shellfish and fish the big deals – mains average around €20. Closed Sun.

Southeast of Ciutadella: Cala Turqueta

Beginning at the traffic island on c/Alfons V, the cross-country **Camí de Sant Joan de Missa** runs southeast from Ciutadella to the remote coves of the south coast. The one to head for is **Cala Turqueta**, a lovely cove flanked by wooded limestone cliffs. About 3km from town, you reach the clearly marked farmhouse of **Son Vivó**, where the road branches into two with the more easterly (signposted) road leading to the **Ermita de St Joan de Missa**, a squat, brightly whitewashed church with a dinky little belltower. There's a fork here, too, but the signs are easy to follow, and you keep straight with the road slicing across the countryside before swerving round the **Marjal Vella farmhouse**. Shortly afterwards, about 4.3km from the church, you turn at the sign, going through the gateway to reach the car park for Cala Turqueta. The beach, a sheltered horseshoe of white sand, slopes gently into the sea and is ideal for swimming – and because there are limited facilities, it's most unusual to find a crowd.

Travel details

(☎807 001 700, ⓦwww.spanair.com) or Air Berlin
(☎902 320 737, ⓦwww.airberlin.com). Inter-island
ferries and hydrofoils are operated by Trasmediterránea (☎902 454 645, ⓦwww.trasmediterranea
.es), Baleària (☎902 191 068, ⓦwww.balearia.com)
and Iscomar (☎902 119 128, ⓦwww.iscomar.com).
Formentera to: Ibiza (13–18 boats daily in
summer, 5–7 in winter; 30min–1hr).
Ibiza to: Palma (9 daily flights, 30min; 2 daily ferries,
4hr; & 2 daily summer-only hydrofoils, 2hr 30min).

Boats from the mainland

Car ferries and catamarans to the Balearics from the
Spanish mainland are operated by Trasmediterránea
(☎902 454 645, ⓦwww.trasmediterranea.es),
Baleària (☎902 160 180, ⓦwww.balearia.com) and
Iscomar (☎902 119 128, ⓦwww.iscomar.com).
Alicante to: Ibiza (May–Sept daily; 3hr).
Barcelona to: Ibiza (3–5 weekly ferries, 9hr; daily
catamaran in summer, 5hr 30min).
Dénia to: Formentera (June–Sept daily; 4hr); Ibiza
(daily; 4hr 30min).
Valencia to: Ibiza (daily ferry in summer, 2 weekly
in winter; 5hr 30min; daily catamaran in summer,
2hr 45min).

Mallorca

Buses

Palma to: Andratx (hourly; 1hr); Deià (3–5 daily;
45min); Pollença (2–5 daily; 1hr 10min); Port de
Pollença (2–5 daily; 1hr 15min); Port de Sóller (via
the tunnel: Mon–Fri hourly, Sat & Sun every 1–2hr,
35min; via Valldemossa: 3–5 daily, 1hr 30min);
Sóller (via Valldemossa: 3–5 daily, 1hr 15min; via
the tunnel: Mon–Fri hourly, Sat & Sun every 1–2hr,
30min); Valldemossa (4–9 daily; 30min).
Port de Pollença to: Palma (2–5 daily; 1hr 15min);
Pollença (every 15min to 1hr; 15min); Port de
Sóller (April–Oct Mon–Sat 2 daily; 2hr 10min);
Sóller (May–Oct Mon–Sat 2 daily; 2hr).
Port de Sóller to: Deià (3–5 daily; 40min); Palma
(via Valldemossa: 3–5 daily, 1hr 30min; via the
tunnel: Mon–Fri hourly, Sat & Sun every 1–2hr,
35min); Pollença (May–Oct Mon–Sat 2 daily; 2hr);
Port de Pollença (April–Oct Mon–Sat 2 daily; 2hr
10min); Sóller (Mon–Fri hourly, Sat & Sun every
1–2hr; 5min); Valldemossa (3–5 daily; 55min).
Valldemossa to: Andratx (weekly; 1hr 15min);
Deià (3–5 daily; 15min); Palma (4–9 daily; 30min).

Menorca

Buses

Ciutadella to: Es Mercadal (Mon–Fri hourly, Sat &
Sun 6 daily; 30min); Maó (Mon–Fri hourly, Sat & Sun
6 daily; 50min).
Maó to: Ciutadella (Mon–Fri hourly, Sat & Sun 6
daily; 50min); Es Mercadal (Mon–Fri hourly, Sat &
Sun 6 daily; 30min).

Ferry and catamaran companies and routings

Journey times and frequencies vary depending on
routings and the time of year.
Acciona Trasmediterranea ☎902 454 645,
ⓦwww.directferries.co.uk or ⓦwww
.trasmediterranea.es.
Barcelona to: Ciutadella, Ibiza, Maó, Palma & Port
d'Alcúdia.
Ciutadella to: Barcelona & Port d'Alcúdia.
Denia to: Formentera, Ibiza & Palma.
Ibiza to: Barcelona, Denia, Formentera, Palma
& Valencia.
Maó to: Barcelona, Palma, Port d'Alcúdia
& Valencia.
Palma to: Barcelona, Ibiza, Maó & Valencia.
Port d'Alcúdia to: Barcelona, Ciutadella & Maó.
Valencia to: Ibiza, Maó & Palma.
Balearia ☎902 160 180, ⓦwww.balearia.com.
Barcelona to: Ciutadella, Maó, Palma & Port
d'Alcúdia.
Ciutadella to: Barcelona & Port d'Alcúdia.
Denia to: Formentera, Ibiza & Palma.
Ibiza to: Denia, Formentera & Palma.
Maó to: Barcelona.
Palma to: Barcelona, Denia & Ibiza.
Port d'Alcúdia to: Barcelona & Ciutadella.
Iscomar ☎902 119 128, ⓦwww.iscomar.com.
Barcelona to: Ciutadella, Ibiza, Maó, Palma &
Port d'Alcúdia.
Ciutadella to: Barcelona & Port d'Alcúdia.
Denia to: Formentera, Ibiza & Palma.
Ibiza to: Barcelona, Denia, Formentera & Valencia.
Maó to: Barcelona, Port d'Alcúdia & Valencia.
Palma to: Barcelona, Denia & Valencia.
Port d'Alcúdia to: Barcelona, Ciutadella & Maó.
Valencia to: Ibiza, Maó & Palma.

⑬

THE BALEARIC ISLANDS | Travel details

Contexts

Contexts

History

The first Europeans of whom we have knowledge lived in southern Spain. A recent series of spectacular discoveries at Orce, 115km northeast of Granada, rocked the archeological world, as the date for the arrival of early humans in Europe was pushed back from around 700,000 years ago to perhaps a million years before this, making Orce – if the findings are scientifically confirmed – the earliest known site of human occupation in Europe by a long way. Other finds of early human remains around 800,000 years old in the Sierra de Atapuerca are further confirmation of early activity on the peninsula. Evidence of occupation by Stone Age societies stretching back some 400,000 years was already known about from discoveries at Venta Micena, close to Orce, where early inhabitants hunted elephant and rhino and left behind tools and camp fires. Some of the earliest human fossils found on the Iberian peninsula were unearthed inside the Gibraltar caves, with evidence of Neanderthals dating from around 100,000 BC.

In the Paleolithic period, the first **homo sapiens** arrived on the Iberian peninsula from southern France, settling around the Bay of Biscay as well as in the south. They were cave dwellers and hunter-gatherers, and, at **Altamira** in the Cordillera Cantábrica near Santander, and the Pileta and Nerja caves near Málaga, left behind remarkable **cave paintings** and deftly stylized cave murals depicting the animals they hunted. The finest examples (created about 12,000 BC) are at Altamira – now closed for general visits, though you can see similar paintings at Puente Viesgo nearby. During the later Neolithic phase, a sophisticated material culture developed in southern Spain, attested to by the finds of *esparto* sandals and baskets as well as jewellery in the **Cueva de los Murciélagos** in Granada. This period also saw the construction of **megalithic tombs** (dolmens) along the perimeter of the Iberian peninsula, including the superbly preserved examples at Romanya de la Selva, in Catalunya, and **Antequera**, near Málaga.

Subsequent prehistory is more complex and confused. There does not appear to have been any great development in the cave cultures of the north. Instead, the focus shifts south to Almería, which was settled around 5000–4000 BC by the "Iberians", **Neolithic** colonists from North Africa. They had already assimilated into their culture many of the changes that had developed in Egypt and the Near East. Settling in villages, they introduced pastoral and agricultural ways of life and exploited the plentiful supply of copper. Around 1500 BC, with the onset of the **Bronze Age**, they began to spread outwards into fortified villages on the central *meseta*, the high plateau of modern Castile. At the turn of the millennium, they were joined by numerous waves of **Celtic** and **Germanic** peoples. Here, Spain's divisive physical make-up – with its network of mountain ranges – determined its social nature. The incoming tribes formed distinct and isolated groups, conquering and sometimes absorbing each other but only on a very limited and local scale. Hence the Celtic "urnfield people" established themselves in Catalunya, the **Vascones** in the Basque Country and, near them along the Atlantic coast, the **Astures**. Pockets of earlier cultures survived, too, particularly in Galicia with its *citanias* of beehive huts.

First colonies

The Spanish coast, meanwhile, attracted colonists from different regions of the Mediterranean. The **Phoenicians** founded the port of Gadir (Cádiz) around 1100 BC and traded intensively in the metals of the Guadalquivir valley. Their wealth and success gave rise to a Spanish "Atlantis" myth, based on the lost kingdom of Tartessus, mentioned in the Bible and probably sited near Huelva; the sophisticated jewellery it produced is on display in Seville's archeological museum. Market rivalry later brought the **Greeks**, who established their trading colonies along the eastern coast – the modern Costa Brava. There's a fine surviving site at Empúries, near Barcelona.

More significant, however, was the arrival of the **Carthaginians** in the third century BC. Expelled from Sicily by the Romans, they saw in Spain a new base for their empire, from which to regain strength and strike back at their rivals. Although making little impact inland, they occupied most of Andalucía and expanded along the Mediterranean seaboard to establish a new capital at Cartagena ("New Carthage"). Under Hannibal they prepared to invade Italy, and in 219 BC attacked Saguntum, a strategic outpost of the Roman world. It was a disastrous move, precipitating the **Second Punic War**; by 210 BC, only Cádiz remained in their control and they were forced to accept terms. A new and very different age had begun.

Romans and Visigoths

The **Roman colonization** of the peninsula was far more intense than anything previously experienced and met with great resistance from the Celtiberian tribes of the north and centre. It was almost two centuries before the conquest was complete, and indeed the Basques, although defeated, were never fully Romanized.

Nonetheless, Spain became the most important centre of the Roman Empire after Italy itself, producing no fewer than three emperors, along with the writers Seneca, Lucan, Martial and Quintilian. Again, geography dictated an uneven spread of influence, at its strongest in Andalucía, southern Portugal and on the Catalan coast around Tarragona. In the first two centuries AD, the Spanish mines and the granaries of Andalucía brought unprecedented wealth and Roman Spain enjoyed a brief "**Golden Age**". The finest monuments were built in the great provincial capitals – Córdoba, Mérida (which boasts the most impressive remains) and Tarragona – but across the country more practical construction was undertaken: roads, bridges and aqueducts. Many of the latter were still used well into recent centuries – perhaps the most remarkable being those of Segovia and Tarragona – and quite a few bridges, such as that crossing the Guadalquivir in Córdoba, remain in use even today.

Towards the third century, however, the Roman political framework began to show signs of decadence and corruption. Although it didn't totally collapse until the Muslim invasions of the early eighth century, it became increasingly vulnerable to **barbarian incursions** from northern Europe. The Franks and the Suevi (Swabians) swept across the Pyrenees between 264 and 276, leaving devastation in their wake. They were followed two centuries later by further waves of Suevi, Alans and Vandals. Internal strife was heightened by the arrival of the **Visigoths** from Gaul, allies of Rome and already Romanized to a large degree. The triumph of Visigothic strength in the fifth century resulted in a period of spurious unity, based upon an exclusive military rule from their capital at Toledo, but their numbers were never great and their order was often fragmentary and nominal, with the bulk of the subject people kept in a state of disconsolate servility and the military elite divided by constant plots and factions – exacerbated by the Visigothic system of elected monarchy and by their adherence to the heretical Arian doctrine. In 589, **King Recared** converted to Catholicism but religious strife was only multiplied: forced conversions, especially within the Jewish enclaves, maintained a constant simmering of discontent.

Moorish Spain

In contrast to the drawn-out Roman campaigns, **Moorish conquest** of the peninsula was effected with extraordinary speed. This was a characteristic phenomenon of the spread of Islam – Muhammad left Mecca in 622 and by 705 his followers had established control over all of North Africa. Spain, with its political instability, wealth and fertile climate, was an inevitable extension of their aims. In 711, Tariq, governor of Tangier, led a force of seven thousand Berbers across the straits and routed the Visigothic army of King Roderic; two years later, the Visigoths made a last desperate stand at Mérida, and within a decade the Moors had conquered all but the wild mountains of Asturias. The land under their authority was dubbed "**al-Andalus**", a fluid term that expanded and shrunk with the intermittent gains and losses of the Reconquest. According to region, the Moors were to remain in control for the next three to eight centuries.

It was not simply a military conquest. The Moors (a collective term for the numerous waves of Arab and Berber settlers from North Africa) were often content to grant a limited autonomy in exchange for payment of tribute; their administrative system was tolerant and easily absorbed both Jews and Christians, those who retained their religion being known as "Mozarabs". And al-Andalus was a distinctly Spanish state of Islam. Though at first politically subject to the Eastern Caliphate (or empire) of Baghdad, it was soon virtually independent. In the tenth century, at the peak of its power and expansion, Abd ar-Rahman III asserted total independence, proclaiming himself caliph of a new **Western Islamic empire**. Its capital was Córdoba – the largest, most prosperous and most civilized city in Europe. This was the great age of Muslim Spain: its scholarship, philosophy, architecture and craftsmanship were without rival and there was an unparalleled growth in urban life, in trade and in agriculture, aided by magnificent irrigation projects. These and other engineering feats were not, on the whole, instigated by the Moors, who instead took basic Roman models and adapted them to a new level of sophistication. In **architecture** and the **decorative arts**, however, their contribution was original and unique – as may be seen in the fabulous monuments of Seville, Córdoba and Granada.

The Córdoban Caliphate for a while created a remarkable degree of unity. But its rulers were to become decadent and out of touch, prompting the brilliant but dictatorial **al-Mansur** to usurp control. Under this extraordinary ruler, Moorish power actually reached new heights, pushing the Christian kingdom of Asturias-León back into the Cordillera Cantábrica and sacking its most holy shrine, Santiago de Compostela. However, after his death the caliphate quickly lost its authority, and in 1031 it disintegrated into a series of small independent kingdoms, or *taifas*, the strongest of which was Seville.

Internal divisions amongst the *taifas* weakened their resistance to the Christian kingdoms that were rallying in the north, and twice North Africa had to be turned to for reinforcement. This resulted in two distinct new waves of Moorish invasion – first by the fanatically Islamic **Almoravids** (1086) and later by the **Almohads** (1147), who restored effective Muslim authority until their defeat at the battle of Las Navas de Tolosa in 1212.

The Christian Reconquest

The **Reconquest** of land and influence from the Moors was a slow and intermittent process. It began with a symbolic victory by a small force of Christians at Covadonga in Asturias (722) and was not completed until 1492 with the conquest of Granada by Fernando and Isabel.

The victory at Covadonga resulted in the formation of the tiny Christian kingdom of **Asturias**. Initially just 50 by 65km in area, it had by 914 reclaimed León and most of Galicia and northern Portugal. At this point, progress was temporarily halted by the devastating campaigns of al-Mansur. However, with the fall of the Córdoban Caliphate and the divine aid of Spain's Moor-slaying patron, St James the Apostle, or Santiago (see pp.562–563), the Reconquest moved into a new and powerful phase.

The frontier castles built against Arab attack gave their name to Castile, founded in the tenth century as a county of León-Asturias. Under **Ferdinand I** (1037–65), it achieved the status of a kingdom and became the main thrust and focus of the Reconquest. Other kingdoms were being defined in the north at the same time: the Basques founded **Navarra** (Navarre), while dynastic marriage merged **Catalunya** with **Aragón**. In 1085, this period of confident Christian expansion reached its zenith with the capture of the great Moorish city of Toledo. The following year, however, the Almoravids arrived on invitation from Seville, and military activity was effectively frozen – except, that is, for the exploits of the legendary El Cid (see box, p.424), a Castilian nobleman who won considerable lands around Valencia in 1095.

The next concerted phase of the Reconquest began as a response to the threat imposed by the Almohads. The kings of León, Castile, Aragón and Navarra united in a general crusade that resulted in the great victory at Las Navas de Tolosa (1212). Thereafter, Muslim power was effectively paralysed, and the Christian armies moved on to take most of al-Andalus. Ferdinand III ("El Santo", The Saint) led Castilian soldiers into Córdoba in 1236 and twelve years later into Seville. Meanwhile, the kingdom of Portugal had expanded to more or less its present size, while Jaime I of Aragón was to conquer Valencia, Alicante, Murcia and the Balearic Islands. By the end of the thirteenth century, only the kingdom of Granada remained under Muslim authority, and for much of the following two centuries it was forced to pay tribute to the monarchs of Castile.

Two factors should be stressed regarding the Reconquest. First, its **unifying religious nature** – the spirit of crusade, intensified by the religious zeal of the Almoravids and Almohads, and by the wider European climate (which in 1095 gave rise to the First Crusade). This powerful religious motivation is well illustrated by the subsequent canonization of Ferdinand III, and found solid expression in the part played by the military orders of Christian knights, the most important of which were the Knights Templar and the Order of Santiago. At the same time, the Reconquest was a movement of **recolonization**. The fact that the country had been in arms for so long meant that the nobility had a major and clearly visible social role, a trend perpetuated by the redistribution of captured land in huge packages, or *latifundia*. Heirs to this tradition still remain as landlords of the great estates, most conspicuously in Andalucía. Men from the ranks were also awarded land, forming a lower, larger stratum of nobility, the *hidalgos*. It was their particular social code that provided the material for Cervantes in *Don Quixote*.

Any spirit of mutual cooperation that had temporarily united the Christian kingdoms disintegrated during the fourteenth century, and independent lines of development were once again pursued. Attempts to merge Portugal with Castile foundered at the battle of Aljubarrota (1385), and Portuguese attention turned away from Spain towards the Atlantic. Aragón experienced a similar pull towards the markets of the Mediterranean, although pre-eminence in this area was soon passed to the Genoese. It was Castile that emerged the strongest over this period: self-sufficiency in agriculture and a flourishing wool trade with the Netherlands enabled the state to build upon the prominent military role it played under Fernando III. Politically, Castilian history was a tale of dynastic conflict until the accession of the Catholic Monarchs.

Los Reyes Católicos

Los Reyes Católicos – the **Catholic Monarchs** – was the joint title given to **Fernando of Aragón and Isabel of Castile**, whose marriage in 1469 united the two largest kingdoms in Spain. Unity was in practice more symbolic than real: Castile had underlined its rights in the marriage vows and Aragón retained its old administrative structure. So, in the beginning at least, the growth of any national unity or Spanish – as opposed to local – sentiment was very much dependent on the head of state. Nevertheless, from this time on it begins to be realistic to consider Spain as a single political entity.

At the heart of Fernando and Isabel's popular appeal lay a **religious bigotry** that they shared with most of their Christian subjects. The **Inquisition** was instituted in Castile in 1480 and in Aragón seven years later. Aiming to establish the purity of the Catholic faith by rooting out heresy, it was directed mainly at Jews – resented for their enterprise in commerce and influence in high places, as well as for their faith. Expression had already been given to these feelings in a pogrom in 1391; it was reinforced by an edict issued in 1492 that forced up to 400,000 Jews to flee the country. A similar spirit was embodied in the reconquest of the **Kingdom of Granada**, also in 1492. As the last stronghold of Muslim authority, the religious rights of its citizens were guaranteed under the treaty of surrender. Within a decade, though, those Muslims under Christian rule had been given the choice between conversion or expulsion.

The year 1492 symbolized a fresh start in another way: this was the year that Columbus (Cristóbal Colón in Spanish) discovered America, and the papal bull that followed, entrusting Spain with the conversion of the American Indians, further entrenched Spain's sense of a mission to bring the world to the "True Faith". The next ten years saw the systematic conquest, colonization and exploitation of the **New World** as it was discovered, with new territory stretching from Labrador to Brazil, and new-found wealth pouring into the royal coffers. Important as this was for Fernando and Isabel, and especially for their prestige, their priorities remained in Europe, and strategic marriage alliances were made with Portugal, England and the Holy Roman Empire. It was not until the accession of the Habsburg dynasty that Spain could look to the activities of Cortés, Magellan and Pizarro and claim to be the world's leading power.

Habsburg Spain

Carlos I, a Habsburg, came to the throne in 1516 as a beneficiary of the marriage alliances of the Catholic Monarchs. Five years later, he was elected emperor of the Holy Roman Empire as Carlos V (**Charles V**), inheriting not only Castile and Aragón, but Flanders, the Netherlands, Artois, the Franche-Comté and all the American colonies to boot. With such responsibilities it was inevitable that attention would be diverted from Spain, whose chief function became to sustain the Holy Roman Empire with gold and silver from the Americas. It was only with the accession of **Felipe II** in 1556 that Spanish politics became more centralized. Felipe lived in the centre of Castile, near Madrid, creating a monument to the values of medieval Spain in his palace, El Escorial.

Two main themes run through his reign: the preservation of his own inheritance, and the revival of the crusade in the name of the Catholic Church. In pursuit of the former, Felipe successfully claimed the Portuguese throne (through the marriage of his mother), gaining access to the additional wealth of its empire. Plots were also woven in support of Mary Queen of Scots' claim to the throne of England, and to that end the ill-fated **Armada** sailed in 1588, its sinking a triumph for English naval strength and for Protestantism.

This was a period of unusual religious intensity: the **Inquisition** was enforced with renewed vigour, and a rising of Moriscos (subject Moors) in the Alpujarras was fiercely suppressed. Felipe III later ordered the expulsion of half the total number of Moriscos in Spain – allowing only two families to remain in each village in order to maintain irrigation techniques. The **exodus** of both Muslim and Jew created a large gulf in the labour force and in the higher echelons of commercial life – and in trying to uphold the Catholic cause, an enormous strain was put upon resources without any clear-cut victory.

By the middle of the seventeenth century, Spain was losing international credibility. Domestically, the disparity between the wealth surrounding Crown and court and the poverty and suffering of the mass of the population was a source of perpetual tension. Discontent fuelled regional revolts in Catalunya and Portugal in 1640, and the latter had finally to be reacknowledged as an independent state in 1668.

Bourbons and the Peninsular War

The **Bourbon dynasty** succeeded to the Spanish throne in the person of **Felipe V** (1700); with him began the **War of the Spanish Succession** against the rival claim of Archduke Charles of Austria, assisted by British forces. As a result of the Treaty of Utrecht, which ended the war (1713), Spain was stripped of all territory in Belgium, Luxembourg, Italy and Sardinia, but Felipe V was recognized as king. Gibraltar was seized by the British in the course of the war. For the rest of the century, Spain fell very much under the French sphere of influence, an influence that was given political definition by an alliance with the French Bourbons in 1762.

Contact with France made involvement in the **Napoleonic Wars** inevitable and led eventually to the defeat of the Spanish fleet at Trafalgar in 1805. Popular outrage was such that the powerful prime minister, Godoy, was overthrown and King Carlos IV forced to abdicate (1808). Napoleon seized the opportunity to install his brother, Joseph, on the throne.

Fierce local resistance was eventually backed by the muscle of the British army, first under Sir John Moore, later under the Duke of Wellington, and in the course of the **Peninsular War** the French were at last driven out. Meanwhile, however, the **American colonies** had been successfully asserting their independence from a preoccupied centre and with them went Spain's last real claim of significance on the world stage. The entire nineteenth century was dominated by the struggle between an often reactionary monarchy and the aspirations of liberal constitutional reformers.

Seeds of civil war

Between 1810 and 1813 an ad-hoc Cortes (parliament) had set up a **liberal constitution** with ministers responsible to a democratically elected chamber. The first act of Ferdinand VII on being returned to the throne was to abolish this, and until his death in 1833 he continued to stamp out the least hint of liberalism. On his death, the right of succession was contested between his brother, Don Carlos, backed by the Church, conservatives and Basques, and his infant daughter, Isabel, who had the support of the liberals and the army. So began the **First Carlist War**, a civil war that lasted six years. Isabel II was eventually declared of age in 1843, her reign a long record of scandal, political crisis and constitutional compromise. Liberal army generals under the leadership of General Prim effected a coup in 1868 and the queen was forced to abdicate, but attempts to maintain a republican government foundered. The Cortes was again dissolved and the throne returned to Isabel's son, Alfonso XII. A new constitution was declared in 1876, limiting the power of the Crown through the institution of bicameral government, but again progress was halted by the lack of any tradition on which to base the constitutional theory.

The years preceding World War I merely heightened the discontent, which found expression in the growing **political movements** of the working class. The Socialist Workers' Party was founded in Madrid after the restoration of Alfonso XII, and spawned its own trade union, the UGT (1888), successful predominantly in areas of high industrial concentration such as the Basque Country and Asturias. Its anarchist counterpart, the CNT, was founded in 1911, gaining substantial support among the peasantry of Andalucía.

The loss of **Cuba** in 1898 emphasized the growing isolation of Spain in international affairs and added to economic problems with the return of soldiers seeking employment where there was none. A call-up for army reserves to fight in **Morocco** in 1909 provoked a general strike and the "Tragic Week" of rioting in Barcelona. Between 1914 and 1918, Spain was outwardly neutral but inwardly turbulent; inflated prices made the postwar recession harder to bear.

The general disillusionment with parliamentary government, together with the fears of employers and businessmen for their own security, gave **General Primo de Rivera** sufficient support for a military coup in 1923 in which the king, Alfonso XIII, was pushed into the background. Dictatorship did result in an increase in material prosperity, but the death of the dictator in 1930 revealed the apparent stability as a facade. New political factions were taking shape: the Liberal Republican Right was founded by Alcalá Zamora, while the Socialist Party was given definition under the leadership of Largo Caballero. The victory of antimonarchist parties in the 1931 municipal elections forced the abdication of the king, who went into exile, and the **Second Republic** was declared.

The Second Republic

Catalunya declared itself a republic independent of the central government and was ceded control of internal affairs by a statute in 1932. **Separatist movements** were powerful, too, in the Basque provinces and Galicia, each with their own demands for autonomy. Meanwhile, the government, set up on a tidal wave of hope, was hopelessly divided internally and too scared of right-wing reaction to carry out the massive tax and agrarian reforms that the left demanded, and that might have provided the resources for thoroughgoing regeneration of the economy.

The result was the increasing polarization of Spanish politics. **Anarchism**, in particular, was gaining strength among the frustrated middle classes as well as among the workers and peasantry. The **Communist Party** and left-wing **Socialists**, driven into alliance by their mutual distrust of the "moderate" socialists in government, were also forming a growing bloc. On the right, the **Falangists**, basically a youth party founded in 1923 by **José Antonio Primo de Rivera** (son of the dictator), made uneasy bedfellows with conservative traditionalists and dissident elements in the army upset by modernizing reforms.

In an atmosphere of growing confusion, the left-wing Popular Front alliance won the general election of **February 1936** by a narrow margin. Normal life, though, became increasingly impossible: the economy was crippled by strikes, peasants took agrarian reform into their own hands, and the government failed to exert its authority over anyone. Finally, on July 17, 1936, the military garrison in Morocco rebelled under the leadership of **General Francisco Franco**, to be followed by risings at military garrisons throughout the country. It was the culmination of years of scheming in the army, but in the event far from the overnight success its leaders almost certainly expected. The south and west quickly fell into Nationalist hands, but Madrid and the industrialized north and east remained loyal to the Republican government.

Civil War

The ensuing **Civil War** was undoubtedly one of the most bitter and bloody the world has seen. Violent reprisals were taken on their enemies by both sides – the Republicans shooting priests and local landowners wholesale, the Nationalists carrying out mass slaughter of the population of almost every town they took.

▲ Nationalist infantry battalion in Vilanova de Meia, Catalunya

Contradictions were legion in the way the Spanish populations found themselves divided from each other. Perhaps the greatest irony was that Franco's troops, on their "holy" mission to ensure a Catholic Spain, comprised a core of Moroccan troops from Spain's North African colony.

It was, too, the first modern war – Franco's German allies demonstrated their ability to wipe out entire civilian populations with their bombing raids on Gernika and Durango, and radio proved an important weapon, as Nationalist propagandists offered the starving Republicans "the white bread of Franco".

Despite sporadic help from Russia and thousands of volunteers in the **International Brigade**, the Republic could never compete with the professional armies and massive assistance from Fascist Italy and Nazi Germany enjoyed by the Nationalists. In addition, the left was torn by internal divisions that at times led almost to civil war within its own ranks. Nevertheless, the Republicans held out in slowly dwindling territories for nearly three years, with **Catalunya** falling in January 1939 and armed resistance in **Madrid** – which never formally surrendered – petering out over the following few months. As hundreds of thousands of refugees flooded into France, General Franco, who had long before proclaimed himself head of state, took up the reins of power.

Franco's Spain

The early reprisals taken by the victors were on a massive and terrifying scale. Executions were commonplace, and upwards of two million people were put in concentration camps until "order" had been established by authoritarian means. Only one party, the **Falange**, was permitted, and censorship was rigidly enforced. By the end of World War II, during which Spain was too weak to be anything but neutral, **Franco** was the only fascist head of state left in Europe, one responsible for sanctioning more deaths than any other in Spanish history. Spain was economically and politically isolated and, bereft of markets, suffered

– almost half the population were still tilling the soil for little or no return. When General Eisenhower visited Madrid in 1953 with the offer of huge loans, it came as water to the desert, and the price, the establishment of American nuclear bases, was one Franco was more than willing to pay. However belated, economic development was incredibly rapid, with Spain enjoying a growth rate second only to that of Japan for much of the 1960s, a boom fuelled by the tourist industry and the remittances of Spanish workers abroad.

Increased **prosperity**, however, only underlined the political bankruptcy of Franco's regime and its inability to cope with popular demands. Higher incomes, the need for better education, and a creeping invasion of Western culture made the anachronism of Franco ever clearer. His only reaction was to attempt to withdraw what few signs of increased liberalism had crept through, and his last years mirrored the repression of the postwar period. Trade unions remained outlawed, and the rampant inflation of the early 1970s saw striking workers across Spain hauled out of occupied mines and factories and imprisoned, or even shot in the streets. Attempts to report these events by the liberal press resulted in suspensions, fines and censorship. **Basque nationalists**, whose assassination of Admiral Carrero Blanco had effectively destroyed Franco's last hope of a like-minded successor, were singled out for particularly harsh treatment. Hundreds of so-called terrorists were tortured, and the Burgos trials of 1970, together with the executions of August 1975, provoked worldwide protest.

Franco finally died in November 1975, nominating **King Juan Carlos** as his successor. Groomed for the job and very much "in" with the army – of which he remains official commander-in-chief – the king's initial moves were cautious in the extreme, appointing a government dominated by loyal Francoists who had little sympathy for the growing opposition demands for "democracy without adjectives". In the summer of 1976, demonstrations in Madrid ended in violence, with the police upholding the old authoritarian ways.

The return of democracy

The violent events leading up to and following his mentor's death seem to have persuaded Juan Carlos that some real break with the past and a move towards **democratization** was now urgent and inevitable. Using the almost dictatorial powers he had inherited, he ousted Franco's reactionary prime minister, Carlos Arias Navarro, and replaced him with **Adolfo Suárez**, an ambitious lawyer and former apparatchik in Franco's ruling *Movimiento* party. Taking his cue from the king, in 1976 Suárez pushed a **Law of Political Reform** through the Cortes, reforming the legislature into two chambers elected by universal suffrage – a move massively endorsed by the Spanish people in a referendum. Suárez also passed legislation allowing the setting up of free trade unions, as well as legitimizing the Socialist Party (PSOE) and, controversially, the Communists. Several cabinet ministers resigned in protest, and an outraged military began planning their *coup d'état*.

When elections were held in June 1977, Suárez's own hastily formed centre-right party, the **Unión del Centro Democrático** (**UCD**), was rewarded with a 34 percent share of the vote, the Socialists coming in second with 28 percent, and the Communists and Francoist **Alianza Popular** marginalized at 9 percent and 8 percent respectively. Despite the overwhelming victories in Catalunya and the Basque Country of parties appealing to regional sentiment, this was almost certainly a vote for democratic stability rather than for ideology, something reflected in the course of the parliament, with Suárez governing through "consensus politics", negotiating settlements on all important issues with the major parties.

The first parliament of the "New Spain" now embarked on the formidable task of drawing up a **constitution**, while the Suárez government applied for membership of the then EEC. One of the fundamental components of the new constitution was the concept of **autonomy** – the granting of substantial self-rule to the seventeen *autonomías* (autonomous regions) into which Spain was to be divided. In Franco's time, even speaking regional languages such as Catalan or Basque was banned, and the backlash against this policy ensured that nothing less than some form of independence would be acceptable for regions such as the Basque Country and Catalunya. Each autonomous region was also to have its own president, parliament and civil service, the costs of which have spiralled in the thirty years since. Still, on December 6, 1978, the new constitution was overwhelmingly endorsed in a national referendum and, remarkably, only three years after the death of Franco, Spain had become a full democracy.

Elections in March 1979 virtually duplicated the 1977 result, but when the UCD, a fractious coalition of moderates and extremists, started to crack, **Suárez resigned** in January 1981. This provided the trigger for a **military coup**, launched by a contingent of Guardia Civil loyal to Franco's memory and commanded by the tragi-comic Colonel Antonio Tejero. They stormed into the Cortes with Tejero brandishing a revolver, and sub-machine-gunned the ceiling as *diputados* (MPs) dived for cover. The crisis, for a while, was real; tanks were brought out onto the streets of Valencia, and only three of the army's ten regional commanders remained unreservedly loyal to the government. But as it became clear that the king would not support the plotters, most of the rest then affirmed their support. Juan Carlos had taken the decision of his life and emerged with immensely enhanced prestige in the eyes of most Spaniards.

The González era

On October 28, 1982, the Socialist PSOE, led by charismatic **Felipe González**, was elected with the biggest landslide victory in Spanish electoral history to rule a country that had been firmly in the hands of the right for 43 years. The Socialists captured the imagination and the votes of nearly ten million Spaniards with the simplest of appeals: "for change".

Once in power, however, the Socialist Party chose the path of pragmatism, and a relentless drift to the right followed. Four successive election victories kept the party in power for fourteen years, and by the mid-1990s the PSOE government's policies had become indistinguishable from the conservative administrations of Britain or Germany.

González himself, meanwhile, had also undergone transformation – from a radical young labour lawyer into a careworn elder statesman. Control of inflation had become a more urgent target than reducing unemployment, while loss-making heavy industries (steel and shipbuilding especially) were ruthlessly overhauled and other industries privatized. **European Union** membership came in 1986, and the pride that most Spanish people felt at this tangible proof of their acceptance by the rest of Europe bought the Socialists more valuable time.

The issue of **NATO** (or OTAN, as the Spaniards know it), perhaps more than any other, demonstrated how much González had sacrificed to pragmatism.

During the 1982 election campaign, he had made an impassioned speech at a rally against Spain remaining a member of NATO, which the dying UCD administration had rushed into joining at the behest of the military. When the promised referendum was finally held four years later – which surprisingly turned out marginally in favour of staying in – his was one of the main voices in favour of continued membership. González finally buried the question of NATO as a political issue for the mainstream left when in 1995 he supported the elevation of his foreign secretary and close colleague, Javier Solana, to the post of secretary-general of the organization he had spent most of his political life reviling.

After long years of being hopelessly divided, in the late 1980s the **Spanish right** realigned itself when former prime minister Adolfo Suárez's UCD Christian Democrats merged with the Alianza Popular to form the new right-of-centre **Partido Popular** (PP), which came a respectable runner-up in the 1989 elections; a new far-left coalition, **Izquierda Unida** (United Left), composed of the Communists and smaller leftist parties, came third, albeit with the same number of seats (18) in the Congress of Deputies as the Catalan Nationalists, barely a tenth of the PSOE's representation.

The nation's progressive disillusionment with Felipe González's government in the early 1990s saw the rise to prominence of **José María Aznar** as leader of the PP. A former tax inspector, Aznar was dogged in his criticism of government incompetence in dealing with its own sleaze and the growing economic crisis. This debilitated the PSOE's position still further in the build-up to the **1993 elections**. However, the PSOE confounded the pundits and the opinion polls to hang on to power by the skin of its teeth, albeit as a minority government. But González's victory was a poisoned chalice, for his past now began to catch up with him. As illegal financing of the PSOE and corruption and commission-taking on government projects by party officials and ministers were being exposed, the director of the Guardia Civil (appointed by González) jumped the country with millions of dollars of secret-service funds, and the governor of the Bank of Spain was caught out making a private (and illegal) fortune. But the most serious of all the scandals to beset González was the **GAL affair** (Grupo Antiterrorista de Liberación), when it was discovered that a semi-autonomous anti-terrorist unit had been carrying out a dirty war against the ETA terrorists in the 1980s, which included kidnapping and wholesale assassinations of suspected ETA members. The press – and a later judicial investigation – exposed police participation in these crimes and a clear chain of command reaching up to the highest echelons of the PSOE government. Some Guardia Civil police officers were sent to prison for offences connected with the GAL affair, as were (briefly) two ministers for covering up the plot, before being released on appeal. But despite the efforts of prosecutors, González managed to avoid being hauled before the courts.

The swing to the right

The ailing PSOE administration, immersed in endless scandals, limped on towards what looked likely to be a crushing defeat in the **1996 elections**. The surprise result, however, was another **hung parliament**, making everyone a loser. Aznar, the narrow victor, was denied the "absolute majority" he had believed to be his throughout the campaign, and was forced to do a deal with the nationalist parties (whom he had described as "greedy parasites" on the hustings) in order to secure a workable parliamentary majority. Meanwhile, the PSOE's avoidance of the expected overwhelming defeat was proclaimed as a vindication by González, who hastily dismissed ideas of retirement. However, unable to make any significant impact on changing public opinion, and with the PSOE still in turmoil, early in 1998 **González resigned** the leadership of the party he had dominated for 23 years.

The reasons for Aznar's failure to win an outright majority are equally significant. When Felipe González told the king after the PSOE's first election victory in 1982 that his party's success had completed the transition from dictatorship to democracy, the monarch sagely advised him that the end of the transition would be when the Socialists lost an election to the right. The long and repressive Franco period still casts a heavy shadow across the Spanish political scene, and many voters seemed to have become nervous at the prospect of a right-wing party with a big majority curtailing their new-found liberties and dismantling the social security system – a vital lifeline in poorer regions such as Extremadura and Andalucía. Thus it was that **Andalucía**, one of the largest *autonomías*, performed its habitual role as the *sartenilla*, or frying pan, of Spanish politics – traditionally frying the votes of the right-leaning north – by confounding the opinion polls and turning out to vote for the discredited government, effectively denying Aznar a majority.

Elected on a centre-right platform, during his first term in office following his narrow 1996 victory, Aznar progressively moved his party to the centre, shifting aside the government's remaining hardliners in the hope of gaining the electorate's confidence and a working majority not dependent on alliances with the northern nationalists.

Following the resignation of Felipe González in 1998, the PSOE went into the 2000 election campaign under the leadership of the distinctly uncharismatic **Joaquín Almunia**, a González henchman. Desperate to prevent another Aznar victory, Almunia set up an unlikely electoral pact with the ex-communist Izquierda Unida, thinking that their combined votes could overturn a likely Aznar victory. The outcome of the March 2000 **general election** was a stunning **triumph for Aznar** and the PP, and for the first time since the death of Franco the right was in power with an overall majority. The result was disaster for the left, with the electorate apparently unconvinced by the "shotgun marriage" between the PSOE and the IU (bitter enemies since the Civil War), which smacked more of political opportunism than a government in waiting. Moreover, large numbers of voters seemed unwilling to risk the undoubted economic gains of Aznar's period in office, while many of the left's traditional supporters didn't bother to vote at all. Joaquín Almunia resigned and a relatively unknown young politician was elected leader: **José Luis Rodríguez Zapatero**, a member of the moderate socialist "Nueva Vía" (New Way) group within the PSOE. Zapatero admitted the PSOE's past mistakes, stating emphatically that any government led by him would be radically different. This seemed to go down well with the electorate, and the opinion polls began to move in the PSOE's favour.

The return of the PSOE

In 2001, José María Aznar – ever an enigma to those around him – announced that he would lead the PP up to the next general election but would then resign, and that it must seek a new leader. As leader designate (to take over following the election), the party chose Aznar's nominee, the less prickly, cigar-puffing **Mariano Rajoy**, minister for the interior and deputy prime minister. Despite the highest level of **unemployment** in the EU and a **general strike** in June 2002 caused by controversial government plans to reform social security and labour laws, the opinion polls still showed solid public support for the Aznar administration. Throughout 2003 Aznar relentlessly urged the electorate to back the party that had brought steady economic growth and low inflation. This strategy appeared to work, and early in 2004 all the indicators suggested the following March general election would deliver a comfortable victory for the ruling PP and its new leader, Rajoy.

Then, on March 11, and three days before polling day, a series of **bombs exploded on rush-hour commuter trains** travelling into Madrid, killing 191 people and injuring almost two thousand others. The nation was thrown into shock at the most savage attack seen in Spain since the Civil War. Despite the discovery by police within hours of a van linked to the bombings containing detonators and a Koranic audiotape, the PP leadership decided that the Basque terrorist group ETA had to be the culprits. This was a high-risk tactic for the government, but it seemed convinced that by pinning the responsibility on ETA it would deflect attention away from its support for the Iraq war (ninety percent of Spaniards had been against it) just long enough for the votes to be counted. No mention was to be made of any possible link with Islamic militant groups, and at the same time the blaming of ETA would conveniently vindicate Aznar's hardline stance against Basque terrorism and separatism.

For the three days prior to the election, the heavily state-influenced media and Spanish diplomats around the world attempted to peddle the "ETA is responsible" line. But soon doubts began to surface, and in the hours before the polls opened the electorate seems to have become highly suspicious of the government's tactic of using ETA as a scapegoat to save its skin, believing that the attack – as was subsequently proved – was the work of **Islamic terrorists** and a retaliation for Spain's participation in the unpopular Iraq war.

The nation turned out in force to give its verdict – and Zapatero and the **PSOE an unexpected victory**. Two million new young voters already angered by the government's mishandling of the *Prestige* oil spill (see p.579) and Aznar's unwavering support for the Iraq war appear to have been pivotal to the final result. In Catalunya and the Basque Country, the government's duplicity backfired spectacularly. The Catalans voted overwhelmingly for socialist and Catalan nationalist candidates, reducing the PP to a fringe party, and there was a similar fall in support in the Basque regions. The accusations of lies and distortion hurled at the PP following the election result only intensified when it was revealed that the outgoing government had hired a specialist company to destroy all computer records dealing with the bombings before leaving office.

The first act by Zapatero as government leader was to announce the **immediate withdrawal of Spanish troops from Iraq**, an election promise. This aligned him firmly with the German and French governments in Europe to whom Aznar had been hostile, but incurred the displeasure of US president George W. Bush, who shunned Zapatero for the rest of his presidency and turned down requests by the Spanish leader for a meeting at the White House or in Madrid.

In his first four years of office leading up to elections in 2008, Zapatero's record was competent if unspectacular. It will probably be remembered more for legislation legalizing **gay marriages** than any other government innovation. He also enjoyed the benefit of a favourable economic climate with consistently high growth figures and an economy producing more jobs than any other euro-zone member. International financial number-crunchers declared in 2007 that's Spain's GDP per head had overtaken that of Italy. But in the latter part of 2007, the impact of the world **economic downturn** was also felt in Spain, as one of the major drivers of the Spanish economy, the huge construction industry, went into meltdown. Unemployment figures started to rise as worried consumers put off making major purchases such as cars and homes. The **general election of March 2008** took place against a backdrop of economic uncertainty, and although the result was another **PSOE victory** the reality was that they had scraped home seven seats short of the overall parliamentary majority that Zapatero had stated was the party's main campaign target. The fact that the PSOE had won at all was as much due to the lacklustre campaign fought by opposition leader Mariano Rajoy and the PP, as the PSOE's rather tame appeal to the voters that offered few new ideas. A further worry for the Zapatero government was that without a majority it must again rely on the votes of smaller parties to get its administrative programme through. It may end up regretting a decision not to seek a formal alliance with any of these minor parties. Comprised mainly of nationalist Basques and Catalans (with separatist agendas of their own), they will undoubtedly demand a high price for help in pushing through any unpalatable policies to deal with the nation's economic predicament.

The election result also provided the **PP** with a few headaches. Their support in Catalunya and the Basque Country had drained away (the PP has never been in favour of giving increased autonomy to these regions), and it is difficult to see where a majority of electoral votes is going to be found if the party is ever going to achieve power again. Inevitably, following two successive defeats, Rajoy's leadership was also questioned and throughout the months following the election pressure on him to resign was accompanied by high-level resignations from the party leadership. So far he has managed to weather the storm, but it remains an open question if he will still be the PP's leader come the general election of 2012.

Contemporary politics

Given the unstable economic climate, it is certain that Zapatero's second term will be considerably tougher than his first. As he tries to cope with his first economic crisis (significantly, he refused to use the word "crisis" until after the election), he has still to define a coherent strategy capable of meeting Spain's economic and constitutional problems. The country's **economic difficulties** – accentuated by a decline in tourist income, a construction industry whose bubble has burst, rising unemployment and inflation figures, and faltering consumer spending – are going to need a steady hand and some clearly thought-out policies in the years ahead. The haemorrhaging of foreign investment as multinational companies quit the peninsula to cut costs by moving production to low-wage East European economies has also had a serious impact. The bureaucracy and red tape surrounding business start-ups, and an education system that fails to provide students and redundant workers with new skills, added to an almost total lack of government support for new enterprise and innovation, are yet more contributors to Spain's problems (Spain is the only leading industrialized country where more is spent on gambling every year than on research and development). More worrying still is the fact that as a result of EU enlargement, Spain – until recently the largest recipient of EU aid – has lost around €7 billion in annual grants.

In dealing with the **autonomous regions**, Zapatero has been confronted by the same intransigent nationalist demands as his predecessor Aznar. When the Basque regional president Juan José Ibarretxe announced early in 2005 that the Basque parliament had approved a blueprint for a "**Basque free state**" with its own court system, passports and international diplomatic representation, Zapatero dismissed the proposals as unconstitutional and the plan was thrown out by the Madrid Cortes. But the Basque autonomous government (run by nationalists) refused to accept this decision, and in the spring of 2008, Ibarretxe announced plans to hold a **double referendum** in the Basque Country on whether to start peace talks with ETA and "the right for Basques (rather than Spaniards) to decide" if the *autonomía* remains a part of the Spanish state. The government referred the case to the Spanish constitutional court, which, predictably, ruled the referendum unconstitutional, therefore illegal. Ibarretxe condemned the ruling and announced that the Basque government would now take its case to the European Court of Human Rights. The Spanish government is only too aware that where the Basques lead the Catalans (and possibly the Galicians, too) will wish to follow, which is why they are prepared to give no quarter on an issue that threatens the unity of the state. In October 2005, the Catalan parliament voted overwhelmingly for a similar charter to that of the Basques, defining Catalunya as a "nation" and seeking to distance itself from Spain. Not quite as intransigent as the Basques, in a **referendum in 2006** the Catalans approved a revision of their statute of autonomy, which the Spanish government hopes will keep them satisfied for a few years until the engine of further decentralization is cranked up once more.

Despite the economic storm clouds currently gathering over the peninsula, the larger picture has many positives. Thirty years on from the 1978 constitutional referendum that effectively dispatched the Franco era to the political dustbin, Spain is a confident player on the world stage and a core member of the **European Union**. And while the nation is no longer as starry-eyed as it was two decades ago when it joined the then EEC, most citizens are acutely aware of the benefits that have flooded into the country as a result of huge EU grants funding important infrastructure projects as well as subsidies channelled to the pivotal farming sector. As these funds now dry up, a major challenge for the country is to continue to transform the economy as well as outdated educational and legal systems, all key factors in building the Spain of the new century. Another crucial test for the future is how the country comes to terms with **regional nationalism**, which, if mishandled, could doom the state to disintegration. As with the transition to democracy, Spain often confounds its detractors by finding the inspiration and the energy to carry out necessary changes. There is no reason to believe that it will not do so again.

Wildlife

D espite its reputation as the land of the package holiday, you can't beat
Spain for sheer diversity of landscape and wildlife. When the Pyrenees
were squeezed from the earth's crust they created an almost impenetrable barrier stretching from the Bay of Biscay to the Mediterranean
Sea. Those animals and plants already present in Spain were cut off from the
rest of Europe, and have been evolving independently ever since. In the same
way, the breach of the land bridge at what is now the Strait of Gibraltar, and
the subsequent reflooding of the Mediterranean basin, stranded typical
African species on the peninsula. The outcome was an assortment of wildlife
originating from two continents, resulting in modern-day Iberia's unique
flora and fauna.

Spain is the second most **mountainous** country in Europe after Switzerland.
The central plateau – the *meseta* – averages 600–700m in elevation, slopes
gently westwards and is surrounded and traversed by imposing *sierras* and
cordilleras. To the north, the plateau is divided from the coast by the extensive
ranges of the Cordillera Cantábrica, and in the south the towering Sierra
Nevada and several lesser ranges run along the Mediterranean shore. Where
these southern *sierras* continue across the Mediterranean basin, the unsub-
merged peaks today form the Balearic Islands. The Pyrenean chain marks the
border with France, and even along Spain's eastern shores the narrow coastal
plain soon rises into the foothills of the *sierras* of Montseny, Espuña and los
Filabres, among others. The ancient *sierras* de Guadarrama and Gredos cross the
meseta just north of Madrid, and the Sierra Morena and the Montes de Toledo
rise out of the dusty southern plains. With such an uneven topography, it is not
surprising to find an alpine element in the flora and fauna, with the most
strictly montane species showing adaptations to high levels of ultraviolet light
and prolonged winter snow cover.

The centre of Spain lies hundreds of kilometres from the coast, with a
climate almost continental in character. The summers can be scorching and the
winters bitter, and what rain there is tends to fall only in spring and autumn. To
the east, the Mediterranean Sea moderates this weather pattern, blessing the
coastal lands with mild winters, and summers that become progressively hotter
as you move south towards Africa. With the *costas* representing the popular
perception of the country, first-time visitors are often surprised by the contrast
between the almost subtropical south and the cool, wet, temperate north.
Depressions coming in from the Atlantic Ocean bring high rainfall, persistent
mists and a landscape akin to the west of Ireland. Appropriately named the
Costa Verde (Green Coast), temperatures are mild even in summer, and when
the sun does shine the high humidity can sometimes make it feel
uncomfortable.

These climatic variations have produced a corresponding diversity in Spanish
wildlife. The wet, humid north is populated by species typical of northern
Europe, whilst the southern foothills of the Sierra Nevada have more in
common vegetation-wise with the Atlas Mountains of Morocco. The continental weather pattern of much of the **interior** has given rise to a community
of drought-resistant shrubs, together with annual herbs that flower and set seed
in the brief spring and autumn rains, or more long-lived plants that possess
underground bulbs or tubers to withstand the prolonged summer drought and
winter cold.

Habitat

Like most of Europe, the Iberian peninsula was once heavily forested. Today, though, following centuries of deforestation, only about ten percent of the original **woodland** remains, mostly in the north. Historically, much of the *meseta* was covered with evergreen oaks and associated shrubs such as laurustinus and strawberry tree (*madroño* – the tree in the symbol of Madrid), but the clearance of land for arable and pastoral purposes has taken its toll, as have the ravages of war. Today, tracts of Mediterranean woodland persist only in the *sierras* and some parts of Extremadura. When it was realized that much of the plateau was unsuitable for permanent agricultural use, the land was abandoned, and it is now covered with low-growing, aromatic scrub vegetation, known as *matorral* (maquis). An endangered habitat, the maquis is a haven for many rare and distinctive plant and animal species, some found nowhere else in Europe. The southeastern corner of the *meseta* is the only part of Spain that probably never supported woodland; here the arid steppe **grasslands** (*calvero*) remain basically untouched by man. In northern Spain, where vast areas are still forested, the typical tree species are more familiar: oak, beech, ash and lime on the lower slopes, grading into pine and fir at higher levels – and the appearance is distinctly northern European.

Much of the *meseta* is predominantly flat, arid and brown. Indeed, in Almería, Europe's only true **desert** is to be found, such is the lack of rainfall. But the presence of subterranean water supplies gives rise to occasional **oases** teeming with wildlife. The numerous tree-lined **watercourses** of the peninsula also attract birds and animals from the surrounding dusty plains. The great Ebro and Duero rivers of the north, and the Tajo and Guadiana in the south, have been dammed at intervals, creating **reservoirs** that attract wildfowl in winter.

The Spanish **coastline** has a little of everything: dune systems, shingle banks, rocky cliffs, salt marshes and sweeping sandy beaches. In Galicia, submerged river valleys, or *rías*, are reminiscent of the Norwegian fjords, and the offshore islands are home to noisy sea-bird colonies; the north Atlantic coast is characterized by limestone promontories and tiny, sandy coves; the Mediterranean coast, despite its reputation for wall-to-wall hotels, still boasts many undeveloped lagoons and marshes; and southwest of Seville lies perhaps the greatest of all Spain's coastal wetlands: the Coto Doñana.

While the rest of Europe strives for agricultural supremacy, in Spain much of the land is still **farmed** by traditional methods, and the **landscape** has changed little since the initial disappearance of the forests. The olive groves of the south, the extensive livestock-rearing lands of the north and even the cereal-growing and wine-producing regions of the plains, exist in relative harmony with the indigenous wildlife of the country. It is only since Spain joined the European Union that artificial pesticides and fertilizers and huge machines have made much impact. Even so, compared to its neighbours, Spain is still essentially a wild country. Apart from a few industrial areas in the northeast and around Madrid and large-scale urbanization along parts of the coast, the landscape reflects the absence of modern technology, and the low population density means that less demand is made on the wilderness areas that remain.

Flora

With such a broad range of habitats, Spain's **flora** is nothing less than superb. Excluding the Canary Islands, about eight thousand species occur on Spanish soil, approximately ten percent of that are found nowhere else in the world. The plethora of high **mountains** allows an alpine flora to persist in Spain well beyond its normal north European distribution, and because of the relative geographical isolation of the mountain ranges, plants have evolved which are specific to each. In fact, there are about 180 plants that occur only in the Pyrenees, and over forty species endemic to the Sierra Nevada.

This effect is clearly illustrated by the **buttercup** family. In the Pyrenees, endemic species include the pheasant's-eye *Adonis pyrenaica* and the meadow rue *Thalictrum macrocarpum*; the Sierra Nevada has *Delphinium nevadense* and the monkshood *Aconitum nevadense*, and of the columbines *Aquilegia nevadensis* occurs here alone. *A. discolor* is endemic to the Picos de Europa, *A. cazorlensis* is found only in the Sierra de Cazorla, and *A. pyrenaica* is unique to the Pyrenees. Other handsome montane members of this family include alpine pasqueflowers, hepatica, hellebores, clematis and a host of more obvious buttercups.

The dry Mediterranean grasslands of Spain are excellent hunting grounds for **orchids**. In spring, in the meadows of the Cordillera Cantábrica, early purple, elder-flowered, woodcock, pink butterfly, green-winged, lizard and tongue orchids are ten a penny, and a little searching will turn up sombre bee, sawfly and Provence orchids. Farther into the Mediterranean zone, exotic species to look for include Bertoloni's bee, bumblebee and mirror orchids. Lax-flowered orchids are common on the Costa Brava and high limestone areas will reveal black vanilla orchids, frog orchids and summer lady's tresses a bit later in the year.

The Mediterranean **maquis** is a delight to the eye and nose in early summer, as the cistus bushes and heaths come into flower, with wild rosemary, thyme, clary and French lavender adding to the profusion of colour. The *dehesa* grasslands of southwest Spain are carpeted with the flowers of *Dipcadi serotinum* (resembling brown bluebells), pink gladioli and twenty or so different trefoils in May. In the shade of the ancient evergreen oaks grow birthworts, with their pitcher-shaped flowers, bladder senna and a species of lupin known locally as "devil's chickpea".

Even a trip across the **northern meseta**, although reputedly through endless cereal fields, is by no means a dull experience. Arable weeds such as cornflowers, poppies, corncockle, chicory and shrubby pimpernel add a touch of colour and are sometimes more abundant than the crops themselves. Where the coastal **sand dunes** have escaped the ravages of the tourist industry you can find sea daffodils, sea holly, sea bindweed, sea squill and the large violet flowers of *Romulea clusiana*.

Mammals

The great mammalian fauna that roamed Europe in the Middle Ages today survives only as a relict population in the wildest areas of Spain. Forced to seek refuge from hunters and encroaching civilization, it is perhaps surprising that the only species to have succumbed to extinction is the little-known European beaver. Unfortunately, with elusiveness the key to their survival, the mammal species that remain can be almost impossible to see. Endangered, but common in the mountains of the north, the **wolf** (*lobo*) avoids contact with humans as much as possible. Persecuted for centuries in response to the exaggerated menace portrayed in folk tales, they are still today regarded as a major threat to livestock in some quarters, despite their dwindling numbers. Although afforded official protection, many farmers would not think twice about shooting on sight. Similarly, the omnivorous **brown bear** (*oso pardo*) shows none of the inquisitive boldness exhibited by its American cousins, and with numbers as low as a hundred in Spain, anybody catching a glimpse of one should consider themselves exceptionally fortunate.

In the **northern mountains** – the Pyrenees and the Cordillera Cantábrica – you should get at least a glimpse of chamois, roe and red deer, and possibly **wild boar** (*jabalí*), which can be seen at dusk during the winter conducting nightly raids on village potato patches. The **Spanish ibex** (*cabra montés*), the scimitar-horned wild goat, had represented the main quarry of locals since prehistoric times. However, while it was able to sustain low levels of predation, its agility was no match for modern hunters and it almost disappeared in the early years of the twentieth century. Thanks to effective conservation measures, its numbers are slowly beginning to recover and it is becoming an increasingly common sight in the *sierras* de Cazorla, Grazalema (both Andalucía) and Gredos (Castilla y León). Europe's answer to prairie dogs, **marmots** (*marmotas*) can occasionally be seen in the Pyrenees, where they graze in alpine meadows, while the surrounding pine forests support large numbers of their arboreal relatives – the **red squirrel**. Less well known, and considerably more difficult to see, is the bizarre **Pyrenean desman**, a large, shrew-like creature closely related to moles, which inhabits mountain streams.

The typical mammals of **southern Spain** have more in common with Africa than Europe, the separation of the two continents leaving several species stranded to evolve in isolation. Specialities of African origin include the sleek, cat-like **spotted genet** and the adaptable, intelligent **Egyptian mongoose**, both of which are active mainly at night but can be glimpsed during the day. The undoubted jewel of the south, though, is the **Iberian lynx** (*lincé iberico*), paler, more heavily spotted and less heavily built than the northern European species, in adaptation to the subtropical climate. Highly endangered, and now almost completely confined to parts of the Sierra Morena and Parque Nacional Coto Doñana, its haunting cries on spring nights are sadly becoming more and more infrequent. A breeding programme set up in 2005 in Coto Doñana has now produced a number of cubs, and it is hoped that this will eventually aid the lynx's regeneration.

In the air, no fewer than 27 species of **bat** occupy caves and woodlands throughout Spain. Highly visible and often attracted to artificial light sources by clouds of insects, they are amongst the easiest of wild mammals to see, although identification to species level is best left to experts. Most interesting are the four types of horseshoe bat and Europe's largest bat, the rare **greater noctule**, which, with a wingspan of 45cm, even feeds on small birds.

The most spectacular **aquatic mammals** are the twenty or so species of whale and dolphin, whose presence has encouraged the appearance of numerous boating companies to run trips out to see them. **Pilot whales** and **sperm whales** are common in the Straits of Gibraltar, and **dolphins** will often choose to accompany boat trips in all areas. Isolated and protected coves on the Mediterranean shores shelter some of the last breeding colonies of the **Mediterranean monk seal**, a severely threatened species perhaps doomed to extinction. **Fresh water** also supports a number of mammal species, perhaps the best known being the playful **European otter**, which is still fairly numerous in the north.

Birds

If any country in Europe qualifies as a paradise for **birdwatching**, then it must surely be Spain. Most twitchers head straight for the world-famous Parque Nacional Coto Doñana, where over half of all European bird species have been recorded, but other parts of the country are just as rewarding, even if you have to work a little harder to get a matching list.

Birds of prey are particularly visible, and as many as 25 species of raptor breed here, but it is during the spring and autumn migrations that you will see the most dramatic numbers. Clouds of honey buzzards, black kites and Egyptian vultures funnel across the Straits of Gibraltar, aided by warm currents, followed by less numerous but equally dramatic species such as short-toed and booted eagles. Resident species include the widespread griffon vulture, the surprisingly common red kite and the dramatic Bonelli's eagle. Twitchers, though, are likely to have their sights set on four attention-grabbing species: the Eurasian black vulture, fighting against extinction in Extremadura; the bone-breaking bearded vulture of the Pyrenees; the diminutive but distinctive black-winged kite of the southern plains; and the endangered, endemic Spanish imperial eagle. The latter is most easily seen in Coto Doñana, where guides take great delight in pointing out this emblematic hunter.

There is no less variety in other types of birds. Woodpeckers are most abundant in the extensive forests of the **northern mountain ranges**. While white-backed woodpeckers are confined to the Pyrenees, other such rarities as black and middle-spotted woodpeckers may also be seen in the Cordillera Cantábrica, and the well-camouflaged wryneck breeds in the north and winters in the south of the country. Other typical breeding birds of these northern mountains are the turkey-like capercaillie, pied flycatchers, blue rock thrushes, alpine accentors, citril and snow finches and that most sought-after of all montane birds, the unique, butterfly-like wallcreeper.

In the open **grasslands** and cereal fields of the *meseta*, larks are particularly common. Look out for the calandra lark, easily identified by its chunky bill and the trailing white edge to the wing. More rewarding are great and little bustards – majestic at any time of year, but especially when the males fan out their plumage during the springtime courtship display. In a tiny area of the Mediterranean coast, strange nocturnal mooing calls from low-growing scrub betray the presence of the secretive **Andalucian buttonquail**, a tiny, quail-like bird, more closely related to the bustards than the quails. Look out also for the exotically patterned pin-tailed sandgrouse, one of only two European members of a family of **desert-dwelling birds**, as well as stone curlews and red-necked nightjars, the latter seen (and heard) mainly at dusk.

Olive groves are an ornithological treasure trove playing host to a colourful assemblage of birds – hoopoes, azure-winged magpies, golden orioles, southern grey and woodchat shrikes, bee-eaters, rollers, great spotted cuckoos and black-eared wheatears. On a sunny summer's day, these birds are active and often easy to spot if you are patient.

Fluctuating water levels, particularly in the south, mean that there is no shortage of seasonally flooding **freshwater** habitats positively teeming with bird life. In reedbeds, you may come across the vividly coloured purple gallinule, the high-stepping Bailon's crake, the thrush-sized great reed warbler or localized colonies of sociable bearded reedlings. In winter, large flocks of migrant waterfowl may gather, but it is the resident species that bring more reward: the exotic red-crested pochard, the rare ferruginous duck, the delicate marbled teal and the threatened white-headed duck among the highlights.

Coastal wetlands and **river deltas** are a must for any serious birdwatcher, with common summer occupants including black-winged stilts, avocets, greater flamingos and all but one of the European representatives of the heron family: cattle and little egrets, purple, grey, squacco and night herons, bitterns and little bitterns. In the right conditions and at the right time of year, almost all the species can be seen breeding together in vast and noisy heronries – an unforgettable sight. Wintering waders are not outstandingly distinctive, though wherever you go, even on the Atlantic coast, you should look for spoonbills. Grey phalaropes visit the northwest corner, as do whimbrels, godwits, skuas and ruffs, taking a break from their northern breeding grounds. For **sea birds**, the Illas Cíes, off the Galician coast, are unbeatable, providing breeding grounds for shags, the rare Iberian race of guillemot and the world's southernmost colony of lesser black-backed gulls.

Even **towns** have their fair share of notable species. The **white stork** (*cigüeña blanca*) is a summer visitor that has endeared itself to Andalucía and south central Spain, and few conurbations are without the unkempt nest atop a bell tower, electricity pylon or war monument. Finches such as serin and goldfinch are numerous, and the airspace above any town is usually occupied by hundreds of swifts, martins and swallows; you may be able to pick out alpine, pallid and white-rumped swifts and red-rumped swallows if you're in the southern half of the country, as well as crag martins in the north.

The **Balearic Islands** can provide you with a few more unusual cliff-nesting species, such as Eleanora's falcon, while deserted islets are ideal for hole-nesting sea birds, including Cory's shearwaters and storm petrels.

Reptiles and amphibians

Around sixty species of reptiles and amphibians occur in Spain, including some of Europe's largest and most impressive. Four species of salamander inhabit the peninsula. The brightly coloured **fire salamander**, an attractive patchwork of black and yellow, is perhaps the best known. Named for its habit of seeking solace in woodpiles and later emerging when the fire was lit, the salamander spawned the legend that it was somehow born out of the flames. The 30cm-long **sharp-ribbed salamander** of the southwest is Europe's largest, and bizarrely pierces its own skin with its ribs when attacked. The two remaining species, the drab, misnamed **golden-striped salamander** and the **Pyrenean brook salamander**, are confined to the cool, wet, mountainous north.

Closely related to the salamanders are the **newts**, of which there are only four species in Spain. If you take a trip into the high mountain pastures of the Cordillera Cantábrica, where water is present in small, peaty ponds all year round, you should see the brightly coloured **alpine newt**, while the aptly named **marbled newt** can be seen round the edges of many of Spain's inland lakes and reservoirs. Searches through tall waterside vegetation frequently turn up the tiny, lurid-green **tree frog**, striped in the north and west, but stripeless along the Mediterranean coast.

Two species of **tortoise** occur in Spain: **spur-thighed tortoises** can still be found along the southern coast and on the Balearic Islands, the latter the only Spanish locality for the other species – **Hermann's tortoise**. European **pond terrapins** and **stripe-necked terrapins** are more widely distributed, but only in freshwater habitats. Beware of confusion between these native species and the introduced North American **red-eared terrapin**, the result of the release of unwanted pets following the decline of the Teenage Mutant Ninja Turtle craze. **Marine turtles** are uncommon visitors to the Mediterranean and Atlantic coasts – perhaps the most frequently encountered is the protected **green turtle**, especially in the waters around Gibraltar, but **loggerhead** and **leathery turtles** are very occasionally reported.

The most exotic reptilian species to occur in Spain is the **chameleon**, although again this swivel-eyed creature is confined to the extreme southern shores where its camouflage skills render it difficult to find. **Lizards** are numerous, with the most handsome species being the large **ocellated lizard** – green with blue spots along the flank. Some species are very restricted in their range, such as Ibizan and Lilford's wall lizards, which live only in the Balearic Islands. In the south, the most noticeable species are **Moorish geckos**, large-eyed nocturnal creatures usually seen on the walls of buildings both inside and out. Adhesive pads on their feet enable them to cling perilously to vertical surfaces as they search for their insect prey.

Similarly, **snakes** are common, although few are venomous and even fewer are ever likely to bite. When faced with humans, evasive action is the snake's preferred option, and in most cases a snake will be long gone before the intruder even knew it was there. The **grass snake** will even play dead rather than bite, if cornered. **Asps** and **western whip snakes** occur in the Pyrenees, while the commonest species in the south is the harmless **horseshoe whip snake**, named for the distinctive horseshoe mark on the back of its head.

The most unusual Spanish reptile is undoubtedly the **amphisbaenian**, sometimes misleadingly called the blind snake. Adapted to a subterranean existence, this rarely encountered and harmless creature can sometimes be found by searching through rotten leaves and mulch in forested environments and gardens of the south.

Insects

Almost a hundred thousand insects have been named and described in Europe and an untold number await discovery. In a country with areas where no one knows for sure how many bears there are, insects have barely even begun to be explored.

From early spring to late autumn, as long as the sun is shining, you will see **butterflies**: there are few European species that do not occur in Spain, but by contrast there are many Spanish butterflies that are not found north of the Pyrenees. These seem to be named mostly after obscure entomologists: Lorquin's blue, Carswell's little blue, Forster's furry blue, Oberthur's anomalous blue, Lefèbvre's ringlet, Zapater's ringlet, Chapman's ringlet, Zeller's skipper and many others. You need to be an expert to identify most of these, but the more exciting butterflies are in any case better-known ones: the Camberwell beauty, almost black and bordered with gold and blue; swallowtails, yellow and black or striped like zebras, depending on the species, but always with the distinctive "tails"; the lovely two-tailed pasha, which is often seen feeding on the ripe fruit of the strawberry tree; and the apollo (papery white wings with distinctive red and black eyespots), of which there are almost as many varieties as there are mountains in Spain. Other favourites include the small, bejewelled blues, coppers, fritillaries and hairstreaks that inhabit the hay meadows.

Aside from butterflies, keep an eye open for the largest **moth** in Europe, the giant peacock, which flies by night but is often attracted to outside lights, or the rare, green-tinted Spanish moon moth, a close relative of tropical silk moths. During the day, take a closer look at that hovering bumble bee, as it may be a hummingbird hawkmoth, or a broad-bordered bee-hawk, flying effortlessly from flower to flower. Oleander and elephant hawkmoths (resplendent in their pink and green livery) are often seen around flowering honeysuckle bushes at dusk. Despite the often nondescript appearance of the adult forms, many moths have bizarre caterpillars, for example the lobster moth, which feeds on beech, or the pussmoth, found on willows and poplars.

Grasslands and arid scrub areas are usually good hunting grounds for **grass-hoppers and crickets**, which can be located by their calls. Mole crickets and field crickets live in burrows they have excavated themselves, but look to the trees for the most colourful species, such as the enormous great green bush cricket, about 7–8cm long. French lavender bushes in the maquis are a favourite haunt of the green mantis *Empusa pennata*, identified by a large crest on the back of the head and the familiar "praying" posture. **Stick insects** are harder to spot, as they tend to sit parallel with the stems of grasses, where they are well camouflaged.

Members of the *Arachnidae* (**spiders**) to be found include two species of **scorpion** in the dry lands of southern Spain. Look out also for long-legged *Gyas*, the largest harvest-spider in Europe, with a pea-sized body suspended by ridiculous gangly legs and a diameter of about 10cm. Spanish **centipedes** can grow to quite a size, too. *Scutigera coleoptra*, for example, which often lives indoors, has fifteen pairs of incredibly long, striped legs, which create a wonderful rippling effect when they move across walls. The daddy of them all, though, is the massive *Scolopendra cingulatus*, up to 15cm long and with a vicious venomous bite when molested.

Teresa Farino

Flamenco

Flamenco – one of the most emblematic musics of Spain and its richest musical heritage – has recently enjoyed huge exposure and today is more popular than ever before. Twenty-five years or so ago it looked like a music on the decline, preserved only in the clubs or *peñas* of its *aficionados*, or in travestied castanet-clicking form for tourists. However, prejudice vanished as flamenco went through a tremendous period of innovation in the 1980s and 90s, incorporating elements of pop, rock, jazz and Latin, and today there's a new respect for the old "pure flamenco" artists and a huge joy in the new.

The initial impetus for flamenco's new-found energy came at the end of the 1960s, with the innovations of guitarist **Paco de Lucía** and, especially, the late, great singer **Camarón de la Isla**. These were musicians who had grown up learning flamenco but whose own musical tastes embraced international rock, jazz and blues.

They have been followed by groups such as **Ketama**, **Raimundo Amador** (ex Pata Negra), **La Barbería del Sur**, **Navajita Plateá** and **Niña Pastori**, who have all reached massive audiences that neither de Lucía nor de la Isla could have dreamt of decades before. At the end of the 1990s, there were even successful comebacks from such established artists as **Enrique Morente** and **José Mercé**. Morente – the established king of flamenco – experimentally revisited old styles and combined them with new moves, releasing a spectacular new album, *Omega*, in 1996, with **Lagartija Nick**, one of the most emblematic bands of the Spanish indie rock scene. José Mercé collaborated with **Vicente Amigo** – recognized as the most gifted player of the moment, notably for his sense of syncopation – on *Del Amanecer*. Paco de Lucía acknowledges Amigo as his successor in the innovation of flamenco guitar.

Among others regarded as the best **contemporary singers** are the male singers El Cabrero, Juan Peña El Lebrijano, the Sorderos Fosforito, José Menese, Duquende and El Potito. The most revered women include Fernanda and Bernarda de Utrera, Carmen Linares, Remedios Amaya, Estrella Morente (daughter of Enrique Morente, and the new "star" of Spanish flamenco), Montse Cortés, La Macanita and Carmen Amaya. Until his death **Camarón** – or more fully **Camarón de la Isla** – was by far the most popular and commercially successful singer of modern flamenco. Collaborating with the guitarists and brothers Paco de Lucía and Ramón de Algeciras, and latterly, Tomatito, Camarón raised *cante jondo* to a new art. A legend in his own lifetime, he tragically died of cancer in 1992 at the age of 42, having almost single-handedly revitalized flamenco song, inspiring and opening the way for the current generation of flamenco artists.

Origins

Flamenco evolved in southern Spain from many sources: Morocco, Egypt, India, Pakistan, Greece and other parts of the Near and Far East. Most authorities believe the roots of the music were brought to Spain by gypsies arriving in the fifteenth century. In the following century, it was fused with elements of Arab and Jewish music in the Andalucian mountains, where Jews, Muslims and "pagan" gypsies had taken refuge from the forced conversions and clearances effected by the Catholic Kings and the Church. Important flamenco centres and families are still found today in quarters and towns of *gitano* and refugee origin, such as Alcalá, Jerez, Cádiz, Utrera and the Triana *barrio* of Seville. Although flamenco is linked fundamentally to **Andalucía**, emigration from that province has long meant that flamenco thrives not only there but also in Madrid, Extremadura, the Levante and even Barcelona – wherever Andalucian migrants have settled.

Flamenco *aficionados* enjoy heated debate about the purity of their art and whether it is more validly performed by a *gitano* (gypsy) or a **payo** (non-gypsy). Certainly during dark times, flamenco was preserved by the oral tradition of the closed *gitano* clans. Its power, too, and the despair that its creation overcomes, seem to have emerged from the vulnerable life of a people surviving for centuries at the margins of society. These days, though, there are as many acclaimed *payo* as *gitano* flamenco artists, and the arrival on the scene of musicians from Barcelona such as Vicente Amigo – who has no Andalucian blood but grew up in a neighbourhood full of flamenco music – has de-centred the debate.

The concept of dynasty, however, remains fundamental for many. The veteran singer **Fernanda de Utrera**, one of the great voices of "pure flamenco", was born in 1923 into a *gitano* family in Utrera, one of the *cantaora* (flamenco singer) centres. The granddaughter of the legendary singer "Pinini", she and her younger sister Bernarda, also a notable singer, both inherited their flamenco with their genes. This concept of an active inheritance is crucial and has not been lost in contemporary developments: the members of Ketama, for example, the Madrid-based flamenco-rock group, come from two *gitano* clans – the Sotos and Carmonas.

While flamenco's exact origins are debated, it is generally agreed that its "laws" were established in the nineteenth century. Indeed, from the mid-nineteenth into the early twentieth century flamenco enjoyed a Golden Age, the tail end of which

▲ Flamenco at Plaza de España, Seville

is preserved on some of the earliest 1930s recordings. The musicians found a first home in the **café cantantes**, traditional bars that had their own groups of performers (*cuadros*). One of the most famous was the *Café de Chinitas* in Málaga, immortalized by the poet Gabriel Garciá Lorca in his poem *A las cinco de la tarde* (At five in the afternoon), in which he intimates the relationship between flamenco and bullfighting, both sharing root emotions and flashes of erratic genius, and both also being a way to break out of social and economic marginality.

The art of flamenco

Flamenco is played at *tablaos* and fiestas, in bars and at *juergas* (informal, more or less private parties). The fact that the Andalucian public are so knowledgeable and demanding about flamenco means that musicians, singers and dancers found at even a local club or village festival are usually very good indeed.

Flamenco songs often express pain. Generally, the voice closely interacts with improvising guitar, which keeps the *compás* (rhythm), the two inspiring each other, aided by the **jaleo** – the hand-clapping *palmas*, finger-snapping *palillos* and shouts from participants at certain points in the song. *Aficionados* will shout encouragement, most commonly ¡olé! when an artist is getting deep into a song, but also a variety of other less obvious phrases. A stunning piece of dancing may, for example, be greeted with ¡*Viva la maquina escribir!* (Long live the typewriter!), as the heels of the dancer move so fast they sound like a clicking machine; or the cry may be ¡agua! (water!), for the scarcity of water in Andalucía has given the word a kind of glory.

The encouragement of the audience is essential for the artists, as it lets them know they are reaching deep into the emotional psyche of their listeners. They may achieve the rare quality of **duende** – total communication with their audience, and the mark of great flamenco of any style or generation. Latterly, the word *duende* has been used to describe "innovation", which, while it is significant, does not always capture its real depth.

Flamenco songs

There is a classical repertoire of more than sixty flamenco **songs** (*cantes*) and dances (*danzas*) – some solos, some group numbers, some with instrumental accompaniment, others *a cappella*. These different styles (or *palos*) of flamenco singing are grouped in families according to more or less common melodic themes, establishing three basic types of *cante flamenco*: **cante grande** (comprising songs of the *jondo* type), **cante chico**, and **cante intermedio** between the two. Roughly speaking, the *jondo* and *chico* represent the most and the least difficult *cantes* respectively in terms of their technical and emotional interpretation, although any form, however simple, can be sung with the maximum of complexity and depth. **Cante jondo** (deep song) comprises the oldest and "purest" songs of the flamenco tradition, and is the profound flamenco of the great artists, whose *cantes* are outpourings of the soul, delivered with an intense passion, expressed through elaborate vocal ornamentation. To a large extent, however, such categories are largely arbitrary, and few flamenco musicians talk about flamenco in this way; what matters to them is whether the flamenco is good or bad.

The basic *palos* include **soleares**, **siguiriyas**, **tangos** and **fandangos**, but the variations are endless and often referred to by their place of origin: *malagueñas* (from Málaga), for example, *granaínos* (from Granada), or *fandangos de Huelva*. *Siguiriyas*, which date from the Golden Age, and whose theme is usually death, have been described as cries of despair in the form of a funeral psalm. In contrast, there are many songs and dances such as tangos, *Sevillanas*, *fandangos* and *alegrías* (literally "happinesses"), which capture great joy for fiestas. The **Sevillena** originated in medieval Seville as a spring country dance, with verses improvised and sung to the accompaniment of guitar and castanets (rarely used in other forms of flamenco). In the last few years, dancing *Sevillenas* has become popular in bars and clubs throughout Spain, but their great natural habitats are Seville's *Fería de Abril* and the annual *romería*, or pilgrimage, to El Rocio. Each year wonderful new *Sevillenas* come onto the market in time for the fiestas.

Another powerful and more seasonal form is the **saeta**, songs in honour of the Virgins that are carried on great floats in the processions of *Semana Santa* (Holy Week). Traditionally, they are quite spontaneous – as the float is passing, a singer will launch into a *saeta*, a sung prayer for which silence is necessary and for which the procession will therefore come to a halt while it is sung.

Flamenco guitar

The guitar used to be simply an accompanying instrument – originally, the singers themselves played – but in the early decades of last century it began developing as a solo instrument, absorbing influences from classical and Latin American traditions. The greatest of these early guitarists was **Ramón Montoya**, who revolutionized flamenco guitar with his harmonizations and introduced a whole variety of *arpeggios* – techniques of right-hand playing adapted from classical guitar playing. Along with Niño Ricardo and Sabicas, he established flamenco guitar as a solo medium, an art extended from the 1960s on by **Manolo Sanlucar**, whom most *aficionados* reckon the most technically accomplished player of his generation. Sanlucar has kept within a "pure flamenco" orbit, and not strayed into jazz or rock, experimenting instead with orchestral backing and composing for ballet.

The best known of all contemporary flamenco guitarists, however, is undoubtedly **Paco de Lucía**, who made the first moves towards "new" or "fusion" flamenco. A *payo*, he won his first flamenco prize at the age of 14, and went on to accompany many of the great singers, including a long partnership with Camarón de la Isla. He started forging new rhythms for flamenco following a trip to Brazil, where he was influenced by *bossa nova*, and in the 1970s established a sextet with electric bass, Latin percussion, flute and saxophone. Over the past twenty years, he has worked with jazz-rock guitarists such as John McLaughlin and Chick Corea, while his own regular band, the Paco de Lucía Sextet featuring his other brother, the singer Pepe de Lucía, remains one of the most original and distinctive sounds on the flamenco scene.

Other modern-day guitarists have equally identifiable sounds and rhythms, and fall broadly into two camps, being known either as accompanists or soloists. The former include **Tomatito** (Camarón's last accompanist), Manolo Franco and Paco Cortés, while among the leading soloists are the brothers Pepe and Juan Habichuela; Rafael Riqueni, an astonishing player who is breaking new ground with classical influences; Enrique de Melchor; Gerardo Nuñez; and Vicente Amigo. Jerónimo Maya was acclaimed by the Spanish press as the "Mozart of Flamenco" when he gave his first solo performance, aged 7, in 1984.

Nuevo flamenco

The **reinvention of flamenco** in the 1980s was initially disliked by purists, but soon gained a completely new young public. Paco de Lucía set the new parameters of innovation and commercial success, and following in his footsteps came **Lolé y Manuel** and others, updating the flamenco sound with original songs and huge success. **Jorge Pardo**, Paco de Lucía's sax and flute player, originally a jazz musician, has continued to work at the cutting edge. **Enrique Morente** and **Juan Peña El Lebrijano** were two of the first to work with Andalucian orchestras from Morocco, and the Mediterranean sound remains important today, together with influences from southern India.

Paco Peña's 1991 *Missa Flamenca* recording, a setting of the Catholic Mass to flamenco, with the participation of established singers including Rafael Montilla "El Chaparro" from Peña's native Córdoba and a classical academy chorus from London, has stayed a bestseller since its first appearance, remaining a benchmark for such compositions.

The encounter with rock and blues was pioneered at the end of the 1980s by Ketama and Pata Negra. **Ketama** (named after a Moroccan village famed for its hashish) were hailed by the Spanish press as creators of the music of the "New Spain" after their first album, which fused flamenco with rock and Latin salsa, adding a kind of rock–jazz sensibility, a "flamenco cool" as they put it. They then pushed the frontiers of flamenco still farther by recording the two *Songhai* albums in collaboration with Malian kora player Toumani Diabate and British bassist Danny Thompson. The group **Pata Negra**, a band led by two brothers, Raímundo and Rafael Amador, introduced a more direct rock sound with a bluesy electric guitar lead, giving a radical edge to traditional styles like *bulerías*. Their *Blues de la Frontera* album caused an equal sensation. After splitting, Raímundo Amador has continued as a solo artist.

Collectively, these young and iconoclastic musicians became known, in the 1990s, as **nuevo flamenco** – a movement associated in particular with the Madrid label Nuevos Medios. They form a challenging, versatile and at times musically incestuous scene in Madrid and Andalucía, with musicians guesting at each other's gigs and on each other's records. Ketama have gone on to have massive hits nationally, bringing flamenco fully into the mainstream.

In the 1980s and 90s, the music became the regular sound of **nightclubs**, through the appeal of young singers such as **Aurora** – whose salsa-rumba song *Besos de Caramelo*, written by Antonio Carmona of Ketama, was the first 1980s number to crack the pop charts. Pop singer **Martirio** (Isabel Quiñones Gutierrez) is one of the most flamboyant personalities on the scene, appearing dressed in lace mantilla and shades like a cameo from a Pedro Almodóvar film, recording songs with ironic, contemporary lyrics, full of local slang, about life in the cities. Martirio's producer, **Kiko Veneno**, who wrote Camarón's most popular song, *Volando Voy*, is another key artist who helped open up the scene. A rock musician originally, he has a strongly defined sense of flamenco. **Rosario**, one of Spain's top female singers, has also brought a flamenco sensibility to Spanish rock music. In the mid-1990s, **Radio Tarifa** emerged as an exciting group, leading the exploration of a flamenco-Mediterranean sound with a mix of Arabic and medieval sounds on a flamenco base. They started out as a trio, later expanding to include African musicians.

More recently, the Barcelona-based collective, **Ojos de Brujo**, have given new flamenco fusions hip credibility and a contemporary ethos, making flamenco much more integral to Spanish musical life. Their genius has been their reworking of flamenco styles to incorporate modern musical tendencies, while expressing passionate politics embedded in issues of everyday life, championing anti-corporate concerns and challenging the negative effects of global capitalism on the small community.

Other more identifiably *nuevo flamenco* bands and singers to look out for include La Barbería del Sur (who add a dash of salsa), Wili Gimenez and José El Frances.

**Jan Fairly, David Loscos
and Manuel Dominguez**

Books

L istings below represent a highly selective reading list on Spain and matters Spanish. Most titles are in print, although we've included a few older classics, no longer in print (indicated by o/p); most of them are easy enough to find, though, in secondhand bookshops or on secondhand-book sites such as ⓦwww.abebooks.co.uk. We have also included the names and websites of several smaller publishers whose publications are not available on Amazon and other similar websites.

If you have difficulty finding any title, an excellent specialist source for books about Spain – new, used and out of print – is Paul Orssich, 2 St Stephens Terrace, London SW8 1DH (☎020/7787 0030, ⓦwww.orssich.com). Books marked 🏃 are particularly recommended.

Travel and general accounts

The best introductions

Nina Epton *Grapes and Granite* (o/p). One of the few English books on Galicia – full of folklore and rural life in the 1960s – and well worth trying to get hold of.

🏃 **John Hooper** *The New Spaniards*. This excellent, authoritative portrait of post-Franco Spain was originally written by the *Guardian*'s former Spanish correspondent in the 1980s. A revised second edition published in 2006 is already becoming dated, but this is still one of the best possible introductions to contemporary Spain.

Adam Hopkins *Spanish Journeys: A Portrait of Spain*. Published in the mid-1990s, this is an enjoyable and highly stimulating exploration of Spanish history and culture, weaving its considerable scholarship in an accessible and unforced travelogue form, and full of illuminating anecdotes.

🏃 **Michael Jacobs** *Andalusia*. A well-crafted, opinionated and wide-ranging introduction to Andalucía. It covers everything from prehistory to the Civil War and manages to cram in perceptive pieces on flamenco, gypsies and food and drink. A gazetteer at the back details

major sights. Recently updated, this remains one of the best introductions to the region.

🏃 **Mark Kurlansky** *The Basque History of the World*. A brilliantly entertaining take on this much maligned, misunderstood and misrepresented people. Kurlansky uses history, stories, anecdotes and even recipes to concoct this heady brew.

Edward Lewine *Death and the Sun: A matador's season in the heart of Spain*. Bullfight aficionado Lewine takes on the perilous task of trying to make this Spanish bloodsport comprehensible to non-believers. He spends a year on the road in the company of top *matador* Francisco Rivera Ordoñez – whose great-grandfather was revered by Hemingway – and provides fascinating background on the gruelling routine of long road journeys between towns, often dingy hotels and the bitter recriminations when the "boss" has had a disastrous day in the ring.

Lucy McCauley (ed) *Spain: Travelers' Tales*. It would be hard to better this anthology of writing on Spain, which gathers its stories and journalism predominantly from the last fifteen years. Featured authors include Gabriel García Márquez, Colm Tóibín and Louis de Bernières, whose "Seeing Red", on Buñol's *La Tomatina* festival, is worth the purchase price alone.

🏃 **Cees Nooteboom** *Roads to Santiago: Detours and Riddles in the Land and History of Spain*. This is one of the most literary travel books of recent decades: an almost Shandyesque tale (few of the roads travelled lead anywhere near Santiago), garnished from the notebooks of this quirky, architecture-obsessed Dutch writer.

Paul Richardson *Our Lady of the Sewers*. An articulate and kaleidoscopic series of insights into rural

Spain's customs and cultures, fast disappearing.

🏃 **Giles Tremlett** *Ghosts of Spain*. Tremlett (the Madrid correspondent of the *Guardian*) digs into the untold story of Spain's Civil War dead and the collective conspiracy of silence surrounding the war's terrors, and goes on to peel away the layers of the post-Franco era to present an enthralling and often disturbing study of contemporary Spain.

James Woodall *In Search of the Firedance: Spain through Flamenco*. This is a terrific history and exploration of flamenco, and as the subtitle suggests it is never satisfied with "just the music" in getting to the heart of the culture.

Recent travels and accounts

🏃 **Chris Stewart** *Driving Over Lemons – An Optimist in Andalucía*. A funny, insightful and very charming account of life on a remote peasant farm in the Alpujarras where Stewart and his family set up home. The sequel, *A Parrot in the Pepper Tree*, has more stories from the farm interspersed with accounts of some of the author's earlier adventures as a sheep shearer in Sweden, drummer with rock band Genesis and greenhorn flamenco guitarist in Seville. The saga's latest episode, *The Almond Blossom Appreciation Society*, delivers another cocktail of hilarious, improbable and poignant tales.

Ted Walker *In Spain* (o/p). Until his death in 2004, the poet Ted Walker had lived and travelled in Spain on and off since the 1950s. This is a lyrical and absorbing account of the country and people, structured around his various sorties throughout the peninsula.

Jason Webster *Duende – A Journey in Search of Flamenco* and *Andalus*. Webster sets off on a Spanish odyssey to learn flamenco guitar, which takes him to Alicante, Madrid and finally Granada with quite a few emotional encounters along the way. *Andalus* relates a journey with an illegal immigrant whose precarious toehold in Spain inspires parallels with the current position of Islam on the peninsula.

Twentieth-century writers

Alastair Boyd *The Sierras of the South: Travels in the Mountains of Andalusia*, *The Road from Ronda* and *The Essence of Catalonia*. *Sierras* is a sensitively worked portrait of the Serranía de Ronda, which describes one Englishman's continuing love affair with a region he knew as

home for twenty years. His earlier *The Road from Ronda* is a 1960s view of the same landscape, while *Catalonia* is a laudable part history of, part guide to Spain's northern province: strong on art and architecture.

Gerald Brenan *South From Granada*. An enduring classic. Brenan lived in a small village in the Alpujarras in the 1920s, and records this and the visits of his Bloomsbury contemporaries Virginia Woolf, Lytton Strachey and Bertrand Russell.

Laurie Lee *As I Walked Out One Midsummer Morning*, *A Rose For Winter* and *A Moment of War*. *One Midsummer Morning* is the irresistibly romantic account of Lee's walk through Spain – from Vigo to Málaga – and his gradual awareness of the forces moving the country towards civil war. As an autobiographical novel, of living rough and busking his way from the Cotswolds with a violin, it's a delight; as a piece of social observation, painfully sharp. In *A Rose For Winter* he describes his return, twenty years later, to Andalucía, while in *A Moment of War* he looks back again to describe a winter fighting with the International Brigade in the Civil War – by turns moving, comic and tragic.

James A. Michener *Iberia*. A bestselling, idiosyncratic and encyclopedic compendium of inter-views and impressions of Spain on the brink – in 1968 – looking forward to the post-Franco years. Fascinating, still.

George Orwell *Homage to Catalonia*. Stirring account of Orwell's participation in the early exhilaration of revolution in Barcelona, and his growing disillu-sionment with the factional fighting among the Republican forces during the ensuing Civil War.

Older classics

George Borrow *The Bible in Spain* and *The Zincali* (both o/p). On first publication in 1842, Borrow subtitled *The Bible in Spain* *"Journeys, Adventures and Imprison-ments of an English-man"*; it is one of the most famous books on Spain – slow in places but with some very amusing stories. *The Zincali* is an account of the Spanish *gitanos* (gypsies), whom Borrow got to know pretty well.

Richard Ford *A Handbook for Travellers in Spain and Readers at Home* and *Gatherings from Spain*. The *Handbook* (1845) must be the best guide ever written to any country. Massively opinionated, it is an extremely witty book in its British, nineteenth-century manner, and worth flicking through for the proverbs alone. *The Gatherings* is a rather timid – but no less enter-taining – abridgement of the general pieces, intended for a female audience who wouldn't have the taste for the more cerebral stuff. A recently published biography *Richard Ford, Hispanophile, Connoisseur and Critic* by Ian Robertson places the great man in context and is also recommended.

Washington Irving *Tales of the Alhambra* (published 1832; abridged editions are on sale in Granada). Half of Irving's book consists of oriental stories, set in the Alhambra; the rest of accounts of local characters and his own residence there. A perfect read *in situ*.

George Sand *A Winter in Majorca*. Sand and Chopin spent their winter at the monastery of Valldemossa. They weren't entirely appreciated by the locals, in which lies much of the book's appeal. Local editions, including a translation by late Mallorcan resident Robert Graves, are on sale around the island.

Anthologies

Jimmy Burns (ed) *Spain: A Literary Companion.* A good anthology, including nuggets by most authors recommended here.

David Mitchell *Travellers in Spain: An Illustrated Anthology* (also published under the title *Here in Spain*). A well-told story of how four centuries of travellers – and most often travel writers – saw Spain. It's interesting to see Ford, Irving, Brenan, Laurie Lee and the rest set in context.

History

General

Juan Lalaguna *A Traveller's History of Spain.* A lucid (and pocketable) background history to the country, spanning the Phoenicians to Franco and the emergence of democratic Spain.

M. Vincent and R.A. Stradling *Cultural Atlas of Spain and Portugal.* A formidable survey of the Iberian peninsula from ancient to modern times, in coffee-table format, with excellent colour maps and well-chosen photographs.

Prehistoric and Roman Spain

James M. Anderson *Spain: 1001 Sights, An Archeological and Historical Guide.* A good guide and gazetteer to 95 percent of Spain's archeological sites.

María Cruz Fernandez Castro *Iberia in Prehistory.* A major study of the Iberian peninsula prior to the arrival of the Romans, which surveys recent archeological evidence relating to the remarkable technical, economic and artistic progress of the early Iberians.

Roger Collins *Spain: An Archeological Guide.* Covering just 130 sites, this book's more detailed coverage makes it a more useful guide to the major sites than Anderson's work (left).

John S. Richardson *The Romans in Spain.* A new look at how Spain came to be a part of the Roman world, which also examines the influences that flowed from Spain to Rome as well as vice versa.

Early, medieval and beyond

J.M. Cohen *The Four Voyages of Christopher Columbus.* The man behind the myth; Columbus's astonishing voyages as described by Columbus himself in his log are interwoven with opinions of contemporaries on the great explorer, including his biographer son Hernando. A fascinating collection, superbly translated.

Roger Collins *The Arab Conquest of Spain 710–97.* Controversial study documenting the Moorish invasion and the significant influence that the conquered Visigoths had on early Muslim rule. Collins's earlier *Early Medieval Spain 400–1000* takes a broader overview of the same subject.

John A. Crow *Spain: The Root and the Flower.* Perceptive and shrewdly observed cultural and social history from Roman Spain to the present.

J.H. Elliott *Imperial Spain 1469– 1716*. The best introduction to the "Golden Age" – academically respected, and a gripping tale.

Richard Fletcher *The Quest for El Cid* and *Moorish Spain*. Two of the best studies of their kind – fascinating and highly readable narratives. The latter is a masterly introduction to the story of the Moors in Spain.

L.P. Harvey *Islamic Spain 1250– 1500*. Comprehensive account of its period – both the Islamic kingdoms and the Muslims living beyond their protection.

David Howarth *The Voyage of the Armada*. An account from the Spanish perspective of the personalities, from king to sailors, involved in the Armada.

Henry Kamen *The Spanish Inquisition*. A highly respected examination of the Inquisition and the long shadow it cast across Spanish history. *The Spanish Inquisition: An Historical Revision* returns to the subject in the light of more recent evidence, while Kamen's *Philip of Spain* is the first full biography of Felipe II, the ruler most closely associated with the Inquisition. In *Spain's Road to Empire*, Kamen skilfully dissects the conquest of the Americas and Philippines.

Elie Kedourie *Spain and the Jews: the Sephardi Experience, 1492 and After*. A collection of essays on the three million Spanish Jews of the Middle Ages and their expulsion by Los Reyes Católicos.

John Lynch *Spain 1598–1700* and *Bourbon Spain: 1700–1808*. Two further volumes in the Blackwells project covering Spain from prehistory to modern times, written by the series' general editor and dealing with Spain's rise to empire and the critical Bourbon period.

Geoffrey Parker *The Army of Flanders and the Spanish Road (1567– 1659)*. Although sounding dry and academic, this is in fact a fascinating read giving a marvellous insight into the morals, manners and organization of the Spanish army, then the most feared in Europe.

James Reston Jr *Dogs of God*. An alternative take on the Inquisition from that of Kamen (left), connecting it with the epic year 1492 and linking religious intolerance to the final defeat of the Moors in Spain and Columbus' sudden widening of the Spanish crown's sphere of influence.

Hugh Thomas *Rivers of Gold: The Rise of the Spanish Empire*. Thomas's scholarly but eminently accessible history provides a fascinating snapshot of Spain's most glorious period – its meteoric imperial rise in the late fifteenth and early sixteenth centuries, when characters such as Fernando and Isabel, Columbus and Magellan, shaped the country's outlook for the next three hundred years.

The twentieth century

Phil Ball *Morbo – The Story of Spanish Football* (When Saturday Comes Books, UK). Excellent account of the history of Spanish football from its nineteenth-century beginnings with British workers at the mines of Río Tinto in Huelva to the golden years of Real Madrid and the dark days of Franco. Everpresent as a backdrop is the ferocious rivalry, or *morbo* – political, historical, regional and linguistic – that has driven the Spanish game since its birth. Essential reading for every football aficionado visiting Spain.

Gerald Brenan *The Spanish Labyrinth*. First published in 1943, Brenan's account of the background to the Civil War is tinged by personal experience, yet still makes for an impressively rounded read.

Jimmy Burns *Barça: A People's Passion*. On one level, simply an informative history of the city's famous football team, *alma mater* of Cruyff, Lineker, Maradona, Ronaldo, Figo et al. But like the club itself, the book is so much more than that, as Burns examines Catalan pride and nationalism through the prism of sport.

Raymond Carr *Modern Spain 1875–1980* and *The Spanish Tragedy: the Civil War in Perspective*. Two of the best books available on modern Spanish history – concise and well-told narratives.

Ronald Fraser *Blood of Spain*. Subtitled "An Oral History of the Spanish Civil War", this is an equally impressive – and brilliantly unorthodox – piece of research allowing Spaniards to recount their experiences in their own words.

Ian Gibson *Federico García Lorca, The Assassination of Federico García Lorca* and *Lorca's Granada*. The biography is a compelling book and *The Assassination* a brilliant reconstruction of the events at the end of the writer's life, with an examination of Fascist corruption and the shaping influences on Lorca, twentieth-century Spain and the Civil War. *Granada* contains a series of walking tours around parts of the town familiar to the poet.

Paul Preston *Franco* and *Concise History of the Spanish Civil War*. A penetrating – and monumental – biography of Franco and his regime, which provides as clear a picture as any of how he won the Civil War and survived in power so long. *Civil War* is a compelling introduction to the subject and more accessible for the general reader than Thomas's work (below).

Hugh Thomas *The Spanish Civil War*. This exhaustive thousand-page study is regarded (both in Spain and abroad) as the definitive history of the Civil War.

Gamel Woolsey *Málaga Burning* (Pythia Press, US) and under its original title *Death's Other Kingdom* (Eland, UK). A long-ignored minor classic written in the late 1930s and recently reprinted (and retitled) by a US publisher, in which the American poet and wife of Gerald Brenan vividly describes the horrors of the descent of their part of Andalucía into civil war. The Eland edition includes an interesting biographical afterword by Michael Jacobs.

Art, architecture, photography, film and design

Xavier Barral I Altet *The Romanesque: Towns, Cathedrals and Monasteries*. Concise without stinting on illustrations, this is a highly readable and authoritative introduction to the genre; especially good on townscapes and castles, and more than half the book is focused on Spain.

Marianne Barrucand and Achim Bednoz *Moorish Architecture*. A beautifully illustrated guide to the major Moorish monuments.

Bernard Bevan *History of Spanish Architecture* (o/p). Classic study of Iberian and Ibero-American architecture, including extensive coverage of the Mudéjar, Plateresque and Baroque periods.

Hugh Broughton *Madrid: A Guide to Recent Architecture*. Modern Spanish architecture is at the cutting edge of world design, and this is a fluent and pocketable guide to a hundred of the best examples in Madrid, each with its own photo and directions.

Robert Goff *The Essential Salvador Dalí*. An enjoyable and accessible introduction to Dalí and Surrealism, which examines the artist's bizarre life and obsessions (particularly his intense attachment to Gala, his wife), as well as his most enigmatic paintings.

Godfrey Goodwin *Islamic Spain*. Portable architectural guide with descriptions of virtually every significant Islamic building in Spain, and a fair amount of background.

Gijs van Hensbergen *Gaudí: the Biography*. At last, a worthy biography of one of the world's most distinctive architects. Van Hensbergen puts substantial flesh on the man while also describing the milieu in which he worked, placing his work firmly in context.

Robert Hughes *Goya*. The celebrated author of *The Shock of the New* and *Barcelona* turns his attention to one of Spain's greatest painters in this fabulous biography, a gripping account of Goya's life and work, placed within the context of turbulent eighteenth- and early nineteenth-century Spain.

Robert Irwin *The Alhambra*. A detailed tour of the building by art expert Irwin who – referring to other Islamic monuments – puts the palace in its Islamic context and attempts to determine how it actually functioned as a building. The account concludes with an appraisal of the impact of the Alhambra on modern culture.

Michael Jacobs *Alhambra*. Sumptuously produced volume with outstanding photographs and expert commentary. Authoritatively guides you through the history and architecture of the Alhambra, and concludes with a fascinating essay on the hold the palace has had on later artists, travellers and writers, from Irving and Ford to de Falla and Lorca.

John Richardson *A Life of Picasso*. The definitive biography of one of the twentieth century's major artistic driving forces, currently in three volumes with more to come.

Cristina García Rodero *Festivals and Rituals of Spain* and *España Oculta*. *Festival and Rituals* is a mesmerizing photographic record of the exuberance and colour of Spain's many fiestas by Spain's most astonishing contemporary photographer. *Oculta* is an equally atmospheric collection of black and white pictures celebrating the country's religion and mysticism.

Gabriel Ruiz Cabrero *The Modern in Spain*. This readable book is a clear, comprehensive study of postwar Spanish architecture. The author is an architect and professor in the renowned Faculty of Architecture at Madrid's Politécnica.

Meyer Schapiro *Romanesque Art*. An excellent illustrated survey of Spanish Romanesque art and architecture – and its Visigothic and Mozarabic predecessors.

Fiction and poetry

Spanish classics

Pedro de Alarcón *The Three-Cornered Hat*. Ironic nineteenth-century tales of the previous century's corruption, bureaucracy and absolutism.

Leopoldo Alas *La Regenta*. Alas's nineteenth-century novel, with its sweeping vision of the disintegrating social fabric of the period, is a kind of Spanish *Madame Bovary* (a book that it was in fact accused of plagiarizing at time of publication).

Ramón Pérez de Ayala *Belarmino and Apolonio* and *Honeymoon, Bittermoon*. A pair of tragi-comic picaresque novels written around the turn of the twentieth century.

Emilia Pardo Bazán *The House of Ulloa*. Bazán was an early feminist intellectual and in this, her best-known book, she charts the decline of the old aristocracy in the time of the Glorious Revolution of 1868.

Miguel de Cervantes *Don Quixote* and *Exemplary Stories*. With Spain and the Hispanic world lavishly celebrating the four-hundredth anniversary of publication in 2005, *Quixote* (or *Quijote*) is, of course, *the* classic of Spanish literature and still an excellent and witty read, with much to inform about Spanish character and psychology. J.M. Cohen's fine Penguin translation or a new version by Edith Grossman, published by Harper-Collins, are worth looking out for. If you want to try Cervantes in a more modest dose, the *Stories* are a good place to start.

Benito Pérez Galdós *Fortunata and Jacinta*. Galdós wrote in the last decades of the nineteenth century, and his novels of life in Madrid combine comic scenes and social realism; he is often characterized as a "Spanish Balzac". Other Galdós novels available in translation include *Misericordia*, *Nazarín* and the epic *"I"*.

St Teresa of Ávila *The Life of Saint Teresa of Ávila*. St Teresa's autobiography is said to be the most widely read Spanish classic after *Don Quixote*. It takes some wading through, but it's fascinating in parts. Various translations are available.

Modern fiction

Bernardo Atxaga *Obabakoak*. This challenging novel by a Basque writer won major prizes on its Spanish publication. It is a sequence of tales of life in a Basque village and the narrator's search to give them meaning.

Arturo Barea *The Forging of a Rebel* (o/p). Superb autobiographical trilogy, taking in the Spanish war in Morocco in the 1920s, and Barea's own part in the Civil War. The books have been published in UK paperback editions under the individual titles *The Forge*, *The Track* and *The Clash*.

Michel del Castillo *The Disinherited*. Riveting account of Madrid during the Civil War, written in 1959.

Camilo José Cela *The Family of Pascual Duarte* and *The Beehive*. Nobel Prize-winner Cela was considered integral to the revival of Spanish literature after the Civil War, though his reputation is compromised by his involvement with Franco's government where he worked as a censor. *Pascual Duarte*, his first novel, portrays the brutal story of a peasant murderer from Extremadura, set against the backdrop of the fratricidal Civil War, while *The Beehive*, his best-known work, is set in Madrid at the end of the same war and depicts the poverty and misery of this period through the lives of a multitude of characters.

Ildefonso Falcones *Cathedral of the Sea*. Well-researched and atmospheric historical romp tracing the life of the son of a fugitive serf who makes a new life for himself in the thriving medieval port of Barcelona. The title refers to the glorious Gothic church of

Santa María del Mar, which provides the backdrop to much of the action.

Juan Goytisolo *Marks of Identity, Count Julian, Juan the Landless, Landscapes after the Battle* and *Quarantine*. Born in Barcelona in 1931, Goytisolo became a bitter enemy of the Franco regime, and has spent most of his life in self-exile, in Paris and Morocco. He is perhaps the most important modern Spanish novelist, confronting, above all in his great trilogy (comprising the first three titles listed above), the whole ambivalent idea of Spain and Spanishness, as well as being one of the first Spanish writers to deal openly with homosexuality. The more recent *Quarantine* documents a journey into a Dante-esque netherworld in which the torments of hell are set against reportage of the first Gulf War. Goytisolo has also written an autobiography, *Forbidden Territory*.

Carmen Laforet *Nada*. Written in 1944 but only recently translated, this is a haunting tale of a Barcelona family locked in the violence and despair of post-Civil War Spain. For all the horror, there is beauty also in the portrayal of a teenage girl's longing for consolation.

Javier Marias *Tomorrow in the Battle Think on Me*. There are many who rate Marias as Spain's finest contemporary novelist – and the evidence is here in this searching, psychological thriller, with its study of the human capacity for concealment and confession. Two other Marias novels, *A Heart So White* and *All Souls*, are also available in English translation.

Ana María Matute *School of the Sun*. The loss of childhood innocence on a Balearic island, where old enmities are redefined during the Civil War.

Eduardo Mendoza *City of Marvels* and *The Truth about the Savolta Case*. Mendoza's first and best novel, *City of Marvels*, is set in the expanding Barcelona of 1880–1920,

full of rich underworld characters and riddled with anarchic and comic turns. It's a milieu repeated with flair in *The Truth about the Savolta Case*.

Manuel Vázquez Montalban *Murder in the Central Committee, Southern Seas, An Olympic Death, The Angst Ridden Executive, Off Side* and *The Man of My Life*. Montalban was, until his death in 2003, one of Spain's most influential writers. A long-time member of the Communist Party, he lived in Barcelona, like his great creation, the gourmand private detective Pepe Carvalho, who stars in all of his wry and racy crime thrillers. The one to begin with – indeed, a bit of a classic – is *Murder in the Central Committee*.

Arturo Pérez Reverte *The Seville Communion* and *The Queen of the South*. Pérez Reverte is one of Spain's leading writers, and *Seville Communion* is an entertaining crime yarn played out against the colourfully described backdrop of Seville. Also in translation, *Queen of the South* was another Spanish bestseller and relates the story of a woman drug trafficker running narcotics between Morocco and Cádiz.

Julián Ríos *Larva*. Subtitled *Midsummer Night's Babel*, *Larva* is a large, complex, postmodern novel by a leading Spanish literary figure, published to huge acclaim in Spain.

Javier Tomo *The Coded Letter* and *Dear Monster*. A pair of Kafkaesque tales from one of Spain's leading post-Franco-era novelists.

Carlos Ruiz Zafón *The Shadow of the Wind*. A wonderfully atmospheric novel in which a young boy tries to unravel the truth behind the life and death of a forgotten writer. Set in post-Civil War Barcelona, it is beautifully written and makes for a gripping read. Its follow-up, a prequel called *The Angel's Game*, has recently been translated.

Plays and poetry

Pedro Calderón de la Barca *Life is a Dream and other Spanish Classics* and *The Mayor of Zalamea*. Some of the best works of the great dramatist of Spain's "Golden Age".

J.M. Cohen (ed) *The Penguin Book of Spanish Verse*. Spanish poetry from the twelfth century to the modern age, with (parallel text) translations from all the major names.

Federico García Lorca *Five Plays: Comedies and Tragicomedies*. Andalucía's great pre-Civil War playwright and poet.

Lope de Vega The nation's first important playwright (b.1562) wrote literally hundreds of plays, many of which, including *Lo Cierto por lo Dudoso* (*A Certainty for a Doubt*) and *Fuenteobvejuna* (*The Sheep Well*), remain standards of classic Spanish theatre.

Spain in foreign fiction

Harry Chapman *Spanish Drums*. An engaging thriller, telling of an Englishwoman outsider's entry into the life of a family in Teruel – and her discovery of all the terrible baggage of its Civil War past.

Charles Cumming *The Spanish Game*. The follow-up to Cumming's debut thriller, *A Spy by Nature*, sees one-time British agent Alec Milius living in Madrid, where his past catches up with him. The Le Carré-like thriller twists and turns through the Spanish capital as Basque politics and international intrigue combine to ensnare Milius one more time.

Ernest Hemingway *The Sun Also Rises* and *For Whom the Bell Tolls*. Hemingway remains a big part of the American myth of Spain – *The Sun Also Rises* contains some lyrically beautiful writing, while the latter is a good deal more laboured. He also published two books on bullfighting, the enthusiastic and not very good *Death in the Afternoon* (1932), and *Dangerous Summer* (1959), an overheated account of the contest between Dominguín and Antonio Ordóñez for the title of top-dog *matador*.

Norman Lewis *Voices of the Old Sea*. Lewis lived in Catalunya from 1948 to 1952, just as tourism was starting to arrive. This book is an ingenious blend of novel and social record, charting the breakdown of the old ways in the face of the "new revolution". The same author's *The Tenth Year of the Ship* is a superb tale about the devastating impact modernization and speculative investment have on the mythical Spanish island of Vedra after a steamboat link is established.

Amin Malouf *Leo the African*. A wonderful historical novel, re-creating the life of Leo Africanus, the fifteenth-century Moorish geographer, in the last years of the kingdom of Granada and his subsequent exile in Morocco and world travels.

Colm Tóibín *The South*. First novel by the Irish writer, who spent the early 1990s in Barcelona. The city is the setting for his tale of an Irish woman looking for a fresh start after fleeing her boring, middle-class family for a lover and a new life in Catalunya.

Specialist guidebooks

The pilgrim route to Santiago

Millán Bravo Lozano *A Practical Guide for Pilgrims: The Road to Santiago* (Everest). Colourful, informative guide. Includes separate map pages so you can leave the heavy guide at home.

John Higginson *Le Puy to Santiago – A Cyclist's Guide*. A cyclist's guide to the pilgrim route, which follows as closely as possible (on tarmac) the walkers' path, visiting all the major sites en route.

Edwin Mullins *The Pilgrimage to Santiago* (o/p). This is a travelogue rather than a guide, but is by far the best book on the Santiago legend and its fascinating medieval pilgrimage industry.

Alison Raju *The Way of St James: Le Puy to the Pyrenees* (vol. I) and *Pyrenees-Santiago-Finisterre* (vol. II); *Via de la Plata – The Way of St James* (all Cicerone, UK). Walking guide to the pilgrim route divided between the French and Spanish sections and written by an experienced Iberian hiker. Both books include detailed maps, background on sights en route as well as practical information such as where to stay. In *Via de la Plata* Raju covers the lesser-known pilgrim route to Santiago, starting out from Seville.

David Wesson *The Camino Francés* (Confraternity of St James). Annually updated basic guide to the *camino*, with directions and accommodation. The Confraternity (ⓦ www.csj.org .uk) publishes the most accurate guides to the route, and there's also an online bookshop.

Trekking and cycling

David and Ros Brawn *Sierra de Aracena*. A guide covering this magnificent Andalucian *sierra* in 27 walks, with an accompanying map (sold separately), and all routes GPS waypointed.

Valerie Crespi-Green *Landscapes of Mallorca* (Sunflower Books). Aimed at fairly casual walkers and picnickers. Sunflower Books' *Landscapes* series also includes reliable and well-researched touring and trekking guides on the Canary Islands, Menorca, Catalunya, Andalucía and the Costa Blanca.

Charles Davis *Costa del Sol Walks*, *Costa Blanca Walks* (both Santana, Málaga; ⓦ www.santanabooks.com). Well-written guides to two excellent walking zones describing 34 (32 in *Costa Blanca*) walks of between 3 and 18km; each walk has its own map. The same author's *Walk! the Axarquía* (Discovery, UK; ⓦ www.walking.demon.co.uk) is a reliable guide to this picturesque Andalucía region describing 30 walks between 5 and 22km, all GPS waypointed. *34 Alpujarras Walks* (Discovery, UK), with similar format, details GPS waypointed treks. In both the latter books, each walk has its own map, or there are waterproof 1:40,000 *Axarquía/ Alpujarras Tour and Trail* maps (sold separately) with all walks (and GPS points) marked.

Harry Dowdell *Cycle Touring in Spain*. Well-researched cycle-touring guide, which describes eight touring routes of varying difficulty in the north and south of Spain. Plenty of practical information on preparing your bike for the trip, transporting it, plus what to take.

Teresa Farino *Picos de Europa*. An excellent walking and touring guide in the *Landscapes* series detailing a variety of hikes in this spectacular national park, with special emphasis given to flora and fauna.

Guy Hunter-Watts *Walking in Andalucía*. First-rate walking guide to the natural parks of Grazalema, Cazorla, Los Alcornocales, Aracena and La Axarquía, as well as the Alpujarras and the Sierra Nevada, with 36 walks of various lengths, each with a colour map, and free internet updates.

Jacqueline Oglesby *The Mountains of Central Spain*. Walking and scrambling guide to the magnificent *sierras* de Gredos and Guadarrama by resident author.

June Parker *Walking in Mallorca*. This popular guide is now in its third edition, with many new treks.

Jeremy Rabjohns *Holiday Walks in the Alpujarra* (Sigma, UK; Ⓦwww .sigmapress.co.uk). Excellent small walking guide by Alpujarras resident Rabjohns, describing 24 walks between 3 and 22km in length with clear maps (including many village street maps) and background information. Free updates and corrections available online.

Kev Reynolds *Walks and Climbs in the Pyrenees*. User-friendly guide for trekkers and walkers, though half devoted to the French side of the frontier.

Bob Stansfield *Costa Blanca Mountain Walks*. Two-volume set (sold separately) of walks in this little-known but spectacular area near Alicante. Vol. 1 covers the western Costa Blanca, Vol. 2 the eastern sector.

Douglas Streetfield-James et al *Trekking in the Pyrenees*. The best – and always the most current – English-language west-to-east guide to most of the GR11 and choice bits of the Camino de Santiago, though the GR10 and its variants is half the book. Easy-to-use sketch maps with (brisk) time courses and practical details for overnighting in villages.

Robin Walker *Walks and Climbs in the Picos de Europa* and *Walking in the Cordillera Cantabrica*. The first is a guide to walks and rock climbs in the Picos by an experienced resident mountaineer, the second expands beyond this zone to detail treks in the expansive Cordillera mountain range.

Andy Walmsley *Walking in the Sierra Nevada*. Forty-five walks of varying distance and difficulty, from three-hour strolls in the Alpujarras to the seriously arduous Tres Mils (3000m-plus) peaks. The latest edition also caters for mountain bikers.

The Barcelona-based map publisher **Editorial Alpina** (Ⓦwww .editorialalpina.com) has a good range of 1:25,000 to 1:40,000 walking maps and guides covering Andalucía, Catalunya, the Pyrenees, the Picos de Europa, the Costa Blanca, the Balearics and other parts of Spain.

Wildlife

Teresa Farino and Mike Lockwood *Travellers' Nature Guides: Spain*. Excellent illustrated wildlife guide by two Spanish-based experts (one of whom contributed this guide's wildlife section); conveniently divided into regional groupings with detailed maps, it covers all the peninsula's major habitats for spotting flora and fauna.

Clive Finlayson and David Tomlinson *Birds of Iberia*. Reference work rather than field guide, this book has superb photos of most of the birds to be seen on the Iberian peninsula, with detailed descriptions of species and habitats.

Frederic Grunfeld and Teresa Farino *Wild Spain*. A knowledgeable and practical guide to Spain's national parks, ecology and wildlife.

Oleg Polunin and Anthony Huxley *Flowers of the Mediterranean*. Useful, if by no means exhaustive, field guide.

Oleg Polunin and B.E. Smythies *Flowers of South-West Europe*. Covers all of Spain, Portugal and southwest France; taxonomy is old, but still unsurpassed for its plates, line drawings and keys.

Svensson, Grant, Mullarney and Zetterstrom *The Collins Bird Guide*. The best bird field guide yet published covers (and illustrates) the birds of Europe, including almost everything you're likely to encounter in Spain.

Food and wine

Coleman Andrews *Catalan Cuisine*. The best available English-language book dealing with Spain's most adventurous regional cuisine.

Nicholas Butcher *The Spanish Kitchen*. A practical and knowledge-able guide to creating Spanish dishes when you get back. Lots of informative detail on tapas, olive oil, *jamón serrano* and herbs.

Penelope Casas *The Foods and Wines of Spain*. Superb and now classic Spanish cookbook, covering traditional and regional dishes with equal, authoritative aplomb. By the same author is the useful *Tapas: the little dishes of Spain*.

Alan Davidson *The Tio Pepe Guide to the Seafood of Spain and Portugal*. An indispensable (and pocketable) book that details and illustrates every fish and crustacean you're likely to meet in restaurants and bars along the Spanish *costas*.

Tomás Graves *Bread & Oil: Majorcan Culture's Last Stand*. Written by the son of famous father Robert, this is an intriguing and entertaining book exploring Mallorca via its palate, with sections on what the

islanders eat and how the ingredients end up where they do.

Julian Jeffs *Sherry*. The story of sherry – history, production, blending and brands. Rightly a classic, and the best introduction to Andalucía's great wine. The same author's *Wines of Spain* is an erudite guide to traditional and up-and-coming wine regions, with details of vineyards, grape varieties and vintages.

Jean Claude Juston *The New Spain – Vegan and Vegetarian Restaurants* (available from ⓦwww .vegetarianguides.co.uk). Very useful guide to vegetarian restaurants throughout Spain by the owner/chef of a vegetarian restaurant in the Alpujarras. Catering also for vegans, each listing has its own review and there's lots of background information on Spanish veggie websites and magazines plus details of animal-friendly organizations.

John Radford *The New Spain, The Wines of Rioja*. Lavish coffee-table format disguises *The New Spain's* serious content – a detailed region-by-region guide to Spanish wine with colour maps, *bodega* and vintage evaluations and fine illustrations. *Wines of Rioja* is a comprehensive *vade mecum* to the wines and producers in this emblematic Spanish wine region.

Jan Read *Guide to the Wines of Spain*. Encyclopedic (yet pocketable) guide to the classic and emerging wines of Spain by a leading authority. Includes maps, vintages and vineyards.

🏃 **Paul Richardson** *Late Dinner*. A joyous dissection of the food of Spain, region by region, season by season, nibble of ham by shoot of asparagus. He even squeezes in a meal with top chef Ferran Adriá at culinary shrine *El Bulli*. A celebration of culture and cuisine, this is the best general introduction to what Spanish food – and life – is really all about.

Living and working in Spain

David Hampshire *Living and Working in Spain* (Survival Books, UK; ⓦwww.survivalbooks.net). An excellent and comprehensive guide to moving to, and setting up home in, Spain.

Guy Hobbs & Heleina Postings *Live and Work in Spain and Portugal*. Well-researched handbook full of useful information on moving to the peninsula, buying property, seeking work, starting a business, finding schools and lots more.

David Searl *You and the Law in Spain* (Santana, Málaga; ⓦwww.santanabooks.com). Invaluable, lucid and remarkably comprehensive guide to the Spanish legal and tax system (now in its nineteenth updated edition) and an essential read if you are thinking of buying property, working or setting up a business in Spain.

Learning Spanish

Breakthrough Spanish The best of the tape- and book-linked home-study courses, which aims to give you reasonable fluency within three months. The same series has advanced and business courses.

🏃 **Collins Spanish Dictionary** Recognized as the best single-volume bookshelf dictionary. Regularly revised and updated, so make sure you get the latest edition.

Elisabeth Smith *Teach Yourself Instant Spanish* Good book-based (although CD is available) course that aims to get you from zero to streetwise Spanish in six weeks by studying thirty minutes per day.

🏃 **Get by in Spanish** (BBC Publications, UK; ⓦwww.bbcactive.com/languages; book and CD). One of the BBC's excellent crash-course introductions, which gets you to survival-level Spanish (bars, restaurants, asking the way, etc) in a couple of weeks.

Learn Spanish Now! (Transparent Language, UK/US; ⓦwww.transparent.com). CD-Rom-based (with facility for MP3 use) interactive course incorporating all kinds of gadgets enabling you to compare your pronunciation with a native speaker, access web-based additional learning resources and play skill-improving interactive games.

Rough Guide Spanish Dictionary Good pocket-size dictionary that should help with most travel situations.

Language

Language

Language

O nce you get into it, **Spanish (Castilian)** is the easiest language there is. English is spoken, but wherever you are you'll get a far better reception if you at least try communicating with Spaniards in their own tongue. Being understood, of course, is only half the problem – getting the gist of the reply, often rattled out at a furious pace, may prove far more difficult.

The rules of **pronunciation** are straightforward and, once you get to know them, strictly observed. Unless there's an accent, words ending in d, l, r and z are **stressed** on the last syllable, all others on the second last. All **vowels** are pure and short; combinations have predictable results.

A somewhere between the A sound of "back" and that of "father".

E as in "get".

I as in "police".

O as in "hot".

U as in "rule".

C is lisped before E and I; otherwise, hard: *cerca* is pronounced "thairka" (though in Andalucía many natives pronounce the soft "c" as an "s").

G works the same way, a guttural "H" sound (like the ch in "loch") before E or I, a hard G elsewhere – *gigante* becomes "higante".

H is always silent.

J the same sound as a guttural G: *jamón* is pronounced "hamon".

LL sounds like an English Y or LY: *tortilla* is pronounced "torteeya/torteelya".

N is as in English unless it has a tilde (accent) over it, when it becomes NY: *mañana* sounds like "manyana".

QU is pronounced like an English K.

R is rolled, RR doubly so.

V sounds more like B, *vino* becoming "beano".

X has an S sound before consonants, normal X before vowels. More common in Catalan, Basque or Gallego words, where it's sh or zh.

Z is the same as a soft C, so *cerveza* becomes "thairvaitha" (but again much of the south prefers the "s" sound).

The list of a few essential words and phrases overleaf should be enough to get you started, though if you're travelling for any length of time a dictionary or phrasebook is obviously a worthwhile investment. If you're using a **dictionary**, bear in mind that in Spanish CH, LL and Ñ count as separate letters and are listed after the Cs, Ls and Ns respectively.

In addition to Castilian, many Spaniards speak a second, **regional language** – we've given brief pronunciation rules and condensed glossaries for the three most widely spoken: **Catalan** (*Català*; p.980), **Basque** (*Euskara*; p.981) and **Galician** (*Galego*; p.982).

L

LANGUAGE

Spanish words and phrases

Basics

Yes, No, OK	Sí, No, Vale
Please, Thank you	Por favor, Gracias
Where, When	Dónde, Cuando
What, How much	Qué, Cuánto
Here, There	Aquí, Allí
This, That	Esto, Eso
Now, Later	Ahora, Más tarde
Open, Closed	Abierto/a, Cerrado/a
With, Without	Con, Sin
Good, Bad	Buen(o)/a, Mal(o)/a
Big, Small	Gran(de), Pequeño/a
Cheap, Expensive	Barato, Caro
Hot, Cold	Caliente, Frío
More, Less	Más, Menos
Today, Tomorrow	Hoy, Mañana
Yesterday	Ayer

Greetings and responses

Hello, Goodbye	Hola, Adiós
Good morning	Buenos días
Good afternoon/ night	Buenas tardes/ noches
See you later	Hasta luego
Sorry	Lo siento/disculpéme
Excuse me	perdón/Con permiso
How are you?	¿Como está (usted)?
I (don't) understand	(No) Entiendo
Not at all/ You're welcome	De nada
Do you speak English?	¿Habla (usted) inglés?
I (don't) speak Spanish	(No) Hablo español
My name is ...	Me llamo ...
What's your name?	¿Como se llama usted?
I am English/ Australian/ Canadian/ American/ Irish	Soy inglés(a)/ australiano(a)/ canadiense(a)/ americano(a)/ irlandés(a)

Hotels and transport

I want	Quiero
I'd like	Quisiera
Do you know ...?	¿Sabe ...?
I don't know	No sé
There is (is there)?	(¿)Hay(?)
Give me ... (one like that)	Deme ...(uno así)
Do you have ...?	¿Tiene ...?
the time	la hora
a room	una habitación
... with two beds/ double bed	... con dos camas/ cama matrimonial
... with shower/bath	... con ducha/baño
It's for one person (two people)	Es para una persona (dos personas)
for one night (one week)	para una noche (una semana)
It's fine, how much is it?	¿Está bien, cuánto es?
It's too expensive	Es demasiado caro
Don't you have anything cheaper?	No tiene algo más barato?
Can one ...?	¿Se puede ....?
camp (near) here?	¿... acampar aquí (cerca)?
Is there a hostel nearby?	¿Hay un hostal aquí cerca?
How do I get to ...?	¿Por donde se va a ...?
Left, right, straight on	Izquierda, derecha, todo recto
Where is ...?	¿Dónde está ...?
... the bus station	... la estación de autobuses
... the train station	... la estación de station ferro-carril
... the nearest bank	... el banco mas cercano
... the post office	... el correos/la oficina de correos
the toilet	el baño/aseo/servicio
Where does the bus to ... leave from?	¿De dónde sale el autobús para ...?

Is this the train for Mérida?	¿Es este el tren para Mérida?
I'd like a (return) ticket to …	Quisiera un billete (de ida y vuelta) para …
What time does it leave (arrive in …)?	¿A qué hora sale (llega a …)?
What is there to eat?	¿Qué hay para comer?
What's that?	¿Qué es eso?
What's this called in Spanish?	¿Como se llama este en español?

Numbers and days

one	un/uno/una
two	dos
three	tres
four	cuatro
five	cinco
six	seis
seven	siete
eight	ocho
nine	nueve
ten	diez
eleven	once
twelve	doce
thirteen	trece
fourteen	catorce
fifteen	quince
sixteen	diez y seis
twenty	veinte
twenty-one	veintiuno
thirty	treinta

forty	cuarenta
fifty	cincuenta
sixty	sesenta
seventy	setenta
eighty	ochenta
ninety	noventa
one hundred	cien(to)
one hundred and one	ciento uno
two hundred	doscientos
two hundred and one	doscientos uno
five hundred	quinientos
one thousand	mil
two thousand	dos mil
two thousand and one	dos mil un
two thousand and two	dos mil dos
two thousand and three	dos mil tres
first	primero/a
second	segundo/a
third	tercero/a
fifth	quinto/a
tenth	décimo/a
Monday	lunes
Tuesday	martes
Wednesday	miércoles
Thursday	jueves
Friday	viernes
Saturday	sábado
Sunday	domingo

Menu reader

Basics

Aceite	Oil
Ajo	Garlic
Arroz	Rice
Azúcar	Sugar
Huevos	Eggs
Mantequilla	Butter
Miel	Honey
Pan	Bread
Pimienta	Pepper

Sal	Salt
Vinagre	Vinegar

Meals

Almuerzo/Comida	Lunch
Botella	Bottle
Carta	Menu
Cena	Dinner
Comedor	Dining room
Cuchara	Spoon

Cuchillo	Knife
La cuenta	The bill
Desayuno	Breakfast
Menú del día	Fixed-price set meal
Mesa	Table
Platos combinados	Mixed plate
Tenedor	Fork
Vaso	Glass

Soups (*sopas*) and starters

Caldillo	Clear fish soup
Caldo	Broth
Caldo verde or gallego	Thick cabbage-based broth
Ensalada (mixta/verde)	(Mixed/green) salad
Pimientos rellenos	Stuffed peppers
Sopa de ajo	Garlic soup
Sopa de cocido	Meat soup
Sopa de gallina	Chicken soup
Sopa de mariscos	Seafood soup
Sopa de pescado	Fish soup
Sopa de pasta (fideos)	Noodle soup
Verduras con patatas	Boiled potatoes with greens

Fish (*pescados*)

Anchoas	Anchovies (fresh)
Anguila/Angulas	Eel/Elvers
Atún	Tuna
Bacalao	Cod (often salt)
Bonito	Tuna
Boquerones	Small, sardine-like fish
Chanquetes	Whitebait
Dorada	Bream
Lenguado	Sole
Lubina	Sea bass
Merluza	Hake
Mero	Grouper
Pez espada	Swordfish
Rape	Monkfish
Raya	Ray, skate
Rodaballo	Turbot
Salmonete	Mullet

Sardinas	Sardines
Trucha	Trout

Seafood (*mariscos*)

Almejas	Clams
Arroz con mariscos	Rice with seafood
Calamares (en su tinta)	Squid (in ink)
Centollo	Spider crab
Cigalas	King prawns
Conchas finas	Large scallops
Gambas	Prawns/shrimps
Langosta	Lobster
Langostinos	Crayfish
Mejillones	Mussels
Nécora	Sea crab
Ostras	Oysters
Paella	Classic Valencian dish with saffron rice, chicken, seafood, etc
Percebes	Goose barnacles
Pulpo	Octopus
Sepia	Cuttlefish
Vieiras	Scallops
Zarzuela de mariscos	Seafood casserole

Some common terms

al ajillo	in garlic
asado	roast
a la Navarra	stuffed with ham
a la parrilla/plancha	grilled
a la Romana	fried in batter
al horno	baked
alioli	with garlic mayonnaise
cazuela, cocido	stew
en salsa	in (usually tomato) sauce
frito	fried
guisado	casserole
rehogado	sautéed

Meat (*carne*) and poultry (*aves*)

Callos	Tripe
Carne de buey	Beef
Cerdo	Pork

Choto	Baby kid
Chuletas	Chops
Cochinillo	Suckling pig
Codorniz	Quail
Conejo	Rabbit
Cordero	Lamb
Escalopa	Escalope
Fabada asturiana/ Fabes a la catalana	Hotpot with butter-beans, black pudding, etc
Hamburguesa	Hamburger
Hígado	Liver
Jabalí	Wild boar
Lacón con grelos	Gammon with turnips
Lengua	Tongue
Lomo	Loin (of pork)
Pato	Duck
Pavo	Turkey
Perdiz	Partridge
Pollo	Chicken
Riñones	Kidneys
Solomillo	Sirloin steak
Solomillo de cerdo	Pork tenderloin
Ternera	Beef/Veal

Vegetables (legumbres)

Acelga	Chard
Alcachofas	Artichokes
Arroz a la cubana	Rice with fried egg and tomato sauce
Berenjenas	Aubergine/eggplant
Cebollas	Onions
Champiñones/Setas	Mushrooms
Coliflor	Cauliflower
Espárragos	Asparagus
Espinacas	Spinach
Garbanzos	Chickpeas
Habas	Broad/fava beans
Judías blancas	Haricot beans
Judías verdes, rojas, negras	Green, red, black beans
Lechuga	Lettuce
Lentejas	Lentils
Menestra/Panache de verduras	Mixed vegetables
Nabos/Grelos	Turnips

Patatas	Potatoes
Patatas fritas	French fries (chips)
Pepino	Cucumber
Pimientos	Peppers/capsicums
Pisto manchego	Ratatouille
Puerros	Leeks
Puré	Mashed potato
Repollo	Cabbage
Tomate	Tomato
Zanahoria	Carrot

Fruits (frutas)

Albaricoques	Apricots
Cerezas	Cherries
Chirimoyas	Custard apples
Ciruelas	Plums, prunes
Dátiles	Dates
Fresas	Strawberries
Granada	Pomegranate
Higos	Figs
Limón	Lemon
Manzanas	Apples
Melocotones	Peaches
Melón	Melon
Naranjas	Oranges
Nectarinas	Nectarines
Peras	Pears
Piña	Pineapple
Plátanos	Bananas
Sandía	Watermelon
Toronja/Pomelo	Grapefruit
Uvas	Grapes

Desserts (postres)

Arroz con leche	Rice pudding
Crema catalana	Catalan crème brûlée
Cuajada	Cream-based dessert served with honey
Flan	Crème caramel
Helado	Ice cream
Melocotón en almíbar	Peaches in syrup
Membrillo	Quince paste
Nata	Whipped cream
Natillas	Custard
Yogur	Yogurt

Cheese

Cheeses (*quesos*) are on the whole local,
though you'll get the hard, salty *queso
manchego* everywhere. Mild sheep's cheese
(*queso de oveja*) from León Province or the
Sierra de Grazalema (Cádiz) is widely
distributed and worth asking for.

Standard tapas and *raciones*

Aceitunas	Olives
Albóndigas	Meatballs
Anchoas	Anchovies
Berberechos	Cockles
Boquerones	Anchovies
Cabrillas	Large snails with tomato
Calamares	Squid
Callos	Tripe
Caracoles	Snails
Carne en salsa	Meat in tomato sauce
Champiñones	Mushrooms, usually fried in garlic
Chocos	Deep-fried cuttlefish
Chorizo	Spicy sausage
Cocido	Stew
Empanadilla	Fish/meat pasty

Ensaladilla rusa	Russian salad (diced vegetables in mayonnaise)
Escalibada	Aubergine (eggplant) and pepper salad
Garbanzos	Chickpeas
Gambas	Prawns
Habas	Broad beans
Habas con jamón	Broad beans with ham
Hígado	Liver
Huevo cocido	Hard-boiled egg
Jamón Serrano	Dried ham (like Parma ham)
Mejillones	Mussels
Navajas	Razor clams
Patatas alioli	Potatoes in garlic mayonnaise
Patatas bravas	Spicy fried potatoes
Pimientos	Peppers
Pincho moruno	Kebab
Pisto	Ratatouille
Pulpo	Octopus
Riñones al Jerez	Kidneys in sherry
Salchicha	Sausage
Sepia	Cuttlefish
Tortilla española	Potato omelette
Tortilla francesa	Plain omelette

Catalan

Catalan (*Català*) is spoken in Catalunya, part of Aragón, much of Valencia, the
Balearic Islands and the Principality of Andorra. On paper, it looks like a cross
between French and Spanish, and is generally easy to understand if you know those
two, but, spoken, it has a distinct, rounded sound and is far harder to come to grips
with – the language has eight vowel sounds (including three diphthongs).

The main differences from Castilian in **pronunciation** are:

A as in "hat" when stressed, as in "alone"
when unstressed.

C sounds like an English S: *plaça* is pronounced "plassa".

G before E and I is like the "zh" in "Zhivago";
otherwise, hard.

J as in the French "Jean".

N is as in English, though before F or V it
sometimes sounds like an M.

NY replaces the Castilian Ñ.

QU before E or I sounds like K; before A or O
as in "quit".

R is rolled at the start of the word; at the end,
it's often silent.

TX is like the English CH.

V sounds more like B at the start of a word;
otherwise, a soft F sound.

W sounds like a B/V.

X like SH in most words, though in some it
sounds like an X.

Z like the English Z.

Catalan glossary

one	un(a)
two	dos (dues)
three	tres
four	quatre
five	cinc
six	sis
seven	set
eight	vuit
nine	nou
ten	deu
Monday	Dilluns
Tuesday	Dimarts
Wednesday	Dimecres
Thursday	Dijous
Friday	Divendres
Saturday	Dissabte
Sunday	Diumenge
good morning/hello	bon dia
good evening	bona nit
goodbye	adéu

please	per favor
thank you	gràcies
today	avui
yesterday	ahir
tomorrow	demà
day before yesterday	abans d'ahir
day after tomorrow	demà passat
more	més
a lot, very	força
a little	una mica
left	esquerre(a)
right	dret(a)
near	(a) prop
far	lluny
open	obert(a)
closed	tancat
town square	plaça
beach	praia
where?	¿on?
when?	¿quan?
how much?	¿quant?

Basque

Basque (*Euskara*) is spoken in the Basque Country and Navarra. According to the official estimates in 2008, around thirty percent of the population of the Basque Country and eleven percent of Navarra are "actively bilingual", speaking Euskara as their first language but understanding Castilian.

It's worth noting a couple of **key letter changes**: notably, the Castilian CH becomes TX (*txipirones* as opposed to *chipirones*), V becomes B and Y becomes I (Bizkaia as opposed to Vizcaya). Above all, *Euskara* features a proliferation of Ks: this letter replaces the Castilian C (Gipuzkoa instead of Guipúzcoa) and QU (Lekeitio instead of Lequeitio) and is also used to form the plural and the possessive (eg Bilboko means "of Bilbao").

Basque glossary

one	bat
two	bi
three	hiru
four	lau
five	bost
six	sei
seven	zazpi
eight	zortzi
nine	bederatzi

ten	hamar
Monday	astelehen
Tuesday	astearte
Wednesday	asteazken
Thursday	ostegun
Friday	ostiral
Saturday	larunbat
Sunday	igande
yes, no	bai, ez
hello	kaixo
good morning	egun on

good night	gabon		near	hurbil
please	mesedez		far	urruti
thank you	eskerrik asko		open	ireki
today	gaur		closed	hertsi
yesterday	bihar		town square	enpastantza
tomorrow	atzo		beach	hondartza
more	gehiago		shop	denda
a lot	asko		where?	¿daude?
a little	gutxi		when?	¿noiz?
left	ezker		how much?	¿zenbat?
right	eskuin			

Galician

While superficially similar to Castilian, **Galician** (*Galego*) is closer to Portuguese – in fact, both Galician and Portuguese evolved from a single ancestral tongue – and the main or only language of seventy percent of the population of Galicia.

The most obvious **characteristic** of Galician is the large number of Xs, which in Castilian might be Gs, Js or Ss; these are pronounced as a soft "sh" – thus *jamón* in Castilian becomes *xamón*, pronounced "shamon", in Galician. Similarly, LL in Castilian often becomes CH in Galician. You'll also find that the Castilian "la" becomes "a" (as in A Coruña), "el" is "o" (as in O Grove), "en la" is "na", "en el" is "no", "de la" is "da" and "del" is "do".

Galician glossary

one	un		good night	boas noites
two	dous		thank you	grazas
three	tres		today	hoxe
four	catro		yesterday	onte
five	cinco		tomorrow	mañá
six	seis		more	mais
seven	sete		a lot	moito
eight	oito		a little	pouco
nine	nove		left	esquerda
ten	dez		right	dereita
Monday	Luns		near	preto
Tuesday	Martes		far	lonxe
Wednesday	Mécores		open	aberto
Thursday	Xoves		closed	pechado
Friday	Venres		town square	praza
Saturday	Sábado		beach	praia
Sunday	Domingo		shop	tenda
good morning	bos días		where?	¿onde?
good afternoon	boas tardes		when?	¿cándo?
			how much?	¿cánto?

Glossary of Spanish and architectural terms

Alameda Park or grassy promenade.

Alcazaba Moorish castle.

Alcázar Moorish fortified palace.

Apse Semicircular recess at the altar (usually eastern) end of a church.

Ayuntamiento/ajuntament Town hall.

Azulejo Glazed ceramic tilework.

Barrio Suburb or quarter.

Bodega Cellar, wine bar or warehouse.

Calle Street.

Capilla mayor Chapel containing the high altar.

Capilla real Royal chapel.

Capital Top of a column.

Cartuja Carthusian monastery.

Castillo Castle.

Chancel Part of a church containing the altar, usually at the east end.

Churrigueresque Extreme form of Baroque art named after José Churriguera (1650–1723) and his extended family, its main exponents.

Colegiata Collegiate (large parish) church.

Convento Monastery or convent.

Coro Central part of church built for the choir.

Coro alto Raised choir, often above west door of a church.

Correos Post office.

Corrida de toros Bullfight.

Crypt Burial place in a church, usually under the choir.

Cuadrilla A bullfighter's team of assistants.

Custodia Large receptacle for Eucharist wafers.

Dueño/a Proprietor, landlord/lady.

Ermita Hermitage.

Gitano Gypsy or Romany.

Hórreo Granary.

Iglesia Church.

Isabelline Ornamental form of late Gothic developed during the reign of Isabel and Fernando.

Loggia Covered area on the side of a building, usually arcaded.

Lonja Stock exchange building.

Mercado Market.

Mihrab Prayer niche of Moorish mosque.

Mirador Viewing point.

Modernisme (Modernista) Catalan/Spanish form of Art Nouveau, whose most famous exponent was Antoni Gaudí.

Monasterio Monastery or convent.

Morisco Muslim Spaniard subject to medieval Christian rule – and nominally baptized.

Mozárabe Christian subject to medieval Moorish rule; normally allowed freedom of worship, they built churches in an Arab-influenced manner (Mozarabic).

Mudéjar Muslim Spaniard subject to medieval Christian rule, but retaining Islamic worship; most commonly a term applied to architecture which includes buildings built by Moorish craftsmen for the Christian rulers and later designs influenced by the Moors. The 1890s to 1930s saw a Mudéjar revival, blended with Art Nouveau and Art Deco forms.

Narthex Entrance hall of church.

Nave Central space in a church, usually flanked by aisles.

Palacio Aristocratic mansion.

Parador Luxury hotel, often converted from minor monument.

Paseo Promenade; also the evening stroll thereon.

Patio Inner courtyard.

Plateresque Elaborately decorative Renaissance style, the sixteenth-century successor of Isabelline forms. Named for its resemblance to silversmiths' work (*platería*).

Plaza Square.

Plaza de toros Bullring.

Portico Covered entrance to a building.

Posada Old name for an inn.

Puerta Gateway, also mountain pass.

Puerto Port.

Raciones Large plate of tapas for sharing.

Reja Iron screen or grille, often fronting a window.

Reliquary Receptacle for a saint's relics, usually bones. Often highly decorated.

Reredos Wall or screen behind an altar.

Retablo Altarpiece.

Ría River estuary in Galicia.

Río River.

Romería Religious procession to a rural shrine.

Sacristía, sagrario Sacristy of church – room for sacred vessels and vestments.

Sardana Catalan folk dance.

Seo, Seu, Se Ancient/regional names for cathedrals.

Sidreria Bar specializing in cider.

Sierra Mountain range.

Sillería Choirstall.

Solar Aristocratic town mansion.

Taifa Small Moorish kingdom, many of which emerged after the disintegration of the Córdoba caliphate.

Telefónica The phone company; also used for its offices in any town.

Transepts The wings of a cruciform church, placed at right angles to the nave and chancel.

Tympanum Area between lintel of a doorway and the arch above it.

Turismo Tourist office.

Vault Arched ceiling.

Political parties and acronyms

CNT Anarchist trade union.

Convergencia I Unio Conservative party in power in Catalunya.

ETA Basque terrorist organization. Its political wing is Euskal Herritarrok.

Falange Franco's old Fascist party; now officially defunct.

Fuerza Nueva Descendants of the above, also on the way out.

IU Izquierda Unida, broad-left alliance of communists and others.

MC Movimiento Comunista (Communist Movement), small radical offshoot of the PCE.

MOC Movimiento de Objeción de Conciencia, peace group, concerned with NATO and conscription.

OTAN NATO.

PCE Partido Comunista de España (Spanish Communist Party).

PNV Basque Nationalist Party – in control of the right-wing autonomous government.

PP Partido Popular, the centre-right alliance formed by Alianza Popular and the Christian Democrats. Currently the main opposition party.

PSOE Partido Socialista Obrero Español, the Spanish Socialist Workers' Party. Currently the governing party.

UGT Unión General de Trabajadores, Spain's major union and the equivalent of Britain's Transport and General Workers' Union.

Small print and
Index

A Rough Guide to Rough Guides

Published in 1982, the first Rough Guide – to Greece – was a student scheme that became a publishing phenomenon. Mark Ellingham, a recent graduate in English from Bristol University, had been travelling in Greece the previous summer and couldn't find the right guidebook. With a small group of friends he wrote his own guide, combining a highly contemporary, journalistic style with a thoroughly practical approach to travellers' needs.

The immediate success of the book spawned a series that rapidly covered dozens of destinations. And, in addition to impecunious backpackers, Rough Guides soon acquired a much broader and older readership that relished the guides' wit and inquisitiveness as much as their enthusiastic, critical approach and value-for-money ethos.

These days, Rough Guides include recommendations from shoestring to luxury and cover more than 200 destinations around the globe, including almost every country in the Americas and Europe, more than half of Africa and most of Asia and Australasia. Our ever-growing team of authors and photographers is spread all over the world, particularly in Europe, the USA and Australia.

In the early 1990s, Rough Guides branched out of travel, with the publication of Rough Guides to World Music, Classical Music and the Internet. All three have become benchmark titles in their fields, spearheading the publication of a wide range of books under the Rough Guide name.

Including the travel series, Rough Guides now number more than 350 titles, covering: phrasebooks, waterproof maps, music guides from Opera to Heavy Metal, reference works as diverse as Conspiracy Theories and Shakespeare, and popular culture books from iPods to Poker. Rough Guides also produce a series of more than 120 World Music CDs in partnership with World Music Network.

Visit www.roughguides.com to see our latest publications.

Rough Guide travel images are available for commercial licensing at www.roughguidespictures.com

SMALL PRINT

Rough Guide credits

Text editor: Keith Drew, Lucy White
Layout: Pradeep Thapliyal, Nikhil Agarwal
Cartography: Rajesh Chhibber, Rajesh Mishra
Picture editor: Mark Thomas
Production: Rebecca Short
Proofreader: Jan McCann
Cover design: Chloë Roberts
Editorial: London Ruth Blackmore, Andy Turner, Edward Aves, Alice Park, Jo Kirby, James Smart, Natasha Foges, Róisín Cameron, Emma Traynor, James Rice, Emma Gibbs, Kathryn Lane, Christina Valhouli, Monica Woods, Mani Ramaswamy, Alison Roberts, Harry Wilson, Joe Staines, Peter Buckley, Matthew Milton, Tracy Hopkins, Ruth Tidball; **New York** Andrew Rosenberg, Steven Horak, AnneLise Sorensen, Ella Steim, Anna Owens, Sean Mahoney, Paula Neudorf; **Delhi** Madhavi Singh, Karen D'Souza, Lubna Shaheen
Design & Pictures: London Scott Stickland, Dan May, Diana Jarvis, Chloë Roberts, Nicole Newman, Sarah Cummins, Emily Taylor; **Delhi** Umesh Aggarwal, Ajay Verma, Jessica Subramanian, Ankur Guha, Sachin Tanwar, Anita Singh
Production: Vicky Baldwin

Cartography: London Maxine Repath, Ed Wright, Katie Lloyd-Jones; **Delhi** Ashutosh Bharti, Animesh Pathak, Jasbir Sandhu, Karobi Gogoi, Alakananda Roy, Swati Handoo, Deshpal Dabas
Online: London George Atwell, Faye Hellon, Jeanette Angell, Fergus Day, Justine Bright, Clare Bryson, Áine Fearon, Adrian Low, Ezgi Celebi, Amber Bloomfield; **Delhi** Amit Verma, Rahul Kumar, Narender Kumar, Ravi Yadav, Debojit Borah, Rakesh Kumar, Ganesh Sharma, Shisir Basumatari
Marketing & Publicity: London Liz Statham, Niki Hanmer, Louise Maher, Jess Carter, Vanessa Godden, Vivienne Watton, Anna Paynton, Rachel Sprackett, Libby Jellie, Laura Vipond; **New York** Geoff Colquitt, Nancy Lambert, Katy Ball; **Delhi** Ragini Govind
Manager India: Punita Singh
Reference Director: Andrew Lockett
Operations Manager: Helen Phillips
PA to Publishing Director: Nicola Henderson
Publishing Director: Martin Dunford
Commercial Manager: Gino Magnotta
Managing Director: John Duhigg

Publishing information

This thirteenth edition published April 2009 by
Rough Guides Ltd,
80 Strand, London WC2R 0RL
345 Hudson St, 4th Floor,
New York, NY 10014, USA
14 Local Shopping Centre, Panchsheel Park,
New Delhi 110017, India
Distributed by the Penguin Group
Penguin Books Ltd,
80 Strand, London WC2R 0RL
Penguin Group (USA)
375 Hudson Street, NY 10014, USA
Penguin Group (Australia)
250 Camberwell Road, Camberwell,
Victoria 3124, Australia
Penguin Group (Canada)
195 Harry Walker Parkway N, Newmarket, ON,
L3Y 7B3 Canada
Penguin Group (NZ)
67 Apollo Drive, Mairangi Bay, Auckland 1310,
New Zealand
Cover concept by Peter Dyer.

Typeset in Bembo and Helvetica to an original design by Henry Iles.
Printed and bound in China
© Simon Baskett, Jules Brown, Marc Dubin, Mark Ellingham, John Fisher, Geoff Garvey, AnneLise Sorensen & Greg Ward 2009
No part of this book may be reproduced in any form without permission from the publisher except for the quotation of brief passages in reviews.
1000pp includes index
A catalogue record for this book is available from the British Library.
ISBN: 978-1-84836-034-1

SMALL PRINT

Help us update

We've gone to a lot of effort to ensure that the thirteenth edition of **The Rough Guide to Spain** is accurate and up to date. However, things change – places get "discovered", opening hours are notoriously fickle, restaurants and rooms raise prices or lower standards. If you feel we've got it wrong or left something out, we'd like to know, and if you can remember the address, the price, the hours, the phone number, so much the better.

Please send your comments with the subject line "**Rough Guide Spain Update**" to ⊛mail@roughguides.com. We'll credit all contributions and send a copy of the next edition (or any other Rough Guide if you prefer) for the very best emails.
Have your questions answered and tell others about your trip at
⊛community.roughguides.com

Acknowledgements

Simon Baskett would like to give special thanks to Trini, Patrick and Laura once again for all their hard work and patience. Thanks, too, to all those who gave recommendations or advice for this edition.

Jules Brown would like to thank María Jesús Bernal González at Turismo de Salamanca, Anna Hunt at Keytel and Paradores de Turismo de España for all their kind assistance. And special thanks to John and his indefatigable appetite for the *chuletón*.

Marc Dubin thanks the management of Fonda Rigà in Tregurà, Niki Forsyth and Richard Cash in the Valle d'Echo, David and Consell Bardaji in Taüll, and the Zitara for sharing Catalunya once again.

Geoff Garvey thanks Josep Vergés, Jean-Claude Juston, Bienvenido Luque, Pasqual Rovira, Paco Moyano, Juan Carlos Abalos, Javier Andrade, Pepa Babot, Pam Lalonde and Lindsay Vick for valuable help on the ground in Andalucía; and in London, Raquel Fonseca Cambeiro at the Spanish tourist office and Alan Biggins at the Canning House library.

AnneLise Sorensen thanks all who invited me in, wined and dined me, and shared information, travel tips and lively evenings, including: Maite Vidal, as always, for her splendid hospitality and knowledge of Spain; my entire – and ever-entertaining – Catalan family, including Anna, Miquel (thanks for the Teruel tips!), Jaume and familia; Jaume, Irene and family for a delicious Barcelona dinner; the Ferrer *familia*, including Jaume, for a great night out; all my wonderful Tietas and Tiets, *por supuesto*!; Claire (and *familia*) for being such a special best friend, and for memorable evenings of tapas and *vino*; Juan Peiro and the magnificent *paradores*, from Sos del Rey Católico (cheers to Emilio Mojón) to Tortosa; and the top-notch *turismos* across Catalunya, Aragón, Valencia and Murcia, particularly Maria José Rabadán in Valencia, as well as superb bike guide Josep Alberola; Laura Martinez Moya in Murcia; and Turespaña New York. Thanks to *guapo* and all the wonderful friends in New York for their support and cheery emails. A resounding thanks to the London and Delhi Rough Guides offices, including Katie Lloyd-Jones, Mark Thomas, the excellent typesetting and cartography teams and, above all, to Keith Drew, who is a true editor extraordinaire. Finally, a big *gracias, mange tak* and thank you to the best companion a travel-writer could ask for, Papa Kurt; and to Mama, who welcomed us back, with *truita* and open arms, to the home base in Cervera.

Greg Ward gives many thanks to Marga Sanz of Turgalicia for all her help in Galicia, to Sam Cook for sharing the work, and to Keith for his input and support.

Readers' letters

Thanks to all those readers of the twelfth edition who took the trouble to write in with their amendments and additions. Apologies for any misspellings or omissions.

Keith Allison, Louise Ansari, Carlos Arribas, F. Bird, Tobias Boese, Nigel Bowie, Richard Budden, Nicholas Butcher, Pat Campbell, Alina Congreve, Charles Curran, Thomas Dougan, Isaac Esteban and Zuriñe García, Michael Ford, Andy Gemmell, Jennifer Hainsworth, Remco van der Hoogt, Peter Household, Marieke Ijsselmuiden, Kim Johns, Susan Jones, John and Rose Meech, Catherine Mitchell and Paul Jacob, Lynn Nolan, Sue and Chris Nurse, Paulo Oliveira, Farida Parkyn, Terry Roberts, Bob and Rose Sandham, Vince Smeaton, Jon Stein, Kate Summers, David Swain, Phil Tunstall.

Photo credits

All photos © Rough Guides except the following:

Introduction
Santiago de Compostela Cathedral
© H Marstrand/Axiom
Parc Güell © Marco Cristofori/Getty Images
Flamenco dancer's hair piece © Timothy Allen/Axiom
Plaza de España, Seville © Anthony Webb/Axiom
Castle, La Mancha © Robert Harding/Alamy
La Boqueria market © Hemis/Alamy
Ciudad de las Artes y las Ciencias, Valencia
© Mark Thomas
Plaza Mayor, Madrid © Ian Cumming/Axiom
Calella, Costa Brava © Dosfotos/Axiom

Things not to miss
01 La Mezquita © Getty Images
04 Toledo © Mark Thomas
05 Leon Cathedral © Paul Quayle/Axiom
07 Seafood, San Sebastian © Alex Serge/Alamy
10 Plaza Mayor, Salamanca © Anthony Webb/Axiom
12 Iberian lynx © John Cancalosi/Alamy
13 Sitges Carnival © Oso Media/Alamy
14 Museo Guggenheim, Bilbao © Mark Thomas
16 Prado Museum © Peter Barritt/Alamy
17 Flamenco dancing © Timothy Allen/Axiom
18 Farmer in vineyard, La Rioja © Daniel Acevedo/Alamy

Index

Map entries are in colour.

INDEX

W

X

Y

Z

We speak English, German and Spanish!!!

Map symbols

maps are listed in the full index using coloured text

Motorway	Mosque
Tolled motorway	Monastery
Major road	Synagogue
Minor road	Tram stop
Pedestrianized street	Metro station
Unpaved road track	Cercanías renfe station
Steps	Bus stop
Railway	Statue
Funicular railway	Parking
Cable car	Campsite
Footpath	Eating & drinking
Ferry route	Accommodation
Coastline/river	Mountain refuge
Wall	Church (regional maps)
Chapter division boundary	Monastery
Provincial border	Hospital
International boundary	Tourist office
Point of interest	Post office
Ruins	Internet access
Castle	Telephone office
Mountain peak	Skiing
Mountain range	Swimming pool
Viewpoint	Bridge
Rocks	Market
Lighthouse	Building
Airport	Church (town maps)
Cave	Park
Waterfall	Beach
Gardens	Saltpan
Spa	